# Twentieth-Century Literary Criticism

# Guide to Gale Literary Criticism Series

**When you need to review criticism of literary works, these are the Gale series to use:**

| If the author's death date is: | You should turn to: |
|---|---|
| After Dec. 31, 1959 (or author is still living) | ***CONTEMPORARY LITERARY CRITICISM***<br><br>for example: Jorge Luis Borges, Anthony Burgess, William Faulkner, Mary Gordon, Ernest Hemingway, Iris Murdoch |
| 1900 through 1959 | ***TWENTIETH-CENTURY LITERARY CRITICISM***<br><br>for example: Willa Cather, F. Scott Fitzgerald, Henry James, Mark Twain, Virginia Woolf |
| 1800 through 1899 | ***NINETEENTH-CENTURY LITERATURE CRITICISM***<br><br>for example: Fedor Dostoevski, Nathaniel Hawthorne, George Sand, William Wordsworth |
| 1400 through 1799 | ***LITERATURE CRITICISM FROM 1400 TO 1800*** *(excluding Shakespeare)*<br><br>for example: Anne Bradstreet, Daniel Defoe, Alexander Pope, François Rabelais, Jonathan Swift, Phillis Wheatley<br><br>***SHAKESPEAREAN CRITICISM***<br><br>Shakespeare's plays and poetry |
| Antiquity through 1399 | ***CLASSICAL AND MEDIEVAL LITERATURE CRITICISM***<br><br>for example: Dante, Homer, Plato, Sophocles, Vergil, the Beowulf Poet |

---

**Gale also publishes related criticism series:**

***CHILDREN'S LITERATURE REVIEW***

This series covers authors of all eras who write for the preschool through high school audience.

***SHORT STORY CRITICISM***

This series covers the major short fiction writers of all nationalities and periods of literary history.

ISSN 0276-8178

Volume 28

# Twentieth-Century Literary Criticism

**Excerpts from Criticism of the
Works of Novelists, Poets, Playwrights,
Short Story Writers, and Other Creative Writers
Who Died between 1900 and 1960,
from the First Published Critical Appraisals
to Current Evaluations**

**Dennis Poupard**
**Editor**

**Paula Kepos**
**Marie Lazzari**
**Thomas Ligotti**
**Associate Editors**

**Gale Research Company**
**Book Tower**
**Detroit, Michigan 48226**

## STAFF

Dennis Poupard, *Editor*

Paula Kepos, Marie Lazzari, Thomas Ligotti, *Associate Editors*

Joann Prosyniuk, Keith E. Schooley, Laurie A. Sherman, *Senior Assistant Editors*

Faye Kuzma, Sandra Liddell, Timothy Veeser, *Assistant Editors*

Carolyn Bancroft, Denise Michlewicz Broderick, Melissa Reiff Hug,
Jay P. Pederson, Anne Sharp, Debra A. Wells, *Contributing Assistant Editors*

Sharon R. Gunton, *Contributing Editor*

Jeanne A. Gough, *Permissions & Production Manager*
Lizbeth A. Purdy, *Production Supervisor*
Kathleen M. Cook, *Production Coordinator*
Cathy Beranek, Suzanne Powers, Kristine E. Tipton, Lee Ann Welsh, *Editorial Assistants*
Linda M. Pugliese, *Manuscript Coordinator*
Maureen A. Puhl, *Senior Manuscript Assistant*
Donna Craft, Jennifer E. Gale, Rosetta Irene Simms, *Manuscript Assistants*

Victoria B. Cariappa, *Research Supervisor*
Maureen R. Richards, *Research Coordinator*
Mary D. Wise, *Senior Research Assistant*
Joyce E. Doyle, Kevin B. Hillstrom, Karen D. Kaus, Eric Priehs,
Filomena Sgambati, Laura B. Standley, *Research Assistants*

Janice M. Mach, *Text Permissions Supervisor*
Kathy Grell, *Text Permissions Coordinator*
Mabel E. Gurney, Josephine M. Keene, *Senior Permissions Assistants*
Eileen H. Baehr, H. Diane Cooper,
Anita L. Ransom, Kimberly F. Smilay, *Permissions Assistants*
Melissa A. Kamuyu, Martha A. Mulder, Lisa M. Wimmer, *Permissions Clerks*

Patricia A. Seefelt, *Picture Permissions Supervisor*
Margaret A. Chamberlain, *Permissions Coordinator, Pictures*
Pamela A. Hayes, Lillian Tyus, *Permissions Clerks*

Special thanks to Sharon K. Hall for her assistance with the Title Index.

Library of Congress Catalog Card Number 76-46132
ISBN 0-8103-2410-5
ISSN 0276-8178

Computerized photocomposition by
Typographics, Incorporated
Kansas City, Missouri

Printed in the United States of America

# Contents

# Preface

It is impossible to overvalue the importance of literature in the intellectual, emotional, and spiritual evolution of humanity. Literature is that which both lifts us out of everyday life and helps us to better understand it. Through the fictive lives of such characters as Anna Karenina, Jay Gatsby, or Leopold Bloom, our perceptions of the human condition are enlarged, and we are enriched.

Literary criticism can also give us insight into the human condition, as well as into the specific moral and intellectual atmosphere of an era, for the criteria by which a work of art is judged reflect contemporary philosophical and social attitudes. Literary criticism takes many forms: the traditional essay, the book or play review, even the parodic poem. Criticism can also be of several types: normative, descriptive, interpretive, textual, appreciative, generic. Collectively, the range of critical response helps us to understand a work of art, an author, an era.

## Scope of the Series

*Twentieth-Century Literary Criticism (TCLC)* is designed to serve as an introduction for the student of twentieth-century literature to the authors of the period 1900 to 1960 and to the most significant commentators on these authors. The great poets, novelists, short story writers, playwrights, and philosophers of this period are by far the most popular writers for study in high school and college literature courses. Since a vast amount of relevant critical material confronts the student, *TCLC* presents significant passages from the most important published criticism to aid students in the location and selection of commentaries on authors who died between 1900 and 1960.

The need for *TCLC* was suggested by the usefulness of the Gale series *Contemporary Literary Criticism (CLC)*, which excerpts criticism on current writing. Because of the difference in time span under consideration *(CLC* considers authors who were still living after 1959), there is no duplication of material between *CLC* and *TCLC*. For further information about *CLC* and Gale's other criticism series, users should consult the Guide to Gale Literary Criticism Series preceding the title page in this volume.

Each volume of *TCLC* is carefully compiled to include authors who represent a variety of genres and nationalities and who are currently regarded as the most important writers of this era. In addition to major authors, *TCLC* also presents criticism on lesser-known writers whose significant contributions to literary history are important to the study of twentieth-century literature.

Each author entry in *TCLC* is intended to provide an overview of major criticism on an author. Therefore, the editors include fifteen to twenty authors in each 600-page volume (compared with approximately forty authors in a *CLC* volume of similar size) so that more attention may be given to an author. Each author entry represents a historical survey of the critical response to that author's work: some early criticism is presented to indicate initial reactions, later criticism is selected to represent any rise or decline in the author's reputation, and current retrospective analyses provide students with a modern view. The length of an author entry is intended to reflect the amount of critical attention the author has received from critics writing in English, and from foreign criticism in translation. Critical articles and books that have not been translated into English are excluded. Every attempt has been made to identify and include excerpts from the seminal essays on each author's work.

An author may appear more than once in the series because of the great quantity of critical material available, or because of a resurgence of criticism generated by events such as an author's centennial or anniversary celebration, the republication or posthumous publication of an author's works, or the publication of a newly translated work. Generally, a few author entries in each volume of *TCLC* feature criticism on single works by major authors who have appeared previously in the series. Only those individual works that have been the subjects of vast amounts of criticism and are widely studied in literature classes are selected for this in-depth treatment. F. Scott Fitzgerald's *Tender Is the Night* and Leo Tolstoy's *Voina i mir (War and Peace)* are examples of such entries in *TCLC,* Volume 28.

## Organization of the Book

An author entry consists of the following elements: author heading, biographical and critical introduction, list of principal works, excerpts of criticism (each preceded by explanatory notes and followed by a bibliographical citation), and an additional bibliography for further reading.

- The *author heading* consists of the author's full name, followed by birth and death dates. The unbracketed portion of the name denotes the form under which the author most commonly wrote. If an author wrote consistently under a pseudonym, the pseudonym will be listed in the author heading and the real name given in parentheses on the first line of the biographical and critical introduction. Also located at the beginning of the introduction to the author entry are any name variations under which an author wrote, including transliterated forms for authors whose languages use nonroman alphabets. Uncertainty as to a birth or death date is indicated by a question mark.

- The *biographical and critical introduction* contains background information designed to introduce the reader to an author and to the critical debate surrounding his or her work. Parenthetical material following many of the introductions provides references to biographical and critical reference series published by Gale, including *Children's Literature Review, Contemporary Authors, Dictionary of Literary Biography, Something about the Author,* and past volumes of *TCLC.*

- Most *TCLC* entries include *portraits* of the author. Many entries also contain illustrations of materials pertinent to an author's career, including manuscript pages, title pages, dust jackets, letters, or representations of important people, places, and events in an author's life.

- The *list of principal works* is chronological by date of first book publication and identifies the genre of each work. In the case of foreign authors where there are both foreign language publications and English translations, the title and date of the first English-language edition are given in brackets. Unless otherwise indicated, dramas are dated by first performance, not first publication.

- *Criticism* is arranged chronologically in each author entry to provide a perspective on changes in critical evaluation over the years. All titles by the author featured in the critical entry are printed in boldface type to enable the user to ascertain without difficulty the works being discussed. Also for purposes of easier identification, the critic's name and the publication date of the essay are given at the beginning of each piece of criticism. Unsigned criticism is preceded by the title of the journal in which it appeared. When an anonymous essay is later attributed to a critic, the critic's name appears in brackets at the beginning of the excerpt and in the bibliographical citation. Many critical entries in *TCLC* also contain translated material to aid users. Unless otherwise noted, translations within brackets are by the editors; translations within parentheses or continuous with the text are by the author of the excerpt. Publication information (such as publisher names and book prices) and parenthetical numerical references (such as footnotes or page and line references to specific editions of works) have been deleted at the editors' discretion to provide smoother reading of the text.

- Critical essays are prefaced by *explanatory notes* as an additional aid to students using *TCLC.* The explanatory notes provide several types of useful information, including the reputation of a critic, the importance of a work of criticism, the specific type of criticism (biographical, psychoanalytic, structuralist, etc.), a synopsis of the criticism, and the growth of critical controversy or changes in critical trends regarding an author's work. In some cases, these notes cross-reference the work of critics who agree or disagree with each other. Dates in parentheses within the explanatory notes refer to a book publication date when they follow a book title and to an essay date when they follow a critic's name.

- A complete *bibliographical citation* designed to facilitate location of the original essay or book by the interested reader follows each piece of criticism.

- The *additional bibliography* appearing at the end of each author entry suggests further reading on the author. In some cases it includes essays for which the editors could not obtain reprint rights.

An appendix lists the sources from which material in each volume has been reprinted. It does not, however, list every book or periodical consulted in the preparation of the volume.

## Cumulative Indexes

Each volume of *TCLC* includes a cumulative index listing all the authors who have appeared in *Contemporary Literary Criticism, Twentieth-Century Literary Criticism, Nineteenth-Century Literature Criticism, Literature Criticism from 1400 to 1800, Classical and Medieval Literature Criticism,* and *Short Story Criticism,* along with cross-references to the Gale series *Children's Literature Review, Authors in the News, Contemporary Authors, Contemporary Authors Autobiography Series, Dictionary of Literary Biography, Concise Dictionary of American Literary Biography, Something about the Author, Something about the Author Autobiography Series,* and *Yesterday's Authors of Books for Children.* Readers will welcome this cumulated author index as a useful tool for locating an author within the various series. The index, which lists birth and death dates when available, will be particularly valuable for those authors who are identified with a certain period but whose death date causes them to be placed in another, or for those authors whose careers span two periods. For example, F. Scott Fitzgerald is found in *TCLC,* yet a writer often associated with him, Ernest Hemingway, is found in *CLC.*

Each volume of *TCLC* also includes a cumulative nationality index. Author names are arranged alphabetically under their respective nationalities and followed by the volume numbers in which they appear.

## New Index

An important feature now appearing in *TCLC* is a cumulative index to titles, an alphabetical listing of the literary works discussed in the series since its inception. Each title listing includes the corresponding volume and page numbers where criticism may be located. Foreign language titles that have been translated are followed by the titles of the translations—for example, *Voina i mir (War and Peace)*. Page numbers following these translated titles refer to all pages on which any form of the titles, either foreign language or translated, appear. Titles of novels, dramas, nonfiction books, and poetry, short story, or essay collections are printed in italics, while all individual poems, short stories, and essays are printed in roman type within quotation marks. In cases where the same title is used by different authors, the author's surname is given in parentheses after the title, e.g., *Collected Poems* (Housman) and *Collected Poems* (Yeats).

## Acknowledgments

No work of this scope can be accomplished without the cooperation of many people. The editors especially wish to thank the copyright holders of the excerpted criticism included in this volume, the permissions managers of many book and magazine publishing companies for assisting us in securing reprint rights, and Anthony Bogucki for assistance with copyright research. We are also grateful to the staffs of the Detroit Public Library, the Library of Congress, the University of Detroit Library, the University of Michigan Library, and the Wayne State University Library for making their resources available to us.

## Suggestions Are Welcome

In response to various suggestions, several features have been added to *TCLC* since the series began, including explanatory notes to excerpted criticism that provide important information regarding critics and their work, a cumulative author index listing authors in all Gale literary criticism series, entries devoted to criticism on a single work by a major author, more extensive illustrations, and a title index listing all literary works discussed in the series since its inception.

Readers who wish to suggest authors to appear in future volumes, or who have other suggestions, are cordially invited to write the editors.

# Authors to Be Featured in Forthcoming Volumes

*Twentieth-Century Literary Criticism,* Volume 30, will be an Archive volume devoted to various topics in twentieth-century literature, including the Surrealist and Russian Symbolist movements, the journal *Partisan Review,* and the literature of German émigrés fleeing Naziism during the 1930s and 1940s.

Mikhail Artsybashev (Russian novelist)—Artsybashev was notorious for works promoting the principles of anarchic individualism and unrestrained sensuality. His erotic novel *Sanin* produced an international sensation and inspired cults dedicated to the destruction of social convention.

Henri Bergson (French philosopher)—One of the most influential philosophers of the twentieth century, Bergson is renowned for his opposition to the dominant materialist thought of his time and for his creation of theories that emphasize the supremacy and independence of supra-rational consciousness.

Edgar Rice Burroughs (American novelist)—Burroughs was a science fiction writer who is best known as the creator of Tarzan. His *Tarzan of the Apes* and its numerous sequels have sold over thirty-five million copies in fifty-six languages, making Burroughs one of the most popular authors in the world.

Samuel Butler (English novelist and essayist)—Butler is best known for *The Way of All Flesh,* an autobiographical novel that is both a classic account of the conflict between father and son and an indictment of Victorian society.

Joyce Cary (Anglo-Irish novelist)—Regarded as an important contributor to the trilogy as a literary form, Cary wrote trilogies noted for their humor, vitality, sympathetic characterizations, and technical virtuosity.

Willa Cather (American novelist and short story writer) Cather combined knowledge of Nebraska with an artistic expertise reminiscent of the nineteenth-century literary masters to create one of the most distinguished achievements of twentieth-century American literature. She has been compared to Gustave Flaubert and Henry James for her sensibility, emphasis on technique, and high regard for the artist and European culture, and to the "lost generation" of Ernest Hemingway and F. Scott Fitzgerald for her alienation from modern American society.

Anton Chekhov (Russian dramatist and short story writer) Praised for his stylistic innovations in both fiction and drama as well as for his depth of insight into the human condition, Chekhov is the most significant Russian author of the generation to succeed Leo Tolstoy and Fedor Dostoevsky. *TCLC* will devote an entry to Chekhov's plays, focusing on his dramatic masterpieces *The Seagull, Uncle Vanya, Three Sisters,* and *The Cherry Orchard.*

Stephen Crane (American novelist and short story writer) Crane was one of the foremost realistic writers in American literature. *TCLC* will devote an entry to his masterpiece, *The Red Badge of Courage,* in which he depicted the psychological complexities of fear and courage in battle.

Bernard DeVoto (American historian, critic, and novelist)—A prolific writer in several genres, DeVoto is primarily remembered as a historian of the American frontier, an important scholar of Mark Twain, and a pugnacious literary critic.

Theodore Dreiser (American novelist)—A prominent American exponent of literary Naturalism and one of America's foremost novelists, Dreiser was the author of works commended for their powerful characterizations and strong ideological convictions.

Vicente Huidobro (Chilean poet)—Huidobro was among the most influential South American poets of the twentieth century for his formulation of *creacionismo,* a poetic theory that regarded poetry not as an imitation of nature but as an original creation.

William James (American philosopher and psychologist)—One of the most influential figures in modern Western philosophy, James was the founder of Pragmatism, a philosophy that rejected abstract models of reality in an attempt to explain life as it is actually experienced.

Franz Kafka (Austrian novelist and short story writer) Kafka's novel *The Trial* is often considered the definitive expression of his alienated vision as well as one of the seminal works of modern literature. *TCLC* will devote an entire entry to critical discussion of this novel, which has been described by Alvin J. Seltzer as "one of the most unrelenting works of chaos created in the first half of this century."

Nikos Kazantzakis (Greek novelist)—Kazantzakis was a controversial Greek writer whose works embodied Nietzschean and Bergsonian philosophical ideas in vividly portrayed characters, the most famous of which was the protagonist of *Zorba the Greek.*

Dmitri Merezhkovsky (Russian novelist, philosopher, poet, and critic)—Although his poetry and criticism are credited with initiating the Symbolist movement in Russian literature, Merezhkovsky is best known as a religious philosopher who sought in numerous essays and historical novels to reconcile the values of pagan religions with the teachings of Christ.

George Orwell (English novelist and essayist)—Designated the "conscience of his generation" by V. S. Pritchett, Orwell is the author of influential novels and essays embodying his commitment to personal freedom and social justice. *TCLC* will devote an entry to Orwell's first major popular and critical success, *Animal Farm,* a satirical fable in which Orwell attacked the consequences of the Russian Revolution while suggesting reasons for the failure of most revolutionary ideals.

Luigi Pirandello (Italian dramatist)—Considered one of the most important innovators of twentieth-century drama, Pirandello developed experimental techniques including improvisation, the play-within-the-play, and the play-outside-the-play in order to explore such themes as the fluidity of reality, the relativity of truth, and the tenuous line between sanity and madness.

Marcel Proust (French novelist)—Proust's multivolume *À la recherche du temps perdu (Remembrance of Things Past)* is among literature's works of highest genius. Combining a social historian's chronicle of turn-of-the-century Paris society, a philosopher's reflections on the nature of time and consciousness, and a psychologist's insight into a tangled network of personalities, the novel is acclaimed for conveying a profound view of all human existence.

George Saintsbury (English critic)—Saintsbury has been called the most influential English literary historian and critic of the late-nineteenth and early-twentieth centuries.

Ernest Thompson Seton (American naturalist and author) Best known as the founder of the Boy Scouts of America, Seton was the author of twenty-five volumes of animal stories for children as well as books on woodcraft and natural history.

Italo Svevo (Italian novelist)—Svevo's ironic portrayals of the moral life of the bourgeoisie, which characteristically demonstrate the influence of the psychoanalytic theories of Sigmund Freud, earned him a reputation as the father of the modern Italian novel.

Thorstein Veblen (American economist and social critic) Veblen's seminal analyses of the nature, development, and consequences of business and industry—as well as his attack on bourgeois materialism in *The Theory of the Leisure Class*—distinguished him as one of the foremost American economists and social scientists of the twentieth century.

Thomas Wolfe (American novelist)—Wolfe is considered one of the foremost American novelists of the twentieth century. His most important works present intense and lyrical portraits of life in both rural and urban America while portraying the struggle of the lonely, sensitive, and artistic individual to find spiritual fulfillment.

William Butler Yeats (Irish poet, dramatist, and essayist) Yeats is considered one of the greatest poets in the English language. Although his interest in Irish politics and his visionary approach to poetry often confounded his contemporaries and set him at odds with the intellectual trends of his time, Yeats's poetic achievement stands at the center of modern literature.

# Additional Authors to Appear
# in Future Volumes

Abbey, Henry 1842-1911
Abercrombie, Lascelles 1881-1938
Adamic, Louis 1898-1951
Ade, George 1866-1944
Agustini, Delmira 1886-1914
Akers, Elizabeth Chase 1832-1911
Akiko, Yosano 1878-1942
Alas, Leopoldo 1852-1901
Aldrich, Thomas Bailey 1836-1907
Aliyu, Dan Sidi 1902-1920
Allen, Hervey 1889-1949
Archer, William 1856-1924
Arlen, Michael 1895-1956
Arlt, Roberto 1900-1942
Austin, Alfred 1835-1913
Bahr, Hermann 1863-1934
Bailey, Philip James 1816-1902
Barbour, Ralph Henry 1870-1944
Benjamin, Walter 1892-1940
Bennett, James Gordon, Jr. 1841-1918
Berdyaev, Nikolai Aleksandrovich
  1874-1948
Beresford, J(ohn) D(avys) 1873-1947
Binyon, Laurence 1869-1943
Bishop, John Peale 1892-1944
Blake, Lillie Devereux 1835-1913
Blest Gana, Alberto 1830-1920
Blum, Léon 1872-1950
Bodenheim, Maxwell 1892-1954
Bowen, Marjorie 1886-1952
Byrne, Donn 1889-1928
Caine, Hall 1853-1931
Cannan, Gilbert 1884-1955
Carducci, Giosuè 1835-1907
Carswell, Catherine 1879-1946
Churchill, Winston 1871-1947
Conner, Ralph 1860-1937
Corelli, Marie 1855-1924
Croce, Benedetto 1866-1952
Crofts, Freeman Wills 1879-1957
Cruze, James (Jens Cruz Bosen) 1884-
  1942
Curros, Enríquez Manuel 1851-1908
Dall, Caroline Wells (Healy) 1822-1912
Daudet, Léon 1867-1942
Delafield, E.M. (Edme Elizabeth Monica
  de la Pasture) 1890-1943
Deneson, Jacob 1836-1919
Diego, José de 1866-1918
Douglas, (George) Norman 1868-1952
Douglas, Lloyd C(assel) 1877-1951
Dovzhenko, Alexander 1894-1956
Drinkwater, John 1882-1937
Durkheim, Émile 1858-1917
Duun, Olav 1876-1939
Eaton, Walter Prichard 1878-1957

Eggleston, Edward 1837-1902
Erskine, John 1879-1951
Fadeyev, Alexander 1901-1956
Ferland, Albert 1872-1943
Field, Rachel 1894-1924
Flecker, James Elroy 1884-1915
Fletcher, John Gould 1886-1950
Fogazzaro, Antonio 1842-1911
Francos, Karl Emil 1848-1904
Frank, Bruno 1886-1945
Frazer, (Sir) George 1854-1941
Freud, Sigmund 1853-1939
Fröding, Gustaf 1860-1911
Fuller, Henry Blake 1857-1929
Futabatei Shimei 1864-1909
Gamboa, Federico 1864-1939
Glaspell, Susan 1876-1948
Glyn, Elinor 1864-1943
Golding, Louis 1895-1958
Gould, Gerald 1885-1936
Guest, Edgar 1881-1959
Gumilyov, Nikolay 1886-1921
Gyulai, Pal 1826-1909
Hale, Edward Everett 1822-1909
Hansen, Martin 1909-1955
Hernández, Miguel 1910-1942
Hewlett, Maurice 1861-1923
Heyward, DuBose 1885-1940
Hope, Anthony 1863-1933
Hudson, W(illiam) H(enry) 1841-1922
Ilyas, Abu Shabaka 1903-1947
Imbs, Bravig 1904-1946
Ivanov, Vyacheslav Ivanovich 1866-
  1949
James, Will 1892-1942
Jammes, Francis 1868-1938
Johnson, Fenton 1888-1958
Johnston, Mary 1870-1936
Jorgensen, Johannes 1866-1956
King, Grace 1851-1932
Kirby, William 1817-1906
Kline, Otis Albert 1891-1946
Kohut, Adolph 1848-1916
Kuzmin, Mikhail Alexseyevich 1875-
  1936
Lamm, Martin 1880-1950
Leipoldt, C. Louis 1880-1947
Lima, Jorge De 1895-1953
Locke, Alain 1886-1954
López Portillo y Rojas, José 1850-1903
Louys, Pierre 1870-1925
Lucas, E(dward) V(errall) 1868-1938
Lyall, Edna 1857-1903
Machar, Josef Svatopluk 1864-1945
Mander, Jane 1877-1949
Maragall, Joan 1860-1911

Marais, Eugene 1871-1936
Masaryk, Tomas 1850-1939
Mayor, Flora Macdonald 1872-1932
McClellan, George Marion 1860-1934
Mikszáth, Kálmán 1847-1910
Mirbeau, Octave 1850-1917
Mistral, Frédéric 1830-1914
Monro, Harold 1879-1932
Moore, Thomas Sturge 1870-1944
Móricz, Zsigmond 1879-1942
Morley, Christopher 1890-1957
Morley, S. Griswold 1883-1948
Murray, (George) Gilbert 1866-1957
Nansen, Peter 1861-1918
Nobre, Antonio 1867-1900
O'Dowd, Bernard 1866-1959
Ophuls, Max 1902-1957
Orczy, Baroness 1865-1947
Oskison, John M. 1874-1947
Ostaijen, Paul van 1896-1928
Owen, Seaman 1861-1936
Page, Thomas Nelson 1853-1922
Palma, Ricardo 1833-1919
Papadiamantis, Alexandros 1851-1911
Parrington, Vernon L. 1871-1929
Paterson, Andrew Barton 1864-1941
Peck, George W. 1840-1916
Phillips, Ulrich B. 1877-1934
Pinero, Arthur Wing 1855-1934
Pontoppidan, Henrik 1857-1943
Powys, T. F. 1875-1953
Prévost, Marcel 1862-1941
Quiller-Couch, Arthur 1863-1944
Radiguet, Raymond 1903-1923
Rainis, Janis 1865-1929
Ramos, Graciliano 1892-1953
Randall, James G. 1881-1953
Rappoport, Solomon 1863-1944
Read, Opie 1852-1939
Reisen (Reizen), Abraham 1875-1953
Remington, Frederic 1861-1909
Reyes, Alfonso 1889-1959
Riley, James Whitcomb 1849-1916
Rinehart, Mary Roberts 1876-1958
Ring, Max 1817-1901
Rivera, José Eustasio 1889-1928
Rozanov, Vasily Vasilyevich 1856-1919
Saar, Ferdinand von 1833-1906
Sabatini, Rafael 1875-1950
Sakutaro, Hagiwara 1886-1942
Sanborn, Franklin Benjamin 1831-1917
Sánchez, Florencio 1875-1910
Santayana, George 1863-1952
Sardou, Victorien 1831-1908
Schickele, René 1885-1940
Seabrook, William 1886-1945

Shestov, Lev 1866-1938
Shiels, George 1886-1949
Singer, Israel Joshua 1893-1944
Södergran, Edith Irene 1892-1923
Solovyov, Vladimir 1853-1900
Sorel, Georges 1847-1922
Spector, Mordechai 1859-1922
Squire, J(ohn) C(ollings) 1884-1958
Stavenhagen, Fritz 1876-1906
Stockton, Frank R. 1834-1902
Subrahmanya Bharati, C. 1882-1921
Sully-Prudhomme, René 1839-1907
Sylva, Carmen 1843-1916

Talvik, Heiti 1904-1947?
Taneda Santoka 1882-1940
Thoma, Ludwig 1867-1927
Tomlinson, Henry Major 1873-1958
Totovents, Vahan 1889-1937
Tozzi, Federigo 1883-1920
Tuchmann, Jules 1830-1901
Turner, W(alter) J(ames) R(edfern)
    1889-1946
Upward, Allen 1863-1926
Vachell, Horace Annesley 1861-1955
Van Dyke, Henry 1852-1933
Villaespesa, Francisco 1877-1936

Wallace, Edgar 1874-1932
Wallace, Lewis 1827-1905
Walsh, Ernest 1895-1926
Webster, Jean 1876-1916
Whitlock, Brand 1869-1927
Wilson, Harry Leon 1867-1939
Wolf, Emma 1865-1932
Wood, Clement 1888-1950
Wren, P(ercival) C(hristopher) 1885-
    1941
Yonge, Charlotte Mary 1823-1901
Zecca, Ferdinand 1864-1947
Zeromski, Stefan 1864-1925

Readers are cordially invited to suggest additional authors to the editors.

# William Rose Benét

## 1886-1950

American poet, essayist, critic, short story writer, and editor.

Remembered today primarily as the brother of Stephen Vincent Benét and husband of Elinor Wylie, Benét wrote poetry that illuminated his belief in human dignity and celebrated the national spirit he saw illustrated in the lives of common people. Set in traditional metrical lines praised for their technical precision, Benét's poems present ideals and sentiments more common to the nineteenth century than the twentieth. In addition to fervid patriotism, Benét's work typically reveals his deeply humanistic values as well as his profound religious faith.

Benét was born in New York, the son of a career army officer whose appreciation of poetry inspired each of his three children to become poets. During his youth, Benét planned to follow his father into the military and attended Albany Academy. While there, he began to write, discovering, as he later noted, that he had "inherited from his father a love of French verse-forms, and so began—with the aid of *Tom Hood's Rhymester*—fashioning rondeaus, triolets, and ballads, and printing a little of this very bad verse in the school paper." In lieu of further military schooling, Benét attended Yale University, where he studied science, wrote poetry, and became editor of the *Yale Record*. Benét graduated in 1907 and worked for a variety of periodicals, including the *Century,* the *Literary Review,* and the *New York Evening Post.* His first volume of poetry, *Merchants from Cathay,* appeared in 1911. This collection is noted for an abundance of fanciful details, including references to jeweled temples, glittering swords, gallant heroes, and maidens in distress, and the evocative atmosphere of the title poem has been compared to that of Samuel Taylor Coleridge's "Kubla Khan." The poet Vachel Lindsay declared that "Merchants from Cathay" was his favorite American ballad, and he often recited it before large audiences during the early decades of the twentieth century. Like Lindsay, Benét wrote for a popular audience, believing that the poet "should produce all his poems on single broadsheets and go through the city every week tossing them in doors, like circus or furniture-sale announcements."

During the First World War, Benét volunteered for service and was enrolled in flight school; however, he was honorably discharged in 1918 because of poor eyesight. In that same year *The Burglar of the Zodiac, and Other Tales* appeared, a poetry collection in which Benét confronted more modern subjects than in his earlier poems. While his poems now treated such topics as films, quick-lunch counters, and skyscrapers, he retained his traditional verse forms, explaining that his intention was "to put the splendors of ancientry into the grim of modernity." He also employed classical allusions in poems based on characters in American folklore; for instance, in his most often reprinted poem, "The Horse Thief," a figure from Greek mythology appears in what is essentially a wild-west cowboy yarn. During the 1920s, Benét took on the role of mentor to several poets, including his brother, Stephen Vincent Benét, and a friend's sister, Elinor Wylie. He married Wylie in 1923, the year during which her success in New York's literary and social circles reached its height. Edmund Wilson noted at the time: "When I expressed my doubts about their union, she

[Wylie] said with her harsh and callous laugh: 'Yes, it would be a pity that a first-rate poet should be turned into a second-rate poet by marrying a third-rate poet'." Benét and Wylie lived apart for most of their married life.

After the war, Benét helped to establish the *Saturday Review of Literature,* where he worked as an associate editor for the rest of his life. The poetry he produced during the 1930s earned him a reputation as a poet of mixed talent; as Louis Untermeyer has written: "His poetry was the man: generous, sometimes too lavish, overflowing with forthrightness and brotherly good will." Benét's poetry has frequently been criticized for its sentimentality and melodrama, most notably in Harriet Monroe's 1932 review of the verse novel *Rip Tide,* which derided Benét's portrayal of the deaths of two star-crossed lovers. Nonetheless, his work continued to earn respect, and in 1942 he received the Pulitzer Prize for *The Dust Which Is God,* a collection of autobiographical poems with an optimistic and patriotic emphasis. In "Men on Strike," for instance, he praises America in such exclamatory lines as: "The Country of the Free! Yes, a great land." Benét later wrote patriotic poems attacking Hitler which were distributed by the Office of War Information. He died in 1950 at the age of sixty-four.

Throughout his poetry, Benét often synthesized opposites such as the elevated and the ordinary, the sacred and the sensual, and the lyrical and the prosaic. Joining classical allusions and folk types, he attached legendary significance to daily experience. In "Jesse James," for instance, Benét presents a Missouri outlaw in a mythical aspect, writing: "Jesse James was a Hercules / When he went through the woods he tore up the trees." Although Benét's poems are usually considered didactic, uneven, and derivative, critics have commended his poetry for its technical precision and versatility as well as its lyrical qualities.

(See also *Contemporary Authors*, Vol. 118; *Dictionary of Literary Biography*, Vol. 45: *American Poets, 1880-1945*.)

## PRINCIPAL WORKS

*Merchants from Cathay*   (poetry)   1913
*The Falconer of God, and Other Poems*   (poetry)   1914
*The Great White Wall*   (poetry)   1916
*The Burglar of the Zodiac, and Other Poems*   (poetry) 1918
*Perpetual Light*   (poetry)   1919
*Moons of Grandeur*   (poetry)   1920
*The First Person Singular*   (novel)   1922
*Man Possessed*   (poetry)   1927
*Wild Goslings*   (essays, short stories, and poetry)   1927
*Rip Tide*   (poetry)   1932
*Starry Harness*   (poetry)   1933
*Golden Fleece*   (poetry)   1935
*The Dust Which Is God*   (poetry)   1941
*Day of Deliverance*   (poetry)   1944
*The Stairway of Surprise*   (poetry)   1947

---

**JOYCE KILMER**   (essay date 1913)

[*An American poet and critic, Kilmer is best known for his popular sentimental poem "Trees." In the following review of* Merchants from Cathay, *he praises Benét's adherence to traditional poetic forms.*]

Mr. Benét's book of poems [*Merchants from Cathay*] takes its title from a gay ballad that gave pleasure to many when it appeared several months ago in a leading magazine; a tale of two strange merchants who rode into town on paunchy beasts with golden hooves. They bought sacks of magic merchandise, and they sang a carol in praise of the Grand Chan, "the King of all the Kings across the sea."

Nevertheless, this reviewer will resist the temptation to call Mr. Benét himself a merchant from Cathay. It is true that he brings some strange exotic wares, songs and stories from other lands and other times. But he is not (as many young poets are) wilfully a foreigner. He does not rebel against the noble old traditions of English poetry.

Of late years there has been noticeable among the younger poets a tendency to break deliberately the established rules of rhyme and rhythm and to write the sort of verse which is called "free." Partly this comes from a morbid craving after novelty, partly from laziness. It is good to find that Mr. Benét takes seriously the techniques of his art. There are in the volume now under consideration a number of poems—particularly **"The Halcyon Birds"** and **"The Violin's Enchantress"**—that are remarkable when looked at merely as examples of virtuosity. Not only does Mr. Benét show an enviable sense of verbal

music, he also has an accurate perception of the connection between rhythm and thought, he uses the form conscientiously, but he selects the form with due regard to the idea to be expressed.

So much for his mastery over his tools. He has, it has been stated, that knowledge of the use of words which the public legitimately demands of every maker of verses. Now must be examined that even more important thing, the idea, which is the poem's essential justification. And (contrary to the platitude of the amateur) sincerity is not the quality by virtue of which a poem stands or falls. The idea must first of all be interesting. It may also be sincere, elevating, original. But it must interest the reader before it can display to him its other virtues. Sincerity undecorated and obtrusive makes the work and conversation of many young poets things diligently to be avoided. Well, he must be blasé indeed whom all of these poems fail to interest. For the romanticist here are such strange tales as **"The Bird Fancier"** and **"The Halcyon Birds,"** and ringing tributes to such illustrious vagabonds as Baron Munchausen and Sir John Mandeville. Those (not all of them are gone) who know the difference between Helle and Hades will enjoy such beautiful echoes of the classics as **"The Centaur's Farewell," "The Winning of Pomona,"** and—best of all—**"The Argo's Chanty."**

> Orpheus hath harped her,
> Her prow hath drunk the sea.
> Fifty haughty heroes at her golden rowlocks be!
>    His fingers sweep the singing strings,
>    Her forefoot white before she flings,
>    Out from the shore she strains—she swings—
> And lifts, oh, gallantly!

Mr. Benét has written few "nature poems," but a keen and sympathetic observation of trees, flowers and clouds is manifest throughout his work. There are, of course, many love poems (the beautiful dedication is perhaps the best) and they are poems of real love, not sordid, not feverish, but strongly, whitely passionate. Mr. Benét is not interested in sphinxes, "love" does not invariably suggest "pain" to him, nor does he even once use the dear old rhyme of "lust" and "dust."

Some—but not all—of the poems that are ethical or philosophical in theme, deserve high praise. To take an exception first, **"Remarks to the Back of a Pew,"** is a composition which Mr. Benét probably wrote when he was undergoing some punishment for "cutting" chapel in his freshman days. All of us know that on a hot Sunday morning it is pleasanter to sit under a tree and smoke a pipe than to listen to a long sermon in a poorly ventilated church. Some 8,000 people have put this idea into verse—calling the results "The Cathedral of the Trees" "Nature's Church" or something of the sort, and most of them have done it better than Mr. Benét. Undoubtedly, the back of his pew was very much bored. **"Ritual"** is less trite, but it is evidently the work of one who, for the moment, tries to fix his own limitations on all mankind, who decries what—as yet—he fails to understand. But he will understand.

Having thus patronizingly insulted Mr. Benét, the reviewer desires to call particular attention to three poems, to which, in the course of years, there will come, he thinks, no little fame. These are **"The Anvil of Souls," "Sincerities,"** and **"Umbrae Puellularum."** The poem first named is the splendid expression of a tremendous thought; critics courageous enough to use the term will call this poem "great." The second (refreshing after **"Ritual"**) is full of that abasement before God's works which marks the true poet. The third is an exquisite memorial to the little maids of history and romance, a poem that for its sheer loveliness deserves immortality.

These three poems are things for which to be grateful. For the whole book we may well be grateful; it is a book of real poetry, musical, imaginative, vigorous. There are echoes of other poets— Francis Thompson, Alfred Nowes, Robert Browning, and (possibly) E. A. Robinson; but there is no slavish imitation; there is sure evidence of originality. Mr. Benét's second book will be better, but *Merchants from Cathay* is good enough to make all friends of American poetry glad.

> Joyce Kilmer, "'From Cathay': Mr. Benét's Songs and Stories from Other Lands," in The New York Times Book Review, *November 30, 1913, p. 683.*

**WILLIAM MORTON PAYNE**   (essay date 1914)

[*The longtime literary editor for several Chicago publications, Payne reviewed books for twenty-three years at the* Dial, *one of America's most influential journals of literature and opinion in the early twentieth century. In the following excerpt, he offers an unfavorable review of* Merchants from Cathay, *finding a lack of restraint in Benét's poetry.*]

> I would not be a dogmatist,
> Banging a heavy, hairy fist
> To crack the pint-pots on the table.
> But I would dream as I am able
> And noose God's wonders in a twist
> Of quaintest thoughts and rippled rhyme;
> By happy turns of fortunate phrase
> Would capture Faith, and teach stern Time
>       To mend his ways.

Thus discourses Mr. William Rose Benét, in **"Merchants from Cathay."** He is certainly a master of "quaintest thought and rippled rhyme," although the "happy turns of fortunate phrase" seem to elude him. Gifted with an opulent imagination, and bearing a staggering load of the stuff of poetry on his shoulders, he makes us a little too conscious of the burden, and does not quite succeed in so ordering his expression as to escape turgidity. Now and then he achieves restraint and clean-cut form, as in the sonnet on **"The Guests of Phineus"**:

> Man hungers long. Into his cup is poured
> Wine of pearled brilliance or of flaming dyes
> From gold and silvern ewers of the skies—
> The sun and moon. And on his banquet-board
> Rich lands of romance, glamorous seas, afford
> His vision viands. Yet with upturned eyes
> Like to poor Phineus, he still descries
> The shadows overhead, the birds abhorred.
>
> Ye dark enigmas of this universe,
> Cloud not my feast! God, give me thoughts to face
> And rend despair, as did the wingèd twain
> Who soared above the baffled guests of Thrace
> And hurled the harpies of Jove's ancient curse
> To whirlwind ruin o'er the Ionian main!

Mr. Benét is fond of classical themes, but he usually handles them in the wildest romantic manner. The realms of phantasy are his province, and he delights in the imaginings of Baron Munchausen and Sir John Mandeville. It is not every poet who would be daring enough to write a chanty in Kiplingese for the Argonauts to sing as they plied the oar:

> Lemnos lies behind us
>    And ladies of good grace,
> Home, bring home the oars again and lift the coasts of Thrace!

> Nor yet the Clashing Islands find,
> Nor stark Promethean highlands find,
> But here, of far or nigh lands, find
>    Adventure's very place—
>    Adventure's splendid, terrible, and dear and dafting face!
>
> Then, Orpheus, strike harp for us!
> Oh, Talking Head, speak true for us!
> Lynceus, look you sharp for us!
> And, Tiphys, steer her through for us!
> May Colchis curse the dawn o'day when first she thundered
>       free
> And our golden captain, Jason, in glory put to sea.

Ragged and swinging measures are Mr. Benét's favorites, and they force his volume into a special *format* for their accommodation. But even the widened page is not wide enough, and a small type has to be used which is a serious obstacle to pleasurable reading. . . . Many of Mr. Benét's poems are marred by infelicitous words and halting rhythms, but sometimes he achieves something approaching perfection of form. There is probably no finer poem in the volume than **"The Rival Celestial"**:

> God, wilt Thou never leave my love alone?
>    Thou comest when she first draws breath in sleep,
>       Thy cloak blue night, glittering with stars of gold.
> Thou standest in her doorway to intone
>    The promise of Thy troth that she must keep,
>       The wonders of Thy heaven she shall behold.
>
> Her little room is filled with blinding light,
>    And past the darkness of her window-pane
>       The faces of glad angels closely press,
> Gesturing for her to join their host this night,
>    Mount with their cavalcade for Thy domain!
>       Then darkness. . . . But Thy work is done no less.

(pp. 67-8)

> William Morton Payne, in a review of "Merchants from Cathay," in The Dial, *Vol. LVI, No. 662, January 16, 1914, pp. 67-8.*

*POETRY*   (essay date 1917)

[*In the following review of* The Great White Wall, *the critic praises Benét's poems for their metrical variety.*]

The heroic narrative in verse, in which anthropomorphic gods and brawny heroes stride through countless cantos of hexameter, is necessarily out of vogue in these days of staccato short-stories in *vers libre* and pithy etchings that reduce a life to an epigram. Yet there is something in us that goes behind the vogue, that escapes now and again from the stern censorship of our intellect and revels with a childlike glee in fierce bearded heroes with glittering swords, in lovely maidens in distress, in the color and gleam and swing of a crisp narrative in decorative verse. And as for the *Arabian Nights*, in whatever form we find them, it will be a mercifully long day before we lose our delight in them.

All these elements William Rose Benét has gathered together into a really enchanting tale in his latest book, *The Great White Wall*. He has called for his enchantment on all the ancient sources, on Kublai Khan, on ancient Cathay, on Persia and India and Arabia; but the enchantment remains authentic, and Mr. Benét is at his happiest in evoking it. The lines are everywhere agleam with color, as in these, from the description of the army of Timur the Terrible on the march:

Pheasant feather and peacock plume from many a marching
  headdress glitters.
Bows on backs, a crowd of archers bronzely swings along as
  one.
Herds of antelope, goat, and nihlgao straggle along the armies'
  fringes.
Mimics, sorcerers, and buffoons in parti-colored costumes
  pass.
Dancing girls with golden anklets trip in the desert dust that
  singes.
High upheld above their bearers, banners stream from poles of
  brass.
Over all the embroidered arms of Samarcand, the City
  Splendid:
Lion and Sun and Three Great Circles, threefold realms that
  signify,
Blaze on a banner of gold brocade. And, densely by his troops
  attended,
Odmar, leading the Avant-guard, to a blare of terrible horns
  goes by.

Mr. Benét has avoided with real craftsmanship that pitfall of
the narrative poem, a too regular rhythm. The framework of
heroic measure is here, but so well does he halt and vary it
that nowhere, even to the ear of the sophisticated, is the sense
rocked to sleep in the cradle of the metre; and the ambitions
and the love of Timur stand out almost as starkly as from prose.
In the end too, while not losing the elaborate brightness of the
key, he lends a note of human truth to the tale by having
Timur's spiritual defeat come at the moment of his greatest
physical triumph.

There is a distinct place in American poetry for Mr. Benét's
jewelled stories, and it is to be hoped that he will give us more
of them. (pp. 322-24)

> E. T., *"Cathay Again,"* in Poetry, *Vol. IX, No. 6,
> March, 1917, pp. 322-24.*

### HARRIET MONROE (essay date 1922)

[*As the founder and editor of* Poetry, *Monroe was a key figure
in the American "poetry renaissance" that took place in the early
twentieth century.* Poetry *was the first periodical devoted primarily to the work of new poets and to poetry criticism, and from
1912 until her death, Monroe maintained an editorial policy of
printing "the best English verse which is being written today,
regardless of where, by whom, or under what theory of art it is
written." In the following review of Benét's verse novel* Rip Tide,
*Monroe criticizes Benét for reducing a tragic story to melodrama.*]

In spite of certain lapses, Mr. Benét has made a poem of his
novel [*Rip Tide*]. It is true, as the jacket says the author believes, that "a story may be told in verse with a condensation
and intensification not possible to prose . . . and that it can be
just as natural." But it is also true that the telling in verse
makes a more severe demand upon the writer, not only in the
obvious details of fitting a story to verse technique, but in
lifting and holding the story to the higher levels of the poetic
imagination. Nothing is so prosy as a verse-tale which does
not reach and keep these levels; no one is so mistaken as the
poet who thinks that mere rhyme and metrics will carry him
to these upper ranges and sustain him there.

On the whole Mr. Benét moves securely on his poetic plateau—
not the lofty epic heights, but a mountain meadow where there
are grasses and flowers and views of the sea and icy, steep
declivities. His progress is interrupted now and then by lines,
or even passages, of prose, usually in the dialogue sections;
the most flagrant example being two or three pages of talk

*Stephen Vincent and William Rose Benét on the Yale campus
in 1915.*

between the young Barry and his chum, where the loosely
woven pentameter rhymes make a clever pattern but sadly
stiffen the friendly jargon of youth. Or we may find stylistic
offences like this:

> She wondered now as she had wondered then,
> Grasped by a will to which her will was water,
> Why all young love had meant had not prevailed
> Despite one careless boy who ceased to write.

The poet is happier in descriptive passages, whether of nature
or human character. Here, from the first section of the poem,
is a stanza showing forth the heroine's tragically ineffectual
husband, him of the "burning eyes," the "hawklike face,"
the "ever-restless hands"—an eight-line stanza, rhyming 1-5,
2-6, etc.:

> So he, who lived by fire, famished by fire,
> Changelessly unconsumed and burning ever,
> His passion always razing what he reared,
> His heart a hound hunting to kill his peace
> Though ever tracking beauty with desire,
> Gazed at the wasting prey of one endeavor
> And felt her tugging heart that leapt and veered
> Beneath his hand and quivered for release.

The poet changes his measures and stanza-forms adroitly, slipping in grace notes of extra short syllables to quicken the pace
of the pentameter lines—

> Something fortuitous willed it should find her alone—

Or cutting down to three's and two's:

> Heart lead-encased—
> O difficult breath!—
> Taste as of death
> In the writhing mouth—

and returning to the slower iambics for the final tragedy, ending finally to the sound of the ocean, with which the poem began, when the actors in it

> Heard in their ears, all night, like the drums of fate,
> The far-off surf, the wind that would not abate,
> The roar of the sea, the heavy roll of the tide,
> And thought their ears would hold that sound forever.

The climax of the poem—the discovery to each other of father and son—is skilfully stripped bare of any unnecessary trope or word. It is done with complete competence, with appreciation of dramatic values, with every excellence except the last magic of great poetry.

In his treatment of the theme it would seem that Mr. Benét fumbled his chance at some kind of a really modern development. He surrendered to a romantic temptation to let the tempestuous surf kill off his young hero and thereby save everybody trouble. But this was begging the question, for the situation invited trouble. The poet leads up simply and dramatically to his climax: the house party of young people, with the head of the house, Gordon Powell, away at first, and his daughter falling in love with a tall young guest and getting engaged; Gordon's return and gradual realization that his daughter's suitor is his own son by a secret, brief liaison with a young matron who had died soon after; the young man asking the older one for his daughter's hand, and Gordon answering that the marriage can never take place and bluntly telling the shocked young suitor why.

One is tempted to follow in imagination a number of leads to possible endings. Suppose the poet had made Gordon hold his peace, and suffer horribly as the lovers rushed ignorantly into an incestuous marriage—that might have been an almost Freudian study of a strong man writhing into suicide or insanity, or of a weak one slithering into abysses of despairing secrecy or ultimate revelation; all this involving a presentation of human agony worthy of Jeffers himself. Or the young lover, under the shock of Gordon's terrible revelation, might have killed himself; or he might have told the girl, and made it, sooner or later, a double suicide; or he might have run away and left the girl to shoulder the agony. By any one of a number of endings the poet would have faced the issue raised by his plot, and followed it consistently to a credible modern finale. But an incurable romanticism got in his way; he must needs call in a tempest to kill off his hero, and not only that, but the hero must die a hero's death, must be dashed on the rocks in saving his sweetheart from the undertow.

The result of this concession to romance is a softening of fibre and a relaxing of the reader's interest. Somehow Gordon becomes commonplace when he so bluntly blurts out the terrible truth to the son he had never known, and one does not quite believe in nature's benevolent intercession—the storm and the violent death of the young lover seem manufactured, and thereby the story is lowered from the level of tragedy to that of melodrama.

It is the same poet who wrote **"Merchants from Cathay,"** **"The Horse Thief,"** and other fabulous ballads, only in these poems his romantic imagination moved more freely in its own element, was more at home than in this recent effort to invoke the fates and furies of tragedy.

*Harriet Monroe, "Mr. Benét's Verse Tale," in* The Saturday Review of Literature, *Vol. IX, No. 15, October 29, 1922, p. 203.*

## LOUIS UNTERMEYER (essay date 1923)

[*A poet during his early career, Untermeyer is better known as an anthologist of poetry and short fiction, an editor, and a master parodist. Horace Gregory and Marya Zaturenska have noted that Untermeyer was "the first to recognize the importance of the anthology in voicing a critical survey of his chosen field." Notable among his anthologies are* Modern American Poetry *(1919),* The Book of Living Verse *(1931),* New Modern American and British Poetry *(1950), and* A Treasury of Laughter *(1946). In the following excerpt from* American Poetry Since 1900, *Untermeyer surveys Benét's poetry collections, emphasizing the lyrical quality of his work.*]

The outstanding feature of William Rose Benét's poetry is the fact that his lyrics have an unusually narrative quality and his ballads are intensely lyrical. Less apparent but equally characteristic is his mingling of realism and symbolism; he delights in interpreting the elemental through the incidental. A mystic with his feet firmly fixed in to-day. This is established even in his first volume, *Merchants from Cathay* where Benét has already found his own manner. But his is no thin and sugary mysticism, no Maeterlinckéd sweetness long drawn out; it has a hearty and almost muscular power. The best examples of this mood are **"The Anvil of Souls,"** with its robust swing, **"Invulnerable"** and **"The Wrestlers."** But it reaches its highest pitch in the thumping rhythms of the ballads where Benét is at his best. The title-poem is the epitome of this rollicking gayety. It opens in a crisp tempo:

> Their heels slapped their bumping mules; their fat chaps glowed.
>   Glory unto Mary, each seemed to wear a crown!
> Like sunset their robes were on the wide, white road:
>   So we saw those mad merchants come dusting into town.
>
> Two paunchy beasts they rode on and two they drove before,
>   May the Saints all help us, the tiger stripes they had!
> And the panniers upon them swelled full of stuffs and ore!
>   The square buzzed and jostled at a sight so mad.
>
> They bawled in their beards, and their turbans they wried.
>   They stopped by the stalls with curvetting and clatter.
> As bronze as the bracken their necks and faces dyed—
>   And a stave they sat singing, to tell us of the matter.
>
> *"For your silks to Sugarmago! For your dyes to Isfahan!*
>   *Weird fruits from the Isle o' Lamaree!*
>     *But for magic merchandise,*
>     *For treasure trove and spice,*
> *Here's a catch and a carol to the great, grand Chan,*
>   *The King of all the Kings across the sea!"*

Snatches like these shout from Benét's pages; they have the tone of Lewis Carroll's buoyant nonsense reset by Vachel Lindsay. Turn to a still earlier poem. Nine poets out of ten would have made **"The Argo's Chanty"** a wearisome list of forgotten incidents and half-remembered names. Given such a theme, they would have filled the lines with outworn classic phrases, routine images, Bulfinch's Mythology and dullness *ad lib*. Benét does nothing of the sort. He does not hesitate to use Greek names with the rest of them, but in his sharp measures they do not remain names; they take on ruddy flesh, they glow once more with the thrill of their shining adventure.

This vigor of utterance permeates most of Benét's work; it spurs his pen even when he is not engaged in the making of ballads. It surges beneath such quieter poems as **"Paternity,"** the ironical and intricately rhymed **"Remarks to the Back of a Pew"**; the freshness of **"His Ally,"** the tender strength of **"Charms"** and the fantastic **"Morgiana Dances,"** in which swift movement is cleverly achieved. It makes us condone the instances where his borrowing is unabashed. His love for Keats and Browning is so intense that occasionally he cannot refrain from imitating them—even when he is conscious of it.

In *The Falconer of God* the athletic mysticism grows. And with it grows a more fantastic sense of color and image. Benét has the gift of evoking a strange and spicy music from a combination of seemingly casual words. Interesting as was his earlier work, there was, beneath the bluster and airiness, something overstudious; hovering above the fresh aroma of his poems one caught, not infrequently, a whiff of midnight oil, slightly rancid. Here, even the more scholastic attempts show a sharpened participation, a livelier increase of life. Take, for example, the title-poem of the new book. This has all of Benét's early glamour lifted to a plane of symbolism where it is sustained without ever being forced. These are the first two verses:

I flung my soul to the air like a falcon flying,
I said, "Wait on, wait on, while I ride below!
    I shall start a heron soon
    In the marsh beneath the moon—
A strange white heron rising with silver on its wings,
        Rising and crying
        Wordless, wondrous things;
The secret of the stars, of the world's heart-strings
        The answer to their woe.
Then stoop thou upon him, and grip and hold him so!"

My wild soul waited on as falcons hover.
I beat the reedy fens as I tramped past.
    I heard the mournful loon
    In the marsh beneath the moon.
And then, with feathery thunder, the bird of my desire
        Broke from the cover
        Flashing silver fire.
High up among the stars I saw his pinions spire;
        The pale clouds gazed aghast
As my falcon stoopt upon him, and gript and held him fast.

As more pointed instances of this broadening of perceptions there are the whimsical anger of **"People,"** the macabre music of **"The Cats of Cobblestone Street,"** and the revealing freshness that animates the rather ponderous learning in **"The Schoolroom of Poets,"** where we see the great singers, not as laurel-crowned bards, but as boys in class—pinched little Chatterton oblivious of the rest, Francis Thompson mumbling scraps of Latin, Keats deep in the charms of Marmontel's *Peru*.

Some of the poems in this volume, some of the best poems, in fact, show an unfortunate tendency of Benét's—a tendency to be discursive and run on past the limitations of his themes. **"The Land of the Giants"** is a case in point. It is the sort of ballad that this poet writes so well, a blend of light whimsy and loud protest. G. K. Chesterton, in one of his "tremendous trifles," suggested that, since there are chanties for sailors, we ought to have a set of songs for shopmen, printers and bankers' clerks. In **"The Land of the Giants,"** Benét has done an even more fascinating thing—he has written a marching song for reformers. But this ballad of Jack, the modern iconoclast, defying the ogres of tradition, would have been twice as appealing had it been half as long. Benét excels in the shorter poems where he can curb the prancing imagination that so often runs away with him; it is in the sonnet, where he is compelled to keep his restless steed curvetting inside the palings of fourteen lines, that he is most effective. Here his figures gain in definition and sharpness. In **"The Pearl Diver"** he speaks of

            . . . the bright, bare Day
Like a tall diver poised above the surge
Of ebony night,

that plunged through a spray of stars to pluck a filmy pearl

        And held it high for earth and heaven to mark:—
        The cold globe of the winter-shrunken sun.

Benét's next volume is composed of one long poem interspersed with lyric interludes. *The Great White Wall* differs somewhat in kind but not in color from his previous volumes. Here is the same extraordinary sense of whimsy, a wayward fancy and a deft juggling with the grotesque. None of his compatriots, with the exception of Amy Lowell, Vachel Lindsay and his own younger brother, has his *flair* for the decorative that verges on the diabolic. In the present work, he has lightly turned back a few centuries and lets us revel in the savage glitter of ancient China. True, there are times when, like Swinburne, Benét pulls his reader under as he sinks in a welter of flowing words and inundating figures; but he is a good swimmer, even in the roughest verbal seas. One pictures him, having just plunged through an especially threatening passage; his feet firm but swaying a trifle on the shore; his head thrown back victoriously, still dripping phrases like:

He razed the ramparts of Systan and smote the lords of
    Badukshan,
Whose chepaval and shekaval, wild squadrons, he outrode.
Polonians, barbarians, Udecelains, Hungarians
He gripped and threw, and on to new and vaster triumphs
    strode.

The poet is seldom as rumbling as this. Often he achieves, in the midst of such merely mouth-filling rhymes, a piercing lyrical note. His vivacity and his invention rarely flag; the end where terrible Timur sees his great defeat in the hour of his greatest triumph is a skilful, dramatic climax.

In *The Burglar of the Zodiac* the poet begins to let his fantastic Pegasus run away and frequently unseat him. He seems either afraid or incapable of using the bit. The result is that often what started out as a canter among the stars ends in a scraping of shins on the pebbly earth. One watches this in such poems as the over-long allegory, **"The Seventh Pawn," "The Quick-Lunch Counter"** and **"The Blackamoor's Pantomime."** There are many times when the rhythms are badly cramped and the rhymes seem twisted out of joint.

But all the poet's earlier gifts are combined with new energy in the madcap title-poem, in **"Films"** (particularly the first and third reels), in the amusing **"How to Catch Unicorns"** and **"The Horse Thief."** This last is a prodigal and lively extravaganza. A desperate cowboy, crouching with coiled lariat in the mesquite, sees a snow-white horse, whose mane is mixed with moonlight and silver. He lassos the bright mustang: the rope breaks; he manages to swing up and hold to its glittering mane. Then, as the horse springs from the earth, he hears "a monstrous booming like a thunder of flapping sails," the mustang spreads wings—and he realizes he has caught Pegasus! . . . But the first poem is also the best example of what Benét can rise to. Here is possibly less of the impudent, soaring vivacity, but more of a homelier vision. **"The Singing Skyscrapers"** has the rich combination of daring and nobility toward which Benét's work seems to aim. In the voices of the titanic buildings calling each other across the night, we hear a new sort of mysticism—one that, with its mixture of splendor and stridency, is wholly American. It is impossible to imagine such a conception coming from a graduate of Oxford. The fancy itself is inconceivable except from one to whom skyscrapers are as native as quick-lunch counters, crap-games, doubleheaders and Douglas Fairbanks—all of which make up the chief part of this volume. Here is a fragment from the initial poem:

> *And from far to the South*
> *I heard the Woolworth Tower*
> *Reply from the sky:*
>
> "Aye, cities of power,
> Each a granite flower
> Stamened to unfold
> With towers of ivory,
> Towers of gold,
> Towers of brass
> And towers of iron;
> Towers as many as the hours that environ
> The years of our servitude,
> Our steel and iron yoke.
> In the deep blue skies
> They stand like smoke!"

*Perpetual Light* is a memorial to the poet's dead wife, a series of love poems which, in their very reverence, bar criticism. The first fourteen may be found in Benét's earlier volumes, but there are more than thirty new and lonely tributes. The dedication is especially moving; so is the concluding "**Sealed,**" the sequence "**After**" and the verses which begin:

> By her beauty stayed, by her love empowered,
>     (*Coward! Coward!*)
>   Take the honest light and pray for grace.
> Where her lightning struck, where her presence flowered,
>     (*Coward! Coward!*)
>   Dare to see her face.

These are low melodies played on muted strings. And if some of the strains are over-delicate, they are no less emotional. "Delicacy," says Santayana, "is a finer means of being passionate."

*Moons of Grandeur* contains a little of Benét's worst and much of his best. His worst is to be found in the excessively long monologues which, for all his exactitude of detail and precision of style, Benét fails to infuse with life. The Egyptian and Italian poems are well documented, shaped with an artisan's skill, but none of the characters seems to have the gift of concision and all of them talk in the same lengthy, lifeless monotone. (pp. 235-42)

> *Louis Untermeyer, "The Lyricists—2: William Rose Benét," in his* American Poetry Since 1900, *Henry Holt and Company, 1923, pp. 234-42.*

## LOUIS KRONENBERGER   (essay date 1927)

[*A drama critic for* Time *from 1938 to 1961, Kronenberger was a distinguished historian, literary critic, and author highly regarded for his expertise in eighteenth-century English history and literature. Among his best known critical writings are* The Thread of Laughter: Chapters on English Stage Comedy from Jonson to Maugham *(1952) and* The Republic of Letters *(1955), which contain some of his best literary commentaries. In an assessment of Kronenberger's critical ability, Jacob Korg states: "He interprets, compares, and analyzes vigorously in a pleasingly epigrammatic style, often going to the essence of a matter in a phrase." In the following excerpt, Kronenberger reviews* Wild Goslings, *a collection of Benét's essays, short stories, and poetry.*]

Mr. Benét, who is well known as a poet and well known as a critic and well known as a columnist, has just published in *Wild Goslings* a collection of papers which his publishers call light essays. Mr. Benét, to date, has not been known as a light essayist, and I do not think that *Wild Goslings* should make him so. In form most of these papers are essays, but in spirit they are columns. Most of them originated as columns, most of them still remain the work of a journalist "who writes with taste, but also haste."

Mr. Benét has seized on that timeliness which is the salt of the columnist to give tang to much of his wit and satire. As the columnist on a literary review, he has chiefly literary interest, and these papers have not much range. They are about writing, and writers, and books, and New York, and the sad literary quackery of our time. Mr. Benét takes the correspondence school method of authorship, or he takes the banality of the movie scenario, or he takes the faces advertised in magazines as those of men who succeeded because they took institute lessons or read scrapbooks, and he proceeds to burlesque them. If he is not very subtle, he is often amusing. He reads of the misguided tyro being taught how to secure "emphasis by surprise" and takes the hint to surprise by emphasis:

> Jessica Trent's husband sat down at his pallid face
> and began mechanically to rub his eighteenth birthday
> with Mennen's Shaving Cream.

He takes his poke, no less, at those who misguide themselves. "**Bookman's Diary**" is an amusing record of a writer who intended spending his vacation hard at work, and day after day, for the worst of reasons, put it off until his vacation was over and nothing accomplished. Mr. Benét has a paper on "**The Ten Worst Books**" which doesn't quite come off, and another on "**A Magazine of the '60s**" which tells its own tale, and suggests that some of the writers in the '60s really had something to gain from a correspondence course. "**Five Years of It**" is a confession which all who earn their living by reading books, and long before the lost days when they could read them for pleasure, will agree with. There are many more column pieces on this order.

Mr. Benét has also, at the end of the book, six exhibits of short-story writing—broad burlesques on the short story of mystery, love, war, sport, big business and literature. These, like many other satirical pieces in the book, seem to offer greater possibilities than Mr. Benét makes use of. He has more gusto and sense of fun in him than actual wit and cleverness. He is more appreciative than inventive, a better detector of absurdity in others than creator of absurdity himself. One thing which works against him, of course, is the fact that much of what he laughed at in his column when it was new has become hackneyed in the meantime. Its timeliness is past and it dates. We are almost ready today to befriend the correspondence school methods of writing against further onslaught, and it is difficult to remember that Mr. Benét's onslaughts, and they are numerous, were among the first.

The best things in his book are Mr. Benét's articles of fact and his poetry. It is very interesting to read "**Our Shameless Past**" and consider the six best sellers of 1897—Sienkiewicz's *Quo Vadis,* James Lane Allen's *The Choir Invisible,* Richard Harding Davis's *Soldiers of Fortune,* Barrie's *Sentimental Tommy,* Mrs. Steel's *On the Face of the Waters,* and Ian Maclaren's *Kate Carnegie.* Mr. Benét has a very attractive way of dealing with a subject like this, and it seems superior to his prose fantasies and his more ambitious burlesques. His humorous poems are good also—frequently the level of humor is not so very high, but the versification is remarkably ingenious and complex.

It is impossible to concede that *Wild Goslings* is a book of light essays. Its history belies the term; so do its contents. It is a product of that precarious journalism which races frantically against time, and of that weekly institution, the column, which permits repetition of theme and slight variation of theme. In book form, it is harder to get away with haste and repetitiousness, and it is all but impossible for informal literary satire of the hour to comport itself as a light essay. (pp. 2, 5)

Louis Kronenberger, "Two Adepts in the Art of Airy Persiflage," in The New York Times Book Review, February 27, 1927, pp. 2, 5.

## ROLFE HUMPHRIES (essay date 1934)

[*Humphries was an American poet, translator, and critic. In the following essay, he expresses his disapprobation for Benét's work.*]

Mr. Benét's services to the literary trade are well known. These require the exercise of talents denied the average poet: competence attended by facility; taste easily appreciative for the most part, but nicely discreet against the extremes of popular fashion; a complaisant modesty in disclosing matters of private interest; engaging manners; whimsicality; tone. When, however, the question arises, as it does in the present instance, concerning the immediate poetic merit of our candidate, we are subject to embarrassment by the sum total of our recollections. We may be expecting too much; we may think that by virtue of experience and possession of qualities denied the average poet, he should in proportion surpass the average. Or, we may be too ready with the excuse that professional activities constitute major interference with the possibility of poetic success. The present reviewer's preference for candor obliges him to state that he considers the burden of proving that Mr. Benét is a poet to rest on Mr. Benét, and that the evidence at hand justifies certainly no more than a Scotch verdict.

*Rip Tide* is said to be a novel in verse; novelette would be a better title. The story, told in prose, might or might not be worth the telling. The quality of the verse in which it is presented insufficiently demonstrates the theorem that the poem achieves a condensation and intensity impossible to prose; a feeble variation of rhythm is insufficient warrant for abandoning the medium more conventionally associated with novel-writing. The influence of Jeffers is apparent, but the rather daring themes are handled with a delicacy of which Jeffers is incapable. There is nothing shocking about Mr. Benét's treatment of adultery and incest. The characters, more upper-class than anything in Jeffers, are limned without the compulsive obsession that gives them value as symbols of a private religion; the figures in *Rip Tide* confute the author's estimate of their vital emergence.

*Starry Harness* is as good a title as one might ask for a book of lyric poems that are on the whole a little high-flown. Pretentiousness is a bad quality in art, and Mr. Benét's verse pretends badly. It is for the critic to penetrate pretense, to discover and define the peculiar quality of the pleasure, if any, given us by this writer, to shuck him down to his central reality. But the process of husking is here so continual, the search for the integrity of this poet so tedious and so complicated by his extravagance, that we abandon the pursuit with little remorse.

*Fifty Poets* is an anthology conceived in the belief that there are at least fifty living American poets worth listening to about themselves and a certain one of their poems. It is offered to the public with the unreluctant willingness of many poets conspiring toward that charitable hope. The items that compose this egregious book are not without interest to the mathema-

tician who would discover how eccentric in our time is the pursuit of poetry, nor to the philosopher who yearns to peruse lines upon the vanity of human wishes. For the researcher they may some day possess genuine antiquarian significance; it is a pity that by then the luster of the more gorgeous comic passages will be overlaid by the patina of time.

Let us improve the occasion with one or two general propositions. What ails the poetaster as critic is that, consciously or otherwise, his standards are so set as to include ratification of his own workmanship; conversely, the critic who is habitually lax in venting a generous enthusiasm for other men's verses will not err on the side of the strictness in self-rebuke. What distinguishes the minor from the mediocre poet (if indeed the latter has any existence outside of paradox) is the occasional instance of perfection. (pp. 108-11)

Rolfe Humphries, "Journeyman of Letters," in Poetry, Vol. XLIV, No. 2, May, 1934, pp. 108-11.

## WINFIELD TOWNLEY SCOTT (essay date 1936)

[*Scott was an American poet and critic. In the following review of* Golden Fleece, *he focuses on the variety in form and content of Benét's poetry, which Scott believes results in a lack of synthesis in the present collection.*]

"A collection of poems and ballads old and new," Mr. Benét's new book [*Golden Fleece*] purposes a representative selection (excluding certain narrative poems) of his verse. It brings together, on the author's word, "all the poems I care for." Thus it supersedes his *Man Possessed*—largely by adding to that several new poems and generous selections from the recent volume, *Starry Harness*. And so it presents a reviewer, particularly one convinced that Mr. Benét's lengthy narratives are not among his better works, with an apt basis for attempted judgment on his poetic career.

The most salient quality of his poetry is its variety. This is true not only of its forms but as well of its intentions. Mr. Benét, besides a story-teller, is by turns didactic, lyrical, thoughtful, impressionistic and humorous. And somehow, while he is almost invariably assured and practised in his shifting technics, he is just as invariably something less than distinguished in his completed work. At his worst he writes with immense and uninspired wordiness (as in **"Jaldabaoth"**), and at his best he misses that intensity which is the indefinable yet always recognizable life of genuine poetry.

Mr. Benét approaches this intensity in a few of his personal lyrics, notably those about Elinor Wylie; and this near-success, more clearly than his failures, reveals his true worth. In short, one misses throughout his work the stamp of an individual. That personality, of whose charm one so often hears testimony, is lost in the shuttling variety of a talent which is, after all, more various than profound. What we have here, in *Golden Fleece,* is rather the practice of an art in many of its phases than the work of an artist. There is no synthesis, no created world, no unmistakable expression.

Inevitably then, one must judge Mr. Benét's work as verse. That is to say, his most successful work is completely explicit in the very words on the page; rarely means more, rarely gives off that aura of light which belongs to poetry alone. Such equipment has served Mr. Benét well in his most famous role, that of balladist. At times nearly as bad as Robert Service (**"The Horse Thief"**), at others nearly as good as Vachel Lindsay (**"Harlem"**), he has yarned of tales foreign and American with the essential glibness of balladry. To say that, in ballads, if you save the surface you save all, is not enough; you must also consider that, by this token, the surface is highly important. What I miss in these ballads is, once again, that stamp of individual coloring that one finds only in a very great versifier such as Rudyard Kipling.

On the other hand, Mr. Benét's lighter touch is sometimes charming; best of all in his delightful **"Whale"**:

> The Lord shall say with His Tongue,
>   "Now let all Heaven give hail
> To my Jest when I was young,
>   To my very Whale."

And with a touch just as light but turned to restraint, he has written that wistful lyric, **"Deer in Mooreland."** Occasionally, in poems such as these, he is simple and direct, and these may be remembered as adroit, well-fashioned and honest verse. (pp. 223-24)

*Winfield Townley Scott, "Modern Jason," in* Poetry, *Vol. XLVII, No. 4, January, 1936, pp. 223-24.*

**FRANCES WINWAR  (essay date 1941)**

[*Winwar is an American novelist, translator, and critic who has written several biographical studies of such Romantic poets as Lord Byron, William Wordsworth, and John Keats. In the following excerpt, she discusses Benét's literary development and his place among the poets of his era.*]

In 1913 [Benét's] first book of poems—*Merchants from Cathay*—had won him friends with a public that was becoming aware of the first gleams of a literary renaissance upon which Ezra Pound, Amy Lowell, Harriet Monroe—poet laureate of the World's Fair of the nineties—and other heralds of the dawn had begun to open casements. Miss Lowell's *A Dome of Many-coloured Glass*—a volume of pallid verse which had appeared the previous year—gave as yet small promise of the coming day; but the light was there to emerge, after her study in France of the imagists, in the briliance of *Some Imagist Poets*—an anthology of the poetry of the school. From 1915 to 1917, while Europe bled itself white in the war, literary America was being made aware of a revolution in poetry. "We are not a school of painters," declared the propounders of the imagist gospel, "but we believe that poetry should render particulars exactly and not deal in vague generalities, however magnificent and sonorous."

It was the old feud between classicism and romanticism brought up to date, with the imagists in the ranks of the rebellious young, wresting what they thought a new freedom from the past. Literature gained from the revolt in a demand for exactness in the word, in a broadening of the materials for poetry, and in a clear, hard intellectuality that did much toward laying at last the sentimental, spooky indefiniteness of the writing of the previous decade. In poetry, free verse, partaking of the solidity of prose, was born; in prose there flourished for a time the polyphonic, as practiced by Amy Lowell and her followers. (p. 416)

Appearing when it did, William Rose Benét's *Merchants from Cathay*, therefore, gave the delight of the expected. There was the familiar beat in the golden hooves of the merchants' beasts; their curious merchandise astonished one but did not startle; even their song of praise to the Grand Chan had the nostalgic echo of something heard long ago in some enchanted dream of childhood. But William Rose Benét had more personal mat-

ters to sing of: the joy and passion of love, best expressed, perhaps, in his lovely dedication; the impact of the world upon his poet's sensibility; the wonder in the things of every day which one took for granted; the dreams and aspirations of youth.

In his next volume of verse, *The Falconer of God,* he took leave of the exotic for a closer observation of the world in which he lived. Subjects like **"Poor Girl," "On the Water-front,"** and **"Cats of Cobblestone Street"** dispossessed the apes and peacocks, to the displeasure of the dwellers in the literary Cathay but to the gratification of those who saw more genuine worth in the muse of grief and toil—and humor, for William Rose Benét had a strain of whimsical fantasy which he was only beginning to play upon. His volume *The Great White Wall* followed in 1916, and two years later *The Burglar of the Zodiac*—a collection of contemporary poems on quick-lunch counters, films, smoke, the suffrage procession, night motoring, skyscrapers—a far cry from the gilded patterns of the Amy Lowell school but true to the demands of poetry "to render particulars exactly."

He was clever and observant, brilliant and intensely modern, and, though sometimes trivial, always in love with his art and therefore tender of it. Nevertheless, there was justice in the criticism of Conrad Aiken who, while recognizing in the poet a considerable intelligence, regretted that "his best work is a jargon of approximations" [see Additional Bibliography]. In a sense all but the one perfect thing which it is occasionally given the creative artist to achieve becomes, in the long view, something attempted but not realized; and so clear-sighted a critic as William Rose Benét has proved himself in his writings for the *Saturday Review of Literature* would be the first to grant Mr. Aiken's assertion. In the Preface to his selected poems, *Man Possessed,* Mr. Benét wrote:

> To the potential poet—that is, to any one sensitive to experience—to any one with the curse in his or her blood that intensifies experience and makes moments beautiful or terrible beyond the comprehension of the cool, outside observer. . . . there are a thousand pictures behind the retina that will never be painted, there are a thousand plastic shapes of beauty that haunt dream and waking, there is music that will never be scored and many poems every day that will never be written.

Even when their conception has received form on canvas, harmonious sound in the played score, or expression in the written word, it is all too often the lot of creative artists to remain to the highest criticism merely potential.

In his volume *Starry Harness* William Rose Benét drew from approximation closer to achievement. The fifty-odd new poems, held together by a title from William Blake, had in them some of the quality, in feeling if not in form, of the mystical poet. They were, many of them, on the themes of love and remembered beauty, poems lyrical and personal, removed—or, one might say—treasured apart—from the contemporary scene as too intimate for the electric glare of ordinary living. Though not out of touch with life, since they were compact of its very essence, they had none of the compromise to the modern scene of action which marked his earlier work. One sensed a conflict there—the conflict of the poet who, while possessing, like Shelley, a never sleeping social conscience, yet finds himself by tradition and aesthetic identity of an age removed from his own. That same conflict existed in the poet and novelist Elinor

Wylie, whom William Rose Benét had married in 1923 and whom he lost by her untimely death in 1928.

Elinor Wylie, however, had been able to resolve her conflict by creating a world of her own in which she lived more completely than in the real. It was a world in little—an exquisite microcosm, highly artificial, tidy, perfect, made wholly by her hands and polished and refined until not a brown spot of natural soil showed under the stiff, glazed porcelain flowers with which she decked it. It was inhabited by delicate figures somehow magically endowed with life; by lace-clad beaus and belles of a fastidious century; by Venetian-glass youths and sad, beautiful orphan angels—Shelley with no admixture of human dross; by haunting puppets that nevertheless seemed more substantial and real than one's next-door neighbors. In spite of the overelaboration of the *décor,* the precise, jeweled creatures came warm and alive under the evocative spell of the author's sensory style which achieved what many an imagist strove for in vain. It was in her novels at first that Elinor Wylie captured the most elusive shades of feeling rather than in the poems of her early slight volume *Black Armour,* or even in *Trivial Breath,* published the year of her death. Not until the posthumous appearance of her book *Angels and Earthly Creatures,* with its moving love sonnets and noble long lyrics, did she attain to full poetic stature, the confict of reality and emotional identification effectively solved at last in a warm human approach to experience that is at once personal and universal.

That same approach William Rose Benét put into *Rip Tide,* even though the subject—the love of a young man and a girl, who, unknown to themselves are children of the same father—has more of Byronic romanticism than twentieth-century realism, *pace* Faulkner and others of his school. Mr. Benét wrote the novel in verse to give his story the intensification which would have been impossible in the looser medium of prose. It moves rapidly from the brooding loveliness of the first book, "Sheila," to the third with its tragic though rather incredible denouement when the hero is killed in a hurricane while saving the girl. One feels that Nature interceded too patly as a *deus ex machina* and that, serving morality, Mr. Benét did a disservice to what might have been a noble tragedy. Throughout, however, there are passages of exceptional beauty and power which more than offset the occasional pedestrianism of the narrative sequences and occasionally lift the book to rare poetic heights. Besides his volumes of poetry William Rose Benét has produced a mystery romance, *First Person Singular;* a children's fantasy, *The Flying King of Kurio;* a selection of fugitive pieces, *Wild Goslings;* and has edited a number of anthologies, *Poems of Youth, Fifty Poets,* and *The Oxford Anthology of American Literature,* this last in collaboration with Norman H. Pearson. As a member of the staff of the *Saturday Review of Literature,* he has a devoted following both for his essays and for his literary criticism. (pp. 417-20)

> Frances Winwar, "Two Poets: Stephen Vincent and
> William Rose Benét," in College English, *Vol. 2,*
> *No. 5, February, 1941, pp. 415-27.*

## JOHN GOULD FLETCHER  (essay date 1942)

[*Fletcher was an American critic and poet. Initially associated with Ezra Pound and the Imagists, he later became linked to the Southern Agrarians, a group that sought to preserve the traditional values and rural character of the American South through both literature and political activism. His poetry often incorporated elements drawn from other art forms, such as music and painting, and is considered innovative and influential. In the fol-*

*lowing review, Fletcher presents a mixed appraisal of* The Dust Which Is God.]

First, let me say, and emphatically: Mr. Benét's fictionized autobiography in verse [*The Dust Which Is God*], is one of the great documents of our time. Like other such documents—Mr. Sandburg's *The People, Yes,* Mr. Stephen Vincent Benét's *John Brown's Body,* Mr. Auden's *The Double Man,* it belongs with the most extensive, and most courageous attempts made to achieve great poetry in our day. But that it remains when all is said and done, not great poetry except incidentally, and apart from its main purpose, is manifest to anyone who has read through all its more than six hundred pages. And the reason is chiefly due, not to any lack of skill on Mr. Benét's part, but to insuperable difficulties implicit in the theme, which attempts to cover the age itself.

Since the machine, aided and abetted by science, enthroned itself as god around 1900, there have been two major world-wars, of which the second—of doubtful result and of utterly inconceivable post-war readjustment—is being fought out today. No single organized body of belief has been able to prevent, or even in any measure to control, the incredible brutality and horror of these conflicts: not to mention the innumerable smaller conflicts that have continued to persist on the fringes of the main body. And the reason for such a situation is that—thanks again to applied science—two different and utterly contradictory attitudes towards life dominate today. The first emphasizes success, it exalts the struggle for life and the survival of the fittest, "get while the getting is good," and it leads straight to the mass-man and to the "principle" of the *Führer.* The second emphasizes the mixed legacy of pagan myth and humanism, as well as medieval mysticism and speculation, that first confronted the Renaissance; it exalts the scholar-artist, or the self-detached scientist; it leads straight to expression for expression's sake, and to the deliberate cultivation of states of abnormal consciousness via surrealism.

No poet—not even were his name Dante or Shakespeare—could possibly construct a poem covering both of these self-destroying directions of the human psyche at the present day. The poet requires, far more than most men, a fixed body of beliefs *all tending in one direction,* even if this body is only something for him to react against (I have not forgotten Keats' remark, "What shocks your moralist delights the chameleon poet"). The trouble with this age is not that it lacks beliefs, but that it has two opposing sets of beliefs—between which we are forced to choose at every moment. And this, of itself, destroys the possibility of there being any great and widely-comprehensive kind of poetry today. Indeed, the poets who have been the most successful in our time have been the most severely restricted as to their subject-matter: poets like W. B. Yeats or T. S. Eliot, who have deliberately left out of account whole ranges of human experience, in their ever-renewed search for supernatural or abstract principles.

All this has its bearings on Mr. Benét's attempt to tell the story of the past thirty years, in its incidence upon the world as upon his chief protagonist. The story itself is simple. A young man, with a natural facility for writing but with no particular philosophy, whom Mr. Benét's calls Fernandez, graduates from a University identifiable as Yale, and then—thanks to his lack of economic status—enters the commercial world of our time via free lance journalism. He falls in love with, and eventually marries, a girl called Nora, and there are two children. (It is only about the 100th page that Mr. Benét's story really hits its stride, and begins to engage the reader's full interest, with a scene on an apartment house roof in Manhattan.) The first World War finds them ensconced in a country cottage, and Fernandez has an impulse to join up. He follows the impulse, with the result that he is chained to a desk in Washington for the rest of the war—while wife and children stay with his parents in Carolina. After the armistice, he drifts back to New York, and has to start again from the bottom, writing advertising copy. Suddenly he is summoned to the bedside of his wife, who has caught the post-war influenza and is dying. Her death concludes the first half of the story.

After this tragedy—unmitigated as it is in Fernandez's own mind by any feeling, whether rational or mystical, that it may be all part of some tremendous and overpowering plan on the part of that force we call God—the protagonist is again caught up in the swirl of the sophisticated, speakeasy, cocktail, jazz and gangster era of the twenties. He is helped into it—despite honest and abiding doubts of its validity—by the interposition of another woman, who has already wrecked two other men's lives. After a married life of ups and downs, following on a long separation overseas, the woman suddenly dies: a brilliant poet, but the self-confessed betrayer at last of her own husband's love and loyalty. And Fernandez, apparently now inured to the position of being perpetually used and kicked out, accepts this situation also.

In the last section the protagonist is led—via various casual affairs—to the final acceptance of the God of his childhood, whom he has all along half-admired, half-mistrusted; and in the meantime, the world, in its blundering and confusion, is led into another world-war. Thus the whole book concludes as a modern novel, with the exit of its leading character, and with the underlying moral dilemmas completely unresolved.

The difficulty with all this, it seems at least to me, is that the main plot is not good enough to justify all the skill which Mr. Benét has lavished upon it. How, at this late date, when the whole structure of democracy lies far more than half in ruins, can we have any great sympathy for a victim whose chief downfall came about because he was caught up heart and soul in the swirl of the "sophisticated" era, which should have warned everybody that democracy in itself was far from being perfect? How can we feel that this tragedy, common enough as it is, was other than insignificant? If tragic victims of today are to be found, let them be rather among the lust-crazed, loneliness-warped California ranchers of Mr. Jeffers' imagination, than among Mr. Benét's Manhattan sophisticates! At least, these peasants of the Big Sur region have kept their desires—however crazy—for God. Mr. Benét's attempt to envisage the world, from the standpoint of a modern agnostic who has merely endured and shared the dust-swirl over Manhattan for the past thirty years, must be frankly admitted a failure. The dust-swirl in itself had no point of reference, no object and no goal—nor can Mr. Benét make it relevant to the problems we have to face today.

That is not to say that Mr. Benét is a bad poet. When he ceases discussing the affairs of his main character and concentrates on events and things around him, he can be extremely convincing. His chief technical device—blank verse, written in swift-stabbing phrases, somewhat like a telegram—then does better duty than in the more personal passages of narrative. One could signal out much for attention here: I cite only a few of the best: the apostrophe to America; the picture of New York around 1912; the scene on the apartment house roof; the advertising agency scene and its commentary (really superb); the upsurge of Manhattan under the impact of the boom, mag-

nificently done. And also—though I do not know what it means—the conclusion, "As It was in the Beginning."

And yet, when all is said and done with Mr. Benét's book—and I hope I have made it clear that no one could do better with such a subject—what abides in the mind are a few excellent lyrics. (pp. 213-17)

> *John Gould Fletcher, "Dust Swirl over Manhattan,"*
> *in* Poetry, *Vol. LIX, No. 4, January, 1942, pp. 213-17.*

**HORACE GREGORY** AND **MARYA ZATURENSKA** (essay date 1946)

[*Gregory and Zaturenska are both noted American poets and critics. Since their marriage in 1925, they have coauthored several works, including the important study* American Poetry, 1900-1940. *In the following excerpt from that work, they offer an overview of Benét's career as a poet and man of letters.*]

William Rose Benét's verses touched upon and sometimes passed over many subjects lightly, and the very conditions of his life, his many activities in editing magazines and anthologies of verse seemed to contribute toward a neglect of his own gifts in favor of his ability to encourage and to appreciate the works of others. Like his younger brother, Stephen, he abhorred dullness as nature does a vacuum, and at Yale a decade earlier than Stephen, his training for a professional career included editorship of *The Yale Record* and *The Yale Courant*—and he was markedly of the same restless college "generation" at Yale that produced the novelist, Sinclair Lewis. The same spirit of revolt against an academic reading of literature which led Henry Seidel Canby from the English department at Yale to an assistant editorship of *The Yale Review,* and finally to the chairmanship of the Book of the Month Club in New York, seems to have entered the generation of which Canby, William Rose Benét, and Sinclair Lewis were the forerunners, and of which Archibald MacLeish, Thornton Wilder, and Stephen Benét, and latterly Selden Rodman, poet and editor, were the fortunate heirs. Behind all these, perhaps the example set by William Lyon Phelps exerted a charm that has been underrated by critics of contemporary American letters. Phelps's enthusiasm for current literature in the broadest terms has its analogy only in the adventurous spirit that possessed such Victorians as Sir Richard Burton, the translator of *The Arabian Nights*—and the title of William Rose Benét's first book of poems, **Merchants from Cathay,** has something of the same adventurous character.

William Rose Benét's early verse delighted in fancy for its own sake; it glittered rather than shone, and translated quickly and lightly into its own speech the attractions that Swinburne, Rossetti, Browning, G. K. Chesterton, and Rudyard Kipling held for the young Americans in a generation that saw a "poetic renaissance" in the United States. Like his younger brother and his sister Laura, the true touchstone for the verse that seemed to move with so much ease and skill was of a family heritage—and it seems natural that his first editorial job should have been on the staff of the *Century* magazine which was closely associated (since it was then published by the same firm) with the *St. Nicholas.*

William Rose Benét's abilities turned in the direction of light verse, and his ballad on **"Jesse James: American Myth"** showed the skill with which his facility in writing verse was at its best advantage. The poem's qualities of lightness, brilliance, and metrical speed place it among the best of its kind in American verse and one must turn to Vachel Lindsay's verses to find something of like temper.

Of William Rose Benét's some fifteen books of verse, **Man Possessed** and **Golden Fleece** are the most representative volumes, and within them one clearly sees the reflections of a volatile, gracefully mannered, and erratic talent. His **"The Falconer of God"** has been reprinted in many anthologies, and it has never failed to awaken admiration for its metrical variety and skill. But Benét's verse found its best expression in an elegy, his **"Inscription for a Mirror in a Deserted Dwelling,"** which was written (it is believed) in memory of his second wife, Elinor Wylie, and which justly deserves to be remembered long after his more facile and glittering pieces are forgotten:

> Set silver cone to tulip flame!
> The mantel mirror floats with night
> Reflecting still green watery light.
> The sconces glimmer. If she came
> Like silence through the shadowy wall
> Where walls are wading in the moon
> The dark would tremble back to June.
> So faintly now the moonbeams fall,
> So soft this silence, that the verge
> Of speech is reached. Remote and pale
> As though some faint viridian veil
> The lovely lineaments emerge,
> The clearly amber eyes, the tint
> Of pearl and faintest rose, the hair
> To lacquered light a silken snare
> Of devious bronze, the tiny dint
> With which her maker mocked the years
> Beneath her lip imprinting praise.
>
> (pp. 441-43)

In this poem, Benét's sensibility assumed its own character, and the poem properly distinguishes his talents from those of his younger brother, and indeed from those possessed by all other poets of his generation. His autobiography in verse, **The Dust Which Is God,** showed a man who had participated actively in the years that spanned two world wars, and the reader sees reflected in its pages a busy life that enabled him to work with so much felicity in collaboration with Henry Seidel Canby and Christopher Morley in the founding and editing of *The Saturday Review of Literature*. The book received the Pulitzer Prize for poetry in 1942. In 1944, he published another book of poems, **Day of Deliverance,** whose lines expressed with great sincerity the national feeling of the day in the third year of the Second World War. (p. 444)

> Horace Gregory and Marya Zaturenska, *"The National Spirit of Stephen Vincent and William Rose Benét, with Notes on Lola Ridge and Muriel Rukeyser," in their* A History of American Poetry, 1900-1940, *Harcourt Brace Jovanovich, Inc., 1946, pp. 431-47.*

## ADDITIONAL BIBLIOGRAPHY

Aiken, Conrad. "The Return of Romanticism: Walter de la Mare, John Gould Fletcher, William Rose Benét." In his *Scepticisms: Notes on Contemporary Poetry*, pp. 187-192. New York: Alfred A. Knopf, 1919.
> Unfavorable review of The Burglar of the Zodiac in which Aiken concludes: "Mr. Benét is clever, but mechanical. One detects in him a considerable intelligence working through a shallow and unoriginal sensibility. Neither his rhythms nor his color seem to be peculiarly his own, nor has he apparently any sense of effect. His best work is a jargon of approximations."

Benét, William Rose. "William Rose Benét." In *Portraits and Self-Portraits*, pp. 19-20. Boston: Houghton Mifflin Co., 1936.
> Autobiographical sketch written in the third person.

Canby, Henry Seidel. "William Rose Benét: February 2, 1886-May 4, 1950." *The Saturday Review of Literature* XXXIII, No. 20 (20 May 1950): 8-9.
> Obituary tribute to Benét.

"William Rose Benét." In *The Literary Spotlight*, edited by John Farrar, pp. 195-203. New York: George H. Doran Co., 1924.
> Biographical sketch.

Morley, Christopher. "Ballade of William Rose Benét." *The Saturday Review of Literature* XXXIII, No. 20 (20 May 1950): 11.
> Elegy offering tribute to Benét.

Review of *Merchants from Cathay*, by William Rose Benét. *Poetry* IV, No. 1 (April 1914): 32-3.
> Favorable review.

Review of *The Falconer of God, and Other Poems*, by William Rose Benét. *Poetry* V, No. 2 (November 1914): 91.
> Mixed review.

Review of *The Burglar of the Zodiac*, by William Rose Benét. *Poetry* XV, No. 1 (October 1919): 48-51.
> Praises The Burglar of the Zodiac, comparing Benét's art to that of a magician.

Ransom, John Crowe. "Poetic Strategy." *The Saturday Review of Literature* XII, No. 13 (27 July 1935): 6.
> Describes Benét's approach to poetry as facile and outdated.

Rosenberger, Coleman. "Poet as Public Speaker." *Poetry* LXV, No. 2 (November 1944): 101-04.
> Review of Day of Deliverance in which Rosenberger praises the timeliness of the book. He writes: "It is not . . . merely as a skilled literary practitioner that Benét invites attention here. It is as a man who possesses considerable awareness of the world in which we live, who earlier than many was alert to the menace of fascism, and who says clearly many things which are in need of saying."

Untermeyer, Louis. "The Man in His Work." *Saturday Review of Literature* XXXIII, No. 20 (20 May 1950): 13-14.
> Survey of Benét's work. Untermeyer writes: "Somehow he managed to combine high seriousness and high-flying fantasy with a sure hand."

# George Douglas Brown

## 1869-1902

(Also wrote under the pseudonyms George Douglas, William Douglas, and Kennedy King) Scottish novelist.

Brown is the author of *The House with the Green Shutters*, one of the first works of Scottish literature to depict the baser aspects of life in rural Scotland. The novel, which chronicles the decline of the Gourlay family and the destruction of their green-shuttered house, the symbol of their pride, was written in reaction to the Kailyard school, a term used by critics to describe a group of nineteenth-century writers whose works present a sentimental and idealized depiction of rural Scotland. Unlike these authors, Brown focused on the harsh realities of life and the tragic weaknesses of his characters. While *The House with the Green Shutters* has been criticized for belaboring misery and degradation in nineteenth-century Scottish life, the novel has been cited as a precursor of the predominantly realistic Scottish fiction of the twentieth century.

The illegitimate son of a well-educated farmer, Brown was born in Ayrshire and raised by his mother, who worked to support him. He attended various local schools, including the prestigious Ayr Academy, where he distinguished himself as an excellent student with a particular talent in literature. In 1887 he entered the University of Glasgow to study classics; upon his graduation in 1891, he received a scholarship to continue his education at Oxford University. Brown was older than his classmates and lived in near poverty, and he later maintained that this had been the most miserable period of his life. After completing his final examinations, he settled in London, determined to establish himself as a man of letters.

In London, Brown supported himself as a free-lance journalist, contributing articles, poems, short stories, and book reviews to various publications and writing a juvenile adventure story entitled *Love and a Sword*, which was published in 1899 under the pseudonym Kennedy King. During this time he eschewed steady work in order to concentrate on developing ideas for a novel. In 1901 Brown achieved sudden popular and critical acclaim for his realistic portrayal of Scotland in *The House with the Green Shutters*. With the royalties he received from the novel, he retired to semiseclusion in Haslemere. There he continued work on a critical study of *Hamlet* that he had begun several years before and began writing three more novels: a historical romance set during the era of Oliver Cromwell, a study of the life of a writer entitled *The Novelist*, and a chronicle of an unhappy marriage entitled *The Incompatibles*. None of these works was ever finished. Brown, who suffered from poor health throughout his life, became seriously ill and died in August 1902.

*The House with the Green Shutters* has been praised for its vivid description of Scottish life, its apt characterizations, and its accurate presentation of Scottish dialect, all drawn from Brown's personal experiences. The most striking characteristic of the novel is its grim tone and tragic subject matter. In sharp contrast to the romanticized Scotland of the Kailyarders, Brown's Scotland is a bleak landscape inhabited by spiteful characters. The Kailyarders, most prominently J. M. Barrie, S. R. Crockett, and Ian Maclaren, were noted for their strong feelings of sympathy with their characters; Brown is wholly unsympathetic to the society of Barbie, the small village in which most of the action of his novel takes place, and critics note that the reader is more likely to feel disgust than compassion for his characters. Brown felt that the Kailyarders did not accurately portray the rural Scotland that he had known as a youth, the Scotland from which he felt alienated due to his illegitimate birth and broad education. His aim in writing *The House with the Green Shutters* was to present the darker side of Scottish life that had previously been ignored. Edmund Gosse wrote that Brown, when asked why he had concentrated on moral ugliness, "said that the sentimental gush of the Kailyard dealt with an imaginary moral beauty, and gave no hint of the realities of Lowland village life, with its 'malignancy, hard drinking, and coarse language.' He had determined to paint these qualities, and these only, in his unsparing picture of Barbie." Many critics have written that Brown overemphasized the weaknesses of his characters, allowing his animus toward Scotland to dominate his novel, making it, in the words of William Parker, "too brutal to be wholly artistic." Others have seen Brown's excesses as social criticism of the rural Scottish communities and, alternatively, as an expression of "theological furor" and "profound revulsion" against the petty malignancy of humanity. Propelled by this moral imperative, along with the strength of its characterization and the imaginative force of its narration, *The House with the Green Shutters* brought a new perspective and purpose to Scottish literature.

## PRINCIPAL WORKS

*Love and a Sword* [as Kennedy King]   (novel)   1899
*The House with the Green Shutters* [as George Douglas]
   (novel)   1901

---

### THE BOOKMAN (LONDON)   (essay date 1901)

[*In the following review, the critic extols* The House with the Green Shutters.]

Without actual adventure, without any love interest—if we except the one case of the mother's love for her son—with scarcely a woman in the book, Mr. Douglas has written a strong and impressive piece of fiction [*The House with the Green Shutters*]. It is very quietly done; not till the story nears its close does the tragedy move quickly. When it does move, however, it moves to some purpose; we realise the force which has been accumulating from the outset; and the end is gruesome. The book is not gloomy; indeed, it is the reverse; there is humour in plenty. There are also clever, incisive writing, good phrasing, fine characterization, and true insight. Surely only a Scot would dare to draw such a picture of a Scottish village; it is entertaining, and it is apt in its witticisms, but it is remorselessly cruel—there is scarcely one kind heart in it. Barbie is the village, and John Gourlay, of the House with the

Green Shutters, is the big man of it; a harsh, purse-proud, cheating, unintelligent bully, who wins the detestation (and the fear) of everyone; a man whose downfall anyone with a human weakness for retribution would be glad to see accomplished. And yet—when it is accomplished, when the downfall comes and overwhelms him, one is not glad. The man is great in his way, and the other man who sets to work to accomplish the ruin is so shrewd, so unscrupulous, so mean, that the reader veers; the bully is preferable to the sneak. John Gourlay is the main theme of the book, but he is by no means the only one. John Gourlay's son, with his fine perceptions, his sensitiveness, his brag, his cowardice; Mrs. Gourlay, with her slatternly ways, her sufferings, her apathy, and her piteous love for her boy; even Janet, Gourlay's daughter, so unattractive and so sickly, drawn with so few touches; all are almost terrible in their reality. And terrible is the meeting between father and son, when young John, soaked with drink, comes home, frightened and desperate, expelled from Edinburgh University; when the strong nature plays with the weak with excess of cruelty, till the weak, becoming maddened, ends the scene with catastrophe. Mr. Douglas shows that he can handle strong situations, and his book proves that he is able to write with power and originality.

> *A review of "The House with the Green Shutters," in* The Bookman, *London, Vol. XXI, No. 122, November, 1901, p. 69.*

**W. M. PARKER**   (essay date 1917)

[*In the following excerpt, Parker praises the characterization in* The House with the Green Shutters *while criticizing the overwhelmingly sinister tone of the novel.*]

To the roll of names that have become famous by one work . . . there should be added that of George Douglas Brown by his ***The House with the Green Shutters***. The first thing that strikes one in reading that book is, of course, its uncompromising realism, and in his frank picture of the ways and doings and talk of the inhabitants of a Scottish "nippy locality," as he calls it, he was a herald of revolt against that other, and perhaps less lifelike, view, seen through the rosy spectacles of the "kailyarders." (p. 248)

***The House with the Green Shutters*** is a difficult book to criticize. The sense of impending tragedy is kept well in view from the opening, on a serene summer morning, to the time when Gourlay's son imbibes too freely on his return from the Bacchic roysterings in Edinburgh. The character of the brutal Gourlay is the masterpiece of the book. The tyranny and overweening vanity for his House with the Green Shutters of this bully, a dour bodie whom every one in the neighbourhood detests and fears, are ruthlessly observed. Gourlay "had made dogged scorn a principle of life," and prided himself that he could nearly kill a man "wi' a glower from his een." Only less successful are the scenes of humorous gossip indulged in by the cronies of the village of Barbie; the character of Mrs. Gourlay, slatternly, long-suffering, and too inclined to spoil her son; the son, a sensitive boy who turns out to be a brag, a coward, and a misuser of what little gifts he possessed. . . . The chorus of villagers—Deacon Allardyce; Sandy Toddle; Drucken Wabster; the baker, an enthusiastic Burnsite who quotes the bard on all possible, and on as many impossible, occasions; Johnny Coe; and Tam Brodie, the cobbler—this chorus is introduced just as his quaint peasant choruses are introduced by Mr. Thomas Hardy in his novels, as a relief from the tragedy

of the main theme. It becomes a necessary relief from the sinister tone that is so persistently prominent. The names of places and persons, like Tenshillingland, Irrendavie, Loranogie, and Templandmuir, have a true smack of the Ayrshire soil about them. The end, the complete downfall of the tyrant of Barbie, is grim and terrible rather than gloomy. The atmosphere of Scottish rustic life and character is consistent all through, and the little vignette of the auctioneering at the cattle-market is vividly real. Yet even when all these things have been said in its favour, and they have no doubt contributed largely to the unique success of the book, to the critical mind there is somehow here and there a hiatus that breaks it cohesion and, on account of its overpowering brutality, a want of restraint in its dramatic crises. A later reading confirms my first impression that the novel is too brutal to be wholly artistic. (pp. 250-53)

> *W. M. Parker, "A Herald of Revolt: George Douglas Brown," in his* Modern Scottish Writers, *1917. Reprint by Books for Libraries Press, 1968, pp. 245-55.*

**EDWIN MUIR**   (essay date 1923)

[*Muir was a distinguished Scottish novelist, poet, critic, and translator. With his wife Willa, he translated works by various German authors unfamiliar to the English-speaking world, including Gerhart Hauptmann, Hermann Broch, and, most notably, Franz Kafka. Throughout his career, Muir was intrigued by psychoanalytic theory, particularly Freud's analyses of dreams and Jung's theories of archetypal imagery, both of which he often utilized in his work. In his critical writings, Muir was more concerned with the general philosophical issues raised by works of art—such as the nature of time or society—than with the particulars of the work itself, such as style or characterization. In the following excerpt, originally published in the* Freeman *in 1923, Muir comments on several stylistic and thematic aspects of* The House with the Green Shutters.]

A little over two decades ago, ***The House with the Green Shutters***, . . . attracted the attention of the critics. It was in reality one of the great novels in the English language. . . . That work, full of genius and style, is still read and remembered by people who appreciate imaginative literature; but for a decade now I have not seen it mentioned in any review. Yet in solidity, in form, above all in imaginative power, it is easily greater than anything that has been achieved since, either by the reputations (a little aging) of Mr. Conrad and Mr. Galsworthy, or by later writers such as Mr. Lawrence and Mr. Joyce whom no one can avoid the obsession of taking too seriously. Of Douglas it may be said that the only gift he lacked in comparison with his contemporaries was that of becoming the rage; his other talents were of the kind which are given only to great writers. The novel which ***The House with the Green Shutters*** resembles most is *Wuthering Heights*, and if Douglas was inferior to Emily Brontë in pure imagination, in the capacity to create a world of art which is real and yet is not the world of reality as we see it, he was her superior in many ways: in a power of visualization not like hers, wild and romantic, but exact and solid; in a ripe knowledge, marvelous for his years, of the motives which determine human conduct; in a sense of life which might without exaggeration be compared with that of Scott; and in an architectural completeness which in achieving harmony does not become artificial. Every quality in his novel was genuine and was great, and such as one might have predicted to weather all the accidents of time. (pp. 31-2)

***The House with the Green Shutters*** is, like most first novels in our own time, an autobiographical novel. It is partly the record of the unalleviated life of young John Gourlay (an imaginative portrait of the author), and partly the story of the downfall of the Gourlay family and of the symbol of its pride, the house with the green shutters. These two themes are woven into one, giving the book a unity and an accumulating movement towards disaster. The elder John Gourlay, the chief figure in the book, is one of those Scotsmen of little intellect, brutal will and contemptuous absence of pity who can be found in positions from the highest to the lowest, in Scotland and all over the world. He is stupid, slow of speech, relentless towards his inferiors, without fear of his superiors, giving and taking no quarter; and he is the richest man in the little town of Barbie, where all the small people hate him on account of his wealth, his insolence and his stupidity. Denied by the dullness of his parts, and perhaps by his honesty, the posts of honor which his social position should have gained him (he could not even hope to become Chairman of the Gasworks!), he builds the house with the green shutters, the most prominent house in Barbie, "cockit up there on the brae," as a symbol of his power and superiority. . . . The Provost, the Deacon, and all the other great little men who suffer under Gourlay's power and indifference, are in time corrupted by their hatred towards him and their inability to give it effect. "But, oh no, not he; he was the big man; he never gave a body a chance! Or if you did venture a bit jibe when you met him, he glowered you off the face of the earth with thae black een of his. Oh, how they longed to get at him! It was not the least of the evils caused by Gourlay's black pride that it perverted a dozen characters. The 'bodies' of Barbie may have been decent enough men in their own way, but against him their malevolence was monstrous." These "bodies" act throughout the book as a malignant chorus to Gourlay's drama, acrid and unavailing at the beginning, when he is at the height of his power, but rising in sordid triumph as he sinks beneath the blows of a new competitor in the town, a man more clever but more ignoble, on the whole, than himself. Gourlay falls in the end through an inability to adapt himself to the changes which come with the arrival of the railway at Barbie; through the fecklessness of his wife, "a long, thin, trollop of a woman, with a long, thin, scraggy neck, seated by the slatternly table, and busy with a frowsy, paper-covered novel"; and the failure of his son, a suffering creature, insolent in prosperity and abject in adversity. These causes ultimately bring about the downfall of the house of the green shutters and the death of all the Gourlays by violent means.

A fatality lies on young Gourlay from his birth; the shapes and colors of things are so intensely apprehended by him that they bring him a personal terror before nature and life. "With intellect little or none," the author says briefly, "he had a vast, sensational experience"; and that is the cause of his apparent cowardice, his incapacity to face the world. He was born in circumstances of unusual terror. I quote the passage, both as indicating the artistic *motif* for young Gourlay's life, and as an example of Douglas's exact and vivid powers of description.

> Ye mind what an awful day it was [he makes one of the characters say], the thunder roared as if the heavens were tumbling on the world, and the lichtnin' sent the trees daudin' on the roads, and folk hid below their beds and prayed—they thocht it was the Judgment! But Gourlay rammed his black stepper in the shafts, and drave like the devil o' hell to Skeighan Drone, where there was a young doctor. The lad was feared to come, but Gourlay swore by God that he should, and he garred him. In a' the country-side driving like his that day was never kenned or heard

tell o': they were back within the hour! I saw them gallop up the Main Street; lichtnin' struck the ground before them; the young doctor covered his face wi' his hands, and the horse nickered wi' fear and tried to wheel, but Gourlay stoop up in the gig and lashed him on through the fire.

The mother was never herself again; the boy was born weakly and fretful, and so afraid of the anger of nature that even when he was grown up a thunderstorm sent him hysterical with terror. . . . An absolute clearness of vision into the forms of nature, with a total inability to do anything with it: that is the tragedy of young Gourlay.

If this portrait is autobiographical, as it is almost certainly, it is surely one of the strangest pieces of self-revelation ever written. Such self-loathing combined with such clearness of knowledge and delineation, such a masterly holding of oneself up to contempt, a contempt felt first and led by oneself, have an unusualness that approaches unnaturalness. One can not look upon the portrait with pity, for the mood of the author kills a sentiment which to him, one feels, would have appeared facile. Young Gourlay suffers from beginning to end, yet his sufferings do not awaken compassion in the author, but a mood which one can only call disgust. The human race was disgusting to Douglas as it was to Swift, and its sufferings had generally something ridiculous or mean in them which made them only another circumstance of disgust added to the sum. It was to Douglas, one feels, a metaphysical indignity that the people whom he delineated in *The House with the Green Shutters* should exist; and his novel came clean out of a burning negation of life as he knew it, and with most intensity, therefore, out of a negation of his own being. In this negation there was nothing consoling, no ease from the fact that one had existed, and that in existing one had been vain, vulgar and unreal, as the majority of the human race are. The thing, accordingly, which obsessed him most strongly was not vice or suffering, but the disfiguring touch of vulgarity which he always found upon them. In his portrait of young Gourlay, he revealed this ineluctable vulgarity of existence relentlessly; and inwardly he was appalled by it. This much is sure: only a spirit of the most fine fastidiousness could have apprehended vulgarity so vividly and have hated it so extravagantly. The cowardice of the world, the good sense of the average sensual man, may easily see in such an excess of sensitiveness something pathological; but any one who detaches himself from the conspiracy of mankind will scarcely deny that Douglas spoke the truth. And truths such as his are not profitless; they are, on the contrary, in the highest degree salutary for us, who usually have no very strong sense of the unsatisfactoriness of our existence as we live it. Douglas saw, it is true, the ignobility of life too constantly, too exclusively. Not one or two, but all of his characters are betrayed into some meanness which we feel is ridiculous, into some movement of the body or of the mind which recalls faintly the gestures of the lower animals. But these perceptions gave Douglas no satisfaction; they were, on the contrary, the obsession and the torment of a disappointed spirit to whom human life and the existence of this world were not enough.

There is a kind of imagination which manifests itself in the vivid realization of great scenes; and there is another kind, higher, indeed the highest, which is shown in the unremitting grasp of the passions and conflicts of the characters in a work, from the beginning to the end. Douglas possessed the latter in a high degree; but he possessed the former in a degree greater than any one else since Emily Brontë. There are places in *The House with the Green Shutters* where the conflict between the two wills is held for twenty pages with that intensity of imagination and greatness of truth, which, though common in great literature, always astonish us. The last scene between Gourlay and his son, which ends, because there is no other issue for it, with the murder of the father, is too long to quote. It is one of the greatest scenes in literature. In the realization of the immediacy of the enmity between father and son there is nothing to set beside it; and in this direction tragedy could go no farther.... In his evocation of states such as this, which go to the very limits of human endurance, Douglas is wonderfully sure; and his scenes are full of mastery and vigor as well as of horror. He had the capacity to let himself go, and to let the passions of his characters stand naked before us on the page, as if they had no control over themselves and no choice but to do so.

But his genius was not always on the stretch; his gifts were too solid to manifest themselves in one direction only. He had a capacity not unlike Carlyle's for the vivid phrase. One of his Scotsmen coming back from Paris describes the incense in Notre Dame as "burning stink." Old Gourlay "had a chest like the heave of a hill." After Templandmuir had insulted him and walked away in the darkness, "his blood rocked him where he stood." Logan, the middle-aged tippler who loved the society of youths, "the slow, sly, cosy man, with a sideward laugh in his eye, a humid gleam" was attracted to young Gourlay on their first meeting in Edinburgh. "He sat smiling in creeshy benevolence, beaming on Gourlay, but saying nothing." It is possible that only a Scotsman, who knows the nuances of the adjective, can grasp all the virtues of that inimitable and ignoble picture. Such minor triumphs as these illustrate perhaps better than his great scenes the most remarkable of young Douglas's qualities; his ability to render confidently and unerringly, with hardly one uncertain touch, whatever his imagination attempted; and his imagination rose to the highest themes.

*The House with the Green Shutters* is an autobiographical novel, but it is autobiographical as *Roderick Random* and *David Copperfield* are autobiographical; that is, with a true detachment, a true measure, and an immense realization not only of the chief figure, but of the life which surrounded him, giving to the portrayal that universality and justice which we demand from art. It is not, like the best example in the other genre, Mr. Joyce's *Portrait of the Artist as a Young Man* (a work accomplished and sometimes, indeed, beautiful), a full-length picture of the writer himself seen from within, and of the world only through a sort of secondary vision, as it was observed or felt by the hero; but a vision of life with all the figures in which the author identifies himself by the magnanimity of imagination, in that immense renunciation which is the beginning of art. Mr. Joyce's book, to use a convenient philosophical term, is subjective merely, while Douglas's is objective as well; and this objectivity it is which by its presence distinguishes a true work of art from one which is only partially realized, and by its greater power and soundness distinguishes what we call classical art from the art which is generally termed romantic. The characteristic of classical art is that it is so securely objective that whatever circumstance of grief, of turpitude or of horror it may describe, it raises no echo in our ordinary subjective emotions, and is entirely incapable of corrupting us. The characteristic of romantic art is that, in giving us a picture of the world which is indeed æsthetic, it moves these emotions at the same time, and moves them pathetically and agreeably. But the characteristic of Mr. Joyce's art is, one must say, that it moves these emotions almost exclusively, and that the æsthetic

picture which it leaves is in the last degree fragmentary and unsatisfying. In aspiration, in temper, in his view of life, Douglas was classical, but his classicism was plucked with "forced fingers rude"; and to detach himself from his characters he had to employ a coldness which was almost contemptuous, a harshness so grudging that it is a blot on the book. A spirit of unremitting calculation which, even when he has revealed the worst weaknesses of his characters, makes him go a little farther and discover a more abysmal meanness, gives his book a sense of terrible intimacy, where we feel that the last bounds of decency have been passed, and it is painful to look. Nevertheless we are persuaded in spite of our distaste; Douglas's pen, when it is most savage, is solid and just; and his art convinces us, as classical art does.

Yet *The House with the Green Shutters*, in spite of the greatness and solidity of its qualities, does not strike one as expressing fully the genius of Douglas. It has truth, imagination, style, architecture; and that confidence which, in a man of Douglas's powers of mind, could come only from a sense of his own genius. All his characters are seen with undeviating objectivity, with deliberate justice; yet there is something strained in his justice, and that is perhaps his chief fault. His objectivity was not a thing which had ripened of itself and fallen into his lap; he seized upon it violently, tearing himself, seeing that it was himself, when he tore it from experience. There is no serenity, therefore, in his detachment, but a constant separating struggle, which by its hardness imparts to his characters something hateful, the reflection of the deliberate enmity he had to practice to detach himself from them. In spite of his magnanimity, or rather because of it, and because it was attained with such effort, the mark of his reprobation lies on every one of his characters. As he is without serenity, so he is without pity; and his picture is sometimes unbearably grim and hateful. Yet when his imagination was freed by a great scene, and he was delivered for a moment from the struggle to remain aloof, and was carried into the spaces of art with all his faculties consenting, he was indeed a great writer.

Life was hardly kind to him once from his birth, and was most harsh of all in leaving him when fame and the enjoyment of his unfolding genius seemed to lie before him. But the qualities of his genius were so authentic, so solid, and so clearly not in their full maturity when he wrote his first book, that, with better fortune than he had been accustomed to, he must have lived to be the greatest writer of our time. (pp. 33-46)

        *Edwin Muir, "George Douglas," in his* Latitudes,
        *B. W. Huebsch, Inc., 1924, pp. 31-46.*

### SIR EDMUND GOSSE   (essay date 1925)

*[Gosse's importance as a critic is due primarily to his introduction of Henrik Ibsen's "new drama" to an English audience. He was among the chief English translators and critics of Scandinavian literature and was decorated by the Norwegian, Swedish, and Danish governments for his efforts. Among his other works are studies of John Donne, Thomas Gray, Sir Thomas Browne, and important early articles on French authors of the late nineteenth century. Although Gosse's works are varied and voluminous, he was largely a popularizer, with the consequence that his commentary lacks depth and is not considered in the first rank of modern critical thought. However, his broad interests and knowledge of foreign literatures lend his works much more than a documentary value. In the following excerpt, Gosse characterizes* The House with the Green Shutters *as a reaction to the Kailyarders' sentimental idealization of Scottish peasant life.]*

*The House with the Green Shutters* is a satire, not a parody. It effects its purpose by what it leaves out, not by a burlesque profusion of detail. In fact, the first thing which strikes the reader on reinspection of the tale is its bareness, its severe detachment from all the usual ornaments of fiction. Pathos and religion and humour are excluded, and with still greater austerity all the elements of love. . . . Andrew Lang, greatly admiring the firm draughtsmanship of *The House with the Green Shutters,* nevertheless asked the author why he had concentrated his powers on "moral ugliness," and nothing else.

Brown's answer was direct; he said that the sentimental gush of the Kailyard dealt with an imaginary moral beauty, and gave no hint of the realities of Lowland village life, with its "malignancy, hard drinking, and coarse language." He had determined to paint these qualities, and these only, in his unsparing picture of Barbie. He spoke much to his friends about the "malignancy," of the Scottish peasants, by which he seems to have meant their unfortunate tendency to allow the slightest difference of opinion or interest to breed an implacable animosity. This had been speciously ignored by the sentimental novelists, and it forms the central feature of *The House with the Green Shutters,* where the village, when once displeased with its leading citizen, pursues him and his family with such unyielding and corporate hostility that the prosperity with which the history opens is reduced to ruin at the end. There is not a touch of human pity or of exoneration in the united, slow persecution of the Gourlays by the relentless inhabitants of Barbie, and yet Gourlay himelf is throughout painted in colours which deprive him of our sympathy. What he gets is terrible, yet we feel that he largely deserves it. There is not one chapter in the book which is not thoroughly satisfied with itself and dissatisfied with everyone else. (pp. 342-43)

It is perfectly idle to conjecture what Brown might have done had he lived to maturity. But he will be remembered because of the stern originality and the sincere bitterness of his solitary study of life as he had seen it around him in his childhood. The opening scene of his novel, where Gourlay, in the plenitude of his pride, sends his pomp of carts streaming down the dazzled village, and the final scene, where the House of the Green Shutters closes around its inevitable and awful tragedy, give us reason to believe that Brown would have displayed a mastertouch in everything he afterwards undertook. But what really inspires us most with respect and regret is the unflinching spirit in which he pursued the spirit of Truth in moral observation. (p. 344)

> Sir Edmund Gosse, "The House with the Green Shutters," in his Silhouettes, William Heinemann Ltd., 1925, pp. 339-44.

### JOHN SPEIRS   (essay date 1939)

[*In the following excerpt, Speirs finds* The House with the Green Shutters *important for its social criticism rather than its literary merit.*]

The appearance of George Douglas Brown's single novel *The House with the Green Shutters* as a "World's Classic," suggests that the book has claims both to be regarded as a "classic" and nearly forty years after its first appearance (1901) to be read. Whether or not it has claims to be read is the test; for a classic that will be content to ornament a bookshelf is a classic of very equivocal kind. It was doubtless the vogue half a century ago of idyllic "kailyard" fiction that provoked George Douglas to the prosaic "realism" of his book. But what appears

rather to sustain it is an almost terrifying dissatisfaction with the Scotland itself he had known. The book not merely implies a criticism of certain other books that in any case are no longer read—that it killed the "kailyard" type of fiction is its historical importance—it implies a radical *social criticism* amounting to an indictment, and it is as such that it may have its present importance; for while I would not admit it to the highest rank as a work of the novelist's art—to the rank that is to say of *Wuthering Heights,* the novel with which one immediately compares it in one's mind—its value *as a work of art* seems to me to depend on the values of the social criticism it successfully implies. As a "tragedy" detached from these implications it seems to me at once "conventional" as if its author were striving to conform to some exterior idea of "tragedy" which he supposes himself perhaps to have got from the Greeks. Expectation is preferred to surprise according to the best models; the "bodies" are thought of as filling the role of the "chorus," and so on. The scenes of pity (not weakly indulged) and terror—horror rather—towards the end would appear to justify it as a "tragedy" in this conventional sense. But the source of all that power the book undoubtedly has, can, it seems to me,be shown to exist in reality in the terrible nature of its social criticism.

The novel presents a number of different individuals—centering in the members of the Gourlay family—in the setting of a small local community—that of Barbie—which is in a late phase of disintegration. Whether or not Barbie was characteristic of the Scotland of the nineteenth century must be left to someone other than the literary critic to confirm; in any case "Barbie" has, I think, a general application. "Barbie has been a decaying burgh for thirty years," we are told explicitly in the beginning of the second chapter. To call Barbie a community is indeed to extend the meaning of the word unduly; it has ceased to be an "organic community"; there is no longer a fruitful co-operation between its members. The "bodies" who represent the last of the local public opinion and should have been, without necessarily knowing it, the guiding and controlling centre of the community are—destructive worms bred out of the decaying organism—idly malicious gossipers and backbiters. Yet the "bodies" are in a sense what has become of the past, and as traditional figures are significant, as well as richly comic. The Deacon, and for example . . . David Aird, the City bounder about to return to the City after finding Barbie "too quiet for his tastes" ("Thank God, we'll soon be in civilization") form a significant comic contrast; but it is the Deacon alone who is satirically aware of the others. (pp. 450-51)

There being no longer a community holding together and controlling its members, the sheer individual, Gourlay, of peasant stock, stupid, but of tremendous dourness and brute force of "character" thrusts upward. He builds the House with the Green Shutters on the top of the hill. It represents his attempt at self-sufficiency—the house apart. "It is his character in stone and lime," and it dominates the town. Since the public opinion—as represented by the "bodies"—is important to control him the malevolence of the "bodies" grows monstrous against him. With shakes of the head they judge Gourlay's house as Vanity and "Pride that *will* have a downcome." But the traditional judgment loses most of its force from being made the vehicle of their petty personal spite.

Gourlay maintains his position till the advent of another individual—Wilson—who although a native of Barbie has been—significantly—*away* for an interval of years. (p. 453)

Gourlay, although a type of the individualism which both followed from and contributed to the break-up of the Scottish community, is himself thoroughly Scottish. Wilson is no longer Scottish but nondescript modern commercialism and "progress."

The downfall of the Gourlay family gains in significance from being a particular instance of a more general downfall. The house of Gourlay looks well enough from the outside and in its yard . . . but inside it is in filthy disorder for Gourlay has a sluttish wife and his son and daughter are ailing in mind and in body; the fruit of Gourlay's pride is internally rotten. Gourlay's attempt to found a self-contained house and family dominating Barbie has to come to nothing sooner or later in any case, for young Gourlay, his son and heir, is a "weakling." Yet we are shown clearly enough that brought up in more favourable conditions there is sufficient in young Gourlay to have brought forth some fruit. He is gifted with a wealth of sensuous perceptiveness represented in passages of a prose that in this respect reminds one oddly of Katherine Mansfield's.

But as young Gourlay's schoolmaster and, later, his professor perceive, he is without the mind and character to use this wealth so as to make it something other than an incubus. The difficulties of the sensitive adolescent Scot are dealt with in a way that seems to anticipate what *The Portrait of the Artist as a Young Man* does for the Irish adolescent. In the case of the adolescent Scot there is almost no tradition, no sympathetic understanding community to guide him; prematurely born, he is subjected only to the brutal will of his father and the weak indulgence of his mother. Not that the novelist attempts to invoke our sympathy for him. He is dealt with as unsympathetically as almost everyone else in the book. It is part of the bracing effect of the book that it is almost wholly unsympathetic. Douglas is a stringent moralist, scrupulous searching our moral failure. As a moralist he is perhaps too *explicit* for a novelist. But as that is not a fault of much modern work it is almost to be welcomed here as a sign of health than otherwise. A moral preoccupation in the finest sense of 'moral' may be held to be an essential for a novelist, perhaps for any artist.

Young Gourlay is sent to Edinburgh University to be made into a minister. . . . Old Gourlay has no illusions as to the sacred profession. He wants to put his son into it as an expedient for saving the falling fortunes of his house. At this point then the focus is shifted from a small rural burgh to the very capital of Scotland itself and to what might be expected to be the centre of its cultural life, Edinburgh University. Young Gourlay at Edinburgh is partly a test of what Edinburgh and its university have to offer. It might not have been too much to expect that here if anywhere the youth might have found the conditions lacking in Barbie favourable for the multiplication of his single talent. Douglas's picture of Edinburgh and its university is no flattering one. Edinburgh offers the "weakling" only too much encouragement in his suicidal tendency to whiskey-addiction. The lecture rooms, where as one of a mob of rowdy students he has his sole opportunity of confronting his professor, are twice presented in the condition of a bear-garden. "Auld Tam," the Scots professor, is indeed a figure to be reckoned with. He is representative of the Scots professor of the days before Scots professors were mostly Englishmen from Oxford and Cambridge, and he possesses powers of mind and character (he quells the unruly students with the humorous acerbity of his tongue) which we are bound to respect. Being also a representative of the tradition of philosophy and abstract speculation

which we associate more especially with the Edinburgh of the eighteenth century, he is in general amusingly inadequate when attempting to deal with something so concrete and particular as literature. What effective culture there might seem still to be in Edinburgh is represented by the Allan circle. There seems to me a serious weakness betrayed by Douglas in his portrayal of this circle. The novelist seems to accept it almost as its own valuation. If, as appears, Douglas intends it to be regarded as really "brilliant," he does not succeed in convincingly representing it as such. Could it have been that Douglas, in general so without illusions, was himself impressed by the sort of thing represented by Tarmillan, the most "brilliant" apparently of the Allan circle? The superficial, even vulgar, cleverness of the wit of Tarmillan's conversation is something sadly inferior to the corresponding thing there is reason to believe there was in the Edinburgh of the eighteenth century. "The Howff"—the pub which night after night lures young Gourlay to it out of his dismal room and away from his uncongenial books—represents what had become of the tradition to which at an earlier phase Burns's poetry belongs. It is a survival from the older Scotland. . . . (pp. 454-56)

But for young Gourlay "the Howff" is no longer an expression of the robust enjoyment of bucolic life; it is merely a refuge to shrink into from the terrors that assail his sensitivity. The novel ends, inevitably, on the notes of Insanity, Disease, Murder, Suicide. The tendency is not only in young Gourlay; it is in the whole of the society of which the novel is a grim representation. This seems to me the nature of the tragedy of the novel, by virtue of which it may prove permanently applicable.

What is to be one's final word on the book as a contribution to literature? The quality of a novel is of course that of its prose both locally and as a cumulative organic whole. The passages extracted above give a fair idea of Douglas's prose at its working best. The purple patch about the thunderstorm at young Gourlay's birth might be extracted, together with its echo later that so terrified the truant boy, if the comparison with *Wuthering Heights* is to be insisted on. But Douglas's prose is not always so good. At times it appears insufficiently controlled—emotions "seethe" and "boil"—and on the other hand, while frequently exhibiting a rich particularity, it occasionally drops into something like the journalist being "literary." That the book was Douglas's first (and only) novel may explain its immaturities, as its astonishing power may seem to have offered great promise of future achievement; but it's not easy to believe that the life of a journalist in London would have qualified him to write a greater Scottish novel; and in any case considerations of what he might have done ought not to deflect the critical judgment on what he did do. That Douglas's prose should so consistently preclude sympathy is of course its unusual strength. If that unsympathy could have been converted into a purely artistic detachment and sustained as such the novel would have been a great work of art. Unfortunately, as an examination of its prose at once confirms, the unsympathy is not always that of detached and seriously poised art, but seems at times to proceed from an unresolved personal animus. There is not space to extract the opening passage of the book for examination, but I may perhaps refer to it. It is Douglas's prose at its best, but even here the "silly" of "The silly *tee-hee* echoed up the street" is perhaps a sign of this insecurity. There may be some justice also in the common dismissal of the book as "merely depressing." Douglas does indeed refer to certain positives, . . . but these positives, though referred to, are nowhere strongly and positively realized in the book. If they had been it would perhaps have been a wiser, because more complete, book. Nevertheless if not a great novel it is because of the clarity of the social criticism it implies, a very remarkable one, perhaps the only very remarkable Scottish novel, not excepting the earlier Scottish novels of Walter Scott and John Galt. (pp. 456-57)

> *John Speirs, "Nineteenth-Century Scotland in Allegory," in* Scrutiny, *Vol. VII, No. 4, March, 1939, pp. 450-57.*

### GEORGE BLAKE  (essay date 1951)

[*A Scottish novelist, journalist, and critic, Blake was a member of the movement against the rural stereotypes of Kailyard fiction. In the following excerpt from his study* Barrie and the Kailyard School, *he examines the relationship between* The House with the Green Shutters *and the work of the Kailyarders.*]

We shall have to consider in a moment or two how far *The House with the Green Shutters* was deliberately organized as a counterblast to the excessive sentimentality of the Kailyard men.... In the meantime, it is most interesting to know that the famous novel was first written as a long short story of some 20,000 words, and that it was expanded to its ultimate 80,000 as the result (if we follow Mr. Melrose [see Additional Bibliography]) of earnest discussions among ... friends. This, I think, is the key to certain obvious faults of the technical kind in the completed work. One may at least hazard the suggestion that it might have been a more perfect novel, in both shape and balance of emphasis, if Brown had conceived it as a full-length novel in the first place and worked on it according to his own exclusive lights. (pp. 92-3)

The plot is in the simplest convention of tragedy. John Gourlay, grain merchant and contractor in Barbie, dominates the township and its people, including the Provost and councillors, by his commercial success and the force of a ruthless personality. His house with the green shutters, overlooking the place, is the prized symbol of his brutal sovereignty. The capital for his enterprises came with his wife, but she is a feckless slut by the time we first meet her. The only son, young John, is a cocky coward, spoiled by his mother and mortally afraid, while proud, of his father. There is a daughter of whom Brown makes nothing except a figure of convenience in the last chapter.

A native of Barbie, named Wilson, returns with some commercial experience elsewhere and some capital, and Gourlay grossly insults him at the first encounter. Wilson, thus stung into rivalry, is cleverer than Gourlay by far. Cunningly managed, his new business takes trade from Gourlay until the house with the green shutters is ultimately all the man has left to mask his pride. He is represented as being so fierce in his lust for power and prominence that, when he hears of Wilson's son going to the university, he must send his own John the same way, even if the lad is ill-fitted for the vocation and was destined to be the natural successor to a triumphant business.

Young John makes a mess of things at Edinburgh, learns to drink to almost incredible excess, and is sent down. His return in this disgrace coincides with Gourlay's final realization of his commercial failure and, therefore, the collapse of his pride. There is the inevitable scene between father and son, and a blow is struck with a poker. The death of the old man is represented as a fall on to the edge of the fender, but remorse and fear have their way with young John; he indulges in a bout of drinking and then in a dram of poison. Mother and sister, the latter now a hopeless invalid, discover in their terror that

there is still poison in the bottle and share it in a last pact of death. The house with the green shutters is finally the mortuary of the Gourlays and their pride.

It may read crudely enough in this version, but Brown carried it off. Even if the consumptive daughter, of whom we have heard next to nothing beforehand, is dragged in at the end by the hair of the head to make the fatal decision, the horror of the affair is not abated by that technical consideration. The character of old Gourlay is wildly improbable, we may say in the forenoon, but in the lamplight it frightens as much as it frightened his weakling son. The tale of technical blemishes may be long enough. Brown all too often falls into the beginner's vice of explaining his characters as from author to reader instead of suffering them to explain themselves in thought, speech and action; and, even so, Brown's discourses on his own characters and on the Scottish character in general are packed with arresting aphorisms. Many readers may share my feeling that the passages on young Gourlay's life at Edinburgh University and, in particular, his surrender to extremely large libations of strong drink are both clotted and scamped—probably one of those extensions fitted on to the original short story; but the suspension of disbelief is only mildly shaken. Brown carries it off by a force almost as ruthless as that which he makes us believe old Gourlay to have possessed.

The high merits of the book are clear. First of all, the sheer gift of story-telling, the natural drive of the born novelist, for which there can be no accounting. Next, a surprisingly tender feeling for the "atmosphere" of a small country town, particularly (as the critical and sensitive reader may be interested to note and check) in the early hours of fine spring and summer mornings. Third, an extraordinarily efficient and yet perfectly natural use of dialect, especially in its personal applications. But the supreme literary virtue of the tragedy is Brown's brilliant success in the presentation and characterization of his Greek Chorus—the "bodies" of Barbie. Here we have at once his finest creative success and his most effective criticism of the sentimental tendencies of Crockett and Watson at least. (pp. 94-7)

The "bodies" of any Scottish village are—or, rather, used to be—the equivalent of the "gaffers" in the English tradition. They were those male inhabitants of small places who could afford the time to gather round the village pump or its equivalent, even in the forenoon, watch what was going on, speculate on motives, exchange small rumours, pass on malicious gossip and act in general as the clearing-house of local news....

[Such] people had a curiously powerful influence, often malignant enough, on the social atmosphere of any small and isolated community in the middle decades of the nineteenth century. It is one of the supreme virtues of *The House with the Green Shutters* that Brown gives this social factor prominence, making his group of "bodies" at the Bend o' the Brae participants in the drama as well as spectators of the central tragedy. They watch and speculate and put two and two together (usually making five) and they are a repulsive bunch of small-town malignants, but Brown, handling their snivelling dialect with mastery, shows that the negative force they wield is as much a factor in the downfall of a masterful man as Gourlay's unrelenting pride. (p. 97)

Brown was every bit as guilty as the Kailyard men of holding his fellow-countrymen up to the ridicule of the foreigner: his only possible defence being, in the boyish phrase, "but they started it." It must also be maintained that he is, in one direction, as false to the facts of Scottish life (or any other sort of peasant life) as Crockett. The pity inherent in his tragic conception apart, there is precious little acknowledgment of the kindness, sentiment and tenderness of the ordinary life in *The House with the Green Shutters*. The jests are of the bitterest variety. There is no honest laughter in Barbie, only a nasty whinnying of small persons. We accept Brown's world while he has us in his charge as a storyteller; but we hesitate, in the early hours of the next morning, to accept his premisses.

Now the documentary values of fiction may be nothing as beside the power of the novelist to induce in us that willing suspension of disbelief, but here we must concern ourselves with claims that have been widely made as to the importance of Brown's one novel in relation to the Kailyard success. It is still said, sometimes by people who should know better, that it blasted the Kailyard seedlings overnight; and that is to ignore the clear fact that the Kailyard was bound to wither in the changing social and scientific conditions of the early twentieth century. In his pardonable pride in his influence on Brown while the tale was being written, Mr. Melrose makes it out to have been conceived in almost direct reaction to the Kailyard interpretation of Scottish life. Brown was determined to display the other side of the shield, "the Scot malignant." Therefore, Mr. Melrose implies, his friend wrote *The House with the Green Shutters*.

This is nonsense, surely. One must refuse to believe that any considerable work of the creative order—and *The House with the Green Shutters* is certainly that—can be produced as a sort of polemic, a mere retort like any Letter to the Editor. I am myself confident in the view that, however much Brown's genius may have been stimulated by the success of what he thought to be worthless and false, and by his earnest friends, *The House with the Green Shutters* was the novel he was born and bound to write, the grim story that had long been gestating within a wry and awkward personality: the chunk of convinced, inward truth that fortified a shy man in claiming the title of Man of Letters.

One last thought has its fascination. Of Barrie's attitude to rural life in Scotland one has used that hard word "sadism." Of George Douglas Brown's testimony on the same subject one could reasonably use the word "brutal" or, at the least, "merciless." The distinction is all-important in any understanding of the Kailyard betrayal, as the modern Scot sees it. One writes of Barrie in his Kailyard phase as a sadist because, so obviously the master of technique and understanding, he sniggered, nudged with the elbow, whispered under his hand, and exploited the intimacies of his most private life to make the picture appealing to those who might buy it. Brown was cruel, but he was as honest as the bright mornings he so loved to describe. He was possessed of a savage indignation indeed, but he did not drag the short-coated peasant, who was his mother, into the proceedings. He saw his world from the outside, honestly if clumsily at times, and, though lacking Barrie's exquisite gift of presentation, slugged away to give us what he believed to be a neglected facet of truth. His one novel remains in the classic order of such things. . . . [We] may safely believe that *The House with the Green Shutters* will live as long as literate men are capable of saying: "Yes, but look at this side of the picture." (pp. 98-100)

*George Blake, in his* Barrie and the Kailyard School, *Arthur Barker, Ltd., 1951, 103 p.*

**IAN CRICHTON SMITH**  (essay date 1969)

[*Smith is a Scottish poet, fiction writer, dramatist, and critic who writes in both English and Gaelic. In the following excerpt, he evaluates artistic merits and shortcomings of* The House with the Green Shutters.]

One of the things that George Douglas Brown does in *The House with the Green Shutters* is abolish Scottish history and concentrate on the present and the physical. . . . There are no historical references. What Brown might lose in depth he gains in immediacy. It is true, however, that the section of the book which is set in Edinburgh is weak; he is the novelist par excellence of the small town and not the city. . . .

Instead of describing a landscape for its own sake, Brown creates it only to dismiss it, or rather only to annex it into a specific human consciousness. He makes the observed detail do some work as, for instance, in the following: "The table was littered with unwashed dishes and in the corner of it next him was a great black sloppy ring showing where a red saucepan had been laid upon the bare board. The sun streamed through the window in yellow heat right on to a pat of melting butter." This is a description of Mrs. Gourlay's kitchen but the details have been carefully selected. The last sentence is not poetic; it is telling us about Mrs. Gourlay and is an indirect evocation of her negligence. It is not a fact of landscape; it is a human fact. (p. 3)

Brown has learned to make landscape a function of human psychology. He hardly ever writes about it for its own sake. The book is essentially about human beings, and that is a good thing.

How good is the novel? The most powerful character is, of course, Gourlay, a man of primitive strength and ambition. He is not, however, powerful mentally but he does give an impression of greatness. It is the greatness of an Ajax bewilderedly hacking at sleep. He suffers from the sin of hubris, for this book seems to be modelled on Greek tragedy. The stage full of deaths at the end suggests this. And if we follow this analogy through, we discover that, if there is a chorus in Green tragedy, the chorus of people in this novel—the Deacon, the Provost and so on—are actively hostile to the hero. It is as if the Greek chorus had become, not commentator, but enemy. In Greek drama the chorus is there to pass average human judgment. It is usually neutral or at least not prejudiced against the hero. It works for the playwright since he himself cannot speak. It represents a moral centre. Here we see Gourlay a lot of the time through a chorus that hates him. And the fact that Brown may be thinking in terms of the Greek hero—or at least a legendary primitive hero—is shown by a little incident which happens when Wilson, Gourlay's business rival (a little quick minor cut-price Ulysses), is engaged in attracting a potential customer away from Gourlay.

> Then a strange thing happened. Gourlay had a curious stick of foreign wood (one of the trifles to feed his pride on) the crook of which curved back to the stem and inhered, leaving room for the fingers. The wood was of wonderful toughness and Gourlay had been known to bet that no man could break the handle of his stick by a single grip over the crook and under it. Yet now, as he saw his bargain whisked away from him and listened to Wilson's jibe, the thing snapped in his grip like a rotten twig.

It is typical of Brown that he should signal a psychological setback by a physical gesture, for the power of the book is almost wholly physical: "He went down the street with grinding jaws, the letter crushed to a white pellet in his hand."

Gourlay reveals himself continually through the physical. "Gourlay's jaw clamped. 'Noathing, Peter,' he said sullenly." And later, "'No, no, Peter' and Gourlay gripped him by the shoulder as he turned back to his work."

The book, of course, falls apart at the end. Everyone in the house has to die and there is some unconvincing business with a hammer where Gourlay, I think in an act which sounds psychologically wrong, sets about improving his house. Similarly, in order that the postman—the small town Mercury—may discover the dead bodies, he has to have some reason for entering the house and the pretext supplied by the author is that a letter addressed to Gourlay is insufficiently stamped.

These incidents are perhaps not serious flaws—and we all know how careless even Shakespeare was—but they reveal a negligence which threw away, though it did not demolish, the book.

One is also interested in another question with regard to the novel. Who is telling the story? It is told mostly in the third person and yet near the end an inexplicable "I" narrator emerges briefly. Is this "I" the author?

What, however, is important—indeed crucial—is the fact that the author has not sufficiently withdrawn himself from the events. His own hatred of the society is involved and this muffles the impact of the book, and gives it in places a shrill hectic tone. One feels this partisanship on the very first page where he is describing the chambermaid of the Red Lion (called, significantly enough, Blowsalinda): "Halfway she met the hostler with whom she stopped in amorous dalliance. He said something to her and she laughed loudly and vacantly. The silly tee-hee echoed up the street." The single word "silly" betrays the author. (pp. 4-6)

It is rather a pity that the author should have injected his own emotion and dislike into the book since, in other ways, the society is meticulously and accurately described as if the inhabitants of Barbie were, in fact, an insect species which has learned to use intelligence in the service of a blind instinct of hate. The book would have been much more powerful if the image, scientifically conceived, had been allowed to do its own work. And yet . . . there is no doubt too that the anger of Brown animates the whole structure.

There is also no doubt that there is a terrifying truth in the book, a truth which he has brought to the boil in a small venomous hothouse. And how much healthier it is than the sentimental kailyardism against which he was rebelling!

He describes the Deacon as an "artist in evil." And this also is true. In a sense these people are doing what he himself is doing, that is, meticulously observing and making a story from their observations. They are in truth artists. But the accusation that can be made against them is that they are obsessively one-sided. It is a pity that the same observation can be made against the author. If he had shown the magnanimity which could have insulated himself against their venom he could have written a masterpiece for he had the passion and the equipment to do so.

I consider that the final damaging weakness of a potentially great book is this. If history and religion are abolished in this arena where Gourlay is baited like a bull, where is the moral centre from which judgment is passed? Has the author created one character who stands for what we can admire and who can yet survive as a human being in such an environment?

There is none. The baker shows decency but he is not big enough to affect events. Oedipus recognises the judgment of the gods. But there are no gods for Gourlay to recognise. What we have is a kind of squalid natural history into which no judgment can be inserted. Consequently, at the end, Brown is driven into melodrama and his cruel Mercury postie who discovers the deaths.

The trouble is not so much that events are exaggerated but that there is no resonant depth such that we can know that Gourlay's hubris is wrong. If his hubris is only a reaction against this town who would not excuse him? Gourlay is only doing what is natural in isolating himself from these people. They represent no values either human or divine. He himself represents no values except the courage of a flawed but ultimately barren spirit. If the novel is a kind of Darwinism in action can Darwinism ultimately be the stage on which a tragedy can be played? Certainly not in *Lear* where—in spite of the continuous animal imagery—the King and Gloucester are partially defined by another order—a religious one. There is no order to which Gourlay looks or on which the author can rely.

Nevertheless, when all this has been said, Brown has set down a powerful image of Scottish small town society. We feel it to be true though perhaps exaggerated.

If Wilson is a devious small town Ulysses and Gourlay an inarticulate Ajax they are nevertheless divorced from the anger or concern of the gods. We, the readers, cannot find a place to be at. We hate to see what happens to Gourlay but only as we hate to see a lack of fair play in life. Is this enough for tragedy? Wouldn't true tragedy be more cathartic than this? The enraged Ajax slashing at the sheep is not tragic. It is painful but not ultimately meaningful.

And yet. And yet . . . how close Brown got here to a masterpiece when the writing is about Barbie and its inhabitants! When the book is placed beside Turgenev's *A Lear of the Steppes* we can see what is gained by a distancing and coolness on the part of the author. The image of the Russian Lear tearing apart rafter after rafter of his house shows what happens when a writer follows the logic of his story through and does not step aside in the service of melodrama. (pp. 6-7)

*Ian Crichton Smith, "The House with the Green
Shutters," in* Studies in Scottish Literature, *Vol. VII,
Nos. 1 & 2, July-October, 1969, pp. 3-10.*

## CHRISTIAN CIVARDI   (essay date 1972)

[*In the following excerpt, Civardi studies Brown's treatment of
Scottish social issues in* The House with the Green Shutters.]

Shortly after the publication, in 1901, of his first and only novel, ***The House with the Green Shutters,*** George Douglas Brown wrote to his friend Tom Smith:

> I'm not sure that you'll like the book. There is too
> much black for the white in it. However, the malig-
> nants of rural life in Scotland had never been studied
> and I wished to show them up as they deserved.

His intentions as well as his misgivings are even more evident in another letter, written a few weeks before his sudden death at the age of thirty-three, in August 1902:

> Even so it is more complimentary to Scotland, I think, than the sentimental slop of Barrie, and Crockett, and Maclaren. It was antagonism to their method that made me embitter the blackness. Like old Gourlay I was going to "show the dogs what I thought of them." Which was a gross blunder of course.

Thus, we cannot be blind to the fact that Brown wrote his novel . . . "in reaction to a stereotyped Scotland that needed to be challenged": the Scotland of the spuriously realistic, unashamedly lachrymose, but extremely popular works of the Kailyarders. But Brown's own comments are somewhat misleading, and it should not be too readily assumed, as it has been all too often, that *The House with the Green Shutters* is a mere polemical novel, and that, as Somerset Maugham wrote in his introduction to the 1938 edition:

> George Douglas wrote in anger rather than with sympathy. There is not a single character in his novel that is not base, cruel, mean, drunken, or stupid. In fierce contradiction to the characters of the Kailyard novelists who are all white, he made his all black. . . .

For all its shortcomings—lack of sympathy is certainly not among them—, Brown's novel is a highly elaborate work of art in which the personal, social, and mythical levels are of a piece. John Gourlay and his family are led to their doom by forces springing from what they are meant to embody: the two major conflicting drives of nineteenth century Scotland.

John Gourlay, a fierce, hectoring, but rather stultified grain merchant of the eighteen-fifties, in the full vigour of his prime, has the monopoly of the carrying trade around the fictitious Ayrshire village of Barbie, drawn on the model of Brown's own Ochiltree. . . . Riding roughshod over every potential competitor, Gourlay has managed to hold his sway over the paltry, sleepy little burgh, but only at the expense of breeding hatred, especially among the "bodies"—the "malignant" male gossips, including the provost and the deacon, who keep "wrangling among themselves" but become a "band of brothers . . . (when) they hit on a common topic of their spite in railing at him." Such an all-pervading atmosphere of hatred is bound to bring down tragedy upon the village, and Gourlay will have to reap what he has sown. His downfall starts with the arrival of John Wilson, who, after having "done well for himself" in Aberdeen, comes back to settle down in his native Barbie, with a "fond desire that he, the son of the molecatcher, should get some recognition from the most important man in the locality." But Gourlay rudely slights him, thus paving the way for his own retribution. Nettled into revenge, Wilson soon becomes the champion of the ravenous "bodies"—not so "damn proud" as Gourlay, he is always ready for a "dram" and a "tit-bit"—and launches into business as a direct rival of his offender, whom he quickly outwits. Aware as he is that his fortune is on the wane, Gourlay holds his ground in the face of all, and, though he can hardly afford it, sends his only son John to the burgh high-school and thence, despite John's reluctance, to the University of Edinburgh. The son quickly dashes his father's ill-grounded expectations: completely upset by his new environment, he becomes a hopeless drunkard whom the Barbie bodies sadistically goad into utter profligacy and is finally sent down for misbehaviour at the end of his second session at the university. The bodies are exultant, but Gourlay's demeanour is as overbearing as ever. At this point, the figure of Gourlay unquestionably arouses feelings of pity and admiration—pity that he should thus be let down by his son, admiration as he has "stood up to everything without flinching"—as well as a feeling of fear, as he clearly cannot let John

go unscathed. Indeed, the end of the novel is a rapid succession of scenes in which Brown's "blackness" runs riot: as John, blind drunk and at bay, is cowering at his father's feet, he suddenly hits him with a poker, and Gourlay falls and "smashes his brow on the muckle fender," the pride of his house. Nobody challenges Mrs. Gourlay's explanation that her husband's death was accidental, but John, haunted by his father's wrathful eyes, poisons himself. Unwilling to go to the poorhouse, his mother and sister, both incurably ill, follow suit. Before taking the poison, however, Mrs. Gourlay reads aloud the thirteenth chapter of the first Corinthians, "Charity never faileth." The following morning, the Barbie bodies, sorely in need of this gospel, gaze "with blanched faces at the House with the Green Shutters, sitting dark there and terrible, under the radiant arch of the dawn."

The emblematic quality of the Gourlays is enhanced by a comparison with Stevenson's unfinished masterpiece, *Weir of Hermiston*, in which we have the same family pattern: a ruthless, self-assertive, brainless father, a weak, dithering wife, and a solitary son, coddled by his mother and bullied by his father. But while both fathers, Lord Hermiston and John Gourlay, epitomize the grim Scottish qualities of struggle—sternness, straightforwardness, unity of purpose—, their sons give totally different images of the younger generations: Archie harkens back to Scott and his romantic, chivalric heroes, as is made obvious in his forced retreat from Edinburgh to a Border estate, while John, compelled to leave the Ayrshire countryside for the capital, is quite unable to come to terms with his new environment, and, in a desperate attempt to find his own identity, seeks refuge in profligacy, murder, and suicide. The old Gourlay is an embodiment of the pride and individualism which had for ages sustained the Scots' struggle for existence before precipitating the disintegration of their social life; the son is an embodiment of the fear and escapism which appeared in the nineteenth century, when Scotsmen were brutally confronted with the dire realities of the industrial age. (pp. 194-96)

The proud individualism of [Old Gourlay] is insisted upon from the opening scene of the novel:

> He smoked in silent enjoyment because on a morning such as this, everything he saw was a delicate flattery to his pride. . . . It was the most secret and intimate joy of his life to go out and smoke on summer mornings by his big gate, musing over Barbie ere he possessed it with his merchandise.

These few lines contain the root of the whole problem: the perversion of pride. When the Scots' common foe disappeared with the Union of 1707, their grim qualities of struggle became perverted as they could only find expression within the bounds of small communities. Pride and individualism were turned into envy and censoriousness, and singleness of purpose became sheer stubbornness. These flaws were exacerbated by the "agricultural improvements" of the late eighteenth century, the main effect of which was a new eagerness for profit, due to the tremendous increase of the rental value of land and the ensuing payment of rents in money instead of in kind. This new acquisitive spirit was given a justification and a philosophy by the economists of the industrial age, as well as by many Calvinist theologians, and soon became sheer mammonism. Unlike the English, who could always struggle up the ladder of social, religious, military or political hierarchy, the Scots had no hierarchy to climb, they did not have a vast enough field on which they could vent their pride. When individualism, pride, poverty, and the Calvinist equalitarian dogma were combined within the bounds of small communities, they fostered rampant and all-corrupting greed and envy. . . . What Barrie and the Kailyarders failed to realize, or deliberately ignored, was that all the instances of petty jealousy which they staged in their novels, especially Barrie in *A Window in Thrums,* would gradually built up and end up by poisoning the moral fabric of a community. This was one of the main points that Brown wanted to make. . . .

> For many reasons intimate to the Scot's character, envious scandal is rampant is petty towns such as Barbie. To go back to the beginning, the Scot, as pundits will tell you, is an individualist. . . . From their individualism, however, comes inevitably a keen spirit of competition. . . . and from their keen spirit of competition comes, inevitably again, an envious belittlement of rivals. If a man's success offends your individuality, to say everything you can against him is a recognized weapon of the fight. . . .

He goes on to give an example of the main weapon used to denigrate potential rivals: gossip, especially of the genealogical kind. This is obviously not the apanage of Scotland . . . ; nor is it a feature of the nineteenth century alone. . . . But Brown stresses the point that gossiping is a prerequisite condition of social integration. Gourlay's greatest fault in the eyes of the bodies was that he did not comply with the rules of social conformity when refusing to take part in the gossiping game:

> There was no give and take in the man; he could be verra jocose with the lairds, to be sure, but he never dropped in to the Red Lion for a crack and a dram with the town-folk; he just glowered as if he could devour them! And who was he, I should like to know? His grandfather had been noathing but a common carrier! . . .

Even J. M. Barrie readily admitted that people reluctant to take part in gossip were given the cold shoulder:

> Sam'l was rale liked, for he was saft-spoken to everybody, an' fond o' ha'ing a grossip wi' ony ane 'at was aboot the farm. We did na care sae muckle for the wife, Eppie Lounie, for she managed the farm an' she was fell an' terrible reserved we thocht. . . . Ay, we made a rich mistake.

A similar mistake is related in L. G. Gibbon's short-story "Greenden," an intimation that things had not changed much some thirty years after the writing of *A Window in Thrums.*

There is a great contrast in tone, however, between the gossip of Barrie's characters and that of Brown's and Gibbon's. Although a whole chapter of *A Window in Thrums* is devoted to the tittle-tattle of Jess and Leeby when they see the minister passing on his gig, their comments are not basically malignant; whereas one single page is sufficient for Brown to make us aware that when the bodies are watching the Free Kirk minister going down the Skeighan road, they are intently looking for any opportunity to back-bite him. In the same way, "chit-chat on tales of sweethearting," which sounds quite harmless in Barrie's novel, turns out to be extremely damaging in Gibbon's trilogy [*A Scots Quair*]. In *The House with the Green Shutters,* surprisingly enough for a novel which has often been called "zolaesque," there is absolutely no mention of sexual problems. One may venture as an explanation that Brown's illegitimate birth had made him chary of dwelling on such matters. . . . (pp. 197-99)

A direct corollary of the paramount importance of grossip was the great impact of public opinion in social as well as domestic matters. It is public opinion that matters most to John Wilson

as he is coming back to his native Barbie, "for it is often the favourable estimate of their own little village . . . that matters most to Scotsmen who go out to make their way in the world." Even Gourlay is a slave to public opinion. His whole relationship with the community of Barbie is epitomized in his often repeated words of challenge: "I'll shew them." This attitude will pricipitate his downfall:

> It was strange that a thing so impalpable as grossip should influence so strong a man as John Gourlay to his ruin. But it did. The bodies of Barbie became the chorus to Gourlay's tragedy, buzzing it abroad and discussing his downfall; they became also, merely by their maddening tattle, a villain of the piece and an active cause of the catastrophe.

> The son's success would justify the father's past and prevent it being quite useless. . . . The Gourlays would show Barbie that they could flourish yet in spite of their present downcome. Thus, in the collapse of his fortunes, the son grew all-important in the father's eyes.

Unfortunately, young Gourlay proves utterly unable to come up to his father's standards. While the latter is a proud fighter, a man very much in the tradition of Cameronians, Jacobites, and Wee-Frees, the former, like the Scotland of his time, is incapable of assuming and asserting his individuality. In Barbie, he has been able to come to terms with himself, to acquire a sense of his own personality; whereas in the new world into which he has been launched, he has to pass once again through the whole process of self-discovery:

> The scenes round Barbie, so vividly impressed, were his friends, because he had known them from his birth; he was a somebody in their midst and had mastered their familiarity; they were the ministers of his mind. Those other scenes were his foes because, realizing them morbidly in relation to himself, he was cowed by their big indifference to him, and felt a puny, a nobody before them.

He is so frightened after leaving his native village that he longs for the night so as to escape the terrifying revelations of the day:

> When ensconced in his room that evening, he had a brighter outlook on the world. . . . After the whirling strangeness of the day he was glad to be in a place that was his own; here at least was a corner of earth of which he was the master; it reassured him. The firelight dancing on the tea things was pleasant and homely, and the enclosing cosiness shut out the black roaring world that threatened to engulf his personality.

Obviously, all this is to be related to the collective unconscious of Scotsmen in the nineteenth century, seeking refuge in something that would keep out the "black roaring world" and remind them of "auld lang syne": such a refuge was to be found in the works of the Kailyarders. Of such "silly literature" are Mrs. Gourlay and her son extremely fond. Brown's art is so elaborate here that their identification with the fate of their country can be read at more than one level. First of all, one ought to keep in mind the allegorical maiden name of Mrs. Gourlay, Miss Richmond of Tenshillingland, which represents the noble but poor Scotland half-heartedly marrying into money and so losing dignity. Thus, Gourlay is the embodiment of both the Scottish upstart bourgeoisie and the wealthy England of the Treaty of Union, John Gourlay the bully having obvious links with John Bull. Moreover, the fact that his son tries to forget his problem of adaptation by indulging in heavy drinking is not only relevant to the fact that Scotsmen were trying to forget the same problem by indulging in heavy Kailyard reading, both stupefying drugs. It is also relevant to the fact that Scotland was content to find its individuality among other nations, and especially the nations of Britain, by striking an attitude, by deliberately playing a rôle which did not reveal its true face but which, in spite of the falsification, enabled Scotsmen to be immediately identified wherever they went:

> Scotland was figured to the world at the turn of last century through "Punch's" jokes about golf caddies, ministers, and gawky housemaids, the soft-headed ruralising fiction of the Barrie-Maclaren school, and the century-old genius Burns.

In the same way, young Gourlay realizes that the community tolerates him and grants him an identity only when he accepts to exhibit a personality which will meet what is expected of him:

> Here at last he had found the sweet seduction of a proper pose—that of a "grand homme manqué," or a man who could be a genius were it not for the excess of his qualities.

As a country boy going to the university, John Gourlay could have been portrayed as a typical "lad o' pairts"; but he is the antithesis of the Kailyarders' stereotype of these poor students. (pp. 199-201)

Young Gourlay's stay at Edinburgh enabled Brown to explode another national myth, that of "John Barleycorn." Until him, the Scots overt tendency to heavy drinking had either been regarded as a funny, and, all things considered, rather congenial, idiosyncrasy of theirs, or totally ignored. Scottish laws of hospitality had always made it clear that he was a poor host indeed who let his guests go sober. John Dunlop, the founder of the first temperance society in Scotland, complained in 1829 that people would drink

> When an apprentice entered on his article, when a bargain was struck, when wages were paid. In family life, drink appeared during and between meals, at night, in the morning, as a preventive of cold or damp, as a mark of respect to the visitor, at births, marriages and funerals, great patriotic and social festivals to which had now been added the cult of the national poet.

This situation is evinced in *The House with the Green Shutters*, where every business transaction is struck with a drink at the Red Lion, where every forenoon the bodies assemble for their "morning," and where there are "several public houses," although the town is shown to be a fairly small one. On the contrary, in *A Window in Thrums*, there is not a single mention of alcoholism, not even one reference to the slightest drop of spirits. Barrie and the Kailyarders made a point of writing nothing that might shock their readers. (pp. 202-03)

It goes without saying that George Douglas Brown aimed at shattering the major myths propagated by these people: barren but friendly villages swarming with lads o' pairts and "dour men with hearts of gold and tender women of simple nobility" and ruled over by all-powerful but benevolent ministers. To do so as forcefully as possible he wove together into a tightly-knit composition multifarious elements of Scottish village life, constantly bringing into relief the vivid and the realistic, and entrusted his major characters with highly symbolic roles. Indeed, more than symbols, the Gourlays are the collective embodiment of a myth. Thus, James Baldwin's statement about

Richard Wright's *Native Son*: "Bigger's force comes from his significance as the incarnation of a myth," might be aptly applied to the Gourlay family. This fundamental analogy confronted both writers with the same problem: they felt that their heroes were too feeble-minded, or at least too inarticulate, to be allowed to cope alone with the formidable task of exploding the powerful myths they embodied. Therefore, they resorted to expedients, Wright to a spokesman in the person of Max, and Brown to unstinted moralizing authorial comment: in both cases a major structural flaw in the novel was the outcome.

Unlike *Native Son*, however, *The House with the Green Shutters* is not a politically committed novel. Brown has no new socio-political system to advocate; he is not even trying to alter the existing one. The butt of his satire is not society as the mirror of a socio-political order, it is society as a compound of individuals who are mistaken in their human relationships. The only remedy that is propounded is charity, as is exemplified by Mrs. Gourlay's reading of the Bible. In this respect, one may link Brown's novel with Dickens's *Hard Times* and recall George Orwell's criticism of the latter work:

> The truth is that Dickens's criticism of society is almost exclusively moral. Hence the utter lack of any constructive suggestion anywhere in his work. Of course it is not necessarily the business of a novelist, or a satirist, to make constructive suggestions, but the point is that Dicken's attitude is at bottom not even destructive. . . . For in reality his target is not so much society as "human nature." . . . His whole message is one that at first glance looks like an enormous platitude: If men would behave decently the world would be decent.

(pp. 205-06)

> *Christian Civardi, " 'The House with the Green Shutters': A Chapter of the Moral History of Scotland," in* Recherches Anglaises et Americaines, *No. 5, 1972, pp. 194-206.*

**IAN CAMPBELL**   (essay date 1978)

*[In the following excerpt from an essay written in 1978, Campbell discusses various themes and techniques in* The House with the Green Shutters.*]*

[Since] his searing picture of realistic Scottish country life in *The House with the Green Shutters* Brown had been identified in Ayrshire circles as the man who incorporated Ochiltree into the unflattering picture of Scottish "reality," peopled by the "Scot malignant" whom he believed to be more realistic, more honest to the facts, than the sugary sentimentalities of the "kailyard" popular at the turn of the century, the often able but hopelessly over-romanticised pictures of Barrie, Crockett and MacLaren. Like Lewis Grassic Gibbon two generations later, he seemed to have saved up his unhappiest childhood observations to flesh out the skeleton of his novel, incorporating barbed pictures of people and places which were all the more realistic for being (or so it seemed) not altogether fiction. (pp. 148-49)

Education was an important thing for Brown: it released him from the countryside of his youth, from his upbringing, from the stigma of his illegitimacy sardonically or unfeelingly observed by the community, and from the prospect of living out an existence of drabness, monotony and intellectual dullness intolerable to his morbidly sensitive mind. . . . Never a man at his ease, he found it easy to be outside his community. [As an] educated man, he was set apart . . . both by his own attitude to life and by the attitude of others to his privileged position. One thinks of Thomas Carlyle's father being advised by an acquaintance not to give his son "education": "James Bell (one of our wise men) had told him: 'Educate a boy, and he grows up to despise his ignorant parents.' My Father once told me this; and added: 'Thou hast not done so. God be thanked for it!'" A nice story, but one notices the parenthesis; Carlyle's education allows him the ironic reference to "our"—Ecclefechan's—wise men. He was glad to go back to revisit Ecclefechan for holidays, but notably not to settle again in the village from which education had alienated him. Perhaps he was lucky he was not a woman, for then his chances of emancipation would have been even slimmer. Lewis Grassic Gibbon's Chris Guthrie experiences amply the alienation from her community which "education" brings, but there is no immediate escape. Her mother freshly dead, Chris sits in the family kitchen and sees the ruin of her education.

> You'll be leaving the College now, I'll warrant, education's dirt and you're better clear of it. You'll find little time for dreaming and dirt when you're keeping the house at Blawearie.

And Chris in her pit, dazed and dull-eyed, said nothing. . . . The alienation, interestingly, is a compound of thoughtlessness and cruelty. The remark is monstrously tactless, but it also comes from a social tradition which quite omits subtleties of verbal interchange on this level. Brown underlines this tactlessness, quite brilliantly, in the handling of Gourlay's inarticulacy in *The House with the Green Shutters*. Perhaps this point would bear some closer inspection.

Gourlay (senior) is far from inarticulate. His gifts of character come from enormous self-possession, brute masculine courage, a bigness of presence which earns him the bodies' grudging respect as a "gentleman" in a book where such are woefully few. On his own ground, he can dominate (or domineer) verbally without question: witness his dismissal of Gilmour, and his handling of Templandmuir. That his powers of verbalisation, particularly under stress, have their limitations is painfully obvious at the public meeting which precedes his break with Templandmuir. In a village where modern manners, improving contact with the outside world and a gloss of civilisation mean more and more, his brute strength of character counts for less and less. He is never beaten down, but all too easily outmanoeuvred. Brown makes the point, but is not content to leave it at that—he turns it splendidly to advantage in one of the most subtle points of characterisation.

It is necessary for us to some extent to identify with Gourlay before his tragic downfall: Brown was too well versed in his Greek dramatic studies (both his University degrees were in Greek) not to know the Aristotelian injunction that the tragic character must have elements of good and bad together, not merely bad. There is small tragic pleasure to be had out of watching a purely bad character fall to a deserved punishment. Rather the ambiguous response must be cultivated by showing a potentially good, but flawed, character. Such a man is Gourlay—how are we to bypass Brown's heavy-handed insistence on his limitations, and achieve a genuine rapport with him?

The answer lies in part in his limited powers of verbalisation. "'I was always gude to the beasts at any rate,' Gourlay muttered, as if pleading in his own defence." He didn't have to talk to them, nor could they answer back. Yet the power of the writing Brown brings to bear on this description is undeniable. "For a long time he stared down at the sprawling carcass, musing. 'Tam the powney,' he said twice, nodding his head each time he said it; 'Tam the powney'; and he turned away." The control of emotion is hinted at purely suggestively; the restraint of the writing is its strongest point. There is nothing to say, after all, just a hint of the emotional attachment to a horse which had been, we know, his favourite. Nature's gentleman does not need to make speeches: his silence is more eloquent.

Occasionally he does make speeches, and their effect is closely related to that of the foregoing passage. Particularly is this so when, near to financial ruin, he has to dismiss the last of his servants, the half-wit Peter Riney. Communication between master and man is not difficult between these two, for Gourlay has nothing to fear from willing old Peter. All the more painful when Gourlay parts with this last vestige of his empire; significantly, the day before he had sold "Black Sally, the mare, to get a little money to go on with."

The scene of Riney's dismissal is handled with total economy of dialogue. (pp. 149-52)

There is no patronising in the episode, rather an observation from life. Riney cannot understand for a long time, and he drives Gourlay further and further onto the insecure ground of explaining himself. Peter unwittingly twists a knife in Gourlay's wounds by rambling on. "Man, have ye noathing for us to do?" he asks.

> Gourlay's jaw clamped. "Noathing, Peter," he said sullenly, "noathing," and slipped some money into Peter's heedless palm.
>
> Peter stared stupidly down at the coins. He seemed dazed. "Aye, weel," he said; "I'll feenish the tatties at ony rate."
>
> "No, no, Peter," and Gourlay gripped him by the shoulder as he turned back to his work, "no, no; I have no right to keep you. Never mind about the money—you deserve something, going so suddenly after sic a long service. It's just a bit present to mind you o'—to mind you o'—" and he broke off suddenly and scowled across the garden.

The breakdown of the cash nexus indicates keenly how this hurts Gourlay. With other men he dominates by personality or money: with Peter he can do neither. He is vulnerable. Peter is insensitive to both. Yet he shows his feelings in the unthinkable gesture, presumptuous and touching—he shakes Gourlay's hand.

> Without a word of thanks for the money, Peter knocked the mould off his heavy boots, striking one against the other clumsily, and shuffled away across the bare soil. But when he had gone twenty yards, he stopped, and came back slowly. "Good-bye, sir" he said with a rueful smile, and held out his hand.
>
> Gourlay gripped it. "Good-bye, Peter! good-bye; damn ye, man, good-bye!"
>
> Peter wondered vaguely why he was sworn at. But he felt that it was not in anger. He still clung to his master's hand. "I've been fifty year wi' the Gourlays," said he. "Aye, aye; and this, it seems, is the end o't."
>
> "Oh, gang away!" cried Gourlay, "gang away, man!" And Peter went away.

This is Gourlay at the end of his tether; unable to verbalise his intense feeling, he resorts to swearing (in a quite unmalicious way, but it is the only weapon in his armoury), then to dismissiveness. As in the case of Gourlay with the dead pony, Brown ends with the skilful, brief anti-climactic sentence. Peter went away, and with him the last trace of the Gourlay empire.

The breakdown of communication is one of the most effective ways in which Brown evokes the breakdown of the social contract in Barbie, and by extension in the "real" Scotland which he, partly from memory, tries so hard to recreate in opposition to the sugar-candy picture of the kailyard. That the same attempt was in progress in the Victorian social novel in England needs little underlining here: the gulf is not only between the Deadlocks and the lower ranks, but between the Gradgrinds and Veneerings and those relatively little removed from their social position. (pp. 152-53)

Brown the outsider was ideally suited to observe life from either social level. He felt at home in neither. . . . He chooses the rootlessness of the socially mobile as one major theme of *The House with the Green Shutters,* but treats this difficult, because very personal, subject with startling flexibility. . . . Brown focuses grimly on the inarticulacy of the trapped individual, locked in an uncaring, inflexible, frequently needlessly abusive and hostile society which has the outside trappings of kailyard pleasantness, and is widely held by millions of readers to be an archetype of country calm and virtue. The irony of the situation lends savagery to his treatment of it.

So far this paper has dealt with the generation in power, the businessmen like the Provost, Gourlay, Wilson, Gibson. Yet their power is a transitory one, and even in the brief span of *The House with the Green Shutters* the balance of power in Barbie shifts quite startlingly from Gourlay's hands. At the outset of the novel his house is new, his grip of the carting trade in Barbie iron; he ruthlessly tramples his rivals, he externalises his pride in achievement by the excellence of the house, right down to the fender and poker specially imported from Glasgow, the poker with heavy tragic irony introduced as the murder-weapon which is to strike down its owner. A smaller but a more flexible man, Wilson can undo him when a bigger and more direct man could not; one bigger and more flexible—but not more admirable—like Gibson can out manoeuvre both of them. Change is the great factor operating against Gourlay, the change which brings such transformation to Glenburnie and Dalmailing, yet is largely excluded from Brown's hated kailyard. Change brings the advent of the railway and the coal-mines, the factories and the immigrant workers, the Wilson Emporium and its associated business empire, the redistribution of power which ousts Provost Connell by Provost Wilson (yet fails to unseat the malignant Bodies, the real Town Council). In fiction, change prepares a new generation to succeed the previous one; in *this* fiction, there is no such exception to the general attack on Scottish life. The younger generation will *not,* on the evidence of *The House with the Green Shutters,* be better able to cope with change, and bring about the improvement their elders failed to achieve. Unlike *Grey Granite,* Brown's novel fails to offer this consolation to Scotland: rather, in George Blake's phrase, it "forced a neglected truth upon the Scot." The younger generation share their fathers' faults, the constrictions of their environment and the mean-ness of their lives, without the redeeming feature of learning from their experiences.

A superficial examination of the medium in which young John Gourlay and his contemporaries grow up shows an alarming lack of sustaining or morally improving forces. Each force incorporated in Barbie is the deliberate antithesis of his kailyard prototype. The Established Kirk minister is a pompous and disgusting ass, the Free Kirk Minister—for Gourlay persists in the kailyard habit of playing up to the post-Disruption divided Scotland—a botanising weakling; provost and Doctor are non-entities; perhaps most serious (as Brown would know), the schoolmasters are failures as moral influences. . . . Gemmell, the Barbie schoolmaster, a stern disciplinarian, has little idealism for his task and contents himself with keeping order. McCandlish, a weaker but a more humane man, fails to brace young Gourlay's character and weakly tolerates his truancy from a hated environment. Perhaps most serious of all, though the Barbie schoolmaster follows young John Gourlay's progress and understands him, he fails to intervene when his intervention could have saved not only suffering, but four lives.

Young John Gourlay is in many ways the antithesis of his father; where the older man is straight, bluff, masculine, animal, superb, coarse, the younger is weak, effeminate, unphysical, yet noticing, clever, articulate in an undisciplined way. Brutally domineered by his father, he shelters in his mother's uncritical adoration. Gourlay likes his daughter, the unlovely and neglected Janet; Mrs. Gourlay loves her effeminate and clever, but weak son. So it goes.

Sneered at, repressed, bullied and shouted at, John can hardly express himself freely at home. In his father's presence he is cowed, or easily shouted down. His terror of lightning (shared by his creator), and his pathetic gratitude for the baker's unthinking protective sympathy in the Skeighan station yard during the thunderstorm, show how little affection he has known in the house with the green shutters. Yet he has talent; he *is,* in his mother's fond words, a "noticing boy" for little trifles, though significantly he cannot share his mother's taste for trashy "novelles" since he cannot handle even the limited externalisation of his imaginative world necessary to relive the experiences of any coherent plot. He can handle only flashes, and the immediately memorable is all he can grasp. . . . Human inter-relations hold no interest for him; brutally callous to his mother's sufferings, and apparently unconscious of his own sister's steady decline into tuberculosis, he is as bored by his home life as by the love-interest of fiction. "An Arctic Night" catches his fancy for the Raeburn prize essay title just for the cold purity of its matter, experienced, vivid, uncluttered by messy human beings. To let such a boy loose in the city, to give him an unwanted University education for purely social reasons, to keep up with neighbours, is tantamount to a crime against his developing personality, and the Barbie schoolmaster, in choosing not to become involved, could be thought guilty of a grave dereliction of duty.

> A brooding and taciturn man, he said nothing till others had their say. Then he shook his head.
>
> "They're making a great mistake," he said gravely, "they're making a great mistake! You boy's the last youngster on earth who should go to College."
>
> "Aye man, dominie, he's an infernal ass, is he noat?" they cried, and pressed for his judgement.
>
> At last, partly in real pedantry, partly, with humorous intent to puzzle them, he delivered his astounding mind.
>
> "The fault of young Gourlay," quoth he, "is a sensory perceptiveness in gross excess of his intellectuality."
>
> They blinked and tried to understand.

"Aye man, dominie!" said Sandy Toddle. "That means he's an infernal cuddy, dominie! Does it na, dominie?"

But Bleach-the-boys had said enough. "Aye," he said drily, "there's a wheen gey cuddies in Barbie!"—and he went back to his stuffy little room to study *The Wealth of Nations.*

This is a crucial moment in the book. The bodies would not have lifted a finger to save young Gourlay, indeed they would have refrained from doing so if it could have injured old Gourlay, but the public figure of the schoolmaster should perhaps have had higher ideals. Yet the scene here, in addition to reinforcing the degenerate nature of Barbie's public institutions, is quite in keeping with what has been argued to be the main intention of this novel, to parody the kailyard by incorporating its familiar characteristics, applied in an inverted way. In Maclaren and Barrie the dominie moves heaven and earth for the good of his poor pupils, and to get them to College is the limit of his ambitions; not so Bleach-the-boys. For the sake of a thin joke he breaks off the subject; for a cheap point against the Bodies (hardly worth engaging in verbal battle) he hides his analysis of young Gourlay's trouble in verbiage and walks off, unwilling to become engaged. The system has failed; neither Gemmell nor McCandlish try to talk Gourlay out of sending his son to Edinburgh University, and of course the inarticulacy of young John makes his feeble protests easy to overcome. (pp. 153-57)

If the school system of John's youth fails to diagnose and cure this weakness, so does the University system, with a vengeance. . . . The University cared little for young Gourlay, as it cared little for his creator. Enormous classes seem to have been enlivened by no individualised tutorial discussion. Junior staff barely met the students, except to impose discipline. Outside lectures, the students merely walked to and from lonely digs, or gathered in public houses for discussions which seemed more an escape from, than an extension of, their learning experience. This is not quite fair, for the view of Edinburgh University is as viciously limited by the author's intention (and by his chosen social sample) as is his view of rustic Scotland. Yet when Allan and his cronies attempt the philosophical discussion at the Howff, the sort of scene Brown must have grown accustomed to in Oxford and missed sadly when revisiting his native village, the attempt does not come off given the background of the Scottish cubs, their limited powers of conceptualisation, and above all their halting verbalisation of the unfamiliar. They descend easily to the anecdotal . . . and seek to "cap" each other's stories rather than analyse the reasons behind the subject under discussion—the extraordinary vividness of the Scottish peasant's speech.

> "To hear Englishmen talk, you would think Carlyle was unique for the word that sends the picture home—they give the man the credit of his race. But I've heard fifty things better than 'willowy man,' in the stable a-hame on a wat day in hairst—fifty things better!—from men just sitting on the corn-kists and chowing beans." . . .

"It comes from a power of seeing things vividly inside your mind," is young Gourlay's explanation, piping up from a corner of the dinner table where he has been sitting unperceived. . . .

> "Metaphor comes from the power of seeing things in the inside of your head," said the unconscious disciple of Aristotle,—"seeing them so vivid that you see the likeness between them. . . . A man'll

never make phrases unless he can see things in the middle of his brain. *I* can see things in the middle of my brain. . . ."

So could he; so could his creator. "He was unusually susceptible to the season," wrote one of Brown's student contemporaries ". . . ordinary things which leave no impression on the ordinary mind were to him full of a definite relish." He was, after all, a Scottish peasant, and to this class he attributed a share of "Burns's terrible vividness." Everywhere among them he expected to ". . . find men who can plant a picture in the mind for every single terrible phrase." To add to this the ambition of being a novelist was to put a terrible strain on the writer, the strain of having to live with the gift of the vivid imagination. His imaginary writer in the notes he made called "The Novelist" ". . . ran from note-book to note-book—he left notes half finished in the hurry of inserting others. His mind seemed to tower, to achieve; he was abundantly content." When all was not well, the strain was extreme, as he rushed to put down ideas, then strained to give them shape. The sparking of congruous ideas did not take place; Brown's notebooks are full of half-finished, desperately unfinished work. He honestly admitted to Ernest Barker that his style was "too tense," and young Gourlay "subjected to too much analysis." Wryly he agreed with Balzac's sister, when she diagnosed her brother's problem as "congestion of ideas": ". . . straining on one phase of thought spoils the general satisfying effect of the whole concatenation of thought."

Lucid order, clarity, control lead to relaxation of tension; it was rarely that Brown knew this relaxation, and more rarely still that he permitted it to young John Gourlay, the product of all the stresses and injustices in the Scottish educational system which had plagued his creator, and which are largely responsible for the downfall of *The House with the Green Shutters,* after the more obvious reasons of pride, character defect and personal animus are accounted for. The Scottish system made John Gourlay the man he was, and his interaction with it made Barbie the twisted place it was; his son was educated to that system, and in its highest development the Scottish educational system could not rescue him, nor release him from the inner tensions which, sternly repressed in the father (who only rarely gave way, as when his pony died, or he had to part with Peter Riney) break out and demoralise the son.

Far from helping, the system by uncaring actually hastens the harm to young Gourlay, by the heedless judging and awarding of the Raeburn prize. A minor essay prize . . . , it had been won several times by Barbie men, and by winning it young Gourlay seemed deceptively set on a career of academic success for which he was plainly unfitted. Auld Tam the professor who liked the essay (it is shrewdly hinted) as much for its brevity as for any other quality, should have hesitated before inflating the ego of a weakling like its author by the public award of the prize at the final lecture. Yet, like the dominie in Barbie, he cannot resist making a *bon mot* of the occasion, and his prosy words of advice flow unheeded by young Gourlay, whereas a private admonition would perhaps have changed his whole lifestyle.

> "You know, Jack," said Gillespie, mimicking the sage, "what you have got to do next summer is to set yourself down for a spell of real, hard, solid and deliberate thought. That was Tam's advice, you know."

> "Him and his advice!" said Gourlay.

Tam plainly did not even know who the author was; carelessly he awarded the prize, and set young Gourlay off on a hard-drinking course of several months which culminated in his expulsion, return to Barbie in disgrace, murder of his father, and eventual suicide. Could Tam have prevented it? In no very obvious way. Yet what he *said* from the rostrum was exactly what Gourlay needed to hear.

Tam, in returning the essays, distinguished between the lowest kind of imagination, which "merely recalls something which the eyes have already seen, and brings it vividly before the mind," and a higher kind which "pictures something which you never saw, but only conceived as a possible existence." Beyond this is a kind which can both see and hear another man's experiences "entering into his blood," and the finest, highest imaginative act is both "creative" and "consecrative," and "irradiates the world." It is just this which is lacking in Gourlay's writing, though there is much evidence of nervous perception. "It displays, indeed, too nervous a sense of the external world."

There are very ironic levels of writing here, for Brown clearly saw in this analysis some of the weaknesses of his own hypersensitive character. He wrote, with feeling, the final admonition of the professor. "That almost morbid perception, with philosophy to back it, might create an opulent and vivid mind. Without philosophy, it would simply be a curse. . . . Without philosophy, it would simply distract and irritate the mind." That philosophy is something Gourlay does not attain; his creator is out to make sure we do not sympathise too much with Gourlay as a fallen sage. He cannot, as can Tam, see the value of a "wise indifference." With it, a man is "undaunted by the outer world. 'That, gentlemen, is what thought can do for a man.' 'By Jove,' thought Gourlay, 'that's what whiskey does for me!'" The bathos is calculated; Gourley is a fool and soak as well as a victim of his upbringing. Yet the uncaring professor who swells his head by the award of the Raeburn delivers him into the environment from which he has failed to escape; the bodies love to play on his new arrogance, to inflate his absurd self-importance, and they accelerate his tragedy.

Education in itself, the ultimate goal of the kailyard dominie, is exposed as a chimaera by this novel. The untutored soul in James Carlyle may have been vividly metaphorical, in John Gourlay it was (just as credibly) trapped in inarticulacy, though still possessed of boundless brute courage. After all not all Scots are phrasemakers, even in the kailyard, and most of the Scots in *The House with the Green Shutters* are very poor verbalisers indeed. What little *tendresse* there is in the novel— between the baker and his wife, in their memorable encounter during one of the bodies' gossips—is unspoken and suggested, as is the bond between the baker and young Gourlay. In Barbie public speech-making is cruelly parodied, public exchanges reduced to the spiteful buzzing of the bodies, or the crude raillery of the bar-room or the Skeighan brake. At University the flow of reason is sadly interrupted, and public discourse from the professoriat self-indulgent and unfocussed. Young Aird and Gourlay may come back to Barbie in the vacations to show off, with new clothes and newly Englished vocabularies to match—but they have not learned to communicate, any more than have those who stayed behind in country obscurity. The climactic scenes at the end are all on a level of failed communication. Gourlay tries to inflict mental torture on his son more by calculated silence and half-speech than by command of words; John's attempts to explain his near-insanity after his father's death are whimperingly inarticulate. His moth-

er's magnificent speech on charity is little more than unvarnished Biblical quotation, and only poor, colourless Janet is allowed one splendid speech, in Scots, before she, too, dies. Her achievement is a very partial success; her mother was not even listening. Even outside, when the murder is discovered, the postie surprises Sandy Toddle struggling to tell the bodies (as he had solemnly promised not to do) the Gourlays were "sequestered," instead of "sequestrated."

There are many levels of irony in *The House with the Green Shutters,* all of them worthy of the ironic man who could write as his own epitaph, "Here lies a man whose ideals were so high that he never tried to realise them." If the book is an "honest brute" then it achieves its effect partly through its form (its satire of a dishonestly sentimentalised Scotland), partly through its characters (inversions of a dishonest parody), partly through the life-philosophy it projected *in its characters,* unrelieved by any objective standard which suggests the validity of higher ideals. Moving as Mrs. Gourlay's reading on charity from Corinthians is, on the verge of her suicide, it does not really give the reader much hope that it will be put into effect in Barbie, even that it will be heard by any of the natives who cluster round to witness the House's fall the following morning. There is no honest dominie, no worthy professor, no struggling reforming minister, no ideal parent trying to bring up his children despite the influences of environment. Perhaps Brown's dissatisfactions were so high that he did not try to picture his ideals in this first, angry novel, but this is not to say that the novel is not without ideals implicit in the novel which is there. The book is, it has been suggested, a sustained critique of a Scotland which can subsist without real communication, which can stumble on uncaringly and uncomprehendingly ignoring suffering or actually rejoicing in it, and rejoicing in causing it. It is a plot which touches on tender areas of Brown's own childhood experiences, on the injustices of fathers to sons, the difficulties of working-class schoolchildren trying to get on in a world seemingly quite alien to all they know, the uncaring or hostile reception that success—the outside world's success— meets with in the home town. Wilson's first return to Barbie, and his putting-down by Gourlay, is so bitterly written that it must be intended to relive some experience Brown knew. The University fails to diagnose and cure the weakness in Gourlay, as presumably it fails through indifference to see similar weaknesses in scores of boys from similar, if less restricted, backgrounds. The town fails to diagnose the trouble with the Gourlays, or if it does it opts out of involvement.

Change sweeps through this novel, and the social and economic upheaval of the closing decades of the nineteenth century is vividly recalled by its rapid evolution. George Douglas Brown's concern is not to trace the true social effects of population change, to analyse the breakdown in communication between master and servant, urbanite and countryman; he is not concerned with the work ethic, nor with the aesthetic problems forced on an industrial society by a machine age. George Douglas Brown is an observer, keen, too keen for his own comfort; if *The House with the Green Shutters* is an angry book it is in part because it *does* have ideals, but the anger comes in the way of the ideals. Instead the reader is offered the embittered irony of the outsider, the man alienated from his early Scotland yet fascinated by the very features which embitter. Above all, he is fascinated by the character of the "Scot Malignant," and allows the ironies of his society to speak for themselves, however ambiguously.

> "Tyuts," said the baker, "folk should be kind to folk. There may be a possibeelity for the Gourlays in the youngster yet!"

He would have said more, but at that moment his sonsy big wife cáme out, with oh! such a roguish and kindly smile, and, ''Tom, Tom,'' said she, ''what are ye havering here for? C'way in, man, and have a dish o' tea wi' me!''

He glanced up at her with comic shrewdness from where he sat on his hunkers—for fine he saw through her—and ''Ou aye,'' said he, ''ye great muckle fat hotch o' a dacent bodie, ye—I'll gang in and have a dish o' tea wi' ye.'' And away went the fine fuddled fellow. . . .

If that is the only unquestioned moment of fine interpersonal affection in the book, it is as ambiguous as the only unquestionably ''moral'' moment:

Wylie looked at him for awhile with a white scunner in his face. He wore the musing and disgusted look of a man whose wounded mind retires within itself, to brood over a sight of unnatural cruelty. The Deacon grew uncomfortable beneath his sideward, estimating eye.

''Deacon Allardyce, your heart's black-rotten,'' he said at last.

The Deacon blinked and was silent. Tam had summed him up. There was no appeal.

Of course, Brown's untimely death meant there was no appeal from the picture of Scotland he painted in *The House with the Green Shutters*. Yet with all its errors of overstatement and personal animus, the power of this novel suggests the power of feeling which lay behind Brown's self-picture, and his picture of the Scotland of his youth. To label it ''anti-kailyard'' is as dangerous as to label all kailyard ''sentimental slop'': *The House with the Green Shutters* was a timely warning against false self-analysis, and a timely and welcome reflection of a rapidly-changing Scotland as the country left the nineteenth century behind. (pp. 157-62)

> *Ian Campbell, "George Douglas Brown: A Study in Objectivity," in* Nineteenth-Century Scottish Fiction: Critical Essays, *edited by Ian Campbell, Barnes & Noble Books, 1979, pp. 148-63.*

**FRANCIS RUSSELL HART**   (essay date 1978)

[*In the following excerpt, Hart describes the moral perspective of* The House with the Green Shutters.]

[T. W. H. Crosland wrote that] G. D. Brown's Barbie ''is not of heavenly origin in the least.'' Indeed not: it is hell. Maurice Lindsay is right: ''Kailyardism must satisfy some continuing Scottish need.'' But anti-Kailyardism does too: they are poles, in fact, of the same field. What Richard Chase found to be true of the American romantic imagination is true as well of the Scottish moral imagination: it is theological, but hardly tragic, hardly Christian; rather, it is deeply polarized, Manichean and melodramatic. . . . In Kailyard fiction, the denial of evil itself was allied with an elegiac paralysis of will. In light of such an alliance, we may begin to understand the contrary ferocity of anti-Kailyardism, so vital an impulse of modern Scottish culture.

The three most promising of early modern Scottish novels promulgate a common anti-Kailyard lesson: an enlightened liberalism cannot cope with the Manichean warfare carried on behind man's facade of civility. (pp. 131-32)

Crockett's forced gusto, Maclaren's overwhelming melancholy, and Barrie's elfin cynicism have become George Douglas Brown's anger; and the anger has an instability that Brown's superb rhetoric does not control. Iain Crichton Smith [see excerpt dated 1969] and others have suggested that it was Brown's artistic error to let his animus pervade the book; this is an error if it is distracting or confusing—and it probably is. Brown speaks to a foreign audience as a distanced, knowledgeable interpreter of Scots; his premise is that one who understands a thing cannot sneer at it, yet he sneers constantly. For all his pretense of analytic distance he is deeply implicated in the culture he portrays. His theme, Kurt Wittig finds, is in Mrs. Gourlay's Bible reading: charity is the gospel that Barbie needs. But Brown as narrator shows none. His anti-Kailyardism proscribes all show of gentler virtues. He writes with the wrathful justice of an Old Testament Jehovah, with a classical Greek model, and with a naturalistic ethic. And for all that, his is one of the greatest of Scottish novels. (p. 134)

[Most] late Victorian naturalists are driven by an ethical passion and cannot accept a naturalistic ethic. As they imagine the ruthless strong man conquering his world, they cannot help but fear him and invoke a moral law for his downfall, even though they don't ''believe'' in it. Gourlay's flaw, we are told, is hubris. But hubris is an error in Greek theology, and Brown's animus has nothing to do with man's struggle with gods.

The chief object of hate in *The House with the Green Shutters* is stupidity and weakness. Gourlay is stupid but strong; his son is weak and almost as dumb. For this reason his vivid imagination becomes a curse rather than a source of power. The narrator tells us repeatedly that weaklings are most dangerous, vindictive, and malignant. In his vision of human malignancy the contrast seems to be between a grand, stupid, and strong malevolence, and a weak, cowardly malevolence—and somehow strong evil is preferable to weak. In the logic of Gourlay's downfall, the weak are a means of destroying the strong; only by imitating the strong are the weak ennobled, as when mother and daughter kill themselves: ''Willing her death, she seemed to borrow its greatness and become one with the law that punished her. Arrogating the Almighty's function to expedite her doom, she was the equal of the Most High.'' The one unqualified villain is the most cowardly and mean of the ''bodies'' of Barbie, Deacon Allardyce. He is called ''an artist in spite.'' He uses a feigned sympathy, ''a favourite weapon of human beasts anxious to wound. The Deacon longed to try it on Gourlay. But his courage failed him. It was the only time he was ever worsted in malignity.'' The entire book is a contest in malignity and spite.

Only the baker believes ''folk should be kind to folk''; the baker is ''the only kind heart in Barbie.'' But he also believes Gourlay to be the only gentleman: ''Brute, if you like, but aristocrat frae scalp to heel. If he had brains, and a dacent wife, and a bigger field, oh, man . . . Auld Gourla could conquer the world, if he swalled his neck till't.'' And it almost seems he is right. But we cannot imagine Gourlay under such circumstances, for his circumstances—summed up in Barbie—are his fate. He comes from peasant stock; he does not have the brains; he married for money and helped turn his wife into a slut. And what is a ''bigger field'' in a world made up of Barbie? Edinburgh? Edinburgh is seen as frightful, alien, and equally bad. The only good world present is that of nature, and nature is a pastoral dream from which man in his petty malignity is cut off.

This, then, is the controlling theological vision of the book, and it is familiar to the reader of Scottish fiction from Smollett to Robin Jenkins and Alan Sharp. The book's opening paragraph contrasts the frowsy, sluttish chambermaid and her slovenly postures with the water she throws out, which becomes a smooth round arch glistening in the morning's perfect stillness. The book's last sentence shows the "dark" and "terrible" house "beneath the radiant arch of the dawn." When Gourlay is forced to mingle with the malicious "bodies" on the brake to Skeighan, the theme is sounded: "The brake swung on through merry cornfields where reapers were at work, past happy brooks flashing to the sun, through the solemn hush of ancient and mysterious woods, beneath the great white-moving clouds and blue spaces of the sky. And amid the suave enveloping greatness of the world, the human pismires stung each other and were cruel, and full of hate and malice and a petty rage." This is the book's vision: a profound revulsion at man as an alien in nature, appearing first in mock-heroic satire and finally in horror at diabolical inhumanity. It is more Gothic even than Hogg's in *The Justified Sinner*. There is little reason to see as social criticism what is clearly a theological revulsion. Young Gourlay sees it: "The contrast between his own lump of a body, drink-dazed, dull-throbbing, and the warm bright day, came in on him with a sudden sinking of the heart, a sense of degradation and personal abasement. He realized, however obscurely, that he was an eyesore in nature, a blotch on the surface of the world, an offence to the sweet breathing heavens. And that bright silence was so strange and still. He could have screamed to escape it." He finally does escape—from the horror of his own vision.

Why must the intensity of that vision be a curse? Because the vision itself is devastating, or because he is stupid and weak? The vision is bad enough, but the book expends much energy of hate on his stupidity and weakness, when they are simply the brute given of his fallen nature. The only valid response is the baker's, when told by Drucken Wabster's wife that he was throwing tumblers at his mother: "Puir body! puir body!" Why detest the equally helpless "bodies" of Barbie? "It was not the least of the evils caused by Gourlay's black pride that it perverted a dozen characters. The 'bodies' of Barbie may have been decent enough men in their own way, but against him their malevolence was monstrous." Gourlay's is the chief diabolical presence. It is evident in "the score of wild devilries he began to practise on his son. Wrath fed and checked, in one, brings the hell on which man is built to the surface." The hell on which man is built. Supremely possessed by a devil of malignity, Gourlay is transformed, beyond himself in his art of spite and cruelty. (pp. 135-37)

*Francis Russell Hart, "The Anti-Kailyard as Theological Furor: Stevenson, Brown, Hay," in his The Scottish Novel: From Smollett to Spark, Cambridge, Mass.: Harvard University Press, 1978, pp. 131-39.*

## ALAN BOLD (essay date 1983)

[*Bold is a Scottish poet, critic, translator, and editor whose poetry explores "the insights made available to modern man through scientific research and political change." In the following excerpt, he admires the narrative artistry of* The House with the Green Shutters.]

Chronologically and thematically twentieth century Scottish fiction begins with Brown's *The House with the Green Shutters*. It is not revolutionary in manner but rather a return to the exploratory style used by Stevenson in *Weir of Hermiston*; it is seemingly revolutionary in matter only when considered in a Scottish context where the ambitions of the novelist had been reduced to the confines of the kailyard. (p. 108)

*The House with the Green Shutters* is the work of a careful, self-conscious stylist. There had been nothing quite as structurally shapely as it in previous Scottish fiction. The whole book is contained within a parabola described by the rise and fall of the House of Gourlay. Brown makes sure this shaping principle will not be lost on the reader. He begins the novel with the description of a liquid arch:

> The frowsy chamber-maid of the "Red Lion" had just finished washing the front door steps. She rose from her stooping posture, and, being of slovenly habit, flung the water from her pail, straight out, without moving from where she stood. The smooth round arch of the falling water glistened for a moment in mid-air. John Gourlay, standing in front of his new house at the head of the brae, could hear the swash of it when it fell. The morning was of perfect stillness.

Ezra Pound thought that great literature was "simply language charged with meaning to the utmost possible degree." Brown's opening paragraph therefore qualifies as great literature. It contains the seed of the whole story that is about to unfold—the rise and fall of the arch symbolising the rise and fall of the House of Gourlay, the unlovely nature of Barbie's inhabitants ("frowsy . . . stooping . . .") as represented by the chambermaid, the image of Gourlay standing in front of his imposing new house, the bustling reality behind the rural idyll.

The arch image is crucial so, at the end of the novel, when the psychological and physical House of Gourlay has collapsed, Brown returns to it:

> Their loins were loosed beneath them. The scrape of their feet on the road, as they turned to stare, sounded monstrous in the silence. No man dared to speak. They gazed with blanched faces at the House with the Green Shutters, sitting dark there and terrible, beneath the radiant arch of the dawn.

*Pride comes before a fall,* or as Brown paraphrases it in his novel "Pride *will* have a downcome" that gloating piece of folkwisdom is at the heart of *Green Shutters*. Brown had suffered from malicious gossip in his own life and had formed a bitter impression of Scottish smalltown life. Scots, according to Brown's experience, were motivated by malice: they resented any man who surpassed the situation he inherited. Such a man would, thanks to the workings of a Calvinist God, get his just desserts. A humble man was a Godfearing man; an overbearing man was diabolical. John Gourlay was proud and unbearably overbearing so, to the locals of Barbie (Brown's fictional recreation of Ochiltree), was simply tempting fate. The Greeks had a word for it—*hubris*—and it was to the Greek model that Brown went for his bleak study of a Scottish tragedy. Gourlay's *hubris* invites disaster but he is also destroyed by the bodies; the malicious gossips who comment on his character, proleptically gloat over his downfall, and contribute to the inevitable catastrophe. In elevating a group of Scottish gossips to the status of a Greek chorus, Brown made use of his classical training. In his "Rules for Writing," collected at the end of 1901 and intended to form the basis of a theoretical treatise, he discussed

> The value of The Chorus. (1) It gives the moral environment. (2) In its composite character it is an actor contributing to the final results. The gossips in

*The House with the Green Shutters* act directly on the two Gourlays. (3) It adds a convincing reality to the central characters. . . . (4) To shew the mind of an essential character through the mind of a secondary character.

Brown thought deeply, then, about the structural possibilities of the novel; the finished product demonstrates more architectonic power than any Scottish novel of comparable length. Brown did not see himself in the restricted role of storyteller but as a man with a visionary grasp of the nature of the novel. He set out, quite deliberately, to write a masterpiece and succeeded in doing just that. When reduced to a paragraph-length paraphrase *Green Shutters* sounds like a melodrama; Brown's style, however, informs the story with significance and brings out all its subtleties. It is the story of a divided community and, as such, a microcosm of the story of Scotland itself. As we read it on one level the secondary allegorical level attracts our attention.

John Gourlay is the top man in Barbie. The biggest fish in a little pond, for Barbie is only ''a dull little country town.'' He revels in his position of power as the only carrier in Barbie and, to emphasise his monopolistic power-base, builds the grandest house in the town. All Gourlay's pride is contained in the house and just as the house looks down on the town so Gourlay looks down on the people:

> At the beginning of a new day to look down on the petty burgh in which he was the greatest man, filled all his being with a consciousness of importance. His sense of prosperity was soothing and pervasive; he felt it all round him like the pleasant air, as real as that and as subtle; bathing him, caressing. It was the most secret and intimate joy of his life to go out and smoke on summer mornings by his big gate, musing over Barbie ere he possessed it with his merchandise.

Gourlay has married into money and has nothing but contempt for his wife; she has fulfilled her monetary function and is of no more use to Gourlay. He is incapable of appreciating human nature as an intrinsically loveable quality but prefers to quantify everything from goods to family. Appalled at Gourlay's hostility, his wife has succumbed to squalor, and this provokes the violence in him. After being bested in a business deal Gourlay returns to witness his wife:

> The sight of the she-tatterdemalion there before him, whom he had endured so long and must endure forever, was the crowning burden of his night. Damn her, why didn't she get out of the way, why did she stand there in her dirt and ask silly questions? He struck her on the bosom with his great fist, and sent her spinning on the dirty table.

Gourlay is not only vindictive he is brutal: the archetypal Scottish hardman who strikes first and asks questions later. There are few in Barbie with the character to confront Gourlay face-to-face for he is physically formidable and temperamentally aggressive. Their vindictive grudge against Gourlay is expressed behind his imposing back. Seeking strength in numbers the malicious gossips of Barbie (the bodies) gather together at the Bend o' the Brae to plan their little strategies. Brown's description of the bodies is deservedly famous because it is so devastatingly accurate. . . . (pp. 111-13)

*Green Shutters* is a book fired by conflict just as Barbie is polarised between the forces represented by, respectively, Gourlay and James Wilson—the molecatcher's son whose business acumen breaks Gourlay's monopolistic control of the carrying trade, and initiates his financial ruin. The eponymous House is at once a realistic edifice and a symbol with biblical overtones for ''if a house be divided against itself, that house cannot stand.'' Moreover, in Gothic manner, there is a curse on the House of Gourlay:

> And so, gradually, his dwelling had come to be a passion of Gourlay's life. It was a by-word in the place that if ever his ghost was seen, it would be haunting the House with the Green Shutters. Deacon Allardyce, trying to make a phrase with him, once quoted the saying in his presence. ''Likely enough!'' said Gourlay. ''It's only reasonable I should prefer my own house to you rabble in the graveyard!''

Gourlay, as Brown makes perfectly clear, is a man who lusts after possessions for the power they convey on the possessor. Having attained the heights of personal success, Gourlay falls because of his inherently petty nature (which links him with the bodies he despises) and his soul-destroying environment. His ambition stops at the frontiers of Barbie. For all that he is a more impressive man than the bodies and his tragedy is the tragedy of the Scotsman brought down by a history of acquired inferiority:

> Even if Gourlay had been a placable and inoffensive man, then, the malignants of the petty burgh (it was scarce bigger than a village) would have fastened on his character, simply because he was above them. No man has a keener eye for behaviour than the Scot (especially when spite wings his intuition), and Gourlay's thickness of wit, and pride of place, would in any case have drawn their sneers . . . his repressiveness added a hundred-fold to their hate of him. That was the particular cause, which acting on their general tendency to belittle a too-successful rival, made their spite almost monstrous against him.

Gourlay, always obsessive about his possessions, begins to act hysterically from a desire to get the better of Wilson: ''Wilson and Gourlay were a pair of gladiators for whom the people of Barbie made a ring.'' Events, like the coming of the railway to Barbie, overtake Gourlay and he has to compensate by vicarious triumphs. Because Wilson sends his son to the High School of Skeighan, Gourlay does likewise; because Wilson's son goes to university Young John Gourlay is sent to study for the ministry. Surprisingly enough, Young Gourlay begins auspiciously by winning the Raeburn essay-prize, much thought of in Barbie. Unfortunately Young Gourlay has inherited all his father's arrogance without any of his father's strength of character; he begins to indulge his alcoholic impulses and act accordingly. Eventually he is expelled from university for insulting a lecturer and this is not only an insult to the Gourlay name but an injury to the House of Gourlay. Gourlay himself, owing interest on a mortgage and unable to get a loan, takes his wrath out on his son:

> He had a triple wrath to his son. He had not only ruined his own life, he had destroyed his father's hope that by entering the ministry he might restore the Gourlay reputation. Above all he had disgraced the House with the Green Shutters. That was the crown of his offending. Gourlay felt for the house of his pride even more than for himself—rather the house was himself; there was no division between them. He had built it bluff to represent him to the world. It was his character in stone and lime. He clung to it, as the dull, fierce mind, unable to live in thought, clings to a material source of pride. And John had disgraced it. Even if fortune took a turn for the better, Green Shutters would be laughed at the country over, as the home of a prodigal.

That passage demonstrates the limitations of Gourlay's life; the bodies are the mirror he looks to for approval.

When Gourlay comes to deal with his son his attitude is diabolical and he stands as the absolute and hideous image of the authoritarian Scottish patriarch, the Calvinist God of vengeance on earth. Brown describes this with acute psychological penetration in one of the most powerful passages in a powerful book:

> [Gourlay] meant to sweat punishment out of [Young John Gourlay] drop by drop, with slow and vicious enjoyment. . . . To bring a beaten and degraded look into a man's face, rend manhood out of him in fear, is a sight that makes decent men wince in pain; for it is an outrage on the decency of life, an offence to natural religion, a violation of the human sanctities. Yet Gourlay had done it once and again. I saw him "down" a man at the Cross once, a big man with a viking beard. . . . Gourlay, with stabbing eyes, threatened, and birred, and "downed" him, till he crept away with a face like chalk, and a hunted, furtive eye. . . . to break a man's spirit so, take that from him which he will never recover while he lives, send him slinking away *animo castrato*—for that is what it comes to—is a sinister outrage of the world. It is as bad as the rape of a woman, and ranks with the sin against the Holy Ghost—derives from it, indeed. Yet it was this outrage that Gourlay meant to work upon his son. He would work him down and down, this son of his, till he was less than a man, a frightened, furtive animal. Then, perhaps, he would give a loose to his other rage, unbuckle his belt, and thrash the grown man like a wriggling urchin on the floor.

Gourlay, we see plainly, is a tyrant; a vicious domestic tyrant at that. Brown, who normally keeps a respectful distance from his material, invades that passage with personal opinions and its fervency suggests it harks back to his own experience as a figure of fun in Ochiltree.

Eventually the worm turns and, in front of his mother and sister, Young John Gourlay murders his father. This climactic act is conveyed with rare artistic precision and symbolic resonance: the murder weapon has, in previous pages, insinuated its ominous way into the narrative and Gourlay's last gesture is typical of the man as it shows him looking down from the top of a ladder. Brown mixes realistic with melodramatic modes, classical catastrophe with Gothic effect:

> "By God, I'll kill ye," screamed John, springing to his feet, with the poker in his hand. . . . Mrs Gourlay screamed and tried to rise from her chair, her eyes goggling in terror. As Gourlay leapt, John brought the huge poker with a crash on the descending brow. The fiercest joy of his life was the dirl that went up his arm, as the steel thrilled to its own hard impact on the bone. Gourlay thudded on the fender, his brow crashing on the rim.
>
> As the blow fell there had been a cry as of animals, from the two women. There followed an eternity of silence, it seemed, and a haze about the place, yet not a haze, for everything was intensely clear, only it belonged to another world. One terrible fact had changed the Universe. The air was different now; it was full of murder. Everything in the room had a new significance, a sinister meaning. The effect was that of an unholy spell.

The three remaining Gourlays—mother, son and daughter—attempt to disguise the patricidal catastrophe as an accident but the curse on the House of Gourlay brings its insubstantial presence to bear. Young Gourlay is haunted by the fearsome image of his father and dying of drink; his sister Janet is dying from a lung complaint; and his mother is, as a result of the blow inflicted on her by Gourlay, dying of an abscess of the breast. The three of them have nothing to live for now that Gourlay has gone in dreadful circumstances. Therefore the three of them take their own lives: first Gourlay's son, then his wife, then his daughter take poison. The book ends as the postman spreads the news of the final fall of the House of Gourlay. We can imagine that the bodies will dwell on the events for the rest of their lives.

Thematically Brown's book gathered together all the strands of Scottish realism: it has a domestic tyrant, a downtrodden woman, a drink problem, a group of malicious gossips, an explosive situation, supernatural overtones, and a classical catastrophe. Stylistically it is a model of literary excellence. All the elements are so beautifully integrated into the texture of the book that each new reading reveals different levels. *Green Shutters* was a self-conscious work of art, something Scottish writers could emulate. It was not only an important literary event; it was a precedent acknowledged by succeeding Scottish novelists. *The House with the Green Shutters* is the most seminal novel in modern Scottish literature and its offspring are still appearing. (pp. 114-16)

> *Alan Bold, "'Green Shutters': The New House of Scottish Fiction," in his* Modern Scottish Literature, *Longman, 1983, pp. 108-16.*

### JEFFREY SOMMERS   (essay date 1984)

[*In the following excerpt, Sommers discusses the ways in which Brown reversed the conventions of the bildungsroman in* The House with the Green Shutters.]

George Douglas Brown boasted to his friends that "No one pictures the real Scottish village life. . . . I will write a novel and tell you all what Scottish village life is like." Brown, in satisfaction of that ambition, wrote *The House with the Green Shutters,* and when he is remembered, it is as the author of this grim little book. Recognizing the historical importance of the novel almost immediately, a contemporary reviewer commented, "For a thoroughly surprising book which breaks with every sentimental tradition of the British novel, we have no hesitation in recommending this book." In Walter Raleigh's words, the novel stuck "the Kailyarders like pigs." Clearly, sticking the Kailyarders like pigs was Brown's motive in writing his vitriolic novel, a fact to which his personal letters attest.

Although the novel's protagonist is John Gourlay the elder, Brown's strategy for debunking the Kailyarders' myth of Scotland is significantly bound up in the fate of John Gourlay the younger. Ian Cambell [see excerpt dated 1978] has made note of Brown's methods recently by observing that his "general attack on Scottish life" is not ameliorated by the appearance of a younger generation which will bring about the improvement not achieved by their elders. Campbell concludes that the younger generation in Brown's novel offers no "consolation," for they do not differ markedly from their inadequate and petty elders. These are perceptive remarks, and a closer examination of the career of the younger John Gourlay substantiates Campbell's observations. At the same time, John's career also suggests several other major novels of the period, for the story of the two John Gourlays, father and son, may be the most extreme incarnation of the Oedipal struggle imaginable but that struggle itself is a familiar one to readers of novels of the later Victorian and Edwardian periods. Although George Meredith's Feverels and Samuel Butler's Pontifexes are too civilized for such homicidal activities, they do experience the same sort of conflict and thus, in an important sense, young John's "coming of age" resembles the experiences of Richard Feverel and Ernest Pontifex. Thus Brown's novel displays important features of the *Bildungsroman* which traditionally depicts the formation of character by a maturing young man or woman.

However, an even more germane parallel might be drawn between young John and Thomas Hardy's Jude Fawley. Frank Giordano has called *Jude the Obscure* an "anti-*Bildungsroman*" in that it depicts the conflict of "an innocent young man *against* a dehumanizing society." Brown's story, however, goes well beyond Hardy's in its perversion of the typical pattern of the Victorian *Bildungsroman*. Hardy's concern with criticizing society's hypocrisy lies behind his writing of an "anti-*Bildungsroman*" since clearly Jude cannot achieve the sort of integration of self and society available to inhabitants of the earlier, more harmonious world depicted in the Victorian *Bildungsroman* (*David Copperfield* comes to mind as an example). Brown, who is also quite clearly criticizing an entire society, has similar reasons for writing an "anti-*Bildungsroman*," but his young man is not an innocent in the same way that Jude is—indeed, John is a booby, a boor, a lout—and his paternal character is not overbearing in the civilized, cultured manner that Meredith's Sir Austin Feverel and Butler's Theobald Pontifex are. What more effective way imaginable is there to demolish a mythical, and distorted, view of a society than to "pervert" the literary genre which has traditionally presented society in a positive light? The turbulent transition of the generations should eventually ebb to a soothing and even calm which keeps society flowing along like a river; in *The House with the Green Shutters* the turbulence never ebbs, the river remains a cascading rapid.

My use of metaphors of setting to describe the reasons Brown creates an "anti-*Bildungsroman*" is deliberate, for Brown himself uses setting in his novel as a primary means for explaining just why it is that John the younger comes to such a disastrous fate. The novel's central landmark, and in a sense titular character, is carefully situated in a fully realized larger setting: Barbie, the scabrous little village in which the Gourlays reside. And, in turn, Barbie itself is carefully located by Brown in the context of what he terms in the novel "the careless world." These three aspects of setting—the House, Barbie, and the "careless world"—doom young John, who is particularly susceptible to their influences. John has no concrete opportunity to succeed in the world of Brown's novel because he is, figuratively if not always literally, a prisoner in a series of concentric prisons, none of them of his own making. Brown uses these settings to create just the sort of hate-filled environment which will lend the proper air of inevitability to the bloody resolution of the Gourlays' generational conflict.

The House itself is overtly hostile to young John, its inhospitability symbolized by its lack of a warm hearth. It is not happenstance that the color of Gourlay's shutters is green, for the house is obviously an attempt to build a monument to pride which will provoke the envy of all of Barbie. But the house is merely the innermost of the cold and dehumanizing settings which encircle John and in which he must make his way in life. The town of Barbie is equally devoid of human warmth; the very walls of the houses even reproach young John at one point. The unhealthy relationships between Gourlay and the

bodies, between the almost sentient House and town, are not likely to provide a firm foundation upon which young John can build a successful life for himself.

To further obstruct John's progress through life, Brown depicts the town of Barbie as a part of "the careless world." As the shadows of their domestic disaster begin to darken their lives, the Gourlays can hear the sound of a concertina being played in the town square. "That sound of the careless world came strangely in upon their lonely tragedy," writes Brown. "The careless world" here appears to be an epithet for Barbie, but when John returns from the university, Brown notes that he passes "from the careless world where he was nobody at all, to the familiar circle where he was a somebody, a mentioned man. . . ." One is compelled to read this same epithet, then, as a reference not only to Barbie but at times to something larger than Barbie, perhaps to Scotland itself. The larger society of which all Barbie's inhabitants are a part is clearly "careless" or indifferent to the problems of one family in a decaying burgh. Yet, eventually, even this enlarged view of the careless world seems limiting. It does not seem unreasonable to read "the careless world" literally to mean the entire world, or perhaps figuratively even the universe itself, as being oblivious to the Gourlays and their tragedy.

The indifference of the universe is nowhere more apparent than in the final pages of the novel when, after John, his mother, and his sister lie dead at their own hands, the House remains "gawcey and substantial on its terrace, beneath the tremulous beauty of the dawn. There was a glorious sunrise." The final lines of the book reiterate this ironic contrast: the House sits "dark . . . and terrible, beneath the radiant arch of the dawn." But, as with a Thomas Hardy novel, the world is not truly careless or indifferent, for if it were, then chance itself would decree that an occasional favor be bestowed upon man. Such is not the case here. When the irony of a universe smiling while man suffers is not present, then the universe does not smile at all. Thus spring, the traditional season of rebirth, is "enervating" and "treacherous," and storms fit for Judgment Day itself crash in the skies on the day of John's birth.

To compound John's troubles, he is peculiarly sensitive to his environment. His professor comments on John's writing that it "displays, indeed, too nervous a sense of the external world." This observation is the key to understanding John's character: he is too much affected by and too susceptible to the influences of the world around him. Always sensitive in this manner even as a child, John articulates rather haltingly at a university dinner how the capacity to create metaphor originates, an explanation which also explains how his too nervous sense of the external world operates. He says metaphor comes "from a power of seeing things vividly inside your mind." Although this very quality of John's proves to be the fatal flaw in his character, it nevertheless serves to distinguish him from his father, who is totally devoid of any sensitivity. Brown says of the son that "in his crude clay there was a vein of poetry," and so there is. This crude aesthetic sense is not unfamiliar in the protagonist of a *Bildungsroman* and is not out of place here in the protagonist of an "anti-*Bildungsroman*." It is John himself though who is "out of place," for clearly such an aesthetic sensibility, rudimentary as it may be, cannot thrive in the environment depicted in the novel.

Ill-equipped for success as he is, John nevertheless must stumble along the path trod by all *Bildungsroman* protagonists toward maturity and adulthood. When he is overwhelmed by his perceptions of a threatening world, a not infrequent occurrence in the brutal environment he inhabits, John understandably seeks escape. In fact, the impulse to flee is with him from his earliest years when, as a boy, he routinely seeks refuge from the world in the attic of the House with the Green Shutters (much like George Eliot's Maggie Tulliver in the attic of Dorlcote Mill). Brown rhapsodizes about the garret hiding-place of young John, calling it "the true kingdom of the poet," but John is so hypersensitive that he soon feels threatened even in his hideaway. A pattern of unsuccessful escapes develops throughout the novel as John tries reading, the train depot, the Howff, and alcohol as methods of obtaining release from his fears of the hostile universe. None succeeds.

At root John is trying to escape from the careless world itself, patently an impossibility. The perplexities of such a flight are represented by the image of the labyrinth by John's professor during a lecture on the nature of life. After sketching the typical and understandable fears of the vast, remote, cold universe experienced by an unformed mind, Auld Tam suggests that it is the lack of thought which makes the universe appear so incomprehensible and terrifying. "But the labyrinth . . . the labyrinth cannot appal the man who has found a clue to its windings. A mind that has attained to thought lives in itself, and the world becomes its slave." John, whose mind never progresses to the level of thought mentioned by Auld Tam, remains the world's slave. It is quite easy to imagine John as lost in a labyrinth: he tends to react to the unknown passages before him by backing down familiar dead end corridors behind him. So terrified is he at one point at the idea of leaving for the unknown Edinburgh, that he actually takes solace in being in dismal, vindictive Barbie because it is at least familiar and thus comforting.

Thus the entire pattern of the *Bildungsroman* is perverted: the young man is thrust from the nest by the father quite against his own wishes rather than striving to leave on his own. In fact John's career consists primarily of attempts to return to the family home. To Jerome Buckley, the protagonist of the *Bildungsroman*, his "initiation complete," may return to visit his old home to "demonstrate by his presence the degree of his success or the wisdom of his choice" to leave home for the larger world. Brown's young man, however, returns only in failure, slinking back to the cold home that he so pitifully views as his only "anchorage."

John never does reach full maturity, he never finds a real sense of identity, he never establishes a place in the world. How can he when the only home he knows becomes little more than a haunted house to him only to pass on subsequently to the bankers, no longer belonging to the Gourlays at all? With the House gone, there is no "anchorage" left for John who thus finds a final—and at last successful—escape from the world he cannot tolerate by committing suicide. Brown views this "doom" as "implicit" in John's character. He wrote to one of his readers: "if there is an inevitable law on earth it is the old Greek law which means that we must all bear the consequences of our own action or want of action!"

The most cogent criticism of the novel is directed at the idea behind this disingenuous remark. W. Somerset Maugham complains that Brown has "loaded the dice against the persons of his invention even when, by their own fault, catastrophe has befallen them." Maugham, I believe, is right; Brown has sought to improve upon the "old Greek law" by making certain that the Gourlays come to disaster. Brown's antipathy toward the Kailyarders provides the motivation for such loading of the dice. Ian Crichton Smith's query "who can yet survive as a

human being in such an environment?" [see excerpt dated 1969] is quite apposite. The world in which John must move, as we have seen, is one too harsh for him to be able to adapt to. His flaw, his "sensory perceptiveness in gross excess of his intellectuality," is just the weakness to guarantee his failure. Buffeted by the House with the Green Shutters, Barbie, the careless world itself, John never has a chance in life, and this lack of opportunity mars the realistic qualities of the novel.

But then can we be sure that Brown's ambition is to create a realistic picture of the Scottish village? If the Kailyarders err on the lighter side, then Brown, it cannot be denied, errs on the darker. However, since he offers his novel as a corrective to that rosy-tinted view of the Kailyarders, it is understandable that he has swung the pendulum so far in the opposite direction if only as a matter of balance. His bleak depiction of Scottish village life deliberately offers no consolation: at the close of the novel the family is destroyed, the new generation—the hope of the future—is dead. But throughout the novel in his use of setting Brown has established that he is determined that such will be the inevitable ends of his story, that youth will not be served, that no act of *Bildung* is possible in the world he depicts. There is no place for an artist, a person of any sensitivity, in the brutal Scotland of Brown's novel. The House, once a monument to human pride, survives, now a mausoleum to vanity; Barbie also survives, home to a group of "human pismires"; finally the careless world too remains, still utterly indifferent to those pismires. And that is all Brown wants us to see as remaining. If youth cannot rise up and take its rightful place in society, if art cannot flourish even in its most rudimentary form, then society cannot help but stagnate. Such a society can hardly be deemed anything other than sterile. The "anti-*Bildungsroman*" motif of **The House with the Green Shutters** is intended to make such harsh points about Scottish society—that the novel not only makes these points but pounds them home is undeniable. Although the sun may make a radiant arch over the House with the Green Shutters, there is, clearly, no glorious new dawn for Brown's Scotland. (pp. 252-58)

> *Jeffrey Sommers, in a review of "The House with the Green Shutters," in* Studies in Scottish Literature, *Vol. XIX, 1984, pp. 252-58.*

**DOROTHY PORTER** (essay date 1985)

[*In the following excerpt, Porter analyzes theme and technique in* The House with the Green Shutters.]

The popularity of **The House with the Green Shutters** declined after the death of Brown. Although most subsequent writers of Scottish fiction have been conscious of it, it has until relatively recently been less widely read than known as a phenomenon, not infrequently treated as a sport, compared typically to *Wuthering Heights*. But the initial reception of the book shows that the reviewers of 1901 saw various traditions to which it might be related: the "Kailyard School" (*Manchester Guardian*); Balzac and Flaubert (Andrew Lang in *Longman's Magazine*); Greek tragedy (*New York Evening Sun*).

There is no room to explain Kailyard, nor indeed to do justice to its once maligned writers. To characterize its objectional aspects Edwin Morgan's parody is useful:

> A typical Kailyard theme of the Maclaren-Crockett school at the end of the nineteenth century might show the "lad o' pairts" in some country village who is carefully nurtured by the local dominie and minister, goes to University in a city like Glasgow,

and quickly dies of consumption, perhaps with a ray
of light from the setting sun falling neatly on his calm
white face as he expires.

This helps to clarify Brown's comment in a letter to Barker
shortly after publication of the novel. "... it is more com-
plimentary to Scotland, I think, than the sentimental slop of
Barrie, and Crockett, and Maclaren. It was antagonism to their
method that made me embitter the blackness; like Old Gourlay
I was going 'to show the dogs what I thought of them'." Ian
Campbell [see Additional Bibliography] shows that Brown's
technique is rather subversion than counterblast, achieved through
the appropriation of Kailyard elements which are made to self-
destruct. We may take one version of sentimentality to be the
expression of a belief that a world containing certain recognizable features cannot have much wrong with it: in the case
of the Kailyard these features would include the village, a value
in itself in a debased pastoral tradition, the dominie, the minister, the typical group concern with the affairs of individuals. ... Brown assembles these features and gives them through
an angry, disturbed rather than complacent narrator who shows
that a world that contains them has little that is right with it.

As for the French, we do not need to make too much of this
debt. He may from them have developed an interest in the use
of indirect narrative to render the psychologies of his principals,
but his manipulation of the technique is special. Brown's shifts
from direct to indirect narrative are subtly managed: we have
to be constantly alert to where things are coming from.

And Greek tragedy? Low describes the structural principles of
the book in the terms appropriate for some Greek drama:

> The novel appears to me to be structured in two parts.
> The First Part, up to the end of Chapter 23, seems
> to fall into three movements—the prosperity of John
> Gourlay, the Gourlay-Wilson *agon*, the rise and fall
> of Young Gourlay. The Second Part concentrates on
> the Fall of the House of Gourlay, and takes the form
> of a five-act tragedy with prelude leading to dramatic
> confrontation, the first tragedy, bridging section de-
> picting young John's breakdown, final triple tragedy
> with epilogue.

We need not insist on these terms. We should observe that
from the first chapter Gourlay has no encounter, makes no
decision which is not fateful, which does not contribute to his
downfall. The last real decision he makes is to send his son
to university and he makes it when his own struggle with
Wilson is effectively lost. Brown does not quite overcome the
problem of the book's dual interest with the attendant central
split: there is some loss of concentration in the early Edinburgh
scenes. The subsequent movement between the two localities
is nicely judged; the ending precipitately grim.

Fateful prefiguring is a consistent feature of the narrative. The
arch motif in the water from Blowsalinda's pail, in the lettering
above Wilson's Emporium and in the final metaphor of the
dawn is inescapable. Less obtrusive are the poker with attendant prediction of John's role; Gilmour's warning, "There'll
be dafter folk as me in your hoose yet"; the threat of Gourlay's
ghost which does come back to haunt his son; and Blowsalinda,
associated with Mrs Gourlay through her gaping petticoat, holds
the big bass against her breast—Mrs Gourlay seeks more furtive
protection for her breast.

Classical analogues can be found for at least some of the main
figures. Iain Crichton Smith [see excerpt dated 1969] suggests
Ajax for Gourlay, Ulysses in his scheming role for Wilson and
a Mercury "postie" at the end. Mrs Gourlay is at last both

Cassandra (but we believe her) and sibyl among the scattered
autumn leaves, emblems of her life, which she cannot assemble
into anything as meaningful as even a patch-work quilt.
(pp. 12-13)

The variety of pressures on the narrative may suggest that *The
House with the Green Shutters* requires a flexible reader. And
in truth it does. J. B. Priestley would have us focus on the
"tragic drama" and largely ignore the passages of social realism: it seems better to accept that like Hardy, Brown "claims
the licence which is not invariably available to a novelist but
is normally conceded to a writer of romance." Thus if we call
Brown a realist, then we must equally admit that some of his
incident is not even probable, but it is none the less powerful
for that. Of course the information about railways and quarries
and coal-mining has a firm factual basis. ... But elsewhere
the probable is excitingly flouted for the extraordinary. Here
is Gibson after his foolish attempt at insincere playfulness with
the man he has cheated: "Next instant he was high in air; for
a moment the hobnails in the soles of his boots gleamed vivid
to the sun." It is the humanly impossible that we value as we
succumb to the tricks of perspective that eventually place the
reader on the table beside the bleeding Gibson looking in horror
at Gourlay's face at the jagged rent in the window. Nor will
realism do for Gourlay swinging his black-faced truant son
back to school. "Opposite The Fiddler's Inn whom should they
meet but Wilson! A snigger shot to his features at the sight.
Gourlay swung the boy up—for a moment a wild impulse
surged within him to club his rival with his own son." So
vivid is the possibility the deed is felt to have been done. By
sending John to university Gourlay tries to make his son into
a club to beat Wilson. Instead he prepares the arm that will
batter him to death.

Brown even pulls off the melodrama of the triple suicide. (We
need not use melodrama pejoratively.) He takes great risks,
not least that of repetition, and, I believe, gets away with it
by the alternation of the extreme with the restrained, even the
gentle—we might dare to compare Shakespeare's handling of
Cleopatra's death. John Gourlay dead demands an appalled
response, but the claim is not made through a plethora of violent
adjectives or adverbs: "His legs had slipped to the floor when
he died, but his body was lying back across the couch, his
mouth open, his eyes staring horridly up." Mrs Gourlay's
response chills because it is *not* appalled, "There's twa thirds
of the poison left." The impassioned heights of Janet's pity
and recognition of kinship, Mrs Gourlay's reading of I Corinthians 13, produce an almost intolerable strain. The drop in
pitch is not bathetic: "Maybe the Lord Jesus Christ'll no' be
owre sair on me." The restraint as they withdraw is splendid:
"They went into the parlour." Their deaths are unobserved,
their postures in death never described.

The visions and hallucinations of John Gourlay do not draw
on the strategies of realism, but they have the force of truth.
The vision which he briefly harnesses for the Raeburn seems
to owe something to the landscapes of the accursed Ancient
Mariner. The Mariner violates the natural order by killing the
albatross and is like one who "knows a frightful fiend / Doth
close behind him tread." This too is John's fate. He is enslaved
by the drink that he uses to protect himself from the oppression
of the external world. Perverted versions of that world league
themselves to torture him. At first his eidetic images are still
versions of decay and neglect in the natural world, but "mould-
ering walls" and "stain of lichen" lead into sinister other-
worldly threats in a procession of cowled figures. First and

last is the nightmare of the eyes. For the adolescent, the lightning is "the heavens . . . opening and shutting like a man's eye." His father's gleaming red eyes—"just a pair of e'en"—will not leave him. He walks home to his death "beneath a hundred eyes." (Brown attaches "glower" only to Gourlay until this point. After Gourlay's death "glower" attaches to others, so that John is persecuted within and without.) The human is fragmented. Eyes and glower. Not man looking on man. And John has never known the love that makes it possible for us to bear others' perception of us.

But characterizing the book's strengths does not absolve one from the responsibility of facing what are consistently felt to be its fundamental weaknesses—the things that ensure that it is great without its ever having been good. The questions of balance and of alleged authorial animus await. Brown himself said on more than one occasion that "there is too much black for the white in it." . . . (pp. 14-16)

Gourlay is a brave, insensitive brute; his son and converse a cowardly, sensitive weakling: they are both in different ways inarticulate. Mrs Gourlay is a slattern, silly to the point of imbecility, capable only of doting, not loving; Janet is a death-marked nonentity. The malignity of the bodies needs no rehearsal. Wilson is an inverse pied piper in his light yellow with black patches and dirty white waistcoat who joins and cheats the rats of the Corporation. That his pleasure is more in scheming than power says little.

Representatives of institutions are inadequate or corrupt. Bleach-the-boys beats away and uses his real perception about John Gourlay to feed his self-satisfaction; MacCandlish says, "What can I do?"; the Free Church minister may have an inner life, but seems no part of the village; Struthers is ignorant and pompous; even Auld Tam, possessed of real wisdom, is indifferent to his students as people.

Change in the form of railways and industrial development is going on around Barbie, but although it is discussed and exploited by those like Wilson and Gibson, no radical change effected, say, by a youth equal to the challenges is envisaged, nor is there any sense of a better past that has been betrayed.

The baker's "Tyuts folk should be kind to folk" articulates the plea for charity that is reiterated by Mrs Gourlay and Janet. Yet the baker has no real authority. It is hard to deny the charge of Iain Crichton Smith [see excerpt dated 1969], who admires the novel, that the book lacks a moral centre: "What we have is a kind of squalid natural history into which no judgment can be inserted." Francis Russell Hart points out that the charges Iain Crichton Smith makes can be levelled against naturalistic tragedy in general: post-Darwin, classical and Christian models are still available but the convictions that informed them command no general assent. But this is a question of minding less about the same thing—and if this naturalistic pessimism is supported by loaded dice? Did not Brown admit that "A novelist should never have an axe of his own to grind. If he allows a personal animus to obtrude ever so slightly it knocks his work out of balance. He should be an aloof individual, if possible, stating all sides and taking none."

Brown's narrator has traditionally got up the noses of his audience. He explains too much (Scottish dominie syndrome); charity is preached, he seems to show little; punditry sneered at, is not he a pundit? There are some crude false notes—Blowsalinda (Jeanie would do) and Dian the Queen will not do at all; some of the mock-biblical language is *voulu*. There are venial sins. More radical confusions are more disturbing

and much more interesting. Who is this narrator? A sufficiently educated, sufficiently experienced, sufficiently travelled man who generally understands the springs of human behaviour. On the demeanour of boys; on the weaknesses of Allan (a potential Kailyard narrator) and so on, he speaks with secure authority. Elsewhere the spatter of angry, sarcastic fire seems indiscriminate. It is not reserved for the principals or the malignants: it hits Bleach-the-boys' "astounding mind" or Auld Tam's "inspiring theme" or "savages and Englishmen on Bank Holidays." It even subverts in advance the magical or mythical significance of Gourlay's stick by styling it a trifle. The narrator is often a user of the depreciating sarcastical humour that he deprecates. Gourlay is a "resolute dullard," but they are donkeys who call him donkey.

This violent arm's length is not consistent. It is not simply that Gourlay has moments of greatness or pathos, John of perception and suffering—Brown is too much of an Aristotelian not to know that these are the essential conditions of their presentation. (The narrator's assessment of John in the garret is most unsettled—if he had been the right kind of boy, but he is not, but perhaps he is—in so far, presumably, as he is like the narrator.) But this outsider narrator is uncertain about how much he loses by his separation from the community he chronicles (not, by the way, patiently), and cannot disentangle himself from Scotland or even Barbie. Barbie he dismisses as "usually so poor to see," "a decaying burgh for thirty years," "the mean and the dull," but it is through his eyes that its occasional transfigured loveliness is given. The narrator is wholly implicated in John Gourlay's sense of loss as he bowls away from his native locality: possess though he may the intellectuality John lacks, it is his heart-strings that are being tugged.

In other ways the narrator conveys the uncertainty of his stance. When he recounts the baiting of Wilson for his pretentious use of initials, he remarks, "Ours is a nippy locality." Here, against Wilson, the narrator places himself within the community. Some varieties of stance are displayed at the beginning of Chapter XI where the commercial instincts of the Scot are anatomized. The narrator is at first distanced from his subject, wholly in charge of it. "There is," he concludes, "a megalomaniac in every parish in Scotland. Well not so much as that; they're owre canny for that to be said of them": the sudden shift into the vernacular betrays the narrator's complicit satisfaction with the group from which he had dissociated himself.

There is a direction we might take which will permit the narrator's uncertainty to be characterized as functional rather than helpless. It is not a matter of re-reading but of adjusting emphasis. Community is both necessary and oppressive or impossible. The problem is there from the first. Gourlay stands as the lonely hero, the town's greatest man: but he is stupid, thus his loneliness is as ominous as it is heroic. The figures admiring his procession are really insignificant and even they quickly disperse to their own concerns. Gourlay is isolated from the community on which he is wholly dependent, for he maintains his sense of self in opposition to it, his meaning derives from aggression and antagonism: he is neither a part nor apart.

He has no other resource. He is dead to the natural world (only the narrator comprehends the possibility of a Wordsworthian relationship with the external world). The house, his pride and emblem, is completely unsocial. No children play there; no women gossip; the "birling of the bottle" with Templandmuir, itself a maintenance of power, not an act of friendship, is seen only at its moment of dissolution.

The Gourlays cannot participate in the communal culture of the street. No internal solidarity sustains them. Gourlay oppresses his son; Mrs. Gourlay neglects her daughter; even the natural childish meanness of Janet and John to each other is significantly indicative of a house divided within, whose shutters cannot protect, although they exclude.

John Gourlay's position is the necessary outcome of his father's stance. As his father's son he is disliked, lacking his father's love he is unable to develop the latter's crude strength of resistance. His efforts to achieve a place among his peers result in fight and jeering. The communal life that he believes he reaches in Edinburgh is an illusion born of the false camaraderie of drink and the false self drink produces. It is scarcely necessary to show that Mrs Gourlay and Janet have neither communal life nor inner refuge—with each other they share only a liking for silly books.

The rottenness of the available communities may be briefly dealt with. Those who are of the community of Barbie have no sense of it as an organism. Gourlay is doubtless right about their motives over the water. Platitudes about the good of Barbie scarcely conceal the eye to the main chance. Wilson's accomplice, Gibson, is more disgusting than his "mate." He does not even have the excuse of hatred—he schemes to ruin Gourlay out of disinterested greed. He is the coming man. A hell-broth is brewing in Barbie.

The streets of Edinburgh are little hells to John. The world of men in parlour and pub and lecture theatre is little better. The amiability of Allan's soirées rests on sentimentality and booze; the Howff is more corrupt; student solidarity is a noisy bedlam easily collapsed. (pp. 16-19)

To show the failure and impossibility of community is one thing: to show its necessity another. The narrator's incoherent response is one indication of such need. The uncertainties of the more or less good, more or less educated man articulate the dilemma. "It was not the least of the evils caused by Gourlay's black pride that it perverted a dozen characters." "So the bodies wrangled among themselves. Somehow or other Gourlay had the knack of setting them by the ears." The scenario of *The House with the Green Shutters* has the Gourlay-effect on the narrator: it makes him wisely perceptive and angrily cruel, alternately convinced and confused. A situation that can generate the pity and anger of the narrator awaits redress.

And there is more. There are touches that distract from the blackness and liberate towards possibility. And there is the whole texture of the novel as it conveys loneliness, longing, loss and hence need.

The baker, kindly and mindful of his youthful self, and his wife, wisely cajoling, have been remarked. The imagination of Johnny Coe, whose visualizing faculty, combined with fearfulness, points to John Gourlay, is liberating and awe-inducing. Even the Free Church minister's nature study is a value of sorts. "Puffy Importance" Struthers has a wife who is a six-footer and who leaves the Emporium with a brush in her bonnet—this curiously frees the imagination. It is true that the closeness of the Wilson family smells of corruption, the real stink at the Cross, but the Provost's daughters and Hogmanay parties, Templandmuir's sourly witty wife at least point to questions about how people live. Only the Deacon and Gibson are totally devoid of context. Brown is a great poet of silence and stillness. Thus loneliness and loss are conveyed; thus the frailty of self-integrity offered." The morning was of perfect stillness." "The

street was lonely in the sudden stillness"—into this stillness creeps the solitary figure of John Gourlay. The train stops between stations as John journeys to Edinburgh. There is a sudden quiet. In the "intense quietude" John creates, from a glimpse of a farmhouse, a scene of warm, intimate community. "He wondered who the folk were, and would have liked to know them." Yes, the narrator castigates John for stupidity and incapacity which are the mere facts of his birth and condition, but he is also seen as a creature of longing and loss, destined to fill the silence with the meaningless noise of the Howff, until the two terrible silences. "To Hell wi' ye!" Gourlay says to his lecturer tormentor—"the silence throbbed." His second tormenter he also sends to Hell—"there followed an eternity of silence."

The lonely smell of wallflowers, the threatening smell of varnish, the stillnesses that surround him—these are the beautifully judged means by which a sense of pity is evoked, a pity that survives even the presentation of him as brutish, drunken sot. Is it not pity rather than anger that records this plea: "'It's the only hame I have,' he sobbed angrily to the darkness; I have no other place to gang till'."

Mrs Gourlay, nursing the cancer that is her husband's gift, has least sense of what she lacks. But it is conceded that there is "something tragic in her pose." She was a gay young fliskie once with the hopes and expectations that implies. "I'm Miss Richmond o' Tenshillingland," heroic echoes apart, gives her awareness that she had once a comprehensible place. Janet's recognition of need comes perhaps too late, certainly too late for her, in her confession of hurt, and perception of sisterhood, "But oh, mother, I didna ken *you* were just the same, I didna ken *you* were just the same."

We must not sentimentalize Gourlay. He is diabolic. His treatment of his son *is* the sin against the Holy Ghost. His tormenting skills are at first hideously human, depending on the iron control of his anger which permits the unmanning sneer. In a Satanic disintegration his control collapses into an animality which makes him literally smaller though quite as frightening. "Sometimes Gourlay would run the full length of the kitchen, and stand there glowering on a stoop; then he would come crouching up to his son on a vicious little trot, pattering in rage, the broken glass crunching and grinding beneath his feet."

Yet he has a deep, simple need for the things that his own nature denies him. His house defines him (the narrator admits pride in house as commonly human), but his wife will not permit the definition to be just. Through his eyes we see her violation of the order he desires: he cannot allow his wife to be the wife he needs. He makes his son what he is, then finds he needs to depend on him, discovers that after all he needs the son he has denied himself.

> More and more, as his other supports fell away, Gourlay attached himself to the future of his son. It became the sheet-anchor of his hopes . . . now it was the whole of life to him . . . in the collapse of his fortunes, the son grew all-important in the father's eyes. . . . If that boy would only hurry up and get through, to make a hame for the lassie and the auld wife!

There is even a touch of sentiment in the last wish—Gourlay retains the capacity to surprise.

Among the book's greatest scenes (probably really the greatest) are those which with wonderful tact give Gourlay at moments of loss—the death of Tam "the powney" and the dismissal of Peter Riney. It is an impertinence to anatomize their procedures: no one can miss their power, and no one has. "For a long time he stared down at the sprawling carcass, musing. 'Tam the powney,' he said twice, nodding his head each time he said it; 'Tam the powney'; and he turned away. At last Gourlay truly *sees* Peter:

> Gourlay went out to the big green gate where he had often stood in his pride, and watched his old servant going down the street. Peter was so bowed that the back of his velveteen coat was half-way up his spine, and the bulging pockets at the corners were mid-way down his thighs. Gourlay had seen the fact a thousand times, but it never gripped him before. He stared till Peter disappeared round the Bend o' the Brae.
>
> "Aye, aye," said he, "aye, aye. There goes the last o' them."

Brown reaches emotional depth in a number of other places too through repetition in speech, through doublings and triplets. "It's a pity o' me, it's a pity o' me; my God, aye, it's a geyan pity o' me." In this way Brown exploits an intensity of feeling rooted in the national language itself. There is nothing self-conscious about these locutions, they are essential facts of humanity. Their use provides the bonds of likeness and need that the communal surface of life cannot satisfy.

Man needs community but is not fit for it. It is impossible to stand alone—community means complicity with the despicable and the vicious and may always to some extent so mean. In the procedures of this narrative moral positives are conveyed by the confused pity and anger of the narrator and defined by absence and failure. The necessary outcome would seem to be hopelessness and despair. Is there any possibility of man connecting with man or reaching any relationship with "the radiant arch of the dawn" that is only beautifully indifferent to the stunned figures at the end?

To pull promise out of this would be dishonest. Yet the town is awestruck. "Their loins were loosened beneath them. The scrape of their feet on the road, as they turned to stare, sounded monstrous in the silence." Awe is perhaps a beginning. If it became humility it would be a basis for improvement. But this is not much. Brown reaches an impasse. The arch is no gateway.

Edwin Muir said of Brown, "As he is without serenity, so he is without pity." It is because he cannot rid himself of pity that he is without serenity. (pp. 20-3)

*Dorothy Porter, in an introduction to* The House with the Green Shutters *by George Douglas Brown, edited by Dorothy Porter, Penguin Books, 1985, pp. 7-24.*

---

**ADDITIONAL BIBLIOGRAPHY**

Campbell, Ian. "George Douglas Brown's Kailyard Novel." *Studies in Scottish Literature* XII, No. 1 (July 1974): 62-73.
  Proposes that the traditional view of *The House with the Green Shutters* as a reaction against Kailyard fiction oversimplifies the relationship between Brown's novel and the Kailyard school. Campbell asserts that Brown satirized the Kailyarders by using their own literary conventions to demonstrate the inadequacy of their worldview.

————. "*The House with the Green Shutters:* Some Second Thoughts." *The Bibliotheck* 10, No. 4 (1981): 99-106.
  Describes the publication history of *The House with the Green Shutters* and lists corrections made by Brown on a proof copy of the novel which suggest that he intended to publish a second edition.

Lennox, Cuthbert. *George Douglas Brown: A Biographical Memoir* and *Reminiscences of a Friendship and Notable Novel* by Andrew Melrose. London: Hodder and Stoughton, 1903, 243 p.
  Includes an introduction by Andrew Lang. Melrose's *Reminiscences* presents a thoughtful and informative view of the last and most productive years of Brown's life.

Manson, John. "Young Gourlay." *Scottish Literary Journal* 7, No. 2 (December 1980): 44-54.
  Analyzes the characterization of young Gourlay.

McClure, J. Derrick. "Dialect in *The House with the Green Shutters*." *Studies in Scottish Literature* IX, No. 2-3 (October-January 1971-72): 148-63.
  Analyzes Brown's use of Scottish dialect, concluding that he intentionally introduced inconsistencies either for reasons of dramatic effect or in order to represent the natural inconsistency inherent in the dialect.

Scott, J. D. "Novelist-Philosopher-IX: R. L. Stevenson and G. D. Brown, The Myth of Lord Braxfield." *Horizon* XIII, No. MCMXLVI (May 1946): 298-310.
  Compares Stevenson's novel *Weir of Hermiston* with *The House with the Green Shutters*, focusing on their common representation of a character based on Lord Braxfield, the Scottish archetype of oppressive authority.

Veitch, James. *George Douglas Brown*. London: Herbert Jenkins, 1952, 197 p.
  The most comprehensive biography to date.

# Joseph Seamon Cotter, Sr.

## 1861-1949

American poet, dramatist, and short story writer.

Cotter's *Caleb, the Degenerate* was one of the earliest dramas by a black American. Throughout his career, Cotter also wrote sonnets, folk ballads, and black dialect poems, and in these works he frequently praised black leaders such as Frederick Douglas, Booker T. Washington, and W. E. B. Du Bois for their efforts to overcome racial prejudice. Although not considered a major author, Cotter is regarded as representative of those black writers of the 1890s and early twentieth century who dedicated their work to overcoming negative stereotypes of black Americans, which were perpetuated by such white authors as Thomas Dixon and Thomas Nelson Page. Frequently serving as a form of counterpropaganda, Cotter's work reflects his strong moral and philosophical convictions.

Cotter was born near Bardstown, Kentucky, the illegitimate son of a Scotch-Irishman and his employee, Martha Vaughn. His mother, the freeborn daughter of an American slave, significantly influenced Cotter by sharing her appreciation of literature with him. He described her as "a poet, a story-teller, a maker of plays," and under her guidance Cotter learned to read by the time he was four years old. Cotter's formal education was interrupted when, at the age of eight, he left school and found work in order to contribute financially to the household. In his youth, he developed a talent for storytelling and later utilized this skill to encourage black children to read. While employed over the next decade as a manual laborer, Cotter continued to educate himself, reading the works of such writers as John Milton, Alfred Tennyson, Edgar Allan Poe, and Paul Laurence Dunbar. Cotter returned to school as an adult and eventually became a teacher in an impoverished Kentucky school district, an experience that is believed to have provided the inspiration for his poem "Description of a Kentucky School House." Viewing education as a means of social betterment for black Americans, Cotter wrote: "He who steals or kills may be reformed behind prison bars, but he who fails to educate his children libels posterity."

In 1891 Cotter founded a black community near Louisville that was known as "Little Africa," which he described as "part of the city where the word 'segregation' breeds no terror and conjures up no lawsuits." In 1893, he founded a school he named after the black poet Paul Laurence Dunbar, who visited him the following year and who praised the "ease and beauty" of Cotter's poetry. Cotter's conviction that social and economic reform for black Americans depended on self-determination finds expression in "Dr. Booker T. Washington to the National Negro Business League," a poem published in his collection *A White Song and a Black One,* in which he supported Washington's promotion of the work ethic as a means to economic independence for black Americans. In other didactic poems directed at black readers, such as "Ned's Psalm of Life for the Negro," "The Negro Woman," and "The Negro's Educational Creed," Cotter advocated self-reliance, racial pride, personal initiative, and an optimistic outlook. Cotter's only drama, *Caleb, the Degenerate,* was published in 1901 but was never given a stage production.

On assuming the position of principal of the Samuel Taylor Coleridge school in 1911, Cotter instituted a storytelling contest, an effort that brought him recognition when by 1919 it had become a national movement. About this time, Cotter praised W. E. B. Du Bois, Booker T. Washington's ideological adversary, in the poem "The Race Welcomes Dr. W. E. B. Du Bois as Its Leader." In opposition to Washington's emphasis on vocational training as a means of social advancement for black Americans, Du Bois stressed the right of black Americans to pursue a professional degree based on a liberal arts education. Defending the position of Du Bois, Cotter wrote: "To work with the hands / Is to feed your own mouth / And maybe your neighbor's; / To work with the mind / Is to unleash the feet of millions." Cotter retired from his position as principal in 1942 and published his last collection of miscellaneous work in 1947. He died at the age of eighty-eight.

While some critics have regarded Cotter's work as conciliatory, others have evaluated his apparent adoption of the ideals of white Americans in terms of the black American literary tradition in which messages of social protest were often disguised to avoid antagonizing white readers. In particular, James Hatch and Betty Cain find that earlier critics overlooked the irony or double meanings by which Cotter disguised his real theme in *Caleb, the Degenerate.* Both Hatch and Cain view the drama as an indirect attack on Booker T. Washington's belief that industrial training was sufficient to overcome the obstacles to racial betterment. Hatch contends that "although the surface features of the play were meant for the white and black readers who already believed [in Washington's advocacy of industrial training], there is a subsurface that commands the attention of those aware of the black experience." Epitomizing the modern reassessment of the drama, Cain has written: "Nothing quite like it has been seen in Afro-American drama before or since."

Cotter's work is considered important for its examination of race relations and its foreshadowing of the interests of later black writers such as James Weldon Johnson, Mary McLeod Bethune, and Langston Hughes. Praising Cotter's exploration of the nature of racial relations, Eugene B. Redmond wrote in 1976: "Brilliant, precocious, and enduring, Cotter pursued the complex side of life, daring to examine the often over-simplified phenomena of race relations in America."

(See also *Dictionary of Literary Biography*, Vol. 50: *Afro-American Writers before the Harlem Renaissance*.)

## PRINCIPAL WORKS

*A Rhyming* (poetry) 1895
*Links of Friendship* (poetry) 1898
*Caleb, the Degenerate: A Study of the Types, Customs and Needs of the American Negro* (drama) [first publication] 1901
*A White Song and a Black One* (poetry) 1909
*Negro Tales* (short stories) 1912
*Twenty-fifth Anniversary of the Founding of Colored Parkland or "Little Africa"* (nonfiction) 1934
*Collected Poems of Joseph S. Cotter* (poetry) 1938
*Sequel to "The Pied Piper of Hamelin," and Other Poems* (poetry) 1939
*Negroes and Others at Work and Play* (poetry and short stories) 1947

---

**JOSEPH S. COTTER**   (essay date 1901)

[*In the following excerpt from a preface written for the first edition of* Caleb, the Degenerate, *Cotter explains his intentions in writing this drama.*]

The aim [of *Caleb, the Degenerate*] is to give a dramatic picture of the Negro as he is to-day. The brain and soul of the Negro are rising rapidly. On the other hand, there is more depravity among a certain class of Negroes than ever before. This is not due to anything innate. It is the result of unwise, depraved leadership and conditions growing out of it.

Rahab represents this unwise, depraved leadership. Caleb is his pupil, and represents the depraved class of Negroes referred to. Some may claim that the picture is overdrawn, but both leader and led are with us to-day and speak for themselves.

The Bishop and Olivia represent the highest types of cultivated Negro manhood and womanhood. The Dude represents the so-called educated young Negro politician, of whom something may be made if the right steps are taken in time.

The Negro needs very little politics, much industrial training, and a dogged settledness as far as going to Africa is concerned.

To this should be added clean, intelligent fireside leadership. Much of any other kind is dangerous for the present.

I am a Negro and speak from experience.

> *Joseph S. Cotter, in a preface to his* Caleb, the Degenerate: A Study of the Types, Customs, and Needs of the American Negro, *The Bradley & Gilbert Company, 1903, p. v.*

**ROBERT T. KERLIN**   (essay date 1940)

[*Kerlin was an American poet, educator, and critic. In the following excerpt, he praises Cotter for the technical skill and lyrical quality of his work.*]

In many of Cotter's verses there is a sonorous flow which is evidence of poetic power made creative by passion. Didacticism and philosophy do not destroy the lyrical quality. In **"The Book's Creed"** this teacher-poet makes an appeal to his generation to be as much alive and as creative as the creed makers of other days were. The slaves of the letter, the mummers of mere formulas, he thus addresses:

> You are dead to all the Then,
>   You are dead to all the Now,
> If you hold that former men
>   Wore the garland for your brow.
>
> Time and tide were theirs to brave,
>   Time and tide are yours to stem.
> Bow not o'er their open grave
>   Till you drop your diadem.
>
> Honor all who strove and wrought,
>   Even to their tears and groans;
> But slay not your honest thought
>   Through your reverence for their bones.

Cotter is a wizard at rhyming. His **"Sequel to the Pied Piper of Hamelin"** surpasses the original—Browning's—in technique—that is, in rushing rhythms and ingenious rhymes. It is an incredible success, with no hint of a tour-de-force performance. Its content, too, is worthy of the metrical achievement. I will lay the proof before the competent reader in an extract or two from this remarkable accomplishment:

> The last sweet notes the piper blew
>   Were heard by the people far and wide;
> And one by one and two by two
>   They flocked to the mountain-side.
>
> Some came, of course, intensely sad,
> And some came looking fiercely mad,
> And some came singing solemn hymns,
> And some came showing shapely limbs,
> And some came bearing the tops of yews,
> And some came wearing wooden shoes,
> And some came saying what they would do,
> And some came praying (and loudly too),
> And all for what? Can you not infer?
> A-searching and lurching for the Pied Piper,
> And the boys and girls he had taken away.
> And all were ready now to pay
> Any amount that he should say.

So begins the **"Sequel"**. Another passage, near the end, will indicate the trend of the story:

> The years passed by, as years will do,
>   When trouble is the master,
> And always strives to bring to view
>   A new and worse disaster;

And sorrow, like a sorcerer,
  Spread out her melancholy pall,
  So that its folds enveloped all,
And each became her worshipper.
And not a single child was born
  Through all the years thereafter;
If words sprang from the lips of scorn
  None came from those of laughter.

Finally, the inhabitants of Hamelin are passing through death's portal, and when all had departed:

—a message went to Rat-land. . . .

And lo! a race of rats was at hand. . . .

They swarmed into the highest towers,
And loitered in the fairest bowers,
And sat down where the mayor sat,
And also in his Sunday hat;
And gnawed revengefully thereat.
With rats for mayor and rats for people,
With rats in the cellar and rats in the steeple,
With rats without and rats within,
Stood poor, deserted Hamelin.

Like Dunbar, Cotter is a satirist of his people—or certain types of his people—a gentle, humorous, affectionate satirist. His medium for satire is dialect, inevitably. Sententious wisdom, irradiated with humor, appears in these pieces in homely garb. In standard English, without satire or humor that wisdom thus appears:

What deeds have sprung from plow and pick!
  What bank-rolls from tomatoes!
No dainty crop of rhetoric
  Can match one of potatoes.

The gospel of work has been set forth by our poet in a four-act poetic drama entitled *Caleb, the Degenerate*. All the characters are Negroes. The form is blank verse—blank verse of a very high order, too. The language, like Shakespeare's—though Browning rather than Shakespeare—is always that of a poet. The wisdom is that of a man who has observed closely and pondered deeply. Idealistic, philosophical, poetical—such it is. It bears witness to no ordinary dramatic ability.

"Best bard, because the wisest," says our Israfel. Verily. "Sage" you may call this man as well as "bard." (pp. 77-80)

> *Robert T. Kerlin, "The Present Renaissance of the Negro" and "Dialect Verse," in his* Negro Poets and Their Poems, *third edition, The Associated Publishers, Inc., 1940, pp. 51-138, 234-60.*

## DORIS E. ABRAMSON (essay date 1969)

[*Abramson is an American educator and critic. In the following excerpt, she discusses* Caleb, the Degenerate *as a response to the negative stereotypes of black Americans that were common at the time.*]

Booker T. Washington mapped out a course for his people to follow when he gave a speech at the Cotton States' Exposition in Atlanta, Georgia, in 1895. In this speech he urged his fellow Negroes to cultivate friendly relations with white men. He recommended that Negroes devote themselves to agriculture, mechanics, domestic service, and the professions. He placed more value on acquiring industrial skill than on attaining a seat in Congress. He assured members of the white race that they could rely on eight million Negroes, "whose habits you know,

whose fidelity and love you have tested in days when to have proved treacherous meant the ruin of your firesides." His people, he reminded the whites, had tilled the fields and cleared the forests "without strikes and labor wars." The audience cheered when Booker T. Washington said, "In all things that are purely social we can be as separate as the fingers, yet one as the hand in all things essential to mutual progress."

Joseph S. Cotter's play, *Caleb, the Degenerate*, with the amazing subtitle *A Study of the Types, Customs, and Needs of the American Negro,* is one Negro's way of expressing appreciation of Booker T. Washington's point of view. It is a slight, pretentious play, written in blank verse. The author—at the time of publication principal of the Colored Ward School in Louisville, Kentucky—could read, we are told in the Preface, before he was four years old but had little opportunity for schooling. At twenty-two he went to a night school for colored pupils. It is significant that the Preface was written by Thomas G. Watkins, financial editor of the *Courier-Journal*. The benevolent white man was pleased to praise the wholly self-taught Negro who advocated that Negroes mind the teachings of Booker T. Washington.

Joseph Cotter states the purpose of his play in the Author's Preface:

> The aim is to give a dramatic picture of the Negro as he is today. The brain and soul of the Negro are rising rapidly. On the other hand, there is more depravity among a certain class of Negro than ever before. This is not due to anything innate. It is the result of unwise, depraved leadership and conditions growing out of it. . . . The Negro needs very little politics, much industrial training, and a dogged settleness [*sic*] as far as going to Africa is concerned. To this should be added clean, intelligent fireside leadership.

There is no doubt that Cotter listened attentively to Booker T. Washington's "Atlanta Compromise."

*Caleb, the Degenerate,* which is in four acts, is filled with unbelievable characters spouting incredible lines. There is no moment when they touch reality, even to the extent of . . . early melodramas by white authors writing about Negro characters. There is no minstrel type here, no Cato or Topsy. The characters, forced to speak in blank verse that tries to soar no matter how the vocabulary would pull it down, are merely vessels for ideas. Here Caleb, who is described in the cast of characters as a pupil of a "depraved leader," is speaking to an undertaker who wishes to know if he wants to buy a coffin for his deceased father.

A thirty-dollar coffin! I say no!
Five dollars for a robe? No, death-worm, no!
Four carriages? No, undertaker, no!
Think you a son must curb his appetite
Because a pauper father breathes no more?
The living must have money! I'm alive!
Cold dignity is all the dead require.

None of the characters in the play seem to exist as men but rather to represent types. Caleb and his leader, Rahab, represent wicked types, the degenerate Negroes. Goodness is personified by Olivia and her father, the Bishop. Olivia, in the course of the play, establishes an industrial school for the children of Negroes her father has described as "a people, friendless, ignorant, / living from hand to mouth, from jail to grave." Olivia and the Bishop rise to such an emotional pitch in their enthusiasm for industrial training that they give it credit for "health, wealth, morals, literature, civilization." Somehow one senses that even Booker T. Washington would not have made such extravagant claims.

Two minority views expressed by depraved characters are that Negroes should vote and that they might consider going back to Africa. The playwright did not consider either viewpoint worth much attention. The Bishop refers to his people as "primitive people" and seems to conclude that suffrage is beyond them at the moment. He recognizes, however, that they are Americans—"And this our land shall be our paradise"— not Africans.

The degenerate Caleb is found dead of his profligacy in the woods on the grounds of Olivia's industrial school. His death is represented as being horrible because he followed the wicked Rahab who professed to lead, not to love, his race. Had Caleb listened to Olivia and the Bishop, he might have reaped the benefits of the school, which Olivia says was built with gifts from millionaires. He might at least have been able to go to war with Dude, who at the very end of the play announces:

> I go to war. Some say the Negro shirks
> The tasks of peace. Who says he will not fight?
> I go to war.

Joseph Cotter set out to write a moral tract that would show the dangers of depravity and the values of industrial training over mere book learning—"Go, cage life's life before you pause to read." He put into the play good and bad characters, drew his message, killed off the wicked, rewarded the virtuous, and even, in conclusion, waved the American flag.

Though never performed, *Caleb, the Degenerate* was published and probably read by a number of civic and religious leaders of the period. The copy of the play at the Schomburg Collection was once owned by the Unitarian minister Edward Everett Hale, who became chaplain to the United States Senate in 1903. Joseph Cotter's message on the flyleaf to the Reverend Mr. Hale was: "If you can say a good word for *Caleb,* please do so." Anyone who believed in the Atlanta Compromise probably had a good word to say for *what* the play said. It is difficult to believe that anyone had a kind word for *how* it was said. (pp. 14-18)

The theatre of Joseph Cotter's time was made up of minstrelsy, melodrama, and the beginnings of musical comedy. (Bob Cole's *A Trip to Coon Town,* in the 1898-99 season, is thought to have been the first Negro musical comedy with a story line and something more than skits.) It is unlikely, however, that Cotter visited the theatre. His play, for all that it denounces book learning, reflects only that and not experience in the live theatre of his day. He had probably read Shakespeare and the nineteenth-century English poets, hence the use of blank verse.

When we look for the wellsprings of *Caleb, the Degenerate,* it is not in the theatre but in the fiction of the day that we find them. Between 1890 and 1914, American fiction was extremely race conscious. White writers like Thomas Dixon, Thomas Nelson Page, and Robert Hilliard wrote novels of the hate in which they pictured the Negro as half animal, half child, a threat to the United States. Many Negro writers and some white ones answered their propaganda by glorifying the Negro and exposing those who exploited him. Of these writers of counterpropaganda, Hugh Gloster observed:

> In their counterpropaganda Negro fictionists usually portrayed educated and well-mannered colored characters . . . who often engage in long discussions of racial and political issues and are almost invariably

presented as teachers, clergymen, physicians, lawyers, politicians, or journalists. A favorite practice is the depiction of these individuals attending lectures, literary societies, political councils, and institutions of higher education.

Gloster goes on to say that Negro writers were determined in their fiction to call their audiences' attention to the various repressions experienced by Negroes and to write of their time from a Negro's point of view. If Joseph Cotter's play seems to keep step with the counterpropaganda, it is well to be reminded that he was not with the majority of Negro writers when he took Washington's side in the Booker T. Washington-W. E. B. DuBois debate. According to Gloster, this controversy received a great deal of discussion, and the majority of the writers indicated, either through implication or direct statement, a preference for the militant DuBois rather than for the pragmatic and conciliatory school of race leadership espoused by Washington. Cotter's play did share one thing with most of the turn-of-the-century polemical fiction: melodrama. (pp. 19-20)

> *Doris E. Abramson, "Beginnings," in her* Negro Playwrights in the American Theatre: 1925-1959, *Columbia University Press, 1969, pp. 5-21.*

**JOAN R. SHERMAN**   (essay date 1974)

*[Sherman was an American novelist, editor, and critic. In the following excerpt, she surveys the diverse subjects and themes in Cotter's poetry.]*

During five decades of poetry-writing, Cotter's interests range from industrial education in the 1890's to the "zoot suit" and atom bomb in 1947. In both dialect and standard English verse he urges social and moral reform, sectional reconciliation, and brotherhood. He satirizes the foibles and frailties of blacks but also praises their strengths and accomplishments; he philosophically examines God's ways and mysteries of human nature; he comments on historical events and pays homage to notables like Frederick Douglass, William Lloyd Garrison, Cassius M. Clay, Presidents McKinley, Taft, and Roosevelt, Booker T. Washington, and W. E. B. Du Bois; he extols good literature and his literary idols: Shakespeare, Milton, Tennyson, Riley, Holmes, Swinburne, Poe, and his close friend Dunbar. Finally, Cotter writes story ballads and light verse enlivened by wit and striking imagery.

Cotter's major concern is race advancement, to be gained by a mixture of race pride, humility, hard work, education, and a positive, optimistic outlook. He chides lazy, aggressive, extravagant, and parasitical blacks who will never succeed in **"The Loafing Negro," "The Don't-Care Negro" "The Vicious Negro," "I'se Jes' er Little Nigger,"** and **"Negro Love Song."** He praises those who are moving upward in **"Ned's Psalm of Life for the Negro"** in **"The Negro Woman,"** which charges the female "To give the plan, to set the pace, / Then lead him in the onward race"; and in **"The True Negro"**:

> Though black or brown or white his skin,
> He boldly holds it is no sin,
> So long as he is true within,
>    To be a Negro.

·   ·   ·   ·   ·

> He loves his place, however humbling,
> He moves by walking, not by stumbling,
> He lives by toiling, not by grumbling
>    At being a Negro.

Devoted to the ideology of Washington, Cotter advocates self-help, money-getting, and accommodation in verses like **"Tuskegee," "The Negro's Educational Creed,"** and **"Dr. Booker T. Washington to the National Negro Business League"**:

> Let's spur the Negro up to work,
>     And lead him up to giving.
> Let's chide him when he fain would shirk,
>     And show him when he's living.
>
>             .    .    .    .
>
> What deeds have sprung from plow and pick!
>     What bank rolls from tomatoes!
> No dainty crop of rhetoric
>     Can match one of potatoes.
>
>             .    .    .    .
>
> A little gold won't mar our grace,
>     A little ease our glory.
> This world's a better biding place
>     When money clinks its story.

*Caleb, the Degenerate* a four-act play in blank verse subtitled, "A Study of the Types, Customs, and Needs of the American Negro," dramatizes the credo of Cotter's preface: "The Negro needs very little politics, much industrial training, and a dogged settledness as far as going to Africa is concerned. To this should be added clean, intelligent fireside leadership."

Cotter introduces the characters as archetypal Negroes: Caleb, a money-hungry atheist, murders his father, philosophizes in pun-ridden Elizabethan diction, goes mad, and dies; Rahab, an amoral politician and emigrationist, corrupts everyone. Caleb and Rahab typify "unwise, depraved leadership." In contrast, the "highest types" are a magniloquent Bishop and his daughter Olivia, who teaches in the industrial school and unwisely loves Caleb. The Bishop sprinkles abstruse theological arguments with homilies: "Industrial training is the thing at last," "God's love and handicraft must save the world," "Work is the basis of life's heritage." Olivia, who has written a book, *The Negro and His Hands,* idealizes "hewers of wood and drawers of water" and the true religion:

> Hope is the star that lights self unto self.
> Faith is the hand that clutches self's decree.
> Mercy is oil self keeps for its own ills.
> Justice is hell made present by a blow.

Although *Caleb* is poor drama and mediocre poetry, it is probably the most original tract supporting Washington's policies and as such has considerable sociohistorical interest.

In later years Cotter recognized the value of Du Bois's "Talented Tenth" doctrine in **"The Race Welcomes Dr. W. E. B. Du Bois as Its Leader"**:

> To work with the hands
>     Is to feed your own mouth
> And maybe your neighbor's;
>     To work with the mind
> Is to unleash the feet of millions
>     And cause them to trip
> To the music of progress;
>     We welcome you, prophet,
> You who have taught us this lesson of lessons.

"We welcome you," the poem continues, "Race-called leader of Race . . . Christ-called saver of souls . . . God-sealed brother and prophet." In his subsequent work Cotter supports the combined doctrines of Washington and Du Bois.

Cotter's didactic verse, which appears in every volume, is usually trite in sentiment and style. . . . Using a variety of verse forms which complement their subjects, Cotter's tributes to those he admires are often successful. **"William Lloyd Garrison"** communicates the militancy, courage, and altruism of the "God-like" abolitionist; a tender eulogy, **"To the Memory of Joseph S. Cotter, Jr."** asks with simplicity whether the poet and his son will meet in eternity; and in **"Algernon Charles Swinburne,"** Cotter parodies Swinburne's themes and versification to show his admiration:

> Thy gift was a yearning
> That paradised learning,
> And ended in turning
>     All seasons to Junes
> Through death that caresses,
> Through hatred that blesses,
> And love that distresses,
>     And words that are tunes.
>
> A Milton may ghoul us,
> A Shakespeare may rule us,
> A Wordsworth may school us,
>     A Tennyson cheer;
> But thine is the glory,
> Star-sprung from the hoary,
> Flame-decadent story
>     Of the munificent ear.

Such facile rhyming, musicality, and unorthodox word coinage and word usage distinguish some of Cotter's tales in verse like **"The Tragedy of Pete"** and **"Sequel to the 'Pied Piper of Hamelin'."** The latter, a lively narrative in thirty stanzas of from four to twenty-one lines, recounts the search of the people of Hamelin for their children, lured away by Robert Browning's "Piper." After many years the childless adults of Hamelin die, and "a race of rats" occupies the town:

> They swarmed into the highest towers,
> And loitered in the fairest bowers,
> And sat down where the mayor sat,
> And also in his Sunday hat;
> And gnawed revengefully thereat.
> With rats for mayor and rats for people,
> With rats in the cellar and rats in the steeple,
> With rats without and rats within,
> Stood poor, deserted Hamelin.

Cotter's nursery-rhyme tone and rhythms in this **"Sequel"** are especially effective. A poem of later years, perhaps his most original effort, is reminiscent of Lewis Carroll's lyrical nonsense verse. The twenty-four-stanza **"Love's Tangle"** fascinates as it perplexes, and the tangle escapes definition. The poem begins:

> As Simile to myth and myrrh
>     She led gruff care to slaughter,
> And saw the moonlight vow to her
>     In dimples on the water. . . .

Added to this great variety of poems are several unpretentious observations of human nature from a personal point of view, like Cotter's casual appreciation, **"On Hearing James W. Riley Read (From a Kentucky Standpoint)"** and his colloquial greeting, **"Answer to Dunbar's 'After a Visit'."** Although the aesthetic quality of Cotter's verse is extremely uneven, his catholic tastes and techniques, and his consistent race-consciousness combined with sympathetic regard for the needs, joys, and aspirations of all people, give him well-deserved celebrity among the black poets. (pp. 166-70)

Joan R. Sherman, "Joseph Seamon Cotter, Sr.," in her Invisible Poets: Afro-Americans of the Nineteenth Century, University of Illinois Press, 1974, pp. 164-71.

## JAMES V. HATCH (essay date 1974)

[Hatch is an American poet, dramatist, and critic. In the following excerpt, he finds that Caleb, the Degenerate may be read as both conciliatory to white readers and to followers of Booker T. Washington and as a satirical protest against these groups.]

In the tradition of many self-made men, Joseph Cotter, Sr. gave over much of his writing to urging others to emulate his own success. The first of **"The Negro's Ten Commandments,"** he wrote, is "Thy fathers' God forsake not and thy manhood debase not, and thou shalt cease to say 'I am a Negro, therefore I cannot.'" And toward this end he published poems, stories and, in 1901, one full-length play: Caleb, the Degenerate: A Study of the Types, Customs, and Needs of the American Negro.

Caleb, the main character, is a degenerate and a villain by the standards of 1900. He sells his father's corpse to medical students; he pushes his mother to her death; he smokes, drinks, bullies, lies, steals, and takes cocaine. He raves against God and church:

> They rather worship god whose cruel laws
> are made up wholly of mistakes and flaws.
> The time shall be when they will cease to follow
> Views that are so disgusting and so hollow.
> Let blinded Christians, ere they think or stir,
> Confer with me, their great philosopher.

Caleb's philosophy is to vehemently spurn the Establishment in all its aspects. There is something in his perpetual anger, his bitter wit, his hopelessly destructive life, that makes him a rebel in the modern sense—much as Johnny Williams in No Place To Be Somebody becomes a hero as antihero.

Opposed to Caleb's satanic nature are the Bishop, his stepdaughter, Olivia, and the faculty and children of the Industrial School. These "good Negroes" represent the true course the race is to take—learn a trade, save money, be Christian, and don't get involved in any Back-to-Our-African-Homeland movements. From this simplistic interpretation, it is no wonder that most critics—among those who have bothered to read the play—have not many good works to say for it.

They attack Mr Cotter's verse: "It is dull in the writing," says Fannin S. Belcher, Jr., "chaotic in treatment and unactable." They attack Cotter's characters: "Caleb . . . is filled with unbelievable characters spouting incredible lines. There is no moment when they touch reality," comments Doris Abramson [see excerpt dated 1969].

When the play has been praised, it is often in a tone of condescension. Alfred Austin, poet laureate of England, responded by letter when the play was sent to him: "It affords yet further evidence of the latent capacity of your long maltreated race for mental development." Author Israel Zangwill did not manage much better: "I do not profess to understand it all, but I desire to express my appreciation of the passages of true poetry in which you express the aspirations of the Negro race for salvation by labor."

Before these evaluations are accepted, a question needs to be answered: what audience was Mr. Cotter writing for? Was he simply showing his black brothers a pathway toward economic salvation? Was he showing his white brothers that they need not fear the black man? Finally, was Mr. Cotter writing two plays, an overt and a covert one?

The answer to all these questions is "Yes." Yes, Mr. Cotter is urging the black man to follow Dr. Washington's work ethic. As has been suggested, the race virulence of America was at a crest in Cotter's time. Solutions for survival had to be found. Yes, the play was written with an eye to the white reader. The preface to the play was composed by Thomas Watkins, financial editor of the Louisville Courier-Journal, who wrote, "The author is one of a race that has given scarcely anything of literature to the world." How pleased Mr. Watkins must have been to help a good nigra. But although the surface features of the play were meant for the white and black readers who already believed, there is a subsurface that commands the attention of those aware of the black experience.

The failure of the critics to find much merit in Caleb is a failure to recognize this subsurface of black experience, a powerful intensity created out of Joseph Cotter's own growing up in America. Nowhere is this intensity greater than in the character of Caleb.

For the reader who is attracted by the emotional drive of Caleb, it is intriguing to note the author's belated attempt in the fourth act to explain Caleb's degeneracy by shifting the blame to another man.

> DOCTOR.    . . . His mother sinned ere he was born.
>                      This tainted him, therefore his wicked course.
> BISHOP.    No! No! She did not sin. Caleb was led
>                      To that belief.
> DOCTOR.                              Was led?
> BISHOP.                                              Rahab's the man!

The blame is Rahab's, but the motivation for the crime has only been pushed back, not explained. The nature of the "mother's sin" is not clear. Ten years later, Mr. Cotter made it more explicit when he published a collection of short stories. The lead story is entitled **"Caleb,"** and follows the plot of the play in many respects—except that the mother and father of Caleb were married twice: once before and once after emancipation (the slave marriage presumably was not sanctified by church and state). Caleb was born between the marriages, ergo a bastard. When Caleb learns this in the story, he strikes his father "violently over the heart." The father falls dead.

This story of patricide is followed by a tale entitled **"Rodney."** Mr. Cotter writes:

> Rodney was an illegitimate child. He knew not what
> this meant, but the sting of it embittered his young
> life.

The Negro has as much prejudice as the white man. Under like conditions the Negro would make the same laws against the white. This crept out in the treatment of Rodney. His worst enemies were always Negroes. The Anglo-Saxon blood in his veins made scoffers of some and demons of others.

To be pitied is the boy who has never framed the word "father" upon his lips. Rodney attempted it once, but failed, and never tried again. He stood before his father bareheaded and with the coveted word on his lips.

> "You have a fine head of hair," said the father.
>
> "That's what people say." replied Rodney.
>
> "Are you proud of it?"
>
> "Should I be, Sir?"

"Well, my little man, it's a disgrace to you."

This was the first and last meeting of Rodney and his father. Joseph Cotter himself was the bastard son of a black mother and her "employer," a Scotch-Irishman, "a prominent citizen of Louisville." The fact that young Joseph was not sent to school but put to menial work at the age of ten suggests that the "prominent citizen" did not rejoice in his Negro son. It is fair to speculate that Cotter's black experience as the bastard black son of a white father speaks through both Rodney and Caleb.

There are three fathers in the play: Grandison, who is dead when the play opens; the Bishop, Olivia's adopted father, a man who has a lecherous itch for his ward; and Noah, whose beard Caleb pulls out. Speeches are given over to the value of mother love, but no praises are given to fathers—nor is one ever allowed to merit praise. The Industrial School is saved by Olivia. Joseph Cotter hated his Anglo-Saxon father, and by extension, the country he attempts to praise in act three. A comparison of the Old Man's speeches, as he urges his followers to leave "a country that is one ignoble grave," with those of the Bishop, who is defending America as a paradise, makes the latter appear vacuous. The Back-to-Our-African-Homeland section is powerful. It is of small consequence that the Old Man is slipped into the final tableau to show that he has acquiesced to the Bishop's America.

> In his own preface to the play, the author states: The Negro needs very little politics, much industrial training, and a dogged settledness as far as going to Africa is concerned. To this should be added clean, intelligent fireside leadership. Much of any other kind is dangerous for the present. I am a Negro and speak from experience.

This is hardly a denunciation of those who wish to return to Africa. Militancy is not rejected: it is rejected "only for the present."

How much Mr. Cotter is aware of his own dual attitude regarding white America must be left to the reader—with one final hint. What is the real allegory of the scene in act two between the Bishop, Olivia, and the ministers? Is this a "realistic" scene, or did Mr. Cotter write a surrealistic scene of associative visual and aural images? If the scene were transferred to *Alice in Wonderland* (and it could easily be done), would it not become "significant?"

Perhaps the case that the author was consciously disguising his material can never be proved. Indeed, it may not be possible to show that some of the best scenes of the play sprang "unintended" from his unconscious. However, a fair and sensitive reading will reveal that Joseph Cotter is a black man whose total being is writing out the anguish of his life. It may be enough that he saw early that for the black man to have power he must own the means of distribution and production. And perhaps the fairytale ending was Mr. Cotter's final note of satire on what might be expected from the great white fathers. (pp. 61-3)

> *James V. Hatch, "Yes We Must, Yes We Can: 'Caleb the Degenerate' (1901), Joseph S. Cotter, Sr.," in* Black Theater, U.S.A.: Forty-Five Plays by Black Americans, 1847-1974, *edited by James V. Hatch, The Free Press, 1974, pp. 61-99.*

## BETTY CAIN  (essay date 1978)

[*Cain is an American educator and critic. In the following excerpt, she examines* Caleb, the Degenerate *as disguised social protest.*]

Caleb in the Bible got to the Promised Land because he did not fear the giants in the walled cities and "wholly followed the Lord" (Deuteronomy, 1:25-26). Another Caleb, the protagonist of a strange, enigmatic four-act verse drama by Afro-American poet Joseph S. Cotter Sr., is called in the title "the Degenerate." He is given actions and speeches to show "degeneracy," but other elements in the play strongly suggest the militant power of the Biblical Caleb. This question of intended thematic effect is explored in the following discussion of Cotter's *Caleb, the Degenerate: A Study of the Customs, Types, and Needs of the American Negro,* first published in 1901, and recently anthologized in 1974 in *Black Theater, U.S.A.,* edited by James Hatch and Ted Shine. These editors introduce the play [see excerpt dated 1974] with the suggestion that there may be a hidden message under the surface theme, which is that American blacks of the time needed to turn away from "degeneracy" and devote themselves to the Booker T. Washington work ethic.

That there should be a play with at least two levels of interpretation, with meanings which contradict each other in itself dramatizes the uneasy situation of Black intellectuals at the turn of the century, especially in the South. The Ku Klux Klan was powerful; voting was forbidden to Blacks; Jim Crow laws were stringent—and the only way to exist in peace seemed to be the way of Booker T. Washington. Yet the founder of Tuskegee had set limits on the growth of Black freedom in the so-called Atlanta Compromise, his address at the Atlanta Exposition of 1895:

> Our greatest danger is that in the great leap from slavery to freedom we may overlook the fact that the masses of us are to live by the productions of our hands, and fail to keep in mind that we shall glorify common labor and put brains and skill into the common occupations of life; shall prosper in proportion as we learn to draw the line between the superficial and the substantial, the ornamental gewgaws of life and the useful. No race can prosper till it learns that there is as much dignity in tilling a field as in writing a poem.

The enthusiasm with which whites accepted this speech made Booker T. Washington the most influential Black person in America, with the power of effectively blocking other potential leaders.

It is logical then to assume that Joseph Cotter, Sr., the largely self-educated child of a slave and her white owner, for most of his long life a teacher and school principal in Louisville, should feel the necessity of writing in ways that Washington would approve. Certainly the surface plot of *Caleb, the Degenerate* fits that requirement. (pp. 37-8)

[The play's] reception since its first publication shows that it is a riddle that has never yet been solved. Cotter first asked a white patron, Cale Young Rice, to read *Caleb* in 1898. It was later published in 1901 and 1903 editions, appeared in a little-noticed 1973 reprint from the original publishers, Bradley and Gilbert of Louisville, Kentucky, and was given one public reading. Research so far has not uncovered any evidence of the play being staged. The text apparently circulated, however, because Hatch and Shine give quotations of critical opinions from three diverse sources in their introduction:

> The play brings into sharp contrast the ideas of the cultivated Negroes. . . . a unique and interesting addition to the dramatic literature of America.
>
> —*New York Dramatic Mirror*

... further evidence of the latent capacity of your long-maltreated race for mental development.
—Alfred Austin, then Poet Laureate of England

I do not profess to understand it all, but I desire to express my appreciation of the passages of true poetry in which you express the aspirations of the Negro race for salvation by labor.
—Israel Zangwill, Jewish-American novelist

In the fifties and sixties some brief comments about *Caleb* in histories of Afro-American literature dismiss it as a "problem play" (with no discussion of the problems) [Margaret Just Butcher, *The Negro in American Literature*]; as "terribly inept blank verse" with "incidents and dialogue frequently laughable" but "the closest thing to a folk play ever turned out in the United States"; and as a "slight, pretentious play" with "unbelievable characters spouting incredible lines," reflecting none of the conventions of the live theater of the day [see Abramson excerpt dated 1969].

In an article in *Negro Digest* "First Afro-American Theater" [see Additional Bibliography], playwright and critic Carlton W. Molette III objected to Doris Abramson's disparagements, pointing out that in the oral tradition out of which the Afro-American theater springs, plays can be mixtures of sermons, stories, pageants, and whatever else the theme calls for. Molette does not, however, make any attempt to discuss the puzzle of theme in *Caleb.*

Hatch and Shine, calling Cotter a "disciple" of Washington, may be missing a clue in the playful irony in Cotter's doggerel lines on **"Dr. Booker T. Washington to the National Negro Business League."**

What deeds have sprung from plow and pick!
What bank-rolls from tomatoes.
No dainty crop of rhetoric
Can match one of potatoes.

In the tone of this verse and from the play *Caleb* itself, there is hardly a warrant for identifying Cotter as a "disciple" of Washington.

Another proof that Cotter was capable of using poetry for social criticism was given in a poem of his printed in 1898:

**"To Kentucky"**

Make not a law to rule another
That you yourselves would not obey;
In this, as in the ancient day,
Man is the keeper of his brother.
Let not the states about you see
That you are great in all that goes
To banish friends and harbor foes
Around the base of freedom's tree.

The ambiguity begins with the Preface to the 1903 edition of the play. Cotter himself notes the puzzling use of elevated and often witty Shakespearean blank verse in most of the play. Why did he use the poetry that Booker T. Washington had implied is one of "the ornamental gewgaws of life," in a play seeming to promote manual labor as the panacea for Negro problems? Cotter says, "An author puts poetry into the mouths of his characters to show the possibility of individual human expression." Although somewhat cryptic, this statement seems to indicate human possibilities far beyond Washington's limited accommodationism and hints that we will find these potentials in the play's poetic speeches. Cotter, however, goes on to say, "The Negro needs very little politics, much industrial training, and a dogged settledness as far as going to Africa is con-

cerned." That seems pretty clear, so perhaps we should look no further, and take the surface message of the play at its face value. But that future generations were *not* intended to do that, is strongly suggested by the last two sentences of the Preface: "Much of any other kind is dangerous for the present. I am a Negro and speak from experience." In 1901, in the long period after the Reconstruction, with white power manifest in the form of lynchings and terror and the legalization of Jim Crow, Cotter, I believe, is telling us that the Negro actually *has* much of another kind of need, but to express it openly might mean persecution and even death. His play *Caleb,* I am convinced, is in the tradition of hidden messages in spirituals; Cotter is thus also a precursor of playwrights like Marcel and Sartre, who concealed anti-Nazi propaganda in seemingly neutral plays written and staged during the occupation of France.

From the first scene of the play, *Caleb, the Degenerate,* odd juxtapositions of characters, actions, and dialogue remind us more of the Expressionistic dramas of Strindberg than of any melodrama or tragedy written for the American stage before 1901. The Bishop, "adopted father" to Olivia, inveighs against "Caleb, this hell-builder upon earth" in Shakespearean blank verse. When he stops for breath, Olivia plays a violin, after first getting her bow back from the Bishop, who has seized it. The Bishop speaks of his dead wife, and then says, "I have one more! 'Tis you, Olivia!" We wonder why Olivia needs an "adopted father," when she has a real one, Noah, and sense something slightly sinister in the Bishop's more than fatherly interest in her and in his jealousy of Caleb: "You wed a brute, my child?"

"Caleb's the man!" is Olivia's impudent reply, and she goes out, playing the violin softly. The Bishop calls her back. She responds from offstage, taunting him, as she does throughout the play: "What profits it? A child is never grown." Then she "breaks chord on violin" and says: "A broken chord! Chords break so easily." The "broken chord" is immediately followed by news from Olivia's friend Frony, who is also part of the Bishop's household, that Caleb, in the company of the "libertine" preacher Rahab, has killed his father in an argument. Olivia turns pale, but talks with Frony of love and of hope for Caleb's soul.

In the second scene, in Caleb's cottage, Rahab, called "Caleb's devil's man," is hypocritically preparing a funeral sermon. Caleb strides in "with whip and spurs in hand" and shouts: "No sermon!.... Money! Money! Money!", and soon arranges the sale of his father's body to a medical student.

Even though Caleb's "degeneracy" is thus from the outset laid on heavily, Olivia, the idealistic young teacher, holds to him through the rest of the play—not sexually, not romantically, but intellectually and spiritually. Many long interchanges with the Bishop in later scenes express her perception of Caleb as a hero for future generations. And yet Olivia and Caleb never speak to one another on stage, and meet only once, and then briefly, the directions reading, "As Olivia enters Caleb looks abashed and runs out." Obviously there is some deeper theme here than sentimental romance. Caleb is ambivalently presented as "a hero as antihero," as Hatch and Shine suggest in their introduction. The epithet "the Degenerate" may thus be meant as heavily ironic. Blacks accused of rape were categorized as "degenerate," and therefore, their lynching was justified. Cotter here gives us a man who does not respect his father's body, his mother's love, or his sweetheart's father's white hairs— but his evil is confined to his own people and his acts may be symbolic. Further, he is motivated by a belief that his mother was guilty of adultery, that he himself was not of legitimate birth, sub-themes which were predominant in an earlier crude prose tale, **"Caleb,"** included in a collection, *Negro Tales,* all by Cotter, although the contrast between the early pathetic tale and the full-length play in style and conception is striking.

From the first scenes of *Caleb* referred to above, to the end of the play, the reader is continually intrigued and baffled by tension between the surface story and the dreamlike scenes of symbolic action, the whole effect compounded by the dialogue in archaic blank verse. Nothing quite like it has been seen in Afro-American drama before or since. Certainly the story seems as ridiculous, pretentious, and crude as some critics have said it is. But even in the above skeleton form, strange elements and combinations are apparent, which have no counterparts in the conventional melodramas of the day. Conventionally there were stock characters, action progressing through the machinations of the villain, pathos, sentimentality, "serious" action intended to create suspense, good rewarded, evil punished, and hero and heroine united at the end. *Caleb* departs from all these characteristics in complex and interesting ways.

Close study of the interrelationships of actions and characters and of the long poetic "sermons" in *Caleb* reveals a coded structure that could convey a hidden message to alert readers and audience. The two main characters, Olivia and Caleb, are the keys to the hidden structure. Olivia is central; the others can all be interpreted as they relate to her. Her actions and speeches reveal her to be much like the Shakespearean Olivia. She is brave and determined:

> OLIVIA. 'Twas horrible! 'Twas horrible! Caleb
> Did prove a demon! 'Tis my sober thought
> Great God will hear no prayers that he will make.
> FRONY. You should have seen! You should—
> OLIVIA. I heard enough.
> FRONY. Are satisfied?
> OLIVIA. That I should strive the more.

She is intelligent and imaginative, speaking in the elevated blank verse Cotter defended in his Preface:

> OLIVIA. Past ages toyed with man. He knew it not,
> And made their jest the altar of his praise.
> They thorned his soul with fear, yet asked him why
> He was so slow to sniff the rose of life.
> They dulled his sight by bringing Hell so close,
> They scorned him for not seeing Heaven afar.

She is witty and wily—very much a Shakespearean heroine:

> OLIVIA. As Frony says, your sermons cling to me.
> BISHOP. As you to Caleb?
> OLIVIA. I have no mind to make comparisons.
> Besides the ancient rule of courtesy
> Forbids that you bring up a second point
> When I have introduced a sober first.
> BISHOP. 'Tis true! Go on!

She is compassionate. As she exposes the politician Rahab's falseness, she asks him:

> OLIVIA. You love the race?
> RAHAB. I love the race? I lead.
> Others may do the loving. I look up.
> OLIVIA. I love Rahab. (He turns toward her.) I love Rahab.
> RAHAB. Woman,
> That spurs me on to action.

> OLIVIA. That's your speech
> Upon yourself. It spurs you on—
> BISHOP. To death.

Olivia is a powerhouse of a woman, directing, manipulating, always taking the initiative, setting the philosophical tone, and always more aware of what is going on than any of the other characters. For instance, although she loves Caleb for his intelligence and rebellious assertiveness, she has no illusions of being able to save him. She knows he is doomed—

> OLIVIA. Caleb shall soon find his reward.
> . . . He is the man to expiate his crimes.
> He is secure in the coils of retribution.
> His reward shall be death.

Booker T. Washington's name is nowhere mentioned in the play, although ostensibly the drama appears to promote Washington's philosophy. If Washington is represented at all, however, it is by Olivia, who is running, promoting, and raising money for a trade school for blacks. Why did Cotter make the industrial school principal a woman? We might speculate that this choice made the character so different from Washington himself that no one could claim the two are similar; thus it enabled Cotter to make his idealistic figure a complicated one, pointing beyond industrial training for the Negro and accommodationism. Many accounts of Washington's career indicate, however, that he was not so simple either; some see him as the clever trickster covering up an inner militance in order to get what blacks needed to survive in the white post-Reconstruction world. Cotter's character Olivia does this too, as she implies when she tells how she got money for the school:

> OLIVIA. Chance threw me with a group of millionaires.
> I doubted, fretted, feared. At last I spoke.
> The speech was short and simple. See the checks!
> BISHOP. They lost no time in writing them?
> OLIVIA. A tale
> Our folks oft slumber o'er drew tears from them.

Olivia's relationships with the other characters show, however, that she is much more than a female Booker T. Washington. Her having two fathers seems odd, but can be seen as significant. Her natural father, Noah, is a ridiculous, ineffectual figure; in relation to both Caleb and Olivia, he may represent the backward older generation that the young people must break away from. As for the Bishop, in whose home she lives, we can perhaps assume that he adopted her to give her the education she could not otherwise have afforded. Thematically, Olivia's close relationship to a high church official shows the need to convert a stagnant black clergy interested only in preaching hell fire, to acting for the progress of the Negro. Evidently Cotter is trying to show that the black church can be aroused and lead the race much further than Washington considered possible during his lifetime. The closing lines of the play indicate that the Bishop has come quite far:

> BISHOP. Failure? 'Tis a misfit. Success is what?
> 'Tis a measurement of self. 'Tis measurement of all the forces that encounter self.
> 'Tis fitting these together day by day.
> 'Tis seeing goals with eyes that never blink.
> 'Tis finding desert spots and tending them
> So that their fruitage stars man's ancient lot and links his freedom with the linked spheres.

But why, throughout the play, is Olivia so disrespectful to an august Bishop? Why does she taunt him, mock him, and play tricks on him? Strange behavior for a proper young woman in any age, but especially in the 1890s! Even more strange is the

Bishop's desire to marry his foster daughter. Not so strange, however, in terms of the hidden message, is Olivia's *not* marrying the Bishop or showing any romantic interest in him at all. The members of the younger generation, represented by Olivia, are to arouse the clergy, but they are not to be too closely allied to the church's traditional nonmilitant teachings.

In addition to providing Olivia with two fathers, Cotter has three other women in the play who may be seen as *other selves* of Olivia. One is Caleb's mother, Patsy, a good woman, who was Olivia's early teacher. Her belief in Caleb's potential, which she relates in a dream story, parallels Olivia's. After Caleb kills his father, Olivia commits herself to Patsy's role to regenerate him. Then there is Frony, Olivia's confidante, who abhors Caleb's deeds, but sympathizes with Olivia and expresses the sisterhood of feminism—

> FRONY.  I like not Caleb, but I'll help you out.
> We women must be women! Men are men!

A third variant of Olivia, introduced in Act III at the school, is simply called A Woman. That this mysterious Woman and Frony are both aspects of Olivia's personality becomes apparent in some amazing scenes using surrealistic techniques. First we see Olivia/Frony, in Act II, Scene One, as three ministers are waiting to "say goodbye" to the Bishop. Who they are, where they are going, or why, is not told. Two of the ministers are shown in by Frony. She then brings in Noah, Olivia's natural father. The Bishop asks him to stay, and the following dream-like ritual takes place—

> (*The MINISTERS stand on either side of table and toss ball to each other. OLIVIA and FRONY let their hair so fall that it covers back of head and face. They stand with arms around each other's neck and rock to and fro.*)
> OLIVIA.  Ball! Ball!
> FRONY.  That means a little game. Ha! ha!
> (*They continue to rock and measure first hands and then feet. Ball rolls under table. MINISTERS upset table in getting it. BISHOP's hat falls. FIRST MINISTER rubs his head with one hand and hands hat to SECOND MINISTER, who does same and hands hat to NOAH. NOAH takes it and wipes it reluctantly. MINISTERS whisper again.*)
> BISHOP.  My hat! Is this a game of ball? My hat!
> NOAH.  Stay, Bishop, stay! You see just what you see!
> BISHOP.  I stay! Is this a trick? Then let me learn! Even a sober man may smile at whims.
> FIRST MINISTER. (*lays ball on table*) Here, Bishop!
> SECOND MINISTER. (*puts down doll-shoes*) Here, Bishop!
> THIRD MINISTER. (*enters hurriedly, lays on table doll-toys and loaf of bread*) Bishop, look well!
> FRONY.  The game! The game!
> OLIVIA.  Who'll live to see it out?
> (*FIRST and SECOND MINISTERS run to OLIVIA and FRONY and fan them with their beavers. NOAH puts BISHOP's beaver on table and goes to door*)
> BISHOP.  Noah, you go?
> NOAH.  My wits won't let me stay. (*exit NOAH*)
> (*OLIVIA and FRONY put up their hair*)
> BISHOH.  Things seem to say: "Be philosophical."
> You'd have a game? Let each one take a part.
> (*FIRST and SECOND MINISTERS give their hats to THIRD MINISTER to hold. He bows and holds them with dignity*)
> Draw near! (*all draw near*) Olivia, take you the ball!
> Good Ministers, take each a little shoe!
> The loaf of bread, Frony! (*to THIRD MINISTER*) Some of the toys?
> THIRD MINISTER.  Bishop, I'm toying now with this head-wear
> That wears so well a score of years might fail

> To see its gloss in need of hatter's aid.
> Suppose my grandfather had owned these hats;
> Suppose they came to me as his estate;
> Suppose I brought them to a place like this;
> Suppose I fanned two ladies, side by side;
> Suppose I gave them to a friend to hold;
> Suppose he held them in his sturdy left; (*holds them so*)
> Suppose he drew his right and poised it thus; (*he draws as though to strike*)
> Suppose—
> MINISTERS.  We take our beavers back again.
> (*They take them and lay them aside*)
> (*to THIRD MINISTER*) What would you have?
> We would not slight you, sir.
> THIRD MINISTER. (*walks to FRONY and points to bread*) A slight division of the honors here.
> OLIVIA.  I'll squeeze. (*she squeezes the ball. FIRST MINISTER points to SECOND MINISTER's feet and to little shoes*)
> FIRST MINISTER.  How many pairs will make a pair?
> (*FRONY looks at bread as though she would eat it*)
> FRONY.  My teeth are many years younger than I.
> THIRD MINISTER. (*aside*) I do not ask for a division there.

The Bishop then admits that—

> These trinkets seem to tell a sober tale.

He launches into a sermon on how his "misguided" people need to learn handicrafts.

But what is the significance of Olivia's and Frony's letting their hair fall over their faces and rocking to and fro together? They seem in this action to be prophetesses who know more than they are willing to tell, hiding secrets of the future and also refusing to watch the childish game of the ministers. They know, perhaps, that it is far from the whole story.

Nevertheless, Olivia encourages the Bishop in his interpretations: the ball is progress; the little shoes show "how scant our footing is"; the doll-toys are "the many things we need to learn to make." But Olivia is surely being ironic when she says: How far we looked to learn a truth that's taught by jingling pots and pans. After the ministers and Noah have gone, "OLIVIA holds the BISHOP's beaver and motions him to toss the ball. He does. She catches it in hat."

> OLIVIA.  My hat! Is this a game of ball? My hat!
> BISHOP.  Olivia my child, it is a game
> Of progress that I riddled out for you.
> (*She puts hat on table*)

Then Olivia and the Bishop exchange opposing views of Caleb, and Olivia describes her ideal man, with strong implications that Caleb, at least potentially, has these qualities. The Bishop laughs scornfully and picks up his hat to go. As he puts it on, the ball falls out—so the Bishop really does not have the ball of progress in his hat after all.

This strange scene in Act II is perhaps the most revealing key to a hidden message running counter to the flag-waving glorification of good old American hard manual labor in the final act. That simple solution is here made to seem ridiculous. Yet later Olivia herself espouses it when the Bishop visits her school. Several thematic levels are thus interwoven throughout, as we have seen, and their puzzling juxtaposition was very likely intended to conceal a militance that Cotter hinted in his Preface would be "dangerous."

In another surrealistic, expressionistic scene at Olivia's school in Act III, Frony and the mysterious Woman come in with

Olivia's book entitled *The Negro and His Hands* and go through actions that seem to signify something quite opposed to Olivia's official enthusiasm in the same scene for her pupil's learning useful trades.

> (*Enter FRONY and WOMAN with OLIVIA'S book. They*
> *sit back to back and search books. . . .*)
> FRONY.    (*to WOMAN*) What seek you?
> WOMAN.    What seek you?
> FRONY.    A laugh.
> WOMAN.    Find it!
> (*They search books*)

The pupils go on working and Olivia directs them, paying no attention to her other selves, Frony and the Woman. Then—

> FRONY.    Ha! Ha!
> WOMAN.    You found the laugh? Where?
> FRONY.    Nowhere!
>           I laughed to cheer me up to find the laugh.
> WOMAN.    You might have made me laugh a real laugh.
> FRONY.    Do laugh! A real laugh! 'Twill bring again
>           the bloom—
> FRONY.    and WOMAN (*pointing to each other*) You
>           lost some twenty years ago.
> FRONY.    (*holds up book*) The laugh is here.
> WOMAN.    How know you that?
> FRONY.    The book
>           Was written by Olivia.
> WOMAN.    (*Holds up book and strikes it*) 'Tis here.
>           (*Drops book, laughs, and runs out*)

This "laugh" Frony and the Woman are looking for could have several interesting meanings. It could be making fun of the simplicity of the handiwork ethic. It could signify the ridiculousness of the intelligent Olivia's having written a simple-minded book about that ethic. It could stand for the free enjoyment of life that the dull industrial training is squashing. It certainly shows ambivalence in the Olivia/Frony/Other Woman character.

Caleb is, of course, the other main character, and, in spite of his "degeneracy," comes through as a tragic hero, not quite in the ancient Greek sense, but in many ways close to it.

But what kind of hero is this, who begins by killing his father and then heartlessly sells the body? He says to the undertaker who has come to offer his services:

> CALEB.    A thirty-dollar coffin! I say no!
>           Five dollars for a robe? No, deathworm, no!
>           Four carriages? No, deathworm, no!
>           Think you a son must curb his appetite
>           Because a pauper father breathes no more?
>           The living must have money! I'm alive!
>           Cold dignity is all the dead require.
>           The living must have money! Hear you that!

Caleb's behavior is so outrageous and Olivia's belief in him so unbelievable that we must look for a subtler signification. In the above speech, Caleb may be symbolically asserting the right of the living, new generation to have their needs met, because they will be the doers for the future. It might seem selfish, but it is necessary. After his mother dies later in the play, Caleb repeats this theme by simply saying, "She's dead? Then bury her." Further, can we not see Caleb's killing of his father as not a real murder but a symbol of the need for a courageous young generation to overthrow tradition and the unproductive ways of their fathers?

A parallel, although not so drastic, symbol reinforcing the same theme appears when Caleb pulls off Noah's beard. It is as though the old patriarch, the rescuer and then founder of his people, has lived too long. Caleb deprives him of his strength, just as Samson's strength was in his hair. When Noah cries, "My beard is being wasted," Caleb replies, "My strength is not."

Another motive for Caleb's "degeneracy" is his belief in the teachings of the false prophet, Rahab, who is collecting funds to lead Blacks back to Africa. He is exposed as a scoundrel by Olivia and her followers, and he too dies in what Cotter presents as a well-merited death.

Caleb's self-awareness is expressed in his last speech before he tries to stab himself:

> CALEB.    O, God, if I have sinned because the blood
>           Thou gavest me was tainted ere my birth,
>           Whose is the wrong? Whose is the reckoning?
>           Master, I leave it all with thee—with thee.
>           Men sneer and say: "Be guided by your will!"
>           I have no will! I never had a will!
>           Thy fate, O God, did rob me of my will!

Here Caleb is of course still the rebel, flinging the blame at God, but he recognizes that a lack of will power was his fated and fatal flaw. Here in an interesting variation, is the Greek tragic hero's hubris and his fated punishment for it. Caleb is certainly not a villain of the melodramas popular when this play was written. Neither is he a true Greek tragic hero, but in many ways a full-blooded Shakespearean one with all his complications.

Although the title of the play names Caleb, we earlier identified Olivia as the central character and suggested that all others can be interpreted in relation to her. As we should expect, Olivia's direct and indirect speeches about Caleb give us the strongest indexes to what Cotter wanted to convey in the construction of the complex character of Caleb.

Olivia sets the tone of her feeling about Caleb in the first act, by saying firmly, both before and after the Bishop's objections: "Caleb's the man! Calebs the man!" Even after she hears he has killed his father, she persists in her plans to marry him. Yet, as observed earlier, there is no real romance between Olivia and Caleb, and only the one brief wordless meeting on stage. Their relationship is an expression, rather, of a significant idea about the "Needs of the American Negro" of the subtitle. That idea is made clear in Act II, when Olivia describes her ideal man to the Bishop. He senses that she is speaking of what Caleb might have been had he not misused his gifts. But she is also describing an ideal man quite different from Booker T. Washington's ideal humble manual laborer—

> BISHOP.    Your ideal man?
> OLIVIA.    I have him.
> BISHOP.    Let me hear.

First the sassy Olivia answers with a series of ridiculous paradoxes, but the Bishop persists—

> BISHOP.    That character's impossible! Again!
> OLIVIA.    His is an eye that runs compassion's length.
>            His is a tongue that snares the simplest words
>            Round simplest thoughts in beauty's fadeless
>            mesh.
>            Such art as his the soul of man endears
>            Through all the silences of all the years.
>            Right-fettered and full-faced he halts him by
>            Each column wrong has builded to the sky.
>            He flaws each flaw until proof-laden runs
>            Faith's highest hope past earth and stars and
>            suns.

BISHOP.     That is not Caleb—
OLIVIA.     Well you know 'tis not.
BISHOP.     Again!
OLIVIA.     How many think you I possess?
BISHOP.     Enough to banish Caleb.
OLIVIA.     He's secure.
BISHOP.     What think you of his creed—his atheist's
            creed
            He thundered it into his mother's ears.
            He blurted it above his father's corpse.
OLIVIA.     I think not of it now. I do not wish.
            Accept the creed of strenuous modern life?
BISHOP.     Of strenuous modern life? Well, let me hear.
OLIVIA.     God makes a man. Conditions make his
            creed.
            When reason's torch has once been kindled
            by
            the vicious fancies of the ignorant
            And fueled by the greed and soullessness
            That stamp eternal vengeance everywhere,
            The human in us often scoffs and says:
            "There is no God nor Heaven to be found."
            Hope is the star that lights self unto self.
            Faith is the hand that clutches self's decree.
            Mercy is oil self keeps for its own ills.
            Justice is hell made present by a blow.
            Conditions, therefore, make this creed I hold:
            "God-like I strive, but man-like I rebel!"
            Man is most man, and, therefore, most like
            God
            When he does weigh life's actions in such
            scales
            As balance not for his sufficiency,
            But quiver till the All-intelligence
            Applies a power whose name is very truth.
            Great men, not creeds, will have the right of
            way.
BISHOP.     (he calls as to one far off) Caleb! Caleb!
            You have the right of way.
            A great man, you? Ha! ha!. . . .
            (bows to OLIVIA) Ha! ha!. . . .
OLIVIA.     Great men, not creeds, will have the right of
            way.
            They clash in every age; and clashing strip
            Some worn-out garment from the limbs of
            Truth.
            Should one put forth his eager hand and touch
            Truth's perfect robes they would entangle it
            And hold it captive till God's reckoning time.

This "creed of strenuous modern life" is militant and revolutionary. And above it, having "the right of way," are great men, who clash with creeds "in every age." In Olivia's eyes, Caleb could have achieved that kind of greatness.

These brave words are in the Second Act; Caleb's death (as Washington-imago), the most moving scene in the play, comes much later. Olivia has saved her School for Industrial Arts, but she has lost the "great man" she had sought as her mate. A strong wild man became degenerate, was defeated, then died.

In *Caleb, the Degenerate* Cotter attempted in dramatic form the same strategy that his friend and fellow Afro-American poet Paul Laurence Dunbar wrote of so movingly:

> We wear the mask that grins and lies,
> It hides our cheeks and shades our eyes,—

> This debt we pay to human guile;
> With torn and bleeding hearts we smile,
> And mouth with myriad subtleties.

That the mask Cotter donned was this strangely beautiful and complex drama, *Caleb, the Degenerate,* is an answer to Dunbar's cry, because, as we have seen, it is a mask we can see through, if we will. It is "beauty's fadeless mesh" spoken of by Olivia in her lines about her ideal man—

> His is a tongue that snares the simplest words
> Round simplest thoughts in beauty's fadeless mesh,
> Such art as his the soul of man endears
> Through all the silences of all the years.

(pp. 39-52)

*Betty Cain, "Wearing the Mask: Joseph S. Cotter Sr.'s 'Caleb, the Degenerate',"* in MELUS, *Vol. 5, No. 3, Fall, 1978, pp. 37-53.*

## ADDITIONAL BIBLIOGRAPHY

Jones, Paul W. L. "Two Kentucky Poets." *The Voice of the American Negro* III, No. VII (July 1906): 583-88.
    Descriptive sketch of Cotter's life and work.

Kerlin, Robert T. "A Poet from Bardstown." *The South Atlantic Quarterly* XX, No. 3 (July 1921): 213-21.
    Survey of Cotter's poetry and fiction that finds philosophical, didactic, and lyrical qualities in his work.

Molette, Carlton W. "The First Afro-American Theatre." *Negro Digest* XIX, No. 6 (April 1970): 4-9.
    Argues that *Caleb, the Degenerate* has been unfairly dismissed by critics who evaluated it without taking into account the particular traditions and cultural milieu out of which it arose.

Redmond, Eugene B. "Jubilees, Jujus, and Justices." In his *Drum Voices: The Mission of Afro-American Poetry,* pp. 83-138. Garden City, N.Y.: Anchor Press, 1976.
    Brief overview of Cotter's work, in which Redmond states: "Cotter . . . it must be said, was among the first black poets to represent, without shame and minstrelsy, authentic black folk life. . . . He achieves 'rushing rhythms and ingenious rhymes' when he is at his best; and a quiet, reflective perseverance when he writes introspectively."

Shockley, Ann Allen. "Joseph S. Cotter, Sr.: Biographical Sketch of a Black Louisville Bard." *College Language Association Journal* XVIII, No. 3 (March 1975): 327-40.
    Overview of Cotter's life and works.

Thompson, R. W. "Negroes Who Are Doing Things: Joseph Seamon Cotter." *Alexander's Magazine,* No. 1 (15 August 1905) 25-6.
    Sketch of Cotter's life and literary career. Thompson states: "Cotter was a 'born poet' and a happy storyteller. Every sentiment, incident, or chain of events illustrative of human nature, appeals to his sensitive mind, and is gathered up by his constructive genius into a finite tale or verse."

Watkins, Thomas G. "The Author." In *Caleb, the Degenerate,* by Joseph S. Cotter. Louisville: Bradley & Gilbert Co., 1903.
    Biographical sketch. Watkins praises Cotter for surmounting personal and social obstacles "undreamed of by Burns and other sons of song who struggled up from poverty, obscurity, and ignorance to glory."

# Finley Peter Dunne

## 1867-1936

American journalist.

A prominent journalist at the beginning of the twentieth century, Dunne was the creator of the popular fictional character Mr. Dooley, whose comments on social and political issues were a regular feature of American newspapers for nearly twenty years. Imbued with Dunne's considerable wit and insight, Mr. Dooley's commonsense aphorisms voiced the sentiments of many Americans and, as a result, frequently became popular slogans. At the same time, critics note that the Dooley essays also contain sophisticated indictments of corruption and hypocrisy, a contention that is supported by continuing scholarly interest in both the style and content of Dunne's work.

Born in Chicago, Dunne was the son of Irish immigrants who had achieved a measure of success in the United States. The elder Dunne, a carpenter and active participant in Democratic politics, was able to provide a comfortable living for his eight children, while his well-read wife instilled in them a love of literature. The brightest of the eight, Dunne was the only son to attend high school, but he failed to apply himself to his studies and graduated last in his class of fifty. In light of this poor academic performance, his father decided not to send him to college, advising him instead to find employment.

Dunne's first job was as an office boy for Chicago's smallest newspaper, the *Telegram*. The editor of the *Telegram* soon discovered that Dunne could write as well as anyone on the staff and he made the young man a reporter. Shortly thereafter, Dunne moved to the more prestigious *Chicago News*; during the decade that followed he worked on nearly every one of the major Chicago newspapers, becoming editor of the *Chicago Times* at the age of 21, pioneering the newly created field of sports reporting, and writing political commentaries. He was, therefore, already a seasoned journalist and local celebrity when he began writing the dialect pieces that eventually became the Mr. Dooley series.

The genesis of Dunne's Irish-dialect essays has been variously reported, with Dunne himself maintaining that the first was inspired by the comments of James McGarry, the proprietor of a bar frequented by Chicago reporters, concerning the death of railroad magnate Jay Gould. Dunne found McGarry's comments extremely funny and incorporated them into his editorial for the Sunday *Post* on 11 December 1892, changing McGarry's name to Colonel McNeery and reproducing his Irish accent phonetically. Dunne's editor was enormously pleased with the resulting article, a response shared by readers of the *Post,* and he encouraged Dunne to write more such essays. As the popularity of the series grew, however, McGarry became uncomfortable at being associated with Dunne's mordant political criticism—many readers identified McGarry with McNeery from the first—and he insisted that Dunne stop using the NcNeery character. As a result, in his column for 7 October 1893, Dunne sent Colonel McNeery home to Ireland and introduced a new Irish-American bartender, Mr. Martin Dooley.

Dunne's many Chicago readers readily transferred their affection to Mr. Dooley, and the local popularity of the series increased steadily throughout the 1890s. National attention came

in 1898, when Dunne focused several articles on the events of the Spanish-American War. Editors in several major American cities reprinted Dunne's jibes, and within months his column had begun to appear weekly in newspapers across the country. Dunne's national readership forced him to write essays with wider appeal; after 1898 he shifted the focus of his essays from local to national and international politics. In addition, the phenomenal success of the series encouraged Dunne to issue periodic collections of the Dooley articles, beginning in 1898 with *Mr. Dooley in Peace and War.*

Shortly before the publication of his third collection of essays in 1900, Dunne moved from Chicago to New York, where he wrote for and edited the journal *Collier's Weekly* in addition to supplying his syndicated Dooley editorials. As the decade progressed, the frequency of Mr. Dooley's appearances in print gradually decreased. Dunne stopped the series altogether for the duration of the First World War, declaring that "insanity and racial murder" were inappropriate topics for humor. Yet, despite the gradual demise of the Dooley series, Dunne's reputation as a humorist and political sage continued to increase, and he numbered such eminent figures as President Theodore Roosevelt and Mark Twain among his close friends. Plagued by poor health, Dunne wrote little during the latter decades of his life; Mr. Dooley made a brief reappearance during the 1924 presidential campaign and another in 1926, but he was permanently retired when his creator inherited several million dollars in 1927. Dunne thenceforth devoted his full energies to his crowded social agenda, continuing to entertain lavishly up to the day of his death.

The Dooley essays were formulaic in nature, most often opening with Mr. Dooley's renowned observation, "I see be th' papers . . . ," which would be followed by a discourse upon some current topic or event. Comments were occasionally supplied by Mr. Dooley's most faithful patron and the other central character of the series, Mr. Hennessy, whose social and political naivete represented the unenlightened viewpoint of a large segment of the American population and provided a perfect foil for Dunne's trenchant wit. Despite his characterization as a representative of the working and middle classes, particularly as exemplified by the Irish-American laborers who frequented his bar, Mr. Dooley was in fact the vehicle for the expression of Dunne's more erudite liberal sympathies. Declaring himself the "enemy of pretense," Dunne sought to expose the hypocrisy and greed that he believed had permeated private enterprise and the government. While he hoped that such exposure might help to induce reform, his wide experience of the world led him to be skeptical about both the eventuality and the efficacy of such reform: "A man that'd expect to thrain lobsters to fly in one year is called a loonytic; but a man that thinks men can be turned into angels be an iliction is called a rayformer an' remains at large."

Dunne utilized a number of traditional comic devices in his satires, including understatement, puns, malapropisms, and solecisms, while the dialect feature added a further farcical dimension to the essays. Yet critics agree that the primary sources of humor in Dunne's works are his ironic treatment of subject matter and his unerring sense of the absurd. The combination of these elements results in what one critic has called the "debunking" quality of the Dooley essays, exemplified in the following description of banking and finance: "It ain't burglary, an' it ain't obtainin' money be false pretinses, an' it ain't manslaughter. . . . It's what ye might call a judicious seliction fr'm th' best features iv thim ar-rts." Such criticisms of established institutions and powerful people earned Dunne the respect and affection of many who felt dispossessed, and while Dunne directed his writing toward a more learned audience, his appeal was nevertheless universal.

Dunne's popularity during his lifetime cannot be overemphasized: his Mr. Dooley was one of the best known figures in America, inspiring songs, plays, musical comedies, and a long list of imitators, while Dunne himself enjoyed only slightly less attention. His renown also spread to other English-speaking nations, and he was particularly well-received in England. Critical response was predominantly favorable, with only isolated objections to his absolute irreverence and his identification with what one anonymous reviewer called "slum-dwellers." In the decades immediately following his death, however, Dunne's name rapidly faded from the public memory, and interest in his work was revived only in the 1960s as a result of increasing awareness of the historical importance of popular culture. Since that time, knowledge of Dunne and his writings has grown; a number of his books have been republished and several studies of his works have recently appeared. In addition, many of his essays have been newly anthologized, a fact that attests to the continuing relevance of his humor.

(See also *Contemporary Authors,* Vol. 108; *Dictionary of Literary Biography,* Vol. 11: *American Humorists, 1800-1950;* Vol. 23: *American Newspaper Journalists, 1873-1900*.)

## PRINCIPAL WORKS

*Mr. Dooley in Peace and War* (essays) 1898
*Mr. Dooley in the Hearts of His Countrymen* (essays) 1899
*Mr. Dooley's Philosophy* (essays) 1900
*Mr. Dooley's Opinions* (essays) 1901
*Observations by Mr. Dooley* (essays) 1902
*Dissertations by Mr. Dooley* (essays) 1906
*Mr. Dooley Says* (essays) 1910
*Mr. Dooley on Making a Will and Other Necessary Evils* (essays) 1919
*Mr. Dooley at His Best* (essays) 1938
*Mr. Dooley: Now and Forever* (essays) 1954
*The World of Mr. Dooley* (essays) 1962
*Mr. Dooley on Ivvrything and Ivvrybody* (essays) 1963
*Mr. Dooley on the Choice of Law* (essays) 1963
*Mr. Dooley Remembers: The Informal Memoirs of Finley Peter Dunne* (memoirs) 1963
*Mr. Dooley and the Chicago Irish* (essays) 1976

---

## HARRY THURSTON PECK (essay date 1899)

[*Peck was a prominent American critic and author who was noted for both the quality and the diversity of his writings. A widely respected classical scholar, he also wrote volumes of history, biography, literary criticism, poetry, and children's stories. Peck served as editor of the* Bookman *from 1895 to 1902, and his erudition contributed significantly to the stature of that journal. In the following excerpt, Peck praises the objectivity, rationality, and comic genius displayed in* Mr. Dooley in Peace and War.]

[We] think that Mr. Dooley is a person who will live for a long time in the memories of those who read his words of wisdom as recorded by the pen of Mr. Dunne. Mr. Dooley is a Chicago Irishman past middle age, who lives in the Archey Road, where he presides over a small "saloon." He left Ireland when young, and he has witnessed from his eyrie the events of the world's history and has thought about them deeply and is always ready to impart his impressions of them to his sympathetic friend and comrade, Mr. Hennessy, and to answer the searching questions of his other neighbour, Mr. McKenna. Mr. Dooley is a type. He has all an Irishman's shrewdness, an Irishman's combativeness, an Irishman's independence, an Irishman's underlying appreciation of courage and loyalty, and also an Irishman's keen wit and picturesque phraseology, with that inevitable genius for blundering that is also Irish. He is as individual as [Rudyard Kipling's] Mulvaney, and his philosophy is broader and has to do with a wider field. In reading his short conversations as recorded for us by Mr. Dunne, it is quite impossible for the most serious-minded man to refrain from laughter, and there is much more here than wit and humour only. There is an underlying truth of characterization, an indomitable common-sense and shrewdness that, under all the comicality and farcical exaggeration, strike right home to the reason and reveal at a flash the very root and heart of the matter which is before the mind. To read Mr. Dooley is to get a peep into the universal consciousness of mankind, to come into close touch with clear-sighted reasonableness, wrapped up but not concealed by a hundred whimsical exaggerations.

What gave to Mr. Dooley his national reputation was his comments on the occurrences of the late war, for these were widely copied by newspaper after newspaper throughout the country; yet we are really more impressed with some of his discourses on matters that are always interesting and always in men's minds. (pp. 574-75)

The most amusing thing in [*Mr. Dooley in Peace and War*] is to be found in Mr. Dooley's description of some expert evidence given in a murder trial. It is both amusing and it is also a very fair exposition of the absurdity of our judicial system. A medical professor is put upon the stand and is examined by the lawyers:

> "Prifissor," says th' lawyer f'r th' State, "I put it to ye if a wooden vat three hundherd an' sixty feet long, twenty-eight feet deep, an' sivinty-five feet wide, an' if three hundhred pounds iv caustic soda boiled, an' if th' leg iv a guinea pig, an' ye said yestherdah about bicarbonate iv soda, an' if it washes up an' washes over, an' th' slimy, slippery stuff, an' if a false tooth or a lock iv hair or a jawbone or a goluf ball across th' cellar eleven feet nine inches— that is, two inches this way an' five gallons that?" "I agree with ye intirely," says th' profissor. "I made lab'ratory experiments in an ir'n basin, with bichloride iv gool, which I will call soup-stock, an' coal-tar, which I will call ir'n filings. I mixed th' two over a hot fire, an' left it in a cool place to harden. I thin packed it in ice, which I will call glue, an' rock-salt, which I will call fried eggs, an' obtained a dark, queer solution that is a cure f'r freckles, which I will call antimony or doughnuts or anything I blamed please."
>
> "But," says th' lawyer f'r th' State, "measurin' th' vat with gas—an' I lave it to ye whether this is not th' on'y fair test—an' supposin' that two feet acrost is akel to tin feet sideways, an' supposin' that a thick green an' hard substance, an' I daresay it wud; an' supposin' you may, takin' into account th' measuremints—twelve be eight—th' vat bein' wound with twine six inches fr'm th' handle an' rub iv th' green, thin ar-re not human teeth often found in counthry sausage?" "In th' winter," says the Profissor. "But the sisymoid bone is sometimes seen in th' fut, sometimes worn as a watch-charm. I took two sisymoid bones, which I will call poker dice, an' shook thim together in a cylinder, which I will call Fido, poored in a can iv milk, which I will call gum arabic, took two pounds iv rough on rats, which I rayfuse to call; but th' raysult is th' same." Question be th' coort: "Different?" Answer: "Yis!" Th' coort: "Th' same." Be Misthur McEwen: "Whose bones?" Answer: "Yis." Be Misthur Vincent: "Will ye go to th' divvle?" Answer: "It dissolves th' hair."

A great deal of abstruse philosophical speculation is written and published in these days with regard to Anglo-Saxon superiority. Books have been written on the subject, both by Englishmen and by Frenchmen, but Mr. Dooley in a few paragraphs has put his finger on the secret of the whole thing. We should like to quote the whole discourse, but must content ourselves with a few inadequate extracts:

> 'Tis unforch'nit, but 'tis thrue. Th' Fr-rinch ar-re not steady eyethur in their politics or their morals. That's where they get done be th' hated British. Th' diff'-rence in furrin' politics is the diff'rence between a second-rate safe blower and a first-class boonco steerer. Th' Fr-rinch buy a ton iv dinnymite, spind five years in dhrillin' a hole through a steel dure, blow up th' safe, lose a leg or an ar-rm, an' get away with th' li'bilities iv th' firm. Th' English dhress up f'r a Methodist preacher, stick a piece iv lead pipe in th'

tails iv their coat in case iv emargency, an' get all th' money there is in th' line.

> In th' front dure comes th' Englishman with a coon king on eyether ar-rm that's jus' loaned him their kingdoms on a prom'ssory note, and discovers th' Fr-rinchman emargin' frim th' roons iv th' safe. "What ar-re ye doin here?" says th' Englishman. "Robbin' th' naygurs," says th' Fr-rinchman, bein' thruthful as well as polite. "Wicked man!" says th' Englishman. "What ar-re ye doin' here?" says the Fr-rinchman. "Improvin' th' morals iv th' inhabitants," says th' Englishman. . . . These pore, benighted savidges," he says, "'ll not be left to yer odjious morals an' yer hootchy-kootchy school iv thought," he says, "but," he says, "undher th' binif'cint r-rule iv a wise an' thrue goven'mint," he says, "'ll be thurly prepared f'r hivin," he says, "whin their times comes to go," he says "which I thrust will not be long," he says. "So I'll thank ye to be off," he says, "or I'll take th' thick end iv th' slung-shot to ye," he says.

> The Fr-rinchman is a br-rave man, an' he'd stay an' have it out on th' flure; but some wan calls, "Abase th' Chinnymen," an' off he goes on another thrack. An', whin he gets to th' Chinnymen, he finds th' English 've abased them already. An' so he dances fr'm wan par-rt th' wurruld to another like a riochous an' happy flea, an' divvle th' bit iv progress he makes, on'y thrubble f'r others an' a merry life f'r himsilf.

We wish that we could quote Mr. Dooley's acute observations on books, and also, as an illustration of his more serious moods, what he has to say on the necessity of modesty among the rich. This last shows a certain dramatic power and an undercurrent of pathos that appeal to us very strongly, but after all the best thing that we can do is to advise every one who reads these lines to procure the book for himself and thus to get a first-hand enjoyment of a volume that is full of wit and humour and real philosophy which rank their possessor among those humourists who have really made a genuine contribution to permanent literature. We have found nothing else this season which bears so unmistakably the marks of freshness, originality, and real genius. (pp. 575-76)

> *Harry Thurston Peck, "A New Humorist," in* The Bookman, *New York, Vol. VIII, No. 6, February, 1899, pp. 574-76.*

***THE NATION,*** NEW YORK   **(essay date 1899)**

[*In the following essay, the critic commends* Mr. Dooley in the Hearts of His Countrymen *for its wit and insight.*]

Mr. Dooley won fame in the Spanish war, and it is not to be expected that his comments on peaceful themes should be as successful as his military criticisms. It must be said, however, that there is fighting enough in this book. The air is full of brickbats, and resounds with the whacks of the shillelah. There is bloodshed a plenty, but the wounds are not mortal, and are given and received with the traditional Irish *insouciance*. Perhaps the genial author has somewhat overdone this well-worked theme of Irish pugnacity; but his sketches [in *Mr. Dooley in the Hearts of His Countrymen*] are spirited and clever, and the world seems never to tire of smiling at "the rows and the ructions" to which the natives of the Emerald Isle are supposed to devote all their leisure.

What Mr. Dooley has to say of the careers of sundry local bosses is more instructive than the disquisitions of most writers on political science. To the people of "Archey Road," the issues decided at elections are not related to abstract principles of legislation, but are intensely local and personal. Whether this one shall get a place "on the force," and that one hold his position as bridge-tender, are questions that interest the ordinary voter more than tariffs or constitutions, and no one can listen to Mr. Dooley without obtaining some useful suggestions concerning the nature of government by universal suffrage. As in his comments on the war, Mr. Dooley shows an impartial and penetrating judgment. He "shoots folly as she flies," and allows no humbug to remain unexposed, no cant to pass for genuine feeling. He is too cynical to be compared with Hosea Biglow, but he uses the weapon of ridicule with very telling effect. Possibly this weapon is more serviceable in influencing a democracy than logical argument, or appeals to principle and to history. At all events, the creator of Mr. Dooley knows how to handle it; and, to treat him seriously, he invariably employs it against what deserves contempt and derision. To the canting imperialist we have no doubt that Mr. Dooley's sarcasm appears extremely coarse and vulgar; but there is enough of pure fun in this book to make it acceptable to every one possessing the sense of humor.

> A review of "Mr. Dooley in the Hearts of His Countrymen," in The Nation, *New York, Vol. LXIX, No. 1799, December 21, 1899, p. 476.*

## W. D. HOWELLS (essay date 1903)

[*Howells was the chief progenitor of American Realism and the most influential American literary critic during the late nineteenth century. He was the author of nearly three dozen novels which, though neglected for decades, are today the subject of growing interest. In the following excerpt, Howells notes that Dunne's characterization of Mr. Dooley is strengthened by the element of fallibility.*]

I have been reading the five volumes which [the Dooley] papers now fill, with the impression that there are not so many of them, and with a constant surprise that their very simple formula suffices for the treatment of so many of our social as well as political ills. There is always Mr. Dooley talking to Mr. Hinnessy, with much mention of a Mr. Hogan who never appears on the scene of the dialogue, if in Mr. Hinnessy's strict subordination it is not rather a monologue. The scene is Mr. Dooley's bar, where the action that passes consists of one or other of the friends standing up or sitting down, or folding or unfolding a newspaper. But the whole drama of the nation, and largely the drama of the world, is represented in that simple setting through the comments of Mr. Dooley on passing events. Hardly any of these have escaped his notice in the years that have followed since the Cuban war and our acquisition of the Philippines. Each of the salient facts of the protracted pacification of our Pacific possessions has offered itself for Mr. Dooley to hang some wise or witty remark upon; and the tragicomedy of the Boer war, the novel posturings of the German Emperor in his continuous cake-walk, the saddened circus of the English King's coronation, the bouffe aspects of the Drey-fus Case, the performances of Lieutenant Hobson in his search for his level, the varied activities of Admiral Dewey, the mysterious and difficult nature of anarchism, the Chinese situation and the future of China, the insular decisions of the Supreme Court, Mr. Carnegie's gifts and the Booker Washington incident, are a few of the public interests which have joined with a hundred social and human interests in attracting the censure of the Irish-American sage.

By way of preface to the volume **Mr. Dooley in Peace and War,** Mr. Dunne, in as brilliant a little piece of analysis as I have lately seen (I like to put it modestly for him, or I should say, as I have ever seen), and in as graphic a study of conditions as I presently remember, tells in his own person what he knows of Mr. Dooley's nature and natural history. The humor, vibrant with a certain pride of race, and with a laughing consciousness of race-limitations, gives a captivating quality to this uncommon piece of self-criticism, but is to blame for leaving other criticism not so much to say of Mr. Dooley as it would like to say. It is at least left me, however, to venture upon the safe commonplace that no one but an Irish-American could have invented such an Irish-American, or have invested his sayings with such racial and personal richness. Dooley's characterization is, except in that preface, through his own talk, and the art of the author is felt in nothing so much as in his sensitive respect for Dooley's personality. Dooley is wise and shrewd and just for the most part; but from time to time he reaches a point where he is neither. He gives out, he breaks, and he saves himself from falling down by an effort of pure humor which wins your heart. Mr. Dunne knows Mr. Dooley's limitations, and he does not force him beyond them in the interest of the best purpose. He knows that there are moments when his philosophical spectator of events must lapse into a saloon keeper, and he guards the precious integrity of his creation from the peril of perfunctory humanity. It is upon a review of the whole course of Mr. Dooley's musings on men and things that one recognizes Mr. Dunne as of the line of great humorists who have not failed us in our crises of folly or misdoing. To

*Dunne at the time he was city editor of the* Chicago Times.

have one's heart in the right place is much; it is, in fact, rather indispensable; but to have one's head in the right place, also, adds immeasurably to the other advantage. It was not only because Hosea Biglow had such a good conscience, but because he had such a lot of good sense, that he approved Lowell so fine a humorist; and the generous instinct of Mr. Dunne would have been lost in Mr. Dooley if he had not known how to keep Mr. Dooley strictly within bounds as a character, sometimes sordid and sometimes stupid.

It is this admirable artistic discretion that imparts such exquisite pleasure in some of those quick turns by which Mr. Dunne saves Mr. Dooley from himself. Mr. Dooley starts out with an opinion without always knowing where it will carry him, and then with the flash of his Irish wit lights himself past the peril and goes gayly on again. He had not the least notion when he began how he was going to get out of it, and, to tell the truth, I do not believe Mr. Dunne had. The Irish wit came to *his* help too; and I could fancy with what sympathetic exultation he shared in Mr. Dooley's triumph. This agile suddenness in seizing a disadvantage and making it work for the author's intention, is the difference that distinguishes Mr. Dunne's humor from [George] Ade's. With Mr. Ade there is no arrest and no turning. He has seen the end clear from the beginning, and he has gone for it straightforward and unfaltering. When I read a fable beginning, "Once there was a gum-chewer named Tessie, who ironed up her white dress, and bought seven yards of ribbon, and went on a picnic given by the Ladies' Auxiliary of the Horseshoers Union," I am calmly glad in the security of a fully foreseen passage of life. When I read a Dooley paper I try to prepare myself for the delicious surprises which Mr. Dooley has in store for Mr. Dunne, but I am not sure of any of them till it comes. Then I know that it is of the last effect of subtle irony, and could not be better if it had been meant from the first. (pp. 743-46)

W. D. Howells, *"Certain of the Chicago School of Fiction," in* The North American Review, *Vol. 176, No. 5, May, 1903, pp. 734-46.*

### THE DIAL  (essay date 1910)

[*In the following essay, the critic remarks upon the undiminished humor of Dunne's seventh volume of Dooley essays,* Mr. Dooley Says.]

It is truly surprising how Mr. Dooley's vein of humor holds out. Familiar as we all have long since become with the workings of his spacious intellect, some fresh oddity of utterance is continually dropping from his lips of wisdom, and one is forced to smile in spite of oneself, if not to laugh outright. *Mr. Dooley Says* is the latest collection of his winged words, and in it of course are to be found comments and judgments on a great variety of current questions, such as divorces, the proposed tax on bachelors, woman suffrage, financial panics, expert testimony, and the Japanese war-scare. Even Dr. Eliot and his five-foot book-shelf are brought under Mr. Dooley's scrutiny. Of the works selected to fill that shelf he says: "They are sthrong it is thrue. They will go to th' head. I wud advise a man who is aisily affected be books to stick to Archibald Clavering Gunter. But they will hurt no man who's used to readin'. He has sawed thim out carefully. 'Give me me tools,' says he, 'an' I will saw out a five-foot shelf iv books.' An' he done it. He has th' right idee. He real-izes that th' first thing to have in a libry is a shelf. Fr'm time to time this can be decorated with lithrachure. But th' shelf is the main thing."

His comments on Milton's "Arryopatigica" reveal the breadth and depth of Mr. Dooley's education. On great questions of international significance he has decided opinions of his own. "Hogan says we've got to fight f'r th' supreemacy in th' Passyfic. Much fightin' I'd do f'r an ocean, but havin' taken th' Philippeens, which ar-re a blamed nuisance, an' th' Sandwich Islands, that're about as vallyable as a toy balloon to a horseshoer, we've got to grab a lot iv th' surroundin' dampness to protect thim." Truly, Mr. Dunne's fund of Dooleyisms is inexhaustible. (pp. 336-37)

A review of *"Mr. Dooley Says," in* The Dial, *Vol. XLIX, No. 585, November 1, 1910, pp. 336-37.*

### JAMES A. JOYCE  (essay date 1916)

[*Joyce was the most prominent and influential literary figure of the first half of the twentieth century. Many critics feel that his experiments in prose, particularly his advancement of interior monologue, both redefined the limits of language and recreated the form of the modern novel. Though he wrote little criticism, what he did produce demonstrates a subjective approach to literature with a penchant for psychological realism. Joyce was an admirer of Dunne's work, and when he wrote the following poem, "Dooleysprudence," in condemnation of the belligerents of World War I, he chose Mr. Dooley as the representative of the common man, who easily perceived the foolishness of warfare. The structure of the poem is modeled after the immensely popular "Mr. Dooley Song."*]

Who is the man when all the gallant nations run to war
Goes home to have his dinner by the very first cablecar
And as he eats his canteloup contorts himself in mirth
To read the blatant bulletins of the rulers of the earth?
    It's Mr Dooley,
    Mr Dooley,
    The coolest chap our country ever knew
    "They are out to collar
    The dime and dollar"
    Says Mr Dooley-ooley-ooley-oo.

Who is the funny fellow who declines to go to church
Since pope and priest and parson left the poor man in the lurch
And taught their flocks the only way to save all human souls
Was piercing human bodies through with dumdum bulletholes?
    It's Mr Dooley,
    Mr Dooley,
    The mildest man our country ever knew
    "Who will release us
    From Jingo Jesus"
    Prays Mr Dooley-ooley-ooley-oo.

Who is the meek philosopher who doesn't care a damn
About the yellow peril or the problem of Siam
And disbelieves that British Tar is water from life's fount
And will not gulp the gospel of the German on the Mount?
    It's Mr Dooley,
    Mr Dooley,
    The broadest brain our country ever knew
    "The curse of Moses
    On both your houses"
    Cries Mr Dooley-ooley-ooley-oo.

Who is the cheerful imbecile who lights his long chibouk
With pages of the pandect, penal code and Doomsday
    Book
And wonders why bald justices are bound by law to wear
A toga and a wig made out of someone else's hair?
        It's Mr Dooley,
        Mr Dooley,
        The finest fool our country ever knew
        "They took that toilette
        From Pontius Pilate"
        Thinks Mr Dooley-ooley-ooley-oo.

Who is the man who says he'll go the whole and perfect
    hog
Before he pays the income tax or licence for a dog
And when he licks a postage stamp regards with smiling
    scorn
The face of king or emperor or snout of unicorn?
        It's Mr Dooley,
        Mr Dooley,
        The wildest wag our country ever knew
        "O my poor tummy
        His backside's gummy!"
        Moans Mr Dooley-ooley-ooley-oo.

Who is the tranquil gentleman who won't salute the State
Or serve Nabuchodonesor or proletariat
But thinks that every son of man has quite enough to do
To paddle down the stream of life his personal canoe?
        It's Mr Dooley,
        Mr Dooley,
        The wisest wight our country ever knew
        "Poor Europe ambles
        Like sheep to shambles"
        Signs Mr Dooley-ooley-ooley-oo.

                                        (pp. 246-48)

*James A. Joyce, "Dooleysprudence," in his* The
Critical Writings of James Joyce, *edited by Ellsworth
Maston and Richard Ellmann, The Viking Press, 1959,
pp. 246-48.*

### HENRY SEIDEL CANBY   (essay date 1936)

[*Canby was a professor of English at Yale and one of the founders
of the* Saturday Review of Literature, *where he served as editor
in chief from 1924 to 1936. He was the author of many books,
including* The Short Story in English *(1909), a history of that
genre which was long considered the standard text for college
students. Despite the high acclaim his writings received, Canby
always considered himself primarily a teacher, whose declared
aim was "to pass on sound values to the reading public." In the
following excerpt, Canby comments on the importance of Mr.
Dooley's function as a commentator on American society, lamenting the fact that no author was able to take Dunne's place
in this respect.*]

I was a Yale undergraduate, with a shoulder sore from carrying
a Civil War musket in the old Armory, when I first read Mr.
Dooley. We were drilling then with the general idea that Cer-
vera's flying squadron was likely to blow the top off East Rock
any day, and that patriotic Americans must rush to the defense
of their country. It was an unreal, a romantic patriotism, that
felt warm in the heart but queer in the brain. For there was
something a little phoney about this war. The eagerness of
Spain to give us everything we asked for before we began, did
not seem to square with the blazing headlines of the yellow
press, warning of death and invasion. And the chaos of amateur

soldiers, typhoid camps, heroics, and embalmed beef, the rumors of dynamite cruisers, hay fleets, fat generals with the sun
stroke, and troops everywhere except where they were needed,
suggested a football practice for a Harvard game in which all
the university but the athletes were sent to Yale field and told
to get the ball.

Then came Finley Peter Dunne. Reading over again his *Mr.
Dooley in Peace and War* (much the better of his two important
books), the stir and the laughter and the uneasiness of those
Spanish War months come back vividly; and several ideas
suggest themselves which would have been impossible to our
naïveté then.

To begin with, some sense of humor, some willingness to take
criticism has leaked out of the country since those days. There
are a dozen pieces in this little book whose equivalent could
not have been published in any year since 1916 without landing
the author in court or jail as a pacifist (Mr. Dooley a pacifist!),
a pro-something or another, or a Red. Does anyone remember
the famous charge of the Tampa mules led by "th' biggest
jackass in Tampa today, not exciptin' th' cinsor . . . Says Sampson, . . . 'Form-rm in line iv battle, an' hurl-rl death an' des-
thruction at yon Castilyan gin'ral.' 'Wait,' says an officer, 'It
may be wan iv our own men. It looks like th' Sicrety iv'—
'Hush!' says th' commander. 'It can't be an American jackass,
or he'd speak.'" And so on to "What's needed to carry on
this war as it goes today is an ar-rmy iv jacks an' mules. . . .
Th' ordhers fr'm Washin'ton is perfectly comprehinsible to a
jackass, but they don't mane annything to a poor, foolish
man." . . .

"'I shu'd think,' said Mr. Hennessy, 'now that th' jackasses
has begun to be onaisy'—

"'We ought to be afraid th' cabinet an' th' Board of Sthra-
teejy'll be stampeded,' Mr. Dooley interrupted. 'Niver fear.
They're too near th' fodder.'"

Mr. Dooley was the only man who didn't know what to do
with the Philippines, though he prophesied that Mark Hanna
would organize the Philippine Islands Jute and Cider Co., "an'
th' revoluchinists'll wish they hadn't." Mr. Dooley knew that
"war was hell whin 'twas over." Mr. Dooley knew what ought
to be done with the "fruits of victory." "If 'twas up to me,
I'd eat what was r-ripe an' give what wasn't r-ripe to me
inimy." Mr. Dooley thought that the Porto Ricans who became
pro-American over night had "nawthin' to larn in th' way
iv . . . th' signs in gover'ment, even fr'm th' Supreme Court."

It is a shame to mutilate these marvelous little satires, each
perfectly constructed with a twist at the end as incomparable
as the last line of a sonnet. Read "On the Victorian Era,"
where Dooley celebrates the benefits that have fallen to the
race since he came to earth. But "ye haven't been as far east
as Mitchigan Avnoo in twenty years," Mr. Hennessy objects.
"What have ye had to do with all these things?" "Well," said
Mr. Dooley, "I had as much to do with thim as th' queen."

This is debunking with a difference. Something has changed
in us since this light-hearted rapier play has gone out of use
and perhaps of possibility. But something remains, and as one
reads on through *Mr. Dooley in the Hearts of His Countrymen,*
on reformers and prosperity, on making a cabinet, on the Pop-
ulist convention, and on national expansion ("I know what
they'd do with him [Aguinaldo the rebel] in this ward. They'd
give that pathrite what he asks, an' thin they'd throw him down

an' take it away fr'm him'')—the power of these little papers begins to explain itself.

For Mr. Dooley, in spite of his Irish wit and Catholic tolerance, and Mr. Hennessy, in spite of his Celtic truculence, are American to the bone. It is Dunne, a great American humorist—the best since Twain—speaking in the brogue of Mr. Dooley, choosing the Irish because the Irish then could say anything, because one laughed at the first Irish word. And Mr. Hennessy is the American public. You have only to compare Mr. Dooley with his great contemporary, Kipling's Mulvaney, to see the difference. Mulvaney is witty and Catholic and wise in human nature. But Dooley is all this and more. He has the shrewd skepticism of the Western individualist, the quality of leadership, the power of self-control, though he hates to exercise it against his enemies, the Bohemians and the Dutch. He comes from Missouri. He is the American of whom Kipling wrote while Dooley was still serving beers on Archey Road—

> He turns a keen untroubled face
> Home to the instant need of things.

> Enslaved, illogical, elate,
> He greets the embarrassed Gods, nor fears
> To shake the iron hand of Fate
> Or match with Destiny for beers.

Mr. Dooley is all that. His Irishness is genuine enough (weren't the Irish governing America?), but it is a mask, a dialect, a jester's license. Underneath he is the American who made this country disorderly, self-reliant, shrewdly realistic, and (intermittently) a self-expressive nation able to run itself if not its government. But where are the Dooleys now? In the American Legion? In the D. A. R.? In the Republican old guard? In the Administration? Some blight of unself-confidence has withered them. Maybe they blew off with the dust storms. Maybe immigration swamped them. Or prosperity did them in. Are they all dead?

Mr. Hennessy isn't dead. Mr. Hennessy believed everything he read in the papers. When "day be day th' pitiless exthries come out an' beat down" on Mr. Dooley, Mr. Hennessy followed the headlines just as the Supreme Court followed the election returns. Mr. Hennessy didn't know where the Philippines were, but he knew what to do with them. Mr. Hennessy didn't know what Dreyfus was charged with, but he was sure he was guilty because he was a Jew. Mr. Hennessy was all for William J. O'Brien because he was Irish from the sixth precinct, and when it turned out to be William J. Bryan who was nominated he was still for him because he had been before. Mr. Hennessy knows that we are a great people. "An' th' best iv it is, we know we ar-re," says Mr. Dooley. Mr. Hennessy, who makes $1.25 a day wheeling slag in the steel mill, proves his hatred of capital by quarreling over the price of wheat in the year of the big wind. Mr. Hennessy is all the yes-men and no-men in America. Mr. Hennessy lives by what was said to him last, believes the loudest shouter, can be calmed in a minute by being told he is an Irishman and a Democrat. He is fodder for political cannon, the sawdust stuffing of a dictatorship, the disease of a democracy. Mr. Dooley, who says that anarchists are the sewer gas of a state with bad plumbing, might have described Mr. Hennessy as the ball bearings of a plutocracy. Mr. and Mrs. Hennessy are with us yet, millions strong; but where is Mr. Dooley? (pp. 55-9)

*Henry Seidel Canby, "Estimates of the Dead," in his* Seven Years' Harvest: Notes on Contemporary Literature, *Farrar & Rinehart Incorporated, 1936, pp. 20-59.*

## D. W. BROGAN   (essay date 1936)

[*Brogan was a distinguished Scottish critic and a scholar of American history and culture. In the following excerpt from an essay written in 1936, he contends that the Dooley essays will be preserved as a monument to the turn-of-the-century political and social milieu that they documented.*]

It is nearly forty years since the American and then the whole English-speaking world began to ask "What does Mr. Dooley say?" and in the abounding and confident days of the turn of the century the sage of the "Archey Road" was not only a source of amusement but of enlightenment for his own countrymen and for other people too.

He began, like many great men, in a modest way. F. P. Dunne, a writer on a Chicago paper, had been struck with the sagacity and wit of an obscure saloon-keeper, and with that figure as a basis built up the myth of Martin Dooley, of his patient auditor Hennessy, of the erudite Hogan, of the German rival Schwartzmeister, and the rest of the dramatis personæ.

It was the time of the Spanish-American War, the most comic military enterprise of modern times, of the great Fitzsimmons and Corbett fight, of the first real fame of Theodore Roosevelt (or Teddy Rosenfelt, as he was called in the Archey Road), and of Admiral Dewey, promoted to the rank of "Cousin George." What began as a local joke became, in a few months, a nation-wide institution, to the delight of all except the original of the hero, who was not sure that he was being laughed with and not at.

No American journalist since Artemus Ward had rivalled "Mr. Dooley," and until the rise of Will Rogers no one has rivalled him since. The comparison with Artemus Ward was often made, and it was fair enough, though "the Showman" had a more elaborate background than had the saloon-keeper. But it would be easy to find in Ward dicta that (*mutatis mutandis*) might have been uttered over the bar in the Archey Road.

The comparison with Will Rogers was made even oftener, but was not nearly so appropriate. Will Rogers was a character, a humorist of a mild kind, but his importance was in his representative character; what Will Rogers said the "plain people" were thinking, and so Mr. Coolidge wanted to know what Will Rogers thought. But Mr. Dooley did not say what the plain people thought; he was a wit rather than a humorist, and he was fundamentally far more irreverent than Will Rogers.

It was the intelligentsia who laughed when Mr. Dooley said that Roosevelt's account of the Spanish War ought to have been called "Alone in Cubia," the plain people took the colonel at his own valuation. The description of pragmatism which rejoiced many philosophers, that a lie wasn't a lie if it worked, was not the view of the man in the street. Such jests were more than "wise-cracks"; they were not very obvious truths given the necessary condiment of Attic salt, even if expressed in a barbarian dialect.

"Mr. Dooley" followed the old American comic convention of bad spelling and exaggerated dialect, but at his best he owed nothing to his Irish-American jargon. The famous exposition of the basis of the power of the Supreme Court that "No matter whether the constitution follows the flag or not, the supreem coort follows th' iliction returns" is improved in force by having its jargon removed. Neither Mr. Beard nor Mr. Boudin could express the modern point of view of judicial review better than Mr. Dooley, and Mr. Justice Holmes was not a greater master of language.

Mr. Dooley was not at bottom a humorist, or rather, his real talents were not those of a humorist. Many of his essays today suffer by an elaborate building-up of a rather simple situation, as well as from a lavishness of local and temporal reference that makes annotation necessary.

Not every reader knows who was the great "Carter Haitch," Mayor of Chicago in the good old days. Indeed, that Chicago is remote enough. Promiscuous shooting was then the prerogative of Kentucky and the Far West, and rows in the Archey Road were not settled by sub-machine guns or by pineapples; indeed, the terms as applied to fruit was little known in that street, and as applied to hand grenades not at all.

The Chicago of Dion O'Banion and Al Capone and Studs Lonergan was present in embryo, but when the monstrous growth was visible to all the world "Mr. Dooley" had little to say. During the war and again during Prohibition he wrote a little, but his hand had lost its cunning and his tongue its edge. The petty corruptions of politics that had been exposed with kindly irony (and far more profound understanding than more pompous experts could command) were both out of place in the city in which the gangs from Cicero worked their will, when the old Archey Road saloon was merely a selling agency for the "Big Shot," and where the old moral standards on all sides were shaken.

Was not the Cardinal Archbishop a German? Were not the once dominant Irish struggling desperately to hold their own in a new city full of Negroes and Italians?

And the outside world was no more attractive. It was as a satirist of war and warlike glories that Mr. Dooley had first won fame, but who could joke in face of the European butchery? It is as a monument and a study of American life, of politics and social ideas of the turn of the century, that Mr. Dooley will be preserved. (pp. 47-9)

> *D. W. Brogan, "Mr. Dooley," in his* American Themes, *Harper & Brothers Publishers, 1949, pp. 47-50.*

## ELMER ELLIS (essay date 1941)

[*Ellis is an American critic and historian. In the following excerpt, he discusses Dunne's dual function as both a simple humorist and a social and political satirist.*]

Few things are more difficult to evaluate than the influence of a writer upon the life of his own generation. One qualification must always be kept in mind in attempting to evaluate Dunne's. Undoubtedly there were many levels of appreciation of Mr. Dooley. The lowest of these was the reader who found merely something comic in the fact that the saloon-keeper spoke in a quaint language, a dialect associated with unskilled laborers and household servants, and it was therefore an invitation for smiles to find it in print. How many of these were among Dunne's readers, one can only guess, but one fears there were many. Were it not a matter beyond dispute that he was also read and enjoyed by the best minds in every important field of endeavor, one might be inclined to scale down his influence unreasonably. Even the most bloodless intellectuals such as Henry Adams and Henry James were constant readers of Mr. Dooley, and that is clear proof not only of his varied appeal but also of the penetrating nature of his observations.

These levels of appreciation exist for many writers, although one searches in vain for another with Dunne's widespread appeal. Will Rogers had it at a later date, but only in his stage and radio appearances, as his written product never secured anything like the widespread demand which Mr. Dooley had from 1898 to 1905, and read today, Rogers' comments are far more clearly dated than Dunne's on the events of twenty years earlier.

In his function of censor, this very width of appeal, even leaving out the lower orders of enjoyment, made Dunne the most influential of the editorial writers of his day. Like all social satirists, his influence was discounted by the very human tendency for everyone to read such corrective literature for the enjoyment he gets from the pillory in which he finds an opponent or the manner in which a disliked argument is eviscerated, and this pleasure is not spoiled by equally trenchant blows upon himself and his concepts, because these strokes can be partly ignored or more quickly forgotten. Perhaps the mind should work differently, but it does not, and Dunne himself recognized this tendency as one of the weaknesses of popular satire. But it was far from universal, because of the good temper and humor in which Dunne usually dressed his most destructive blows. A remark that made one laugh, because he recognized the fundamental truth of the idea, was not likely to be forgotten, even if it contradicted a firmly held opinion. At least the holder would have to modify his belief to the extent of justifying his smile to his own conscience. And when one smiles at one of his own political opinions, he is well along the way to re-examine his stock of ideas with some hope of making a more rational framework. This was what was meant when an anonymous reviewer of the second Dooley book wrote ruefully: "If the American people continue to laugh with Dooley they will be Mugwumps before they know it." They were, for Mr. Dooley was a strong factor in reducing the narrow partisanship that had been intensified by the sectional struggle of the sixties and its political consequences.

It is unnecessary, at this point, to list formally all of the traits in American life which Dunne tried to modify or destroy, but one should mention the two major ones. First and most persistently, he was against all demagoguery, whether vicious in intent or from well-meaning but self-deceived humbugs. A people deceived was the worst of all societies, and Dunne used every good opportunity to make clear such deceptions. He persistently labored against permitting the pocketbook interests of individuals or groups to parade as altruism, patriotism, or religion. A great share of his satire is directed at exposing such shams, and making clear to all who would read the underlying reality of personal interest. It was natural of people to use such excuses for their own selfishness. "If ye'd turn on th' gas in th' darkest heart, ye'd find it had a good raison f'r th' worst things it done, a good varchous raison, like needin' th' money, or punishin' th' wicked, or teachin' people a lesson to be more careful, or protectin' th' liberties iv mankind, or needin' th' money." But that was far from saying that the public should accept such testimony. The demagoguery of politician and reformer, of Wall Street operator and educational leader, of newspaper editor and labor leader—none escaped his pillory.

Next only to this, Dunne's greatest object of attack was the group of concepts underlying the definite American feeling of national and racial superiority that was basic to the more dangerous trends in popular thought, from imperialism in 1898 to the Ku-Klux Klan in 1924. Dunne's Irish Catholic background was helpful here in freeing him from some common nativistic emotions, and he struck at these anti-democratic and un-Christian concepts of superiority with a fury that can be explained only by the sudden strength they assumed during and after the Spanish-American War. It was not so much the Anglo-Saxon allegiance tea-talk, for that was a private feud, but it was the whole basic imperialistic policy as upheld by Lodge and Roosevelt, and more unblushingly maintained by Mahan and Beveridge. When the latter would talk about shedding blood for "our imperial destiny," strikingly like a Hitler or Mussolini of forty years later, it is not surprising that a democrat who understood people and their weakness for such intoxicants would try to laugh him and his kind out of countenance. And Dunne had notable successes in this field, as has been shown. "We're a great people," said Mr. Hennessy, earnestly. "We are," said Mr. Dooley. "We are that. An' the' best iv it is, we know we are." These same claims of superiority were attacked as vigorously when they appeared as the claims for class privilege by Mr. Baer or Mr. Worldly Wiseman. Intolerance of all kinds stemmed directly from the fiction of superiority of class, creed, or race. Dunne recognized it among all sorts of people, finding it in its most vicious forms in supposedly select circles. To him it seemed the most explosive and cruel element in American society, and he struck at it with his strongest weapons at every opportunity.

It should be recalled also that Dunne's satire on aspects of our national life was not only influential because of its effect upon the mind of the reading public, but it was also potent directly upon the leaders in all walks of life. Between 1898 and 1910 at least, presidents, Cabinet members, and congressman read Mr. Dooley, and absorbed as much as their own characters and their fears of public reaction made necessary. Nor did it stop there. Prominent leaders in all walks of life read Mr. Dooley with some trepidation, fearing to find themselves being discussed in the Archey Road barroom. Theodore Roosevelt's assiduous cultivation of Dunne was probably not alone due to his appreciation of wisdom and humor. Certainly there could be few more unpleasant happenings to the high and mighty than to be made to strut before the world morally and mentally undressed as only Mr. Dooley could perform that revealing task. Not the least of Mr. Dooley's threat was that his exposure of hollowness and sham was so good-natured that one dare not risk resentment. Certainly one of the greatest pleasures of living, when Dunne was at his best, was the confidence one might have that the powerful of the world would be held immediately accountable for meanness and folly. Fortunate is an age and a nation so blessed!

Nearly as important a function in American life as being its satirist was Dunne's role as its humorist and wit. Conceiving of democracy as a form of society in which the conflicts of interests are compromised by peaceful means, Dunne's function here was one of lubricating the cog-wheels of peaceful adjustment. Compromise is made easier by laughter, especially when one can be made to laugh at himself. And after one has laughed at himself, it is not so easy to be led into the belief that an issue which concerns part of his personal income is a cause for which governments should be overthrown and mankind slaughtered. Mark Sullivan, who has made extremely intelligent use of Mr. Dooley in his history of the period, describes the influence of Dunne's humor in this manner: "Most useful of all, Mr. Dooley supplied the softening solvent of humor to the American atmosphere in times of acute controversy. Just when we were getting worked up into factional passion, with everybody searching the cellar of his vocabulary for verbal lumps of coal, Mr. Dooley would come out in the Sunday papers with a picture of the situation that made every reader laugh at it, and at himself." Charles A. Beard, who

would emphasize Dunne's role as a critic more, likewise agrees that the Dooley essays "relaxed the tension of the 'moral overstrain'" of public controversy.

These two functions—the satirist and the humorist—frequently came into conflict in practice. As a satirist Dunne had to have Mr. Dooley possessed of a point of view and excoriate the other side. He might also satirize some of the arguments which his own side used, but with all his good humor there could be no real doubt as to where his heavy blows were falling. In every case of effective satire which Dunne wrote, this is clear. Imperialism, militarism, smug corruption in government and business, pretentious nonsense in education or religion, the protective tariff, fake reformers, self-deified aristocrats, and dishonest journalists—all of these he could and did satirize in his masterly fashion. And although each essay contained some other humorous elements, none of them was directed at easing the conflicts within society. They were aimed at influencing action. For real achievement in his second role, Mr. Dooley had to take a position above or beside the battle, as he did in each political campaign; and while he could satirize the methods of all parties without limit, he could not become partisan to the immediate struggle itself. To do so immediately rendered his writing useless for lessening the friction of the struggle, but those who wanted him firing on the enemy from their side of the battlefront—and who did not?—naturally resented these lapses from satire. But forty years after the struggles one begins to suspect that the other function was just as significant to Dunne's readers and to American life of his day. As has been seen, the humorist function tended to encompass more and more of Dunne's writing as time went on, and after 1910 there is little of the satire in Mr. Dooley that had made him a modern scourge of princes. Most of what remains is directed against harmless popular pastimes. Perhaps, as some thought, this was a natural result of moving in the society of some of these very princes; perhaps it was a mellowness which came with greater age and a growing disinclination to throw bricks where they would do the most good in the old Archey Road manner. Or perhaps it was merely a greater personal pleasure from the humorous type of comment. At any rate the change was there. (pp. 288-95)

> *Elmer Ellis, in his* Mr. Dooley's America: A Life of Finley Peter Dunne, *Alfred A. Knopf, 1941, 310 p.*

## WALTER BLAIR   (essay date 1942)

[*Blair is an American critic who has written numerous studies of American humorists. In the following excerpt, he explores the character of Mr. Dooley.*]

What really made a national figure of [Mr. Dooley] was the way he talked about the Spanish-American War in 1898. There was plenty of material for good satire in that contest. Americans, after many decades of coveting Cuba, decided that they had a holy inspiration to go to the aid of that downtrodden island. There were amusing discrepancies between the contempt in this country for the Spaniards and the fear that, after all, the American army and navy might be as inefficient as the American government in general. There was a laughable contrast between the desperate valor summoned up before the fighting and the ease with which what John Hay called "a splendid little war" was won. Finally, there was the contrast between the holy aims of the United States and the imperialistic plunder they gained by fighting.

*Dunne (far left) and other members of the Whitechapel Club in one of their meeting rooms.*

All these matters were grist for Mr. Dooley as he chatted in his saloon on Archey Road with his old friend, Mr. Hennessy. Dunne thought that the pieces setting down the talk possibly were as popular as they were because they "reflected the feeling of the public about this queer war," and his guess was probably a pretty good one. Having caught the attention of a large audience, the Irish saloonkeeper chattered on in piece after piece for many years, and his remarks were printed in numerous newspapers and magazines. Although the period, roughly, from 1898 to 1910 was the time of his greatest success and although the articles and books came less often as the years passed, Dooley kept commenting on all sorts of contemporary subjects down into the 1920's. The issues of four decades, therefore, were discussed over the counter in his humble saloon.

Dooley's creator gave a good characterization of the old fellow in the Preface to the first book about him. He was, said Dunne, a

> traveller, historian, and social observer, saloon-keeper, economist, and philosopher, who had not been out of the ward for twenty-five years "but twict." He read the newspapers with solemn care, heartily hated them, and accepted all they printed for the sake of drowning Hennessy's rising protests against his logic. From the cool heights of life in the Archey Road, uninterrupted by the jarring noises of crickets and

cows, he observed the passing show, and meditated thereon. His impressions were transferred to the desensitized plate of Mr. Hennessy's mind, where they could do no harm. . . . He was opulent of advice, as became a man of his station; for he had mastered most of the obstacles of a business career, and by leading a prudent and temperate life had established himself so well that he owned his own house and furniture, and was only slightly behind on his license. . . . He has served his country with distinction. His conduct of the important office of captain of his precinct (1873-75) was highly commended, and there was some talk of nominating him for alderman. . . . But the activity of public life was unsuited to a man of Mr. Dooley's tastes; and while he continued to view the political situation with interest and sometimes with alarm, he resolutely declined to leave the bar for the forum. His early experience gave him wisdom in discussing public affairs. "Politics," he often said, "ain't bean bag. 'Tis a man's game; and women, children, and pro-hybitionists would do well to keep out of it."

This was the man who gave Mr. Hennessy the low-down on everything as it happened. Hennessy, a fool character "who had at best but a clouded view of public affairs" and who suffered badly from credulity and horrible logic, asked an innocent question now and then to get the Sage started and to keep his tongue wagging, and Dooley held forth on anything close to his heart.

The old Irishman was in many ways a victim of his limited environment. Since Archey Road was his universe, he reduced every problem to the terms of life in that bedraggled section of Chicago—and in his mind a major general or a queen was as easy to understand as a shanty Irishman who now and then came to the saloon. Since life on Archey Road was friendly and informal, he did not see anything strange about calling President McKinley "Mack" and Admiral Dewey "Cousin George." Even the czar of Russia was pictured with great familiarity when the barkeeper said:

> The Hague conference, Hinnissy, was got up by the Czar of Rooshya just before he moved his army against the Japs. It was a quiet day at St. Petersburg. The Prime Minister had just been blown up with dinny-mite, the Czar's uncle had been shot, and one of his cousins was expirin' from a dose of prussic acid. All was comparative peace. In the warm summers afternoon the Czar felt almost drowsy as he sat in his royal palace and listened to the low, monotonous drone of bombs bein' hurled at the Probojensky guards. . . . The monarch's mind turned to the subjeck of war and he says to himself: "What a dreadful thing it is that such a beautiful world should be marred by thousands of innocent men bein' sint out to shoot each other for no cause whin they might better stay at home and work for their royal masters," he says. "I will disguise mesilf as a moojik and summon a meetin' of the Powers," he says.

This Dooleymorphism was matched by other limitations on his knowledge. Entirely unread in anything but the newspapers, knowing nothing of the world of books, he was likely to call an acolyte "an alkali," an encyclopedia "a bicyclopedia," and when he quoted what he thought was the German national anthem, it came out "Ich vice nit wauss allus bay doitan." His ignorance of books led him to ascribe all sorts of fine sayings to his friend Hogan, giving him credit for all the phrases he had quoted. "Oh," Dooley would say, "as Hogan says, why should the spirit of mortal be proud?" or "Onaisy, as Hogan says, is the head that wears the crown." His ethical standards, worked out during a rough life in his ward, were those of the wrong side of the tracks—he might use loaded dice or pass bad money at times to cheat a neighbor he disliked; he had a liking for a good hard brick to settle an argument; he accepted vote-buying and crookedness as normal parts of politics. An Irishman from the top of his white head to the tips of his toes, he had all the prejudices, whether justifiable or not, of his race.

But in his long life he had seen men come and go, and he was well acquainted with their ways. Hence he knew much of human nature—both its grandeurs and its depravities. His democracy was a fine thing, and so was his tolerance and sympathy. Sometimes his heart worked better than his head, as when he practiced charity on the sly, although his thinking had caused him to condemn it.

William Dean Howells, well read though he was in the great literatures of Europe, paid high compliments to the way Dunne made his hero a believable character [see excerpt dated 1903]:

> Dooley's characterization is. . . . through his own talk, and the art of the author is felt in nothing so much as in his sensitive respect for Dooley's personality. Dooley is wise and shrewd and just for the most part; but from time to time he reaches a point

when he is neither. . . . Mr. Dunne knows Mr. Dooley's limitations, and he does not force him beyond them in the interest of the best purpose. He knows that there are moments when his philosophical spectator of events must lapse into a saloon keeper, and he guards the precious integrity of his creation from the peril of perfunctory humanity.

As a personality, then, a richly complicated character in spite of resemblances to older characters, he stood out from the hosts of humorous figures who had preceded him. There were two other things about him which made him different from most of his predecessors—his sense of humor and the doctrines which (often without knowing it) he preached.

Strange though it may seem to casual readers of comic writings, his sense of humor was an unusual gift for an American humorous character to enjoy. Jack Downing, Major Jones, and almost the whole army of their followers had been as solemn as owls and as blind to the funny sides of things they were saying as they were to the knowledge contained between the covers of books. Artemus Ward, on the lecture platform, saying excruciatingly funny things but looking as woebegone as an undertaker, was a type of the average hero of native humor.

But Dooley could crack a joke with a point to it. He had a liking for a pun—as when he said that all the powers of Europe sent delegates to a peace conference "and a great many of the weaknesses did so too" or that "Gin'ral Miles is preparin' to destroy the Spanish at one blow—and he's the boy to blow." He had a flair for a phrase which painted a funny picture, as when he told how a drunken man was "comin' home a little late and tryin' to reconcile a pair of round feet with an embroidered sidewalk." At times he could be ironic. When he had told how an Irish revolutionary plot had failed because newspapers had been notified of it and how the leader, Tynan, had then led a parade of conspirators and unloaded explosives in the sight of everyone, the dumb Hennessy said brightly, "There must have been a spy in the ranks." Then—

> "Sure thing," said Mr. Dooley, winking at Mr. McKenna [another customer]. "Sure thing, Hinnessy. Ayether that or the accomplished detictives at Scotland Yards keep a close watch in the newspapers. Or it may be—who knows?—that Tynan was indiscreet. He may have dropped a hint of his intintions."

At times this talent of the Irishman for fun gave the Dooley papers passages in which there were amusing contrasts between the minds involved—Dunne pretending to be Dooley, and Dooley acting like a fool.

The doctrines the good-natured saloonkeeper gave voice to were also distinctive. He evidently had an interest in almost everything that got into the columns of the daily press, so his talk was far from specialized. He treated not only war but political battles of all sorts, family life, sports, literature, education, and enough other subjects to make his collected monologues quite encyclopedic. Wittingly or unwittingly he threw light on this great variety of subjects in such sayings as:

> There's only one thing that would make me allow mesilf to be a hero to the American people, and that is it don't last long.

> If a man is wise, he gets rich and if he gets rich, he gets foolish, or his wife does.

> There are no friends at cards or world politics.

> Here's the pitchers of candydates I pulled down from the window, and just knowin' they're here makes me

that nervous for the contints of the cash drawer I'm afraid to turn me back for a minute.

I guess a man niver becomes an orator if he has anything to say, Hinnessy.

The Supreme Court follows the iliction returns.

In a gineral way, all I can say about golf is that it's a kind of a game of ball that you play with your own worst inimy which is yourself, and a man you don't like goes around with you and gloats over you, and a little boy follows you to carry the clubs and hide the ball after you've hit it.

As far as Martin Dooley was concerned, this wide variety in his talk was inspired by his great interest in the many things he found in newspapers. As far as his creator was concerned, Dunne could put pertinent remarks into the saloonkeeper's words because he himself had more than average interest in the affairs of the day and more knowledge of them than most men. The wry wisdom and the scorn for sham that so often stir in the minds of big-city reporters were his. In addition he happened to fall in with a crowd of people in Chicago who were beginning to become excited over social and political changes. He was a member of the newly organized White Chapel Club, which a fellow-member, George Ade, said, is

> . . . still remembered as a collection of harum-scarum irresponsibles who scorned the conventions and shared an abiding enthusiasm for alcoholic liquors. It was more than that. It was really a round-up of interesting intellectuals whose opinions and doctrinal beliefs were far in advance of the Chicago environment of that time, although they have since come into favor and received governmental endorsement. Not all of what they stood for will ever be approved by popular vote, because they were irreligious and probably might have been classified as agnostics. They had such scathing contempt for the self-seeking political bosses and the stuffed shirts of the millionaire aristocracy of their own town, and such a tyranny of wealth, that they probably might be called socialists, with a leaning toward outright anarchy.

Mr. Ade thought the Dooley articles were "merely truth concealed in sugar-coated idiom and dialect"; and it is true that they said more harsh things about the United States and its people in general than a writer could have said—and have remained popular—a few years before Mr. Dooley started to make his pronouncements. But though Dunne adopted the device he did because he wanted a safe way to say biting things about certain politicians without risking libel suits, it is wrong to think that the sugar coating was necessary for the expounding of doctrines such as the humorist wanted to preach. The period of Dooley's reign in humor was one during which social revolt flourished. After 1896, William Jennings Bryan (on whom Dooley at times affectionately bestowed the Irish name O'Brien) was a beloved leader of dissatisfied common people of the prairies and the mining country. William Allen White was shouting his Kansas version of liberal doctrine. Such a poem as Edwin Markham's "The Man with the Hoe" (1899), complaining about the woes of the worker and dimly hinting at the possibility of revolution if things did not straighten out, could, in those days, stir the nation. It was the time of the rise of Teddy Roosevelt (Rosenfelt to Dooley), who lashed out fiercely at "the malefactors of great wealth." The early 1900's saw, too, the great success of the muckrakers—popular magazine writers whose fame was based on sensational attacks upon graft and corruption in the city, the state, and the nation. Mr. Dooley, in other words, was a humorous ally of a group of crusaders who shared many of his liberal views and made good money by putting them into print.

Yet it is striking to see how many of the old Irishman's comments, in the light of discoveries made by historians long after the days of his talking, have turned out to be sound. As Mr. John Chamberlain has pointed out,

> Certainly a dandy course in pre-war American history could be taught by taking Mr. Dooley as a three-times-a-week plain English text. His comments on the conduct of the Spanish-American War, for example, anticipated Walter Mills' sanely comic *The Martial Spirit* by some thirty years. His description of William McKinley, the praying President who got the tip direct from Jehovah that the United States owed it to Christianity to take the already Catholic Philippines, turned up a generation later in Thomas Beer's *Hanna* as the "mature" judgments of the nineteen-twenties. His title for Theodore Roosevelt's book on the Rough Riders—*Alone in Cubia*—made Hermann Hagedorn look silly even before Hermann Hagedorn had constituted himself chief T. R. hagiographer. And his remarks on the Dreyfus case might have served as the text for Matthew Josephson's *Zola*.

Some proof of the aptness of the Archey Road sermons is the number of times they turn up in good histories of the Dooley era—especially in one of the best of them, Mr. Mark Sullivan's *In Our Times*. There is at least some justice in the claim of Thomas L. Masson: "If all the newspaper files and histories were destroyed between the years 1898 and 1910 and nothing remained but Mr. Dooley's observations, it would be enough."

And it is also striking to note how much of the talk, early and late, of Mr. Dooley, without change or, at most, with that of a few names, has the sting of satire on the affairs of the present day. Professor Pattee's claim that "satire . . . , no matter how biting or sparkling, perishes with its own generation" does not hold good for the Irishman's talk—for much of it, at all events—if touches of dialect too hard for modern readers are deleted.

The experience Martin Dooley had when he visited Mary Ellen Cassidy's kindergarten has more than a little lasting value as comment on various contemporary educational fads. The children were sitting around on the floor, or sleeping, or dancing, and he noticed one lad pulling another lad's hair.

> "Why don't you take the coal shovel to that little barbaryan, Mary Ellen?" says I. "We don't believe in corporeal punishment," says she. "School should be made pleasant for the childer," she says. "The child whose hair is bein' pulled is larnin' patience," she says, "and the child that's pullin' the hair is discoverin' the futility of human indeavor," says she. . . . "Put them through their exercises," says I. "Tommy," says I, "spell cat," I says. "Go to the devil," says the cherub. "Very smartly answered," says Mary Ellen. . . . "They don't larn that till they get to college . . . , sometimes not even then." . . . "And what do they larn?" says I. "Rompin'," she says, "and dancin'," she says, "and independence of speech, and beauty songs, and sweet thoughts, and how to make home home-like," she says.

Mr. Dooley's talk about the value of the crusader to political reform also has lasting value:

> As a people, Hinnissy, we're the greatest crusaders that iver was—for a short distance. On a quarter mile track we can crusade at a rate that would make Hogan's friend, Godfrey the Bullion look like a crab.

But the trouble is the crusade don't last after the first sprint. The crusaders drops out of the procession to take a drink or put a little money on the ace, and by the time the end of the line of march is reached the boss crusader is alone on the job and his former followers is hurlin' bricks at him from the windows of policy shops. The boss crusader always gets the double cross. If I wanted to send my good name down to the ginerations with Cap. Kidd and Jesse James I'd lead a movement for the suppression of vice. I would so.

What he thought about the cost of the Spanish-American War does not seem dated yet:

"And so the war is over?" asked Mr. Hennessy.

"Only part of it," said Mr. Dooley. "The part that you see in the pitcher papers is over, but the tax collector will continyoo his part of the war with relentless fury. Cavalry charges are not the only ones in a real war."

Nor is his account of his harrowing experiences during the horrible conflict without a good deal of point:

This war, Hinnissy, has been a great strain on me. To think of the suffrin' I've endured! For weeks I lay awake at nights fearin' that the Spanish armadillo'd leave the Cape Verde Islands, where it wasn't, and take the train out here, and hurl death and destruction into my little store. Day by day the pitiless extras came out and beat down on me. You hear of Teddy Rosenfelt plungin' into ambuscades and Sicrity of Wars; but did you hear of Martin Dooley, the man behind the guns, four thousand miles behind them, and willin' to be further? . . . I'm what Hogan calls one of the mute, inglorious heroes of the war; an' not so dam mute, ayther.

How long Mr. Dooley will continue to sound as apt as he does now it is, of course, impossible to say. So far, however, as Hogan says, age has not withered nor custom staled his infinite variety. (pp. 245-55)

> Walter Blair, "Imported Horse Sense—Mr. Dooley," in his Horse Sense in American Humor from Benjamin Franklin to Ogden Nash, *The University of Chicago Press*, 1942, pp. 240-55.

**JOHN V. KELLEHER**  (essay date 1946)

[*In the following excerpt, Kelleher discusses the element of social criticism inherent in the Dooley essays, noting that the opinions of Mr. Dooley must be viewed as distinct from those of Dunne.*]

It is now twenty years since Mr. Martin Dooley, then proprietor of a speak-easy, was last heard from. It is nearer forty years to the time when he had the daily attention of millions of Americans, and when his words, spoken in the relative seclusion of his barroom to his silent auditor, Mr. Malachi Hennessy, were re-echoed admiringly throughout the United States and the United Kingdom. You, gentle reader, may never have heard of him, or only vaguely, as you have heard of Bill Nye or Petroleum V. Nasby; yet, just forty years ago, some one of your relatives was singing:—

> For Mister Dooley, for Mister Dooley,
>   The greatest man the country ever knew,
> Quite diplomatic and democratic
>   Is Mister Dooley-ooley-ooley-oo.

It was a silly song. It heaped praises on Mr. Dooley for things he had never done, and could not be imagined attempting:—

> He drove the Spaniards back to the tanyards . . .

Those who sang it knew very well how silly it was, but they sang it in tribute and gratitude to the man whose wisdom was more than helpful to a nation still trying to recover its self-possession after having fought the War with Spain. In that United States, still full of men who had survived Spanish bullets and American embalmed beef and the Montauk Point hospital camp,—a country headed by Theodore Roosevelt, the hero of San Juan Hill,—Martin Dooley, self-described as "th' man behind th' guns, four thousan' miles behind thim, an' willin' to be further," easily held his own in popularity. It was one of those rare moments in history when venerable wisdom is given the palm over youth and vigor.

If your interest is aroused by this and you turn to any recent American history to find out more about Martin Dooley, the chances are that you will find his words quoted in the text, but you will not find his name in the index. His creator, Finley Peter Dunne, will be listed there, a proof of the weakness of current historical method, which readily accepts Plato's Socrates but draws the line at our American philosopher, presumably because he is not mentioned in so poor an authority as the Chicago city directory. There is no denying the substantive existence of Finley Peter Dunne, or his influence in American politics and journalism; but to use that as an excuse for relegating Mr. Dooley to the limbo of once popular fictions, with Private Miles O'Reilly and the Lady from Philadelphia, is as foolish as it is bigoted.

The admirers of Mr. Dooley are now a small and select group, gently asserting the merits of *good* dialect writing; yet you will never hear one of them say, "Wait till I read you what Finley Dunne has to say about that." The idea is preposterous. One might as readily quote what William Shakespeare said when he decided that his royal uncle had killed his royal father. Let the historians grasp the larger realities. It was Mr. Dooley, and not Dunne, to whom the American people listened lovingly. And it was the old and wise Dooley who gave the historians the indispensable observation with which they high-light the politics of our emergence as an imperial power: "Whether th' constitution follows th' flag or not, th' Supreme Coort follows th' iliction returns." When Dooley said that, Dunne was a mere stripling of thirty-three.

Proceeding conventionally, one would admit that Dunne, the author, takes standing over Dooley, the character, and begin with a sketch of Dunne's life and works. Neither, however, is a conventional figure in literature. Dooley is a unique invention: the only mythical philosopher I can think of with a philosophy. He is also Dunne's only major character. With the exception of Hennessy, who somehow manages a vivid existence on little more than silent bewilderment, the other people in the essays are as shadowy as the fall guys in Plato's dialogues: they exist only through Dooley's quotations or descriptions of them. Hogan, the gullible intellectual; Father Kelly, the humane and humorous priest; Dock O'Leary, the agnostic; Schwartzmeister, the foreign element and Dooley's German rival; the various cops, plumbers, misers, lovers, housewives, aldermen, reformers, and bums, who are mentioned transiently—all exist to feed Dooley information it would be out of character for him to find in his newspaper, or to enable him to point and illustrate a moral.

Nor is it simply Dooley's singularity that gives him precedence. Other authors have spoken through their characters, or invented them only to discover that, once alive, they would go their own ways and do their own work. But Dooley was so large that Dunne could live inside him unnoticed and endowed with a freedom that Dunne, the citizen, would never be permitted. No one could serve a warrant on Dooley; nor could any enemy impugn his motives. His probity and fairness and tolerance, the modesty of his living, were as unquestioned as George Washington's honesty. Hence, when Dooley struck at a malefactor, the victim had no redress except to answer Dooley back in kind with as good as he gave. It is a matter of history that no one ever managed that.

The great of the nation—industrial barons, leaders of reform, generals of the army; indeed, the President of the United States himself—tiptoed past that Archey Road barroom with placating smiles. No one willingly drew on himself the whip of Dooley's scorn. Those who did wished they hadn't. Imagine being poor Andrew Carnegie, who, every time he opened his mouth, got Dooley's foot in it. Or Theodore Roosevelt, whose bulliest bravery was no protection against potshots from behind the bar—"I'd like to tell me frind Tiddy that they'se a sthrenuse life an' a sthrenuseless life"—though it was as an author that Roosevelt suffered most. Dooley's review of his *Rough Riders*, a regimental history in the first person, began with a discussion of suitable subtitles:—

> 'Tis "Th' Biography iv a Hero be Wan Who Knows." 'Tis "Th' Darin' Exploits iv a Brave Man be an Actual Eye Witness." 'Tis "Th' Account iv th' Desthruction iv Spanish Power in th' Ant Hills," as it fell fr'm th' lips iv Tiddy Rosenfelt an' was took down be his own hands.
>
> (pp. 119-20)

The personal history of Martin Dooley was known to all. Like Socrates he made one brief excursion into office—as precinct captain (1873-1875)—but after that retired to philosophy. (When asked to remain in politics, he refused and gave his reasons: "As Shakespere says, 'Ol' men f'r th' council, young men f'r th' ward.'") His occupation was saloonkeeper, though in his earlier years he had worked at heavier manual employment as street laborer and drayman. Born in County Roscommon, Ireland, he had emigrated to the United States before the Civil War and had worked his way west to Chicago. He was a mature observer of the Chicago Fire of 1871. His age, when he first became a national figure, in 1898, was unknown, but was commonly believed to be at least in the late sixties. What his age was when he last appeared, in 1926, is anybody's guess.

Dooley's barroom was on Archey Road (Archer Avenue) in Chicago, in a neighborhood once purely Irish and still, in 1898, Irish enough so that it made little difference in the essays. "The barbarians around them," we are told in Dunne's description of the area, "are moderately but firmly governed, encouraged to passionate votings for the ruling race, but restrained from the immoral pursuit of office." (p. 120)

It was far easier to create Dooley in charcter than to keep him there. Much of Dunne's quality as an artist can be measured by his success in doing just that. The difficulties were innumerable. Many of the earlier essays written between 1893 and 1898 were concerned with Chicago politics, a subject obviously within Dooley's experience. Others were observations on general topics, or tall stories, or little homilies on practical virtue and everyday vice. But with national syndication the politics

had to become national or international, and the localisms either universal or unintelligible.

Dunne managed it beautifully. The newspapers still accounted for the bulk of Dooley's information; and Hogan and Father Kelly and Dock O'Leary supplied subjects for literary, theological, and scientific discussion. Hogan was the most useful. He read everything, believed everything, and followed every fad from infant care to golf. Hogan came very close to being enthusiastic, progress-minded America. He is an appealing, understandable, and—in his full implications—rather a terrifying character.

There were other dangers for Dooley—the worst, perhaps, that he would become a fossil, with only a fossil's powers of entertainment, and lose his value as an interpreter. Such fossils abound in all professional humor. An American example, to which you can easily add a dozen others, is the chin-whiskered farmer, with cowhide boots and a catgut twang, dear to fifth-rate cartoonists. It would have been all too easy for that to happen to Dooley, for he represented a factor in American life that changed very nearly out of recognition during the thirty-three years he appeared in the newspapers and magazines. That Dooley did not fossilize, that he remained fresh and alive to the last, is due to Dunne's objective sensitivity to social change.

It would be foolish to offer the eight volumes of essays as a sociological document on the thens and nows of the American-Irish scene. The primary interest of both Dunne and his readers was in his political or social comment; his attention to background was purely literary. Yet the essays do record many of the most significant permutations of Irish life in America, as and when they took place.

The change of tone over the years is very broad. In the late nineties, for example, Dooley waxed sardonic over golf, that social-silly pastime of the idle rich. In 1919, he followed Hogan and Larkin out to the links to watch them play. He was as ironic as ever, but now in everyday language. The game had become just another foolish fact—no longer a Sunday-supplement, lobsters-and-champagne myth. "There's nawthin' more excitin' to th' mother iv siven at th' end iv a complete wash-day thin to listen to an account iv a bum goluf game fr'm th' lips iv her lifemate. 'Tis almost as absorbin' as th' invintory iv a grocery store." That Dooley or Hogan should be on the links in 1895 might not have been impossible, but at any rate it wouldn't have happened. In 1919 it would not lift an eyebrow.

Golf is one example, and not particularly a central example, of the change represented. The whole process needs a history by itself, and none is yet written. The essays indicate it by progressively relaxing the belligerence with which the characters, Dooley included, face the smug and wealthy world. More and more their angry sarcasm is softened by indifference, their irony by amusement. This is not growing weakness or old age or an access of gentleness—just that a battle has been won and the victors are letting down their stiffly assumed defense. To put it more briefly still: the pressure is off.

The pressure let up in numberless ways, about that time, as the first generation of American-born Irish took over from their parents. Think of it in concrete terms. Families that had struggled along for years—God knows how—on the father's uncertain wages of, say, eight to ten dollars a week suddenly found themselves with five or six times that amount as the boys and girls grew up and got jobs their parents could never dream of. They marched into Canaan land and the walls toppled in the onrush. The "No Irish Need Apply" signs were broken up for firewood. It was a happy, marvelous time—a time for them to wonder at and enjoy—and it was enjoyed.

After fifty years of low wages, high immigration, and few opportunities, the American dream came true for the Irish with a bang. People with Irish names might, if they chose, be irritated by a last social sniper or two, but there was no serious obstacle left. Like the Yankees before them, they were now free to camp on the higher pastures and throw rocks at the foreigners below—for the *Mayflower* had meanwhile discharged another enormous boatload.

This last aspect of the change did not escape Dunne's attention, and though he had always been avowedly partisan as far as the Irish were concerned, he let these new recruits to smugness have a well-directed volley. Know-Nothingism was a form of mental decrepitude he disliked in anybody. (pp. 121-22)

For the most part, however, Dunne let his people enjoy their prosperity in quietness, and added his benediction. His own prosperity, considerable as it was, had, I believe, very little to do with the increasing gentleness of his comment. He was far too objective for that, and his natural kindliness, combined with a bitter hatred of hypocrisy, did not lend itself to jeremiads on the evils of having enough. The observation was as fundamental with him as with Shaw that the trouble with the poor is poverty. In his later years he had fewer occasions to attack the comfortable proponents of salutary poverty, but if we go back to 1894, the year of the Pullman strike, we can see the color of his fury.

After months of conflict, the strike against the company had been suppressed with use of Federal troops, and starvation was a daily fact in Pullman, Illinois. Dunne, then on the editorial staff of the *Chicago Evening Post,* had punched at Pullman's head from time to time, but when it seemed that the company's policy toward the beaten men was to be one of cold-blooded retaliation, he let go with both hands and both feet and the pavement, and did not smile as he worked. The essay shows Dunne at his most Irish, using wit coldly as a bludgeon, savaging his victim with it. It shows too what Dunne could do when he felt himself called upon to champion a cause—for his action in such a case was that of a champion. You could hardly call it defending the weak. It was slaughter:—

> Go into wan iv th' side sthreets about supper time an' see thim, Jawn—thim women sittin' at th' windies, with th' babies at their breasts an' waitin' f'r th' ol' man to come home. Thin watch him as he comes up th' sthreet, with his hat over his eyes an' th' shoulders iv him bint like a hoop an' dhraggin' his feet as if he carried ball an' chain. Musha, but 'tis a sound to dhrive ye'er heart cold whin a woman sobs an' th' young wans cries, an' both because there's no bread in th' house. Betther off thim that lies in Gavin's crates out in Calv'ry, with th' grass over thim an' th' stars lookin' down on thim, quite at last. An' betther f'r us that sees an' hears an' can do nawthin' but give a crust now an' thin. . . .
>
> (p. 122)

As the editorial writer at twenty-seven had had nothing but contempt for a tycoon befuddled by his own power, so at thirty-one, when Dunne lifted his sights from Chicago to the world of nations, he found no bigger game. Dooley was fazed by no man's pretensions. Statesman or alderman, man of war or man of God, it was all the same; "man" without its modifiers was the meaningful word—and, be it noted, the dignified word.

Though his hero-worship was not even microscopic, his respect for human worth was as ready as his understanding of human nature.

Like every writer worth his salt, Dunne had his vision of evil, profound and thoroughgoing, and what is less usual, balanced by an equally searching vision of decency. He could never write a *Utopia.* The complexity of the human spirit was his starting point, and his philosophy was bounded by an intensely felt perception that all souls are alike before man as before God. "All men are ME. Th' little tape line that I use f'r mesilf is long enough an' acc'rate enough to measure anny man in th' wurruld, an' if it happens that I'm ladlin' out red impeeryalism at tin cints th' glass instead iv breakin' stone at Joliet or frinds in Wall Sthreet it's because I started th' way I did." The same applied to Joe Chamberlain and Oom Paul Kruger, to Father Kelly and to Carey, the young criminal in "The Idle Apprentice." It was, I think, largely because of this perception that people recognized in Dooley the peculiar authority of the man who has been there and knows. Applicability is an attribute of the classics. Dooley navigated in the world with his map of Archey Road: he traveled Archey Road by the signposts of the human heart.

"It must be a good thing to be good," he said, "or ivrybody wudden't be pretendin' he was. But I don't think they'se anny such thing as hypocrisy in th' wurruld. They can't be. If ye'd turn on th' gas in th' darkest heart ye'd find it had a good raison for th' worst things it done, a good varchous raison, like needin' th' money or punishin' th' wicked or tachin' people a lesson to be more careful, or protectin' th' liberties iv mankind, or needin' the money." Hypocrisy and the money motives it concealed were often his theme—sometimes illustrated by an example drawn from Archey Road, but more usually by a direct attack on the conniving interests, whether individual or national.

Imperialism he counted the biggest hypocrisy of all, and the most vicious. And though his friend Theodore Roosevelt wrote him argumentative letters on the subject, he hit at it repeatedly, scoring his most effective shot when he readjusted the imperialistic slogans of the day to "Hands acrost th' sea an' into somewan's pocket" and "Take up th' white man's burden an' hand it to th' coons." In this work he rarely let his personal sympathies interfere with his vision. As an Irishman he loved the United States, hated England, and had a soft spot in his heart for France, but he knew all too well that greed has no nationality.

The protests that Dunne leveled against British methods in South Africa merge inevitably with his open disgust at the cruelty used in suppressing the Filipino Insurrection. Read his discussion of American use of the water torture in his essay on "The Philippine Peace," an almost Swiftian satire in which his pity and indignation vent themselves in lacerating wit. Or his personalization of nineteenth-century diplomacy, in which both the Englishman and the Frenchman are represented as thieves—the Frenchman the more amiable, but not enough to matter much to the victim. (pp. 122-23)

In view of the lambasting they took from him, it is difficult to understand Dooley's immense popularity with the English. The likeliest explanation is that they knew that his fair-mindedness cut both ways. He flailed into them as hard as any other American journalist in his protests about the Boer War, but he was the first to admit the safety-first quality of American sympathy.

"Don't ye think th' United States is enthusyastic f'r th' Boers?" asked the innocent Hennessy.

"It was," said Mr. Dooley. "But in th' las' few weeks it's had so manny things to think iv. Th' en-thusyasm iv this counthry, Hinnissy, always makes me think iv a bonfire on an ice-floe. It burns bright so long as ye feed it, an' it looks good, but it don't take hold, somehow, on th' ice."

(p. 123)

Dunne's admirations were as catholic as his resentments. Ready to applaud at a hero's popular triumph, he was yet like William James, who found most cause to wonder at those "great examples of sustained endurance" found readily in "thousands of poor homes where the woman successfully holds the family together and keeps it going by taking all the thought and doing all the work." James saw that from a distance. Dooley lived on the same block with it.

The distance or nearness of the point of vantage does not matter: it takes like genius to make a selection from the obvious. All Dooley's personal heroes are kin to the woman James described. They appear in different guises—a good cop, a hard-working father of a large family, a washerwoman whose tenderly reared only son turns out a bum, a Union veteran who never marches in a parade or waves the bloody shirt. In one of his finest heroic tales the hero is a fireman. It never disqualified a man, to Dooley's thinking, that he got paid for his bravery by the week. (p. 124)

The suggestion is regularly made that the time has come to revive Dooley, and not infrequently some small attempt at it is made. One of the essays, peculiarly applicable to some present crisis, is reprinted in a newspaper or magazine, or an editorial is written, liberally spiced with pertinent quotations. The result is only a vague wonder and amusement, not the hoped-for stirring of a new interest. As a method it is too piecemeal to succeed. Dooley's credit with his readers was long-term. He held them by his continuous provision of apposite wisdom; by his wit, and its varied rhythm which is not to be learned in one day; and above all, by his personality, which was thoroughly loved and as thoroughly understood. His clientele was trained to him and stayed with him for years. Besides, they knew how to read dialect. Strange as it may seem, they even liked to read it.

The present reading public has a firmly settled aversion to dialect writing, which is not likely soon to be shaken. If taste should turn again in that direction, it will not be towards the dialect of Dooley's all but vanished generation of immigrant Irish, but to some vernacular as readily heard now as that was then. Meanwhile, with every year, his obscurities increase. As unfamiliarity makes his language difficult, so the fading memory of topicalities that were the occasions of his wit darkens the wit itself and makes what was catholic and clear seem merely abstruse.

Rendition into straight English has been tried and, to my taste, fails. As well translate Chaucer—though that has been done. Translation precipitates some of the wit out of the essays, but it destroys their artistic compaction and it dissolves Martin Dooley altogether. Dooley without Dooley is inexcusable. He must be read in the original and at length. That will never be done again by a great many. But there will, I believe, always be a scattering of people in whose estimation he will be secure. The need for study and a glossary to read it has rarely killed a specimen of wisdom; and of witty wisdom—never. (p. 125)

*John V. Kelleher, "Mr. Dooley and the Same Old World," in* The Atlantic Monthly, *Vol. 177, No. 6, June, 1946, pp. 119-25.*

## NORRIS W. YATES   (essay date 1964)

[*An American critic, Yates is the author of several studies of American humor. In the following excerpt, he examines those facets of Mr. Dooley's characterization that distinguish him from the creations of other humorists of the period.*]

The migration of millions of people from country to city carried American humor along with it, but rural humor did not change its overalls for a boiled shirt when it moved into the city. Despite his urban background and his distrust of the country, where he once spent a night with "dogs an' mosquitos an' crickets an' a screech-owl," Mr. Dooley is rightly designated a crackerbox philosopher. Elmer Ellis, the biographer of Mr. Dooley's creator, Finley Peter Dunne, has said that Dooley's saloon "was in a village-like area of one-story business buildings, shanties, cabbage patches, and goat pastures." Neighborliness—the neighborliness of the small town—was the word for Archey Road and its oracle. (pp. 81-2)

The crackerbox tradition, even including the use of immigrant dialect, does not account for all of Mr. Dooley's characteristics. As Dunne describes Martin in the preface to [*Mr. Dooley in Peace and War*], there emerges a neighborhood oracle who is also a businessman—small but independent—and a respected citizen:

> Among them [the Irish] lives and prospers the traveller, archaeologist, historian, social observer, saloon-keeper, economist, and philosopher, who has not been out of the ward for twenty-five years "but twict." He reads the newspapers with solemn care, heartily hates them, and accepts all they print for the sake of drowning Hennessy's rising protests against his logic. . . . His impressions are transferred to the desensitized plate of Mr. Hennessy's mind, where they can do no harm. . . .
>
> He is opulent in good advice, as becomes a man of his station; for he has mastered most of the obstacles in a business career, and by leading a prudent and temperate life has established himself so well that he owns his own house and furniture, and is only slightly behind on his license. . . . His conduct of the important office of captain of his precinct (1873-75) was highly commended, and there was some talk of nominating him for alderman. . . . But the activity of public life was unsuited to a man of Mr. Dooley's tastes; and, while he continues to view the political situation always with interest and sometimes with alarm, he has resolutely declined to leave the bar for the forum. . . . "Politics," he says, "ain't bean bag. 'Tis a man's game; an' women, childher, an' prohybitionists'd do well to keep out iv it." Again he remarks, "As Shakespeare says, 'Ol' men f'r th' council, young men f'r th' ward.'"

The irony with which the author indicates Dooley's self-importance suggests that here is a clown who is not to be taken seriously. But despite the irony, he appears as a fusion of oracle and citizen. Dunne's variations in creating this blend are important in giving Dooley's ideas their mixture of sympathy and critical severity. First, Dooley is a bachelor (like many crackerbox sages), and his age is indefinite but great—indeed, in the number of his years, Dooley verges on the larger-than-life, on the mythical. This bachelorhood and his age lend him a degree of detachment in viewing the social scene, as does also the independent nature of his business and the fact that it is not quite respectable. On the other hand, this slight lack of respectability and the additional fact that he belongs to two minority groups, the Irish and the Catholic, put Dooley closer to the underside of life in America than any other humorous spokesman, with the possible exception of Archy the cockroach. Hennessy is a common laborer in a steel mill and Dooley patronizes him a good deal, but their man-to-man relationship is not seriously impaired thereby. The lives, loves, griefs, and joys of Archey Road, with its firemen, policemen, and other small wage earners, are important to the saloonkeeper, and he suggests that in this area a visiting dignitary such as the Kaiser may find as valid a cross section of the "real" America as anywhere. Dooley may be ignorant of much of America, but there is more truth than he knows in his pompous suggestion. The reader can see that in the tour offered by Dooley and his mates, the visiting VIP would meet a number of small-businessmen like the saloonkeeper himself and would look into establishments where he would view many workingmen like Hennessy. . . . (pp. 83-5)

The fact that his license fees are not quite paid up suggests that Dooley is not much more secure economically than Hennessy, who shovels slag. Further, Dooley's trade depends primarily on the manual laborers of the area—he could not afford to lose touch with them even if he wanted to. However, his freehold status, precarious though it may be, puts him in a position to lecture his customers from a slight psychological point of vantage. And lecture he does, one of his frequent targets being the ignorance and fickleness of the public as a whole, regardless of social classes. "Jawn, ye know no more about politics thin a mimber iv this here Civic Featheration [for reform]," he says to Mr. McKenna when that specimen of the people has been fighting in the streets for his candidate. On the inertia with which the public, recently so strongly for the Boers, now received a Boer mission seeking aid against the British, Dooley says, "The enthusyasm iv this counthry, Hinnissy, always makes me think iv a bonfire on an ice-floe. It burns bright so long as ye feed it, an' it looks good, but it don't take hold, somehow, on th' ice." When the plain folk vent certain prejudices born of ignorance, Dooley scourges them with irony—without losing his identification with them. Hennessy, referring to Captain Dreyfus, declares, "I think he's guilty. He's a Jew." Whereupon Dooley goes into a wise-clownish parody of the Dreyfus trial: "'Jackuse,' says Zola fr'm th' dureway. An' they thrun him out. . . . That's all I know about Cap Dhry-fuss' case, an' that's all anny man knows. Ye didn't know as much, Hinnissy, till I told ye." Hennessy then asks in bewilderment, "What's he charged with?"

> "I'll niver tell ye," said Mr. Dooley. "It's too much
> to ask." "Well, annyhow," said Mr. Hennessy, "he's
> guilty, ye can bet on that."

In his ignorance and narrow-mindedness, Hennessy resembles Ade's "Plain People," Mencken's *homo boobiens,* and Lardner's average man. Dooley in part conceals his own ignorance, but he knows he is ignorant, and this alone is enough to set him off from the herd, with Ade's more sensible patriarchs, Mencken's skeptical *persona,* and Lardner's Gullible, after that character has become not quite so gullible. In all four authors, two types of "ordinary" American—mass-man and thinking citizen—are contrasted.

The conscientious, thoughtful type of citizen was a postulate of the Wilsonian-Progressive spokesmen. Richard Hofstadter says of the Progressives:

At the core of their conception of politics was a figure quite as old-fashioned as the figure of the little competitive entrepreneur who represented the most commonly accepted economic ideal. This old-fashioned character was the Man of Good Will, the same innocent, bespectacled, and mustached figure we see in the cartoons today labeled John Q. Public—a white collar or small business voter-taxpayer with perhaps a modest home in the suburbs. William Graham Sumner had depicted him a generation earlier as "the forgotten man," and Woodrow Wilson idealized him as "the man on the make. . . ."

The leading trait of this ideal citizen was rationality; ". . . he would study the issues and think them through, rather than learn about them through pursuing his needs. Furthermore, it was assumed that somehow he would really be capable of informing himself in ample detail about the many issues he would have to pass on, and that he could master their intricacies sufficiently to pass intelligent judgment." Dunne, in causing Dooley to admit his own ignorance of complex issues, is debunking the Progressive ideal of the intelligent, "well-informed" citizen at the same time as he satirizes the other type of common man in the person of Hennessy. Not only does Mr. Dooley's reason desert him at times—as when he wants to throw bricks at various old enemies—but he can't possibly keep well informed. All he reads is the "pa-apers," and the data in his mind are a weird mixture of truth and misinformation. Here, suggests Dunne, is the "ideal" citizen of the liberals as he really is.

Dunne's personal history of participation in the journalism of reform shows that he was not a cynic, and in his humor he was merely trying to show that the social education of the man in the street was far more difficult than most of the Progressives believed. In causing Dooley at least to recognize his own limitations at times, Dunne implied that the intelligence of the better sort of common man is not enough; it must be accompanied by humility as well as by information. A skeptical point of view toward all politics, Dunne suggested, is also helpful in piercing the smoke of "patented political moralities." Part of this skepticism consists in seeing the economic issues underlying the political surface. Using the old technique of twisting a familiar maxim, Dooley says, "I tell ye, th' hand that rocks th' scales in the grocery store, is th' hand that rules th' wurruld." Dooley also knows that the real issue beneath the wrangle over the tariff status of Cuba *libre* is American beet sugar vs. Cuban cane sugar—"We freed Cubia but we didn't free annything she projooces."

The reformers had also better learn that what little relationship politics has to the laboring poor is that of the wolf to the lamb. Some of Dooley's most caustic quips are merely different ways of pointing out this relationship:

> If these laws ar-re bad laws th' way to end thim is
> to enfoorce thim. Somebody told him that Hinnissy.
> It isn't thrue, d'ye mind. I don't care who said it,
> not if 'twas Willum Shakespere. It isn't thrue. Laws
> ar-re made to throuble people an' th' more throuble
> they make th' longer they stay on th' stachoo book.

> Di-plomacy has become a philanthropic pursoot like
> shopkeepin', but politics, me lords, is still th' same
> ol' spoort iv highway robb'ry.

> Th' modhren idee iv governmint is "Snub th' people,
> buy th' people, jaw th' people."

(pp. 85-8)

Dooley thus may not be exactly the kind of citizen who could easily be "educated" to vote a straight Progressive or liberal-Democratic ticket, but he does have political insight and a social conscience. That Dunne himself had a social conscience is attested by his crusade against crooked politicians in Chicago—it was during such a crusade that Mr. Dooley was conceived—and by his writing for the *American Magazine* during its muckraking days and for the *Metropolitan* after that magazine had become a moderately socialist periodical. However, Dunne also made his small-businessman tell the Good Government reformers that the vast majority of working people have too hard a struggle with poverty and the day's work to bother about far-off and complicated questions like the "Nicaragoon Canal," the Monroe doctrine, Roosevelt's Janus-faced attitude toward the trusts, irrigation in the West, the Indian question, and expansion of the merchant marine. Identifying himself with these workers, Dooley says, "None iv these here questions inthrests me, an' be me I mane you an' be you I mane ivrybody. What we want to know is, ar-re we goin' to have coal enough in th' hod whin th' cold snap comes; will th' plumbin' hold out, an' will th' job last." When Seth Low, president of Columbia University, rode into the mayoralty of New York on an anti-Tammany ticket in 1902, Dooley warned that candidates are not elected because of their fancy platforms, reform or otherwise. A man is 'ilicted because th' people don't know him an' do know th' other la-ad; because Mrs. Casey's oldest boy was clubbed be a polisman, because we cudden't get wather above th' third story wan day, because th' sthreet car didn't stop f'r us, because th' Flannigans bought a pianny, because we was near run over be a mail wagon, because th' saloons are open Sundah night, because they're not open all day, an' because we're tired seein' th' same face at th' window whin we go down to pay th' wather taxes. Th' rayformer don't know this."

In this analysis of why the masses vote irrationally, their precarious lot is given heavier weight than their petty envy and dissipations. Occasionally Dunne even suggests that the working masses, despite their ignorance, are the backbone and hope of the nation. Behind the fool's mask, Dooley says of the stockmarket panic of 1907, "I wanted to rush to th' tillygraft office an' wire me frind J. Pierpont Morgan: 'Don't be downcast. It's all right. I just see Hinnissy go by with his shovel.'" And he advises Hennessy to "be brave, be ca'm an' go on shovellin'. So long as there's a Hinnissy in th' wurruld, an' he has a shovel, an' there's something f'r him to shovel, we'll be all right, or pretty near all right." Though foolish in pretending that he and Morgan are on familiar terms, Dooley is sensible in warning the rich not to think the country as a whole is ruined and in neatly summing up the labor theory of value. At another time he suggests that "Ohio or Ioway or anny iv our other possissions" don't make headlines "because they'se nawthin' doin' in thim parts. Th' people ar-re goin' ahead, garnerin' th' products iv th' sile, sindin' their childher to school, worshipin' on Sundah in th' churches an' thankin' Hiven f'r th' blessin's iv free governmint an' th' protiction iv th' flag above thim." (pp. 89-91)

The quest for wealth and status was not flatly rejected by Dunne, any more than by Ade, as a valid goal for the common man, but like Ade, Dunne stressed its limitations as an achieved goal. In the city of "Bathhouse John" Coughlin, "Hinky Dink" Kenna, and "Big Bill" Thompson, Dooley's comments on successful men were likely to concern shanty Irish who had risen by the traditional method of the immigrant Celt—politics. Dooley tells how Flanagan, starting at one end of a shovel,

fights his way to wealth and power in the wards, and stays on top through a blatant but courageous hypocrisy that cows lesser men. Flanagan's career is a study worthy of Ade in how far amorality and audacity may carry one. In another such study, Dooley's emphasis falls on how the boss somehow lost the love and companionship of his woman, who remained a plain laborer's housewife while her husband rose beyond her. In telling this story, Dooley remarks on the relativity—and therefore the ultimate inconsequence—of class status: "Aristocracy, Hinnissy, is like rale estate, a matther iv location. I'm aristocracy to th' poor O'Briens back in th' alley, th' brewery agent's aristocracy to me, his boss is aristocracy to him, an' so it goes, up to th' czar of Rooshia." Dunne's sympathies in this case are with the woman, but he did not forget that women's heads too may be turned by success—"If a man is wise, he gets rich an' if he gets rich, he gets foolish, or his wife does."

Dooley has not done badly as an entrepreneur, but he has little hope of getting rich. Consequently he can afford a middle attitude in which he does not reject wealth and power as undesirable goals but sees clearly the penalties they exact. With compassion he satirizes the pretensions of the rich, as he does those of the poor, frequently emphasizing the basic humanity of both. He points out the single-mindedness of Higgins the "millyionaire" who gets no enjoyment out of luxury: "He mus' be up an' doin'. An' th' on'y things annywan around him is up an' doin' is th' things he used to get paid f'r doin' whin he was a young man." The well-to-do don't often land in court, but when they do they must "stand in th' clear sunlight iv American justice, . . . an' be smirched," whereas the humble may not get justice, but they at least escape widespread persecution by the press—"No wan cares to hear what Hogan calls: 'Th' short an' simple scandals iv th' poor.'" Of the socialites at Newport, Rhode Island, Dooley says that, ". . . they ain't much diff'rence between th' very rich an' th' very poor. . . . No, sir, they ain't th' breadth iv ye'er hand's diff'rence between Mrs. Mulligan and Mrs. Ganderbilk." Both must have a social circle of which they can feel a part, or their lives aren't worth living. Without sentimentalizing poverty, then, Dooley sharply questions those among both the rich and the poor who think wealth important in itself, and he does not reject the success-philosophy wholly, but counsels against its whole-hog acceptance. This may be a reasonable attitude for almost all men, but it seems especially appropriate for a citizen who has had a little success and who has to work steadily just to keep that, let alone gain more.

When he touched on the struggle between management and labor, Dooley likewise expressed views acceptable to citizens who felt themselves in the middle brackets. There were three such groups of citizens: skilled workers who hoped to rise into management or at least into the white-collar ranks; the new middle class of salaried white-collar workers, and the old middle class—the self-employed managers of small enterprises, a class which included Dooley himself. All three groups had reasons for feeling disengaged from the strife between union labor and corporate management. Despite his compassion for the laborers in industry, Dooley often says things that may have pleased some large employers but must surely have pleased many people in these three categories. Dooley deplores strikes, sympathizes with the nonunion man who cannot strike, informs McKenna that, "A prolotoorio, Jawn, is the same thing as a hobo," and says of capital and labor, "They're so close together now that those that ar-re between thim ar-re crushed to death." "Abe Martin," the crackerbox sage of Indianapolis, implied a similar view, and one thus sees how attitudes appropriate to the crackerbarrel philosopher and his rural audience might also fit the solid citizen and his urban readers. One sees further how Dooley could make shrewd comments in the role of the levelheaded citizen even though at times he betrays the ignorance and confusion that, Dunne felt, too often impeded this levelheadedness as a social force. One sees finally that this citizen may speak for other middle groups besides the small entrepreneur, though he speaks most obviously for that class.

Besides the comments on politics, labor, and reform, Dunne has something to say about history, science, progress, Ireland, the Negro question, medicine, progressive education (Dooley was against it), music (Dooley's views on grand opera resemble those of the middlebrow narrators depicted by Bangs, Ade, and Lardner), sports, the wild West, family life, and many other topics. But not all of Dunne's views are voiced through Mr. Dooley; minor characters also play their parts. These characters populate Archey Road and thus give it reality; they are also foils for the saloonkeeper's wit and humor—his "straight" men. In addition, they represent humorous types other than the crackerbarrel philosopher. Hennessy and McKenna embody the less admirable traits of the plain people; Hogan is the eternal pedant, "who's wan iv th' best-read an' mos' ignorant men I know." Hogan is Archey Road's version of Ichabod Crane and of Dr. Obed Battins (in James Fenimore Cooper's *The Prairie*). Father Kelly, the parish priest, is a common-sense philosopher in his own right, and often is quoted when Dunne wishes to stress Dooley's ignorance or narrow-mindedness rather than his shrewdness. Father Kelly is also used to make Dooley more convincing as an individual. William Dean Howells had said of Dunne, "He knows that there are moments when his philosophical spectator of events must lapse into a saloon keeper. . . ." When this occurs, the priest is there to provide whatever wisdom Dooley lacks. Since the priest is an educated man, he can do this, especially when cultural matters are concerned, and Dunne, the author, need not take a definite stand. (pp. 91-4)

Dunne's attitudes often seem ambiguous and inconsistent. He was skeptical of reform and reformers, but in Chicago he crusaded against municipal and financial evils, singling out in particular the city's perpetual crime wave; bosses Frank Lawler, "Bathhouse John" Coughlin, and "Hinky Dink" Kenna; gambler Mike McDonald; traction magnate Charles T. Yerkes (later to be used by Dreiser in *The Financier* as the basis for Frank Cowperwood), and the excesses of the Pullman company in the great strike of 1894. Sometimes Dunne struck at these targets through editorials written in his own person; sometimes through Mr. Dooley in sketches never collected in book form. In fact, one reason for Mr. Dooley's leap into being was Dunne's desire to hit corruption hard and yet not alarm the timid publisher of the Chicago *Post*. He could accomplish both ends by putting his criticism into the mouth of a comic Irishman, resentment of whom would not easily be transferred to an author who kept himself out of these pieces.

In later years, Dunne, usually through Dooley, slashed at crooked life-insurance executives, exposed by Charles Evans Hughes and Louis D. Brandeis, as zealously as he ridiculed the over-earnest crusader against vice, Theodore Parkhurst. He satirized "Idarem" (Ida M. Tarbell), "Norman Slapgood" (Norman Hapgood), and other muckrakers for their sensationalism—and shortly thereafter, joined Miss Tarbell, Lincoln Steffens, and others in the purchase of the *American Magazine* for muckraking purposes. He wrote in both correct English and in the

dialect of Dooley for the *American* from 1906 to 1910, and in 1911 he contributed editorials in correct English regularly to the *Metropolitan*, another organ of protest, yet he was the most conservative member of the editorial staff on both magazines. As a result of his palpable hits on Roosevelt's egocentric book *The Rough Riders*, Dunne acquired a personal friendship with the volatile President, a friendship not abated by Dunne's joining the muckrakers. He compared business to murder and highway robbery, but could also say of the businessman, "He is what Hogan calls th' boolwarks iv pro-gress, an' we cudden't get on without him even if his scales are a little too quick on th' dhrop."

Actually Dunne's views were not so much inconsistent as cautious—skeptical, if one prefers. Neither he nor his colleagues on the *American Magazine* wanted or expected any radical changes in society. To some extent, Dunne shared the self-made businessman's belief in the trinity of self-reliance, opportunity, and progress, but he was too close to the working poor to expect any startling benefits therefrom for "the Hennessys of the world who suffer and are silent." The future might bring "a great manny changes in men's hats an' the' means iv transportation but not much in annything else." One will "see a good manny people still walkin' to their wurruk." Even those workingmen who did "get on" might not behave so much like the "new citizen" of reform propaganda as like the common man of Ring Lardner. If Hennessy were to get rich, says Dooley, here's what would happen:

*Mr. Dooley as drawn by E. W. Kemble (left) and James Montgomery Flagg.*

''Ye'd come back here an' sthrut up an' down th' sthreet with ye'er thumbs in ye'er armpits; an' ye'd drink too much, an' ride in sthreet ca-ars. Thin ye'd buy foldin' beds an' piannies, an' start a reel estate office. Ye'd be fooled a good deal an' lose a lot iv ye'er money, an' thin ye'd tighten up. Ye'd be in a cold fear night an' day that ye'd lose ye'er fortune. Ye'd wake up in th' middle iv th' night dhreamin' that ye was back at th' gas-house with ye'er money gone. Ye'd be prisidint iv a charitable society. Ye'd have to wear ye'er shoes in th' house, an' ye'er wife'd have ye around to rayciptions an' dances. Ye'd move to Mitchigan Avnoo, an' ye'd hire a coachman that'd laugh at ye. Ye'er boys'd be joods an' ashamed iv ye, an' ye'd support ye'er daughters' husbands. . . . Ye'd be a mane, close-fisted, onscrupulous ol' curmudgeon; an', whin ye'd die, it'd take half ye'er fortune f'r rayqueems to put ye r-right. I don't want ye iver to speak to me whin ye get rich, Hinnissy.''

''I won't,'' said Mr. Hennessy.

This could have been a paraphrase in Irish dialect of one of Ade's more pessimistic fables *Ecce homo boobiens!* In such passages about the common man, Dunne has irony and pity but no sentimentality. Dooley, the solid citizen, may advise Hennessy, but little hope is offered that he will influence him. Even if he does, this influence will not necessarily be sound. (pp. 97-9)

> Norris W. Yates, ''Mr. Dooley of Archey Road,'' in his The American Humorist: Conscience of the Twentieth Century, *Iowa State University Press, 1964, pp. 81-99.*

**JESSE BIER** (essay date 1968)

[*Bier is an American critic and novelist. In the following excerpt, he discusses Dunne's place in the development of American satirical writing.*]

In our perspective today, [Finley Peter] Dunne comes almost midway in the American saga between the folly of Brackenridge's Teague O'Regan and the wit and charm of John F. Kennedy, between the immigrant scapegoat and the Irish-American President. Dunne left all obsequiousness and folderol behind him but still took querulous, alienated exception to practically all of the terms of American life. The Dooley papers are filled with insurgency, as they also are with vitality, all of a piece as acidic satires against fraud and American pretense, richly comic exercises in archskepticism.

Dooley sets himself firmly against the economic system and all its patriotic blandishments, as in his report ''On the Victorian Era.''

> I have seen America spread out fr'm th' Atlantic to th' Pacific, with a branch office iv the Standard Ile Comp'ny in ivry hamlet.

He mightily loosens the connection between Business and Progress.

> An' th' invintions,—th' steam-injine an' th' printin'-press an' th' cotton-gin an' the gin sour an' th' bicycle an' th' flyin'-machine an' . . .—crownin' wur-ruk iv our civilization—th' cash raygisther.

In *Mr. Dooley in Peace and War* and in all of his turn-of-the-century fusillades, he fires incessantly and with extra glee upon the imperialism that was the shameful consequence of our aggressively expansionist industrial system at home.

> An' afther awhile, whin he gits tired iv th' game, he'll write home an' say he's got the islands; an' he'll tur'rn thim over to th' gover'ment an' go back to his ship, an' Mark Hanna'll organize th' Flip-ine Islands Jute an' Cider Comp'ny, an' th' rivolutchinists'll wish they hadn't.

> (p. 179)

It may well be that Dunne's steady opposition to American business, militarism, politics, and custom is a displacement of both his Irish and Catholic hostility to the English, who left the brand of WASP on this new world. For when, in ''On the French Character,'' he reviews the record of French and English imperialism wreaked upon darkest Africa and Asia, Dooley sides with the French as the lesser of two evils because they are partly Celtic and honest, and two qualities more or less equatable. The English, like the American come-latelies, are all hypocritical moralism and religiosity. . . . But liberated from the dominant pietism of the English-speaking world, Dunne is also alienated from the whole question of religion and is Shavian in observations prompted by the Spanish-American War in ''On Prayers for Victory.''

> Th' Lord knows how it'll come out. First wan side prays that th' wrath iv Hiven'll descind on th' other, an' thin th' other side returns th' compliment with inthrest. Th' Spanish bishop says we're a lot iv murdherin', irreligious thieves, an' ought to be swept fr'm th' face iv th' earth. We say his people ar-re th' same, an' manny iv thim. . . . We have a shade th' best iv him, f'r his fleets ar-re all iv th' same class an' ol' style, an' we have some iv th' most modhern prayin' machines in the warruld. . . .

And so Dooley presides as bartender and critic behind his bar on Archey Road. The great and leading questions suffer reduction to the ward level, but the narrowed scope gives him and some of his customers their telling insights, too. (pp. 181-82)

All of which prompts the question of provincialism in the humor of this period and in Dunne peculiarly. On one side in the matter is George Ade, who proceeds in many of his fables to expose deep-seated mid-western provincialism; he does so good-naturedly but unmistakably. On the other side is Will Rogers, who makes the issue into a personal tenet. Paris, he defines, as ''the Claremont, Oklahoma, of France.'' It is part of his charm, though when he slowly but surely became a professional American, he hardened his comic attitudes into serious values and became too literally an isolationist. Between the two is Dunne's Dooley, at loose ends. Severely provincial as only some urbanites can be, yet he is ferocious in discountenancing every telltale sign of national imperialist provincialism on a world stage. He is comically and sublimely unaware of the resulting disparity.

Such comic doubleness, duplicity even, stands in contrast to the monolithic integrity, catastrophic perhaps but grand and somewhat superhuman, of the classic tragic figure. Mr. Dooley lives in the Sixth Ward of Chicago but projects a higher self to Washington, Havana, and Manila, split into several comic alter egos. A certain unintegration probably, rather than disintegration, recommends the comic spokesman. Of course Dunne is at pains to create a comic character of some objective fascination. And contradiction, a form of internal conflict, is a prime means to the artistic end. But in doing so, almost by the way, he uses Dooley's provincialism, in contrast to the character's liberating imagination otherwise, in a manner that is profoundly instructive.

It is not primarily that Dunne removes himself from Dooley, though that also is true enough. Dooley's anti-intellectualism, for instance, together with his provincialism, keeps him separate from the author. We find Dooley arguing out the question of books with the parish priest. "What ar' ye goin' to do with thim young wans? We're goin' to make thim near-sighted an' round shouldered." But Dunne has the good priest, with a wild catechistic logic of his own, have rather the best of it. So that once again we feel Dooley's adamant position at variance with his good sense. Dooley is only, but supremely, human, a parvenu with stubborn prejudices that he can voice with the same breath he gives to his amazing perspectives and insights. He is variable enough to be one of the ideal representatives of comic human diversity, which always defies strict formulation—and which has always been dearer to our American experience than its opposite. Which means that, in our depths, we believe that we certainly perish as tragic whole men but that we endure in comic bits and pieces.

In these days of renewed American interventionism and tragical heroic saviorism, Dooley recaptures more and more interest as archcritic and satirist. But his topicality will pass, too, and Dooley must abide on the intrinsic grounds of his comic human nature: paradoxically provincial and broad-minded, anti-intellectual but thoughtful, pugnacious but humanitarian, a marvel of self-division but capable of the most concerted singularities of insight and feeling. Dunne's conception of him is one of the finest creations we have after Twain's Huck and Roxy. His portrayal of Dooley alone, all other characters and themes and techniques aside, is both a clue to the essence of humor and one of the triumphs of American practice.

Still, there was evidently more to Dunne's practice than the characterization of Mr. Dooley. His techniques, predominantly verbal, were varied and expert. Apart from being one of the country's greatest dialecticians, Dunne may still be regarded as one of our most tough-headed but flexible technicians.

He is a specialist in anticlimax.

> Winsdah night a second ar-rmy iv injineers, miners, plumbers, an' lawn tinnis experts, numberin' in all four hundherd an' eighty thousan' men, ar-rmed with death-dealin' canned goods, was hurried to Havana to storm th' city.
>
> . . . . .
>
> "Sure," said Mr. Hennessy, sadly, "we have a thing or two to larn oursilves."
>
> "But it isn't f'r thim to larn us," said Mr. Dooley. "'Tis not f'r thim wretched an' degraded crathers, without a mind or a shirt iv their own, f'r to give lessons in politeness an' liberty to a nation that manny-facthers more dhressed beef than anny other imperyal nation in th' wurruld." . . .

His antiproverbialism is less active than [Ambrose] Bierce's but is apparent. "There's only one thing that would make me allow myself to be a hero to the American people," says Dooley, "and that is it don't last long." We might deduce the tendency from his proud and truculent urban cynicism, but it is also a consequence of general reversalism and opposition, as in every other humorist who tries it. In this light, the inveterate enmity between Dooley and the County Mayo man, Dorsey, is deliberate antithetic reversal of Christian, or Protestant, charity and loving-kindness. . . . We may observe, incidentally, the instinctive role of aggression, as Dunne furnishes it to us. This is the deepest kind of cultural and philosophic reversal. One

can't love well if he does not hate well, too . . . sane Irish candor made to rectify the simple, if not hypocritical, midwestern American fairy tales of mutual adoration.

> Whin England purrishes, th' Irish'll die iv what Hogan calls ongwee, which is havin' no wan in the weary wurruld ye don't love.

The corrective is a legacy of the brawling Old World, one of the ways in which America has been vitally dependent on first-generation immigrants, who will not dissolve readily into the seething mindlessness and indiscriminate, chummy conformity of any Melting Pot.

Dunne is weaker at literalism than we would expect, though he has his moments. He cribs "Dooley the Wanst" from Artemus Ward, and he puns with unmerciful simplicity. He does not care if Queen Victoria has reigned or "snowed." Typically, however, he talks about a young man, another "bum vivant," on the make for a rich woman as his "financée." He deflects to the easy literalist pun in almost any circumstance, as in a political rally exchange.

> "'Th' inimies iv our counthry has been cr-rushed,' he says, . . . 'Now,' he says, 'th' question is what shall we do with th' fruits iv vichtry?' he says. [A voice, 'Can thim.']"

His best gibes, however, have to rise out of some difficulty, like an extravagant literal war of mules that he describes in Cuba, during which someone observes, "It can't be an American jackass, or he'd speak."

Dunne's verbal comedy was a compound of the greatest brilliance at dialect we have, after Joel Chandler Harris, and much lower forms of oral technique. Like the earlier Billings and his contemporaries, Dunne sometimes labored his orthographic humor unnecessarily, spelling "foot" as "fut," etc. He is not above simple malapropism, as when he describes Chicago after the fire rising "felix-like" from its ashes. And he seeks out the comedy of the misquote: "he's as thrue as th' needle in th' camel's eye, as Hogan says." But his surprising talent at what we have come to call "Dooleymorphisms" is just as much a special technical gift as it is a matter of over-all characterization. Dooley's anti-imperialism extends to the Boer War as well as to the Spanish-American War, and he takes out his scorn for the Dutch and Germans in his contempt for the Barvarian butchershop owner on Archey Road. But Dooleymorphisms also account for the way Dooley's brain works in sheer comic metaphor, so that his description of the universal drunk is inimitably local.

> . . . wanst in a while a mimber iv th' club, comin' home a little late an' thryin' to riconcile a pair iv' r-round feet with an embroidered sidewalk. . . .

Dunne is, of course, a partisan of the talltale, his Irish extravagance making him susceptible to the gross and fanciful exaggeration. His comic catalogues often function exuberantly to this point, climaxing a tale that mixes one part blarney to one part frontier-ism (even if we have to go north to get there now).

> "What ta-alk have ye?" Mr. Dooley demanded. "A walrus don't fly, foolish man!"
>
> "What does he do, thin?" asked Mr. Hennessy. "Go 'round on crutches?"
>
> "A walrus," said Mr. Dooley, "is an animal something like a hor-rse, but more like a balloon. It doesn't walk, swim, or fly. It rowls whin pur-suin' its prey.

It whirls 'round an' 'round at a speed akel to a railroad injine, meltin' th' ice in a groove behind it. Tame walruses are used be th' Eskeemoyoos, th' old settlers iv thim parts, as lawnmowers an' to press their clothes. Th' wild walrus is a mos' vicious animal, which feeds on snowballs through th' day, an' thin goes out iv nights afther artic explorers, which for-rms its principal diet. Theyse a gr-reat demand among walruses f'r artic explorers, Swedes preferred; an' on account iv th' scarcity iv this food it isn't more than wanst in twenty years that th' walrus gets a square meal. Thin he devours his victim, clothes, collar-buttons, an' all.''

Inevitably there are marks of the outré in such interludes.

To march well, a man's feet have to be mates; an' if he has two left feet both runnin' sideways, he ought to have interference boots to keep him fr'm setting fire to his knees.

Now and then the outlandish and slightly macabre come together.

''Why, man alive,' I says, 'Charter Haitch was assassinated three years ago,' I says. 'Was he?' says Dugan. 'Ah, well, he's lived that down be this time. He was a good man,' he says.''

Dunne's greatest departure from Bierce, who is really the exception in the period, lies in his democratic attitudes. Dooley is a triumphant commoner, and all tirades against generals and monarchs and the like are of a piece with his democratic bias and the deflationism it breeds. He is also inclined, as Bierce is not, to self-deprecation (simultaneous with Queen Victoria's Diamond Celebration is Dooley's ''rhinestone jubilee''). And quite separate from Bierce's high style, against which Bierce like the southwesterners had to defend himself, is the totally democratic vocabulary, rhythm, and tone of Dunne's language. The Irish American's antirhetorical thrusts are pure and genuine parodies, as when he travesties McKinley's oratory.

'''We can not tur-rn back,' he says, 'th' hands iv th' clock that, even as I speak,' he says, 'is r-rushin' through th' hear'rts iv men,' he says, 'dashin' its spray against th' star iv liberty an' hope, an' no north, no south, no east, no west, but a steady purpose to do th' best we can, considerin' all th' circumstances iv the case,' he says.''

An avowed admirer of Bill Nye, Dunne was probably influenced by the whole deflationary technique of the literary comedians. But there is so much his own in his immigrant, urban, and democratic talent that there is less value than usual in pointing out influences except to indicate the continuity of American humor. (pp. 183-90)

> *Jesse Bier, ''Intercentury Humor,'' in his* The Rise and Fall of American Humor, *Holt, Rinehart and Winston, 1968, pp. 162-207.*

## BARBARA C. SCHAAF  (essay date 1977)

[*In the following excerpt, Schaaf emphasizes the importance of Mr. Dooley's urban, immigrant background in explaining his enormous popularity.*]

[Mr.] Dooley's national popularity has amazed and puzzled many, including his creator.

Why, indeed, should the views of a Bridgeport barkeep interest and amuse so many who were neither Irish, nor Chicagoans, nor Democrats, nor immigrants? Without diminishing in any

way Dunne's personal talents and gifts, which were splendid indeed, the answer lies to some extent in the urban history of the period.

Much of the modern city as it is known today, its advantages as well as its problems, originated at the turn of the century: the great population growth of major cities, including the role of immigration; the change in appearance of the cities due to building projects, erection of landmarks, and the like; the development of cultural pursuits—the founding of operas, ballets, orchestras, and museums; technological advances, such as the automobile, electrified street lighting, the telephone system, roads, bridges, and tunnels.

Uplifting as these achievements may be, the seamier aspects of city life, many of which still disfigure our cities today, were also taking shape: crime and corruption; political chicanery made possible by manipulation of ethnic, immigrant blocs; labor activity and its violence; radical agitation.

Chicago's place in this rapidly urbanizing landscape was unique. Its desolation by fire coupled with a semifrontier audacity released an almost frantic burst of energy. So eager were the Chicagoans to rebuild that they did not even pause to enact zoning codes that would prevent the reconstruction of inflammable wooden buildings, despite the fact that they were literally standing in the ashes of their city.

The determination to revive Chicago brooked no interference. Results were what counted, and Chicagoans of the period had no time to waste on niceties of method or unfortunate side effects. And if this opened wide the way to the exploiter, the criminal, the corrupt, the boodler, it was an inevitable price of progress.

Chicago, in truth, was every growing American city. This is not to say that it was a paradigm; on the contrary, each city had its own peculiar development and destiny. But the problems and solutions, successes and failures, inspirations and disasters that occurred or would occur in other cities as they pursued their individual fate all were concentrated and magnified in Chicago. If other cities boasted commercial enterprise, Chicago was the player with the nation's railroads. If other cities had labor troubles, Chicago had Pullman. If other cities had corrupt politicians, Chicago had raised graft to a high art.

At the center of this ferment was Mr. Dooley, keeping a skeptical and humorous eye on the view from his Bridgeport saloon. And behind Dooley was Finley Peter Dunne, both creator and creature, firmly fixed in the urban environment and influenced by it. More than a quintessential Chicagoan, Dooley was a quintessential urbanite, who drew his examples, anecdotes, and knowledge from city surroundings. Whether the issue was silver coinage or the Spanish-American War, Dooley, the city dweller, could apply the mental tools of Archey Road and find that other urbanites would get the message, irrespective of issue, dialect, or locale.

Dooley had a comment on every significant phase of urban life and thereby struck a responsive note with new-landed urbanites everywhere. But the Dooley columns also imparted the flavor of life in the city. Mr. Dooley's Chicago was a fast-paced and exciting place to live. Something was always going on, a world's fair, a speech, a strike, or a political movement. Moreover, the columns were liberally dashed with subtle qualities of the urban lifestyle, for instance, the necessity for coexistence among ethnic groups. Most of the immigrants in Chicago and in other cities had come from rural areas of the Old Country. In America's cities they were thrown together cheek by jowl. They clustered in ethnic neighborhoods, but at some point, usually a very definable line, the neighborhood ended and some sort of co-operation or truce had to begin. Dooley could relate with pride, in one column, how he evened a score with "the Polacker swinging the red bridge," by rolling a beer keg at the man and breaking his leg. Yet, in another column on the Pullman strike, he would tell how Irish workers lucky enough to have a little money in the house during the strike contributed food to their Polish working-class brethren who were not so fortunate. Such small beginnings, growing out of the "same boat" situation that ethnic urbanites found themselves in, formed an important early underpinning of the broad ethnic coalitions that play such a large role in modern city politics.

Dooley's awareness of the ethnic and rural heritages in the city may have, paradoxically, assured his acceptance by America's new urbanites. Many were neophytes at city life and still clung to the traditions of the rural folk. One of those traditions, which has attained the status of myth, is the cracker-barrel philosopher—the wise, unsophisticated commentator who punctures the overblown with humor, exposes evil with irony, but never loses his tolerance for human weakness. Dooley was in this great line. Had Dunne offered his thoughts on his own, in his own speech, they probably would have generated no more than a mild interest in the views of a newsman from an energetic, but on the whole rather vulgar, city. Dooley, however, bridged the gap between rural and urban, homespun and sophisticated. Dunne's significant contribution was to have made Dooley a cracker-barrel philosopher with a crucial difference; his cracker barrel was not at the general store, but at city hall.

It would be mistaken for us to consider Dooley only a humorist or an advance man for the muckrakers. He was more, but assessing his influence is not something that can be done objectively by reference to numbers, reforms, legislation, or monuments. His monuments exist, but they are of a different order.

What Dooley said was remembered and often repeated by the high and the low, his observations became bon mots, his insights a standard of awareness. How deep and long such influences may run perhaps can be judged by an incident that occurred in Chicago not long before the writing of this book. Chicago Mayor Richard J. Daley was engaged in a dispute with Illinois Governor Daniel Walker, the details of which are not relevant here. Governor Walker endorsed anti-Daley candidates in Chicago aldermanic elections, but Daley called forth his precinct legions and they delivered the mayor's vote with a vengeance. Asked to comment on the soundness of the thrashing received by the Walker-backed candidates, Daley responded with a quote from Mr. Dooley that "politics ain't bean bag."

This, more than fifty years after the publication of the last Dooley column! How much more influence on other men Dooley exerted during the flower of his popularity can only be estimated, but that influence went deeper than the mere parroting of what Dooley said. Those who adopt another man's language also adopt, however thinly or fleetingly, his frame of mind. Obviously, not everyone who quoted Dooley or imitated him was a Dooley himself, but it cannot be denied that through the accumulation of points well taken, issues refined to a memorable epigram, and social commentary vivified by example, Dooley educated the attitudes of many. He exemplified and raised urban consciousness; he helped countless thousands of his readers find or keep their bearings during a period of uprooting social change; he expressed what many felt

but all could not say; he was among the first and best transmitters of American urban culture. (pp. 375-79)

> *Barbara C. Schaaf, in her* Mr. Dooley's Chicago, *Anchor Press/Doubleday, 1977, 399 p.*

## CHARLES FANNING (essay date 1978)

[*Fanning is an American critic who specializes in the study of Irish-American literature. In the following excerpt, he discusses the nature and importance of the Dooley essays within the context of American humorist traditions.*]

It would be foolish to deny that Dunne was limited by his chosen form [in creating the Mr. Dooley essays]: a weekly newspaper column of roughly 750 words is too slight and too time-serving ever to constitute crafted literature of the first rank. The pieces are true sketches, and at the most they provide telling glimpses into character and motive, particular places and times. No synthesis can bring into being what was never there to start with: that is, the coherent, rounded wholeness of fiction. Yet there is more of a realized world in these scattered pieces than Dunne has been given credit for, and its creation in his severely constricted form is a minor miracle of American letters. . . .

[In addition to big-city journalism], Dunne seems to have borrowed in various ways from three other oral and literary traditions. . . . First, there is the indigenous American tradition of the crackerbox philosopher, or wise fool, the low-caste and unlettered dispenser of wisdom in dialect who was a fixture on the American scene throughout the nineteenth century. Mr. Dooley shares with the Nasbys, Wards, and Downings the stock verbal tricks of the dialect humorist. Also, Dunne's critical commentary on the war against Spain is part of a dialect tradition of realistic/humorous evaluation of American military involvement that includes Lowell's Hosea Biglow, Browne's Artemus Ward, and Locke's Petroleum V. Nasby. Mr. Dooley differs importantly from his predecessors, though, in being both the first immigrant and the first city-dweller to achieve sustained identity in this tradition. Morever, he is a fully developed character who has been placed in a definite social and geographical context; in this he is unlike the isolated, shadowy figures—little more than disembodied rural voices—of his predecessors. (p. 219)

Second, Dunne seems consciously to make use of the American tall-tale tradition. His memorable anecdotes from Bridgeport's early, brawling days as a canal port are worthy of Mike Fink, the king of the bargemen: for example, the canalside fist fight between "Con Murphy, th' champine heavyweight iv th' ya-ards" and "th' German blacksmith," which begins at four in the morning and ends after dark, "whin Murphy's backer put a horseshoe on th' big man's fist." Throughout his Chicago career, tall-tale hyperbole is one of Mr. Dooley's favorite devices. Among the gems are his description of Chicago air as "so thick with poisonous gases that a wagon loaded with scrap iron wud float at an ilivation iv tin feet"; and of the "Great Hot Spell," during which "the sthreet-car thracks got so soft they spread all over th' sthreet, an' th' river run dhry," and "th' fire departmint was all down on Mitchigan Avnoo, puttin' out th' lake."

Third, Mr. Dooley seems to echo the literary and folk traditions of Ireland. Dunne probably listened to Irish storytellers from his parents' generation, and he may have been influenced by the upsurge of interest in Irish folklore in the 1890s generated by Yeats, Hyde, and Lady Gregory. We know that news of the Irish folk movement reached him in Chicago, because Colonel McNeery spends a column in 1893 explaining to John McKenna that "folk-lore" is "di'lect pothry." At least one Dooley piece deals directly with an Irish folk plot—a man's ghost returning to cause trouble for his remarried wife and her new husband. When the ghost of big Tim O'Grady wafts into his old home, "in th' mos' natural way in th' wurruld, kickin' th' dog," he is summarily ejected by his successor, O'Flaherty the tailor, who declares that "I'll make th' ghost iv a ghost out iv ye. I can lick anny dead man that iver lived." The same embarrassing situation occurs in the traditional Irish tale, "Leeam O'Rooney's Burial," which Douglas Hyde translated into English in his seminal collection, *Beside the Fire,* of 1890. Moreover, both stories point the same moral: it is plain bad form to come back after having been decently buried. " 'Tis onplisint iv thim, annyhow, not to say ongrateful," says Mr. Dooley:

> F'r mesilf, if I was wanst pushed off, an' they'd waked me kindly, an' had a solemn rayqueem high mass f'r me, an' a funeral with Roddey's Hi-bernyan band, an' th' A-ho-aitches, I have too much pride to come back f'r an encore. I wud so, Jawn. Whin a man's dead, he ought to make th' best iv a bad job, an' not be thrapsin' around, lookin' f'r throuble among his own kind.

In Hyde's tale, O'Rooney's wife chides him similarly: "I can't let you in, and it's a great shame, you to be coming back again, after being seven days in your grave. . . . doesn't every person in the parish know that you are dead, and that I buried you decently."

A particular convention of Irish storytelling that Dunne always uses is the repeated interjection of "he says . . . I says . . . he says," by which he is able to control the pace and rhythm of Mr. Dooley's conversation, often for lyrical, humorous, or satiric emphasis. Dunne's ear for the rhythms, contractions, and occasional rolled "r's" of Irish-American common speech is everywhere remarkable. His ability to transfer these tones still living onto the page is central to the perennial freshness of the Dooley pieces; even in the least successful of them, we hear a real human voice.

Actually, Dunne's persistent concern for the spoken language may loosely be labeled "Irish," for, as Oscar Wilde once told Yeats, "We Irish are too poetical to be poets; we are a nation of brilliant failures, but we are the greatest talkers since the Greeks." A major Dooley theme is the abuse of political speech for selfish ends. Mr. Dooley exposes rhetorical excess on every possible political level: in his own Bridgeport precinct, in Chicago municipal affairs, in the camps of the Irish nationalists, in the 1896 presidential campaign, and in the self-justifying speeches of the apologists for American imperialism in Cuba and the Philippines. Moreover, the determined deflation of the high-falutin is one of Dunne's favorite means of cutting through to the deeper duplicity of character whose exposure is at the core of so many Dooley pieces.

Dunne's love of the language and fascination with its potential come through even more in Mr. Dooley's continual verbal playfulness, more sophisticated, by and large, than that of his fellow American practitioners of dialect humor. There are enough ingenious double-entendres and portmanteau words scattered through the Dooley pieces to warrant at least passing comparison with Joyce, the master wordsmith. "Jackuse," screams Emile Zola at the trial of Captain Dreyfus, "which is a hell of a mane thing to say to anny man." Admiral Dewey cables home from Manila that "at eight o'clock I begun a peaceful blockade iv this town. Ye can see th' pieces ivrywhere," while on the Cuban front "Tiddy Rosenfelt" lays single-handed siege to "Sandago." And when the smoke clears, and President McKinley asks "What shall we do with th' fruits iv victhry?", a voice from the audience answers "Can thim." Meanwhile, in Chicago, a city which rose "felix-like" from the ashes of the 1871 Fire, the river flows backward toward its "sewerce," the German "Turnd'-ye-mind" meets in Schwartzmeister's back room, and Lake Shore millionaires marry to the strains of "th' Wagner Palace Weddin' March fr'm 'Long Green,'" after exchanging vows before "Hyman, which is the Jew god iv marredge."

There are, in addition, sustained flights of wit and linguistic inventiveness in pieces such as Mr. Dooley's paradoxical juxtaposition of the healthful city and the contaminating countryside, or his exposure of military unpreparedness on President McKinley's Strategy Board. One of the very best of these, in which Dunne gives free rein to his verbal imagination, is Mr. Dooley's wild commentary on the use of "expert testimony" in the trial of Chicagoan Adolph Luetgert, accused of murdering his wife and mingling her remains with the raw materials in his sausage factory. (pp. 219-22)

This may be stretching for a point, but I see one other affinity with literary modernism in the ironic perspective of the piece in which Mr. Dooley compares the fallen state of modern Greece (currently besieged by Turkey) to the decline of Bridgeport's "fightin' tenth" precinct. "Leonidas an' th' pass iv Thermometer" are compared to Bridgeport's old-time heroes, most of whom "come fr'm th' ancient Hellenic province iv May-o." The glory that was Bridgeport has faded, having given way to an influx of "Polish Jews an' Swedes an' Germans an' Hollanders," and when "a band iv rovin' Bohemians fr'm th' Eighth Ward" swoops down on the precinct, old Mike Riordan, "th' on'y wan iv th' race iv ancient heroes on earth," stands alone against them; and "if it wasn't f'r th' intervintion iv th' powers in th' shape iv th' loot an' a wagon-load iv polismin, th' Bohemians'd have devastated as far as th' ruins iv th' gashouse, which is th' same as that there Acropulist ye talk about." The Fisher King of Eliot's *The Waste Land* is a similarly incongruous, ironic figure in a similar urban landscape, complete with gashouse.

Dunne's accomplishment can be measured on its own terms also, in the context of Chicago journalism, for a rival Irish dialect series, "Officer Casey on the City Hall Corner," ran in the *Chicago Times-Herald* for five months in 1895. In this series two Irish patrolmen, Casey and "the Connemara cop," discuss Chicago and Irish affairs, concentrating primarily on politics. There is little to compare between them. The Dooley pieces are invariably shorter and more focused than the Casey columns, which often become rambling catalogs of Chicago political names, most of which have little significance now. Casey's dialect is strained and inconsistent, a mixture of forced Irishisms, incongruous slang terms, and overly formal, uncontracted "ing" forms. Most important, where the Dooley pieces begin solidly rooted in Bridgeport and move easily and naturally into general applicability, the typical Casey piece is a static compendium of flat, provincial, dated gossip, and goes nowhere.

One last strength of the Dooley form that must be mentioned here is Dunne's control of his endings. In the satirical pieces, the ending often constitutes a startling ironic reversal that turns over our perspective on the subject at hand. At its best, the effect is abruptly clarifying, as a window shade in a darkened room flips up to let in a shaft of light. Just when Mr. Dooley appears to have been seduced out of a gloomy contemplation of Bridgeport poverty by thoughts of approaching spring, he concludes that "Th' spring's come on. Th' grass is growin' good; an', if th' Connock man's children back iv th' dumps can't get meat, they can eat hay." Similarly, after McKinley's victory in 1896, Dooley overturns John McKenna's sententious moralizing message that "we must all work," by concluding "Yes, . . . or be wurruked." Dunne's touch is equally sure in the best of the dark vignettes, which he often ends with haunting images of solitary suffering: Petey Scanlan's mother sitting with her hoodlum son's first communion picture in her lap; or Fireman Mike Clancy's wife waiting at the door for her husband's body; or old Shaughnessy with his elbows on his knees, staring into the fire on his last daughter's wedding night. In these minor-key tragedies we forget the limitations of the Dooley form and respond directly to the flash of common humanity revealed to us.

The Chicago Dooley pieces need, finally, to be examined in terms of Peter Dunne's contributions in three roles: as a historian, as a literary realist, and as a philosopher.

As to historical interest, . . . [the] Chicago Dooley pieces provide a detailed picture of an Irish-American working-class community caught in the throes of assimilation, a picture which contributes to our understanding of nineteenth-century urban and immigrant life. The pieces also provide for the political historian new perspective on the phenomenon of urban boss rule in America, of which Bridgeport in the nineties was a perfect microcosm. In addition, they give us insight into Irish-American nationalism, a curious, tragicomic passion that has been rekindled in our time by the terrors of the crisis in Ulster. And lastly, Mr. Dooley's treatments of the Spanish-American War and the origins of American imperialism reverberate against our latter-day criticisms of foreign policy and unpopular war. In short, Dunne speaks directly to many of our most salient historical interests.

Dunne's importance to American literature needs to be explained more fully. He has not been given his due as a significant contributor to the realistic movement. In the first place, the Chicago Dooley pieces are part of the realistic reaction against genteel strictures of both language and subject matter. Because they were of real literary merit, they constituted weekly exempla all through the middle nineties of the potential for legitimate literature of the common speech and the common lives of American working-class immigrant city-dwellers. William Dean Howells, realism's champion, partially recognized Dunne's contribution in a 1903 review of "Certain of the Chicago School of Fiction" [see excerpt dated 1903], in which he linked Dunne with George Ade, whose "Fables in Slang" were also attempts to salvage for literature the special languages of city streets. Howells, however, missed some of Mr. Dooley's point, for he called on Dunne to shed his persona and "come into the open with a bold, vigorous and incisive satire of our politicians and their methods." To my knowledge, Dunne has not since been called a literary realist. But he does belong in that company, and in a special position that can be defined in terms of two related concepts: place and community.

Eudora Welty has defined "place in fiction" as "the named, identified, concrete, exact and exacting, and therefore credible, gathering-spot of all that has been felt, is about to be experienced, in the novel's progress." She sees "place being brought to life in the round before the reader's eye" as "the readiest and gentlest and most honest and natural way" to begin to do the writer's job of making "the world of appearance . . . *seem* actuality." Welty further remarks on the "mystery" of place, which lies in "the fact that place has a more lasting identity than we have, and we unswervingly tend to attach ourselves to identity." Also, "the magic" lies "partly too in the *name* of the place—since that is what *we* gave it," thereby putting "a kind of poetic claim on its existence. . . . The truth is," she contends, "fiction depends for its life on place. Location is the crossroads of circumstance, the proving ground of 'What happened? Who's here? Who's coming?'—and that is the heart's field."

As surely as Welty and the other Southern writers, Dunne knew instinctively the value of place. He has located Mr. Dooley in Bridgeport by evoking the "identified, concrete, exact and exacting" details of that neighborhood, and by invoking the magic of names. Mr. Dooley defines all movement in relation to the "r-red bridge," which joins Bridgeport to the rest of Chicago. "Archey Road" is a vivid, realized main street—from Dooley's place to Schwartzmeister's "down the way" to the political capital of Bridgeport at Finucane's Hall. Questions of social status hinge on the proximity of one's home to the gashouse and the rolling mills, and every new person to appear in Mr. Dooley's running conversation is given this defining placement. Finally, the waters of that swampy Chicago River run-off, Haley's Slough, provide a meandering backdrop for nearly every scene. Thus, moving the St. Patrick's Day parade downtown to Michigan Avenue is little less than sacrilege, and the irony is only partial in Mr. Dooley's lament at the takeover by newer immigrant groups of Bridgeport's "sacred sites." One must truly belong somewhere to convey the loving sense of place that comes across in the Dooley pieces; and it is a part of Dunne's accomplishment to have created sketches which convey the feeling of the city as a familiar, potentially comfortable, unthreatening place to live.

It is in this perspective of grounded familiarity that Dunne's Chicago work differs most emphatically from that of the two great American pioneers of urban fiction, Stephen Crane and Theodore Dreiser, neither of whom is ever at home in the city. Beginning with *Maggie: A Girl of the Streets*, his 1893 first novel, Crane observes city life as an explorer; he surveys a strange land for archetypal examples of human fear and suffering. Because he never really lived in the city (except as a bohemian tourist) and because his aim in fiction was "to show that environment is a tremendous thing in the world and frequently shapes lives regardless," Crane cannot present Maggie's New York as a home where real people lead real lives. Either the city remains a static tableau against which Crane works out several acts of his private vision of man as victim of fear and circumstance, or else it comes alive as a malignant force—for example, in the description of Maggie's tenement house as a threatening beast with tenants as devoured victims "stamping about in its bowels." The city is a jungle to Crane, and he imposes this impressionistic, warped perspective on us too; fear, alienation, and helplessness are the only allowable reactions.

The same thing happens in Dreiser's fiction. The Chicago of *Sister Carrie* (1900) is the archetypal city as alien environment. From the beginning to the end of the book, the dominant reaction of downstate villager Carrie Meeber to the city streets is detached fascination—which is to say, they never become familiar to her. Home is the place that Dreiser's American villager leaves behind when moving to the city, and she never finds another. Thus, Carrie's first impression of downtown Chicago as a confusing jumble of "wall-lined mysteries . . . all wonderful, all vast, all far removed" is telling and lasting. She is no closer to New York as she rocks and dreams in a plush apartment above Central Park in the novel's final image. Dreiser's heroine can learn to ignore her sense of the city as an alien organism, by subjugation to mind-dulling routine or, if she is lucky, by escaping into diversion and luxury. But she can never make the city a home. She remains outside.

Both Crane and Dreiser are locked into their private visions of urban man as a stranger in a strange land. Thus, the cities they describe are invariably cold, bleak, and killing to real social life. Community in such settings is impossible. On the other hand, Mr. Dooley's Bridgeport is a real community. The difference is, of course, in point of view: Crane and Dreiser are detached, ironic observers, while Mr. Dooley speaks to us directly, as a committed member of the community he is describing. Crane's admitted purpose in writing *Maggie* was "to show people to people as they seem to me," and both the abstractness of "people" and the impressionism of "me" are revealing. Although the characters of *Maggie* and his related New York City sketches are ostensibly Irish-Americans, Crane makes no attempt to describe them as such; their background meant as little to him as the names of the streets on which they lived, most of which also remain anonymous. But Dunne's purpose was to show Bridgeporters to people as they seem to a fellow Bridgeporter. And so the closest we come to hearing a story like Maggie's is when Mr. Dooley brushes quickly over the moral ruin of old Shaughnessy's first daughter: "She didn't die; but, th' less said, th' sooner mended." Instead of the whole story, we get truth to the Dooley persona. To this end, Dunne musters his sense of place and Irish character and his ear for common speech. The result is unique: the literary evocation of a late nineteenth-century urban ethnic neighborhood where the residents have strong attachments to the place and to one another. Mr. Dooley is one of the first characters in American literature for whom the city is a real home. (pp. 223-28)

We come now to the placement of Mr. Dooley as a philosopher. John Kelleher has called him "a unique invention: the only mythical philosopher I can think of with a philosophy" [see excerpt dated 1946]. And it is true that over the long haul the Chicago Dooley pieces do embody a consistent view of the world—one that, I think, helps to explain two apparently contradictory facts about them: first, that they are still so readable today, and second, that Dunne in effect stopped writing them when he moved on to syndication and New York. The amputation of Mr. Dooley from his life-giving Chicago context was complete by at least 1902, when a survey of "New Humor" for *The Critic* stated that "Mr. Dooley . . . has no place in this list [of humorous creations based on distinctive American character types]. He is not the study of a type,—simply the mouth-piece of his author in the expression of theories on many subjects." Having lost his cultural grounding in Bridgeport, Mr. Dooley still has something to say to us in the later pieces only because of his consistent philosophical stance, which Dunne never abjured. It can be described as a kind of skepticism/relativism, rooted both in the pervasive cultural revolution that Henry May has called "the end of American innocence" and in Dunne's own Irish background.

"American relativism," in May's words, was "a rejection on one ground or another of the mid-nineteenth-century cosmos, the familiar combination of adapted Christianity, science, industrialism, and middle-class mores. In England and America,

the revolt was directed particularly against the world of Herbert Spencer, a world of progress *toward* moral perfection." May describes America's turn-of-the-century relativists as fence-straddlers who had rejected the old simplistic certainties of the Victorian world view without stepping out of the mainstream of nineteenth-century American thought, itself predominantly optimistic. William James defines the type: eminently cheerful, he looked both ways at once, "toward skeptical practicality and even materialism, and also toward an acceptance of the promptings of intuition and faith. . . . Moral to the core, with deep idealistic tendencies, devoted to standard culture though impatient of its stuffier tendencies, progressive above all, James was clearly a part of the surviving nineteenth-century American civilization we have described, and he died just before the crucial phase of its disintegration."

Certainly Dunne was affected by the winds of change described here; on the other hand, he really doesn't belong with May's cheerful questioners because Mr. Dooley's philosophy is shot through with prominent dark veins of cynicism, pessimism, and grim fatality. These can be traced to Dunne's position as the child of an already fragmented culture. His roots are in Ireland and in the experience of immigration; which is to say, in a subject nation whose history has been one long lamentation and in an experience of displacement, prejudice, and alienation. In creating Martin Dooley, Dunne was electing to bring in the minority report of the immigrant Irish, rather than allowing himself to be assimilated into the milder skepticism of the dominant American intellectual frame in his time.

Putting Dunne in an Irish philosophical context also helps to explain why the Chicago Dooley pieces demonstrate Eudora Welty's principle of place, so important to the literary achievement of the great Southern writers. As defeated cultures, Ireland and the American South have much in common. C. Vann Woodward has pointed out that the "irony of Southern history" has been its "thoroughly un-American" preoccupation "with guilt, not with innocence, with the reality of evil, not with the dream of perfection." The tragic experiences of slavery, defeat in civil war, and Reconstruction had kept the South "basically pessimistic in its social outlook and its moral philosophy," even "in that most optimistic of centuries in the most optimistic part of the world." What Woodward says of the South is in large part true of Ireland and of the Irish in America: "It had learned to accommodate itself to conditions that it swore it would never accept, and it had learned the taste left in the mouth by the swallowing of one's own words. It had learned to live for long decades in quite un-American poverty, and it had learned the equally un-American lesson of submission." In both cultures the literary preoccupation with place may be a matter of sanity and survival: when everything else is flying apart, the mind and heart can be steadied by concentration on locality, on named, palpable landmarks. Faulkner's having been able to map his mythical county for Malcolm Cowley is of a piece with Joyce's boast that a stranger could negotiate Dublin with a copy of *Ulysses* as guide.

At any rate, Dunne remains most Irish in his consistently dark perspective. Hamlin Garland came close to describing this quality in declaring that "he had the somber temperament of the Celt. I felt in him a sadness of outlook, a fatalistic philosophy which was curiously at variance with his writing." Of course, Garland was speaking of Dunne's later syndicated work; like the rest of Mr. Dooley's audience in the years of celebrity, he never felt the combined pressure of the many Chicago pieces in which Irish background and philosophical skepticism come together so powerfully. Having now felt that pressure, we can grant Dunne his unique position as a philosophical hyphenate: an Irish-American relativist. (pp. 232-34)

> *Charles Fanning, in his* Finley Peter Dunne & Mr. Dooley: The Chicago Years, *The University Press of Kentucky, 1978, 286 p.*

**JAMES DeMUTH**   (essay date 1980)

[*In the following excerpt, DeMuth examines Mr. Dooley's attitudes, finding their origin in the urban yet highly parochial atmosphere of turn-of-the-century Chicago.*]

The popularity of Dunne's comic Chicago barkeep, Martin Dooley, was due both to the outspoken comments he made and to the familiar mold in which Dunne had cast his character; he was the novel embodiment of the crackerbarrel philosopher. Like such predecessors as Jack Downing, Hosea Biglow, Artemus Ward, and Josh Billings, Mr. Dooley exemplified the pride and self-assurance of a satisfied American villager. But unlike the earlier comic characters whom he closely resembled, Mr. Dooley was not a rustic. His crackerbarrel wisdom expressed the world of a Chicago tavern, and his "village," though as parochial as any New England village or midwestern county seat previously invoked in American popular humor, was the Irish-American Sixth Ward on Chicago's industrialized South Side.

The Sixth Ward, or "Bridgeport," as it was (and still is) more commonly known, was the original settlement of Chicago's Irish, who had come to work on the Illinois and Michigan Canal and had stayed to labor in the mills, foundries, and factories of South Side Chicago. In the preface to his first collection of Mr. Dooley essays, Dunne emphasized for his readers those traditional and unique qualities of Irish culture which distinguished Bridgeport as a community within Chicago:

> In this community you can hear all the various accents of Ireland, from the awkward brogue of the "far-downer" to the mild and airy Elizabethan English of the Southern Irishman, and all the exquisite variations to be heard between Armagh and Bantry Bay, with the difference that would naturally arise from substituting cinders and sulphuretted hydrogen for soft misty air and peat smoke. Here also you can see the wakes and christenings, the marriages and funerals, and the other fetes of the ol' country somewhat modified and darkened by American usage. The Banshee has been heard many times in Archey Road. On the eve of All Saints' Day it is well known that here alone the pookies play thricks in cabbage gardens. In 1893 it was reported that Malachi Dempsey was called "by the other people," and disappeared west of the tracks, and never came back.

(pp. 28-9)

The Chicago experience which had first inspired Dunne to write comic essays in Irish dialect was the World's Columbian Exposition of 1893. In the weeks when preparations for the fair were at their peak, Dunne created Col. McNeery, Mr. Dooley's loquacious predecessor. As Dunne presented him, Col. McNeery was keenly amused with the fair because, as the neoclassic "White City," it stood in ironic contrast to the actual city of its builders. While acknowledging Chicago's stupendous and admirable effort in building the fair, Col. McNeery waggishly noted the realities of life in Chicago which the fair planners could not adequately disguise. The fair was broadly and en-

thusiastically advertised as Chicago's cultural debut; Col. McNeery, however, unerringly perceived the coarsened features of mercantile Chicago beneath the new, ill-fitting fancy dress: "Divvle a word about pothry," he dourly concluded after attending the fair's premier "Lithry Congress." "It was like a meetin' iv th' Bricklayer's Union, it was, so it was, with all th' talk about how th' dirty old book publishers was thrown it into th' poor potes an' grindin' thim down in th' ground."

Just as the "Lithry Congress" convinced Col. McNeery that the World's Fair would not produce Chicago poets where none had been before, a meeting of the "Lady Managers" left him skeptical about the fair's lasting contribution to the movement for women's rights. As Col. McNeery reports this meeting, Chicago's women, notably the committee's chairwoman, Mrs. Potter Palmer, are woefully unsuited for managerial responsibility. The meeting of these newly enfranchised women delegates quickly degenerates into a peevish dispute, replete with tears, between "the 'Naypoltan' ice-crame woman and the 'tooty-frooty' Lady Manager":

> "Who'se old?" says th' old lady. "Ye minx," says she. "Ye'er a dishturber iv th' peace," she says. "Set down," says all th' ladies that do be on th' side iv th' Naypoltan ice-crame lady, an' "Thrun her out," says all them that's with th' lady with th' white hair. "Ladies," says Mrs. Pammer. "Ordher," she says, wallopin' th' table with a fan. "Will ye set down," says th' white-haired wan. "Niver," says th' Naypoltan ice-crame wan, "till I gets me rights, an' whin I gets home," she says, "I'll be tillin' me husband—boo-hoo," says she, cryin' "what a horrid way I've been threated."

Broad burlesques of suffragettes, poets, scholars, and other unconventional people reassured Col. McNeery's readers that Chicago was securely immune from the artistic and social renaissance advertised by the promoters of the World's Fair. (pp. 31-2)

For Mr. Dooley and his neighbors on Archey Road, the Midway was the World's Fair's significant legacy. The literary congresses, women's committees, learned symposiums, and grandiose buildings were all ridiculously foreign to their lives, and the many exhibits celebrating the progress of mechanical science were too uncomfortably close:

> a wurruld's fair is no rollin'-mills. If it was, ye'd be paid f'r goin' there. 'Tis not th' rollin'-mills an' 'tis not a school or a machine-shop or a grocery store. 'Tis a big circus with manny rings an' that's what it ought to be.

On the Midway, away from the stately order of boulevards, temples, and vistas, the common folk from Bridgeport—"thim that was n't annybody"—could relax and enjoy themselves. There they were not edified, patronized, or threatened; they were simply entertained.

The contrast between the vital Midway and the stultifying fair is broadly analogous, in the Mr. Dooley essays, to the general contrast Dunne draws between Bridgeport and Chicago. In Bridgeport, the Irish-Americans had evolved a relaxed, satisfying and tolerant social life which Protestant, Republican Chicagoans tried repeatedly to reform and uplift. The inviting quality of Bridgeport's social life is perhaps best illustrated by the balance its citizens comfortably maintain between their saloons and their church. They see this balance as natural and necessary for a healthy society; "Father Kelly," Mr. Dooley's pastor, frequently visits Dooley's saloon, and even in his absence the men in the saloon often discuss the social activities of their religious fraternities. This easy accommodation, though, offends the moral sensibilities of reform-minded Chicagoans. In their opposition to the alien culture of the immigrant, as it is represented in the Mr. Dooley essays, they reveal, ironically, their own contempt for the civil liberty and democratic equality essential to the American way of life which they purport to defend:

> Th' rayformer . . . thinks you an' me, Hinnissy, has been watchin' his spotless career f'r twenty years, that we've read all he had to say on th' evils iv' pop'lar suffrage befure th' society f'r th' Bewilderment iv th' Poor, an' that we're achin' in ivry joint to have him dhrag us be th' hair iv th' head fr'm th' flowin' bowl an' th' short card game, make good citizens iv us an' sind us to th' pinitinchry. So th' minyit he gets into th' job he begins a furyous attimpt to convart us into what we've been thryin' not to be iver since we come into th' wurruld. . . . His motto is "Arrest that man."

The threats to Bridgeport's social equanimity come not only from the crusades of Chicago's self-righteous reformers, but also, and more insidiously, from the frivolous fashions of Chicago's urban sophisticates. One strange mode after another is born in Chicago, but nearly all are squelched in the Sixth Ward. Bloomers and bicycles were particularly conspicuous examples of Chicago's strange modes. In one Mr. Dooley essay, Molly Donahue begins riding a bicycle and wearing bloomers, to the shame of her family and outrage of her neighbors. Her odd behavior, though, is easily suppressed by Father Kelly. The worldly-wise priest simply observes, in complimenting Molly on her attractive bloomers, that he had never before known that she had bowed legs.

There are many other comic incidents in which the Irish-American ward confidently deflects the modern challenges to its traditional life. The "Univarsity Settlement," particularly, is frequently ridiculed as a source of patently absurd ideas and values:

> "Th' question befure th' house is whin is a lie not a lie?" said Mr. Dooley. "How's that?" asked Mr. Hennessy. "Well," said Mr. Dooley, "here's Professor E. Bimjamin Something-or-Other insthructin' th' youth at th' Chicago Univarsity that a lie, if it's f'r a good purpose, is not a lie at all. There's th' grreat school down there on the Midway. Ye can larn anything ye have a mind to in that there siminary an' now they'll have a coorse in lyin."

By confidently ridiculing the strange ideas of the University of Chicago or the curious fashions of high society, Mr. Dooley warmly affirmed, for Chicago's ordinary citizens, the contemporary relevance of their commonsense, conventional tastes and orthodox morality. It is no surprise, then, that he enjoyed immediate and enduring popularity from Chicago newspaper readers and, later, the broad audience of his nationally syndicated newspaper columns and nationally distributed books.

Mr. Dooley's blithe confidence in his ward's resiliency could, though, be shaken. The violent criminality of "Petey Scanlan," eldest son of a pious, sober Irish-American family, for example, prompts Mr. Dooley to remark, with uncharacteristic resignation, "Sometimes I think they'se poison in th' life iv a big city." Or, on another occasion, the desperate suicide of "Timothy Grogan," an unemployed meat packer, and the degrading poverty into which his widow and children are thrown, spur Mr. Dooley to bitter denunciations of Philip Armour and his co-conspirators in the "beef thrust." But these denunciations are infrequent. Far more often, Mr. Dooley views Chicago with genial tolerance, tempering his satire of unconventional Chicagoans with broad reassurances to the many ordinary Chicagoans who resembled his neighbors in Bridgeport. In the 1930s, a far different time from the 1890s Chicago of Mr. Dooley, Dunne looked back, nostalgically, to the Chicago he had known to observe that "humor, especially political humor, is a privilege of the innocent and secure."

Dunne perceived innocence and security as the normal conditions of American life at the turn of the century. In the comic essays he wrote, these qualities were most evident in the intimate neighborliness of Bridgeport, but they were also characteristic of the general culture of Chicago. Though he represents Bridgeport as a distinct community within Chicago, it is not a separate, isolated society. For Dunne, the Irish immigrants had found in Chicago the opportunities to build a community which had been denied them in Ireland as the impoverished tenants of landlords. He often contrasts the degradation the Irish had suffered in Ireland with the security and dignity they discovered as Americans. Most frequently he satirizes those exceptional Americans who envy the Old World privileges of Irish landlords and British imperialists. (pp. 33-6)

Unlike the other topics on which Mr. Dooley commented, politics allowed no easy contrast between provincial Bridgeport and urban Chicago; in politics, Brideport was inextricably welded to Chicago. The ward's politicians were conspicuous figures in the general and persistent corruption of Chicago's political life. As a property owner and "member of the onforchnit middle class," Mr. Dooley dispassionately observed Chicago's tangled political web and followed its various strands of culpability to their sources in the downtown council chambers and in his own ward's back rooms.

The most significant political contest for the straight-ticket Democrats of Bridgeport was the biennial aldermanic race; as Mr. Dooley wryly noted, "Out here we have to pay thim two dollars apiece at important ilictions f'r aldhermen an' wan dollar whin some minor office like prisident is bein' ilicted." Chicago's aldermen, particularly those representing the immigrant wards, had been publicly criticized for many years for their open and persistent corruption. They had connived with the various business interests seeking public contracts, most notably the streetcar entrepreneur Charles Yerkes, to sell out Chicago's eminent domain for a pittance. "Sandbagging" was their favorite method of reaping personal profit from public business. Whenever a Chicago business sought an economic privilege from the council, the "grey wolves," as the corrupt aldermen were known, would organize a rival company and award the desired privilege to it. This maneuver forced the legitimate company to buy out the council's paper corporation at great profit to the incorporators. By these flagrant means, the city council had bankrupted Chicago's treasury and, through long-term, low-rent leases, had forfeited the city's political authority for decades to come.

Despite repeated calls for reform, the grey wolves kept returning to their lair; they served a legitimate political need. For the poor and immigrant wards, which they represented, political reform held little appeal. Under civil service reform, to choose the most striking example, the poor and ill-educated could never compete for public jobs. But, with a corruptible alderman to bargain for them, they might expect to win a place on the public payroll or a job with a company which was courting the alderman's favor; as "Bathhouse John" Coughlin, alderman from Chicago's notorious Levee, arrogantly explained: "You know, if you ain't a lunkhead, that in wards where the poor have the cinch, next to the priest, the alderman is their guardian angel."

Bridgeport's alderman, in life and in the Mr. Dooley essays, was William J. O'Brien. Mr. Dooley viewed "Willum J." with tolerant respect. And through Mr. Dooley, Finley Peter Dunne educated Chicagoans in the political obligations which Alderman O'Brien diligently fulfilled. In one essay, "On Oratory in Politics," Mr. Dooley illustrates Alderman O'Brien's political function by contrasting him with a high-minded, enthusiastic, and confident reformer. "I'll not re-sort," the reform candidate naively pledges, "to th' ordin'ry methods." "Th' thing to do," he says, "is to prisint th' issues iv th' day to th' voters. I'll burn up ivry precin't in th' ward with me iloquince." (pp. 39-40)

William J. O'Brien does not try to reform his ward; he accepts it, demonstrates his loyalty by attending its picnics, dances, and church fairs; he then works, with what political power he can muster, to sustain his neighbors with jobs, pocket money, and favors. At the campaign's conclusion, he consoles the defeated reformer with this political advice: "Whin ye've been in politics as long as I have, ye'll know,' he says, 'that th' roly-boly is th' gr-reatest or-rator on earth,' he says." (pp. 40-1)

For Dunne, the immigrant wards had developed political techniques appropriate to their needs. In his editorials and in his Mr. Dooley essays, Dunne did not indict Irish-Americans in his criticism of their aldermen. The immigrant ward shared in the alderman's "roly-boly," but it did not provide his funds; aldermen, Mr. Dooley often reminds his readers, were bought downtown.

While defending the rough political accommodations which Chicago's immigrants had made, Mr. Dooley repeatedly drew attention to the real culprit responsible for Chicago's impoverished civic life: the privilege-seeking businessman. The moral issue in the corruption of Chicago's politicians by Chicago's "responsible" businessmen is perhaps best drawn in Dunne's parable of "Martin Dochney":

> 'Tis not Hinnissy, that this man Yerkuss goes up to an aldherman an' says out sthraight, "Here Bill, take this bundle, an' be an infamyous scoundhrel." That's th' way th' man in Mitchigan Avnoo sees it, but 'tis not sthraight. D'ye mind Dochney that was wanst aldherman here?

Martin Dochney, Mr. Dooley explains, was a small contractor on Halsted Street, "an honest an' sober man" and very popular in the ward. In his first days on the city council, he is asked to support a "sandbag" ordinance. When offered a bribe of five thousand dollars, he angrily assaults his tempter. The next day, though, a close friend seeks him out to again recommend the ordinance.

> "'Tis a plain swindle," Dochney protests. "'Tis a good thing f'r th' comp'nies," his friend replies, "but look what they've done f'r th' city," he says, "an' think," he says, "iv th' widdies an' orphans," he says, "that has their har-rd earned coin invisted."

That night Alderman Dochney ponders the relation between his five-thousand-dollar bribe and Chicago's deserving widows and orphans. The money would pay his mortgage and the debt on his new contract. It would buy a new dress for Mrs. Dochney, and besides, he rationalizes, the ordinance will obviously benefit widows and orphans:

> "No wan'd be hurted, anyhow," he says; "an', sure, it ain't a bribe f'r to take money f'r doin' something ye want to do, annyhow," he says. "Five thousan' widdies an' orphans," he says, an' he wint to sleep.

The next day, Alderman Dochney calls on his banker to renew the notes on his outstanding contract. The banker warmly recommends the pending ordinance and implies that Dochney's affirmative vote will satisfy his debt. Dochney votes for the ordinance and continues in his political career to become a notorious council grey wolf. At the parable's end, Dunne points the moral of the ward's innocence and Chicago businessmen's guilt in the corruption of Alderman Dochney: "He was expelled fr'm th' St. Vincent de Pauls, an' ilicted a director iv a bank th' same day."

To Mr. Dooley, the crowning irony of Chicago's political life was the identification of reform politics with business methods and ethics: "When a rayformer is ilicted he promises ye a business administhration. Some people want that but I don't." A politician, Mr. Dooley reminds us, usually understands his obligation to serve the immediate needs of his constituents; he may not fulfill this responsibility, but he is aware of it. A businessman, though, in Mr. Dooley's simple contrast, is obliged only to the specific demands of his individual economic interest; serving the dollar, he cannot serve the people. . . . Though Mr. Dooley often contrasted politicians and businessmen, he did not exempt politicians, or any class of Americans, from the criticism he regularly leveled against businessmen. His criticism of businessmen is frequent and sharp; they often exemplify, in their selfish materialism, moral hypocrisy, and social irresponsibility, the distortion of the democratic spirit which should, ideally, distinguish America as a nation. When Mr. Dooley criticizes other classes of Americans, especially politicians, he criticizes them for emulating or even for tolerating the alien class consciousness of America's new plutocrats. Thus he regularly condemns the war policy of President McKinley ("Mack th' Wanst, or Twict, iv th' United States an' Sulu") for promoting class elitism as a national principle:

> "In our former war," he [McKinley] says, "we had th' misfortune to have men in command that didn't know th' diff'rence between a goluf stick an' a beecycle; an' what was th' raysult; We foozled our approach at Bull R-run," he says. "Ar-re ye a mimber iv anny clubs?" he says. "Four," says Willie. "Thin I make ye a major," he says. "Where d'ye get ye're pants?" he says. "F'rm England," says Willie. "Gloryous," says McKinley. "I make ye a colonel," he says. . . . "Thank Gawd, th' r-rich," he says, "is brave an' pathriotic," he says.

With similar broad lampoons of public figures like President McKinley, Dunne vigorously affirmed, for two decades, the contemporary relevance of his traditional, crackerbarrel humor. In assessing his political satire, one must conclude that his conscious restoration of such a traditional comic style was commercially successful and artistically advantageous. It allowed him a coherent, familiar moral standard by which to confidently and persuasively measure the men, events, and ideas of his time. By invoking Mr. Dooley's conventional wisdom, Dunne could easily isolate and ridicule those attitudes, ambitions, and principles which were alien to accepted American traditions. He could, for example, decisively separate the imperial ambitions of America's war leaders in the Spanish-American War from the commonplace, domestic concerns of Bridgeport's workers and merchants, or he could sharply contrast the exceptional "public-be-damned" arrogance of some

American industrialists and financiers with the ordinary ethical habits expected of Bridgeport's Catholics. By characterizing Bridgeport as a village and Mr. Dooley as its crackerbarrel philosopher, Dunne recovered for his urban audience the familiar values of American tradition: economic self-reliance, informal neighborliness, honest, blunt expression, simple religious faith, and firm community loyalty. Dunne's affirmation of these traditional virtues seemed especially relevant to his time because Mr. Dooley was an immigrant; the Irish barkeep's orthodox patriotism and conventional social attitudes were not the mere residue of habit. They were, rather, the conscious choices of a mature adult.

However, though immediately successful, Dunne's efforts to conserve a traditional comic style were not long sustained. By defining Mr. Dooley as an elderly, opinionated village moralist, Dunne restricted him to social attitudes which became increasingly archaic and eccentric. Mr. Dooley was an independent neighborhood merchant who believed that the bonds of personal obligations, family affiliations, political loyalties, and friendships were sufficient to preserve the economic and social order of his small community. As the urban economy became more large-scaled and technologically sophisticated, and as citizens of cities, towns, and farms became, or aspired to become, more mobile in seeking educational and vocational opportunities, Mr. Dooley's modest social vision of the stable, multigenerational community became less relevant. (pp. 41-5)

> James DeMuth, "Finley Peter Dunne," in his Small Town Chicago: The Comic Perspective of Finley Peter Dunne, George Ade, Ring Lardner, *Kennikat Press, 1980, pp. 24-45.*

## GRACE ECKLEY (essay date 1981)

*[In the following excerpt, Eckley discusses the structure and content of the Dooley essays.]*

The thirty-odd years which span the Dooley essays brought into existence exciting developments for the future: in 1893 Karl Friedrich Benz and Henry Ford built motor cars; in 1895 Wilhelm Röntgen discovered X-rays, Marconi invented the radiotelegraph, Auguste and Louis Lumière invented the movie camera, H. G. Wells wrote *The Time Machine,* and Sigmund Freud and Josef Breuer wrote *Studies in Hysteria;* in 1896 Antoine Henri Becquerel discovered radioactivity in uranium; and in 1897 Joseph John Thomson discovered the electron; in 1898 Wells wrote *War of the Worlds;* in 1903 the Wright brothers made the first powered flight; in 1905 Albert Einstein published the "Special Theory of Relativity"; in 1907 Henri Bergson published his *Creative Evolution,* and Ivan Pavlov made his famous studies in conditioned reflex; in 1912 Victor Franz discovered cosmic rays; among 1913's several scientific developments, Niels Henrik Bohr presented his theory of atomic structure, and Hans Geiger developed his radium counter; in 1914 Robert Hutchins Goddard began his rocket experiments, and the first open-heart surgery on a dog was performed by Alexis Carrel; in 1917 Carl Jung published his *Psychology of the Unconscious.*

During this period also occurred the sinking of the *Titanic* (1912), the discovery of the Piltdown man (also 1912 but not proved a hoax until 1953), and the opening of the Panama Canal in 1914, the same year as the beginning of World War I. The Constitution was amended radically four times, with Articles 16 through 19 establishing the income tax, prohibition, and women's suffrage. In the decade of the twenties, the first commercial radio station was opened, simultaneously with the invention of television (1920), Tutankhamen's tomb was discovered (1922), Joseph Stalin rose to power (1924), the Scopes Trial on evolution began in Tennessee (1925), and Robert Goddard flew the first liquid-fuel rocket (1926). Dunne stopped writing just before Charles Lindbergh flew across the Atlantic Ocean (1927).

Into this kind of perspective must be placed Dunne's "Mr. Dooley" essays, especially as they recorded the social—even more so than the scientific—impact of these developments. The era of rapid change was inaugurated with the Chicago Fair, or the World Columbian Exhibition, as it was formally known (1893); Dunne wrote "On the Midway" to express for many the opportunities presented by this and succeeding spectacles of similar nature. The people react, predictably, with as much skepticism, indifference, and boredom as awe. Dooley says, for example, "Th' printin'-press isn't wondherful. What's wondherful is that annybody shud want it to go on doin' what it does." Sturdy qualities of independence, ego, and self-preservation act as strong bumpers against "future shock."

On the subject of progress in general Dunne wrote "Machinery," but the saving grace of this and other essays—once more—is that Mr. Dooley maintains his usual reductionism and skepticism; for the saving of mankind will be in its refusal to be overwhelmed. Moreover, Dunne could recognize how quickly the opening statement, "Niver befure in th' histhry iv th' wurruld has such pro-gress been made," can become exceedingly trite. At the ordinary human level, Mr. Dooley finds "a taste iv solder in th' peaches," though they were scientifically improved; and he knows that science has done little to improve him: "amidst all these granjoors here am I th' same ol' antiquated combination iv bellows an' pump I always was. Not so good. Time has worn me out. Th' years like little boys with jackknives has carved their names in me top. Ivry day I have to write off something f'r deprecyation." To sum it up, he says, "Mechanical science has done ivrything f'r me but help me." He lists several remarkable developments and the fate of the developers which their ingenuity did not forestall. Extending the discoveries to union with matters of the cosmos, Mr. Hennessy wants to know what Dooley thinks of the man who has announced himself and the Lord as partners in a coal mine. Dooley asks, "Has he divided th' profits?"

On the other hand, social progress seemed always to continue its rearward trek, and many magazines and newspapers made their livings by intentionally alarming the public. The title of Dunne's essay, "National Housecleaning," parodies *Good Housekeeping* magazine, and the essay accents our puritanic instincts to root out faults. By contrast, Dooley says, "A Frinchman or an Englishman cleans house be sprinklin' th' walls with cologne; we chop a hole in th' flure an' pour in a kag iv chloride iv lime."

As for theories of the construction of the universe, Mr. Dooley in "The Intellectual Life" rendered his verdict: "I dismiss with a loud laugh th' theory that [the world] was created in six days. I cud make such a poor wurruld as this in two days with a scroll saw. Akelly preposterous is th' idee that it wasn't made at all, but grew up out iv nawthin'. Me idee is that th' wurruld is a chunk iv th' sun that was chipped off be a collisyon with th' moon, cooled down, an' advertised f'r roomers. As to its age, I differ with th' Bible. Me own opinyon iv th' age iv th' arth is that it is about twenty-eight years old. That is as far as I go back." The same topic could appear in an unexpected place. Writing on the American stage, Dunne listed several possibilities of works for adaptations to drama. All are extremely entertaining Dooley witticisms, among which he expects soon the bible "undher th' direction iv Einstein an' Opperman."

With allusion to George Ade, Mr. Dooley calls a newspaper article "On the Descent of Man" a "fable in slang," his term for scientific language. Dooley says he always knew that man is better than the other animals because of what is in his head. Darwin came along and "made a monkey iv man," showing that we have lost our tails in the bamboo trees "where our fam'ly had spint so many happy millyons iv years," from which we came down to earth to be men. Having lost his tail, our ancestor lost at once "his manes iv rapid thransit an' his aisy chair," and the "old gintleman" had to go to work. Monkeys have been laughing at people ever since. But Dooley sees the descent theory as an improvement over the earlier idea that man is "a fallin' off fr'm th' angels." Another theory that man has descended from the jumping shrew he finds insulting to the earlier ancestors, such as the lobster, the oyster, the jelly fish, all the way back to the microbe, "an' before that th' viggytables, an' befure thim th' mud at th' bottom iv th' sea."

Dunne continued this topic in 1926, when Mr. Dooley announced that the Scopes trial had "found Darwin guilty, an' voted to hang him th' nex' time he set foot in Chattanooga." He recognizes in Darwin a superiority over contemporary scientists, for Darwin at least wrote "'mebbe' or 'p'raps' afther ivry line." Of the transfers among species, he explains, "Life was more promiscus in thim days thin it is now, an' it was a wise boa consthrictor that knew its own father." He learns now that the body is mostly water and that "Hootch an' hormones makes life what it is." The descent from the Cro-Magnon man means a terrible drop "to th' lower ordher iv mammals an' invertebrates that infest th' Capitol at Wash'nton at prisint."

Spiritism as a science, as distinguished from spiritualism as a religion, began with the rappings of the Fox sisters in Hydesville, New York, in 1848. It spread to England, where, in 1882, the Society for Psychical Research was founded with a similar society founded in 1885 in the United States. The society in Europe enrolled many members famous in literature and science, including William James, Henri Bergson, Gilbert Murray, and Camille Flammarion. The American society's motto was Gladstone's statement: "Psychical research is the most important work which is being done in the world—by far the most important." These developments, too, Dunne took into account in "Things Spiritual," which evidences a great deal of knowledge. He begins with the discovery of the weight of the human soul and uses it as his theme, knowing that people would fear for their own esteem to have their souls weighed. Without naming Bergsonian time, he comments on it, saying that "Scales an' clocks ar-re not to be thrusted to decide annything that's worth deciding." He discusses himself in terms of multiple identities, saying "to me I'm a millyon Dooleys an' all iv thim sthrangers to ME," and in this refers to ideas publicly prominent from such works as Madame H. P. Blavatsky's *Secret Doctrine* (1888), in explanation of the Linga-Sharîri of Hindu philosophy, and in P. D. Ouspensky's *Tertium Organum* (1912). The astronomer Percival Lowell had published *Mars and its Canals* (1906), and Dooley explains faith by citing the discoveries of Columbus and Lowell. He ends the discussion by recognizing the psychic phenomena of ghosts and of telepathy, with the latter known to him through a Spiritualist friend.

Anything threatening in the environment Dooley could reduce to terms by which people could handle it; anything remote he brought near, making the affairs of the world the affairs of Archey Road. His topics ranged from the far past in such Greek heroes as Miltiades, into the nineteenth century in his Irish origins, and into the immediate past in essays such as "Times Past" and "A Winter's Night," both of which can be read for sheer nostalgia. The latter begins like a novel set in the 1890s: "Any of the Archey Road cars that got out of the barns at all were pulled by teams of four horses, and the snow hung over the shoulders of the drivers' big bearskin coats like the eaves of an old-fashioned house on the blizzard night." "Times Past" recalls now-outlawed election tactics—the use of force, the stuffed ballot box, the withholding of votes for the opposition (in this case the feeding of Schwartzmeister's ballots to Dorsey's goat), and the rise and fall in local politics of one friend who quickly becomes a former friend.

The structure of the essays reveals why Dunne never succeeded in a sometimes-tendered ambition to write a novel or a play; for the qualities of both those art forms, and to a certain extent, their techniques, appear in random selections. One other type of art Dunne essayed, for which he seems to have been given no recognition by critics, is the tall story. "The Great Hot Spell," in great purity of form, is a tall story. Throughout the essays, the use of dialect varies, its inconsistency perhaps reflecting typesetters' difficulties as much as Dunne's lack of commitment to it. *Haut finance*, for example, appears as "hawt finance" in one essay and as "ho finance" in another. Dunne's careful use of the subjunctive in the midst of dialect—not the impossibility of Dooley's knowing about a particular person or topic—betrays Dooley's origins in the mind of a master of language.

The structure of the essays can be seen, generally, to move through several distinct stages: (1) a "generating circumstance," in which an item in the newspaper or a comment by Hennessy begins the discussion; (2) Dooley's monologue, beginning with opposing views of a given issue presented with heavy irony so that blind prejudices are exposed as ignorant while sounding intelligent or at least popular; (3) a "reversal," in which Dooley continues the monologue but his own moderate view emerges; (4) a conclusion in which Mr. Hennessy confirms, rejects, or moderates as necessary. Often, especially in the example of a national or international issue, the "reversal" turns the discussion to a personal example in Dooley's memory and/or on Archey Road. In the conclusion, Hennessy offers a comment in the form of a brief penultimate paragraph, usually composed of a single sentence. Dooley then makes the last comment in the last paragraph, also extremely brief; and this last comment acts as a "punch line." The epigrammatic nature of the conclusion has rendered many of these popular for quotation, but the epigrams may actually occur in any part of the essay. Throughout the several hundred essays, Dooley specializes in imaginative flights with lists of exaggerated examples of human fallacies. (pp. 142-47)

Readers of James Joyce (1882-1941) will recognize in Dunne's work several constructions which have become better known as Joycean. In Joyce's *Ulysses* (1922), for example, Leopold Bloom puns on "poached eggs on toast" when he remarks of Howard Parnell, "Poached eyes on ghost"; but Dooley said it first, when Dunne was writing about microbes "with eyes like pooched eggs." Joyce had his Stephen Dedalus look at the mystic poet A. E. (George Russell), remember that he owed A. E. some money, and think "A.E.I.O.U."; but Dooley had earlier described an aged millionaire approaching Newport in his yacht, inquiring, "An' is that where Mr. A.E.I.O.U. an' sometimes W. an' Y. Belcoort lives an' has his bein'?" Dunne and Joyce draw upon a background in Irish folklore which makes several details the property of the people, and not any writer exclusively, for example, turning a picture to the wall or using a potato cure against rheumatism (which Joyce used in place of the magical herb "moly" in *Ulysses*). Dunne was fond of turning king's titles into Dooley's dialect, so that he spoke of Cousin George as "Dooley the Wanst"; and on his return from Ireland Dunne wrote "Americans Abroad," saying that William Waldorf Astor, in his applying for British citizenship, had "renounced fealty to all foreign sovereigns, princes an' potentates an' especially Mack th' Wanst, or Twict [should McKinley be elected to a second term as president], iv th' United States an' Sulu an' all his wur-ruks." Joyce adapted Mack the Wanst to his Mark, referring to him, for example, as "Moke the Wanst."

The most striking comparison between Dunne and Joyce, however, concerns the use of language, for Dunne's bilingual puns provide excellent background for Joyce's multilingual puns; what Walter Blair called "Dooleymorphisms" [see excerpt dated 1942] occasionally call to mind Joyce's verbal polymorphisms and portmanteau words. Perhaps the best of these occurs in "Insanity as a Defense." Here the doctor testifies, "He suffered fr'm warts whin a boy, which sometimes leads to bozimbral hoptocoliographophilloplutomania or what th' Germans call tantrums."

Joyce was interested in pairs of opposites, of which Dooley and Hennessy provide an excellent example; and he introduced the two of them into *Finnegans Wake* in the Wellington episode in which he refers, as did Mr. Dooley, to the reputed saying of the Duke of Wellington about the playing fields of Eton. In this scene, the old woman Kate as janitrix and guide conducts visitors through a museum and points out pictures of the Battle of Waterloo and other Wellington memorabilia hung on the walls: She says, "This is hiena hinnessy laughing alout at the Willingdone. This is lipsyg dooley krieging the funk from the hinnessy. This is the hinndoo Shimar Shin between the dooley boy and the hinnessy."

Joyce was still in Dublin when Dunne visited there in 1899 and must have read reports of Dunne's visit, of which Elmer Ellis writes, "His reputation had preceded him there, and at his hotel in Dublin reporters called to see Mr. Dooley. To one who asked how Mr. Dooley liked Ireland, Dunne replied: 'You may say Mr. Dooley felt at home when he arrived in Dublin for the first time since he left Chicago.'"

There is evidence that Joyce continued to read Dunne's work. The war in Europe put Joyce on the defensive for his pacifism and he left Austrian Trieste in 1915 to go to neutral Switzerland; he wrote his irritation with the war into a poem called "Dooleysprudence," a parody of the "Mr. Dooley Song," in which he declared his opposition [see excerpt dated 1916]. Among several approximations to Dooley's work, Joyce's fifth stanza, for example, begins,

> Who is the man who says he'll go the whole and perfect hog
> Before he pays the income tax or licence for a dog,

and reflects details from Dunne's essay "The Bachelor Tax," which appeared in *Mr. Dooley Says*.

Joyce's attention to Dunne gives Dunne just one more kind of immortality, as evidenced in the next stage of the Dooley-Dooleysprudence history. The two poems were revived on Broadway in 1975 in the award-winning play *Travesties* by Tom Stoppard, in which Joyce as a character in the play recites twenty-two lines from his poem, introducing it as "my version of Mr. Dooley." (pp. 148-50)

The test of all great writing may well be its prophetic qualities, and certainly much of Dunne's work has this quality. Philip Dunne, when collecting his father's memoirs in 1962, asked to be permitted to believe that "if Mr. Dooley had been lurking in ambush, piece loaded and cocked, Mr. Nixon wouldn't have made his 'Checkers' speech at all. Such power, indeed, had the Irish bards who sat next to the king and kept him in check with the threat of their satire. The breakdown of amenities after President Carter's Camp David agreement between the Israelis and the Arabs underscores once more the truth of Dunne's essay on "International Amenities": "Unforchunitly diplomacy on'y goes as far as the dure. It is onable to give protection to th' customer, so whin he laves th' shop th' sthrong arm men iv th' Sinit knocks him down an' takes fr'm him ivrything he got inside an' more too." Discussing the modern explosive lyddite, Dooley predicted much of what became in its destruction of defenseless citizens, a reality with the atomic bomb: "I can see in me mind th' day whin explosives'll be so explosive an' guns'll shoot so far that on'y th' folks that stay at home'll be kilt, an' life insurance agents'll be advisin' people to go into th' ar-rmy."

The endurance, as well as the prophetic qualities, of the essays springs from the similarity in human existence throughout the fleeting decades. The problems remain the same; only the customs and manners change—and even those not very much. (p. 151)

> *Grace Eckley, in her* Finley Peter Dunne, *Twayne Publishers, 1981, 173 p.*

## ADDITIONAL BIBLIOGRAPHY

Bander, Edward J. *Mr. Dooley and Mr. Dunne: The Literary Life of a Chicago Catholic*. Charlottesville, Va.: Michie, 1981, 321 p.
    Demonstrates Dunne's journalistic intentions through analysis of significant quotes from the Dooley essays.

Cosgrove, Cornelius. "Mr. Dooley and the Reformers." *American History Illustrated* VI, No. 6 (October 1971): 23-30.
    Discusses Dunne's ambivalent attitude toward political reform and his involvement in several major political controversies.

Filler, Louis. "The First Muckraker." In his *Crusaders for American Liberalism*, pp. 55-67. Yellow Springs, Ohio: Antioch Press, 1939.
    Describes Dunne's contributions to turn-of-the century muckraking journalism.

Foster, Roy. "The Punditry of Mr. Dooley." *The Times Literary Supplement*, No. 4904 (18 September 1981): 1056.
    Assesses Mr. Dooley's importance in the development of American satirical writing.

Gibson, William M. "TR and Finley Peter Dunne, 'Mr. Dooley'." In his *Theodore Roosevelt among the Humorists*, pp. 43-65. Knoxville: University of Tennessee Press, 1980.

Traces the evolution of Dunne's attitude toward the Roosevelt presidency.

Harrison, John M. "Finley Peter Dunne and the Progressive Movement." *Journalism Quarterly* 44, No. 3 (Autumn 1967): 475-81.
Maintains that the Dooley essays manifest Dunne's "moderate progressivism."

Mann, Georg. "Call for Mr. Dooley." *Eire-Ireland* IX, No. 3 (Autumn 1974): 119-27.
Biographical essay in which Mann calls for a revival of satirical writing in the style of the Dooley essays.

Masson, Thomas L. "Finley Peter Dunne." In his *Our American Humorists*, pp. 110-19. 1931. Reprint. Freeport, N.Y.: Books for Libraries Press, 1966.
Reprints quotes from the Dooley essays to demonstrate Dunne's comic excellence.

Pattee, Fred Lewis. "The Decade of Strenuous Life, 1901-1909." In his *The New American Literature, 1890-1930*, pp. 103-20. New York: Cooper Square, 1968.
Considers the satire of the Dooley articles highly topical and too closely linked to the era to remain popular.

Shannon, William V. "The Changing Image." In his *The American Irish*, pp. 131-50. New York: Macmillan, 1963.

Considers the attitudes expressed in the Dooley essays as a transition between condemnation and acceptance of Irish immigrants in America.

"A New American Satirist." *The Spectator* 82, No. 3689 (11 March 1899): 344-45.
Review of *Mr. Dooley in Peace and War* in which the critic commends Dunne's wit but notes that "he omits, with the solitary exception of Admiral Dewey, to say a good word where good words are due."

"Mr. Dooley." *The Spectator* 105, No. 4299 (19 November 1910): 862-63.
Positive review of *Mr. Dooley Says*, quoting "enough to show that Mr. Dooley is in as good form as ever."

Thogmartin, Clyde. "Mr. Dooley's Brogue: The Literary Dialect of Finley Peter Dunne." *Visible Language* XVI, No. 2 (Spring 1982): 184-98.
Analysis of dialect in the Dooley essays. Thogmartin contends that Mr. Dooley's dialect is "an accurate representation of certain features of Anglo-Irish speech" and that "the Mr. Dooley pieces obtain a particular force and authenticity from being written in Anglo-Irish dialect."

Way, W. Irving. "Mr. Martin Dooley of Chicago." *The Bookman* LX (May 1899): 215-19.
Biographical sketch outlining the genesis of the Dooley articles.

# F(rancis) Scott (Key) Fitzgerald

## 1896-1940

American novelist, short story writer, essayist, screenwriter, and dramatist.

The following entry presents criticism of Fitzgerald's novel *Tender Is the Night*. For a discussion of Fitzgerald's complete career, see *TCLC* Volumes 1 and 6; for a discussion of his novel *The Great Gatsby,* see Volume 14.

*Tender Is the Night* examines the Jazz-Age generation's search for the elusive American dream of wealth and happiness and scrutinizes the consequences of that generation's adherence to false values. Set against the backdrop of expatriate life in Europe in the 1920s, the novel presents the story of a brilliant young psychiatrist, Dr. Richard (Dick) Diver, and his schizophrenic wife Nicole. The victim of rape by her father when she was fifteen, Nicole steadily recovers through the care of her husband, who suffers disillusionment and emotional deterioration under the demands of the complex roles he must serve in the marriage as doctor, husband, and father. Diver's collapse, while not strictly regarded as allegorical, is seen as Fitzgerald's rendering on an individual level of the collapse of the Jazz Age era and of the onset of disillusionment with the American dream.

Shortly after *The Great Gatsby* was published in 1925, Fitzgerald began working on the manuscript which, after numerous drafts and revisions, appeared ten years later as *Tender Is the Night*. The work was initially titled "The Boy Who Killed His Mother" and focused on a matricide committed by an American film technician visiting the Riviera with his domineering mother. Although the plot of the original story was never fully worked out, the extant manuscript is often examined by critics for the seminal elements of Fitzgerald's later novel. Francis Melarky, the central character of the draft, encounters several situations that Fitzgerald retained in *Tender Is the Night*, including the shooting incident in the Gare St. Lazare and the beating at the hands of the police in Rome.

In the years between *Gatsby* and *Tender Is the Night,* Fitzgerald's wife Zelda suffered at least three severe nervous breakdowns, and Fitzgerald abandoned his novel-in-progress to arrange for her psychiatric care and to write short stories to pay for it. In 1932, after several false starts on the novel, Fitzgerald devised a general plan for the work. In these notes, he wrote: "The novel should do this. Show a man who is a natural idealist, a spoiled priest, giving in for various causes to the ideas of the haute Burgeoise, and in his rise to the top of the social world losing his idealism, his talent and turning to drink and dissipation." The character of Dick Diver is often seen as a combination of traits belonging to Fitzgerald and his friend Gerald Murphy, whom the Fitzgeralds met while living in Europe during the mid-1920s. Murphy and his wife Sara, to whom the novel is dedicated, provided the models for the glamorous expatriate couple Dick and Nicole Diver, and their home, the Villa America on the French Riviera, served as the model for the Villa Diana, the Divers' home in *Tender Is the Night*.

As the novel opens, the Divers and the world that Dick has created around them are viewed through the ingenuous eyes

of Rosemary Hoyt, a seventeen-year-old film star who has lately arrived on the Riviera with her mother. Rosemary sees the glittering surface of the Divers' existence without recognizing their secret—Nicole's madness—and falls in love with what she perceives as their charmed life. Critics consider the opening chapters masterful in their depiction of the cultured leisure class of the period. In an early review, C. Harley Grattan offered typical praise for the presentation in *Tender Is the Night* of the "feverish beauty of a class in decay, the polished charm of a decadence that is not yet self-conscious, the exciting insecurity" of the wealthy expatriates. The second section of the novel looks back on the Divers' meeting and courtship, revealing to the reader the nature and causes of Nicole's madness. The third section portrays the disintegration of the Divers' marriage as Dick sacrifices his powers and ambitions as a psychiatrist in the single-minded cause of his wife's recovery, while Nicole ultimately outgrows the need for her husband's psychic ministrations, leaving him exhausted as both man and doctor. At the end of the novel Diver, now only a shadow of his personal and professional self, has retreated to live out a relatively obscure existence in upstate New York.

Fitzgerald considered *Tender Is the Night* his greatest work, but the novel met with mixed reviews when it was published in April 1934. While praising its effective writing, many early critics complained that the novel lacked focus due to its non-chronological plot sequence. At the time Fitzgerald defended his structure, charging that the reviewers had simply missed his intentions in the novel, but when Scribner's later approached him about publishing a new edition of *Tender Is the Night* in the Modern Library series, Fitzgerald devised a plan to rework the material, and his notes were subsequently used by Malcolm Cowley to revise the work in 1951. While some admirers consider Cowley's to be the "Author's Final Version" of the novel, the revised edition has never gained preeminence over the 1934 edition. The most prominent reason for this lack of acceptance is that in the revised edition the Rosemary section is placed later in the novel; as a result, the reader does not share her initial ingenuousness, and with this change in viewpoint an element of mystery and revelation is lost.

Nevertheless, Cowley's edition served as an early stimulus to the revival of interest in Fitzgerald's work that began in the 1950s, specifically initiating a new phase in the critical reputation of *Tender Is the Night*. Commentators of the 1930s had generally viewed the work as a poorly executed autobiographical novel, and throughout the 1940s it suffered the same neglect as Fitzgerald's other works. With the appearance in the early 1950s of newly edited versions of Fitzgerald's major novels, and of Arthur Mizener's *The Far Side of Paradise*, the first full-length study of Fitzgerald's life and work, critics began to discuss *Tender Is the Night* as a work far more complex in theme and calculated in narrative structure than had formerly been perceived. Most prominently, the social and historical scope of the novel is regarded as more ambitious than autobiographical readings could discern. Later examinations of *Tender Is the Night* conclude that the circle of wealthy expatriates that Fitzgerald so knowledgeably depicted attains symbolic status as a microcosm of the Western world in decline. In such readings the breakdown of Dick Diver's idealistic personality is often viewed as Fitzgerald's metaphorical rendering of the failure of the American dream. As Milton R. Stern has noted: "Dick's boundless hope and dedication were those of his nation's dream. And as his cure of Nicole took form in circumstances bitterly different from his dream-vision, so too America's dream-liberation from history shattered against its own realities—history's obdurate and endless restatements of mortal limitation, hypocrisy, selfishness, corruption, and lies—even for America—in a fallen world. No less than this is the subject of *Tender Is the Night*."

In the progress of his disillusionment, Dick Diver resembles the protagonist of Fitzgerald's earlier masterpiece, *The Great Gatsby*, which is considered a greater artistic achievement than *Tender Is the Night*, although one that was accomplished within a more limited context. According to Marvin J. LaHood: "Dick Diver's life lacks that sharply etched tragic climax of Gatsby's, but his world contains more things than Gatsby's philosophy ever dreamed of. Gatsby's past consists of a dream of youthful love on the veranda of a Louisville mansion, Diver's past consists of all that we cherish in Western Civilization. His defeat signifies more than the impossibility of repeating the past, it stands for the defeat of much that was valuable in the cultural legacy of the twenty-five centuries." Reflecting this greater thematic range and ambition is a more complex narrative structure in which Fitzgerald dealt with an impressive diversity of characters and backgrounds. Ultimately, however, such differences between the two novels prevent rather than facilitate any conclusions that would place one work above the other. Brian Way has explained that "the two novels exemplify quite distinct approaches to the art of fiction. *Gatsby* uses the

method of poetic concentration which Henry James—more than anyone else within the American tradition—had developed; *Tender Is the Night* has the extended scope and the richness of detail which one associates with classic European realism. In both novels, Fitzgerald is equally successful in achieving the complexity of meaning and artistic truth."

*Tender Is the Night* was Fitzgerald's last completed novel. At the time of his death in 1940 he was working on *The Last Tycoon*, which is based on his frustrating and unfruitful years in Hollywood. Published posthumously, this unfinished novel clearly demonstrates that, however much critical and popular interest in his fiction had declined, Fitzgerald continued to develop as an artist. Today, his two major works, *The Great Gatsby* and *Tender Is the Night*, are recognized as classics of American literature that transcend their Jazz-Age background. *Tender Is the Night* is especially celebrated as the work in which Fitzgerald integrated his personal traumas with those he observed in Western society in general and American life in particular.

(See also *Contemporary Authors*, Vol. 110; *Dictionary of Literary Biography*, Vol. 4: *American Writers in Paris, 1920-1939*; Vol. 9: *American Novelists, 1910-1945*; *Dictionary of Literary Biography Yearbook: 1981*; *Dictionary of Literary Biography Documentary Series*, Vol. 1; and *Authors in the News*, Vol. 1.)

---

**F. SCOTT FITZGERALD** (essay date 1932?)

[*The following is Fitzgerald's "General Plan" for the novel that became* Tender Is the Night. *Arthur Mizener has suggested that Fitzgerald's notes, excluding the "Summary of Part III," which seems to have been written later, were written at the same time, but that "none of this material is dated, so that it is only a guess . . . that the main outline of the story and the character sketches were made at La Paix in 1932, when, for the last time, he started over again to write the book." Fitzgerald's misspellings are reproduced in the text.*]

The novel should do this. Show a man who is a natural idealist, a spoiled priest, giving in for various causes to the ideas of the haute Burgeoise, and in his rise to the top of the social world losing his idealism, his talent and turning to drink and dissipation. Background one in which the leisure class is at their truly most brilliant & glamorous such as Murphys.

•  •  •  •  •

The hero born in 1891 is a man like myself brought up in a family sunk from haute burgeoisie to petit burgeoisie, yet expensively educated. He has all the gifts, and goes through Yale almost succeeding but not quite but getting a Rhodes scholarship which he caps with a degree from Hopkins, & with a legacy goes abroad to study psychology in Zurich. At the age of 26 all seems bright. Then he falls in love with one of his patients who has a curious homicidal mania toward men caused by an event of her youth. Aside from this she is the legendary *promiscuous* woman. He "transfers" to himself & she falls in love with him, a love he returns.

After a year of non-active service in the war he returns and marries her & is madly in love with her & entirely consecrated to completing the cure. She is an aristocrat of half American, half European parentage, young, mysterious & lovely, *a new character*. He has cured her by pretending to a stability &

belief in the current order he does not have, being in fact a communist—liberal—idealist, a moralist in revolt. But the years of living under patronage ect. & among the burgeoise have seriously spoiled him and he takes up the marriage as a man divided in himself. During the war he has taken to drink a little & it continues as secret drinking after his marriage. The difficulty of taking care of her is more than he has imagined and he goes more and more to pieces, always keeping up a wonderful face.

At the point when he is socially the most charming and inwardly corrupt he meets a young actress on the Rivierra who falls in love with him. With considerable difficulty he contains himself out of fear of all it would entail since his formal goodness is all that is holding his disintegration together. He knows too that he does not love her as he has loved his wife. Nevertheless the effect of the repression is to throw him toward all women during his secret drinking when he has another life of his own which his wife does not suspect, or at least he thinks she doesn't. On one of his absences during which he is in Rome with the actress having a disappointing love affair too late he is beaten up by the police. He returns to find that instead of taking a rest cure she has committed a murder and in a revulsion of spirit he tries to conceal it and succeeds. It shows him however that the game is up and he will have to perform some violent & Byronic act to save her for he is losing his hold on her & himself.

He has known slightly for some time a very strong & magnetic man and now he deliberately brings them together. When he finds under circumstances of jealous agony that it has succeeded he departs knowing that he has cured her. He sends his neglected son into Soviet Russia to educate him and comes back to America to be a quack thus having accomplished both his burgeoise sentimental idea in the case of his wife and his ideals in the case of his son, & now being himself only a shell to which nothing matters but survival as long as possible with the old order.

## *Approach*

*The Drunkard's Holiday* will be a novel of our time showing the break up of a fine personality. Unlike *The Beautiful and Damned* the break-up will be caused not by flabbiness but really tragic forces such as the inner conflicts of the idealist and the compromises forced upon him by circumstances.

The novel will be a little over a hundred thousand words long, composed of fourteen chapters, each 7,500 words long, five chapters each in the first and second part, four in the third— one chapter or its equivalent to be composed of retrospect.

### DICK

The hero was born in 1891. He is a well-formed rather athletic and fine looking fellow. Also he is very intelligent, widely read—in fact he has all the talents, including especially great personal charm. This is all planted in the beginning. He is a superman in possibilities, that is, he appears to be at first sight from a burgeoise point of view. However he lacks that tensile strength—none of the ruggedness of Brancusi, Leger, Picasso. For his external qualities use anything of Gerald, Ernest, Ben Finny Archie Mcliesh, Charley McArthur or myself. He looks, though, like me.

The faults—the weakness such as the social-climbing, the drinking, the desperate clinging to one woman, finally the neurosis, only come out gradually.

We follow him from age 34 to age 39.

The actress was born in 1908. Her career is like Lois [Moran] or Mary Hag—that is, she differs from most actresses by being a lady, simply reeking of vitality, health, sensuality. Rather gross as compared to the heroine, or rather *will be* gross for at present her youth covers it. . . .

We see her first at the very beginning of her carreer. She's already made one big picture.

We follow her from age 17 to age 22.

The Friend was born in 1896. He is a wild man. He looks like Tunte and like that dark communist at the meeting. He is half Italian or French & half American. He is a type who hates all sham & pretense. (See the Lung type who was like Foss Wilson) He is one who would lead tribesmen or communists— utterly aristocratic, unbourgeoise king or nothing. He fought three years in the French foriegn legion in the war and then painted a little and then fought the Riff. He's just back from there on his first appearance in the novel and seeking a new outlet. He has money & this French training—otherwise he *would* be a revolutionist. He is a fine type, useful or destructive but his mind is not quite as good as the hero's. Touch of Percy Pyne, Denny Holden also.

We see him from age 28 to age 33.

ACTUAL AGE OF

DICK

| September | 1891 | Born |
|---|---|---|
| " | 1908 | Entered Yale |
| June | 1912 | Graduated Yale aged 20 |
| June | 1916 | Graduated Hopkins. Left for Vienna (8 mo. there) |
| June | 1917 | Was in Zurich after 1 year and other work. Age 26 |
| June | 1918 | Degree at Zurich. Aged 26 |
| June | 1919 | Back in Zurich. Aged 27 |
| September | 1919 | Married—aged 28 { after his refusing fellowship at University in neurology and pathologist to the clinic. Or does he accept? |
| July | 1925 | After 5 years and 10 months of marriage is aged almost 34. |
| | | Story starts |
| July | 1929 | After 9 years and 10 months of marriage is aged almost 38. |

NICOLE'S AGE
Always one year younger than century.

Born July 1901

courtship for two and one half years before that, since she was 13.

Catastrophe June 1917 Age almost 16
Clinic   February, 1918 Age 17
          To middle October bad period
          After armistice good period
          He returns in April or May 1919
          She discharged June 1, 1919. Almost 18
          Married September 1919. Aged 18

Child born August 1920
Child born June 1922

2nd Pousse almost immediately to October 1922 and thereafter

Frenchman (or what have you in summer of 1923 after almost 4 years of marriage.

In July 1925 when the story opens she is just 24

One child almost 5 (Scotty in Juan les Pins)
One child 3 (Scotty in Pincio)

In July 1929 when the story ends she is just 28

The heroine was born in 1901. She is beautiful on the order of Marlene Dietrich or better still the Norah Gregor-Kiki Allen girl with those peculiar eyes. She is American with a streak of some foreign blood. At fifteen she was raped by her own father under peculiar circumstances—work out. She collapses, goes to the clinic and there at sixteen meets the young doctor hero who is ten years older. Only her transference to him saves her—when it is not working she reverts to homicidal mania and tries to kill men. She is an innocent, widely read but with no experience and no orientation except what he supplies her. Portrait of Zelda—that is, a part of Zelda.

We follow her from age 24 to age 29

*Method of Dealing with Sickness Material*

(1) Read books and decide the general type of case
(2) Prepare a clinical report covering the years 1916-1920
(3) Now examine the different classes of material selecting not too many things for copying.

(1) From the sort of letter under E
(2) "   "   "   "   "   " F

(In this case using no factual stuff)

(3) From the other headings for atmosphere, accuracy and material being careful not to reveal basic ignorance of psychiatric and medical training yet not being glib. Only suggest from the most remote facts. *Not like doctor's stories.*

Must avoid Faulkner attitude and not end with a novelized Kraft-Ebing—better Ophelia and her flowers.

*Classification of the Material on Sickness*

A.  Accounts
B.  Baltimore
C.  Clinics and clipping
D.  Dancing and 1st Diagnoses
E.  Early Prangins—to February 1931
F.  From Forel (include Eleuler Consultation)
H.  Hollywood
L.  Late Prangins
M.  My own letters and comments. . . .

(pp. 307-13)

Summary of Part III (1st half)

The Divers, *as a marriage* are at the end of their rescources. Medically Nicole is nearly cured but Dick has given out & is sinking toward alcoholism and discouragement. It seems as if the completion of his ruination will be that fact that cures her—almost mystically. However this is merely hinted at. Dick is still in controll of the situation and thinks of the matter practically. They must separate for both thier sakes. In wild bitterness he thinks of one tragic idea but controlls himself and manages a saner one instead.

His hold is broken, the transference is broken. He goes away. He has been used by the rich family and cast aside.

Part III is as much as possible seen through Nicole's eyes. All Dick's stories such as are *absolutely necessary*: Edwardo, father, auto catastrophe (child's eyes perhaps), Struppen quar-

rel?, girls on Rivierra, must be told without putting in his reactions or feelings. From now on he is mystery man, at least to Nicole with her guessing at the mystery. (pp. 313-14)

*F. Scott Fitzgerald, "Appendix B," in* The Far Side of Paradise: A Biography of F. Scott Fitzgerald *by Arthur Mizener, Houghton Mifflin Company, 1951, pp. 307-14.*

**HENRY SEIDEL CANBY**   (essay date 1934)

[*Canby was a professor of English at Yale and one of the founders of the* Saturday Review of Literature, *where he served as editor in chief from 1924 to 1936. He was the author of many books, including* The Short Story in English *(1909), a history of that genre which was long considered the standard text for college students. Despite the high acclaim his writings received, Canby always considered himself primarily a teacher, whose declared aim was "to pass on sound values to the reading public." In the following essay, he considers* Tender Is the Night *an occasionally brilliant novel that is ultimately flawed by Fitzgerald's lack of stylistic, structural, and thematic control.*]

It is clear enough now that Scott Fitzgerald's **This Side of Paradise** was a pioneer book. Sketchy, a little incoherent, youthful, it was nevertheless the introduction in fiction to that "younger generation," demoralized by war or the repercussions of war, which was later called the "lost" generation, and is now said to be "recovered," although upon evidence not entirely convincing. What he has to say about life in the second era of demoralization is naturally interesting.

It is interesting and in the opening chapters of [*Tender Is the Night*] brilliant. In theme, in setting, in characterization, and in the difficult art of narrative writing, there is the promise of a book of first importance. The hero of this novel, Dr. Diver, has "recovered," and has furthermore achieved that simplicity of perfectly sophisticated culture which makes his natural charm irresistible. Of the two heroines, one, a "baby star" of the movies, is also happily compounded of charm (innocent this time) and hardness. She has been brought up to be economically a boy. The other, Dr. Diver's wife, is, like him, a product of conditioning by civilized pleasure-seeking, but she has been once literally "lost"; an incestuous attack upon her in girlhood has split her personality, and it is her husband who has brought her back. Both women are "men's women," and the description of their type is admirable of its kind. What could be done with this subtly varied triangle is obvious. For if the lovely Nicole should come to feel that her dependence upon her husband for mental health was in its own way a slavery, so that once healed, rebellion was inevitable; or if the fresh and innocent Rosemary should step from the screen into this intensely difficult relationship and shatter both its charm and its permanence; why then a plot of unusual quality would be sure to unfold itself. And it does, and its background of the Riviera, the clinic in Zurich, and night-and-bar life is vivid, and their flotsam of cosmopolitans is described with so much originality, with such a firmer dry point, than the Paris-Mediterranean novels of the baser sort, that one gladly admits the skill of this first witness to the new generation. But not the art—or at least not the sustained art. Alas, this promising novel is promising only in its first brilliant chapters. Part way through the author loses his grip upon the theme. The central figures change, the focus of the plot shifts, the story rambles, the style drops to the commonplace and even the awkward and ungrammatical. What begins as a study of a subtle relationship ends as the accelerating decline into nothingness of Dr. Diver—not for no reason, but for too many reasons, no one of which is dominant. This book may be life with its veil over causality, but it is not art which should pierce that veil.

And here is a writer capable of paragraphs that one reads twice for their incisiveness, their wit, or their wisdom, letting his story shamble through episodes, shifting his stance as if he wearied of a theme that required concentration, tossing clever but irrelevant digressions into a plot already growing confused because its focus is constantly changing, and making a novel which is too good and, in spite of all these strictures, too interesting, to escape the criticism which consistent mediocrity might escape. Any second-rate English society novelist could have written this story better than Scott Fitzgerald, though not one of them could have touched its best chapters. Is it laziness, indifference, a lack of standards, or imperfect education that results in this constant botching of the first-rate by American novelists? (pp. 630-31)

> *Henry Seidel Canby, "In the Second Era of Demor-*
> *alization," in* The Saturday Review of Literature,
> *Vol. X, No. 39, April 14, 1934, pp. 630-31.*

## PHILIP RAHV   (essay date 1934)

[*A Russian-born American critic, Rahv was a prominent and in-fluential member of the Marxist movement in American literary criticism. For thirty-five years he served as co-editor of* Partisan Review, *the prestigious literary journal T. S. Eliot once called "America's leading literary magazine." During the 1940s and 1950s* Partisan Review *was a significant force in American culture, providing a forum for intellectual debate, actively cultivating an audience for literary modernism, and, largely through the efforts of Rahv, promoting the talents of such young writers as Saul Bellow, Delmore Schwartz, Bernard Malamud, and Elizabeth Hardwick. Rahv's criticism usually focuses on the intellectual, social, and cultural milieu influencing a work of art. His approach was intellectually eclectic and non-ideological: according to Richard Chase, "what one admires most about Rahv's critical method is his abundant ability to use such techniques as Marxism, Freudian psychology, anthropology, and existentialism, toward his critical ends without shackling himself to any of them." Noted for his "moral intelligence," Rahv attributed much of his critical perspective to his Marxist training. He asserted that he had acquired from Marxism "a certain approach, a measure of social and intellectual commitment and, I make bold to say, a certain kind of realism, not untouched with hope and expectancy, in my own outlook on society and the human potential as articulated in the constructs of the imagination." In the following excerpt, Rahv focuses on the wealthy and deteriorating society Fitzgerald depicted in* Tender Is the Night.]

F. Scott Fitzgerald made a name for himself in the literature of the past decade as the voice and chronicler of the jazz age. This, in a sense, was his strength, as he showed himself capable of quickly responding to features of American life that other writers assimilated rather slowly; but it also proved to be his greatest defect, since he failed to place what he saw in its social setting. He himself was swept away by the waste and extravagance of the people he described, and he identified himself with them. Hence the critics who, at his appearance on the literary scene, saw in him a major talent in post-war American literature, soon realized that here was another creative promise petering out. The fever of the boom days settled in his bones. In the end he surrendered to the standards of the *Saturday Evening Post.*

In these days, however, even Fitzgerald cannot escape realizing how near the collapse of his class really is. In his new work

he no longer writes of expensive blondes and yachting parties, lavish surroundings and insane love-affairs from the same angle of vision as in the past. These things are still there, but the author's enthusiasm for them has faded, giving way to the sweat of exhaustion. The rich expatriates who trail their weary lives across the pages of the novel breathe the thin air of a crazy last autumn. The author is still in love with his characters, but he no longer entertains any illusions concerning their survival. Morally, spiritually, and even physically they are dying in hospitals for the mentally diseased, in swanky Paris hotels and on the Riviera beaches. Yet, having immersed himself in the atmosphere of corruption, Fitzgerald's eye discerns a certain grace even in their last contortions. The morbid romance of death sways his mind, and signs are not wanting that instead of severing the cords that bind him to their degradation, he prefers to stick out with them to the end. Even while perceiving their doom, he still continues to console and caress them with soft words uttered in the furry voice of a family doctor pledged to keep the fatal diagnosis from his patients.

A number of things happen in *Tender Is the Night.* First, let us introduce Mr. Warren, a Chicago millionaire who rapes his sixteen-year old daughter Nicole. This non-plebeian act drives the girl out of her mind, and she is sent to a sanatorium in Switzerland, where she is partially cured and where she meets Dick Diver, a young American psychologist who marries her. Nicole is extremely wealthy and the Divers lead a model parasitic life, flitting from one European high spot to another, accompanied by a varied assortment of neurotics and alcoholics. Wherever they go they are intent on smashing things up. Dick Diver's strength and charm fall apart in the insufferable atmosphere of sophisticated brutality. In the course of time he realizes his role as a live commodity bought by the Warren family to act as husband-doctor to their crazy daughter. And Nicole, sensing Dick's growing despair, flies from him to the arms of Tommy Barban, the stylized young barbarian who is potentially an ideal leader of a Nazi storm-troop.

When the plot is thus bluntly stated, stripped of its delicate introspective wording, of its tortuous style that varnishes rather than reveals the essential facts, we can easily see that the book is a fearful indictment of the moneyed aristocracy. But Fitzgerald's form blunts this essence, transforming it into a mere opportunity for endless psychologizing. And on account of it many a reader will let himself float on the novel's tender surface, without gauging the horror underneath.

The reviewer is inclined to think that in creating the figure of Dick Diver, Fitzgerald has created—perhaps unconsciously— the image of a life closely corresponding to his own. The truth is that Nicole can be understood as a symbol of the entire crazy social system to which Fitzgerald has long been playing Dick Diver.

> *Philip Rahv, "You Can't Duck Hurricane Under a*
> *Beach Umbrella," in* Daily Worker, *May 5, 1934,*
> *p. 7.*

## C. HARTLEY GRATTAN   (essay date 1934)

[*An American economist as well as a social and literary critic, Grattan was a prolific contributor of articles to national magazines and was considered a well-informed literary critic. His professional career began in 1924, when one of his essays appeared in H. L. Mencken's* American Mercury; *afterward, like Mencken, he earned a reputation as an outspoken opponent of the moralistic New Humanism movement in American letters. In the following excerpt, he proclaims* Tender Is the Night *a success in its portrait of "a class in decay."*]

[*Tender Is the Night*] has called forth more than the usual quota of discussion allowed these days for the works of writers definitely identified with the dead and gone pre-depression era. This alone should serve to indicate that it is an uncommonly interesting piece of work and one which makes plain, strange as it may seem to those who remember only the frothy brilliance of *This Side of Paradise,* that Fitzgerald has grown steadily and now definitely promises to emerge as one of the really important interpreters of the upper middle class in our time. Unusually sensitive to the charm and excitement of the life of the idle and semi-idle rich and near-rich and the vast army of hangers-on they attract to them, he has slowly moved toward a position which allows him to abate very little his sympathetic attitude while definitely taking up the position of an observer rather than a participant in their revels. *Tender Is the Night* exploits to the full the feverish beauty of a class in decay, the polished charm of a decadence that is not yet self-conscious, the exciting insecurity of our betters.

The integral significance of the opening pages of the book has been missed by most reviewers. Almost to a man they have complained that the stress laid upon Rosemary, the beautiful cinema star, is unjustified by the future action of the story, that the pages devoted to building her up are really wasted effort, and that they "throw the reader off." Rather I should say that in these pages Fitzgerald is presenting the type of girl who, in the past, has always been foreordained to absorption into the world of his characters. She is the typical outsider who, moonstruck by glamor, can be quite sure that some man will select her from the host of the beautiful and innocent as his particular contribution to the seraglio of physically charming females. She is obviously not a female hairy ape, excluded, downtrodden, and exploited. She can and will belong. For it is indisputable that this process of absorbing beautiful women from the outside has been going on from time immemorial and is a characteristic of all the "aristocracies" of history. It always goes on to the end. Not gifted with insight into social processes (and why on earth should she be anyhow?) Rosemary does not realize that she has come a bit too late and that on penetrating the world she will find it already in decay and dissolution. Seen through her eyes, however, what glamor remains can legitimately be exploited and by the same token, the tragedy of its actuality can be all the more accentuated.

And so we come to the central characters, Dr. Richard Diver and his wife Nicole, beautiful daughter of a wealthy household whose life has been distorted and made precarious by incestuous relations with her father. Fitzgerald has tried to use this situation, this extreme (according to our tabus) example of decadence, to symbolize the rottenness of the society of which Nicole is a part. This is well-nigh impossible. It is always difficult to argue from the individual to the social and when the social issues are so tremendous as they are here, the chances are that any individual will turn out to be an inadequate symbol. Nevertheless Fitzgerald has done as well as possible. Dr. Diver's relation to his wife is more than that of a man to a woman he has loved enough to marry; it is also that of a psychiatrist to a patient. First encountering her in a sanitorium, he is gradually persuaded by his emotions and his technical interest and against his better judgment, to undertake her cure as her husband as well as her physician. He is, therefore, in much the same relationship to her as the reformer is to the sick society which he wishes to cure because he cannot bring himself to

abandon it and which in the end forces him either to accept it on its own terms or reject it and with it his life. That the reformer should fail and in the process be corrupted by the poisons flowing through the social veins, is as inevitable as the slow corruption of the charming Dick Diver. And when he finally abandons the task, the chances are as good that he will plunge into an even more complete obscurity than overtakes those who reject the task from the first in favor of the more drastic cure of revolution as that he will go over to the masters and become at one with them in the tacit or self-conscious support of the corrupt values. Dick Diver when he finally realizes that his task of rehabilitating Nicole is accomplished and that he can do no more without abandoning the few remnants of physician's values he retains and accepting all those of her world, chooses the way to obscurity, the corruption that follows on the realization of a wasted life, and death from the cultivation of that corruption. He is divorced by Nicole and disappears into upper New York State. No one knows what has become of him but "in any case he is almost certainly in that section of the country, in one town or another." This fate is so close to that of unstable personalities in any place and time that it has been perversely misread by those critics anxious to avoid the implications of the whole book.

For it would be folly to ignore the fact that society always produces its misfits and no-goods and that many of them can and do move in leisured society until the inevitable disintegration takes places and they disappear into obscure saloons, shabby rooming houses and out of the way towns, there to nurse their vices to the death. It is even possible that no higher percentage of each college generation today goes down to obscurity and extinction than heretofore. But if this were all that Fitzgerald had intended to say he would not have been so careful to introduce overtones of a larger purpose into his book. In the light of the plainly indicated larger purpose, we are not straining the facts of the narrative to see in these miscellaneous and sometimes highly entertaining ascents and descents, mere symbolic reflections of a larger corruption. One passage which makes that perfectly clear is the following:

> Nicole was the product of much ingenuity and toil. For her sake trains began their run at Chicago and traversed the round belly of the continent to California; chiclet factories fumed and link vats grew link by link in factories; men mixed toothpaste in vats and drew mouthwash out of copper hogsheads; girls canned tomatoes quickly in August or worked rudely at the Five-and-Tens on Christmas Eve; half-breed Indians toiled on Brazilian coffee plantations and dreamers were muscled out of patent rights in new tractors—these were some of the people who gave a tithe to Nicole, and as the whole system swayed and thundered onward it lent a feverish bloom to such processes of hers as wholesale buying, like the flush of a fireman's face holding his post before a spreading blaze. She illustrated very simple principles, containing in herself her own doom, but illustrated them so accurately that there was grace in the procedure and pleasantly Rosemary would try to imitate it.

This is perceptive writing and I should like to stress for the benefit of those austere individuals who see in the bourgeois world nothing but filth and corruption the significance of the words "feverish bloom" and "grace." Only a person utterly insensitive to the grace and beauty of the way of life open to the leisured will fail to see that even in decay these people are infinitely charming, insidiously beguiling to all but sea-green incorruptibles. (pp. 375-77)

*Fitzgerald in his study at La Paix, where most of* Tender Is the Night *was written. From* Scott Fitzgerald and His World, *by Arthur Mizener. Thames and Hudson, 1972. © 1972 Arthur Mizener.*

C. Hartley Grattan, in a review of "Tender Is the Night," in The Modern Monthly, Vol. III, No. 6, July, 1934, pp. 375-77.

### D. W. HARDING  (essay date 1934)

[*An English literary critic and psychologist, Harding has stated that in his writings he has "hoped to bring something of the discipline of scientific psychology to bear on literature without falsely simplifying complex issues." In the following excerpt, he argues that* Tender Is the Night *is dependent on narrative "tricks" that Fitzgerald used to insure the plausibility of his characters' emotions and behavior.*]

Many of the features that go to making *The Great Gatsby* as fine as it is are also present in [*Tender Is the Night*]. There is still his power of seeming to lose himself in incident and letting the theme emerge by itself, there is his sensitiveness (occasionally touching sentimentality) and his awareness of the brutalities in civilized people's behaviour, and there is simultaneously his keen appreciation, not entirely ironic, of the superficies of the same people's lives. This last is the feature that is most nearly lost in the new book. Here there is no more gusto, but right from the start an undercurrent of misery which draws away even the superficial vitality of the Euramerican life he depicts.

The story is the acutely unhappy one of a young psychiatrist, brilliant in every way, who gradually deteriorates. In place of plot there is a fine string of carefully graduated incidents to illustrate the stages of the descent. Rather than tragedy, however, the book appears to me to be one variety of the harrowing, if this can be taken to mean that as we read it our feelings are of misery and protest, and that, unlike tragedy, it can give no satisfactions to those who wish to go on living. On the other hand, it is so effectively and sincerely harrowing that its mechanisms deserve close examination.

In the first place the doomed hero is offered as the most admirable kind of modern man we can reasonably ask for, and throughout the novel he is made to stand out as superior to all the other personæ. This being so we look for some explanation of his collapse, and the first mechanism of misery appears in the ambiguity here. Various possible explanations are hinted at but none is allowed to stand. His wife's wealth, with its heavy burden of smart leisure, Dick deals with like a disciplined artist; he shows himself heroically adequate to the strain of her recurrent mental trouble; and he has as full an insight into himself and the strains his work imposes as he has into his patients. Everything that we could hope to do he is shown doing better, and—apparently as a consequence—he cracks up. The gloomy generalization is made by Dick himself in commenting on a man who precedes him to ruin: "Smart men play close to the line because they have to—some of them can't stand it, so they quit.'' But the pessimistic conviction of the book goes deeper than that, and its puritan roots are suggested by Dick's misgivings over his good fortunes and achievements in his heigh-day. He soliloquises: ''—And Lucky Dick can't be one of these clever men; he must be less intact, even faintly destroyed. If life won't do it for him, it's not a substitute to get a disease, or a broken heart, or an inferiority complex, though it'd be nice to build out some broken side till it was better than the original structure.'' Scott Fitzgerald sees to it that life *will* do it for him.

But in addition to the puritan conviction, there is also present a curious mingling of a childish fantasy with an adult's attempt to correct it, and much of the harrowing effect of the book depends on this. On the one hand, Dick is the tragic fantasy hero who is so great and fine that everyone else expects to go on taking and taking from him and never give back; and so he gets tired, so tired; and he breaks under the strain with no one big enough to help him, and it's terribly pathetic and admirable. The vital point of this childish fantasy is that he should remain admirable and (posthumously) win everyone's remorseful respect. But the story is too obviously sentimental in those terms. To try ruthlessly to tear out the sentimentality, Scott Fitzgerald brings in a much more mature bit of knowledge: that people who disintegrate in the adult world don't at all win our respect and can hardly retain even our pity. He gets his intense painfulness by inviting our hearts to go out to the hero of the childish fantasy and then checking them with the embarrassment which everyone nearest him in the story, especially Nicole his wife, feels for the failure.

The question is whether the situation could in fact occur. Not whether the main events could be paralleled in real life, but whether all the elements of action and feeling could co-exist in the way they are presented here, whether we are not being trapped into incompatible attitudes towards the same events. In short, is an emotional trick being played on us?

There seem to me to be several tricks, though without extensive quotation they are hard to demonstrate. Chief among them is the social isolation of the hero, isolation in the sense that no one gives him any help and he has no genuinely reciprocal social relationships; he remains the tragic child hero whom no one is great enough to help. Even towards the end he is made to seem superior to the others so that they are inhibited from approaching him with help. That this should be so is made plausible by the continual returns of his old self amongst the wreckage, returns of self-discipline and willingness to shoulder responsibility that amount almost to alternations of personality. He explains it himself: ''The manner remains intact for some time after the morale cracks.'' But it seems highly doubtful whether anyone could remain so formidable spiritually during a process of spiritual disintegration, especially to someone who had been as close to him as Nicole had been. But here another trick appears in the interests of plausibility: the patient-physician relationship between the two of them is now emphasized, and Nicole's abandonment of Dick is interpreted as an emergence from fixation, whereas much of the misery of the collapse springs from its wrecking what has earlier been made to seem a genuine and complete marriage.

Once achieved, Dick's isolation permits of the further device of making his suffering dumb. Reading the aquaplane episode in particular is like watching a rabbit in a trap. The story begins to become less harrowing and more like tragedy when, once or twice, Dick is articulate about himself. This happens mo-

mentarily when he comments on the manner remaining intact after the morale has cracked: but no other persona is allowed to be big enough to hear more, and '''Do you practise on the Riviera?' Rosemary demanded hastily.'' At one point the cloud of dumb misery lifts again for a moment, when he thinks he is unobserved and Nicole sees from his face that he is going back over his whole story, and actually feels sympathy for him; but this episode only introduces the final harrowing isolation. His position at the end is the apotheosis of the hurt child saying ''Nobody loves me,'' but the child's self-pity and reproaches against the grown-ups have largely been rooted out and in their place is a fluctuation between self-disgust and a fatalistic conviction that this is bound to happen to the nicest children.

The difficulty of making a convincing analysis of the painful quality of this novel, and the conviction that it was worth while trying to, are evidence of Scott Fitzgerald's skill and effectiveness. Personal peculiarities may of course make one reader react more intensely than another to a book of this kind, and I am prepared to be told that this attempt at analysis is itself childish—an attempt to assure myself that the magician didn't really cut the lady's head off, did he? I still believe there was a trick in it. (pp. 316-9)

> D. W. Harding, ''Mechanisms of Misery,'' in Scrutiny, *Vol. III, No. 3, December, 1934, pp. 316-19.*

### MALCOLM COWLEY  (essay date 1951)

[*Cowley has made several valuable contributions to contemporary letters with his editions of important American authors (Fitzgerald, Nathaniel Hawthorne, Walt Whitman, Ernest Hemingway, William Faulkner), his writings as a literary critic for the* New Republic, *and above all, with his chronicles and criticism of modern American literature. Cowley's literary criticism does not attempt a systematic philosophical view of life and art, nor is it representative of a neatly defined school of critical thought. Rather, Cowley focuses on works that he considers worthy of public appreciation and that he believes personal experience has qualified him to explicate, such as the works of the "lost generation" writers whom he knew. The critical approach Cowley follows is undogmatic and is characterized by a willingness to view a work from whatever perspective—social, historical, aesthetic—that the work itself seems to demand for its illumination. In the following excerpt from his introduction to the 1951 edition of* Tender Is the Night, *a revision of the novel based on Fitzgerald's notes, Cowley examines Fitzgerald's intended revisions and their effect on the reading of the novel.*]

To the end of his life Fitzgerald was puzzled by the comparative failure of **Tender Is the Night,** after the years he spent on it and his efforts to make it the best American novel of his time. . . . Nine years of his life had gone into the writing and into the story itself. Reading closely one could find in it the bedazzlement of his first summer at the Cap d'Antibes—for he could picture himself as Rosemary Hoyt in the novel, besides playing the part of Dick Diver; then his feelings about money and about the different levels of American society; then his struggle with alcoholism and his worries about becoming an emotional bankrupt; then his wife's illness and everything he learned from the Swiss and American doctors who diagnosed her case; then the bitter wisdom he gained from experience and couldn't put back into it, but only into his stories; then darker things as well, his sense of guilt, his fear of disaster that became a longing for disaster—it was all in the book, in different layers, like the nine buried cities of Troy.

When another writer went to see him at Rodgers Forge, near Baltimore, in the spring of 1933, Fitzgerald took the visitor to his study and showed him a pile of manuscript nearly a foot high. "There's my new novel," he said. "I've written four hundred thousand words and thrown away three-fourths of it. Now I only have fifteen thousand left to write and—" He stood there with a glass in his hand, then suddenly burst out, "It's good, good, good. When it's published people will say that it's good, good, good."

*Tender* was published in the spring of 1934 and people said nothing of the sort. It dealt with fashionable life in the 1920s at a time when most readers wanted to forget that they had ever been concerned with frivolities; the new fashion was for novels about destitution and revolt. The book had some friendly and even admiring notices, but most reviewers implied that it belonged to the bad old days before the crash; they dismissed it as having a "clever and brilliant surface" without being "wise and mature." Nor was it a popular success as compared with Fitzgerald's first three novels, which had been easier to write. . . . (pp. ix-x)

Fitzgerald didn't blame the public or the critics. It was one of the conditions of the game he played with life to accept the rules as they were written; if he lost point and set after playing his hardest, that was due to some mistake in strategy to be corrected in the future. He began looking in a puzzled fashion for the mistake in *Tender Is the Night*. There must have been an error in presentation that had kept his readers from grasping the richness and force of his material; for a time he suspected that it might merely be the lack of something that corresponded to stage directions at the beginning of each scene. (p. x)

[Within a couple of years] *Tender* seemed to be forgotten, although it really wasn't; it stayed in people's minds like a regret or an unanswered question. "A strange thing is that in retrospect his *Tender Is the Night* gets better and better," Ernest Hemingway told Maxwell Perkins, of Scribners, who was the editor of both novelists. In scores of midnight arguments that I remember, other writers ended by finding that they had the same feeling about the book. Fitzgerald continued to brood about it. In December 1938, when he was in Hollywood and was drawing near the end of his contract with Metro-Goldwyn-Mayer, he wrote to Perkins suggesting that three of his novels might be reprinted in one volume. *This Side of Paradise* would appear with a glossary that Fitzgerald planned to make of its absurdities and inaccuracies. *Gatsby* would be unchanged except for some corrections in the text. "But I am especially concerned about *Tender*," he added, "—that book is not dead. The *depth* of its appeal exists—I meet people constantly who have the same exclusive attachment to it as others had to *Gatsby* and *Paradise,* people who identified themselves with Dick Diver. Its great fault is that the *true* beginning—the young psychiatrist in Switzerland—is tucked away in the middle of the book."

The first edition of the novel had opened with the visit to the Cap d'Antibes of a young moving-picture actress, Rosemary Hoyt, and her meeting with the circle that surrounded the Richard Divers. It was the summer of 1925 and Antibes was enjoying its days of quiet glory. Rosemary had been entranced with the Divers and their friends, had fallen in love with Dick in a pleasantly hopeless fashion, and had become aware that there was some mystery about his wife. Then, on pages 151-212, the story had gone back to wartime Switzerland in order to explain the mystery by telling about Doctor Diver's courtship and marriage. Fitzgerald now proposed to rearrange the book

in chronological order. "If pages 151-212 were taken from their present place and put at the start," he said in his letter to Perkins, "the improvement in appeal would be enormous."

It must have been about the same time that Fitzgerald made an entry in his notebook, outlining the changed order and dividing the novel into five books instead of three. The entry reads:

> Analysis of *Tender*:
>
> I   Case History 151-212 61 pps. (change moon) p. 212
> II  Rosemary's Angle 3-104 101 pps. P. 3
> III Casualties 104-148, 213-224 55 pps. (—2) (120 & 121)
> IV  Escape 225-306 82 pps.
> V   The Way Home 306-408 103 pps. (—8) (332-341)

I haven't been able to find the moon that was to be changed in Book I; perhaps Fitzgerald gave some special meaning to the word, and in any case it doesn't occur on 212. That was of course the last page of "Case History" and it had to be revised in order to prepare the reader for 3, which was the first page of Book II and also needed minor revisions. The page numbers in parenthesis—(120 & 121), (332-341)—were passages that the author planned to omit. All these changes were made in Fitzgerald's personal copy of *Tender Is the Night*, which is now in the manuscript room of the Princeton University Library. . . . On the inside front cover Fitzgerald has written in pencil:

"This is the *final version* of the book as I would like it."

The words "final version" are underlined, but they have to be taken as a statement of intention rather than as an accomplished fact. It is clear that Fitzgerald had other changes in mind besides his rearrangement of the narrative and the minor revisions already mentioned: he also planned to correct the text from beginning to end. One can see what he intended to do if one reads the first two chapters of the Princeton copy. There he has caught some of his errors in spelling proper names, has revised the punctuation to make it more logical, has sharpened a number of phrases, and has omitted others. Small as the changes are, they make the style smoother and remove the reader's occasional suspicion that the author had hesitated over a word or had failed to hear a name correctly. Near the end of Chapter II there is a pencilled asterisk and a note in Fitzgerald's handwriting: "This is my mark to say that I have made final corrections up to this point." Beyond the mark are a few other corrections but only of errors that happened to catch his eye. (pp. xi-xiii)

The question remains whether the final version as Fitzgerald would like it is also the best version of the novel. I was slow to make up my mind about it, perhaps out of affection for the book in its earlier form. The beginning of the first edition, with the Divers seen and admired through the innocent eyes of Rosemary Hoyt, is effective by any standards. Some of the effectiveness is lost in the new arrangement, where the reader already knows the truth about the Divers before Rosemary meets them. There is a mystery-story element in the earlier draft: something has passed between Nicole Diver and Mrs. McKisco that is shocking enough to cause a duel, and we read on to learn what Nicole has done or said. There is also the suggestion of a psychoanalytical case study: it is as if we were listening behind the analyst's door while his two patients, Nicole and Dick, help him to penetrate slowly beneath their glittering surfaces. But the mystery story ends when Rosemary discovers—on page 148 of the first edition—what Violet

McKisco had seen in the bathroom at Villa Diana. The psychoanalytical case study is finished by page 212, when the reader has all the pertinent information about the past life of the Divers; but meanwhile half of the novel is still to come. The early critics of *Tender* were right when they said that it broke in two after Rosemary left the scene and that the first part failed to prepare us for what would follow. By rearranging the story in chronological order Fitzgerald tied it together. He sacrificed a brilliant beginning and all the element of mystery, but there is no escaping the judgment that he ended with a better constructed and more effective novel.

One fault of the earlier version was its uncertainty of focus. We weren't quite sure in reading it whether the author had intended to write about a whole group of Americans on the Riviera—that is, to make the book a social study with a collective hero—or whether he had intended to write a psychological novel about the glory and decline of Richard Diver as a person. Simply by changing the order of the story and starting with Diver as a young doctor in Zurich, Fitzgerald answered our hesitation. We are certain in reading the final version that the novel is psychological, that it is about Dick Diver, and that its social meanings are obtained by extension or synecdoche. Dick is the part that stands for the whole. He stands for other Americans on the Riviera, he stands for all the smart men who played too close to the line, he even stands for the age that was ending with the Wall Street crash, but first he stands for himself. The other characters are grouped around him in their subordinate roles: Rosemary sets in operation the forces waiting to destroy him, Abe North announces his fate, and Tommy Barban is his stronger and less talented successor. From beginning to end Dick is the center of the novel.

All this corresponds to the plan that Fitzgerald made early in 1932, after working for years on other plans and putting them aside. At first he had intended to write a short novel about a young man named Francis Melarky, a movie technician who visited the Riviera with his possessive mother. He met the Seth Pipers, a couple much like the Divers; he fell in love with the wife, followed them to Paris, went on a round of parties, and lost control of himself. The last chapters of this early draft are missing—if Fitzgerald ever wrote them—but it seems that Melarky was to kill his mother in a fit of rage, run away from the police, and then meet his own death—just how we aren't certain. In later versions of the story Melarky was somewhat less the central figure, while Abe Grant (later Abe North) and Seth Piper moved into the foreground. Then, at the beginning of 1932, Fitzgerald drew up the outline of a more ambitious book. "The novel should do this," he said in a memorandum to himself that was written at the time [see excerpt dated 1932]: "Show a man who is a natural idealist, a spoiled priest, giving in for various causes to the ideas of the haute bourgeoisie, and in his rise to the top of the social world losing his idealism, his talent and turning to drink and dissipation. Background one in which the leisure class is at their truly most brilliant and glamorous. . . ." In finishing the book Fitzgerald changed and deepened and complicated his picture of Dick Diver, but his statement of purpose is still the best short definition of the finished novel. His final revision brings the book even closer to the plan made in 1932.

It has to be said that Fitzgerald could never have revised *Tender* into the perfect novel that existed as an ideal in his mind. He had worked too long over it and his plans for it had changed too often, just as the author himself had changed in the years since his first summer on the Riviera. To make it all of a piece

he would have had to start over from the beginning and invent a wholly new series of episodes, instead of trying to salvage as much as possible from the earlier versions. No matter how often he threw his material back into the melting pot, some of it would prove refractory to heat and would keep its former shape when poured into the new mould. The scenes written for Francis Melarky, then reassigned to Rosemary or Dick, would retain some marks of their origin. The whole Rosemary episode, being rewritten from the oldest chapters of the book, would be a little out of key with the story of Dick Diver as witnessed by himself and by his wife. But a novel has to be judged for what it gives us, not for its defects in execution, and *Tender* gives us an honesty of feeling, a complexity of life, that we miss in many books admired for being nearly perfect in form.

Moreover, in Fitzgerald's final revision it has a symmetry that we do not often find in long psychological novels. All the themes introduced in the first book are resolved in the last, and both books are written in the same key. In the first book young Doctor Diver is like Grant in his general store in Galena, waiting "to be called to an intricate destiny"; meanwhile he helps another psychiatrist with the case of Nicole Warren, a beautiful heiress suffering from schizophrenia, and learns that the Warrens have planned to buy a young doctor for her to marry. In the last book he finishes her cure, realizes that the Warrens have indeed purchased and used him—"That's what he was educated for," Nicole's sister says—and is left biding his time, "again like Grant in Galena," but with the difference that his one great adventure has ended. The Rosemary section of the novel no longer misleads our expectations; coming in the middle it simply adds fullness and relief to the story.

Although the new beginning is less brilliant than the older one, it prepares us for the end and helps us to appreciate the last section of the novel as we had probably failed to do on our first reading. That is the principal virtue of Fitzgerald's new arrangement. When I read *Tender* in 1934 it seemed to me as to many others that the Rosemary section was the best part of it. The writing there was of a type too seldom encountered in serious American fiction. It was not an attempt to analyze social values, show their falseness, tear them down—that is a necessary attempt at all times when values have become perverted, but it requires no special imaginative vitality and Fitzgerald was doing something more difficult: he was trying to discover and even create values in a society where they had seemed to be lacking. Rosemary with her special type of innocence offered the right point of view from which to reveal the grace and manners and apparent moral superiority of the Diver clan. The high point of her experience—and of the reader's—was the dinner at Villa Diana, when "The table seemed to have risen a little toward the sky like a mechanical dancing platform, giving the people around it a sense of being alone with each other in the dark universe, nourished by its only food, warmed by its only lights." Then came the underside of the Divers' little world, as revealed in Abe North's self-destructiveness and in what Violet McKisco had seen in the bathroom at Villa Diana, and everything that followed seemed a long anticlimax or at best the end of a different story.

Coming back to the novel afterward and reading it in the new arrangement I had a different impression. The Rosemary section had its old charm and something new as well, for it now seemed the evocation of an age first condemned, then forgotten, and finally recalled with pleasure in the midst of harsher events; but the writing seemed to be on a lower level of intensity than the story of the hero's decay as told in the last section of the novel. That becomes the truly memorable passage: not Dick as the "organizer of private gaiety, curator of a richly incrusted happiness"; not Dick creating his group of friends and making them seem incredibly distinguished—"so bright a unit that Rosemary felt an impatient disregard for all who were not at their table"; but another Dick who has lost command of himself and deteriorates before our eyes in a strict progression from scene to scene. At this point Fitzgerald was right when he stopped telling the story from Dick's point of view and allowed us merely to guess at the hero's thoughts. Dick fades like a friend who is withdrawing into a private world or sinking to another level of society and, in spite of knowing so much about him, we are never quite certain of the reasons for his decline. Perhaps, as Fitzgerald first planned, it was the standards of the leisure class that corrupted him; perhaps it was the strain of curing a psychotic wife, who gains strength as he loses it by a mysterious transfer of vitality; perhaps it was a form of emotional exhaustion, a giving of himself so generously that he went beyond his resources, "like a man overdrawing at his bank," as Fitzgerald would later say of his own crack-up; or perhaps it was something far back in his childhood that could only be discovered by deep analysis—we can argue about the causes as we can argue about the decline of a once-intimate friend, without coming to any fixed conclusion; but the point is that we always believe in Dick and in his progress in a circle from obscurity to obscurity. With our last glimpse of him swaying a little as he stands on a high terrace and makes a papal cross over the beach that he had found and peopled and that has now rejected him, his fate is accomplished and the circle closed. (pp. xiv-xviii)

> *Malcolm Cowley, in an introduction to* Tender Is the Night: A Romance *by F. Scott Fitzgerald, revised edition, Charles Scribner's Sons, 1951, pp. ix-xviii.*

## A. H. STEINBERG  (essay date 1955)

[*In the following excerpt, Steinberg examines the presentation of psychiatry in* Tender Is the Night.]

If F. Scott Fitzgerald's **Tender Is the Night** is remembered at all, one recalls the Riviera beach, since this backdrop furnishes imagery so eminently suited to the subject matter. The proud hotel cooled by deferential palms mirrors the relations of the flesh-and-blood characters, whose status must be defined with the exactitude of the "thin, hot line" of sea and sky. Between the "nice" people around the Divers and the "not nice" around the McKiscos exists a difference as plain as between good and poor swimmers. The same sharp division between people reappears later in the Swiss inn where the acoustics permit the patrons along the wall to converse easily, unheard by those in the middle. Relentlessly final is the distinction between Dick ascendant and Dick fallen: once he could perform an aquaplane stunt, later he cannot.

Not quite as hard and fast as the distinctions themselves are the criteria underneath. A touch of petulance is directed at those foreigners who fail to uphold American standards of physical cleanliness and at the Italians who violate American canons of fair play. Such colored people as are here presented are best kept at arm's length and serve only to complicate Dick's life. It is not clear whether the sympathetically drawn Abe North is conceived as Jewish, but the nauseating Von Cohn Morris unmistakably is. Nevertheless the prevailing

chauvinistic snobbery is flexible enough to admit the existence of unpleasant Americans and worthwhile Europeans.

Although Fitzgerald has a special reverence for the big money and a special disesteem for penny-pinching, a trait he ascribes to the French, even the possession of wealth does not guarantee automatic acceptance. Women are as a matter of course expected to be beautiful and men brave, but the greatest virtue is hardness: "It was good to be hard, then; all nice people were hard on themselves." By hardness is meant self-control and self-discipline, Rosemary's own virtues which she finds in Dick, virtues well personified in the metallic Nicole.

But even Nicole's hard and lovely face betrays a pitiful aspect. For all the veneration of hardness, the nice people are characterized by a certain tenderness, "a special gentleness" apparent in their abandoned, uncontrolled living. As the sharp outlines of the beach begin to dazzle and dance in the intense daylight, so the rigid code which so neatly disposes of people tends to dissolve in the basic aimlessness it is meant to camouflage, so Nicole's set and controlled loveliness aims "straight ahead toward nothing." The requirements for acceptability cannot be stated explicitly because they are determined by Dick's whim. His personality binds the wild and delicate spirits around him into a family who remain under his beach umbrella even after the scene shifts to Paris. Outside of his circle the beach appears blank and deserted, apparently devoid of life.

His hardness he reserves for those outside his sway, his tenderness for those within. When he first comes into view, he is "giving a quiet little performance," his every antic calling forth a burst of laughter. Circulating among his intimates with "a bottle and little glasses," he doses his friends with his private brand of excitement, forming around himself "a single assemblage of umbrellas." Such is his typical method of relating (or not relating) to others, to transform them into his enthralled audience and cater to their desires with charming and titillating entertainment, demanding in return an acknowledgment of preeminence.

This unspoken bargain he puts into words in a discussion of acting which is really an exposition of his own way of life. The actress, he feelingly declares, should suppress her own desires in order to surprise the audience by acting hard when they expect softness and soft when they expect hardness, tossing them their sop of excitement in return for the chance to redirect their attention to herself. Yet in spite of the intensity of his interest in dramatics, he refuses an offered screen test: "My God, they can't photograph me. I'm an old scientist all wrapped up in his private life." His sensitized blindness to the fact that he keeps playing the actor in real life is based on a conscious contempt for actors as empty persons: "The strongest guard is placed at the gateway to nothing . . . because the condition of emptiness is too shameful to be divulged."

For the actor the wishes of his auditors assume precise shape while his inner self remains blank. Dick cannot be photographed because he has no real picture of himself, although as a scientist he is precisely certain about the actions of others. Assuming as the occasion warrants the various roles of doctor, lover, father, or partygoer, Dick is at bottom so unsophisticated about himself that his drinking, brawling, and unproductiveness loom up as so many externally caused events, if he thinks of them at all. In typically exhibitionistic demonstration at Voisins, he proves that only he has "repose," because unlike everybody else who comes in, he alone does not raise his hand to his face.

Superficial as his self-knowledge is his comprehension of the dynamics of the illnesses in which he is presumably a specialist. That emotional disturbance fills him with distaste is everywhere apparent, although his dislike does not keep him from kissing one of his attractive patients and marrying another. Certain of his charges he takes under his umbrella, others he excludes. His patients can afford to be humored, but they are more the victims of self-indulgence than of disease: "We're a rich person's clinic—we don't use the word nonsense," but nonsense adequately describes those "shell-shocks who merely heard an air raid from a distance." The cure, then, is to clamp down hard, like nice people everywhere. Dick's way of bringing Nicole out of a spell is to bark commands at her to control herself. Nicole is intelligent, let her read Freud. If the Spanish homosexual wants to be cured, let him control his sensuality. If Von Cohn Morris were any sort of a man, he would get a grip on himself.

Incurred by a traumatic episode, Nicole's insanity is grudgingly admitted, but the event is taken as something that just happened in an unguarded moment. Nicole's father is distinguished, prominent, magnificently successful; but hard as are these daylight values they do not cover the disgusting, incestuous tenderness of his night mind. To make the connection between the symptomatic event and the person is beyond Dick's power, for he is too ashamed of the paternalistic ingredient in his own behavior to do anything but condemn this kind of softness in others. How his unresolved fears color his expectations is apparent in his reaction to the closing shot of *Daddy's Girl,* a movie showing "Rosemary and her parent united at the last in a father complex so apparent that Dick winced for all psychologists at the vicious sentimentality."

Now it is true that Rosemary is all too eager to obey her consummate mother, even requiring her permission to go after Dick. Rosemary's interest is spiced by the knowledge that, like her father, Dick is a doctor, a man "all complete" and qualified to replace her all-perfect mother. But this does not absolve Dick, whose implied promise that "he would take care of her" gives evidence of his own "paternal interest" in Rosemary. Another glimpse of the goings-on inside Dick is disclosed later when, in trying to think of Rosemary, a comparison with his own daughter springs to mind.

With Nicole Dick has set up a similar relationship in the guise of doctor and patient. Playing doctor allows him to maintain a detached, scientific superiority which cloaks the fact that he cannot participate as husband on an equal basis with his wife in the marriage relation. What Dick wants is a love involvement in which he is not involved, and when Nicole first voices her awareness of this truth during their courtship, her "impertinence, the right to invade implied, astounded him." To partake of her money is to refute his self-sufficiency, to expose a softness in the armor of this distant god, laying open perhaps his silent and carefully shielded need to clutch at people. And so he reverts to his pose of undesiring desirability, treating Nicole like a patient who might contaminate him, until she finally bursts out: "You're a coward! You've made a failure of your life, and you want to blame it on me."

*"L'amour de famille."* With this sneer Tommy Barban writes off Dick's attachment to Nicole. One wonders about the truth of this allegation, recalling perhaps the joke which temporarily reunited the Divers in uproarious laughter, Dick's pretended threat to divorce his son—"Did you know there was a new law in France that you can divorce a child?" If this kind of feeling is in fact the groundwork of the family happiness,

progressive deterioration would not be unexpected. The question next arises, and Dick asks it, "If you and Nicole married won't that be *'l'amour de famille'?"*

This question Tommy chooses to ignore. Neither does the author supply any answer, and for the best of possible reasons: he does not know one himself. *Tender Is the Night* is Fitzgerald's inadvertent version of Dick's unpublished treatise, *A Psychology for Psychiatrists.* In this system the emphasis on status allows little room for human growth, and the novel similarly exhibits a curiously static quality in spite of the surface motion, a blankness beneath the precision. In accord with the author's tenets, Nicole becomes well as she removes herself from dependency on Dick. In the process she learns that "she hated the beach, resented the places where she had played planet to Dick's sun"; having grown hard as "Georgia pine, which is the hardest wood known, except lignum vitae," she is ultimately able to dethrone her doctor-husband. But we are left wondering whether she is drawn to Barban the man or to Barban harder and more barbarous than Dick, Barban the more efficient parental protector of her soft core of insanity. Who will say whether Nicole is really liberated or simply embarked on another pointless, joyless round of "l'amour de famille?"

For a while it seems that Fitzgerald might, in the Gregoroviuses, depict a love in which the conflicts of childhood have been more successfully overcome, but his heart fails him. Afraid this kind of portrayal would mark him as soft, he is also afraid to hear others espouse any cure less rigorous than his own; in a fit of adolescent bravado he has consequently christened his hero with a name whose slang meaning amply conveys the author's contempt for softness. In this topsy-turvy world world it is no wonder that the patient flees such a doctor to regain her health, just as her father breaks out of the hospital to live on in defiance of his doctor's ministrations. In the end Dick Diver leaves the field in defeat to his patients because he is softer than they.

Had Fitzgerald accepted his own psychology at face value, this novel might fairly be dismissed as a faded chronicle of the high jinks of a forgotten cafe society, a curious footnote to the jazz age. But one must be insensitive indeed to miss the pulse beneath the glittering surface, the shy, sympathetic questions behind the toughness. Behold what has happened to this resplendent creature on the beach: Why? What did Dick do wrong? These wistful searchings prove that the author has managed, despite the constrictions of a limited and distorted point of view, to invest something of himself in honest creation. An effort of this type invariably carries with it an intrinsic dignity, on which must rest the slender but secure claim this novel makes as literature. (pp. 219-22)

*A. H. Steinberg, "Fitzgerald's Portrait of a Psychiatrist," in The University of Kansas City Review, Vol. XXI, No. 3, March, 1955, pp. 219-22.*

**ROBERT STANTON** (essay date 1958)

*[In the following excerpt, Stanton analyzes the incest motif in* Tender Is the Night *as a major artistic device that Fitzgerald used to unify his novel.]*

[*Tender Is the Night*] contains a large number of "incest-motifs," which, properly understood, take on symbolic value and contribute to the thematic unity of the novel. The term "incest-motifs" may seem ill-chosen at first, since most of these passages allude, not to consanguineous lovers, but to a mature

*Pages from the manuscript of* Tender Is the Night. *Copyright © 1963 by Matthew J. Bruccoli. Reprinted by permission of Harold Ober Associates, Incorporated.*

man's love for an immature girl. I have used the term chiefly because the first of these passages concerns Devereux Warren's incestuous relation with his fifteen-year-old daughter Nicole, so that whenever Fitzgerald later associates a mature man with an immature girl, the reader's reaction is strongly conditioned by this earlier event. Devereux's act is the most obvious, and the only literal, example of incest in the novel. It is of basic importance to the plot, since it causes Nicole's schizophrenia and thus necessitates her treatment in Dr. Dohmler's clinic, where she meets Dick Diver. Nicole's love for Dick is in part a "transference" caused by her mental disorder; the character of their marriage is dictated largely by the requirements of her condition.

In spite of the importance of Devereux' act, the use of incest as *motif* is more evident in the fact that Dick, Nicole's husband and psychiatrist, falls in love with a young actress whose most famous film is entitled *Daddy's Girl*. As this coincidence suggests, Fitzgerald deliberately gives an incestuous overtone to the relationship between Dick Diver and Rosemary Hoyt. Like Rosemary's father, Dick is of Irish descent and has been an American army doctor, a captain. At his dinner-party on the Riviera, he speaks to Rosemary "with a lightness seeming to conceal a paternal interest." He calls her "a lovely child" just before kissing her for the first time, and in the Paris hotel he says, again with a "paternal attitude," "When you smile . . .

I always think I'll see a gap where you've lost some baby teeth." Dick is thirty-four, twice Rosemary's age, and to emphasize this, Fitzgerald continually stresses Rosemary's immaturity. When she first appears in 1925, her cheeks suggest "the thrilling flush of children after their cold baths in the evening"; "her body hovered delicately on the last edge of childhood—she was almost eighteen, nearly complete, but the dew was still on her." She and her mother are like "prize-winning school-children." Even Nicole pointedly refers to Rosemary as a child.

By the time of Abe North's departure, Dick admittedly loves Rosemary; now, "he wanted to . . . remove the whole affair from the nursery footing upon which Rosemary persistently established it"; but he realizes that Rosemary "had her hand on the lever more authoritatively than he." Helpless as he is, he remains conscious—even over-conscious—of the incongruity of the situation; he tells Rosemary, "When a child can disturb a middle-aged gent—things get difficult." Finally he tells Nicole that Rosemary is "an infant. . . . there's a persistent aroma of the nursery."

After Rosemary leaves the Riviera, Dick begins to exaggerate the immaturity of *other* women as well. He is uneasy when Nicole suggests that he dance with a teen-age girl at St. Moritz, and protests, "I don't like ickle durls. They smell of castile soap and peppermint. When I dance with them, I feel as if I'm pushing a baby carriage.'' He looks at a pretty woman, and thinks, ''Strange children should smile at each other and say, 'Let's play'.'' Gradually an obscure sense of guilt appears. When Nicole accuses him, falsely and irrationally, of seducing a patient's daughter—''a child,'' she says ''not more than fifteen''—he feels guilty. When he is being taken to court after the taxi-driver fight, a crowd boos him, mistaking him for a man who has raped and slain a five-year-old child; later that day Dick cries, ''I want to make a speech. . . . I want to explain to these people how I raped a five-year-old girl. Maybe I did—.''

As his decline continues, Dick's attitude toward his own children, Topsy and Lanier, begins to change. In Rome, he decides that Rosemary ''was young and magnetic, but so was Topsy.'' When Nicole realizes that his aquaplaning at the Riviera is inspired by Rosemary's ''exciting youth,'' she remembers that ''she had been seen him draw the same inspiration from the new bodies of his children. . . .'' Earlier, Dick has exclaimed, ''What do I care whether Topsy 'adores' me or not? I'm not bringing her up to be my wife,'' apparently assuming that the love of a child does not differ essentially from the love of an adult; he jokes with Lanier about ''a new law in France that you can divorce a child.'' Finally, late in the novel Nicole notices his ''almost unnatural interest in the children.''

The presence of these incest-motifs may be explained in several ways. First, they may have been suggested, if only slightly and indirectly, by Fitzgerald's own ambivalent attitudes toward his mother and his daughter. He vacillated between being ashamed of his mother and devoted to her; one of the early titles for **Tender Is the Night** was *The Boy Who Killed His Mother*. According to his biographer, with his daughter Scottie, Fitzgerald was alternately ''the severe father, the difficult alcoholic, and the man who loved his child intensely.'' But opposing this explanation is the fact that incest is not mentioned in his other works, and only **''Babylon Revisited''** and **''The Baby Party''** concern the love of father for daughter.

In any case, the incest-motifs may be fully accounted for by **Tender Is the Night** itself. Most of them grow logically out of Dick's relationship to Nicole. When Nicole first begins writing to Dick, she still pathologically mistrusts all men; her first letter to him speaks of his ''attitude base and criminal and not even faintly what I had been taught to associate with the rôle of gentleman.'' Gradually Dick begins to take the place once occupied by her father, as a center of trust and security. As a psychiatrist, Dick realizes the value of this situation; he also realizes that Nicole must eventually build up her *own* world. After her psychotic attack at the Agiri fair, for example, he says, ''You can help yourself most,'' and refuses to accept the father-role into which she tries to force him. But this sort of refusal costs him a difficult and not always successful effort of will. First, loving Nicole, ''he could not watch her disintegrations without participating in them.'' Second, he is by nature a ''spoiled priest,'' the father for all of his friends; he creates the moral universe in which they live. His nature and his love oppose his profession. It is therefore plausible, once his character begins to crumble, that he compensates for his long self-denial by falling in love with a girl literally young enough to be his daughter; that after the crowd has booed him for raping a five-year-old girl, he makes a mock-confession; and that when Nicole accuses him of seducing a patient's fifteen-year-old daughter, ''He had a sense of guilt, as in one of those nightmares where we are accused of crime which we

recognize as something undeniably experienced, but which upon waking we realize we have not committed.''

Ironically, although Dick's fascination with immaturity gives him an opportunity to be both lover and father, it also reveals his own fundamental immaturity. Like Nicole, who responds to Tommy Barban because she sees her own hardness and unscrupulousness reflected in his character, and like Rosemary, who responds to Dick at first because of his ''self-control and . . . self-discipline, her own virtues,'' Dick is attracted to Rosemary's immaturity partly because of a corresponding quality within himself. Behind his facade of self-discipline, this central immaturity appears in the obsessive phrase, ''Do you mind if I pull down the curtain?'' Rosemary calls him ''Youngster,'' ''the youngest person in the world,'' and while he waits for Rosemary outside her studio, he circles the block ''with the fatuousness of one of Tarkington's adolescents.'' When Abe North talks to Nicole in the railroad station, Fitzgerald says, ''Often a man can play the helpless child in front of a woman, but he can almost never bring it off when he feels most like a helpless child''; similarly, when Dick talks to Mary Minghetti just before leaving the Riviera, ''his eyes, for the moment clear as a child's, asked her sympathy. . . .''

The significance of the incest-motifs is not limited to Dick's personal disaster. After all, they do not all *issue* from him. It is not of Dick's doing that a patient accuses him of seducing her fifteen-year-old daughter or that a crowd boos him for raping a five-year-old girl. And except for Devereux Warren's act, the most conspicuous incest-motif in the novel is the motion picture for which Rosemary is famous, *Daddy's Girl*. Everyone, we are told, has seen it; and lest we miss the point of the title, we are given Dick's reaction to the final scene of the picture, ''a lovely-shot of Rosemary and her parent united at the last in a father complex so apparent that Dick winced for all psychologists at the vicious sentimentality.'' As the universal popularity of *Daddy's Girl* suggests, the incest-motifs symbolize a world-wide situation. In 1934, C. Hartley Grattan wrote of the relation between Nicole and her father [see excerpt dated 1934], ''Fitzgerald has tried to use this situation, this extreme (according to our tabus) example of decadence, to symbolize the rottenness of the society of which Nicole is a part.'' But the meaning of the repeated motif is both broader and more precise than this.

During the 1920's, the relationship between the prewar and postwar generations was curiously reversed. In Mark Sullivan's words [in *Our Times: The United States 1900-1952*],

> The Twenties, reversing age-old custom, Biblical precept and familiar adage, was a period in which, in many respects, youth was the model, age the imitator. On the dance-floor, in the beauty parlor, on the golf course; in clothes, manners, and many points of view, elders strove earnestly to look and act like their children, in many cases their grand-children.

And Frederick Lewis Allen notes [in *Only Yesterday*] that ''the women of this decade worshipped not merely youth, but unripened youth. . . .'' That Fitzgerald agreed with this interpretation of the period is evident from a late essay in which he described the Jazz Age as ''a children's party taken over by the elders. . . . By 1923 [the] elders, tired of watching the carnival with ill-concealed envy, had discovered that young liquor will take the place of young blood, and with a whoop the orgy began.''

Here, on a world-scale, is Dick Diver's fascination with immaturity; and since the younger generation is the child of the elder, here is a situation to which the incest-motifs are relevant. Dick Diver's generation is older than Rosemary's, and he is the product of an older generation still, his minister-father's, with its stress upon "'good instincts,' honor, courtesy, and courage." Rosemary is the product of Hollywood, with its emphasis upon the future, and we are told that in *Daddy's Girl* she embodies "all the immaturity of the race." In embracing Rosemary, therefore, Dick Diver is a symbol of America and Europe turning from a disciplined and dedicated life to a life of self-indulgence, dissipation, and moral anarchy—a symbol of the parent generation infatuated with its own offspring. Dick's collapse, appropriately, occurs in 1929.

Even aside from Dick's relationship with Rosemary, there are many hints that he is gradually shifting allegiance from the past culture of his father to an unworthy future. In the beginning, he exhibits dignity and self-discipline, unfailing courtesy, and a firm (if unexpressed) moral code; before the novel is over, he has been beaten in a brawl with taxi-drivers, has insulted his friend Mary Minghetti, and, at the very end, has been forced to leave Lockport, New York, because he "became entangled with a girl who worked in a grocery store." To clarify this change, Fitzgerald underlines it in several passages. The most memorable example is Dick's remark at his father's grave, "Good-bye my father—good-bye, all my fathers"; later, as he enters the steamship to return to Europe, he is described as hurrying from the past into the future. But this is only his formal farewell to something he has long since left behind. Most of the allusions to the shift occur four years earlier, during the episode in which Dick falls in love with Rosemary. At the battlefield near Amiens, he tells Rosemary that the "whole-souled sentimental equipment" of the past generations was all spent in World War I. Next day, he takes her to the Cardinal de Metz's palace: the threshold of the palace connects the past without (the stone facade) to the future within (blue steel and mirrors), and crossing that threshold is an experience "perverted as a breakfast of oatmeal and hashish." Just after leaving the palace, Dick admits for the first time that he loves Rosemary. Next day, his attempt to visit Rosemary at her studio is explicitly labelled "an overthrowing of his past." And on the following day, in the hotel dining room, although Dick sees in the gold-star mothers "all the maturity of an older America," and remembers his father and his "old loyalties and devotions," he turns back to Rosemary and Nicole, the "whole new world in which he believed." It is worth noticing that at both the beginning and end of this episode, Fitzgerald emphasizes Rosemary's significance by placing her beside the memory of World War I.

One reason for the broad applicability of the incest-motif is its inherent complexity: it simultaneously represents a situation and expresses Fitzgerald's judgment of it. First, it suggests how appealing youth can be (whether as person or as quality) to the adult in whom the long-opposed edges of impulse and self-restraint have begun to dull. He longs not only for youth's vitality but for its innocence, which apparently confers moral freedom. In the first flush of love, Dick and Rosemary seem to share

> an extraordinary innocence, as though a series of pure accidents had driven them together, so many accidents that at last they were forced to conclude that they were for each other. They had arrived with clean hands, or so it seemed, after no traffic with the merely curious and clandestine.

Similarly, most of the rebels of the Twenties sought not merely to discard the Victorian morality but to do so without any

aftermath of guilt—to recapture the amorality of youth. But the incest-motif also suggests decadence and the violation of a universal taboo—particularly since in *Tender Is the Night* it appears first as the cause of Nicole's insanity—and thus indicates that the unconscious innocence of youth is forever lost to the adult, and that in searching for it he may find disaster: "that madness akin to the love of an aging man for a young girl." (pp. 136-42)

The incest-motifs . . . help to unify the novel on several levels, as well as to show how those levels are interrelated. First, these motifs function literally as one result of Dick's relationship to Nicole; they are symptoms of his psychological disintegration. Second, they both exemplify and symbolize Dick's loss of allegiance to the moral code of his father. Finally, by including such details as *Daddy's Girl* as well as Dick's experience, they symbolize a social situation existing throughout Europe and America during the Twenties. Fitzgerald's ability to employ this sort of device shows clearly that he not only felt his experience intensely, but *understood* it as an artist, so that he could reproduce its central patterns within the forms and symbols of his work. His experience transcends the historical Fitzgerald who felt it and the historical Twenties in which it occurred, and emerges as art. (p. 142)

*Robert Stanton, "'Daddy's Girl': Symbol and Theme in 'Tender Is the Night'," in* Modern Fiction Studies, *Vol. IV, No. 2, Summer, 1958, pp. 136-42.*

## JOHN LUCAS  (essay date 1963)

*[Lucas is an English poet and critic who writes primarily on nineteenth- and twentieth-century fiction. In the following excerpt, he discusses Fitzgerald's presentation of personal and societal "breakdowns" in* Tender Is the Night.*]*

***Tender Is the Night*** is about breakdowns: breakdowns in marriages, friendships, and individuals; breakdowns suggestive of a larger breakdown which, in the last analysis, involves the whole of Western Society. In 1927, about the time he was starting his novel, Fitzgerald was reading Spengler's *Decline of the West,* and according to Turnbull: "In the prosperous luxury-loving America of 1927 Fitzgerald thought he saw new evidence of Western man's decay." This must not be misunderstood: I am not trying to say that *Tender Is the Night* is the sort of novel whose characters function at a strictly symbolic, let alone allegorical, level: Dick no more "stands for" the collapse of American values than Tommy Barban or Franz Gregorovius "stand for" the collapse of European ones, or Lady Caroline Sibley-Biers for the collapse of British ones. But the larger significances which underlie the various personal and social failures are there and they can be felt; and it is worth remembering that Fitzgerald at one time intended calling his novel *The World's Fair.*

The characters in *Tender Is the Night* move from success to failure, or from large possibilities to smaller ones: the collapse of each has to do with a failure to realize his own promise, and the only alternative to collapse is to come to terms with, and accept, a shrunken world whose possibilities begin and end in compromise. At the beginning of the novel it is said of Dick that he knew that "the price of his intactness was incompleteness," and the phrase provides a key to the novel's primary concern. The characters in *Tender Is the Night* are either intact or complete, the one is to be had only at the expense of the other. And the word which more than any other defines the quality of their intactness is "hard." Baby Warren is hard, so hard that Dick feels there is "something wooden and on-anistic about her." And indeed this sexual reference can be extended to take in all her inconclusive love affairs: her sexual loneliness is the price she pays for staying "intact"; and her virginity is intimately associated with her hardness. And as with Baby, so with others. When Rosemary first meets Dick she feels the "layer of hardness in him," and we are told of her that her mother "had made her hard." Nicole tells her "I'm a mean, hard woman," and although this is only partly true at the time—periodically her hard casing is fractured—it indicates what she is in the process of becoming. By the end of the novel she is intact, and it is then that Dick tells Tommy Barban: "Nicole is now made of—of Georgia Pine, which is the hardest wood known, except lignum vitae from New Zealand—." Encased in this new hardness she settles for the incompleteness of marriage with Barban, and the shrunken world which is all he can offer her.

To use the terms "intactness," and "completeness," however, is to raise the problem of personal identity, and indeed this offers another approach to discussion of *Tender Is the Night*, for in a real and very terrible sense various of the characters do lose their identities. (And here, of course, it becomes fatally easy to take Nicole's schizophrenia as the central symbol of the novel, and although this would be not wrong it might well lead to critical evasions, for what matters is the way in which the breakdowns are presented.) In this novel an individual's identity is recognized through and defined by, his function: it is Dick's function to be a doctor, this is his identity, his nature; Abe North's function is to be a musician, it is *his* identity, *his* nature: when their functions are usurped their identities are shattered, and they break down.

The most exhaustively examined breakdown in the novel is that of the marriage between Dick and Nicole, with the parallel but opposed movements of his breakdown and her return to health; his loss of identity and her assumption of one. When we first meet him, Dick is a brilliant young psychiatrist of immense ambition, who admits that he wants to be the greatest doctor in the world. His intellectual brilliance is not, perhaps, convincingly shown, but the aspect which inspires his admission is. For he is vain, a flaw which he interprets to himself as wanting "to be loved," and which plays an integral part in his gradual collapse. Fitzgerald told Edmund Wilson that Dick was not only "un homme manqué," but "un homme epuisé," which helps us understand why he admitted to a partial failure with him, for it is never fully certain to what extent Dick's fall is his own fault, and to what extent the Warren money and the sapping effect of Nicole's illness must take the blame; sometimes it seems the one, sometimes the other, and judgement wavers. Yet this failure is comparatively slight, I think, and Fitzgerald himself over-stated it in his effort to account for the novel's unpopularity.

The complex motives that push Dick into marriage with Nicole are operating from the outset, and his love for her is partly a realisation that she loves him and depends on him for her health. In fact, he takes on himself the responsibility of restoring her to permanent sanity, for he has the chance to fade out of her life, is advised to do so by her doctors who are also his friends. So his decision to marry her, a decision aided by Baby's tactical manoeuvres—she wants a doctor for Nicole—means that he chooses to be responsible for what happens to her; he has to create a world for her, one in which she can find security. The decision also means that his intactness is lost. Nicole realises this when she thinks to herself of him: "You are no longer

insulated; but I suppose you must touch life in order to spring from it." How he springs from it is, of course, indicated by his name; the course of his life is that of the "diver's brilliant bow." But it is he who has chosen to forfeit his intactness, so that his struggle against being owned involves us in a moral judgement of him, for although Baby Warren uses her money to hold him, he has put her in the position of being able to do so. Of Nicole it is said that "she led a lonely life owning Dick, who did not want to be owned," and the criticism is of him, not her.

It is from Rosemary's angle that we first see the Divers as a family. They are on their beach, the "tanned prayer-mat" that Dick has created out of rubble as he has created Nicole's life out of rubble. And through Rosemary's eyes we see Dick at his most vital and attractive, his powers at their zenith. That this should be so is of the greatest importance, for we have to realise that Fitzgerald is not allowing us to assess directly those powers, and that because we see them only as they are refracted through the eyes of an immature girl, an actress, they show themselves ambiguously and our judgement is taxed accordingly. What Rosemary sees tells us a good deal about her, but it does not tell us anything straightforward about Dick, and we should not be beguiled into accepting her valuation of him. A good instance of the obliquity of valuation which is being demanded of us occurs at the famous dinner-party, which Rosemary attends thinking of Dick's villa as "the centre of the world."

> The table seemed to have risen a little towards the sky like a mechanical dancing table, giving the people around it the sense of being alone with each other in the universe, nourished by its only food, warmed by its only lights. And, as if a curious hushed laugh from Mrs. McKisco were a signal that such detachment from the world had been attained, the two Divers began suddenly to warm and glow and expand, as if to make up to their guests, already so subtly assured of their importance, so flattered with politeness, for anything they might still miss from that country left well behind.

This is a crucial scene, and it is important that we do not misunderstand the ironic tone which controls its ambiguities, and which can be pinned down in the description of the "mechanical dancing table"; that phrase alone should warn us against accepting the account of the dinner-party as one in which Fitzgerald solicits our unqualified admiration for the Divers. For the scene is being viewed from Rosemary's angle, and it is particularly apt that she should think of the mechanical dancing table as being part of it: Hollywood offers for her the highest form of enchantment, of glamour, of taste, so that it is inevitable she should see the dinner-party in terms of an early Hollywood musical, a world of fake romance. Which is not to say that the enchantment of the Diver dinner-party *is* fake, but that its possible meretriciousness has been allowed for. Once this is realised it becomes evident that the inherent worth of Dick's qualities is not the same as Rosemary's valuation of them, and we should not confuse the two: we see a good deal through Rosemary's eyes, but we see more than she does; our standpoint is not hers.

I may seem to have attached undue importance to this point, but I have done so because what writing there is on *Tender Is the Night* has assumed that Fitzgerald is endorsing Rosemary's view of Dick, and so it has quite failed to take account of the very great skill which he reveals in his use of her. Dick is a finer man than ever Rosemary can know, but—and it is a bitter paradox—she is the only one who can uncritically respond to what he is and does.

Not surprisingly she falls in love with him. We shall not understand the nature of their relationship unless we remember that Rosemary is an actress, and that what she does is determined by what she is, by her identity. So her love for Dick is not only an adolescent emotion, but something for which her career has especially created her, and with Dick she finds a kinship in career to which she responds; she thinks she can understand him on her own terms, and it is a criticism of him that she should be so successful. Her love must be compared to a teenager's admiration for a film-star: "I think you're the most wonderful person I ever met—except my mother" she tells him, and we take the confession for what it is worth. But the film-star analogy goes further than may at first seem, for this is the kinship she finds with Dick. Judging, as she is forced to do, by the standards of her Hollywood world, what she responds to most fully is his ability as an actor, this is the side of him she can understand. When she first sees him on the beach she realises he is its chief entertainer, and so she offers us the opportunity of understanding something about Dick that none of the others can. For Dick's new role is that of entertainer, and he acts it because it is now his function; he has set out to create Nicole's world for her, and is playing the lead part in it. The occasion of Rosemary's arranging a screen test for him and her asking him to be the leading-man in her next picture is indicative of how she regards him, and that his life permits this interpretation is something to which we should be alive.

Their affair is an act in which Dick self-consciously plays a role, the opportunity for which has been created by his new identity and in which his vanity has greater scope. From the time Rosemary first tells him of her love he is aware of what their relationship amounts to, aware of "the too obvious appeal, the struggle with an unrehearsed scene and unfamiliar words." Rosemary is aware of it too. When she asks Dick to make love to her:

> She was astonished at herself—she had never imagined she could talk like that . . . Suddenly she knew too that it was one of her greatest rôles and she flung herself into it the more passionately.

But for Rosemary it is not—as it is for Dick—a matter for moral concern that their love should be an act, and the nearest approach she makes to any moral perception is when she says to him, "Oh, we're such actors—you and I." It is, we are told, her most sincere remark, but it is not certain how aware of this she is. What is certain is that her identity is defined by her being an actress, and that her shallowness in love springs from what she *is*; acting at love is for her the extreme of sincerity, and so she has no proper comprehension of the crime she allows Dick to commit against Nicole; to the end she regards them as "darling people."

Dick on the other hand, has the self-awareness which is the product of intelligence if not its equivalent. For him to act at love is to attempt to deny his true identity, and from this truth he cannot escape. Indeed it has to be said that Dick always reveals a degree of self-awareness that sets him apart from the others and gives him the stature which allows for a tragic element in his fall. What makes it possible for him to fail Nicole is his inability to retain a grip on the two identities of doctor and actor: it is as actor that he has his affair with Rosemary, and the doctor is powerless to save Nicole the effects of this. Thus the breakdown in the Paris Hotel, a finely achieved

scene, involves a severe judgement of Dick. he and Rosemary are in her apartment and about to make love when Abe North disturbs them. They all adjourn to the Divers' apartment—just along the corridor—where Dick tries to sort out Abe's tangled story of a negro he insulted whilst drunk. After they have been talking for several minutes Rosemary returns to her own apartment, and there discovers a dead negro on her bed. It is a moment of irrational violence, a prelude to the storm about to burst. She calls Dick, and he, wanting to avoid scandal, dumps the negro in the corridor, and gives the bedspread, stained with the dead man's blood, to Nicole, telling her to clean it off. Minutes later he asks Rosemary where Nicole is.

> "I think she's in the bathroom."

> . . . he went into the bedroom and towards the bathroom. And now Rosemary, too, could hear, louder and louder, a verbal inhumanity that penetrated the keyholes and the cracks in the door, swept into the suite and in the shape of horror took form again. . . .

> Nicole knelt beside the tub swaying sidewise and sidewise. 'It's you.'' she cried, ''—it's you come to intrude on the only privacy I have in the world—with your spread with red blood on it. . . .''

> "Control yourself, Nicole."

> "I never expected you to love me—it was too late—only don't come in the bathroom, the only place I can go for privacy, dragging spreads with red blood on them and asking me to fix them."

When he and Rosemary do finally become lovers, Dick knows that they are not in love, and his jealousy over possible rivals is that of the vain man who fears his powers are fading. This fear, and its justification, is brilliantly revealed in the incident, late in his marriage, where he attempts to perform the feat of carrying a man on his back whilst balancing on a ski-board—a trick which previously he has managed with ease, but which now defeats him. This is a particularly fine piece of writing: Nicole's contempt at Dick's vanity, his anger at failing in front of Rosemary, her "tact," and the bewilderment and scorn of the young people who are watching from the boat, are all brilliantly shown. And through the entire scene run reminders of the promises with which Dick had started out as the creator of Nicole's world, and their corruption through the passage of years. He and Nicole go on the beach to look for Rosemary, and she watches him with detachment—the indication of a new intactness.

> Probably it was the beach he feared, like a deposed ruler secretly visiting an old court . . . Let him look at it—his beach, perverted now to tastes of the tasteless; he could search it for a day and find no stone of the Chinese wall he had once erected around it, no footprint of an old friend.

And as she watches Dick flattering Rosemary, she notices that he is bringing out his old expertness with people, "a tarnished object of art."

The water-stunt is the ageing actor's last attempt to impress the teenage worshipper, and it fails. But it underlines the essence of Dick and Rosemary's relationship, and this he acknowledges to himself, and to Nicole. He leaves her for a few nights when their marriage is at breaking-point, and on his return admits that he has been with Rosemary.

> "I wanted to find out if she had anything to offer—the only way was to see her alone."

> "Did she have anything to offer."

"Rosemary didn't grow up," he answered.

Finally, there is the last view that Dick takes of the beach he had built before he leaves it for ever; the beach which has come to stand as an important symbol of the world he created for Nicole, and in which he no longer has any place. And as he stands looking at it we have our last glimpse of him, and it is one that goes far to explain how he has lost that world, and with it his identity. He meets Mary Minghetti, and they sit down.

> Dick felt fine—he was already well in advance of the day, arrived at where a man should be at the end of a good dinner, yet he showed only a fine, considered, restrained interest in Mary. His eyes, for the moment clear as a child's, asked her sympathy and stealing over him he felt the old necessity of convincing her that he was the last man in the world and she was the last woman.

That is superb and it carries its own judgement; and if Fitzgerald did put a good deal of himself into the portrait of Dick, that moment alone should be sufficient to dismiss the accusations of self-pity.

So far I have spoken of Dick's collapse in terms of his vanity, and I have tried to show that the valuation of him we are meant to form is different from, but dependent on, what Rosemary sees him as, and what he sees himself as through her. But there is another aspect to be considered, which Fitzgerald was referring to when he called Dick "un homme epuisé": we have to take account of the "lesion of vitality" that results from his efforts to restore Nicole's health, the effect of which she notices when she says to him, "you used to want to create things, now you want to smash them up." As Mizener has noticed, a lesion of vitality was a possibility which Fitzgerald himself dreaded, and which in *The Crack-Up* he refers to as "emotion bankruptcy." Dick, when he acknowledges to Rosemary how much he has changed, uses words almost identical to those his creator was later to use of himself: "The change," he tells her, "came a long way back—but at first it didn't show. The manner remains intact for some time after the morale cracks." This cracking of Dick's morale is worth considering in a little detail, because it is intimately associated with his loss of identity, the crumbling of his nature which results from the pressures of Nicole's ownership.

The outward sign of his crumbling is, of course, his heavy drinking, and it is this more than anything that points the way to his failures as a doctor. This is well shown in the hectic removal from his and Gregorovius' clinic of the Australian Von Cohn's son who, himself an alcoholic, has smelt drink on Dick's breath. And it is shortly before this that Kaethe Gregorovius has told her husband that "Dick is no longer a serious man."

The attempt to function as both husband and doctor produces a state of mind where Dick can no longer be sure of his love for Nicole. This, and the gradual decay of their love and marriage, comes out as he reflects how difficult it is to distinguish between his protective professional detachment for her, "and some new coldness in his heart."

> As an indifference cherished or left to atrophy, becomes an emptiness, to this extent he had learned to become empty of Nicole, serving her against his will with negations and emotional neglect. . . . There are open wounds, shrunk sometimes to the size of a pinprick, but wounds still. The marks of suffering are more comparable to the loss of a finger, or the sight

of an eye. We may not miss them, either, for one minute in a year, but if we do there is nothing to be done about it.

Dick does become aware of what he has lost, however, when he goes on holiday by himself, after the climactic and brilliant chapter which ends with another eruption of violence as Nicole tries to kill the whole family by driving their car over a cliff.

> But Dick had come away for his soul's sake, and he began thinking about that. He had lost himself—he could not tell the hour when, or the day or the week, the month or the year.

And this awareness of his lost identity emerges in a remark he makes to Nicole, when they are staying with the children at Mary Minghetti's house. Dick gets drunk at dinner.

> Nicole reproved him when they were in their room alone. "Why so many highballs? Why did you use the word spic in front of him?"
>
> "Excuse me, I meant smoke. The tongue slipped."
>
> "Dick this isn't faintly like you."
>
> "Excuse me again. I'm not much like myself any more."

And it is his drunkenness, plus a deliberate tactlessness, which helps force the breakdown of the Divers's long friendship with Mary Minghetti—herself now settled for the intactness of marriage to a Count.

It is an especially savage irony that although Baby has bought Dick as a doctor for Nicole, his own abilities to function as a doctor are progressively denied by the marriage; the lesion of vitality affects the doctor who, in the deepest sense, *is* Dick. In an obscure way Baby realises this when she gets him out of a jail after his drunken fight with the Italian taxi-men.

> It had been a hard night but she had the satisfaction of feeling that, whatever Dick's previous record was, they now possessed a moral superiority over him for as long as he proved of any use.

And the irony is insisted on. As Dick loses his ability to function, so increasingly he is referred to as Doctor Diver and Doctor Richard Diver, the name now completely at odds with his nature.

At the very end, when Nicole struggles free of him, Fitzgerald notes laconically, "The case was finished. Doctor Diver was at liberty." It is a crushing moment, the understatement containing all the forces of a final judgement. To refer to the marriage as a "case" is to define the empty husk it has now become, something that need be seen merely in medical terms. And Doctor Diver is similarly a husk and an empty name, he cannot return to the liberty which once provided his intactness, his identity, for that has been broken by Nicole's ownership, his true nature usurped by his acting husband to her; he has created her world, she has destroyed his. The design of the novel from this point of view is masterly: Dick's gradual collapse is perfectly balanced by Nicole's climb to health; the lesion of his vitality is the source from which she takes strength; the intact hardness of his identity crumbles as and because she builds hers.

The central breakdowns in *Tender Is the Night* are those of Dick and his marriage, but they are not the only ones. I said earlier that the novel's characters are either intact or incomplete, that they stay—or become—intact, only if they accept a shrunken world whose possibilities do not allow for completeness. What I have said about Rosemary shows, I hope, the truth of this. She retains her hardness at the cost of remaining an adolescent, and at the end she is still the "Daddy's Girl" of her first picture. It is because of this that she and her world can be intact, and some measure of how we are meant to judge that world can be got from comparing the enacted adolescence of Rosemary with the factors of Nicole's early life: taken together they carry a criticism of society which contributes to the atmosphere of breakdown and decay of which the book is redolent. (pp. 134-42)

That Fitzgerald should have found breakdown for his theme is not, perhaps, surprising at a time when *The Waste Land*, the great war Memoirs, and *But It Still Goes On* had all been written. But he is unique, I think, in making a great novel out of such a theme, and in the way he accomplishes it. It is true that in its pages can be found mention of cosmopolitan society, and the names of unidentifiable internationality. . . . But *Tender Is the Night* is not a chronicle novel: it does not attempt to give a panoramic view of society, nor is its focus predominantly social. It is a novel about individuals, and whatever typicality they have it is not with their representative qualities that Fitzgerald begins; the suggestions of a breakdown on a vaster scale arise out of the failures and compromises of the individuals, and not the other way round. So it is right that the book should close anti-climactically with the reports of Dick's return to America, their distancing effect suggesting his tired emptiness of ambition and vitality, his being at the lowest curve of his brilliant bow.

> In the last letter she (Nicole) had from him he told her that he was practising in Geneva, New York, and she got the impression that he had settled down with someone to keep house for him. She looked up Geneva in an atlas and found it was in the heart of the Finger Lakes section and considered it a pleasant place. Perhaps, so she liked to think, his career was biding its time . . . ; his latest note was postmarked from Hornell, New York, which is some distance from Geneva and a very small town; in any case he is almost certainly in that section of the country, in one town or another.

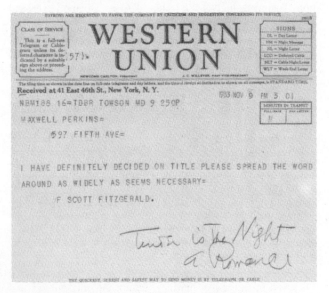

*A telegram to Maxwell Perkins from Fitzgerald, with Perkins's notation of the novel title chosen by Fitzgerald. Reproduced courtesy of Random House, Inc.*

It is a very moving ending and a supremely tactful one. (pp. 146-47)

John Lucas, "In Praise of Scott Fitzgerald," in Critical Quarterly, Vol. 5, No. 2, Summer, 1963, pp. 132-47.

## ARTHUR MIZENER   (lecture date 1964)

[*Mizener is an American educator and critic who is chiefly recognized for his biographies of Fitzgerald and Ford Madox Ford. In the following excerpt from a lecture on* Tender Is the Night *delivered in February 1964, Mizener discusses Fitzgerald's presentation in the novel of wealthy, imaginative, and self-disciplined individuals and the emotional price they pay to maintain their way of life.*]

The whole opening section of **Tender Is the Night,** I mean the opening section of the novel in its original form, which for all the deepest and most moving meanings of the novel is far the best form, the whole of this opening section is written to show us how people of great wealth, great imagination, and great self-discipline can create a magnificent life.

As is fairly well known Fitzgerald had actually observed this life. The little society that gathers on the beach of the Riviera and dines with the Divers is modeled closely on the group that actually lived there in the early twenties, around the Gerald Murphys, to whom *Tender Is the Night* is dedicated. That dedication, if you remember, reads "To Gerald and Sara Murphy." That remark, that dedication, referred to an observation Picasso once made after visiting the Murphys when he said, "Whatever Sara is, there's always a fête."

We see this beautiful life of the Divers through the eyes of Rosemary Hoyt who had learned what personal creativity is and, even more important, what self-discipline is from her experience as an actress. But she is still young enough not to understand what it costs to maintain these things all one's life. Thus she is aware of all the beauty of the dinner party at the Divers' when "the table seemed to have risen a little toward the sky like a mechanical dancing platform, giving the people around it a sense of being alone with each other in the dark universe." Then the Divers "began suddenly to warm, and glow and expand, as if to make up to their guests already so subtly assured of their importance, so flattered with politeness, for anything they might still miss."

What we see in the first part of **Tender Is the Night** is the ideal beauty of this life, the achieved perfection of this civilization (in the highest sense of that word) because that is all Rosemary Hoyt had the understanding to see. What we do not see is the cost in emotional energy, in selflessness, in self-discipline, because Rosemary is not experienced or old enough to understand that. Thus, this is the ideal opening for a book that wishes to make us feel the value of the fully imagined and completely civilized life. Nevertheless, even here in this first part, behind the intelligence and the controlled grace of the Divers that so dazzled Rosemary Hoyt, are hints of the cost. Afterward when Rosemary asked Dick Diver the time of day he said, "It's about half-past one. It's not a bad time. It's not one of the worst times of the day." For in fact Dick Diver has already begun to exhaust his emotional and imaginative nature. He has been carrying this world on his shoulders for six long years. Now he is approaching emotional exhaustion exactly as he approaches literal physical exhaustion at the end of the book, when he tries to lift a man on his shoulders on an aquaplane. "Did you hear I had gone into a process of deterioration?" he asks Rosemary. And when she denies it he says, "It's true. The change came a long way back, but at first it didn't show. The manner remains intact for some time after the morale cracks."

The reasons the task is so exhausting are also there for us to see in the book's first part if we only look. These are reasons that are represented for us by individual characters. But these characters are in turn carefully chosen to project something about a civilization. Not just American civilization, but Western culture as a whole. Where else could so representative a group of characters have been gathered as on the Riviera? There's the American social climber of another generation, Mama Abrams, "preserved," as Fitzgerald says, "by imperviousness to experience and a good digestion, into another generation." There is Luis Campion, the Spaniard, letting his monocle drop into the hair on his chest and saying to his friend, "Now, Royal, don't be too ghastly for words." There is the American McKisco who is writing a novel on the idea of *Ulysses* which "takes a decayed old French aristocrat and puts him in contrast with the mechanical age"; the McKiscos are belligerently anxious to keep up with what they called "what everybody intelligent knows." But McKisco is hopelessly defeated in his dinner-table argument by Tommy Barban, the extremely sophisticated, anarchic, European barbarian, who says with ruthless pleasantry, "I'm a soldier. My business is to kill people." He does it very well. There, finally, like a foreshadowing of what Dick Diver will become when his emotional energy is exhausted and his purpose in life gone, is Abe North, the brilliant musician who has written nothing for seven years and who is always with great dignity quite drunk. Abe North is, incidentally, modeled after Fitzgerald's close friend, Ring Lardner. "I used to think until you're eighteen nothing matters," his wife says at one point. "That's right," Abe agrees, "and afterwards it's the same way." There, finally, is Nicole Diver's sister, Baby Warren, who concentrates in herself all the Warren arrogance and imperception. These are the rich from all parts of the Western world, representing all the characteristic types the West has produced, free to do anything they choose, and they choose to honor lack of moral imagination until they reduce all but the perverted and the stupid to despair.

These are the people who are gathered about the Divers. They are, by the heroic trick of the heart that Dick Diver works over and over again, lifted up as if by magic to something beautiful. "It was themselves," Fitzgerald says, "[Dick] gave back to them, blurred by the compromises of how many years."

But Fitzgerald does not leave to implication what this all means for the society as a whole. He tells us directly what has happened to Western civilization by showing us a scene of the battlefield of the First World War and by letting us listen to Dick Diver talk about that war. Dick says,

> "See that little stream; we could walk to it in two minutes. It took the British a month to walk to it— a whole empire walking very slowly, dying in front and pushing forward behind. And another empire walked very slowly backwards a few inches a day, leaving the dead like a million bloody rugs. No Europeans will ever do that again in this generation. . . . This kind of battle was invented by Lewis Carroll and Jules Verne and whoever wrote *Undine,* and country deacons bowling and marraines in Marseilles and girls seduced in the back lanes of Wurtemburg and Westphalia. . . . Why, this was a love battle— there was a century of middle-class love spent here."

This is a society that has spent its emotional capital and is living off borrowed energy—the inherited recollection of the honor, the courtesy, the courage of the previous age; keeping, as Dick says about himself, the manner intact for a little while after the morale has cracked.

A little later in the novel, Dick sees a group of elderly American women in a restaurant, a group of Gold Star mothers who have come over to visit the graves of their dead sons. Watching them, Fitzgerald says, "he perceived all the old maturity of an older America. They made the room beautiful, and almost with an effort he turned back to his two women, [that is, to Rosemary and Nicole] at the table, and faced the whole new world in which he believed." A little later again, at Gstaad, Dick, according to Fitzgerald, "relaxed and pretended that the world was all put together again by the gray-haired men of the golden nineties," and "for a moment . . . he felt they were in a ship with a landfall just ahead."

In moments like this Dick Diver remembers his father, an impoverished, beautifully mannered southerner who, above all, "had been sure of what he was," as Dick never has been. As the society of which Dick was a part had exhausted the accumulated energy of its culture in the First World War, so Dick was using up the emotional energy, the expenditure of which gives meaning to his life and a reason for his exercise of self-discipline and his powers of bringing out all that is best in the people around him.

Ultimately, Dick cracks up, to use the word Fitzgerald himself used when he came to describe his own personal experience with this kind of disease. Dick suffered what Fitzgerald called in *Tender Is the Night* a lesion of vitality. He had, as Fitzgerald puts it, "lost himself—he could not tell the hour when, or the day or the week, the month or the year. . . . between the time he found Nicole flowering under a stone on the Zurichsee and the moment of his meeting with Rosemary the spear had been blunted."

This crack-up first shows as little fissures. Dick notices a pretty, but insignificant girl at Gstaad and plays to her. He is appealed to in a random way by an unknown woman at Innsbruck; he lets his heretofore submerged unconscious judgments of the people around him come to the surface in bitterness, as when he says to Mary North, "You've gotten so damn dull, Mary." He does that because he is now drinking in an uncontrolled way. There are still occasional flashes of his old will to exercise his charm on people so that they become their best selves. One comes the last time he sees Rosemary on the beach; another comes when he talks for a last time there to Mary North; but he can't keep it up. "The old interior laughter," as the book says, "had begun inside him and he knew he couldn't keep it up much longer."

The greatest of all Dick's efforts to remake people into their best selves has been his struggle with Nicole. After six years, just about as he has exhausted himself, she is cured of her schizophrenia. Becoming whole again she becomes a more intelligent version of her sister, a Warren "who welcomed the anarchy of her lover," Tommy Barban, who can, when she chooses, speak in her grandfather's voice, slowly, distinctly, insultingly. The one thing Dick Diver can save from the wreckage of his own exhaustion is, he believes, Nicole. All that remains—now she is well—is to free her from her dependence on him. By a supreme effort of will, as he sits quietly on the terrace of their house, he drives her from him. When she finally walked away, a free woman, "Dick waited until she was out of sight. Then he leaned his head forward on the parapet. The case was finished. Dr. Diver was at liberty.''

This is, I think, very beautiful. We remember that Baby Warren's idea had originally been to *buy* a doctor for Nicole until Nicole got well again: Dick had laughed helplessly at that idea originally, seeing everything that was going on in Baby's mind and knowing she would never see anything of what was going on in his. Twice during the engagement only his deep love for Nicole keeps him from throwing the marriage in Baby's face, as Fitzgerald says. But now at the end, Baby and her world have won. Dick's epitaph is pronounced by Baby Warren when Nicole says, ''Dick was a good husband to me for six years. . . . He always did his best and never let anything hurt me.'' Baby sticks her jaw out in good arrogant Warren style and says, ''That's what he was educated for.''

Thus the hard, brutal, anarchic world of the unimaginative rich has won and the representative of the good life, of awareness, of kindness, of understanding, has been set adrift to wander like a ghost of his former brilliant self through the little towns of upstate New York. . . . ''In any case,'' as the last sentence of the book says, ''he is almost certainly in that section of the country, in one town or another,'' as are perhaps all the heroes of transcendentalist American idealists. *Tender Is the Night* is a book filled with despair because Fitzgerald begins it with such a high ideal of what the American individual and American society might be if they'd only take full advantage of their opportunities. (pp. 26-32)

Arthur Mizener, ''On F. Scott Fitzgerald,'' in Talks with Authors, *edited by Charles F. Madden, Southern Illinois University Press, 1968, pp. 23-38.*

### SERGIO PEROSA (essay date 1965)

[*Perosa is an Italian educator and critic whose works reflect his long career as a professor of American literature. In the following excerpt, he traces the development of* Tender Is the Night *through its several distinct versions.*]

If *The Great Gatsby* is a dramatic *tour de force*, *Tender Is the Night* might be described, in a Jamesian sense, as a ''loose and baggy monster.'' It presents so many characters and such a complex of motives and themes that there is difficulty in establishing its exact value and its artistic significance. But the difference between the two novels is less substantial than we are made to believe. Fitzgerald himself thought that he had used different canons and had written a different type of novel. But he managed, through whole series of endless modifications, to bring *Tender Is the Night* within the more congenial ''line'' of development which runs from *Gatsby* to *The Last Tycoon*. As we read it today, *Tender Is the Night* does not represent a deviation from the main line of his fiction, but constitutes a bridge passage, showing an unquestionable continuity of themes and inspirations. Even in the complexity of its motives and the variety of its thematic variations, the informing idea seems to be the same as in the preceding novel. In the same way, it is the precise structural disposition of the plot that accounts for its artistic achievement. At least superficially, the theme is once more provided by the concept of the young, sentimental idealist corrupted and ruined by contact with the carelessness and selfishness of the leisure class, by involvement in the world of the very rich. And once more, a careful plot contrivance is responsible for bringing to light the latent and symbolic possibilities of that theme, even if in this case it was laboriously achieved.

The novel bristles with episodes and characters, in an ambitious attempt to give the ''picture'' of a whole world and to follow closely, in their gradual developments, the life stories of a group of characters without relying too much on principles of economy and structural tightness. A depth of realization is combined with an extensive treatment of the subject matter, explored and illustrated in its details and organized according to its inner growth. Only at the very last, and not conclusively, did Fitzgerald manage to tighten the structure and to get a firm grasp of the theme.

As Fitzgerald published it in 1934 after seven or eight years of painstaking composition, *Tender Is the Night* gives the impression of a vast and chaotic fresco, written in compliance with the ''pictorial'' method advocated by James in his early writings. The main concern seems to be for the ''creation of imaginary psychologies'' according to the formula advocated by Ortega y Gasset, and the manner of presentation apparently goes back to the well-established tradition of the nineteenth-century novel. A group of characters is set in a well-defined and recognizable historical and social situation, and their psychological reactions are followed until these give substance to, and provide a development for, the story—determining and illustrating it at the same time. Charged with philosophical implications, this kind of novel presupposes the necessity of the ''long story''; there is no foreshortening, and depth is achieved through an exhaustive analysis of the characters' motivations. It *was* a new departure in Fitzgerald's fiction. But he did not seem to be satisfied with it and revised and reorganized the novel according to a different structural perspective, which stressed the linear development of the story. In this ''final version,'' published posthumously in 1948, Fitzgerald restored the dramatic quality of the novel at the expense of its pictorial vividness. In this way both its informing idea and its fictional achievement were made clearer and brought closer to his main ''line'' of fictional development.

The road which leads to this result is as long as it is complex. (pp. 102-03)

The very first idea, conceived in the summer of 1925, was to write a novel dealing with ''an intellectual murder on the Leopold-Loeb idea,'' ''about Zelda and me and the hysteria of last May and June in Paris.'' The tentative title was *Our Type*. Right from the start the idea was to make the protagonist representative of an entire social class. Fitzgerald began working on it in the fall of 1925, and he completed one-fourth of it by the next April, when he announced to his agent, Harold Ober, that he would complete twelve chapters by the end of the year. But he had already changed his original concept, and he wrote that the book ''will be . . . concerning tho this is absolutely confidential such a case as that girl who shot her mother on the Pacific coast last year.'' The ''intellectual murder'' has been replaced by a matricide—a murder whose motivation can only be emotional or psychological, and the fact is important for a writer like Fitzgerald, who was more open to the charm and suggestion of emotions than to the stimulus of ideas.

The first draft of the novel, of which we have only four chapters, is known as the ''Melarky Case.'' Francis Melarky, a young Hollywood technician touring Europe with his mother, arrives on the Riviera. He has already been involved in a drunken brawl in Rome, and we learn that he has been dismissed from West Point for insubordination; he has a violent temper, and his inborn dissatisfaction and latent rebellion will be released in the Europe of the expatriates. His father is serving a prison term, and he can hardly suffer his dominating mother;

he is caught in an impossible situation, and it is easy to foresee that he will revert to desperate means. Of the two titles that the novel might have taken, the first, *The Boy Who Killed His Mother*, admits of no doubt; the second, *The World's Fair*, emphasizes the importance of the setting and the environment which determine Francis' violent actions, indicating at the same time that he was to be representative of a larger collapse of moral values.

The first chapter shows Francis in Rome, disgusted with himself and the "natives," exasperated by the city which seems "corrupt" to him. At the end of a wild night he is beaten by some taxi drivers and then by the police. This episode will be reworked later to show Dick Diver's final deterioration; at this point, it is Francis' mother who manages to get him out of jail. She has for the first time a clear indication of his exasperation and can assert her moral superiority over him, as Baby Warren will later do in *Tender Is the Night*. It is a dark and gloomy beginning, marked by an atmosphere of violence and disorder. Even the airy landscape of the Riviera, in the second chapter, cannot dispel the gloom. Francis arrives on the Mediterranean beach just as Rosemary does and is taken up by a group of carefree expatriates led by Seth and Dinah Piper (originally Roreback). The episodes in this second chapter were for the most part retained in the novel, but here Francis, in contrast to Rosemary, is still disgusted and dissatisfied: life in France seems to him as "empty and stale" as it was in Rome, and there is premonition of disaster when he tells his mother: "I thought I could go to pieces better if we had a car." His meeting with the Pipers (a first incarnation of Dick and Nicole Diver), however, seems at first to give a certain order to his life and to stimulate his willingness to work: "He wanted desperately to get back into pictures."

In the third chapter, during a party in the villa of the Pipers, Francis gives way to the temptation to make love to Dinah. This ill-advised behavior only heightens his state of inner tension, and he is driven to thoughtless and irresponsible acts which speed his ruin. He acts, for instance, as second in a duel between Gabriel Brugerol and Albert McKisco and shows his willingness to take part in the duel—to give or receive the *coup de grace*—when he is not concerned in the quarrel: "All right"— he says—"but this time it's me. And eight paces." He is prevented by the bystanders; but when he misses the chance of going back to work for an American film company in France, owing to his mother's opposition and to his indecision, it becomes clear that his destiny is marked. Faced with the possibility of leaving and thus saving himself, he remains instead entangled in the dubious and dangerous game of the expatriates, and when Seth goes to see him, he gets the impression that "he looks exactly like a man planning a murder." Francis accepts the invitation to go to Paris with the Pipers to see Abe Grant off to America, and there he flirts with Dinah (Chapter four) as they take long taxi rides through the city. His behavior becomes more and more irresponsible: he goes to a homosexual hangout, attacks a Negro and beats him, despising himself at once for his weakness, and then throws himself into a disastrous escapade with a girl named Wanda Breasted, who turns out to be a lesbian and attempts suicide.

The "Melarky Case" stops at this point, although Fitzgerald at various times wrote his friends and his agent that he had "nearly finished" the novel; and it stops at the very point when Francis realizes that he is disgusted and disillusioned by every woman he has met: "God damn these women!" is his final comment, and his mother seems to be included in his curse.

There is no indication of how he was to murder his mother, but it is worth noting that one of the characteristics of *Tender Is the Night* is already present: an insistent imagery of corruption and sexual disorder, of uncontrollable violence and crude realism—which is at the same time the background and a reflection of the protagonist's decay. The writer's interest, however, wavered between the two elements. The interplay between Francis' dissipation and the corrupted world around him is not clearly defined. The motivation of Francis' behavior seems to lie only in his pathological predisposition to violence and disorder. He figures, furthermore, as the only protagonist; the Pipers remain in the background, and although they hasten his deterioration, they remain marginal and external. (pp. 104-06)

The transformation of Francis into Rosemary begins to take shape in the second draft, known as the "Rosemary Version," or as the "Kelly-shipboard Version," of which only a single chapter and fragments of the second remain. The action begins here at an earlier stage and is set on a liner bound for Europe. Fitzgerald wrote Perkins in 1929 that he was working night and day on the novel "from a new angle," and as the second draft has points in common with both "The Rough Crossing" and "One Trip Abroad," it is safe to infer that Fitzgerald worked at it for a short time in 1929-30. The general concept of the breakdown of the protagonist in contact with Europe remains unchanged, but the relationships between the various characters undergo a definite modification.

A brilliant young movie director and his wife, Lewellen and Nicole Kelly, move gradually into the foreground. He is leaving America for Europe because he feels drained and must take a vacation. A symptomatic episode takes place at the very beginning: a young American named Curly jumps overboard to meet the challenge of two college girls and to perform a gratuitous act of protest "out of weariness with it all." Although he is rescued, his plunge into the abyss can be taken as a symbol of an abdication from life as it will be later exemplified in the novel. It is significant that Kelly is attracted by him, going to the extent of providing him with liquor after the captain has expressly forbidden it. This detail might suggest that he is ready for "experimenting"; and it means that he will not refrain from any temptation that Rosemary might offer him. Rosemary is here a young actress whose mother gets her to sneak from tourist class into first class to meet Kelly and extract, if possible, a contract from him. She is introduced to Kelly, but Kelly is "sick with everything" as much as Francis was; he is weary of his neurotic wife, who is given to drinking, just as Francis was weary of his mother. Going to Europe, he is running away from impotence and decay, and probably trying to run away from himself as well: "He didn't know what relation he bore to Nicole or to the world," we are told. And it can be expected that in Rosemary he will find a factor that will hasten his process of deterioration.

This draft is interrupted before any actual development of the story. But we can see that the general atmosphere evoked in this brief fragment is again one of moral disorder and corruption, and it is important to perceive that the role of protagonists is taken up by the married couple, while Francis-Rosemary is relegated to a secondary position. The draft represents an unmistakable transitional stage toward the completed novel; Kelly himself prefigures Dick (his name, originally Francis, shows Francis' link with Dick, too), while Rosemary and Nicole will gradually develop into the characters of the novel, even if Rosemary's dubious behavior will be toned down. But the whole conception of the novel underwent a radical change in

1931-32 after Fitzgerald's own collapse and his wife's hospitalization. The idea of a compact, dramatic novel gave way to the idea of "a double decker novel," which would rely more and more for subject matter on his personal experiences and for form on the "pictorial" method. (pp. 107-08)

Fitzgerald estimated that he would write fourteen chapters divided into three parts ("Part I From outside mostly. II Nicole and Dick. III Dick"), but he wrote the whole story in twelve chapters, and this third version brings us to the very threshold of *Tender Is the Night.* The two working titles which Fitzgerald had adopted were both discarded: *Doctor Diver's Holiday* because he found the reference to Dick's profession depressing, *The Drunkard's Holiday* because it gave away most of the contents. This version is therefore best known as the "Dick Diver Version," both because it is centered on Dick's story and because the method of presentation tends to focus as much as possible on Dick, who was to be called Dick ("the gentleman of leisure," as M. J. Bruccoli rightly suggests) in the first part, Dr. Diver in the second ("husband and physician"), and Diver in the third ("the emotional bankrupt and spoiled doctor"). Of the two suggested titles, however, the second would be more to the point, because in this version the protagonist's disposition to drinking plays an all-important and prepossessing role.

The informing idea of the natural idealist corrupted by the *haute bourgeoisie* remains latent in the background, while Dick's ruin is brought about by his pathetic weakness and by his drunken disposition. Here Dick does not seem properly a victim of "the compromises forced upon him by circumstances" but rather a victim of his very "flabbiness," of his lack of "tensile strength," and of his "secret drinking," which he had begun during the war. It is a substantial difference from *Tender Is the Night* because the outer forces are less destructive here than they will be in the published novel.

The main line of the plot is already that of *Tender Is the Night* as it was published in 1934. It opens with the arrival of Rosemary on the Riviera and her meeting with Dick and Nicole; the duel between Barban and McKisco (this time due to Barban's wish to keep Nicole's secret hidden) follows, and then the trip to Paris to see Abe off, with the beginning of Dick's love for Rosemary and Nicole's collapse. Next is a retrospective chapter (the fifth), as foreseen in Fitzgerald's notes for the "General Plan," which reveals Dick's and Nicole's past, Dick's flight in search of Rosemary and of himself, his trip to America for the death of his father, his drunken brawl in Rome, his encounter with Rosemary, ending in complete breakdown and in his failure as a man and as a psychiatrist, and his final separation from Nicole, who has become Barban's mistress. The order of the main episodes is the same as in the published version, even if this version has a few marginal episodes that will be cut or compressed in the novel. But the general tone and significance of the story—on account of a number of minor details—are substantially different.

To begin with, Dick is not the *brilliant* scientist that he is in the novel, although his personal charm is unquestionable and he is willing to risk his career for Nicole. His first book, for instance, is published at his own expense: "his book which upon consideration of $150.00 help from Dr. Diver, Messrs. etc. etc. were to present this autumn to the German speaking psychiatric world." From the very start his desire to be loved and admired is accompanied by a kind of sentimental weakness and emotional complacency, and he has begun drinking, we remember, "during the war." During his flight from Nicole

(Chapter VIII) he is attracted by quite a number of women. He dreams of the girl-friends of his youth, flirts without a moment's hesitation with an "undifferentiated" girl, indulges in a thoughtless adventure with a woman whom he takes for a governess and who is in fact the mistress of his friend; on the ship on which he returns from America after his father's funeral he spends afternoons in the cabin of a lady, and when he finally meets Rosemary in Rome his efforts are clearly directed to the egotistical purpose of seducing her ("to make her," as we read in this text). His moral deterioration is clearly defined in sexual terms and indicated by his urge to pick up women as soon as he sees them. He seduces Rosemary in a rather detached way, realizing immediately that she means very little to him; he does not abandon himself to the illusion, at least, of redeeming and refreshing love. It is not yet a question of achieving "poetic justice," as in the novel, and Rosemary is not seen as the girl "that crowns the other girls with meaning"—she is simply one more conquest, and it is Dick himself who manages with skeptical cynicism to get rid of her after the short-lived affair: "She would have come up to him but he pretended to be tying his tie." There is no sign here of his emotional involvement, and very little suffering on his part, at least as far Rosemary's destiny is concerned; and the lack of a moral, dramatic dilemma on his part disqualifies him in our eyes.

Just as Kelly had done, Dick finds it natural in this version to sympathize with Curly, the young man who has jumped overboard, and to give him liquor; the episode marks his growing disinterest as a psychiatrist in a case which is apparently neurotic. His only reaction to incumbent ruin is to take more and more to drinking, and this congenital weakness becomes the most important determining factor of his deterioration, if it is true that the external pressures are less active here than in the novel. Nicole, in fact—and this is another very important feature of this version—does not so much act on him as a disrupting force as assist him in an attempt to strengthen his resistance and to preserve his integrity. Nevertheless, her repeated attempts at reconciliation are met by Dick with coldness and disinterest, or even with needless accusations and abuse; and it is Dick that almost drives her to adultery with his detached and insufferable behavior. (pp. 109-11)

Summing up . . . we can see that Dick's story was presented in a particular light in this version. The abyss beneath his feet is opened by his obstinate refusal of any moderation, by his contempt for moral and social values, even by his ill-nature—all of them aggravated by his immoderate drinking. And if he falls pathetically into the abyss, he is not pushed into it by a concurrence of inexorable tragic forces. Responsible for his predicament to a great extent, he has not the justification of having been crushed by the weight of a psychological and social conflict which he could not escape. Fitzgerald's statement of purpose, therefore, is only partly carried out. The difference from *The Beautiful and Damned* is not so marked as he would have it. Only in the fourth and notably in the fifth version was this imperfection of focus gradually eliminated and the balance between the external factors and Dick's inborn weakness reestablished according to the original plan.

In the fourth version, published serially in four numbers of the *Scribner's Magazine* (January-April 1934), some stylistic and structural modifications begin to bring the story back to the right track. Some cuts were probably due to a moralistic concern with the possible reactions of the magazine's readers—Fitzgerald omitted for instance Warren's confession of his incestuous relation with Nicole, Dick's interview with the Chilean homosexual, and smaller details. But he also omitted Dick's conversation with Mary on the terrace after his "dismissal" from the beach, which has nothing to do with sexual matters but only serves to stress Dick's self-pity at his failure. This cut clearly had the effect of quickening the pace of the narration and thus might have been suggested by structural reasons. In fact, the writer now was trying to attain a kind of dramatic intensity in the single scenes by tightening the episodes as much as possible. But this cut has also the effect of presenting Dick in a slightly different light by removing at least one pathetic aspect of his final surrender.

This process is continued in the fifth version, which appeared in book form in the same year. The scenes cut for moralistic purposes were reintegrated into the text, but a number of different scenes were cut from the serial, with the result of hastening the pace of the story, of placing the pathetic aspect of Dick's failure in the background, and of stressing the determining value of the social pressures at work to destroy him. Working feverishly on the galley proofs, which had eventually to be reset for the most part, Fitzgerald cut out six scenes: two dealing with Abe North at the Ritz bar, the episode of Dick's involvement with the governess at Innsbruck, his affair with the woman on the ship, the episode of the boy who jumps overboard, and finally Nicole's calling with Tommy Barban at the retired bootlegger's at the end of book. He also inserted some new material and revised carefully, from a structural and stylistic point of view, the whole texture of the book. (pp. 112-13)

Dick's deterioration is presented here with more equanimity (his sexual disorder is toned down and his drinking is not so much insisted on), while part of the blame is transferred to his wife Nicole and, above all, to the world of careless corruption that she represents and personifies. Dick's plight is seen from a more sympathetic point of view, and the corruption of the *haute bourgeoisie* becomes not only a catalytic agent, but a determining factor of his individual ruin. Through an elaborate interplay of psychological and social conflicts, clearly defined in the book version, the story can develop on the double level of Dick's personal *épuisement* and of his defeat "forced upon him by circumstances." These two levels are strictly interrelated and interdependent, since Dick's *épuisement* is determined by his devotion to Nicole, who is herself part and parcel of the *haute bourgeoisie,* and since the defeat of the idealist is prepared by his psychological condition of *épuisement.* (p. 113)

Malcolm Cowley edited the *"final version"* in 1948. Not everyone accepts it as legitimate or useful, but there can be no doubt as to Fitzgerald's intentions regarding his book. Whoever sees Fitzgerald's own copy feels that Malcolm Cowley followed to the letter his intention. As a working text, moreover, this "sixth" version *is* extremely useful: by toning down the brilliancy and the suspense of the 1934 edition, and by developing the story in a linear way without the possibility of misunderstandings as to its real purport, it gives further consistency, unity, and symmetry to the book. It enhances its dramatic quality at the expense of its pictorial value and thus brings it closer to the main "line" of Fitzgerald's fiction. (p. 116)

The subject matter is woven into recurrent patterns, embroidered as it were on the counterpoint of thematic motives, exhausted in all its implications by a detailed documentation and an underlying comment. It was, as suggested, and as Fitzgerald himself wanted to make clear, a typical nineteenth-century tradition that he had in mind, a shifting from the dramatic

convention to the pictorial ideal. There are, therefore, no "marginal" episodes in the book, if practically all of them serve to illustrate a widespread condition of moral disorder and social corruption, for the most part represented in sexual terms: Nicole's incest, Baby Warren's uncleanliness, the ghostlike reappearance of their father at the end, Collis Clay naked and drunk in bed before Baby Warren, the homosexuals in the clinic, the girls who greet the sailors with their panties from the room where Nicole has given herself to Barban, the disgusting reappearance of Mary Minghetti with Lady Caroline shut up in jail for having picked up girls, and so on. If Dick's sexual exploits are remarkably toned down in the last versions of the novel, even Rosemary seems to be tainted by this prevailing atmosphere: not only because of her adventure in the train with her young friend, but because she cannot give herself to Dick in Rome since, as she puts it, "those things are rhythmic." Abe North's deterioration or McKisco's cheapness are none the less revealing for not being strictly related to sexual matters.

We are confronted with a wealth of details and episodes which make up the "pictorial" background and are at the same time strictly functional from a thematic point of view. The imagery is overwhelmingly sexual or woven in with suggestions of violence and disorder: Barban's exploits as a military leader or as a lover, the Negroes in Paris, the murder at the station, Nicole's homicidal tendency, the brawl in Rome, and so on. The wolves are present everywhere, roving undisturbed through Europe. Rosemary has a passing contact with them, and she might still save herself. But if the idealists like Dick succumb to such an array of disrupting forces, it is because the times themselves are "out of joint." And this thematic implication is made clear in the novel exactly because its pictorial quality allows the writer an extensive documentation.

In his way, therefore, Fitzgerald complied with the precepts of the Thirties. The danger for him was that the "tempo" of the narration, "so harrowing and highly charged," might also be "out of joint." This danger was still present in the 1934 edition of the book; and one might claim that the new chronological disposition of the "final version" helped quite a bit to remove it, or at least to obscure it as much as possible. In this new disposition everything seems to find its proper place and to harmonize with the general trend of the story. All the motives gradually introduced in the first book are resolved in the last, and the tone of the narration is made uniform; what is lost in brilliance is gained in clarity and simplicity.

The first book is written on the key of Nicole's psychic disorder, in an atmosphere of postwar dissolution which might recall Thomas Mann's *The Magic Mountain* or *Death in Venice.* The fifth book is written on the key of Dick's psychic and moral *épuisement.* In the first the action is chiefly seen through the sane and steady eyes of Dick and filtered through his conscience as he scrutinizes Nicole's illness and his own involvement. In the fifth book the action is filtered through Nicole's restored sensibility, to which Dick's breakdown is gradually revealed. If in the first book Dick stands up "like Grant in Galena, waiting to be called to an intricate destiny," in the fifth he is shown in the same attitude, "biding his time again like Grant in Galena." If in the first book the movement slowly rises toward the climax of the wedding, in the last it ends its downward course, which had already begun at the end of the second book, with a dizzy descent. In the second book the action is seen "from without," filtered through Rosemary's eyes, and the young girl, dazzled by her love for Dick and by the brilliance of the Divers cannot see the horror that lies behind

*Zelda and Scott Fitzgerald at the time* Tender Is the Night *was written. Reprinted by permission of Harold Ober Associates, Incorporated.*

the fascinating façade of their life on the Riviera. The movement is for awhile suspended, almost as if in a dance or ballet, until it gradually resumes speed and precipitates to the conclusion. In the third book the rhythm becomes broken and nervous; the unity of the point of view is lost, as though the events themselves were no longer under control, while the movement begins its downward course until it becomes precipitous and fractured in the fourth book. The last book marks then the completion of the waning parable until it reaches a disconsolate conclusion "not with a bang but a whimper," as T. S. Eliot had prophesied. "You felt—Fitzgerald had written to Hemingway—that the true line of a work of fiction was to take a reader up to an emotional pitch but then let him down or ease him off. You gave no aesthetic reason for this—nevertheless, you convinced me." He had more than learned a lesson: he had mastered his technical means in a perfect way. (pp. 126-28)

A literary masterpiece, as Valéry once stated, is never "finished"—it is only abandoned. *Tender Is the Night,* after so many years of revision and reworking, was somehow "abandoned" by Fitzgerald; he was prevented from "finishing" it either by weariness or by his early death. But the reasons for its greatness and for its validity are unimpaired; one might even say that the writer stopped reworking it at the right moment. (p. 130)

*Sergio Perosa, "The 'Intricate Destiny'," in his* The Art of F. Scott Fitzgerald, *translated by Charles Matz and Sergio Perosa, The University of Michigan Press, 1965, pp. 102-31.*

## MILTON R. STERN   (essay date 1970)

[*Stern is an American educator and critic specializing in American literature. In the following excerpt from his study* The Golden Moment: Novels of F. Scott Fitzgerald, *he discusses* Tender Is the Night *as an essentially social, rather than psychological or philosophical novel.*]

[In a letter to his daughter Scottie written six months before his death, Fitzgerald wrote]: "What little I've accomplished has been by the most laborious and uphill work, and I wish now I'd *never* relaxed or looked back—but said at the end of *The Great Gatsby:* 'I've found my line—from now on this comes first. This is my immediate duty—without this I am nothing.'"

The broken decalogues, disobeyed and trampled on, led to nights of despair, days of the locust—always Fitzgerald felt that his generation's departure from the good, gone world of the old commandments of work and discipline and politeness was a symptom of a general breakdown and insanity in Western civilization. Intrigued as he was by Spengler's *Decline of the West,* which he had begun to read in 1926, he had come to see Zelda's insanity and his own alcoholism as private, painful symbols of the disintegration of a time and a nation. His own jazz-age golden moment was a brief, insular American idyll that turned out to be a sordid corruption of its own promise. (pp. 289-90)

"Often I have encouraged [your being an old-fashioned girl]," he told Scottie, "because my generation of radicals and breakersdown never found anything to take the place of the old virtues of work and courage and the old graces of courtesy and politeness. But I don't want you to live in an unreal world or to believe that the system that produced Barbara Hutton can survive. . . ." The broken decalogues. The old virtues and the old graces, work and courage, courtesy and politeness, came from a dream-filled past that also somehow produced "Barbara Hutton." In the history of an entire people the golden commandments from a lost Sinai were replaced by gilded calves in the promised land. That's what *Tender Is the Night* is all about, and to see it as a "psychological novel" is to miss what Fitzgerald himself meant when he said, using confusing terminology, that the book is a "philosophical, now called psychological novel."

He meant by that term that unlike *The Great Gatsby,* which he called a "dramatic" novel, *Tender Is the Night* is not a lyrical organization of dramatic moments, but a Jamesian, scenic arrangement of dramatic moments, a visual novel whose scenes are to suggest a philosophy of history. The history of manners, in what Fitzgerald meant by the "philosophical novel," becomes a cultural clue to the meaning, the moral development, of an era. An entire civilization can be tested and evaluated in the values that surround the fate of the hero of the novel. Fitzgerald thought of *Tender Is the Night* as his *Vanity Fair,* even calling it *The World's Fair* in one draft. In technique, as well as in "classification," the novel is one of scenes rather than lyrical, "elaborate and overlapping blankets of prose." The novel reflects what Fitzgerald learned in Hollywood, and the difference in voice between his two greatest novels is immediately discernible when you reflect that you tend to remember great poetic passages, or at least a sense of poetic prose, from *The Great Gatsby* but that you don't recall many, if any, such passages from *Tender Is the Night.* What you tend to remember is scenes, movie stills almost, of the action. Unquestionably, a "dramatic" novel can also be a "philosophical" or "psychological" novel, but the extent to which the prose of *Tender Is the Night* insists upon scene and action creates a question that provides a most fruitful critical clue to the nature of the novel: in the development of the book, version after version, what did all the scenes provide as consistent elements, regardless of change of characters, plot, and even specific scenes? What kinds of elements did Fitzgerald keep and re-create in the various changes and deletions and rewritings? They were most decidedly not elements focusing on case history, on psychiatry, on psychological analysis of behavior, normal or abnormal. Those elements crept into the story with the onslaught of Zelda's illness, but they never became the focus of the story. The elements common to all versions in the development of the plot are exposing scene after exposing scene of high social life, either in Hollywood or on shipboard or among American expatriates in Europe. That life is presented constantly as the flashing world of broken decalogues most likely to unhinge and undo the innocent seeker or whatever is left of the responsible, polite personage in a society in which the old virtues and graces no longer define people, success, or social life itself. Consistently, over the years, as Fitzgerald tried to discover what his book was about—what *story* he was telling—he focused on scenes in which the relationships of characters became vehicles for the delineation of the corrosion of the personage among destructive, significantly expository, social types. Without question, Zelda's emotional collapse provided material for the final version of *Tender Is the Night,* but, as in the earlier versions, disease leads outward to the social heritage which it sums up rather than inward to a causal analysis of individual psyche. Fitzgerald's "philosophical, psychological" novel is a social novel if it is anything, and if it is anything it is a great social novel which demonstrates how the intricacies of psychology can describe, in dramatic form, the effects of an eroded society on human personality. (pp. 290-92)

[What] is more important in the growth of the novel than the chronicle of the materials is a recognition of what remains unchanged. In all seventeen drafts, it is clear that what Fitzgerald is concerned with is a presentation of the glittering golden world in its effect on the yearning, searching American, on the bitter arrivist, on the dewy *naif,* on the strong and callous rich, but most of all, on the innocent, expectant idealist. The famous note he wrote to himself [see excerpt dated 1932] . . . is not so much an explanation of the many complex changes in the various versions of the novel as it is an explanation of what increasingly summed up the revisions as they undulated and surged toward the final draft: "The novel should do this," the note said: "Show a man who is a natural idealist, a spoiled priest, giving in for various causes to the ideas of the haute bourgeoisie, and in his rise to the top of the social world losing his idealism, his talent and turning to drink and dissipation. Background one in which the leisure class is at their truly most brilliant and glamorous."

The dedication of the novel,

To
GERALD AND SARA
Many Fêtes

is a dedication to people who were near, dear, and very valuable to Fitzgerald, and who, for him, were sparklingly representative members of "the leisure class" at its "truly most brilliant and glamorous." Gerald and Sara Murphy, among the most cultured and gracious of the American expatriates in Europe, were, for Scott, living examples of the old virtues and the old graces, of civilization wrought to an exquisite turn through work and courage, courtesy and politeness. They were the older, vanished, promising America. At the same time, they were representative to him of the new world that emerged from the ruin of the Victorian time that in self-deluded ways opened the doors to "Barbara Hutton," to gaudy cosmopolitanism, graceless money, and callous power that supplanted and destroyed—paradoxically was fostered by—the graciousness the Murphys personified. (pp. 294-96)

The Murphys epitomized the world Fitzgerald wanted to capture in all the versions of his novel, and in his relationship to them of envy and belonging, of hostility and love, and of constant fascination, Fitzgerald saw in them everything that his underdog sense of "work as the only dignity" repudiated and to which his romantic sense of life's charmed possibility as an extended golden moment drew him. As the Murphys dispensed grace and fun to the new, young postwar world and were, in turn, sustained within it, Fitzgerald, wistful and envious, saw that what was needed was a touch of the ruin which, neglected in the sunny world of money and culture and gaiety and independence, was the personal and international reality which alone could turn fairyland into a paradigm of the actuality of human limitations. Dick Diver was to know "that the price of his intactness was incompleteness."

"'The best I can wish you, my child,' so said the Fairy Blackstick in Thackeray's *The Rose and the Ring,* 'is a little misfortune.'" One part of the Murphys that went into Dick Diver was the association between taste and ruin, charm and lesions of vitality, civilization and defeat. It was hardly that the Murphys' charming life was also a charmed one. They had deep and real misfortunes of their most personal own. It was that they *seemed* to live in grace because they lived in graciousness, and Fitzgerald wished to capture them in all the tensions and ambivalences of "the old virtues and the old graces" and the "Barbara Hutton" world of broken decalogues. His immersion in ruin (and his often being ostracized by it) was, finally, what set Fitzgerald off from the Murphys and gave him a full, evaluative overview of the world that, for him, they represented. He analyzed and analyzed them, straining his relationship with them to the breaking point and causing them to assert, by gesture and by direct statement, that they could not tolerate Fitzgerald's company as long as he was either drunk, rude, and sophomoric or analytic, "objective," and probing. In his own identification of himself as both failure and outcast on the one hand, and on the other hand both spiritual descendent of the Murphy's world and crown prince of the world of broken decalogues, he fashioned his most problematical and complex composite self, Dick Diver. By injecting his own increasingly chaotic and catastrophic experience, as an index to the morally chaotic state of the new young world, into Gerald Murphy's impeccable and apparently enviable life on the Golfe Juan, he was once more able to turn his autobiographical impulse into the impersonality of an art which allowed him to express his most personal statements. Drunk or sober, on a spree or remorseful, he found the meaning of his own experience in his novel and its hero. And though he said more than once that he was sometimes drunk when he wrote ("I would give anything if I hadn't had to write Part III of *Tender Is the Night* entirely on stimulant"), he insisted fully as often that his constant revising made writing for him not merely an act of alcoholic sensibility but also, and finally, a sober, disciplined, and rational act of will. (pp. 296-98)

Drink, the euphoric sense of making it, the excitement of ever-promised new chances, both highlighted and mediated between Fitzgerald's ambivalences as the intoxication of wealth and power did his nation's. The morning after demanded sober self-examination as both Fitzgerald and his nation dived from the spree of the twenties into the cold Depression years in which *Tender Is the Night* was published. But regardless of these generalizations and speculations, the plain fact is that as he was caught—often drunkenly—between the ambivalences, Fitzgerald did come to identify his own disintegration with his nation's disintegration of the old decalogues beneath the weight of its own wealth and power: the "times" of "the happy ending" have "changed," and "I don't want you to . . . believe that the system that produced Barbara Hutton can survive."

By the time he came to the Dick Diver version of *Tender Is the Night,* working out of the themes implicit in *This Side of Paradise* and *The Beautiful and Damned* and artistically solidified in the motifs that expressed those themes in *The Great Gatsby,* Fitzgerald had complete amalgams of associations in his imagination. They were amalgams in which the corrupt new world of soulless wealth becomes identified with the new America as the new America spreads over the world, is internationalized, and loses its old unique identity; amalgams in which, in a completely contrasting set of associations, the destroyed, old world of our Gatsby-youth, Dick Diver's lost "safe, beautiful world" of promise, hope, passion, charm, virtues, and graces, is identified with an older America that is forever buried as, with Dick, we say goodbye to all our fathers. In short, in *Tender Is the Night,* Fitzgerald supplied an international setting whose series of scenes allowed him a Jamesian "philosophical" perspective of the two Americas. His "philosophical novel" thus allowed him a broader canvas and more complex contrasts than ever before with which to present a moral picture of the two Americas that had appeared as "the actuality" and "the dream" in *The Great Gatsby.* Dick Diver, the spoiled priest intricately and inextricably associated with both Americas, like Fitzgerald with his worlds of personage and personality, significantly is not only the drunk ruined by wealth and power, but is also the potential world-redeemer self-ruined by his own responses, by his deepest need to be liked and loved. Like Gatsby, he lives in both worlds and has a real home, "these days," in neither. As composite fictive character, he is his creator and his creator's nation. "I am part of the race consciousness," Fitzgerald told his secretary. "I take people to me and change my conception of them and then write them out again. My characters are all Scott Fitzgerald," fully as much as the characters that Dick "took to him" and "worked over" were all Diver creations of the composite moment. Fitzgerald restored people to an essential meaning as he remade them into part of a character, as Dick restored people to an essential identity in his creative moments: "It was themselves he gave back to them, blurred by the compromises of how many years." (pp. 301-02)

*Milton R. Stern, in his* The Golden Moment: The Novels of F. Scott Fitzgerald, *University of Illinois Press, 1970, 462 p.*

### GEORGE D. MURPHY   (essay date 1973)

[*In the following excerpt, Murphy examines the reasons for Dick Diver's psychological collapse.*]

Ever since 1934, readers of F. Scott Fitzgerald's *Tender Is the Night* have had difficulty in perceiving a cause adequate to its hero's catastrophe. It is not, as Henry Seidel Canby remarked when he reviewed the book [see excerpt dated 1934], that there

are no reasons provided for Dick Diver's fate, but rather that "there are too many reasons, no one of which is dominant." Whether there should be one dominant reason is an arguable point; but, alternatively, Fitzgerald does not suggest any clear combination of causes which can be seen to account synergistically, as it were, for the velocity and extent of Dick's decline.

Over the years, however, readers have easily seen that the many more or less discrete reasons for Diver's collapse can be arranged under two broad categories. The first is socioeconomic: An idealistic, middle-class hero is used and discarded by a rich and careless leisure class. But Fitzgerald was more subtle and more honest than to confine himself to such a baldly dialectical motivation, and provided a second, psychological category of motivation by ascribing to Dick some flaw of character which made him extraordinarily susceptible to the fate which overtook him. This psychological flaw has been designated by most of the critics of the novel as a compulsive addiction to charm—which Dick himself was aware of and ruefully dismissed as a "trick of the heart"—or as a fatal vulnerability to the need to be loved. Both psychological deficiencies are abundantly demonstrated in the novel, but they are, I think, only the symptoms of a deeper flaw which has gone unremarked by the critics.

"I loved my father—always deep in my subconscious I have referred judgments back to him, to what he would have thought or done." Fitzgerald wrote this about his own father when he died in 1931, and readers of *Tender Is the Night* may recall that he used essentially the same words in describing the psychological significance of the death of Dick Diver's clergyman father: "—again and again he referred judgments to what his father would probably have thought or done." In these passages, Fitzgerald was not only displaying his inveterately autobiographical bent, but stating a literal truth, a truth, moreover, which is an elementary principle of psychoanalytic theory and one which can shed a good deal of light on the vexed matter of Dick Diver's motivations. The "deeper flaw" in Dick's personality—to use jargon, which, as a psychiatrist, he might himself have used—was the failure of his super-ego to come effectively to terms with the disruptive, libido-charged impulses of his id and ego.

The super-ego was what Freud, when he constructed his structural hypothesis of the personality, called that part of the mind which serves the function of censorship; that is, it resists the emergence from the unconscious of those impulses which would engender conscious conflict. The super-ego derives its attributes from the behavioral ideas of the child's parents, which become incorporated into the developing child's personality. A constituent portion of the super-ego is the ego ideal, which is an idealized picture of what one wants to be, while a very small portion of the super-ego is experienced in consciousness as conscience. When the super-ego fails or falters in its task of keeping in check the predominantly sexual impulses pervading the unconscious, the consequences are highly disruptive to the personality. Now, the operative points to be made here are that the super-ego is basically nothing more than an internalized parent, that *Tender Is the Night* is largely concerned with the disruption of personality, and that it is much involved with both explicit and symbolic variations on the relationship of parent to child.

One way in which Dick Diver had patterned his life after his father's example is by his choice of profession, for his practice of psychiatry can be taken as the secular equivalent of his father's cure of souls, and this parallel lends considerable irony to the "papal cross" with which Dick blesses Gausse's beach at the novel's end. And, as Abraham Steinberg has perceptively noted, what little Fitzgerald allows us to see of Dick's actual practice of psychiatry suggests that his professional manner owes less to the tolerant objectivity of Vienna than it does to an authoritarian paternalism. For example, when Dick is confronted at the end of Book I with the pathetic spectacle of Nicole in full, schizophrenic cry, all he can do is say again and again, "Control yourself!"

Franz Gregorovius, Dick's partner in the Swiss clinic, complains at one point about the difficulty he has had in breaking away from the shadow of his father's and grandfather's scientific eminence and becoming his own man. Dick too bears the weight of a paternal tradition, a genteely Christian tradition of self-abnegation and "good instincts, honor, courtesy, and courage," learned from his father who had in turn imbibed it from "the two proud widows who had raised him." Dick was consciously—and uncomfortably—aware of the ineffective incongruity of those values for him, values derived from a father dismissed by his own contemporaries as "very much the gentleman, but not much get up and go about him." Fitzgerald's own father was in fact a gentlemanly and occasionally drunken failure, and Fitzgerald had been aware of this since childhood. There is even reason to suppose that his father's weakness accounted for Fitzgerald's notable concern with the theme of failure in his fiction.

One aspect of his father which seemed to have particularly struck Fitzgerald was his capacity for ingratiation and self-abnegation. After his father died in 1931, Fitzgerald recalled a story that the father had told of himself and which disarmingly reveals these qualities: "'Once when I went into a room as a young man I was confused, so I went up to the oldest woman there and introduced myself and afterwards the people of that town thought I had good manners.'" The anecdote appears almost word for word in *Tender Is the Night,* where it is attributed to Dick's father, and Fitzgerald may, of course, simply have been employing the husbandry of a hard-pressed freelance of letters by transplanting material virtually unchanged from an unpublished eulogy to his novel. Yet, the story had had a long-term fascination for Fitzgerald, for he had used it, unaltered in its particulars, to apply to the father of Stephen Palm, the hero of "The Romantic Egoist," which was, of course, the ur-version of his first novel, *This Side of Paradise.* The ingratiating aspect of the paternal personality revealed by these three, practically identical, reminiscences, seems not notably different from Dick Diver's impulse to charm others—a trait which Fitzgerald himself notoriously shared.

Psychologically, Dick's compulsion to solicit love and approval from others can be interpreted as a maneuver to gain the approval of his internalized parent, or ego-ideal. This is to say that Dick does what his father did and what his father approved, and in gaining the admiration of others, he presents his ego-ideal with tangible evidence of his fidelity to its standards and, in turn, gains its approval.

The trouble, however, is that Dick, even on a conscious level, seems not to have entirely approved the standards of that internalized parent, regarding them as outmoded, ineffectual, and, most importantly, ego-denying: "A part of Dick's mind was made up of the tawdry souvenirs of his boyhood," Fitzgerald wrote as he had Dick remember the Sundays passed in his father's church. "Yet," Fitzgerald went on, "he had managed to keep alive the low painful fire of intelligence." Not

surprisingly, then, Dick's super-ego, under fire as it were from Dick's id, ego, and ambivalent consciousness, proves inadequate to its censorial task, and Dick indulges in behavior of a sexual and aggressive nature which is repugnant both to his internalized parent and to that portion of his conscious mind which still ruefully submits itself to the domination of that parent.

A psychological equation is worked out just beneath the surface texture of *Tender Is the Night*: a super-ego which seeks to impose unrealistic controls upon the unconscious simply compounds the violence with which that unconscious will assert itself once the weakness of its censor is discovered. We catch a glimpse of this violent formula early in the novel as Dick conducts his sightseeing party around the battlefield at Amiens. This passage, one of Fitzgerald's most justifiably famous set-pieces, is often cited as neatly emblematic of the differences between the pre- and post-war generations, but it also relates to the conflict going on within Dick and which will soon be destructively resolved: "Why, this was a love battle—there was a century of middle-class love spent here. This was the last love battle."

The control which Dick had exerted over himself during his "heroic period" as a student of psychiatry in Vienna and Zurich before the war was costly. Even then he knew that "the price of his intactness was incompleteness," which is to say that he was aware of the danger of so rigorously repressing emotion in favor of such conscious virtues as "memory, force, character—especially good sense." Denying the representations of his unconscious, he managed for a while to anesthetize emotion and attain to "the fine quiet of the scholar, which is nearest of all things to heavenly peace." But this, Fitzgerald wrote, "had to end," implying that Dick's personality was too fragilely perfect, that it would be better to be "faintly destroyed" and to "build out some broken side (of the personality?) till it was better than the original structure." The result of this heroic asceticism was that, when his conscious values came under serious attack, they were incapable of incorporating and dealing with unconscious impulse and instead dramatically collapsed. And the source of these inadequate values was, as Fitzgerald put it, a number of "Achilles' heels," illusions about reality which, he implied, were parentally transmitted— "the lies of generations of frontier mothers who had to croon falsely that there were no wolves outside the cabin door," or, one might extrapolate, beneath the threshold of consciousness.

The picture of the "frontier mothers" transmitting their unreal values reminds us that *Tender Is the Night* began in 1925 as a tale of matricide, having for a while the explicit working title of "The Boy Who Killed His Mother." It dealt then with Francis Melarky, a young man with much of the charm Dr. Diver was to have, who, in a rage, murdered his mother because she stood between him and the enjoyment of the glamorously sensual life typified by the Riviera. From its very inception, then, the book was centrally involved with a pathologically expressed opposition of generational values. But in the 1934 version, it is the father who is the symbol of parental repression, and it is, I feel, much more than coincidental that the disintegration of Dick's personality should accelerate at the point where he learns of his father's death.

For that is precisely the point where it does begin. There have been cracks in the facade before, intimations of the decline to come, and much of the novel's appeal derives from our growing sense of the discrepancy between the serene luxury of the world we first glimpse with Rosemary on Gausse's beach and the realities of madness and drunkenness, of lubricity and violence that luxury disguises. But Dick's facade really crumbles when, at Innsbruck, he learns of his father's death. (pp. 314-18)

Indeed, how does that death affect Dick Diver? Within thirty pages, Fitzgerald compresses the father's funeral, the consummation of the affair with Rosemary, the drunken aggressiveness of the following hours in Rome, the fight with the taxi drivers, Dick's arrest, the fight with the police and his release from prison by the despised Baby Warren, who then "possessed a moral superiority over him for as long as he proved of any use." On these words Book II ends; the disintegration of Dick's personality is fairly underway, and there only remains for Fitzgerald the task of charting its consequences in Book III.

As I suggested above, Dick's compulsion to exert charm and play the self-effacing "paternal" role can be interpreted as an oblique stratagem to gain the love and approval of others as a surrogate for the approval of his father. The intrusion of sexuality into that role by the consummation of his affair with Rosemary is a violent betrayal of it. It is significant, then, that when he finds that he is no longer loved by her, he plunges into violent, drunken despair. His real father is dead, and even substitute affection has been withdrawn from him.

As Dick passed through the crowd outside the Roman police station, he suggested the depths to which he felt that he had descended by crying out, "I want to explain to these people how I raped a five-year-old girl. Maybe I did—." He had not, of course, but his speech indicates the extent at that moment of his preoccupation with sexuality, and with sexuality of a perverse sort. Once the super-ego has ceased, as it has by this time, to exert an effective control over the unconscious, it is hardly surprising that sexual material of a polymorphous nature should begin to obtrude into consciousness.

A paradox about Fitzgerald is that, despite his reputation as a chronicler of "flaming youth," his fiction contains little explicit sexuality. In this respect, his art exhibits more than a touch of puritanism, as did, in fact, his personal life, save of course, for when he had been drinking. Then his conduct was very apt to undergo a startling reversal. But *Tender Is the Night* is more directly concerned with sexuality than all his other work.

In addition to heterosexual encounters, such as the bedroom episode, between Nicole and Tommy Barban (which, for Fitzgerald, is rather graphically sketched), homosexuality plays a sizeable role in the novel. One thinks, in this connection, of Royal Dumphy and Luis Campion, who are first encountered on Gausse's beach, the beach where Dick himself has played the "pansy's trick" with the black lace drawers; of the Sapphic masquerade of Mary North and Lady Caroline Sibly Biers; and of Dick's professional encounter with Francisco Pardo y Cuidad Real, the "Queen of Chili." Young Francisco's case parallels Dick's own situation: Dick urges him to control his "sensuality—and, first of all the drinking which provokes it." It is a prescription he might well have written for himself. As a matter of fact, Dick is strangely drawn to the troubled young man, feeling that he was as close as he "had ever come to comprehending such a character from any but the pathological angle." Both men have the trick of charm, the charm which made it possible for "Francisco to perpetrate his outrages," and they have fathers—Francisco's alive and Dick's but recently dead—who have tried ineffectually to censor the "outrages" of their sons. They differ, of course, in the nature of their "sensuality," for Dick is heterosexual. Yet, it is a matter

of record that Fitzgerald had been almost obsessively troubled at times by the worry that he might have been at least latently homosexual since Zelda had accused him of having a sexual interest in Hemingway back in 1926—an accusation which apparently had no foundation in anything save jealous expatriate gossip and Zelda's incipient madness. Nevertheless, the accusation disturbed Scott, and it is possible to view Dick Diver as an authorial projection paired off against the mirror-image of an epicene Francisco, having in common ineffectually monitory fathers, alcoholism, charm, and the potential for sensuality of one kind or another.

But incest is the most thematically important sexual variation encountered in *Tender Is the Night*. Robert Stanton, the first critic to address himself to the book's incest motif [see excerpt dated 1958], rightly contended that he had no need to persuade his readers of the importance of that motif as it had been recognized from the beginning. That the precipitating cause of Nicole's psychosis was a literally incestuous relation with her father; that there is a variety of metaphorical incest implicit in the therapeutic transference Nicole must make to her husband/psychiatrist; that there are incestuous overtones to the connection between Dick and the barely nubile Rosemary, star of "Daddy's Girl," are facts that cannot escape the attention of even the most determinedly innocent reader.

Incest occurs nowhere else in Fitzgerald's work. *Tender Is the Night* is in most respects conspicuously autobiographical in its inspiration (there exists, for example, a chart on which Fitzgerald had carefully paralleled the cases of Zelda and Nicole). Yet, there seems to have been nothing in Fitzgerald's experience to account for the intrusion of the incest motif into this novel. Zelda's psychosis was not precipitated by incest, and Fitzgerald seems to have deliberately invented this detail. Why, then, in the composition of this particular book should the incest theme exert such a powerful attraction upon a writer whose treatment of sex had heretofore been characterized by a rather romantic diffidence?

I submit that it was because incest was the most compelling metaphor available to him for the radical breakdown of the relation between parent and child, and, by extension, of the relation between the super-ego and the rest of the personality.

*The Fitzgeralds on the Riviera, 1929. Reprinted by permission of Harold Ober Associates, Incorporated.*

Psychoanalytically, Dick's involvement with incest on a met-aphorical level can be glossed in at least two ways, and they are not necessarily contradictory.

Dick's choice of a life role was deliberately imitative of his father's, and it was a role which emphasized a charming so-licitude for others at the expense of ego-gratification, a role which compelled him to act as a kind of self-effacing parent for Nicole and for others. If Dick was ambivalent about that role, a violation of the role through incest would be a dramatic repudiation of the father and a resolution, dramatic in propor-tion to its perversity, of that ambivalence. Also, Dick's in-volvement in a kind of emblematic incest can be interpreted as a consistent extension of the father-role in terms of the dream logic of the unconscious. This is to say that it can be seen as the acting out of long-repressed Oedipal hostility: the child who admires and imitates the courteous gentility of his father is simultaneously aware of that father's concealed sexuality. Thus, when in adult life the child carries the father-role to the grotesque conclusion of incest, he exposes, in the most hideous manner conceivable to him, the hypocrisy of the father.

The drama of a breakdown of the father-child relationship ex-pressive of the dysfunction of a vital censor in the psyche animates much of the action in *Tender Is the Night,* and, if its readers have traditionally complained of the difficulty of as-signing a cause adequate to Dick Diver's collapse, they do so because it cannot be seen to immediately and obviously or-ganize that action. Though it pervades the book, it does so in an oblique and appropriately "unconscious" way, and this is an important, if not fatal, lapse of Fitzgerald's craft. It is, however, an understandable lapse. *Tender Is the Night* is the most nakedly self-revealing of all Fitzgerald's basically auto-biographical fictions, and Dick Diver's collapse is a troubled foreshadowing of Fitzgerald's imminent "crack-up" in 1935-36. Fitzgerald proved as unable to portray explicitly this dysfunc-tion in Dick's personality as he was unable to confront directly its symptoms in his own. (pp. 318-21)

> *George D. Murphy, "The Unconscious Dimension of 'Tender Is the Night'," in* Studies in the Novel, *Vol. V, No. 3, Fall, 1973, pp. 314-23.*

**BRUCE L. GRENBERG**   (essay date 1978)

[*In the following excerpt, Grenberg considers the relationship between the characters in* Tender Is the Night *and the historical events that form the background to their lives.*]

At the outset I would like to disclaim wholly the all too prev-alent view that in Fitzgerald's works historicity functions merely as glossy topicality, serves merely as an enhancing background to "popular" fiction. Rather, Fitzgerald is a "critical," a "philosophical," and, if you will, a "moral" historical nov-elist, intent on comprehending and explaining in rational terms the motives and implications of human events, viewed simul-taneously as personal experience and public phenomena. In-deed, Fitzgerald has little sympathy for those who conceive of history as a simple sequence of recorded events; for him history holds the most profound meaning. In a passage once intended for *Tender Is the Night,* he defined history as "a figured curtain hiding that terrible door into the past through which we all must go." Thus conceived, history in fact conceals its truth from those who passively view the "figured curtain" of human events as some sort of fascinating, but uninterpreted hiero-glyph. But for those who penetrate the hieroglyph and draw

aside the curtain, history reveals the deepest, if the darkest, truths.

Fitzgerald's historical concerns in *Tender Is the Night* are, indeed, both deep and dark. The ten-year period which the book illuminates is summarily and explicitly defined by him in **"Echoes of the Jazz Age"**: "The ten-year period that, as if reluctant to die outmoded in its bed, leaped to a spectacular death in October 1929, began about the time of the May Day riots in 1919." And this metaphorical personification of his-torical events is persistent in Fitzgerald's mind. He character-izes the 1919 riots themselves as springing from the universal feeling that "something had to be done with all the nervous energy stored up and unexpended in the War"; he characterizes the "golden boom" of the 1920s as the release of that unex-pended human energy in "the greatest, gaudiest spree in his-tory." This precise historical period, with "its splendid gen-erosities, its outrageous corruptions and the tortuous death struggle of the old America," is the informing essence rather than the topical background of *Tender Is the Night.* Throughout the novel Fitzgerald interprets history's curtain and takes us through that door to our past—gently, with the artist's "trick of the heart"—as he charts his generation's strangely hopeful passage from World War I to the Great Depression.

To appreciate Fitzgerald's consummate skill in fusing person-ality and history we must first recognize that when he centered the novel's motivation and action in Nicole's schizophrenia, he was thinking in metaphorical as well as in clinical terms. Explicitly, his notes on Nicole [see excerpt dated 1932?] reveal his conception of her character in specific historical terms, for in trying to define her role in the novel, he concentrated not upon her psychiatric development *per se,* but upon the sequence of significant dates in her life. She is born in 1901; in 1914 her courting begins; in June 1917, the "catastrophe" occurs; and in February 1918, she takes up residence in the Clinic. Then,

> To middle October bad period
> After armistice good period
> He returns in April or May 1919
> She discharged June 1, 1919. Almost 18
> Married September 1919. Aged 18

These particular dates cannot be viewed merely as an author's memory log to aid in keeping the narrative straight. Their most salient feature is their uncanny correspondence with the most significant dates of the first two decades of the twentieth cen-tury. Even more explicitly, the significant dates in Nicole's personal history correspond to those marking America's in-volvement in *the* great event of the early century—World War I. Nicole is born precisely with the twentieth century (1901), and her sexuality, which proves so disturbing and rife with conflict, emerges in 1914, coincident with the beginnings of the war. Nicole is raped by her father in June 1917, the exact month in which American troops first landed in France, perhaps the first historical event discomfiting America's traditional pos-ture of splendid isolation from European affairs. Yet Nicole doesn't seem to realize the full horror of her experience and doesn't enter the Clinic until February 1918, just as America didn't realize the implications of her commitment to the war until American soldiers made their delayed entry into the fight-ing on the Western Front on 31 January 1918.

The analogy between Nicole's sickness and America's partic-ipation in the war is extended and quite precise. Nicole suffers a "bad period" from February until October 1918: the Germans launched their last great offensive in March 1918, and American troops, who first appeared in the front lines 31 January 1918, fought intensely, impressively, but indecisively until October, when Germany began the general retreat which was to end with her surrender. The Armistice, of course, came in November, at which time Nicole inexplicably recovers from her illness and begins a "good period." To be sure, the twentieth century is "Nicole's Age," Fitzgerald's title for the note on her character; her experience and her suffering typify rather than merely illustrate the experience and suffering of an immature America in the opening decades of the twentieth century.

For Devereux Warren, in his role as Nicole's father, virtue is but a mask to his true self-interest just as for France, Germany, England, and Russia alike the patriotic virtues of courage, honor, duty, and loyalty cloaked the naked truth of *Realpolitik* and imperialism. . . . Devereux Warren's rape of Nicole has the immediacy and shock of personal experience, to be sure, but at the same time it dramatizes and specifies the emotional reality behind the larger trauma of the war. Incestuous rape is an apt metaphor for the intra-familial, self-destructive conflict of World War I, a war in which two opposing nations were led by grandchildren of Queen Victoria, a war in which no nation was really victorious.

The effect of the rape upon Nicole is most clearly and directly expressed in her letters (1918-1919) to Captain Dick Diver, written while she is a patient at Dohmler's Clinic and while Dick serves his military duty in a psychiatric unit at Bar-sur-Aube. And though these letters are of considerable psychiatric interest, their more comprehensive purpose lies in their identification of Nicole's personal trauma with the broader cultural trauma of the war. Again Fitzgerald is explicit: he divides the letters "into two classes, of which the first class, *up to about the time of the armistice,* was of marked pathological turn, and of which the second class, *running from thence up to the present* [i.e. 1919], was entirely normal, and displayed a richly maturing nature" (my emphasis). From their inception then, these letters are not intended as expressions of a literal lunatic; rather, they are Ophelian utterances, burying sense within nonsense, essence within evanescence. They define not merely the pained and frightened soul of an eighteen-year-old girl in a Swiss asylum; they define all the pain and fright of a century only eighteen years old but already at the edge of despair.

Unlike the merely suggestive ravings of Ophelia, Nicole's letters do yield a consistent theme: her pain and disorientation originate not so much with the rape itself as with her awareness that her father had bred her a victim to his lies. Her trust in him and in his self-proclaimed, selfless love had made her vulnerable to unexpected attack. Thus Nicole, like so many of the participants in the war, sees herself as having been betrayed by her own inherited ideals—"what I had been taught to associate with the role of gentlemen." She finds herself in "what appears to be a semi-insane-asylum, all because nobody saw fit to tell me the truth about anything. If I had only known what was going on like I know now I could have stood it I guess for I am pretty strong, but those who should have, did not see fit to enlighten me."

Appropriately enough, the letters begin with a reference not to madness, but to the military and the war: "I thought when I saw you in your uniform you were so handsome. Then I thought Je m'en fiche French too and German." And though Nicole knows Dick is a doctor, she continues throughout her correspondence to address him as "Mon Capitaine," "Captain Diver," "Dear Captain Diver," and finally as "Dear Capi-

taine"—a polyglot salutation fitting to an American in France in 1918.

Such pointed, cumulative details virtually demand that we read Nicole's letters as a personal paradigm for the larger madness of the Western world. Indeed, in mid-1918 Nicole's words to Diver might well have served as the A.E.F.'s motto: "I am lonesome all the time far away from friends and family across the Atlantic I roam all over the place in a half daze." And the fluctuations in Nicole's health during her last weeks at the clinic correspond to the vicissitudes of the last stages of the war. Shortly before getting better Nicole relapses into the uncertainty and frustration of one who has been cut off from her cultural roots:

> I think one thing today and another tomorrow. That is really all that's the matter with me, except a crazy defiance and a lack of proportion. I would gladly welcome any alienist you might suggest. Here they lie in their bath tubs and sing Play in Your Own Backyard as if I had my backyard to play in or any hope . . . which I can find by looking either backward or forward.

(In the summer of 1918 the Germans again drove to the Marne in a frantic last effort to break through to Paris, and the A.E.F. found itself at Chateau Thierry and the Meuse-Argonne, far removed from the safe "backyards" of nineteenth-century American idealism.) After this uncertainty there is a month with no word from Nicole, and then "suddenly the change"— that is, to the "entirely normal, richly maturing nature." Her "acute and down-hill" schizophrenia comes to a clinically improbable, but metaphorically poignant end; Nicole "recovers" as the war ends. . . . (pp. 106-10)

Neither the war's end nor Nicole's "recovery" can be intended as a complete resolution of conflict. Rather, each represents a subtle remission of continuing trauma and disorientation, and a bewildered longing for a security that once existed, or at least had been thought to exist. For inherent in Nicole's situation is the question that haunted the Western world after 1918: if the old ideals of order, love, propriety and property, honor, and social responsibility were irrevocably lost in the war, and the "true" nature of society was revealed to be irrational chaos springing from man's aggressive self-interest and amoral will to survive, could the war's survivors find or invent *any* principles to govern individual and social behavior?

Fitzgerald's fictional portrayal of this paradoxical desire within denial is characteristically original, and, it seems to me, psychologically as well as artistically convincing. True to the metaphor of schizophrenia in the novel, Nicole and the war generation she represents can neither assent to the nineteenth-century values which had deceitfully concealed their own hollowness nor accommodate the destructive chaos that had been born out of that hollowness. But such a suspension of belief can lead only to a complete paralysis of being, and Nicole and her generation find themselves forced into a pragmatic choice of the lesser evil. In terms of the novel's psychiatric metaphor, Nicole can "transfer" to Dr. Dick Diver her remembered affection for her father and the ideals he represented prior to the catastrophe; in terms of the novel's historical analogue, the survivors of the war find themselves reverting to an uneasy faith in nineteenth-century idealism simply because in 1919 there is no other faith possible.

As the character embodying these contradictory nineteenth-century ideals in a world which at best can grant them only conditional assent and ultimately must abandon them altogether, Dick Diver is, understandably, resistant to easy explanation. (pp. 110-11)

Whether defining Dick as a ruined idealist or a fraudulent psychiatrist, all the interpretations of his character, and consequently of the whole novel, rest on the assumption that Nicole typifies and represents the American leisure class exclusively, that she is, in brief, merely rich and merely neurotic. But insofar as Nicole represents young, naive America in the twentieth century, disillusioned in her ideals and shattered by the unforeseen violence of World War I, Dick's efforts to bring her back to wholeness must be interpreted in a very different light. Dick in this context does become a truly believable culture "hero" like Grant, embodying his society's highest aspirations in spite of his own human shortcomings: "It was themselves he gave back to them, blurred by the compromises of how many years." And his ultimate failure to "cure" Nicole in this larger context is nothing less than the tragic failure of American idealism in the twentieth century. As in *The Great Gatsby*, **"May Day," "The Diamond as Big as the Ritz,"** and so many of his stories from the Twenties, Fitzgerald in *Tender Is the Night* depicts an America whose ideals, noble in themselves, are becoming untenable, whose idealists, by the very virtue of their ideals, are being corrupted, or crushed and cast out by a new culture progressively giving itself over to material, amoral pleasure.

Dick's nineteenth-century ideals and sensibilities survive well into the twentieth century simply because they are not exposed directly to the shock of World War I. Young and inexperienced in 1917, Dick is buoyed up by "illusions of eternal strength and health, and of the essential goodness of people; illusions of a nation, the lies of generations of frontier mothers who had to croon falsely, that there were no wolves outside the cabin door." And though Switzerland is "washed on one side by the waves of thunder around Gorizia and on another by the cataracts along the Somme and the Aisne," Dick remains safe in his insular innocence: "the war didn't touch him at all." Even when Dick returns to Zurich in 1919, supposedly having "been to war" for two years, he reaffirms his innocence by telling Franz, "I didn't see any of the war."

Thus, Fitzgerald characterizes in Dick's "innocence" the residual force of nineteenth-century idealism which survived the war. (As well as the punitive Versailles Treaty, the war's end did give birth to the idealized League of Nations.) Such innocence and such idealism of course *are* impossible illusions to those who have felt and seen the "Batter of guns and shatter of flying muscles" Wilfred Owen describes in his poem "Mental Cases." "These are men whose minds the Dead have ravished," says Owen; theirs is the world in which Nicole, agonizingly, amazingly, lives. But in Dick, Fitzgerald creates the psychiatrist-healer of such torment.

When Dick returns in 1919 to Zurich, to Nicole, and to his "intricate destiny," his hubristic determination "to be a good psychologist—maybe to be the greatest one that ever lived" defines the greatness of his vision and at the same time foreshadows the inevitability of his failure. For Dick demands too much of his "psychiatry." Unlike Dr. Dohmler and Franz Gregorovius, whose clinical method offers only a sanitized "refuge for the broken, the incomplete, the menacing, of this world," Dick through his psychiatry attempts to regenerate the survivors of nightmare and recreate a world of purpose and order in which meaning, not mere existence, is possible. Thus, Dohmler and Franz ultimately can only treat Nicole. Dick marries her.

Dick's commitment to Nicole, therefore, is whole and personal—metaphorically rather than narrowly therapeutic. With his nineteenth-century ideals of courage, honor, courtesy, loyalty, and love, Dick attempts to lead Nicole out of Switzerland's unreal sanity, first to the half-safe, half-controlled, half-real world of the Villa Diana, then back through the remembered horrors of Beaumont Hamel and Thiepval to the naked reality of Paris, Rome, and Naples, reality fraught with endless danger, endless possibility.

Nowhere else in his fiction does Fitzgerald depict so clearly or so forcefully the antinomies of mind and character that for him define the modern man, paradoxically driven by the "sense of the futility of effort and the sense of the necessity to struggle; the conviction of the inevitability of failure and still the determination to 'succeed'—and, more than these, the contradiction between the dead hand of the past and the high intentions of the future." Further, in Dick's tortured efforts to rekindle light and purpose in Nicole's world Fitzgerald dramatizes what he defines elsewhere as the mark of a "first-rate intelligence": "the ability to hold two opposed ideas in mind at the same time, and still retain the ability to function"; Dick *is* "able to see that things are hopeless and yet be determined to make them otherwise." And if Dick's nineteenth-century will to believe that life can be made coherent and rational appears as historical fiction to the twentieth century, Fitzgerald dramatizes it as a noble, a tragic, perhaps even a necessary and "supreme" fiction.

From beginning to end, Dick and Nicole's marriage is a contest, compressing within itself all the uncertainties and paradoxes of the 1920s. Although the sobriquet "Dicole" suggests the inseparability of Dick and Nicole "in the first days of love," is soon becomes clear that their union is one of uneasy confluence and embattled wills. To prevail over Nicole's madness, Dick must perpetually attract, woo, and win her to his idealizing vision. She, to be sure, is momentarily charmed by the correspondence between Dick's promise of love and peace and her own recollections of childhood's innocent dreams: "When I get well I want to be a fine person like you, Dick." But she is also persistently seduced by the power of the Warren family and its money: "They were an American ducal family without a title—the very name written in a hotel register, signed to an introduction, used in a difficult situation, caused a psychological metamorphosis in people." And under the influence of this amoral vision, which sees power as antecedent to value, Nicole (like her sister, Baby) can only view Dick's idealism, no matter how qualified, as an inversion of reality: "You used to say a man knows things and when he stops knowing things he's like anybody else, and the thing is to get power before he stops knowing things. If you want to turn things topsyturvy, all right, but must your Nicole follow you walking on her hands, darling?"

Furthermore, Dick's relationship to Nicole is essentially flawed by the contradictions inherent in his attempt to be both husband and doctor to her. In both roles, of course, Dick is trying to reaffirm the ideal of selfless love which Devereux Warren had virtually destroyed, marriage serving as an apt metaphor for the elevation of self-interest (sexual desire) into a social ideal (the family). But Dick knows, and we know, that the desires of a husband and the responsibilities of a physician are scarcely more compatible than the desires of a lover and the responsibilities of a father. And Dick is aware, further, that his commitment to curing Nicole prevents him to a considerable degree from living with her. In fact, the ideal of selfless love which

Dick prescribes for Nicole's cure is in the very act of prescription self-defeating, for he can win Nicole over to himself only at the cost of her independent selfhood. And, as we shall of course see, if he allows her complete self-determination, he loses her absolutely.

From 1919 to 1925, "from Woolloomooloo Bay to Biskra," Nicole reveals her "schizophrenic" inability to live with reality or to escape from it, to trust in ideals or to disbelieve them. Her interior monologue which recounts the period reveals an essential confusion of identity, polarized significantly (in terms of subsequent events) between Dick and Tommy Barban: "When I talk I say to myself that I am probably Dick. Already I have even been my son, remembering how wise and slow he is. Sometimes I am Doctor Dohmler and one time I may even be an aspect of you, Tommy Barban." And her desire to flee to an inner sanctum of unknowing innocence—"Life is fun with Dick;" "We'll live near a warm beach where we can be brown and young together"—is opposed with equal force by a desire to grasp her experience, however horrible—"I am tired of knowing nothing and being reminded of it all the time." It is at this point of perfect but unstable balance between contrary and warring values that Dick and Nicole move to the Riviera. It is at a critical point of no return for western civilization that the novel begins—truly *in medias res*. It is June 1925; the crucial decade of the 1920s is half past, half future. (pp. 111-14)

By 1925, however, Dick's view of Nicole and the generation for which she is the synecdoche has undergone a "qualitative change"; his assured confidence of 1919 has been replaced by a more mature, but also a more ambivalent vision—less sure in its definition. Including old generation and new, sun-browned and moon-pale, experienced, naive, and those drones "preserved by an imperviousness to experience and a good digestion into another generation," Dick's party is seen to be a "desperate bargain with the gods," one of his "performances" to insure that each day be "spaced like the day of the older civilizations to yield the utmost from the materials at hand, and to give all the transitions their full value." As such, the party is a monument to Dick's nineteenth-century ideals of rational order and purpose. But his ideals include a commitment to truth as well, and since he cannot deny the existence of violence and chaos, Dick wishes his party to be "really *bad*," to include "a brawl and seductions and people going home with their feelings hurt and women passed out in the cabinet de toilette." Dick's "bad party," as its rubric suggests, is a reflection of his ambivalence, for through it he is not trying to eliminate chaos so much as he is trying to give it a manageable form; he is trying to subdue man's worse nature by a simple, direct appeal to his better self.

The party begins very well indeed. The markedly heterogeneous group of Abe and Mary North, Tommy Barban, the McKiscos, Campion, Dumphry and Abrams, Rosemary Hoyt, and the Divers had been at table but half an hour when "a perceptible change had set in—person by person had given up something, a preoccupation, an anxiety, a suspicion, and now *they were only their best selves and the Divers' guests*" (my emphasis). For the moment, at least, Dick makes the world "safe" for this lost generation, gives the party a seeming wholeness and security which the real world lacks. (p. 115)

For Dick the two most important people at the party are Nicole and Rosemary, for together they embody the complex object of his passionate idealism. Enough has been said about Nicole seen as the synecdoche of the war generation; by analogy, Rosemary compresses within her character all the salient features of the postwar generation. In one sense she is a mid-decade reincarnation of Nicole, a "Daddy's Girl" anachronistically possessing a prewar innocence: "Her body hovered delicately on the last edge of childhood—she was almost eighteen, nearly complete, but the dew was still on her." But the "raw whiteness" of her body identifies her with the McKiscos, Campions, *et al*, whose imperviousness to experience she shares; in the entire novel she does not comprehend, properly speaking, any one or any thing. And if from the mid-decade perspective of 1925 Nicole has become the dark past within whom Dick tries to rekindle light, Rosemary (now eighteen, notably the same age as Nicole when Dick first met her) stands as the pale future seeking her color and definition in the uncertain origins which only Dick can explain.

Within this metaphorical context, Nicole's relapse and Rosemary's hysteria at the end of the party define Dick's failure to provide new hope for the war generation and understanding for the generations that follow. Structurally and thematically this initial failure of the party prefigures Dick's repeated failures; throughout the novel violence does erupt, irrationally yet persistently, out of good feelings and the best of intentions—in the train station, in the hotel, in the police station and clinic, in kitchen and bathroom. And Dick more and more clearly becomes the man who can explain, but not explain away, the world's ugliness.

Immediately after the Riviera party with its absurd duel, Dick takes Nicole, Rosemary, and Abe and Mary North to Paris, the image and substance of modern, postwar life-in-death, as we shall see. But to define this world most precisely, Fitzgerald takes us back, with Dick, Abe, and Rosemary, to the world of Beaumont Hamel and Thiepval, the world of 1916 and the Battle of the Somme. And here at the *locus classicus* of the war's mindless futility, as we listen to Dick's poignant interpretation of the century's greatest trauma, we recognize just how profound, yet how helpless, he truly is.

Dick's interpretation of the war is intensely symbolic rather than military or narrowly political; it is philosophical rather than nationalistic. Indeed, looking out upon Beaumont Hamel and Thiepval, Dick is stricken by the likeness of the opponents, the similarity of their motivations, the identity of their fates. Throughout his resume he refuses to distinguish between French, English, and German, seeing them all simply as mutual participants in the battle. To fight at the Somme on whatever side, he says,

> "You had to have a whole-souled sentimental equipment going back further than you could remember. You had to remember Christmas, and postcards of the Crown Prince and his fiancee, and little cafes in Valence and beer gardens in Unter den Linden and weddings at the mairie, and going to the Derby, and your grandfather's whiskers."

Ultimately, the Somme is "the last love battle" in Dick's historical view; in it the virtues of "religion and years of plenty and tremendous sureties," wedded to the unrestrained imaginative force of "Lewis Carroll and Jules Verne and whoever wrote Undine," paradoxically gave birth to grotesque horror. In short, Dick's interpretation of the Somme conflict stands as a definition of the European tragedy which America willingly, if mistakenly, accepted for her own. And this battle, standing as archetype to the war's horrifying consumption of life and sanity, makes Dick's sense of *complete* loss rhetorically and emotionally true: "*All* my beautiful lovely safe world blew itself up here with a great gust of high explosive love'' (my emphasis). (pp. 116-17)

Thus, western idealism carried the seeds of its own destruction. But for Fitzgerald the war didn't happen ''over there'' or ''back then''; his concern in the novel is not with those who died at the Somme but with those who lived beyond that moral point of no return. And Dick's interpretation of the war is immediately and equally valid as a diagnosis of Nicole's traumatic experience, in which ''love,'' ''tremendous sureties,'' and ''years of plenty'' also gave way to eruptive violence. Thus, in the disheartened and cynical Abe, once a composer now just a drinker, we see all the creative energy irrevocably destroyed in the war, and in the feckless Rosemary we find all the pointless energy of the generation born too late for disillusionment, whose members in their self-concentration can conceive of no loss greater than a personal desire unfulfilled.

For Abe, who ''had seen battle service,'' Beaumont Hamel and Thiepval hold no dreamy, philosophical reminiscences; he responds to complex, ineluctable reality with simplistic, self-destroying pessimism: ''There are lots of people dead since and we'll all be dead soon.'' Even more disappointing is the response of Rosemary, for whom Dick recreates history in order to make a bridge between their ages. She is carried momentarily by the intensity of Dick's concern—if he had said ''they were now being shelled she would have believed him that afternoon.'' But ''I don't know'' is her persistent refrain, and she doesn't. She doesn't know whether Dick's lovely safe world blew itself up in 1916, 1919, or any other time. For her the battle is not a trauma, but a ''thrilling dream'' arousing not anguish, but warm, uninformed sentimentality: ''altogether it had been a watery day, but she felt that she had learned something, though exactly what it was she did not know.''

Within this context of Abe's conscious withdrawal and Rosemary's blissful ignorance, Dick's ambivalence is delicately yet firmly defined. Dick has seen too much of Abe's world to succumb to Rosemary's naive sentimentalities (''Later she remembered all the hours of the afternoon as happy''). But born with the end of the 19th century (1891 according to Fitzgerald's notes), Dick is the last surviving devotee of that era's ideals. And he must live by his faith, however futile it might prove, for he has no other: ''The silver cord is cut and the golden bowl is broken and all that, but an old romantic like me can't do anything about it.'' The proper image of Dick is that of Icarus flying to the sun though he knows the wings made by his father are fatally waxen. . . . To be sure, Dick cannot splice the silver cord nor mend the golden bowl of the world's fact. But tragically determined to nurse his own vision to the last, he can render the meaning of history into a ''whole affair'' in the alembic of his ordering mind, thus creating from horror ''a faint resemblance to one of his own parties.'' He can charm Rosemary, and he can support Abe. He can even sustain—for the moment—Nicole, abstracted and restless, moving closer and closer to reality's true heart of darkness.

When the action returns to Paris from the Somme battlefield, we see just what the modern world can be, and is, without Dick's controlling moral energy. The pattern of this new world is set by the Parisian house ''hewn from the frame of Cardinal de Retz's palace in the Rue Monsieur.'' Explicitly the house is said to ''enclose the future,'' and its inmates are perfect types of the species, postwar man: ''They were very quiet and lethargic at certain hours and then they exploded into sudden quarrels and breakdowns and seductions.'' Indeed, throughout the remainder of the novel aimless violence will continue to explode out of just such dazed preoccupation and lethargy.

It is thoroughly appropriate that Abe, not Dick, dominates the Parisian scene. Possessed merely of a ''survivant will, once a will to live, now become a will to die,'' Abe has ''given up about everything'' and is tired—even of friends—to the point of death. Hence, his departure from Paris clearly signals the end of life, not a new start: for him, ''it was such a long way to go back in order to get anywhere.''

Fitzgerald is emphatic. Just as the train whistles and moves, just as Abe waves and Dick responds, ''the sound of two revolver shots cracked the narrow air of the platform.'' And these shots fired by Maria Wallis, ''the young woman with the helmet-like hair,'' effectively mark the turning point in the novel's thematic development. As ''echoes of violence,'' the shots serve as a remembrance of things past, of the war and the original ''concussions that had finished God knew what dark matter''—as one observer notes, there is ''assez de sang pour se croire a la guerre.'' But the shots also foreshadow the events of 1928, the year in which Dick must say good-by to Abe for the last time, must say good-by to his father forever, must say good-by, finally, to *all* his fathers. Most subtly and perhaps most significantly, the shots and their aftermath foreshadow the only world that will remain to Dick after 1928— the world of Rosemary, Baby, and Nicole, a world in which Dick learns painfully what it means to live long after he has been shot ''through his identification card.''

As the last remnant of an older America in a changed world, Dick does not cope well with modern, senseless violence— even in 1925. He sees no causes, no goals, no meaning at all in Maria Wallis's action, and for the first time in the novel he can think of nothing to do or say. Nicole, of course, is already more acclimatized to a valueless world, and, as Milton Stern points out, she for the first time ''takes over and firmly prevents Dick from acting as savior, party-director, doctor.'' From this point on, in fact, Nicole will always adjust more readily than Dick to the world. Yet Fitzgerald makes clear that with the waning of Dick's energy and vision, something of value is being lost. At the end of the Wallis affair both Nicole and Rosemary (''who was accustomed to having shell fragments of such events shriek past her head'') want Dick ''to make a moral comment on the matter and not leave it to them.'' And when he is unable to ''resolve things into the pattern of the holiday,'' they are aware of the missing element: ''so the women, missing something, lapsed into a vague unhappiness.'' In that simple understatement whereby the complex inheritance of Dick's moral force becomes merely ''something'' missing, Fitzgerald captures the paradox of that force seen as essential, yet forever lost.

The scene in the Gare St. Lazare points ahead to a world in which expressive force must and will operate devoid of any moral purpose; the nineteenth-century American ideal of power and moral purpose indissolubly joined has been shattered. Dick himself is clearly aware of the ''turning point in his life.'' He knows that his survival and dignity can come ''only with an overthrowing of his past, of the effort of the last six years,'' knows that after 1914-1918 neither Nicole nor America can ever be truly innocent again. It is perhaps worth noting here, even as a supposition, that had Dick been able to accept a world without innocence he might have been able to come to terms with Nicole's and his own imperfections; beyond supposition, it is Dick's essential tragedy that his ideals allow for no re-vision. Like his predecessor, Jay Gatsby, Dick is trapped by the irresistible beauty of his own remembered dreams. From the memorable scene in Voisins to the end of the novel, whatever "repose" Dick has serves wholly as self-insulation from a world inimical to his dreams; whatever happiness he has must take the dubious form of fading memories. (pp. 118-20)

Dick's love affair with modernity, his infatuation with Rosemary, can be but a momentary fling. Naturally enough, he loves Rosemary's newness: "'You're the only girl I've seen for a long time that actually did look like something blooming'" he tells her at the Cote d'Azur. But he can only wince at the "vicious sentimentality" of her parodic innocence in the role of *Daddy's Girl*. And though on the one hand he wishes to "remove the whole affair from the nursery footing upon which Rosemary persistently established it," he also realizes that the affair is founded on precisely those "brave illusions" of the "nursery"—"tremendous illusions . . . that the communion of self with self seemed to on a plane where no other human relations mattered." In love with Rosemary's promise, Dick tells her so, but he tells her in the same breath: "Nicole and I have got to go on together. In a way that's more important than just wanting to go on." For ultimately Dick is committed to continuity of purpose and action in his own life and in the lives of others, even though he knows that continuity, philosophically and historically, is not possible.

Committed to the unyielding past and attracted to the implacable future, Dick at the end of Book I is the living persona of anxiety, fully occupied in controlling himself—his chin dominating "the lines of pain around his mouth, forcing them up into his forehead and the corner of his eyes, like fear that cannot be shown in public." As a moral idealist in 1925, Dick is a charming, admirable, but archaic remnant of an older civilization, struggling to maintain himself in a thoroughly alien world.

This mid-decade America introduced by the war-echoing shots in the Gare St. Lazare is defined conclusively in the events at the Hotel Roi George which end Book I. Abe, avatar of all that is lost, desperate, and failing, reappears, bringing with him the incredible figure of Jules Peterson, Afro-Scandinavian inventor of shoe-polish. In this comedy of errors, Fitzgerald avoids the ludicrous only by translating it into the grotesque; bad burlesque and mock melodrama become bloody murder. And Nicole relapses again. But her demands of 1925 are no longer susceptible to Dick's assurances of 1919. Dick has been weakened by the expenditure of his own moral energy and must appeal to Nicole's strength: "Control yourself!" he repeats three times as Book I closes on 1925.

Of course Nicole cannot control herself completely—yet. In Fitzgerald's concept of historical dialectic, the old nineteenth-century idealism, which in 1925 was strangling itself with uncertainties and inherent weaknesses, had yet another four years before its course was to be fully run. And in Dick's career and life from 1925 to 1929 Fitzgerald depicts the final, tragic act of this idealism, fighting an heroic but futile rearguard action against modernity. The shallowness of Rosemary's vanity, the hardness of Tommy's self-gratification, and the all-consuming selfishness of Nicole's lust for things and for power ultimately triumph over Dick's vision of what *ought* to be, for his moral idealism no longer answers the needs of an age intent merely on survival. Yet, in spite of its inherent flaws and its ultimate failure, it is Dick's vision which haunts our memory of the novel as surely as the remembered ideals of our "naive"

fathers haunt us, as surely as the nightingale's song haunted Keats:

> Was it a vision, or a waking dream?
> Fled is that music:—Do I wake or sleep?

History to Fitzgerald is, indeed, a highly "figured curtain," no more simple than the complex, ambivalent persons who create it. (pp. 121-22)

With emphatic suddenness Fitzgerald leaps from the decisions and indecisions of 1925 to the events of 1927, which in turn serve as general commentary and prelude to the novel's climax and conclusion in 1928-1929. The drama of 1927 begins as Dick awakes "after a long dream of war" and goes to the bedside of the pathetic woman suffering from neuro-syphilis, diagnosed as "nervous eczema." Ravaged and rapidly decomposing through the inheritance of a corrupt love, this sensitive soul is indeed correct in seeing herself "as a symbol of something." Consistent with the book's imagery, her illness is described as a lost battle; truly her innocent beauty, imagination, youth and charm are fled. But as she is thus being compared implicitly with Nicole and Abe North, we also see that her failure is Dick's. For like her, Dick is "fine-spun, inbred," and lacks that "measure of peasant blood" necessary to those explorers who perforce must "take punishment as they took bread and salt, on every inch of flesh and spirit." The suffering, unnamed woman is quite clearly a symbol of both aspects of the modern trauma, of all Nicole's innocence capriciously destroyed, and of all Dick's idealism, terribly futile. How touching, yet how futile, and how tragic a picture it is as Dick stoops to kiss the dying artist; how poignant his farewell: "We must all try to be good."

In 1927 Dick does not try to save his broken patients. He "makes his rounds." He now admits there is "nothing much to be done" for the fifteen-year-girl whom we readily identify with the young Nicole, this mad girl "brought up on the basis that childhood was intended to be all fun." Like the wasted parent of a mad child once docile, now grown to be overpowering, Dick finds it harder and harder to muster his tired, paralyzed faculties. He also realizes now that in the six years with Nicole "she had several times carried him over the line with her . . . had succeeded in getting a point against his better judgment." And haunting Dick ultimately is his self-reflection in the "collapsed psychiatrist," to whom Dick croons falsely "that he was better, always better." As an experienced explorer into the wilderness of the human heart, Dick in 1927 knows that the wolves not only are at the door, they are inside the house itself. In 1927, in Switzerland *deja vu*, the question is no longer one of "curing" Nicole; the question now is whether Dick can save himself. (pp. 123-24)

In 1927 Dick's commitment to reason and his hope for its supremacy are equally futile. . . . Dick's values, Dick's dreams, Dick's life have not prevailed, and power has become the world's only reality, exertion of power man's only grip upon existence.

Avatar of the new order is Tommy Barban, who reenters the novel in the singularly fitting setting of "the Marienplatz in Munich" where "The air was full of politics, and the slap of cards." In this cynical, aggressive world of *Realpolitik* Tommy is a "ruler" and a "hero," characterized essentially by his "martial laugh." He is, most of all, Dick's antagonist, the antithesis to all his ideals.

Tommy's narration of Prince Chillicheff's escape from Russia and his bringing to light Abe North's death in a New York speakeasy reflect at once the decline of the old order and the birth of the new. Both the Prince and Abe are "parched papier mache relic[s] of the past"; both have necessarily yielded to overpowering force—whether it be that of the Red Guard or of New York thugs is of little consequence.... His attitude is as simple and uncluttered as it is inhuman: "Well, I'm a soldier.... My business is to kill people." Amoral and self-indulgent, Tommy worships the power of money, which can bring him his dreams of good food, good clothes, and "good" women, and his only church is the stock market, where "everybody . . . is making millions." Caring no more for Abe lying dead in New York than for the "three Red Guards dead at the border," Tommy is ultimately committed only to himself—to his own survival and self-indulgence.

In direct contrast, Dick is stricken by Abe's death and mourns the irrecoverable past.... Dick's intricate destiny is entering its final phase—of precipitous decline. It is 1928.

For Fitzgerald the years 1928-1929 are the years of crisis defining the modern phase of America's history. The period is signally defined by the death of Abe and the death of Dick's father. It is then marked by the sudden death of the long lingering neuro-syphilitic artist and by the contrasting, miraculous deathbed "recovery" of Devereux Warren, by Dick's unfeeling, sterile seduction of a careless Rosemary and by his irrevocable loss of Nicole to Tommy. It is marked by Dick's descent into the Roman city of dreadful night, where he is saved only by his persistently dark angel, Baby, and marked by Nicole's ascent to power. Ultimately, the period is defined by Dick's recognition of his own inability to make people happy. (pp. 124-26)

Dick's response to this alienating world is less heroic perhaps, but certainly more human than that of Hemingway's Jake Barnes, Frederic Henry, or Robert Jordan, for Dick cannot indefinitely maintain his "purity of line through the maximum of exposure." Dick is a man subject to history and human change like the rest of us, and when history's stream changes course, leaving him to flounder in a drying channel, he, like the rest of us, strikes out blindly in panic and frustration. In this light Dick's bigotry toward the French and the Italians, his drunkenness, his violence with the cabmen, and his pointless baiting of the police do not mark his acquiescence to the calculated violence of Baby's world; they mark his violent, but futile protest against her world's recalcitrance to moral order. But violence in the service of virtue is nevertheless violence, and Dick's personal vision of a lovely safe world blows itself up in 1928 as surely as his larger Victorian world blew itself up in 1914-1918.

Though Dick is an extraordinarily complex character, as we have seen, Fitzgerald makes clear that his conception of Dick is essentially tragic. Amid the defeat and hopelessness of his experience in Rome, Dick is identified with Keats, the genius prematurely withered in a world of crass materialism and cheap pleasure. The picture that Rome lastingly imprints on Dick's mind is "the walk toward the American Express past the odorous confectioneries of the Via Nationale, through the foul tunnel up to the Spanish Steps, where his spirit soared before the flower stalls and the house where Keats had died."

Book III of *Tender Is the Night* is the story of sane crooks and one mad puritan. Set in 1929, it chronicles the end of the decade in which heartless money and amoral force carry the day at the expense of moral values and purposive behavior. Like a final fade out in a spurious Hollywood epic, rude self-interest joins with the glamour of wealth to seduce America's taste and desires with a travesty of her original dreams of endless moral expansion, making the nation of Jefferson and Lincoln and Wilson merely the most powerful nation in the world. Dick's waning energy is viewed against the background of the general social chaos generated by Mary Minghetti, Lady Caroline Sibly-Biers, T. F. Golding, and the rest of the "new crowd" on the Riviera; his defeat is assured when Nicole deserts him in favor of Tommy Barban.

The Divers' return to the Villa Diana in the summer of 1929 signals the final retrenchment of Dick's original vision. (pp. 127-28)

For Fitzgerald the historical issue of 1929 could be stated summarily as the conflict between the pursuit of self-gratification and the maintenance of moral principles and propriety; dramatically, the crisis centers upon a small bottle of camphor rub. This small bottle of balm is provocatively and irresistibly symbolic. "It's American," and Dick "believes in it;" yet it is also "extremely rare" and Dick has only the one bottle left. In so few remarks the bottle of rub is invested with all the values Dick has stood for throughout the novel—healing love, care, and what Fitzgerald once called the definitive American characteristic—"a willingness of the heart." Tossing the bottle to Tommy with a cautionary "Now catch it," Nicole is fully aware that she is betraying Dick, his principles, his love, his work, and his devotion. Her final remark to him is worthy of Baby: "We can always get another jar—." (pp. 128-29)

The precise nature of Dick's diminished position in the changed world of 1929 is dramatically compressed in the aquaplaning scene. Unlike Nicole, who "refused her turn" on the board, and unlike Rosemary, who "rode the board neatly and conservatively, with facetious cheers from her admirers," Dick can still muster the energy "to try his lifting trick." Desperately he tries three times to lift a man upon his shoulders, "then he was simply holding his ground, then he collapsed . . . and they went over, Dick's head barely missing a kick of the board." Though Nicole considers Dick to be showing off for Rosemary, we clearly view the scene as a synecdoche of Dick's longtime efforts to lift everyone—especially Nicole. In the larger context Dick has indeed "put his heart into the strain, and lifted," but what "he had done . . . with ease only two years ago" leaves him now "floating exhausted and expressionless, alone with the water and the sky."

Dick *is* beaten. In fact, as he tells Rosemary after the aquaplane fiasco: "The change came a long way back—but at first it didn't show. The manner remains intact for some time after the morale cracks." Dick has been slowly but irresistibly crushed by the same force giving ascendance to Nicole—by the "billions" and "trillions" of the booming stock market, by the "plenitude of money" which became "an absorption in itself." How appropriate it is that Nicole's new transference—from Dick to Tommy—should be initiated on the "Margin," the yacht of T. F. Golding. This scene of reunion between Nicole and Tommy is redolent of wealth tentatively gained and tenuously held, of lives bordering upon each other, but not bonding: "Golding's cyclonic arms blew them [Dick and Nicole] aft without touching them." From this point of transference, all Dick has left of himself is his poise, stretched taut over the hollow laughter and despair within. What Tommy offers Nicole is hard confidence, "good stocks in the hands of friends" and "all the old Languedoc peasant remedies." Truly the day of the barbarian has come. (pp. 129-30)

Corollary to Nicole's regeneration is Dick's return to his origins—to the obscurity of the Finger Lake region in New York State, to the withering green breast of the once New World. But Nicole's ascendance over Dick is itself founded upon a fateful illusion and fraught with a controlling irony that would have been painfully obvious to readers of 1934, had any recognized Fitzgerald's historical purposes. For if only with the accuracy of hindsight, the reader of that year could have seen the imminent disaster awaiting those who in July 1929 followed the creed of "Why shouldn't I?" The reader of 1934 could have seen that the arrogant dreams of a sunny July beach—dreams of permanent wealth, endless power, and the right to do what one was tempted to do and pay no penalty for it—had led to the nightmare of October's Black Friday and to the grim years of the Great Depression.

For Fitzgerald the issuing events of history are thus as complex as their origins, both springing from the incalculably wrought human heart. The human passion for self-determination which made "idealism" the dominant force in nineteenth-century philosophy and politics inevitably had overextended itself and in World War I could scarcely bear the horror of its own creations. Dick's "beautiful lovely safe world" did blow itself up, and in 1929, with no one to love and no left to love him, Dick retreats deeper and deeper into upper New York State, a Keatsian wood of indefinite place and uncertain time. But Nicole's acceptance of aggression and self-indulgence as the basic principles of her behavior doesn't rectify the excessive errors of the earlier idealism so much as ratify their failure. And her future, as Fitzgerald clearly implies, will be written in a hard, but cramped hand, and will tell the story of hollow men: "New vistas appeared ahead, peopled with the faces of many men, none of whom she need obey or even love." Her world, unlike Dick's, will not blow itself up with a "great gust of high explosive love"; it will linger on in the discontent of those whose wants are insatiable—it will end, we are assured, with a whimper.

In every sense *Tender Is the Night* marks the culmination of Fitzgerald's art. It is nurtured by the same vision and techniques we find in **"May Day," "The Diamond as Big as the Ritz,"** *The Great Gatsby, The Beautiful and Damned,* and **"Babylon Revisited,"** but it is a riper, more mature work, founded upon a maturity and historical perspective that could come to Fitzgerald only with the passage of time. His long struggle with the writing of the book, the many changes and alterations he incorporated into it as his imagination feasted upon the decade-long struggle between Old and New America, all testify to his patient determination to capture honestly the complex essence of an era. To finish *this* novel, he had to wait, as it were, for history to declare itself definitively. And it did—in October 1929.

More than any other work, *Tender Is the Night* makes it clear that Fitzgerald's creative vision and expression required the presence of moral questions—if not necessarily answers, required a conception of history founded upon purposive human activity—if not necessarily "manifest destiny." And finally, *Tender Is the Night* presents with the clearest intensity Fitzgerald's profoundly paradoxical conception that man's nobility lies in his unyielding efforts to be his *best* self—even when faced with certain defeat, that man's tragedy lies in his failure to recognize his own limitations and live with them. (pp. 131-32)

Bruce L. Grenberg, "Fitzgerald's 'Figured Curtain': Personality and History in 'Tender Is the

*Night'," in* Fitzgerald/Hemingway Annual: 1978, *1979, pp. 105-36.*

**JEFFREY BERMAN**   (essay date 1985)

*[In the following excerpt, Berman discusses Fitzgerald's portrayal of Dick Diver as a psychiatrist and the rendering of psychoanalytic concepts in* Tender Is the Night.*]*

Dick's psychiatric expertise . . . is less than convincing. One of Fitzgerald's problems is the banality of Dick's medical advice to his patients. Whenever the psychiatrist speaks, he sounds more like a moralist than a therapist. "I won't lecture to you," Dick says to Nicole, and then proceeds to do just that. ". . . it's only by meeting the problems of every day, no matter how trifling and boring they seem, that you can make things drop back into place again." Despite his immodest aim to be a "good psychologist—maybe to be the greatest one that ever lived," he remains indifferent to the distinctions in terminology among psychology, psychiatry, and psychoanalysis. Nor does Fitzgerald explain the dynamic basis of Dick's psychiatry except to note his avoidance of hypnosis. Yet, even here, the explanation is curious. Dick avoids hypnosis not because of its failure to bring repressed material to the surface but because of its perceived theatricality.

The question of psychiatric authenticity also occurs in Dick's understanding of Nicole's mental illness. Fitzgerald's description of Nicole's illness evokes Dr. Forel's diagnosis of Zelda. "She's a schizoid—a permanent eccentric," Dick tells Baby Warren, "You can't change that." Forel had considered Zelda "a constitutional, emotionally unbalanced psychopath—she may improve, never completely recover." So too does Dick's characterization of Nicole as a "schizophrene" or "split personality" recall Dr. Bleuler's diagnosis of Zelda. Fitzgerald cannot be faulted for the imprecision of Zelda's eminent psychiatrists; yet there is a deep pessimism toward Nicole's intellectual equipment that surprises us in light of her apparent recovery at the end of the novel. "A 'schizophrêne' is well named as a split personality—Nicole was alternately a person to whom nothing need be explained and one to whom nothing *could* be explained. It was necessary to treat her with active and affirmative insistence, keeping the road to reality always open, making the road to escape harder going." The definition of Zelda's mental illness in *Tender Is the Night* implies that self-discovery and psychological insight are of little value in effecting any therapeutic cure. Fitzgerald views the psychiatrist as one who actively intervenes to prevent the patient from lapsing into insanity rather than one who, as Freud argues, adopts a more passive but analytical role as interpreter of the patient's symptoms and resistance to recovery. Despite the case-study approach of the novel, the descriptions of the sanitariums evoke an image of the rest cure rather than the talking cure. Patients and psychiatrists do not talk to each other; Nicole never seems to do anything. Her recovery at the end remains a mystery to us.

Toward Freud, Fitzgerald reveals a contradictory attitude of vague admiration and suspicion. Franz's statement that Dr. Dohmler had given Nicole "a little Freud to read, not too much, and she was very interested" conveys Fitzgerald's limited tolerance for psychoanalytic theory. Dick's decision to attend the "Psychiatric Congress" in Berlin confirms the novel's strong hostility toward psychotherapy. Fitzgerald satirizes, in the following passage, the motives of psychiatrists, condemning what he perceives to be the theatricality, hollowness, greed, and ineffectuality of the profession:

> He had no intention of attending so much as a single session of the congress—he could imagine it well enough, new pamphlets by Bleuler and the elder Forel that he could much better digest at home, the paper by the American who cured dementia praecox by pulling out his patients' teeth or cauterizing their tonsils, the half-derisive respect with which this idea would be greeted, for no more reason than that America was such a rich and powerful country.

Dick's developing cyncism toward his own profession is primarily moral rather than intellectual; in the same paragraph he mocks the "dozens of commercial alienists with hang-dog faces, who would be present partly to increase their standing, and hence their reach for the big plums of the criminal practice, partly to master novel sophistries that they could weave into their stock in trade, to the infinite confusion of all values." Although Bleuler and Forel are spared from Fitzgerald's most withering criticism, the entire profession is condemned in the most categorical terms. It is as if the author of *A Psychology for Psychiatrists* has become disgusted with the entire field and is ready to denounce his own colleagues in a single jeremiad.

Oddly enough, Fitzgerald does not confront the one psychoanalytic concept that offers the greatest insight into Dick's catastrophic fall: transference love. The word "transference" appears three times in *Tender Is the Night,* each time in a clinical context. Referring to Nicole's growing emotional attachment to Dick, Franz exclaims: "It was the best thing that could have happened to her . . . a transference of the most fortuitous kind." Dr. Dohmler later uses the word in a similar context, warning Dick about the dangers of emotional involvement with his patient. But the tone of Dohmler's remarks suggests that, unlike Franz, he is more qualified in his endorsement of the term. ". . . this so-called 'transference' . . . must be terminated. Miss Nicole does well indeed, but she is in no condition to survive what she might interpret as a tragedy." The word also appears near the end of the novel when Nicole, falling in love with Tommy Barban, tries to detach herself from her husband. Feeling her old love for Dick reawakening, she "struggled with it, fighting him with her small, fine eyes, with the plush arrogance of a top dog, with her nascent transference to another man, with the accumulated resentment of years. . . ." Additionally, the word appears three times in Fitzgerald's notes to *Tender Is the Night:* the hero "'transfers' to himself and she falls in love with him, a love he returns"; "Only her transference to him saves her"; and "His hold is broken, the transference is broken. He goes away. He has been used by the rich family and cast aside."

References to transference confirm that Fitzgerald is using the term not in its dynamic psychoanalytic context—the projection of essentially primitive experiences and emotions onto other people—but in the more general sense of an absorption or incorporation of one individual by another in a shifting love relationship. Despite the mechanistic connotations, Fitzgerald's use of transference does coincide with the psychoanalytic definition to the extent that Dick cannot maintain emotional detachment from entangling human alliances. Dick's integrity and wholeness are constantly threatened by the "egos of certain people, early met and early loved," who undermine his independence:

> His love for Nicole and Rosemary, his friendship with Abe North, with Tommy Barban in the broken universe of the war's ending—in such contacts the personalities had seemed to press up so close to him that he became the personality itself—there seemed some necessity of taking all or nothing; it was as if for the remainder of his life he was condemned to carry with him the egos of certain people, early met and early loved, and to be only as complete as they were complete themselves. There was some element of loneliness involved—so easy to be loved—so hard to love.

The language intimates a desire to love so intensely as to both engulf and be engulfed. Although the passage implies that the people who are oppressing Dick are figures from the present—Nicole, Rosemary, Abe North—psychoanalytic theory would suggest that these relationships are repetitions of much earlier relationships dating back to Dick's past. The pattern recalls the pre-Oedipal stage of the mother-child relationship when the form of nurturing creates the archetypes of identifications, the basis of future interaction. Dick's insatiable quest for love paradoxically drains him, rendering him broken and incomplete. Emotional involvement proves disastrous because it threatens the distinction between self and other. The loved object always becomes menacing to Dick because, in absorbing others, he finds himself absorbed, depleted, violated. At the center of the male-female relationship in *Tender Is the Night* looms the spectre of transference, with its ominous implications of the repetition-compulsion principle. Of all the characters who endanger Dick, it is Nicole whom Fitzgerald accuses of sapping his hero's strength and creativity. "He could not watch her disintegrations without participating in them." To understand further the meaning of Dick's fear of absorption in *Tender Is the Night* we must explore the psychoanalytic theory of transference.

Freud's most complete definition of transference is given in *An Autobiographical Study,* published nine years before Fitzgerald's novel. Since it is impossible to improve upon Freud's description, we may quote it in full:

> In every analytic treatment there arises, without the physician's agency, an intense emotional relationship between the patient and the analyst which is not to be accounted for by the actual situation. It can be of a positive or of a negative character and can vary between the extremes of a passionate, completely sensual love and the unbridled expression of an embittered defiance and hatred. This *transference*—to give it its short name—soon replaces in the patient's mind the desire to be cured, and, so long as it is affectionate and moderate, becomes the agent of the physician's influence and neither more nor less than the mainspring of the joint work of analysis. Later on, when it has become passionate or has been converted into hostility, it becomes the principal tool of the resistance. It may then happen that it will paralyse the patient's powers of associating and endanger the success of the treatment. Yet it would be senseless to try to evade it; for an analysis without transference is an impossibility.

Transference love arises when the patient becomes infatuated with the analyst. The love affair is fraught with dangers, Freud observes, and he proceeds to elaborate upon them as if he were indeed writing *A Psychology for Psychiatrists.* "This situation has its distressing and comical aspects, as well as its serious ones. It is also determined by so many and such complicated factors, it is so unavoidable and so difficult to clear up, that a discussion of it to meet a vital need of analytic technique has long been overdue. But since we who laugh at other people's failings are not always free from them ourselves, we have not so far been precisely in a hurry to fulfill this task.'' (pp. 69-73)

How . . . should the analyst confront a patient's love? Each alternative, Freud says, has its difficulties. Rarely do circumstances allow the analyst to marry his patient, even if he desires to, and besides, this would result in the breakdown of the therapeutic relationship—as *Tender Is the Night* illustrates. If the analyst breaks off therapy to defuse the affair, as Breuer did with Anna O., then this too would signal the collapse of the treatment. For the analyst to carry on an illicit affair with his patient would be unthinkable, both for reasons of morality and professional dignity. ''If the patient's advances were returned it would be a great triumph for her, but a complete defeat for the treatment.'' What then must the analyst do?

He must, argues Freud, resist succumbing to whatever unconscious tendencies toward countertransference may be lurking within him. ''He must recognize that the patient's falling in love is induced by the analytic situation and is not to be attributed to the charms of his own person; so that he has no grounds whatever for being proud of such a 'conquest', as it would be called outside analysis.'' (p. 74)

Yet ambiguities continue to surround transference love. How does it differ, for example, from genuine love? Freud's answer is surprising, for he acknowledges the overlapping between the two forms of love. . . . What is different between the two forms of love, Freud points out, is that transference love is provoked by the analytic setting, intensified by clinical resistance to recovery, and less concerned with reality than genuine love. The patient certainly cannot be expected to see this distinction, but the analyst must; otherwise, the gravest consequences will occur.

One final observation must be noted. Freud insists that analytic treatment be conducted in a state of ''abstinence,'' which is not limited to a narrow sexual context. Insofar as it was a frustration that made the patient ill, ''It is possible to observe during the treatment that every improvement in his condition reduces the rate at which he recovers and diminishes the instinctual force impelling him towards recovery.'' Favorable external changes in the patient's life may give the impression of effecting a therapeutic cure while in reality retarding psychological progress. ''Cruel though it may sound, we must see to it that the patient's suffering, to a degree that is in some way or other effective, does not come to an end prematurely.'' The analysis should be carried out, Freud emphasizes, *''as far as is possible, under privation—in a state of abstinence.''* What example does he cite of external changes endangering the complete recovery of a half-cured patient? Apart from bodily infirmity, an unhappy marriage poses a particularly severe danger. For by gratifying unconscious guilt, the unhappy marriage becomes a form of self-punishment in which the patient's neurosis takes on new symptoms or substitute gratifications.

One of the ironies of *Tender Is the Night* is that, had Dr. Dick Diver fully understood the psychoanalytic dynamics of transference love, he would have indeed been successful in writing the definitive *A Psychology for Psychiatrists*. And he would have immeasurably aided Nicole Warren's therapeutic recovery, succeeding where greater psychiatrists had failed. Instead, Dick never does solve the meaning of Nicole's illness. His own research into psychology never progresses beyond *Studies on Hysteria,* which offers intriguing parallels to *Tender Is the Night.* Both Dr. Breuer and Dr. Diver find themselves in the presence of hysterical women who project their incestuous fan-

tasies upon father figures. To be sure, Breuer's hasty retreat from Anna O.'s advances is in contrast to Dick's ambivalent surrender to Nicole; yet, both women appear to be acting out imagined or real seduction fantasies. And in both case studies, treatment fails largely because of the psychiatrists' unawareness of the link between transference love and resistance. Dick's blindness to transference love deprives him of the most powerful instrument for Nicole's recovery. Worse, it ensnares him in a marital relationship built upon the similar psychological weaknesses of husband and wife.

Dick's sin is that he is too loving and loved for his own good. Nowhere is Fitzgerald more successful than in portraying the complexity of his hero's dark love, with its lust for power and possessiveness. There is something terrible about Dick's need for adulation, a narcissistic hunger that can never be fulfilled. ''Save among a few of the tough-minded and perennially suspicious, he had the power of arousing a fascinated and uncritical love. The reaction came when he realized the waste and extravagance involved. He sometimes looked back with awe at the carnivals of affection he had given, as a general might gaze upon a massacre he had ordered to satisfy an impersonal blood lust.''

Dick's ''impersonal blood lust'' evokes the blood imagery surrounding Nicole and the ''bathroom mystery'' in which an unspeakable act is hinted at but never described. Waste, self-indulgence, and futility characterize Dick's carnivals of affection. His desire to ''give a really *bad* party'' identifies him as the archetypal Fitzgerald hero. The motives behind the party call into question his attitude toward life. ''Maybe we'll have more fun this summer but this particular fun is over. I want it to die violently instead of fading out sentimentally—that's why I gave this party.'' The comment betrays his similar feelings about marriage: the need to end love relationships with a bang, not a whimper; the assumption that relationships with violent endings are less ''sentimental'' than those which slowly fade or remain loyal and permanent; the hint, later magnified, of Dick's self-destructive tendencies. Fitzgerald returns to the dark side of Dick's character, though the murky syntax and strained psychological interpretation do little to illuminate the problem. ''And Lucky Dick can't be one of these clever men; he must be less intact, even faintly destroyed. If life won't do it for him it's not a substitute to get a disease, or a broken heart, or an inferiority complex, though it'd be nice to build out some broken side till it was better than the original structure.'' Oddly enough, when Fitzgerald does attempt to analyze—or psychoanalyze—Dick's problem, the narrative distance breaks down and the explanation only deepens the mystery. The novelist seems as bewildered and defenseless here as his character. Nor does Dick's next thought cast further light on his situation. ''He mocked at his reasoning, calling it specious and 'American'—his criteria of uncerebral phrase-making was that it was American. He knew, though, that the price of his intactness was incompleteness.'' Cannot one be both intact and complete?

Whence arises Dick's overwhelming need to love and be loved? The novel offers a few clues. At the core of his unconscious feelings toward psychotherapy lies a rescue fantasy in which he desires to cure his patients through love, not self-awareness. Hence the impossibility of clinical detachment from his female patients, even those who are strangers to him. ''Yet in the awful majesty of her pain he went out to her unreservedly, almost sexually. He wanted to gather her up in his arms, as he so often had Nicole, and cherish even her mistakes, so deeply were they part of her.'' The love from which his identifications spring contains both regressive and compulsive features, violating the necessary space between self and other and compelling Dick's romantic attachments to conspicuously younger women. Dick's natural protectiveness toward women evokes his paternal nature, yet he fails to accept responsibility for awakening sexual desires he cannot possibly fulfill. Paradoxically, there is an infantile quality to his ''father complex''; his paternalistic power over women is one of the most dangerous aspects of his countertransference. For example, he receives a letter from a woman recently released from his clinic which ''accused him in no uncertain terms of having seduced her daughter, who had been at her mother's side during the crucial stage of the illness.'' Dick had ''in an idle, almost indulgent way'' kissed her, though he goes no further than this despite the girl's desire to deepen the affair.

Indeed, the pattern of Dick's romantic relationships invariably involves a much younger woman. *Tender Is the Night* opens in 1925, with Dick ten years older than his wife—a substantial difference (he is 34)—and 16 years older than Rosemary, with whom he later has an affair. Two additional incidents confirm the age inequality. When he is brought to the Italian courtroom at the end of Part II to face the charge of assaulting one of the carabinieri, the crowd confuses him with a native of Frescati who has raped and slain a child. Himself out of control, Dick yells: ''I want to a make a speech. . . . I want to explain to these people how I raped a five-year-old girl. Maybe I did—''. In the penultimate paragraph of the novel, Fitzgerald hints at Dick's entanglement with a young woman who worked in a grocery store. According to Bruccoli, Fitzgerald had specified in the serial version of the novel that the clerk was 18, but he deleted her age in the final form of the story. Dick's history thus seems to be a depressing pattern of recurring affairs with women half his age and younger.

Consequently, Dick has taken a prolonged ''leave of abstinence''—to use the ''Freudian slip'' that Franz makes on two separate occasions. Franz has become increasingly critical of his colleague's decision to marry Nicole, and when Dick announces his plan to take a leave from the clinic—ostensibly to allow his troubled marriage to heal—Franz responds: ''You wish a real leave of abstinence?'' Without commenting upon the meaning of the slip of tongue, Dick replies: ''The word is 'absence'.'' Franz's remark proves prophetic in that Dick's leave from home sets into motion his renewed and altered relationship with Rosemary. Later, Franz makes the identical verbal slip. ''Why not try another leave of abstinence?'' to which Dick again mechanically replies: ''Absence.'' Franz's error continues to be prophetic; this time Nicole proves unfaithful.

These Freudian slips, which Fitzgerald deliberately structures into the novel, emphasize Dick's inability to control the transference love relationship arising both in and outside of therapy. They also suggest the incestuous nature of his love for Nicole and the others. Several critics have pointed out the importance of incestuous love in *Tender Is the Night*. In [''The Significance of F. Scott Fitzgerald''], published in 1952, D. S. Savage draws a parallel between Devereux Warren's incestuous relationship with his daughter Nicole and Dick Diver's unconscious recapitulation of that earlier experience. ''Since Nicole's condition is the consequence of physical seduction at the hands of her own father, it is impossible to evade the conclusion that Dick is unconsciously implicated in the very incestuous regression which is at the root of her psychopathic (schizophrenic)

condition.'' Robert Stanton published a similar interpretation in 1958 [see excerpt dated 1958]. Exploring the subject of *Daddy's Girl*, the film in which Rosemary stars, Stanton defines the incest motifs in *Tender Is the Night*. . . . ''First, these motifs function literally as one result of Dick's relationship to Nicole; they are symptoms of his psychological disintegration. Second, they both exemplify and symbolize Dick's loss of allegiance to the moral code of his father. Finally, by including such details as *Daddy's Girl* as well as Dick's experience, they symbolize a social situation existing throughout Europe and America during the Twenties.''

Other critics have confirmed these conclusions. Biographical evidence also supports Fitzgerald's interest in incestuous love. ''There is no help for it,'' D. S. Savage remarks, ''what emerges most patently from Fitzgerald's biography is his character as a mother's boy.'' He also cites Arthur Mizener's observation in *The Far Side of Paradise:* ''His mother's treatment was bad for a precocious and imaginative boy, and as Fitzgerald confessed to his daughter after she had grown up, 'I didn't know till 15 that there was anyone in the world except me. . . .''' (pp. 75-9)

There is a darker side to incestuous love. The notes to *Tender Is the Night* demonstrate that Fitzgerald had originally intended the story to deal with the subject of matricide, with the title *The Boy Who Killed His Mother*. He must have felt terribly ambivalent about the subject. He began working on the matricide theme in 1925, discarded it in 1929, returned to it again in 1930, and finally abandoned it. Although he omitted the overt matricide element from *Tender Is the Night,* he did not entirely succeed in disguising the misogyny that underlies the story. In perceiving Nicole and Rosemary as images of ''Daddy's Girl,'' Dick views them and the ''Amazonian'' Baby Warren as part of a conspiracy to drain his creativity and emasculate him. Dick's submerged hostility toward women may be interpreted, according to the dynamics of ego psychology, as a turning around or denial of incestuous love. Matricide and misogyny come into existence when sexuality and aggression are fused together, usually as a defense against incestuous love. The result is an intolerable ambivalence toward women—which exactly defines Dick's attitude toward the women in his life.

Fitzgerald's critics have been reluctant to acknowledge the presence of misogyny in his fiction, although they do concede that women are dangerous to his male characters. Matthew J. Bruccoli [in his *Some Sort of Epic Grandeur*] voices a representative opinion. . . . ''Fitzgerald created a procession of female destroyers of men, but his judgment was not misogynistic. His women—even at their most destructive—are warmly attractive.'' Yet misogyny, of course, can exist alongside of heroine worship. If Dick is only partly aware of the incestuous implications of his acting out, he is blind to his fear and mistrust of women. There are simply too many passages reflective of Dick's—and Fitzgerald's—anger toward women:

> Baby Warren shifted her knees about—she was a compendium of all the discontented women who had loved Byron a hundred years before, yet in spite of the tragic affair with the guards' officer there was something wooden and onanistic about her.

> Women are necessarily capable of almost anything in their struggle for survival and can scarcely be convicted of such man-made crimes as ''cruelty.''

> It would be hundreds of years before any emergent Amazons would ever grasp the fact that a man is vulnerable only in his pride, but delicate as Humpty-

Dumpty once that is meddled with—though some of them paid the fact a cautious lip-service.

> . . . the American Woman, aroused, stood over him; the clean-sweeping irrational temper that had broken the moral back of a race and made a nursery out of a continent, was too much for him.

Fitzgerald can condemn Albert McKisco as a pretentious writer and Tommy Barban as a brutal soldier without condemning all men; but, by contrast, his attack on Baby Warren and to a lesser extent Mary North, Rosemary, and Nicole is generalized to include all women. The distinction is important. Even during the depths of Dick's self-degradation, Fitzgerald reminds us of the husband's anguish for his wife and the tragic consequences of a psychiatrist's love for his patient. Nicole, in contrast, can harden herself to Dick. Unlike him, she begins to "slight that love, so that it seemed to have been tinged with sentimental habit from the first. With the opportunistic memory of women she scarcely recalled how she had felt when she and Dick had possessed each other. . . ."

Compared to Dick, all the women in *Tender Is the Night* remain harder, less vulnerable, armorial. The name he secretly whispers to himself—"Lucky Dick, you big stiff"—gives way to Fitzgerald's fear of unmanly softness as his hero drifts toward a nosedive. Indeed, Dick's nose actually is broken by a policeman, suggesting symbolic castration. Dick's name also has a phallic connotation; as one critic has pointed out about Fitzgerald, "in a fit of adolescent bravado he has consequently christened his hero with a name whose slang meaning amply conveys the author's contempt for softness." And Leslie Fiedler has noted the fluid and shifting sexual distinctions in *Tender Is the Night,* including the inversion of roles. "Indeed, the book is shot through with a thematic playing with the ambiguity of sex: Dick Diver makes his first entrance in a pair of black lace panties, and homosexuals, male and female, haunt the climaxes of the novel." Fitzgerald implies that between the time Dick met and married Nicole, and his acquaintance with Rosemary, his "spear had been blunted." The embodiment of phallic hardness in the novel is Rosemary's mother, whose last name—"Speers"—betrays the women's capture of an increasingly limp Dick.

Moreover, there is a curious coincidence behind the "Mary" element of three characters: Rosemary, who sees life from a rose-colored point of view; Mary North, whose successful remarriage after the death of her first husband arouses Fitzgerald's uneasiness; and Maria Wallis, who shoots to death an Englishman. Along with Nicole and Baby Warren, these women serve as a variation on the theme of Mary Magdalene, though without achieving final redemption. Dick becomes what Fitzgerald calls in the notes to *Tender Is the Night* a "spoiled priest," pursuing and pursued by the "legendary *promiscuous* woman."

Fitzgerald's attitude toward Nicole fluctuates between sympathy and criticism. Although obviously a portrait of Fitzgerald's wife, Nicole—unlike Zelda—has been sexually traumatized by her father's advances. In inventing this detail, the novelist had difficulty in deciding whether it was rape or seduction. In the notes to the novel he views the incest with her father as nothing less than a rape: "at fifteen she was raped by her own father under peculiar circumstances—work out." In the novel, however, Nicole consents to sexual intercourse. The change is obviously significant in that now she must assume partial responsibility for the act, along with the consequent blurring of innocence. What Fitzgerald thus imagined

initially as a rape now becomes Nicole's acting out of an infantile seduction scene. Yet Fitzgerald could have gone one step further by completely eliminating the objective basis of Nicole's seduction. If she had only imagined seduction, the novelist would have had to deal with her wishes and fears, and the extent to which her imagination had distorted reality into mental illness. This was precisely what Freud had to confront when he reluctantly gave up his seduction theory—the belief that his neurotic patients were actually seduced by their fathers—in favor of the idea that they only imagined incestuous acts. Psychical reality need not correspond to objective reality, Freud taught us; fantasized seduction can seem as real as if it actually happened. We may question Fitzgerald's implication that the incest directly precipitated Nicole's schizophrenia. Indeed, she hardly appears schizophrenic at all. Unlike the female patients of other fictionalized psychiatric case histories—the heroines of "The Yellow Wallpaper," *The Bell Jar, I Never Promised You a Rose Garden*—Nicole rarely seems mentally ill to us and never psychotic except for perhaps a few moments. We certainly do not receive an inside account of her madness. The few symptoms she manifests suggest hysteria and obsession compulsion, especially during the "bathroom mystery."

However obscure the bathroom mystery must remain, it appears to have something to do with Nicole's menstruation, seduction, and horror of blood-stained sheets. Her swaying back and forth beside the bathtub may also hint at masturbation. Nicole seems to be obsessed with "blood lust" (Fitzgerald's simile to describe Dick's power to arouse a fascinated and uncritical love): the blood on the sheets of the dead black man, the blood from Dick's broken nose, and the menstrual blood of Rosemary when she and Dick make love for the first time, all seem thematically to coalesce around the bathroom scene. The entire drama has a play-within-a-play quality, reproducing the symbols and symptoms of Nicole's psychic conflict. Fitzgerald evokes a theme of the rites of passage through the expression "What time is it?" which becomes a major leitmotif in Part I. According to Freud, behind every neurotically inhibited activity lies an instinctual wish; Nicole's seduction fantasy evokes dread and desire. The hysteria during the bathroom scene may reflect the emotions accompanying her incestuous relationship with her father. Nicole's love for Dick has its source in her tangled feelings toward her father; but whereas she allows the father to seduce her, she reverses the situation with her psychiatrist. Despite Nicole's horror of sexuality, she proves to be the aggressor with Dick. It is she who is seducing him. Dick's command—"Control yourself"—becomes ironic in that he too conspires in the incestuous regression. The impossibility of purgation may be suggested in the "dirty bathtub water" scene in Part III, in which the children appear implicated in the evil.

Nicole's desertion of Dick for Tommy Barban raises the question of the motives behind her present affair: Do these motives differ from those behind her attraction toward Dick when she was his patient? That is, is there an element of resistance in her transference love? She enters into her affair with Barban quite calculatingly, unlike the indecision and guilt with which Dick begins his affair with Rosemary. Before Nicole can commit herself irrevocably to the affair, she does a great deal of rationalizing, as Fitzgerald makes clear:

> Nicole did not want any vague spiritual romance—she wanted an "affair"; she wanted a change. She realized, thinking with Dick's thoughts, that from a superficial view it was a vulgar business to enter, without emotion, into an indulgence that menaced all of them. On the other hand, she blamed Dick for

> the immediate situation, and honestly thought that
> such an experiment might have a therapeutic value.

Nicole's reasoning includes the desire both to hurt her husband and to release herself from his power. Because she allies herself with the morally hollow Barban (whose name suggests his barbarian qualities), we lose sympathy for her. Why then does she commit herself to a man she does not love? Barban offers her the possibility of rescue from an increasingly destructive husband. She senses that the new union will complete the therapeutic cure initiated by her preceding rescuer. The affair with Barban thus allows her to end the enforced dependency upon another man and to exact a fitting revenge for his marital infidelity.

Although Fitzgerald recognizes the complex motives underlying Nicole's relationship to Barban, there is little evidence to suggest the novelist's awareness of her similar motives for loving Dick. This is not to reduce Dick's generous character to Barban's, nor to debase her love for Dick, but to suggest that Nicole's psychological needs dictate the nature of her relationships with men. This returns us to the element of resistance behind her transference love for Dick. It is disingenuous for Fitzgerald to tell us that Nicole is thinking with Dick's thoughts in the passage above. Nicole's motives for pursuing Barban do not seem very different from her initial pursuit of Dr. Dick Diver in the Swiss sanitarium: to effect a change in her life and to exert her sexual attractiveness over a man. To this extent, Nicole has not changed at all—she is thinking not Dick's thoughts but her own. In another sense, however, Nicole is Fitzgerald's own creation, quite apart from her indebtedness to Zelda's biography. Nicole's role as exploiter of men reaches back to Dick's deepest fears and ultimately Fitzgerald's as well.

The structure of Nicole's love relationships to the three men in her life—father, husband, lover—reveals an element of aggression directed toward the previous man, from whom the successful rival promises to free her. Dick offers to rescue her from the mental illness triggered off by her father's incestuous advances. Barban promises to liberate her from her husband's incurable alcoholism. Love thus represents to Nicole an escape from an unhappy situation engendered by the abandonment of an earlier man in her life. She is astonishingly successful as a survivor. What we rarely see in *Tender Is the Night* is the full-blown marital warfare that inevitably accompanies the subtle betrayal of love. The rage and painful recriminations found in the Fitzgerald correspondence are largely absent from the novel. That part of the story may have been too terrible for Fitzgerald to write.

As *Tender Is the Night* draws to a conclusion, we are left wondering about the reasons for Nicole's miraculous recovery and Dick's hopelessness. The novel is unclear here, but Fitzgerald implies that the patient's health depends somehow on the psychiatrist's dissipation, as if he has mysteriously absorbed her suffering and absolved her from guilt. Yet the "spouse" seems to be guilty of inflicting a lethal injury to the doomed protagonist. . . . Fitzgerald's notes to the novel make clear that the patient's cure results in the psychiatrist's terminal illness, as if madness is contagious. "The Divers, *as a marriage* are at the end of their resources. Medically Nicole is nearly cured but Dick has given out and is sinking toward alcoholism and discouragement. It seems as if the completion of his ruination will be the fact that cures her—almost mystically."

The explanation for this probably lies in Fitzgerald's biography—his deep guilt over Zelda's illness, the fear she would not recover, and the wish to sacrifice himself for her sake. "I left my capacity for hoping on the little roads that led to Zelda's sanitarium," he wrote in his notebooks. The hopelessness of her situation contributed to the bleakness of his. Why then does Fitzgerald grant Nicole complete and permanent recovery, contrary both to biography and to the pessimistic statements about schizophrenia earlier in the novel? The conclusion seems inevitable: in curing Nicole and condemning Dick, Fitzgerald is punishing himself for complicity in Zelda's illness. He may also have been trying to heal Zelda's illness through the magic of fiction. But the element of wish fulfillment in *Tender Is the Night* may be viewed, psychoanalytically, as a denial of the novelist's unconscious aggression toward the woman perceived as responsible for the hero's collapse. Masochism and sadism, most therapists agree, are the sides of the same coin. There is one passage in the novel that ominously hints at Dick's death wish toward his wife. "Certain thoughts about Nicole, that she should die, sink into mental darkness, love another man, made him physically sick." This is one of the few clues that Dick's self-destructive behavior derives from guilt over his hostile feelings toward Nicole. But this idea is too terrifying for Fitzgerald, and, like his fictional psychiatrist, the novelist retreats from these murky depths. Yet, Dick is literally killing himself over his "ambivalence" toward Nicole—ironically, it was Zelda's psychiatrist, Dr. Bleuler, who first coined the word.

It is not Freud whom Fitzgerald and his fallen hero invoke at the end of *Tender Is the Night* but Christ. Releasing Nicole from the strangulation hold he has momentarily wished to exert, Dick "raised his right hand and with a papal cross he blessed the beach from the high terrace." Fitzgerald thus casts off his doomed hero, though not without conceding him a vestige of dignity and grandeur. Nicole's future with Tommy Barban remains uncertain: She seems destined to reenact a pattern of falling in and out of love in a futile effort to remain "Daddy's Girl." But Fitzgerald's main focus rests on Dick, who gives up psychiatry, we are told, for general medicine. Nor is this surprising. After all, Dick has never displayed an interest in parent-child relationships, the interpretation of dreams, symptomatology, ego defenses, or transference. The talking cure has never informed his therapy. Fitzgerald mentions the "big stack of papers on his desk that were known to be an important treatise on some medical subject, almost in process of completion." No longer practicing the art of psychiatry nor what had been for him the more valuable art of writing, the author of *A Psychology for Psychiatrists* succumbs in the end to his own shrinking vision, a victim of the love he never quite understands and the once heroic commitment to work that has now taken a permanent leave of abstinence. (pp. 80-6)

> *Jeffrey Berman, "'Tender Is the Night': Fitzgerald's
> 'A Psychology for Psychiatrists',"* in his The Talking
> Cure: Literary Representations of Psychoanalysis, *New
> York University Press, 1985, pp. 60-86.*

---

## ADDITIONAL BIBLIOGRAPHY

Allen, Joan M. "The Lost Decade, 1924-1934: *Tender Is the Night*." In her *Candles and Carnival Lights: The Catholic Sensibility of F. Scott Fitzgerald*, pp. 124-31. New York: New York University Press, 1978.

> Discusses Catholic references in *Tender Is the Night*. According to Allen: "An underlying moral seriousness, Dick's priestly role, and the carnival imagery [in the novel are] . . . perhaps all products of Fitzgerald's Catholic orientation."

Bruccoli, Matthew J. *The Composition of "Tender Is the Night": A Study of the Manuscripts.* Pittsburgh: University of Pittsburgh Press, 1963, 252 p.

Seminal study of the plot, characterizations, structure, and themes through various preliminary versions of *Tender Is the Night.*

———. "The Long Way Out, 1931-1934." In his *Some Sort of Epic Grandeur: The Life of F. Scott Fitzgerald,* pp. 319-84. New York: Harcourt Brace Jovanovich, 1981.

Chronicles Fitzgerald's life during the period in which he completed and published *Tender Is the Night.*

———, and Duggan, Margaret M., eds. *Correspondence of F. Scott Fitzgerald,* pp. 179ff. New York: Random House, 1980.

Includes numerous references to *Tender Is the Night* in letters from Fitzgerald to George Jean Nathan, Maxwell Perkins, Louis Bromfield, T. S. Eliot, Samuel Marx, and Bennett Cerf, among others, and in letters to Fitzgerald from Robert Benchley, Malcolm Cowley, John Dos Passos, Zelda Fitzgerald, Dr. O. L. Forel, Gertrude Stein, and others.

Bryer, Jackson R., ed. "*Tender Is the Night* (1934)." In his *F. Scott Fitzgerald: The Critical Reception,* pp. 283-336. New York: Burt Franklin & Co., 1978.

Gathers over three dozen early reviews of *Tender Is the Night,* including those by Henry Seidel Canby, Malcolm Cowley, Clifton Fadiman, C. Hartley Grattan, Horace Gregory, Philip Rahv, Gilbert Seldes, and Edward Weeks.

Buntain, Lucy M. "A Note on the Editions of *Tender Is the Night.*" *Studies in American Fiction* 1, No. 2 (Autumn 1973): 208-13.

Compares the original 1934 edition with Malcolm Cowley's 1951 revised edition, concluding that "the two structural arrangements provide two quite different novels, each with a different focus, each with a different theme. *Tender Is the Night* must stand with *The Last Tycoon* as a second 'unfinished' Fitzgerald novel. Though physically complete, the competing editions of *Tender* indicate Fitzgerald's painful indecision about what his novel should ultimately mean."

Burton, Mary E. "The Counter-Transference of Dr. Diver." *ELH* 38, No. 3 (September 1971): 459-71.

Analyzes the deterioration of Diver as he accepts the role Nicole transfers to him, becoming "psychically . . . Devereux Warren— the pathetic and criminal American rich man who has committed incest with his daughter."

Callahan, John F. *The Illusions of a Nation: Myth and History in the Novels of F. Scott Fitzgerald.* Urbana: University of Illinois Press, 1972, 221 p.

Presents an extended analysis of *Tender Is the Night.*

Chamberlain, John. Review of *Tender Is the Night. The New York Times* (13 April 1934): 17.

Praises the novel as an "exciting and psychologically apt study in the disintegration of a marriage."

Coindreau, Maurice Edgar. "College Life and the American Novel: Part One, 1920-1945." In his *The Time of William Faulkner: A French View of Modern American Fiction,* edited and translated by George McMillan Reeves, pp. 171-91. Columbia: University of South Carolina Press, 1971.

Finds *Tender Is the Night* "a miscarried novel." According to Coindreau: "Fitzgerald could sing only one kind of music. *Tender Is the Night* is a terrible false note."

Cowley, Malcolm. "Breakdown." *The New Republic* LXXIX, No. 1018 (6 June 1934): 105-06.

Describes the strengths and weaknesses of *Tender Is the Night,* concluding that "it has a richness of meaning and emotion—one feels that every scene is selected among many possible scenes and that every event has pressure behind it. There is nothing false or borrowed in the book" [see excerpt dated 1934 in *TCLC,* Vol. 1].

Dahlie, Hallvard. "Alienation and Disintegration in *Tender Is the Night.*" *The Humanities Association Bulletin* XXII, No. 4 (Fall 1971): 3-8.

Sees the pattern of isolation and alienation in the novel as "one of the most significant structural and thematic elements."

Doherty, William H. "*Tender Is the Night* and 'Ode to a Nightingale'." In *F. Scott Fitzgerald,* edited by Harold Bloom, pp. 181-194. New York: Chelsea House Publishers, 1985.

Explores Fitzgerald's inspiration in John Keats's "Ode to a Nightingale" for themes and motifs central to *Tender Is the Night.*

Dudley, Juanita Williams. "Dr. Diver, Vivisectionist." *College Literature* II, No. 2 (Spring 1975): 128-34.

Focuses on Dick's wish in Book I of *Tender Is the Night* to "give a really *bad* party. . . . [Where] there's a brawl and seductions and people going home with their feelings hurt and women passed out in the cabinet de toilette" as "an architectonic device for ordering the novel and insuring unity between parts."

Ellis, James. "Fitzgerald's Fragmented Hero: Dick Diver." *The University Review* XXXII, No. 1 (October 1965): 43-9.

Examines the psychological state of Dick Diver in an attempt "to understand the reasons for his seemingly sudden collapse." Ellis concludes that Diver is psychically fragmented by his dissatisfaction with his profession, his demanding roles as doctor, father, and husband to Nicole, his failed affair with Rosemary, and his realization that he has wasted his youth.

Fahey, William A. "Love Battle." In his *F. Scott Fitzgerald and the American Dream,* pp. 89-114. New York: Thomas Y. Crowell, 1973.

Considers *Tender Is the Night* a "book about the ethical significance of cultural differences between Europe and America," noting that the novel "turns upon the question of the meaning of integrity and the problem of innocence in a world that . . . has lost the ability to articulate public codes in meaningful private terms."

Fiedler, Leslie A. "The Revenge on Woman: From Lucy to Lolita." In his *Love and Death in the American Novel,* rev. ed., pp. 291-336. New York: Dell Publishing, 1966.

Asserts that Fitzgerald's "outrage and self-pity constantly break through the pattern of his fiction . . . [making] even an ambitious attempt like *Tender Is the Night* finally too sentimental and whining to endure" [see excerpt dated 1966 in *TCLC,* Vol. 1].

Fitzgerald, F. Scott. *The Letters of F. Scott Fitzgerald,* edited by Andrew Turnbull, pp. 127ff. New York: Charles Scribner's Sons, 1963.

Includes Fitzgerald's comments on *Tender Is the Night* to his wife, his editor, John Peale Bishop, Ernest Hemingway, Gerald and Sara Murphy, and Edmund Wilson. Also included is his well-known letter of 13 August 1936 to Bennett Cerf regarding the revision of the novel for the proposed Modern Library edition.

Foster, Richard. "Time's Exile: Dick Diver and the Heroic Idea." *Mosaic* VIII, No. 3 (Spring 1975): 89-108.

Finds that "Dick Diver both knew and did not know, or refused to acknowledge that he knew, that he had been exiled by history's redefinition of the qualities of the hero. As a hero of tradition born in a post-heroic age, Dick was perhaps also a tragic hero because he found himself cut off, finally from both his duty and his fulfillment in it."

Gallo, Rose Adrienne. "Plagued by the Nightingale: *Tender Is the Night.*" In her *F. Scott Fitzgerald,* pp. 57-81. New York: Frederick Ungar, 1978.

Plot summary, structural analysis, and discussion of Fitzgerald's inspiration for the novel in Keats's "Ode to a Nightingale."

Grube, John. "*Tender Is the Night:* Keats and Scott Fitzgerald." *The Dalhousie Review* 44, No. 4 (Winter 1964-65): 433-41.

Examines Keatsian imagery and mood in *Tender Is the Night.*

Hall, William F. "Dialogue and Theme in *Tender Is the Night.*" *Modern Language Notes* LXXVI, No. 7 (November 1961): 616-22.

Finds the theme of the novel revealed primarily through the dialogue. According to Hall, in *Tender Is the Night* Fitzgerald concentrated on "the hidden roots of adult relationships; and with the waste that results from the characters' misunderstanding of themselves and of each other."

Hemingway, Ernest. *Ernest Hemingway: Selected Letters, 1917-1961,* edited by Carlos Baker, pp. 305ff. New York: Charles Scribner's Sons, 1981.

Includes Hemingway's initial reaction to *Tender Is the Night* recorded in May 1934, as well as several later references to the novel, which he came to consider Fitzgerald's greatest work.

Higgins, Brian, and Parker, Hershel. "Sober Second Thoughts: Fitzgerald's 'Final Version' of *Tender Is the Night.*" *Proof* 4 (1975): 129-52.

Surveys critical views of the novel focusing on the varying editions. Maintaining that the "experience of Dick's collapse is more vivid, more painful, and more overwhelming in the 1934 edition," Higgins and Parker conclude that Fitzgerald's chronological arrangement, "caused great damage in the long run, to all parts of the novel. Rewriting, reshaping parts of *Tender Is the Night* might indeed have produced a better novel; reordering it caused far more problems than it solved."

Hindus, Milton. "Tender Is the Night." In his *F. Scott Fitzgerald: An Introduction and Interpretation,* pp. 50-69. New York: Barnes & Nobel, 1968.

Deems the novel a failure. According to Hindus: "The weakness of the novel as a whole cannot be detected readily in any of the details because they are disguised by some very effective writing."

Huonder, Eugen. "*Tender Is the Night.*" In his *The Functional Significance of Setting in the Novels of Francis Scott Fitzgerald,* pp. 77-102. Bern, Switzerland: Herbert Lang & Co., 1974.

Analyzes the functions of various settings in the revised edition of the novel, including locations in Austria, Germany, and Switzerland, as well as the battlefield near Amiens, the beach, Nice, Paris, and Rome.

Kinahan, Frank. "Focus on F. Scott Fitzgerald's *Tender Is the Night.*" In *American Dreams, American Nightmares,* edited by David Madden, pp. 115-28. Carbondale and Edwardsville: Southern Illinois University Press, 1970.

Sees the central concern of the work as "the tension between the [American] Dream and the harsh reality underlying it." According to Kinahan, this theme "is developed primarily in terms of the personality of Dick Diver. Indeed, the contradictions inherent in his character are the same as those of the Dream as a whole; the Dream evaporates and Dick dies for much the same reasons and with the same inevitability" [see excerpt dated 1970 in *TCLC,* Vol. 1].

LaHood, Marvin J., ed. "*Tender Is the Night*": *Essays in Criticism.* Bloomington: Indiana University Press, 1969, 208 p.

Collects critical essays by William Hall, Kent and Gretchen Kreuter, John Kuehl, and G. C. Millard, among others, and reprints LaHood's own essay "Sensuality and Asceticism in *Tender Is the Night.*"

Lehan, Richard D. "*Tender Is the Night.*" In his *F. Scott Fitzgerald and the Craft of Fiction,* pp. 123-48. Carbondale and Edwardsville: Southern Illinois University Press, 1966.

Offers background and explication of the novel.

Lowry, Malcolm, and Lowry, Margerie Bonner. *Notes on a Screenplay for F. Scott Fitzgerald's "Tender Is the Night."* Bloomfield Hills, Mich.: Bruccoli Clark, 1976, 84 p.

Background and notes to the Lowrys' 1950 treatment of the novel, in which they envisioned several changes from the original story, including the death of Dick Diver at the end of the proposed film.

McCay, Mary A. "Fitzgerald's Women: Beyond Winter Dreams." In *American Novelists Revisited: Essays in Feminist Criticism,* edited by Fritz Fleischmann, pp. 311-24. Boston: G. K. Hall & Co., 1982.

Finds more hostility toward women in *Tender Is the Night* than in any other work by Fitzgerald.

McNicholas, Sister Mary Verity, O. P. "Fitzgerald's Women in *Tender Is the Night.*" *College Literature* IV, No. 1 (Winter 1977): 40-70.

Analyzes the characters Nicole Diver, Kaethe Gregorovius, Rosemary Hoyt, Violet McKisco, Mary North/Mary Minghetti, Lady Caroline Sibly-Biers, Elsie Speers, and Baby Warren, concluding that Dick Diver's downfall is effected through his relationships with this "gallery of formidable women."

Mencken, H. L. *Letters of H. L. Mencken,* edited by Guy J. Forgue, pp. 194 ff. Boston: Northeastern University Press, 1981.

Includes several letters to Fitzgerald, most notably Mencken's response to Fitzgerald's letter of 23 April 1934 complaining that the critics had misunderstood his intentions in *Tender Is the Night.* In his letter dated 26 April 1934 Mencken agreed that reviewers "usually miss the author's intentions completely. I think your own scheme is a capital one, and that you have carried it out very effectively in [*Tender Is the Night*]."

Miller, James E., Jr. "Creation." In his *F. Scott Fitzgerald: His Art and His Technique,* pp. 127-58. New York: New York University Press, 1964.

Finds *Tender Is the Night* "more complex in conception than . . . *The Great Gatsby*—but *Tender* never gives the impression of absolute certainty of control that *Gatsby* gives" [see excerpt dated 1964 in *TCLC,* Vol. 1].

Mizener, Arthur. "Chapter XIII." In his *The Far Side of Paradise: A Biography of F. Scott Fitzgerald,* pp. 238-51. Boston: Houghton Mifflin Co., 1949.

Concludes that "the scope of *Tender Is the Night* is such that, for all the book's faults, its 'philosophical' impact is unforgettable. It makes *The Great Gatsby . . .* seem neat and simple."

———. "F. Scott Fitzgerald: *Tender Is the Night.*" In his *Twelve Great American Novels,* pp. 104-19. New York: New American Library, 1967.

Includes introductory commentary on the plot, characters, themes, and distinctive traits of the novel.

Nelson, Gerald B. "Dick Diver." In his *Ten Versions of America,* pp. 43-60. New York: Alfred A. Knopf, 1972.

Considers Fitzgerald's treatment of American ethics, manners, and values in *Tender Is the Night* by focusing on the characterizations of Dick Diver and the events surrounding him.

Piper, Henry Dan. "*Tender Is the Night*: 1932-1934." In his *F. Scott Fitzgerald: A Critical Portrait,* pp. 205-28. New York: Holt, Rinehart and Winston, 1965.

A biographical and critical essay discussing Fitzgerald's intentions for the novel and the prominent issues, motifs, and themes of the work.

Prigozy, Ruth. "From Griffith's Girls to *Daddy's Girl*: The Masks of Innocence in *Tender Is the Night.*" *Twentieth Century Literature* 26, No. 2 (Summer 1980): 189-221.

Compares the image of child-women presented in popular films of the era with Fitzgerald's characterization of Rosemary Hoyt in *Tender Is the Night* and examines Fitzgerald's sources in the films of D. W. Griffith.

Rascoe, Burton. "Esquire's Five-Minute Shelf." In *Esquire* 1, No. 5 (April 1934): 133, 159, 161-62.

A favorable review calling *Tender Is the Night* "superb" and noting that "the rich, Celtic, romantic imagination of F. Scott Fitzgerald which has flowered so tropically in the short story and novel. . .has in this, the maturest novel he has written, been subjected to the discipline of reflection and selection."

Roulston, Robert. "Dick Diver's Plunge into the Roman Void: The Setting of *Tender Is the Night.*" *The South Atlantic Quarterly* 77, No. 1 (Winter 1978): 85-97.

Focuses on the section of Book III set in Rome. According to Roulston, "[Because] in *Tender Is the Night* all narrative and thematic roads lead to Rome, the section devoted to Dick's ordeal in the Eternal City assumes an importance utterly disproportionate to its length.''

Samsell, R. L. ''Won't You Come Home, Dick Diver?'' *Fitzgerald/ Hemingway Annual: 1970*, edited by Matthew J. Bruccoli and C. E. Frazer Clark, Jr., pp. 34-42. Washington, D. C.: NCR/Microcard Editions, 1970.
    Analyzes Diver's charm and egoism, noting that throughout the novel ''there are numerous examples of Dick's sub-surface which reveal him to be just another assembly line American.'' Samsell concludes that Diver is ''an egocentric phony, surrounded by dolts even duller than himself.''

Sklar, Robert. ''Chapter Ten.'' In his *F. Scott Fitzgerald: The Last Laocoön*, pp. 249-92. New York: Oxford University Press, 1967.
    Comprehensive examination of plot, characterization, and prominent characteristics of *Tender Is the Night*. According to Sklar: ''In *Tender Is the Night* Fitzgerald created a work of fiction rare in American literature, a novel uniting romantic beauty and also historical and social depth; and he proved by his creation that his art, and his identity as an artist, could survive the death of the society which had nurtured and sustained him.''

Stanley, Linda C. *The Foreign Critical Reputation of F. Scott Fitzgerald: An Analysis and Annotated Bibliography*. Westport, Conn.: Greenwood Press, 1980, 276 p.
    Lists British reviews and editions of *Tender Is the Night*, numerous translations, and Danish, Dutch, French, Indian, Italian, Japanese, Norwegian, and Swedish reviews.

Stark, John. ''The Style of *Tender Is the Night*.'' In *Fitzgerald/Hemingway Annual: 1972*, edited by Matthew J. Bruccoli and C. E. Frazer Clark, Jr., pp. 89-95. Washington, D.C.: NCR/Microcard Editions, 1973.
    An analysis of Fitzgerald's prose style in *Tender Is the Night*, focusing on the opening paragraphs of that novel. According to Stark, this is a fascinating passage because in it ''meanings are conveyed by an authorial voice that speaks clearly to the reader, and because that voice expresses attitudes very much like the ones usually attributed to Fitzgerald.''

Stavola, Thomas J. ''*Tender Is the Night*: Dick Diver.'' In his *Scott Fitzgerald: Crisis in an American Identity*, pp. 145-65. New York: Barnes & Noble Books, 1979.
    Studies Diver's personal identity and the conflict between ''his own notion of the Self rooted in the traditional virtues. . .'honor, courtesy, and courage','' and the society ''that has abandoned its former values.''

Stern, Milton R., ed. *Critical Essays on F. Scott Fitzgerald's ''Tender Is the Night.''* Boston: G. K. Hall & Co., 1986, 280 p.
    Collects important reviews and essays from the 1930s to the 1980s.

Trachtenberg, Alan. ''The Journey Back: Myth and History in *Tender Is the Night*.'' In *Experience in the Novel: Selected Papers from the English Institute*, edited by Roy Harvey Pearce, 133-62. New York: Columbia University Press, 1968.
    According to Trachtenberg: ''*Tender Is the Night* submits American myths to the test of time. . . . The reader's work is to assemble the materials of the novel into a fictive history which, once attained, is surely one of the most remarkably illuminating experiences in American literature.''

Troy, William. ''The Worm i' the Bud.'' *The Nation* CXXVIII, No. 3592 (9 May 1934): 539-40.
    An unfavorable review. According to Troy: ''Dick Diver turns out to be Jay Gatsby all over again, another poor boy with a 'heightened sensitivity to the promises of life' betrayed by his own inability to make the right distinctions. And the repetition of the pattern turns out to be merely depressing.''

Way, Brian. ''*Tender Is the Night*.'' In his *F. Scott Fitzgerald and the Art of Social Fiction*, pp. 119-48. New York: St. Martin's Press, 1980.
    Discusses violence, decay, and suffering in *Tender Is the Night* as reflections of Fitzgerald's attitudes toward the decadent society that he depicted in the novel.

White, Eugene. ''The 'Intricate Destiny' of Dick Diver.'' *Modern Fiction Studies* VII, No. 1 (1961-62): 55-62.
    Views Dick Diver as ''a man who because of his deep love for Nicole Warren makes a deliberate choice with full realization of the dilemma which it will eventually force upon him. And when the dilemma must be resolved, he chooses what is best for Nicole even though it brings heartbreak to him.''

Whitehead, Lee M. ''*Tender Is the Night* and George Herbert Mead: An 'Actor's' Tragedy.'' *Literature and Psychology* XV, No. 3 (Summer 1965): 180-91.
    Analyzes *Tender Is the Night* in terms of the social psychology delineated by Mead in his *Mind, Self, and Society* (1934).

Wilson, Edmund. *Letters on Literature and Politics: 1912-1972*, edited by Elena Wilson, pp. 129ff. New York: Farrar, Straus and Giroux, 1957.
    Includes several references to *Tender Is the Night*. Notable are Wilson's comments in a letter of 1951 to Malcolm Cowley: ''[The] weakness of *Tender Is the Night* was that Scott, when he wrote the first part, was thinking only about Gerald Murphy and had no idea that Dick Diver was a brilliant psychiatrist. It is hard to believe in him as a scientist—also, I think, hard to believe that such a man as Scott tries later to imagine should eventually have sunk into obscurity instead of becoming a successful doctor with a fashionable practice in New York or attached to an expensive sanatorium.''

# (Sir) Edmund (William) Gosse

## 1849-1928

English biographer, autobiographer, critic, essayist, translator, poet, dramatist, and novelist.

Gosse was a prolific man of letters whose lasting fame rests on a single and quite atypical volume: *Father and Son,* an account of his childhood that is often considered a prominent example of Victorian spiritual autobiography. At one time Gosse was most highly regarded as a literary historian, biographer, and critic. However, a widely publicized scandal concerning deficiencies in his scholarship did lasting damage to his reputation. Although disregarded as a serious scholar, Gosse was well known as an effective popularizer who was praised for his ability to vividly and entertainingly convey a wide range of information to his readers. Of his many works, only *Father and Son* excites much discussion today. Variously described as biography, autobiography, memoir, and even as a novel, *Father and Son* is frequently regarded as an amalgamation of literary elements that combined to form a unique work which is a classic of English literature.

Gosse was the only child born to Emily Bowles Gosse, then forty-three, and Philip Henry Gosse, a noted and widely traveled zoologist of thirty-nine. Both of Gosse's parents were devout members of the Plymouth Brethren, a strict Calvinist sect for whom the Bible was a literal document and the Day of Judgment imminent. The middle-aged Gosses pledged their son at birth to the service of the Lord—a pledge that was renewed seven years later at his mother's deathbed. In 1857, the year after Emily Gosse's death, the elder Gosse published *Omphalos,* an attempt to reconcile the scriptural account of creation with the scientific discoveries that were then shaping the theory of evolution. The book was universally derided, and Philip Gosse, still distraught over the loss of his wife and further distressed over the decline in his professional standing, moved with his son to the small seaside town of Marychurch in Devon. Here the elder Gosse assumed leadership of the community's small congregation of Plymouth Brothers, and administered adult baptism rites to his son when Edmund was ten. This ceremony was, Gosse wrote in *Father and Son,* "the central event of my whole childhood. Everything, since the earliest dawn of consciousness, seemed to have been leading up to it. Everything, afterward, seemed to be leading down and away from it." Gosse depicts his childhood in *Father and Son* as a time of almost unrelieved bleakness, and much critical discussion centers on Gosse's claim that the book is "scrupulously true," offered "as a *document,* as a record." It is most likely that Gosse selectively recorded only that which supported the artistic theme that supplied the book's subtitle: "A Study of Two Temperaments," that of the father, unquestioningly devoted to his faith, and that of the son, doubtful in matters of religion and attracted to worldly pleasures. Religion dominated the Gosse household and so filled the family's purview that as a child Gosse enjoyed few secular amusements: for example, he was never told a fairy tale, and claimed that he did not understand the concept of fiction until he was at least eleven. His formal education was limited to local primary schools and a boarding school chosen by his father for the piety

of the administrators. Gosse's schooling ended when he was about sixteen.

As he grew older, Gosse increasingly questioned his father's beliefs, privately repudiating many of the tenets of the Brothers' faith. At seventeen he was settled in London, living at a rooming house selected by his father and working at a position secured by his father, that of cataloger at the British Museum. Many of his fellow library workers were aspiring poets and critics, and Gosse was soon writing poetry himself, as well as publishing book reviews and critical essays in periodicals such as the *Spectator, Academy,* and *Fraser's Magazine.* His father's letters at this time were full of concern about Edmund's spiritual state. In 1873 Gosse made a decisive break with his past and established a secondary career for himself: he published the poetry collection *On Viol and Flute,* which was well received, and formally replied to his father's many anxious inquiries with the statement that he no longer shared his father's faith. Despite this enormous rift, Gosse father and son maintained a respectful relationship for the rest of their lives. *The Life of Philip Henry Gosse F.R.S.,* the biography that Gosse wrote after his father's death, is a sympathetic work that gives no indication of the conflict that he would later detail in *Father and Son.*

It is often suggested that Gosse deliberately set out to become famous. Returning from a vacation in Norway in 1871 with a volume of Henrik Ibsen's poems, Gosse, according to biographer Ann Thwaite, was advised that the fastest way to secure renown was to specialize in some obscure literary field. Acting on this advice, he reviewed Ibsen's *Digte* for the *Spectator,* thus publishing the first English review of a work by Ibsen. Whatever Gosse's intent, his articles on Ibsen and other Scandinavian authors—later collected in *Studies in the Literature of Northern Europe*—not only established him as an expert in this field, but also helped to popularize Scandinavian literature in England. In 1875 he began working as a translator for the Board of Trade, and he remained in civil service for the next twenty-nine years. In the 1870s Gosse continued to publish critical essays as well as poetry. He moved increasingly in society, and counted among his close friends such prominent writers as Robert Browning, Thomas Hardy, Henry James, and William Dean Howells. Many commentators maintain that Gosse cultivated these relationships in order to advance his own career. Others have noted, however, that many of these friendships endured for Gosse's lifetime, and he was generally remembered as loving, generous, and steadfast in his relationships. For example, Algernon Swinburne was a frequent houseguest of Gosse long after Swinburne's erratic behavior had led to his ostracism elsewhere.

Within a decade after the appearance of *On Viol and Flute* in 1873, Gosse was widely known as a competent minor poet, an expert in Scandinavian literature, and one of the foremost commentators on English letters. He succeeded Leslie Stephen as Clark Lecturer at Trinity College, Cambridge, in 1884, and conducted a highly successful American lecture tour in the winter of 1884-85. In 1885 Gosse published his Trinity lectures as *From Shakespeare to Pope*—a volume that resulted in a widely bruited literary scandal. Gosse was already known for occasional inaccuracies in his works. Reviewers of his edition of Thomas Gray, for example, noted that some important dates were rendered incorrectly. This was just one sort of error, however, that was found in abundance in *From Shakespeare to Pope* by a anonymous reviewer who was quickly identified as John Churton Collins. According to Phyllis Grosskurth, Collins, like Gosse, had striven to make a name for himself in literary London. Unlike Gosse, he possessed a formal background of scholarship, having graduated from Oxford; also unlike Gosse, Collins met with little success. His meticulously researched volumes of literary history and criticism attracted scant notice, and his social ineptitude made him personally unpopular. He had already published vituperative critical attacks on Alfred Tennyson, John Addington Symonds, and Swinburne, but the attack on Gosse and *From Shakespeare to Pope* was characterized by Grosskurth as "more virulent than any he had yet devised." Collins's chief objection was that Gosse claimed familiarity with many literary works that Collins maintained he knew only secondhand. Citing multiple examples of Gosse's "habitual inaccuracy with respect to dates," Collins went on to charge that "almost all Mr. Gosse's statements and generalizations, literary and historical alike, are on a par with his chronology." Gosse was found guilty of mistaking the genres of works, confusing the identities of historical figures with similar names, and making broad generalizations based upon insufficient historical data.

"Although the review caused a flurry of interest and excitement," Janet Malcolm wrote, "it brought Collins no real glory, and, in fact, shoved him the more decisively and irrevocably off to the side of the arena in which late-nineteenth-century literary life was being played out." Collins was in the awkward position of being "right at the expense of another," and public

opinion was largely with Gosse, who may have been careless in his scholarship, but at least was not guilty of ungentlemanly behavior. Gosse had the official backing of Cambridge, as well as comforting letters and public statements of support from his many influential literary friends. His professional standing, however, shaken by the merciless exposure of what Collins called his scholarly "delinquencies," suffered further when Ibsen enthusiasts William Archer and Bernard Shaw noticed that Gosse's translations of Ibsen were less than satisfactory and his volumes of criticism riddled with countless minor errors. Gosse's currency with the reading and book-buying public and his place in society, however, were unaffected: he continued to publish books and to increase in personal popularity until his death in 1928. "Gosse would continue to be read and admired for his fluency, his wit, his wide-ranging acquaintance with so much literature," Thwaite has written. "But in his continued attempts to establish himself as a serious scholar, he was now irrevocably handicapped. . . . The contemptuous verdict of Churton Collins would never be forgotten."

Gosse's most distinguished and important contribution to literature, *Father and Son,* in many ways resembles traditional autobiography. However, its striking differences were immediately apparent. "It was biography and autobiography in one hand," wrote Gosse biographer Evan Charteris. "There was no model and no predecessor in literature. . . . There was something here so new, and so different in its nature and the scope of its achievements from any previous work of the writer that it called for a fresh estimate of his place in English literature. He was no longer assembling facts and valuing the ideas of others, but calling into existence a work of art deep in its humanity, humor, and emotion." In *Father and Son* Gosse presents a vivid picture of a peculiarly Victorian childhood, circumscribed by stringent religious conventions and deeply affected by the powerful personality of his father. While earlier authors had written about their experiences of antipathy between generations, Gosse is considered the first to write about his own early life with a sense of the historical significance of the generational conflict in which he and his father were embroiled. Philip Gosse was representative of a rapidly disappearing group: fanatical Puritans who, commentators agreed, blighted the early years of their offspring with their repressive creed. Edgar Johnson termed the book "the story of a relationship and a struggle" told "with all the unerring craftsmanship of a masterly novelist," and many commentators have noted Gosse's introduction of such novelistic devices as symbolism and dramatic structure and have praised his skillful treatment of intensely personal themes. Brian Finney has identified *Father and Son* as the prototype of an important subgenre of autobiography: one that focuses upon the subject's childhood as a period of conflict with a parent of disproportionate influence.

Late twentieth-century evaluations of Gosse remain mixed. It is common to find modern commentators adopting a slightly derogatory tone, taking their lead, perhaps, from some of Gosse's contemporaries, who observed with distaste Gosse's propensity for snobbish behavior and sometimes based evaluation of his work on perception of his personality. In addition, the view of Gosse as unsound in his scholarship has persisted to the present day. Nevertheless, many commentators, including both contemporaries and critics writing in later years, have set such considerations aside to note Gosse's ability as a literary biographer who skillfully selected anecdotes and biographical details to compose vivid portraits of his subjects. Further, in *Father and Son*, Gosse offered an insightful expression of the spiritual crises of Victorian society, creating a work that has earned a lasting place as one of the landmarks of autobiographical literature.

(See also *Contemporary Authors*, Vol. 117 and *Dictionary of Literary Biography*, Vol. 57: *Victorian Prose Writers after 1867*.)

## PRINCIPAL WORKS

*Madrigals, Songs and Sonnets* [with J. A. Blaikie]   (poetry) 1870

*On Viol and Flute*   (poetry)   1873; also published as *On Viol and Flute* [revised edition], 1883

*King Erik*   (drama)   [first publication] 1876

*Studies in the Literature of Northern Europe*   (criticism) 1879; also published as *Northern Studies* [revised edition], 1890

*Gray*   (biography)   1882; revised edition, 1889

*Seventeenth Century Studies*   (criticism)   1883

*Firdausi in Exile*   (poetry)   1885

*From Shakespeare to Pope*   (lectures)   1885

*Raleigh*   (biography)   1886

*Life of William Congreve*   (biography)   1888; revised and enlarged edition, 1924

*A History of Eighteenth Century Literature, 1660-1780* (criticism)   1889

*The Life of Philip Henry Gosse F. R. S.*   (biography) 1890

*Robert Browning*   (biography)   1890

*Gossip in a Library*   (essays)   1891

*The Jacobean Poets*   (criticism)   1894

*Critical Kit-Kats*   (criticism)   1896

*A Short History of Modern English Literature*   (criticism) 1898; revised edition, 1924

*The Life and Letters of John Donne.* 2 vols.   (biography) 1899

*English Literature: An Illustrated Record.* 4 vols. [vol. 2 with Richard Garnett]   (criticism)   1903

*French Profiles*   (criticism)   1904

*Jeremy Taylor*   (biography)   1904

*Coventry Patmore*   (biography)   1905

*Sir Thomas Browne*   (biography)   1905

*Father and Son: A Study of Two Temperaments*   (memoir) 1907

*Ibsen*   (biography)   1907

*The Collected Poems of Edmund Gosse*   (poetry)   1911

*Two Visits to Denmark: 1872, 1874*   (essays)   1911

*Portraits and Sketches*   (essays and criticism)   1912

*The Life of Algernon Charles Swinburne*   (biography) 1917

*Three French Moralists*   (essays)   1918

*Some Diversions of a Man of Letters*   (essays and criticism) 1919

*Books on the Table*   (criticism)   1921

*Aspects and Impressions*   (essays and criticism)   1922

*More Books on the Table*   (criticism)   1923

*Silhouettes*   (essays and criticism)   1925

*Leaves and Fruit*   (poetry)   1927

*The Correspondence of André Gide and Edmund Gosse: 1904-1928*   (letters)   1959

*Sir Edmund Gosse's Correspondence with Scandinavian Writers*   (letters)   1960

*America: The Diary of a Visit*   (journal)   1966

*Transatlantic Dialogue: Selected American Correspondence of Edmund Gosse*   (letters)   1966

*\*The Unequal Yoke*   (novel)   1975

\*This novel was first published serially in the journal *English Illustrated Magazine* in 1886.

---

**A[NDREW] LANG**   (essay date 1874)

[*One of England's most influential men of letters during the closing decades of the nineteenth century, Lang is best remembered today as the editor of the "color fairy books," a twelve-volume series of fairy tales introduced with* The Blue Fairy Book *in 1889 and concluding with* The Lilac Fairy Book *in 1910. A romantic vision of the past imbued Lang's writings and is evident in his work as a translator, poet, and historian. In the following excerpt, Lang notes the technical excellence but derivative nature of Gosse's poetry in* On Viol and Flute.]

Mr. Gosse's poems [in *On Viol and Flute*] are mainly remarkable for the striking examples they afford of the advantages and disadvantages which attend the existence of something like a school in modern English poetry. The disadvantages lie most obviously on the surface, and do his verses much wrong. Borrowed rhythms, borrowed mannerisms, expressions which once had the beauty of the *bizarre*, but which are now neither strange nor sweet, are unpleasant themes to dwell on, and must be noticed as briefly as possible. It is a violence to speak of "the sunset, with her warm red flesh," to talk of a woman's mouth as the "rose-tree of the world's great rose!" the rose of the world's great rose-tree would have been intelligible. And it is surely a mistake to write verses so provocative of parody as **"Guinevere,"**

> When the autumn nights were hot,
> (*Peach and apple and apricot,*)

and so on, with a refrain rhyming on the names of all sorts of fruit. To end our list of objections the poem called **"Renaissance"** is too close an echo of Mr. Swinburne's "Laus Veneris," which has been written once for all, and loses by repetition.

These are faults which cannot be overlooked, and which are traceable to the study of one phase of English poetry. But the beauties of Mr. Gosse's verses, beauties often due to the same influences, are as much a wider theme as they are a pleasanter one to treat of. And first of the beauty of form specially manifest in these sonnets. It is not easy to praise too highly their careful structure, their music and colour. Only a few years ago such sonnets would have been, for their perfection and form, almost a new thing in English verse. It is owing to the revived study of Italian art . . ., that a collection of fourteen casually rhymed lines is no longer considered good enough to call a sonnet, and that what is done in this way is done well. Mr. Gosse's sonnets are so much on a level of excellence that it is difficult to know which to select for quotation. Perhaps that which closes the series on **"Fortunate Love"** is as good an example as any other.

## "Epithalamium"

High in the organ-loft, with lilied hair,
    Love plied the pedals with his snowy foot,
    Pouring forth music like the scent of fruit,
And stirring all the incense-laden air;
We knelt before the altar's gold rail, where
    The priest stood robed, with chalice and palm shoot,
    With music men, who bore citole and flute,
Behind us, and the attendant virgins fair;
And so our red Aurora flushed to gold,
    Our dawn to sudden sun, and all the while
The high-voiced children trebled clear and cold,
    The censer boys went swinging down the aisle,
And far above, with fingers strong and sure,
Love closed our lives' triumphant overture.

It would be scarcely possible to surpass this blending of the triumphant passion of music with the colour and quiet of painting. Other sonnets, which it is a temptation to call masterpieces, are **"Experience," "Perfume," "D. G. R.,"** and **"Old Trees."** **"Perfume,"** especially, is worthy of one who loves sweet scents, and can trace and express their mystic "correspondences" with delicate emotions as subtly as Baudelaire.

Mr. Gosse's other lyrics are less perfect in form than his sonnets, but they have the interest of expressing a philosophy of life, which is perhaps as useful as any other mental anodyne of our time. In his eclecticism there is a good deal of Goethe and of Walt Whitman, of Marcus Aurelius, and of Théophile Gautier. This philosophy is most definitely expressed in the prelude—

I clasp, as bees do flowers, with amorous wings,
The spirit of life in moving, joyous things;
    Whereër desire receives the boon it craves,
A new Athene from my forehead springs.

Lovers behind the haystacks, out of sight,
Lovers behind the haystacks, out of sight,
And peasants dancing in a barn at night,
    Rough fishers chanting as they haul the net,
And whistling mowers in the fading light.

All these are more than my own life to me;
I haul the moonshot fishes from the sea,
    I fiddle on the village green, I dance,
I thrill with others in their honest glee.

The same feeling is expressed in **"Lying in the Grass,"** a poem which embodies those effects of evening light, and the contemplation of peaceful labour. . . .

Obviously, any one who thinks it a demerit in literature to be literary, who wants to be "grand, epic, homicidal," will find no pleasure in Mr. Gosse's book. But he shows every promise of becoming a poet whose verses may well be read to loungers beneath the trees, like those whom Mr. W. B. Scott has designed for the frontispiece. There are, however, blemishes enough, and irritating affectations to be cleared away before listeners will be as complacent as the *Auditor* addressed in the interludes.

"You do not stir? you will not rise and go?
Then listen longer, *if it must be so.*"

*A[ndrew] Lang, in a review of "On Viol and Flute,"*
*in* The Academy, *January 31, 1874, p. 108.*

## GEORGE COTTERELL   (essay date 1885)

[*In the following excerpt from a review of Gosse's poetry collection* Firdausi in Exile, *Cotterell tempers his positive comments with the qualification that the poems in this volume do not bear out Gosse's initial promise as a poet.*]

A high reputation is not an unmixed advantage to an author. If he has done much good work he may produce a little that is not good without harm to his popularity; but if his fame depends rather on promise than on performance, he is under the constant necessity of excelling himself. Mr. Gosse has been regarded, whether rightly or wrongly, as a poet of great promise, and it is a misfortune for him that [*Firdausi in Exile*] cannot altogether satisfy the expectation which that promise has aroused. There are parts of it that are as good as any of Mr. Gosse's previous work—some of the sonnets, indeed, show a marked advance—but other parts are of quite inferior merit. It is to be regretted that at least two of the poems of greater length, and the two which Mr. Gosse himself appears to regard as of most importance, are decidedly poor.

**"Firdausi in Exile"** is one of these. This poem has been published before, and the episode of Persian story to which it relates is generally known. Mr. Gosse tells the tale in very bald verse, with scarcely any attempt at imaginative treatment. Stanzas which might otherwise have had the merit of plain prose are deprived even of that by the presence of forced rhymes and inversions. . . .

**"The Island of the Blest"** is the longest composition in the volume. The subject, if an old one, affords ample material for poetic treatment; and though among this material Mr. Gosse seems to have chosen the poorest, his treatment of it is not unpoetic. Some northern mariners lose the control of their ship in a storm, and the vessel finally drives upon an island which is thus picturesquely described:

A craggy isle it seemed, of wanton shape,
    Rounded with woodland, scarped by peaks on high,
With many a curve of brave fantastic cape,
    And bright bare ridge of rock against the sky.

Landing here, the wanderers are received by a grave people who are strange to them; and again Mr. Gosse describes the scene in apt and excellent lines:

The forms that crowded round us all were Greek,
    Yet by some marvel of the shifty brain
Their tongue seemed ours when they began to speak,
    And ours seemed theirs when we replied again.

The inhabitants of the Island of the Blest were once the denizens of the old world of Greek history and fable. Instead, however, of their virtues and heroisms being reproduced in nobler forms, they appear only in a sort of burlesque. . . . The *dénouement* of the poem consists in the flirtation and subsequent elopement of one of the northern wanderers with Helen—an incident which caused the banishment of all the strangers, for whom the magic isle and its delights were thenceforth no more. Such an incident is, indeed, highly disillusionary; and a reader who possesses any poetic sensibility may be excused if he resents upon the poet his employment of so excellent a theme to so worthless a purpose.

It is pleasant to turn from these ambitious but unsatisfactory poems to others of less pretension and greater merit. **"A Ballad of the Upper Thames"** is a charming piece of homely rural description, clever in form and bright and happy in tone. (p. 386)

Two or three of the sonnets may be said to be perfect. There have been great poets who have written indifferent sonnets, but nobody who is not a genuine poet can write a good sonnet. In so far, therefore, as the production of this form of verse with success is a test of poetic capacity Mr. Gosse entirely justifies his calling. . . .

The merits [of this volume], which are not small, are found in poems of the affections, of domestic and rustic life, in pictures of simple natural beauty and quiet cultivated grace. Within these limits Mr. Gosse's work is admirable, and it is only when he attempts something beyond that he fails. Any estimate of his powers which is based on the quality of his best work, and takes no account of the limited range of that work, would be misleading. It is due to Mr. Gosse himself that too much be not expected from him, and that the standards by which his work shall be judged be not those of the great poets, by whose side he would inevitably appear dwarfed to less than his rightful stature. He lacks their imagination, their power to project bold outlines and fill them, to invest dry bones with life, to sound the depths and reach the higher levels of human nature. He can produce polished verse, but he cannot "build the lofty rhyme." His powers of observation are wide, keen, and sympathetic; he has facility and grace of expression, undoubted cleverness, a refined taste, a cultivated and scholarly mind; but all these do not make up genius. (p. 387)

> *George Cotterell, in a review of "Firdausi in Exile, and Other Poems," in* The Academy, *Vol. 28, No. 710, December 12, 1885, pp. 386-87.*

### [JOHN CHURTON COLLINS]   (essay date 1886)

[*The following excerpt is taken from Collins's famous attack on Gosse's scholarship in* From Shakespeare to Pope. *Collins had been a friend of Gosse, but the two had not met for several years when Collins published his lengthy expression of outrage at the errors appearing in a volume issued by a university press. Gosse's reply to Collins (see excerpt below) stirred a controversy that brewed in the letters columns of several literary magazines.*]

That such a book as [*From Shakespeare to Pope*] should have been permitted to go forth to the world with the *imprimatur* of the University of Cambridge, affords matter for very grave reflection. But it is a confirmation of what we have long suspected. It is one more proof that those rapid and reckless innovations, which have during the last few years completely changed the faces of our Universities, have not been made with impunity. (p. 289)

[It is] with the greatest regret that we have had placed in our hands, dated from Trinity College, Cambridge, and published by the University Press, a work which we do not scruple to describe as most derogatory to all concerned in its production. Whether this volume is an indication of the manner in which the important subject with which it deals is studied at Cambridge, we do not know. We sincerely trust that it is not. But of two things we are very sure; first, that a book so unworthy, in everything but externals, of a great University has never before been given to the world; and secondly, that it is the bounden duty of all friends of learning to join in discountenancing so evil a precedent.

Not the least mischievous characteristic of the work is the skill with which its worthlessness is disguised. From title to colophon there is, so far as externals are concerned, everything to disarm suspicion, everything to inspire trust. An excellent index; unexceptionable type; unexceptionable paper. . . . (p. 295)

In the course of the work we learn that many "eminent friends" have been anxiously consulted; for "in an enquiry of this nature," observes the author, "exact evidence, even of a minute kind, outweighs in importance any expression of mere critical opinion." As we are not concerned with Mr. Gosse's eminent friends, but only with Mr. Gosse himself, we shall merely remark that we quite absolve Professor Gardiner and Mr. Austin Dobson from all complicity in Mr. Gosse's delinquencies.

Of all offences of which a writer can be guilty, the most detestable is that of simulating familiarity with works which he knows only at second hand, or of which he knows nothing more than the title. That a Lecturer on English Literature should not know whether the *Arcadia* of Sidney, and the *Oceana* of Harrington, are in prose or verse, or, not knowing, should not have taken the trouble to ascertain, is discreditable enough; but that he should, under the impression that they are poems, have had the effrontery to sit in judgment on them, might well, in Macaulay's favourite phrase, make us ashamed of our species. And yet this is what Mr. Gosse has done. . . . It is easy to see what has misled him with regard to the *Oceana*, and his error certainly furnishes a very amusing illustration of his method of investigation. He has confounded James Harrington, the prose writer, who was born in 1611, with Sir John Harrington, the poet, who was born in 1561; and the title *Oceana* having a very poetical sound, he has jumped to the conclusion that it is a poem. (pp. 295-96)

But these are not the only examples of Mr. Gosse's offences on this score. On page 102 he describes Daniel's *Cleopatra* and *Philotas* as "choral tragi-comedies." If he had consulted them, he would have seen that they are pure tragedies in the most monotonously stilted style of pure classical tragedy. Again on page 102 we are told that Denham's *Sophy* "remains a solitary specimen of the Seneca tragedy amonst the English dramas of the age, just as the curious play of Tyr et Sidon remains a solitary experiment in romantic tragedy in 17th-century French." Will our readers credit that the play thus confidently asserted to be a "specimen of Seneca tragedy" has absolutely no point in common with Seneca's plays? It is a drama as purely romantic as Lear or Hamlet. It does not observe the unities, except perhaps the unity of place; it has no Chorus; one of the characters is obviously modelled on the Shakspearian Clown; part of it is written in rhyme, part of it in prose, and part of it in blank verse so loose and straggling as to be scarcely distinguishable from prose. But to proceed. Mr. Gosse speaks on page 118 of Fanshawe's "little epic of *Dido and Æneas*"; Fanshawe's little epic, as he would have seen if he had turned to it, is neither more nor less than a translation of Virgil's Fourth Æneid in the Spenserian stanza. (pp. 297-98)

There are many things in Mr. Gosse's volume, as we shall presently show, which prove his utter incapacity for the task he has undertaken, but nothing is more derogatory to him than his habitual inaccuracy with respect to dates. However limited a man's reading may be, however treacherous his memory, however slender his abilities, he has no excuse for making blunders of this kind. It is plain that Mr. Gosse, so far from attempting to verify his dates, has not even troubled himself to consult the title-pages of the works to which he refers. We will give a few examples. . . . Mr. Gosse tells us that Oldham died in 1684. Oldham died in December 1683. He informs us that certain verses quoted from Fenton were "sung" by that poet in 1730. The verses occur in the dedication of Fenton's well-known edition of Waller's *Poems*, which was published in 1729. He informs us that in 1684 Roscommon "threw off the constraint of rhyme in his *Art of Poetry*." Roscommon's *Art of Poetry*, or rather his translation of Horace's *Ars Poetica*, the work to which Mr. Gosse with characteristic slovenliness alludes, appeared in 1680. Speaking of the year 1642, he says: "Ford and Massinger were resigning the art which they had received," &c. Massinger had been dead two years, he died in March 16³⁹/₄₀, and it is probable that Ford died about the same time. On page 11 it is confidently asserted that Philips's *Cyder* was written in 1699. Philips's *Cyder* was published in 1708, and all that is known about the time of its composition is that it was begun at Oxford and completed in the year before its publication. That the first book could not have been composed before 1705, and the second before 1706, is proved by internal evidence. . . . We are told on page 210, that John Norris's Miscellanies were brought out in 1678. John Norris brought out his Miscellanies in 1687. Indeed, Mr. Gosse appears to be incapable of transcribing a date correctly, even when it must have been before his very eyes. On page 55, for example, he twice asserts that Waller's verses "To the King on his Navy" were written in 1621, when the date 1626 is given under the title of the poem. . . . We shall not weary our readers by multiplying instances of these blunders, for we have cited quite enough to show how far Mr. Gosse's chronological statements are to be depended on. But the following is so exquisitely characteristic, not only of Mr. Gosse himself but of the Dilettanti School generally, that we cannot pass it by. "Late in the summer, one handsome and gallant young fellow"—Mr. Gosse is speaking of the death of Sidney Godolphin—"riding down the deep-leaved lanes that led from Dartmoor . . . , met a party of Roundheads, was cut down and killed." Now Sidney Godolphin was killed at the end of January 164⅔, when the lanes were, we apprehended, not deepleaved; he was, it may be added, not handsome, for Clarendon especially enlarges on the meanness of his person; he was not "cut down and killed," he was shot dead by a musket ball; he was not meeting a party of Roundheads in the lanes, he was pursuing them into Chagford.

We are sorry to say that, bad as all this is, worse is to come. Almost all Mr. Gosse's statements and generalizations, literary and historical alike, are on a par with his chronology. There is not a chapter—nay, if we except the Appendices and index, it would be difficult to find five consecutive pages which do not swarm with errors and absurdities. And the peculiarity of Mr. Gosse's errors is, that they cannot be classed among those to which even well-informed men are liable. They are not mere slips of the pen, they are not clerical and superficial, not such as, casually arising, may be easily excised, but they are, to borrow a metaphor from medicine, local manifestations of constitutional mischief. The ignorance which Mr. Gosse displays of the simplest facts of Literature and History is sufficiently extraordinary, but the recklessness with which he exposes that ignorance transcends belief. Will our readers credit that Mr. Gosse attributes the pseudo-classicism of the diction of the eighteenth-century poetry to the influence of the writings of Anthony Ashley Cooper, first Earl of Shaftesbury; that he asserts that "it was Waller's duty to seize English Poetry by the wings, and to shut it up in a cage for a hundred and fifty years"; that Cleveland and Wild were the leaders of a reaction against the classical school; and that he accounts for the fact, that it was Waller who "revolutionized" poetry in England, and not Milton "because Milton was born three years later than Waller?" (pp. 298-301)

On page 165 we find the following amazing statement. Speaking of Dryden's employment of the heroic quatrain in the *Annus*

*Mirabilis* (1667), Mr. Gosse goes on to inform us, that the heroic quatrain "was not again employed all through the Restoration or the Augustan age, nor again until, in 1743, the Earl of Chesterfield brought out the posthumous *Elegies* of his young cousin Hammond." The heroic quatrain was employed habitually by poets between 1667 and 1743. It was employed by Aphra Behn; it was employed by Blackmore; it was employed by Wycherley, by Sheffield, by Walsh, by Garth, by Prior, by Swift, by Hughes, by Rowe, by Gay, not reckoning the continuation of Gondibert, which is probably not genuine; it was employed by Pope, by Parnell, by Savage, by Aaron Hill.

But this is nothing to what follows. Our readers will probably believe us to be jesting when we inform them that Mr. Gosse deliberately asserts, that between 1660 and "about 1760" Milton and Roscommon were the only poets who employed blank verse:—

> "From 1660 onwards to about 1760 the exact opposite was the case (that is, that the couplet superseded blank verse). A poet of decent abilities was sure of readers if he would write in the couplet." Then, in a note, he adds: "Milton would stand absolutely alone in his preference of another form if Roscommon, also in 1684, in emulation of *Paradise Lost*, had not chosen to throw off what he calls the restraint of Rime in his Art of Poetry."

Has Mr. Gosse ever inspected the *All for Love* and the *Don Sebastian* of Dryden; the *Mourning Bride* of Congreve; the *Julius Cæsar* of Sheffield; the blank verse tragedies of Crowne; the later dramas of Davenant; the tragedies of Otway, Lee, Southern, Rowe, Lillo, and Thomson; Addison's tragedy of *Cato;* Smith's tragedy of *Hippolytus;* Hughes's *Siege of Damascus;* Johnson's *Irene*? Has he ever read Roscommon's own parody of Milton, inserted in the "Essay on Translated Verse''; or Addison's Ovidian translation in Miltonic verse; or Lady Winchelsea's *Fanscomb Barn;* or Philips's *Splendid Shilling*, Blenheim, and Cyder; or Aaron Hill's *Cleon to Lycidas?* Can he be unaware that within those years were published Thomson's *Seasons* and *Liberty;* Dyer's *Ruins of Rome*, and *Fleece;* Akenside's *Pleasures of Imagination;* Armstrong's *Art of Preserving Health;* Somerville's *Chace*, and *Hobbinol;* Glover's *Leonidas*, Mallet's *Excursion*, Blair's *Grave*, Young's *Night Thoughts*, not to speak of innumerable other poems less celebrated? (pp. 306-07)

But the recklessness with which Mr. Gosse displays his ignorance of the very elements of literature is, if possible, exceeded by the recklessness with which he displays his ignorance of the commonest facts of history and biography. We will give one or two examples. In the life of Waller, Mr. Gosse finds this sentence: "Mr. Saville used to say that no man in England, should keep him company without drinking but Ned Waller." This becomes, in Mr. Gosse's narrative, "George Savile, Lord Halifax, the famous *viveur*, and a pupil of Waller's, in verse, said," &c. It would be difficult to match this. Nearly every word is a blunder. Indeed, we will boldly say that, if our own or any other literature were ransacked, it would be ransacked in vain for a sentence which condenses so many errors and so much of that *crassa negligentia*, which is as reprehensible in writers as it is in lawyers and doctors. George Savile, Lord Halifax, who is apparently known only to Mr. Gosse as "the famous *viveur*," was, as we need scarcely say, one of the most distinguished statesmen of the seventeenth century. He was in no sense of the word a *viveur*. He was not a pupil of Waller. He never, so far as is recorded, wrote a line of verse in his life. But there was another Lord Halifax, who might perhaps be known to Mr. Gosse only in connection with his convivial habits and his bad poetry, but who is known to everyone else as the Originator of the National Debt, as the Founder of the Bank of England, and as the most eminent financier in English history. It is this Lord Halifax who might, as the author of a copy of verses on the death of Charles II., be described as a pupil of Waller. And it is of this Lord Halifax that Mr. Gosse is probably thinking. But the name of this Lord Halifax was, unfortunately for Mr. Gosse, Charles Montague. The "Mr. Savile" alluded to, was in truth neither George Savile, Marquis of Halifax, nor Charles Montague, Earl of Halifax, but Henry Savile, a younger son of Sir William Savile, and a younger brother of the Marquis.

"When the Queen fled from Exeter," says Mr. Gosse, "with the new-born Princess of Wales in July 1644." If Mr. Gosse had consulted his "eminent friend," Professor Gardiner, he would have learned that the younger daughters of English Kings are not Princesses of Wales; and as he appears to be fond of picturesque touches, he might, had he pushed his enquiries, have ascertained that to this particular child a peculiar interest is attached. If too, when writing the lines which follow, he had taken the trouble to turn to the Biographia Britannica, he would have discovered that "the young Duke of Newcastle," who "fled from defeat at Marston Moor," was in his fifty-third year, and that he was, moreover, not a Duke, but a Marquis.

We proceed to something much more serious. To the historian of Literature nothing should be so sacred as the reputation of the Dead, and on no point is he bound in honour to be more sensitively scrupulous than when he is called upon to discuss anything which may reflect unfavourably on that reputation. Now on the same page (p. 113) we find a statement which, unless Mr. Gosse is prepared to produce his authority for it, we do not scruple to designate a gross and shameful libel on the memory of as worthy a man as ever lived, "James Shirley, who had left a starving wife and children behind him, was in attendance (at Paris) upon his Royal Mistress." This is repeated on pp. 117, 118. Speaking of the "balls, comedies and prom-enades," with which "the English exiles were regaled at Fon-tainebleau," in 1646 and 1647, Mr. Gosse says that Shirley was "certainly" present at them, Waller and Hobbes probably, but Shirley "certainly." Now our only authority for the life of Shirley is Anthony Wood, and what Wood says is this:— "When the rebellion broke out Shirley was invited by his patron, Newcastle, to attend him in the war." This Shirley appears to have done. But after the King's cause declined— we give Wood's own words—"he, following his old trade of teaching, not only gained a comfortable subsistence, but ed-ucated many ingenious youths, who afterwards proved most eminent in divers faculties." In this honourable drudgery, un-dertaken for the support of his wife and children, all Shirley's life between about 1644 and 1660, appears to have been passed, and his conduct has elicited just praise from his biographers. If Mr. Gosse is in possession of documents hitherto unknown, it was his duty to have specified them, and it is his duty to produce them. Till he does so we shall continue to believe that this is only one of his many other loose and random assertions, and to protest against such unwarrantable liberties being taken with the biographies of eminent men.

We have by no means exhausted the list of Mr. Gosse's blun-ders, but we have, we fear, exhausted the patience of our readers. What further remarks, therefore, we have to make shall be brief. We have given a few specimens of Mr. Gosse's method of dealing with facts; we will now give a few specimens of his criticism. That excellent man, Mr. Pecksniff, was, we are told, in the habit of using any word that occurred to him as having a fine sound, and rounding a sentence well, without much care for its meaning, "and this," says his biographer, "he did so boldly and in such an imposing manner, that he would sometimes stagger the wisest people, and make them gasp again." This is precisely Mr. Gosse's method. About the propriety of his epithets, so long as they sound well, he never troubles himself; sometimes they are so vague as to mean anything, sometimes they have no meaning at all, as often they are inconsistent with each other. What is predicated of a work in one place is directly contradicted in another. Thus (p. 34), Drayton's "Barons' Wars" is described as "a serene and lovely poem"; on the very next page we are told that a "passionate music runs through it"; and on page 75 this same "serene and lovely poem" is described as "possessing various brilliant and touching qualities, irregular force, and sudden brilliance of style." Thus, on page 158, Davenant's *Gondibert,* coupled with Southey's *Epics,* is compared to "a vast sapless trunk, one of the largest trees in girth and height, but the deadest of them all, with scarcely a cluster of green buds here and there''; at the bottom of the same page we are told that it owed its popularity "to its gorgeous and exotic imagery." . . . Mr. Gosse's observations are, it may be added, never so amusing as when he touches on points of classical learning, and the extraordinary self-complacency with which they are enunciated, adds to their absurdity. "When a young fellow," he says, "prefers Moschus to Homer, and Ausonius to Virgil, we know how to class him." Whether such a young fellow has ever existed, or if he does exist, whether he is worth classing at all, is probably a reflec-tion which will occur to most people. But when a young fellow, or an old fellow, talks of "the grace of Latinity," or tells us that it was the property of hellebore to produce forgetfulness, or informs us that Aristotle and Horace have left rules for the composition of a "straightforward prosaic poetry," it is not, we apprehend, very difficult to class him. (pp. 307-10)

If we turn from the matter of Mr. Gosse's volume to the style and the diction, it is equally surprising that any University could have sanctioned its publication. How even the reader for the press could have allowed such words as "preciosity," "recrudescence," "solidarity," "rejuvenescence," "alem-bicated," or such phrases as "the lively actuality of a news-letter," "a personal sympathy with vegetation," "the excite-ment of resuscitation," and the like, to pass unchallenged, is to us inexplicable. Was there no one who could save Mr. Gosse from making himself ridiculous by such eloquence as this: "We who can see this Orpheus-like Charles torn to pieces by the outraged liberties of England, and that comely head floating down the Hebrus of the Revolution"? Could the Delegates of the Cambridge Press have been blind to the ludicrous impro-priety of permitting what was intended to be a serious treatise on English Literature to be prefaced by a copy of silly verses, in which the author—an official of the University—assures his readers that he is—

> Less than bird or shell,
> More volatile, more fragile far than these.

Nor does the bad taste—to call it by no harsher name—which is conspicuous throughout the book, less jar on us. Speaking, for example, of Waller's "Battle of the Summer Islands," Mr. Gosse observes, "My own belief is that the astute Waller, having property on the Islands, wrote his heroic poem and circulated it among wealthy and noble friends as an advertise-ment." Can Mr. Gosse possibly be ignorant that Waller was a gentleman? So again, when he talks of the "tattling monkey-tongue" of Pope, we have an example of one of the most detestable fashions of modern times—we mean the pert irreverence with which very little men are in the habit of speaking of great men.

And now we bring to a conclusion one of the most disagreeable tasks which it has ever been our lot to undertake. Our motives for undertaking it have already been explained. Had Mr. Gosse's volume been published in the ordinary way, we need scarcely say that we should not have noticed it. Had its errors and deficiencies been pointed out in the literary journals, we should probably have comforted ourselves with the thought, that what had been done once need not be done again. But when we saw that it came forth, carrying all the authority of a work published by a great University, and under the auspices of the most distinguished community in that University, and that so far from the literary journals estimating it at its true value, and placing students on their guard against its errors, Review vied with Review in fulsome and indiscriminating eulogy, we felt we had no choice. It was simply our duty, our imperative duty, in the interests of literature and in the interests of education, to speak out. That duty we have endeavoured to perform temperately and candidly. We have perverted nothing. We have coloured nothing. Had it been our object to make game of the book, it would not, we can assure Mr. Gosse, have been very difficult. Though we have, we own, been strongly tempted to comment as severely on his delinquencies as they certainly deserve, we have deliberately forborne. We have even refrained from discussing matters of opinion. We have confined ourselves entirely to matters of fact—to gross and palpable blunders, to unfounded and reckless assertions, to such absurdities in criticism and such vices of style as will in the eyes of discerning readers carry with them their own condemnation. When we consider the circulation secured to this volume from the mere fact of its having issued from so famous a press, and under such distinguished patronage, it is melancholy to think of the errors to which it will give currency. We only hope that our exposure of them will have the effect of serving in some degree to counteract the mischief. (pp. 310-12)

But whatever be the faults of Mr. Gosse's book, it will not, we hope, be without its use. If it illustrates comprehensively the manner in which English literature should not be taught, it may, on the "lucus a non lucendo" ["explanation of contraries"] principle, direct attention to the manner in which it should be taught. . . . (p. 312)

[*John Churton Collins*], *"English Literature at the Universities," in* The Quarterly Review, *Vol. 163, No. 326, October, 1886, pp. 289-329.*

## EDMUND GOSSE (essay date 1886)

[*In the following excerpt, Gosse responds to Collins's attack on* From Shakespeare to Pope *(see excerpt above). Gosse later admitted privately in letters to John Addington Symonds and others that he had in fact been guilty of carelessness in the volume.*]

As a rule I think that the most proper way of taking adverse criticism is to bow the head, and determine to profit by it when it is honest and to ignore it when it is the reverse. It is generally best not to reply at all. The article, however, entitled "English Literature in the Universities," which opens the current number of the *Quarterly Review,* and which takes the form of an extremely severe criticism of a volume of lectures which I published last year, cannot be ignored in this way. It is due to my

colleagues at Cambridge, and especially to the Council of Trinity College, that an article which is not merely harsh, but utterly contemptuous, and which accuses me of incompetence and even of imposture, should not be allowed to pass unchallenged. The *Quarterly* reviewer, with great ability, gathers all his thunders for the purpose of crushing me, and a good many people will think that I am crushed. I should be the charlatan he accuses me of being if I were silent.

I would say, in the first place, that severe as the review is I desire to draw from it what benefit I can. I have been hitherto very indulgently treated by the critics; I have eaten, perhaps, too many sweets, and the inevitable julep is here in a monstrous dose. I have always desired to secure accuracy; this stringent lesson of my fallibility will make me seek it still more. If my reviewer had kept within the bounds of moderation, had he shown less heat, had I thought him honest in his assumption of "a painful duty," I should have borne a reasonable punishment with resignation. But he has passed all bounds of moderation, and no one needs be surprised if I turn to defend myself.

Briefly, then, I charge this attack upon me with dishonesty because it accuses me of ignorance which my other publications alone would be sufficient to disprove; because it wilfully strains my words, not once or twice, but habitually, to meanings which they do not legitimately bear; because it dogmatically states that I show incompetence in matters of pure controversy, wherever my view may be held as fairly as the reviewer's; and because it wraps up in rhetorical garments of abuse little statements of mine which research may have proved to be inexact, but the importance of which the reviewer knows perfectly well can only be estimated by specialists.

I may be allowed to remind your readers that my volume is not a handbook, but a dissertation. It attempts to expound a certain theory, and to support it by several hundreds of allusions or illustrations taken from the most varied fields of literature. Most of these allusions are as brief as possible—mere momentary touches. Among this multitude of illustrations my reviewer has toiled with extraordinary patience, and in the face of his onslaught I am not so much surprised that he should have found so many errors as that he should have found so few. Among these there is only one for which I have truly to do penance.

In repeating an anecdote about Waller I had to mention a certain Savile as the hero of the tale. I rashly took for granted that George Savile, the delightful author of the *Anatomy of an Equivalent,* was the gentleman intended; and in reference to certain verses I thought of him, as Lord Halifax, as their author. My *Quarterly* reviewer is perfectly right in pointing out that these verses were written by the other contemporary Lord Halifax, Charles Montague, and that the hero of my little anecdote was not George Savile, but his brother Henry Savile. These Saviles and Halifaxes make rather a tangled web, and I confess that here I am guilty of a double-barrelled mistake. I regard this as the most serious error on which the *Quarterly Review* has put its finger.

I will cap this bad blunder of mine with one of my reviewer's which is at least as gross. He finds that I have alluded to the *Oceana,* without mentioning the name of its author, in a passage which may be a little ambiguous, although I confess it seems clear enough to me. The reviewer jumps to the conclusion that I suppose this prose romance to be a poem, builds up an elaborate theory to show why I have confounded James

Harrington with Sir John Harington the Elizabethan poet (whose name he misspells), and then exults for a whole page over his discovery. If he had not been in such a hurry to destroy me he might have perceived that the *Oceana* is mentioned once again in my book, and this time with the Christian name of its author, James Harrington.

Let me now give an example of sheer misrepresentation. The *Quarterly* reviewer charges me with what would have been indeed a monstrous error, the statement that between 1660 and 1760 only Milton and Roscommon used blank verse. Now what I do say is that during that period ''a poet of decent abilities was sure of readers if he would write in the couplet; he had to conquer them if he presumed to stray from it.'' That is to say, in non-dramatic verse (for I had spoken elsewhere of the dramatic verse of the same period) the fashionable tendency of the age was in favour of the couplet. Was it not? and so long as the seventeenth century lasted was not Roscommon the only poet of the Restoration, besides Milton, who rebelled against the restraint of rhyme? What is the use of swelling up an enormous list of names like Dryden, Otway, Lee, Rowe, Southerne, to attack a statement which I never had the absurdity to propound?

The *Quarterly* reviewer quotes against me an array of errors which he asserts to be of a very grave importance. His own knowledge of the period is exceedingly extensive, and he follows me sometimes like my own evil conscience. For instance, it gave me a start to find that he pounced on my too-confident conjecture that Phillips wrote his *Cider* in 1699. Ever since my book appeared I have had inward qualms about this unlucky guess. Yet who but my reviewer and myself cares much about Phillips's *Cider*? Another class of mistake about which he is very severe can surely be pardoned by those who consider that I was dealing with the little writers of a somewhat obscure period, whose bibliography is notoriously full of pitfalls. For instance, my reviewer is very sarcastic because I dated a certain poem of Elijah Fenton's 1730 instead of 1729. In this case I had nothing to guide me but my own copy of the book, which lies before me at this moment, dated 1730, and with no sign on the title-page of being a second edition. It is quite true that there has since come into my hands a copy dated 1729, and my reviewer is technically correct. But this is surely fishing with a very close net. A third class of blunders is exemplified by the instance that my book dates the *Miscellanies* of John Norris of Bemerton 1678. The date should be 1687, but every writer for the press is aware that this inversion of figures is one of the very commonest of misprints. That an error in correcting proofs should be construed into ignorance shows a strange forgetfulness of a misfortune to which all writers are exposed. Nevertheless, on all these points I am ready to be grateful for correction, even if I feel like the boy in Mr. Sala's delightful novel, who was so much hurt by the pence which the lady threw in his face that he forbore to thank her.

By far the most serious charge, however, which the *Quarterly* reviewer brings against me is one under which I will not sit down for a moment. He says (and it is almost the only point on which I agree with him) that ''of all offences of which a writer can be guilty, the most detestable is that of simulating familiarity with works which he only knows at second hand.'' This is most true; but when he goes on to accuse me of never having read this and the other common English classic, he leaves my withers entirely unwrung. I have said that one of his manoeuvres is to represent me as solely known by the volume under notice, the ***From Shakespeare to Pope***. He might,

however, have reflected that when he accused me of not knowing whether the *Arcadia* is in prose or verse, of confounding James Harrington with Sir John Harington, of never having inspected Dryden's and Otway's tragedies, his readers might be inclined to glance at some other portion of my critical work. The *Quarterly* reviewer, in fact, puts himself out of court by pretending that I have obtained my information second hand, and have not read the books I write about. He knows perfectly well that this is not true. I can let this accusation pass without further notice; my criticism may have every fault, but it is certainly based on independent research and first-hand reading.

One instance, however, of this particular charge may be given as a specimen of the reviewer's ingenuousness. He says: ''Will our readers credit that Mr. Gosse attributes the pseudo-classicism of the diction of the eighteenth century poetry to the influence of the writings of Anthony Ashley Cooper, first Earl of Shaftesbury?''

Will the readers of the *Athenaeum* credit that my words are: ''Shaftesbury introduced this exaggerated elegance of diction into the field of prose''? This is all I say about Shaftesbury. When, in a purely literary treatise, Shaftesbury is mentioned, the third Earl, the author of the *Characteristics*, is intended as a matter of course. The reviewer introduces the words ''first Earl'' and changes ''prose'' into ''poetry'' of his own accord, and then pretends to think that I mean the politician. There is no arguing with such an antagonist.

In a great number of instances my reviewer charges me with making blunders when the mistake is certainly his own. Of Denham's *Sophy* I have said that it is ''a solitary specimen of the Seneca tragedy amongst the English dramas of the age.'' The reviewer says: ''Will our readers credit that the play . . . has absolutely no point in common with Seneca's plays? It is a drama as purely romantic as *Lear* or *Hamlet*.'' If your readers will read the *Sophy* they will find that I am absolutely right, and the reviewer absolutely wrong. Again, the reviewer says that if I had turned to Fanshawe's *Dido and Æneas* I should never have called it a little epic. I am perfectly familiar with this poem, and if it is not ''a little epic'' I do not know what it is. . . . In all these instances the *Quarterly* reviewer must be perfectly aware that I am as instructed as he is on the points in question, which are quibbles in nomenclature; he thinks that these are matters of which the general public knows little, and on which simple bold assertion will pass unchallenged.

One other instance of the peculiar way in which the reviewer deals with my text may now be given. He says: ''Mr. Gosse tells us that Oldham died in 1684. Oldham died in December, 1683.'' Of course he did; but what I really say is that Dryden sang his early death in 1684, which is strictly true; I at least know no earlier edition of Dryden's *Elegy* than that of 1684. The reviewer in the same way roundly attacks me for saying that Roscommon made English Horace's *Art of Poetry* in 1684, not in 1680. It is true that some books of reference give the date 1680, but this is an error. I have the first edition before me at this moment, and it is dated 1684. In matters of Restoration bibliography the *Quarterly* reviewer, if I may say so without immodesty, should be careful in attacking me. I believe I possess one of the fullest private collections of Restoration poetry and drama in the country; I have not neglected it, and in this matter the reviewer's assumption of superiority is entirely out of place. (pp. 534-35)

The quarrels of authors are proverbially bitter, and proverbially, too, the world stands by and laughs. But it is no laughing matter to the antagonists. In the present case we all know who my *Quarterly* reviewer is; his name is an open secret. There are no stabs like those which are given by an estranged friend. My *Quarterly* reviewer was once my intimate companion; no one has accompanied me more closely into the special field of seventeenth century study which we have both loved than he. The arrow comes barbed with the belief that no one, perhaps, is so able as he to give what seems a mortal wound to the old fellow student whose studies he used to share. But when he devotes a page and a half to ingeniously persuading the reader that I am such an impostor as to describe Garth's poem of "Claremont" without having read it, I marvel that even indignation should have so short a memory, and his used to be miraculous. Yet the first copy of Garth's "Claremont" which I ever possessed I bought in the Euston Road in 1878 for a few pence in company with my *Quarterly* reviewer. . . . And I first read Garth's "Claremont" in the company of my *Quarterly* reviewer that same summer, in the garden of a Berkshire house where he was staying as my guest. (p. 535)

> *Edmund Gosse, "The 'Quarterly Review' and Mr.*
> *Gosse," in* The Athenaeum, *No. 3078, October 23,*
> *1886, pp. 534-35.*

### WALTER PATER   (essay date 1890)

[*Pater was an English novelist and critic associated with the pre-Raphaelites and with the "art for art's sake" movement in English arts and letters. In his criticism and his philosophical romances—of which* Marius the Epicurean (1885) *is the best known—Pater advocated approaching life itself as an art. In the following excerpt from an essay originally published in 1890, he praises Gosse's modern approach to traditional poetic themes in* On Viol and Flute.]

Perhaps no age of literature, certainly no age of literature in England, has been so rich as ours in excellent secondary poetry; and it is with our poetry (in a measure) as with our architecture, constrained by the nature of the case to be imitative. Our generation, quite reasonably, is not very proud of its architectural creations; confesses that it *knows* too much—knows, but cannot do. And yet we could name certain modern churches in London, for instance, to which posterity may well look back puzzled.—Could these exquisitely pondered buildings have been indeed works of the nineteenth century? Were they not the subtlest creations of the age in which Gothic art was spontaneous? In truth, we have had instances of workmen, who, through long, large, devoted study of the handiwork of the past, have done the thing better, with a more fully enlightened consciousness, with full intelligence of what those early workmen only guessed at. And something like this is true of some of our best secondary poetry. It is the least that is true—the least that can fairly be said in praise of the poetic work of Mr. Edmund Gosse.

Of course there can be no exact parallel between arts so different as architecture and poetic composition. But certainly in the poetry of our day also, though it has been in some instances powerfully initiative and original, there is great scholarship, a large comparative acquaintance with the poetic methods of earlier workmen, and a very subtle intelligence of their charm. Of that fine scholarship in this matter there is no truer example than Mr. Gosse. It is manifested especially in the even finish of his varied work, in the equality of his level—a high level—in species of composition so varied as the three specimens which follow.

Far away, in late spring, "by the sea in the south," the swallows are still lingering around "white Algiers." In Mr. Gosse's **"Return of the Swallows,"** the northern birds—lark and thrush—have long been calling to them:—

> And something awoke in the slumbering heart
>   Of the alien birds in their African air,
> And they paused, and alighted, and twittered apart,
>   And met in the broad white dreamy square,
> And the sad slave woman, who lifted up
> From the fountain her broad-lipped earthen cup,
>   Said to herself, with a weary sigh,
>   "To-morrow the swallows will northward fly!"

Compare the following stanzas, from a kind of palinode, **"1870-1871,"** years of the Franco-German war and the Parisian Commune:—

> The men who sang that pain was sweet
>   Shuddered to see the mask of death
> Storm by with myriad thundering feet;
>   The sudden truth caught up our breath,
>   Our throats like pulses beat.
>
> The songs of pale emaciate hours,
>   The fungus-growth of years of peace,
> Withered before us like mown flowers;
>   We found no pleasure more in these
>   When bullets fell in showers.
>
> For men whose robes are dashed with blood,
>   What joy to dream of gorgeous stairs,
> Stained with the torturing interlude
>   That soothed a Sultan's midday prayers,
>   In old days harsh and rude?
>
> For men whose lips are blanched and white,
>   With aching wounds and torturing thirst,
> What charm in canvas shot with light,
>   And pale with faces cleft and curst,
>   Past life and life's delight!

And then Mr. Gosse's purely descriptive power, his aptitude for still-life and landscape, is unmistakably vivid and sound. Take, for an instance, this description of high-northern summer:—

> The ice-white mountains clustered all around us,
>   But arctic summer blossomed at our feet;
> The perfume of the creeping sallows found us,
>   The cranberry-flowers were sweet.
>
> Below us through the valley crept a river,
>   Cleft round an island where the Lap-men lay;
> Its sluggish water dragged with slow endeavour
>   The mountain snows away.
>
> There is no night-time in the northern summer,
>   But golden shimmer fills the hours of sleep,
> And sunset fades not, till the bright new-comer,
>   Red sunrise, smites the deep.
>
> But when the blue snow-shadows grew intenser
>   Across the peaks against the golden sky,
> And on the hills the knots of deer grew denser,
>   And raised their tender cry,
>
> And wandered downward to the Lap-men's dwelling,
>   We knew our long sweet day was nearly spent,
> And slowly, with our hearts within us swelling,
>   Our homeward steps we bent.

"Sunshine before Sunrise!" There's a novelty in that, for poetic use at least, so far as we know, though we remember one fine paragraph about it in *Sartor Resartus*. The grim poetic sage of Chelsea, however, had never seen what he describes:

not so Mr. Gosse, whose acquaintance with northern lands and northern literature is special. We have indeed picked out those stanzas from a quiet personal record of certain amorous hours of early youth in that quaint arctic land, Mr. Gosse's description of which, like his pretty poem on Lübeck, made one think that what the accomplished group of poets to which he belongs requires is, above all, novelty of motive, of subject.

He takes, indeed, the old themes, and manages them better than their old masters, with more delicate cadences, more delicate transitions of thought, through long dwelling on earlier practice. He seems to possess complete command of the *technique* of poetry—every form of what may be called *skill of hand* in it; and what marks in him the final achievement of poetic *scholarship* is the perfect balance his work presents of so many and varied effects, as regards both matter and form. The memories of a large range of poetic reading are blent into one methodical music so perfectly that at times the notes seem almost simple. Sounding almost all the harmonies of the modern lyre, he has, perhaps as a matter of course, some of the faults also, the "spasmodic" and other lapses, which from age to age, in successive changes of taste, have been the "defects" of excellent good "qualities." He is certainly not the—

> Pathetic singer, with no strength to sing,

as he says of the white-throat on the tulip-tree,

> Whose leaves unfinished ape her faulty song.

In effect, a large compass of beautiful thought and expression, from poetry old and new, have become to him matter malleable anew for a further and finer reach of literary art. And with the perfect grace of an *intaglio,* he shows, as in truth the minute *intaglio* may do, the faculty of structure, the logic of poetry. **"The New Endymion"** is a good instance of such sustained power. Poetic scholar!—If we must reserve the sacred name of "poet" to a very small number, that humbler but perhaps still rarer title is due indisputably to Mr. Gosse. His work is like exquisite modern Latin verse, into the academic shape of which, discreet and coy, comes a sincere, deeply felt consciousness of modern life, of the modern world as it is. His poetry, according with the best intellectual instincts of our critical age, is as pointed out recently by a clever writer in the *Nineteenth Century,* itself a kind of exquisite, finally revised criticism.

Not that he fails in originality; only, the graces, inborn certainly, but so carefully educated, strike one more. The sense of his originality comes to one as but an after-thought; and certainly one sign of his vocation is that he has made no conscious effort to be original. In his beautiful opening poem of the **"White-Throat,"** giving his book [*On Viol and Flute*] its key-note, he seems, indeed, to accept that position, reasons on and justifies it. Yet there is a clear note of originality (so it seems to us) in the peculiar charm of his strictly personal compositions; and, generally, in such touches as he gives us of the soul, the life, of the nineteenth century. Far greater, we think, than the charm of poems strictly classic in interest, such as the **"Praise of Dionysus,"** exquisite as that is, is the charm of those pieces in which, so to speak, he transforms, by a kind of colour-change, classic forms and associations into those— say! of Thames-side—pieces which, though in manner or subject promising a classic entertainment, almost unaware bring you home.—No! after all, it is not imagined Greece, dreamy, antique Sicily, but the present world about us, though mistak-

able for a moment, delightfully, for the land, the age, of Sappho, of Theocritus:—

> There is no amaranth, no pomegranate here,
> But can your heart forget the Christmas rose,
> The crocuses and snowdrops once so dear?

Quite congruously with the placid, erudite, quality of his culture, although, like other poets, he sings much of youth, he is often most successful in the forecast, the expression, of the humours, the considerations, that in truth are more proper to old age:—

> When age comes by and lays his frosty hands
>     So lightly on mine eyes, that, scarce aware
> Of what an endless weight of gloom they bear,
> I pause, unstirred, and wait for his commands.
> When time has bound these limbs of mine with bands,
>     And hushed mine ears, and silvered all my hair,
>     May sorrow come not, nor a vain despair
> Trouble my soul that meekly girdled stands.
>
> As silent rivers into silent lakes,
> Through hush of reeds that not a murmur breaks,
>     Wind, mindful of the poppies whence they came,
> So may my life, and calmly burn away,
> As ceases in a lamp at break of day
>     The flagrant remnant of memorial flame.

*Gosse with Thomas Hardy, 1927. From* Edmund Gosse: A Literary Landscape 1849-1928, *by Ann Thwaite. By permission of the Syndics of Cambridge University Library.*

Euthanasia!—Yet Mr. Gosse, with all his accomplishment, is still a young man. His youthful confidence in the perpetuity of poetry, of the poetical interests in life, creed-less as he may otherwise seem to be, is, we think, a token, though certainly an unconscious token, of the spontaneous originality of his muse. (pp. 107-15)

> Walter Pater, "Mr. Gosse's Poems," in his Essays from "The Guardian," Macmillan and Co., 1906, pp. 107-18.

### THE ATHENAEUM  (essay date 1908)

[*In the following excerpt,* Father and Son *is praised for its revelations of a child's developing mind and for its depiction of the conflicting philosophies represented by Gosse and his father.*]

It is idle to pretend ignorance of the identity of the distinguished author [of *Father and Son*]. So much has been said already by the "rapid" reviews that no apology is needed for noticing this book in the light of Mr. Gosse's other works, which are sufficiently known to the literary public, though indeed that public is less wide than reviewers are apt to imagine. Premising thus much, one may say that if the writer should achieve anything like lasting remembrance, it will be due to this work rather than to any of the studies, essays, or verse in which his learning and versatility have won praise. This book is unique. It is at once a profound and illuminating study in the concrete of the development of a child's mind, and also an historical document of great value. At least its value will be great for the age, not so far distant, to which Puritanism, Plymouth Brethren, and pre-Darwinian science will seem as prehistoric as the "fossils" which men like "Mr. G." believed to have been stuck in the rocks in order to try men's faith.

In spite of what has been said on the question of taste, we cannot see that the writer is to be blamed for this account of his father; it seems to us neither disrespectful nor untender, but eminently delicate and fair; nor do any of the jokes seem to us ungenerous. It is, of course, possible that the writer's literary skill has embellished some of the incidents, and that his feelings at the moment were not always of that elaborately self-conscious character which he now believes them to have been. But we must remember that an event includes its consequences in the mind; that what we think of it in memory is as much a part of it as what we feel at the moment. This is at once the justification of many physical evils—

> Forsan et hæc olim meminisse juvabit—
> ["'Perchance someday it may be a pleasure to remember even these things."]

and the condemnation of those attempts to crush the soul-life which a book like this displays. Further, it is our own experience that the thoughts of youth are "long, long thoughts," and that the child-mind is far more self-conscious and analytic of those thoughts which interest it than elders, busied with affairs and occupied with action, are apt to imagine. It is the hustling manhood of the Western world that is truly irresponsible; childhood, like old age, is "the age of reflection."

The home described is probably familiar to some of us. As the author says, what is unique is his father's position as a man of science, not his opinions. Those opinions are simply the narrowest form of individualist Protestantism, which makes of religion outwardly the barest and least human of any creed that has ever had practical effect; is opposed to culture, to art, to poetry; regards Shakspeare as a devil to be shunned; is blind to the beauty and the joy of earth, but has for its rare and elect spirits a fountain of joy and peace which is none the less real for the hideous form in which it is commonly expressed.

*Father and Son* shows all this in a concrete instance, portrayed with extraordinary accuracy, skill, and humour. . . .

The two facts which stand out from this book are the incapacity of Puritanism to deal with children, and its affinity to the scientific rather than the romantic temperament. In the first place, Puritanism never has known, and never will know, how to deal with children except by making them prigs. We yield to none in admiration for the grandeur of Puritan faith at its best, its magnificent vision, its splendour of strength, and its unsurpassable appeal to the lonely conscience. But at one point it breaks down—the child. Puritanism has in fact very little sense of religion as a process, a life; it is always the miracle, the instantaneous, the conversion, at which it aims; it can only reach its aim by treating the child as an adult. The tragedy of this book lies not in its attempt to make the boy a religious boy, but to make him a mature saint at the age of ten. That great event is symbolized here by his baptism. (He tells us that afterwards he put out his tongue at other boys to show his superiority as a saint.) After that he is on a level with his elders, and though his education must go on, he is really no longer a child. Before it he is not a child, he is merely an animal. In both ways Puritanism misconceives childlife. It is a faith for adults, and adults only, and in this it is like every other creed or religion which occupies the educated world, with the exception of the system of the Church. We fancy a good deal of the education controversy really hinges on the fact that it is not so much two opposing views of religion, as on the one hand two views of the State, and on the other two views of the child, which are in internecine and irreconcilable conflict. (p. 6)

Secondly (and we learn this from *Father and Son*), the Puritan scholasticism, like all scholasticism, is, as we have said, far more akin to the scientific than the artistic temperament. It was not only because one man was orthodox and rigid, and the other irresistibly modern, that the two temperaments clashed; but also because one had the artistic, the other the scientific temperament. . . . The son was emphatically a poet, an artist, an impressionist, sensitive to every breath of beauty and aspect of delight; and hence [his] opposition [to his father] was, as he says, irreconcilable and (when realized) final. It is the clash not of two creeds only, not even of two temperaments, but of two whole universes of thought and feeling, which is presented in this work, and will make it deeply illuminating long after the echoes of its controversies and the forms of its expression, and even the names of the combatants, are as silent and forgotten as are at this moment the scientific apology of the "Father," or the pietistic tracts of the mother.

> Oh, East is East, and West is West, and never the twain shall meet.

And it is the spirit of the East (we fancy we have read a poem called "**Firdausi in Exile**") which is shown in this single concrete case in one of the phases of the age-long struggle that will, we suppose, go on "as long as the sun and moon endureth." Religion is only one of its many phases, though it is probably the most important, because it is the most comprehensive. That is why the book is so interesting. Its nominal material is detailed, particular, local. Its real subject is a difference as great as that between light and darkness, a conflict no less profound and eternal than that typified in Oriental dualism as existing from the dawn of things. (pp. 6-7)

*A review of "Father and Son," in* The Athenaeum, *No. 4184, January 4, 1908, pp. 6-7.*

**ELEANOR CECIL**  (essay date 1908)

[*In the following excerpt, Cecil focuses upon the "struggle between two temperaments"—one directed by religious fanaticism and the other ruled by aesthetics—as central to* Father and Son.]

That very remarkable work *Father and Son* has been presented to the world as "a document, a record of educational and religious conditions which, having passed away, will never return," and further, as "the diagnosis of a dying Puritanism." We may also, if we are so inclined, read the work more simply as "the record of a struggle between two temperaments, two consciences, and two epochs." Wise readers will probably confine their attention to the latter aspect of the book, to the dramatic conflict between religious fanaticism and a temperament driven by equally imperative instincts to rule its tolerant course through life by "æsthetic junctures." No one who has read *Father and Son* will need to be reminded of the exquisite touch with which the author has unfolded a story tragic in its essence, though humour predominates on the surface. The drama, to be candid, is more satisfying than the "diagnosis," which concerns itself chiefly with obvious symptoms rather than with any deep underlying cause. One can partly sympathise with this procedure, for the symptoms of the mental disease under consideration are undeniably picturesque, as indeed they have already been very generally recognised to be, in many fields of literature.

The author, in a few words of apology at the outset, guards himself against misunderstanding with regard to the element of humour contained in his presentment of a dying Puritanism. The precaution seems unnecessary. There must be few now who have not been taught to recognise absurdity in Puritanism, and perhaps to recognise in it little else. The Puritanism of early and mid Victorian days is as much out of fashion as the horsehair sofa against which this father and son of the early 'sixties knelt seeking enlightenment as to whether it was or was not the Lord's will that the younger petitioner should attend the Browns' party. Puritanism of this kind, and perhaps of all kinds, has long been in the trough of discredit; indeed, we are not yet wholly recovered from some of the effects attending violent reaction, as more than one page of this book unconsciously testifies.

The faculty of private judgment seems to have been developed to an abnormal degree in both the author's parents. One by one every organised form of Protestant religion came under the ban of their disapproval, until at length they subsided into the little community of extreme Calvinists known to the world at large as the "Plymouth Brethren." By occupation and repute both belonged to the literary world, but were immeasurably removed from it in aims and ambitions and by the rigours of their creed. "My parents," says the author, "lived in an intellectual cell bounded at its sides by the walls of their own house, but open above to the very heart of the uttermost heavens." Such were the surroundings of the only child of the marriage, whose nature from the first prompted him to examine the rational walls of the intellectual cell rather than to explore the heart of the uttermost heavens. Very early we hear of searching questions on delicate points of theological doctrine. The five-year-old son of the house has been taught that we should pray for the things we need, and he will demand good reasons why he should not pray for a certain humming-top,

since he is confident he needs the humming-top far more than the conversion of the heathen or the restitution of Jerusalem to the Jews. Or he will put to a practical test the "jealousy" of his parents' God by the solemn invocation of an image of wood, composed of a chair hoisted on to one of the drawing-room tables. (pp. 344-45)

Obviously a child of this disposition will be far from comfortable under a "dedication" sealing him from birth to the peculiar service of the Lord. That no open revolt took place until childhood had already passed, may, one supposes, be attributed on the one side to a genuine fatherly tenderness underlying the spiritual severities and apparent inhumanity of his home life, and, on the other, to a passion for imitation which succeeded the child's early instinctive revolt against the Law and the Prophets. At this point in the story, the author—in a passage which reminds one that spiritual tyrannies have given place to other arbitrary demands on youthful nature of which not the least oppressive is: "Thou shalt be original"—pauses to explain that originality in early youth shows itself most clearly by close imitation of things said and done near at hand. This child at all events evinced his originality in an orthodox manner by sedulous imitation not only of his father's scientific monographs and drawings, but of the sentiments and phraseology of the Saints, so that we find him in his eleventh year, with monitory vigour and effect, cross-examining his parent as to the religious standing of the lady who is coming to be his stepmother: "Is she one of the Lord's children? Has she taken up her cross in baptism? Papa, don't tell me that she is a Pædobaptist!" It is hardly surprising that a little boy capable of discoursing in so edifying a manner should have already been made, as one by circumstances and nature peculiarly elect, an "adult" member of the "Brethren." The public baptism which celebrated this event was the central point of the author's childhood. "Everything since the earliest dawn of consciousness seemed to have been leading up to it. Everything afterwards seemed to be leading down and away from it." The author's first experiences of fiction, of secular poetry, of the wonders of Greek art (the last occasion drawing from parental authority the ruthless dictum that there is "nothing in the legends of these gods or rather devils that it is not better for a Christian not to know"), his first taste of liberty in the London world, these were the steps which led rapidly and inevitably to the final parting between two natures holding incompatible points of view. (pp. 345-46)

No one will grudge the author the plain-speaking in the end to which, he pleads, his long patience and forbearance entitle him. Whether the plain-speaking is precisely to the purpose is another matter. It would be difficult, one imagines, to support by historical proof the author's singular theory that the inclusion of philanthropic activity in the category of saintliness is a comparatively late invention. . . . Plain-speaking, however, as an expression of personal opinion has always its value. "It often amazed me, and I am still unable to account for the fact, that my father, through his long life, or till nearly the close of it, continued to take an eager pleasure in the text of the Bible," writes the author in his epilogue, and the remark may be taken to sum up the limitations implied in the sub-title of the book.

Hardly less remarkable than the central figures in this drama of culture and fanaticism is the background against which they stand. That Puritanism has a fine flower as well as a bitter fruit is shown in the author's mother, who moves through the early chapters, a presence severe but lovely, Puritan in grain, of an inflexible, daring spirit, but gentle in speech and ways, sometimes even "extremely gay, laughing with a soft merry sound." Later, in the remote Devonshire village, we have an incongruous medley of human beings united by a common spiritual need. There is Mary Grace Burmington, the crippled spinster, who plays benevolence to the author's childhood, "a very charming person." There is James Sheridan Knowles, ex-comedian and poet, ending his days as a Baptist minister; there is Mrs. Jones, who sees Hell open beneath her feet at the wash-tub and the Devil holding out a long scroll inscribed with the record of her sins; there is a sprinkling of retired professional men, an Admiral even (what is the subtle connection between Puritanism and the sea?), and pious rustics, artisans, domestic servants, mostly in feeble health. Finally, at the very base of the little community of rigid sectarians, rests a tradition of certain storm-driven, soul-hungry Cornish fishermen, a romance of youth and beauty and religion, haunting the mind with its strange pathos like some old Irish saga.

All these things the author describes with inimitable skill and a quiet amused curiosity, such as might have been brought by an intelligent layman to a survey of the minute sea-creatures which in those days lined the tidal pools on the Devonshire coast, but have now long since vanished beneath the prying fingers of science and the conscientious collector. No less odd, no less insignificant, and no less ephemeral are the fragments of humanity gathered together on an obscure spot inland. Strange, frail, and on the whole harmless manifestations of a vagary of the human mind, which, growing rank, swells sometimes into "religion in a violent form," a thing dreadfully disturbing to the domestic amenities and the comfort of small boys, dreadfully harassing to young men about to embark on the business of life. That is one way of looking at it. Or shall we see in these ignorant villagers, with their uncouth beliefs, a moral fervour, a strong sense of human obligation to the infinite and of the power of will over circumstance, which the world will not easily do without? By their "oddities" these peasants have become significant, valuable, part of the main stream—linked also in a way, strangely enough, to the matters of that mythology which contains "nothing that it is not better for a Christian not to know." Puritanism is perhaps not altogether vanished like the rare sea anemones of the English sea-coast, or at least, unlike those relics of the past, may return in another shape. Perhaps also in the final estimate of nineteenth-century Puritanism something more will be found to say for it than that it exercised a destructive influence on the faith of a younger generation. (pp. 346-48)

> Eleanor Cecil, "The Book on the Table: 'Father and Son'," in *The Cornhill Magazine*, n.s., Vol. 24, No. 14, March, 1908, pp. 344-48.

**ALFRED NOYES**  (essay date 1912)

[*Noyes was an English poet and critic who advocated the use of traditional poetic themes and techniques. He opposed modern movements in literature, and his* Some Aspects of Modern Poetry *(1924) is a virulent attack on modernism in poetry. In the following excerpt, Noyes calls Gosse's poetry a valuable contribution to English literature.*]

*The Collected Poems of Edmund Gosse*, which have just been published in a single volume, form perhaps the most completely representative work of one of the most interesting periods in our modern literature. They are the chief product of a distinct poetic "school," as the word is understood in modern French literature, rather than in our own; and though Mr. Gosse suggests in his preface that fashions have altered in poetry since

these poems were written, they are as fresh to-day as ever. For it is not the originators of the fashion that are deciduous. It is only the imitators that fall—and not even the imitators if they develop and create in imitating, and so take their place in that organic evolution of literature of which Mr. Gosse in this country is the chief critical exponent. At a time when all traditions and standards are being attacked, it is well that those who guard the flame in Art and Life should have a clear consciousness of the scientific basis of their creed. Such a consciousness in literature, at any rate, is our sole barrier against a relapse into formless chaos and barbarism. And it is this consciousness which makes the poetry of Mr. Gosse so particularly valuable. (p. 297)

[Mr. Gosse's] poems represent a school which has now a permanent place in the history of English verse. Incidentally it is, of course, to this school that we owe most of those modern experiments with French verse-forms which have wearied us, perhaps, in the hands of those who have imitated without developing. But those verse-forms have, nevertheless, permanently raised the standard of technique in English verse, and have made life impossible for all future Robert Montgomeries.

But the poetry of Mr. Gosse has much more than this value. It has one very weighty quality which one associates more with the work of such poets as Leconte de Lisle than with the lighter and more airy work of Théodore De Banville. Underlying it all there is that scientific consciousness, a more organic form of what Rossetti called "fundamental brainwork." The lines are loaded with the golden logic of beauty.

Some sentences in Mr. Gosse's preface are interesting on this point. "If I am a poet at all," he says, "I belong to the age of the Franco-German War, of the introduction of Japanese art into Europe, of the discoveries of Huxley and Häckel, and of the Oxford lectures of Matthew Arnold.". . .

Such certainly is the "intellectual topography" of poems like **"Palingenesis"** and **"Monad and Multitude.".** . . (pp. 298-99)

Again and again in reading this volume we realise that the intellectual method of true poetry is a weapon of precision and of an edge not to be matched by the mere flint weapons of prose. It flashes, but only because it is of steel. And it strikes home, because it has behind it the whole strength of a man, not merely this or that intellectual impulse.

All the more satisfying for their inner logic are those poems in which Mr. Gosse sets forth his conception of the poet's task, and guards "the memorial fire," as in **"Alere Flammam."** A grave and beautiful conception of the functions of literature informs all this side of his work. Sometimes it is manifested simply in the chiselled beauty of the verses themselves, as in that exquisite poem, **"Lying in the Grass,"** which he dedicates to Thomas Hardy:—

> And see that girl, with pitcher on her head,
> And clean white apron on her gown of red,—
> Her even-song of love is but half-said:
>
> She waits the youngest mower. Now he goes;
> Her cheeks are redder than a wild blush-rose;
> They climb up where the deepest shadows close.
>
> But though they pass and vanish, I am there;
> I watch his rough hands meet beneath her hair;
> Their broken speech sounds sweet to me like prayer.
>
> Ah, now the rosy children come to play,
> And romp and struggle with the new-mown hay;
> Their clear high voices sound from far away.

Fragmentary quotation utterly destroys the golden thread of thought connecting these detached stanzas; but that is only another tribute to Mr. Gosse's care for form. In another mood, what could be more delicate than that piece of metrical tapestry entitled a **"Dream of November"**? (pp. 299-300)

It is difficult, in this hour of hasty work, and sometimes barbarous misuse of the English tongue, to overestimate the value of [Mr. Gosse's] care for technique and form. Mr. Gosse himself passes an interesting criticism on his own school when he says:—

> If we could dare to write as ill
> As some whose voices haunt us still,
> Even we, perchance, might call our own
> Their deep enchanting undertone.
>
> We are too difficult and nice,
> Too learned and too over-wise,
> Too much afraid of faults to be
> The flutes of bold sincerity.

But there is as little doubt of the sincerity that is bold enough to question itself thus as there is of the value of these poems to a literature which shows signs, once more, of the usual blind reaction against form, order, and proportion, without which there is neither Art, nor Beauty, nor Truth.... In no way clashing with the reverence for a great literary heritage, for "famous men and our fathers that were before us," there shines through the poems in this volume . . . the light of an intellect at once creative and keenly critical.

The epilogue to Mr. Gosse's latest work nobly takes up the burden of the epilogue to his first. At the end of his early book, *On Viol and Flute,* he struck the key-note of all his work, with his lines to those who "disdain the sacred Muse":—

> The moving heavens, in rhythmic time.
>   Roll, if thou watch them or refrain;
> The waves upon the shore in rhyme
>   Beat, heedless of thy loss or gain;
>   Not they, but thou, hast lived in vain
> If thou art deaf and blind and dumb,
>   Parched in the heat of morning rain,
> And on the flaming altar numb.

And, at the end of his latest work he expresses in perfection just that wide sane view of literature which is so necessary at the present day, expresses it with a noble eagerness and an intellectual curiosity that our conventional rebels would do well to emulate:—

> Before my tale of days is told,
>   O, may I watch on reverent knees,
> The Unknown Beauty once unfold
>   The magic of her mysteries!
>
> Before I die, O may I see
>   Clasp'd in her violet girdle, Spring;
> May April breezes blow to me
>   Songs that the youngest poets sing!. . .
>
> New arts, new raptures, new desires,
>   Will stir the new-born souls of men;
> New fingers smite new-fashioned lyres,—
>   And O, may I be listening then. . . .
>
> Shall I reject the green and rose
>   Of opals, with their shifting flame,
> Because the classic diamond glows
>   With lustre that is still the same.

> Change is the pulse of life on earth;
>   The artist dies, but Art lives on.
> New rhapsodies are ripe for birth
>   When every rhapsodist seems gone.
>
> So, if I pray for length of days,
>   It is not in the barren pride
> That looks behind itself and says
>   "The Past alone is deified!"
>
> So to my days' extremity
>   May I, in patience infinite,
> Attend the beauty that must be,
>   And, though it slay me, welcome it.

Only in such a fine and lofty air can literature prosper. I am not writing this for the mere stupidity that does reject the shifting opal. I am writing, or trying to write, for those who have intelligently accepted the opal, and at the same time are rejecting, a little stupidly, the classic diamond, and are even desirous of destroying it. We must have both; and to each its proper place must be assigned. That, and that alone, is the function of criticism. This broad and scientific view of literature is manifest in all the work of Mr. Edmund Gosse; so that, over and above their intrinsic beauty, his poems are a contribution of permanent value to the literary history of our time. Many of them are records of the author's adventures among masterpieces; and taken together, they are a confession of faith in the future of English poetry by a true guardian of the fire. (pp. 301-03)

*Alfred Noyes, "The Poems of Edmund Gosse," in* The Fortnightly Review, *n.s. Vol. 92, No. DXLVIII, August 1, 1912, pp. 297-303.*

## PATRICK BRAYBROOKE   (essay date 1925)

[*In the following excerpt, Braybrooke discusses Gosse's stature in English letters.*]

There is a vast difference between a man of letters and one who merely writes books. The novelist does not want to bother about his permanent position, he knows well enough that after a few years it will in all probability be oblivion, his output must be ephemeral it if is to get hold of the novel reading public. But the man of letters is a very serious person, he has a sincere wish to live when he is dead, he likes to think that students will read him when his body has long turned to dust, he writes not for the passing moment but with an eye on the years that lie many ages ahead. Assuming then that Gosse is a man of letters of this latter description, what we have to ask and to ask at once is, has he a permanent position in the world of letters?

It has been said by a good many critics that a man who writes studies of other people cannot hope to be remembered to the same extent as the writer who gives to the world creative work of an original genius. To a certain extent this may be true, but the criticism really requires modification. What the literary critic has to expect, is not so much recognition of himself as an original thinker but remembrance by those who turn to his books when they are in need of enlightenment on the particular personalities he has written of. The great part of Gosse's activity has, of course, been purely literary critical work of a very high order. His original work though considerable and certainly meritorious cannot I think expect to find any large place in the ages that are to come. It is his critical output that must be examined . . . if we wish to establish Gosse's place in the world of letters. Whatever critics may think as regards the bulk of Gosse's work, I am certain that the volume that deals with Congreve will always be the standard work upon that great playwright who in this twentieth century seems at last to be coming in for his proper share of praise and attention. Because Gosse's *Life of Congreve* is the only one is not my reason for giving it permanence. In its way this biography is all that such a volume should be.

A good deal of biographical work in these days is far too official. We have great difficulty in realising that the subject of the book has ever been a live person at all. Much biographical production seems to be born on a coffin as though the person written of had always been but a mass of dust and bones with no soul whatever. In the case of Gosse's critical work, such a complaint cannot be made with any accuracy. If he writes of Congreve, it is not a perfunctory life or a mere scholarly exposition of his plays. We are introduced to a live person, we can almost hear him speak, we realise that here was a man who like ourselves was assailed by the ordinary trials and troubles of life. Again, though much has been written of Swinburne, either violently for him or angrily against him, in the writer's opinion, Gosse has produced the best biography that has been written or will be written of that most extraordinary poet. As we read Gosse's work on Swinburne, we can almost see the little man with the enormous head hurrying across the Theobalds Road or wandering along the vastnesses round Putney, intent on his own thoughts, oblivious of the curious stares of the passers-by. Or if we detach the more personal side of Swinburne and ask what is the value of Gosse's criticism of him as a poet, we have no hesitation in saying that none of the critics have a tenth part of the understanding of his genius that we find in Gosse's brilliant estimate.

If we leave our own country for a little and proceed to the country that produced one of the greatest of dramatists, Ibsen, none can give a better or more accurate picture of his melancholy genius, than Gosse. For with his profound knowledge of the background of the *Literature of Northern Europe,* Gosse can tell us why Norway should have produced Ibsen and why Ibsen should have been able to take such advantage of his surroundings, even though at times they might have appeared to be such as to have killed even the most brilliant literary spark. Gosse gives not only a remarkable study of the dramatic skill of Ibsen, he manages at the same time to present an extraordinarily interesting portrait of the man himself. Not the least fascinating being the peculiar incident when Ibsen, an old man, fell in love with a sweet and charming girl, who was too ordinary to be aware that she had caused the cold, almost dead heart of the great Dramatist, to beat with an ecstasy, that when it ceased, left behind a sense of everlasting loss.

For perhaps if we look rather generally for a characteristic of excellence in Gosse's work, it is to be found in the fact that he harmonises delightfully in his critical studies, both the person of the subject and his achievement. In this Gosse stands out almost as unique, so seldom is this dual combination successfully mastered. I am not sure that it is an exaggeration to say that the study of Ibsen is the best thing Gosse has done, though I am aware that the life of Congreve is a good second, and to many it may quite well be that this volume would claim the prior place. Perhaps as good a reason as any for putting the Ibsen study in the forefront of Gosse's books is that it is that most valuable thing in literature, a masterly study of a famous foreign dramatist. And I have said before, nothing is so scandalously neglected as the great literary lights of other lands.

When, then, I say Gosse's book on Ibsen is his best, I mean that it is to my mind his most important work. (pp. 149-55)

When Gosse studies men like Sir Thomas Browne and Jeremy Taylor he is not nearly so happy. He is evidently a little afraid of the theology of Taylor, and not quite at home with the piety and curious psychology of Browne. It is with his purely literary and critical studies that Gosse gives all the genius of his pen.

I have then not the slightest hesitation in prophesying immortality for Gosse with his literary critiques of such men as Swinburne, Gray, Patmore, Ibsen and Congreve. To deny Gosse permanence with such volumes would be as futile as denying Napoleon or Hannibal immortality in the realms of military art. By these delightful and important studies, Gosse will live long after the tombstone over his grave has lost its new look.

Having then established our first proposition that Gosse will live by his critical studies we have to ask what is his position among his contemporaries, or rather in more popular language, what is his place to-day?

Undoubtedly to the general public which reads books very largely to pass away railway journeys, Gosse's name is but a name. Though I cannot believe there are many educated people, who would confess, as a very modern woman confessed to me, that she had never heard of him! That this particular lady had a profound liking for sex novels and the monthly magazines was but little excuse for never having heard of Gosse. But those who read that they may learn something a little more useful than money getting and robbing one's neighbour look upon Gosse as one of the greatest literary critics of the day. To attempt any comparison of him with other writers is but waste of time. It is absurd to say that Gosse is not so great a writer as Shaw, for Mr. Shaw is brilliant and Gosse is sound. To suggest that there is any comparison between Gosse and Chesterton is to argue that a paradoxical, whimsical, eccentric, knockabout genius has affinity to a polished, dignified and extremely scholarly critic. Again, though Belloc and Gosse both deal with outstanding figures, their methods are completely different. Belloc is always political, he is always under the eye of the priests, Gosse is never political, he probably is not even aware that politics or even religion have anything to do with such questions as he delights in, to wit the poetry of Swinburne or the melancholy of Gray.

There is perhaps a very small similarity between Gosse and the late Lord Morley. In my book on Lord Morley, I said that his fame would rest on his critical studies of men like Voltaire, Rousseau and Diderot. Of course, the methods of Lord Morley and Gosse are not exactly alike though there is a considerable amount of the same method of approach in each writer. Both Gosse and Lord Morley aptly combine the personal side of the subject and the literary side. (pp. 153-55)

If there is one essential difference between the two, it is that Lord Morley allows more of his own personality and convictions to take their place in the study, than does Gosse. For though Gosse has certain well defined likes and dislikes, there is much more in Morley's methods which may be termed didactic. Gosse is almost entirely concerned with the literary position of his subjects, their poetical progress or their dramatic progress is what interests him. He does not try to get too much of his own feelings into what he writes of.

Probably, Gosse occupies in the world of letters to-day a unique position. Whatever he says is accepted as being backed up by sufficient authority to allow of little questioning. I do not wish to do more than touch upon his work as a journalist. For a long time now Gosse has regularly delighted the literary readers of the *Sunday Times* with his charming book gossip. It is a Sunday delight in itself and to many these columns that Gosse fills week after week are their choicest possession. For it is on a Sunday of all other days that people who like books, like to read of them. They may *like* books on week days, but they have no time to like *reading* of them. The Sunday public is really of two kinds. The kind that reads book columns in a villa after roast beef and roast potatoes will find Gosse in the *Sunday Times* their great joy. (pp. 156-57)

We come really then to the conclusion that Mr. Gosse has a place in literature all his own. He is the best literary critic of the 20th century. His criticisms are emblasoned by a scrupulous fairness and a sincere effort to present a clear and convincing picture of the subject of his critique. Probably, Gosse is mostly read by students and not only by those who are just reading for exams. I do not think we are likely to see his books in the position of "best sellers" for the very good reason that they are much too good and far too anti-ephemeral. For though "best sellers" denote a certain and convincing genius, that genius is of a kind that rather dies when the problem of the hour has arrived, at the end of its sixty minutes of striving. But when Gosse writes his critical biographies, he writes them for all time, he writes that they may be read when the rain drives us to the library, he writes that they may be perused when tyrannical examiners determine that we shall know all we don't want to know of English Literature. He writes for those who, older in years have become by long watchings, what we all become sooner or later, students, when the word means not an irresponsible young man or woman "up" at the University, but a looker on at life, a watcher, one who strives to understand in little, the troubled waters through which his own ship so hesitatingly drives.

So far in this attempted summing-up of Gosse's niche in literature I have concentrated on his purely critical work, which though it is of course, original, is not quite original in the sense that the word has come to mean. Original production in our day seems to be that which is really new, entirely a point of view; critical work is rather, specialisation.

I have concentrated on Gosse as a critic for three reasons, one, that his books deal in large part with critical activity; secondly, because I am convinced Gosse will find permanence for his books in the critical direction; and thirdly, because he is known first and foremost as a critic. Before I deal with the trend of his work along general lines, I must consider very briefly his original output, when the word is used in the popular sense of this century. Probably, Gosse's best original work is his poetry, which though falling short of greatness has considerable merit, especially in its rich and natural spontaneity. His other original books, which are mostly Essays, are characteristic of the man who really loves letters, but that they will have any very permanent vogue is extremely doubtful. They are too ordinary without ever being commonplace, they do not appeal necessarily to the student, and books which do not, unless they have outstanding genius, are likely to be pretty speedily forgotten.

Pleasant, polished books, written by a real lover of literature, gives them a place of merit while their author is alive, but after, I should not care to predict them much notice.

I must now discuss my third proposition concerning the general trend of Gosse's writings. When we say what is the general trend of a writer I suppose it is inferred that some literary movement or "motive" is meant. Taking, for instance, the general trend of fiction to-day. It would be surely a movement towards realism with a fair sprinkling of psycho-analysis and sex. . . . If we ask what is the trend of serious literature in this century, it is undoubtedly towards Essay writing and critical studies. Apart from these two movements, the fiction energy and the essay and critical study movement, there is a third, all its own and apparently the monopoly of our era. That is, of course, a whole gamut of autobiography which describes how celebrities eat their eggs and bacon, propose to or are proposed to, or how they spend their last moments. What place then does Gosse occupy in the three movements that seem to me to be the main eddies of contemporary literature? Without any doubt, Gosse is a disciple of the second movement, which is generally, the advance along a channel which leads literature to being entirely a serious thing.

Apart from this general position that to Gosse literature is a serious thing (as it always was to Lord Morley) I find two other tendencies in his literary outlook. I will examine each of them separately. It seems perfectly obvious that Gosse is much distressed, as all students of comparative literature must be, at the colossal ignorance concerning the drama and poetry of other nations. Such a state is not only to be deplored for its own sake, but from a national point of view and from an international standpoint, this ignorance constitutes a grave danger. For I need not enlarge upon the obvious fact that the best way to know a nation is to be conversant with its literary aspirations and achievements, nor need I do more than mention the painfully apparent fact that the Englishman who is normal, cares for little outside his own house, his own red brick church or tin chapel and his highly respectable wife and moderately intelligent children. In opening up in some measure the *Literature of Northern Europe,* Gosse has quite evidently given expression in the best way, to the sorrow he has at our appalling national ignorance of foreign literature. I say then that a subsidiary movement to be found in his work is the importance he attaches to the literature of other lands.

The other tendency is perhaps one that is not very easy to discover without a special knowledge of Gosse's books. It is what I should call a "policy of encouragement.". . . It seems to be really that literature is worth while for its own sake, not for the sake of the reward or fame it may bring. This is a highly useful thought for we are much inclined to-day to place value on the writing of a book, not so much for its intrinsic worth, as for its commercial return. In writing of unknown playwrights and poets, Gosse has given voice to this "policy of encouragement," for though their value did not and does not command much attention, there was something in all of it worth while. And this is entirely apart from my suggestion that the work of ordinary people is one of the best ways of learning history of other days.

To sum up then the general trend of the work of Gosse. Firstly, it has as its ideal the seriousness of literary work, secondly, it does much to open up foreign literature, thirdly, it supports a "policy of encouragement."

Sir Edmund Gosse is now an old man, he has by several years exceeded man's allotted threescore years and ten. He is acknowledged by practically all book-lovers to be the leading critic of the day. His new *Life of Congreve,* which has been but recently published, shows no signs that Gosse's pen has lost any of its power.

Naturally, when a man has passed the seventy mark, it must be certain that the bulk of his work is done. Gosse has rendered immense services to literature. His books adorn any library that cares for good work. We live in times when unrest and turmoil are the order of the day. But when we require rest and refreshment we shall lock the door, we shall turn our backs on the busy world, we shall, instead, dwell with the great minds of the past, and we shall let Gosse interpret them for us, for indeed none can do this better than he. (pp. 157-62)

> *Patrick Braybrooke, in his* Considerations on Edmund Gosse, *Drane's Limited, 1925, 162 p.*

## HAROLD NICOLSON (essay date 1927)

[*In the following excerpt, Nicolson finds that* Father and Son *is of all Gosse's biographical works the one least concerned with the theory and practice of "pure" biography.*]

[When he wrote *Father and Son*, Sir Edmund Gosse] had long been an expert both in the theory and practice of biography. The article which he contributed on the subject to the *Encyclopædia Britannica* is a lucid exposition of what, in effect, is "pure" biography. For him biography is "the faithful portrait of a soul in its adventures through life." For him again "the peculiar curiosity which legitimate biography satisfies is essentially a modern thing, and presupposes our observation of life not unduly clouded by moral passion or prejudice." He lays no stress upon the literary element in biography. He would contend, I presume, that the essential element in biography is actuality, individuality; that the form of a biography is less important than its content. Here I agree. It is strange, however, that the author of *Father and Son,* which I consider to be the most "literary" biography in the English language, should not have grappled more closely with this problem of content *versus* form. For it is on the rocks of this problem that pure biography is doomed to split. In his other biographies Sir Edmund Gosse has relieved the pressure of facts, the explosive force of the scientific element, by the safety-valve of innuendo. He hints. This is all very well, and has enabled him to produce several highly graceful biographies and portraits in which, while not denying truth, he allows the extreme pressure of truth to evaporate and to escape. These works will for long remain as models of grace and dexterity, but they will not live as models of biography. Sir Edmund Gosse as a biographer will be judged by *Father and Son.* For to this work he brought great courage, great originality, and consummate literary art.

Consider, in the first place, his courage. A combination of circumstances had given him the privilege of witnessing, in a tragically concentrated form, the clash between the age of belief and the age of reason, the death struggle of Puritanism in its battle with science. He felt impelled to place on record his observation of that tragedy. It happened, however, that the struggle as he witnessed it had taken an acutely personal form, had resolved itself into the clash between his own temperament and that of his father. The full flow of convention, disguised as "good taste," ran counter to his purpose: yet he knew that his book was necessary, that it would do enormous good. He persisted, and by his persistence not only gave posterity a masterpiece, but won a signal victory for intellectual liberty. Let it not, moreover, be supposed that public opinion in 1907 was prepared for the shock occasioned by *Father and Son.* Victorianism only died in 1921. So late as 1911 we find Sir Sidney Lee speaking of the function and ethics of biography in a fully nineteenth-century spirit. Biography, for him, was essentially commemorative: it must be serious, it must possess a quality "which stirs and firmly holds the attention of the

earnest-minded"; while aiming at "the truthful transmission of personality," it must deal with exploits as well as character, it must deal with important people. "Character," writes Sir Sidney, "which does not translate itself into exploit is for the biographer a mere phantasm"; or again, "the life of a nonentity or a mediocrity, however skilfully contrived, conflicts with primary biographic principles."

It was in disregarding superstitions such as these that Sir Edmund Gosse demonstrated his originality. He set out, not to write a life, but to present "a genuine slice of life." The character of Philip Henry Gosse is displayed not through his zoological exploits, but in his domestic behavior over a period of some twenty years. We have no record of the early struggles at Carbonear, in Canada, or in Alabama; we have but slight references to the happy Jamaica period; we are told nothing of the final period from 1870 to 1888. The book is not, therefore, a conventional biography; still less is it an autobiography. It is something entirely original; it is a triumphant experiment in a new formula; it is a clinical examination of states of mind over a detached and limited period. From one point of view the book is "a diagnosis of a dying Puritanism." From another point of view it is "a study of the development of moral and intellectual ideas during the progress of infancy." Yet it is far more than this. Underlying the story is a conflict of the utmost intensity. We have the clash of wills; the constant hidden presence of a malignant deity; the intellectual blindness with which the father is afflicted and which impels him to the destruction of his own dearest hopes. There is all the apparatus of a Greek tragedy, and yet this tragic element is implicit only; it is never expressed. Sir Edmund Gosse's detachment from the tragedy in which he was so closely implicated is indeed amazing. He writes of it gently, humorously, ironically, pathetically; he is never sentimental, never angry, never intense. The texture of the book is uniform and soothing, like that of the finest velvet; and yet, essentially, the book is scientific. We are shown a curious and indeed singular specimen of human character; this specimen is beautifully prepared for us and all irrelevant material is cleared away; we are provided with an easy-chair, and the softest cushions are afforded for our backs; the microscope is there ready to hand; and, thus accommodated, thus reclining, we listen to that soft and brilliant exposition. It does not last a moment longer than is necessary; it has all been tremendously interesting, and instructive too, and Sir Edmund through it all has been so wise, so witty, and so nice. Do we have a slight reaction? Do we feel, on looking back, that the Eumenides have, for the occasion, been dressed in sun-bonnets? Such reactions are not very enlightened and are not permanent. The permanent impression left by *Father and Son* is that of a masterpiece in which, by consummate power of selection, the author has been able to combine the maximum of scientific interest with the maximum of literary form.

Sir Edmund Gosse achieved his synthesis by processes of exclusion. Not only did he reject all such material as was irrelevant to his immediate purpose, but he rejected forty-eight years of his father's span of life. He thus limited his field of inquiry both in time and space, and was able to reduce his scientific investigation to manageable proportions. His father throughout the book remains fixed and rigid. Such development as occurs, occurs in the psychology of the observer, not in that of his subject. By this means the scientific interest is enormously enhanced, for it is through autobiography, and not through biography, that the development of character can most convincingly be conveyed. (pp. 143-48)

*Harold Nicolson, "The Present Age," in his* The Development of English Biography, *1927. Reprint by Harcourt, Brace and Company, 1928, pp. 132-58.*

## EDMUND WILSON (essay date 1928)

[*Wilson, considered America's foremost man of letters in the twentieth century, wrote widely on cultural, historical, and literary matters, authoring several seminal critical studies. He is often credited with bringing an international perspective to American letters through his widely read discussions of European literature. In the following excerpt, Wilson pronounces upon Gosse as a critic.*]

[**Leaves and Fruit,** by Sir Edmund Gosse; *Aspects of the Novel,* by E. M. Forster; and *The Classical Tradition in Poetry,* by Gilbert Murray] seem fairly to represent the top level of English criticism today. Edmund Gosse's [book] is the least important: it is merely a collection of brief weekly articles on miscellaneous subjects. Yet this is not the only reason why the author does not carry quite the weight which his intelligence and learning seem to warrant. On the paper jacket of **Leaves and Fruit** there is an unusually fatuous quotation from some article or review: "Gosse occupies in the world of letters today a unique position. He is the best literary critic of the twentieth century." We reflect on this and we ask ourselves why we decline to believe that Sir Edmund is the best literary critic even of his own generation in England. Why, for example, do we prefer George Saintsbury? We come to the conclusion that, if we are reluctant to grant Gosse a high place in literature, it is simply because that does not seem to be precisely the kind of high place at which he himself has aimed. Where Saintsbury is a connoisseur of books, with some prejudices but an incorruptible palate, who writes about literature as candidly, as eagerly and as freely as he does about wine, Edmund Gosse appears to be haunted, in his practice of criticism, by irrelevant fears and inhibitions. His taste for literature is genuine and his familiarity with it complete; and he has not only read and enjoyed, but has understood. When in the present volume, for example, he writes of Mallarmé, or even of Edith Sitwell, it is with an intelligent appreciation of modern poetry of a kind quite uncommon in contemporary English criticism: he understands the issues which these poets raise, and these issues do not terrify him. He is, however, a little afraid that they may terrify other people. Before he will go so far as to take Mallarmé seriously, he is insistent to make us understand that he is not to be classed with those "literary snobs" who have said so many "vain and foolish things in praise of Mallarmé"; and he is careful to let us know that he considers many of Miss Sitwell's extravagances in very poor taste. When it is a case of naughty morals, even so far back as the seventeenth century, though he may profess a lively admiration for the intelligence or charm of his subject, he would not have us believe for a moment that he approves of his dissolute courses: the decorous tone which he adopts in dealing with Rochester or Ninon de L'Enclos is almost ludicrous: the latter was certainly a woman of admirable character from any except the most prudish standards, and she would certainly, in any case, seem to have been long enough dead to relieve Sir Edmund Gosse from the necessity of behaving so coyly about her for the benefit of his British readers. But Sir Edmund cares what people say; that is a concern never far from his mind. He has aimed all his life, perhaps, at becoming not so much a first-rate writer as a distinguished institution. He has rarely allowed a preoccupation with beauty or with truth to confuse an instinct for respectability. And once we have read George Moore's *Avowals,* we

are never afterward able to read Gosse without remembering the faintly comic role which he is made to play in it. (p. 21)

*Edmund Wilson, "Three English Critics," in* The New Republic, *Vol. LIV, No. 690, February 22, 1928, pp. 21-2.*

## VIRGINIA WOOLF (essay date 1931)

[*Woolf is considered one of the most prominent figures of twentieth-century English literature. Like her contemporary James Joyce, she is remembered as one of the most innovative of the stream of consciousness novelists. Also a discerning and influential critic, Woolf began writing reviews for the* Times Literary Supplement *at an early age. Her critical essays, which cover almost the entire range of English literature, contain some of her finest prose and are praised for their insight. Along with Lytton Strachey, Roger Fry, Clive Bell, and others, Woolf and her husband Leonard formed the literary coterie known as the "Bloomsbury Group." In the following excerpt from an essay originally published in 1931, Woolf comments on some of Gosse's qualities as a critic.*]

To be oneself is . . . an achievement of some rarity, and Gosse, as everybody must agree, achieved it, both in literature and in life. As a writer he expressed himself in book after book of history, of biography, of criticism. For over fifty years he was busily concerned, as he put it, with "the literary character and the literary craft." There is scarcely a figure of any distinction, or a book of any importance in modern letters, upon which we cannot have Gosse's opinion if we wish for it. For instance, one may have a curiosity about Disraeli's novels and hesitate which to begin upon. Let us consult Gosse. Gosse advises on the whole that we shall try *Coningsby.* He gives his reasons. He rouses us with a suggestive remark. He defines Disraeli's quality by comparing him with Bulwer, with Mrs. Gore and Plumer Read. He tells an anecdote about Disraeli that was told him by his friend the Duke of Rutland. He breaks off a phrase here and there for our amusement or admiration. All this he does with perfect suavity and precision, so that by the time he has done Disraeli is left glowing and mantling like an old picture lit up by a dozen bright candles. To illumine, to make visible and desirable, was his aim as a critic. Literature to him was an incomparable mistress and it was his delight "to dress her charms and make her more beloved." Lovers of course sometimes go further and a child is the result. Critics too sometimes love literature creatively and the fruit of their devotion has a toughness and a fibre that the smooth strains of Sir Edmund's platonic devotion are entirely without. Like all critics who persist in judging without creating he forgets the risk and agony of childbirth. His criticism becomes more and more a criticism of the finished article, and not of the article in the making. The smoothness, the craftsmanship of the work rouse his appreciation and he directs our attention only to its more superficial aspects. In other words, he is a critic for those who read rather than for those who write. But then no creator possesses Gosse's impartiality, or his width of reading, or his lightness and freedom of mind, so that if we want to hold a candle to some dark face in the long portrait gallery of literature there is no better illuminant than Edmund Gosse. (pp. 91-2)

*Virginia Woolf, "Edmund Gosse," in her* The Moment and Other Essays, *1947. Reprint by Harcourt Brace Jovanovich, Inc., 1948, pp. 84-92.*

**EDGAR JOHNSON** (essay date 1937)

[*Johnson is an American critic and theoretician of biography as well as a noted biographer. His monumental biographies* Charles Dickens: His Tragedy and Triumph *(1952) and* Sir Walter Raleigh: The Great Unknown *(1970) are regarded as definitive lives of these figures as well as models of the genre. They were described by C. P. Snow as "supreme examples of American literary scholarship at its best." In his* One Mighty Torrent: The Drama of Biography, *Johnson discusses the principles of biographical art and demonstrates the value of biography in understanding both the past and the future. In the following excerpt from that study, Johnson discusses the revolutionary nature of* Father and Son, *finding Gosse unique in seeing historical significance in the conflict that was central to his own life.*]

Although he has written other biographies, Sir Edmund Gosse will be remembered pre-eminently for but one excursion into the realm of biography. In that single foray, though, he wrote himself more significant as an artist, more striking as an innovator, than either Harris or Whibley. Few people can have realized, when *Father and Son* was published anonymously in 1907, what a portent glowed before them.

That it was a fascinating book anyone could see—fascinating as a most brilliant novel. Two people were there—a sober, earnest, and desperately devoted man and an instinctively rebellious little boy—in all the sharpness and shading of life; and they were surrounded by a group of brightly sketched minor figures. There were drama, comedy, pathos; a strange mixture of hilarity and bitterness, seen as in life, and yet suffused with understanding, reflected in the serene mirror of the past. There was the spectacle of a spirit being enslaved, almost reduced to unresisting dust, by the kindliest and most noble-hearted affection; and then, by the queerest of chances, a source of strength and resistance unwittingly presented by the benevolent oppressor.

All these things might be clear enough to any reader. But the revolutionary nature of the book came from other qualities. It was hard to classify, as biography or autobiography, for in almost equal degrees it mingled the two, the narrator being the little boy so nearly crushed by his father's love. It was not the story of the father's life, and still less of his son's, but the story of a relationship and a struggle. Its details were selected with all the unerring craftsmanship of a masterly novelist, deepening the atmosphere with wash after wash of color, touched with sparkling highlights, and the crucial scenes marched with ever-increasing drama to the ultimate flare-up of defiance.

Not until twenty years later, in Strachey's *Elizabeth and Essex*, was anything like this conflict of two entangled, devoted, and yet antagonistic personalities to command the whole attention of a biography, and even then it could not have the curious insight derived from one of the contestants being the teller of the story. Clarence Day, in his reminiscences of his father, narrates the explosive but not rancorous guerilla warfare between Father and his family, but the continual outbursts of the elder Day are fireworks rather than conflict, and his son's sketches are episodic not climactic.

In all these ways the genius of Gosse has been exploratory, opening new realms with quiet authority, and, so far, transcending any of those who have followed him. The tense psychological struggle, the dramatic structure, the mingling of biography and autobiography, the stringent limitation of theme: here were blazes of new light illumining undreamed-of deeps.

And although Gosse was not alone in regarding his experience as historically significant, representative of his age (for Mill and Henry Adams . . . so rated the importance of their own lives), he is unique in finding its significance precisely in a conflict. "This book," he begins, "is the record of a struggle between two temperaments, two consciences, and almost two epochs." That struggle marked the dividing line between the non-conformist, evangelical conscience—"a state of soul once not uncommon in Protestant Europe"—and the modern mind. It is "the diagnosis of a dying Puritanism" that Gosse presents us.

His parents were extreme Calvinists, austerely withdrawn from all ritual and ceremony. . . . These two believed in the absolute truth of everything in the Bible; for them, "nothing was symbolic, nothing allegorical or allusive . . . except what was, in so many words, proffered as a parable or a picture." They lived absolutely alone, in the most rigid poverty, dividing their time between zoology (the profession of the elder Gosse) and the discussion of theology. To this literal-minded couple, already middle-aged when they were married, "the advent of a child was not welcomed, but was borne with resignation," and the unconscious infant was dedicated to the Lord.

The child was not allowed to hear or read stories: the stern conscience of his parents debarred all fictions as lies. "I was told about missionaries, but never about pirates; I was familiar with humming-birds, but I had never heard of fairies." It would be erroneous, however, to think of the household as a gloomy one for a child. . . . [They] were a cheerful family. His mother was ethereally pretty, with gold hair and white skin, and his parents "were playful with one another," his mother "sometimes extremely gay, laughing with a soft, merry sound." They were full of guileless mirth, and so indifferent to forms that they could even joke mildly about the surroundings of their religion.

But God, omniscient and absolute, was always with them, unseen but as solid as father, with whom the childish mind, in fact, confused Him. Not until his sixth year did the child realize that his father did not share God's knowledge. One morning his father announced some fact to them. "I was standing on the rug, gazing at him, and when he made this statement, I remember turning quickly, in embarrassment, and looking into the fire. The shock to me was as that of a thunderbolt, for what my Father had said *was not true*." It was merely an error of fact, but to the child it revealed the appalling discovery that his father did not know everything.

Worse was to follow. The heathen in their blindness bowed down before objects of wood and stone, and his father assured him that God would be very angry indeed if anyone in a Christian country were guilty of the sin of idolatry. When his parents were safely out of the house, "with much labour," he hoisted a small chair on to a table, and, his heart in his throat, knelt and prayed to it, "O Chair!" What would God do? "I was very much alarmed, but still more excited; I breathed the high, sharp air of defiance." But nothing happened. He had committed idolatry, and God did not care. It did not make him question the existence and power of God; but it did "lessen still further my confidence in my Father's knowledge of the Divine mind."

In his seventh year his mother fell ill. When he asked the meaning of the word that told her cruel disease, he saw his parents "gazing at each other with lamentable eyes." In terrible pain she met her death serenely, saying to her husband, "I

*Gosse, age eight, with his father.*

shall walk with him in white. Won't you take your lamb and walk with me?'' Dazed with grief, he failed to understand, and growing agitated she repeated several times, ''Take our lamb, and walk with me!'' Then the child was pressed forward, and the dedication begun in his cradle was sealed at her death-bed. ''But what a weight, intolerable as the burden of Atlas, to lay on the shoulders of a little fragile child!''

In their lonely life after his mother's death, when his father would often fold him closely in his arms, the child turning up his face wonderingly ''while the large, unwilling tears gathered in the corners of his eyelids,'' it became the parent's greatest desire that the child should be received into the community of the ''Saints,'' the small band of brethren with whom he prayed. (pp. 460-63)

The congregation proved a little restive at the suggestion: ''each of themselves, in ripe years, had been subjected to the severest cross-examination'' before being admitted to communion. But finally opposition was overborne. The child was submitted to examination by two of the elders, and his answers were so clear, his acquaintance with Scripture so amazing, his testimony to the principles of salvation so exhaustive, that they felt confounded.

In the midst of intense excitement, at the age of ten, he was publicly baptized. His father's joy was pathetic. . . .

Despite this external triumph, there was no native ardor in the boy's heart. He was sincere in desiring to be good and holy, he did not doubt that his father indicated to him the good life, he was not lacking in candor, but there was never any spiritual joy in surrender. There was nothing but resignation, and a

desperate clinging, deep within, ''to a hard nut of individuality,'' almost destroyed and shrivelling away. (p. 464)

Then, suddenly, by a wild caprice, his father ''gratuitously opened a little window'' in the prison-tower, ''and added a powerful telescope.'' The boy had become fascinated by the geography of the West Indies; his father presented him with an old copy of *Tom Cringle's Log,* saying, ''You'll find all about the Antilles there.'' It was the first work of fiction he had ever had; at first he did not realize that it was not literally true; but when his father advised him to read the descriptions of sea and mountain and skip the noisy amorous adventure, of course he did not do so. They filled his horizons with radiant glory.

When his father married a second time the boy was aided to a further gasping plunge into beauty. As a pretty kind of aftermath to courtship his father read aloud to his bride some of the poems of Scott, and, unobserved, a shudder floated down the boy's backbone when he heard the resounding words:

> A sharp and shrieking echo gave,
> Coir-Uriskin, thy goblin cave!
> And the grey pass where birches wave,
> On Beala-nam-bo.

Insensibly the stern prohibition melted away. The novels of Dickens were permitted, on the ground, somewhat odd in a newly married husband, that they expose ''the passion of love in a ridiculous light''; and the boy's shouts of laughing at the richer passages in Pickwick were almost scandalous. ''I felt myself to be in the company of a gentleman so extremely funny that I began to laugh before he began to speak; no sooner did he remark 'the sky was dark and gloomy, the air was damp and raw', than I was in fits of laughter.''

But worldly gaieties were still frowned upon. Imaginative horizons, however, were widening, doors being thrown open, and they gave the boy courage to resist. When he was invited to ''tea and games'' by some neighboring Browns, he evinced so strong a desire to go that his father was obliged to make it an occasion for prayer. With great fervor he asked the Lord to reveal whether or not it was his will that the boy should go to the Browns' party. ''My Father's attitude seemed to me to be hardly fair, since he did not scruple to remind the Deity of various objections to a life of pleasure and of snakes that lie hidden in the grass of evening parties.'' Finally, ''in a loud wheedling voice,'' his father asked him, ''Well, and what is the answer which our Lord vouchsafes?'' He had no doubt of the reply, he was already planning, his son believed in later years, some little treat to make up for the loss. ''But my answer came, in the high, piping accents of despair: 'The Lord says I may go to the Browns.''' Speechless with horror, his father was nevertheless caught in his own trap, and there was no way for him but to retreat. ''Yet surely,'' Gosse adds demurely, ''it was an error in tactics to slam the door.''

Slowly but inevitably his father's prestige and infallibility thenceforth declined. . . . And there came a moment at last when the youth broke out in open revolt. To his father's anxious questioning as to whether he was ''walking closely with God?'' he responded with violence and hysteria. ''I desire not to recall the whimpering sentences in which I begged to be let alone . . . in which I repudiated the idea that my Father was responsible to God for my secret thoughts.'' . . .

It was the end. To London he hurried, followed close by a letter in which his father reviewed with sorrow the stages of his breaking away from God. He prayed that his son might be restored to grace, and then "Oh! how joyfully should I bury all the past, and again have sweet and tender fellowship with my beloved Son, as of old." It was an ultimatum that allowed no truce or compromise, and none was made. Then and there, "as respectfully as he could," the young man "took a human being's privilege to fashion his inner life for himself." Neither Father nor Son, "to the very last hour, ceased to respect the other, or to regard him with a sad indulgence"; but "sweet and tender fellowship" was beyond all yearning lost.

It is unusual, as Gosse says, to find a story of spritual struggle so mingling merriment and tragic pathos. It is not only true, however, that such minglings are the very nature of life—they may have as well the unity and perfection of art. Nothing is clearer than that Gosse is telling *a story:* not a chance series of events, but a development, steady, inevitable, logical, climatic, in which all that he had to do with the materials that life presented to him was to subdue the irrevelant and bring out the dramatic movement. The scenes of comedy were no mere "comic relief"; they were an irreducible datum of the very character and structure of his tale. Only by portraying them could he give us the full human depth and flavor of that childhood scene.

There is an immeasurable gain in realizing it in no stage-caricature rendering of a blue-nosed and strait-laced Puritanism, of mean hypocrisy and thick gloom, but as a living thing, shot through by gleams of lightness and laughter. The cheerful sereneness possible in Evangelical religion is as logical a necessity in Gosse's narrative as the series of revelations by which his spirit is led to freedom. Fate presented him with brilliant finds, but there is not one out of which Gosse's art does not wring the last drop of significance, from the hot embarrassment of the little boy looking into the fire on realizing that his father is not as God to the young man's whimpering rebellion in the orchid-perfumed hothouse. Nature had enacted a work of art, and Gosse had the power to seize and shape to lasting form what nature had provided.

In less significant only because less inventive ways Gosse is quite as noteworthy. No one who ever reads the book will forget its scenes and episodes; no one will forget the characters of the father and the mother and the little boy, although the more fluid and rapidly changing character of the youth, as is inevitable in those years when the personality is changing sometimes with airplane speed, grows less sharply defined. No one will forget the deepening sense of conflict, from the quaintness of the little boy's early skepticism about idolatry to the obsessive struggle against what is, for all its sacrificial purity, almost a spiritual vampirism. But unless we stop to reflect upon it we may not have realized the blinding new biographical possibilities that are thus thrown open in releasing biography from the leading-strings of the entire-life, birth-to-death formula, and at the same time giving it more force than the mere anecdote-enlivened character sketch. They are possibilities that few biographers have yet seen, but they are end-lessly fruitful.

The deepest significance of all in *Father and Son,* as Gosse indeed realized, is its historical meaning. Not only were his parents "perhaps among the latest consistent exemplars" in Protestant Europe of the iron Calvinism that had been so powerful a force in earlier days: their religion was to join in battle with the modern age. They were vigorous-minded people, both of distinguished accomplishment—it is these facts that give significance to "the contrast between their spiritual point of view and the aspect of a similar class of persons today." The

elder Gosse was to find that, both in science and in the heart of his son, he was flung into desperate warfare to preserve a waning creed.

The impact of scientific materialism upon the father's career as a zoologist is told in some brilliant pages of Gosse's book. The strong mingling of pathos and absurdity so often running through it is nowhere richer than in the story of his father's unhappy "Omphalos" theory, which a hasty press coarsely defined as being "that God hid the fossils in the rocks in order to tempt geologists into infidelity." But if his conflict with the modern world embittered his professional life, he found the conflict even more painful when he was obliged to wage it over the soul of his son.

The interplay of pragmatism, paganism, and poetry in the son were like the innocent-looking waves of the sea; but they sucked and tore at the stone foundations of faith, crumbled gradually and remorselessly the joints in the rock; and in vain did the elder strive to save the edifice by damming or by striking at the individual symptoms: he might as well strike the waves on the shore. Freedom, science, skepticism, a more flexible morality, an emancipated art: against all these tendencies of the contemporary world the elder Gosse was dashing himself in vain. It was indeed a struggle between two ages, and as such we can almost see the world-process being enacted symbolically in these narrow little London lodgings and country cottages.

The great intellectual realms of politics and philosophy and sociology are almost entirely offstage, not in the center of things as they are in the autobiographies of Mill and Henry Adams, but the swirl of conflict is no less there. In *Father and Son,* quite as much as in *The Education of Henry Adams,* we are observing a world in transition, in struggle and defeat. . . . Gosse enables us to understand, and even sympathize with the hopes he leaves behind, and then flings us on the threshold of a life, looking forward to the new. He finds the meaning of those mid-nineteenth-century years in the conflict. The meaning is as much victory as it is defeat. (pp. 464-68)

*Edgar Johnson, "Turn of the Century (Biography),"
in his* One Mighty Torrent: The Drama of Biography, *Stackpole Sons, 1937, pp. 441-68.*

### RUTH ZABRISKIE TEMPLE   (essay date 1953)

[*Temple is an American educator and critic specializing in English literature of the late Victorian and early Edwardian periods. Her critical history* The Critic's Alchemy: A Study of the Introduction of French Symbolism into England *is considered one of the most informative and illuminating works on fin-de-siècle writing. In the following excerpt from that work, she discusses Gosse's role as a literary critic who introduced French literature and literary forms to English readers.*]

[Of the critics Edmund Gosse, Matthew Arnold, Algernon Swinburne, Arthur Symons, and George Moore,] Gosse is probably the one who in his own time had the widest public. Symons, though he wrote for some journals of wide circulation, incurred the odium of association with the Decadence, that poisonous French importation. This disability he shared with Swinburne and with Moore. Gosse, like Arnold, was above reproach, and was indeed less susceptible than Arnold to objection on religious or political grounds, as in print he refrained from the expression of any but literary opinions. Being guiltless, also, of propagandist purpose, he was easier to read. These were, no doubt, some, though not all, of the reasons for the enormous prestige which for many years Gosse enjoyed as contributor to the *Times*. He was, we are told, the regular sequel to Sunday roast beef and roast potatoes for all the villa dwellers [see Patrick Braybrooke excerpt dated 1925]. His critical reputation has of course by now declined much more than Arnold's has. The second-rate is nearly always found out. But for the influence he once wielded he must be reckoned with. Moreover, his critical method provides the link between Sainte-Beuve and the syndicated literary gossip column. (p. 185)

As intermediary between France and England, Gosse must be credited with three different sorts of accomplishment. He encouraged by precept and practice the imitation in England of Old French verse forms. He was among the first of the critics writing for a large audience to study French and English literature from a comparative point of view and without initial prejudice. His criticism, like that of Arthur Symons, tended to keep those of the English public who were readers of fairly popular journals abreast of French literature. Of his somewhat hysterical championship of France during the First World War, there is no need to speak here. His writing at that time, for example in the volume *Inter Arma,* was only ostensibly concerned with literary values. (pp. 190-91)

For the record of how [the revival in England of French verse forms of the Middle Ages or the Renaissance] came about we are indebted chiefly to Gosse. He tells of reading in 1874 the French work in which these forms were defined, the *Petit traité de poésie française* by the French poet Théodore de Banville. This treatise served also the other English poets who practiced these forms, Swinburne, Henley, Robert Louis Stevenson, Dobson, and Lang, and indeed a common acquaintance with it initiated the lifelong friendship of Gosse and Austin Dobson. Gosse does not claim the honor of being first to publish poems in all these forms. That honor he divides with the others of the group. But he did write the first English essay defining the forms and advocating their use, and this appeared as an article in the *Cornhill Magazine* in July, 1877. Here the forms are not merely described, but are historically traced through French, and in some cases English, literature. Gosse had used in his preparation of the article other sources besides Banville's treatise. The plea for imitation in England of the triolet, the rondeau, the ballade, the villanelle, in addition to the sonnet, already well established in English poetry, is based on the necessity which Gosse sees for reaction against the excessive practice of blank verse, a fashion for which he holds Tennyson and Browning accountable. In versification, he says, law is better than anarchy, and it may reasonably be supposed that these particular laws, consecrated by the use of our ancestors, are effective in producing certain kinds of art. The article contains, as illustrations, poems in these forms by French poets, by Swinburne, Dobson, and Robert Bridges, and, where other examples are wanting, by Gosse himself. A few of these poems were here printed for the first time. Gosse had already published (imperfect) rondels, in the sequence **"Fortunate Love,"** and the rondeau **"If Love Should Faint,"** in *On Viol and Flute,* and a virelay, in the *Athenaeum* (November 14, 1874). The villanelle and the chant royal of his which appear in the article had not previously been published. (pp. 193-94)

It is probable that Gosse cannot be given much of the credit for initiating or perpetuating this revival. His *Cornhill* article had not the celebrity of Dobson's similar exposition published soon after, and his experiments in the fixed forms were less accomplished as well as less conspicuous than those of the other exponents, Swinburne, Lang, Dobson, and Henley. Yet

his participation in this restricted movement is interesting, because it marks his only alliance with an artistic élite. Very rapidly he became a critic speaking to a wide and varied audience and dealing in his reviews with the most diverse forms of literature, in English, in the Scandinavian languages, in French. He had little personal connection and less sympathy with the nineties writers. But for a brief period in his literary youth, he, too, belonged to a little chapel and preached its doctrine seriously. ". . . I am half in despair," he wrote to Swinburne, sending him the *Cornhill* article. "In all this battle for form and for pure literature, we fight as a mere handful against the whole army of Philistia."

Even more significant, perhaps, for his future criticism of French literature is this early enthusiasm for the rigorously formal poetry described and practiced by Théodore de Banville. The centenary article on Banville, written for the Sunday *Times* in 1923, recaptures the charm which this richly-rhymed and technically dazzling verse had for the young Gosse. That experience furnished a literary standard from which the critic never thereafter seriously deviated. His preference—insofar as it can be distinguished from his expression of decorous and suitable opinion—was for classical French verse, from Malherbe to the Parnassians.

The "comparative" emphasis, which is one of the special characteristics of Gosse's criticism, is to be noted incidentally in nearly all his articles on French poets and determines the topic and presentation of some. Two examples of the latter sort were destined not for English but for French audiences. **"The Influence of France on English Poetry"** was read before the Société des Conferences in Paris in 1904. **"France et l'Angleterre: l'avenir de leurs relations intellectuelles"** [**"France and England: The Future of Their Intellectual Relations"**] is the topic of an essay written, though with reluctance, in French for the *Revue des deux mondes,* in 1916, at the request of its editor, René Doumic. In each of these, the general text is the beneficent effects to be derived from a knowledge of French literature by the English people and of English literature by the French people. But in both Gosse adds a note of caution: these effects are conditional on *judicious* borrowing and careful exportation.

In the lecture Gosse traces in their broad outlines the parallel histories of French and English poetry, indicating the points at which, for better or worse, French poetry reflected upon English. The account gains in force but loses in accuracy by the author's readiness to indulge in picturesque generalization. It is curious that a journalist, whose concern had been, since the 1870's, with contemporary poetry, should have failed to observe any marked influence of French poetry on English after Shelley and Keats. Gosse does concede a debt of the English "Parnassians" to Gautier and Banville, by which he presumably intends a reference to the imitations of Old French forms, but this is to take no account of the English disciples of Baudelaire and Symbolism. Apart from poetry, however, Gosse rightly found a conspicuous influence of French upon English literature since 1870.

In the 1916 essay he traces the reception of French literature in England, this time confining himself to the nineteenth century, and remarking justly upon the causes for the English neglect of French romantic literature at the moment of the latter's appearance. He betrays, unfortunately, not a little of that insular prejudice he deplores in Thackeray's strictures on George Sand, when he cautions the French against exporting certain of their books—books which, because of the subject or the "special conventions" of the French language, will not bear translation—and when he advises French authors to avoid certain themes or recommends a more careful separation in France of true literature from *"marchandise de mauvais aloi"* ["merchandise of inferior quality"] masquerading as the novel. This caution is the more necessary, he says, because at the moment there is a disposition in England to regard everything French as no less than perfect. Gosse was quite right in discerning the extent of contemporary English admiration for things French. He was curiously wrong in appraising the current English debt to French poetry. At the very moment when French poetry was the dominant influence on young poets in England, all that Gosse finds to say of French poetry in England is that Mallarmé, whose character Gosse had always esteemed more than his work, has fathered in England a bastard family of poetasters. No failure in critical illumination on the part of Gosse is more remarkable than this.

The French qualities which he particularly recommends for English emulation are those which Arnold had advocated many years before: order, measure, and elegance. To know French, he declares, is to know the value of logic and precision even in audacious imaginative flights. Occurring in an address to a French public, this has the value of compliment rather than of counsel.

The relations of particular French poets with English poetry and the comparisons with English poetry which their work suggests—to Gosse—are the principal themes of certain of his articles. To write these, Gosse had, of course, to have equipment not in the possession of the ordinary reviewer. He needed not only full biographical information—easily available, it is true—but also the less obvious details on which his case for the special English relationships of his authors was based. The enterprise is that of popularizing the materials of literary scholarship, and in this Gosse takes his cue from Sainte-Beuve. In erudition he was, of course, vastly inferior to Sainte-Beuve, as in the assiduity with which he prepared his articles, but the method was rarely enough exhibited in English reviewing, when he began his career, to render its use a just claim to distinction. (pp. 194-97)

Comparisons with English authors are frequent even in the articles on French poets whose relations with English literature are not important enough to form the substance of special study. It is Gosse's belief that a foreigner reviewing any literature must either be content to echo native criticism, since the foreigner can never hope to rival the native critic on major issues, or adopt a special province and point of view. He must in the latter case select for comment what will interest and benefit his own public; and thus his estimate of the value of French authors will not necessarily duplicate the native estimate. This is a plausible policy and might produce excellent results when applied by a critic of unusual discernment. It is based, of course, on the assumption that there is no universal criterion of taste or absolute standard of literary value, an assumption which Gosse, as we shall see later, was reluctant to acknowledge and on which very little of his criticism is actually based. It would justify the "moral" fulminations of a Gifford as well as the mild appraisals of a Gosse. On the whole, it is probably less safe as a critical principle than the determination to discover and "echo" the best native opinion. The results which Gosse had from his application of the principle are a fairly accurate indication of its value.

The disreputable poets had small attraction for Gosse. Of Villon and Verlaine he deplored the lives too thoroughly to be a convincing champion of their poetry for English audiences. Stevenson's denunciation of Villon's career has his full approval. For too long, in their belief, the vagabond poet had been regarded as the mere unhappy victim of circumstance, and Stevenson in a *Cornhill* article (1877) set about correcting this sentimental attitude. Gosse does not make the crude mistake, common in earlier English criticism, of detesting the man's work because of his character. Villon, he admits, was a very great poet, but the review does not go beyond this admission. . . . Elsewhere Gosse shows some acquaintance with the poetry of Villon, but it was not the sort of poetry to which he recurred in his eminently decorous articles. (pp. 199-200)

"I am the disciple of one man, and of one man only—Sainte-Beuve." Thus Gosse wrote in 1924 to Professor Roe, who had inquired, no doubt in the interest of his forthcoming book, how much Gosse owed to Taine. Gosse rejects all indebtedness to Taine, whose "idea" regarding literature he did not at any time find attractive. (p. 219)

Gosse was, as he says, more affected by Sainte-Beuve than by any other critic, although the fact of influence does not bring him close, in rank, to the man he designated as the Prince of Critics.

On Sainte-Beuve, Gosse bestows one of his rare unqualified superlatives [in *More Books on the Table*]: "He had imperfections, prejudices, limitations, but when we have recognized them all, he remains the greatest literary critic that the world has seen." . . . Though Gosse does not specify the short-comings of Sainte-Beuve, he enumerates some of his virtues: "His insatiable curiosity, the width of his comprehension, the wonderful dexterity of his mental processes." . . . For none of these was Gosse remarkable.

Like Sainte-Beuve, he wrote, to be sure, on a wide variety of topics, but he does not appear to have had either the scholar's anxiety to number accurately the streaks of the tulip or a Boswell's determination to achieve understanding of his quarry. His curiosity was always bounded by decorum. Decorum, again, limited his tolerance (of Verlaine, of Villon), and he seldom wrote with comprehension beyond the range of his personal preferences, which were invariably discreet. After his daring adventure into the New Movement of the seventies, the Revival of Old French forms, he settled down to write with approval of those writers already consecrated by some public recognition, rarely and with tempered praise of the obscure. It was, of course, one of Sainte-Beuve's precepts that the critic should discover new talent, although it was a branch of criticism in which he distinguished himself less than, for example, Baudelaire.

The most notable exhibition of mental dexterity on the part of Gosse is his adaptation to the demands, the capacities, and the fluctuations in taste of his wide public. If he is undulating and diverse, it is in this sense only. And this rendered him unlikely to imitate Sainte-Beuve in another article of the latter's originality, which Gosse notes as an attempt to judge by "pure, frank impression as naïve as possible."

Gosse is no more an Impressionist than Matthew Arnold—either in his response to literature or, the usual definition of the term, his transcription of its effect on him. What he did principally imitate in Sainte-Beuve was the combination of biographical with literary study.

It was this method, informally practiced by Sainte-Beuve, which Taine systematized into a new dogma to replace the classical grounds of judgment, and, in conformity with the scientific spirit of the age, the system was calculated not so much to evaluate as to explain. For Sainte-Beuve, of course, it was no system but merely one of several techniques for approaching literature, and as such it was acceptable to the English mind which resisted Taine. Gosse imitated the letter rather than the spirit of Sainte-Beuve's biographical method, and it is unlikely that he understood its theoretical justification. Much less often and less skilfully than his master does he use biography to illuminate literature. More often the biographical material distracts the critic—and the reader—from the work at hand. This, no doubt, is the basis for the charge that Gosse debased the method of Sainte-Beuve to the gossip column. The contemporary purveyor to the public of what porridge had John Keats is far below Edmund Gosse but is nevertheless in his line of descent from Sainte-Beuve. On the whole, however, we cannot regret that the biographical element of Gosse's criticism is so prominent, for in this, if nowhere else, he excelled. He had a gift not much inferior to Sainte-Beuve's for seizing and formulating in a phrase the characteristic gestures of his subjects, dead or living. Had he, besides this gift, possessed the speculative mind which would have enabled him to perceive significant relationships, he might have practiced with some distinction the historical criticism which he highly valued. (pp. 220-21)

Happily, Gosse has declared himself to be incapable of speculative thought. It thus becomes our pleasant duty simply to find corroboration for his own statement. There is no lack of evidence. If one tries to discover what theory of criticism Gosse applied—and Gosse wrote that the historian of literature must form his own opinions on a series of aesthetic principles—one is forced to conclude that no man who had so little idea what theory was could consciously have entertained a theory of his own. And indeed Gosse admits that his essays are simply the result of his desire to share the pleasure which literature has given him. He protests, however, that the critic's continued interest in literature can only be justified by the assumption that there is a positive norm of excellence. Yet he asks of books only that they amuse him. The history of literary expression should be regarded, he believes, as part of the history of a vast, living organism directed in its manifestations by a definite, though obscure and inscrutable, law of growth. Yet he asserts that art does not progress, develop, or improve from age to age; it only differs.

To juxtapose these various statements of Gosse's is to do him no injustice, for there was no development in his thought on the business of the critic; there was perhaps not even complete consciousness of change of opinion from one pronouncement to the next.

If his theory is amoeboid, his criticism is not less so, and this, perhaps, in the absence of more distinguished virtues, is its excellence. He wrote on a great variety of subjects, and each one in some way he surrounded, taking possession of it not with a firm grasp but by a gradual process of almost insensible advance balanced by retreat, of expansion and retraction, until assimiliation was achieved and there remained no subject but simply an essay by Mr. Edmund Gosse.

This is not to suggest that his critical essays were formless. They are, on the contrary, recognizable as their author's almost by form alone. The device of including biography with criticism he managed less variously than his master, Sainte-Beuve, and his essays were arranged nearly always in one pattern: the biography preceding discussion of the works. Shaping his es-

says carefully, he exercised equal care in the phrasing of them. Here at least his reach did not exceed his grasp.

Although his most persistent motive in criticism was, we may conclude, to communicate the pleasure he found in books, his method was not that of the impressionistic critic. He seldom (and more seldom in the later years) attempted or managed to evoke the quality of the work of art itself. *Placing* seemed to him of extreme importance, in the world of books as in society, and he multiplied comparisons, introducing also, wherever possible, superlatives, most often guarded. To assign places in the hierarchy of the literary world, was, however, to judge. And as he possessed, and indeed wished to possess, no set of principles, this might, had he recognized the dilemma, have proved embarrassing. He did not, however, recognize it.

Although there was no development in his critical theory, it is not quite exact to say that there was none in his criticism. The earlier essays, those written for periodicals in the last decades of the century, are more forthright, are notably less urbane, and display more interest in general issues. The habit of caution grew on him proportionately, one may suppose, with his sense of responsibility to a widening audience and to his own increasing social eminence. The mellowing effect of years enabled him to praise, to dispose of, and to condescend to authors with equal grace and with the careful courtesy which consists in never giving unintentional offense.

Naturally, the general characteristics of Gosse as critic obtain of Gosse as critic of French literature. But certain differences are to be remarked.

Gosse had a principle to which he generally adhered in his criticism of French literature. This principle, a logical and legitimate application of romantic relativism, was that the foreign estimate of a given writer will and should differ from the native one. One estimate is not truer than the other; they are merely different. This, as we have seen, gave Gosse, on occasion, the temerity to contradict a current French evaluation. Arnold also had taken leave to disagree with French judgments of value, though declaring (sometimes) that the foreign critic would naturally know best. In this matter Gosse has at least the modest virtue of consistency. . . . He was, unlike the others but like Sainte-Beuve, a popularizer. That Englishmen should know French literature was an article of his creed as of Arnold's. He would have called it his pleasure, but I suspect that it seemed to him a pleasant duty, to act as intermediary for the literature of the country he loved. Didactic literature was abhorrent to him, and he would not have it thought that his criticism aimed at more than communicating pleasure. But, oddly enough, his criticism of French literature is of all that of the period most apt to have instructed, by pleasing, its readers. His persistent emphasis on which French poetry should be read by English readers and which French poets copied by English poets is significant. Other critics wrote—like Symons and Moore, Pater and Swinburne—for an artistic élite or—like Dowden and Saintsbury—for an audience of students or amateurs of French literature. Gosse alone did not take for granted in his readers a preliminary acquaintance with that literature. He used by preference comparisons with English authors to convey the character and status of French authors, helped to this, perhaps, by his own hard-won and incomplete knowledge of French literature. It is probable that Gosse reached a wider audience than even Saintsbury and Dowden, his fellow-contributors to several periodicals, for articles by Gosse read easily and his felicity of style was much admired. (The assiduities of the French government to him were not miscalculated.) And, even if Gosse did not reach a wider audience than his colleagues in criticism, he may very well have reached more nearly the audience he shared with them. For their flattering assumption of the general reader's sophistication in French literature was plainly unjustified.

That Gosse should have undertaken the defence of French classical literature and of poetry in the most austere French tradition is therefore of great importance. There had been few to plead the cause of Racine, of Malherbe, of Banville and Heredia and Leconte de Lisle to a wide British audience. Also, his misjudgments and dislike of certain symbolist poets are the more regrettable, for, although these poets had their own lively advocates, Gosse might have done more than they could to hasten general appreciation of the new poetry.

In conveying information unobtrusively, Gosse was almost unrivaled. In that other part of the critic's function, which is to send his reader directly to the books, it is less certain that he was successful. Curiously enough, although he certainly took constant joy in literature and believed that his criticism was the record of his pleasure, he had a mediocre gift for communicating the quality of a book and tempting his reader to partake of it. And this is a useful and necessary function of the critic in an age when nearly everybody reads and almost no one grasps the import of his reading. Then criticism, as Carlyle said, "stands like an interpreter between the inspired and the uninspired." This service good impressionist criticism notably performs, and here Moore and Symons excel. Writing neither impressionistically nor dogmatically, Gosse had not the positive support of any system for his opinions, and to supply this deficiency he had not even the endowment of unfailing taste. Perhaps this explains his careful abstention from enthusiasm and surprise, and, especially in later years, his habit of almost universal moderate approval. "The truth is," Robert Lynd comments, "Mr. Gosse is always doing his best to balance the pleasure of saying the best with the pleasure of saying the worst." The result is, despite his excellent intention, that he may not have encouraged the reading of French literature so much as critics who spoke out and spoke from an uncompromising temperament.

His habit of arranging his views for publication and of urging on his audience the literature that in his estimation was good for them makes his public utterance more important, as well as easier to come at, than his private preferences. If we try to determine the extent of his own enjoyment of French poetry, we find the evidence as contradictory and baffling as that we found in examining his theory and practice of criticism.

Here was an Englishman with no pretensions to being partly French in spirit, having no close personal connections with France. That he valued especially the classical tradition in French poetry seems to be proof enough that such appreciation was not impossible in England. But certain of his statements and omissions cast some doubt on his understanding of the classical tradition.

There is in all his criticism very little comment on French versification. He did not explain the character of classical versification or comment in detail upon the technical innovations of the Romantics. He did not, although he had abundant opportunity for doing so, explain the technical experiments of the Symbolists but contented himself with accusing them of an attempt to "deliquesce" French poetry. There is indeed evidence that he did not fully understand the nature of their experiments. In the first review of Régnier he complained of

the poet's use of eccentric rhymes, which he cannot believe satisfactory to the French ear: *fontaines* and *même, hautes* and *roses.* This is, of course, not rhyme at all but assonance, and it is one of the principal devices of the Symbolists. (pp. 222-27)

His observations on the differences between French and English poetry are significant. He does not simply dismiss French poetry as inferior; he recognizes that each of the two has its own excellences. English has the peculiar magic and melody of a Coleridge or a Keats (found also by exception in Vigny's poem "Le Cor"). There is also in the English tradition a tendency to obscurity and to confusion of poetry with prose. French poetry has the virtues of order and proportion, of logic even in imaginative effects. Although he nowhere remarks on a greater fitness of one or of the other language for the purposes of poetry—which is an omission greatly to his credit—neither does he notice the contrasting systems of versification which language differences entail. One might have expected comment on a difficulty which English practitioners of the Old French forms would encounter and which French exponents of those forms were spared: namely, a scarcity of rhyming words. There is no detailed analysis of the reasons why certain French poets do or do not appeal to English audiences.

Admiring *finish* more than any other single literary quality, he naturally delighted in the obvious formal perfection of the French classicists and Parnassians. Whether he had more than a superficial idea of the means by which this finish was secured and of the subtleties which composed the obvious effect, is doubtful.

Gosse established his reputation in the years between 1865 and 1900, the period that has been called the golden age of English reviewing. He did most of his work in the period of decline from that happy age to the low level of the twenties and after. The change came about with the advent of newspaper reviewing, with the adoption of the signed review, and with the increased production of merely entertaining fiction designed for the larger and less literate reading public. Gosse did little to divert the current, for he indulged his own taste for whimsical pronouncements and he encouraged the tendency to dwell on the man at the expense of his book. . . . [If] not erudite or meticulous in scholarship, he was widely read and exacting in the matter of style. Adapting himself to his expanding audience just enough to catch their ear, he may have led them a little nearer tolerance for some French poetry. . . . In the appreciation of this poetry, however, Gosse was never absolutely right, if he was seldom absolutely wrong. In this, as in other literary matters, his discrimination was not fine and his penetration not profound. Neither by temperament nor by critical method was he equipped to serve the cause of French poetry in England as did the aesthetic critics Swinburne, Moore and Symons. (pp. 227-28)

*Ruth Zabriskie Temple, "Sir Edmund Gosse," in* The Critic's Alchemy: A Study of the Introduction of French Symbolism into England, *Twayne Publishers, Inc., 1953, pp. 185-228.*

## V. S. PRITCHETT  (essay date 1964)

*[Pritchett is a highly esteemed English novelist, short story writer, and critic. Considered one of the modern masters of the short story, he is also one of the world's most respected and well-read literary critics. Pritchett writes in the conversational tone of the familiar essay, approaching literature from the viewpoint of a lettered but not overly scholarly reader. In his criticism, Pritchett*

*stresses his own experience, judgment, and sense of literary art,
rather than following a codified critical doctrine derived from a
school of psychological or philosophical speculation. In the following excerpt, Pritchett discusses Gosse's depiction of his father
in* Father and Son.]

When we read Edmund Gosse's **Father and Son** which describes the remarkable life of a family of Plymouth Brethren,
we see that an insufferable ennui drove the son from his father's
faith. Extreme peculiarity in a religious sect is exciting, even
stimulating and enlarging to a child; it isolates him, and in
doing so gives him a heady importance, an enormous lead (in
some respects) over his more orthodox fellows. But the experience is too fierce. It creates that "chaffiness"—so quickly
burned out—which the early Quakers were always talking about.
The real reason for the boredom to come lies in that war against
the imagination which all puritan sects—the political and scientific it should be observed, as well as the religious—have
undertaken. Sir Edmund Gosse's parents would not allow their
child to read or hear stories. Fact, yes; but stories were not
true, therefore they were lies. The young Gosse, whose father
was a scientist, was familiar with birds, insects, the creatures
of the sea, and with books of scientific travel; but he had never
heard of Jack the Giant Killer or Little Red Riding Hood.

> So far as my "dedication" was concerned [he writes]
> I can but think that my parents were in error thus to
> exclude the imaginary from my outlook upon facts.
> They desired to make me truthful; the tendency was
> to make me positive and sceptical. Had they wrapped
> me in the soft folds of supernatural fancy my mind
> might have been longer content to follow their tra-
> ditions is an unquestioning spirit.

Yet it would be hard to call the elder Gosse a totally unimaginative man. As a scientist he was unimaginative, and so
nipped the promise of his own intellect and career; but as a
religious man he was riotously imaginative. He lived in the
Eastern imagery of the Bible; he believed in it literally; he
apprehended the instant end of the world and prepared himself
for a literal flight upwards into the air toward the arms of the
angels. His was simply an intense and narrow imagination.
And there is a comment by the son here which is very suggestive. We might assume that Gosse senior was a typical middle-
class Victorian scientist and Nonconformist, presumably conditioned by his class and his age and bent on the general purpose
of practical self-improvement; but, as the son points out, the
father's religious life really sprang from a far earlier period.
Gosse senior was not a nineteenth-century man; his Calvinism
had survived, intact, from the seventeenth-century. Conduct,
which meant everything to the nineteenth-century man, meant
little to the elder Gosse; vision, the condition of grace, was
everything. Later on, when the boy grew up and went to live
in London, the father was worried very little by what the boy
did; but was in agony about what he might think or feel. Was he
still a dedicated soul, had he fallen from grace? To such
questions the elder Gosse might bring the exhausting and pet-
tifogging inquiry of a lawyer, rather than the imaginative
anxiety of the religious mystic; but the attitude, as the son says,
is nearer Bunyan's or Jeremy Taylor's than it is to the nineteenth
century. (pp. 148-50)

What was it that prolonged the seventeenth-century stamp upon
the elder Gosse? A possible explanation is that, on both sides,
the family was a genteel one of steadily declining fortune, and
no family is more tenacious of the past, more prone to fixation
than the declining family. We have only to compare Gosse's
quarrel with Butler's to see the difference between two con-

temporaries. Gosse was fortunate; for Butler's nineteenth-century father had become a kind of practical Jehovah who thrashed
prayer and Latin into his son indifferently. Gosse never hated
his father. There was a break, a tragic and passionate break,
not a clash of wills so much as a division of principles; and,
since the breach was tragic, its agony was without resentment.
Butler and his father, in their common hatred, were vituperative
to the end; the Gosses gazed helplessly, emotionally across the
gulf of history between them. Centuries separated them. The
violence of the revolutionary nineteenth century did not possess
them; and so it was the scorn, the satire and hatred of Butler
and not the scrupulous, unavailing sympathy and impartial
regret of Gosse that were to whip up the violent reaction against
the Victorian family, and especially the Victorian father.

Gosse's attitude to his father is acquiescent and almost Gib-
bonian. If Gosse's imagination had been fed in childhood he
might have used his father as a starting point for one of those
imaginative libels, like Dickens's portrait of Micawber, which
are fatherhood's vicarious and unwilling gift to literature. But
from Gosse, the ex-puritan and melodious prig, we get instead
a positive, literal, skeptical document. What an incredible story
the mere facts make. Nothing fixes the fantastic note like the
episode of the moth. The naturalist, his wife and his child were
at prayer one morning in 1855:

> . . . when through the open window a brown moth
> came sailing. My mother immediately interrupted the
> reading of the Bible by saying to my father, "Oh,
> Henry, do you think that can be *Boletobia*?" My
> father rose up from the sacred book, examined the
> insect, which had now perched, and replied "No! It
> is only the common *Vapourer Orgyia antiqua*!" re-
> suming his seat and the exposition of the Word, with-
> out any apology or embarrassment.

I said earlier that Gosse senior could not be called unimaginative, but as the son points out, he was certainly deficient in
sympathetic imagination. In one sense his fanatical religion
was scientific, an exhaustive classification and checking up.
There was, for example, the question of Prophecy. The father
said that no small element in his wedded happiness had been
the fact that he and his wife were of one mind in the interpretation of Sacred prophecy. They took to it as profane families
take to cards or the piano. They played with the Book of
Revelation as if it were Happy Families or Snap:

> When they read of seals broken and of vials poured
> forth, of the star which was called Wormwood that
> fell from Heaven, and of men whose hair was as the
> hair of women, and their teeth as the teeth of lions,
> they did not admit for a moment that these vivid
> mental pictures were of a poetic character, but they
> regarded them as positive statements, in guarded lan-
> guage, describing events which were to happen, and
> could be recognized when they did happen. It was
> the explanation, the perfectly prosaic and positive
> explanation, of all these wonders which drew them
> to study the Habershons and the Newtons whose books
> they so much enjoyed. They were helped by these
> guides to recognize in wild Oriental visions direct
> statements regarding Napoleon III and Pope Pius IX,
> and the King of Piedmont, historic figures which they
> conceived as foreshadowed, in language which ad-
> mitted of plain interpretation, under the names of
> denizens of Babylon and companions of the Wild
> Beast.

The conviction that the last days of the queenly arrogance of
Rome had come so affected Gosse's mother that her husband

wrote in his diary that it "had irradiated her dying hours with an assurance that was like the light of the Morning Star." As the years went slowly by—and how slowly they passed for the bored and ailing child who was expected to live at this pitch— it began to dawn on him that there was something incredibly trivial about such convictions. The elder Gosse could swallow one Eliot's stuff about prophecy and yet reject Darwin. He was an educated man, yet he could say that Shakespeare, Marlowe and Ben Jonson endangered the soul and that Dickens was preferable to Scott "because Dickens showed love in a ridiculous light." The child of such a man was obliged to develop two selves. One assented, got itself publicly baptized and dedicated at the age of ten, and confounded the wise with his theology and unction; the other quietly built up a very different mind—and as the sons of puritans will—an inveterate irony. This came out at the time when his father was thinking of marrying again. The father (the child sharply detected) was put, for once, in the position of the penitent. One was required, the child remembered, "to testify in season and out of season." Was the lady (he therefore asked) "one of the Lord's children"? Had she, he pressed, "taken up her cross in baptism"? The father had to admit that the lady had been brought up in the "so-called Church of England." "Papa," said the little prig, wagging his finger, "don't tell me that she's a pedobaptist?"

Gosse was encouraged to draw this portrait by the revolt of the times. He was faced by the difficulty that at the moments when narrow or peculiar religion is behaving most ludicrously, it is also providing its adherents with emotions or intentions that one must respect. Nothing could have been more intellectually disgraceful and spiritually disastrous than the boy's public dedication; nothing more dingily farcical; or more humiliating when one considers that Gosse's father was, after all, an educated man. Yet one must respect the emotions that the participant felt. There is, as Gosse said, something comic and tragic, really tragic, in the theme. On a similar subject Mark Twain became savage; he was driven to a kind of insulting nihilism. Gosse, in the end, was rather more bored than outraged by his father, for he understood the defect of character that had caused the malady. He saw that the sin was the denial of the imagination and the pestering of the judgment. He saw that, at the time of the Darwin crisis, his father had really sold his intellect and perhaps his soul. That flight to Devonshire was a flight from the society of his equals, who would challenge his faith every day, into a society of rustics who could be guaranteed to swallow everything he said. We smile with amusement and irony at the two figures; the father examinig his insects under the naturalist's microscope, the son applying the lens of the biographer and producing one of the most brilliant specimens of his century. (pp. 150-54)

                    *V. S. Pritchett, "A Plymouth Brother," in his* The
                    Living Novel & Later Appreciations, *revised edition,
                    Random House, 1964, pp. 147-54.*

## WILLIAM J. GRACIE, JR.   (essay date 1974)

[*In the following excerpt, Gracie discusses sections of* Father and Son *in which Gosse unconsciously reveals much about himself while discussing his father.*]

Soon after the publication in 1907 of Edmund Gosse's *Father and Son,* George Moore wrote to Gosse to report that he had read the book with pleasure and had found that his friend's autobiographical narrative had "more than truth in it." In what may have been a deliberate comment on Gosse's claim in the preface to *Father and Son* that his work was "scrupulously true," Moore wrote that *Father and Son* told his story "beautifully as well as truthfully, and with beauty and truth the life of a writer is indefinitely prolonged." Moore's remarks apply directly to Gosse's decision to combine a partial biography of his father with his own autobiography and to bind together this potentially unwieldly amalgam with devices more common to the novel than to traditional autobiographical writing—symbolism, elaborate metaphorical language, and a dramatic structure. It is difficult and probably unnecessary to dispute Gosse's decision or Moore's judgment, but it is important to note just how Gosse's choice of form in his autobiographical study tells us more about Gosse than he may have wished, or—to give Moore's words another reading—"more than truth." I suggest that Gosse's choice of form enabled him to write one of the more interesting and careful documents in autobiographical literature but it also enabled him to reveal more of his attitude towards his paternal adversary than he may have wished—or even realized. In some respects, therefore, *Father and Son* remains more valuable for what it suggests than for what it states.

As a biography as well as an autobiography, *Father and Son's* defects derive from its virtues. It is clearly one of the most skilfully drawn portraits of childhood and adolescence in autobiographical literature, and in its subtle self-recrimination . . . it successfully escapes the aura of egotism and vanity so often common to autobiography. The trouble with *Father and Son* concerns the matter of truth. As we have seen, Gosse could scarcely have made clearer his claim for truth in his autobiography than in his prefatory remarks; indeed, he had made a similar claim in his *Life* of his father. That Gosse should make his claim for truthfulness so emphatic should not be surprising. He was certainly aware that a book-length portrait of his relations with his father as well as a concomitant critique of the same might raise more than one suspicious eyebrow, so it is therefore only fair to regard his prefatory remarks as his first defense against criticism. I shall suggest, then, that our problem does not involve truth of fact but a kind of truth of experience. We cannot avoid the problem, because it is inherent in the form Gosse has chosen for his autobiographical recollections.

As skilful as Gosse's blend of biography and autobiography may be, it necessarily involves its author in at least two "kinds" of truth: truth of fact and truth of experience. There is little enough evidence that Gosse's *Father and Son* is not factually true. There may be minor flaws in the narrative, but the usual cause for such slips—faulty memory—can be hardly called reprehensible. As was the case with John Stuart Mill in his claim that he read Coleridge during his first mental crisis (he actually read Coleridge much later), the entire narrative does not stand or fall on the matter of factual accuracy. But Gosse introduces into his narrative some of the devices of the novelist—especially symbolism and dramatic structure—and once he does so, he necessarily involves his narrative in something clearly beyond factual accuracy. The perceptions, insights, and interpretation of character which invest and control Edmund and Philip Henry Gosse involve the biographer-autobiographer in what we may call, lacking a better phrase, a kind of truth of experience.

Now all this is obvious enough in any autobiography which sets out, as Gosse's does, to be consciously artistic. In all such cases we must regard both what the narrator says of himself and how he chooses to say it as the so-called truth of his experience. What makes an assessment of *Father and Son* so difficult is Gosse's basic decision to raise his father to a level of equal importance with himself. Edmund Gosse and Philip Henry Gosse become protagonist and antagonist, and, like parallel lines, their roles are constant in the narrative until the lines unexpectedly bisect at young Edmund's baptism, and the father recedes in importance as the son rises. What we are left with is a good enough dramatic structure and a serious question regarding truth, because we must necessarily regard Philip Gosse through his son's eyes. The validity of the father's character is consequently compromised. This basic problem of Gosse's book seems not to have occurred to him, but it in no way suggests that the book is without value. . . . What Edmund Gosse seems not to have seen in his father is actually more interesting than what he reports.

*Father and Son* begins with the birth of Edmund Gosse and ends with his settling in London in his twenty-first year. The narrative therefore covers Gosse's life until his majority and his father's life from age thirty-nine to sixty. Clearly, the book must deal with the father at the height of his powers and, correspondingly, with the emergence of young Edmund Gosse to independence and selfhood. If nothing else, we have here the ingredients of conflict and perhaps a ready-made plot for the novelist: a prosaic father hurt severely at the apex of his career by his publication of *Omphalos*, an earnest refutation of Charles Lyell, and—juxtaposed to this—a sensitive boy emerging into manhood, religious doubt and aestheticism. It would seem under such circumstances that some kind of father-son conflict would be wellnigh inevitable. It was inevitable, of course, but what makes Gosse's treatment of the conflict so interesting is his feeling that father-son conflict is virtually inherent in the race. This is why we are introduced so early in the narrative to Gosse's idea that he and his father were "assailed by forces in comparison with which the changes that health or fortune or place introduce are as nothing."

The "forces" are various: discoveries in geology and biology which were rapidly making his father's fundamentalism untenable, the growth of scepticism, and perhaps even the gradual erosion of the Victorian idea of the family as an autonomous unit of society. Forces so closely related make it virtually impossible to single out one or two as primarily responsible for Edmund's break from his father, but Gosse complicates the matter by suggesting that forces even greater than those just mentioned and infinitely more mysterious than any of them were somehow or other responsible for the conduct of his father and himself. For example, in the opening paragraph of the first chapter, we are told that Gosse's father "was born to fly backward" while Gosse himself "could not help being carried forward." A sentence such as this is full of interesting possibilities, but it is typical of *Father and Son* that they remain no more than suggestive. Gosse will not elaborate. It is certainly possible, however, for us to take the sentence as a good example of Gosse's method and style. It is clear enough in a sentence like this that Gosse is fond of suggestion; there will be more examples of this suggestive manner later, but for the moment let us simply note this single example. It is also true of this sentence that it introduces us to Gosse's method of implicating the social and spiritual environment in the actions of his major characters. What this means is that Gosse seems to regard his father and himself as innocents acted upon by forces much greater than themselves. Like so many other aspects of his book, this concept of human behavior is closely related to Gosse's style; for *Father and Son* is the story of the emergence of an aesthetic soul from a hostile environment.

Though he is consistently characterized in the autobiographical narrative as a stubborn antagonist, it would be a mistake to regard Philip Henry Gosse as an ignorant and severe man. Neither in his son's *Life* nor in *Father and Son* is the elder Gosse described in any such way. As a matter of fact, both books characterize him as a man of immense self-will, courage and energy. As a zoologist, he was largely self-taught, and as a writer he seems to have been blessed with amazing stamina and an attractive style. His essential flaw, however, was related to his energy and perseverance—he was firmly committed to what he believed to be the rightness of his opinions. It is true of course that many of these opinions were religious, but it is no less true that his unswerving devotion to his conscience caused him to be stubborn and cold when he should have been—especially in the company of his son—flexible and warm. Gosse underlines this aspect of his father's character early in his *Life*: "His conscience was a law to him, and a law that he was prepared to obey in face of an army of ridicule drawn up in line of battle." If he was firm in his convictions, he was also firm in his devotion to work. This fact is brought out clearly in *Father and Son* in the recollection of Philip Gosse's behavior at the birth of his son. The elder Gosse's diary entry for that day is severely brief: "E. delivered of a son. Received green swallow from Jamaica." Edmund Gosse interprets the entry as an example of "my Father's extreme punctilio": "The green swallow arrived later in the day than the son, and the eariler visitor was therefore recorded first; my Father was scrupulous in every species of arrangement."

While not occupying as crucial a place in the narrative as her husband, the character of Emily Gosse nevertheless gives her son the opportunity to add perspective and depth to his recreation of the Gosse household. We are perhaps not surprised to learn that the religious beliefs of both Philip and Emily did much to bring them together as husband and wife; nor are we surprised to learn that the couple soon "found themselves shut outside all Protestant communions, and at last they met only with a few extreme Calvinists like themselves. . . ." To say the least, the Gosse household was brought into being by religious beliefs and was run in accordance with strict Calvinist teachings. Gosse sums up his account of the home: "Here was perfect purity, perfect intrepidity, perfect abnegation; yet there was also narrowness, isolation, an absence of perspective, let it be boldly admitted, an absence of humanity. And there was a curious mixture of humbleness and arrogance; entire resignation to the will of God and not less entire disdain of the judgment and opinion of man."

As an account of Gosse's home, this description amounts almost to an indictment, and the claim that there was an "absence of humanity" in the small home in London seems exaggerated. The description does not, however, invalidate Gosse's essential point that he was a virtual alien in his own home. The important thing to recognize here is that Gosse almost immediately juxtaposes the severe picture of his home with his first venture in the book into elaborate symbolism. The chapter closes with an extended account of an unmistakably alienated soul:

> This, then, was the scene in which the soul of a little child was planted, not as in an ordinary flower-border or carefully tended social parterre, but as on a ledge, split in the granite of some mountain. The ledge was hung between night and the snows on one hand, and the dizzy depths of the world upon the other; was furnished with just soil enough for a gentian to struggle skywards and open its stiff azure stars; and offered no lodgment, no hope of salvation, to any rootlet which should stray beyond its inexorable limits.

The preceding describes Gosse's earliest years, though the elaborate floral imagery of the first chapter obviously represents recollection in tranquillity. Because the symbolism in *Father and Son* is remarkably consistent, it is worth mentioning here that the choice of floral imagery to describe Gosse's infant character is not accidental. He not only turns frequently to floral imagery, but he seems to have been well aware of the imagery's connotations. In a self-portrait of his thirteenth year, for example, we find that he "was like a plant on which a pot has been placed, with the effect that the centre is crushed, and arrested, while shoots are struggling up to the light on all sides." Taken out of context, such effects seem forced, but they indicate that Gosse conceived of himself as a sensitive and delicate being who, in struggling toward some kind of sustenance not found in his family, was thwarted and often blocked. In keeping with the imagery already established, Gosse seems to have felt that he was starved of imagination, poetry, and beauty in his youth. Again, it is no accident that he describes the imaginative adventures and conversations of Michael Scott's *Tom Cringle's Log* as the "flower of the book"; likewise, it is significant that his father advised his young son to skip all such passages and to concentrate instead on the descriptions of the mountains and sea of Jamaica. An unpublished letter from Philip to Edmund now in the University Library, Cambridge, reveals that the father was as capable as the son in employing appropriate imagery. During one of their frequent quarrels in the late 1860's, Philip writes Edmund to offer that the latter's recent conduct puts him in mind "of those aromatic herbs, which give out their fragrance with peculiar intensity when they are bruised." The similarity of imagery employed by father and son is uncanny.

Involved and mannered as Edmund Gosse's symbolism may be, it is undoubtedly appropriate for his purposes. It is difficult to escape the feeling, for instance, that he wishes his readers to see in all his floral imagery the elements of struggle against confinement. This much, at least, seems clear from the very consistency of the imagery, and surely a writer as careful as Gosse would recognize the imagery's connotation. What complicates matters, however, is connotation itself. It is all very well, we may suppose, to equate one's emergence into mature life with the struggles all flowers must wage with the elements and other hostile forces, but it is quite another thing to imply an analogous relationship between those alien forces and one's father. Although Gosse never actually makes this equation, he implies that his father's stubbornness and rigidity were in many ways similar to all such things that would unintentionally crush a flower. As mentioned earlier, Gosse's ability to suggest and to imply is evident throughout the book. What is not so evident is his recognition that he was telling more of himself through his powerful use of suggestion than he realized.

The analogies suggested by the floral imagery are complicated enough matters to ponder, but there is an even more complicated analogy presented in Gosse's early recollection of his father as God. Gosse recalls that in his sixth year he came to the sudden realization that his father was not God. Before that time, he tells us, "I confused him in some sense with God; at all events I believed that my Father knew everything and saw everything." It seems that one day Philip Gosse made some error of fact and was corrected by his wife. Gosse admits that the incident meant nothing to his parents, but to the sensitive youth it meant "an epoch": "Here was the appalling discovery, never suspected before, that my Father was not as God, and did not know everything. The shock was not caused by any suspicion that he was not telling the truth, as it appeared

*Gosse with his cat, Mopsy, 1906.*

to him, but by the awful proof that he was not, as I had supposed, omniscient." Gosse's identification of his father as God is hardly unusual. The elder Gosse was the recognizable figure of authority in the household, and his young son knew scarcely anyone outside his own family. But young Gosse had, in fact, experienced his first religious doubt in the incident of his father's "loss of infallibility," and from this point in the narrative to the conclusion, Gosse's Evangelical faith steadily weakens.

The fallibility incident has an important corresponding episode which must not be overlooked. It could rightly be said that the curious experience of Gosse's sixth year was a discovery of his father's weakness and, correlatively, a discovery of the son's own inner strength. What this means is that the young boy found that by turning within himself he could find the sympathy and solace which he felt his father, as a fallen god, could not offer. Gosse calls this discovery of his own inner and sustaining strength "the consciousness of self" and relates its effect: "But of all thoughts which rushed upon my savage and undeveloped little brain at this crisis, the most curious was that I had found a companion and a confidante in myself. There was a secret in this world and it belonged to me and to somebody who lived in the same body with me. There were two of us, and we could talk with one another."

It is very important to recognize in Gosse's statement his discovery of selfhood—that is, an individuality, and to some degree a sense of purpose in himself. It is just as important to recognize that the discovery is made a result of his loss of faith in his father. In other words, Gosse makes it appear that his father unintentionally set in motion the various series of events and discoveries which ultimately severed him from his only child. Thus Edmund Gosse, recalling the opening paragraph of the book, is more acted upon than acting. (pp. 176-82)

Always solicitous for his son, Philip Gosse had determined in a typical burst of Evangelical fervor to have Edmund baptized publicly at the age of 10. The proposal was as unprecedented as it was unwise. For one thing, it violated the Evangelical doctrine of adult baptism, and as a consequence it caused much dissension within the Plymouth Brethren. Nevertheless, Philip was determined, and when a man as zealous as he was so determined, there was little his fellow saints could do to stop him. Edmund's interpretation of his father's motives is severe: "He wished to secure me finally, exhaustively, before the age of puberty could dawn, before my soul was fettered with the love of carnal things. He thought that if I could now be identified with the 'saints,' I could stand on exactly their footing, a habit of conformity would be secured." Whatever the case may have been, young Edmund dutifully submitted to the ordeal of baptism. He felt in later years that the event nearly marked a turning point in his life, but he was too young at the time to experience anything more than vague unease. Underlining forcefully the dramatic importance of the event for his life as well as the structure of his autobiographical study, Gosse reports, "Everything, since the earliest dawn of consciousness, seemed to have been leading up to it. Everything, afterwards, seemed to be leading down and away from it."

Gosse describes the ceremony itself with some amusement. The elder Gosse, for example, appears pedantically orthodox in his interpretation of a young woman's deliberate fall into the baptismal font:

> It was found that she herself had wished to be a candidate and had earnestly desired to be baptized, but that this had been forbidden by her parents. On the supposition that she fell in by accident, a pious coincidence was detected in this affair; the Lord had preordained that she should be baptized in spite of all opposition. But my Father, in his shrewd way, doubted. He pointed out to us, next morning, that, in the first place, she had not, in any sense, been baptized, as her head had not been immersed; and that, in the second place, she must have deliberately jumped in, since, had she stumbled and fallen forward, her hands and face would have struck the water, whereas they remained quite dry.
>
> (p. 182)

Gosse's irreverent recollections amount to comic relief in the midst of incorrigibly sober proceedings, for no amount of humor can gainsay the fact that the young boy's life was significantly altered by his baptism. What makes the change so painful is our recognition that father and son had interpreted the significance of baptism so differently. To Philip, his son had been chosen and should now be ready to serve. To Edmund, his father was forcing him to fit a way of life which seemed increasingly foreign and intolerable. Very nearly like the discovery of his father's fallibility and the consequent turning in to himself, baptism causes a further breach between father and son and a further dialog on Edmund's part with the self. Once again Gosse indicates that his father's understanding of his son was compromised by his "too-anxious love," and once more he implies that his father was blocking his son's natural development:

> My father was very generous. He used to magnify any little effort that I made, with stammering tongue,

to sanctify a visit; and people, I now see, were accustomed to give me a friendly lead in this direction, so that they might please him by reporting that I had "testified" in the Lord's service. The whole thing, however, was artificial, and was part of my Father's restless inability to let well alone. It was not in harshness or in ill-nature that he worried me so much; on the contrary, it was all part of his too-anxious love. He was in a hurry to see me become a shining light, everything that he had himself desired to be, yet with none of his shortcomings.

Again, following the pattern of the fallibility incident, Gosse turns further from his father and closer to his imaginative, poetic, mysterious self: "Meek as I seemed, and gently respondent, I was always conscious of that innermost quality which I had learned to recognize in my earlier days in Islington, that existence of two in the depths who could speak to one another in inviolable secrecy." Taken together, then, the incidents of discovery—of his father's fallibility and stubbornness—as well as the consequent turning in to the self of each episode clearly indicate that Edmund Gosse saw his struggle into manhood as one of emergence from repression. Moreover, he seems to have felt that his father's actions made both his struggle and his break inevitable: "There was an extraordinary mixture of comedy and tragedy in the situation which is here described, and those who are affected by the pathos of it will not need to have it explained to them that the comedy was superficial and the tragedy essential."

Were it not for the fact that Gosse himself raises the matter of truth in his autobiographical narrative, we could end our remarks here. From beginning to end, **Father and Son** does indeed seem to be "scrupulously true," and the skill displayed in its form and style ought to persuade us to rest our case with an uncritical acceptance of all the book offers. But, as previously mentioned, Gosse makes a wholesale acceptance of the truth of his work rather difficult. To put the matter as simply as possible, Gosse's problems with truth arise directly from his choice of form. He related his father's biography as it coincided with his own autobiography with the result that the character of Philip Gosse is blurred by the co-presence of his son's autobiography. Indeed, Gosse's authorship does not prejudice the account of his father nearly so much as the mere fact that the autobiography runs parallel with the father's biography. While we cannot justifiably quarrel with so colorful, incisive, and ultimately so rewarding a display of imaginative skill as Gosse's, we may, however, question the efficacy of the son's judgments upon his father; or, to put it another way, we may wonder whether Gosse's choice of form has compromised a sense of objectivity and detachment which would make his judgments of his father more acceptable and much more convincing. To suggest that Edmund Gosse was too close to his subject matter to render disinterested comment would be close to the truth were it not for the fact that such a suggestion overlooks the complexity of the autobiographer's character. Rather, what seems to be the case here is that Edmund Gosse was too close to Edmund Gosse to make his interpretation and judgment of his father scrupulously true. Ultimately what is wrong with Gosse's vision is not that it was not wide enough but that it was not deep enough.

The symbolism and imagery of **Father and Son** certainly serve a valuable purpose. They permit Gosse to display what he felt to be his true self—his aesthetic nature—and they are in large part responsible for his attractive prose. Curiously enough, however, they reveal certain blind spots in Gosse's manner which seriously challenge the veracity of his narrative. The floral imagery mentioned earlier is a case in point. Gosse's choice of floral imagery to express his budding aesthetic consciousness seems appropriate enough, but we may question whether the implication that Gosse's father impeded such growth is altogether fair. To be fair to Gosse himself we should be careful to note that he never specifically charges his father with deliberately setting obstacles in his way, but his imagery suggests that such was the case.

Another special case of imagery in *Father and Son* tells a similar story. Gosse portrays himself in the book as a young child who was trapped within a hostile environment, and, significantly enough, the most extended example of such imagery closely follows the account of the baptism:

> I felt like a small and solitary bird, caught and hung out hopelessly and endlessly in a great glittering cage. The clearness of the personal image affected me as all the texts and prayers and predictions had failed to do. I saw myself imprisoned forever in the religious system which had caught me and would whirl my helpless spirit as in the concentric wheels of my nightly vision. I did not struggle against it, because I believed that it was inevitable, and that there was no other way of making peace with the terrible and ever-watchful "God who is a jealous God." But I looked forward to my fate without zeal and without exhilaration, and the fear of the Lord altogether swallowed up and cancelled any notion of the love of Him.

The imagery of the trapped bird at least implies the presence of a keeper. But if this is not clear from the above passage, Gosse himself spells out the implication near the close of the book. He speaks of the inquisitorial correspondence from his father which hounded him daily after his removal to London:

> As time went on, and I grew older and more independent in mind, my Father's anxiety about what he called "the pitfalls and snares which surround on every hand the thoughtless giddy youth of London" became extremely painful to himself. By harping in private upon these "pitfalls"—which brought to my imagination a funny rough woodcut in an old edition of Bunyan, where a devil was seen capering over a sort of box let neatly into the ground—he worked himself up into a frame of mind which was not a little irritating to his hapless correspondent, who was now "snared" indeed, limed by the pen like a bird by the feet, and could not by any means escape. To a peck or a flutter from the bird the implacable fowler would reply.

What all this indicates is an unconscious tipping of the scales in favor of Edmund Gosse—and away from Philip Gosse. Such a shift of sympathy should be expected, we suppose, in any account of a son's emergence from dependence and his assertion of selfhood. It remains to say, however, that Gosse has made his father more obstinate and crueller than he seems to have intended. Indeed, he has accomplished such an unenviable feat because he lacked the sympathy and understanding needed in an assessment of a biographical character who also happened to be his father.

The key to our understanding of Gosse's unconscious revelations as well as the source of the prejudicial characterization of Philip stems unquestionably from Edmund's inability to understand his father's religious beliefs. While we cannot fairly expect Edmund to have accepted his father's religion, we expect more understanding of that religion from one who seeks to be scrupulously truthful in his portrait of his father. Instead

of understanding, however, we find candid admissions of puzzlement and lack of understanding. Recalling his mother's prolonged death agony, for example, Gosse admires his parents' patience but is baffled by their equanimity:

> As I look back upon that tragic time, it is for him that my heart bleeds,—for them both, so singularly fitted as they were to support and cheer one another in an existence which their own innate and cultivated characteristics had made little hospitable to other sources of comfort. This is not to be dwelt on here. But what must be recorded was the extraordinary tranquility, the serene and sensible resignation, with which at length my parents faced the awful hour. Language cannot utter what they suffered, but there was no rebellion, no repining; in their case even an atheist might admit that the overpowering miracle of grace was mightily efficient.

Similarly, Gosse could not understand his father's ability to read his Bible not simply for its scriptural truth but for its apparently abundant pleasures: "It often amazed me, and I am still unable to understand the fact, that my Father, through his long life—or till nearly the close of it—continued to take an eager pleasure in the text of the Bible."

In the episode of the mother's death and in the matter of Biblical pleasure, Gosse so clearly reveals an inability to understand the religious views on which parental conduct was based that we may fairly question the entire portrait he draws of, particularly, Philip Henry Gosse. Our understanding of the father is unfortunately precluded by the son's own lack of understanding. Further, it is of more than passing interest to note that the father had actually counselled his son during the sharp epistolary exchange between Sandhurst and London to try to understand opposing, even hostile viewpoints:

> . . . I strenuously beseech *you,* before you read any further, solemnly to kneel down and ask that, in reading [this letter], you may be kept from pride, & self-justifying, & anger; & that you may be enabled with calmness and candour, at least to *understand* my feeling; to stand, at least hypothetically, on my stand point. . . . I know that you *must* think for yourself; you *must* answer for yourself at the bar of God; I cannot take His solemn & most weighty responsibility from you, if I would. But have I not rights too? You are yet a youth. I am your parent. Have not I the right to counsel, to suggest, to entreat; & if I see you choosing fatal error, have I not the right to remonstrate? Have I not the right to *grieve?*

Whatever we may feel of Philip Henry Gosse in *Father and Son,* we may say with certainty that we know a great deal of Edmund Gosse. This is, of course, to be expected, but what may not be expected are Gosse's unintentional revelations. It seems doubtful that he had portrayed his father as a man deliberately crushing his son's innate gifts of artistic consciousness and expression. But Gosse has given us in *Father and Son* something we anticipate in autobiography but do not always receive—that is, the unconscious revelation of the autobiographer himself.

In Gosse's sense of the words, *Father and Son* is not "scrupulously true." By all accounts it is factually true, and its character interpretation is without question sincere. *Father and Son,* however, tells a truth about Edmund Gosse which actually transcends the truth of which he spoke in his preface. It reveals some of Gosse's blind spots—curiously reminiscent of his father's—in its evidence of bias, unfair implication, and want of understanding. And it reveals, as a result, that there were elements in his own character that Gosse does not seem fully to have understood. Therefore when we suggest that *Father and Son* is not "true," we must not assume that it is false. It is true in the sense that it conveys Gosse's recollection of his first twenty-one years—as true an account, that is, as Gosse perceives. It does not matter that Gosse's portrait of his father is at times unfair, for what matters is that Gosse felt the portrait to be true. His flaws, however, are apparent in his work. They tell us a good deal more of Edmund Gosse than he may have wished us to know, or, indeed, knew himself. (pp. 183-87)

William J. Gracie, Jr., "Truth of Form in Edmund Gosse's 'Father and Son'," in The Journal of Narrative Technique, Vol. 4, No. 3, September, 1974, pp. 176-87.

**JAMES D. WOOLF**   (essay date 1978)

[*Woolf is an American educator and critic. In the following excerpt, he discusses the development of Gosse's aesthetic sense in* Father and Son.]

Edmund Gosse's masterpiece, his autobiographical *Father and Son: A Study of Two Temperaments,* has experienced a wide reception from its first appearance and has been the subject of much important study and criticism; but its central meaning, the aesthetic sense in the son, has only been noticed and never explored or evaluated. In a study of the development of this aesthetic sense, one may clearly observe the author's quest for and definition of self, prime evidence that the book belongs essentially to the genre of autobiography. Scholars and critics have produced important writings on how *Father and Son* can be classified in this or that genre but have left practically untouched how the book qualifies as autobiography—a study which has as its chief characteristic a definition of self.

*Father and Son* has been analyzed variously, and with defensible reasons, as biography, as a novel, and as tragedy. . . . [Gosse] gives a clue to the importance of tragedy in his narrative when he says that in the "mixture of comedy and tragedy in the situation which is here described," the tragedy is the "essential" quality; and [Harold] Nicolson observes that there is "intellectual blindness" in the father (suggestive of both Oedipus and Lear, one might add) and that Gosse employs "all the apparatus of a Greek tragedy" [see excerpt dated 1928]. These generic forms in *Father and Son,* major aesthetic values, are the flowerings in adulthood of the aesthetic sense in the youth of the author, the development of which in his youth is the central meaning in the autobiography.

Recognition of some ingenious techniques, innovative in nature, related to the novel genre in *Father and Son* will also illuminate the significance of the aesthetic sense in the narrative. Employing the fictional device of the objective author as narrator, Gosse enters unobtrusively into the life of his boyhood and youth. This objective stance, fictional nonetheless, is so effective that one major critic declared that the "narrator [is] the little boy" [see Edgar Johnson excerpt dated 1937]. The technique of narration is indeed a remarkable achievement. The device is definitely more skillful than that of Butler in *The Way of All Flesh* (1903) who makes Ernest Pontifex's alter-ego, Overton, the narrator. Butler dilutes the force of his autobiographical expression by dividing it between two voices; Gosse concentrates his in one voice. Gosse is also ingenious, and indeed innovative, in the depiction of his main characters, who assume fictional qualities over and above their historical origins: the fictional Puritan in the father, the Pre-

Raphaelite beauty in the mother, and a British Tom Sawyer pose with its dandy overtones in the son. And the main plot in this epic-like narrative centers directly on the son through the creation of a series of episodes and impressions without any real climax, which constitute essentially an aesthetic growth.

Gosse's concept of aesthetics in *Father and Son,* only informally expressed, is in the tradition of Romantic aesthetics, in which beauty or pleasure functions as a harmonizing faculty between material and spiritual values, and fashions a cultural concept which includes material and social pleasures, as well as pleasures of the mind and spirit. For example, Gosse says he once experienced a marked exhilaration from viewing pictures of some ancient Roman deities, which infuriated his father; he states further that a "notion that beauty palliates evil budded in my mind" and then describes the whole episode as "this aesthetic juncture" in his youth. This position on aesthetics is consonant with the Romantic concept of beauty as a harmonizing principle between the formal or spiritual and the sensuous or material worlds. (The term "this aesthetic juncture" implies a series of such junctures in the book, which actually constitute an aesthetic growth). In another instance, Gosse mentions a "grip in the throat" from listening to his father read rhythmic prose from the Bible and defines the feeling as "in its essence a purely aesthetic emotion"—in other words, a heightened feeling of joy, which is the chief, and a specific, identifying feature in all the aesthetic junctures. Gosse's informal concept of aesthetics is premised only as a working definition and as a part of the strategy for study of the son's aesthetic development in the narrative.

The father's Puritanism, which the son's aesthetic nature reacted against, is in the tradition of English Puritanism, a religion whose main origin is John Calvin's theology. Gosse characterizes his parents as "extreme Calvinists." In a letter to his father in 1873, he defines the Calvinistic Puritanism which his father subscribed to as a religion with four main doctrines: infallibility of the Scriptures, conversion in crisis, asceticism, and election. In the practical application of the religion in their home, delineated in *Father and Son,* Gosse depicts such conditions as effusions of anger from his father, a dismal household spirit, fanaticism, very limited social intercourse, and an absolutist egocentrism in his father. Gosse rejects this concept of Puritanism in the letter of 1873 and in the autobiographical narrative.

The sharp dichotomy posited in the two cultural concepts—aestheticism and Puritanism—affords the author an opportunity to fashion a very effective structural device—a dramatic conflict with tragic overtones. This dichotomy is alluded to in the subtitle of the narrative, "a study of two temperaments," which may be interpreted as a study of the conflict of the aesthetic temperament in the son with the Puritanical temperament in the father. (pp. 134-36)

[William J. Gracie, Jr.] recognizes the significance of the aesthetic nature of the son in the narrative when he declares that *"Father and Son* is the story of the emergence of an aesthetic soul from a hostile environment" [see excerpt dated 1974]. But Gracie does not say anything about the development of the proposition which is premised in the phrase, "emergence of an aesthetic soul from a hostile environment." Eleanor Cecil goes a step further by clearly envisioning the significance of the aestheticism in the son: she recognizes the conflict between the father's "religious fanaticism" and the son's "equally imperative instincts to rule [his] tolerant course through life by 'aesthetic junctures'" [see excerpt dated 1908]. But Cecil does not define an aesthetic experience in the son nor explore its development in the autobiography.

Foreshadowings of the aesthetic junctures appear early in the narrative in remarks about his mother's artistic bent, in a satirical lament of the absence of children's stories in the home, in an ironical delight in seeing as a small boy Puritanical street drama in a description of the almost overpowering natural beauty of the Devonshire coast near the Gosse home, and in the "jolly presence" that Charles Kingsley brought with his Devonshire visits. Once while sitting with his ill mother, Gosse says he read a mediocre religious poem, "The Cameronian's Dream," and had awakened in him for the first time "the sense of romance . . . the kind of nature-romance which is connected with hills, and lakes, and the picturesque costumes of old times."

A short time after his mother's death, Gosse states that a visit he made to his aunt and cousins in Clifton was "a blessed interval in my strenuous childhood"—an early instance of joyous living in which his emotions were allowed expression, in contrast to the dismal atmosphere of his own Puritanical home where rational theology prevailed. Gosse describes this visit (during which he was allowed to say his nightly prayer "under the bed-clothes instead of kneeling at a chair") as an "enchanting period of respite" and a "happy breathing-space." (pp. 136-37)

Gosse was only ten years of age when he had his first genuine aesthetic experience through poetry. He reports that one evening his father, taking a respite from his stern Puritanism, took a copy of Virgil from his book shelf, read silently for a while, and then after closing the book "began to murmur and to chant" the poetry from memory. Gosse declares: "I stopped my play, and listened as if to a nightingale. . . . [A] miracle had been revealed to me, the incalculable, the amazing beauty which could exist in the sound of verses. My prosodical instinct was awakened, quite suddenly that dim evening, as my Father and I sat alone in the breakfast-room after tea, serenely accepting the hour, for once, with no idea of exhortation or profit." The Puritanical father inadvertently introduced his son to the fascination of poetry, which he says "took hold of my heart for ever." The son ends the episode by declaring that afterwards as he walked about in the garden "all my inner being [would] ring out with the sound of 'Formosam resonare doces Amaryllida silvas'." At this early stage in the son's education, aesthetic emotion clearly rivals the didacticism and discipline of the father's Puritanical principles.

The son's first experience with novel reading, which occurred soon after hearing his father read Virgilian poetry, prevented the Puritanical father from overpowering a ten-year-old boy who possessed an aesthetic inclination. This experience occurred in connection with the father's teaching the son geography. Since the father had never been as adamantly opposed to novel reading as the mother, who had died four years previously, he handed the son a long narrative of the West Indies, Michael Scott's *Tom Cringle's Log,* and advised him "to read the descriptions of the sea, and of the mountains of Jamaica" and to skip the "imaginary adventures and conversations." Gosse says that he did not take his father's counsel, but states rather that "these latter were the flower of the book to me. I had never read, never dreamed of anything like them, and they filled my whole horizon with glory and with joy." He declares that reading and re-reading *Tom Cringle's Log* "did more than anything else, in this critical eleventh year of my life, to give

fortitude to my individuality," which was beginning to succumb to Puritanical "pressure" from his father.

If there is one outstanding juncture in Gosse's early aesthetic development, it is his introduction to Shakespeare, which occurred as a result of a social encounter. Among the inhabitants of the Devonshire community where the Gosses lived was the aged James Sheridan Knowles who had been a playwright in his young days. He met young Gosse, marveled at his knowledge of theology and geography, but counseled him to ask the schoolmaster to read some Shakespeare plays in class. The boy relayed the information to the teacher who liked the idea and set his boys to reading aloud, in recitation fashion, successive passages in *The Merchant of Venice.* Gosse declares ecstatically that he was "in the seventh heaven of delight" as he participated in the event, but that the readings abruptly ceased at the end of the first act; he theorizes that his father, who boasted that he had never read a line of Shakespeare, suggested that the schoolmaster return to the "ordinary" curriculum. Nevertheless, young Gosse had been introduced to Shakespeare and had experienced a highly significant aesthetic juncture.

After the father's second marriage, he read during spring evenings to his new bride from a volume of Sir Walter Scott's poetry, which was in the collection of books that the lady had brought with her. These readings led, inadvertently from the viewpoint of the father's Puritanism, to young Gosse's introduction to Dickens, another highlight in the son's aesthetic maturation. . . . Gosse declares that he was allowed to read *Pickwick* "by which I was instantly and gloriously enslaved. My shouts of laughing at the richer passages were almost scandalous, and led to my being reproved for disturbing my Father while engaged, in an upper room, in the study of God's Word. I must have expended months on the perusal of *Pickwick,* for I used to rush through a chapter, and then read it over again very slowly, word for word, and then shut my eyes to realize the figures and the action." Young Gosse thereby experienced another major juncture in his aesthetic development. He says he was probably "the latest of the generation who accepted Mr. Pickwick with an unquestioning and hysterical abandonment"—an aesthetic reaction which is in direct conflict with the dismal outlook that resulted from his father's strictly rational principles of Puritanism. (pp. 137-38)

The stepmother's book collection was the source not only of poetry for the son but also of art materials, from which he learned a principle in aesthetic philosophy that came into direct conflict with a Puritanical doctrine of his father—that the Puritan God is the only means of ridding man of evil. Gosse says he discovered a book in his stepmother's collection which contained pictures of "steel engravings" of some "old Greek" [sic] deities. "These attracted me violently," Gosse continues, "and here for the first time I gazed on Apollo with his proud gesture, Venus in her undulations, the kirtled shape of Diana, and Jupiter voluminously bearded." He reports that his father's "face blazed white with Puritan fury" and that he appeared as one who had just "escaped with horror from some Hellenic hippodrome," when he learned of the son's experience and berated the statues as indicative of the "vices of the heathen"— an example of the novelistic Gosse picturing his father as a fictional Puritan in contest with foes. Gosse says he "bowed" to his father's remarks but did not accept his "condemnation of the Greeks." Rather, he concludes: "The dangerous and pagan notion that beauty palliates evil budded in my mind." . . . At this juncture in his education, the breach widened markedly between the father's narrow Puritanism and the son's newly developing aesthetic philosophy.

Fortified with a major principle in aesthetic philosophy, the son was better prepared to defend his literary pursuits in the face of Puritanical opposition. His continued reading in Shakespeare, during which he says he became "intelligently" acquainted with the poet-dramatist, afforded a test of his newly-acquired knowledge and became indeed an important juncture in his aesthetic maturation. . . . At this aesthetic juncture, when he was "under the full spell of the Shakespearean necromancy," Gosse states that his father took him to London to attend an Evangelical conference. Here he heard Shakespeare denounced as a "lost soul" and concluded, in confusion, that literature tempted him to stray "at right angles to that direct strait way which leadeth to salvation." But he brings his "casuistry" and propensity for magic into play by imagining that when "Shakespeare wrote any passage of intoxicating beauty . . . he was beginning to breathe the rapture that faith in Christ brings." . . . Magic and beauty combine to counteract the dismal effect of the Puritanical condemnation of Shakespeare and to allow young Gosse further aesthetic maturity.

A conspicuous juncture in the son's aesthetic development was his surreptitious purchase of the combined "poetical works of Ben Jonson and Christopher Marlowe." He states that he could make nothing of Ben Jonson but that when he turned to Marlowe's *Hero and Leander,* he was "lifted to a heaven of passion and music. . . . [It] all seemed to my fancy intoxicating beyond anything I had ever even dreamed of, since I had not yet become acquainted with any of the modern romanticists." This volume also got Gosse into "sad trouble," he reports, because his father learned of the book, burned it subsequently, and then "with a pale face and burning eyes" (the fictional element again) denounced his son for bringing such an "abominable" work into the house. At this stage in his development, the son's aesthetic exuberance and maturing mind are able to parry successfully his father's Puritanical admonishment.

Gosse declares that during his sixteenth year his aesthetic interests became intense and multiple: he "read with unchecked voracity, and in several curious directions. Shakespeare now passed into my possession entire. . . . I made acquaintance with Keats, who entirely captivated me; with Shelley, whose *Queen Mab* at first repelled me from the threshold of his edifice; and with Wordsworth, for the exercise of whose magic I was still far too young. My Father presented me with the entire bulk of Southey's stony verse, which I found it impossible to penetrate, but my stepmother lent me *The Golden Treasury,* in which almost everything seemed exquisite." Gosse states that this extension of his "intellectual powers" did not lessen his religious faith. Rather, he says he diligently searched the Scriptures on his own initiative and discovered, "without animosity [a truly Christian note], the strange narrowness of my Father's system, which seemed to take into consideration only a selected circle of persons, a group of disciples peculiarly illuminated, and to have no message whatever for the wider Christian community." Gosse's cultural vision, now centered in aestheticism and aided by a maturing intellect, has finally overshadowed the narrow Puritanism of his father.

Shortly before he moved to London in his seventeenth year for a position in the British Museum, Gosse states that his brain was a "huddled mixture of 'Endymion' and the Book of Revelation, John Wesley's hymns and *Midsummer Night's Dream.* . . . In my hot and silly brain, Jesus and Pan held sway together, as in a wayside chapel discordantly and impishly consecrated to Pagan and to Christian rites. . . . I had been reading a good deal of poetry, but my heart had translated Apollo and Bacchus into terms of exalted Christian faith." He states that at this juncture in his education he prayed to Christ to take him to Himself in Paradise. Receiving no reply but the dancing of branches in a tree, he declares that the "extravagant faith" of his father "began to totter and crumble" and that thenceforth he and his father "walked in opposite hemispheres of the soul." Here the son's aestheticism has clearly become independent of his father's Puritanical influence.

During his first two or three years in London, Gosse continued in his father's faith, even taught Sunday School a while, and translated from Dean Alford's edition of the Greek New Testament, which his father had presented him as a gift. Although he promised his father that he would read and translate regularly from the New Testament, he soon failed to keep the promise, and a "growing distaste for the Holy Scriptures began to occupy my thoughts, and to surprise as much as it scandalised me. My desire was to continue to delight in those sacred pages, for which I still had an instinctive veneration. Yet I could not but observe the difference between the zeal with which I snatched at a volume of Carlyle or Ruskin—since these magicians were now first revealing themselves to me—and the increasing languor with which I took up Alford for my daily 'passage'." At this stage of his education, Gosse has fully centered his cultural interest in aesthetic literature and has achieved aesthetic maturity.

Reading Carlyle and Ruskin is the last of the aesthetic junctures which Gosse presents from his objective authorial stance, but the evidence is clear and overwhelming that the son's inner self points to a life of literary endeavor in adulthood rather than Puritan theology. This inner self is synonymous with "individuality," which is related to a strain of psychology in the son running through the narrative. The individualist psychology has a direct bearing on the process of aesthetic growth in the son. When he discovers privately that his father is not infallible and like God, he also discovers that he "found a companion and a confidant in myself" and that there "was a secret in this world [which] belonged to me and to a somebody who lived in the same body with me"—suggestive of a harmony in his inner being involving self, happiness, and "God." This inward self coupled with the outward self that conformed to the demands of his father's Puritanism he calls his "dual individuality." . . . In the conclusion to the narrative, Gosse alludes again to this "dual individuality" by declaring that the son "took a human being's privilege to fashion his inner life for himself." This last statement is not only concluding but also summarily thematic in the book—thematic in the allusion to the aesthetic focus of his "inner life" or his "innate and persistent self."

Near the end of *Father and Son,* Gosse for a brief moment steps out of the role of objective narrator and speaks openly as his subjective self in a manner which might be interpreted as an artistic flaw but which actually reinforces the autobiographical quality of the work. He writes:

> Let me speak plainly. After my long experience, after my patience and forbearance, I have surely the right to protest against the untruth . . . that evangelical religion, or any religion in a violent form, is a wholesome or valuable or desirable adjunct to human life. It divides heart from heart. It sets up a vain, chimerical ideal, in the barren pursuit of which all the tender, indulgent affections, all the genial play of life, all the exquisite pleasures and soft resignations of the body, all that enlarges and calms the soul, are exchanged for what is harsh and void and negative.

This is a humanistic position (stated as effectively in the subjective person as in the objective) which supports the validity of the aesthetic sense by characterizing it as a wholesome human attribute. The inner self in maturity, aesthetically centered, has developed to the extent that it can speak out openly—so that the "subjective" and "objective" selves are merged. The aesthetic self is as mature as the intellectual or objective self. (pp. 139-42)

Gosse makes two important statements in *Father and Son* which express faith in both original and traditional Christianity. Contrasting the narrowness of Puritan concerns with genuine Christian charity, Gosse declares with telling understatement that "the moral and physical improvement of persons who have been neglected . . . seems to have formed some part of the Saviour's original design." He also states that as a youth he "longed to attend the Anglican and Roman services," but knew that his father would be wounded if he entered "the fine parish church of our village, or the stately Puginesque cathedral which Rome had just erected at its side."

*Father and Son* is indeed genuine autobiography; it is in the tradition of Mill and Newman who in autobiography extend the dimensions of Victorian culture. Mill in his *Autobiography* moves from an exclusive rationalism to a philosophical position which provides for human emotions—a recognition of the therapeutic value of the aesthetic sense. Newman in *Apologia* moves from an Evangelical Protestant theology, emphatically rationalistic, to a Roman Catholicism which recognizes aesthetic and emotional, as well as intellectual and spiritual, characteristics in the human personality. Gosse in *Father and Son* moves from a narrow Puritanism to a profound Christianity which provides for material and aesthetic, as well as for intellectual and spiritual, values in human life. The main methods in all three autobiographies, processes of escape from the fetters of unsuitable cultures, are similar, and so are the results—three great definitions of self that respectively expand the dimensions of philosophy, religion, and aesthetics in Victorian England. In the case of Gosse, as with the earlier Mill and Newman, the details of the method and the final results appear to be what Roy Pascal means by the "structure of truth" of the inner self in genuine autobiography. (pp. 142-43)

> *James D. Woolf, "'In the Seventh Heaven of Delight': The Aesthetic Sense in Gosse's 'Father and Son',"* in Interspace and the Inward Sphere: Essays on Romantic and Victorian Self, *edited by Norman A. Anderson and Margene E. Weiss, Western Illinois University, 1978, pp. 134-44.*

**BRIAN FINNEY**  (essay date 1985)

[*In the following excerpt, Finney examines Gosse's relationship with his father and his depiction of their conflict in* Father and Son.]

Edmund Gosse first wrote a book-length biography of his father shortly after the father's death in 1888. His death was in keeping with his life, being the result of bronchitis which he contracted from studying the stars on a succession of cold winter nights in expectation of the personal coming of the Lord. *The Life of Philip Henry Gosse F.R.S.* appeared in 1890. In it Gosse wrote of his father in that curiously ambiguous tone that was to characterize the later *Father and Son*: "He was not one who could accept half-truths or see in the twilight. It must be high noon or else utter midnight with a character so positive as his."

If George Moore is to be believed it was he who first suggested to Gosse the idea of *Father and Son* after reading *The Life of P. H. Gosse*. "I missed the child," he told Gosse. "I missed the father's life and your life as you lived it together—a great psychological work waits to be written . . ." Gosse demurred at the time on the grounds that too many of the individuals concerned were still alive. Much later George Moore claims to have suggested telling the father's life in the first-person voice of the son. Gosse, according to Moore, agreed that that would overcome the final difficulty lingering in his mind and proceeded to write the book in 1906. (pp. 141-42)

[The book is both by the nature of its] inspiration (Moore's suggested use of the first person) and of its viewpoint (that of the son) autobiographical. It covers the first sixteen years of the life of Edmund Gosse, from his birth in 1849 to his departure from the family home in Devon for London in 1865. An Epilogue briefly continues the narrative for a further five years to his final break with his father in 1870. Both his parents were extreme Calvinists, members of the Plymouth Brethren. The father was a zoologist of repute who became a Fellow of the Royal Society. However his Calvinist beliefs led him to refute the new theories of evolution making themselves felt in the 1850s. His stand brought ridicule on him in scientific circles and left him in a backwater of his profession. Gosse's mother was a writer of religious verse and popular tracts who died of cancer when the son was seven. On her deathbed his mother's dying words sealed the young boy's dedication to God, a task the father proceeded to devote himself to with the utmost vigour, especially after their move to Marychurch in Devonshire where the father took charge of the local band of the Plymouth Brethren. When his schooling ended Gosse left home for London where his father's friend Charles Kingsley found him an opening in the cataloguing section of the British Museum. But Gosse was still subjected for a further five years to what he calls the daily "torment of the postal inquisition" from his father. He didn't manage to break this extenuated form of parental control until he was twenty-one, when he claimed to have finally freed himself "to fashion his inner life for himself."

How successfully he separated himself from his father can best be judged by *Father and Son* itself, written in his late fifties. One's first impression is of a remarkably balanced and impartial account of a childhood warped and constricted by an inhumanly severe upbringing. Natural resentment and anger appear to have been supplanted by love, forgiveness and understanding on the part of the ageing and reflective son. The distance and seeming impartiality which he maintains from his painful memories leave the feeling that here is a highly civilized and humane individual who has had to overcome unusual impediments to reach the calm state of mind in which he recalls his earlier life. It is one of the literary achievements of the book that Gosse contrives to establish this perspective on such emotionally charged material. The strategy was essential if he was to win acceptance from the Edwardian public for a story which up to 1907 could be told only fictionally—as in Samuel Butler's *The Way of All Flesh* (1903). Despite a few outraged reviews, Gosse's book won widespread approval judging from its sales during the first year.

However closer examination of the subtext reveals a more ambiguous and simultaneously a more fascinating picture of the relations prevailing between father and son. The book is at one and the same time more subversive of the father's role than Gosse pretends to be the case, and yet reflects a greater continuing dependence of the son on the father figure than its author seems to realize. Both Gosse and his Edwardian readers appear to be communicating at a second subconscious level where his anti-paternalistic feelings are voiced more strongly and found acceptable by his readers partly because of the way in which the father is seen to live on in the son. By embodying within the book those emotionally ambivalent feelings towards his father which, according to Freud, are inherent in human nature, Gosse instinctually struck a chord that reverberated in all his readers.

These deep conflicting feelings towards his father are buried in a narrative that ostensibly seeks to attribute the primitive conflict between father and son to the impersonal forces of historical change, a moment in the evolutionary time scale on which the father turned his back. Both protagonists are presented as passive agents blown in opposite directions by the winds of historical necessity. The Preface characterizes these winds as "educational and religious conditions which, having passed away, will never return." Chapter I places father and son in two epochs, their mutual affection "assailed by forces in comparison with which the changes that health or fortune or place introduce are as nothing." The son, it suggests, cannot help being carried forward on the stream of modern progress. The book is offered as no more than a "document," "record," "diagnosis" or "study" which is "scrupulously true." It quotes at intervals from objective documents such as his mother's diary and his father's notes and letters to his son. Gosse adopts the tone and approach of a naturalist observer—modelled primarily on his father. Gosse, the conscious author, sincerely believed that these wider forces justified the more personal material on which he drew. At one point he catagorically denies that he is writing an autobiography, a curious claim unless one appreciates the extent to which he needed to think that his own experiences were only illustrations of larger historical movements. Shortly after publication he informed one correspondent that the core of the book lay in its "exposure of the modern sentimentality which thinks it can parade all the prettiness of religion without really resigning its will and its thought to faith." He clearly is genuine in believing that this is the central theme of the book. Four years before his death he informed another correspondent that his aim in the book had been "to set down a perfectly faithful and unadorned picture of a succession of moral and religious incidents which can, in all probability, never recur." It is as if he had convinced himself in the course of writing **Father and Son** that this was his subject— not his father in person so much as "the puritanism of which he was perhaps the latest surviving type." What "divides heart from heart," he asserts in the Epilogue, is not individual temperament but "any religion in a violent form." His father just happened to offer the best instance he knew of such religious fanaticism, this implies.

But one has only to continue reading the passage from which the last quotation is taken to realize that this lofty stance allows Gosse to discharge emotions which far exceed the pretext for their release. His diatribe against extreme Calvinism hides from him (though not from an alert reader) his need to release more personal feelings against his father's oppression than he can consciously admit to. He goes on to assert that evangelical religion sets up a "vain chimerical ideal" which can lead only to the "barren pursuit" of "what is harsh and void and negative," and proceeds to call it "stern," "ignorant," "sterile," "cruel" and "horrible" all in the same paragraph. These emotive epithets are more likely to have originated in what David Grylls has called a surviving animus against the father [in *Guardians and Angels* (1978)], an animus which he has long since repressed and now surfaces indirectly. On only one occasion does he admit to a child's patricidal impulse towards his father. Whipped by the father for a misdemeanour he can no longer remember, he experienced such "a flame of rage," he writes, that he "went about the house for some days with a murderous hatred" of him locked in his heart. Normally one has to look to the subtext and especially to the imagery which constitutes a vital component of it to appreciate how much anger and resentment Gosse unconsciously harboured towards his father.

Gosse was born on the same day as his father received a green swallow from Jamaica. Betraying no special emotion, the elder Gosse recorded both events consecutively in his diary for that date. In the autobiography Gosse repeatedly uses images of birds and plants to present himself as another product of nature whose freedom and growth has been inhibited by his naturalist father's interference. On at least three occasions Gosse compares himself to "a small and solitary bird, caught and hung out hopelessly and endlessly in a great glittering cage," "a bird fluttering in the network of my Father's will," "'snared' indeed, and limed . . . like a bird by the feet." By extension the image turns the father into a cruel captor who heartlessly inhibits another's life force for his own ends. The same charge emerges from Gosse's comparisons of his situation to a plant, growing on a rocky ledge with just sufficient soil to flower alone on the rarified heights or to one "on which a pot has been placed, with the effect that the centre is crushed and arrested, while shoots are straggling up to the light on all sides." What is worse, although his father was aware of his contorted growth, "all he did was try to straighten the shoots, without removing the pot which kept them resolutely down." If the pot represents religious fanaticism then it has been placed there in the first instance by his father and mother.

Read metaphorically, these passages reveal that Gosse's subconscious charge against his father is that he made of his son an extension of his ego. The victim of an overdeveloped moral conscience, the father unconsciously spread his load of guilt among those most subject to his influence, pre-eminently his son. Because he was convinced that his failure to win approval for his anti-evolutionary book was due to some hidden sin within himself, "act after act became taboo, not because each was sinful in itself, but because it might lead others into sin." Yet behind his father's evangelical zeal lurked a streak of vanity which expressed itself by seeking the advancement of his son. The most obvious example of this is his insistence on having the ten-year-old boy baptized and admitted to communion as if he had attained an adult's state of grace through conversion. A letter written by Gosse at this time refers to his public baptism as "an initiation into every kind of publicity and glory," which suggests that the son had at least temporarily caught from his father his narcissistic attitude towards the ceremony. In the book after the ceremony the father indulges his son quite uncharacteristically, only warning him against spiritual pride. But it is personal pride that is responsible for the father's usurpation of a child's customary privileges, depriving him of pictures, all forms of fiction and, above all, companions of his own age.

Adding to the father's power over his son is the fact that he is a fanatical minister of an extreme Protestant sect. As such his authority becomes identified in the young boy's mind with the Divine Will whose guidance the father is for ever seeking. (pp. 142-46)

At the age of five or six Gosse is still identifying with the father's powers, trying to reproduce them by "an infantile species of natural magic" that involves bringing dead animals back to life and other such fantasies which "approached the ideas of savages at a very early stage of development." Even more illuminating is the six-year-old's attempts to flout his father's and God's commands by praying to a wooden idol—a chair. When no divine punishment follows, his confidence in his father's knowledge of the Divine Will, already shaken earlier, is further undermined. But instead of following the usual pattern of introjecting parental authority in the form of a super-ego, Gosse invents an alter ego, as Roger Porter has shown [see Additional Bibliography]. Porter points out how "the twin roles of this second self—analytical and aggressive—suggest Gosse's desire both to imitate his father and to transcend him by expressing a forbidden mode of behaviour." But what Porter does not say is that these patterns of behaviour conform to a psychosocial phase of development normally associated with a one–three-year-old child. At the age of nine Gosse is still seeking to identify with his father by writing childish imitations of his father's monographs on seaside creatures. The father's constant supervision is responsible for his son's retarded development and for his emotional ambivalence towards this patriarchal figure. Right up to the end of his son's adolescence the elder Gosse continues to suspect, like Job, that his son might have sinned, rejoicing in the excuse this gives him to come nearer to his God, supposedly on his son's behalf.

Equally Gosse is subconsciously driven to express the other side of this ambivalence towards his father in his autobiography. Patricidal fantasies are matched by a desire to earn his father's love and approval that survives even the actual father's death. What else impelled him to write not one but two books about his father? It is highly significant that Gosse's memory fails him whenever he breaks out of what he calls their "Calvinist cloister" and temporarily becomes a normal child surrounded by other children or adults happy to allow him to pursue a child's usual preoccupations. After his mother's death he spends three idyllic months with relatives in Bristol, "relapsing, to a degree that would have filled my Father with despair, into childish thoughts and childish language." But, he admits, "of this little happy breathing-space I have nothing to report." During his eleventh year his new stepmother encourages him to become one of a gang of eight to ten local boys of his own age. Gosse notes how once again his memory of that summer spent in their company loses all distinctions. "I have no difficulty in recalling, with the minuteness of a photograph, scenes in which my father and I were the sole actors within the four walls of a room, but of the glorious life among wild boys on the margin of the sea I have nothing but vague and broken impressions, delicious and illusive."

The theatrical metaphor in the last quotation highlights the fact that for Gosse his solitary encounters with his father had a glamour and gave him a sense of his own importance as leading co-actor besides which his life outside the home seemed pale and insignificant. Was it not his father's ban on works of imaginative literature that lent them such excitement that he felt compelled to make his living from them as an adult? At the same time he recounts with unbelievable indulgence his father's reason for not agreeing with a fellow member of the Plymouth Brethren that Shakespeare was a lost soul in hell. How are we to know, the father tells his delighted son, that Shakespeare was not converted late in life? Unable to maintain his separate adult identity from that of his father, Gosse within a paragraph assumes full responsibility for this blatant piece

of sophistry, claiming that "it was with a like casuistry that I condoned my other intellectual and personal pleasures." His first attempts to write poetry took the form of pietistic verse, the only form likely to prove acceptable to his father. Nor was his break with his father as decisive as the book makes it seem by positioning it on the final page. As Gide and others have testified, Gosse continued to imitate his father long after his death, assuming the same authoritarian and puritanical attitudes, showing the same discomfort in company, the same tendency towards pedantry in his literary writings. But it is not really necessary to cite such biographical evidence to show how dependent he had grown on his father's actual or remembered company. But for his piety, Gosse concludes, his father would have been "a charming companion," "a delightful parent" and "a courteous and engaging friend." Gosse seizes on this dichotomy to express his own ambivalence towards his father, exposing extreme evangelicism to ridicule so as to be able to preserve the charming companion of his childhood for his life-long admiration and love. It is this half-buried emotional content, complex and paradoxical, that imbues *Father and Son* with its true fascination. (pp. 147-49)

> *Brian Finney, "Parents and Children," in his* The Inner I: British Literary Autobiography of the Twentieth Century, *Oxford University Press, 1985, pp. 138-61.*

## ADDITIONAL BIBLIOGRAPHY

Arana, R. Victoria. "Sir Edmund Gosse's *Father and Son:* Autobiography as Comedy." *Genre* 10, No. 1 (1977): 63-76.
    Defines the "true nature" of *Father and Son* as intentionally comic.

"Literary Gossip." *The Athenaeum,* No. 4185 (11 January 1908): 44-5.
    Anonymous correspondence suggesting that an early essay by Philip Henry Gosse on his own childhood reveals that he may not have been "quite so severe or mirthless" or as lacking in understanding as a reader of *Father and Son* would be led to believe.

Baring, Maurice. "Ibsen." In his *Punch and Judy & Other Essays,* pp. 245-50. Garden City, N.Y.: Doubleday, Page & Co., 1924.
    Credits Gosse with introducing Ibsen's works to English audiences in 1872 and praises Gosse's biography of Ibsen.

Baylen, Joseph O. "Edmund Gosse, William Archer, and Ibsen in Late Victorian Britain." *Tennessee Studies in Literature* 20 (1975): 124-37.
    Details Archer's role as a popularizer of Ibsen's dramas in England, and examines the disputes between Gosse and Archer regarding their respective translations, published editions, and copyrighted performances of Ibsen's plays.

Bourne, Randolph. "The Morality of Sacrifice." *The Dial* XLV, No. 775 (19 October 1918): 309-10.
    Finds that Gosse presents a limited but appealing historical understanding of France's role in World War I in his *Three French Moralists*.

Caserio, Robert L. "Plot, Purpose, and the Modern Self." In his *Plot, Story, and the Novel: From Dickens and Poe to the Modern Period,* pp. 167-97. Princeton: Princeton University Press, 1979.
    Characterizes Gosse's purpose in *Father and Son* as an attempt to discredit his father's religious convictions.

Charteris, Evan. *The Life and Letters of Sir Edmund Gosse.* New York: Harper & Brothers, 1931, 524 p.
    Earliest life of Gosse, comprising biographical chapters interspersed with chronologically arranged letters.

"Mr. Gosse's Edition of Gray." *The Critic* n.s. III, No. 59 (14 February 1885): 74-5.
Commends the scholarship evident in *The Works of Thomas Gray in Prose and Verse*.

Dobson, Austin. "Edmund Gosse's Poems." *The Living Age* 272, No. 3529 (24 February 1912): 474-77.
Favorable review of Gosse's *Collected Poems*, noting also Gosse's estimable reputation as a literary critic and the place he secured in English literary history through his use of French verse forms.

Drinkwater, John. "The Poetry of Edmund Gosse." *The Bookman* (London) 63, No. 5 (July 1926): 536-43.
Favorable appraisal of Gosse's poetry.

Fleishman, Avrom. "Turning Figures." In his *Figures of Autobiography: The Language of Self-Writing in Victorian and Modern England*, pp. 275-309. Berkeley: University of California Press, 1983.
Discusses *Father and Son* as exemplary of the emphasis in late nineteenth- and early twentieth-century autobiographical works on secular rather than spiritual development.

Folkenflik, Vivian, and Folkenflik, Robert. "Word and Language in *Father and Son*." *Biography* 2, No. 2 (Spring 1979): 157-74.
Analyzes the language of *Father and Son* as a supporting element of what the critics call the book's central claim upon the reader's attention: its factual accuracy.

Freeman, John. "Edmund Gosse." In his *English Portraits and Essays*, pp. 149-74. London: Hodder and Stoughton, 1924.
Praises Gosse as a literary critic who is especially accomplished at creating verbal sketches of his subjects.

Grosskurth, Phyllis. "Churton Collins: Scourge of the Late Victorians." *University of Toronto Quarterly* XXXIV, No. 3 (April 1965): 254-68.
Details some of Collins's more notorious critical attacks upon literary figures, including Gosse, Alfred Tennyson, Algernon Swinburne, and John Addington Symonds.

Henderson, Archibald. "The Ibsen Harvest." *The Atlantic Monthly* CII, No. 2 (August 1908): 258-62.
Considers Gosse's role in interpreting Ibsen's life and works to English-speaking readers and audiences, together with discussion of other notable Ibsen critics, translators, and biographers.

Mais, S. P. B. "Edmund Gosse." In his *Some Modern Authors*, pp. 204-10. New York: Dodd, Mead and Co., 1923.
Considers *Father and Son* among the finest of literary and spiritual biographies, ranking it with Samuel Butler's *The Way of All Flesh*.

Malcolm, Janet. "The Unreliable Genius." *The New York Times Review of Books* XXXII, No. 4 (14 March 1985): 7-8, 10-12, 14.
Biographical and critical sketch of Gosse and a favorable review of Ann Thwaite's *Edmund Gosse: A Literary Landscape, 1849-1928*.

Mattheisen, Paul F., and Millgate, Michael. "Introduction" to *Transatlantic Dialogue: Selected American Correspondence of Edmund Gosse*, by Edmund Gosse, edited by Paul F. Mattheisen and Michael Millgate, pp. 3-55. Austin: University of Texas Press, 1965.
Biographical and critical discussion dealing with some of the chief events and controversies in Gosse's life.

Moore, Rayburn S. "A 'Literary-Gossippy Friendship': Henry James's Letters to Edmund Gosse." *The Southern Review* 20, No. 3 (July 1984): 570-90.
Reprints some letters from James to Gosse, with an introductory essay commenting on their long friendship.

Morrissette, Bruce A. "Early English and American Critics of French Symbolism." In *Studies in Honor of Frederick W. Shipley*, pp. 159-80. St. Louis: Washington University Studies, 1942.
Includes discussion of Gosse's contributions to English-language explications of French Symbolism.

"Gray's Works." *The Nation* XL, No. 1027 (5 March 1885): 204-05.
Largely favorable review noting some editorial errors in Gosse's edition of Thomas Gray's works.

Panichas, George A. "A Family Matter." In his *The Courage of Judgment: Essays in Criticism, Culture, and Society*, pp. 245-49. Knoxville: The University of Tennessee Press, 1982.
Compares *Father and Son* with *My Father and Myself* (1969) by J. R. Ackerley, finding Gosse's volume "the more classically executed in its dignity" and more attuned to larger social issues.

Peterson, Linda H. "Gosse's *Father and Son*: The Evolution of Scientific Autobiography." In her *Victorian Autobiography: The Tradition of Self-Interpretation*, pp. 156-91. New Haven: Yale University Press, 1986.
Maintains that *Father and Son* is essentially a sophisticated parody of traditional autobiography.

Porter, Roger J. "Edmund Gosse's *Father and Son*: Between Form and Flexibility." *The Journal of Narrative Technique* 5, No. 3 (September 1975): 174-95.
Examines the strategies that Gosse depicted himself using to gain independence from his father's narrow view of the world. Porter's discussion assumes that *Father and Son* is as balanced and unbiased as Gosse claimed in his introduction.

Shepherd, Henry E. Review of *From Shakespeare to Pope*, by Edmund Gosse. *PMLA* 1 (1884-85): 149-55.
Calls *From Shakespeare to Pope* "pleasing" and "lucid" as a popular introduction for students of English literature, but maintains that it lacks depth and breadth of scholarship.

Sitwell, Sir Osbert. "Sir Edmund Gosse." In his *Noble Essences: A Book of Characters*, pp. 40-76. Boston: Little, Brown, and Co., 1950.
Chatty, sympathetic reminiscence.

Squire, J. C. "Mr. Gosse's Criticisms." In his *Books Reviewed: Critical Essays on Books and Authors*, pp. 109-15. 1920. Reprint. Port Washington, N.Y.: Kennikat Press, 1968.
Favorable review of *Books on the Table*, a collection of Gosse's periodical essays on literature.

Swinnerton, Frank. "Edmund Gosse." In his *Critics Who Have Influenced Taste*, pp. 63-5. London: Geoffrey Bles, 1965.
Discusses Gosse's alleged "unsoundness" as a critic.

Thwaite, Ann. *Edmund Gosse: A Literary Landscape*. Chicago: University of Chicago Press, 1984, 567 p.
Excellent biography covering every aspect of Gosse's life and career with extensive documentation from contemporary sources, including unpublished Gosse family papers.

Review of *Father and Son*, by Edmund Gosse. *The Times Literary Supplement*, No. 305 (14 November 1907): 347.
Questions the propriety of exposing "the weaknesses and inconsistencies of a good man who is also one's father."

Waugh, Alec. "Edmund Gosse." *The Virginia Quarterly Review* 32, No. 1 (Winter 1956): 69-78.
Reminiscence based on Waugh's childhood memories of Gosse and on the recollections of Waugh's father, Arthur Waugh.

West, Rebecca. "Gosse." In her *Ending in Earnest: A Literary Log*, pp. 91-5. Garden City: Doubleday, Doran & Co., 1931.
Sketch of Gosse that attempts to explain his fondness for praise and for close association with eminent figures.

Woolf, James D. *Sir Edmund Gosse*. New York: Twayne, 1972, 180 p.
Biographical and critical study.

———. Introduction to *The Unequal Yoke*, by Edmund Gosse, pp. 1-12. Delmar, N.Y.: Scholars' Facsimiles & Reprints, 1975.
Critical discussion of Gosse's first, anonymously published novel.

———. "The Benevolent Christ in Gosse's *Father and Son*." *Prose Studies* 3, No. 2 (September 1980): 65-75.
Examines Gosse's religious beliefs, placing him within a context of nineteenth-century theological liberalism.

# Pauline Elizabeth Hopkins

## 1859-1930

American novelist, dramatist, short story writer, editor, and biographer.

A minor black author of the late nineteenth and early twentieth centuries, Hopkins was one of the first writers to introduce racial and social themes into the framework of traditional nineteenth-century romance novels. In her most important work, *Contending Forces: A Romance Illustrative of Negro Life North and South,* published in 1900, she propounded the ideology of W. E. B. Du Bois, an early advocate of liberal education and political rights for black Americans, within the literary conventions of the romances that were popular during her era. Throughout her work, Hopkins represented racial injustice, challenged widely held notions about her race, and emphasized self-reliance as an important component of social advancement for black Americans.

Hopkins was born in Portland, Maine, and grew up in Boston, where she attended public schools and graduated from Girls' High School. She was twenty-one when her musical drama *Slaves' Escape; or, The Underground Railroad* was produced, with Hopkins and members of her family in the cast. For several years following this production, Hopkins toured as a singer with her family's performing group, the Hopkins' Colored Troubadors. During the 1890s she worked at various clerical jobs and as a public lecturer. In 1900 Hopkins's short story "The Mystery Within Us" appeared in the first issue of the *Colored American* magazine, and that same year her first novel, *Contending Forces,* was published. During the early 1900s Hopkins served on the editorial staff of the *Colored American* and eventually became the magazine's literary editor. Her subsequent novels, short stories, and nonfiction appeared primarily in the *Colored American* between 1901 and 1903. She may also have published fiction under the pseudonym Sarah A. Allen, but the authorship of these works remains uncertain. Ill health caused Hopkins to leave the magazine's staff in 1904, but she continued writing and occasionally published fiction and nonfiction in black-owned journals, while supporting herself largely through clerical work. She died in a fire in 1930.

*Contending Forces* is a historical romance tracing the experiences of one black family throughout the nineteenth century, from slavery in the West Indies and the American South to freedom in Boston and New Orleans. The novel illuminates the political, economic, and social problems encountered by black people in antebellum America. Hopkins stated that she wrote *Contending Forces* in order to "faithfully portray the inmost thoughts and feelings of the Negro with all the fire and romance which lie dormant in our history," and to help "raise the stigma of degradation" from her race—something that she maintained black people had to do for themselves. *Contending Forces* earned Hopkins neither literary fame nor financial success during her lifetime, and it began to receive critical attention only after her death. In an early survey of black American authors, Vernon Loggins considered *Contending Forces* overly complicated and sensational. In 1948 Hugh M. Gloster also pronounced Hopkins an untalented narrator, but commended *Contending Forces* for providing "interesting sidelights on the struggles of a middle-class Negro family for education, em-

ployment, and social adjustment in post-bellum Boston." Most recent critics agree that *Contending Forces* is overplotted and confusingly constructed; nevertheless, they consider it an important historical and sociological document that portrays the effect of Du Bois's social and educational programs on the black community and the role of black women in nineteenth-century America.

Throughout her career Hopkins protested the inequities suffered by her race, advocating assimilation and integration with the white community as a remedy to racial injustice. Hopkins's presumption of the superior value of white culture and her advocacy of assimilation have been of particular interest to modern critics. Gwendolyn Brooks has criticized Hopkins for her assimilationist outlook and her admiration for the dominant culture, and Joseph Rosenbaum has commented that in *Contending Forces* "beauty and success are judged by the white man's standard." However, Robert Bone has noted that the "ideology of success" in the terms of white society was a common theme among early middle-class black writers, and according to Judith Berzon, it was not until the 1920s that black writers began to glorify self-images and the achievements of their own culture. Even Brooks has commented that Hopkins "would have been very remarkable indeed if, enslaved as she was by her special time and special temperament, she had been forward enough'' to consider black culture preferable for black Americans to the dominant white culture of her time.

Hopkins remains an obscure figure in American literature. The critical neglect of her work has most often been attributed to her unexceptional narrative technique, although the unavailability of her works and the general neglect suffered by female authors have also been cited as reasons for her obscurity. Nevertheless, a number of commentators have argued that her fiction merits wider attention, and especially praise *Contending Forces* as a poignant reflection of her era.

(See also *Dictionary of Literary Biography,* Vol. 50: *Afro-American Writers before the Harlem Renaissance.*)

## PRINCIPAL WORKS

*Slaves' Escape; or, The Underground Railroad*　(drama)
　　1880
*Contending Forces: A Romance Illustrative of Negro Life North and South*　(novel)　1900
"The Mystery Within Us"　(short story)　1900; published in journal *The Colored American*
*Famous Men of the Negro Race*　(biographical sketches) 1901-02; published in journal *The Colored American*
*Famous Women of the Negro Race*　(biographical sketches) 1901-02; published in journal *The Colored American*
*Winona: A Tale of Negro Life in the South and Southwest* (novel)　1902; published in journal *The Colored American*
*Of One Blood; or, The Hidden Self*　(novel)　1902-03; published in journal *The Colored American*
*Topsy Templeton*　(novella)　1916; published in journal *New Era*

---

### PAULINE E. HOPKINS　(essay date 1900)

[*In the following excerpt, Hopkins discusses her purposes in writing* Contending Forces.]

In giving this little romance [*Contending Forces*] expression in print, I am not actuated by a desire for notoriety or for profit, but to do all that I can in an humble way to raise the stigma of degradation from my race.

While I make no apology for my somewhat abrupt and daring venture within the wide field of romantic literature, I ask the kind indulgence of the generous public for the many crudities which I know appear in the work, and their approval of whatever may impress them as being of value to the Negro race and to the world at large.

The colored race has historians, lecturers, ministers, poets, judges and lawyers,—men of brilliant intellects who have arrested the favorable attention of this busy, energetic nation. But, after all, it is the simple, homely tale, unassumingly told, which cements the bond of brotherhood among all classes and all complexions.

Fiction is of great value to any people as a preserver of manners and customs—religious, political and social. It is a record of growth and development from generation to generation. *No one will do this for us; we must ourselves develop the men and women who will faithfully portray the inmost thoughts and feelings of the Negro with all the fire and romance which lie*

*dormant in our history,* and, as yet, unrecognized by writers of the Anglo-Saxon race. (pp. 13-14)

In these days of mob violence, when lynch-law is raising its head like a venomous monster, more particularly in the southern portion of the great American republic, the retrospective mind will dwell upon the history of the past, seeking there a solution of these monstrous outbreaks under a government founded upon the greatest and brightest of principles for the elevation of mankind. While we ponder the philosophy of cause and effect, the world is horrified by a fresh outbreak, and the shocked mind wonders that in this—the brightest epoch of the Christian era—*such things are.*

Mob-law is nothing new. Southern sentiment has not been changed; the old ideas close in analogy to the spirit of the buccaneers, who formed in many instances the first settlers of the Southland, still prevail, and break forth clothed in new forms to force the whole republic to an acceptance of its principles.

"Rule or ruin'' is the motto which is committing the most beautiful portion of our glorious country to a cruel revival of piratical methods; and, finally, to the introduction of *Anarchy.* Is this not so? Let us compare the happenings of one hundred—two hundred years ago, with those of today. The difference between then and now, if any there be, is so slight as to be scarcely worth mentioning. The atrocity of the acts committed one hundred years ago are duplicated today, when slavery is supposed no longer to exist.

I have tried to tell an impartial story, leaving it to the reader to draw conclusions. I have tried to portray our hard struggles here in the North to obtain a respectable living and a partial education. I have presented both sides of the dark picture—lynching and concubinage—truthfully and without vituperation, pleading for that justice of heart and mind for my people which the Anglo-Saxon in America never withholds from suffering humanity. (pp. 14-15)

I have introduced enough of the exquisitely droll humor peculiar to the Negro (a work like this would not be complete without it) to give a bright touch to an otherwise gruesome subject. (p. 16)

> *Pauline E. Hopkins, in a preface to her* Contending Forces: A Romance Illustrative of Negro Life North and South, *1900. Reprint by Southern Illinois University Press, 1978, pp. 13-16.*

### CORNELIA A. CONDICT　(essay date 1903)

[*In the following excerpt from a letter written to the* Colored American *magazine, Condict addresses the prevalence of interracial love affairs in the magazine's fiction and recommends a different focus. Hopkins, the magazine's literary editor, replied to Condict's letter in the same issue (see excerpt below).*]

I have been taking and reading with interest the *Colored American* magazine.

If I found it more helpful to Christian work among your people I would continue to take it.

May I make a comment on the stories, especially those that have been serial. Without exception they have been of love between the colored and whites. Does that mean that your novelists can imagine no love beautiful and sublime within the range of the colored race, for each other? I have seen beautiful home life and love in families altogether of Negro blood.

The stories of these tragic mixed loves will not commend themselves to your white readers and will not elevate the colored readers. I believe your novelists could do with a consecrated imagination and pen, more for the elevation of home life and love, than perhaps any other one class of writers.

What Dickens did for the neglected working class of England, some writer could do for the neglected colored people of America. (pp. 398-99)

> *Cornelia A. Condict, in a letter to the editor, in* The Colored American Magazine, *Vol. VI, No. 5, March, 1903, pp. 398-99.*

## PAULINE E. HOPKINS   (essay date 1903)

*[In the following excerpt, Hopkins replies to a letter from Cornelia A. Condict to the* Colored American *magazine (see excerpt above), challenging Condict's perspective and explaining her rationale for the subject matter of her own fiction.]*

My stories are definitely planned to show the obstacles persistently placed in our paths by a dominant race to subjugate us spiritually. Marriage is made illegal between the races and yet the mulattoes increase. Thus the shadow of corruption falls on the blacks and on the whites, without whose aid the mulattoes would not exist. And then the hue and cry goes abroad of the immorality of the Negro and the disgrace that the mulattoes are to this nation. Amalgamation is an institution designed by God for some wise purpose, and mixed bloods have always exercised a great influence on the progress of human affairs. I sing of the *wrongs* of a race that ignorance of their pitiful condition may be changed to intelligence and must awaken compassion in the hearts of the just.

The home life of Negroes is beautiful in many instances; warm affection is there between husband and wife, and filial and paternal tenderness in them is not surpassed by any other race of the human family. But Dickens wrote not of the joys and beauties of English society; I believe he was the author of *Bleak House* and *David Copperfield.* If he had been an American, and with his trenchant pen had exposed the abuses practiced by the Southern whites upon the blacks—had told the true story of how wealth, intelligence and femininity has stooped to choose for a partner in sin, the degraded (?) Negro whom they affect to despise, Dickens would have been advised to shut up or get out. I believe Jesus Christ when on earth rebuked the Pharisees in this wise: "Ye hypocrites, ye expect to be heard for your much speaking"; "O wicked and adulterous (?) nation, how can ye escape the damnation of hell?" He didn't go about patting those old sinners on the back saying, "All right boys, fix me up and the Jews will get there all right. Money talks. Divy on the money you take in the exchange business of the synagogue, and it'll be all right with God." Jesus told the thing as it was and the Jews crucified him! I am glad to receive this criticism for it shows more clearly than ever that white people don't understand *what pleases Negroes.* You are between Scylla and Charybdis: If you please the author of this letter and your white clientele, you will lose your Negro patronage. If you cater to the *demands* of the Negro trade, away goes Mrs. ——. I have sold to many whites and have received great praise for the work I am doing in exposing the social life of the Southerners and the wickedness of their caste prejudice.

Let the good work go on. Opposition is the life of an enterprise; criticism tells you that you are doing something. (pp. 399-400)

> *Pauline E. Hopkins, in a reply to a letter in* The Colored American Magazine, *Vol. VI, No. 5, March, 1903, pp. 399-400.*

## HUGH M. GLOSTER   (essay date 1948)

*[Gloster, an American author and critic, was a contributing editor of the periodical* Phylon *from 1949 to 1953, and is the author of* Negro Voices in American Fiction *(1948). In the following excerpt from that work, Gloster terms* Contending Forces *unsuccessful as a novel but of value for its insights into middle-class black family life.]*

In *Contending Forces: A Romance Illustrative of Negro Life North and South* Pauline E. Hopkins, actuated by the desire to do all she could "in an humble way to raise the stigma of degradation from my race," followed Mrs. Harper and J. McHenry Jones in placing the case of worthy but oppressed Negroes before the American bar of justice. The author thus expressed her belief in fiction as an instrument of racial uplift:

> Fiction is of great value to any people as a preserver of manners and customs—religious, political and social. It is a record of growth and development from generation to generation. No one will do this for us; we must ourselves develop the men and women who will faithfully portray the inmost thoughts and feelings of the Negro with all the fire and romance which lie dormant in our history, and, as yet, unrecognized by writers of the Anglo-Saxon race [see excerpt dated 1900].

The overplotted action of the novel follows the experiences of Charles Montfort, his near-white British wife Grace, who recalls Cora Munro of Cooper's *The Last of the Mohicans,* and their descendants. Moving from Bermuda to a North Carolina plantation with his wife and two sons, Charles and Jesse, Montfort decides to liberate his slaves within twenty-five years and retire with his family to England. Learning of Grace's Negro blood and of Montfort's intention to free the bondmen, Anson Pollock, a white neighbor, takes steps which lead to the murder of Montfort, the suicide of Grace, the hiring of Charles to an English mineralogist, and the reduction of Jesse to slavery. After escaping to New England, Jesse marries mulatto Elizabeth Whitfield and thus joins "that unfortunate race, of whom it is said that a man had better be born dead than to come into the world as part and parcel of it." The rest of the novel traces the love affairs and economic struggles of Jesse's grandchildren, Dora and William Smith.

In an introductory note Mrs. Hopkins . . . stated that she had "tried to tell an impartial story, leaving it to the reader to draw conclusions." This effort was unsuccessful, however, for *Contending Forces,* like [Frances E. W. Harper's] *Iola Leroy* and [J. McHenry Jones's] *Hearts of Gold,* is characterized by the usual exaggerations of its genre. Perhaps the best comment that may be made about the book is that it provides interesting sidelights on the struggles of a middle-class Negro family for education, employment, and social adjustment in post-bellum Boston. (pp. 33-4)

> *Hugh M. Gloster, "Negro Fiction to World War I,"* in his *Negro Voices in American Fiction, 1948. Reprint by Russell & Russell Inc., 1965, pp. 23-100.*

## GWENDOLYN BROOKS   (essay date 1978)

*[Brooks is an American poet, novelist, and educator whose second volume of poetry,* Annie Allen *(1949), won the Pulitzer Prize in*

*1950. In the following excerpt, she compares Hopkins with other twentieth-century black writers, examines Hopkins's view of the dominant white culture of her time, and criticizes her assimilationist outlook.*]

No, [*Contending Forces*] is not *Native Son, Invisible Man, Jubilee, Roots.* Pauline Hopkins is not Richard Wright, Ralph Ellison, Margaret Walker, Alex Haley. Unlike Margaret Walker, in the fire of *For My People,* Pauline Hopkins is not . . . urging that "martial songs be written"; she is often indignant, but not indignant enough to desire Margaret's "bloody peace." It is true that Pauline Hopkins can and does involve herself with black anger, but the texture, range, scope, the slashing red and scream and curse and *out-there* hurt that overwhelm us as Wright, Ellison and Haley deal with us, are not to be found in *Contending Forces.* I am not prepared to say that they are not "necessary." However, this quaint little "romance"—as the author likes to call it—keeps us with it, keeps us trotting, with quite some tension, too, down its elder dust, and through its quizzical mist.

Words do wonderful things. They pound, purr. They can urge, they can wheedle, whip, whine. They can sing, sass, singe. They can churn, check, channelize. They can be a "*Hup* two three four." They can forge a fiery army out of a hundred languid men. Pauline Hopkins, had we met, might have said in answer to my questions that her interest was *not* in Revolution *nor* exhaustive Revision. But it is perfectly obvious that black fury invaded her not seldom and not softly, and if she has not chosen from her resources words and word jointures that could make changes in the world, she has given us a sense of her day, a *clue* collection, and we can use the light of it to clarify our understanding and our intuition. We can take the building blocks she does supply us and use them to fill in old gaps. After association with her, some of our concepts won't be quite as wobbly.

Pauline Hopkins had, and this is true of many of her brothers and sisters, new and old, a touching reliance on the dazzles and powers of anticipated integration. But she would have been remarkable indeed if, enslaved as she was by her special time and special temperament, she had been forward enough to instruct blacks not to rely on goodies coming from any source save personal heart, head, hand. To ask them, to entreat them to address themselves, rather than whites, to cherish, champion themselves, rather than whites, to trust, try, traipse with themselves, was not her inspiration nor motivation.

Often doth the brainwashed slave revere the modes and idolatries of the master. And Pauline Hopkins consistently proves herself a continuing slave, despite little bursts of righteous heat, throughout *Contending Forces.* She tells us, for example, what she really thinks of "black beauty" over and over again, in passages like this description of our paper-doll heroine, Sappho Clark: "Tall and fair, with hair of a golden cast, aquiline nose, rosebud mouth, soft brown eyes veiled by long, dark lashes which swept her cheek, just now covered with a delicate rose flush . . . a combination of 'queen rose and lily in one'." To which vision an *ordinary* black, Sarah Ann, (fat, colloquial, ebony-hued), responds: "That's somethin' *God* made, honey." (The accepted understanding being that one of the lower devils made the ilk of Sarah Ann.) We are also treated to such outrages as "there might even have been a strain of African blood polluting the fair stream of Montfort's vitality"; and "In many cases African blood had become diluted from amalgamation with the higher race"; *and* "that justice of heart and mind for

my people which the Anglo-Saxon in America never withholds from suffering humanity."

In her preface, the author suggests that *her* desire is to give us the kind of "simple, homely tale . . . which cements the bond of brotherhood among all classes and all complexions." But like most blacks, of whatever persuasion, self-delusion, perverse ambition, or approximate "transformation," Pauline is unable to keep a certain purely "native" rage *steadily* stomped down. Certain things she does not mind us suffering through, any more than does Alex Haley or Margaret Walker. We get "cruelties . . . such as to sicken the most cold-hearted and indifferent. For instance: causing a child to whip his mother until the blood ran; if a slave looked his master in the face, his limbs were broken; women in the first stages of their accouchement, upon refusing to work, were placed in the treadmill where terrible things happened, too dreadful to relate." And she is able to make Will say—calmly—that agitation—never Revolution—"will do much. It gave us freedom; it will give us manhood. The peace, dignity, and honor of this nation rises or falls with the Negro."

As she says, and with more desperate truth than she knows she says or feels, the reader is left to "draw conclusions." (pp. 403-06)

> *Gwendolyn Brooks, in an afterword to* Contending Forces: A Romance Illustrative of Negro Life North and South, *by Pauline Elizabeth Hopkins, Southern Illinois University Press, 1978, pp. 403-09.*

### JUDITH R. BERZON (essay date 1978)

[*In the following excerpt, Berzon compares* Contending Forces *with G. Langhorne Pryor's* Neither Bond nor Free (1902), *considering their political ideologies, literary qualities, and importance as historical documents.*]

G. Langhorne Pryor's 1902 novel, *Neither Bond nor Free* and Pauline E. Hopkins's 1900 novel, ***Contending Forces: A Romance Illustrative of Negro Life North and South,*** are both vehicles for their authors' political views—Pryor's a plea for Washingtonian "conservatism," Hopkins's a dramatization of the ideology of W. E. B. Du Bois and the "radical" faction.

Pryor uses his novel not only to promote the conservative point of view but to attack the priorities of the radicals. Throughout the novel Washington's program of moral uplift, industrial education, cooperation with southern whites, and gradualism and conciliation—as opposed to political agitation—are stressed. In addition to the numerous passages of political debate to be found in the novel, Pryor uses his major characters to embody political principles. (p. 200)

All of the key ideas espoused by Booker T. Washington are to be found in Pryor's novel. Like [Francis E. W. Harper's] *Iola Leroy* and ***Contending Forces, Neither Bond nor Free*** is dreadfully written: the style is stilted; the novel is "preachy"; the characters are totally unconvincing and lifeless. But these novels are documents of historical, if not literary, importance. In the writings of these black authors we gain some notion of how the ideas of Washington, Du Bois, and others were being received in the black community. Many of the novels present dialogues rather than one-sided polemics. Thus, while more attention is paid to presenting Washingtonian political principles in *Neither Bond nor Free,* Du Boisean attitudes are also given eloquent expression. (p. 201)

# Shall The Race Have a Fair Chance?

# Contending Forces.

## A Romance of Negro Life

### NORTH AND SOUTH

BY

## PAULINE E. HOPKINS,

The Popular Colored Writer.

Author of "Talma Gordon," "General Washington," etc.

With original illustrations and cover design by R. Emmett Owen.

Over 400 pages, 8vo.  Price, $1.50.

"*The civility of no race can be perfect whilst another race is degraded.*" — EMERSON.

A most fascinating story that is pre-eminently a race-work, dedicated to the best interest of the Negro everywhere.  It holds you as by a spell, from start to finish.

A book that will arouse intense interest wherever shown, as it is the most powerful narrative yet published, of the wrongs and injustice perpetrated on the race.  Startling in the array of facts shown and logical in the arguments it presents.

The incidents portrayed HAVE ACTUALLY OCCURRED, ample proof of which may be found in the archives of the Court House at Newbern, N. C., and at the seat of government at Washington, D. C.

The author tells an impartial story, leaving it to the reader to draw conclusions.  She has presented both sides of the dark picture — lynching and concubinage — truthfully and without vituperation, introducing enough of the exquisitely droll humor peculiar to the Negro to give a bright touch to an otherwise gruesome subject.

It is a book that will not only appeal strongly to the race everywhere, but will have a large sale among the whites.  The book mailed postpaid to any address on receipt of $1.50.

### AGENTS WANTED EVERYWHERE.  LIBERAL COMMISSION.

Many of our Agents are making from $15.00 to $25.00 a week.  You can do the same.  Address at once for full particulars and special territory,

## The Colored Co-operative Publishing Company,

### 5 Park Square, BOSTON, MASS.

*Magazine advertisement for* Contending Forces.

*Contending Forces: A Romance Illustrative of Negro Life North and South* has all of the faults of Pryor's novel plus an incredible and incredibly complicated plot. There is far less debate, but Hopkins's ideology is as distinctly Du Boisean as Pryor's is Washingtonian. Sappho, Hopkins's beautiful golden-haired "black" heroine, is opposed to industrial education exclusively. She insists that political rights are essential for any genuine advancement for blacks: "Temporizing will not benefit us; rather, it will leave us branded as cowards, not worthy of a freeman's respect—an alien people, without a country and without a home." Another spokesman for the author argues that "Blacks must unite and not destroy each other's self-respect and just try to make a buck in the white man's world. *These are the contending forces that are dooming this race to despair!*" (p. 202)

> *Judith R. Berzon, "The Mulatto as Race Leader,"*
> *in her* Neither White nor Black: The Mulatto Character in American Fiction, *New York University Press,*
> *1978, pp. 190-217.*

## JOSEPH ROSENBLUM   (essay date 1979)

[*In the following excerpt, Rosenblum offers a negative appraisal of the literary qualities of* Contending Forces.]

The first four chapters [of *Contending Forces*], set some sixty years before the remainder of the book, reveal no understanding of the antebellum South. Nor do they serve any function except to bestow a large sum of money on Will Smith three hundred pages later. The remainder of the novel, set mostly in Boston during the late 1890's, does provide insights into the black culture of the period. But the stories of the Smiths, Sappho Clark, John P. Langley, and Dr. Lewis, potentially interesting, are buried beneath political pamphleteering and lengthy digressions. Thus, for thirty-six pages the reader leaves an agonizing Sappho Clark to attend to the rivalry between Sisters Robinson and Davis over the sale of tickets at a church fair.

A failure as a novel, *Contending Forces* does suggest, as Gwendolyn Brooks observes . . . , the degree to which at least some blacks in 1900, including Pauline E. Hopkins, accepted the values of the white society in which they lived [see excerpt dated 1978]. Beauty and success are judged by the white man's standards. While recognizing the genetic fallacy of the race concept, Hopkins can still refer, without apparent irony, to the "inferior black race" and the "superior (white) race." Never in the work does Hopkins show anything laudable about black culture. This novel is therefore likely to interest the sociologist rather than the literary critic or general reader. Libraries seeking or having extensive collections of black Americana will want to acquire this book. All others may allow this volume in the Lost American Fiction Series to become lost again.

> *Joseph Rosenblum, in a review of "Contending Forces," in* The Reprint Bulletin Book Reviews, *Vol. XXIV, No. 1, 1979, p. 35.*

## CLAUDIA TATE   (essay date 1985)

[*In the following excerpt, Tate discusses the ways in which Hopkins adapted nineteenth-century literary conventions to document black concerns.*]

Pauline Hopkins was an important writer who deserves serious attention because, in being both black and female, she documents the cross section of the literary concerns of two major groups of American writers: turn-of-the-century black writers, who primarily dramatized themes of racial injustice, and mid-to late-nineteenth-century white women writers, some of whom wrote sentimental and domestic novels that acclaimed Christian virtue. In some of these novels, a young girl is deprived of the family assistance she had depended on to sustain her throughout her life. The popular success of white women in depicting their heroines' necessity of making their own way in the world despite injustice provided a ready and fertile context within which black women writers might also place their fair-haired black heroines and dramatize racial protest. For many black women writers embellished the plot line of their white predecessors and contemporaries. They include Amelia Johnson, Sarah Allen, Emma Kelley, Ruth Todd, Marie Burgess Ware, Frances Harper, and J. McHenry Jones. In their work we find that the youth is black and may be male but is more often female. She believes herself to be white, obviously having no knowledge of her African ancestry. This knowledge is withheld so that she can enjoy the privileged life afforded her by her white father. Circumstances lead to his death, and as a result the child and her mother are subjected to the horrors of slavery. Both are abused by cruel slave masters, despite the fact that they are as white and as noble as any one of their former caste and more handsome than most. The child survives and eventually marries well, thereby concluding the tragedy of her plight. This marriage is not only based on love but forms a partnership for continued work in racial advancement and, thus, gives the union a high and noble purpose. But practically every one of these writers has been lost in out-of-print books and periodicals which have long ceased to be available. Their work must be retrieved in order to correct the now longstanding misconception that Phillis Wheatley and Frances Harper were the lone literary women of the eighteenth and nineteenth centuries, who all by themselves brought forth the generation of black women writers of the Harlem Renaissance.

*Contending Forces,* Hopkins's first and best-known novel, conforms to the basic plot structure I have outlined. The story begins in 1790 on the island of Bermuda, when Charles Montfort decides to move his family to North Carolina to invest in a cotton plantation in order to secure his fortune. All goes as planned until a jealous neighbor, Anson Pollock, suspects that Montfort's beautiful wife, Grace, has black blood. He conspires to kill Montfort, claim Grace as his slave mistress, make her two children—Charles and Jesse—chattel slaves, and steal a portion of Montfort's estate. The conspiracy is successful, and after Montfort's murder, Grace commits suicide in order to escape her fate. Charles is sold to an Englishman who subsequently frees him and takes him to England, while Jesse suffers under the abuse of Pollock, until he manages to escape to New England. He eventually marries the daughter of his black benefactor and fathers a large family in Exeter, Massachusetts. These events comprise the background for the novel's central story, which concerns Jesse's grandchildren, Will and Dora Smith.

The central story is set in Boston. Will Smith is a philosophy student at Harvard College, and Dora assists her mother in running the family-owned rooming house. Among the roomers are Sappho Clark and John Langley. Will falls in love with Sappho, a beautiful, virtually white young woman with a mysterious, southern past. John Langley, who is engaged to Dora, also falls in love with Sappho, but his intentions are not honorable. He plots to force Sappho into becoming his mistress, while planning to marry Dora. Sappho escapes Langley, but in so doing she must abandon her lover Will. She leaves behind a letter for him, explaining Langley's intentions as well as her mysterious and tragic past. Will shares this information with Dora, who immediately breaks off her engagement to Langley. Will then tries to find Sappho, but she has left without a trace. In an effort to heal his broken heart, Will goes abroad to continue his studies after graduating from Harvard. Dora eventually marries her former childhood friend, Dr. Arthur Lewis, who is the head of a large industrial school for Negroes in Louisiana. The newlyweds move to Louisiana, and while Will is paying them a visit, he unexpectedly finds Sappho. They are united in marriage a few weeks later on Easter Sunday. Thus, the virtuous are rewarded with happy marriages, made even more fulfilling because of their commitments to racial progress, while the villainous John Langley dies in a mining accident, after having repented much too late for his "sins."

Hopkins's characters conform, as we would expect, to nineteenth-century conventions in that their inner virtues are reflected in their outward appearances. Dora Smith is described as an "energetic little Yankee girl" with a "delicate brown face" and "smooth bands of dark-brown hair." Will Smith, Hopkins's DuBois-like hero, is "tall and finely formed, with features almost perfectly chiseled, and a complexion the color of an almond shell. His hair is black and curly, with just a tinge of crispness to denote the existence of Negro blood." John Langley, on the other hand, is "shorter in stature and very fair in complexion. His hair is dark and has no indication of Negro blood in its waves; his features are of the Caucasian cut. . . . (But) . . . the strong manhood and honesty of purpose which existed in Will Smith are lacking in John Langley. He was a North Carolinian—descendant of slaves and Southern 'cracker' blood." Hopkins accounted for Langley's ignoble character as an inherent result of his poor ancestry, and in so doing, she further qualified the nineteenth-century notion that the mulatto was a degenerate by making degeneration the result not of miscegenation in and of itself but of poor-quality white blood.

When we turn our attention to the beautiful Sappho Clark, we find that her appearance conforms more readily to that of the mulatto heroine: "Tall and frail, with hair of a golden cast, aquiline nose, rosebud mouth, soft brown eyes veiled by long, dark lashes." Although Sappho is fair enough to pass into the white world and secure herself a rich, handsome, white husband, she chooses instead to unite her plight to that of her black brethren. Her most important role, however, is not that of the "tragic mulatto" but that of Hopkins's spokeswoman for the political rights of black Americans. When her argument is combined with Will's contention that "No Negro college . . . ought to bestow a diploma upon a man who had not been thoroughly grounded in the rudiments of moral and natural philosophy, physiology, and economy," we have their combined social program for the advancement of the Negro. Their program is a fictionalized version of DuBois's position in the DuBois-Washington controversy. Washington, his opponent, argued for industrial education for the Negro and believed that this program could be best accomplished by not antagonizing whites over the black vote. Hopkins dramatized Washington's position through the character of Dora's admirer, Dr. Arthur Lewis. Whereas the real-life controversy was never resolved, Hopkins resolved her fictionalized version quite easily by joining the two programs in marriages at the novel's conclusion. As a consequence, we find that the Lewises promote industrial education for the Negro, while their in-laws, the Smiths, promote liberal academic education for the Negro and agitate for his political rights as well.

It is not surprising to find that Hopkins, being both black and female complemented her racial argument with her concern for women's issues. In the chapter entitled "The Sewing Circle," Hopkins characterized a "race woman" by the name of Mrs. Willis who is a proponent for the "evolution of true womanhood in the work of the 'Woman Question' as embodied in marriage and suffrage." Hopkins, through this spokeswoman, contends that women should chart their advance within the domain of marriage and with the assistance of the vote. Mrs. Willis further says that "the advancement of the colored woman should be the new problem in the woman question," and in order to pursue this inquiry she supports "the formation of clubs of colored women banded together for charity, for study, and for every reason under God's glorious heavens that can better the condition of mankind."

The advancement of the black woman was certainly an area of concern at the time of the publication of *Contending Forces*. No doubt the women's clubs which were chartered in the late nineteenth century provided stimulation for the black women's development, although Hopkins had little more than tentative programs to propose, theories to assert, and positions to state. But she did have her spokeswoman, Mrs. Willis, insist that women construct their advancement on virtue and duty within the domain of marriage and with the responsibility of the vote. In addition, Hopkins had Mrs. Willis further reiterate an underlying theme of the entire novel, namely that blacks and women, especially, must be on constant guard to subdue the growth of any passion: "Enthusiasm for any one object or duty may become a passion. I believe that in some degree passion may be beneficial, but we must guard ourselves against a sinful growth of any appetite." Therefore, if we view *Contending Forces* as Hopkins's dramatized expression of a tentative program for the advancement of black Americans in general and black American women in particular, we can surmise that black men and women must be responsible for the course of their own advancement and that duty, virtue, carefully controlled emotions, the institution of marriage, and the vote are the key components for directing social progress and achieving results. (pp. 54-9)

Like *Contending Forces*, *Winona* conforms to the basic plot structure I have described. In 1849 an unknown white man joins the Indian tribes around Buffalo, New York, and eventually becomes their chief, taking the name of White Eagle. Buffalo is the last and, therefore, most important stop in the underground railroad, and as a result many fugitive slaves arrive there in pursuit of freedom. One such fugitive is a mulatto slave woman whom White Eagle marries and who dies shortly after the birth of their daughter, Winona. Another fugitive slave woman also dies shortly thereafter, leaving her small son, Judah, in White Eagle's care. The children grow up as brother and sister, totally unaware of their racial origin; in fact, they believe themselves to be Indians. They spend their days fully enjoying the adventures afforded by the forest, but they also heed the importance of securing a public-school education. In 1855 Warren Maxwell, an Englishman, comes to America in search of the heir to the Carlingford estate. On the first night of Maxwell's arrival, White Eagle is murdered by an unknown assailant. Maxwell learns of his death from Winona and Judah, to whom he immediately becomes attached, so much so that he plans to take them to England with him. But before they can leave, Maxwell has to complete his search, which will take him to another location. When he returns to make arrangements for their trip, he finds that the children have been claimed as chattel slaves by their mothers' owners under the Fugitive Slave Act of 1850 and subsequently have been taken to Missouri.

Two years later Maxwell, still searching for the missing Carlingford heir, visits Colonel Titus's plantation in Missouri, where he finds Winona and Judah in bondage. They plan an escape, and while Maxwell is awaiting their arrival, he meets Maybee, a friend, who is on his way to Kansas to join John Brown and his militia. When Winona and Judah arrive, they are taken to Brown's camp and left in his care. The next night Maxwell is taken prisoner by Thomson, who was White Eagle's murderer. Thomson subsequently tries Maxwell for inciting slave escapes and ultimately sentences him to be hanged. While he awaits his fate, Brown's men discover his whereabouts and he is rescued. The story comes to a quick conclusion when Maxwell learns that White Eagle was the missing Carlingford heir. As a result Winona and Judah, who are now both young adults, inherit his legacy. By this time, as we might have expected, Maxwell has fallen deeply in love with Winona and she with him. They return to England, a nation which Hopkins described as being beyond American caste prejudice, and they are married. Judah, who also accompanies them to England, is eventually knighted by the Queen. He grows prosperous and marries a woman from an old English family. Thus, the story concludes with both couples thriving in domestic bliss.

The structure of this novel conforms to basic conventions. But *Winona* is even more sensational than *Contending Forces* in that there are more incredible coincidences, swashbuckling adventures, and exaggerated heroic descriptions, all held together with a very sentimental love story. Winona's appearance, as we might expect, conforms to the tragic mulatto mold: ''Her wide brow, about which the hair clustered in dark rings, the beautifully chiselled features, the olive complexion with a hint of pink.'' And her hero, Maxwell, is equally as handsome, though fair: ''. . . a slender, well-knit figure with a bright, handsome face, blue eyes and a mobile mouth slightly touched with down on his upper lip.'' The virtuous pair are rewarded with prosperity and happiness, while the villain suffers a painful death.

Hopkins placed this novel into the genre of the fugitive slave story and identified her protest as that against the arbitrary segregation and subjection of black Americans:

> Many strange tales of romantic happenings in this mixed community of Anglo-Saxons, Indians and Negroes might be told similar to the one I am about to relate, and the world stand aghast and may try to find the dividing line supposed to be a natural barrier between the whites and the dark-skinned race.

Thus, as is the case with *Contending Forces*, the central issue of *Winona* is its protest against racial injustice, but unlike *Contending Forces*, *Winona* outlines no program of social reform other than that offered by escape. Whereas escape offered a possible resolution to the slave's dilemma prior to 1864, Hopkins's contemporary scene of 1901 afforded virtually no ostensible reason for her to write an abolitionist novel. Perhaps she wrote the novel as an exercise in nostalgia, intended to arouse sympathy for oppressed black Americans. There was, however, more than sufficient reason to condemn the practices of employment and housing discrimination, separate public accommodations, mob violence, and lynching, as she had done in *Contending Forces*. Whereas her first novel was very sensitive to the racial issues of 1900 and consequently addressed each of them, *Winona* seems to be essentially an escapist, melodramatic romance in which Hopkins used sentimental love

as a means for supporting an appeal for racial justice. Though, granted, Hopkins does dramatize the fact that being black in America means being subjected to racial abuse, she offers little hope to those who cannot escape like Winona and Jude.

Women's issues, which were central to the argument of *Contending Forces,* have been abandoned entirely in *Winona.* Although marriage is depicted as woman's ambition in both *Contending Forces* and *Winona,* in the latter novel a woman's role is seen exclusively as finding a suitable husband and tending to his needs. Love is translated singularly into duty, and duty finds expression only on the domestic front. We do not see women, like Mrs. Willis of *Contending Forces,* who are their husbands' helpmates in the struggle for racial advancement. On the contrary, marriage offers women its own blissful escape in *Winona,* and marital love is portrayed as the balm which soothes their worldly wounds. When we turn our attention to the subject of the advancement of black women, we find no discussion of this topic at all. Although Hopkins was, nevertheless, a product of the nineteenth century's rising consciousness of women's concerns, it is surprising to find that this issue appears so inconsistently in her work.

The change in argument and setting in *Winona* may be a signal for Hopkins's own growing frustration with the effort to improve both the American racial climate and the quality of life for black American women. In 1899, when *Contending Forces* was written, Hopkins's argument concerned the advancement of black Americans in general and black American women in particular. In 1901, when *Winona* was written, her argument seems to focus on escape. Whereas escape is an incident of plot in *Winona* and love is, likewise, translated into domestic duty, both the themes of escape and love evolve into even more limited contexts in Hopkins's third novel, *Of One Blood, or the Hidden Self,* published in 1902/03. Here, the effort to escape becomes total and comprehensive, as the story moves beyond the American social scene to a mysterious Atlantis-like region of an underground city in Africa. And love is translated into racial imperatives on one hand and perversion on the other. Thus, instead of finding urgent social problems dramatized in a somewhat realistic fictional setting, we find the remote landscape of science fiction. Although it can be argued that much of this genre provides critical observations and predictions about the real world, in Hopkins's case, however, her science fiction novel seems almost entirely gratuitous. *Of One Blood* is, nonetheless, an extremely intriguing, imaginative, and provocative novel. (pp. 59-62)

*Of One Blood* is set in the stimulating climate of early twentieth-century scientific discoveries. William James and Sigmund Freud were advancing theories about the nature of the subconscious, while archaeological finds in Egypt were uncovering modern man's racial and cultural history. In this setting we find Reuel Briggs, a young black medical student who is particularly interested in mysticism and the powers of the subconscious mind. The story begins on one evening when he sees the face of a beautiful woman, whom he cannot seem to forget. A few days later, he attends a Negro concert with his best friend, Aubrey Livingston, and who should appear but the beautiful woman, singing a haunting melody. In this manner her racial identity is uncovered. Soon thereafter, Briggs is called upon to assist the victims of a railroad accident at a local hospital, and who should he find but this same young woman, who is presumed dead but who is actually in a catatonic sleep. Briggs succeeds in restoring her consciousness, although she can remember nothing of her past life. As we would expect,

Briggs falls in love with the woman, whose name we learn is Dianthe Lusk. He marries her, but his financial situation is so strained that he decides to postpone its consummation until he can secure his fortune and make a name for himself as a member of an archaeological expedition headed to Meröe, Ethiopia. He leaves her care entrusted to his friend Livingston. But soon after Briggs's departure, Livingston expresses his passionate love for Dianthe, who finds that she is unable to resist the mysterious power he has over her. He plans to take her away, but he must first rid himself of his fiancee, Molly Vance. He conspires to arrange a boating accident in which Molly is drowned. He and Dianthe are presumed dead, although their bodies are never found.

Meanwhile the expedition arrives in Ethiopia, and Briggs is very uneasy because he has not heard from Dianthe. His concern grows to the point that he experiences a clairvoyant trance of the boating accident. As a result, Briggs is brokenhearted, and he becomes seriously ill. When his strength returns, he wanders into a mysterious pyramid in the hope that a man-eating beast may release him from his grief. While exploring the pyramid, he loses consciousness, and when he awakens he finds himself in a mysterious underground city. The populace proclaim him as their long-awaited monarch, King Ergamenes, and he is subsequently betrothed to Queen Candace. Together they are to bring forth a long line of monarchs who will reclaim Ethiopia's former glory. Despite his new life, Briggs cannot forget Dianthe, and while having another trance, he learns that she is still alive.

Meanwhile, Livingston has married Dianthe, who is distraught when she learns that Briggs is not dead, as Livingston has told her. She tries to escape but gets lost in the woods. An old black woman by the name of Aunt Hannah rescues her and immediately recognizes that she is her daughter Mira's child and, therefore, her own granddaughter. Hannah tells Dianthe that Mira was also the mother of Briggs and Livingston; hence, Dianthe learns in the span of a few moments that she, Livingston, and Briggs are all "of one blood" and that she has married not one but both of her brothers. As a result of this knowledge, Dianthe loses her mind and attempts to poison Livingston, but he discovers her plan and makes her drink the poison instead, which she does without regret. When Briggs finally traces the whereabouts of Dianthe and Livingston, he arrives only to find Dianthe dead. Soon afterward, Livingston commits suicide, and Briggs returns to the Hidden City with Aunt Hannah, his grandmother. There he spends the rest of his life with his Queen Candace, doing God's work to prove that "Of one blood has (God made) all races of men."

Like *Contending Forces, Of One Blood* has an early twentieth-century setting. No sooner has the story begun than we find the Fisk Jubilee Singers presenting a concert to a Boston audience, which provides the occasion for Dianthe's introduction. In addition, the startling scientific discoveries in psychology and archaeology of that era provide a launching point for the fantastic events which follow. In fact, the entire intellectual milieu from which the story arises gives Hopkins the opportunity to display the breadth of her knowledge in the arts and the sciences, as if she were using her own writing in a self-conscious attempt to prove that the inherent intellectual capacity of black Americans was equal to that of their Anglo-Saxon counterparts. Moreover, the archaeological expedition is the means by which Hopkins underscores her contention that the biblical references to Ethiopia as a former world power could have been, indeed, factual rather than mythic. In this regard, she spends considerable effort describing Ethiopia's past glory, in addition to arguing her underlying point that there is no scientific basis for the arbitrary separation of the races. Hopkins further contends that knowledge is a serious impediment to racial prejudice, and although readers of today may detect the naiveté of such a position, Hopkins and her contemporaries firmly believed that knowledge would eliminate social injustice of all kinds and improve the quality of human life.

Although most Afro-Americans came from West Africa and not East Africa, this geographical oversight does not offset Hopkins's basic argument that "Afro-Americans are," as she wrote, "a branch of the wonderful and mysterious Ethiopians who had a prehistoric existence of magnificence, the full record of which is lost in obscurity." Hopkins did not appear to be fundamentally concerned with providing a genealogical tree for modern-day American blacks but with presenting broad notions of cultural and racial origins for them specifically and for mankind in general. In this regard, the ambition to retrieve Ethiopia's lost record of glory provides the impetus for the unfolding story and forms the foundation for Hopkins's racial argument.

Hopkins focused most of her attention on dramatizing the racial argument in *Of One Blood,* and as a consequence little emphasis falls on women's issues. There are, however, references to two issues which are related topically to women. The first concerns Queen Candace's physical appearance, and the second concerns Hopkins's mandate that passion must be subjected to reason. Turning our attention first to Candace, we find that, although her name seems peculiarly inappropriate for an Ethiopian queen, her physical portrayal marks a very early appearance of the "brown" heroine in Afro-American fiction. Instead of the conventional olive-skinned heroine, Queen Candace, though she resembles Dianthe, has a "warm bronze complexion; thick black eyebrows and great black eyes." Interestingly enough, she is the means by which pigment is reintroduced into the royal line, inasmuch as Ergamenes (alias Reuel) lost that trait as a result of American miscegenation. Hence, pigment becomes a positive physical attribute measured in terms of feminine beauty more than sixty years prior to the coinage of the slogan "Black is Beautiful." The second issue which finds repeated expression is Hopkins's admonition for restraining passion with reason and for not equating passion to love. This theme consistently appears in all of Hopkins's work, as well as in that of her female contemporaries. Its repeated expression measures the extent of their concern that women avoid being viewed merely as passionate creatures but be seen instead as rational human beings capable of serious thought. Hopkins also makes repeated references to marriage as the proper social domain for both men and women. In this regard, marriage is characterized as the distinctly harmonious setting in which good works abound, and Omnipotence directs good works, in her novels, toward the elimination of caste prejudice and the elevation of racial pride.

*Of One Blood* brings Hopkins's major themes, which were dramatized in her earliest play to this her last novel, full circle. In each work we find that she habitually insisted that black men and women be responsible for the course of their own advancement and that duty, virtue, carefully controlled emotions, and the institution of marriage are the key components for directing social progress. Her excessively episodic and melodramatic techniques resulted in her failure to meet twentieth-century critical standards; nevertheless, she was a serious writer, who wrote three novels at the turn of the century. This fact, alone, demands that we retrieve her work from obscurity. (pp. 62-5)

*Claudia Tate, "Pauline Hopkins: Our Literary Fore-mother," in* Conjuring: Black Women, Fiction, and Literary Tradition, *edited by Marjorie Pryse and Hortense J. Spillers, Indiana University Press, 1985, pp. 53-66.*

---

## ADDITIONAL BIBLIOGRAPHY

Bone, Robert. "Origins of the Early Novel." In his *The Negro Novel in America*, pp. 11-28. New Haven: Yale University Press, 1958.
    Early critical survey of black American novelists containing passing references to Hopkins.

Review of *Contending Forces: A Romance Illustrative of Negro Life North and South. Choice* 15, No. 11 (January 1979): 1518.

Maintains that *Contending Forces* is significant for its content despite Hopkins's adherence to outdated nineteenth-century literary conventions.

Rush, Theressa Gunnels; Myers, Carol Fairbanks; and Arata, Esther Spring. "Pauline Elizabeth Hopkins." In their *Black American Writers Past and Present: A Biographical and Bibliographical Dictionary*, Vol. 1, pp. 389-90. Metuchen: Scarecrow Press, 1975.
    Sketch of Hopkins's life and career, including a bibliography of primary and secondary works.

Setnick, Susan E. Review of *Contending Forces. Kliatt* XIV, No. 6 (September 1980): 7.
    Comments favorably on *Contending Forces.*

Shockley, Ann Allen. "Pauline Elizabeth Hopkins: A Biographical Excursion into Obscurity." *Phylon* XXXIII, No. 1 (Spring 1972): 22-6.
    Surveys Hopkins's life and career.

Smith, Albreta Moore. "Editorial and Publishers' Announcements." *The Colored American Magazine* III, No. 6 (October 1901): 478-79.
    Praises *Contending Forces* as "undoubtedly the book of the century. . . . It is all absorbing from first to last. . . . In point of composition, plot and style of writing it cannot be excelled."

# Muhammad Iqbal

## 1873-1938

(Also transliterated as Mohammad and Mohammed) Indian poet, essayist, and philosopher.

One of the leading Muslim intellectual figures of the first half of the twentieth century, Iqbal is primarily remembered for innovative poetic works written in Persian in which he espoused the revitalization of Islam through the development of the individual personality. Considered one of the first to publicly propose a sovereign Muslim state formed from sections of northwest India, he is celebrated as the spiritual founder of Pakistan, created in the decade after his death. Recognizing him as ''a genius and a commanding one,'' E. M. Forster pronounced Iqbal one of the ''great cultural figures of modern India,'' but noted further that ''our ignorance about him is extraordinary.''

Born into a deeply religious family in Sialkot in the Punjab, Iqbal was educated in local schools before moving to Lahore to study philosophy and languages at Government College. Following graduate studies, he lectured in history and philosophy at the college, becoming a prominent figure in the academic and literary circles of Lahore. Iqbal gained an extensive reputation in the region for his mystic, lyric poetry written in the Urdu language. In 1905 he traveled to England, where he continued his studies at Cambridge and completed a law degree. He was granted a Ph.D. from the University of Munich in 1907 for his thesis *The Development of Metaphysics in Persia*. On his return to India in the following year, Iqbal established a legal practice in Lahore, which he maintained while continuing to publish his poetry until ill health forced his retirement in 1934. He was knighted in 1922 for his service to literature. Much of his later career was devoted to politics; he presided over conventions of the Muslim League in 1930 and 1932, delivering perhaps his most famous speeches on the topic of Muslim separatism. He died in April 1938 after a long illness.

Iqbal used his poetry and prose writings as vehicles for a philosophy promoting social and religious reform. He based his teachings on the Koran and the writings of Eastern mystics, formulating a system of thought that also incorporated the ideas of Western thinkers, including the ancient Greeks, Immanuel Kant, Friedrich Nietzsche, and Henri Bergson. Central to Iqbal's philosophy is his doctrine of *khudi* (ego), which stresses the importance of the individual personality. Through the continued development of the self, Iqbal saw the evolution of the Perfect Man, the highest state attainable by an individual. Critics often compare his notion of the Perfect Man with Nietzsche's concept of the Superman. However, one notable difference is their relationship to religion: Nietzsche's Superman exists in a godless universe while religion is vital to the Perfect Man.

In Iqbal's view, the Perfect Man can only be created within a society that promotes activism over passivity and meditation, and he proposed a system of ethics designed to produce the necessary environment: Good is that which nurtures the Self; evil is that which diminishes the Self. For instance, love, courage, tolerance, and artistic expression are advocated, while fear, mendicancy, slavery, and concern for worldly rewards

are discouraged. Art too can be judged by these standards, according to Iqbal. He rejected the philosophy of ''art for art's sake'' because it failed to provide spiritual or ethical guidance. In Iqbal's view all art should be judged according to its ability to strengthen and inspire the individual, and creative activity is seen as the representation of an individual's struggle to understand and overcome the difficulties of his or her existence. Iqbal illustrated the importance of these efforts, comparing human creativity with God's, in the following lines, translated by S. A. Vahid: ''Thou didst create night and I made the lamp. / Thou didst create clay and I made the cup. / Thou didst create the deserts, mountains and forests, / I produced the orchards, gardens and groves; / It is I who turn stone into a mirror, / And it is I who turn poison into an antidote!''

Parallel to the idea of the evolution of the individual ego is Iqbal's conviction that humanity as a whole must function and develop in the same way as an individual. Society, according to Iqbal, will pass through three stages of development, each bringing it closer to God: 1) obedience to law; 2) self-control; 3) vicegerency to God. In keeping with Iqbal's view of society is his expression of pan-Islamism—including his advocacy of an independent Muslim state in northwestern India—which is based on his conviction that shared religious beliefs embody a better requisite for statehood than national boundaries determined by race or geography.

Most critical examinations in English of Iqbal's works reflect the abundant interest in his philosophical principles rather than his poetic style or technical innovations. His prose works are rarely discussed except as expressions of his philosophy. As one critic wrote: "Iqbal himself was deadly opposed to art for art's sake and therefore we cannot study his art or his style or his theme or his other poetic qualities in isolation from his theme because even though there is steady progression in his style, even though he wrote in different styles yet all these styles were fashioned according to the themes which he was trying to put across." During his lifetime Iqbal's poetry achieved widespread fame among Muslim and non-Muslim readers in India, while Western readers knew him primarily for his prose studies *The Development of Metaphysics in Persia* and *The Reconstruction of Religious Thought in Islam*. In addition to his reputation as a literary artist and philosopher, he was widely known and respected as a political activist and religious reformer. In the decades since his death Iqbal has been recognized by Western scholars as an important intellectual figure, and among Islamic readers he continues to represent something even greater. As Iqbal Singh proclaims, Iqbal "accelerated the transition of the Muslim mind from a feudal to the modern frame. As a prophet, no less than as a poet, he bridges the gulf between yesterday and today."

## *PRINCIPAL WORKS

*The Development of Metaphysics in Persia*  (essay)  1908
*Asrar-i khudi*  (poetry)  1915
    [*The Secrets of the Self*, 1920]
*Ramuz-i-bekhudi*  (poetry)  1918
    [*The Mysteries of Selflessness*, 1953]
*Payam-i mashriq*  (poetry)  1923
    [*The Tulip of Sinai*, 1947]
*Bang-i-dara*  (poetry)  1924
    [*Complaint and Answer*, 1955]
*Zabur-i ajam*  (poetry)  1927
    [*Persian Psalms*, 1948]
*Javid-namah*  (poetry)  1932
    [*The Pilgrimage of Eternity*, 1961; also published as
    *Javid-Nama*, 1966]
*Six Lectures on the Reconstruction of Religious Thought in
    Islam*  (lectures)  1934
*Bal-i Jibril*  (poetry)  1936
*Musafir*  (poetry)  1936
*Pas cha bayad kard ay aqwam-i sharq*  (poetry)  1936
*Zarb-i kalim*  (poetry)  1936
*Armaghan-i hijaz*  (poetry)  1938

*All titles are listed as originally written and published in Persian, Urdu, or English.

---

*THE ATHENAEUM*  (essay date 1908)

[*In the following excerpt, the critic favorably reviews* The Development of Metaphysics in Persia.]

[In *The Development of Metaphysics in Persia,* Iqbal] has produced a really valuable résumé of the history of Persian metaphysics, inevitably sketchy and incomplete, but sound in principle, and trustworthy as far as it goes. In this field the labourers are so few that every one must rely, to a large extent, on his own researches. The materials have to be collected from num-

berless manuscripts preserved in the great libraries of Europe, and it is only after long and tiresome research that any attempt can be made to reconstruct. To review the work in detail is impossible, on account of the enormous range of speculation which it covers—from Zoroaster and Mani to modern Babism. Naturally there are points to which exception might be taken. In discussing the origin of Sufiism the writer claims to have treated the subject in a more scientific manner than previous investigators:—

> They seem completely to have ignored the principle that the full significance of a phenomenon in the intellectual evolution of a people can only be comprehended in the light of those pre-existing intellectual, political, and social conditions which alone make its existence inevitable. Von Kremer and Dozy derive Persian Sufiism from the Indian Vedanta; Marx and Mr. Nicholson derive it from Neo-Platonism, while Prof. Browne once regarded it as Aryan reaction against an unemotional Semitic religion. It appears to me, however, that these theories have been worked out under the influence of a notion of causation which is essentially false. That a fixed quantity A is the cause of or produces another fixed quantity B is a proposition which, though convenient for scientific purposes, is apt to damage all inquiry, in so far as it leads us completely to ignore the innumerable conditions lying at the back of a phenomenon.

We are sure that the scholars mentioned in this passage recognize, as unreservedly as Shaikh Iqbal himself, that Sufiism, like all great spiritual and intellectual movements, was ultimately the result of a certain environment, the nature of which is well known to every student of Islam. Their reasons for not laying stress on this fact are obvious enough. The conditions of which the Shaikh speaks enable us to explain the appearance of mysticism in Islam towards the end of the eighth century A.D., but that is all. We cannot hope, by examining these general conditions, to learn how it came to pass that the mystical tendency assumed a particular form, or how the special doctrines which we find in early Sufiism arose. No wonder, then, that European Orientalists should have preferred a more fruitful line of inquiry, which has demonstrated the influence of other religions in moulding the *development* of Sufiism. Those who derive it from Neo-Platonism do no more than assert that the early Sufis actually drew their leading ideas from that source; but had these Sufis been ignorant of Greek philosophy, they might still have produced a mysticism of the same type. To suppose that Sufiism was *created* by foreign influence is an absurdity so palpable that its refutation, even in the most scientific manner, hardly constitutes a claim to originality. We have dwelt upon the author's treatment of this question because it illustrates the one weak spot in his admirable survey. He is rather deficient on the historical side, and is apt to forget that a theory will carry greater conviction if it comes to close quarters with all the relevant facts.

The present work, however, is mainly concerned with elucidating the various systems of Persian thought and their relations to each other. Any one at all versed in the subject will perceive the appalling difficulty of the author's task when he undertook to give a coherent account in less than two hundred pages of the subtle and complex problems which have formed, during thousands of years, the favourite pabulum of a race that has always been distinguished by its passion for metaphysical speculation. Moreover, for a great part of his journey the traveller finds himself on virgin soil, which he must explore and delineate as well as he can without the help of guides. Shaikh Iqbal deserves high praise for what he has accomplished. The immediate result of his labour is considerable, and he has laid a solid foundation for further research. The most notable sections of the volume are perhaps those which describe the *Hikmat al-Ishrâq,* or "Philosophy of Illumination," expounded by Shihâb al-Din al-Suhrawardî, the famous Sufi thinker who was put to death as a heretic by order of Malik al-Zâhir, a son of Saladin; and the *Insân al-Kâmil,* or "Perfect Man," of al-Jîlî, whose system in some points curiously anticipates the views of Hegel and Schleiermacher.

We have found a few misspellings of Oriental names, and also one or two statements which we are inclined to question; but there can be no doubt as to the competence of the author's scholarship and the importance of his work. (pp. 601-02)

> A review of "The Development of Metaphysics in Persia," in The Athenaeum, No. 4229, November 14, 1908, pp. 601-02.

## MUHAMMAD IQBAL   (letter date 1921)

*[In the following letter to R. A. Nicholson, Iqbal comments on the political, social, and philosophical bases of his works.]*

I was very glad to learn from your letter to Shafi (Principal Md. Shafi of Oriental College, Lahore) that your translation of the *Asrar-i-khudi* had been favourably received and excited much attention in England. Some of the English reviewers, however, have been misled by the superficial resemblance of some of my ideas to those of Nietzsche.

The view of the writer in the *Athenaeum* is largely affected by some mistakes of fact for which, however, the writer does not seem to be responsible. But I am sure if he had known some of the dates of the publication of my Urdu poems referred to in his review, he would have certainly taken a totally different view of the growth of my literary activity. Nor does he rightly understand my idea of the Perfect Man which he confounds with the German thinker's Superman. I wrote on the Sufi doctrine of the Perfect Man more than twenty years ago, long before I had read or heard anything of Nietzsche. This was then published in the *Indian Antiquary* and later in 1908 formed part of my ***Development of Metaphysics in Persia.*** The English reader ought to approach this idea not through the German thinker, but through an English thinker of great merit—I mean Alexander—whose Gifford lectures delivered at Glasgow were published last year. His chapter on Deity and God . . . is worth reading. . . . [He] says—

> Deity is thus the next higher empirical quality to mind, which the universe is engaged in bringing to birth. That the universe is pregnant with such a quality—we are speculatively assured. What that quality is we cannot know; for we can neither enjoy nor still less contemplate it. Our human altars still are raised to the Unknown God. If we could know what Deity is, how it feels to be Divine, we should first have to become as gods.

Alexander's thought is much bolder than mine.

I believe there is a Divine tendency in the universe, but this tendency will eventually find its complete expression in a higher man, not in a God subject to Time, as Alexander implies in his discussion of the subject. I do not agree with Alexander's view of God, but it is clear that my idea of the Perfect Man will lose much of its outlandishness in the eye of the English

reader if he approaches it through the ideas of a thinker of his own country.

But it was Mr. Dickinson's review which interested me most, and I want to make a few remarks on it. (pp. 313-14)

(1) Mr. Dickinson thinks . . . that I have deified physical force in the poem. I am afraid he is mistaken in his view. I believe in the power of the spirit, not brute force. When a people is called to a righteous war, it is, according to my belief, their duty to obey the call; but I condemn all war of conquest (the story of Mianmir and the Emperor of India). Mr. Dickinson, however, is quite right when he says that war is destructive whether it is waged in the interests of Truth and Justice, or in the interests of conquest and exploitation. It must be put an end to in any case. We have seen, however, that Treaties, Leagues, Arbitrations and Conferences cannot put an end to it. Even if we secure these in a more effective manner than before, ambitious nations will substitute more peaceful forms of the exploitations of races supposed to be less favoured or less civilized. The truth is that we stand in need of a living personality to solve our social problems, to settle our disputes, and to place international morality on a surer basis. How very true are the last two paragraphs of Prof. Mackenzie's *Introduction to Social Philosophy.*

> There can be no ideal society without ideal man: and for the production of these we require not only insight but a motive power; fire as well as light. Perhaps, a philosophic understanding of our social problems is not even the chief want of our time. We need prophets as well as teachers, men like Carlyle or Ruskin or Tolstoy, who are able to add for us a new *severity to conscience or a new breadth to duty. Perhaps we want a new Christ . . . .* It has been well said that the prophet of our time must be a man of the world, and not merely a voice in the wilderness. For indeed the wilderness of the present is in the streets of our crowded cities, and in the midst of the incessant war by which we are trying to make our way upwards. It is there that the prophet must be.
>
> Or perhaps our chief want is rather for the poet of the new age than for its prophet—or for one who should be poet and prophet in one. Our poets of recent generations have taught us the love of nature, and enabled us to see in it the revelation of the Divine. We still look for one who shall show us with the same clearness the presence of the Divine in the human. . . . We still need one who shall be fully and in all seriousness what Heine playfully called himself "Ritter von dem Heiligen Geist," one who shall teach us to see the working out of our highest ideals in the everyday life of the world, and to find in devotion to the advancement of that life, not merely a sphere for an ascetic self-sacrifice, but a supreme object in the pursuit of which "all thoughts, all passions, all delights may receive their highest development and satisfaction."

It is in the light of the above thoughts that I want the British public to read my description of the ideal man. It is not our treaties and arbitrations which will put an end to the internecine wars of the human family.

(2) Mr. Dickinson further refers to my "Be hard." This is based on the view of reality that I have taken in the poem. According to my belief, reality is a collection of individualities tending to become a harmonious whole through conflict which must inevitably lead to mutual adjustment. This conflict is a necessity in the interests of the evolution of higher forms of

life, and of personal immortality. Nietzsche did not believe in personal immortality. To those desiring it, he ruthlessly says, "Do you wish to be a perpetual burden on the shoulders of time?" He was led to say this because he had a wrong notion of time, and never tried to grapple with the ethical issue involved in the question of time. On the other hand, I look upon immortality as the highest aspiration of man on which he should focus all his energies, and consequently, I recognise the need of all forms of activity, including conflict, which tend to make the human person more and more stable. And for the same consideration, I condemn speculative mysticism and inactive quietism. My interest in conflict is mainly ethical and not political, whereas Nietzsche's was probably only political. Modern physical science has taught us that the atom of material-energy has achieved its present form through thousands of years of evolution. Yet it is unstable and can be made to disappear. The same is the case with the atom of mind-energy, *i.e.*, the human person. It has achieved its present form through ions of incessant effort and conflict; yet, in spite of all this, its instability is clear from the various phenomena of mental pathology. If it has to continue intact it cannot ignore the lessons learnt from its past career, and will require the same or similar forces to maintain its stability which it has availed of before. It is possible that in its onward march nature may modify or eliminate altogether some of the forces (*e.g.*, conflict in the way of mutual wars) that have so far determined and helped its evolution, and introduce new forces hitherto unknown to mankind to secure its stability. But, I confess I am not an idealist in this matter and believe this time to be very distant. I am afraid mankind will not, for a very long time to come, learn the lesson that the Great European War has taught them. Thus it is clear that my purpose in recognizing the need of conflict is mainly ethical. Mr. Dickinson has unfortunately altogether ignored this aspect of the "Be hard."

(3) Mr. Dickinson further remarks that while my philosophy is universal my application of it is particular and exclusive. This is in a sense true. The humanitarian ideal is always universal in poetry and philosophy, but if you make it an effective ideal and work it out in actual life, you must start, not with poets and philosophers, but with a society exclusive in the sense of having a creed and well-defined outline, but ever enlarging its limits by example and persuasion. Such a society, according to my belief, is Islam. This society has so far proved itself a more successful opponent of the race-idea which is probably the hardest barrier in the way of the humanitarian ideal. Renan was wrong when he said that science was the greatest enemy of Islam. No, it is the race-idea which is the greatest enemy of Islam—in fact, of all humanity, and it is the duty of all lovers of mankind to stand in revolt against this dreadful invention of the Devil. Since I find that the idea of nationality based on race or territory is making headway in the world of Islam, and since I fear that the Muslims, losing sight of their own ideal of a universal humanity, are being lured by the idea of a territorial nationality, I feel it is my duty, as a Muslim and as a lover of all mankind, to remind them of their true function in the evolution of mankind. Tribal or national organizations on the lines of race or territory are only temporary phases in the unfoldment and upbringing of collective life, and as such I have no quarrel with them; but I condemn them in the strongest possible terms when they are regarded as the ultimate expression of the life of mankind. While I have the greatest love for Islam, it is in view of practical and not patriotic considerations, as Mr. Dickinson thinks, that I am compelled to start with a specific society (*e.g.*, Islam) which, among the societies of the world, happens to be the only one suitable to

my purpose. Nor is the spirit of Islam so exclusive as Mr. Dickinson thinks. In the interests of a universal unification of mankind the Quran ignores their minor differences and says, "Come let us unite on what is common to us all!"

I am afraid the old European idea of a blood-thirsty Islam is still lingering in the mind of Mr. Dickinson. All men and not Muslims alone are meant for the Kingdom of God on earth, provided they say goodbye to their idols of race and nationality, and treat one another as personalities. Leagues, mandates, treaties, like the one described by Mr. Keynes, and Imperialisms, however draped in democracy, can never bring salvation to mankind. The salvation of man lies in absolute equality and freedom of all. We stand in need of a thorough overhauling of the aims of science which has brought so much misery to mankind and of a total abandonment of what may be called esoteric politics which is ever planning the ruin of less clever or weaker races.

That Muslim peoples have fought and conquered like other peoples, and that some of their leaders have screened their personal ambition behind the veil of religion, I do not deny; but I am absolutely sure that territorial conquest was no part of the original programme of Islam. As a matter of fact, I consider it a great loss that the progress of Islam as a conquering faith stultified the growth of those germs of an economic and democratic organization of society which I find scattered up and down the pages of the Quran and the traditions of the Prophet. No doubt, the Muslims succeeded in building a great empire, but thereby they largely repaganized their political ideals, and lost sight of some of the most important potentialities of their faith. Islam certainly aims at absorption. This absorption, however, is to be achieved not by territorial conquest but by the simplicity of its teaching, its appeal to the common sense of mankind and its aversion to abstruse metaphysical dogma. That Islam can succeed by its inherent force is sufficiently clear from the Muslim Missionary work in China, where it has won millions of adherents without the help of any political power. I hope more than twenty years' long study of the world's thought has given me sufficient training to judge things impartially.

The object of my Persian poems is not to make out a case for Islam; my aim is simply to discover a universal social reconstruction; and in this endeavour, I find it philosophically impossible to ignore a social system which exists with the express object of doing away with all the distinctions of caste, rank and race; and which, while keeping a watchful eye on the affairs of this world, fosters a spirit of unworldliness so absolutely essential to man in his relations with his neighbours. This is what Europe lacks and this is what she can still learn from us.

One word more. In my notes which now form part of your introduction to *Asrar-i-khudi,* I deliberately explained my position in reference to Western thinkers, as I thought this would facilitate the understanding of my views in England. I could have easily explained myself in the light of the Quran and Muslim Sufis and thinkers, *e.g.,* Ibn Arabi and Iraqi (Pantheism), Wahid Mahmud (Reality as a Plurality), Al-Jili (the idea of the Perfect Man) and Mujaddid Sarhindi (the human person in relation to the Divine Person). (pp. 314-18)

I claim that the philosophy of the *Asrar* is a direct development out of the experience and speculation of old Muslim Sufis and thinkers. Even Bergson's idea of time is not quite foreign to our Sufis. The Quran is certainly not a book of metaphysics, but it takes a definite view of the life and destiny of man, which must eventually rest on propositions of a metaphysical import. A statement by a modern Muslim student of philosophy of such propositions, especially when it is done in the light of religious experience and philosophy invoked by that great book, is not putting new wine in old bottles. It is only a restatement of the old in the light of the new. It is unfortunate that the history of Muslim thought is so little known in the West. I wish I had time to write an extensive book on the subject to show to the Western student of philosophy how philosophic thinking makes the whole world kin. (pp. 318-19)

> Muhammad Iqbal, in a letter to Dr. R. A. Nicholson on January 24, 1921, in The Poet of the East: The Life and Work of Dr. Sir Muhammad Iqbal, the Poet-Philosopher, with a Critical Survey of His Philosophy, Poetical Works and Teachings by A. Anwar Beg, second edition, Khawar Publishing Cooperative Society, 1961, pp. 313-19.

## A. YUSUF ALI   (lecture date 1938)

[In the following excerpt from a lecture delivered in 1938, Ali discusses the major tenets of Iqbal's philosophy as presented in his poetry.]

Poet-philosophers are more usual in the East than in the West. But may we say that the trend of modern post-War poetry in the West also is in the direction of philosophizing? Is not Eliot a mystic, and Auden a singer of "a turning globe," which "has thrust us up together"?

However that may be, certainly the two greatest poets of modern India are philosophers. Rabindranath Tagore represents the contemplative, devotional, Bhakti philosophy of Vaishnava Hinduism. Take passages like the following:—

> Dream is a wife who must talk,
> Sleep is a husband who silently suffers.
>
> (Stray Birds)

> I carry in my world that flourishes the worlds that
> have failed.—
>
> (Stray Birds)

Their haunting poetic beauty, their epigrammatic terseness, yet sum up a whole inner world of human Personality, about whose truth or application philosophers will dispute to the end of time.

Iqbal's world is no less subtle, but it is altogether different, both in tone and tempo, in the source of its inspiration and in the struggle which it seeks to incite in his readers. Courage, Power, Action are the Ideals he would point to. Swiftness, forcefulness, unflinching assertion of Personality are the watchwords which he would din into the ears of a lethargic world. (pp. 89-90)

The source of his inspiration is the Qur-ān and the religious and poetic traditions of Islam in its most vigorous days. In form and substance he has based himself on Maulāna Jalāl-ud-din Rūmī, whose voluminous "mathnavi" is one of the treasures of Persian literature, indeed of the world's literature. But Iqbal is also steeped in modern philosophy, not as a follower but as a critic,—one might almost say, as a fierce assailant of its conclusions. His denunciations of Plato show little sympathy with that philosopher, and—I hesitate to say it—little understanding of his philosophy or of its influence on early Islamic thought. Nietzsche and Karl Marx are referred to, but on the whole they are rejected as smacking of Western materialism. A number of modern names are drawn upon to illustrate the arguments. Eastern names, like those of Jamāl-ud-dīn Afghāni

and Halīm Pasha serve to illustrate the idea of the universal non-national, non-racial Society of Islam, while Western names, such as that of Kitchener, are used to illustrate Western Imperialism. The League of Nations is described in these extraordinary terms: "A few grave-clothes-snatchers have made an association for the division of graves (among themselves)" (Kafan duzdé chand bahr i taqsīm i qubūr anjumane sakhta and). I do not know how far the most rabid enemies of the League would recognize their bête noire in that caricature. The most usual indictment of the League is that it is a model of utter idealistic futility.

In Iqbal's world we are to seek struggle and tension, not peace and calm. Life, to use his own words in illustration of his poetical philosophy, is ever "a forward assimilative movement." Personality is "a state of Tension," and it is the state of tension that "tends to make us immortal." The struggle which we should make is to maintain this tension, to absorb the whole world into ourselves, not to be absorbed. "Love is the desire to assimilate, to absorb," not to lose ourselves in the object of our love. He would dissent from Tennyson's lines:

> Love took up the Harp of Life,
>     and smote on all the chords with might,
> Smote the chord of Self that, trembling,
>     passed in music out of sight.

Nor would he approve of the Sūfi ideal, to be lost in God. For he uncompromisingly attacks the Sūfi mystics, especially Hāfiz and Sa'dī, for preaching the renunciation of the Self in order to reach God.

We must clearly take in the general atmosphere before we can fully understand Iqbal and his doctrine of Personality. (pp. 90-1)

Iqbal began to write poetry quite early. He wrote a number of short pieces in Urdu, which have been collected under the titles of Bāng i darā . . . , Bāl i Jibrīl . . . , and Zarb i kalīm. . . . His fame, however, will rest on the works which he published in Persian. Among these may be mentioned the following:

1. Asrār i khudi, Secrets of the Self (or the Ego). . . .
(p. 92)

2. Rumūz i be-khudi, Mysteries of Self-Denial, a pendant to the Asrār. It develops a philosophy of Society based on the eternal Ummat of Islam.

3. Payām i mashriq, The Message of the East, a series of poems in imitation of Goethe's 'West-Östlicher Diwan.' It assumes that the West is sunk in materialism and intellectualism, without a goal or purpose, and invites it to look more within.

4. Zabūr i 'ajam, The Psalmody of Persia. Here a number of philosophical ideas are discussed. The last two pieces are characteristic. They are entitled "The Religion of Slaves" and "The Art of Building up Free Men." A line may be quoted:

> In Slavery Love and Religion are separated:
> The honey of Life becomes nauseous in Taste.

5. Jāwīd nāma, The Book of Jāwīd, that being the name of his youngest son. This is a mystic Allegory, somewhat in the style of Dante's Divine Comedy, but in an expressly Muslim setting. There is also in it a reminiscence of some of the Mi'rāj Poems of medieval Islam, which, according to Asin, in some sort suggested the form of Dante's Poem. In Iqbal's journey through the various heavens of the Solar System and beyond, his guide is the Persian mystic Jalād ud din Rūmī, and he meets various friends and enemies of Islam, from Abū Jahl the relentless persecutor

of the Prophet Muhammad, to Nietzsche the Superman Philosopher, and Farzmarz the extreme and wicked feminist. Each of them talks dramatically, expounding his or her own views. As Nietzsche's doctrine of the Superman and the will to power has many points of contact with Iqbal's ideas but leaves out God, Nietzsche is described as the Root without the Fruit.

In my opinion, the *Asrār* and the *Rumūz,* though they are themselves somewhat loose in texture, present the leading ideas of Iqbal in a connected form, while the other works are variations on similar themes. (pp. 93-4)

He judges everything by the touchstone of Islam, not as expounded by its doctors, ancient or modern, but as understood by Iqbal in its philosophical, social, political, and personal aspects. While taking the great Sūfi Jālal-ud-din Rūmi as his master and guide, he rails against the Sūfi schools as too otherworldly, as sapping the strength and virility of Islam. Against ascetic Sūfiism in all its forms he wages an unceasing war. He considers it to be a form of freethought and in alliance with Rationalism. This dictum can hardly be accepted as historically true. On the other hand, his protest against the exploitation of Sūfiism, in modern India (and elsewhere) by selfish and ignorant men is both reasonable and effective, and finds an echo in a great deal of current literature in India.

The contrast between the East and the West, much to the spiritual and moral disadvantage of the West, is almost an obsession in Iqbal. It colours his views on many questions, social, political, and economic. In this, perhaps, he is expressing the general sentiments of the educated rising generation in India—and not in India only, but throughout what we may call the Near East. Iqbal delighted in such books as Spengler's *Decline of the West.* He imagined that thinkers in the West were agreed that the days of the West were done, and elicited loud applause when he expressed such sentiments. Political conditions explain the paradox that those who have received western education are, as a class, the bitterest critics of the West. Slavery and Freedom, Capitalism and Socialism or Communism, Materialism and Spirituality, the Inward Eye and the Worship of the Outer Good, Imperialism and the Spirit of Submission, Modernism and Wholesome Tradition,—such are some of the slogans through which the contrast is sought to be expressed. Iqbal's *Zarb i kalīm* has a sub-title on the title-page—*A Declaration of War against the Present Age.* In the same book we have the following poem on **"Woman and Education"**:

> If European civilisation
> Is the death of the Nation,
> Death is its fruit also
> For the Individual Man.
> The education whose influence
> Makes a woman unwomanly,—
> Far-seeing people
> Call such education Death.
> If the schooling of woman
> Is divorced from Religion,
> Then, as regards Love and Affection,
> Knowledge and Art are but Death.

We have thus a strong vein of innate conservatism combined with the most revolutionary doctrines for the Individual and for Society. It is doubtful whether such a combination is either logical, consistent or practicable. Elsewhere I have called Iqbal's philosophy a "mystical protest against mysticism." The form, the tone, the spirit is mystical. The content can only be described as Iqbalism. He is conscious of that. His spirit took a wide sweep. It wandered, as a poet's spirit should, over worlds beyond ken. But all the time he felt he was alone. "In the midst of the Assembly, I am solitary," he cries in the *Asrār* and he repeats the cry towards the end. He has to free himself from Yesterday and To-morrow, and behold another world in his own heart. . . .

To Iqbal the doctrine of Personality is not mere metaphysical speculation. It is an important secret vouchsafed to him, to be rehearsed to a sorrowful world. He has the urge of a prophet, and he invites the world to listen and profit by it:

> Come, if thou wouldst know
> The secret of everlasting life!
> Come, if thou wouldst win
> Both earth and heaven.
>
> [*Asrar*]

What is this Khudī, this Self, this Personality?

> My being was
> As unfinished statue,
> Uncomely, worthless,
> Good for nothing.
> Love chiselled me:
> I became a man
> And gained knowledge
> Of the nature of the universe.
>
> [*Asrar*]

Seven propositions implicit in Iqbal's argument may be first stated categorically, and then considered in detail. They are: (1) that man, in his unregenerate state, is but dust; (2) that there is yet in him a potentiality, which opens up to him the highest destiny in the universe; (3) that the unfolding of that potentiality is through the Khudi, the Self; (4) that that Self or Personality requires to be constantly exercised and developed through Love; (5) that the channel for that development is the Gospel of Tauhīd or Unity, the mystic personality of Muhammad the Prophet; (6) that Intellect, modern knowledge, common virtues like humility or contentment,—anything that is "shackled in the senses". . . is a mere blind and leads away from Perfection; and (7) that the Inner Light in the Self is creative; the pith of Life is action . . . and strength. . . . The Nietzschean tendency is evident, especially in the statement that Life's "mainspring is the desire for victory, and mercy out of season is a coldness of blood." . . . The only difference between Nietzsche and Iqbal is that Iqbal brings in his own idea of religion, of Islam, and of God, as the basis of the whole agreement, while Nietzsche rejects God altogether.

As he frequently refers to Rūmi as his guide, let us glance at Rūmi's idea on the subject of "Khudi." The germ of the "Khudi" idea can be found in three couplets of Rūmi; but its growth, development, and conclusions appear to me to be entirely different—almost at opposite poles—from those of Iqbal. Rūmi, towards the end of his *Mathnavi,* describes three types of men—the wise man, the half-wise man, and the fool. The wise man has personality and light; the half-wise man learns from him; the fool learns from nothing. Let me quote from Rūmi:

"The wise man is he who has a torch: he is the guide and leader of the caravan. He goes in the van, following his own Light *(pairawe Nur e Khud ast)* and obeying his own Self, while the others follow other than their Selves. He believes in himself and his faith in the Light on which his soul feeds." This is the doctrine of the Inner Light or Conscience as illuminated by God. . . . The Sūfis went on developing this doctrine. Two centuries after Rūmi, Jāmi wrote in his 'Lawā'ih:

> Make my heart pure, my soul from error free,
> Make tears and sighs my daily lot to be,
> And lead me on Thy road away from Self,
> That lost to Self I may approach to Thee.
>                     (Whinfield's translation.)

We may observe the remarkable way in which the stream of the Sūfi doctrine of Self has been diverted by Iqbal from its original trend through the intervention of Nietzsche until it runs almost in the opposite direction.

But let us return to Iqbal. If we only look to man's physical nature, man is no more than clay and water. But, according to Quranic phraseology, God breathed His spirit into him. He has now, therefore, to become the vicegerent of God in God's Creation. He has to conquer his body, and let his thought reach to the skies. There is a danger that mere thought, mere mind, mere intellect may make not-Self appear as the Self. Therefore the real Self should be strengthened and asserted, even though it may involve pain and anguish to others. There may be much "wastefulness and cruelty in the shaping and perfecting of spiritual beauty." . . .

Rejecting the Buddhist injunction to kill Desire, Iqbal would on the contrary "set Desire dancing in the breast." . . . Desire enriches life. "We live by forming ideals; we glow with the sunbeams of Desire." . . . Desire became Love; the highest love is the love of God and His Prophet. But do not ask or beg. That is weakness. "Pray God for Courage; wrestle with Fortune." . . . "Desire is Love's Message to Beauty," . . . and Beauty creates Desire. Hence arises the Poet's duty to sing of Beauty and fire the hearts of men. Hence the need for a reform of Islamic literature.

How came it that the doctrine of strength and the assertion of self gave place to the doctrine of self-denial and self-negation? The latter was invented by subject-races to weaken the character of rulers and conquerors. The wakeful tiger was thus called to slumber. Poverty and humility were exalted, and strength and independence declined. The decline was called "Moral Culture." . . . The only case in which the Individual should subordinate his personality arises in relation to the ideal Society of Islam, which is expounded in Iqbal's **Rumūz**.

While the Individual must push forward and conquer, he can only do so by obeying the Law of Islam. He must learn self-command and self-control. He must abjure fear. He must give up "love of riches and power, love of country, love of self and kindred and wife," . . . because of that higher Love, the love of God and of the Law of Islam. Thus is obtained the divine vicegerency. Such a vicegerent "wakes and sleeps for God alone." . . . He is the perfect Man, the rider of Destiny. "Nature travails in blood for generations, to compose the harmony of his personality." . . . The Prophet's cousin 'Ali was such a man.

The Coal in the mine and the Diamond are similar in origin and composition. Yet Coal is held in low esteem, while the Diamond shines in splendour and becomes "the light of a monarch's eye." . . . Why is this? The Diamond thus explains it to the Coal:

> "Dark earth, when hardened,
> Becomes in dignity as a jewel.
> Having been at strife
> With its environment,

> It is ripened by the struggle
> And grows hard like a stone.
> 'Tis this ripeness that has endowed
> My form with light
> And filled my bosom
> With radiance.
> Because thy being is immature,
> Thou hast become abased;
> Because thy body is soft,
> Thou art burnt.
> Be void of fear,
> Grief, and anxiety.
> Be hard as a stone;
> Be a diamond!
> Whoever strives hard
> And grips tight,
> The two worlds
> Are illumined by him."
>                                   [*Asrār*]

It then comes to this. Personality is power, striving, the resistance to the presence of outside circumstances of all kinds. But, as we saw, the Self is not exempt from the Law of Islam. It is a perfect Law, an eternal Law, and in itself it makes for strength and the building-up of the Self. It reconciles the categories of permanence and change, as the Self in striving is always developing, expanding, and in motion. If you understand eternal principles to exclude all possibilities of change, you produce the immobility which has gripped Islamic peoples for the last 500 years. On the other hand, if you have no eternal principles to regulate your collective life, you go on changing and changing, but you fail, as Europe has done, says Iqbal, in her political and social science. The law of change and adaptation, subject to eternal principles, being admitted, it is difficult to follow Iqbal's plea that each community should remain attached to itself to follow its ancestral traditions. Even the idol-worshipper need not abandon his idols. If he is a Brahman, he should be worthy of his sacred thread. "O trustee of an ancient culture, turn not away from the ways of thy fathers." . . . This seems to me to be inconsistent both with the law of Islam *(Qur-ān)* and with Iqbal's own philosophy of Life.

The Self, then, is to Iqbal the fundamental fact of the universe. (pp. 94-102)

There are a few questions that remain unanswered. Is every individual man capable of becoming an *Insān i Kāmil*, a Perfect Man? What becomes, then, of the Unique Individual? For in Iqbalian philosophy man is not finally absorbed in God: on the contrary, he absorbs God into himself. This cannot happen to every individual man as a separate entity. Then, if there is no final cessation of the struggle, this world with its imperfections must be eternal; but Islam denies this *('Qur-ān)*. Again, if for the sake of a single Rose, the Self destroys a hundred rose-gardens . . . , or, if the flames of the Self have to burn a hundred Abrahams that the lamp of one Muhammad may be lighted . . . , what becomes of the souls unsuccessful in the struggle? And if there are no failures, how can we conceive of millions and millions of perfect ones? But perfection itself can only be reached when the struggle ceases, just as prophecy, to use Iqbal's own words, "reaches its perfection in discovering the need of its own abolition." How, then, can the struggle be unceasing? (p. 103)

The last three-quarters of a century have seen revolutionary changes in Indian Muslim thought. The Indian Muslims had been declining in power as well as original thought for over a century and a half. But the Indian Mutiny marks the definite close of the period of their work as an active striving factor in leadership. After that, three great names stand out pre-eminent among the Muslim poets in India, viz. Ghālib, Hāli and Iqbal. Every one of them wrote in Persian as well as in Urdu. (pp. 103-04)

In texture of thought the three poets stand out distinct and apart. Ghālib had to face the disastrous sequels of the social and political revolution which he so bitterly lamented. But he interpreted the inner revolution which was less patent to the ordinary mind. From the note of despair which he sounded, the Aligarh educational movement aimed at rescuing the Indian Muslims by directing them to the modern tendencies of the world at large, which now came from the West. Hāli was associated with that movement and with its founder, Sir Saiyid Ahmad Khan. He, therefore, in reviewing the past found these very tendencies in early Islam, and made an impassioned appeal to his people to adopt them and march forward to progress. In Iqbal's generation the pendulum has swung the other way. Mainly because of political movements, the West was very much out of favour, and Iqbal accentuated that attitude. But he did a real service to his people in calling them back to the more manly virtues of their ancestors. His talent lay in a searching criticism, sometimes carried to extremes, of the false standards of his age. His message was to condemn apathy, timidity, and obscurantism, and put activity, courage and practical achievement in the forefront of his programme. To this end he wrote with the enthusiasm and emotional *élan* of the mystic Sufis whom he condemned. He was after all a mystic in the war which he waged against mysticism. His doctrine of Personality is really a doctrine of activity, with an unbounded field of thought and action in the world of Islam. (pp. 104-05)

> A. Yusuf Ali, *"Doctrine of Human Personality in Iqbal's Poetry,"* in Essays by Divers Hands *n.s., Vol. XVIII, 1940, pp. 89-105.*

### E. M. FORSTER   (essay date 1946)

[*Forster was a prominent English novelist, critic, and essayist whose works reflect his liberal humanism. His most celebrated novel,* A Passage to India *(1924), is a complex examination of personal relationships amid the conflicts of the modern world. Although some of Forster's critical essays are considered naive in their literary assessments, his* Aspects of the Novel *(1927), a discussion of the techniques of novel writing, is regarded as a minor classic in literary criticism. In the following excerpt from an essay written in 1946, Forster introduces Iqbal to Western readers.*]

Iqbal was an orthodox Moslem, though not a conventional one. He was highly educated, and partly in Europe; he was not cosmopolitan, and the basis of his culture remained Oriental. By profession he was a lawyer. He wrote both prose and poetry. The poems are mostly in Urdu, some are in Persian, and a few in Punjabi. As for his politics, he was once in sympathy with a united India, but in later life he changed, and adherents of Pakistan now claim him as a prophet. Whatever his opinions, he was no fanatic, and he refers to Hindus and to Christians with courtesy and respect.

All the same he was a fighter. He believed in the Self—the Self as a fighting unit—and his philosophy is not an enquiry into truth but a recommendation as to how the fight should be carried on. Fight we must, for man is the vice-regent of God upon earth. We must fortify our personalities. We must be hard. We must always be in a state of tension and try to be

supermen. In one poem, Satan complains to God that men are not worth tempting because they are weak and have never discovered their Selves:

> O master of all . . .
> Association with mankind has debased me.
> Take back from me this doll of water and clay.

So might the button-moulder in Ibsen's play complain of Peer Gynt. Iqbal reminds us of Nietzsche too. Renunciation of the Self is a form of cowardice, and therefore a crime. We cannot bear one another's burdens, and we must not expect to be redeemed.

Now he combines this doctrine of hardness and of the Self with a capacity for mysticism. The combination makes him remarkable as a poet. Even in a translation, one can see the sudden opening-up of vistas between the precepts. It is not the mysticism that seeks union with God. On this point the poet is emphatic. We shall see God perhaps. We shall never be God. For God, like ourselves, has a Self, and he created us not out of himself but out of nothing. Iqbal dislikes the pantheism which he saw all around him in India—for instance, in Tagore—and he castigates those Moslem teachers who have infected Islam with it. It is weakening and wrong to seek unity with the divine. Vision—perhaps. Union—no.

Such—if an outsider may summarise—is his philosophy. It is not a philosophy I like, but that is another matter. There is anyhow nothing vague about it, nothing muzzy. It gives us a shock and helps us to see where we are. It is non-Christian. It is, in a sense, anti-humanitarian. It inspires him to write poems. They follow the orthodox forms, but they contain matter which is excitingly modern. Take, for instance, this poem in which Man defiantly addresses God on the ground that Man has proved the better artist of the two:

> Thou didst create night but I made the lamp.
> Thou didst create clay but I made the cup.
> Thou didst create the deserts, mountains, and forests,
> I produced the orchards, gardens and the groves:
> It is I who make the glass out of stone
> And it is I who turn a poison into an antidote.

Or consider this strange poem on the subject of Lenin. Lenin has died, and finds himself in the presence of the deity whom he had supposed to be an invention of the priests. He is not intimidated, but speaks his mind. God exists, to be sure. But whose God is he? The starving peasant's? The God of the East, who worships the white men? Or of the West, who worships the Almighty Dollar?

> Thou art All-Powerful, O Lord, but in thy world
> The lot of the hapless labourer is very hard!
> When will this boat of Capitalism be wrecked?
> Thy world is waiting for the Day of Reckoning.

The angels are moved by the dead Bolshevik's bluntness, and they sing to their Lord like the angels at the opening of Goethe's *Faust*, but not in the same strain:

> Intellect is still unbridled. Love is not localised.
> O painter divine, Thy painting is still imperfect.
> Lying in ambush for mankind are the vagabond, the exploiter
>   and the monk.
> In thy universe the old order still continueth.

The Almighty is moved in his turn. He bows to the criticism of Lenin, and he orders the angels to burn every cornstalk in the field which does not nourish the cultivator, to give the sparrow strength to fight the falcon, and to smash up the glasshouse of modern civilisation. Iqbal never identifies hardness with oppression, or the Self with selfishness. The superman he seeks may come from any class of society.

Here is an uncontroversial lyric, **"Loneliness."** The poet is speaking, and his words gain pathos when we remember his creed of hardness:

To the sea-shore I went and said to a restless wave,
"Thou art always in quest of something. What ails thee?
There are a thousand bright pearls in thy bosom,
But hast thou a heart like mine in thy breast?"
It merely trembled, sped away from the shore, and said
    nothing.

I betook myself to the presence of God, passing beyond the
    sun and the moon, and said:
"In thy world not a single particle knows me,
The world has no heart, and this earthly being of mine is all
    heart.
The garden is charming, but is not worthy of my song."
A smile came to his lips, but he said nothing.

Mohammed Iqbal is a genius and a commanding one, and though I often disagree with him and usually agree with Tagore, it is Iqbal I would rather read. I know where I am with him. He is one of the two great cultural figures of modern India, and our ignorance about him is extraordinary. (pp. 289-91)

*E. M. Forster, "Mohammed Iqbal," in his* Two Cheers for Democracy, *Harcourt Brace Jovanovich, Inc., 1951, pp. 288-91.*

### SACHCHIDANANDA SINHA  (essay date 1947)

[*Founding editor of the periodical* Hindustan Review, *Sinha was an Indian statesman and critic. In the following excerpt, he assesses Iqbal's importance in Indo-Muslim literature.*]

Has Iqbal presented Islam in his works "in a true perspective," and "in accordance with its true spirit"—to adopt the words of Sir Sikandar Hayat Khan. Not minding the poet's deliberate mistake in choosing, for composing by far the greater and the more important part of his poetical works, the language of Persia in preference to that of India—for the reason stated by him that "Persian suits best by nature for expressing my lofty thought"; or his pedantry and sesquipedalianism in interlarding his Urdu verses with uncouth and unfamiliar words and phrases, borrowed unjustifiably from Arabic and Persian, which makes his diction stilted, turgid, and inflated; or his unwarranted tirades against western civilisation and culture, and all that they stand for in religion, morals, economics and politics; or his indifference to the ancient and, on the whole, glorious civilisation, and wonderful culture, of his own country—while proud of his having mastered the secrets of the religion and philosophy of some foreign lands; or his frankly low estimate of his country to the effect that "in the land of Hind the voice of life is ineffective, for the dead body does not come to life through the song of David"—thus betraying a sense of frustration, and offering a counsel of despair in connection with the great movement for the renaissance of India; or last but not least, his wholly mistaken judgment on the effect and influence of his Persian poems on Muslim lands outside India, and especially in Iran—in spite of his wishful thinking "my voice has enkindled the old fire of Persia," in support of which claim there is not a tittle of reliable evidence; but to hark back to the main question (propounded by Sir Sikandar Hayat), what about Iqbal's interpretation and exposition of Islam? Did he perform his task "in a true perspective and in accordance with the true spirit of Islam?" We know that Iqbal took himself

rather seriously as an interpreter and expositor of Islam; for did he not say of himself:—

I am waiting for the votaries that arise at dawn
Oh, happy they who shall worship my fire,
I have no need of the ear of today,
I am the voice of the poet of tomorrow.

But tomorrow is on the knees of the gods, and we can forecast it only in the light of the past and the present—the past which has been the builder of the present, and the present which shall be the builder of the future. Leaving, therefore, the question of "the poet of tomorrow," let us judge of Iqbal's position in the world today. Did the poet offer any interpretation of Islam which might appeal to the non-Muslims in India, or elsewhere, which might attract them to its great spiritual and noble idealism, and which might modify, even partly, the traditional exposition of this sublime religion, which hinders its acceptance by non-Muslims? The answer is that not only it does not, but it makes the task of non-Muslims more difficult in appreciating Islam at its true worth, by reason of the poet's retreating in the twentieth century the differences and distinctions between *iman* and *kufr,* between monotheists and polytheists, and several others of the same kind and type, which have been the weakest point—to put it mildly—of much of Indo-Muslim literature, produced both in Persian and Urdu. Iqbal cannot also be credited with having made any contribution, worth the name, to the liberalisation of the mind of the Indian Muslims, by far the larger number of whom, while professing admiration for his works, are still far behind the times, as compared with their religious compatriots not only in Turkey, Egypt, and Iran but even with those in comparatively backward countries like Iraq and Syria. What then can we place to Iqbal's credit on a careful consideration of his life's work? In the domain of politics and administrative affairs one can but recall his favourite theory of harking back to the polity of early Islam (of the seventh century), and his attempt at its restoration, or re-establishment, in the twentieth century Muslim countries, which he advocated strenuously in his poems, but which (in the words of Mr. Ghulam Sarwar) "offers no more than another Utopia to the world," for which reason, as remarked by Mr. Abdullah Yusuf Ali "his (Iqbal's) influence was negligible." As regards his influence as a poet, . . . I [quote Yusuf Ali's views] to the effect that Iqbal was "an isolated figure," since "he founded no school of literary thought," with the result that his literary influence "is silent in literature and daily life."

In his critical study of a great Bengalee novelist, called *Sarat Chandra Chatterjee,* Mr. Humayun Kabir (a well-known Indo-Muslim scholar) makes some remarks, which are apposite and relevant to the point under discussion. He writes: "Bankim Chatterjee was not only a writer with a purpose: he was a partisan and a propagandist. Purpose is a necessary condition of great art, but propaganda destroys its essence by tying it down to a narrow and definite end. Labels are ruinous for an artist, and so far as Bankim Chatterjee can be labelled, he loses in artistic stature. Sarat Chandra Chatterjee shares with Tagore his artistic detachment. Both are purposive writers, but their purpose is never allowed to degenerate into mere propaganda." Readers . . . will form their own opinion as to whether Iqbal is to be regarded as a purposive "artist," or "propagandist." If they accept the view that he was not so much an "artist" as a "propagandist," they will then agree to the consequential deduction that even in the most important sphere of literary activities Iqbal's failure, as a great poet, is established on the testimony of the duly qualified authorities I have quoted in support of that view, which cannot be, therefore, seriously questioned by dispassionate and unprejudiced critics. To the question, therefore, whether Iqbal's poems—whether in Persian or Urdu—will survive the ravages of Time, the most optimistic answer that can be given, at present, is "wait and see." It will all depend on the growth and development of the mind of the Muslim masses in India, as the years roll by.

But a critic, if fair-minded and impartial, should not omit to add that it will remain to the credit of Iqbal . . . that the outstanding feature of the message embodied in his poems was to place action in the forefront of human activities, in the sense that he preached that life is not to be merely contemplative but to be assertive; that is, to be lived passionately, and strenuously, since the goal of mankind is to be supremacy in preference to that of submission. One finds the same sentiment expressed by Emile Verhaeren (1855-1916), the famous Belgian poet and patriot, in the words: "Life is to be mounted and not be descended; the whole of life is in the soaring upwards." It is this robust and muscular philosophy—which coupled with the poet's denunciation of capitalism, and a suggestion for its replacement by an emotional but not a well-reasoned-out system of socialism—had appealed to a fairly large section of his readers among Indian Muslims. Hence it is that uninformed and uncritical socialists, and also aggressive reactionaries seek and find both consolation and inspiration in the message of Iqbal—since his teachings, as enshrined in his poems are (like much of the later Hindu scriptures) a mass of unsystematic and un-coordinated effusion, in which almost every seeker after support of his own ideals and aspirations not only looks for but finds whatever he wills or requires. Yet when all is said and done, credit must be justly given to Iqbal for having popularised, if not evolved, a form of thinking which appeals to a fairly large section of his co-religionists in India—though, from a critical standpoint, it may not stand the test of scrutiny. This aspect of Iqbal's message should be given due weight in a critical estimate of the poet's works; and I gladly testify to it. (pp. 455-59)

> Sachchidananda Sinha, in his Iqbal: The Poet and
> His Message, Ram Narain Lal, 1947, 512 p.

**IQBAL SINGH** (essay date 1951)

[Singh is the author of The Ardent Pilgrim: An Introduction to the Life and Work of Mohammed Iqbal. In the following excerpt from the conclusion to that work, he assesses Iqbal as "the last in the chain of classical poets of the Indo-Persian order and first of the Moderns."]

[How] is one to sum up a multidimensional personality like that of Iqbal, a personality so rich, so complex, so full of glaring contradictions? To every summing up there must always be something to add. A variety of interpretations are possible; they are even necessary. With a man whose writings are so provocative, so assertive, so dogmatic even, there is bound to be a wide margin of controversy in the assessment of the worth of his work.

There are, obviously, two broadly demarcated, though interrelated, aspects of his personality. There is the poet; and there is the prophet of Indo-Muslim renaissance. These two aspects may, and perhaps should be, considered separately. As a poet his reputation is based on far less controversial grounds than his reputation as a prophet of Pan-Islamic ideas. For his achievement in the sphere of poetry is so monumental that no matter how much we subtract from it there still remains enough,

and more than enough, to sustain his preeminent position among the Urdu and Persian poets of our time.

Yet here a striking paradox has to be noted. Notwithstanding this monumental achievement, Iqbal has exercised singularly little influence on the generation of poets who have followed him. Most of them have admired him for one reason or another; most of them have been willing to acknowledge his supremacy; but hardly anyone among them has followed in his footsteps and their work shows no direct and palpable traces of having been influenced by Iqbal. This is an astonishing contrast to the case of Tagore. For whereas Tagore became the literary glass of fashion and mould of form for a whole generation of Bengali writers, and not only Bengali writers, this cannot be claimed of Iqbal. He has left behind him no school of poetry to carry on his tradition. The younger Urdu poets, Muslim as well as non-Muslim, have been inclined to worship other outlandish poetic gods—not Iqbal.

Possibly the explanation for this paradox is furnished by the fact that he was never preoccupied with formal and technical problems as such. He never experimented with new techniques and new forms in verse. He was not, in form and technique, fond of innovations. He broke no new ground in so far as poetic media are concerned. He was perfectly happy working within the framework of conventional patterns and rhythms. Though he had been influenced by the European Romantics and was temperamentally akin to them in many respects, he adhered to orthodox and traditional modes of poetry. The younger generation of Urdu poets, on the other hand, have been in revolt against these traditional moulds and forms. They have primarily been concerned with breaking away from orthodox patterns and conventions and only incidentally with discovering new content. They can, therefore, derive little direct stimulus from Iqbal.

Iqbal used the conventional patterns of Urdu and Persian poetry; he employed the well-established rhyming schemes and cadences; he remained for the most part faithful to the old symbols, metaphors, similies, imagery and allusions. But it would be a mistake to conclude from this that his poetry is merely a variation on old themes and breaks no new ground. For this is not the case. The surprising as well as the important quality of his poetry is that, though remaining strictly within conventional limits of form, it communicates an urgent and undeniable sense of originality. More than that: it succeeds in vastly expanding the scope and limits of existing forms, in making these forms infinitely more elastic and comprehensive than they had been in the hands of his predecessors. The old metaphors and similies in his hands acquire not only wider but a different kind of meaning; the traditional imagery and symbolism become completely transformed and carry new significations and fresh nuances in his usage; and allusions which superficially are derivative of the classical Persian poetry on closer scrutiny reveal themselves as being instinct with a deeper suggestiveness which can directly be related to contemporary awareness and experience. It is, indeed, a case of new wine in old bottles and there is great substance in the claim which Dr. M. D. Taseer makes in his introduction to Aspects of Iqbal that Iqbal's verse "is not topical but contemporary."

It is in precisely this highly individual use of existing poetic forms and materials that Iqbal was original. He took these forms and materials and lifted them to a higher level, translating them to a new imaginative purpose. Before him Urdu and Persian poetry had largely been either purely descriptive, or purely technical in the sense of reducing itself to verbal virtuosity, or an expression of moods in the language of lyricism. True, there had been Hali and some of his less successful disciples. Hali had redeemed Urdu poetry from the morass of subjectivity and personal expressionism, revived it, and restored to it some of its higher functions such as criticism of social and cultural values, expression of a point of view, and preoccupation with living problems. But it was left to Iqbal to take poetry right into the arena of life and to revitalize it to a point where it could adequately perform these higher functions. With him poetry became true critique of life; it took upon itself the task of moulding social outlook—of "ordering human responses and impulses," if we prefer the scientific language of Dr. Richards; it became able-bodied and adult enough to affirm a world-view. Whether that world-view was valid or not, whether the kind of ordering of our responses and impulses which Iqbal desired was in fact in conformity with the present needs, and whether his critique of life was correct or false—these are separate questions which are not germane to our argument at this stage of the discussion. What is germane is that he, more than any recent poet in India, was responsible for making poetry an effective vehicle by re-establishing its organic connection with social and historic processes. That is his distinctive contribution as a poet.

And it is a very great contribution. For in a sense he had a sharper and deeper appreciation of the functions of poetry than some of the experimentalists and innovators who came after him. He never succumbed, philosophically at any rate, to the lure of the ivory tower. He rejected vehemently the dogma of "Art for Art's sake." In his little note on **"Our Prophet's Criticism of Contemporary Arabian Poetry"** he declares: "There should be no opium-eating in Art. The Dogma of Art for the sake of Art is a clever invention of decadence to cheat us out of life and power."

Thus far, it will be observed, he was entirely on the side of the angels, not *fin de siècle* aestheticism with its doctrine of social irresponsibility of the artist. But, of course, he chose his own special angels on whose side he wanted to be; and his choice is not likely to be universally approved because it is a highly individualistic choice. He brought to poetry a modern approach as well as a vast new content of ideas which it had hitherto lacked; he handled contemporary themes as few before him had dared to handle them. But at this point his modernity ends; a regressive tendency begins to assert itself; and an unresolved duality becomes manifest. For, though he dealt with modern problems and themes in his verse, his interpretations are not necessarily in conformity with the contemporary spirit. There are reasons to believe that he was not unaware of this divergency in himself. True, he could boast that he had "no need of the ear of to-day" since he was "the voice of the poet of tomorrow." But he also admitted in one of his poems his essential difficulty:

> I see tomorrow in the mirror of yester night.

This would be even truer if we substitute the word to-day for tomorrow. He saw the present in the mirror of yesterday. This divergency between the reality and the image is at once the principle of development in relation to his imaginative problems and the reason for the baffling translucency of his vision. It is the principle of development in the sense that there is in Iqbal the ever-present and insistent urge to eliminate the divergency, to make the image conform to the objective reality; and it is the cause of the translucency in his vision in that, because of his upbringing, his position in the society of his time, his inhibitions and complexes, he was unable to take the

one step which would have solved the problem—namely changing the mirror.

Had he done so, however, it is also possible that he might have ceased to write poetry as has sometimes happened. For poetry is in the quarrel, in the tension and contradiction of an imaginative conflict. That is, at least, the case with Iqbal. He belongs to two different worlds, of to-day and of yesterday. His poetry is of both: it forms a kind of bridge between the past and the present. Across that bridge others will pass, if they have not already passed, wholly into the present—one hopes into the future, too. But that passage was not for him. That is the nature of a bridge, whether it bridges a gulf of space or of time: it forms a link, but it is not the road. Iqbal is the link. Standing on the edge of two epochs, it can be claimed, he represents the last in the chain of classical poets of the Indo-Persian order and first of the Moderns. That is his significance.

The perspective is not so clear when we come to treat of him in his prophetic rôle and consider the social, political, and philosophical ideas which he propagated or with which he has become identified. It is not so clear because it is impossible to trace through his work any coherent, systematic and lucid schema of arguments on any of these planes. What we get, instead, is a turbid eclecticism, often brilliant and provocative, but which, in the very nature of things, could never acquire consistency of texture. His was not, despite many claims to that effect, a synthesising intellect. Like most social, political and cultural eminences of India during the past hundred years, from Raja Rammohan Roy through Sir Saiyad Ahmed Khan to Gandhi, his mental background consisted of a mixture of all kinds of ideas; and this mixture constantly approaches a quality of synthesis but never quite achieves a synthesis. The pattern of thought that is projected is not, consequently, an integral whole, but a mosaic of variegated elements, though certain elements are more accentuated than others. And this is so, once again, because the essential dichotomy is the same in the case of the prophet as it is in the case of the poet. For as a prophet, too, Iqbal stands between two epochs, the old feudal and patriarchal and the modern capitalist-bourgeois. He belongs partially to both and wholly to neither, sharing the excellences no less than the defects, the illusions no less than the certitudes of both. (pp. 226-33)

The contradictions and the inconsistencies are manifest through the whole fabric of his social and political ideas. He was a bitter critic of the liberal democratic tradition of the West based on the equality of stomach as he claimed it to be. Yet he found it possible to participate in the mock democracy of the Montford Reforms, which did not go as far even as stomachs. He lamented that the soul of Mir Jafar, who had betrayed India to the foreigner, was still alive; yet he felt no qualm of conscience in accepting knighthood of the Empire which the Mir Jafars of India had been instrumental in bringing into being. He raised his voice in loud protest against the inequities and injustices of a society based on capitalist values. Yet he became the President of an organisation which included some of the biggest capitalists of his community and was prepared to do political deals on the basis of percentages, division of spoil, demarcation of spheres of influence. More than that: the ardent critic of imperialism was prepared to assure the British Empire that the Muslims of North West India would be prepared, at a price, to become "the defenders of India against a foreign invasion," be that one of ideas or bayonets (shades of Cold War twenty years before the event). These may all have been tactical moves, but his philosophy recognised no such duality of ends and means.

To stress these contradictions and inconsistencies is not to prepare the ground for an adverse judgement, nor even to suggest that he was doing something morally reprehensible. The moral question, in any case, is not under discussion. What is at question is the relation of theory to practice. In this case the practice that flowed from a theory which was couched in the most idealistic terms was no different to the practice of the liberal social reformers and politicians of his time and class. It represents merely the continuation and development of the Aligarh tradition.

Related to the question of his critique of existing social and political values is his attitude to socialism. Dr. Taseer has claimed that Iqbal "became avowedly a Muslim socialist." And in support of his claim he has argued that while in the *Payam* he had placed Lenin no higher than Kaiser Wilhelm II in *Bal-i-Jibril* he honours Lenin sufficiently to take him in the presence of the Heavenly Host. There is substance in this argument to the extent that during the last few years of his life Iqbal felt increasingly the impact and challenge of socialist ideas as nobody could fail to do in the present age. It is true also that he wrote a number of poems during this last phase which strike a deceptive revolutionary note. There is, for instance, the oft-quoted "God's fiat to his Angels" in which God commands the angels:

Arise and awaken the disinherited of my earth,
Shake the dwellings of the rich to the very foundations.
That field from which the peasant derives no livelihood
Burn every ear of corn from that field.

Such sporadic emotional outbursts, however, cannot be taken seriously as socialism, or even as "Muslim Socialism," whatever that ambiguous term may imply. For the fact is, as W. Cantwell Smith in his brilliant book *Modern Islam in India* has rightly pointed out, "he never knew what socialism is" though "towards the end of his life some of his friends were able to convince him that he really did not understand socialism, and he was preparing to remedy this ignorance when he died." One might add, speculative though such an assertion must be, that had he lived long enough to complete his study of socialism, he would have still rejected socialism because he would have found its basic assumptions to be destructive of the dogmas on which he built his airy structure of a theocratic charitable social order.

His critique of capitalist social relations, and the inequities and injustices arising from these relations, was essentially from the standpoint of a Utopian—but a very special kind of Utopian. For his Utopianism was not of the same order as that of the 18th and 19th century thinkers like Rousseau, Saint-Simon, Fourier, which started from concrete analysis of society in terms of concrete urgencies and forces which create and destroy social patterns, even though this analysis did not go far enough and got mixed up with strong elements of wishful fantasy. His Utopianism was abstract, metaphysical, closer in spirit, if not in form, to the kind of Utopianism implicit in St. Augustine's *De Civitate Dei*. It was rooted in his emotional and intellectual fixation on the idyllic relations of a precapitalist, feudal social order. To equate it with socialism, in any of its modern forms, is completely to misrepresent socialism and Iqbal's social philosophy.

The relation of Iqbal's ideas to Humanism is equally negative. Admittedly, there is a humanistic urge behind his attempt to reinterpret and reconstruct Islamic polity and ideals in an historical perspective, to claim for these a validity in terms of modern necessities, and to rationalise their dogmatic structure.

But this urge is sub-conscious, involuntary. The avowed aim of his philosophy is to give a "spiritual interpretation of the universe." This, in other words, signifies that a purely human destiny and the making of man "the measure of the universe" did not satisfy him. It is true that he asked man to raise and develop his ego to such a point that:

Before every decision of fate
God would ask of man
Tell me: "What's your will."

But this affirmation which is his closest approach to Humanism merely envisages the possibility of convergence of God's will and man's at some point and under exceptional circumstances. It does not equate the two, much less eliminate the former from the scheme of reality. It still recognises God's will as the ultimate and transcendental arbiter of the human situation. A world-view based on such a premise must inevitably fall within the orbit of the metaphysical rather than humanistic philosophies of our time.

Finally, there remains the problem of Iqbal's ethical and spiritual ideals. It is in truth only another aspect of his philosophical position; and the self-division is even more manifest, more poignant on this level. It could not be otherwise. Iqbal's spiritual and intellectual development, as has been noted, falls into two distinct phases. The thought-pattern of the one is in some respects almost the complete antithesis of the other—at least in its overt signification. During the first phase the matrix of his thought was represented by Sufi mysticism, with its doctrine of Immanence, linked on the one side to Neo-Platonism and on the other to Vedantic Idealism. He felt strongly the fascination of the ecstacy of contemplation, the rapture of the individual self merging in the Universal. During the second phase, however, he completely and even passionately repudiated this ideal. Instead he affirmed the perfection of "the ego" or selfhood as the value of all values, the *summum bonum* of the life-process; and he went on to preach "action" and "desire" as the basic means of realising that perfection. Rising in the still waters of quietist and contemplative philosophies, his thought ultimately reaches a doctrine of unlimited dynamism.

It is clear that a mind which traversed so abrupt a trajectory of thought and belief could not but create for itself almost impossible problems of readjustment and reorientation. The mental conflict, in fact, was never wholly resolved; and behind and beyond the conflict, as we have suggested, there were sharp pangs of doubt, uncertainty, and even regrets which account for the strange, Rilke-like elegaic note which runs through his later verse. With such a translucent spiritual and intellectual background, it is inevitable that the ethical ideals at which he arrived should partake of that translucency. They oscillate between an ambivalent moral eclecticism and a self-hypnotic, didactic dogmatism. But that is not the whole point. The point is that ideals, in the last analysis, must be judged in terms, not just of their facial import and intentions, but of their actual results. The word, indeed, acquires its true character and reveals its real, inward nature only in the process of becoming flesh.

Iqbal's word in the process of becoming flesh reveals its paradoxical and contradictory nature in a startling measure; and it does so because these paradoxes and contradictions are inherent in its very nature. The exalted ethical and spiritual ideals preached so vehemently by the most idealistic thinker produced by modern Islam, on closer scrutiny, appear to be highly suitable for conversion to purely practical, materialistic ends. His philosophy of dynamism, his ideal of the "Ego" or "Self" which must be developed to the uttermost limits of its possibilities and beyond those limits, his doctrine of "assimilation" or "absorption," were precisely the intellectual and spiritual stimuli which his group and his class needed in its struggle for the advancement of its material ambitions and interests, for a better political and economic destiny. These were the psychological and moral ingredients of the new attitude, the new world-view which was essential if it was to pull itself out of the slough of despondent passivity and fatalism, to gain self-confidence, and to stir itself to activity in a deliriously active world where the devil took the hindmost. These ideals were the perfect equipment suited to the needs of a rising capitalist society anxious to make up for lost centuries of opportunity, to consolidate its base of operation, and to achieve the maximum of expansion in the minimum of time. In a very different way, and given the vast differences of historical context it could not but be a very different way, Iqbal's doctrine of individual perfection has had, and was bound to have, the same liberating influence on the Muslim mind as the individualistic doctrine of the thinkers of the Renaissance had on the Christian mind. For his perfect "Ego," the superman of his conception, who can not only claim "divine vice-regency" but even "absorb" God into himself, may have Quranic antecedents, but he is also of the contemporary world where we meet him as the busy, bustling entrepreneur, the pioneering capitalist, the enterprising captain of industry and finance, the masterbuilder of the modern bourgeois social order. The democracy of "more or less unique individuals, presided over by the most unique individual possible" which is Iqbal's idea of the kingdom of God on earth is but an idealised version of the existing order of things and it almost reminds one of some of the Wellsian fantasies about the ideal order of society. The last great metaphysical poet and philosopher of Islam was also, strange and sacrilegious though it may sound to some of his admirers, perhaps the first of the bourgeois ideologue of the Muslim world who is worth listening to.

At this point the connection between Iqbal's ideas and the movement of what is known as Indo-Muslim renaissance becomes demonstrable. It was not a fortuitous and incidental connection, but fundamental. And it is of great importance. Without him this movement would be a movement without a soul, certainly without self-consciousness. And the posthumous popularity leading to canonisation which he enjoys among the Muslim intelligentsia becomes intelligible—inevitable. W. Cantwell Smith has explained Iqbal's remarkable influence among the Muslims of India in the following words:

> Almost everyone found something in him to applaud, something which stirred him to renewed Islamic vigour. There were those, of the liberal school, who read Iqbal, and were merely proud of him—were proud that modern Islam had produced so great a man. Others, however, were incited by Iqbal's message to some degree of activity in the name of their Lord. They could not but see that the world about, or within, them was less good than it might be; and the poet's eloquence stirred them to do something about it—and to co-ordinate their doing it, more or less precisely with their Islam. Islam as a religion has produced no intellectual modernisation of its idea of righteousness more explicit than Iqbal's. He is great because he said with supreme eloquence, and convincing passion, what his fellows were beginning to feel, but were unable to formulate. Any modern Muslim who would talk about religion must begin where Iqbal left off; otherwise he is not worth listening to.

This is an excellent and succinct summing up of the nature and reason of Iqbal's influence. But it needs qualification. In some directions it needs clearer specification; in others amplification. For instance, when it is said that everyone found in him something to applaud, it means obviously every Muslim intellectual and in general the middle class. For though Iqbal was a popular poet whose reputation went far beyond the educated classes, for the masses it could not but be a legendary reputation—as in fact most reputations during the past fifty years in India have been legendary. But to the Muslim middle class and to the Muslim intelligentsia he meant something very definite; he gave them a faith and a doctrine which corresponded to their objective and subjective needs. He objectified and articulated their aspirations and ambitions. He did more: he provided the necessary veneer of idealisation and rationalisation even for their confusions. He was able to do so because he himself shared these confusions; for it is impossible to win a popularity, as he has achieved posthumously, without striking a chord of emotional identity. That is why Iqbal's popularity will endure as long as the confusions of our age will endure.

What will come after? The answer is a truer appreciation of his personality and his work. When that comes it will probably be seen that notwithstanding his revivalism, notwithstanding even his profoundly religious outlook, he prepared the ground for his people to be able to transcend the very outlook which he so passionately wanted to revive. For he accelerated the transition of the Muslim mind from a feudal to the modern frame. As a prophet, no less than as a poet, he bridges the gulf between yesterday and to-day. And that gulf had of necessity to be bridged in order that there could be a tomorrow. That is the summing up of his contribution which is immense. But, in the nature of things, there will always be something to add. (pp. 235-46)

> *Iqbal Singh, in his* The Ardent Pilgrim: An Introduction to the Life and Work of Mohammed Iqbal, *Longmans, Green and Co., 1951, 246 p.*

## ALESSANDRO BAUSANI    (essay date 1955)

[*Bausani is an Italian educator and critic whose career has been devoted to the study of Islamic religion and literature in India and Indonesia. In the following essay, he discusses Iqbal's philosophy of religion and compares his religious ideas with prominent concepts in Western theology.*]

Iqbal does not like the term "God"; this word can have a plural, "gods." Better for him is *Allah*, the personal name the Holy Koran gives to God, as Yahweh is the personal name for God in the Bible. In the Greek world, on the contrary, God in the general sense was an abstraction, *to theion*, "divinity," the Divine Principle or Substance, only the different gods having personal names (Jupiter, Venus, etc.) All the philosophical and theological work of the great Pakistani thinker is centred on a defence—conducted on modern and original lines—of the Semitic idea of *God as personality*, against the Greek and classical one of *God as substance*. In other words we could describe his position as that of *theism versus pantheism*, if these terms were not too vague. "The result of an intellectual view of life—says Iqbal in his **Reconstruction of Religious Thought in Islam**—is necessarily pantheistic." In his philosophy, then, "heart" plays a very important role, heart not in the European sense but rather, as Persian *dil*, considered as the centre of intuition.

Modern thought developed following the lines chiefly of Greek spiritual experience. The "substance" of the ancient world—called *God* in the Middle Ages—became an all-embracing and all-producing "idea" in Hegel. The Semitic idea of a *personal* God, which could have given a different direction to European thought and which made its appearance with Christianity, was very early distorted by interpretations based on concepts borrowed from Hellenistic culture, and the great Prophet of God as Loving Father became a Greek hypostasis, an incarnation of something divine. Islam—especially early Islam, more near the Koranic world of thought—gave a powerful impulse again to the idea of God as supreme personality with which man can come in contact, rather than a vague force with which it is impossible to come face to face—but, unfortunately even the thinkers of Islam fell under the magic spell of purely intellectual philosophy, transforming the creative power of the Living and Ever-working God (. . . "Every day He is in a new work," says the Holy Koran) into an abstract pattern of a fixed universe. In this way many of the wonderful possibilities Islam had, to change the world, were lost. In any case Muslim thinkers were comparatively less affected by classical thought than the Christians, and Iqbal justly points out the importance of the Ash'arite "atomistic" school of thought and of other champions of the purely Koranic conception of God against any compromise with static pantheistic thought. I wonder whether in our Occidental world such purely monotheistic conceptions were ever defended by a theologian or a philosopher as was done by Ibn Taymiyya. Aristotelian philosophy, adapted by St. Thomas Aquinas (d. 1274) to Christian theology has been since then the official philosophy of the Roman Catholic Church, being even openly declared as such by Pope Leo XIII (1878-1903). The rebellions against "classical" thought in our world were of a mystic rather than prophetic character, like the remarkable Franciscan school in the Middle Ages—God remaining always on absolute principle or a rational ordainer of the Cosmos, rather than a creator, or, at the best, something very sweet in which the human soul wanted to be dissolved.

Perhaps a more frontal attack on the Greek thought was the great Protestant Reformation, opposing the Semitic Bible to the philosophy of the schools. And this gave indeed good results: the reconquered personal and living God aroused again the spirit of activity in man and the so-called "modern" world was born. But, the Greek germs contained in the New Testament (I mean especially St. Paul's Epistles and the Fourth Gospel) constrained orthodox Protestantism into the fixed conception of personal atonement, giving sometimes to it a very narrow mental intolerance; and, on the other hand, the so-called liberal school became more and more a simply rationalistic theory on the main lines of the current philosophy of the age. This is now based chiefly on Hegel's thought, one of the most rigorous and perfect forms of intellectual pantheism which gave birth both to modern absolute idealism (taken to its logical conclusion by the Italian Philosopher G. Gentile, d. 1943) reducing all reality into "thought thinking of itself," and to Marxism—a powerful giant with feet of clay, with "believing heart and atheist brain," as Iqbal wrote in his *Javednama*.

The last attack on classical thought in Europe is represented by "existentialism." To some of the existentialists the same words Iqbal used for Nietzsche (considered by themselves one of their precursors) could be applied; they threw themselves away from God and so they cut away from themselves their own self, and they too, like Iqbal's Nietzsche, soar in a void space singing desperately: "No Gabriel, no paradise, no huri, no God, only a handful of clay burnt by the eternal longing of the heart!" (*Javednama.*)

Iqbal's religious philosophy represents—in my opinion—the most radical modern revindication of the old prophetic idea called "monotheism," and at the same time, implicitly, a radical criticism of the entire trend of European thought from Plato to Gentile and existentialism. Iqbal's philosophy of religion offers to us a new direction to choose. Against the ever-living instinctive polytheism of our souls he offers the alternative of *iman* (Faith): Iqbal calls his Superman a *mu'min*, a believer, and here lies his basic difference from Nietzsche's rebellion and from all the modern Occidental anarchisms.

But let us now enunciate the chief points of Iqbal's criticism of Greek thought, or better of classical thought and hence of the whole trend of modern thought.

Against abstract dualism: "Plato despised sense perception which, in his view, yielded mere opinion and no real knowledge." "With Islam the ideal and the real are not two opposing forces which cannot be reconciled." "Islam says yes to the world of matter and points the way to master it."

The dualism between profane and spiritual is still very strong in our world. For Iqbal "*all is holy ground . . . the state, from the Islamic standpoint, is an endeavour to transform these ideal principles into space-time forces. It is in this sense alone that the state in Islam is a theocracy, not in the sense that it is headed by a representative of God on earth*," a typically pre-Christian idea adopted by the Roman Catholic Church and in more profane forms by dictatorial states. With perhaps the sole exception of the Jewish people previous to the establishment of monarchy by Samuel and the early Islam, humanity never experienced this original form of theocratic democracy, which—developed on new lines—could offer the only concrete alternative to the disorder of modern democracy and the tyranny of modern dictatorships.

*Against the Greek idea of the immobility of God:* "The Universe is so constituted that it is capable of extension. 'God adds to His creation what He wills' (Koran 35/1). It is not a clock universe, a finished product immobile and incapable of change. Deep in its inner being lies perhaps the dream of a new birth: '. . . hereafter will He give it another birth' (Koran 29/19)." This, of course, is an ideal European thought borrowed from the Semitic religions, Christianity and Islam, only transferring the attribute of motion from God to the World. It is in any case interesting to remark that for Islam the idea of a moving God, living, even changing his mind (this is the deeper sense of such concepts as the shi'ite *bada'*, or the principle of *an-nasikh wa 'I-mansukh*, or the successive prophethood) is an orthodox one, whereas the dominating Aristotelianism of the Christian churches, fixing God as an almost impersonal substance and giving to Christ a unique and fixed position in the series of the revealers of God, made of the idea of the "changing God" almost a blasphemy.

*Against the classical proofs of the existence of God:* Modern anti-religious thought profits by the obvious philosophical criticism of the classical "five proofs" of St. Thomas in order to deny God. Iqbal, following in this the most traditionalist theological schools of Islam—denies that God, the living God of the Koran, may be proved by means of the Cosmological, Teleological and Ontological arguments. "The cosmological argument . . . tries to reach the infinite by merely negating the finite. But the infinite reached by contradicting the finite is a false infinite." "The teleological argument—he says—gives us a contriver only and not a creator." "All that the ontological argument proves is that the idea of a perfect being includes the *idea* of his existence."

The living God of the Koran (and, I add, of the Bible too) is always something different from the purely intellectual God reached through those arguments, which would acquire life "only if we are able to show that thought and being are ultimately one." Iqbal doesn't give us an elaborate proof of the existence of God, the true God, but he only establishes the basis for a working proof. "What we call Nature," he says, "is only a fleeting moment in the life of God . . . in the picturesque phrase of the Koran it is *the habit of Allah*." Therefore proofs taken only from Nature do not prove anything about the true creator. "But . . . intuition reveals Life as a centralizing Ego."

*Personality of God:* God is then not a substance but an Ego. "In order to emphasize the individuality of the ultimate Ego the Koran gives him the proper name of Allah. But does not individuality imply finitude? The answer is that God cannot be conceived as infinite in the sense of spatial infinity." True infinity does not mean infinite extension which cannot be conceived without embracing all available finite extensions. Its nature consists in intensity and not extensity. "The infinity of the Ultimate Ego consists in the infinite inner possibilities of His creative activity of which the Universe as known to us is only a partial expression." This is a very important point as—in contrast to the classical conception of God—it emphasizes the idea of a changing God, of a God for which Nature is a habit or—to put it as a paradox—a juvenile exercise of the creating God, in preparation of more and more wonderful works. In this lies also hidden a new solution of the old problem, the crux of theism, i.e., the problem of Evil. Nature is neither bad nor good in itself, it is one of the first exercises of God, who "hereafter will give it another birth."

*Creativeness of God:* Among the attributes, *sif at,* of the Koranic God the most important is creativeness. Most of the modern European philosophers agree in admitting that the idea of the creativeness of Spirit is a great contribution of Semitic thought to Western philosophy, as it was unknown to Greek philosophy. But the Christian philosophers of the Middle Ages, imbued with Aristotelian ideas, accepted the idea of a created world only because it was stated in the Bible, without deducing from it the necessary philosophical consequences. St. Thomas even frankly admits that this idea is logically difficult to accept and believable only relying on the Bible. Muslim thought on the contrary has always given the utmost importance to creation, even going so far as to consider human acts as created in order to save the idea of the absolute creativeness of God. The Ash'arite school, with the aim of completely abolishing all those Aristotelian *causae secundae* which could compromise the freedom of the creative act of God, elaborated the highly interesting theory of atomism "the first important indication of an intellectual revolt against the Aristotelian idea of a fixed universe." "According to the Ash'arite school of thinkers . . . the world is composed of what they call *jawahir,* infinitely small parts or atoms which cannot be further divided. Since the creative activity of God is ceaseless . . . fresh atoms are coming into being every moment and the universe is therefore constantly growing. . . . Existence is a quality imposed on the atoms by God. . . . What we call a thing . . . is in its essential nature an aggregation of atomic acts." "Nothing has a stable nature." This idea of a casual and atomically discontinuous universe, moving by jumps rather than by rational

evolution, is considered as the best adapted for God as a free creator and it is not only strangely similar to what some modern scientists think of the Cosmos, but, once admitted, forms a further step for the proofs of the existence of the true personal God: for only an "artistic personality" could bring forth from a casual and purely fortuitous aggregation of atoms results impressing our souls as "beauty." This can be done by that supreme Ego in which "thought and being are ultimately one" and to whom belong *amr* and *khalq: khalq* meaning the creative act of God in relation to the universe of extension (the world of matter) and *amr* the creative relation of God with the world of Spirit. All this, together with the Iqbalian idea of man as creator . . . gives to Man a sound aggressiveness towards things. The non-existence of things as hard and stony realities given for ever, and the possibility for the truly spiritual man (*mu'min,* the believer) to create new counter-things, considering the existing ones as habits or juvenile exercises of God, abolishes in Man every kind of melancholic and romantic passivity, which always results from considering the actual reality as definitive, and constitutes a true spiritual *jihad* (holy war). Man then, if centred in God, becomes a founder of ever new and unforeseeable realities.

*Man and his destiny:* The idea of risk, so emphasized by modern existentialism, is clearly present in the Koran; ". . . man," says Iqbal, "is the trustee of a free personality which he accepted at his peril." "Verily we proposed to the heavens and to the earth and to the mountains to receive the trust, but they refused the burden and they feared to receive it. Man undertook to bear it" (Koran 33/72). "The Ego had its beginnings in time and did not pre-exist its emergence in the spaciotemporal order. According to the Koranic view there is no possibility of return on this earth. Finitude is not a misfortune. . . . It is with the irreplaceable singleness of his individuality that the finite Ego will approach the infinite Ego. . . ." "The Koran does not contemplate complete liberation from finitude as the highest state of human bliss. . . ." This point is connected with the Koranic and Biblical idea of the "reality of Time and the concept of Life as a continuous movement in time, whereas the Greek time was either unreal as in Plato and Zeno, or moved in a circle as in Heraclitus and the Stoics," but "the movement itself, if conceived as cyclic, ceases to be creative." The Protestant theologian, O. Cullman, in his highly interesting book *Christus und die Zeit (Christ and Time)* discovered—independently of Iqbal—this very interesting anti-cyclical "tension of time" in the prophetic religion, only giving it a peculiar Christian turn. In any case, from this point of view (and it is really strange that only now the modern world begins to appreciate this living thought so clearly represented—if not literally stated—in those Holy Scriptures which ought to be and are not the basis of life for Christian people) the whole problem of "immortality" presents itself in a new light. "And then shall be a blast on the trumpet and all who are in the heavens and all who are on the Earth shall faint away (no special rights, then, even for celestial beings in front of the personal power of God!) save those in whose case God wills otherwise" (Koran 39/69). "Who can be the subject of this exception—Iqbal adds—but those in whom the Ego has reached the very highest point of intensity?"

In his typical conception of Reality as a complex of egoes (matter itself being "a colony of egoes of a low order") Iqbal clearly shows himself a disciple of the spiritual pluralism (very near to Leibnitz) of the former Hegelian McTaggart who was his master in philosophy. But McTaggart's arguments in defence of self as elementally immortal are weak. From the mere fact that the individual ego is a differentiation of the eternal Absolute Ego (Koranically speaking, *an-nafsu min amri rabbi,* the soul is from the direction of my Lord) it by no means follows that the human self retains the character which belongs to his source alone. According to Iqbal "Personal immortality . . . is not ours as of right; it is to be achieved by personal effort. Man is only *a candidate* for it."

Immortality is not something which can be proved—as in Plato's Phædon—but a state to be conquered: here is the proof. For our modern world, which, abandoning God, is frantically looking for a cheap and sure personal immortality often through the most strange channels (spiritism, modern magics, etc.), Iqbal's warning is very strong; the idea that not all are immortal is in perfect agreement, I think, also with the spirit of the Old Testament which—according to modern critics—ignored the typically Greek thought of the "immortality of the soul." The old-fashioned Christian and Muslim dogma of the resurrection of the body is—in its deep respect for our physical frame which is called by Iqbal in Zabur-i-Ajam *hal az ahval-i hayat*—one of the states of life, a symbol of the idea of an immortality of the *entire* self.

A modern Western mind can find in Iqbal's philosophy of religion not only an interesting mental or purely theoretical outlook on life and the universe and God, but, more than this, concrete proposals for a change of direction for building the future world on new lines. The rediscovering of the pure Koranic and Biblical God can and must be a new point of departure for the construction of a new history, a religious beginning of new realities.

"Man is a creator." This idea of Iqbal has strong attraction for modern Western minds, and could be given as the essence of Iqbal's philosophy of religion. Iqbal even defends it by quoting the famous verse of the Holy Koran *fatabaraka' Ilahu ahsanu'l-khaliqin,* "Blessed be God, the best of creators." Of course modern Occidental thinkers had already proclaimed some of the ideas of Iqbal: names like those of Leibnitz, Nietzsche, Bergson, James Ward, McTaggart come naturally to our minds. But they did so from an essentially "profane" point of view. Owing to the too strict connection between Biblical personal monotheism and Greek philosophy in Europe, the revolt to a "fixed universe" in Western countries meant also a rebellion against the idea of the Biblical God: so that nobody in Europe recognized the great progressive and modern values implied in a really pure monotheism, which, I think with Iqbal, even in post-Koranic thought did not succeed in affirming itself completely. A "really pure monotheism" means totally divesting the forces of Nature of that divine character with which not only "earlier cultures" (as Iqbal says) but even—in different and more perfectioned forms—all modern cultures too have clothed them. It means moreover the radical invalidity and impossibility of every worldly "authority," inasmuch as only God is the real Lord; giving at the same time to democracy that organic character and unitarian enthusiasm which only Faith can give and which unfortunately purely profane democracies lack. In this really *pure* theocracy (I repeat this: the authority of the Pope, certain forms of Caliphate, etc., *are not* pure theocracies, because it is not only God who reigns in them) the "slave of God"—in the words of Iqbal's *Javed-nama*—"can dispense of any state and position. He has no servants; and he is servant of nobody. The slave of God is no more than a perfectly free man: his kingdom and law are given to him by God, by nobody else. . . ."

In this way, that is by adopting the standpoint of God, by being, in the words of the Koran, God's *khalifa* (vicegerent) on earth, man can develop a tremendous revolutionary force and yet avoid that frantic hysterical explosion peculiar to anarchic atheistic movements, and can in this way substitute the civilization of science as creation of values for one of simple vision of values. Obedience, *ita'at,* (to God of course and to his laws) means very much for Iqbal: an entire section of *Asrar-i-khudi* (*The Secrets of the Self*) is dedicated to it. Not man *as he is now,* but man purified through obedience, self dominion, and detachment, can reach the high station of *niyabat-i-ilahi,* Divine Vicegerency. One could say that—contrary to Occidental practice—revolution is for Iqbal a final aim, not a means. The means consist in submitting himself to a strong and austere spiritual discipline. Be detached from the material world—Iqbal says—in order to become a real revolutionary! The sense of "spiritual discipline"—after the too other-worldly period of medieval asceticism—has been completely lost by Europe. For Iqbal it lies in obedience to the simple laws enjoined by God in the Holy Koran. Only afterwards can man exercise the creative power he shares with God. And then unprecedented things may happen. Because, in the words of the Koran, man's limit is not in the direction of the stars: *"and verily towards God is thy limit"* (Koran 53/43). (pp. 131-41)

*Alessandro Bausani, "Iqbal: His Philosophy of Religion, and the West," in* Crescent and Green: A Miscellany of Writings on Pakistan *by Alessandro Bausani and Others, Cassell & Company Ltd., 1955, pp. 131-41.*

## SYED ABDUL VAHID (essay date 1959)

[*An eminent Iqbal scholar, Vahid is the author of numerous studies, including* Iqbal: His Art and Thought *(1944; rev. English ed. 1959) and* Introduction to Iqbal *(1964). Describing his many years of Iqbal scholarship, he wrote: "To me the study of Iqbal has been a source of great strength and happiness. In him I have always found that which confers healing and refreshment alike upon mind and spirit." In the following excerpt from Iqbal: His Art and Thought, Vahid compares Iqbal's philosophical views with those of Western thinkers, including Friedrich Nietzsche, Henri Bergson, Albert Einstein, and James Ward.*]

> Though Europe is radiant with the splendours of Arts and
>    Sciences,
> It is the Valley of Darkness without the Fount of Life!

Iqbal was a keen student of Western philosophy and all his life studied the works of Western thinkers. That these studies influenced him to a certain extent was inevitable, but as he was essentially what Bertrand Russell calls a "practical philosopher" the real advantage he derived from his Western studies was that by watching the conflict of ideas and creeds in the West he learnt to appreciate the value of creeds and movements of thought to practical life. However, his Western studies did influence his thought and philosophy, and it will be interesting to trace the points of affinity between his ideas and those of prominent Western thinkers. (p. 82)

The influence of the Greeks upon modern European thought cannot be over-emphasised. "We Europeans are children of Hellas," says [H. A. L. Fisher in *A History of Europe*], and the beginning of Western thought must be traced to the galaxy of brilliant Greek thinkers. Greek thought also exercised a profound influence on Islamic thought, but Iqbal considered this influence harmful in important respects, and he continually emphasised that Islamic culture is essentially and fundamentally different from Greek culture. Of all the Greek thinkers,

Aristotle earned Iqbal's greatest admiration. In a brief note to some verses in which he criticises Plato's Theory of Ideas, he refers to Aristotle's criticism of Plato with approval. He also mentions Fārābi's vain attempt in *Al Jama bain ar-ra'ain* to prove that there is no essential difference between the views of Plato and Aristotle. There is some resemblance between Iqbal's Superman and Aristotle's Ideal Man. Aristotle thus defines his Ideal Man:

> He is of a disposition to do men service, though he is ashamed to have a service done to him. To confer a kindness is a mark of superiority; to receive one is a mark of subordination. . . . He never feels malice, and always forgets and passes over injuries. His carriage is sedate, his voice deep, his speech measured; he is not given to hurry, for he is concerned about only a few things; he is not prone to vehemence for he thinks nothing very important. . . . He bears the accidents of life with dignity and grace, making the best of his circumstances, like a skilful general who marshals his limited forces with all the strategy of war . . . [Ethics, IV, 3].

Although Aristotle's Ideal Man differs from Iqbal's Perfect Man, some of his phrases irresistibly remind us of Iqbal's. For instance, "he is of a disposition to do men service, though he is ashamed to have a service done to him" brings to mind Iqbal's well-known line: . . .

> Beware of incurring obligations, beware!

Then "his carriage is sedate, his voice deep, his speech measured" may be compared with: . . .

> Gentle in speech, fierce in action.

Leaving Greek thought we come to modern European thinkers. Modern European thought begins with Bacon, who learned the inductive method from the Arabs. Descartes, Spinoza, Leibniz, and the outstanding thinkers who followed, enriched his thought by developing deductive methods. Descartes established the independence of matter. Berkeley contended that matter was only a form of mind. Hume gave a phenomenalist interpretation to mind. Then came Kant. Kant's greatness lies in his teaching that all knowledge is not derived from the senses. Kant demonstrated the utter futility of intellectual effort when faced with the ultimate problems of life, and thus proved the philosophic necessity of faith. Proceeding on the basis of pure metaphysical argument, he found at the end of his *Critique of Pure Reason* that the existence of God, the freedom of the Will and similar problems are not capable of proof or disproof. (pp. 82-4)

Iqbal also started with faith but he did not have to reason this out. The ceaseless activity of the ego can only be explained in terms of faith in the ultimate result of that activity. As regards scientific experiment, Iqbal starts with intuition and mystic experience as the only way to inner knowledge. Whereas Kant postulates the moral law as a sort of external command, for Iqbal the moral law arises out of the inner necessity of the ego's life. Thus while both Kant and Iqbal believe in faith and moral law, they recognise the necessity of these fundamental factors in different ways and for different reasons. For Iqbal, personality provides the measure of all things: that which fortifies personality is good, and that which tends to weaken it is bad.

Another difference may be noted between the standpoints of Iqbal and Kant. For Iqbal, freedom and immortality are rewards for ceaseless striving and come only to those who never relax their efforts. Kant brings in freedom and immortality in order

to be able to think that ours is a just Universe, and that there is no fundamental discord between actions and their ultimate results. Kant is thrown back on religious orthodoxy, Iqbal is not.

After Kant we find some resemblance between Iqbal and Fichte. Fichte's system of philosophy arose out of his criticism of Kant's analysis of our process of knowing. Kant looked upon this as a construction of the mind's activity in relation to an element which is quite alien to it, called the "thing-in-itself." Fichte rejects this alien element, and is thus left with the knowing mind alone, the self. Thus according to Fichte there must be a self that knows; in other words the ego posits itself. But if ego is to know it follows that there must be something to be known, and thus the ego posits non-ego. But non-ego which the ego contemplates and which is necessary to make knowledge possible is not something alien to the ego, its source is self itself. The non-ego is posited by the ego to render evolution possible through moral struggle and interaction. Beyond this conception of ego there is complete divergence between the views of Iqbal and Fichte. While Iqbal insists on the ego maintaining its individuality, according to Fichte "There is but a single virtue—to forget oneself as individual. There is but a single vice—to look to oneself."

The next great thinker between whose thought and Iqbal's philosophy there appears to be a resemblance is Nietzsche. In fact several writers have gone so far as to assert that Iqbal derived his whole philosophy from Nietzsche. For instance, Professor E. G. Browne [in *A Literary History of Persia*] says: "Muhammad Iqbal has set forth his own doctrines (which as I understand them, are in the main an Oriental adaptation of Nietzsche's philosophy) in a short *mathnawi* poem entitled *Asrār-i-khūdi*. . . ." (pp. 84-5)

Before tracing any resemblance between Iqbal's and Nietzsche's thought, what is, briefly, Nietzsche's philosophy? "Dionysus, Recurrence, Superman; these ideas, and those dependent upon them, make up the most important part of Nietzsche's constructive philosophy, or, if one prefers it, of his religion," writes [A. H. J. Knight in his *Some Aspects of the Life and works of Nietzsche, Particularly of His Connection with Greek Literature and Thought*]. . . . Most people, among whom there are many who have never studied Nietzsche and do not understand him, know that he talked about the Superman. A few years later Iqbal wrote on the same subject; so it was easy for those who had studied neither, or only one, of these great thinkers to imagine a connection between the philosophies of the two. We have to ascertain what kind of Superman Nietzsche wants to produce. The main characteristics of Nietzsche's Superman are admirably summed up by Knight as follows: "Freedom from ethical restrictions, for great ends; active, creative greatness; joy; these shall be good. Fetters shall be thrown off and authority denied. This life shall be accepted as the only life, and as good, though terrible. All that impedes greatness, power, beauty, shall be abolished. The fears of sin, hell, death, conscience shall be exorcised. As there is no soul without body, there can be no spiritual greatness where the body is sick: therefore, health is immeasurably valuable. Pity is a sickness or a selfishness. It hinders action, or serves to give an unhealthy pleasure to the pitier. Hardness is a virtue beyond all price." (p. 86)

In a passage in *Ecce Homo* Nietzsche tries to lay down the distinguishing features of his Superman; studying them, we can see where his Superman differs from those conceived by Darwin and Carlyle. While discussing the characteristics of the Superman, Nietzsche deliberately uses provocative language, for example, when he says that the Superman is the enemy of pity and is the embodiment of hardness and suffering. According to Nietzsche, those who preach pity look only to the ''creature'' side of man and fail to appreciate that man has also another side, the ''creator'' in him. ''In man there is both creator and creative'' *(Beyond Good and Evil)*. Having failed to appreciate the ''creator'' side of man these people fail to realise that for self-perfection man does not need pity, but only hardness and suffering. To pity others or to be pitied by others, when one is undergoing suffering and tribulations, means for Nietzsche the defeat of the wholesome effect of suffering. In fact, it is the denial of life itself. Pity is opposed to the tonic passions, which serve to enhance the energy and feeling of life: pity's action is depressing. ''A man loses power when he pities'' *(Antichrist)*. According to Nietzsche the ideal Superman would be ''the Roman Caesar with Christ's soul.''

It will be seen that there is much in Nietzsche's characterisation of Superman with which Iqbal agrees. But owing to his atheistic outlook and materialistic background Nietzsche failed to comprehend that only by affirming the spiritual basis of life can man realise the highest ideal of perfection. For Iqbal's Perfect Man religion plays an important part, but it ceases to be a mere dogma or ritual. Rather does it become a matter of personal assimilation of life and power. The Perfect Man acquires a free personality, free not in the sense that he is no longer subject to law, but free in the sense that he discovers the ultimate source of law within the depths of his own consciousness.

He no longer needs any persuasion that there is a justification for this world; his own creative activity convinces him.

As in the case of Nietzsche's Superman the greatest task before the Perfect Man is to fight the existing order of things, but this fight does not spring out of any resentment or hatred.

The Perfect Man is the embodiment of a power which he uses ruthlessly to crush and exterminate all those who obstruct him, but unlike Nietzsche's Superman he is at the same time sympathetic and kind to those who deserve his sympathy or kindness. In short, the Perfect Man employs power as well as compassion, force as well as persuasion to achieve his mission, but unlike the Superman he is not beyond the sphere of good and evil.

Now we come to the second chief idea in Nietzsche's philosophy of life: the idea of Eternal Recurrence. . . . (pp. 87-8)

This is not the moment to consider the merits of the idea of Eternal Recurrence, as we are here mainly concerned with what Iqbal thinks of it. But before doing this we have to be clear about the idea itself. When properly analysed, it really means that man's progress is not in an ascending line but in a circle. Whatever progress we may have attained while producing the Superman, the same process must be gone through again; man will again have to start from the same point from which he originally started and he will have to pass through the same stages of development. Thus the idea makes the future of mankind sombre and the whole outlook mainly fatalistic. Whatever we may do, whatever we may achieve counts for little. The circle of human development, culminating in the production of the Superman, must be repeated mechanically. The whole prospect is gloomy and pessimistic. Thus the idea is most demoralising and depressing. If we have to go back to the point from where we started, there is no ground for excitement.

Now let us see what Iqbal thinks of the idea of Eternal Recurrence. According to Iqbal:

> It is only a more rigid kind of mechanism, based not on an ascertained fact but only on a working hypothesis of science. Nor does Nietzsche seriously grapple with the question of Time. He takes it objectively and regards it merely as an infinite series of events returning to itself over and over again. Now Time, regarded as a perpetual circular movement, makes immortality absolutely intolerable. Nietzsche himself feels this, and describes his doctrine, not as one of immortality, but rather as a view of life which would make immortality endurable. And what makes immortality bearable, according to Nietzsche? It is the expectation that a recurrence of the combination of energy-centres which constitutes my personal existence is a necessary factor in the birth of that ideal combination of energy-centres which he calls ''Superman.'' But the Superman has been an infinite number of times before. His birth is inevitable; how can the prospect give me any aspiration? We can aspire only to what is absolutely new, and the absolutely new is unthinkable on Nietzsche's view, which is nothing more than a Fatalism worse than the one summed up in the word *Qismat*. Such a doctrine, far from keying up the human organism for the fight of life, tends to destroy its action-tendencies and relaxes the tension of the ego [*The Reconstruction of Religious Thought in Islam*].

We can pass on to the third head of Nietzsche's philosophy, the Dionysian principle. Dionysus was the God of wine and fertility. His worship was orgiastic and used to be performed at intervals with disgusting excesses of savagery, such as are described in the *Bacchæ*. According to legend, he was torn to pieces by the women of Thrace but he rose again, and mystery rites were performed mainly founded upon this martyrdom and resurrection. (pp. 89-90)

In aphorism 370 *''Was ist Romantik?''* Nietzsche further explains what Dionysiasm is:

> But there are sufferers of two kinds, in the first place those who suffer from the overfullness of life. . . . He who is most right in the fullness, the Dionysiac god and man cannot only permit himself to see what is frightful and questionable, but can even permit himself frightful actions and every luxury of destruction, disintegration, denial, where he is concerned, that which is evil, senseless and ugly seems, so to speak, permitted, in consequence of an excess of creative, fructifying powers, which would be able to make a luxuriant land of fruit out of any desert. . . . The longing for destruction, change, growth, may be the expression of a power that is overfull and pregnant with the future (my term for it, as is known, is the word Dionysiac).

So far as the affirmative answer to life is concerned, Iqbal agrees with Nietzsche that in spite of all the evil one finds in life one has to make the best of it. Similarly with creating a ''land of fruit'' out of desert, the missions of Nietzsche and Iqbal lead to the same goal. But beyond this there is nothing in Iqbal corresponding to Dionysian *Weltanschauung* and we can leave the matter at that. It is safe to say that there is nothing Dionysian in Iqbal.

Now we can consider some of the main ideas dependent upon the three-headed philosophy of Nietzsche described above: such ideas as immoralism, the inversion of values, the will to power; Herrenmoral and Sklavenmoral, the position of women and a united Europe. As regards immoralism and the inversion of values, Nietzsche's polemic against Christianity and Christian morals is mainly directed against false conceptions introduced by Christian priests. Nietzsche adopts an attitude of moral relativism: that only is good which leads to enhancement of the will to power, and because in different times and climes it is possible to achieve this result with the help of different moral devices, he did not see any point in prescribing a universal code of morals. Nietzsche insisted on the inversion of values because he saw in the prevailing Christian values nothing but nihilism and decadence. While both Nietzsche and Iqbal agree regarding the evil effects of prevailing values, Iqbal does not believe in moral relativism; for him all moral values are eternal. That the main reason for Iqbal adopting this attitude was his religious background is in a way admitted by Nietzsche when he says, "If Islam despises Christianity it is justified a thousand times over, for Islam presupposes men" *(Antichrist).*

As regards the Will to Power, we must first try to understand what it actually is. (pp. 90-1)

By the Will to Power Nietzsche does not mean mere physical and brute strength; he includes intellectual and moral strength also. A man of strong impulses, who succeeds in controlling them, will be, according to Nietzsche, a man possessing the Will to Power. Mere political ascendancy or possession of wealth or physical power does not constitute power for him. "Where I found a living thing, there found I Will to Power; and even in the will of several found I the will to be master." *(Zarathustra.)* Iqbal agrees with Nietzsche so far as to say that power is synonymous with truth and determines the standard of values. He who is strong and powerful is on the right side, and he who is weak is destined to be reckoned as false.

Nietzsche distinguishes two kinds of morality—master morality (Herrenmoral) and slave morality (Sklavenmoral). The master morality is fundamentally active and positive, while the slave morality treats evil as the primary concept. The promulgators of master morality were strong, noble, full of vitality, brave and adventurous. Master morality calls those traits good which make a man respected and even feared: power, pride, freshness and ability to be a good friend and noble enemy. In the slave morality whatever the noble aristocrat possesses is called bad, and here a good man is a safe man, who is good-natured and easily deceived. Nietzsche emphasises that Herrenmoral is not meant for the common people. This means that Nietzsche is an inveterate hater of Socialism, while Iqbal is a firm believer in Socialism. There is no doubt that Herrenmoral leads to power, progress and happiness, while Sklavenmoral leads to mediocrity and pathetic contentment, but there seems to be no reason why slaves should not become the Herrenvolk by adopting their morals. Iqbal claims that every human being, master or slave, is a finite centre of possibilities which can be improved and evolved under healthy influences. (pp. 92-3)

Concerning the attitude to women, there is no getting away from the fact that in spite of Nietzsche's well-known statement that the highest woman is a higher being than the highest man, though rarer, he had a very poor opinion of the fair sex. Iqbal on the other hand sees in woman the hope for mankind and wants to pay divine honours to Hadrat Fātima. No doubt Iqbal holds that the place of men and women in the world can never be quite the same and it must be admitted that from the modern standpoint his attitude towards woman could not in certain respects be regarded as progressive; still he recognises the essential nobility of woman's part in life.

While Nietzsche talks of a good European and a united Europe, Iqbal talks of a united humanity.

Thus it will be seen that there is fundamentally no coincidence between the basic ideas of Iqbal and Nietzsche. The two present entirely different views of life which are poles apart. One believes in a division of humanity into water-tight compartments, resembling Manu's caste-system; the other wants to abolish all such distinctions. As remarked before, those writers who have talked of resemblance between the two have not taken the pains to study either, and most of them can be ignored. (pp. 93-4)

[It] will be interesting to see what Iqbal himself has to say about Nietzsche. It has been frequently remarked that Iqbal disliked Nietzsche intently. Whether this is a fact can be seen by referring to what Iqbal has said. In a poem written a few years before his death, Iqbal said: . . .

> Had that *Majdhūb* of Europe been alive today,
> Iqbal would have explained to him the place of God.

It will be seen that Iqbal calls Nietzsche, *Majdhūb.* Now *Majdhūb* in Muslim mysticism is a person in a stage of spiritual development, characterised by a constant state of ecstasy and rapture. This stage is, in some cases, due to direct illumination, and in others attained as a result of vigorous discipline. Iqbal does not think that Nietzsche was insane in the accepted sense of the term. Nietzsche certainly denied the existence of God, but that was, according to Iqbal, Nietzsche's loss. Legend says that St. Paul on his journey to Rome turned aside to visit Virgil's tomb near Naples, and that weeping over it he claimed:

> What a man would I have made of thee
> Had I found thee alive
> O greatest of the poets.

Iqbal's sentiments for Nietzsche bear a close resemblance to those St. Paul is said to have experienced on visiting Virgil's tomb.

In *Payām-i-mashriq,* Iqbal says: . . .

> If thou dost desire the melodious tunes, away from him,
> In the scratch of his pen is the noise of the thunder.
> He put a dagger in the breast of the West,
> His hand is besmeared with the blood of the Church.
> He constructed a temple on the lines of the Ka'ba;
> His heart is *Momin* but his mind is steeped in disbelief.

There is ample evidence to show that Iqbal had, during his stay in Europe, studied Nietzsche and was considerably attracted and impressed by his ideas, especially where he agreed with the Muslim thinkers. He has also acknowledged Nietzsche's contribution to human thought. In fact he gives him credit for much, but at the same time points out the main defects of his *Weltanschauung.*

Summing up, it can be stated that while Iqbal and Nietzsche agree on several points, they also differ on some fundamental concepts. While Nietzsche was an atheist, Iqbal was deeply religious; while Nietzsche was an aristocrat, Iqbal was for the masses; while Nietzsche was anti-socialist, Iqbal was socialist. Thus their philosophies differed. (pp. 98-9)

Iqbal's ideas on theism show affinity with those of the English philosopher James Ward. As we have seen, Iqbal conceives Ultimate Reality as Ego mainly because He responds to our call. From such an Ego other egos proceed. Thus Iqbal arrives at spiritual pluralism. Starting from experience Ward also believes in pluralism, which assumes that the world is made up of individuals, each distinguished from others by his characteristic behaviour. But pluralism cannot explain the ordered world in which we live, it cannot give us any clue to the understanding of the relationship which each ego or monad bears to others. To explain this we have to believe in "inevitable contingency" not only in human affairs, not in animated nature alone, but also in the psychic world. Yet we find that there is a tendency to replace this mere contingency by a definite progression. As we rise higher in the scale of being we find that there is greater and greater guidance and direction. From this Ward concludes that there is some relationship between the monads, depending upon the stage of being. The lowest are most contingent, while the highest are most purposive. These considerations led Ward from pluralism to theism. There are monads higher than ourselves, and above all there is the Supreme Monad—God. But Ward does not conceive God as severed from us. According to him He is one among many and not the Absolute including them all. The world is the joint product of the innumerable free agents working and striving together towards the creation of a stable system. According to Ward, though God is the creator of the world yet in the creation of human beings He has actually created creators, possessing freedom and power of initiative. In this He has imposed limits on Himself. This self-limitation by God means a living God with a living world. Iqbal is in complete agreement with the theistic monadism of Ward and he further maintains that it is compatible with the spirit of the Qur'ān.

After Ward the closest parallel with Iqbal in Western thought is Henri Bergson. Bergson starts with the fact that change is the fundamental reality of the Universe. Life is a continuous stream of change all round, but our intellectual vision gives us the impression that Life is made up of isolated states and things. Our outward perceptions also mislead us, because they are meant to equip us not with a knowledge of Reality but with practical guidance in everyday life. Intellect concerns itself with the appearance of life, which is space and serial time, while the Reality reveals itself in the unity of our consciousness which is known to us intuitionally and which exists in "pure time" or *"la durée."* Reality thus known is in the nature of a Creative Impulse, the *"Élan Vital,"* which is a creative change. This tremendous push forward drives man and beast before it, but its path is absolutely unpredictable. According to Bergson, the forward push exists for its own sake, and has no implications of future purpose. Iqbal also believes in the reality of change, but does not agree with Bergson's creative impulse. Reminiscent of Schopenhauer's blind Will, such a principle leaves no scope for personality. Indeed it seems absurd to think of the human ego under Bergson's system. Iqbal and Bergson both believe in the reality of "pure time" as distinguished from "serial time." But as Iqbal says: "I venture to think that the error of Bergson consists in regarding time as prior to self, of which alone pure duration is predicable." There are numerous differences between the thought of Iqbal and Bergson. In Bergson the conflict of mind and matter means a dualism in the whole universe, which is never resolved into a unity. In Iqbal we have the all-embracing Ego which is God. Similarly Bergson's uncompromising condemnation of Intellect finds no parallel in Iqbal. Iqbal's *'Ishq* is a more vital assimilative process than Bergson's intuition. Iqbal assigns to Intellect a position subordinate to *'Ishq*, but visualises a perfect harmony of the two. (pp. 99-101)

[We] must refer once more to Iqbal's conception of Time and Space, and trace here the connection between Iqbal's thought and that of European thinkers. Iqbal disagrees with Newton's objective view of Time. He also criticises Nietzsche's views of Time and Space, which were expressed mainly in connection with his doctrine of Eternal Recurrence. Iqbal has a great admiration for Einstein and dedicates a whole poem to him in *Payām-i-mashriq.* (p. 101)

Einstein has shown that the conception of an absolute Time and an absolute Space is untenable both on theoretical and experimental grounds. According to the Theory of Relativity, Time and Space are not absolute and separate from each other, but relative and mutually dependent. (p. 102)

Iqbal is in general agreement with the Theory of Relativity, but he raises an objection to the Theory regarding Time as a fourth dimension of Space. According to Iqbal this would mean that the future is as indubitably fixed as the past, and Time would cease to be a free creative movement. This is not a correct view of the Theory of Relativity, for it does not regard Time as a fourth dimension of Space, but of the Space-time continuum. But Iqbal proceeds to analyze further aspects of Time which the theory does not consider. For instance, he agrees with Bergson about duration in Time. One point worth noting here is that Iqbal arrived at his conclusions regarding Time long before the Theory of Relativity was known by any but a small circle of mathematicians and scientists.

Some European thinkers like McTaggart have been misled in assuming the unreality of Time by not differentiating serial time from non-serial. They assume that serial time is final. In this connection Iqbal says [in *The Reconstruction of Religious Thought in Islam*]:

> If we regard past, present and future as essential to Time, then we picture Time as a straight line, part of which we have travelled and left behind, and part lying yet untravelled before us. This is taking Time not as a living creative movement, but as a static absolute, holding the ordered multiplicity of fully shaped cosmic events revealed serially like the pictures of a film to the outside observer.

According to Iqbal the future exists only as an open possibility and not as a fixed reality. Here the modern quantum theory supports his opinion. (pp. 102-03)

While we have indicated above the points of agreement between Iqbal's philosophy and the thought of prominent European philosophers, enough has been said to demonstrate clearly that in several respects Iqbal's philosophy of ego is essentially original. But, as in the case of Plato, some of his thoughts bear close resemblance to those of other thinkers. It could not be otherwise; he owes much to the thought of his predecessors.

To sum up, Iqbal shows some points of affinity with several European thinkers, notably Fichte, Nietzsche, Bergson, Ward and Einstein. The conception of the ego is common to Fichte and Iqbal, and in his idea of Time Iqbal agrees with Einstein and Bergson. But we must bear in mind that Time occupies only a minor place in Iqbal's philosophy of the ego, and the origin of Iqbal's theory of Time can be traced to Muslim thought. The fact that he published his conception of Time, mostly in agreement with Einstein's Theory of Relativity, long before much was known about the Theory beyond the limited circle of mathematicians, provides an indication of his originality. (p. 103)

*Syed Abdul Vahid, in his* Iqbal: His Art and Thought, *John Murray, 1959, 254 p.*

**FAIZ AHMAD FAIZ** (essay date 1967)

[*Faiz was a Pakistani poet and journalist. Considered one of the most important Urdu poets of the twentieth century, he is remembered for traditional* ghazal *verses as well as a number of contemporary poems in which he espoused his leftist political views. In the following excerpt, Faiz discusses stylistic elements of Iqbal's poetry.*]

Iqbal himself was deadly opposed to art for art's sake and therefore we cannot study his art or his style or his theme or his other poetic qualities in isolation from his theme because even though there is steady progression in his style, even though he wrote in different styles yet all these styles were fashioned according to the themes which he was trying to put across. Therefore the evolution of his style is parallel to the evolution of his thought and it would be superficial and misleading to study one in isolation from the other. Keeping that in mind, if you look at Iqbal's works, the first thing that strikes you is a very strong contrast between the style and the expression of his earlier works and the style and expression of his nature and later works. But at the same time the second thing that strikes you is that in spite of these differences there is a continuity, I think, which is due to two reasons. Apart from his juvenile and very early works, even the things that he wrote in his youth are imbued with a sense of solemnity and earnestness which persist throughout his works. The second aspect of this continuity is the element of quest and inquiry—a persistent desire to know and to explore the secrets of reality, the secrets of existence. Now these two subjective elements provide continuity to his works while the stylistic element provides the element of evolution. Now how does this evolution take place? What are the elements in this evolution? I would say there are four elements, each determined by the progression in his thought. Firstly, the style of his earlier works . . . is ornate, florid, Persianised, obviously under the influence of Baidil, Nazir, and Ghalib and the school of Persian poets which was popular with our intelligentsia in the 19th century and the beginning of the 20th. . . . This is generally the style which is a bit florid, a bit diffused, a bit undefined. So you find that so far as the pure style is concerned the progression in his work is from ornamentation to austerity, from diffuseness to precision, from rhetoric to epigram. It does not require any great elaboration because it so obviously strikes one. In his later works all the ornamentation has been cut out. There is no imagery or hardly any imagery. There is hardly any element of the sensory or the perceptive which is purely cognitive, intellectual, austere and precise. This is a process of reduction, or what I might call contraction. The other is the process of expansion. This process is in the thought, in the theme; because Iqbal begins with himself in his very early works, in the works that he wrote in his youth. He talks about himself, about his love, about his grief, about his loneliness, about his disappointments. Then from himself, he progresses to the Muslim community, to the Muslim world, in the later half of *Bang-i-dara*. From the Muslim world he goes further to mankind and from mankind to the universe. So beginning with himself his thought progresses to the cosmos and his thought determines the style, and the expression which he uses. In his earlier works when he is talking about disjointed things, about sensations, about perceptions, about experiences, about subjective bits and pieces, the style is also disjointed; it is varied, sometimes simple, sometimes it is ornate. Later on when his own whole thought is welded into one monolithic entity his style also becomes monolithic. It becomes almost uniform, having no ups and down, practically keeping the same pace and the same level. That is the second progression. The third progression is a process or what you might call integration. In his earlier works, for instance, there are a number of poems on the sun, the moon, the clouds, the mountains, the rivers, cities, but there is no connection between these.

Later on when he developed his thought, then everything, the whole universe, is really welded together by this single thought that Iqbal has with regard to the role of man in the universe and his destiny. When he has determined this role then everything falls into place. In his later works if you find poems about natural phenomena and external objects like his "**Kirmak-i-Shab Taab**," "**Shaheen**," the Moon, and the Sun, then they are no longer external phenomena; they are purely symbols to illustrate some inner subjective themes which Iqbal wanted to illustrate through these symbols. They are no longer things in themselves. He is not interested in the Eagle as such. I don't think he has ever described how the Eagle looks like. He is not interested in the fire fly as such; he does not describe what the fire fly ("**Kirmak-i-Shab Taab**") or the eagle or the moon or the sun is, for they are no longer for him external objects but merely symbols to illustrate certain themes. This is the third progression in his works and the style, the progression which integrates disjointed phenomena, disjointed experiences into a single whole which is both intellectual and emotional. And fourthly there is a transition in emotional climate. In his earlier works you will see that the word he is fond of is *Mohabbat;* whereas in his later works, as you are all aware, his main burden of the song is *Ishq*. . . . But you hardly find this word *Mohabbat* later on in his mature works where the word used is always *Ishq*. So this is the progression from sentiments to passion. A progression from a purely external attachment to something which comes from within, something which is the essence of your being, something which is not an acquired trait that merely makes you love certain things or hate certain things but which is an innate fire which is all-consuming.

I want to emphasize another point. When Iqbal attained to his matured style, a style which is unadorned, which is austere, which is unornamented, then how does he heighten the statement? How does he compensate for the absence of the other ornaments that the poets generally use, the thrills with which the poets generally attract attention? This, I think, is a very fascinating subject and very little study has been done on this. Three or four things are very obvious which no one has done in Urdu poetry before. For instance, one thing which is completely his addition to the poetic style in Urdu is the use of proper names, apart from one or two names which have been traditionally used like Majnoo, Farhad, Laila and Shirin. . . . You will see such names as Koofa, Hijaz, Iraq, Furat, Ispahan, Samarqand, Koh-e-Adam, Nawah-i-Kazima, Qurtuba, etc. Knowing the poetic implication of these, when you come across a proper name like this, you do not need any simili or any metaphor. This word by itself evokes a sense of distance, a sense of time, a sense of remoteness and what you might call a sense of romance because romance after all is the sense of distance, of distance either in space or in time. So this use of the proper name is something which compensates for the absence of other ornamentation in Iqbal. The second thing which he does, which again is rather new, is the use of words which are simple but unfamiliar, words which are neither difficult nor obscure, words which are very crystal clear and yet were never used before—words like *Nakheel, Tailsan,* and *Parnian* which last in Persian is very common but is not used in Urdu. (pp. 120-22)

[The] third element which he employs is to use unfamiliar meters, as, for instance, the meter of **"Masjid-i-Qurtuba."** He has used at least half a dozen meters which were not used in Urdu poetry before and which he introduced for the first time. Then he creates a sense of unfamiliarity by unfamiliar sound, by unfamiliar words, by use of proper names and above all, by a very contrived pattern of sounds. I don't think any poet in Urdu has used the patterns of consonantal and vowel sounds deliberately as Iqbal has done. He does not go after the obvious tricks like onomatopoea and resonance. You will find that a sound arrangement of consonants and of vowels is very deliberate. The only other poet who does it in that way is as far as I know Hafiz. But in Urdu it was not known before. Before Iqbal, the people did use words with similar sounds, onomatopoea, resonance, and things like that but nobody has used the whole thing. These, I think, are some of the stylistic elements which are very characteristic of Iqbal. If you study Iqbal you find that this was the only style which could fit the ultimate theme which he evolved during the course of his poetic career. This ultimate theme, so far as I know, has many aspects and one can choose any aspect that he likes. But I think the final theme that Iqbal arrived at was the world of man, man and his universe, man against the universe, man in the universe or man in relation to the universe which I would call the world of man. I might point out that in spite of Iqbal's deep devotion to religion he never mentions the other world or hardly ever mentions the other world. There is no talk of the hereafter in his poetry. There is no mention of any rewards or any punishments. Rewards and punishments are here according to him, for the very simple reason that since he is the poet of struggle, of evolution, of fight against the hostile forces, the forces hostile to the spirit of man, the hereafter in which there is no action, in which there is no struggle, is entirely irrelevant to his thought and therefore he has never mentioned or hardly ever mentioned it. Anyway the final thing is this theme, the theme of man and the universe of man, of Man's loneliness and of Man's grandeur. He speaks of Man's loneliness because he is pitted against so many enemies. First against the forces within him like the forces of greed, cowardliness, of selfishness, exploitation and secondly the forces outside him like the forces of hostile nature. So he has the small atom of passion set against the entire universe. He speaks of man's greatness, in that he accepts this challenge, he accepts this microcosm of pain, accepts the challenge of stars and the moons and the suns and the universe. It is this greatness which elevates the verse of Iqbal, towards the end of his days, from the beautiful to the sublime. (pp. 123-24)

> *Faiz Ahmad Faiz, "Iqbal Day at Karachi: Iqbal as a Poet," in* Iqbal Review, *Vol. VIII, No. 1, April, 1967, pp. 119-33.*

## HADI HUSSAIN (essay date 1971)

[*In the following excerpt, Hussain examines Iqbal's conception of poetry and the role of the poet in society.*]

No poet, not even Milton, ever took his art more seriously than Iqbal did; none, not even Shelley or Dante, claimed for it a higher place among human activities or employed it in the service of a more far-reaching purpose. In the midst of his multifarious pursuits—philosophy, religion, mysticism, even politics—poetry was Iqbal's real vocation all his life. In fact, his excursions in these and other realms were all in the nature of explorations for ore to be refined into poetic gold. His approach to everything was that of a poet, for poetry was the core of his being. His whole *Weltanschauung*, his vision of God, man, and the universe, is a poet's vision illumined by a fiery heart at its center. His God is the archetypal poet, the supreme creative artist, incessantly creating out of a grand passion of self-expression.

Iqbal's ideal man is God's apprentice and helpmate in this creative activity, always adding to the Master's work and daring even to improve upon it, because he has a personality of his own to express. His universe is that perfect poem yet to be written, which God and man are writing in collaboration, as some of the great epics of ancient times are written, but which will never be completed; for it will continue to grow in the very process of being composed. This is the essence of poetry, no matter by what name it is called.

Iqbal's conception of poetry is of a piece with his cosmology. In a poetic universe poetry is life and life poetry, and both are endless creation. The creative impulse, originating in God's self, which is the primal source of all being, flows through innumerable human selves into the sea of becoming which is life.

> Life is a boundless sea,
> Whose every drop's heart is a restless wave,
> It knows no tranquil state,
> Because it must continually create.

The most restless drop in life's sea is the poet's heart. For one thing, the poet has more than the ordinary human need of self-expression, which is the fountain of all creative activity; for it is what generates, sustains, and multiplies life. For another, it is not merely an individual human heart beating in the poet's breast, but the universal heart; also, his is the voice of the whole humanity. He forges links of sympathy between man and the things that surround him, reveals to him the mysteries that lie behind the obvious and the familiar, and gives him an insight into the secrets of his own self. He creates things by naming them, for by doing so he invests essence with attributes and brings them within man's ken. He imparts to man a vision of the unity that underlies the diversity of phenomena and an awareness of the coherence behind the apparent incoherence of things. (pp. 327-28)

Thus the poet helps in shaping the human personality and human destiny, both within the span of the individual life and in the perspective of history—and in both cases against the background of eternity. Speaking for the poet in his own person, Iqbal claims:

> The destinies of worlds are shaped behind
> The awnings of my mind,
> And revolutions are brought up
> In my heart's lap.
> I spent a moment in my inner solitude,
> And there emerged a world which knows no finitude.
> I witness life and death engaged in transitory strife,
> But have my eyes fixed firmly on eternal life.

In short, the poet is a leader, a teacher, a reformer, a sage—all these together. The unifying principle that activates this composite personality is poetic passion, the passion to create ever new, ever more beautiful and perfect forms embodying man's ever-growing aspirations. Another name for this poetic passion is love. It is a heightened state of the soul, which raises man above his ordinary self, increases his powers of perception, refines his feelings, broadens his sympathies, animates his imagination, and, above all, makes a sense of power well up from within him. This sense of power is a dynamic, outgoing urge to take hold of things and remodel them so as to make them better than they are. Iqbal maintains that love beautifies, sublimates, and idealizes. . . . (pp. 329-30)

Such being their origin, poetic creations are not mere slavish imitations of nature, lifeless reproductions of things in the external world, but living images of things as they exist in the poet's perfection-seeking soul and as they ought to be in nature. Whether poet or painter, the artist who merely imitates nature is untrue to his vocation. . . . (p. 330)

The truth of the poetic creations is a higher form of truth than mere literal faithfulness to appearances; it is an unveiling of reality, residing neither in the world of sense perception nor in its abstraction, the world of the intellect, but in the world of the soul, the world of essence. The power to perceive this essential reality is not given to ordinary mortals, not even to the philosopher or the scientist, who are concerned only with rationally analyzable or empirically verifiable data. The only persons besides the poet who are vouchsafed knowledge of the truth that lies beyond proof or verification are the prophet and the saint—like the poet, men of passion, whose souls are aflame with love. The prophet embodies his vision of reality in the poetry of action, and the poet in the poetry of words; the saint absorbs it in himself, thus becoming a living poem. The poet is closer to the prophet than to the saint in that, like the former and unlike the latter, he transforms subjective into objective reality—his own inner states of being into concrete facts and situations, adding new dimensions to life. Although the media of the prophet and the poet are different, their product is the same—man's moral and spiritual regeneration or, in concrete terms, a morally and spiritually regenerated society—and this product is clearly envisaged and consciously willed by both of them. Their activities are, therefore, fully purposive, notwithstanding the fact that they are the outcome of inspiration, divine in the case of the prophet and intuitive in that of the poet.

The charismatic character of poetic activity and the messianic role assigned to the poet entail a high degree of moral responsibility. In entrusting him with a gift of such vital importance to humanity, God has chosen the poet as an instrument for the fulfillment of His high purpose, which, on the temporal plane, is the advancement of humanity and, on a supratemporal plane, the creation of the perfect man, who is the *beau idéal* of all created things and is destined to be God's comate in eternity. The poet should, therefore, so exercise his art as to help man forward on his journey to perfection. His life's work should itself form a stage of that journey. In other words, he should himself be the forerunner and prototype of the perfect man— rebel, iconoclast, revolutionary, hero of mortal strife, champion of high ideals, and prophet of human progress.

It bears eloquent testimony to Iqbal's belief in this sublimated role of the poet that he sees himself in it, in much the same way as, for example, Homer, according to Longinus, often sees himself to live the great lives of his heroes or as Milton enjoins that one who hopes to write "of laudable things ought himself to be a true Poem." Iqbal's frequent claims of divine frenzy, inspired wisdom, intuitive foresight, and heroic courage are not mere braggadocio or attitudinization in the rather naïve tradition of Persian poetry. On the contrary, they sound like genuine appeals to the reader to take him for a serious poet, one who has something more to offer than mere entertainment. Conscious of the presence of these qualities in himself, he is anxious to make sure that the reader takes them into account so that he approaches him in a receptive frame of mind. His hieratic role not only entitles him, but makes it necessary for him, to speak in an oracular manner. His claims are not

the pretensions of a pseudoprophet or a mystagogue, but the manifesto of a man with a mission who cannot afford to let false modesty prevent him from stating his qualifications. (pp. 332-33)

Similarly, when Iqbal denounces poets and poetry, he is thinking of poets and poetry not deserving of their name because they are decadent, life-negating, and subversive of human progress. Not to speak of poetry which addresses itself to the baser side of human nature, he condemns even poetry which is technically excellent but yields nothing more than mere aesthetic pleasure; for such poetry weakens the will to action and is therefore immoral. For instance, although he was a great admirer of Hāfiz as a master craftsman of Persian poetry, who, he acknowledged, could pack into single words meanings which others could not express in whole *ghazals* (lyrics), he inveighed against him for his quietism, his epicureanism, his libertinism, his indifference to the great historical events that were taking place around him and the soporific effect of his mystical eroticism. It is this kind of poetry which Iqbal intends to disavow; but he disavows it in words which convey the impression that he has no use for poetry of any kind. Here, for example, is a specially violent outburst:

> No good will ever come from any churlish boor
> Who lays the charge of versifying at my door.
> I do not know the alley where the poet's sweetheart dwells;
> I have no lovelorn heart which someone's coldness ails.
> Mere humble dust, I yet do not lie on the street
> To be a carpet under beauty's feet.
> Nor is there in my dust
> A heart made clamorous by lust.

The disclaimer is aimed at the *fin-de-siècle* erotic poetry which was fashionable in Urdu when Iqbal started his poetic career; but Iqbal seems to be repudiating all poetry, although actually intending only to repudiate this one kind. In the passage quoted below, however, he is more specific: the target is unmistakably decadent poetry, the poetry of people on the downgrade, as were the Indian Muslims of that period, whom he particularly had in mind:

> Woe to the nation which regales itself
> On death, whose poet has no zest for life.
> He holds the mirror up to ugliness,
> Presenting it as beautiful. His song
> Is like a poisoned lancet in the heart.
> His kiss drains roses of their youthful bloom.
> He robs the nightingale's heart of the joy
> Of soaring while it sings. His opium dulls
> Your mind. His entertainment costs you dear:
> The price you pay for it is life itself.
> He warps the cypress's tall stateliness.
> He turns proud eagles into timid quails.
> His Muse is a seductive nymph; beware
> Its fatal siren song, which will allure
> You into the depths of the sea to drown.
>
> (pp. 335-36)

It would be wrong to conclude from the foregoing quotations that Iqbal has an ambivalent attitude toward poetry and that he is rent by a conflict between the poet and the moralist in him. The conflict is there, but it is only on the surface. At bottom it has been resolved by a belief in the inherent moral value of true poetry. Poetry and ethics, in their higher reaches, are for Iqbal both motivated by a quest for human perfection. In this quest these traditional opposites find their synthesis by a Hegelian dialectic, acquiring the name of great poetry, and the distinguishing mark of the great poet, the poet dedicated to this quest, is the aura of the perfect man which encircles him. (p. 337)

> Hadi Hussain, "Conception of Poetry and the Poet," in Iqbal: Poet-Philosopher of Pakistan, edited by Hafeez Malik, Columbia University Press, 1971, pp. 327-46.

## JOHN L. ESPOSITO (essay date 1983)

[Esposito is an American educator and critic whose writings reflect his vast study of Islamic religion and society. In the following excerpt, he examines the relevance of Iqbalian philosophy in modern Islamic civilization.]

Some forty years since his death, Muhammad Iqbal continues to be important not only in South Asia but also in the Middle East. Arab writers from the late Sayyid Qutb to the contemporary Sadiq al-Mahdi acknowledge his influence. Since he wrote in Persian as well as Urdu and English, his writings were also accessible to Iranian reformers such as Ali Shariati, a hero and ideologue of Iranian youth and the Islamic left during the Iranian revolution.

Writing during the early decades of this century, Iqbal showed his perceptiveness and genius in identifying and addressing many of the problems and concerns that characterize the contemporary Islamic revival: disillusionment with the West tempered by a recognition of its scientific and technological accomplishments; awareness of the pressing need for the renewal of Muslim society through a process of reinterpretation and reform; affirmation of the integral relationship of Islam to politics and society; espousal of an Islamic alternative; and reaffirmation of the transnational character of the Islamic community.

Iqbal's poetry has moved millions; his life and work have inspired literally thousands of books and articles as well as Iqbal societies and journals. Because of his stature as spiritual father of Pakistan and the popularity of his poetry among educated and uneducated alike, political activists and Muslim intellectuals of every persuasion have sought to proclaim him as their source and master. Indeed, because of Iqbal's widespread influence upon such divergent groups, it becomes necessary to return carefully to his writings in order to distinguish his thought from that of those who claim his influence. This study will demonstrate the relevance of Muhammad Iqbal's thought to the contemporary revival of Islam, focusing on his understanding of the nature and purpose of Islamic society and how such a society might be realized today. (p. 175)

Drawing upon his Islamic heritage and Western studies, Muhammad Iqbal responded to the weakened condition of Indian Muslim society, which he viewed with deep concern. Iqbal lived amidst a Muslim minority which had once ruled India but which now faced co-existence not only with a Hindu majority but also with British colonial rule. The proud days of Islamic ascendancy were no longer. Furthermore, he believed that Hindu intellectualism and Sufi pantheism had severely lessened the Muslim community's capacity for action. He viewed the quietism of the Indian Muslims as a radical departure from the true spirit of Islam, that of dynamic movement and creative evolution. Rejecting the static universe of Plato and those aspects of Muslim mysticism which denied the affirmation of the self in the world, Iqbal, basing himself on the Quran, developed a dynamic Weltanschauung in his theory of selfhood (egohood) which embraced all of reality, self, society, and God.

The individual self, the basic component of Muslim society, enjoys a special, exalted status. Following the Quran, Iqbal emphasized man's chief end or mission as God's vicegerent. It is the Muslim's God-given task to carry out His will on earth:

> . . . this world of colour and scent is your empery—grain by grain gather the jewels from its soil, falcon-like seize your prey out of its skies, smite your axe against its mountain ranges, take light from yourself and set it all afire . . . hew out a new world to your own desire.

Man must mould the matter of the universe in space-time to shape and direct the forces of nature. In this sense, man shares in an ongoing process of creation, ". . . inasmuch as he helps to bring order into at least a portion of the chaos." For Iqbal, then, man is the committed Muslim believer (mumin) who assumes his Quranically mandated responsibility for the world and endeavors to produce the model society which is to be emulated by others, Muslim and non-Muslim alike. Self-realization and personal fulfillment necessitate the Muslim's societal involvement. In *Rumuz-i bekhudi* (*The Mysteries of Selflessness*), Iqbal describes the self's relationship to society:

> All his [man's] nature is entranced
> with individuality,
> Yet only in Society he finds security
> and preservation.

And again we read:

> The link that binds the Individual
> To the Society a Mercy is,
> His truest Self in the Community
> Alone achieves fulfillment.

Due to his strong need and desire for association, the individual forms the basic unit of the *millat* ("community," nation). An interdependence exists between the two: the individual is elevated through the community while the community is organized by individuals. In mystical language, Iqbal spoke of the individual losing his "self" in the community and thus discovering that his personality had become an embodiment of past traditions and a bridge between his past and future. . . . (pp. 176-77)

The human need for society is satisfied by Islam. For the Muslim, Islam is more than a creed: it is his community, his nation, the locus in which he will attain his true individuality (selfhood). The Islamic community (ummah) is a society based upon common belief. However, it encompasses more than the notion of religious community as understood in the Judeo-Christian tradition for it includes the notion of the state as well. There is no bifurcation of the spiritual and the temporal. It is not correct to speak of Church and State as two sides or facets of the same thing, for Islam is a single unanalyzable reality "which is one or the other as your point of view varies."

The purpose of the Islamic state is to take Islamic principles and endeavor to realize them in a definite human organization in history. Basing himself upon the Prophet's saying, "The whole of this earth is a mosque," Iqbal could assert that in Islam: "All that is secular is therefore sacred in the roots of its being" for "All this immensity of matter constitutes a scope for the self-realization of spirit."

The twin pillars of Islamic state and society are the prophethood of Muhammad and, most importantly, the doctrine of tawhid. Muhammad came as the final messenger or "Seal" of all the prophets and taught the community that faith which gives it unity. Thus Iqbal wrote in his *Rumuz-i bekhudi*:

... through his wisdom flows the lifeblood of the
whole community. . . . His was the breath that gave
the people life . . . his Apostleship brought concord
to our purpose and our goal.

Muhammad was not only God's messenger but also the model
or exemplar for the Muslim community. Indeed, his Sunna had
become normative. Traditions (hadith) about the Prophet's words
and behavior from earliest times had been preserved and collected and, with the Quran, had provided the material sources
of Islamic law. Moreover, it was Muhammad who had served
as the Prophet-Statesman of the early Islamic community at
Medina. As such, he reflected the union of religion and state
in his life. Muhammad, who came to a world of men subject
to temporal and spiritual tyrants, rejected the privileged class,
priesthood and caste alike, and founded a society based upon
freedom, equality and brotherhood.

*Tawhid,* the "Unity of God," affirms the radical monotheism
of Islam. God is one; there are no other gods and nothing else
should be valued in His place. The Islamic doctrine of *tawhid*
extends to all of creation, for the Creator sustains and governs
all of His creation. Therefore, God's will is to be realized in
every area of life. For Iqbal, *tawhid* is the principle that brings
the community together, the source of its equality, solidarity,
and freedom: *tawhid* "is the soul and body of our Community." Such is its force that the community of believers is as
a brotherhood of equals (regardless of race, national or geographic origin): "Sharing in one speech, one spirit and one
heart." This very unity of thought should serve as the motivating force for action leading to the advancement of God's
will in space-time.

The constitution of the Islamic state, reflecting the doctrine of
*tawhid,* rests upon two basic propositions: the supremacy of
God's law (the *shariah*) and the absolute equality of its members. Islamic law is a comprehensive law which provided the
blueprint for Muslim society. The law encompassed all areas
of life: duties of God (e.g., worship, fasting, pilgrimage) and
duties in society (civil, criminal, and family laws).

From the nineteenth century on, Muslim countries, under the
influence of colonial rule, adopted Western (European) inspired
legal codes, and thus with the exception of family law, Islamic
law was displaced. In the Indian subcontinent, the interaction
of British and Islamic law in the nineteenth century produced
Anglo-Muhammadan law. Again with the exception of Muslim
family law, British-based codes in civil, criminal, and penal
law were enacted. Iqbal, like Islamic revivalists today, recognized the need to reaffirm the centrality of Islamic law to
the unity and life of the Muslim community:

> When a Community forsakes its Law
> Its parts are severed, like the scattered dust.
> The being of the Muslim rests alone
> On Law, which is in truth the inner core
> Of the Apostle's faith.

In 1937, in a letter to Muhammad Ali Jinnah, the leader of
the Muslim League and the founder of Pakistan, Iqbal stressed
the importance of Islamic law as fundamental to the survival
of Islam and the Muslim community's role as a political and
moral force in Southeast Asia. Enforcement of the law required
a Muslim state: ". . . endorsement and development of the
Shariah of Islam is impossible in this country without a free
Muslim state or states."

Iqbal's second basis for Islamic state and society is absolute
equality, rooted in the doctrine of *tawhid* (unity of God) and

the mission of the Prophet and based upon the Quran, "The
noblest among you are those who fear God most." Any notion
of aristocracy is inimical to Islam. Rather, Islam is a unity
without class distinctions established through a common faith
or conviction. Iqbal saw this principle of equality, which gave
the individual Muslim a sense of his "inward power," as the
source of Muslim political power. The early history of Islam
which saw the Muslim community emerge as "the greatest
political power in the world" provided validation for this belief.

Surveying contemporary Indian Muslim society, Iqbal maintained that it was this same "elevation of the down-trodden"
that should be the secret source of Muslim power. However,
he found just the opposite to be the case. The Muslims of India
had, in fact, "out-Hindued the Hindu himself" by developing
a double caste system: religious (sectarianism) and social. The
remedy for this situation, then, must be a return to the true
egalitarian spirit of Islam which transcended all distinctions,
Wahhabi, Shia, or Sunni in Islam.

Iqbal's central emphasis upon equality and brotherhood led to
his conclusion that democracy was the most important political
ideal in Islam. For this form of government (rooted in the
Islamic principle that the interests of Islam are superior to those
of the Muslim) allowed man the necessary freedom to develop
all the possibilities of his nature while limiting his freedom
only in the interests of the community.

This democratic ideal, which existed for the first thirty years
of Islamic history, had disappeared with Islam's political expansion. The fostering of this democratic spirit is one of the
duties of the Islamic community which historical circumstances
had prevented. Iqbal praised England for embodying this
"Muslim" quality:

> Democracy [which] has been the great mission of
> England in modern times . . . it is one aspect of our
> own political ideal that is being worked out in it. It
> is . . . the spirit of the British Empire that makes it
> the greatest Muhammaden Empire in the world.

However, Iqbal's recognition of democracy as an ideal form
should not be equated with a wholesome acceptance of democracy as it existed and functioned in the West. He believed
that the success of a democratic system was contingent upon
the preparedness of its members. A democratic system might
be less than ideal given the constituents of the society. Thus,
Iqbal did not accept the absolute democracy of undeveloped
individuals. This is at the heart of his criticism of modern
Western democracy: "Democracy is a system where people
are counted but not weighed."

The existence of a society whose members are undeveloped
individuals necessitated for Iqbal the guidance of great leaders
(supermen): "The ethical training of humanity is really the
work of great personalities, who appear, from time to time,
during the course of human history."

The idea of a superman or Perfect Man is not a totally new
concept in the history of thought. It was a favorite theme of
Nietzsche in the West and had also been taught by Muslim
mystical metaphysicians, as the "perfect man" (*insan-i-kamil*), like ibn Arabi, Rumi, and Jili. All were men who influenced Iqbal's thought and were praised in his poetry. However,
Iqbal did not simply follow their thought uncritically. Rather
a new synthesis resulted: "The perfect and godly man of Rumi
embraces the superman of the unbelieving Nietzsche and becomes the Iqbalian man."

For Iqbal, the ideal Muslim is the Quranic "man of belief" (*mard-i-mumin*) or the "perfect man" (*insan-i-kamil*) called to realize his full potential in Muslim society. Iqbal's goal was a democracy of "more or less unique individuals, presided over by the most unique individual possible." Speaking of democracy as the most important aspect of the Islamic state on the one hand and yet ruled by supermen on the other created an apparent inconsistency as when Iqbal wrote:

> Keep away from Democracy: Follow the Perfect Man,
> For the intellect of two hundred asses cannot bring forth a
> single man's thought.

However, as previously noted, for Iqbal the functioning of a true democratic system was contingent upon the preparedness of individuals and was always subject to God's law. Given the decay of the Muslim community, the democratic ideal in Islam was an ideal yet to be realized. Thus, the need for the guidance of a great leader. Unfortunately, Iqbal does not suggest how in a modern state that leader would gain power. The "perfect man" of Islamic mysticism applied to the prophets as well as the Sufi saint (*wali*, "friend" of God). How this concept is to function effectively regarding the political leadership of the Muslim community remains unanswered.

The preservation and protection of the Islamic state and a desire to respond to Western perceptions of Islam as militaristic necessitated Iqbal's consideration of the question of jihad. He denied the claim that jihad represented an offensive attack of the Muslim community for self-aggrandizement. Returning to the sources of Islam, he argued that all the wars waged under the Prophet Muhammad's leadership were defensive.

Moreover, while defensive war is permitted, aggressive warfare is contrary to the Quran. The only justifiable excuse for warfare is the exaltation of God, not the acquisition of land or any other end:

> War is good if its object is God.
> If God be not exalted by our swords,
> War dishonours the people. . . .
> Whoso shall draw the sword for anything except Allah,
> His sword is sheathed in his own breast.

Contrary to the Western caricature of Islam as a "religion of holy war" Iqbal maintained that according to the Quran it is a religion of peace: "All forms of political and social disturbance are condemned . . . the ideal of Islam is to secure social peace at any cost." He concluded that any attempt at social change through the employment of violence is impossible and approvingly cited Tartushi, a Muslim lawyer from Sapin, who had written: "Forty years of tyranny are better than one year of anarchy."

Iqbal did not discuss the criterion for implementing his Islamic ideal of a just war. Since governments often use religion to justify waging war, how does the Muslim determine that the real motive is Allah? More importantly, if "war is good if its object is God," then how justify "social peace at any cost"? The answer may lie in Iqbal's intention to respond to the distorted picture of Islam presented by its European critics. He was responding to the needs of Muslim community at that time. One can only wonder what he would say to those Islamic movements today in Afghanistan, Iran, Pakistan, Egypt, Syria who argue that the establishment and/or preservation of Islamic society requires political and social upheaval.

Iqbal's understanding of the Islamic state as a community whose membership is based on common religious belief and whose purpose is to realize freedom, equality, and brotherhood in history led quite logically to his rejection of territorial nationalism as contrary to the universal brotherhood established by Muhammad:

> Our Master, fleeing from his fatherland,
> Resolved the knot of Muslim nationhood.
> His wisdom founded one Community
> The world its parish—on the sacred charge to civilize.

Iqbal rejected any understanding of the nation-state as a foundation of the Islamic community. Nationalism was the tool used by colonialism to dismember the Muslim world: "to shatter the religious unity of Islam in pieces." Its results are the estrangement of man from his fellow man, the disunity of nations, and the separation of religion and politics that had led to the downfall of Christianity.

In **"Political Thought in Islam,"** Iqbal wrote that the "political ideal of Islam consists in the creation of a people born of a free fusion of all races and nationalities." The inner cohesion of this community issues not from geographic or ethnic unity but from the unity of its political and religious ideal. Membership or citizenship is based upon a declaration of "like-mindedness" which terminates only when this condition has ceased to exist. Territorily, the Islamic polity is transnational, embracing the whole world. Though the Arab attempt to establish such a pan-Islamic order through conquest failed, its establishment still remains an ideal to be realized. The ideal Islamic state does, in fact, exist in germ form:

> The life of modern political communities finds expression, to a great extent, in common institutions, Law and Government, and the various sociological circles . . . are continually expanding to touch one another.

Meeting the objections of those who fear the loss of individual states' sovereignty, Iqbal pointed out that this need not occur since the structure of the Islamic state will be determined not by physical force but by the spiritual force of a common ideal.

Although Iqbal had devoted a good deal of his thinking and writing to his understanding of the political theory of Islamic society and had expressed a pan-Islamic spirit, he realized that the exigencies of his times necessitated adaptation and patience:

> In order to create a really effective political unity of Islam, all Moslem countries must first become independent, and then in their totality they should range themselves under the Caliph. Is such a thing possible at the present moment? If not today, one must wait.

Thus, for Iqbal, the Muslim community must pursue an immediate as well as a long-range goal. First, each Muslim nation must gain its independence, turn in on itself and put its own house in order. This would bring each to the strength and power necessary to realize the second goal, to come together and establish a living family of republics whose unifying bond would be their common Islamic spiritual heritage:

> It seems to me that God is slowly bringing home to us the truth that Islam is neither Nationalism nor Imperialism but a League of Nations which recognize artificial boundaries and racial distinctions of reference only and not for restricting the social horizon of its members.

The poet/philosopher, applying the logic of his thought to his own Indian/Muslim situation, concluded that the Muslims of India were in danger of losing the freedom necessary for development. As noted earlier, Iqbal maintained that every Muslim needed the Islamic community for his development. While many advocated a secular Indian state to incorporate Hindu and Muslim alike, Iqbal rejected any notion that Islam could be reduced to a private ethical code separated from the socio-political sphere:

> The religious ideal of Islam, therefore, is organically related to the social order which it has created. The rejection of the one will eventually involve the rejection of the other.

Iqbal saw the displacement of Islamic solidarity as a real possibility facing the Muslim minority in India.

Reviewing the history of India, Iqbal recognized that the Hindu and Muslim communities had guarded their collective existence and identities jealously and had shown no inclination toward absorption into a larger whole. Moreover, all attempts at discovering a principle of internal harmony had failed. Therefore, for Iqbal, communalism seemed to be absolutely necessary for Muslims to preserve their identity and way of life: "the Indian Muslim is entitled to full and free development on the lines of his own culture and tradition in his own Indian Homelands." He distinguished this from a narrow communalism which deprecated other communities and their customs. Since he viewed the units of Indian society as communal and not territorial (as in Europe) he could agree with Muslims' demand for the creation of a Muslim India within India. However, Iqbal went beyond this resolution of the All-Parties Muslim Conference of Delhi and in his now famous "Presidential Address" of 29 December, 1930, called for the formation of a separate Muslim state:

> I would like to see the Punjab, Northwest Frontier Province, Sind and Baluchistan amalgamated into a single State. Self government within or without the British Empire, the formation of a consolidated North-West Indian Muslim State appears to me to be the final destiny of the Muslims, at least of North-West India.

Using his Islamic perspective, Iqbal sought to assess capitalism and socialism, the two major ideologies dominating the twentieth century and vying for power in the Muslim world. His criticism of Western democracy followed from his belief that the Western capitalist system suppressed the individual and his growth and made true democracy an impossibility:

> The Democratic system of the West is the same old instrument
> Whose chords contain no note other than the voice of the Kaiser,
> The Demon of Despotism is dancing in his democratic robes
> Yet you consider it to be the Nilam Peri of Liberty.
>
> (pp. 178-85)

In *The Pilgrimage of Eternity* (the *Javid Nama*), Iqbal ultimately finds the fundamental faults of capitalism and communism to be the same:

> Both fail to recognize the Lord, deceive
> Mankind. The one for revolution thirsts,
> The other for tribute: they're two millstones
> That pulverise the human kind.

He condemns the gross materialism and godlessness of both systems:

> The soul of both is impatient and intolerant, both of them know not God and deceive mankind. One lives by production, the other by taxation and man is a glass caught between these two stones.

Iqbal was attracted by several Marxist teachings insofar as they exemplified Islamic social principles. This explains his seem-ingly naïve enthusiasm for the Russian revolution and his citation of the Soviet Union as proof that some Islamic social principles could be applied in practice in modern times:

> From the behaviour of nations it appears to me
> That the rapid progress of Russia is not without gain . . .
> Perhaps at this time it demonstrates the truth
> That is hidden in the words "Say: The Surplus."

It is important to remember that Iqbal was not well versed in Marxist theory. His socialist tendencies are best understood within his own religious tradition; his socialism was rooted in Islam's social teachings based on Islamic principles such as the equality and brotherhood of believers and the social welfare obligation of all Muslims to their fellow believers exemplified by the *zakat* (tithe, wealth tax). (p. 185)

Iqbal's underlying concern, which motivated and informed all of his thought, writing, and activity was the revival of Islam. He saw himself as standing in the great tradition of Islamic renewal and reform (*tajdid* and *islah*) which stretched across the centuries and was epitomized by men such as Muhammad Ibn Adb al-Wahhab, Shah Wali Allah, and modern reformers like Jamal al-Din al-Afghani and Muhammad Abduh. These Islamic revivalists reformed their Muslim community through the reapplication of the pristine principles of Islam to the needs of their age. As a result the dynamic, creative spirit of Islam was reaffirmed while preserving that which was essential, immutable. Iqbal's life-long intention was to call for and contribute to the development of a new Islamic synthesis for his age. The title of one of his last works, *The Reconstruction of Religious Thought in Islam*, summarizes his purpose quite clearly.

Iqbal asserted the need for both permanence and change in a living, developing Islamic state, a belief which originates in his interpretation of the Quranic view of God and its relationship to Islamic society. God or Ultimate Ego has creative, dynamic life which is both permanent and changing. Iqbal understood creation to be the unfolding of the inner possibilities of God (Ultimate Ego) in a single and yet continuing act: "The Ultimate Ego exists in pure duration wherein change ceases to be a succession of varying attitudes, and reveals its true character as continuous creation."

If this element of permanence and yet change is true of God, the "ultimate spiritual basis of all life," then it must be true at every level of His creation. Thus, the Islamic way of life as found in the *shariah*, the blueprint for Muslim society, is itself dynamic and open to change. Iqbal rejected the centuries-long tendency of the majority of Muslims to view law as fixed and sacrosanct. The Quran's legal principles were not comprehensive and thus "the early doctors of law taking their cue from this groundwork evolved a number of legal systems. . . . But with all their comprehensiveness these systems are after all individual interpretations and as such cannot claim any finality." Although the eternal, immutable principles of the *shariah* are necessary for the regulation of its collective life, yet the Islamic state includes a principle of change by which it can adapt itself to all the possibilities arising from that which is "essentially mobile in its nature." This principle of movement is *ijtihad*. The failure to appreciate and utilize *ijtihad* was judged by Iqbal as the cause for the immobility of Islam during the preceding 500 years. While acknowledging the role of ulama (religious scholars) in the past, he blamed them for the conservatism which had characterized Islam since the fall of Baghdad (1258). With their acceptance of the dictum: "The door of *ijtihad* is closed," these self-proclaimed scholar-guardians of Islam, who had developed the schools of Islamic law and the system of education, stopped a dynamic process of reinterpretation and reapplication of Islamic principles to new situations. They were content to serve simply as the protector—perpetuators of established traditions. Indeed, while *ijtihad* had been accepted in theory by the Sunnis, ''in practice it has always been denied ever since the establishment of the schools, inasmuch as the idea of complete *ijtihad* is hedged round by conditions which are well-nigh impossible of realization in a single individual.'' Iqbal aligned himself with men like Ibn Taimiya, ibn Hasm, Suyuti, and especially Muhammad ibn Abd al-Wahhab—whom he viewed as the father of ''all the great modern movements''—and called for the opening of the gates of *ijtihad*.

Furthermore, Iqbal extended or developed the function of *ijtihad*. Noting the growth of the republican spirit, he accepted the importance of modern legislative assemblies and advocated the transfer of the right to interpret and apply the law from the domain of individual ulama to that of the legislatures. This collective or corporate *ijtihad* would then constitute the authoritative consensus (*ijma*) of the community. Traditionally, *ijma* referred to community consensus or agreement, one of the four sources of Islamic law. In fact, the consensus was that of religious leaders/scholars of the community. However, given the needs of modern society, Iqbal called for the transfer not only of legal interpretation (*ijtihad*) but also of community authority (*ijma*) from the ulama to a Muslim legislative assembly, the vast majority of whom, he believed, possessed the requisite knowledge of modern affairs: ''In this way alone we can stir into activity the dormant spirit of life in our legal system and give it an evolutionary outlook.''

While acknowledging the ulama's creative contribution during the early Islamic centuries, he stressed that ''a false reverence for past history and its artificial resurrection constitute no remedy for a people's decay.'' Undue dependence upon the ulama's traditional education could lead to inadequate understanding of and response to the demands of modernity. In addition, Iqbal argued that the complex nature of many modern problems required wisdom derived from the polling of experts representing various disciplines—traditional and modern.

Muhammad Iqbal lived during the period between two epochs, the old feudal society and modern capitalism. Given the station of his birth, his education, and his travel in Europe he could appreciate the pluses and minuses of both systems. The poet—for certainly he was first and foremost a poet by temperament—saw and responded to the quietism of the Muslim community and the internal crises which faced Islam. He could admire the achievements of the West—its dynamic spirit, intellectual tradition, and technological advances. However, he was equally critical of the imperialism of European colonialism, the moral bankruptcy of secularism and the economic exploitation of capitalism. Therefore, he advocated a return to Islam in order to construct an Islamic alternative for modern Muslim society.

Like most Muslim revivalists, Iqbal attributed the weakening of Islam to the Muslim community's departure from Islamic principles. His political theory, like all of his thought, is characterized by a conscious turning to the past to rediscover those principles and values which could provide a model for the present as well as the future.

Iqbal's great contribution was his rekindling of an awareness of the dynamic spirit of Islam. He represented to the community those Islamic ideals that could bring new life to the Islamic polity. He reconstructed fundamental principles in a poetry that could move his fellow Muslims, literate and illiterate, to an intuition of what ought to be and fire their minds with a desire to find ways of realizing such ideals.

It is possible to speak of an earlier Pan-Islamic ideal in Iqbal's political thought which would have necessitated a caliphate. However, political events during his lifetime called for some modification. This did not mean a total abandonment of a Pan-Islamic ideal. It was the goal of his counsel, that each Muslim nation should look within and strengthen and rebuild itself so that the Muslim nations might enter into a ''League of Nations''-like relationship. Such a ''League'' would be rooted in the common ideal of its members. This common ''like-mindedness'' would spring from their Islamic traditions with their common ideals of equality, fraternity, and solidarity and their common law—the *shariah*. Thus, Muslim nations could avoid the divisive pitfalls of nationalism with its tendency toward the disintegration of society into rivaling tribes.

Iqbal, like most men, was limited by his temperament. A poet draws heavily upon his feelings and emotions as he attempts to convey his intuition of reality. He could write of social injustice or political ideals while at the same time moving his reader to an experience which enabled him to empathize with the victim of injustice or to be aroused by the nobility of the ideal. However, neither poetic temperament nor the poem itself is concerned with the practical implementation of social reforms or the realization of the ideal.

Muhammad Iqbal articulated those Islamic political principles which he believed were fundamental for a rejuvenation of the Islamic community while leaving the practical implementation to the politicians, sociologists, economists, etc. He expressed the need of the Muslim community when he called for the formation of Pakistan but its practical implementation was to fall to Jinnah and others. Still there is a place in our world for the idealists. To have clothed his insights in poetic form and thus to have fired the hearts and minds of millions to pursue and implement these ideals is an extraordinary achievement, one which more than justifies the great esteem that Muhammad Iqbal had enjoyed. (pp. 186-89)

*John L. Esposito, ''Muhammad Iqbal and the Islamic State,'' in* Voices of Resurgent Islam, *edited by John L. Esposito, Oxford University Press, 1983, pp. 175-90.*

---

## ADDITIONAL BIBLIOGRAPHY

Anand, Mulk Raj. ''Muhammad Iqbal.'' In his *Wisdom of the East: The Golden Breath—Studies in Five Poets of the New India*, pp. 61-85. London: John Murray, 1933.
    Biographical and critical essay.

Baig, M. Safdar Ali. ''Poet Iqbal's Dynamism.'' *Triveni: A Critical Quarterly* XXXVI, No. 3 (October 1967): 35-41.
    Discusses Iqbal's philosophical writings on the nature of humanity.

Bausani, Alessandro. ''Dante and Iqbal.'' In *Crescent and Green: A Miscellany of Writings on Pakistan*, pp. 162-70. London: Cassell & Co., 1955.
    Compares Iqbal's ''Celestial Poem'' with Dante's ''Dark Wood.''

Bilgrami, H. H. *Glimpses of Iqbal's Mind and Thought: Brief Lectures on Iqbal Delivered at London, Cambridge, and Oxford.* Lahore: Orientalia, 1954, 124 p.

Studies Iqbal's life and philosophy, his significance among Islamic writers, and his inspiration in the Koran. According to Bilgrami: "To Iqbal, poetry was not an end in itself. It was only a means to a higher goal which he ever had in view prominently."

Coppola, Carlo. "Nationalism and Urdu Literature of India and Pakistani." *Essays on Nationalism and Asian Literatures*, No. 23 (1987): 35-68.
Survey that includes a discussion of Iqbal's life and works. According to Coppola: "Iqbal viewed his calling as rekindling the Muslim's self-confidence in and awareness of his religion, its past glories, and its mission and status in the contemporary world, by means of a philosophy which can be characterized as a curious and complex blend of radical modernism and arch conservatism."

Harré, R. "Iqbal: A Reformer of Islamic Philosophy." *The Hibbert Journal* 56 (July 1958): 333-39.
Examines Iqbal's metaphysical and theological principles in the context of Muslim intellectual history.

Hussain, Arif. "Iqbal and Casely-Hayford: A Phase in Afro-Asian Philosophy." *Ibadan* 29 (1971): 45-52.
Discusses the similar philosophical beliefs of Iqbal and his contemporary, Ghanian novelist and political thinker J. E. Casely-Hayford. According to Hussain the phase of Afro-Asian thought represented by Iqbal and Casely-Hayford "contains a philosophy which established the self-respect of the Afro-Asian world through faith and reason. It gave a justification for the freedom movements, a justification which is indigenous and original."

Maitre, Luce-Claude. *Introduction to the Thought of Iqbal*, translated by Mulla Abdul Majeed Dar. Karachi: Iqbal Academy, 1961, 53 p.
Studies Iqbal's life, works, and ideas, comparing his philosophy with those of prominent Eastern and Western philosophers.

Maruf, Mohammed. "Allama Iqbal on 'Immortality'." *Religious Studies* 18, No. 3 (September 1982): 373-78.
Maintains that Iqbal's views "present an all-life picture of incessant and continuous struggle—one which is to continue even after death—for the attainment of the highest level of unity and integration of personality."

———. "Iqbal's Concept of God: An Appraisal." *Religious Studies* 19, No. 3 (September 1983): 375-83.
Concludes that "Iqbal's premises warrant a notion of God who is rational and intelligent, possessing knowledge of the particular events beforehand; in whom the Power is limited by wisdom. Iqbal has made a great attempt at explaining God philosophically which failed precisely for the reason for which his contemporaries and predecessors failed—i.e. for approaching the concept first by picking it to pieces and then trying to synthesize it."

Naim, C. M., ed. *Iqbal, Jinnah, and Pakistan: The Vision and the Reality*. Syracuse, N.Y.: Syracuse University, 1979, 216 p.
Reprints papers delivered in April 1977 at a conference sponsored by the Committee on Southern Asian Studies, University of Chicago and occasioned by the centenaries of Muhammad Iqbal and Pakistani statesman Muhammad Ali Jinnah (1876-1948).

Qureshi, I. H. "The Muslim Search for Freedom." In his *Sources of Indian Tradition*, pp. 749-68. New York: Columbia University Press, 1958.
Appreciative introductory sketch followed by excerpts from Iqbal's prose and poetic works. According to Qureshi: "Next to the Qur'an, there is no single influence upon the consciousness of the Pakistani intelligentsia so powerful as Iqbal's poetry. In his own time it kindled the enthusiasm of Muslim intellectuals for the values of Islam, and rallied the whole Muslim community once again to the banner of their faith."

Smith, Wilfred Cantwell. *Modern Islam in India: A Social Analysis*. Lahore: Muhammad Ashraf, 1963, 396 p.
Examines the "progressive" and "reactionary" sides of Iqbal's philosophy in a study of Muslim intellectual and political movements in India.

Symonds, Richard. "The Muslim Renaissance." In his *The Making of Pakistan*, pp. 28-37. London: Faber and Faber, 1950.
Discusses Iqbal's political ideals, including his vision of a separate Indian-Muslim state, for which he is often considered the "father of Pakistan." According to Symonds: "He was a Muslim first and last, who was concerned with the transformation of Islamic society, irrespective of national boundaries, rather than with creating a nation."

Talib, Gurbachan Singh. "Iqbal's Poetic Achievement: An Estimate." *The Indian P.E.N.* 41, No. 2 (February 1975): 6-9.
Concludes that while Iqbal's message is now dated "his moral inspiration is indeed still alive in the minds of all those who understand Urdu—non-Muslims no less than Muslims. His poetic mode has reigned in Urdu for half a century, and is still a very potent force. His Persian poetry, which is over two-thirds of the whole . . . is a fine *tour de force*, but of value mainly to the specialist."

"Islam and the Modern World." *Times Literary Supplement*, No. 1676 (15 March 1934): 178.
Review of *The Reconstruction of Religious Thought in Islam*. According to the critic: "The book is the product of an exalted, poetical and subtle mind, and few leaders will lay it down without a sharpened understanding of the reality of religious experience and a freshened sense of life's spirituality."

Whittemore, Robert. "Iqbal's Pantheism." *The Review of Metaphysics* IX, No. 4 (June 1956): 681-99.
Presents a detailed examination of Iqbal's philosophy.

Ya'acob, Tunku. "Homage to Iqbal." *Asian Review* LVII, n.s. No. 210 (April 1961): 199-200.
Tribute to Iqbal delivered by the High Commissioner for the Federation of Malaya in the U.K. on Iqbal Day, May 1961, in London.

# Horace (Stanley) McCoy

## 1897-1955

American novelist, screenwriter, short story writer, and journalist.

McCoy is remembered primarily as the author of the novel *They Shoot Horses, Don't They?*, an unrelentingly grim portrayal of the destructive and corrupting influence of Hollywood in the 1930s. Like many other American novelists, McCoy used this setting to expose the false promise of effortless fame held out by the motion picture industry, and *They Shoot Horses* is often compared to Nathanael West's *The Day of the Locust* (1939) for its indictment of Hollywood. Somewhat ironically, *They Shoot Horses* is best known as a movie, filmed fourteen years after McCoy's death. McCoy was also the author of hard-boiled gangster and adventure thrillers, and is highly regarded by aficionados of this genre for his creation, in the novel *Kiss Tomorrow Good-Bye*, of a wealthy and cultured protagonist who consciously chooses a life of crime because he enjoys the sensations it offers him.

McCoy was born in Pegram, Tennessee, and grew up in Nashville, where he began high school but dropped out at sixteen to work at a variety of jobs. When he was in his late teens his family moved to Dallas; there he joined the Texas National Guard and received aviation training. During World War I, McCoy served in France as a member of the American Air Service and was decorated for bravery. After the war he returned to Dallas and began working as a journalist, starting as a sports and crime reporter with the *Dallas Dispatch* and becoming sports editor of the *Dallas Journal* in 1920, a position he held for more than nine years. During this time he married and became active in Dallas Little Theatre stage productions. Because McCoy's salary as an editor was insufficient to support his family as well as his penchant for expensive clothing and cars, he began to supplement his income in 1927 with short story sales to pulp magazines, the most famous of which was Joseph T. Shaw's *Black Mask*. Shaw had assumed editorship of the magazine in 1926 and was soliciting "hard-boiled" adventure and detective stories from contributors, who in the 1920s and 1930s included James M. Cain, Raymond Chandler, Erle Stanley Gardner, and Dashiell Hammett. Between 1927 and 1934, McCoy's work appeared regularly in *Black Mask*, and Shaw's careful editing was instrumental in shaping McCoy's writing style.

By late 1929 McCoy's marriage and his job at the *Journal* had ended. After a brief period of editing the *Dallasite*, a short-lived literary magazine modeled on the *New Yorker*, McCoy lived entirely on his earnings from short story sales to *Black Mask*, as well as to *Battle Aces, Action Stories, Detective-Dragnet Magazine, Man Stories, Western Trails*, and *Detective Action Stories*. A brief second marriage to a wealthy debutante was quickly annulled by her parents. In 1931 McCoy left Dallas for Hollywood, seeking work as an actor and hoping to find a market for a screenplay he had written about a marathon dance contest. For about a year he lived as a vagrant, taking odd jobs and besieging the motion picture studios for work. He eventually was cast in some minor movie roles, but, disillusioned with the prospect of an acting career, signed as a contract writer with RKO. Unable to interest any studio in his original screen-

*Photograph by Patricia O'Meara Robbins*

play, he adapted it as a short story and then as a novel, which was published in 1935 as *They Shoot Horses, Don't They?*

Although the novel was favorably received and sold well, *They Shoot Horses* did not make McCoy financially independent, and he continued to work as a screenwriter of what he termed "hack" or "B" movies for several studios: *Queen of the Mob* and *Parole Fixer* were two of his screenplays. During 1936 he completed a second novel, for which he was unable to find an American publisher, and it appeared in England as *No Pockets in a Shroud*. A third novel, *I Should Have Stayed Home*, was published in the United States but attracted little notice. By the end of 1946, McCoy, who had married for a third time and had two children, was in financial difficulty and was struggling with the manuscript of a fourth novel, with which he intended to establish himself as a serious literary artist. At about this time McCoy learned that his novels were highly regarded in France, where the adventure, detective, and gangster fiction of such American authors as McCoy, Cain, Chandler, and Hammett had a large following. According to William F. Stanley: "This sudden wave of critical acclaim from overseas gave McCoy the ego boost he desperately needed," and he completed *Kiss Tomorrow Good-Bye* in 1948. He began commuting between Los Angeles and New York, planning, he told an interviewer, to leave California for good, give up screenwriting, and ''by living modestly and working hard . . . become a literary figure of major importance.'' Although *Kiss Tomorrow Good-Bye* was not enthusiastically reviewed, a film studio purchased the rights, and the James Cagney film of the same name, released in 1950, further boosted McCoy's currency within the Hollywood community he wanted to leave behind him. He sold an original story idea about a brilliant surgeon to a film producer in 1951, and in 1952 used the same material for the novel *Scalpel*, a slick best-seller that brought him the greatest financial return of any of his works. McCoy, however, spent money as quickly as he earned it, and he was deeply in debt and working on a new novel when he died of a heart attack in 1955.

*They Shoot Horses, Don't They?* is McCoy's most critically discussed work. It is the story of two young people, Robert Syverton and Gloria Beatty, who dream of finding success in Hollywood, Robert as a director, Gloria as an actress. Together they enter a dance marathon, attracted by the promise of free board for the duration of the contest, the possibility of winning the prize money, and the remoter chance that publicity generated by the dance will aid their careers. When a murder in the audience leads to the cancellation of the marathon after thirty-seven gruelling days, the defeated and cynical Gloria asks Robert to ''pinch hit for God'' and kill her, which he does. The novel was well received and continues to be highly regarded. Early reviewers were impressed by McCoy's powerful, concise narrative—''as stripped-for-action as a racing car,'' in William Rose Benét's phrase—and by the detached, dispassionate tone of the writing. McCoy employed an unusual framing device to structure the novel: each chapter is headed with a phrase spoken by the judge who is sentencing Robert for Gloria's murder. Thus the narrative present of the novel is some time after the marathon; Robert's thoughts are rendered in italics, and the main events of the novel—the meeting of Gloria and Robert, their decision to enter the marathon, and the events of the dance—are told in flashbacks. ''The technique of this form of narrative could not be bettered,'' wrote T. D. Wilson in an early review, and subsequent commentators have agreed that McCoy hit upon an interesting and effective narrative device.

In *They Shoot Horses, Don't They?* the brutal routine of the marathon dance is vividly portrayed, as is the cruelly exploitive conduct of the contest manager and the sordid behavior of many of the contestants and the members of the ghoulish mob who come to watch. The character of Gloria is cited by many commentators as especially well drawn. McCoy ''never moralizes; he simply records'' the events, according to one reviewer. As David Fine has noted, the lives of Robert and Gloria fall into a bleak ''pattern of hope giving way to frustration and violence'' that is characteristic of McCoy's novels and of much 1930s California fiction. McCoy's second novel, *No Pockets in a Shroud*, has been referred to as an idealized autobiography. The protagonist, Mike Dolan, is a hard-drinking, crusading newsman, superlative amateur actor, and superhuman lover of numerous women. While *No Pockets in a Shroud* was McCoy's most popular work abroad, it is generally regarded by American commentators as hopelessly melodramatic, weakly plotted, and badly written. The pattern of violently terminated prospects that critics found in *They Shoot Horses* is prominent as well in McCoy's next novel, *I Should Have Stayed Home*, which is also set in Hollywood. This work, while lacking the objectivity of *They Shoot Horses*, clearly condemns the decadence of the film community and explicitly blames the dreams fueled by Hollywood for the destruction of several young lives. Con-

trasting *I Should Have Stayed Home* with *They Shoot Horses*, Fine called McCoy's third novel ''a blunter indictment of the meretriciousness of the dream, a weaker, more discursive, and more confused work, both a satire on the dream factory and a farce riddled with movie colony stereotypes.''

According to Thomas Sturak, McCoy intended his forth novel, *Kiss Tomorrow Good-Bye*, to be ''the acid test of his creative genius and artistic talents—to prove . . . both to himself and to the world that his first novel had not been a fluke and that his revival abroad was not merely a Frenchman's fancy.'' Tom Newhouse has noted that McCoy used this novel to extend the possibilities of traditional gangster fiction. To the almost gratuitous violence that was becoming common to the genre in the 1940s, for example, McCoy added ''the psychological aspect of his protagonist,'' a well-educated, upper-class criminal mastermind. Nevertheless, Wilson Follett, in an early review of *Kiss Tomorrow Good-Bye*, dismissed the novel's psychological element as extraneous, while other reviewers rejected the book as ''a gutter-minded, gutter-tongued shocker,'' ''the literature of men's-room walls,'' a novel that ''fails to carry any conviction of artistic integrity or value as a work of literature.'' McCoy's last novel, *Scalpel*, featured his typically troubled, introspective protagonist, and, atypically, a leisurely, stylized narrative. Reviewers of the novel were puzzled by the change in McCoy's formerly terse writing style and the absence of hard-boiled pessimism; Sturak has maintained that *Scalpel* is merely *Kiss Tomorrow Good-Bye* ''turned upside-down,'' with personal success and professional triumph replacing the utter destruction that befell the earlier novel's protagonist.

Since his death, McCoy's novels have been discussed as either typical examples of, or innovative departures from, established genres. For example, *Kiss Tomorrow Good-Bye* has been analyzed as a variation on gangster fiction traditions, and *No Pockets in a Shroud* as a tribute to the fearless muckraking journalists who were instrumental in uncovering and eliminating corruption from local and state governments. Nevertheless, *They Shoot Horses, Don't They?* remains McCoy's best known and most highly regarded work, both for its bitter indictment of Hollywood and for the artistic portrayal of its characters' desperate lives.

(See also *Dictionary of Literary Biography*, Vol. 9: *American Novelists, 1910-1945*.)

## PRINCIPAL WORKS

*They Shoot Horses, Don't They?* (novel) 1935
*Parole Fixer* [with Kubec Glasmon] (screenplay) 1936
*No Pockets in a Shroud* (novel) 1937; revised edition, 1948
*I Should Have Stayed Home* (novel) 1938
*Parole Fixer* [with William J. Lipman] (screenplay) 1939
*Queen of the Mob* [with William J. Lipman] (screenplay) 1940
*Gentleman Jim* [with Vincent Lawrence] (screenplay) 1942
*Kiss Tomorrow Good-Bye* (novel) 1949
*Scalpel* (novel) 1952
*The Turning Point* (screenplay) 1953
*Corruption City* (novel) 1959

**FRED T. MARSH** (essay date 1935)

[*In the following excerpt from an early review of* They Shoot Horses, Don't They?, *Marsh compares McCoy's novel with Nathanael West's* Miss Lonelyhearts *(1933), finding it less successfully executed.*]

You will recall the era of the marathon dances. Such phenomena come and go. Only the six-day bicycle races go on forever. Well [*They Shoot Horses, Don't They?*] is a mere slip of a story of the hard-boiled-newspaper-man-with-a-sob-in-his-throat school of fiction about a couple in a marathon dance, an institution which, apparently, is still a part of the Hollywood cultural sphere of influence. And Hollywood is only the absurd side of American life and manners in microcosm, with lighting effects and a bit of nicely timed and nicely placed distortion. . . .

McCoy turns his marathon dance into a dance macabre, a dance of death. It is a brilliant idea and one that might have been made into a powerful and illuminating novel of certain aspects of American life passing through the so-called depression. But the author and his publishers, between them apparently, have reduced it to a not overlong long short story which you'll read through in an hour and forget nearly as soon. It is entertaining all right enough. McCoy knows the racket; there is no question about that; and you'll learn in this tale how such things are run. His boy and his girl are typical products, too. But why the boy shoots the girl (this is not giving away the plot, for the story starts out as sentence is being passed on the boy for murder) is pretty feebly built up. In short, the story gets no grip on you as tragedy. It is interesting because you get the low-down, the dope on the marathon dance racket. It fails where that extraordinary little novel of a year or so ago, *Miss Lonelyhearts,* succeeded. The two tales are superficially comparable, but *Miss Lonelyhearts* is a bit of creative writing that transcends its material.

In your own imagination you can help the author out. Here are these two youngsters hanging on to the fringes of the Hollywood "movie" world. The boy is still fresh and eager. The girl has been through the mill and her bitter disillusionment, her will to die, her hatred of life and new birth provides the theme of the story. The cataleptic state of the dance marathon goes on and on, broken by intervals of excitement when exacerbated nerves give way, when detectives pick up a man wanted for murder from among the contestants, when the woman's purity league interferes, when a pregnant girl collapses. You see what the author has meant to do, what he is driving at, the significance of his tale. He has fallen short of making us feel with his people, appearing callous through fear of letting himself be caught in some uncompromising philosophical approach.

*Fred T. Marsh, "Marathon Dance Racket," in* New York Herald Tribune Books, *Vol. 11, No. 47, July 28, 1935, p. 8.*

**EDITH H. WALTON** (essay date 1935)

[*In the following review of* They Shoot Horses, Don't They?, *Walton comments on McCoy's terse, unsubtle narrative which renders the novel vivid and effective.*]

Even from perfunctory newspaper accounts one can form an opinion of the typical dance marathon. It is, undeniably, a sordid and brutalizing affair, ruthlessly commercial and catering to the more degraded instincts. To recognize this from a distance is, however, a different thing from having it brought uncomfortably close, and no dim, scattered knowledge of marathon contests will protect one from the shock of Mr. McCoy's story. *They Shoot Horses, Don't They?* is as bitter and disquieting a book as any that the hard-boiled school has produced. In pace and violence it may be inferior to the Cain-Hammett opuses, but its implications are far more deadly.

By a device which is tricky but effective the boy whose story this is recapitulates the past during the delivery of his death sentence. He has killed the girl who was lately his partner throughout a Hollywood marathon, and he has been able to make no one believe that the shot was fired out of kindness and by her own request. Gloria, who had drifted so casually across his path, was one of life's hopeless derelicts. His association with her had been fatal to the boy, so infecting him with her own poison of defeatism that to kill her, he had come to agree, was "the only way to get her out of her misery."

Both the boy and the girl, when they accidentally met, had been hanging round the fringes of the Hollywood studios. It was not Gloria's charm which persuaded Robert to enter the marathon with her, but the lure of "free food and free bed as long as you last and a thousand dollars if you win." Their partnership was born of mutual despair and completely impersonal. Though the boy felt kindly toward her, it was a matter of indifference to him when she indulged her sensuality during the ten-minute rest periods. His chief concern, and hers, was that she should keep sufficiently fresh to remain on her feet.

The marathon dance was held on an amusement pier stretching out over the ocean. Night and day the radio or the orchestra pounded monotonously on, interrupted only by the rest periods in which the dancers were groomed like animals for further endurance. Night and day the surviving couples swayed and reeled across the floor, making obedient spurts now and then for the benefit of visiting movie stars. As the weeks lengthened conditions were stiffened. The cruel, taxing institution of the derby was introduced, by which the nightly elimination of one couple was assured, Greedy for publicity and profits, the management also arranged for a marriage on the dance floor and canvassed the contestants peremptorily for a couple that would consent to the mockery.

In this atmosphere—with the promoters acclaiming "these marvelous kids" and a perverted audience staring at them greedily—Robert and Gloria drag through the weeks in a fevered haze of weariness. They come to know the various contestants—the girl who is going to have a baby, the Italian who is nabbed by the detectives for murder, the couple who have been winners in other contests. More importantly, they come to know each other. Robert, a fairly decent boy, is slowly infected by Gloria's viciousness and despair.

It is open to doubt whether Mr. McCoy was wise in choosing so melodramatic a structure for his story, and in spacing his chapters artificially between the phrases of the death sentence. The effect, though theatrical, is, however, arresting, and there can scarcely be two opinions about his powerful picture of the marathon. Despite a clipped, bare, nervous prose, Mr. McCoy gives one all the needful details and achieves an impression of burning reality. When he is writing, for instance, of the derby, one can almost feel the clogging weariness in one's own feet and experience, personally, the terrible anxiety of the contestants.

*They Shoot Horses, Don't They?* is inevitably a stylized book. More akin to a long short story than to a novel, everything in it is directed toward a single effect and all the non-essentials have been stripped away. One cannot expect richness of incident nor complexity of motive from a book such as this. It is sufficient that one should carry away an unforgettable, flashing glimpse of human degradation and a sense that the boy's killing of his partner is nothing like so improbable as it may at first seem. In choosing the fashionable hard-boiled technique Mr. McCoy has probably chosen the best possible method to tell this particular story. Certain subtleties he has sacrificed, but his book makes a hard, clean, driving impact.

> *Edith H. Walton, " 'They Shoot Horses, Don't They?' and Other Recent Works of Fiction," in* The New York Times Book Review, *July 28, 1935, p. 6.*

**WILLIAM PLOMER**   (essay date 1935)

[*In the following excerpt, an English reviewer of* They Shoot Horses *commends McCoy's narrative concision.*]

[We] may accept Mr. Horace McCoy as a guide to modern barbarism in one of its acutest forms. He invites us to attend a dancing marathon on the amusement pier at Santa Monica. The date is 1935, and we are chiefly concerned with a couple named Robert Syverten and Gloria Beatty. We gather at the very beginning that Robert is being sentenced to death for the murder of Gloria, and this is enough to hold our attention while he reviews the preliminary circumstances. Add to this that Mr. McCoy has the rare merit of brevity and is a follower of the Then-He-Hit-Me-Again school of fiction, and it will be guessed that even the most exhausted novel-addict need make little mental effort to follow him. Actually everybody is so tough in [*They Shoot Horses, Don't They?*] that it might almost be taken as a parody, except that much of it has the stamp of horrid truth. Poor Gloria feels that she has nothing to live for, and one would not venture to contradict her:

> "It's peculiar to me," she said, "that everybody pays so much attention to living and so little to dying. Why are these high-powered scientists always screwing around trying to prolong life instead of finding pleasant ways to end it? There must be a hell of a lot of people in the world like me—who want to die but haven't got the guts————."

She suddenly presents Robert with a pistol and asks him to put her out of her misery, and he, remembering that animals—horses, for instance—are often shot when in pain, is kind and rash enough to oblige her. Mr. McCoy was determined to be short and snappy and has made his marathon rather too eventful though suitably degraded. His exercise in a method of getting the maximum effect in the shortest space should be taken as a shining example by some of our own novelists who would take five times the space to give us a tenth of the matter. His book is, of course, a sad one. People used to say that Russian novels were gloomy, but they were riots of fun compared to some of these modern American examples, with their deathly wisecracks popping like revolver-shots.

> *William Plomer, in a review of "They Shoot Horses, Don't They?," in* The Spectator, *Vol. 155, No. 5588, August 2, 1935, p. 200.*

**TIME**   (essay date 1948)

[*The following is a negative review of* Kiss Tomorrow Good-Bye.]

If one of the dead-end kids were to write a novel, with the aid of an unabridged dictionary, the result might be something like *Kiss Tomorrow Good-Bye.* It is one of the nastiest novels ever published in this country.

Literary Caveman Horace McCoy has driven to an absurd extreme the hard-boiled, feel-my-muscles style of James Cain and Dashiell Hammett, and, to add cultural tone, has dipped into the bowely bathos of the wasn't-Bix-wonderful, oh-blow-that-beautiful-horn school. The result is a gutter-minded, gutter-tongued shocker of alley-cat sex, sadism and unmourned murders—relieved only by odes to Satchmo's and Muggsy's horn blowing.

Author McCoy, a Hollywood hand, keeps firing words out of the side of his mouth as if they were bullets, though often enough when they land they seem more like spitballs. Occasionally, to show he knows his way around a dictionary (or beyond it), he tosses in a word like "propliopithecustian." But most of the time he sticks to the literary method which assumes that the height of human expression can be reached in a monosyllabic grunt.

Among some Parisian café thinkers, who seem to believe that Chicago is run by Al Capone and that New Yorkers live in nightclubs, McCoy has been honored as the peer of Hemingway and Faulkner. The trash he writes is closer to the literature of men's-room walls.

> *"Tough Guy," in* Time, *New York, Vol. LI, No. 19, May 10, 1948, p. 116.*

**W. R. BURNETT**   (essay date 1952)

[*Burnett was the author of* Little Caesar *(1929), a novel about Chicago gangsters that was made into a popular movie. In the following review of* Scalpel, *Burnett finds fault with McCoy's deviation from his former terse writing style.*]

Mr. McCoy's new novel is a far cry from that excellent, terse, and well-known stunner of the Thirties, *They Shoot Horses, Don't They?*—and I am not at all certain that I feel at ease with the new Mr. McCoy and his leisurely, mannered course.

*Scalpel,* basically, is the story of a man in search of his soul. That he happens to be a high society doctor who has made a painful upward climb from the poverty and dirt of a small Pennsylvania coal town, is merely incidental to the main theme; as is the somewhat over-elaborate and rather too neatly worked-out plot.

The protagonist, Dr. Tom Owen, is the book. The other characters are hardly more than convenient shadows. Mr. McCoy has put all of his eggs into one basket—and that can be a very dangerous procedure for a novelist.

I can't quite make up my mind whether this is an old-fashioned novel or a new-fashioned one. Current novels deal largely with dupes and victims. Mr. McCoy's protagonist is a long way from being either; he is, in fact, a rugged individualist, and as many-sided as a Man of the Renaissance—a sort of Pittsburgh DaVinci.

Let me tell you about him. He is big, strong, handsome, virile. He is a graduate of the University of Pennsylvania, a fraternity man, and a great athlete—he personally defeated Cornell once with a well-placed place-kick. Not only that, he is an amateur poet, well versed in literature, and can quote obscure passages from some of Baudelaire's lesser known works. He is an expert on expensive automobiles, from Cadillacs to Hispano-Suizas. He can quote Skira on Utrillo—and it appears that he was once a personal friend of Picasso's. He was awarded the DSC for extraordinary bravery in World War II, and presented with a pair of pearl-handled pistols by General Patton—a pal. He is a gourmet; he is knowledgeable about women's clothes, well aware of the difference between a Mainbocher and a Dior; and he is a connoisseur not only of women but of wine—and he drinks Heidsick '38 and Moet et Chandon in his more expansive moments. On top of all this, he is a great surgeon, a genius with a scalpel, and is ultimately invited, in fact, implored, by the august Dean of Medicine, to become a full professor at Harvard.

When I inform you that this rather amazing protagonist tells the story in the first person I think you will see that here we have something very unusual indeed. In novels told in the first person, the narrators are almost without exception vague, colorless figures, modest, retiring. But our narrator, Dr. Tom Owen, makes Sir Willoughby Patterne seem like a very humble and self-effacing fellow. And yet this magnificent Renaissance figure suffers badly, if intermittently, from self-doubt; he has qualms; he even considers himself to be a dubious character at times, a hustler, a name-dropper (though you'd think, from the data given, that people would be dropping *his* name)—in short, he is frightened that he is a "phony" . . . and from this weird disparity arises the real, it might even be said, the hidden drama of this strange and at times vivid and compelling book.

Of most current novels it can be said that there is less in them than meets the eye; with Mr. McCoy's novel it is definitely the reverse; and what is below the surface is the most important; but the difficulty seems to be that Mr. McCoy can never quite succeed in making us understand precisely what it is.

> W. R. Burnett, *"Under the Knife,"* in The Saturday Review, *New York, Vol. XXXV, No. 25, June 21, 1952, p. 23.*

**THOMAS STURAK** (essay date 1968)

[*Sturak is an American educator and critic. In the following excerpt, he discusses McCoy's novels, focusing on the existential nature of the conflict portrayed in* They Shoot Horses, Don't They?]

Horace McCoy—considered simply as a hard-boiled or tough guy novelist—would have to stand at the head of his class. If, like all writers, the so-called "poets of the tabloid murder" ultimately failed, then McCoy made the best failure because he tried hardest to say the most. But it should be evident that his five novels do not submit to such limited categorization, either by subject matter or approach.

In terms of his career as a novelist, McCoy's own experiences in the down-and-out world of the Hollywood extra during the early thirties were crucial and determinative. Besides providing him with raw materials for two books, the initial shock of failure and the struggle for success set the emotional bent of his creative imagination in all of his subsequent serious fiction. . . . From his beginnings as a writer (even in his pulp stories), McCoy showed signs of an inward-turning artistic sensibility whose thematic preoccupations and stylistic aims reflected the major impulse of twentieth-century literature. The real subjects of his fiction are the existential conflicts arising out of an acute self-awareness and the inevitable consequences of self-division. Like that of many another modern novelist,

McCoy's work comprises an emotional autobiography; his fictional world becomes a symbol of his creative imagination.

Following the publication of his first novel, *They Shoot Horses, Don't They?* . . . , McCoy landed his first major film-writing assignments. In his twenty-year career as a Hollywood writer, he contributed to approximately one hundred filmed screenplays. His second novel, *No Pockets in a Shroud,* was written in fits and starts between 1935 and 1936, and "touched up" in the same manner over another year in an unsuccessful quest for an American publisher. Accepted by Arthur Barker of London, it was further revised and emasculated to meet the demands of England's "invisible censorship." Barker was optimistic about the book's prospects "of making a real hit" in England—"assuming," he wrote to McCoy, "we don't go to gaol on it and in spite of having had to cut a certain amount out." How extensive was this cutting we can't know; but it may have further weakened a plot already notorious for its lack of depth and failure to correlate adequately external acts and motives. In the years prior to World War II, this fast-paced but unevenly inspired story of a crusading journalist's fatal battle against crime, corruption, and a Klan-like organization of native fascists became McCoy's most translated and best known work abroad. (pp. 137-38)

In its anti-Fascism, anti-Hearst passages, *No Pockets in a Shroud* bears a seeming resemblance to certain "proletarian novels" of the thirties. For McCoy, as for the majority of American artists and intellectuals, the Communist movement of the 1930's was an inescapable influence. But this is not a "leftist" novel, because its hero, Michael Dolan, is neither sinister nor subversive politically. He is simply a very angry young man. Created during an era of social consciousness, he is nonetheless drawn in the image of the disillusioned individualist of the twenties, and ultimately postures like "the young reformer" of pre-World War I muckraking novels. . . . Though the book's nominal heroine, Myra Barnovsky, is a Communist, she functions as little more than a vaguely symbolic Doppelgänger; her fatal influence upon Dolan seems more occult than ideological. That so much space is given to his affairs with two wealthy debutantes suggests that the individual acts of rebellion arising from what he calls his "social phobia" are as operative in his destiny as any crusading idealism or love for downtrodden humanity.

Privately, McCoy called *No Pockets in a Shroud* the closest thing to an autobiography that he ever wrote. (It is his only novel written in the third-person.) To an extent, it is a *roman á clef* based upon his own activities as an editor in Dallas during the late twenties. Published when he had already turned forty, it reads very much like an immature and early book by a talented writer. . . . (pp. 138-39)

McCoy's next novel, *I Should Have Stayed Home,* was also hurriedly written and expediently revised under pressure from its editors. Closely patterned after *They Shoot Horses, Don't They?* (e.g., in the submitted manuscript, the hero committed suicide), this brutally realistic story concerns the hapless lot of two young movie extras, Mona Matthews and Ralph Carston. The latter's monolithic simple-mindedness—he is surely one of the most "soft-boiled" heroes in American fiction—undercuts the book's effectiveness as propaganda about what he calls "the most terrifying town in the world." If McCoy were pointing the moral, "keep away from Hollywood," he was not only warning gulls like his incredibly naive hero, but also empathizing with "sellouts" like the minor (but most vibrant) character, Johnny Hill, an idealistic writer turned cynic, who evidently served as his *persona*. As the *Saturday Review* recognized, "Horace McCoy hates Hollywood, not enough to stay away from it but enough to get all the bile out of his system in a short, bitter, name-calling novel" [see Rothman entry in Additional Bibliography].

McCoy himself struck no tragic figure as a Hollywood writer; his public image was hardly that of an *artiste manqué*. Privately, however, he felt himself intrinsically a failure. But during the years following the publication of *I Should Have Stayed Home*, when he was submerged in (as he put it in a letter to Victor Weybright) "the bottomless muck" of Hollywood, his work in translation won a following abroad. During World War II, his first two novels enjoyed an underground—literally—fame on the continent, particularly in France. In 1946, the open publication by Gallimard of *On achève bien les chevaux (They Shoot Horses, Don't They?)* sent his reputation skyrocketing, especially among the existentialists (inevitably he was called "the first American existentialist"). The following year a new translation of *No Pockets in a Shroud (Un linceul n'a pas de poches)* was issued as the fourth volume—and the first by an American—in the extremely popular *Série Noire*. Word began to drift back to the United States that in Paris "everyone in the knowledgeable world talks about American writers, about a curious trinity: Hemingway, Faulkner, and McCoy" [see Talmey entry in Additional Bibliography]. Another report described McCoy as "the most discussed American writer in France." (pp. 139-40)

McCoy made his fourth novel, *Kiss Tomorrow Goodbye*, the acid test of his creative genius and artistic talents—to prove, as it were, both to himself and to the world that his first novel had not been a fluke and that his revival abroad was not merely a Frenchman's fancy. As its publishers advertised, this book is "a kind of success story"—at its simplest, an example of the popular drama of the rise and fall of a gangster. But it is also, to use a phrase of Malcolm Cowley's, "an inquisition into the unknown depths" of McCoy's own mind; subliminally, it is his most damning novel about himself in Hollywood.

In 1947 McCoy told his literary agent, Harold Matson, that he had been thinking about *Kiss Tomorrow Goodbye* "for a long, long time." The shadowy prototype for its Phi Beta Kappa killer briefly appears in his last *Black Mask* story, published in 1934. Five years later, when he was working on a series of "supporting features" (i.e., B movies) based on FBI cases against notorious criminals of the thirties, he seems to have begun his "psychological story of a pathological killer." In its final form, *Kiss Tomorrow Goodbye* became McCoy's most intriguing and ambitious novel. In its thematic preoccupations with states of awareness, failure and success, death and rebirth, and the quest for self-identity, it reflected a period of crisis in his own life which was dominated by a mood of disintegration and complicated by a promising turn of fortune so sudden and unexpected that it was, he wrote to Matson, "something like a miracle, to be revived after all these years with such a fanfare." Time and again in his personal letters, he spoke of his new book's importance to him "as a symbol" of his regeneration as a writer. In itself this novel stands as both the climax of his career and a paradigm of his creative imagination.

*Kiss Tomorrow Goodbye*'s unique first-person protagonist, who goes under the dual alias of Ralph Cotter and Paul Murphy, has been understandably called "one of the most brutal of the hard boiled characters in American fiction." At the same time, he narrates his violent story with a peculiar brand of lyricism that in the book's climactic stream-of-consciousness passage

and poetic and haunting final paragraphs exceeds, strictly speaking, the limits of objectivity. Before *Kiss Tomorrow Goodbye* went to press, McCoy appealed to Random House, as he had with each of his previous publishers, that they take a strong stand to disassociate his work from "the 'James Cain' school." In reassuring McCoy, Editor Allan Ullman remarked in 1948, "you have given me the best kind of clue when you talk about the 'lyricism' of your own brand of brutality." Unfortunately, McCoy's letter to Ullman is lost; but we know that this peculiar stylistic concept had engaged his creative imagination since at least the time of *They Shoot Horses, Don't They?* In 1937, he wrote "there were decadence and evil in the old walkathons—and violence. The evil, of course, as evil always has and always will, fascinated the customer and the violence possessed a peculiar lyricism that elevated the thing into the realm of high art" (quoted in an unidentified Dallas newspaper clipping). Shortly after the publication of his first novel, he explained his "literary aims," in an informal lecture, "dwelling on the lyrical quality that lies in any dramatic action and the transfer of that lyrical quality to the pages of a book by means of graphic and telling words" ("Writer Is Heard / In Informal / Address / Horace McCoy Talks / to Shakespeare / Club Juniors," *Pasadena Star-News*).

In 1945 Raymond Chandler had written that "the possibilities of objective writing are very great and they have scarcely been explored." Three years later, only a few readers of *Kiss Tomorrow Goodbye* sensed that in attempting a lyrical, first-person, psychoanalytical novel about a "master-mind" criminal, McCoy had tried those possibilities to the limits. In 1949, however, Philip Durham asserted that in *Kiss Tomorrow Goodbye* McCoy had carried "the objective technique" (America's "most original contribution to the art of fiction") "to its furthest development." In doing so, he had enhanced the coherence and complexity of both a traditional American fictional manner and a modern American popular drama.

McCoy had hoped that *Kiss Tomorrow Goodbye* would buy his escape from what he called "this whoring" in Hollywood. But in the end, his one-way ticket proved to be a "brass check." In 1949, a paperback abridgment (made with his permission by an editor) sold well; and the story was soon bought by the movies. Try as he would, he had never before been able to interest film makers in any of his novels. Of *Kiss Tomorrow Goodbye*, he had written to his agent: "I do not think there is a picture in the book." With this ironic success, McCoy, financially strapped (as always) and in poor health, once again resigned himself to his destiny as "a Hollywood hack." In his last novel, *Scalpel*, he reversed his course as a creative writer in more ways than might be evident from a reading of this "popular" story of an incredibly successful surgeon who on the final page thinks to himself, "God was in His Heaven and all was right with the script writer." We can read *that* as a sardonic authorial commentary on the only novel McCoy ever "made" from one of his screen stories. Early in 1951, he had sold an original "treatment" of a "medical yarn" to Hal Wallis Productions for something between fifty and one hundred thousand dollars. This "book" was bought by Appleton-Century-Crofts, who commissioned McCoy to turn it into a novel. (The posthumously published *Corruption City* is an unaltered screen treatment which McCoy wrote for Columbia Pictures in 1950. Originally titled *This Is Dynamite*, it was screened as *The Turning Point*. (pp. 140-43)

McCoy's longest book and only "best-seller" in hard covers, *Scalpel* epitomizes Albert Van Nostrand's phrase, "the denatured novel.'' Despite the uncharacteristic leisurely manner and over elaborate and too neatly worked out plot, it nonetheless displays all of the familiar signs of the characteristic McCoy fable. In fact, a collection of selected passages—amounting to perhaps 1500 of its 150,000 words—would comprise a virtual compendium of his major themes, character types, and dramatic conflicts. For example, from time to time the narrative is interrupted for explicit glosses on ambition, success, self-doubt, self-division. Similarly, the conflict is merely—but repeatedly—asserted. In a word, everything has been stylized— and ''stylization exaggerates gestures and attitudes'' [Van Nostrand, *The Denatured Novel*]. In padding out his original screen story, McCoy imitated and borrowed from his previous work, most of all from *Kiss Tomorrow Goodbye*. We need only scratch the surface to discover, for example, that ''genius'' surgeon Doctor Thomas Owen and ''genius'' criminal Cotter-Murphy are blood brothers under the skin. In substance, *Scalpel* is *Kiss Tomorrow Goodbye* turned upside-down. Whereas the latter is a bitterly black parody of the Horatio Alger myth, the former is cynically rosy revival. (pp. 143-44)

Published during a grim period for the American book trade, *They Shoot Horses, Don't They?* was an unquestionable *succès d'estime*, but hardly a best seller. Despite some impressive reviews, it soon slipped into the limbo of neglected books, beyond the grace of established criticism. In 1940 Edmund Wilson, rising from ''a long submergence in the politics and literature of the nineteenth century,'' took a quick look into what ''people were reading.'' The results were some uneven and often inaccurate ''notes'' on ''the California writers''— the infamous ''boys in the back room''—in which a few general remarks were devoted to McCoy's two novels about ''the miserable situation of movie-struck young men and women who starve and degrade themselves in Hollywood'' [see Wilson entry in Additional Bibliography]. Wilson found *They Shoot Horses, Don't They?* ''worth reading for its description of one of those dance marathons that were among the more grisly symptoms of the early years of the Depression'' (''The Boys in the Back Room''). This faint praise—the sum and total of serious American criticism of the book—has been piously re-echoed down to the moment. (p. 145)

Wilson also laid the mark of James M. Cain and the onus of ''writer for the studios'' on McCoy's fiction. Both of these insinuations were undiscerning and unenlightening. *They Shoot Horses, Don't They?* was not one of those books ''which apparently derived'' from Cain's sensational first novel, *The Postman Always Rings Twice* (1934). By November of 1933 McCoy had completed a first draft, which was essentially an amplification of an unpublished short story of the same title that he had written no later than August 1932. McCoy himself always inveighed, justifiably, against the specious, ''almost obligatory'' comparison to Cain's *Postman*. In 1948 he wrote to his paperback publishers (who also reprinted Cain's books), ''I do not care for Cain's work, although there may be much he can teach me. I know this though—continued labeling of me as of 'the Cain school' (whatever the hell that is) and I shall slit either his throat or mine.''

If it can be said that McCoy ever belonged to any school of fiction, it would have to be as a wayward member of Joseph T. Shaw's boys in the *Black Mask* during the late twenties and early thirties (when Cain was still an essayist and closet dramatist for Mencken's *American Mercury*). Editor Shaw himself in 1932 named McCoy among ''the older writers who helped establish the *Black Mask* standard.'' But despite the implied

parity with the work of such so-called ''hard-boiled'' classicists as Carroll John Daly, Raoul Whitfield, and Dashiell Hammett, McCoy's contributions—when measured against Shaw's own avowed aims—are most interesting for their violations of the *Black Mask* ''formula'' that demanded character in constant action. Moreover, he often indulged in symbolistic and lyrical techniques that Shaw once told him were ''almost too fine writing.'' Unlike almost every other *Black Mask* regular who ''graduated'' to hard-cover publication, McCoy did so extra-curricularly. Writing under the patient and encouraging tutelage of Joe Shaw taught McCoy much about the craft of fiction, and sharpened his techniques of objective writing; but he never directly used or adapted any of his pulp materials in his subsequent short stories and novels. Significantly, he persuaded Simon and Schuster not to use either the word or the idea ''hard-boiled'' in the promotion and advertising copy for his first novel.

In writing *They Shoot Horses, Don't They?* (and also his third novel, *I Should Have Stayed Home*) McCoy drew upon his own early experiences and observations in Hollywood. He had come to California from Dallas—leaving behind him a ten-year career as a newspaperman and a national reputation as a little theatre actor—early in 1931, full of self-confidence and the highest ambitions. But until well into 1933, while striving to break into motion pictures as an actor and writer, he shared the hardships, disappointments, and anxieties common to the 20,000 extras reportedly out of work during these cruelest years of the Great Depression. The story that he actually worked as a bouncer in a marathon dance contest is apocryphal, though there is evidence that he may have *acted* the role in a film. He definitely witnessed such contests, which were regular attractions in dance halls on the ocean piers in nearby Venice and Santa Monica. According to his widow, he was always deeply disturbed by the bestiality of these spectacles. All of which is not enough, of course, to explain the evolution of his marathon-dance story into a novel of considerable artistry. As Sartre has said: ''The writer makes books out of words, not out of his sorrows.''

Marathon dancing, which had originated in the twenties as another zany fad, became in the thirties a vicious racket. Whether or not it was part of McCoy's conscious intention to write a ''sociological novel''—as some of his admirers still view *They Shoot Horses, Don't They?*—condemning by implication the social and economic system responsible for such brutalization of human beings, the work certainly rises above mere calculated sensationalism. McCoy's latent reformist tendencies— revealed in a brief fling as the editor of a crusading magazine in Dallas—were suited to the ''mood of social evangelism'' so strong ''among writers and critics and the intellectual elite generally'' during the thirties (Frederick Lewis Allen, *Since Yesterday*). But by any meaningful definition (i.e., ideological commitment), he was never a proletarian writer. The doctrinaire left-wing reviewers of the day ignored *They Shoot Horses, Don't They?* although one English critic thought that the book (''emphatically not just another example of that fake American, romantic tough writing'') implied ''a condemnation of American civilization severe enough to satisfy the standard of the Third International.'' From a perspective of thirty years, however, it is clear that the enduring radicalism of the novel resides in no political program or ethical system; its implied message is perhaps best summed up in Clifford Odets' plea, ''Life should have some dignity.''

In great part, the continuing interest in *They Shoot Horses, Don't They?* is a result of McCoy's lack of commitment to a priori literary or political theories. In writing the novel he consciously minimized topical allusions to the Depression, consistently cutting explicit references, for example, to "bread lines" and the plight of "people who work in factories," which had appeared in the original short story. Always, in this compact narrative, the descriptive details and motifs contribute to the creation of a dominant effect and the elucidation of the human drama.

Technically, *They Shoot Horses, Don't They?* is a brilliant tour de force—but not one without serious purpose and significant implications. In the unpublished original short story (c. 1931-32), the central narrative of the marathon dance was set within the frame of a courtroom trial at the climactic moment of sentencing. In drafting the novel McCoy retained this structure, but carefully reworded the judge's pronouncement which runs through the text in cadenced fragments preceding each of the thirteen chapters, with the last page of the book bearing the final phrase "MAY GOD HAVE MERCY ON YOUR SOUL." The book's designer, Philip Van Doren Stern, thought this idea such a good one that he attempted to make (he wrote to McCoy) "the typographical treatment an integral part of the story" by setting these fragments in black capitals which progressively increase in each section one degree in point. His notion that the final phrase "in huge type" would hit "the reader with a terrific bang—as it must have hit the prisoner at the dock" is questionable on both counts; but the effect is startling, and in a way these scareheads seem to fit the tabloid sordidness of the subject matter and the rising intensity of the story's action. Certainly, the device heightens both the dramatic and ironic contrast between the clipped, colloquial urgency of the narrated events of over a month's duration and the measured, pompous rhetoric of the legal formula spoken in a matter of seconds. Nietzsche somewhere remarked that in the courtroom he would acquit everyone but the judge. By implication in McCoy's minor American tragedy, a condemning society shares in the guilt for the transgressions which precipitate the destruction of two human beings. On this level, the plot of the novel is in the conflict between the "criminal" facts of the narrator's case and another set of "facts" or extenuating circumstances.

The book's first words "THE PRISONER WILL STAND"—standing alone on a page—graphically preamble the narrator's *de trop* situation as he briefly recalls in vivid detail how he shot "*Gloria . . . in the side of the head . . . out there in that black night on the edge of the Pacific. . . . She did not die in agony. She was relaxed and comfortable and she was smiling. It was the first time I had ever seen her smile. . . . And she wasn't friendless. I was her very best friend. I was her only friend.*" No such exposition as this appeared in the short-story manuscript. It is a dramatic prologue—told within the condemned man's mind (indicated by italics)—portraying the protagonists at the catastrophe of their tragic relationship. Immediately in the next one-page chapter we learn that the boy—who remains nameless until the judge intones (before chapter 8), "YOU ROBERT SYVERTEN, BE DELIVERED"—has killed the girl as "a personal favor." The crime is against not only society but seemingly also against nature.

*They Shoot Horses, Don't They?* is obviously no murder mystery. Without a complete sacrifice of suspense, however, McCoy set himself the task of making this killing-out-of-friendship understandable and inevitable. He applied, as it were, Joseph Shaw's dicta to subject matter beyond the range of any popular magazine formula: as in the best *Black Mask* detective stories, the emphasis is on "character and the problem inherent in

human behavior"—the "crime, or the threat" being "incidental."

Gimmicky as the novel's design may appear, it serves in many ways, as suggested above, to integrate the various motifs and themes. For example, within Robert's recital of events there occur several critical passages (always italicized) which momentarily either thrust the narrative back into his childhood or tie it to his present position in the courtroom. These textual in-turnings are concomitant with the repetitive, circular movement permeating the story on all levels—e.g, the monotonous routine and incessant motion of the dancing and the "derby" races; the singsong introductions of celebrities; Robert's ludicrous pirouetting to follow the moving spot of sunlight each afternoon; his habit of psychological reversion, which in the end triggers his bemused but fatal decision to help Gloria off their futile "merry-go-round" existence.

These brief, italicized, reversed flashbacks within the narrative, together with the interpolated phrases between chapters, remind us that Robert is for a minute or two standing in court listening to a judge pronounce sentence. But only if we should choose to force our interest away from the developing drama and onto the set frame must we imagine that the related happenings of thirty-seven days are literally passing through his mind. In fact, *They Shoot Horses, Don't They?* reads easily and seems a simple story told simply. It speaks highly of McCoy's handling of point of view that the typographical and structural devices neither blur nor support the drama, but instead help to hold our attention and to heighten our sense of inevitability and of what Camus called the "secret complicity that joins the logical and the everyday to the tragic" (*The Myth of Sisyphus*).

With a boldness characteristic of all his writing, McCoy overrides certain difficulties inherent in employing a first-person narrator who is also a main actor, and succeeds in gaining immediacy and authenticity of expression without sacrificing plausibility. Unlike the vernacular hero of *The Postman Always Rings Twice,* for example, we are not in the end asked to believe that Robert Syverten is literally *writing* his own story. For that matter, most of the time we are less aware of him as a narrator *of* than as a participant *in* the action. In creating a first-person narrator who is at once both outside and inside the story, McCoy is able to command, direct and, in this case, literally frame the reader's attention. All we read of the experiences which constitute the novel's subject is filtered through Robert's rather limited sensibility. It follows almost of necessity that McCoy would use dramatic scenes as the principal device to objectify this indirect approach and give it self-limiting form. Jamesian as all of this may sound, it is also a refinement of the old *Black Mask* "formula." Certainly from Robert's point of view, the story is not so much about what happened as what he feels about what happened.

Through the *persona* of Robert, McCoy selects and organizes his realistic observations for effect rather than for proof. Patently lacking weight of naturalistic "documentation," the undeniable power of this short novel resides in its intensity of mood. Indeed, atmosphere is of the greatest importance—as the narrative progresses it creates the characters. The crime immediately laid bare, the only interest lies in the how and why of the circumstantial "threats"—the physical and psychological forces—which bear unrelentingly upon the protagonists, in particular upon the central figure of Gloria Beatty.

Among American fictional females, Gloria is unique in her unremitting, evil-tempered, nihilistic despair and total estrangement. Metaphorically, her existence is the point of the title's terrible question. It is *her* story Robert tells; the fact that as he unfolds it he is being condemned to death fuses the intricately patterned ironies of theme and drama.

> IS THERE ANY LEGAL CAUSE WHY SENTENCE SHOULD NOT NOW BE PRONOUNCED?
>
> What could I say? . . . All those people knew I had killed her; the only other person who could have helped me at all was dead too.

The "only other person" being old Mrs. Layden, the wealthy and eccentric "champion marathon dance fan of the world," who takes such an unusual interest in Robert and his future, and whose accidental killing by a stray bullet is the death blow to the marathon and a foreshadowing of Gloria's resolution to have herself shot.

Morbid and ineffectual as she is, Gloria is nonetheless the *anima* and from the outset the seeming arbiter of the world of the novel. As a minor character sarcastically says, she does Robert's "thinking for him." She also dictates his fate, as well as her own, and to an extent even that of the marathon dance. By the end of the book we accept her character and condition because McCoy has succeeded in creating a protagonist who is at once the dramatic matrix of the narrative and the embodiment of the novel's theme.

Since Gloria literally dominates Robert, what he tells us of the setting and action is largely determined by her reactions to their surroundings and activities, or otherwise serves to emphasize their predicament, and their physical and spiritual deterioration. By extension, her character sets the pervading mood of the novel. The Sisyphean routine of the marathon dance itself is clearly symbolic of her view of life in which the one value of existence supersedes all others. In an amoral world nothing is immoral; nothing is meaningful. Robert says he feels sorry for a contestant picked up by detectives for a murder. "'Why,' said Gloria, 'what's the difference between us?'" There is literally no exit out of their absurd world—to open an outside door is to risk disqualification; no chance of getting anywhere, either inside or out. "This whole business is a merry-go-round," Gloria tells Robert. "When we get out of here we're right back where we started."

Gloria's predicament is, however, only in part of her own making, and even that part is shown to be the result of her having been born an orphan into a world she never made—the fact that constitutes her character. Estranged and ineffectual, she is engulfed in a universal amorality. "I wish God would strike me dead," she says. But any sign of God is literally shut out of this insulated dancehall world. When, after the marathon's closing, she and Robert finally walk out onto the pier, he looks back at the building and says, "Now I know how Jonah felt when he looked at the whale." In the end, under the moonless, starless sky, Gloria tells him to "pinch hit for God."

The climactic episode, in terms of Gloria's tragedy, occurs in the tenth chapter, when she confronts two dowager representatives of the Mothers' League for Good Morals and, in a scene that is the emotional high-point of the novel, routs them with the terrible force of all her pent-up frustration and bitterness. Her castigation of the women reformers—delivered in the most notorious four-letter terms—is grounded upon her own experience which has proven "morality" an empty word, always dependent upon circumstances, e.g., dancing in a marathon is better than starving. At the end of her tirade she slams the door

behind the routed ladies, sits down, and for the first and only time in the story begins to cry: "She covered her face with her hands and tried to fight it off, but it was no use. She slowly leaned forward in the chair, bending double, shaking and twitching with emotion, as if she had completely lost control of the upper half of her body. For a full moment the only sounds in the room were her sobs and the rise and fall of the ocean which came through the half-raised window." At this moment in the narrative, McCoy brings together the sum total of the amoral environment—the dancehall, the social system, an indifferent nature—that envelopes Gloria, smothering her last hope, reducing her to whimpering despair. The Mothers' League instigates a public campaign against the contest that makes its demise inevitable. The sound of the ocean, a recurring image suggestive of death, foreshadows Gloria's final resolution. The next time we hear its rise and fall she is dead.

Much more could be said about this critical episode in which the cumulative forces of character and environment at last break Gloria's resistance to her fate. (Nothing even remotely like this incident occurred in the original short-story.) Shortly afterward, Gloria makes the explicit declaration: "This motion picture business is a lousy business. . . . I'm glad I'm through with it." The irony is, of course, pathetic. At this point in his narration, Robert, standing in the courtroom listening to the closing phrases of his death sentence, thinks, *"I never paid any attention to her remark then, but now I realize it was the most significant thing she had ever said."* In the night, out on the pier, Gloria looks "down at the ocean toward Malibu," where, as Robert has pointed out a moment before, "all the movie stars live": "Oh, what's the use in me kidding myself—," she says. "I know where I stand."

"The embodiment of the outcast, unemployed and unemployable, miserable, cynical, foul-mouthed, without faith in anything or anybody, very nearly worthless"—as the *TLS* reviewer characterized Gloria—she is nonetheless "to some small extent redeemed by honesty and pitiless self-knowledge" [see Additional Bibliography]. And also by a lucidity denied to her bemused partner: Robert, looking at the same distant lights of Malibu, still can only think about Hollywood, "wondering if I'd ever been there or was I going to wake up in a minute back in Arkansas." Though near the end, he petulantly complains to Gloria that before meeting her he didn't see how he "could miss succeeding" and "never thought of failing," it is not simply by the sheer force of her passionate unhappiness that she is able to draw him into her fatal orbit. She is obviously no villain. A melodramatic or moralistic interpretation would have to ignore the details and nuances of the relationship between the protagonists, and consequently miss altogether the novel's telling psychological import. In this respect, the scant ten pages of chapter 3—the beginning of the narrative proper—are critical to an understanding of how Gloria is able to exercise such mastery over Robert, and how *They Shoot Horses, Don't They?* expresses a universal human dilemma.

Robert begins, "It was funny the way I met Gloria." The vernacular idiom not only pegs his social caste and suggests the limitations of his comprehension, but also strikes a note of mordant humor which counterpoints his essentially grim narrative throughout, down to its final line, "They shoot horses, don't they?" Gloria accidentally runs into his life in a sardonic burlesque of a *Saturday Evening Post* or *Collier's* story opening—on a streetcorner in Hollywood, yet—swearing at a missed bus and interrupting his childish daydreaming of riding in a Rolls Royce, "the greatest director in the world." The blending of stark realism and grotesque drollery produces an ironic tension which is almost Kafkaesque—as do other features of this nightmare story told by a confused man on trial for "trying to do somebody a favor." "How it all started . . . seems very strange" to Robert, and he can't "understand at all" as he stands and waits for the judge to sentence him to death. Good-natured and basically decent, he is also a fool (in the Jamesian sense) whose constant muddlement promotes a "comicality"—but, in this case, of a distinctly modern distemper.

The morning Robert meets Gloria he isn't "feeling very well" and is "still a little sick" from intestinal flu, which had made him "so weak" he had had "to crawl." Images of sickness and physical disorders quite naturally arise throughout the story and function on many levels, especially those tied to Robert. In more ways than one he is weak and susceptible to contagion. About Gloria there is, almost literally, a faint odor of corruption. In an early rough draft of chapter 3 McCoy had Gloria describe a "laughable" fact concerning her sexual history ("I've never been laid on a bed in my life, . . ."), and Robert "began to feel a little like heaving" while at the same time fascinated enough to think of her as being like "an unpleasant odor that was very interesting" (Typescript held by author). The degradation of her past life and circumstances have inoculated her irremediably with a moral taint as contagious as a disease. Significantly, she tells Robert how she had gotten "the idea of coming to Hollywood . . . from the movie magazines" while recuperating in a hospital from an attempt at suicide by poison. He doesn't say so directly, but we gather that his naive ambitions had been "poisoned" back on the farm in Arkansas from much the same source. Both of them are sick, so to speak, with the same disease and suffer the common hallucinatory hope of "discovery" in Hollywood.

The central scene of the third chapter takes place at night in a stage-like setting of a small, secluded park where Robert takes Gloria to sit and talk. In a few pages of dramatic exposition, mainly dialogue, the two unemployed extras confide in each other with that queer, precipitant intimacy which so often transpires between chance acquaintances who are lonely and share a common predicament. Compact in the extreme, the episode moves naturally, but at one and the same time directly and indirectly, to introduce the characters and to establish the pattern and tone of their relationship. Dramatically this is Robert's big scene—or, more significantly, it *should* be. Armed with money "made squirting soda in a drug store" for a friend who "had got a girl in a jam" and had to take her out of town "for the operation," Robert diffidently asks Gloria "if she'd rather go to a movie or sit in the park." Directly and decisively she takes command: "I got a bellyful of moving pictures. . . . If I'm not a better actress than most of those dames I'll eat your hat—Let's go sit and hate a bunch of people." She dominates the ensuing conversation, and we hear most about her background and what she thinks—about Hollywood in particular and life in general. Since Robert is the narrator, we discover his character by indirection and apposition; and since he is a hypersensitive and dreamy fellow, it is doubly appropriate that we learn most about him through his heightened and emotional internal responses to events, actions and, in particular, his surroundings.

Unaffected by Gloria's caustic outburst, Robert is only "glad she wanted to go to the park." This "very dark and very quiet" place "filled with dense shrubbery" and surrounded by tall palm trees gives him "the illusion of security." He imagines the palms are "sentries wearing grotesque helmets: my own private sentries, standing guard over my own private island." For him the park is a regenerative oasis in a desert of hard knocks and fading mirages, to which he retreats "three or four times a week" to fantasize: "Through the palms you could see many buildings, the thick, square silhouettes of apartment houses, with their red signs on the roofs, reddening the sky above and everything and everybody below. But if you wanted to get rid of these things you had only to sit and stare at them with a fixed gaze . . . and they would begin receding." Gloria, looking at the same "red, vaporish glow," recalls that West Texas, where she comes from, is "a hell of a place." Unable, like Robert, to stare reality out of countenance, she leads him out of his private square-block Eden into the hell of "an enormous old building that once had been a public dance hall . . . built out over the ocean."

Interestingly enough, the characterizations of both Robert and Gloria in the short-story version were more "round" (e.g., in the park, he speaks of failure; she smiles often and says the park is "lovely"); they seemed more like people in real life—inconsistent and often, perhaps paradoxically, less interesting. Given the objective manner and dramatic structure in which McCoy chose to write his novel, he inevitably was forced to delineate his characters in bold, theatrical strokes. Gloria, in particular, is "foreshortened" (in Henry James's phraseology) "to within an inch of her life"; but few readers, I think, would deny that she is thoroughly alive and memorable. McCoy avoids caricaturizing either protagonist by maintaining an "exquisite chemical adjustment" of the psychological affinities which inexorably draw these two dispossessed people together into a tragic, almost sado-masochistic, trap. Though their personalities differ, we sense that fundamentally they have more in common than their social and geographical origins and bad luck in Hollywood. Given their individual limitations of intelligence and sensibility, Robert's self-centered enthusiasm and Gloria's inverted egotism effectively block any chance of mutual insight or understanding—until after it is too late. When next these two sit and talk together at night, looking at distant lights, external forces of degradation will have eroded away all vestiges of balance and control. (pp. 146-58)

In *They Shoot Horses, Don't They?* the characterizations of Robert and Gloria, taken together, reveal a dramatic particularization of the common dilemma of young and naive ambition up against a frustrating, hobbling, and even destructive world in which the truths of existence run contrary to all logic, morality, and dreams. As previously noted, despite the inescapable threatricalness and sensationalism of locale and setting—which are to the very point of the story—McCoy has not written a simplistic melodrama. Robert and Gloria—Couple No. 22 in the dance contest—are not antithetical types in a modern morality play. In the original short-story version, Robert liked Gloria "because she talked to me the way I would talk to a boy if I were a girl." His obsessive ambition and her obsessive despair are opposite sides of the same overvalued coin.

If, as Van Nostrand says, "fiction is the fashioning of an occasion appropriate to one's deepest need, which is to justify oneself," then *They Shoot Horses, Don't They?* can be read as McCoy's first serious attempt to resolve the inner tensions of his own actions and ambitions in Hollywood. (In this and the following paragraph I have found Van Nostrand's general critical terminology useful.) Any fiction is, of course, "a bizarre exaggeration of mere actuality"; but the uniqueness and force of this book are in part due to the fact that the actualities of Hollywood and of a marathon dance are to begin with bizarre.

However, because McCoy exercised such controlled and dispassionate objectivity, we are satisfied that these things could not have happened otherwise (given what we learn about the characters); and we recognize that their implicit meanings transcend the narrative. The necessity of inevitability which rules this novel resides to a great extent in the natures of the characters in conflict—i.e., if we accept the underlying divided-personality motif, in the nature of the conflict within a limited individual driven by an internal compulsion abetted by external corruption. As in any serious novel, the essence of *They Shoot Horses, Don't They?* lies "in the way it repeats and amplifies its substance to appraise it"; and in the way it "represents by metaphor, by analogy to things known," in particular by the metaphor of conflict which is held to be the substance of all narrative fiction.

We should not, of course, hold to any rigorous set of criteria for "the novel" in evaluating such a unique work as *They Shoot Horses, Don't They?* Lacking largeness and breadth, it falls within the dominant tradition of "the best American writing," which is characterized, as Malcolm Cowley has noted, "by narrowness and intensity." Like so many short contemporary American novels, it is more akin to a long short story, from which it derived. More properly, perhaps, we should call it a novelette. But more to the point is the degree to which McCoy develops his subject matter, within his self-imposed limits of size and form, into an intricate system of analogues. Close attention to certain patterns of images and arrangement of incidents reveals a "developing of involvement," that makes "the most of the least material."

For example, there is much to do about intimate man-woman relationships throughout the novel (but not in the short story version), especially the institution of marriage. From Robert's viewpoint, marriage seemingly would be Gloria's only salvation short of "discovery" (but she is, he says, "too blonde and too small and looked too old" for the films)—though, he assures Mrs. Layden, *he* is not going to marry Gloria "or anything like that." But her childhood environment and adult experiences and observations have long since conditioned her to fear and reject this natural solution: "I've thought about it plenty," she tells Robert. "But I couldn't ever marry the kind of man I want. The only kind that would marry me would be the kind I wouldn't have. A thief or a pimp or something." When the dance promoters offer the two a chance to be married in a public wedding—"it don't have to be permanent . . . it's just showmanship"—Gloria adamantly refuses.

All the variations on the motif of marriage culminate in the travesty of the public wedding in the climactic penultimate chapter. This grotesque scene is a dramatic nexus in which the various themes of the novel are self-reflexively appraised: "The entire hall had been decorated with so many flags and so much red, white and blue bunting that you expected any moment to hear firecrackers go off and the band play the national anthem." To the howling, sellout crowd, the master of ceremonies announces: "Remember, the entertainment for the night is not over when the marriage is finished. That's only the beginnin'. . . . After the wedding we have the derby——." Before the grand march of the contestants—who have been costumed in rented tuxedos and dresses—begins, the local merchants "who have made this feature possible" are introduced in the same tedious Academy Awards manner used in previous episodes for visiting Hollywood celebrities. The wedding-ceremony finale to this sordid, almost surrealistic parody of a Busby Berkeley musical-comedy film is performed by the Reverend Oscar Gilder.

"—And I now pronounce you man and wife—" Dr. Gilder said. He bowed his head and began to pray: *The Lord is my shepherd. . . .*

Set all in italics, the Twenty-third Psalm at this moment in the narrative reminds us that Robert, standing in court, has just heard the judge pronounce sentence of death. This funereal hymn would be blatantly inappropriate, of course, to any real wedding ceremony (except, perhaps, at a marathon dance near Hollywood), but in the context of the novel it is a brilliant stroke of indirect commentary, structural fusion, and ironic mood music. As the minister finishes the prayer, a gunfight breaks out in the dancehall's beer garden ("the Palm Garden") and Mrs. Layden—the epitome of the perverted audience—is shot in the head by a stray bullet. Looking upon the dead body, Gloria says under her breath, "I wish it was me——." In an "afterword" to the most recent edition of *They Shoot Horses, Don't They?*, Robert M. Coates found himself concerned over "the tendency to equate" McCoy's first novel with Nathanael West's *Miss Lonelyhearts* (1933), "though the outlook of both was thoroughly pessimistic, West's approach was basically and deeply poetic, while McCoy's was stringently matter-of-fact throughout." I would agree that McCoy can not be superficially equated with West (though this has never been done "so often" as Coates suggested)—or, for that matter, with any other contemporary American novelist. But if by a poetic approach is implied an attempt by a writer to express his most imaginative and intense perceptions of his world, himself, and the interrelationships of the two, then McCoy possessed a profoundly lyrical creative imagination. The deep strain of "symbolism" in *They Shoot Horses, Don't They?*—and not the hard-boiled surface—is its dominant aesthetic characteristic.

Surely, in his first novel Horace McCoy stepped out in new directions. Chandler once wrote of "little lost books . . . which are not perfect, evasive of the problem often, side-stepping scenes which should have been written . . . but somehow passing along crystalized, complete, and as such things go nowadays eternal, a little pure art." In the long run, the atmospheric intensity and inevitable fatality of *They Shoot Horses, Don't They?* speak more convincingly for McCoy's artistry than any amount of categorizing or close analysis. With bold originality and a high degree of literary skill, he imbued his story with the bitter and disquieted mood from which he wrote, creating one of the most original works of contemporary American fiction.

Beyond any conscious intention and artistic control—with the power of intuition that always distinguishes an original creative imagination—McCoy's handling of his story's unique setting and *in extremis* resolution projected it beyond the social and ethical preoccupations of its time and place. Much more than a documentary of a grisly symptom of the early years of this country's Great Depression, more than an objective correlative of the world of Hollywood's extras, McCoy's marathon *danse macabre* has become an universally applicable parable of modern man's existential predicament. Its grotesque and morbid fantasia has echoed with meaning through the literal and spiritual undergrounds of the past quarter-century—among the existentialists of occupied France, the disaffiliated of postwar America. "There is but one truly serious philosophical problem," Camus argued in *The Myth of Sisyphus* (1942), "and that is suicide." Its corollary, he pointed out elsewhere, is the problem of killing others. It should no longer be difficult for American critics to understand how *They Shoot Horses, Don't They?* has received the serious attention of writers and intellectuals abroad, for both its literary techniques and implicit meanings. As Sartre explained twenty years ago: "What we looked for above all else in the American novel was something quite different from its crudities and its violence." (pp. 158-62)

Thomas Sturak, "Horace McCoy's Objective Lyricism," in Tough Guy Writers of the Thirties, edited by David Madden, Southern Illinois University Press, 1968, pp. 137-62.

## LEE J. RICHMOND (essay date 1971)

[Richmond is an American educator and critic. In the following excerpt, she examines the existential themes of isolation and estrangement in They Shoot Horses, Don't They?]

The theme of isolation and estrangement in existential writings which reached a peak of popularity with readers in the 1950's and 1960's through a revival of interest in Kafka's work and in the fiction and plays of Sartre, Camus, and Ionesco (to this list might be added a reassessment at that time of Dostoevsky, Kierkegaard, and Nietzsche) has been traced largely in the productions of these European writers. Latter-day examinations of the existential dilemma of modern man incline toward identifying it in such diverse American writers as T. S. Eliot, Auden, Hemingway, and in European writers not usually regarded as members of the tradition, such as Joyce, Greene, Orwell, and Huxley. A work to receive all but the scantiest attention is Horace McCoy's 1935 novel They Shoot Horses, Don't They? With the exception of Nathanael West's Miss Lonelyhearts (1933) and The Day of the Locust (1939), McCoy's novel is indisputably the best example of absurdist existentialism in American fiction. Dismissed in America essentially as a "penny dreadful" at its first appearance, it nevertheless found, as did West's works, popularity among a small band of French existentialists who recognized its beauty and power. (p. 91)

At its initial American appearance, it should be admitted, a few reviewers anticipated what the French were to glean more perceptively from Horses. William Rose Benét conceded to its "inevitable fatality" [see Additional Bibliography]; and William Plomer intimated its more ambitious design: "People used to say the Russian novels were gloomy, but they were riots of fun compared to some of these modern American examples, with deathly wisecracks popping like revolver-shots" [see excerpt dated 1935]. (p. 92)

A simplistic approach to the novel invites the reader to regard it as a satire on the exploitation by racketeers of a desperate, debilitated society, or as a scathing parody of the Hollywood dream-factory, or, worse, as a severe reproof of the social system that produced bread lines and relief agencies during the Great Depression. Though these motifs are peripheral to McCoy's meaning, none provides proper access to the author's timeless emphasis. Nor does the outline of the action stand as his central propulsion to relate the down-and-out condition of the novel's anti-heroes. In a few words, the story relates Robert Syverten's fortuitous and ultimately fatal meeting with a hard-boiled girl-turned-waif named Gloria Beatty. In desperation, she recruits him as her partner in a 1930's dance-marathon on the California ocean-front. Slowly her tormented outbursts and the terror of the contest undermine Robert's once-optimistic dreams of fame and fortune. The book records with an unsparing tone the wretchedness of the dancers in their undaunted attempts to beat their competitors. The plot proceeds for 879 hours of fictional time to delineate the throes (one is almost tempted to say death-

throes) of the participants. Gloria becomes more and more unhinged (in a philosophical, rather than strictly psychological sense) by the human rubbish she sees strewn about the dance-floor, by the folly of human reason, and by her own nihilism; finally, she requests—almost demands—that Robert kill her. In terror and pity, he executes what would seem only superficially a reckless gesture—he puts a bullet through her head. For this action, he is tried, found guilty, and sentenced to die. That Horace McCoy is capable of rescuing this melodramatic plot is evidenced in his artistic abilities to invent a taut continuity of feeling and theme which obviates a sentimental or impassive response. What impelled the French during World War II to name McCoy "the real founder of Existentialism" can be justified by an acute examination of the novel. Such analysis fixes him securely in a tradition usually associated with European writers such as Céline, Michaux, Camus, Beckett, and Sartre, none of whom is limited to sociological diatribe. (pp. 92-3)

The erratic structure of McCoy's book—which reminds one of Eliot's "heap of broken images"—complies precisely with its emphasis on the senseless, often brutal, gestures of the contestants in the marathon-dance craze of the 1930's. Like the fleet vignettes West employs to hold together Miss Lonelyhearts, the quick-moving scenes in They Shoot Horses, Don't They? are meant to underscore the piecemeal existences of its characters. Gloria Beatty, and not the novel's narrator, Robert Syverten, is the central spokesman for the author's vision of a broken world. One of her speeches, parodied by a fellow-dancer, is a cliché which out of context is laughable, but embodies in the total conception of the book its critical truth:

> "I'm tired of living and I'm afraid of dying," Gloria said. "Say, that's a swell idea for a song," said Robert Bates, who had overheard her. "You could write a song about a nigger down on the levee who was tired of living and afraid of dying. He could be heaving cotton and singing a song to the Mississippi River. Say, that's a good title—you could call it Old Man River—"

Gloria's motives for joining the dehumanizing contest are, it would appear, to land a Hollywood contract, to be provided seven meals a day, clothing, and shelter, and to cash in on the prize money. In its broader significance as an emblem, however, her participation in the dance is consistent with her view that nothing makes sense, that as a fugitive from life the contest is the last, most absurd posture of Angst. Her action could hardly be construed as a token of the "courage of despair." Gloria's speeches are, for the most part, clipped, bare testimonies of her dread of life, of death, of Nothingness:

> ". . . I may get to be a star overnight. Look at Hepburn and Margaret Sullivan and Josephine Hutchinson. . . . But I'll tell you what I would do if I had the guts: I'd walk out of a window or throw myself in front of a street car or something."

> "I don't think it's very nice of you to razz me," I said to Gloria. "I don't ever razz you."

> "You don't have to," she said. "I get razzed by an expert. God razzes me . . .".

> ". . . Anyway, I'm finished. I think it's a lousy world and I'm finished. I'd be better off dead and so would everybody else. I ruin everything I get around . . .".

In a sense, her flat statements of anguish connect the disjointed barrage of incidents in the thirteen sections of the novel. Why she is disenchanted is not because of the Depression doldrums

entirely; to assume so is to reduce McCoy's novel to a sociological commentary akin to the proletariat literature of the
Thirties. Exposition of Gloria's past is frugal, but not irrelevant: her sordid homelife, her luckless associations with men,
and her present poverty all fortify her commitment (for, ironically, it is a commitment) to the proposition that life is an
absurd sequence of events. How, she implies, can death be
more absurd?

> Gloria was fumbling in her purse. When her hand
> came out it was holding a small pistol. I had never
> seen the pistol before, but I was not surprised. I was
> not in the least surprised.
>
> "Here—" she said, offering it to me.
>
> "I don't want it. Put it away," I said. "Come on,
> let's go back inside. I'm cold—"
>
> "Take it and pinch-hit for God," she said, pressing
> it into my hand. "Shoot me. It's the only way to get
> me out of my misery."
>
> "She's right," I said to myself. "It's the only way
> to get her out of her misery."

This passage reveals another important distinction: Gloria does
not, like the atheistic existentialism of Sartre or Camus, deny
God and wished to go on facing the abyss with stoic fortitude.
That would in itself be a bizarre form of salvation. But Gloria
can find nothing to save—either in herself, in others, or in the
world of things. She is the most tough-minded heroine in absurdist literature. Her only request of a fellow-human being is
made to Robert when she asks that he "pinch-hit for God."
Nor does she manifest inner revolt: only revulsion for what
life *does not* mean. God to her is as abstract as is life. He is
an inherited idea which finds no concrete emanation in anything
palpable. He is the absent God. Gloria's death at Robert's hands
is anti-climactic: her spiritual suicide is prefigured in Chapter
Three when she tells him of her unsuccessful attempt at poisoning herself. Her denial of Ruby Bate's desire to have a baby
is a veiled wish for her own extinction. With equal vehemence,
she disavows old Mrs. Layden's reason for living and intimates
her strong death-urge.

> ". . . My God, can you feature that old lady? She's
> a nut about these things. They ought to charge her
> room rent." She shook her head. "I hope I never
> live to be that old," she said again.

The proposal by Rocky Gravo, the master of ceremonies, of
a fake marriage with Robert and the pious platitudes of the
Mothers' League for Good Morals elicit from Gloria a most
vociferous rejection of conventional morality as sham ritual.
They are, to her mind, gaudy spectacles that signify the social
animal man pretends to be. Like Sartre's Roquentin, Gloria
intimates that a "system" of social values disguises man's
terror at realizing he is a victim in an absurd universe. It is
possible to speculate at the end of *La Nausée* that Roquentin,
too, commits suicide as a final sign for his rejection of the
senseless pageant of the human condition. In Chapter Twelve,
we are to take literally Gloria's answer to Robert's insistent
questioning:

> All day Gloria had been very morbid. I asked her a
> hundred times what she was thinking about. "Noth-
> ing," she would reply.

Of course, she has been dwelling on death—which, like life,
to her is "nothing." *Néant*, too, is a key word in the vocabulary
of the absurdist thinkers of the 1940's. In the same chapter,
Mrs. Layden is accidentally killed by a stray bullet. Gloria

says, "I wish it was me—." This incident, the gesture of the
willy-nilly workings of chaotic life, foreshadows Gloria's death
in the final scene, except that her "suicide" presents the illusion of choice.

Robert's killing of Gloria is followed immediately by a flashback from him which summarizes by metaphor her whole agonizing quarrel with the great void. In it Robert recalls when
as a little kid he watched his grandfather shoot Old Nellie the
horse after she has stepped in a hole and broken her leg.

> *I heard a shot. I still hear that shot. I ran over and*
> *fell down on the ground, hugging her neck. I loved*
> *that horse. I hated my grandfather. I got up and went*
> *to him, beating his legs with my fists. . . . Later that*
> *day he explained that he loved Nellie too, but that*
> *he had to shoot her. "It was the kindest thing to do,"*
> *he said. "She was no more good. It was the only*
> *way to get her out of her misery . . ."*.

McCoy's characterization of Gloria is purposefully elliptical.
Her speeches—many of them *non sequiturs* and expletives—
are direct, simple, and yet fierce evidence of her refusal to say
"Yes." Paradoxically, it is her retention of subjectivity amongst
the dehumanizing dance that keeps us from roundly denouncing
her negativism. Her name—Latin for "glory"—is clearly a
sardonic epithet. But by Chapter Thirteen she will not be reduced to a victim any longer, and her self-immolation is, at
least in her psychology, bitter testimony to her retreat from
irrationality.

It is obvious that Robert Syverten's first-person narration is
credible only in terms of his relationship to Gloria, the girl he
meets quite by chance near the Paramount studios and who
cajoles him into joining the macabre dance. His story is, we
can assume, a personal rumination, for in Chapter Two—quoted
here in its entirety—he appears to remain speechless before
the courtroom:

> What could I say? . . . All those people knew I had
> killed her; the only other person who could have
> helped me at all was dead too. So I just stood there,
> looking at the judge and shaking my head. I didn't
> have a leg to stand on.
>
> "Ask the mercy of the court," said Epstein, the
> lawyer they had assigned to defend me.
>
> "What was that?" the judge said.
>
> "Your Honor," Epstein said, "—we throw our-
> selves on the mercy of the court. This boy admits
> killing the girl, but he was only doing her a personal
> favor—"
>
> The judge banged on the desk, looking at me.

The passages from the legal proceedings which preface every
chapter (each is printed in bolder type, until the final page
where the words ". . . May God Have Mercy On Your Soul . . ."
occupy an entire page) serve both to remind us that Robert's
story is secretly uttered to himself as the judge sentences him
and, more dramatically, to underpin the potent irony of his
innocence. Robert's most important thoughts are italicized, as
in Chapter One where the conclusion is presented inversely,
as if to regulate the reader's reactions to the events which
follow:

> *The Prosecuting Attorney was wrong when he told*
> *the jury she died in agony, friendless, alone except*
> *for her brutal murderer, out there in that black night*
> *on the edge of the Pacific. He was wrong as a man*
> *can be. She did not die in agony. She was relaxed*

*and comfortable and she was smiling. It was the first time I had ever seen her smile. How could she have been in agony then? And she wasn't friendless. I was her very best friend. I was her only friend. So how could she have been friendless?*

Like Camus' Meursault, Robert is not a criminal. Why, then, is the novel's big question, does he kill Gloria, and why does he not struggle to acquit himself? In Chapter Three, as he begins to recall to himself everything which lead up to Gloria's death, he says in a kind of aside:

> *They are going to kill me. I know exactly what the judge is going to say. I can tell by the look of him that he is going to be glad to say it and I can tell by the feel of the people behind me that they are going to be glad to hear him say it.*

This admission that others will savor his punishment must be recalled as we see Robert's character develop in the remaining ten chapters. Initially, he has ambitions of becoming a film director: his hopes betray a guileless trust that he can perfect himself, be somebody. His simplicity extends to an admiration of nature as a soothing agent to his struggles and disappointments. The Eden-like park to which he leads Gloria, the tranquil sea towards which he is drawn time and again, and the sunlight from a broken window pane in which he dances at the hall all qualify in his imagination as symbols of peace and harmony. This romantic notion of a gentle nature is rebuffed constantly by Gloria until near the end when she plants in his mind finally its indifferent character:

> "You're hipped on the subject of waves," Gloria said.
>
> "No, I'm not," I said.
>
> "That's all you've been talking about for a month—"
>
> "All right, stand still a minute and you'll see what I mean. You can feel it rising and falling—"
>
> "I can feel it without standing still," she said, "but that's no reason to get yourself in a sweat. It's been going on for a million years."

Robert's answer is revealing of his blighted vision by the story's end:

> "Don't think I'm crazy about this ocean," I said. "It'll be all right with me if I never see it again. I've had enough ocean to last me the rest of my life."

Robert's simple-minded response to life is counter-balanced dramatically at first, as well as through the greater part of the work, by Gloria's unyielding reproaches. Robert sometimes ignores her, sometimes scolds her for her disspiriting remarks, and sometimes listens without comment. When James Bates slaps Gloria for her merciless hints to his wife that an abortion would be best for her, Robert comes inexplicably to Gloria's defense. Probably his protection of her is a social reflex-action, the sign of his holding with the code of honor which demands that a gentleman defend a lady. Robert explains in his naive fashion Gloria's character as he defines it early in their encounter: "She's all right. She's just sore on the world, that's all." We first see him as romantic, vulnerable, and a victim of his society's behavioral patterns. Nor is he envious or jealous of others' success. When Miss Alice Faye comes to the ballroom he is unduly impressed:

> "Come on," I said to Gloria, "clap your hands."
>
> "Why should I applaud for her?" Gloria said. "What's she got I haven't? . . . "

"You're jealous," I said.

> "You're goddam right I'm jealous. As long as I am a failure I'm jealous of anybody who's a success. Aren't you?"
>
> "Certainly not," I said.
>
> "You're a fool," she said.

Elsewhere Robert encourages a fellow-competitor to keep faith:

> "Can I pick 'em?" said Kid Kamm. He shook his head, disgusted.
>
> "Boy, am I hoodooed! I been in nine of these things and I ain't finished one yet. My partner always caves in on me."
>
> "She'll be all right," I said, trying to cheer him up.

By Chapter Six, then, we observe Robert Syverten as a young man not without hope, humanity, and a sense of conventional morality. The savage competition of the dance and Gloria's annihilating rejection of the world, however, gradually undermine his innocent-eye view. The arrest of Mario Petrone, the escaped murderer; Rocky Gravo's bloodthirsty appeals to the kids to compete to the death; the promiscuous sexual acts that are described as animal functions; the second arrest of a murderer, Giuseppe Lodi; the torturous foot-derby; the commercial exploitation of Robert and Gloria by Jonathan Beer; Pedro Ortega's attempted knifing of Lillian Bacon; the sadistic energy of the spectators, among whom are the movie stars, those glamorous chimeras opportunistically promoting their studios; the violent shootings of Monk which end in the accidental slaying of Mrs. Layden—all these reflect the microcosmic structure of McCoy's world. The impressions which these events make upon Robert's tender sensibility prepare for his merciful killing of Gloria. In the midst of these cruel circumstances, she warns him: "This whole business is a merry-go-round. When we get out of here we're right back where we started."

In Chapter Twelve, Robert admits:

> All day Gloria had been very morbid. I asked her a hundred times what she was thinking about. "Nothing," she would reply. *I realize now how stupid I was. I should have known what she was thinking. Now that I look back on that last night I don't see how I possibly could have been so stupid. But in those days I was dumb about a lot of things.*

Then he continues:

> *. . . The judge is sitting up there, making his speech, looking through his glasses at me, but his words are doing the same thing to my body that his eyesight is doing to his glasses—going right through without stopping, rushing out of the way of each succeeding look and each succeeding word. I am not hearing the judge with my ears and with my brain any more than the lenses of his glasses are catching and imprisoning each look that comes through them. I hear him with my feet and my legs and torso and arms, with everything but my ears and brain. With my ears and brain I hear a newsboy in the street shouting something about King Alexander, I hear the warning bells of the traffic semaphores, in the courtroom I hear people breathing and moving their feet, I hear the wood speaking in a bench, I hear the light splash as someone spits in the cuspidor. All these things I hear with my ears and my brain, but I hear the judge with my body only. If you ever hear a judge say to you what this one is saying to me, you will know what I mean.*

At this point it is clear that Robert, like Meursault, cannot defend himself to a court which recognizes a code of law based upon a rational interpretation of human life and of the universe. His killing of Gloria is automatic, is, in keeping with her absurdist position, as meaningless as anything else in the scheme of things. Gloria's premonitional speech just before her death is crucial to Robert's growing acceptance of her negativism:

> "This motion picture business is a lousy business," she said. "You have to meet people who don't want to meet and you have to be nice to people whose guts you hate. I'm glad I'm through with it."
>
> "You're just starting with it," I said, trying to cheer her up. *I never paid any attention to her remark then, but now I realize it was the most significant thing she had ever said.*

Just before Gloria and Robert leave the ballroom "to get some air," the Rev. Oscar Gilder who officiates at the arranged dancefloor wedding of Vee Lovell and Mary Hawley recites the Lord's Prayer. It comes as a sour footnote to the wasteland vision which has gone before. And, of course, it is a more chilling prelude to the following scene when Robert delivers Gloria from her agonies on the pier. The concluding scene in the police car ends with Robert's question, which caps his belated awareness of the world as "the valley of the shadow of death":

> "Why did you kill her?" the policeman in the rear seat asked.
>
> "She asked me to," I said.
>
> "You hear that, Ben?"
>
> "Ain't he an obliging bastard?" Ben said over his shoulder.
>
> "Is that the only reason you got?" the policeman in the rear seat asked.
>
> "They shoot horses, don't they?" I asked.

Like the fatally-lamed horse of his Arkansas childhood, Gloria and Robert are beyond cure. Robert's words in Chapter Two as he awaits judgment: "I don't have a leg to stand on" and Gloria's reference to herself as a horse in the merry-go-round of life relate to the horse's as well as their inevitable death. Their spiritual lameness ends only in the deliverance of death—the final stroke of absurdism.

*They Shoot Horses, Don't They?* has no winners. McCoy has the police close the dance hall because of a shooting that occurs there. This suits his thematic contention exactly; there are no winners in the marathon of life. His metaphor is as spare as his style. The archetypal image of the dance of life—or, is it the dance of death?—is rendered realistically in historic context—the Great Depression. McCoy's pun on "depression" is apt: but, to be sure, the novel's meaning transcends a local historical phenomenon in 1932. It is through the image of the eternal, meaningless dance—with its reminder of the futile rhythm of existence—that Gloria and Robert are ultimately stripped of their particularity and become symbolic projections of the absurdist man and woman. Gloria's "world pain" is seized by Robert in the throes of his dance-movements: his physical exhaustion is a tangible correlative for his spiritual weariness. But Gloria only underscores what he comes to understand in the terror of the ballroom environment which is Horace McCoy's trope for the world. Robert's psychic paralysis is registered in his rejection of protest in court. In Camus' terms, he is doomed to an absurd end through having sensed

*"l'absolu ou l'absurde."* Like Kafka's K. in *The Castle*, Robert can sense, if not definitively articulate, the absolute otherness of God. And like later existential anti-heroes, such as Roquentin and Meursault, he discerns, if only vaguely, the flimsy illusions which men retain to deceive themselves that life is purposeful. Each of these characters is contained in a symbolical hallucinatory setting where the mergence of man, nature, and God is impossible. ". . . May God Have Mercy On Your Soul . . ." rancorously shouts the novel's final page. But God is on leave. Robert's refusal to speak in court is his private declaration of disavowal. (pp. 93-9)

> Lee J. Richmond, "A Time to Mourn and a Time to Dance: Horace McCoy's 'They Shoot Horses, Don't They?'," in Twentieth Century Literature, *Vol. 17, No. 2, April, 1971, pp. 91-100.*

## L. W. MICHAELSON (essay date 1971)

[*In the following excerpt, Michaelson evaluates McCoy as primarily a reform novelist working to point out injustice and corruption.*]

Horace McCoy, author of the marathon-dance novel, belatedly made into a film, got the Hollywood runaround, much as the central character, Gloria Beatty, of his *They Shoot Horses, Don't They?* got shafted both by "life" and Central Casting. That is to say, it's a McCoy-type irony that Movie-Land, *circa* 1935, was too cautious to make the picture when McCoy was alive and active and needed, not so much the money, but artistic fulfillment and public recognition. . . .

Indeed, 1935 was a very painful time for the American business culture, and to make a film of the marathon dance days (as seen through McCoy's eyes) would salt everyone's wounds: The Great Depression was too close to us all. Thus, perhaps some off-the-cuff wisdom or box-office shrewdness can be placed at Hollywood's door in this matter. McCoy died in semi-obscurity, somewhat guilt stricken that he had been, after all, a Hollywood hack, a scenario writer second-class, dependable, well-paid but never top-flight. It's hard to understand this delay of almost thirty-five years, and hard to understand why Hollywood kept him under wraps.

Hitler and World War II muddied the entertainment waters for a good while in the 1940's: a marathon dance film would certainly have been a dud when *Mrs. Minniver* was the ticket. And then the late 1940's had J. Parnell Thomas and the Hollywood purge of suspected Commie writers such as Dalton Trumbo, Albert Maltz, and A. Bessie. Actually, McCoy was never touched by the Hollywood purge, being pretty much politically non-committed, but the sarcasm in *Shoot Horses* and the muckraking in *No Pockets in a Shroud* might have put McCoy under suspicion, or at least on the famous Hollywood "grey list"—if the scripts had been filmed at that time.

After World War II, very likely, the movie-going public was in the mood for such "epics" as *Best Years of Our Lives, The Egg and I, et al*, and later on, grim war pictures came on strong such as *Naked and the Dead*. But surely, sometime between the years 1935 and 1955 (the date of McCoy's death), *Shoot Horses* could have been squeezed into a shooting schedule. Steinbeck's *Grapes of Wrath*, published some three years after, was made into a film fairly quickly; the American public apparently enjoyed it. (p. 15)

Surely, along with *Grapes of Wrath*, McCoy's novel is one of the most graphic and important accounts of our Depression Days ever written. Let us hope now there will be a modest McCoy revival, on the order of Henry Roth's *Call It Sleep*, at least. Certainly, *Shoot Horses* should inch its way to the college freshman reading list to give added pertinence to such journalistic accounts of the order of Allen's *Since Yesterday*, a report on the Roosevelt era. The novel will help to show our affluent young college students of today that the 1930's were no pink tea, and that there were other aspects to our Depression than the agricultural one. (p. 16)

McCoy's later works (*No Pockets in a Shroud, I Should Have Stayed Home, Kiss Tomorrow Goodbye,* and *Scalpel*) might be adjudged on the whole, inferior works of art. He didn't write nearly as well about Hollywood (or anything) as Nathanael West. In fact, N. L. Rothman commenting on McCoy's third effort, *I Should Have Stayed Home,* seems to pin point his later talents. Rothman says,

> McCoy hates Hollywood, but not enough to stay away, but enough to get the bile out of his system. It (the novel) may be a true picture, but an institution that can display both Paul Muni and Shirley Temple, would seem to need a fuller explanation. [see excerpt dated 1938].

To be sure, novels with a deeper, if not a fuller explanation, were forthcoming almost immediately: West's *Day of the Locust,* Fitzgerald's *Last Tycoon,* and Bemelman's *Dirty Eddie,* to name a few. Rothman, a bit later on his review, did admit that McCoy had confined his pen to a rather limited subject: "But McCoy is talking to kids who come in flocks to be stars, but never read McCoy."

Therefore, all of his works (with the possible exceptions of *Scalpel*—although even here there is a touch of propaganda in

*Magazine ad for* Kiss Tomorrow Good-Bye. *Reproduced courtesy of Random House, Inc.*

the matter of mine safety—and *Kiss Tomorrow*), are reform novels, written to correct some injustice and corruption, or at least expose them. But, as someone has said when art mounts the sermon rostrum to preach, artistry is apt to fly out of the window. Nevertheless, *Shoot Horses* is a minor masterpiece; the other novels belong more in the muck-raking class, sugar-coated or perhaps acid-coated Lincoln Steffens stuff, for the most part, plus a touch of Upton Sinclair, and a dash or two of Cain and Hammett. Witness this Lincoln Steffenish beginning of *No Pockets in a Shroud*:

> When Dolan got the call to go up to the editor's office he knew this was going to be the blow-off, and . . . he kept thinking what a shame it was that none of the newspapers had any guts anymore. He wished he'd been living back in the days of Dana and Greeley, when a newspaper was a newspaper and called a sonofabitch a sonofabitch, and let the devil take the hindmost. It must have been swell to have been a reporter on one of those old papers. Not like now when the country was full of little Hearsts . . . beating the drums . . . and saying Mussolini was another Ceaesar (only with planes and poison gas) . . . and selling patriotism at cut-rate prices and not giving a good goddam about anything but circulation. . . . Or: oh yes, sir, Mister Delancy, we understand perfectly. Those two women *wandered* in front of your son's car. Oh yes, sir, haha! That alcoholic odour on his person was from somebody *spilling* a cocktail on his suit.

However, Thomas Sturak in an essay in Madden's collection, "McCoy's Objective Lyricism," denies that McCoy can be neatly pigeonholed with James Cain and Dashiell Hammett. Sturak, rather academically, says:

> The real subjects of his fiction are the existential conflicts arising out of an acute self-awareness and the inevitable consequences of self-division.

In France, during the 1940's McCoy was hailed as the "first American existentialist," partly for his blast against Hitler and Mussolini in *No Pockets,* and partly for the suicidal tendencies of Gloria in *Shoot Horses,* and his name was placed alongside Hemingway and Faulkner in a rather surprising trinity. But certainly the reformer, do-good and Sinclair-Steffens element in McCoy's books predominate over Camus and Sartre. "Do-goodism," aligned with despair was an ailment contracted by many writers who ran full tilt against the 1930 Depression days. (pp. 16-17)

The major thing one can note about McCoy is that he was primarily a Lincoln Steffens in a flamboyant pair of California slacks, sun glasses and a loud sports coat. His basic sermon, both in *Shoot Horses,* and *I Should Have Stayed Home* is that life, also Scott Fitzgerald, is pretty much rigged for the rich; that fickle fate smiles upon the "lucky ones"—others might just as well shoot themselves, that Central Casting, and Fate's great Central Casting in the sky is whimsical, and movie magazine editors who inspire young squirts from Ohio to hitch-hike to Sunset Boulevard to try their luck in a very hard and exacting profession, are guilty of murder, at least in the second degree.

Mona, one of the main characters in *I Should Have Stayed Home,* dramatically throws a number of lurid movie magazines over the dead body of Dorothy, the film-struck kid who commits suicide—suicide being a major *leit motif* in almost all of McCoy. And Mona, who is only another cynical Gloria of *Shoot Horses,* might just as well have strewn the *Reader's*

*Digest,* and similar success-tale oriented periodicals and books on Dorothy's bier. For we all, McCoy insists, have been oversold on some Dale Carnegie or Ben Franklin success pitch, and we all should stay home in our little Kansas town and take a job delivering milk—unless, of course, we are prepared to compromise drastically with our ideals. Such compromise in a McCoy novel usually means sleeping with an aged nympho if we are male, or a corrupt dance hall manager, if we are female, or like Dolan in *No Pockets,* take a bullet in the brain. (p. 19)

> L. W. Michaelson, *"They Shoot Writers, Don't They?"* in The English Record, *Vol. XXII, No. 1, October, 1971, pp. 15-19.*

**THOMAS STURAK** (essay date 1972)

[*In the following excerpt, Sturak examines McCoy's development as a short story writer, traced primarily through numerous letters from* Black Mask *editor Joseph T. Shaw.*]

It would be impossible to track down all the stories that Horace McCoy may have sold to pulp magazines during the Twenties and Thirties. From the time he quit work on a Dallas newspaper in the fall of 1929 until his departure for Hollywood in May 1931, he probably averaged one sale per month, including at least nine to *Black Mask.* He was barely making a living as a writer of fiction. According to a person on the scene in Dallas, McCoy's "greatest creative effort" toward the upkeep of a communal house he shared with six other aspiring writers and artists "was in phoning the editors of *Black Mask* (collect), reeling off the plot of a story, and getting an advance on it."

From its beginnings, *Black Mask* was no run-of-the-mill pulp. Founded in 1920 by H. L. Mencken and George Jean Nathan to help support their financially foundering *Smart Set,* it enjoyed immediate success, with a large circulation, many eminent readers, and wide distribution to newsstands throughout the United States, Canada, and Great Britain. In the early Twenties, *Black Mask* began to publish a few American writers of detective fiction who generated an air of realism through the use of laconic dialogue, literal description of violence, and fast action. By 1923, George W. Sutton, Jr., then editor, had printed stories by Carroll John Daly (whose Race Williams is the progenitor of all "hard-boiled" detectives) and Dashiell Hammett.

But it was under the editorship of Joseph Thompson Shaw (1926-1936) that the *Black Mask* attained the distinction and force that affected American letters. For veteran pulp writers, to speak of *Black Mask* is still to speak of Joe Shaw. The magazine under Captain Shaw (as he was familiarly known) was the major force that made the modern detective story universally popular. Its influence extended even further. As Ernest Borneman has pointed out, the *Black Mask* not only was the training ground for such writers as Hammett and Chandler, but also "contributed to the development of what Mencken called 'the American language'—a prose style which, by transcending the limits of the crime story, has become part and parcel of the serious American novel."

Although this language—the "hard, brittle style" that Chandler said belonged to everybody and to no one—was the most widely imitated characteristic of the *Black Mask* "formula," it was not its essential constituent (for example, the differences among the writing styles of, say, Chandler, Gardner, Hammett, and McCoy are apparent). The critical qualities were of intention and emphasis; and herein the *Black Mask* writers anticipated the existential trend of serious twentieth-century fiction.

"We held that action is meaningless unless it involves recognizable character in three-dimensional form," Shaw later wrote (*The Hard-Boiled Omnibus,* 1946), summarizing his editorial manifesto of June 1927. Out of the pages of his magazine evolved a detective story radically different in tone and intent from what he called "the old, wornout formula sort of gruesome-murder-and-clever-solution" deductive type (stemming from Poe) "lacking human emotional values." *Black Mask* emphasized "character and the problems inherent in human behavior over crime solution. . . . Character conflict is the main theme; the ensuing crime, or the threat, is incidental." This tenet was the core of the editorial policy during McCoy's fitful seven-year relationship with Shaw and the *Black Mask.*

As the story goes, McCoy quit the *Dallas Journal* the day in September 1929 that he received a check from *Black Mask* for 600 or 650 dollars. This money probably was payment for the story **"Dirty Work"** (published in September) and an advance on one, or perhaps both, of his next two "novelettes," **"Hell's Stepsons"** (October) and **"Renegades of the Rio"** (December). Though McCoy had published nothing in *Black Mask* since December 1927 (**"The Devil Man,"** a bizarre tale of the tropics, apparently his first sale to Shaw), and only a few stories to other magazines in the interim, he may have received as much as three cents a word (*Black Mask's* standard rate to established authors, according to Erle Stanley Gardner). Like most of the better pulps, *Black Mask* paid on acceptance; and by the end of the year, McCoy had received checks for four more stories that appeared the following January, March, July, and August. Another accepted story, not published until the December 1930 issue, made his first year as a *Black Mask* regular his best. Sometime during the winter of 1929-1930, he visited New York and met Shaw at a get-together of *Black Mask* writers.

Between September 1929 and October 1934, Shaw published at least 16 stories by McCoy. All but two feature the heroics of one Captain Jerry Frost, a flying Texas Ranger who is also something of a detective. Embodying traits of both the romantic paragons of popular Western fiction and the mechanical supermen of air-war stories, Jerry Frost quickly attracted a loyal following of readers and eventually took his place in the pantheon of favorite *Black Mask* characters. (pp. 139-41)

Shaw launched McCoy (and Frost) off to a flying start by running **"Dirty Work"** as the second story in the September issue, following the opening installment of Hammett's *The Maltese Falcon.* The next title, **"Hell's Stepsons,"** and McCoy's name emblazoned the October cover, a dramatic vignette painting of an aviator, his levelled revolver held chest-high, standing before an airplane. **"Renegades of the Rio"** led off the December number, ahead of the third part of *The Maltese Falcon* and stories by regulars Raoul Whitfield and Erle Stanley Gardner.

Considered among the general run of stories published in *Black Mask,* McCoy's show defensible merit. Except for Hammett's work and, later, Chandler's, his pieces are on a par with the productions of other regular contributors such as Daly, Whitfield, Gardner, Frederick Nebel, and Nels Leroy Jorgensen. Indeed, in sheer expertise and versatility, McCoy was superior to most. He knew his locale (the Texas border country), and enough about flying and air warfare from first-hand World War I experience to satisfy the demands of accuracy in detail and plausibility of action so sacred to pulp-story fans. For example, Frost, engaged in a dogfight, can't hear his guns over the roar of the motor and the scream of the wind in the strut-wires, "but he saw the crank arms jumping and he knew they were working." Too frequently, however, passages are marred by clichés and abstract commentary:

> [Frost] held his dive until within five hundred feet and slowly pulled it up, leveled off and went into a climb. He looked down. The troops were scattered. Some of them were flat on their backs beside the road, with their rifles trained on him. He saw one or two puffs of smoke and laughed. Then he rolled over and dived again. He held his fire a long time, then he saw them fall like ten pins. It was ludicrous. He could not conceive a lone pilot wreaking so much havoc. It bordered on the ruthless. But it was a ruthless land. One man's life was no safer than his neighbor's.

The last five sentences intrude and violate what Chandler years later called "the demand for constant action" in such stories. A more careful workman—or a more ruthless editor—would have cut them. However, this particular story, **"The Trail to the Tropics,"** though not published until March 1932, was in fact the first Jerry Frost tale McCoy had written. Shaw had bought it in 1929, perhaps among a batch of manuscripts, but had held back its publication. Later he returned the manuscript, suggesting: "there is such an excellent bit of characterization in that fat president . . . that I am hoping it can be saved." From the start, Shaw was attracted to McCoy's work by the range and variety of characterizations and incidents.

Two of McCoy's early stories, **"Dirty Work"** and a subsequent Frost adventure, **"The Little Black Book"** (January 1930), were ranked in the *O. Henry Memorial Award Prize Stories of 1930*. Only one other *Black Mask* author (Reynard Lester) was so honored in the listing of 1300-odd stories selected from among 97 magazines. At this distance, it is difficult to appreciate the appeal that McCoy's two stories may have had for a critical reader, especially in the case of **"Dirty Work."** **"The Little Black Book"** is the better piece, full of fast action, ironic incident, and lively characterizations.

**"The Little Black Book"** concerns an "open city" run by a Little Caesar named Flash Singleton who has the chief of police under his thumb. All alone, Capt. Jerry Frost of the Texas Air Patrol comes to town to evict the thugs. They don't scare, but attempt to machine-gun Frost down from a bulletproof limousine. Frost calls for Hell's Stepsons, who move in on Singleton's headquarters, a nightclub named El Algeria (complete with a concealed, steel-walled strongroom), and shoot it out with the gangsters. One of the henchmen is killed and Frost takes a black notebook from the body. In the confusion, Singleton slips out and escapes to a hidden plane. An air chase culminates in a dogfight, Frost riddling the gangster's aircraft and forcing it to land. Singleton has been mortally wounded; but, before dying, he pleads with Frost to destroy the little black book, with its information about an international smuggling ring. Frost, of course, keeps the book, which promises to lead to something big (and to another story). The cast of characters in this story also includes one honest cop, a crooked police commissioner, a rival mobster (named Vito Petrone), a brash young newspaper reporter behind hornrims, and Singleton's two lieutenants—a slender and wiry Sicilian who can handle a knife, and a square-faced, broad-shouldered "chopper" expert.

Except for the air action, this is surely the synopsis of a thousand-and-one gangster epics; an apparent *tour de force* by a Cliché Master of "hard-boiled" fiction. We should remember, however, that when this story appeared, Dashiell Hammett's first two novels had been in hardcovers only a matter of months, and Sam Spade was known only to readers of *Black Mask*. (The final installment of *The Maltese Falcon* appeared in the same issue with **"The Little Black Book."**) Also, the realistic gangster films of the Thirties were still around the corner. McCoy's subject matter was topical and the treatment still fresh. . . . McCoy was in the right place at the right time with the right goods.

Late in December 1929, Shaw wrote that he was "getting lots of favorable" comments on McCoy's work and that "one of the best" had recently come from Eltinge F. Warner, *Black Mask*'s publisher. This fact may have accounted for Shaw's continuing professional patience with these often carelessly written and uneven stories—though he himself was unquestionably McCoy's most loyal champion. In 1933, Shaw wrote to McCoy: "From way back, long before you created Jerry Frost, I always thought you had the promise of doing things in writing, and I still believe it." Moreover, he fully appreciated what he called Jerry Frost's "popular points": "his manhood and the romantic (not love) and glamorous atmosphere that always surrounded him. He was the sort of . . . man in fiction which most readers would like to be in real life." But in a curious way, Jerry Frost often seems too much like most real-life readers—or, at least, like Horace McCoy—contradictory and inconsistent. Already, McCoy's pulp fiction reflected not only the conflicting interests of his everyday life, but the emotional self-division that was at once the source, subject, and undoing of his creative imagination.

If not schizophrenic, Jerry Frost is at least two characters in search of harmonious identity. When we first meet him, he comes walking through the rotunda of the Texas State Capitol and "into the deep-toned offices of the Adjutant-General," reflecting upon the reason for his summons: "Hell, of course he knew. What did trips to this office usually mean? Dirty work—that's what. . . . He just didn't have any illusions about the romance of criminal work. That was a lot of applesauce that looked good in print and nowhere else." A recognizable type of "hard-boiled" hero. Then McCoy gives us Frost's background: "won his wings . . . in the old Lafayette Escadrille"; did a "hitch with the Kosciusko Squadron in Poland"; spent "four years down in the Guatemalan banana country"; known throughout Latin America as El Beneficio, "a bold, roistering Americano who could handle women and a machine-gun like nobody's business." We sigh—McCoy seems to be writing out his fond boyhood memories of Richard Harding Davis and Jack Harkaway. In a letter to McCoy about another early Frost story, Shaw pointedly criticized such authorial paeans to the hero: "I think we discussed this before and my impression is that you agreed that it would give a stronger punch to a character to have his strength brought out by his acts rather than by the writer's statement."

Happily, Frost on foot does act and think realistically, showing at times flashes of that "sardonic dandyism which was," as veteran pulp writer Bill Brandon noted, "a *Black Mask* trade mark." For example, later in the course of his dirty work, Frost finds the Adjutant-General "in another rage," and remarks to himself, "this was getting to be the best thing the Adjutant-General did." But once aloft, Captain Frost comes on like a Galahad of the Planes: "Had it come to the point where there was as much evil in the air as on the ground? God forbid. The air was the last outpost of chivalry. Of romance. It was dead as hell everywhere else." Such careless writing suggests that McCoy wasn't paying attention. (pp. 141-46)

Frost, we are told, "hadn't a lot of imagination"; nor was he a scientist or criminologist or even, "in the technical sense of the word, a detective at all. But he had a fair amount of luck,... was perfectly willing to work hard, and he knew his intuition had stood him in good stead before." Thus McCoy answers Shaw's continual demands for logical plot development. Frost frequently "has a hunch" that just as frequently solves a case or saves his life. Or, if there's time, he may sleep on it all night—or try to: "Writing people and artists know how that is. You can't tear those things out of you. They weigh you down like an anvil. Sometimes you can't breathe comfortably. You think of it for hours and then very suddenly it comes, clear and clean, like big hand-writing. All you have to do then is sit down and copy it." Not the kind of fast action one might expect in a *Black Mask* story, though it perhaps tells us something about McCoy's writing habits.

McCoy, however, seems to have spent few sleepless nights waiting for his pulp stories to come clear and clean. According to a Dallas crony, he wrote them "at night or in the mornings and was evidently a fast worker" who never did "much re-writing or polishing." No one knew this better than Editor Shaw. With characteristic tact, he wrote to McCoy in 1930: "You know, I have an idea that you write so easily and fluently that you are apt to give less thought to the logic of the plot and action than the man who does not write so well." (pp. 146-47)

[In] 1929 and 1930 it is understandable that McCoy, in the midst of a *New Yorker*ish venture editing a short-lived slick called *The Dallasite* and living among six young men pursuing art, would not have taken very seriously his *Black Mask* stories or Shaw's repeated admonition that his "greatest handicap" was possibly "the ease and fluency" with which he wrote. He submitted manuscripts that were little better than rough first-drafts. Shaw invariably returned these with suggestions, often detailed, for changes. Typically, he found no fault with the "excellent writing style"; but there usually was "a little some-thing wrong with a point of the story that is rather vital"—"unfortunate details" or a "slip in the structural workout." The story would be accepted, and perhaps a check sent—along with "a list of queries" for McCoy "to look at" and to think about.

McCoy thought little beyond the level of "your suggestion is my command," and would quickly return an altered manuscript without argument. The editing process might still continue. Concerning a second draft of **"Frost Rides Alone"** (March 1930), Shaw wrote that he thought the story "immeasurably improved," stating his "pleasure and appreciation for the man-ner" in which McCoy "took the criticism": "You understood perfectly my purpose in sending it to you and I think that means a lot." A check was promised (and sent the next day), but Shaw added, almost as if by second thought: "Before sending this to the press, I should like your further thought on several points which should be cleared up to round out your excellent revision." These points amounted to some dozen specific "lit-tle obstacles" (listed by page and line numbers) that required another full typewritten page to outline. Two weeks later a check went out to McCoy "for the extra wordage brought about by the revision."

Shaw might be so charmed by "sweet writing" or by a story that ran "so smoothly" that it tended to make him "forget—

but not quite—our purpose of sticking to the plausible." "It is not that I like continually to ask you for changes," he wrote McCoy, "but I do hate to see a potentially effective story weakened by part of its action which is bound to strain the credulity of a whole lot of its readers. Particularly, if it can just as well be done otherwise." His standard of craftsmanship was "Dash Hammett . . . one of the most careful and pain-staking workmen I have ever known." McCoy, on the other hand, was known in these days for his "nervous nature" and impulsiveness, and "seemed to be taking his local career"—including *Black Mask* publication—"with a grain of salt, pend-ing the big break." In January 1930, Shaw, in reply to an inquiry from McCoy, explained that the magazine purchased only first serial rights, adding: "I am very much interested in the leads you have from the movie people and sincerely hope that you may place some of these stories with them."

By February 1930, after five stories, McCoy seems to have wanted to get rid of Captain Frost and his Flying Texas Rang-ers, perhaps to concentrate on detective tales. Shaw hedged on the question (at least eight more Frost stories were published), but because of McCoy's demonstrated "wide versatility," left the door open for "any stories of the so-called detective va-riety" that he might create. By summertime, McCoy had been seriously ill. Then, early in August, Shaw rejected a story, despite "the excellence of the writing," because of "its sim-ilarity with the preceding yarns, especially in basic plot."

This outright rejection, his first in almost a year, threw McCoy into a month-long funk. By the end of September, however, he was back with another manuscript—and more complaints, apparently, of "another run of hard luck." Shaw could proffer only some fatherly advice about "sacrifices" contributing "di-rectly to the strength" of a writer's work (alluding to Ham-mett's tuberculosis and debts), and of the value in maintaining "an unshakeable sense of humor—a rare and mighty gift."

In this same letter, Shaw explained that he had delayed re-porting on McCoy's latest manuscript because "if I had been obliged to pass on it immediately, I would have undoubtedly returned it at once because of conditions not directly affecting the merit of this story. As you undoubtedly know, the whole magazine field has experienced during the past months one of the very worst situations in its whole history." *Black Mask* was beginning to feel the Great Depression, which Shaw grandly euphemized as "the universal retrenchment." The magazine's new policy was "to draw on the surplus rather than to acquire stories of a similar type that could not find place for months to come."

Shaw read McCoy's next offering "with vivid interest in your work and your situation at this time." Despite "some splendid writing," however, the story relied excessively on "a fabulous eventuality" too reminiscent of "the Falcon of Malta." He prophesied that such "extraordinary and unexpected turns,... when bound to reasonable lines," would make a name for McCoy. Shaw felt that the answer to McCoy's problem lay in doing all the writing his situation would permit. "General conditions," he summarized, were "so adverse" and had "got-ten so near to the bottom that there seems only one way in which they can move." For McCoy, they seemed to move only downhill. In a letter dated 27 December 1930, Shaw rejected two manuscripts at once—both "good jobs of their type," but not "one we are playing at the present time."

McCoy took the hint and began to concentrate on the less fastidious—and less profitable—"pulpwood factories."...

Unlike Shaw, other pulpwood editors worked on a laconic, strictly business, accept-or-reject basis—and paid on publication. (pp. 148-50)

Editors responded to his obvious talents, especially in creating interesting characters and lively incidents, but consistently urged him to submit shorter tales, in the 5000-to-6500-word range. His air stories, in particular, were in demand. *Black Mask,* too, Shaw wrote, was now "concentrating on tales packed with H. E. [high explosives] and short on trimmings, emphasizing economy of expression and swift story telling." In January 1931, he rejected another manuscript as too lengthy for *Black Mask,* but thought that it would sell elsewhere "very readily." McCoy, however, succeeded in "doing wonders" with cutting the story, **"The Mopper Up,"** and Shaw bought it the next month.

Not published until November 1931, **"The Mopper Up"** is one of McCoy's better *Black Mask* efforts. A "complete novelette" (i.e., approximately 9500 words) about the cleansing of a corrupt boom town by a lone Texas Ranger, it was his first break away from the Jerry Frost series. Shaw was taken with the story's impressionistic opening and what he called its "word pictures"; but he realized that the trend in pulps toward shorter stories packed with action was antithetical to McCoy's creative temperament. McCoy himself wanted "to get out a book"; and in February 1931, Shaw suggested that perhaps a number of Jerry Frost stories could be put together "into a straight novel." McCoy apparently thought little of this idea; at any rate, he left Captain Frost up in the air and took himself by automobile to Hollywood. (pp. 150-51)

Typescripts survive of a half-dozen stories written by McCoy after his arrival in California, bearing such titles as "Murder by the Master" and "Death in Hollywood." The latter story directly alludes to Hammett; and, with one exception, all these tales feature a sort of Continental Op in Movieland. Hammett was currently drawing top money at the studios, and McCoy may have been directly inspired by his ex-*Black Mask* colleague's success. A few of these typescripts are carbon copies, but there is no other evidence to suggest that any were published—though most are better-than-average compositions in the by-then crystallized "hard-boiled" manner. One 15,000 word "novelette" called "Murder is Murder" is a remarkable example of its type—carefully constructed and well written in a clean, terse style. But its moments of eroticism and lack of violence (traits common to several of these stories) may have kept it out of the pulps. No matter how good their craftsmanship, however, these stories are obviously imitative; and their narrow range of subject matter seems inimical to the expansiveness of McCoy's creative imagination.

By 1933, McCoy was writing dialogue for Columbia Pictures and at the same time desultorily working at his pulp stories. His New York agent was urging him to fulfill earlier promises, as many new magazines were appearing and the demands for good short-short material were great. No doubt depressed at the state of things in general and his progress as a writer in particular, McCoy turned again to Shaw as a sounding board for his complaints. To his credit, the latter pointed out the obvious in his reply: If McCoy "would take and keep the proper mental attitude towards writing, and would . . . settle down to the inevitable hard work of it," he would be "right alongside" the likes of Frederick Nebel, Raoul Whitfield, and Dashiell Hammett. "It's funny," Shaw went on, "every time I start to write to you I seem unconsciously to fall into the attitude of urging you on, of bolstering up your belief in yourself. . . . I

shouldn't do that, but I should like to see another Jerry Frost and observe from that what you are doing in the writing game today."

McCoy apparently had higher flights in mind than another Jerry Frost story, and did not respond. Early in November 1933, to his congratulations on McCoy's second marriage, Shaw postscripted another teaser for a Frost story. McCoy must have graciously demurred, for a few days later Shaw again wrote: "The other fellows are going ahead fast and there is no reason in the world why you shouldn't be right along with them, and even although you have been working in another medium in the interim I have an idea that you will find you have not lost a single trick in the trade, but on the other side may have acquired a new and even more effective technique." At last, in January 1934, after several more entreaties, McCoy delivered up the manuscript of **"Flight at Sunrise."**

Shaw telegraphed receipt of the story, and four days later wired again: "JERRY OFF TO PRETTY GOOD START." Within another four days, he had sent a check, along with a left-handed compliment: "I observe . . . some of your old touches and although it is not all the story I should like, I feel that it establishes the ground work . . . from which you can start a new series, bringing in all of Jerry Frost's old dynamic character." Some of the old McCoy touches are exactly what obstruct the story's action and corrupt Frost's old dynamism: allusions to Rupert Brooke's poetry; Frost conversationally remarking, *"Honor virtutis praemium";* a "soft and mellifluous" whistle sounds in the distance and "Frost irrelevantly wondered if that train went to New York, thinking if it did he'd like to be on it." In the story's violent climax, Frost, escaping from a burning house, comes upon a "mortally wounded" criminal he himself had shot down a short while before:

> A tongue of fire reached out every second or so and touched his hair, almost playfully. The man was dying; he couldn't move his arms or legs; but his brain was clear and alert and he knew what was happening. His mouth kept opening and closing like a fish's, saying nothing; but his eyes were eloquent, pleading that he be permitted to die in a manner befitting a human being.

Frost goes back to get him.

Shaw had a "hunch," he wrote optimistically, that the next Jerry Frost story would "be back in full swing." But in March 1934, after reading the manuscript of **"Somebody Must Die,"** he wrote McCoy that "frankly," it was "not as good a story" as **"Flight at Sunrise."** The writing, as usual, he found "pretty swell." It was "the story itself"—the action and, as often before, the structure—that bothered him, and he just didn't "know what to do about it." He honestly felt, he wrote, that publishing this story would "not reflect the greatest credit" on McCoy, who he hoped was doing another. In the meanwhile, he would hold this one—which he did until June, when, in order "to put a bit of dynamite" under McCoy and to rid his mind "of any reluctance" to turn out "a great Jerry Frost story," he mailed a check for **"Somebody Must Die."** He reiterated that this piece contained much good writing. "In fact, I think one of the criticisms that might be made against it from our angle is that in parts it runs to almost too fine writing. I don't like to use the word 'arty,' but in certain passages it has a bit of that suggestion." This sort of thing, of course, would "have to be changed," he added, "delicately, but at least to rid the readers of any impression that it attempts to be over their heads. Readers of this type are finicky." Also, the story would "have to be smoothed out a bit to care for some pretty radical sudden [Shaw had crossed out "stunt"] changes and jumps."

These same criticisms might have been made with equal justice against "The Devil Man" in 1927 and, as we have seen, against other of McCoy's *Black Mask* stories. Shaw had not been blind, but he had been indulgent—perhaps as much to his own tastes as to McCoy's wayward talents. In 1934, however, the economics of publishing a magazine that depended greatly on newsstand sales could no longer underwrite indulgence or nonconformity. In July, Shaw wrote McCoy: "So far as our present needs are concerned, don't be in a hurry for the next Frost. As a matter of fact, I am pretty well filled up through November and, outside of the general run of stories along our regular line, I'm making a few small experiments in hopes of gauging a new trend." **"Somebody Must Die"** was finally published in October 1934, and the title turned out to be unusually apt: this was Jerry Frost's—and Horace McCoy's—last appearance in *Black Mask*.

Captain Shaw himself in an editorial of December 1932 had honored McCoy as "one of the older writers who helped establish the *Black Mask* standard." Despite these kind words and the implied association with the likes of Hammett, the truth is that McCoy's contributions are for the most part interesting for their violations of the *Black Mask* manifesto that demanded character in constant action. "If you stopped to think," Chandler recalled, "you were lost. When in doubt have a man come through a door with a gun in his hand" ("The Simple Art of Murder"). Compared with stories by such writers as Daly, Whitfield, Jorgensen, Nebel, and Gardner, even the Jerry Frost tales were not always in the "regular line" of *Black Mask* offerings.

McCoy too often has his heroes stopping to muse on a situation or action. Extraneous descriptive passages frequently intrude. There are tendencies toward stylistic impressionism and lyricism; interests in social and human concerns beyond the demands of casting characters in action; proclivities toward "psychologizing," the grotesque, and the occult. Too often in these stories McCoy commits the unpardonable artistic sin for any writer of fiction: he fails to maintain a consistent tone. Not that such intrusions dominated his pulp stories, or that other *Black Mask* writers were never guilty of similar breaches of convention and decorum. But whereas the most successful craftsmen in this field (for example, Hammett or Chandler) subtly reshaped the mould and impressed on it their stylistic hallmarks, McCoy only succeeded in breaking the pattern. The force and range of his intellectual interests and emotional drives increasingly demanded and received more space. No wonder that his last *Black Mask* story, **"Somebody Must Die,"** is the most ambitious and the least disciplined.

In spite of Shaw's criticisms of this story, it stands up as one of McCoy's best in *Black Mask*. It reveals, as do most of its predecessors, a gradual overall improvement in style and structure. At the same time, the main narrative action is frequently short-circuited by such intrusions as an aerial panorama of Northern Mexico, some satire of Babbittry, a mild romantic note (a first for the hitherto chaste Captain Frost), and the portrait of a curious nonfunctional criminal character who sports an M.A. and Phi Beta Kappa key from M.I.T. [The critic adds in a footnote that this character "would reappear nearly fifteen years later, fully developed, as the protagonist of McCoy's fourth novel, *Kiss Tomorrow Good-bye.*"] These irrelevant and unintegrated intrusions keep what is otherwise the best of McCoy's *Black Mask* efforts (at least in the Frost series) from being what Shaw liked to call good "rough paper" stuff: an action-packed story about a hard man doing hard, dangerous work, who with gun in hand is never at a loss to kick open a closed door.

Somebody must and almost always does die in a *Black Mask* story, sometimes damn near everybody—except, of course, the hero. . . . The dark and sinister world of Sam Spade and Philip Marlowe and Jerry Frost is one of violence and terror and death. The only "philosophical" problem faced by the hero is that of existence—which he is rarely given time to think about. He is first and last a man of action kept busy at staying alive in a ruthless world. As Frost is made to say while strafing enemy troops during the course of his first adventure, "One man's life was no safer than his neighbor's."

The imagination of the Twenties, says Leslie Fiedler [in *Not In Thunder*], lived off the remembered feast of world-war terror, "as well as the mythology of murder and nighttime pursuit bred by Prohibition"; and that of the Thirties "subsisted in the social violence always present in our life but exacerbated by the Great Depression." Despite their stylistic excesses and limitations in subject matter, the stories published in *Black Mask*, though often derided as a subliterary form of "inverted romanticism," embody a world-view that is close to the social realities of the modern scene and to the psychological causes of the modern distemper.

Moreover, these "hard-boiled" fables often contain poignant moments of non-violence, which W. H. Auden, for example, found captivating in Chandler's writings. Memorable incidents involving what Ernest Borneman has called "the nameless melancholy of the man of action who sees the shadow of thought on the wall." Such a moment occurs in the concluding scene of **"Somebody Must Die"**: "A crash of thunder rocked the world. Frost pushed up the window, thinking what an ugly thing physical violence was. The rain beat against his face, wetting his shirt."

These words are the last of Horace McCoy's ever printed in *Black Mask;* and when we look to his first novel, **They Shoot Horses, Don't They?,** already written and soon to be published, it is tempting to read into them an "intentional fallacy" to explain the qualitative disparity between the pulp stories and the book—to suggest, in effect, that the latter is superior because it is built around the idea of *why* somebody must die, whereas in the stories the main concern was with the plotting of *how* and *when* somebody must die. But intention—"the total conscious and unconscious experience during the prolonged time of creation" [René Wellek and Austin Warren, *Theory of Literature*]—is something we can never know. What we *do* know is that (despite its title) **They Shoot Horses, Don't They?** is not a "hard-boiled" detective novel. Nor is it remotely like any pulp story McCoy ever wrote. Unlike Hammett and Whitfield and Chandler and almost every other writer of the *Black Mask* "school" who "graduated" to hardcovers, McCoy did so extracurricularly. He applied the critical lessons learned under Captain Shaw to original themes and novel techniques beyond the range of any popular magazine formula. (pp. 151-56)

> *Thomas Sturak, "Horace McCoy, Captain Shaw, and the 'Black Mask'," in* The Mystery and Detection Annual, *1972, pp. 139-58.*

### MARK ROYDEN WINCHELL   (essay date 1982)

*[Winchell is an American educator and critic. In the following excerpt, he discusses some of the major themes of* They Shoot

Horses, Don't They? *and offers extensive comparison between the novel and the short story on which it was based.*]

**They Shoot Horses, Don't They?** is undoubtedly Horace McCoy's greatest and most famous novel. Never again was he able to achieve the tone of authenticity and the power of the metaphor which pervade this minor masterpiece. Like so many brilliant first novels, it was a promise never redeemed. . . . [McCoy] will finally be remembered—if at all—for this one work. . . . (p. 35)

What little critical attention this novel has received has tended to focus on its existentialist overtones. For example, Lee J. Richmond argues that "With the exception of Nathanael West's *Miss Lonelyhearts* and *The Day of the Locust,* McCoy's novel is indisputably the best example of absurdist existentialism in American fiction" [see excerpt dated 1971]. Also, it is clear that McCoy relished his reputation among continental intellectuals and probably altered the style of his last two novels in order to fit the role assigned to him as "the first American existentialist" [see Sturak excerpt dated 1968].

It is just as clear, however, that McCoy was not a conscious philosopher in the mold of Sartre and Camus. Instead, he was an artist who imaginatively anticipated many of the perceptions which would later become central to the existentialist worldview. Thus, existentialism can provide a useful, but limited, perspective from which to examine **They Shoot Horses, Don't They?**. Indeed, the very limitations of an existentialist critique bring into focus the critical problems which must be solved if we are to attain a full understanding of McCoy's novel.

The dance marathon is obviously meant to be more than just a grisly reminder of the historical period in which this story transpires. McCoy clearly did not intend to write a mere period-piece. In fact, we find that in the finished version of the novel, he has eliminated a number of the socio-economic allusions which appeared in an earlier short story on which the novel was based.

For example, in the short story, when Robert first meets Gloria, he asks her whether she wants to go to a movie or sit in the park. When she indicates that she would prefer the latter, he tells us that he is glad, "because I could live for three or four days on what two movie tickets cost." In the novel, we find no reference to the cost of movie tickets, only the assertion that "it was always nice in the park."

A bit later in the short story, Gloria learns of Robert's ambition to become a movie director. When she asks him what kind of pictures he would make, he tells her, "Pictures about people like us. People who live in dark little rooms and work in factories." And when he decides to enter the marathon, Robert leaves his few possessions and extra clothing with his landlady: "until I could pay her all I owed her," he says. "She wasn't happy about it, but what else could she do?" The novel, however, contains neither the exchange with Gloria nor the reference to Robert's landlady.

Since **They Shoot Horses**—in its various revisions—became less identifiably the product of a particular historical situation, McCoy apparently wished to address himself to a universal human condition. The dance marathon is a sort of organic metaphor which movingly depicts the folly of all human endeavor when measured against the inexorable forces of time and mutability. (pp. 36-8)

Incapable of altering the circumstances of his life, the existential victim can nevertheless act purposefully by courting the annihilation of that life. For this reason, the significance of death is a primary concern of existentialism. The heroic existentialist believes that one knows the value of life only by risking death; while those who have despaired of finding meaning anywhere in life see suicide as the ultimate act of freedom. The Hemingway code hero falls into the former category; Gloria Beatty (and perhaps Hemingway himself) into the latter.

Unlike Nathanael West's Faye Greener, Gloria is too defeated and cynical to be a Hollywood coquette. Instead, she articulates an explicitly perverse view of romance and sexuality. During her first encounter with Robert, Gloria remarks: "I don't know whether the men stars can help me as much as the women stars. From what I've seen lately I've about made up my mind that I've been letting the wrong sex try to make me." Later in the same conversation, she describes her former liaison with a Syrian hot dog vendor:

> "He chewed tobacco all the time. . . . Have you ever been in bed with a man who chewed tobacco?" (ellipsis in text)

. . . . .

> "I guess I might even have stood that," she said, "but when he wanted to make me between customers, on the kitchen table, I gave up. A couple of nights later I took poison."

In the midst of the marathon, however, Gloria is not above spending her ten-minute rest periods copulating with the master of ceremonies under the bandstand.

For Gloria, economic considerations take precedence over humanistic ones. Just as she entertains a relatively debased view of sexuality, so too does she see fertility as a curse rather than a blessing. Early in the novel, she advises a pregnant dance contestant to have an abortion. "What's the sense of having a baby," Gloria says, "unless you got dough enough to take care of it?" Although one might argue that Gloria is simply being realistic, she seems to raise the death-wish to the level of a metaphysical principle.

As is the case with normal sexuality, religious faith is also among those traditional forms of meaning which have been corrupted in the meretricious ambience depicted in the Hollywood novel. Such a corruption is evident in the tawdry funeral rituals of Evelyn Waugh's *The Loved One* and in the proliferation of exotic cults described in West's *The Day of the Locust.* But few displays of bogus religiosity can compare with the marriage of Vee Lovell and Mary Hawley in **They Shoot Horses, Don't They?**

Far from being whimsical matchmakers, the promoters of the marathon are hard-headed businessmen. When one of them approaches Robert and Gloria with the idea of a public wedding, he says: "you can get divorced if you want to. It don't have to be permanent. It's just a showmanship angle." Although Gloria balks at the plan, Couple 71 (Vee and Mary) are persuaded to go along with it. And so a wedding takes place—complete with flowers, ushers, bridesmaids, and a minister named Oscar Gilder. In the chaotic, inverted world of McCoy's novel, it is ironically fitting that the Reverend Gilder's benediction be the twenty-third Psalm.

Curiously enough, Gloria is no atheist; however, the God in whom she believes is no benevolent deity. Instead, He is the force responsible for the world's being the way it is. About midway through the novel, Gloria says: "I wish God would strike me dead"; and when she entreats Robert to shoot her, she tells him to "pinch-hit for God." Here, one is reminded of Gloucester's declaration in *King Lear:* "As flies to wanton boys, are we to th' gods, / They kill us for their sport."

Albert Camus once characterized suicide as being the "one truly serious philosophical problem." For him, "judging whether life is or is not worth living amounts to answering the fundamental question of philosophy" (*The Myth of Sisyphus*). When Gloria answers that question in the negative, her decision is a conscious response to the Sisyphean dance of life. And her plight can be adequately understood in existentialist terms.

The case of Robert, however, raises some difficulties. At the beginning of McCoy's novel, Robert is down-and-out but optimistic. He does not share Gloria's nihilistic view of life and it is difficult to find a point in the novel when he consciously adopts her philosophy of defeat. And yet, by killing Gloria he is also turning himself over to the state for execution. To contemplate why Robert does so is to address oneself to a primary critical issue of this novel.

In McCoy's earlier short story, Gloria says to Robert: "Look—you've wanted to kill yourself, you've admitted it. You're just like I am, you haven't got the nerve. All right, you kill me and then the law'll kill you and neither one of us'll kill ourselves." By excluding this passage from the finished version of his novel, McCoy reduces Robert's consciousness of his fate. It seems to me that his virtual suicide is less a deliberate statement about the futility of life than an impulsive response to physical, mental, and even spiritual fatigue. Robert is a rather conventional fellow whose behavior is conditioned largely by external forces. To view his situation in any other light is to see his act of self-destruction as merely gratuitous.

There is another variation between the short story and novelistic versions of *They Shoot Horses* which I think bears on the question of Robert's consciousness. In the short story, Robert observes: "I think that's a lot of applesauce about people changing their destinies. You're put in a rut when you're born and you never get out of it. It's just like a fish. A fish is a fish when he is born and a fish when he dies. He can't make himself into an octopus by thinking hard, can he?" Such a declaration, complete with biological imagery, is clearly naturalistic in implication; however, it is somewhat anomalous for Robert to see his own condition quite so clearly. In a sense, the circumstances of McCoy's novel verify the determinism which his short story more baldly articulates. But in the novel, we do not encounter the contradiction of a character who *decides* that his fate is determined.

Though never explicitly discussed, the pall of determinism hangs very heavily over *They Shoot Horses*. The very structure of the novel sacrifices suspense for inevitability. We are apprised of the plot's climax on the first page of the text. What follows is largely explication and elaboration. Also, by rendering the judge's sentence in tabloid print—line-by-line, between each chapter, and increasing incrementally in point size—McCoy underscores the impersonal immensity of those leviathan-like forces which have overwhelmed Robert. Although he is not a victim exclusively of "society," Robert is destroyed by powers just as intractable as those which pronounce legal judgment upon him.

By choosing to tell his story from Robert's point of view, rather than from Gloria's, McCoy has deprived us of access to Gloria's consciousness. To a great extent, her function in the novel is determined by her actions toward Robert. Her attitude toward life and death, then, is simply the most im-

portant of many factors which influence her partner's fate. If Gloria can be viewed as a hard-core existential victim, Robert is just a naive country boy who has come to Hollywood in pursuit of the American Dream.

And it is precisely in this lack of singularity that Robert differs most from an existential figure. The striking surface parallels between Robert's perceptions in court and those of Camus' Meursault . . . serve only to accentuate the crucial difference between these two characters. Meursault is tried less for murder than for eccentricity. Robert, however, is an ordinary individual who finds himself capable of an extraordinary action. In this respect, his situation is quite similar to that of the typical naturalistic protagonist. As Donald Pizer points out, naturalism is "an extension of realism . . . in the sense that both modes often deal with the local and contemporary"; however, the naturalist discovers in the commonplace "the extraordinary and excessive in human nature" (*Realism and Naturalism in Nineteenth-Century American Literature*).

In addition to his economic plight, one of Robert's greatest misfortunes is his inability to maintain any life-giving contact with the natural world. As a boy he had lived in pastoral surroundings on his grandfather's farm in Arkansas. Now he is confined, seemingly in perpetuity, to a dance-hall which epitomizes the worst excesses of a commercial, urban civilization. And yet, he compulsively searches out whatever sunlight becomes visible in that dance-hall, at one point even losing himself in a beautiful sunset.

Later he recalls:

> I lay there, thinking about the sunset, trying to remember what color it was. . . .
>
> Through the legs of my cot I could feel the ocean quivering against the piling below. It rose and fell, rose and fell, went out and came back, went out and came back. . . . (this second ellipsis is in the text)
>
> I was glad when the siren blew, waking us up, calling us back to the floor.

The sun can be seen as a symbol of time, the ocean of eternity. However, in the world of the dance marathon, time and eternity are hideously and frighteningly fused. Days and nights seem meaningless as time is measured in terms of "hours elapsed"; and the endlessness of time means only the endlessness of futile suffering.

Robert Syverton ultimately is done in by an accidental conjunction of circumstances. Although it may appear simplistic to say that he probably would have behaved differently had he had a good night's sleep, a square meal, and the promise of a job, no other explanation is nearly so consistent with the facts of the novel. It is the unconsciously victimized Robert, not the deliberately self-destructive Gloria, whose misery—like a dumb beast's—is terminated before he can realize its full horror. If suicide poses a philosophical problem, then it is one which sometimes is resolved for us. (pp. 38-43)

*Mark Royden Winchell, in his* Horace McCoy, *Boise State University, 1982, 50 p.*

**DAVID FINE** (essay date 1984)

[*Fine is an American educator and critic. In the following excerpt, he examines a "pattern of hope giving way to frustration and violence" in* They Shoot Horses, Don't They? *Unexcerpted por-*

*tions of the essay discuss the same theme in James M. Cain's novel* The Postman Always Rings Twice *(1934).*]

[James M. Cain and Horace McCoy both arrived in Los Angeles] in 1931. Both came from backgrounds in journalism—Cain in Baltimore and New York, where he wrote for such ranking journals as *The American Mercury,* the *Baltimore Sun,* and the *New York World;* and McCoy in Dallas, where in addition to his work as a reporter he acted with the Dallas Little Theatre (hoping, in coming to Hollywood, to break in as an actor as well as a screenwriter).

Neither had yet published a novel, but within a few years of their arrival on the coast each published a short novel that steered Los Angeles fiction onto the path it was to follow in the years ahead. Anticipating Nathanael West's *The Day of the Locust,* Raymond Chandler's *The Big Sleep,* and Aldous Huxley's *After Many a Summer Dies the Swan*—all published in 1939, a kind of *annus mirabilis* in Los Angeles literary production—Cain's *The Postman Always Rings Twice* (1934) and McCoy's *They Shoot Horses, Don't They?* mark the real starting place of the Los Angeles novel, a regional fiction obsessively concerned with puncturing the bloated image of Southern California as the golden land of opportunity and the fresh start. For Cain and McCoy, Southern California was not the place of new beginnings but of disastrous finishes. Dissolution and collapse have been the essential themes of the L.A. novel ever since. (p. 44)

Inevitably, Cain's four L.A. novels, written between 1934 and 1941, just before the heyday of American *film noir* and European new realism, found their way quickly to the screen. Like McCoy, Cain found a more admiring audience in Europe, and the first screen adaptations, significantly, were continental. As early as 1930 *Postman* was the basis for a French film *Le Dernier Tournant* and three years later was the source for Luchino Visconti's first film, *Ossessione,* the progenitor of Italy's neorealist cinema. Hollywood followed the European lead, filming *Double Indemnity* in 1944, *Mildred Pierce* in 1945, and *Postman* in 1946. (pp. 45-6)

So Cain, who came to Los Angeles from the East Coast to write for the movies and remained a studio hack, had the peculiar fate of becoming a writer whose works not written for the screen exist most memorably on the screen. (p. 46)

Some of this same fate is shared by his contemporary Horace McCoy, whose 1935 novel *They Shoot Horses, Don't They?* is known today thanks largely to Sydney Pollack's 1969 screen version. While the popularity—and critical success—of the film may have contributed to some interest in McCoy's novel, it is likely that only a few of the people who saw the film had even heard of the author or the novel. McCoy, who remained in Hollywood for twenty years and contributed to about a hundred films, survives for his American audience chiefly through the movie rendition of his first novel, made fourteen years after his death and thirty-four after its initial publication.

With the almost back-to-back publication of the two novels, the two writers were quickly linked—both to each other and to the new hard-boiled school of fiction that was surfacing on the West Coast. Edmund Wilson included them among his "boys in the back room" in a 1940 group portrait of the West Coast tough-guy writers, wrongly naming Hemingway as their chief source and wrongly describing McCoy as a follower of Cain [see entry in Additional Bibliography]. Although Wilson gave only a few lines to McCoy—an equivocal judgment buried in a paragraph on Cain—it was the Cain linkage, echoed by

other critics, that rankled the author: "I do not care for Cain's work," McCoy wrote, "although there may be much he can teach me. I know this, though—his continued labeling of me as of 'the Cain school' [whatever the hell that is] and I shall slit either his throat or mine." McCoy, in fact, had written the unpublished story upon which his novel would be based as early as 1932 and completed a draft of the novel in 1933, before *Postman* appeared. McCoy's real kinship is with the group associated with *Black Mask,* a mystery tabloid whose contributors included Dashiell Hammett, Raymond Chandler, and Erle Stanley Gardner. Between 1927 and 1934 McCoy published sixteen stories in *Black Mask,* and Captain Joseph Shaw, the journal's editor, named McCoy as among "the older writers who helped establish the *Black Mask* standard."

In fact one writer did not influence the other; rather both began their writing careers at a time when a tough, detached, cynical stance had taken strong hold in American writing. *Black Mask* fiction and the hard-boiled detective novels of Hammett, the proletarian fiction of Mike Gold and others, and Cain's and McCoy's own experience as journalists were certainly influential. So, too, was the new tough attitude emerging in drama and film—in plays like Eugene O'Neill's *The Hairy Ape,* Ben Hecht and Charles MacArthur's *The Front Page,* and Robert Sherwood's *The Petrified Forest;* and, even more significantly, in gangster films, like Mervyn LeRoy's *Little Caesar,* the first talking gangster movie (1930—based on W. R. Burnett's 1929 novel), William Wellman's *The Public Enemy* (1931), and Howard Hawks's *Scarface* (1932). When Cain and McCoy wrote their first novels they were joining what had become by the mid-1930s a clearly established tough-guy tradition in American narrative writing.

The similarities between the two first novels not only make comparison inevitable but throw the very substantial differences into relief. To begin with the similarities, both are stories of collapsed hope—a theme that would preoccupy more than one generation of L.A. novelists. Both focus on the violent shattering of the dreams of a pair of seekers who have come to the West Coast chasing its fabled promise. Like their authors—and about 70 percent of the Southern California population in the 1930s—the protagonists of both books are newcomers. Frank Chambers is a drifter and con man with a criminal trail stretching across the county. Cora Papadakis is an Iowa girl named Smith who came to Hollywood after winning a high school beauty contest and wound up working in a hash house before settling into a dull marriage. The principals in *They Shoot Horses,* Robert Syverten and Gloria Beatty, are migrants from small towns who hope to break into movies as extras. In both works the male has been condemned to execution for the violent death of the female, but the "murder" in each case is conceived ironically—a deed resulting from an act of intended kindness or compassion. Frank is rushing the pregnant Cora to a hospital after a threatened miscarriage when the car hits a culvert wall and she is killed instantly; Robert accedes to Gloria's wish to be dead, expressed again and again in the novel, and puts a bullet in her head, the only way, he realizes, she can be taken out of her unending misery. Both stories, moreover, are told in first-person flashbacks by the condemned males, a confessional narrative stance that has the effect of implicating the reader as confidant and arousing some sympathy for the doomed men.

As narrators the two men are very different. Except for a few lapses into sentimentality which in context are almost comical and plain silly (e.g., "I kissed her. Her eyes were shining up at me like two blue stars. It was like being in church.''), Frank remains tough, detached, and dispassionate. Robert, by contrast, is romantic and naively optimistic. He daydreams about being discovered by a talent scout, becoming a famous director, and driving a fancy car. The tough quality of McCoy's novel derives not from the language and tone of its narrator, but from the unremitting hardness and cynicism of Gloria and the relentless brutality of its subject matter.

There is another significant difference in the way the tales are narrated. Cain's narrator tells his story in straight, unframed chronological flashback; it is only in the last chapter that the death-row perspective of the telling is revealed. McCoy's novel is framed from the beginning by the murder trial—the present tense of the novel. It opens on the judge's words, printed alone on the page in capitals: THE PRISONER WILL STAND. Each of the thirteen chapters or episodes of the narrative is preceded by another fragment of the judge's sentence in increasingly larger type face until the final words of the book, MAY GOD HAVE MERCY ON YOUR SOUL, are printed boldly across the whole page. The chapters themselves, beginning with the third, are reflections, acts of memory by the condemned man as he stands before the judge. The events of the thirty-seven days of the marathon leading up to the killing and arrest are compressed into the moment of actual sentencing. There are also a number of italicized passages throughout the text that signal Robert's present-time reflections interrupting his replaying of the past. The effect is that of overhearing the thoughts of a condemned man, not of being told a story. We read Cain's novel as a series of events leading to a resolution held back from the reader; we read McCoy's with the knowledge that everything has already happened. Sydney Pollack remarked that the structure of *They Shoot Horses* is almost that of ''flashforward,'' an effect he tried to achieve in the film by making the marathon the present and using flashforwards to the trial.

Whatever the narrative differences, however, the novels are structurally alike in their persistent circularity. In McCoy's the circularity is achieved by the back and forth shifts in time and by the endless back and forth movement of the marathon dancers, accompanied by the relentless ebb and flow of the ocean beneath their feet. ''The whole business is a merry-go-round,'' Gloria says at one point. ''When we get out of here we're right back where we started.'' As the lame horse on that merry-go-round, however, Gloria will end not where she started but in her sought after death. (pp. 46-9)

In Horace McCoy's two L.A. novels the women are less destructive than self-destructive. More pessimistic, cynical, and consistently more aware than their male partners, they turn their aggressiveness inward, into suicidal impulses. If Phyllis Nirdlinger [in Cain's *Double Indemnity*] is the deadliest of the females in the period's fiction, Gloria Beatty in *They Shoot Horses, Don't They?* is the most nihilistic, the most death-obsessed. Her thoughts constantly turn on death. Just after meeting Robert Syverten, she says to him: ''Why are all these high-powered scientists always screwing around trying to prolong life instead of finding pleasant ways to end it? There must be a hell of a lot of people in the world like me—who want to die but haven't the guts—.''

Gloria is . . . one of the Hollywood dream chasers, but her past has already molded her in a cynicism that Hollywood can only harden. In Texas she had been the victim of an uncle's sexual advances, lived miserably with a number of men, and attempted suicide. Recovering from the effects of poison in a hospital, she began reading movie magazines—another source of infec-

tion—and migrated to Hollywood in a desperate last gesture. Although the narrative comes to us through the courtroom reflections of Robert, Gloria's vision dominates the novel and determines its outcome. It is a nihilistic vision; nothing matters, nothing is immoral, nothing meaningful. Lee Richmond, one of the novel's recent critics, remarked that with the exceptions of West's *Miss Lonelyhearts* and *The Day of the Locust* McCoy's novel is ''indisputably the best example of absurdist existentialism in American fiction,'' anticipating Sartre's *La Nausée* (1938) and Camus' *L'Etranger* (1942) in France [see excerpt dated 1971]. Indeed, as Richmond documents, the novel was wisely discussed in France, and McCoy's name was linked with Hemingway's and Faulkner's on the continent in the late thirties and early forties.

The contrast between Robert and Gloria is that between traditional native optimism and absurd existential awareness. Robert brings to the West Coast an innocent hopefulness, a literal belief in the Gospel of Hollywood; and she the debilitating awareness that the world doesn't square with hopes, logic, or conventional morality. Like the other participants, they join the dance marathon for the meals and lodging, the possibility of prize money, and the hope (which Gloria sees as a ruse) of being discovered by a producer. The cumulative exhaustion has the effect, though, in Robert's case of subverting a too-easily-held optimism, and in Gloria's of corroborating and intensifying her death wish. When Robert, ''out there on the black night on the edge of the Pacific,'' obliges Gloria by putting a bullet in her head, he is indicating that if he has not quite come around to her nihilistic vision, he has come a long way toward it.

The dance marathon serves McCoy as a symbol of deception, of the betrayed Southern California promise. On one level it is pure theater—an elaborate, staged spectacle cynically manipulated by its gangster-promoters to draw crowds of thrill seekers. It is almost a parody of the Hollywood dream factory. On another level it is a potent metaphor for the end of the road. Like the highway that circles back on itself for Frank Chambers, the dance floor represents movement without progress.

Dance, traditionally a celebration of life, becomes in the novel a rite of death. There are no celebrants and no winners, only an abrupt and crashing halt after thirty-seven days, 879 hours of futile movement. The futility is underscored by the insistent presence of the ocean ''pounding, pounding against the pilings all the time.'' Robert feels it whether he is moving across the floor or resting on his cot during the ten-minute break the dancers have every two hours. ''Through the legs of my cot I could feel the ocean quivering against the pilings below. It rose and fell, rose and fell, went out and came back, went out and came back.''

The ocean is the perfect accompaniment to the *danse macabre*, its relentless ebbing and flowing the cosmic counterpart to the drugged movement of the dancers. The pier, ''rising and falling and groaning and creaking with the movements of the water'' is almost an extension of the bodies of the dancers. The once hopeful Robert recalls how previously he romanticized the ocean:

> I used to sit for hours looking at it, wondering about the ships that had sailed it and never returned, about China and the South Seas, wondering all sorts of things. . . . But not any more. I've had enough of the Pacific.

As mental construct or physical presence the Pacific Ocean persists as an image in L.A. fiction, one which evokes a sense of arriving at the end of the line, the border of dreams, the place where the road and the hope run out. In the crime novels of Cain, Chandler, and Macdonald, and in Robert Towne's *Chinatown* script, the edge of the Pacific, the site of the elaborate homes of those who have made it, is the recurring scene of brutal murder. In *Postman* Nick is killed on a cliff above Malibu Beach, lured there by Cora's desire to see where the movie stars live. When Robert and Gloria emerge from the dance hall onto the pier after the marathon is shut down, Robert points to the lights of Malibu up the coast, "where all the movie stars live."

At this point in the narrative two fishermen pass, dragging a four-foot hammerhead shark. "This baby'll never do any more damage," one says to the other. The appearance of the dead predator comes almost as an echo of Robert's remark seconds earlier. He had been looking back at the dance hall where they had spent the last thirty-seven days. "So that's where we've been all the time. . . . Now I know how Jonah felt when he looked at the whale." The dance hall is the demon which has swallowed, then expelled them. The image is claustrophobic, reflecting Robert's constant feeling of entrapment. During the marathon, to open the door and face the sun was to risk disqualification. Every day he tried to steer Gloria into a triangle of sunlight that came through the double windows of the beer garden above the dance floor for ten minutes a day. The sun functions as a counterimage to the ocean, an evocation of life:

> I watched the triangle on the floor get smaller and smaller. Finally, it closed up altogether and started up my legs. . . . When it got to my chin I stood on my toes, to keep my head in as long as possible. . . .
> In a moment it was gone.

Robert has been trying desperately to keep his head above water. The cliché is intentional: the dance hall is not only the belly of the whale but also a sinking ship, the dancers a desperate crew seized increasingly by exhaustion and impotence. Whatever hope Robert has brought to the dance has been undercut by the endless round of meaningless movement, the brutalizing competition of the derbies, and the senseless and degrading extravaganzas engineered to titillate a thrill-seeking audience. When Gloria urges Robert to "pinch hit for God," he does so without reflection, recognizing at least some part of himself in her black despair. Early in the novel, before they enter the marathon, he had responded glibly to her expressed wish to be dead: "I know exactly what you mean." But he *doesn't* know until the night of the killing. One of the arresting policemen asks him why he did it, and he replies, "They shoot horses, don't they?" Gloria is the suffering horse of the title, but while Robert is her executioner, her mercy killer, his act also gives expression to his own growing estrangement from the world in which he had placed all his hope, a point underscored by his refusal to offer any legal defense at his trial or even to listen to the words of the judge.

McCoy's other L.A. novel, *I Should Have Stayed Home,* is a blunter indictment of the meretriciousness of the dream, a weaker, more discursive, and more confused work, both a satire on the dream factory and a farce riddled with movie-colony stereotypes. The leads are again a young pair of seekers who begin with opposing expectations and attitudes. Ralph Carston is hopeful and romantic in temperament; Mona Matthews is tough and disillusioned. One difference, though, is that Ralph, unlike Robert Syverten, never loses his optimism, his expectation that he will be a star. Another is that Mona, while possessing some of Gloria Beatty's cynical and embittered vision, has none of

her paralyzing hopelessness. She remains hard but opportunistic. A third character, Dorothy Trotter, takes on Gloria's consummate despair. Arrested for shoplifting, Dorothy escapes prison, steals a car, and is rearrested. Soon after, she hangs herself with a stocking in her cell. A reporter taking pictures at the morgue asks for the death instrument, and Mona places some fan magazines in the dead girl's hand: the Hollywood publicity network with its small-town-girl-makes-good message is the death instrument.

Ralph and Mona share (chastely) a bungalow on Vine Street. Nearby on Hollywood Boulevard a giant sign reads: "All Roads Lead to Hollywood—And the Pause that Refreshes!" In a tiny neighborhood park, Ralph sees a middle-aged woman dressed in black lay a wreath at a shrine to Valentino. Ralph, who has come west on the strength of a promised screen test and then never hears again from the producer, continues to dream of his big chance. The novel takes on some comic life when he is ensnared by the rich, nymphomaniacal widow Ethel Smithers, setting up McCoy's burlesque version of the film capital. Mrs. Smithers is Mrs. Layden, "the champion dance marathon fan" of *They Shoot Horses,* carried to an extreme of explicit lust. A collector of young men, she tries to seduce the simpleminded hero by showing him pornographic movies in her private screening room. The Hollywood denizens attached to Mrs. Smithers are the stock figures of movieland folklore—homosexual actors and lesbian screen goddesses, nymphomaniacs and their troup of gigolos, cynical, hard-drinking writers and tyrannical producers. They are the people West, Fitzgerald, Schulberg, and Mailer would later portray with considerably more subtlety.

Although very different in tone and ambience from *They Shoot Horses, I Should Have Stayed Home* has something in common with the earlier novel. There are, among other similarities, the constant display of theatrics and showmanship, the exploitative use of sex, and the failure of traditional sources of authority and morality in the competitive drive for status and fame. Most important, it shares with the earlier work the sense of the West Coast as the place not of new beginnings but of disastrous finishes. Dorothy is dead, and Mona, at the end, signals her surrender by accepting a magazine ad proposal and marrying a Central California farmer. Only Robert continues to dream of success in Hollywood. His persistent guilelessness mars the book's effectiveness as an indictment, frustrating our every effort to muster some identification with him as narrator.

There are, it should be added, two interesting characters in the novel—the writer Heinrich, who can't find work until he discovers he can attract attention by continually playing the clown, and the studio publicist Johnny Hill, a quasi-radical and disillusioned idealist who sells out at the end and becomes Ralph's successor as Mrs. Smithers's gigolo. In their political savvy, both are foils to the naive narrator. But they aren't enough to redeem the book.

*I Should Have Stayed Home* might have been saved by a controlling metaphor with the potency of the dance marathon; loose and sprawling, it lacks the tautness, the symbolic compression, of the earlier novel. Both Cain and McCoy in their tougher and leaner first novels were able to do what they could not do as successfully in their subsequent novels—concentrate their fables in powerful images drawn from the built environment, images which would help carry the weight of their themes. The haphazard Twin Oaks Tavern spread along the California highway and the old dance hall pitched over the edge of their

Pacific provided them with symbolic landscapes they were not to find again.

In *Postman* and *They Shoot Horses* Cain and McCoy gave a literary identity to Los Angeles. They made available to their successors the principal metaphors for deception, illusion, and loss. For Nathanael West, Raymond Chandler, Ross Macdonald, Norman Mailer, Joan Didion, Alison Lurie, and John Gregory Dunne, among others, the betrayed promise of the West Coast would be expressed in images of deceptive, fraudulent architecture; highways that dead-end against the Pacific; rootless characters engaged in compulsive, aimless, and futile motion; and human relationships that dissolve in greed, lust, and violence. (pp. 57-62)

> David Fine, "Beginning in the Thirties: The Los Angeles Fiction of James M. Cain and Horace McCoy," in Los Angeles in Fiction: A Collection of Original Essays, *edited by David Fine, University of New Mexico Press, 1984, pp. 43-66.*

## TOM NEWHOUSE (essay date 1985)

[*In the following excerpt, Newhouse provides a close study of* Kiss Tomorrow Good-Bye.]

Whenever the school of hard-boiled writers is discussed, the name of Horace McCoy . . . is bound to be mentioned. Though he never gained the recognition accorded the great triumvirate of tough guys—James M. Cain, Dashiell Hammett, and Raymond Chandler—McCoy was a gifted writer whose literary career spanned a twenty year period in which he produced five novels and numerous short stories. Still, despite his productivity, McCoy seems fated to be remembered by that one slim masterpiece *They Shoot Horses, Don't They?,* his most famous and decidedly best work.

McCoy shared many techniques and attitudes with the acknowledged masters of the idiom, including a fast-paced, simplified narrative style which told only what the characters said and did, and a fictional world which emphasized violence and the physical life. Similarly, he even shared the experience of being a Hollywood scenarist with them, a factor which probably contributed to the verbal leanness of this particular method of storytelling. What is seldom taken into account, however, though no one would argue that there are not substantial differences among the practitioners of the hard-boiled novel, is the extent to which the divergences have determined originality, vision, and personal statement. A close look at the works of Horace McCoy reveals a man who wrote so intuitively that he sometimes violated the limits of the simple method of expression that he had chosen, thus revealing many deeper preoccupations than the tight form permitted. A bold and original prose stylist, McCoy continues to evade critical labels, and while all of his books may offer examples of his obsessions with personal masks, problems of identity, and various other metaphysical notions, no work stands out in this regard more than the culminative novel of his career, *Kiss Tomorrow Goodbye.*

Just as McCoy's first book *They Shoot Horses, Don't They?,* with its dance marathon setting, appears to reflect some of the bleak concerns of its period's literature, although without making specific references to the Depression in a didactic manner, *Kiss Tomorrow Goodbye* may be said to tangentially reflect some of the ideas prevalent in the culture of the forties. Despite numerous suggestions that the hero of the novel, Cotter-Mur-

phy, is a contemporary of John Dillinger and other notorious outlaws that would place its setting squarely in the thirties, the book is otherwise far removed from the aesthetic framework of that decade, and is only in the most simplistic terms a return to the prewar days of the gangster novel. By 1948 the gangster had undergone several metamorphoses both in print and in film, and an eager audience awaited the manifestations. In the gloomy psychological aftermath of the Second World War a deep skepticism was beginning to dominate the pages of the tough novel, the clearest indication of which was a heightened emphasis on violence and spiritual alienation. One of the writers who was significantly emblematic of this new development was Mickey Spillane; his novel *I, the Jury* (1947), the first of many tales of revenge and mayhem noted for their wise-cracking misogyny, clipped prose and furious pace, helped initiate the trend. While violence had of course always been an essential property of the tough novel, Spillane took it a step further. Through the adventures of his hero Mike Hammer, a crude and sadistic extension of the private eyes of Hammett and Chandler, Spillane presented a type of violence which was so concentrated, so excessive and gratuitous, that it seemed closer to fantasy than to realism, thus literally straining the limits of objective realism that had always been the central defining element of the hard-boiled novel.

McCoy's book also reflects this inclination to accentuate violent events and was probably influenced to some extent by Spillane's success. However, McCoy extends the realistic tradition in yet another and perhaps more intriguing way. McCoy was fascinated by psychoanalysis, which had its major impact on America in the forties, and it was this interest that predominantly led him to fashion his "psychological portrait of a pathological killer" [see Sturak excerpt dated 1968]. Thus McCoy allows the psychological aspects of his protagonist, who indulges in all sorts of neurotic reflections, to dominate his narrative. The result is an effective brand of poetic impressionism not often associated with the hard-boiled novel.

That McCoy ventured on this project with the utmost seriousness is asserted by Thomas Sturak when he reports in his essay, "Horace McCoy's Objective Lyricism," that *Kiss Tomorrow Goodbye* was to be the "acid test of his creative genius and artistic talents." McCoy's book, however, was greatly disliked by the critics and was eventually turned into a mediocre movie which could obviously do no justice to the intentions of a novel that dwells so heavily on states of consciousness. Ironically, this was the only film based on a McCoy novel that was ever produced during his lifetime. A James Cagney vehicle, bought by Cagney Productions, it appeared in 1950 and was quickly forgotten, having been seemingly patterned after the great *White Heat* (1949), itself probably influenced to some extent by the McCoy book, particularly in its portrayal of a pathological hood with Oedipal fixations. The irony looms all the greater when one thinks that McCoy had made many unsuccessful attempts to interest producers in doing a version of *They Shoot Horses, Don't They?,* a story which ultimately proved to be one of the most cinematically conceived of all his novels, and which was finally turned into an excellent and very successful film in 1969.

While McCoy's primary objective was to satisfy his desire to write a psychological thriller, it is almost certain that his subject matter was influenced by the unexpected acclaim he was receiving in France. McCoy's books were popular sellers in the serie noire paperback series, and he was often referred to by the postwar philosophers as "the first American existentialist."

Indeed, the protagonist Ralph Cotter, alias Paul Murphy, emerges from the story as, at least superficially, something of an existential figure. He is a sensitive, intelligent man who has chosen with his own free will a life of crime, insisting that he has not been led into it as a result of his environment. Most toughs from the previous decade who had achieved success from violent acts, from Rico Bandello of W. R. Burnett's *Little Caesar* to Bill Trent in Benjamin Appel's *Brain Guy,* have come to it as a result of some environmental or social failure. McCoy's portrait significantly breaks from the socially conscious tradition of the gangster begun in the thirties and presents a man who is as ruthless and ambitious as these men, but with notably different impulses. McCoy, perhaps a bit too urgently, tells us outright that his cold-blooded criminal genius chose his infamy:

> I came into crime through choice and not environment. I didn't grow up in the slums with a drunk for a father and a whore for a mother and come into crime that way. I hate society too, but I don't hate it because it mistreated me and warped my soul. Every other criminal I know who's engaged in violent crime is a two-bit coward who blames his career on society. I need no apologist or crusader to finally hold up my lifeless body to the world and shout to them to come and observe what they have wrought. . . . Use me not as a preach—in your literature or your movies. This I have wrought, I, and I alone.

McCoy, with a token nod to the existentialists, a fascination for violence and evil, and an interest in psychological melodrama, will, through one of his most intriguing creations, subvert the implications of Cotter-Murphy's analysis of his own motives in typically pessimistic fashion, but without yielding to the sociological overtones.

But the fact that Cotter-Murphy has become a criminal by choice is not the only violation of the gangster tradition, and it may be useful here to contrast McCoy's portrait of a ruthless killer with the prototypical gangster hero, Rico Bandello, from W. R. Burnett's tough-guy classic *Little Caesar* (1929). Rico, the ultimate killer, is nothing if not a professional. One of the most single-minded villains in the history of popular literature, the key to his success appears to be his total lack of humanity. He is, in the words of George Grella in his analysis of the gangster novel, "a mere killing machine, a negative creator with absolutely no redeeming human qualities" ["The Gangster Novel" in *Tough Guy Writers of the Thirties*]. With no regard for anything but his own obsessions with power, Rico, as befits his character, is wary for instance of the debilitating effect a woman may have on an unfeeling professional. . . . True, by the late forties, likely as a result of Cain's lurid potboilers, the gangster novel would seem rather empty without the presence of a femme fatale—someone, in fact, to whom much of the violence can be directed, and who may become the ultimate cause of the protagonists demise. This is very explicitly the case with Cotter-Murphy, who, had he been as apprehensive as Rico, might have tumbled to different circumstances rather than be undone by the spitting, clawing nymphomaniac Holiday, or the enervating rich girl Margaret Dobson. Still, in *Kiss Tomorrow Goodbye* the entire situation has become more complex. By his own admission, Cotter-Murphy is well aware of the dangers inherent in his feisty accomplice Holiday.

> She's a goddamn savage, this dame is, a real primitive, and the only way to teach her something is to knock her on her ass.

Yet one senses early that, despite Cotter-Murphy's self-encouraging bravado, there are forces at work which will thwart all simple formulas. Evidence of this is his willing involvement, which is nearly mystically induced, with the mysterious Margaret Dobson, with whom he will be fatalistically linked until the end. This combination of an all-too-human character with an ambition to be deadly inhuman will repeatedly create weaknesses. At one point he is made aware of the shortcomings that his liaison with Holiday potentially creates, while at the same time he realizes his enslavement by her:

> You fools, you mere passers of food, I was thinking. I shall not be saddled with you for longer than is absolutely necessary, and then, swiftly exploding that, and the color of the fragment was mauve, came the image of Holiday naked in the bed, in the tub, in the shower, on the floor, in the car, in the open, pulsing with a lust straight from the cave, and my navel fluttered, mocking me, and I knew that what I was thinking was indeed crap, truly crap, that if only for this she would be absolutely necessary.

McCoy's interest here is not in drawing a portrait of a successful killer, or even an unsuccessful one for that matter, so much as it is to demonstrate the contradictions within his protagonist, the existence of the irrational, the flaw that refuses to right itself even as the mind is conscious of it. This implied paradox takes McCoy beyond earlier examples of the genre in that he has exercised the form of the psychological novel, plumbing the depths of his hero's psyche, and yet has presented a character who is more shadowy, more contradictory, more complex, wholly more incomplete and elusive, and, most important, ultimately more vulnerably human than Burnett's Rico. If Little Caesar is drawn clearly and never falters along the way, as is emblematic of all folk heroes, it is McCoy's intention to discover and define his character as he goes and, in the end, say something of his own about the mythmaking process.

To some extent, these conflicts and dualities are at the heart of all McCoy's novels, and they create the tension and value for us. From the very first page of *Kiss Tomorrow Goodbye,* we are immediately struck by the lyrical quality of the writing—the biggest and most glaring departure from the tradition out of which it has emerged. On that first page an as-yet unnamed narrator discusses such abstractions as displaced souls, the vulnerability of the waking state, and, most importantly, he focuses on the keen concentration of the senses, particularly that of smell, which will remain a constantly repeated image throughout the novel and will become the primary vehicle by which the past intrudes upon the present, ultimately serving to undo the master criminal. As he awakes, Cotter-Murphy seems absolutely without the outward brutality we come to identify him with a page later:

> I always awoke to greet these fragments, hungrily smelling what little freshness they had left by the time they got back to me, smelling them frugally, in careful precious sniffs, letting them dig into the vaults of my memory, letting them uncover early morning sounds of a lifetime ago; bluejays and woodpeckers and countless other birds met like medieval knights and thrusting at each other with long sharp lances of song, the crowings of roosters, the brassy bleats of sheep and the mooing of cows saying, "N-o-o-o-hay, N-o-o-o-milk. . . ."

But the narrator's Proustian recall becomes increasingly negative as knowledge of his present condition as an inmate in a prison farm takes over and indicates the single harsh reality. As the sounds of other men remind him of his confinement, he notes: "You could smell the movement; the pillar of stink which had been lying in laminae like the coats of an onion, was now being peeled, and a little of everybody was everywhere." McCoy's metaphor is an effective one and, since it is Cotter-Murphy's encroaching awareness that generates the major dramatic conflict and ultimately spoils his youthful memories, it becomes the central motif of the novel. In addition, it emphasizes the essential dichotomy which distinguished McCoy's nostalgic gangster with the soul of a romantic, from a more traditional and calculating professional like Rico Bandello. Without telling us directly, McCoy has, with sufficient subtlety, begun his portrait of a jaded but complex and sensitive man who will demonstrate further his affection for things which a man like Rico innately rejects. All the marks of the educated dilettante are subsequently brought into play: historical images, a knowledge of Greek myth, a taste for culture, are eventually introduced into McCoy's narrative in the most unlikely contexts, a tactic which provides frequent dramatic incongruence. For instance, Holiday's womanhood is metaphorically referred to as "Atlantis, the Rout to Cathay, the Seven Cities of Cibola," and "all of Bach essenced into a single note." During lovemaking with her he hears the "moaning of the strings of the corpora cavernosa."

Apart from using music as a sexual metaphor, moreover, Cotter-Murphy is at various stages literally moved by it, especially Jazz. At one point, as he waits for Margaret Dobson in her car, he is swept away by the rhythms of Muggsy Spanier's "I Found a New Baby" as it plays on the radio, and he is compelled to comment that Ira Sullivan's solo is "impeccable." Later he will interrupt the narrative briefly to comment on certain matters of taste regarding Jazz. As he celebrates one of his criminal victories with Cherokee Mandon and Holiday, he mentions that the sweet dance orchestra is "not to my taste," though he will dance to it anyway, since the gracefulness of the dance holds some significance for him. This is the same man who thinks "how nice it would be to stick that acetylene torch down Mason's throat and burn a hole in the back of his head big enough to push my foot through." All of this might be inconsistently ludicrous perhaps, had the utterances not come from a man of good education, good family, and the possessor of a phi beta kappa key, whose major aspiration in life is to outdo "the achievements of bums like Karpis, Floyd and Dillinger, who were getting rich off crackerbox banks, bums who had no talent at all, bums who could hardly get out of the rain."

It is, in fact, these opposite sides of Cotter-Murphy's character that intrigued McCoy and make the downfall of this desperate man so inevitable. Even a cursory glance at McCoy's masterpiece *They Shoot Horses, Don't They?* reveals that the dramatic action of the novel is propelled and made believable by the coming together of Robert's naive optimism and Gloria's all-encompassing pessimism, the intensity of which will dominate the action as well as defeat the former's ambition. There is a conflict of this sort going on in *Kiss Tomorrow Goodbye* as well, and it is made all the more explicit by McCoy's presentation of a man whose nature suggests a near-schizophrenic duality. Most important of all, he is a man who, on one hand thinks too much—this being the natural outcome of his intellect—but on the other, who is determined, based on the exigencies of his profession, to be a man of action. The exploitation by McCoy of this internal-external dialectic of will, then, gains momentum as the novel goes and will be reiterated and heightened by several ironic developments.

Midway through the novel we learn that the very first service rendered by Cherokee Mandon is to wipe away every trace of Ralph Cotter by obliterating his police record (interestingly, the name Ralph Cotter is also an alias) and to create a man named Paul Murphy: "Without this card the police had nothing to go on. My past was wiped clean. I had no past." This accomplishment even impels the cool and pragmatic professional Mandon to marvel, "It is not every man's privilege to be reborn. From this point on, you have nothing to worry about so long as you let me handle things." Later we will witness yet another transformation or possible fulfillment of identity, when Cotter-Murphy is made the biggest offer yet by the millionaire Ezra Dobson, and his destiny will be made to seem limitless. But the reader knows about the dream visions of the past, and in both cases the evidence will preclude any such rebirth. As suits the method of gradual discovery, Cotter-Murphy received these visions in fragments, the whole meaning of which he has obliterated at least until the end when his dissolution becomes complete. In fact, the little control that he does have over the intrusions of his past is exercised in "fighting desperately from seeing the whole thing" as the nostalgia of early innocence turns ugly. Appropriately, a walking confusion of identities like this character, is able to romanticize his criminality only when it is conceived of as a fall; when the corollary to his corrupt but presumably chosen present is that of youthful purity. Making this assumption, Cotter-Murphy therefore glories in his ability to be several people in one. He believes that his "genius" lies in an unlimited potential, the thrust of which resolves itself in behavior that can, on one hand, be brutally violent, or on the other, fairly normal. For instance, it is with a sort of arrogant pride that after his escape from the prison farm he looks "in the windows at electrical supplies and boats and fishing tackle, and secondhand typewriters, and adding machines, just like any other guy." Later he even philosophizes about these little performances he must give in order to remain inconspicuous to the average person toward whom he inevitably feels estranged, and for whom he has contempt:

> I got off the bus at the corner feeling a small curious pleasure that I was able to do this in the easy habitual manner of a man who had been getting off the same bus at the same corner for years, a veteran; for there is nothing more inconspicuous than an expert in anything, even getting off a bus.

In the same passage he emphasizes his estrangement from common humanity by petulantly defining its limitations:

> These are the cheap, common, appalling people a war so happily destroys. What is your immediate destiny, you loud, little unweaned people? A two dollar raise? A hamburger and a hump?

So it is only natural that this man with his battery of identities can feel most comfortable with false ones. In fact, success is managed only through the manipulation of the fake: he manages to lure the chief of police into his clutches by constant playacting; because of their privileged association with the police, Cotter-Murphy and his henchmen don police disguises to accomplish the holdup of the bookies; time and again Cotter-Murphy's words are the direct opposite of his feelings and serve to hide his real purposes, which the reader alone is privileged to know through the protagonist's many asides and reflections. To be sure, in such a self-reliant enterprise as the criminal life, in such a totally amoral world as the one that McCoy presents to us, that source of Cotter-Murphy's pride, his underhanded professionalism, may indeed by the only way to survive, the essential key to success. Thus the real individual assumes that his objectives and stratagems alone are complex while everyone else's are quite apparent. This applies to motivation as well, since Cotter-Murphy's are decidedly abstract, while everyone else's may be reduced to sex and money. These elemental temptations in themselves are formidable enough to corrupt everyone in the novel, from the lowest of crooks like Nick Mason to the highest of city officials like Chief of Police Webber, who, in Cherokee Mandon's initial refusal to believe that Cotter-Murphy had him "caught in the ringer," it is implied, had at one time at least been honest enough to gain a wholesome reputation. Cotter-Murphy may be the last gangster hero simply because in his world it is no longer adequate to adopt the code of toughness that was appropriate enough for the preceding decade. Toughness itself must be subsumed into an anonymous and bottomless duplicity.

The world that McCoy presents, then, is one where, despite total corruption, distinctions cannot be easily made. It is a world of hallucination and nightmare where certainty is hard to come by, whatever else Cotter-Murphy believes are the rules of the game. The hard-boiled novel generally relies on at least the world of the senses to compensate for the absence of values. In *Kiss Tomorrow Goodbye,* even the primary image which imparts the buried secret in a whirlwind of conflicting impressions—that of smell—proves unreliable. Shortly after the escape, as Holiday bakes a loaf of bread, Cotter-Murphy comments, "God! By what mysterious alchemy had my grandmother's bread-baking secret been transmitted way out here. This had the same smell, the loaf was different and the color was different, but this had the same smell. The little old lady humped over an oven. . . ." Likewise, the smell of the perfume that reminds him of the Huele de Noche bushes around the house where he grew up opens the door to the past; yet we soon learn that Margaret Dobson was not wearing any perfume at all, and it is simply the physical resemblance between her and his dead grandmother that triggers the impression.

> Great Heavenly God! I thought, fighting to get my breath. This is what I smelled. It was not the perfume the girl was wearing at all; she was right. It was my imagination. Her face was of the same blackness and there was a sameness in the cast of features too, and this is what had done it, this sameness, that goddamned sameness.

Thus, appearances are deceiving as well, and nothing can be really counted on. Our first introduction to Holiday has her dressed like a man at the spot of the prison break. The objective technique serves McCoy well here as he presents the nightmare to us, always in flux, always unstable:

> The shock of seeing a man there instead of Holiday froze me. I felt as if someone had hit me in the navel with a blizzard. He wore a cap and a bow tie and a blue suit, and he was standing on the edge of the thicket, full in the open, his left forearm against a sapling so young and slender that it trembled with the recoils, moving the machine from side to side in a short, straight line, like a man patiently watering a strip of lawn.

Of course, soon afterward Cotter-Murphy learns who it really is as she literally strips down naked in the car, thus ending a scene already loaded with images of violence counterbalanced with innocence, with a symbol of the action to come, in which Cotter-Murphy himself will be psychologically stripped down and the real will spring forth, free from the false exterior, and

he will be engulfed with "grown-man fright" which he finds more "annihilative" than "little-boy fright."

This stripping down to bare essentials where the ambiguity of the senses, the confusion of past and present, will ultimately lead to a final unraveling of the truth, parallels the direction of the novel. Cotter-Murphy, who sees himself as a logical successor in a pantheon of criminals, is in fact attempting to possess what is for him—and if we accept the implications that the gangster is a sort of contemporary folk hero, for the reader too—a part of the American dream; to become a mythic figure, the ultimate rebel in a corrupt world, or, in the words of Robert Warshow in his celebrated essay, "The Gangster as Tragic Hero," the expression of "that part of the American psyche which rejects the qualities and dreams of modern life, which rejects Americanism itself." McCoy's savagely damning ironies lie in the progression of Cotter-Murphy's movements from swaggering hoodlum to a trembling and pathetic psychotic just as he is closest to the fulfillment of his greatest dream. As the outer movements of the protagonist reveal near-magical accomplishments, the inner drift reveals just the opposite, and the closer he comes to madness and death. It is significant, once again, that the past intrudes on the present only in snatches. Hallucinations and smells remind Cotter-Murphy of his childhood on the farm which is at first revealed to us with a kind of imagistic, pastoral beauty that contrasts with the vague malevolence of the city where the ambulatory killer practices his crimes and deceptions. Even the prison farm, where the novel begins, suggests a more peaceful mood and causes him to remark later on.

> I'm sorry I ever crashed out of the prison farm, I was thinking. That was torture too, but torture of a different sort, much easier to stand. When I was on the prison farm what I remembered of a lifetime ago was pleasant, not like this. Would those foul memories never be expiated?

These juxtaposed urban and rural symbols come full circle when they are brought into focus in the culminative scene on the golf course at Ezra Dobson's country club, where Cotter-Murphy is thrust back into recollections which threaten his vaunted invulnerability. At this point, where, "off in the distance I could see the lights of the city, far, far away—farther than that—and I had a quick thought of Holiday and the others who were waiting," he longs to return to his aggressive role as a criminal. Naturally, when confronted with his own inner truth, which he has throughout the novel attempted to deny, he yearns to focus on his current triumphs with a jeroboam of champagne and the sultry Holiday beside him in order to insure that "Oedipus is dead, and the sepulchre is sealed." He tells Holiday earlier, "You must burn the echoes of those memories, you must purify me in the crucible of your lust." But it is when the pieces fall into place in this natural environment, surrounded by trees and images that are more in keeping with that earlier time than with the corrupt America of concrete and asphalt, the gangster's habitat, that Cotter-Murphy's freely chosen life of crime pales beside his discovery that he had killed his grandmother at the age of six, after having attempted to sexually molest her. It is when Cotter-Murphy discovers that his early years, which he presumed innocent, were in truth actually tainted by murder and evil that his disintegration is complete. Realizing that Margaret Dobson will always be a reincarnation of his grandmother for him, he must reject the offer of a million dollars from her father to marry her, and depart "on legs that were not mine." Not surprisingly, in the very next scene, he will face without the mainstay of his vitality—his gun—the wrath of Holiday who has discovered Cotter-Murphy's responsibility in the death of her brother during the prison break, the most fatal exposure from the past. Cotter-Murphy's sudden catatonic quiescence assures his vulnerability by making it impossible for him to resolve his conflicts in physical terms. His schism of intellect versus action has been reduced to passivity. The mythic images through which Cotter-Murphy has, in part, been able to sustain his power and dominance have evaporated, the most traditional of which is boyhood in the country. McCoy, in his most pessimistic manner, dismisses all possibilities of redemption.

Consistent with the outrageous sexuality in this novel, it is interesting that, in Oedipal fashion, the self-immolation of Cotter-Murphy is almost voluntary. As he is faced with the offer of a million dollars from Ezra Dobson, Cotter-Murphy's imminent demise is made all the more dramatically tantalizing when the possibilities of his final disintegration, the full knowledge of his private demons, clash with his greatest motivating factor, his ambition.

> Can I? Can I? Can I fight my way out of this trap? Here is what I always wanted, now created especially for me alone—it never could be offered to anyone else, it would be too fantastic, it is being offered to me, this world, because the axis of it is the symbol of my guilt, and the tempting God dares me to face it because he knows it is but a short cut to destruction. But why should it be? Myth and memory retreat before intellect.

His ambition wins and he decides to tempt the odds; "... it is certainly audacious enough to appeal to me." The result of the pursuit of this challenge, finally is that, rather than gain success, he will be led to the most shattering of realizations.

The implications of his failure are clear. The knowledge of earlier evil and, worst of all, unnatural behavior—the perversion of a remembered paradise—deprives him of the potential to be anything else than what he is and invalidates every previous artificial pose and deception, thus making the conceit that he became a criminal by choice his biggest and most unforgivable illusion. He becomes, suddenly, conscious of his limitations, a fact which undermines his earlier assertions about freedom and free choice. These turnabouts are made even more plausible by McCoy's objective method in which his protagonists interpret the meaning of reality as they see it. Thus, Cotter-Murphy is led to perceive the intrinsic dangers of situations which otherwise might lead him to the ultimate success and, as measured against the impudence of his character, he must fall by them. In much of McCoy's fiction it is the stark revelation of the irrevocable truth of reality clashing with an assumed identity or world vision which reduces man, betrays his ambitions for success, and leads him to doom.

McCoy's conscious bid to be regarded as a serious artist resulted in some extremely bold narrative attempts of which **Kiss Tomorrow Goodbye** is his most ambitious. Because of this, his novels generally prove to lie outside genre and are, in fact, strikingly original works that were only marginally related to the murder mystery (**They Shoot Horses, Don't They?**), the Hollywood novel (**I Should Have Stayed Home**), the call of the proletariat (**No Pockets in a Shroud**), the rise and fall of the gangster (**Kiss Tomorrow Goodbye**), and the slick medical story bestseller (**Scalpel**). In **Kiss Tomorrow Goodbye,** it is precisely this quality of a genre running away from itself that gives the book its intriguing quality. The insistence on its bizarre, dreamlike plot, its lyrical prose, its daring introspection, its emphasis

on personal obsession that delivers the hero to his end rather than the machination of an impersonal law force, liberates the material from its usual constrictions and gives it an undeniable vitality. In this regard, Cotter-Murphy's own words bear a remarkable relevance to his creator when he remarks, "It was audacious enough to appeal to me." So, too, Horace McCoy would have had it no other way. (pp. 15-29)

> *Tom Newhouse, "Horace McCoy's Introspective Gangster," in* Clues: A Journal of Detection, *Vol. 6, No. 1, Spring-Summer, 1985, pp. 15-30.*

## ADDITIONAL BIBLIOGRAPHY

Barry, Iris. Review of *I Should Have Stayed Home*, by Horace McCoy. *New York Herald Tribune Book Review* (20 February 1938): 8, 10.
> Considers *I Should Have Stayed Home* "in every way less remarkable" than McCoy's first novel, *They Shoot Horses, Don't They?*

Benét, William Rose. "Life Is a Marathon." *The Saturday Review* XII, No. 13 (27 July 1935): 5.
> Favorable review of *They Shoot Horses, Don't They?*, praising it as "a story of great power . . . as stripped-for-action as a racing car."

Connolly, Cyril. Review of *They Shoot Horses, Don't They?*, by Horace McCoy. *The New Statesman and Nation*, n.s. 10 (3 August 1935): 166.
> Terms *They Shoot Horses, Don't They?* "first rate holiday reading—one of those tales of horror and sentiment which America is turning out every week, and which proves it definitely a land fit for halfwits to live in."

Follett, Wilson. "Jailbird." *The New York Times Book Review* (13 June 1948): 26.
> Review of *Kiss Tomorrow Good-Bye,* calling it "a straight crime thriller of the fast, tough school" but wondering "if we actually need two James M. Cains."

Lardner, Rex. "Society Surgeon." *The New York Times Book Review* (22 June 1952): 14.
> Comments on the anomalous behavior of the protagonist of McCoy's novel *Scalpel*, and writes that the believability of this contradictory character "is a tribute to the writing."

Lehan, Richard. "The Los Angeles Novel and the Idea of the West." In *Los Angeles in Fiction*, edited by David Fine, pp. 29-41. Albuquerque: University of New Mexico Press, 1984.
> Considers *They Shoot Horses, Don't They?* in a discussion of California regional fiction, including F. Scott Fitzgerald's *The Last Tycoon* (1941), Nathanael West's *The Day of the Locust* (1939), John Gregory Dunne's *True Confessions* (1977), and Thomas Pynchon's *The Crying of Lot 49* (1966).

Miller, Gabriel. "Marathon Man/Marathon Woman." In his *Screening the Novel: Rediscovered American Fiction in Film*, pp. 64-83. New York: Frederick Ungar, 1980.
> Discusses McCoy's skillful handling of detached, objective narrative in *They Shoot Horses, Don't They?* An analysis of Sydney Pollack's film version of the novel concludes that the movie lacks the dramatic intensity of the book.

Nathan, Paul S. "Books into Films." *Publisher's Weekly* 153, No. 23 (5 June 1948): 2391.
> Recounts that McCoy, "this novelist of the brass knuckles school," intends to give up screenwriting and, "by living modestly and working hard . . . says frankly he expects to become a literary figure of major importance." Nathan quotes McCoy's claim that he is the real founder of Existentialism.

''Success Story.'' *New York Herald Tribune Book Review* (7 September 1952): 14.

> Review of *Scalpel,* calling it a ''fast-paced story'' with ''action . . . suspense, and pretty good character drawing . . . written in such a self-consciously terse style—a Hemingway-Cain-Chandler mixture—that it is much harder to read than it should be.''

Poe, James. ''Trials and Traumas: James Poe, an Interview with Michael Dempsey.'' In *The Hollywood Screenwriters,* edited by Richard Corliss, pp. 181-204. New York: Discus Books, 1972.

> Interview with Poe, whose screenplay for the 1969 film version of *They Shoot Horses, Don't They?* was extensively rewritten by Robert E. Thompson and by the film's director, Sydney Pollack.

Rothman, N. L. ''Hollywood Hater.'' *The Saturday Review of Literature* XVII, No. 17 (19 February 1938): 4.

> Reviews *I Should Have Stayed Home,* calling it McCoy's bitter expression of hate for Hollywood.

Stanley, William F. ''Lost Among the *Black Mask* Boys.'' *The Armchair Detective* 17, No. 2 (Spring 1984): 137-43.

> Chronologically arranged account of McCoy's career, focusing on his early short story contributions to *Black Mask* magazine.

Talmey, Allene. ''Paris Quick Notes: About Sartre, Gide, Cocteau, Politics, the Theatre, and Inflation.'' *Vogue* CIX (15 January 1947): 92, 143-45.

> Report from Paris that McCoy, little known in the United States, ''has a wide public of French literary fans.''

Review of *They Shoot Horses, Don't They?,* by Horace McCoy. *The Times Literary Supplement* (1 August 1935): 488.

> Calls *They Shoot Horses, Don't They?* ''a brilliant but sordid specimen of what has been called the 'hard-boiled' school of American fiction'' and ''a dispassionate but none the less scathing indictment of certain phases of modern civilization with special reference to the cult of sensation in the United States.''

Warshow, Paul. ''The Unreal McCoy.'' In *The Modern American Novel and the Movies,* edited by Gerald Peary and Roger Shatzkin, pp. 29-39. New York: Frederick Ungar, 1978.

> Close study of the motion picture version of *They Shoot Horses, Don't They?*

Wilson, Edmund. ''The Boys in the Back Room.'' In his *Classics and Commercials: A Literary Chronicle of the Forties,* pp. 19-56. New York: Farrar, Straus and Co., 1950.

> Mentions McCoy in a discussion of a new school of California writers influenced by Ernest Hemingway and Dashiell Hammett—including James M. Cain, Richard Hallas, John O'Hara, William Saroyan, John Steinbeck, and Hans Otto Storm—a group that Wilson terms ''the boys in the back room.'' Wilson calls *They Shoot Horses, Don't They?* ''worth reading'' but finds it contains flaws of characterization and motivation that are magnified in McCoy's second novel, *I Should Have Stayed Home.* This interpretation has been questioned by critics who maintain that Wilson displays an inadequate understanding of hard-boiled detective and adventure fiction.

Wilson, T. D. Review of *They Shoot Horses, Don't They?,* by Horace McCoy. *Life and Letters To-day* 13, No. 2 (December 1935): 201.

> Favorable review of McCoy's first novel, praising especially the characterization of Gloria and the unusual structure of the narrative.

# John Muir

## 1838-1914

Scottish-born American naturalist, essayist, diarist, and auto-biographer.

Among the most colorful of nineteenth-century naturalists, Muir was a strident proponent of wilderness preservation who wrote descriptive essays intended to increase public awareness of the beauty of the American West. The philosophical heir of Transcendentalists Ralph Waldo Emerson and Henry David Thoreau, Muir regarded contact with the natural world as both wholesome and sanctifying, and he spent much of his life exploring uncharted portions of the Sierra Nevada. Unlike Emerson and Thoreau, however, Muir considered himself primarily an explorer; he turned to writing relatively late in life as part of his effort to prevent unlimited commercial exploitation of the California wilderness. Muir also waged his land-use struggle on the political front, eventually becoming one of the foremost advocates for the growing conservationist movement, and he succeeded in having vast expanses of land designated as national wilderness preserves.

Muir was the third of eight children born to a grain merchant in Dunbar, Scotland. Muir's father, a sternly pious man, was active in a newly formed Calvinist sect known as the Disciples of Christ, and in 1849 he decided to take his family to the United States, where the sect had originated and was still flourishing. Settling in Wisconsin, the elder Muir established a farm with the help of his children, who were expected to perform the work of adult laborers as soon as they were able; as the oldest male child, Muir was responsible for the most arduous tasks, and it was he who felled the trees, plowed the fields, and dug the well. Because Muir's father was contemptuous of nonscriptural knowledge, he did not allow his children to attend school, but instructed them in the practical skills and biblical lessons he believed would serve them best. Muir, however, obtained books from the private libraries of friends and neighbors, and he rapidly developed an interest in science and literature.

Beginning in adolescence, Muir also designed and constructed unique wooden machines, including a bed that would wake its sleeper at a predetermined hour and an immense grandfather clock, and this hobby eventually provided the means for his escape from endless labor on his father's farm. In 1860, a family friend encouraged Muir to exhibit his machines at the State Fair in Madison. At the fair, Muir was offered a job as a mechanic, and he spent the next several years working at a succession of factories, as well as attending four semesters at the University of Wisconsin. He disliked factory work, however, and after an accident in the spring of 1867 temporarily deprived him of his sight, he became determined to see as much of the world as possible.

Muir traveled first to Florida, collecting plant specimens and carefully recording his observations concerning the inhabitants, landscape, and wildlife of the areas through which he passed, observations which were later published as *A Thousand-Mile Walk to the Gulf*. He then visited New Orleans, Texas, and Cuba. Arriving in northern California in 1868, he became so enamored of the region that he abandoned his plans to continue

traveling and settled there. Working at odd jobs when he needed money, Muir explored the Yosemite Valley and adjacent portions of the Sierra Nevadas, and he quickly became an expert on the geology and biology of the region. Urged by his friends to write about his discoveries, he published his first essay in 1871, announcing the discovery of a "living" glacier in Yosemite and thus substantiating his controversial suggestion that the features of the valley had been carved not by a cataclysm, as had been thought, but by the erosive power of a receding glacier. Muir's first essay collection, *The Mountains of California,* also dealt primarily with the geography of the Sierra Nevadas, although it included descriptions of plant and animal life and meteorological phenomena as well. As his reputation grew, Muir was frequently invited to publish essays describing his experiences in the California wilderness, but, hampered by his lack of education, he found writing for publication extremely difficult, and he complied with such requests only because he felt compelled to "entice people to look at nature's loveliness."

In 1880 Muir married Louise Strentzel, the daughter of a wealthy rancher, and during the last three decades of his life he was occupied primarily with the management of his father-in-law's large estate. He nevertheless continued to travel widely, visiting many of the places he had planned to see in his youth, including the Himalayas, the Amazon River, Egypt, and Australia. It was during this latter portion of his life that Muir became most active in the conservationist cause; he served as guide and consultant to several federally appointed land-use commissions and wrote numerous hortatory newspaper articles. In the most dramatic conflict of these years, Muir joined in the fight to prevent the city of San Francisco from flooding the Hetch Hetchy Valley to create a reservoir, but in the end the city's need for an adequate source of fresh water outweighed other considerations and the requisite dam was constructed. Muir's public image was damaged by the excessive vehemence of his attacks upon the citizens of San Francisco, whom he denounced as "satanic," and following the Hetch Hetchy incident, Muir retired to his ranch to edit his journals for publication. He died of pneumonia one year later.

Muir's writings manifest a high degree of reverence for nature, reflecting their author's essentially pantheistic philosophy. Although he rejected his father's Calvinist teachings when he reached maturity, Muir retained a strong religious faith throughout his life, gradually coming to believe that divinity had been bestowed not only upon the human species, as taught in most Western religions, but upon all of the natural world. As a result, Muir regarded close contact with nature as the best possible means of comprehending the divine, and he considered appreciation of natural beauty a form of worship. Such convictions are clear in Muir's essays, where descriptive passages frequently culminate in a crescendo of lyrical praise.

While Muir's ideas parallel those of the Transcendentalists in many ways, reflecting his interest in and respect for those authors, critics note that Muir's personal philosophy differed from theirs. Unlike Emerson and Thoreau, who acknowledged that natural phenomena at times appeared to be unpleasant or morally ambiguous, Muir considered all natural objects and events to be inherently benign and he attributed contrary attitudes to simple ignorance of physical laws. This attitude is overtly expressed in Muir's account of an earthquake, where he describes his pleasure at witnessing one of nature's most dramatic occurrences and admonishes those who are afraid. Muir's own understanding of physical laws was comprehensive, and his writings are praised as often for their accuracy as for their style.

Despite his avowed preference for field work, Muir became widely respected as an author during his lifetime. A popular success in part because they satisfied Americans' hunger for literature about the West, his books garnered critical acclaim for their stylistic clarity, descriptive power, and forthright sincerity. Some critics, however, were irritated by what naturalist John Burroughs termed Muir's exaggerated piety, and Muir's essays are today esteemed in spite of rather than because of their reverential tone. Moreover, in the opinion of most observers, the primary importance of Muir's writings lies not in their literary quality but in the fact that they persuaded a large number of Americans to regard scenic wilderness areas as irreplaceable natural resources which must be protected and preserved.

## PRINCIPAL WORKS

*The Mountains of California* (essays) 1894
*Our National Parks* (essays) 1901
*Stickeen* (nonfiction) 1909
*My First Summer in the Sierra* (essays) 1911
*The Yosemite* (essays) 1912
*The Story of My Boyhood and Youth* (autobiography) 1913
*Letters to a Friend* (letters) 1915
*Travels in Alaska* (essays) 1915
*A Thousand-Mile Walk to the Gulf* (journals) 1916
*The Writings of John Muir.* 10 vols. (essays, nonfiction, autobiography, journals, and letters) 1916-24
*The Cruise of the Corwin* (journals) 1917
*Steep Trails* (essays) 1918
*John of the Mountains: The Unpublished Journals of John Muir* (journals) 1938
*\*Studies in the Sierra* (essays) 1950
*To Yosemite and Beyond: Writings from the Years 1863 to 1875* (essays) 1980

*These essays first appeared in the *Overland Monthly* in 1874 and 1875.

---

***THE NATION*** (essay date 1894)

[*In the following excerpt from a review of* The Mountains of California, *the critic commends Muir's exploration and documentation of the California wilderness.*]

Mr. Muir's delightful volume [*The Mountains of California*], which comes to jaded city-prisoners like a breeze from a mountain cañon, will at once take its place as a California classic by the side of Whitney's book on the Yosemite Valley, and Clarence King's *Mountaineering in the Sierra Nevada*. More than any other Californian of the past or present is he qualified by knowledge, sympathy, and personal experience, combined with the habit of scientific observation and the gift of a poetic style, to write a monograph on what he pronounces the "most divinely beautiful" of all the mountain chains he has seen. For a quarter of a century the Sierra Nevada Mountains have been his haunt in summer, often in winter, too. "Going to the mountains" is to him "like going home"; sometimes, even as the bees and butterflies, he is "too richly and homogeneously joy-filled to be capable of partial thought"; at other times he finds in regard to the influence of these surroundings that "instead of producing a dissipated condition, the mind is fertilized and stimulated and developed like sun-fed plants." He is his own guide and cook; his outfit consists of a bag of bread, a package of tea, a cup, an ice-axe. No need of blankets or hammocks where one can, in the meadows, lie down almost anywhere. "And what glorious botanical beds I had!" he exclaims. "Oftentimes on awaking I would find several new species leaning over me and looking me full in the face, so that my studies would begin before rising." In the higher regions there are natural pine thickets, or one can make beds of the boughs of the red fir, compared with which, "even in the matter of sensuous ease, any combination of cloth, steel-springs, and feathers seems vulgar"; in these alone one can enjoy the "clear, deathlike sleep of the tired mountaineer." The pine thickets, where the branches form a roof overhead and are bent down around the sides, "are the best bed-chambers the high mountains afford—snug as squirrel-nests, well ventilated, full of spicy odors, and with plenty of wind-played needles to sing one to sleep." In the highest regions he takes a hint from the animals and their choice of the dwarf pine as a dormitory: "During stormy nights I have often camped snugly beneath the interlacing arches of this little pine. The needles, which have accumulated for centuries, make fine beds, a fact well known to other mountaineers, such as deer and wild sheep, who paw out oval hollows and lie beneath the larger trees in safe and comfortable concealment.''

These details regarding the author's personal habits are scattered incidentally throughout the book. Mr. Muir never poses like Thoreau, whom he otherwise resembles in his worship of nature and intimacy with wild animals; he keeps his personality in the background, nor does he, like Thoreau, constantly drag in human analogies, and moralizings on man and his ways. The beauties and sublimities of the California mountains have for him such an absorbing fascination that man is crowded out, and even the writer usually disappears from sight. We have here nature pure and unadulterated, in chapters on the chain as a whole, the glaciers, the snow, the passes, the glacier lakes, the glacier meadows, the forests, the Douglas squirrel, windstorms in the forests, the river floods, Sierra thunder-storms, the water-ouzel, wild sheep, the foothills, the bee pastures—sixteen chapters, each a gem of landscape or animal painting.

Mr. Muir believes that the Yosemite Valley was once a lake, and that it was carved originally, like all the Sierra scenery, by the ice which in the last glacial age covered this region perhaps more than a mile in average depth. The glaciers carved the mountain sides and the passes, and in gradually receding they left the glacier lakes, whose place, again, was taken by the glacier meadows, looking smooth as cultivated lawns, yet without their "painful, licked, nipped, repressed appearance"; for their graceful grasses and flowers respond to the caresses of every breeze. Until the discovery of the Black Mountain glacier by Mr. Muir in 1871, it was not known that there were any glaciers left in the Sierra. Now it is known they exist all the way down from the great Muir glacier, in Alaska, with its two hundred tributaries, to the much smaller ones of the Sierra, Mt. Shasta having three. The highest of all the peaks, nevertheless, Mt. Whitney, has not been able to preserve any of its ice-rivers from the rays of the southern sun, even at its altitude of 14,898 feet. Summer after summer did Mr. Muir hunt for new glaciers, driving in stakes to measure their rate of motion, which he found to be very slow—in the Maclure Glacier only an inch a day, whereas that of the Muir Glacier in Alaska is from five to ten feet. The lowest Sierra glacier is at an elevation of 9,500 feet.

Most of the sublime phenomena witnessed by Mr. Muir are accessible to any one who will spend a summer and a winter in the Sierra Nevada. But there are some of which he only can make sure who is willing, like our author, to give up half his life to intercourse with the mountains. Ninety-nine tourists in a hundred see the Sierra only in summer, but Mr. Muir used to "look forward with delight to the approaching winter, with its wondrous storms," when he would be warmly snow-bound in his Yosemite cabin, with plenty of bread and books. Thus it happened that (in 1873) he witnessed a perfect display of what he pronounces the most magnificent of all storm phenomena he ever saw—silvery banners of snow dust attached to the peaks of the Merced group like streamers at a masthead, each "from half a mile to a mile in length, slender at the point of attachment, then widening gradually as it extended from the peak until it was about 1,000 or 1,500 feet in breadth." Some of these snow banners extended from peak to peak, while others overlapped. (p. 366)

**"A Wind-Storm in the Forests"** is one of the most delightful prose-poems ever penned. Mr. Muir describes what he saw and felt during a violent storm when he had climbed, on a Douglas spruce, a hundred feet high, to the summit of a lofty

ridge, clinging to its elastic top for hours, describing with it arcs of twenty to thirty degrees. What he saw in his "travels on a tree top," and what he heard—each tree "singing its own song, and making its own peculiar gesture"—the reader must look for in the book itself; but we cannot refrain from quoting his admirable analysis of Sierra mountain air—the delicious fragrance that intoxicates all the fortunate visitors to the Yosemite:

> The fragrance of the woods was less marked than that produced during warm rain, when so many balsam buds and leaves are steeped like tea: but, from the chafing of resiny branches against each other, and the incessant attrition of myriads of needles, the gale was spiced to a very tonic degree. And besides the fragrance from these local sources there were traces of scents brought from afar. For this wind came first from the sea, rubbing against its fresh, briny waves, then distilled through the redwoods, threading rich, ferny gulches, and spreading itself in broad, undulating currents over many a flower enamelled ridge of the coast mountains, then across the golden plains, up the purple foothills, and into these piny woods with the varied incense gathered by the way.

Twenty illustrations of various mountain trees—ranging from the graceful, slender *Pinus tuberculata* to the giant Sequoia—add to the interest of the long chapter on the forests, in which the section on the Big Trees occupies a prominent place. In the opinion of Mr. Muir, these Big Trees might continue to excite the awe and admiration of man for ever, were it not for man's own depredations. Their vitality is practically inexhaustible. They produce abundance of seeds, millions being ripened annually by the same tree; he has found eighty-six saplings in the soil of an uprooted tree; groups are widely scattered—as widely as ever, as he gives good reason for believing; drought does not hurt them, as they withstand it best of all trees; but they suffer most of all trees from fires, especially those set by the sheep-herders; and unless protective measures are speedily taken, in a few decades nothing but scarred monuments will be left.

Mr. Muir defends the mountains of California from the charge that there is hardly any animal life in them. The dusty tourist who goes to the Yosemite in a noisy stage will, indeed, see little of life. But if he will, Thoreau-like, or Muir-like, make his home in the woods, he will soon find himself surrounded by animal friends. He will make the pleasing discovery that wild sheep are less timid than the tame. Mr. Muir was once snowbound on Mount Shasta for three days, and when the storm abated he found that a band of wild sheep had weathered the storm under a group of dwarf pines a few yards above his storm nest. To these animals he devotes a separate chapter, and another to the water-ouzel, which makes its home near the waterfalls, never leaving them, and which, like the mocking-bird, always has new strains in its song. Very amusing is his biography of the bold and omnipresent Douglas squirrel, who handles one-half of all the cones; he throws them on the ground, and is often obliged to hasten down and drive away lazy pilferers below. He is not good for food: "eating his flesh is like chewing gum." Then there are the humming-birds, woodpeckers, grouse, quails, crows, jays, and many other birds; deer, bears, beavers digging chambers in the glacier meadows, etc. Of bears Mr. Muir has no fear—like them, going through thickets on all fours; and in following the bear trails he "often found tufts of hair on the bushes, where they had forced themselves through." Indians, too, he has met occasionally—Mono Indians, clad in geological dirt and rabbit skins, begging whiskey and tobacco, on their way to the Yosemite to get acorns and a trout supper; or gathering the wild rye, which grows to a height of six to eight feet, or the pine nuts, of which one man can gather thirty to forty bushels in a season—food for man, horse, dog, as well as for birds and squirrels. The crop is larger than the State's wheat crop, but hardly a bushel in a thousand is ever gathered. White men have been killed by Indians for cutting down these bread trees—a penalty which would have been more justifiable in the case of the murderers of the venerable Sequoias. (p. 367)

*"A Mountain Enthusiast," in* The Nation, *Vol. 59, No. 1533, November 15, 1894, pp. 366-67.*

### THE ATHENAEUM (essay date 1895)

[*In the following review of* The Mountains of California, *an English critic condemns Muir's prose style, denounces his theory of glacial erosion, and questions the value of his aggressive approach to wilderness exploration.*]

Mr. Muir has published a most irritating volume. [*The Mountains of California*] is not, like so many books of travel, the diary of a tourist, filled out with insignificant personal detail, but an account of the highlands of California, their bold peaks and ridges, splendid forests, and fertile foot-hills, written by one who has wandered among them for years, and unites keen enjoyment of scenery with a strong taste for natural history. Unfortunately, Mr. Muir has spoilt his material and made his pages very hard of digestion—at any rate for English readers—by his constant indulgence in an unbridled luxury of language. These are specimens, taken at random, of his descriptive style: "It is easy to find the bright lake-eyes in the roughest and most ungovernable-looking topography of any landscape countenance." Rocks have "an expressive outspokenness"; cañons "maze wildly through the mighty host of mountains"; they are "Nature's poems, carved on tables of stone, the simplest and most emphatic of her glacial compositions." We fear the author has studied Mr. Ruskin to bad purpose. He has also, as is indicated by the last quotation, framed all his ideas of the part played by glaciers in mountain erosion in accordance with the wildest form of the glacial hypothesis. He believes that every lake basin, every valley, is the work of the ice-spade. So far he is in respectable company; but he must needs go further (or higher) still. According to Mr. Muir the passes in the watershed are "simply those portions of the range more degraded by glacial action than the adjacent portions." "The glaciers are the pass-makers. Without exception every pass in the Sierra was created by them without the slightest aid or predetermining guidance from any of the cataclysmic agents." This crude dogmatism is thrust on his reader without a hint that in North America as in Europe the balance of recent evidence and of scientific opinion, while acknowledging the work of ice in surface abrasion, tends to confine within comparatively narrow limits its power of erosive action.

As an observer Mr. Muir is more instructive than as a theorist. He points out very clearly the conservative part played by ice in protecting the concavities of the mountain from the inroads of landslips and fluvial deposits. The lakes and tarns are found on the higher part of the chain, from which the glacial covering has been comparatively recently removed; lower down the basins are choked and meadow platforms take their place. A similar process is now going on in many parts of the Alps, and, owing to the greater rapidity of denudation, has been almost completed in the Caucasus and on the southern slope of the Himalaya.

Since the early days when Mr. Clarence King climbed an icicle, mountaineering methods and incidents in the Far West have never been commonplace or lost anything in the description. Mr. Muir's chief adventure is a singular confession of an unsuccessful attempt at suicide.

In the middle of October . . . Mr. Muir left his companions a day's march from the foot of the mountain, to attempt alone "the untouched summit" of Mount Ritter. The height of the peak is, we are told, about 13,300 ft., and "it is fenced round by steeply inclined glaciers and cañons of tremendous depth and ruggedness." After a night in the forest, the climber, with a "hard durable crust" in his pocket by way of provision, set out for the climb. At first all went well. He "strode on exhilarated as if never more to feel fatigue, limbs moving of themselves, every sense unfolding like the thawing flowers to take part in the new day harmony." Before long, however, the tune was interrupted. A snowfield which had suffered itself "to be scampered over in fine tone" rose up so steeply in the climber's face that he found himself "in danger of being shed off like avalanching snow." Nevertheless Mr. Muir continued to ascend "by creeping on all fours and shuffling up the steepest places on my back"! . . . After all, Mr. Muir's shuffling was unsuccessful, and he had to descend, traverse a ridge, and cross "a chasm" and a crevassed glacier to the mouth of "a narrow avalanche gully" through which he began to climb. The rocks were "glazed in many places with a thin coating of ice," which he had to hammer off with stones. For the man was all the time axeless. But the worst was still to come. At a height estimated as 12,800 ft. the gully was broken by a cliff some 50 ft. high and inadequately provided with footholds. The climber, after reflecting, like Edward Lear's Mr. and Mrs. "Discobbolos," that he should "never go down any more" by the way he had climbed, faced the cliff. The situation is thus described:—

> After gaining a point about half-way to the top I was suddenly brought to a dead stop with arms outspread, clinging close to the face of the rock unable to move hand or foot either up or down. My doom appeared fixed. I *must* fall. There would be a moment of bewilderment, and then a lifeless rumble down the one general precipice to the glacier below. When this final danger flashed upon me I became nerve-shaken for the first time since setting foot on the mountains, and my mind seemed to fill with a stifling smoke. But this terrible eclipse lasted only a moment, when life blazed forth again with preternatural clearness. I seemed suddenly to become possessed of a new sense. The other self, bygone experiences, Instinct or Guardian Angel—call it what you will—came forward and assumed control.

Persons on whose nerves the immediate prospect of travelling in "a lifeless rumble" has so decided an effect should not, it is obvious, climb alone. The new sense that came to Mr. Muir's relief proved a very abiding guardian angel, for on the descent we find him threading his way through the slippery mazes of a crevassed icefall by digging—how we are not told—hollows for the feet "in the rotten portions of the blocks." After that he lapsed into "a confident saunter"!

Mr. Muir, we feel sure, had a fine climb. But is this how they like their climbing done in the New World? Doubtless, as Emerson puts it, the climate "rears purer wits, inventive eyes." And then they have no effete body of "podgy barristers and overfed parsons''—to quote the definition of the Alpine Club once given by a criticized author—to set up an academical standard of self-preservation and discourage the romance of mountain travel!

Mr. Muir's volume is naturally not all so entertaining as the chapter we have imperfectly analyzed; but it is far more generally interesting and instructive than might be gathered from these extracts. In dealing with the forests and the life of the creatures which inhabit them,—the wild sheep, the fascinating Douglas squirrels, and beautiful water ouzels—he shows the spirit of a true naturalist. He makes us long to visit the open glades and noble groves of gigantic pines, where no undergrowth, as in moister regions, impedes the free enjoyment of the woodlands. He suggests curious speculations as to the influence of ancient glaciers in determining the habitat of some of the trees. In conclusion, he condescends to the wild gardens of the foot-hills, where man has not yet extirpated an exquisite indigenous flora, and bee-farming is practised on a scale unequalled in any other region.

We must conclude as we began. The book is a provoking one. An author who had much to tell has spoilt his story in the telling. (pp. 77-8)

> *A review of "The Mountains of California," in* The Athenaeum, *Vol. 105, January 19, 1895, pp. 77-8.*

### JOHN BURROUGHS (essay date 1912)

[*Burroughs was an American poet and naturalist who, like Muir, was profoundly influenced by the writings of Transcendentalists Ralph Waldo Emerson and Henry David Thoreau. In the following excerpt, he discusses some strengths and weaknesses of* The Yosemite.]

Mr. Muir knows his Yosemite like a book, and the book he has written about it leaves little more to be said on the subject. [*Yosemite*] is an exhaustive survey of all the principal features of the famous valley, giving a detailed description of the waterfalls, the towering rocks, the trees, the birds, the wild flowers, the storms, the floods, the climate, with some account of its history and of the pioneers whose names are closely associated with the valley, with the addition of guide-book features for the benefit of tourists, laying out routes for one-day, two-day, and three-day trips, enlivened now and then with episodes from his own personal adventures during his life of three or four years amid those stupendous scenes. I think that most of his readers will wish that he had continued, through the entire work, the personal-narrative form with which he opens the volume, and thus strung his descriptions upon the thread of his own life there, to a much greater extent than he has done. The personal element was one great source of the charm of his recent book, *My First Summer in the Sierra*. Still his reader has not much reason to complain on this score.

While making a guide-book to Yosemite, he has given us a pretty good guide to John Muir. It is a Muir book, and no other man could have written it. Probably no other man in this country has his enthusiasm for mountains and glaciers and waterfalls and big trees united with so rare a literary gift. We get many vivid glimpses of the Sierra-smitten Scot in these pages. We tremble for him when we see him peering over the dizzy brink of Yosemite Falls, clinging to a shelf of rock three inches wide with his audacious heels. And again when he climbs the high, hollow ice-cone formed by the spray of the falls, in order to get a look inside of it. This cone was four or five hundred feet

high and the crater-like mouth into which the water poured was over one hundred feet in diameter. After many drenchings and hair-breadth escapes from fragments of falling ice, he gained a point where he could look down one hundred feet into the interior of this ice volcano, and his adventurous soul was satisfied. With an uneasy feeling we see him again climbing South Dome while it is covered with a fresh fall of snow, following in the footsteps of George Anderson, another Scot who had, reached the summit by means of eye-bolts inserted in holes which he drilled in the rock as he progressed up an almost vertical surface for a distance of four or five hundred feet. Anderson tried to dissuade Muir from making the attempt under the unfavorable conditions that then existed, but Scot could not discourage Scot, and Muir gained the summit. "It was one of those brooding, changeful days that come between the Indian summer and winter, when the leaf-colors have grown dim and the clouds come and go among the cliffs like living creatures looking for work; now hovering aloft, now caressing rugged rock-brows with great gentleness, or wandering afar over the tops of the forest, touching the spires of fir and pine with their soft silken fringes, as if trying to tell the glad news of the coming of snow." Of course, "the first view was perfectly glorious." But the most surprizing, if not the most "glorious," sight he saw from the summit of South Dome, was the "Specter of the Brocken"—his own shadow "clearly outlined, about half a mile long," thrown upon "the glorious white surface" of a vast sea of cloud beneath him. "I walked back and forth," he says, "waved my arms, and struck all sorts of attitudes to see every slightest movement enormously exaggerated." During all his gazing from mountain tops this was the only time he ever saw the startling "Specter of the Brocken." . . .

Mr. Muir is a nature-lover of a fine type, one of the best the country has produced. But it may be the reader gets a little tired at times of the frequent recurrence in his pages of a certain note—a note which doubtless dates from his inherited Scottish Presbyterianism. Whatever else wild nature is, she certainly is not pious, and has never been trained in the Sunday-school. But, as reflected in Mr. Muir's pages, she very often seems on her way to or from the kirk. All his streams and waterfalls and avalanches and storm-buffeted trees sing songs, or hymns, or psalms, or rejoice in some other proper Presbyterian manner. One would hardly be surprised to hear his avalanches break out with the Doxology. The sugar-pine "spreads his arms above the yellow pine in blessing," while the latter "rocks and waves in sign of recognition." In contrasting the sugar-pine with the silence and rigidity of the juniper, he says: "in calm, sunny days the sugar-pine preaches like an enthusiastic apostle without moving a leaf." "A little more than a little" of this sort of thing in the description of the various phases of nature "is by much too much," and there is often too much of it in Mr. Muir's pages and conversation. Just as there is at times too much of another element which is much less Scottish and much more Western—I refer to his "glorious experiences," his "glorious views," his "glorious canopies," his "glorious floods," and his "glorious" this, that, and the other, rivaling our Fourth-of-July orators in his over-use of this cheap epithet. However, such things are but specks in the clear amber of his style, but they are all the more noticeable because they are flies in the amber.

One finds just the right touch in such an account as this of the snow-plant: "The entire plant—flowers, bracts, stems, scales, and roots—is fiery red. Its color should appeal to one's blood; nevertheless, it is a singularly cold and unsympathetic plant. Everybody admires it as a wonderful curiosity, but nobody loves it as lilies, violets, roses, daisies are loved. Without fragrance it stands beneath the pines and firs lonely and silent, as if unacquainted with any other plant in the world; never moving in the wildest storms; rigid as if lifeless, tho covered with beautiful rosy flowers.'' (p. 1165)

Mr. Muir is never more eloquent than when he writes about the glaciers. I must give myself the pleasure of quoting the fine passage with which he ends his discussion of the work of the ancient glaciers: ''Water rivers work openly where people dwell, and so does the rain, and the sea, thundering on all the shores of the world; and the universal ocean of air, tho invisible, speaks aloud in a thousand voices, and explains its mode of working and its power. But glaciers, back in their white solitudes, work apart from men, exerting their tremendous energies in silence and darkness. Outspread, spirit-like, they brood above the predestined landscape, work on unwearied through immeasurable ages, until, in the fulness of time, the mountains and valleys are brought forth, channels formed for the rivers, basins made for lakes and meadows and arms of the sea, soils spread for forests and fields; then they shrink and vanish like summer clouds.'' (p. 1168)

*John Burroughs, ''John Muir's 'Yosemite','' in Literary Digest, New York, Vol. XLIV, No. 22, June 1, 1912, pp. 1165, 1168.*

*Muir and Theodore Roosevelt at Glacier Point, in the Yosemite valley.*

**MARK VAN DOREN**  (essay date 1922)

[*Van Doren was one of the most prolific men of letters in twentieth-century American writing. His work includes poetry (for which he won the Pulitzer Prize in 1939), novels, short stories, drama, criticism, social commentary, and the editing of a number of popular anthologies. Van Doren's criticism is aimed at the general reader, rather than the scholar or specialist, and is noted for its lively perception and wide interest. Like his poetry and fiction, his criticism consistently examines the inner, idealistic life of the individual. In the following excerpt, he compares Muir with other prominent nature writers.*]

The spectacle of what we are in the habit of calling Nature has produced almost as many species of observer as there are species of wind, rock, animal, and plant to be observed. There are idiotic animals and plants, and we have been plagued with idiotic Nature-writers, plagued until we incline to shy at new ones, fearing that if we encourage them they will strike an attitude or babble a gospel. Still, there are the eagle and the bluebird, the otter and the fox; there are Audubon, Thoreau, Burroughs, Hudson, Muir.

Burroughs said once, with characteristic modesty and accuracy: ''Thoreau . . . has a heroic quality that I cannot approach.'' Muir is one of the heroes. There is an excitement in his books such as we do not get from Izaak Walton, Gilbert White, Richard Jefferies, Burroughs of course, Fabre, or even Hudson, much as we may love those men in their respective times and places. He was no worker in pastoral prose like the immortal angler, nor was he immovable in a parish like the naturalist of Selborne, soaking up Nature as a turtle soaks up the sun. He did not have the pathological dependence on field and hedgerow that the lonely Jefferies had; he did not concentrate upon the fascinating minutiae with which the books of Burroughs are methodically filled; he did not do his looking with the almost insect eyes of Fabre. And he lacked—as who does not?—the genius of Hudson for telling tales, the beautiful, baffling gift of a simplicity that never on two pages is the same. Muir belongs with Audubon and Thoreau. Not that he is anything like either, or that anyone is like Thoreau. But he shares their peculiar energy. Audubon careering through deep forests and along wide rivers after birds, Thoreau vaunting his anarchy among the hickories and woodchucks of Walden, Muir keyed by the sublimities of the Sierra to a forty years' ecstasy: these are substantially the same. (p. 431)

[Muir's] books have the virtue of variety. There was every chance for them to be monotonous. Clarence King, mountaineering in the later 1860's, found comic relief from the exaltation of the Sierra in pack-mules and the squalid Digger Indians whom he met and occasionally camped with. If the readers of Muir grow tired of the ''high, cool, green pastures'' where he feeds their minds, it can never be for long, because relief is near in the animals which he inimitably describes, the shepherds and the Indians he hits off. No pages of Burroughs or Thoreau or Fabre are livelier than those of Muir on bears, on bees, on mountain sheep, on rattlesnakes, on the Douglas squirrels, and on those equally living things, the redwoods and the valley flowers. (pp. 431-32)

Muir's two Arctic volumes, **Travels in Alaska** and **The Cruise of the Corwin,** are triumphs of the same sort. The danger in their case was that too much should be said about ice and snow. Muir, whose constitution after all was of the purest and coldest stuff, who looked upon the universe with veritably ''glacial eyes,'' got all the whiteness possible into his report, but when he had got that in, resorted to Eskimos and reindeer, seals and polar bears, for entertainment. The Arctic volumes, like all the others that he stole good time from nature to assemble from old notes, have every sign that they will seem refreshing and important as long as there are persons to read them. (p. 433)

Mark Van Doren, "John Muir," in The Nation, *New York, Vol. CXIV, No. 2962, April 12, 1922, pp. 431-33.*

**NORMAN FOERSTER** (essay date 1923)

[*Foerster was an American critic who wrote numerous studies of American literature. In the following excerpt, he discusses Muir's personal philosophy and his style of nature writing.*]

[Nature], to John Muir, was vastly more than matter permeated with law. Had he looked upon it so, he might have been a more productive scientist; but he regarded it, instead, as the unspeakably beautiful work of a loving creator, and consequently produced books that are only secondarily scientific, and primarily literary. More and more, as time goes on, and as later botanists, geographers, physiographers, and geologists supplement Muir's studies till they are covered over with accretions, as if they belonged to an earlier geological age, we shall go to such books as *The Mountains of California, Our National Parks,* and *My First Summer in the Sierra* for a living and accurate picture of the Great West such as no one else is likely soon to duplicate.

Muir emphasized several causes that make it impossible for most men to look upon nature, with him, as the unspeakably beautiful work of a loving creator, the temple of God in which man may worship. One cause is fear. Men are afraid of nature. They will sometimes venture into the wilderness when they can lean on each other, but to entrust their precious selves to cruel nature alone is too much. Yet, as Muir points out, all the "dangers" of the wilderness—all the colds, fevers, Indians, bears, snakes, "bugs," impassable rivers, jungles of brush, and quick and sure starvation—are either imaginary or grossly exaggerated, and even if they are not, amount to nothing in comparison with the dangers of living indoors in crowded cities. . . . A wise man will perceive that frightful canyons and glacier crevasses are part of an orderly whole; that a great storm is "a cordial outpouring of Nature's love"; that all, indeed, "that we in our unbelief call terrible" is really an expression of the divine love.

Another cause for the blindness of men is the mistaken conception of nature as existing for man's use. Blandly asserting that nature was made for man's material needs—sheep for his clothing, oil for lighting his dark ways, lead for his bullets— most men cherish a curious view of the importance of man. Man is only one of many creatures, and the Lord loves them all. "The creation of all for the happiness of one" seems to this fellow-countryman of Adam Smith an inequitable arrangement of the universe: instead he proposes as the probable object "the happiness of each one of them," and goes on to confute his opponents by pointing out that this earth-ship on which we proudly sail had made many a successful journey round the heavens before *Homo sapiens* was created, and that things may be conducted very satisfactorily after man has disappeared from the world. Why, then, he asks, should man value himself as more than one small part of the great whole? Man is not distinct from, not above nature, but a part of it with his brother winds and rocks, all alike "fashioned with loving care" and all equally admirable.

Still another cause is the meanness of man. Man has desecrated not only nature but himself. More and more men live in cities, dirty, ugly, and morally impure cities. If they live in the country it is perhaps only to seek wealth in sheep, and the shepherd type is produced, living in many-voiced nature but hearing only "baa"! "Even the howls and ki-yis of coyotes might be blessings if well heard, but he hears them only through a blur of mutton and wool, and they do him no good." Or they become gold miners, hardy, adventurous, blazing a trail to nature's utmost fastnesses in disregard of dangers innumerable, as bold as Muir himself tracing his glaciers to their lairs in the mountains—but always blind to the beauty they desecrate, utterly deaf in their immorality, to the celestial love-music of nature. Beholding what God has made of nature, we may indeed deplore what man has made of man. One of the noblest of men, Emerson, Muir terms the sequoia of the human race, yet makes us feel that compelled to choose between the two, he would have discarded the man and kept the tree. The same choice he made more broadly in constantly quoting, as his ministerial friend Young tells us he did, Wordsworth's famous stanza:

> One impulse from a vernal wood
> May teach you more of man,
> Of moral evil and of good,
> Than all the sages can.

Beauty and love in nature, then, we shall see only if emancipated from fear, utilitarianism, and meanness of soul. That Muir was never threatened by any one of the three is manifest from his books and the story of his life. Others have responded to nature more profoundly, but none with more rampant enthusiasm. The wealth of one mountain day was enough to make him run home in the moonlight happy beyond words, and he recorded such days in his journal with a lover's abandon. According to Young, his constant exclamation on beholding a fine landscape was, "Praise God from whom all blessings flow!" It was a never-failing cause of surprise and gratitude to him "to think that He should plan to bring us feckless creatures here at the right moment, and then flash such glories at us." In his first summer in the Sierra, upon seeing a certain view he shouted and gesticulated so extravagantly that the sheep-dog Carlo came up to him with the most ludicrous puzzled expression in his eyes, and a brown bear in the thicket ran away in a panic, tumbling over the manzanita bushes in his haste. He was so enamoured of the Sierras that he asserted that he would be content among them forever if tethered to a stake; and with more literal truth, he said that, if it were not for the need of bread, civilization would never see him again. In his enthusiasm for all of God's handiwork he refused to kill animals for food, and even spared the rattlesnakes that he encountered—after all, they were not *his* snakes.

Rapt away by his enthusiasm, Muir enjoyed many hours when his scientific pursuits were laid aside, together with the whole of his rational impedimenta, and his personality was freely immersed in the landscape. Like the bees and butterflies, he would "lave in the vital sunshine, too richly and homogeneously joy-filled to be capable of partial thought," till he became "all eye, sifted through and through with light and beauty." Intoxicated with the champagne water, distilled air, and his own glad animal movements, it seemed to him that beauty entered, not through the eyes alone, but through all his flesh, like heat radiating from a camp-fire, "making a passionate, ecstatic pleasure-glow not explainable," as if his flesh-and-bone tabernacle were transparent as glass to the beauty surrounding it, "truly an inseparable part of it, thrilling with the air and trees, streams and rocks, in the waves of the sun—a part of all nature, neither old nor young, sick nor well, but immortal''—immortal because life now seemed neither long nor short, and time meant no more to him than to the trees and stars. In such hours Muir was impressed with the familiarity of natural objects, their human warmth; ''no wonder,'' he says, ''when we consider that we have the same Father and Mother.'' Yet he never went so far as to maintain that, in such hours, he was laid asleep in body and became, with Wordsworth, a living soul privileged to ''see into the life of things.'' It was not spiritual insight that he enjoyed, but a pleasure-glow, a pure sensation, not a sensation exalted by thought; his body, deliciously alive, pulsed with nature. What we might call the human element in man had not been transcended but simply omitted. Muir was inclined to think that man is at his best, not when he is most human, but when he is most natural.

But one does not go to John Muir for a criticism of life. He understood neither the heights and depths of his own nature, which he avoided as most of us avoid the dizzy heights and depths of the material world, nor the complexities of social life—the boundless results of man's being a gregarious animal. When Emerson said of him that he was greater than Thoreau, he must have been thinking, not of Thoreau the moralist, but of Thoreau the naturalist. It is as a literary naturalist that Muir is perhaps greater than Thoreau and certainly equal to Burroughs. Knowing his facts perfectly, he had the capacity to present them not only with truth but also with charm. His description of nature—and most of his writing is merely description—has a degree of vividness that reminds one of those ocularly-minded masters of his day, Carlyle and Ruskin.

His sensuous perception, like Thoreau's, was unspoiled by tobacco or liquor—he drank only tea and mountain water. Then, he had a good plastic sense, saw the compositions of nature with an artist's eye, throwing up his arms for a frame, and often sketching in order to commemorate a scene or to bolster up his geological notes. But far more important than his sensuous alertness and æsthetic appreciation was his enthusiasm—his passionate absorption in nature's law and nature's beauty. He had, as we began by saying, the ecstasy of both the scientist and the poet, and it is this ecstasy, more than anything else, that gives power to his account of natural appearances.

Everywhere his enthusiasm revealed to him the principle of life. His landscape is ever ''filled with warm God''; it is a living, breathing, moving landscape, rather than so much expressionless matter outstaring the beholder. His clouds, his very rocks, are instinct with life. A primrose by the river's brim was to him far more than a primrose. An ordinary drop of rain was no less than this: ''a silvery newborn star with lake and river, garden and grove, valley and mountain, all that the landscape holds reflected in its crystal depths, God's messenger, angel of love sent on its way with majesty and pomp and display of power that make man's greatest shows ridiculous.'' In imagination he followed each drop, some penetrating to the roots of meadow plants, some shivered to dust through the pine needles, some drumming the broad leaves of veratrum or saxifrage, some plunging straight into fragrant corollas, or into the lake, dimpling it daintily, some flinging themselves into the wild heart of falls or cascades eager to take part in the dance and the song. He remembered without an effort that everything called ''destruction'' in nature is really creation, a passage from one use to another, one form of beauty to another. The immobile and changeless face of nature, which appals the

unimaginative visitor, was to him replete with fascinating alteration.

Partly for this reason his descriptions of moving water, and storms, and the aurora borealis are usually his best work. The rain-storms of Alaska and the thunder-storms of the Sierras he described with power again and again; perhaps the best of his storm descriptions, however, is the wonderful chapter on **''A Wind-Storm in the Forests,''** which bathes the reader with thrilling light, intoxicates him with piny fragrance, and exhilarates him with pure air and swaying, straining motion. Perched for hours in the top of a Douglas spruce ''with muscles firm braced, like a bobolink on a reed,'' swaying backward and forward, round and round, describing every capricious curve in the air, closing his eyes now and then to enjoy the music the better, or to drink in the tonic fragrance of chafed pine boughs, Muir experienced novel sensations—became, for the time, a pinecrest passive but thrilled by the booming wind. He watched the play of light over the forest billowing like summer grain, he listened to the orchestra of the pines—the deep bass of the naked branches, the shrill hiss and silken murmur of the needles. And he described what he saw and heard with a combination of accurate perceptiveness and bounding emotion that is truly memorable.

Nor does one soon forget the supernal beauty of the aurora at the close of *Travels in Alaska.* Wrapped in his blankets, lying on a glacial moraine, Muir spent an entire night watching ''a glowing silver bow spanning the Muir Inlet in a magnificent arch right under the zenith . . . the ends resting on the top of the mountain walls'':

> so brilliant, so fine and solid and homogeneous in every part, I fancy that if all the stars were raked together into one windrow, fused and welded and run through some celestial rolling-mill, all would be required to make this one glowing white colossal bridge. . . . At length while it yet spanned the inlet in serene and unchanging splendor, a band of fluffy, pale gray, quivering ringlets came suddenly all in a row over the eastern mountain-top, glided in nervous haste up and down the under side of the bow and over the western mountain-wall. . . . Had these lively auroral fairies marched across the fiord on the top of the bow instead of shuffling along the under side of it, one might have fancied they were a happy band of spirit people on a journey making use of the splendid bow for a bridge.

And so on through several pages of delicately sensitive description.

Where there is action, where there is a narrative element in description, as in Muir's account of moving water, roving storms, and evanescent Northern lights, the picture is held together by the cohesive quality of the subject itself. But, as Lessing demonstrated long ago, where this chronological thread is wanting, the picture easily falls apart, one group of details canceling another group, so that the total impression is a blur or a blank. Sheer description in literature is indeed dangerous, now as in the eighteenth century, and yet the suffusion of modern descriptive passages with imagination—not a conspicuous commodity in the age of prose and reason—has gone far to justify ''pen portraits'' and literary landscape-painting. In Muir's writing, thanks to his kindling imagination, one rarely feels that he is going beyond the boundaries of literature and foolishly competing with the painter; a principle of life animates all his work—life in the thing seen, life in the seer.

Nowhere does this principle of life manifest itself more strikingly than in the fresh, free-ranging figures of speech that are nearly certain to illuminate his scenes wherever they are in danger of being darkened with words. The muddy floods that rush down the gorges and gulches during a shower roar "like lions rudely awakened, each of the tawny brood actually kicking up a dust at the first onset." The mountain tarns in early summer "begin to blink and thaw out like sleepy eyes." The hairs of the squirrel's tail quiver in the breeze "like pine-needles." In the dry weather of midsummer in the lower part of the Sierra "the withered hills and valleys seem to lie as empty and expressionless as dead shells on a shore." Muir's metaphors and similes are abundant, new, and apt; they reveal because they proceed from the poet in him.

Life, too, results from his frequent use of onomatopœia. His very words become sentient and mimic the mood of the moment. There are obvious instances everywhere, and also subtle ones that easily escape notice. This is obvious (the topic is icebergs on the Pacific coast):

> Nearly all of them are swashed and drifted by wind and tide back and forth in the fiords until finally melted by the ocean water. . . .

In the following, the contrast between two types of motion is emphasized by the word sounds:

> Butterflies, too, and moths . . . ; some wide-winged like bats, flapping slowly and sailing in easy curves; others like small flying violets shaking about loosely in short zigzag flights.

One more, in which the style reflects perfectly the quiet grace of the deer:

> Deer give beautiful animation to the forests, harmonizing finely in their color and movements with the gray and brown shafts of the trees and the swaying of the branches as they stand in groups at rest, or move gracefully and noiselessly over the mossy ground about the edges of beaver-meadows and flowery glades, daintily culling the leaves and tips of the mints and aromatic bushes on which they feed.

This means of adding to verisimilitude is not rare in Muir's style, but is, rather, a normal method. In all his description he seems to have felt, more than most writers do, that the sound of his phrases and sentences must carry a large part of the sense, and this is clearly one reason why his description is impressive.

Finally, he attained life through speed. His language does not emerge soberly, but flings itself out and hastens on as if word pursued word, sentence pursued sentence, like the pouring notes of a musical composition that rush over every obstacle to their triumph. This is not to say that he wrote with facility, since we know that he did not. "Very irksome" he pronounced "this literary business"; he worked laboriously, rewriting many of his most poetical chapters repeatedly. Hard writing often makes easy reading, and indeed no style could be much simpler than Muir's. It is perhaps too simple, too unvaried, too coördinated, too breathless in its persistent predication, so that one longs to stop, now and then, to rest and muse. At times his style has the melody and the imaginative magnificence of Ruskin, but the melody is rarely swelling, the magnificence rarely deep and reserved. Both Muir and Ruskin were nourished on the Bible and knew most of it by heart, and both became ardent admirers of nature and described her beauties with a lover's eye for detail; but whereas Muir became a scientist,

Ruskin became a critic of life in several distinct fields; his work is therefore reflective. It is Muir's lack of reflection, betrayed by his restless, hurried style, that prevented his attaining a high position in our literature. Accurate and enthusiastic description of nature will go far, but no matter how remarkably accurate and enthusiastic, it cannot reach preëminence without the deeper elements infused by the mind and the spirit.

Even as description, then, his work suffers from its comparative superficiality. Yet who has described *what* Muir described *as* he described it? The human life of the West has been frequently pictured in our literature, most notably perhaps by Parkman and Bret Harte and Joaquin Miller. Their West is, however, a thing of the past, recognized as such by Muir decades ago; those trying times of the pioneers, he exclaims, have already become "dim as if a thousand years had passed over them." Parkman, Harte, and Miller, moreover, did not present the physical aspect of the West adequately—the physical West is exacting because it is so wonderful. Perhaps John Muir's treatment of it, persistently divorced from the human life of the region, is also inadequate; perhaps in time it will be superseded. Yet to-day it remains the most telling description we have of a part of America that has become steadily more important in the development of our continental democracy.

Whoever would know the Far West, from Alaska to Mexico, from the Coast to the Rockies, must know John Muir. Of course, he could scarcely master and reveal with equal distinctness all of this tremendous area. But the part that he knew by heart and described with greatest power is itself large—the National Parks, and the Sierras from giant Whitney to giant Shasta, his beloved "Range of Light," as he preferred to call it, the most beautiful mountains he had climbed in all his wanderings. The purple and gold of the valley flowers massed as perhaps nowhere else in the world; the lovely foothills penetrated with water coursing from the glaciers and snowbanks above; the breathless sublimities of the high mountains, whether storm-shrouded, or shining in the white light with a clearness surpassed nowhere, or flushing with the tender rosy alpenglow as if awaiting a vespertine benediction; the wild, tossing landscape seen from above, with only the sky overhead, a nerve-trying chaos unless one's conviction of nature's order and goodness be like Muir's; the roaring of many waters, the crack and boom of avalanches, the many-mooded winds, singing or flowing softly or beating with passion; the naked rocks, weather-worn through ages, their recorded history opening up the procession of time; the wild sheep, demonstrators of the impossible, "unworn and perfect as if created on the spot"; the brave little water ouzel, Muir's darling comrade in the wildest canyons and gorges, living unconcerned and singing sweetly in the spray of thunderous waters; the Douglas squirrel of the pine woods, vibrant in every atom, the accomplished mockingbird of squirrels; the wonderful trees, the sugar pine, the nut pine, the Douglas spruce, the white silver fir, the red fir, all of them as beautiful and grand as any in America, and the monarch of them all, the famous *Sequoia gigantea*, over three hundred feet high, swaying in the Sierra winds when Christ walked in Palestine.

In his *Mountains of California, Our National Parks, The Yosemite, My First Summer in the Sierra,* Muir gave this region to the country—both to those who could not go to see and to those who, having eyes, saw not. That is his foremost achievement. And in a more literal sense may it be said that he gave this region to the country, for it was he, more probably than any other one man, who was responsible for the adoption of our policy of national parks. (pp. 250-63)

*Norman Foerster, "Muir," in his* Nature in American Literature: Studies in the Modern View of Nature, *1923. Reprint by Russell & Russell, 1958, pp. 238-63.*

### HENRY CHESTER TRACY (essay date 1930)

[*In the following excerpt, Tracy discusses the development of Muir's prose style.*]

[John Muir's] gift of anecdote was notable, and [John] Burroughs found his talk more entertaining than the work of his pen; but it is the pen that will live. Take away the humorous banter, the fervor, the sparkle and easy flow of his conversation you still have something, imperishable and serene and satisfying preserved in his prose. There he does not seek to divert you, or dazzle, or even persuade you but gives you those simplicities which are so like the very air of the Sierras that you are persuaded he has no conscious art.

It was unconscious, naïve, at the first; was impulsive even when mature. We have proofs. The first is from a childish period when, I suppose, nature is at least faintly alive as an experience, in all of us. There was certainly nothing, at that time, to distinguish ten-year-old John Muir from Willie Chisolm or Bob Richardson of the same age. All three sought birds and nests and listened with enthusiasm to the skylarks; but one remembered and recorded the fact.

> Oftentimes on a broad meadow near Dunbar we stood for hours enjoying their marvellous singing. . . .
>
> To test our eyes we often watched a lark until he seemed a faint speck in the sky and finally passed beyond the keenest-sighted of us all. "I see him yet!" we would cry, "I see him yet". . . . as he soared. And finally only one of us would be left to claim that he saw him. At last he, too, would have to admit that the singer had soared beyond his sight, and still the music came pouring down to us in glorious profusion, from a height far above our vision. . . .

—and he dilates on the power of flight, the power and richness of the song. The next is from a period when galling and almost stunting farm-labor at the first Wisconsin homestead was relieved by refreshing contacts and penetrating observations of wild animals and birds—the frozen spermophile that would not revive by hearth-heat as the frozen pickerel had done; the flock of quail found frozen in a circle in the thicket, where they had packed for warmth; the gray squirrel kept clandestinely in the spare room—a wealth of reminiscence, from which I quote only one.

> Once I found a poor snipe in our meadow that was unable to fly on account of difficult egg-birth. Pitying the poor mother, I picked her up out of the grass and helped her as gently as I could, and as soon as the egg was born she flew gladly away.

The next is more illuminating because from a mind more mature, more imaginative which, at the age of twenty-five, has been quickened by a chance encounter with a botanist on the steps of North Hall. (A few words from M. S. Griswold, anent the relationship of the locust tree, whose blossoms hung over their heads as they talked, wakened an interest that never flagged through the remainder of his days.) About a year after that incident he wandered alone, in the forests of Canada, equipped

as a plant-student and financed by a few dollars earned in summer work at his brother-in-law's farm. The interest in botany is not surprising. That he should take his interest in the shape of an enthusiasm was like him. But no collector's infatuation with strange plants, and no student's enthusiasm for new species and names accounts for the tenor of this memorandum on an orchid which Gray's Manual, in the chaste language of pure science, describes as having "sepals and petals similar, ascending, spreading oblong-lanceolate, acute, magenta-crimson, rarely white." In contrast, the intensity of this nature-experience for young Muir, his naïveté in describing it, will appear so incomprehensible to many that it seems almost wiser to pass it by as private lore; yet of what use are words of a naturist unless they reveal nature as perceived by him—person and mind, with emotions intact, not sterilized and processed by an intellectual cult? It had been a long lonely ramble in an arbor-vitæ and tamarack swamp, with much wading of bogs and difficult forcing of tangles among heaps of fallen trees. Faint and hungry, fearing he must pass the night among these glooms and windfalls, almost at sun-down he met his charmer, a flower named after the Grecian nymph:

> I found beautiful Calypso on the mossy bank of a stream, growing not in the ground but on a bed of yellow mosses in which its small white bulb had found a soft nest and from which its one leaf and one flower sprung. The flower was white and made the impression of the utmost simple purity like a snow-flower. No other bloom was near it, for the bog a short distance below the surface was still frozen, and the water was ice-cold. It seemed the most spiritual of the flower people I had ever met. I sat down beside it and fairly cried for joy.
>
> It seems wonderful that so frail and lowly a plant has such power over human hearts. This Calypso meeting happened some forty-five years ago, and it was more memorable and impressive than any of my meetings with human beings except Emerson and one or two others.

We read the account as a reminiscence, but feel it as a present thing. Such experiences, on the face of them trifling and sentimental, are in reality unforgettable and lose none of their immediacy by an interval of forty-five years. After this episode with Calypso, John Muir *Odysseus* walked to the Gulf, out of pure exuberance and will to know his world. Thence to California by boat.

Sheer physical exuberance marks much of the early writing done in California. Cautious folk have a right to discount it, since health and a state bordering on intoxication—Muir was particularly susceptible to the bracing air of the mountains—are not guarantees of that serene perception which we look to a naturist to share. However, this writing was for his friends, or it went down in his journal, and was only published when the demand for all of Muir became keen. Thus, *My First Summer in the Sierra* did not appear in print till 1911, built of journal notes.

That journal was not all enthusiasm either. Sobered by the privations of sheep-herding John Muir was obliged to write, on June 3rd, 1869, of "the poor dust-choked flock," and a few days later, of himself, in a tone not like the newly arrived immigrant, inspired by the mere act of breathing, after having lived "for nearly thirty years on common air." Instead we find, after a month's unrelieved diet of mutton,

> July 7.
> Rather weak and sickish this morning, and all about

a piece of bread. Can scarce command attention to my studies, as if one couldn't take a few days saunter in the Godful woods, without maintaining a base on a wheatfield and gristmill.

In the years that followed Muir never complained of want or weakness if he could have bread. "Just bread and water and delightful toil is all I need" expressed him well. But the toil, it appears, must be either in or concerned with "the Godful woods," whose quality he feels so securely even when sick with the unaccustomed flesh of sheep.

Writing, as we noticed before, was not easy for him, and could therefore be called a toil. That it was performed faithfully and with honest fidelity not merely to fact but to finer feeling, is what we should expect. That it would have enduring value and a quality unknown to ordinary literature of "travel and exploration" is perhaps more than we had cause to hope.

Up to the time of Emerson's visit Muir had not become known as a writer.

It was not his vocation. So far as he knew, he had none. It should have troubled him. It troubled his friends. To him Emerson himself wrote (acknowledging letters and a gift of fragrant incense-cedar flowers):

> I have been far from unthankful—I have everywhere testified to my friends, who should also be yours, my happiness in finding you—the right man in the right place—in your mountain tabernacle and have expected when your guardian angel would pronounce that your probation and sequestration in the solitudes and snows had reached their term, and you were to bring your ripe fruits so rare and precious into waiting society . . . also, solitude, who is a sublime mistress, is an intolerable wife. So I pray you to bring to a close your absolute contract with any yet unvisited glaciers or volcanoes, roll up your drawings, herbarium and poems and come to the Atlantic coast. Here in Cambridge Dr Gray is at home, and Agassiz will doubtless be, after a month or two, returned from Terra del Fuego—perhaps through San Francisco—or you can come with him. At all events, on your arrival, which I assume is certain, you must find your way to this village, and my house. And when you are tired of our dwarf surroundings, I will show you better people.
>
> I send you two volumes, collected essays, by book post.

It is interesting to see this contact between them, and the esteem which the letter shows; between Emerson, who had known so much of Thoreau, and Muir, drawn by solitude in much the same way. Perhaps Emerson mistook his new friend's affinities when he aligned him with Asa Gray and Agassiz.

Muir was then thirty-three years old, and Emerson sixty-eight. Not till two years later did John Muir undertake his first extended engagement to write. Only after the memorable Kings-Kern-Tahoe excursion over a thousand miles of wilderness, and major mountain-climbings, did the first of his Sierra studies appear; in the *Overland Monthly,* in May, 1874. This, and the six following and consecutive **"Studies"** may be said to have launched him as a writer.

Of the peculiar and very personal difficulty to him, of the task, we learn something from a letter to Mrs. Carr, written about this time. It was she that had urged upon him the writing of *Studies in the Sierra.*

His affinities, as hinted earlier, were not with the scholarly Gray or the genial Swiss biologist. Imagine either of those two men making a complaint like this:

> Book-making frightens me because it demands so much artificialness and retrograding. Somehow up here in these fountain skies (of Yosemite) I feel like a flake of glass through which light passes, but which, conscious of the inexhaustible sun, its fountain, cares not whether its passing light coins itself into other forms or goes unchanged—neither charcoaled nor diamonded! Moreover, I find that though I have a few thoughts entangled in the fibers of my mind, I possess no words into which I can shape them. You tell me I must be patient and reach out and grope in lexicon granaries for the words I want. But if some loquacious angel were to touch my lips with literary fire, bestowing every word of Webster, I would scarce thank him for the gift, because most of the words of the English language are made of mud, for muddy purposes, while those invented to contain spiritual matter are doubtful and unfixed in capacity and form, as wind-ridden mist-rags.

The artist in a Muir who could write that was scarcely yet born, was in swaddling clothes, but with a young fist that gripped his enemy as infant Hercules the snakes. And what was this paralyzing foe? *Animal utterance* is the name I propose; and if two serpents, then *mechanical speech.* A creeping utterance could not content him, nor the "angular factiness" of a botanical language. He caught meanings above calculation and contrivance; but he did not yet know the transforming power of art upon words.

His best meanings would never be caught. They were above speech, as all must know who have been alone and glad in the high mountains, whether of California or any other land. One may think like an archangel, then—and fail of words. But this same Muir, who despaired of expression had already learned more than he was aware. Long and free-flowing thoughts on paper, to his friends, had taught him those essentials where lay his special writing-grace and charm. To Mrs. Carr, especially, he had written his most intimate joyousness in the presence of Sequoias, glaciers, falls. To McChesney he wrote with facetious exuberance; even dared to write of moonshine to Asa Gray. But the letters to Mrs. Carr, recording as they did a spiritual evolution, sometimes attained a level of literature in themselves; as when (working, like Emerson, to wean him from his mountains) she wrote disparagingly of glaciers and of ice. Not divining her ulterior purpose he was tempted to be annoyed—he could not be angry—and rallied warmly to the defence of ice-sheets and the age of cold:

> But glaciers, dear friend ice is only another form of terrestrial love. I am astonished to hear you speak so unbelievingly of God's glorious glaciers. "They are only pests" and you think them wrong in temperature, and they lived in "horrible times" and you don't care to hear about them "only that they made instruments of Yosemite music." You speak heresy for once, and deserve a dip in Methodist Tophet, or Vesuvius at least.
>
> I have just been sending ice to LeConte, and snow to McChesney and I have nothing left but hailstones for you, but I don't know how to send them—to speak them. You confuse me. You have taught me here and encouraged me to read the mountains. Now you will not listen; next summer you will be converted—you will be iced then. . . .

> You like the music instruments that glaciers made, but no songs were so grand as those of the glaciers themselves, no falls so lofty as those which poured from brows, and chasmed mountains of pure dark ice. Glaciers *made* the mountains and ground corn for all the flowers, and the forests of silver fir, made smooth paths for human feet until the sacred Sierras have become the most approachable of mountains. Glaciers came down from heaven, and they were angels with folded wings, white wings of snowy bloom. Locked hand in hand the little spirits did nobly; the primary mountain waves, unvital granite, were soon carved into beauty. They bared the lordly domes and fashioned the clustering spires; smoothed godlike mountain brows, and shaped lake cups for crystal waters; wove myriad mazy cañons, and spread them out like lace. They remembered the loud-songed rivers and every tinkling rill . . . saw all the coming flowers, and the grand predestined forests. . . .

Was ever geological hypothesis of glacial erosion so unglacially expressed? The *Letters,* which Dr. Badè has so ably edited, are full of illuminations like this. From them we know more of the personal, spontaneous, heightened and intensified Muir than we could know from any other written source.

It is pretty certain that the things Muir longed to say in his heightened person are things the world does not care to hear. The many, so far as they read him, read to hear of adventures of grandeurs, of playgrounds and the wild life in the nation's sublimest woods. The few who care for more and finer food discover it in imagery and metaphor and prose rhythms.

But he wished both to enjoy and to give, more than that. He had a grand passion for the planet Earth, the "fountained" sky. He could and did experience this object of his passion with a complete, a *quasi* physical response; but in responding he spiritualized even the muscular sense. It taught him to cross rock-faces of danger where his brain told him it would be folly to seek a hold; thus he forgot all such things as physical fear and made a comrade of the tissues and nerves of his frame. But he taxed them, too. Three days' climbing he would do in a day. When bread was wanting his body went unfed. Where night overtook him he slept, despising the hardship of summit cold. He was a spendthrift of the spirit and of the physical flesh, equally.

And what came of it? It is hard to know. I have not heard that the citizens of Dunbar, Scotland, have erected a monument to his memory, as those of Paisley did for another naturist who won fame in the States. Wilson's achievement (and the very name "American Ornithology") savors of erudition, which the Scotch have always admired. It would be difficult to persuade a body of burgesses to vote funds to commemorate some good and graceful volumes in praise of forests and of icy fields.

We can spare the kind of commemoration that rears monuments. There is something about John Muir that challenges. He is not John the Divine but John the Baptist—curiously reminiscent of a "voice crying in the wilderness," facetious though his language sometimes is:

> Come to these purest of terrestrial fountains. Come and receive baptism and absolution from civilized sins. You were but sprinkled last year.

A strange character, and a little wild, a little angelic; never has lost that young rapt look the face wore in 1870 when he set out on his Odyssey: a child in his eyes—and he a man of thirty-three. And why went he out into the wilderness? To live a life, not serve in a prison all his years . . . serve wheels.

Muir's enduring contribution to literature belongs to his middle life, his period of poise. Separate from the work of this period any merely popular papers and journals of adventure, any light descriptive sketches such as those contributed to the *San Francisco Evening Bulletin,* in the summer of 1877 ("**Mormon Lilies**" and "**The San Gabriel Mountains**" are examples.)

But among the papers written for the *Bulletin,* or for the *Overland Monthly* one comes upon superior work. "**Nevada's Dead Towns**" rises to the level of literature, not merely as diction but because of a grave sweep of the imagination gathering past and present into one view. And in "**Wild Wool**" one finds a true and fine essay, not only freighted with original and fresh observation but full of penetrating comment on nature and culture. It is the work of a thinker, and not of an enthusiast. For lucidity and illumination it reminds us of essays by Thomas Huxley, on the relation between nature and man. Muir's theme here is the wild, contrasted with the cultivated. He wisely concludes that neither one is "better" but the two different and by no means interchangeable, to be judged alike, from a user's view. "No dogma," he says, "taught by the present civilization seems to form so insuperable an obstacle in the way of right understanding of the relation which culture sustains to wildness as that which regards the world especially made for man. Every animal, plant and crystal controverts it in the plainest terms. Yet it is taught from century to century as somthing ever new and precious, and in the resulting darkness the enormous conceit is allowed to go unchallenged."

There are no "enormous conceits" in John Muir, and to bring light in places where was darkness was as much his mission as that of any writer. The light is different, that is all, and brings a breath with it, of out of doors. At times the light is so subtle and the air so rarefied that he seems a mystic, treating nature as an abode of gods.

No doubt Muir was a mystic by temperament, and saw more in mountains, breathed more in woods and waterfalls than it is given most men to see or breathe; but he was one without superstition and, I think, without illusion. The things he sensed were real things, and his whole organism seemed to be sensitized to perceive the reality. His body was like that of some forest animals, alive to light, breath and faint sound; but more alive to the sum of them than animal. Thus, in the falls, at night, brain and sense combined, mind stooped and partook of a physical harmony, which it irradiated with thought. In the swirling veils of falling mist, in the moon-ray and darkness and silver, he felt presences. What if they were of his own mind's making? That is ecstasy rather than illusion. All this time, and in all his wanderings, he was consciously storing up experiences worthy of one who, in his first journal, wrote himself down as

> *John Muir, Earth-Planet, Universe*

He had at that moment no other address, but was to sleep for many weeks wherever night should find him, without set destination, and accepting chances that might easily free him even from the first half of his stated address. In the walk to the Gulf he was driven by unformulated compulsions and by a vast hunger to see and know the warm Southern world. In the Sierras he was at first "bewitched, enchanted." He never wholly outgrew this state which, we agree, is a handicap to calm interpretations of nature in prose.

It is a handicap: and yet those who have never known it cannot tell us much that is humanly important about an earth which, without something of enchantment in it, quickly fades to a workhouse and barren holding in which we, the helpless tenants, are confined and exploited against our will.

There is no absentee landlord or task-master in Muir's world. Divinity is immediate because directly felt. Being so felt, and to saturation, it is often communicable in prose. Do not look there for a philosophy, look for an experience. Be led by Muir and you may hope, if you yield to the leading, to walk, sometimes, with his awareness, in "the Godful woods."

It takes something more than, or other than literary criticism to find and assay the chief values of John Muir's prose. In part, it takes knowledge and appreciation of that special human variation, in our own evolution, which gives the world from time to time a mutant like Muir, like W. H. Hudson, like H. D. Thoreau. These men are not quite like other men. They have great talent, but are not made to work. Viewed from a quite common angle their lives seem wasted. Even as writers they do not achieve what we think they might have done. We class them as eccentrics. We query what or how much other and more compressed beauty they might have put into words. It is like querying how many wild sheep it would take to give the hired man a suit of clothes.

Muir, like Thoreau, was a lover and word-treasurer of the wild. It was this he wished to show Emerson, and to that end won his promise to camp out overnight; but this plan Emerson's friends overruled. It was typical, and the friends of literature will sometimes send a reader indoors when he might better be *out* in a Muir book. And does the reader know that one of the most charming essays (and satisfying from any viewpoint, however literary) is **"The Water Ouzel"**? In it much waste of wandering is restored as value, by an art of words. That art, in this essay, loses nothing by the fact that there is behind it a wealth of experience which could only be gathered through wasted time: endless wanderings through canyons and among torrents and crags with an ouzel ever flitting ahead through the spray and mist or mingling its song with the roar of the stream. For each stream or cascade or fall, its complementary ouzel, "that never sings in chorus with other birds, nor with his kind, but only with the streams." It is a symbol, for Muir, of that perfect adaptation which is also a perfect harmonization. It is the thing he loves, and he loves the ouzel for embodying it in every motion of its alert and active frame; for braving the swirl and danger in perfect assurancce and self-possession and for celebrating its life with a perfect song—even though, as he puts it, "some of our favorite's best song blossoms never rise above the surface of the heavier music of the water''; they are there, and he knows it by the motions of the bird's throat and breast.

John Muir is known as a mettlesome mountaineer, explorer, known for tireless endurance in the pursuits he loved best; known for his interpretations of the Yosemite, for his appreciation of our parks and their splendid trees—for many descriptions of things great and sublime in nature: but he has written nothing better than his essay on one small foam-flitting, water-haunting bird. (pp. 100-15)

*Henry Chester Tracy, "John Muir," in his* American Naturists, *E. P. Dutton & Company, Inc., 1930, pp. 100-15.*

*The Hetch Hetchy Valley.*

**JOHN LEIGHLY** (lecture date 1958)

[*In the following excerpt, Leighly discusses the most significant characteristics of Muir's work and provides an assessment of its literary and scientific importance.*]

[John Muir's] most conspicuous part in the scientific and literary conquest of the West was the description and celebration, and in part the scientific explanation, of areas that were not yet subjugated to settlement, which in Muir's eyes was nearly synonymous with their defilement. Aside from his discovery of the existing glaciers of the Sierra, his most important scientific contribution is contained in a series of papers published in *The Overland Monthly* in 1874 and 1875 under the general title *Studies in the Sierra*.

Much of the content of these solid contributions to the geomorphology of glaciated mountains has become a commonplace part of the content of textbooks. This fact, while it reduces their interest when one reads them now, testifies to their permanent value. Their most important content is detailed evidence of the control exercised over the sculpture effected by glaciers, especially over plucking, by the jointing of the rocks. This principle was one that Muir insisted upon: "The most telling thing learned in these mountain excursions is the influence of cleavage joints on the features sculptured from the general mass of the range." The first of his *Studies in the Sierra* reaches a fuller and more forcible conclusion:

> . . . when we say that the glacial ice-sheet and separate glaciers *molded* the mountains, we must remember that their molding power upon *hard granite* possessing a strong physical structure is comparatively slight. In such hard, strongly built granite regions, *glaciers do not so much mold and shape,* as *disinter forms already conceived and ripe.* The harder the rock, and the better its specialized cleavage planes are developed, the greater will be the degree of controlling power possessed by it over its own forms, as compared with that of the disinterring glacier; and the softer the rock and more generally developed its cleavage planes, the less able will it be to resist ice action and maintain its own forms. In general, *the grain of a rock determines its surface forms. . . .*

There is other excellent material in these studies, but also conclusions that are unacceptable, such as Muir's great overestimation of the depth of erosion by glaciers.

Never again did Muir attack a scientific question of any magnitude. He traveled widely and wrote copiously, but he never spent enough time in any other region than the Sierra Nevada to discover or solve a significant problem. "Patient observation and constant brooding above the rocks," he wrote to Mrs. Carr, "lying upon them for years as the ice did, is the way to arrive at the truths which are graven so lavishly upon them." He had no opportunity to brood thus over any other region. In fact, his prolonged and intense attention to the Sierra was an obstacle to his understanding of landscapes having different histories. The Sierra became for him the model and norm for all mountains, so that wherever he went—among the basin ranges of Nevada, the Cascade Mountains of Oregon and Washington, or the coastal mountains of Alaska and northeastern Siberia—he saw glacially smoothed uplands, Yosemites more or less complete, and summit sculpture by cirque glaciers. "Go where we will," he wrote in Alaska, "all the world over, we seem to have been there before." The mental image he had formed of the past and present forms of the Sierra was so complete and detailed that all the mountain forms he saw could

be fitted into it. He clambered about Mount Shasta and explored other parts of the volcanic northeastern part of California; but the land forms produced by vulcanism did not arouse his wonder. He missed completely the nature of the relief of the Great Basin, seeing in the basin ranges drumlinoid forms that to him were evidence of a general glaciation. On the west coast of Alaska he recorded some observations of ground ice exposed in a wave-cut cliff that would have been new and interesting if adequately discussed and interpreted. We may excuse Muir for not investigating these exposures closely, for he was ashore at the site only a few hours. But within this short time he found an all too easy explanation of the largest mass of ground-ice he encountered: he diagnosed it as the last remnant of a glacier preserved against a north-facing slope, identifying it with the remnant cirque glaciers he knew in the Sierra. His eyes were still keen to see and his pen diligent to record; but he scarcely acquired a single new insight after his first few fruitful years in the Sierra Nevada.

It can scarcely be doubted that Muir had enough scientific competence to enable him to contribute more to the natural history of the West than he did. But even in his productive years in the seventies he published many more descriptive articles addressed to the general reader than solid additions to scientific knowledge. One reason for his doing so was certainly economic; writing about the country he loved was a more congenial way of supporting himself than the work he did in his first years in California. But later, when his economic position was secure, he made no effort to reach any other than a general audience.

I do not wish to make an invidious distinction between Muir's *Studies in the Sierra* and his other writings. The contrast between avowedly scientific and so-called "popular" writing has been vastly sharpened in the past eighty years, with the decline of the literate monthly magazines. Muir's articles intended for the general public are as carefully written and contain as detailed and accurate observation as any scientific writing. They differ in that the evidence carefully marshaled is not focused on an objective intellectual problem, but rather on the reader. In them Muir is attempting to share with the reader his emotional reactions to his observations. The data of observation themselves might as well have been used for a more strictly scientific purpose.

The characteristic form of any one of these essays was evidently given by a coherent block of material in one of Muir's notebooks. Its nucleus might be a scene or an incident. About the framework of factual report Muir wrapped a covering of interpretation drawn from his emotional experiences in the presence of the phenomena observed, and these experiences were what he was most eager to report to his readers.

It was not merely shallow sentiment that Muir invited his readers to share. He was convinced that the emotional rewards of association with nature increase with intellectual understanding, and his writings confirm that conviction: his own efforts are least successful when he is writing about things he did not understand, such as certain meteorologic phenomena and the movements of water. The reader of Muir's works must inevitably take a position with reference to the emotion that informs them. Some may reject these writings out of hand because Muir's subjective attitude toward nature is distasteful, and some may reject his interpretations and reflections while appreciating the factual material he recorded. But there is much to be gained from a sympathetic examination of the point of view from which he looked upon the world. I would suggest that in the study of nature the pursuit of ends other than those called "scientific," if done in spirit and in truth, is intellectually just as praiseworthy and rewarding as the search for strictly rational connections.

As is true of all of us, what Muir saw and reported depended at least as much on the mind that received and assimilated his observations as on the objects observed; and his interpretative reflections provide insights into the mind on which these observations impinged. Henry Fairfield Osborn, who had enough personal association with Muir to justify his speaking with some authority, wrote of him: "I have never known anyone whose nature-philosophy was more thoroughly theistic at the same time as he was a thorough-going evolutionist. Osborn, using terms made familiar by the great controversy of the latter part of the nineteenth century, appears to suggest that these two aspects of Muir's view of nature were in conflict. I find no conflict whatever in his writings. His "theism" was very close to pantheism. The God whose name he frequently uses is not one that would find a place in any dogmatic theology. This God, who in Muir's writings presides over the universe, is often replaced, in a neighboring paragraph or sentence, by a more or less personified, maternally solicitous Nature. In other passages these personifications are attenuated to an "eternal, invincible Harmony" among natural processes and their material products. In most instances the presiding entity is scarcely distinguishable from what is often called by the more colorless term "ecologic balance." The attribution of personality to the principle of continuity and balance in nature gives a warmth to Muir's descriptions and interpretations that his emotional constitution evidently demanded. He saw the matrix of natural events as divine love, extended particularly toward living things. "God's love covers His world like a garment of light," he wrote in his journal. This love is foresighted, teleologic: the glaciation of the Sierra Nevada, for example, was a device by which suitable habitats were prepared for the great variety of plants that range upward from the valleys through the belt of forests to the raw moraines in the glacial cirques; and for the animals that accompanied the plants on their march upward as the glaciers receded. Osborn should not have been astonished that in Muir's eyes such a farsighted and solicitous love could use evolution as easily as glaciation to achieve its ends.

Muir parted company with most contemporary evolutionists in his insistence on the quality of benevolence in the processes of nature. He rejected Darwin's word "struggle" (forgetting Darwin's own qualification of the term in *The Origin of Species*) as "ungodly." I have found in his writings only one account of a creature he could not fit into the scheme of harmony he saw in nature. This is his description of certain small, savage black ants whose acquaintance he made during his first summer in the Sierra. Of these "fearless, restless, wandering imps" he writes that:

> . . . they fight anywhere and always wherever they can find anything to bite. As soon as a vulnerable spot is discovered on man or beast, they stand on their heads and sink their jaws, and though torn limb from limb, they will yet hold on and die biting deeper. When I contemplate this fierce creature so widely distributed and strongly intrenched, I see that much remains to be done ere the world is brought under the rule of universal peace and love.

This questioning of the universal rule of divine love is, however, highly exceptional if not unique. Muir used this pervasive love as the basic organizing concept of his interpretation of the natural world. Few of the naturalists of his generation appealed to it, though many of them recognized a moral obligation toward nature. In the fundamental set of his mind Muir was to a substantial degree an anachronism, carrying into Brown Decades attitudes that belonged to the Golden Day or even earlier times. He owed much to Emerson and Thoreau, and something to the romantics of the first half of the nineteenth century.

He had received good instruction in the sciences at the University of Wisconsin, and had pursued the study of nature independently for several years before coming to Californiia. He had set his aim high. "How intensely I desire to be a Humboldt!" he had written to Mrs. Carr in September, 1866. It was this ambition that led him to California, even though as a second choice after his intention to follow Humboldt's footsteps into South America was thwarted. He had the bodily strength and agility required for the exertions he undertook, and habits that made him nearly independent of other human beings. He simplified the techniques of travel in the mountains so as to reduce the amount of gear he carried with him to a minimum that most persons would consider inadequate. On the one occasion when he took a pack animal with him when traveling alone—his excursion, undertaken in the autumn of 1875, to determine how far southward the sequoia extended in the Sierra—he found the mule Brownie, whose services had been urged upon him, more of a hindrance than a help. As Emerson said of Thoreau, "he chose to be rich by making his wants few and supplying them himself." By inuring himself to prolonged travel on foot with a light pack, he freed himself to observe and record. "You are all eyes, sifted through and through with light and beauty."

Muir's works abound in evidence of a consummate power of observation. Rocks, clouds, trees, flowers, animals, the great and the small, attracted his attention and found their way into his notebooks. (pp. 310-13)

The latter-day reader is likely to linger most appreciatively over those passages in which Muir describes things that are not ordinarily noticed. His accounts of some of his feats of observation, such as his view of the behavior of a Sierra forest in a windstorm from the swaying top of a tree, have been reproduced often enough to become widely familiar. I shall call your attention to some less spectacular examples. There are, for example, his remarks on the beads of dew seen on spider webs in the morning, which, he asserts, "are of all the forms of water the most delicate and beautiful I have ever seen." There are his notes on the spray above the surface of a cascading stream, formed by the bursting of bubbles of air caught in the water. "These drops rise in curves, often meeting at the top just before they begin to descend, and forming a series of interlacing arches." Observing a cloud of insects in Alaska, moving "in giddy whirls and spirals," he noted that they circled "mostly from left to right, with the sun, into which they are geared in some mysterious way." While he was exploring the southern parts of the sequoia belt, he encountered a forest fire. He tethered Brownie, the mule, at a safe distance, and watched at close range the behavior of the fire. (pp. 313-14)

The reader also finds, especially in the introductory paragraphs of articles, descriptions of general views from high points. These inclusive views are the ones most likely to stimulate Muir to reflection, and the more inclusive the view the more general the reflection. Having climbed to the peak of Mount Ritter, and looking over an expanse that stretched westward and eastward from the Coast Ranges far into the Great Basin, he wrote:

Here are the roots of all the life of the valleys, and here more simply than elsewhere is the eternal flux of nature manifested. Ice changing to water, lakes to meadows, and mountains to plains. And while we thus contemplate Nature's method of landscape creation, and, reading the records she has carved on the rocks, reconstruct, however imperfectly, the landscapes of the past, we also learn that as these we now behold have succeeded those of the pre-glacial age, so they in turn are withering and vanishing to be succeeded by others yet unborn.

This parallel sweep of the eye through space and of the imagination through time is characteristic. In his journal Muir complained, "Alas, how little of the world is subject to human senses!" He exacted the utmost of his senses; and labored to supplement their incomplete testimony by the exercise of his imagination.

Perhaps the most significant observation that Muir made was the one that led to his first discovery of an existing glacier in the Sierra, which was, moreover, the first glacier he had ever seen. The following account of this discovery is the first one he published; it is more spontaneous than the later, soberer one included in *The Mountains of California*:

> On one of the yellow days of October, 1871, when I was among the mountains of the "Merced group" following the footprints of the ancient glaciers . . . , reading what I could of their history, . . . I came upon a small stream that was carrying mud of a kind I had never seen. In a calm place, where the stream widened, I collected some of this mud, and observed that it was entirely mineral in composition, and fine as flour, like the mud from a fine-grit grindstone. Before I had time to reason, I said, "Glacier mud—mountain meal."
>
> Then I observed that this muddy stream issues from a bank of fresh quarried stones and dirt, that was sixty of seventy feet in height. This I at once took to be a moraine. In climbing to the top of it, I was struck with the steepness of its slope, and with its raw, unsettled, plantless, new-born appearance. . . .
>
> When I had scrambled to the top of the moraine, I saw what seemed to be a huge snow-bank, four or five hundred yards in length, by half a mile in width. Imbedded in its stained and furrowed surface were stones and dirt like that of which the moraine was built. Dirt-stained lines curved across the snow-bank from side to side, and when I observed that these curved lines coincided with the curved moraine, and that the stones and dirt were most abundant near the bottom of the bank, I shouted "A living glacier!"

Though often expressed in exuberant words, Muir's descriptions are full of precise numerical determinations: "arithmetic for clothing my thoughts," as he wrote to Mrs. Carr. In the letter in which he described the glory displayed by the San Joaquin Valley when he first saw it, he proved how flowery it was by counting and reporting to Mrs. Carr the number of orders, species, and individual plants, and finally the number of flowers, he found on one square yard of ground. While he was looking after sheep in the foothills of the Sierra in the winter of 1868-69, he recorded in his journal an estimate, based on the exposure of the roots of plants, of the rate at which the surface of the hills was being lowered by erosion. Though he traveled light, he seems always to have had with him a tape measure, an aneroid barometer for measuring elevation, and frequently a thermometer. In his study of trees, which he pursued through all his travels, he regularly measured their di-

ameter and height, and counted annual rings on stumps and logs. As soon as possible after his discovery of living glaciers in the Sierra, he planted a row of stakes across one of them in order to measure the rate of its motion.

He exposed himself freely, even foolhardily, to extreme discomfort and danger in order to observe. He climbed down into the bergschrund of the first glacier he found in the Sierra, and into the marginal crevasse of the first fiord glacier he had a chance to examine in Alaska, where he saw "not only its grinding, polishing action, but how it breaks off angular boulder-masses."

Muir wrote in his journal of two ways in which living creatures may be observed:

> The man of science, the naturalist, too often loses sight of the essential oneness of all living beings in seeking to classify them into kingdoms, orders, families, genera, species,. . . while the eye of the Poet, the Seer, never closes on the kinship of all God's creatures, and his heart ever beats in sympathy with great and small alike as "earthborn companions and fellow mortals" equally dependent on Heaven's eternal love.

Yet his sense of kinship with all of earth's creatures did not extend to many of his fellow humans. The satisfaction he derived from his solitary communion with nature was paired with an aversion toward most of mankind. At times he expressed his disgust and abhorrence in words worthy of Swift. The inhabitants of towns seemed to him particularly degraded: "All are more or less sick; there is not a perfectly sane man in San Francisco." And elsewhere he speaks of "the deathlike apathy of many town-dwellers, in whom natural curiosity has been quenched in toil and care and poor shallow comfort," contrasting them with a group of Alaskan Indians about a campfire on the shore of Glacier Bay.

But he did not romanticize the American aborigines. The human beings he describes in the most Swiftian terms are the Mono Indians he encountered on his first trip through Bloody Canyon in the summer of 1869, and whom he dismissed by saying that "somehow they seemed to have no right place in the landscape, and I was glad to see them fading out of sight down the Pass." He viewed the Indian and Eskimo he met with the same critical reserve with which he regarded everyone else, and wrote of them with the same praise, scorn, pity, or indifference, as occasion demanded. His attitude toward human beings was strongly colored by a fastidiousness that was outraged by slovenliness and dirt. He repeatedly contrasts the cleanness of wild animals with the dirtiness of men. "Strange that mankind alone is dirty." "Man seems to be the only animal whose food soils him." "Pollution, defilement, squalor are words that never would have been created had man lived conformably to Nature."

What life conformable to nature might be we can only guess. But certainly one important element in the proper relation of man to the rest of life on earth that Muir envisaged is the recognition that all creatures have an equal right to life and enjoyment, a recognition granted by few human beings. Contemplating the fossil record of life on earth, Muir found it "a great comfort to learn that vast multitudes of creatures, great and small, and infinite in number, lived and had a good time in God's love before man was created." And again: ". . . if a war of races should occur between the world's beasts and Lord Man, I would be tempted to sympathize with the beasts."

In his early days in California Muir was able to avoid town life for the most part, and did not have much occasion to record the discomfort he experienced when visiting Oakland or San Francisco, "diving into that slimy town sea-bottom," as he said in a letter to Mrs. Carr. But even in the Sierra he could not escape the destruction wrought by the predatory inhabitants of the lowlands. The earliest example of such destruction that he had occasion to see was the damage inflicted by sheep driven up into the mountains for summer pasture. Fortunately he was soon able to escape from the hateful occupation of caring for these animals, to which necessity had driven him in his first year in California. But he never ceased to bewail the depredations of these "hoofed locusts," as he always called sheep; and a good part of the motivation of his later work for the preservation of the forests of the West was his knowledge of the damage done to the mountain vegetation by them. Yet he did not vent his loathing primarily on the "poor, helpless, hungry sheep"; he saw them as "in great part misbegotten, without good right to be, semi-manufactured, made less by God than by man, born out of time and place." When he became acquainted with the wild mountain sheep, he compared them drastically and invidiously with the domestic breeds: "These are clean and elegant, the others dirty and awkward. These are guarded by the great Shepherd of us all, those by erring money-seekers."

A second kind of depredation that Muir learned to know early in his sojourn in the Sierra was wasteful lumbering, with its accompanying destructive fires. The forests of the Sierra—the finest in the world, as he often said—were particularly dear to him, and it was primarily in their behalf that he engaged in strenuous propaganda in the latter part of his career. But though he condemned "the invading hordes of destroyers called settlers," though he lamented the destruction, in his own lifetime, of the blanket of golden and purple flowers with which the San Joaquin Valley had greeted him when he first saw it, he could imagine, at least late in his career, a use of the land that would accord with his principles. . . . (pp. 314-16)

The great moral imperative that recurs in Muir's writings is that man respect the rest of the natural world. It excludes absolutely the "enormous conceit" "that the world was made especially for the uses of man." Against this pernicious doctrine he inveighs again and again. There is a certain irony in the linking of Muir's name with the movement loosely called "conservation," for the doctrine of subordination of nature to man has been central in our official conservational policies. In Muir's last and unsuccessful struggle to preserve nature from depredation, to prevent the use of Hetch Hetchy Valley, supposedly safe within the bounds of Yosemite National Park, from use as a water reservoir for the city of San Francisco, the decisive influence that moved Congress to permit the Park to be thus despoiled was apparently exerted by that paladin of "conservation," Gifford Pinchot.

Of the naturalist proper Muir demanded more than passive recognition of the rights of all living things to access to the sources of life on the earth. The naturalist must also be animated by a positive love of nature. This is the quality he admired most in the naturalists he had occasion to praise: in Linnaeus, for example, whose great influence he ascribes to Linnaeus' love of nature and natural things. He attributes the same love to Charles Sprague Sargent, author of the great *Silva of North America*. To his regret, he found less of it in Asa Gray, when he made Gray's personal acquaintance, than he had expected to find.

Muir's intense devotion to nature gives a pathos to his writings that is denied to more restrained observers. At times he expresses it with so much warmth that we are embarrassed when reading his words as, according to report, his more reticent associates were sometimes embarrassed by his conversation. On rare occasions the vehemence of his words carries him beyond the bounds of good taste. Yet if I apply to his writings the test for false sentiment suggested by P. G. Hamerton, that if the character of a landscape evokes emotions "it is only a part of veracity to describe these effects on the mind," I find no evidence that he exaggerated his sentiments. At least he confided to his journal and to private letters expressions as warm as any he wrote for publication, expressions that in most of us would seem gross exaggerations of our actual feelings. His capacity for sympathy with nature was obviously far greater than most of us possess, as was his capacity for close and concentrated observation and for hard physical exertion and endurance of prolonged and intense discomfort. Without these traits he would not have been able to perform the work he did. They are good traits, whose excess is less to be deplored than their deficiency.

Muir's attitude toward nature was singularly balanced, combining inseparably and harmoniously intellectual, esthetic, and ethical constituents. The immediate profit of his observations was esthetic; his writings are as much a hymn to beauty as to divine love. "Beauty is universal and immortal, above, beneath, on land and sea, mountain and plain, in heat and cold, light and darkness." Intellectual inquiry adds intensity to the perception of beauty, and the recognition of beauty sharpens the senses and quickens intellectual curiosity. Finally, the recognition of order and coherence in nature—"When we try to pick out anything by itself, we find it hitched to everything else in the universe"—provides a guide to action through a sense of the common origin we share with the rest of nature, and of our responsibility toward it.

The ultimate appeal that Muir makes in his descriptions of the West is "Come to the mountains and see." This is a generous and noble invitation. I invite you to contemplate Muir's serene and harmonious view of nature, a veritable "higher Sierra" of the human spirit. We may not be able to climb to this exalted height, as few of us would be able to follow Muir to the peaks of the physical mountains of the West; but our own less aspiring minds can not avoid receiving some ennobling influence from it. "Doubly happy," wrote Muir, "is the man to whom lofty mountain-tops are within reach, for the lights that shine from there illumine all that lies below." (pp. 316-17)

> *John Leighly, "John Muir's Image of the West," in*
> Annals of the Association of American Geographers,
> *Vol. 48, No. 4, December, 1958, pp. 309-18.*

### HERBERT F. SMITH (essay date 1965)

[*In the following excerpt, Smith discusses the moral aspects of Muir's nature writings.*]

In his excellent chapter on John Muir in *Nature in American Literature*, Norman Foerster wrote that "one does not go to John Muir for a criticism of life. He understood neither the heights and depths of his own nature, which he avoided as most of us avoid the dizzy heights and depths of the material world, nor the complexities of social life—the boundless results of man's being a gregarious animal" [see excerpt dated 1923]. In a sense it is true that Muir did not even understand the complexities of many of the causes he espoused. His view on conservation was, to say the least, one-sided. Furthermore, if we are to consider adjustment to the complexities of society the foremost good of literature, Muir must be a damaging influence. His position is an extreme one. It seems, from his writing, that he abandoned his birthright of gregariousness to pursue a lonely course of absorption in nature. His example is, according to this view, like Thoreau's: it is inapplicable to the situation of common, garden-variety man.

Such observations are suggested by consideration of his work alone. Actually, Muir lived a full social life, including marriage, the making of money, and, as I have shown, a nagging loneliness which never totally deserted him, no matter how high the peak or how isolated the glacier. These incidents are hardly mentioned in his works. Why? Because they were to him the least important aspects of his life. The casual events of life, it must have seemed to him, were not proper material to be emphasized by inclusion within his works. In fact, throughout his writings there is much less emphasis on human processes than in the writings of any other naturalist, certainly less than in Thoreau. No one will ever learn to be a mountain climber by reading John Muir, while one easily perceives the mysteries of camping-out from *Walden*. Muir may describe the summit of Mount Shasta and the panorama visible from it in great detail, but he relates only casually the technique of his journey thither. Effects, processes of nature he fully describes, but his own actions, unless they are exceptional or contribute to the sublimity of the result, are left to the reader's imagination.

Part of the reason for his neglect of description of his own processes is a function of his difficulty with himself as autobiographical hero, but much more important is his moral purpose in writing. Foerster says we must not go to Muir for a criticism of life. He is quite correct that we must not look in him for a criticism of the subtleties of life, but Muir's works do present an ideal of behavior and appreciation which mutely announces "go, thou, and do likewise." Whether aimed at the specific of preservation of natural beauty or as general inspiration to teeming masses to seek some solitude of wilderness for communion with nature, his writings are specifically moral and didactic. In this respect, he is again like Thoreau.

Foerster continued in his summary of Muir that, "when Emerson said of him that he was greater than Thoreau, he must have been thinking of Thoreau the naturalist. It is as a literary naturalist that Muir is perhaps greater than Thoreau and certainly equal to Burroughs." I think there can be little doubt that Muir was a better naturalist than Thoreau, but I do not believe that he was a better moralist. Thoreau, a better writer than Muir, urged his moral program in *Walden* with greater subtlety than Muir was capable of. Emerson's comment meant, however, that he found Muir's moral position more coherent, more considered, and more ideally suited to the life of the soul than Thoreau's.

Muir's morality was founded on a scientific knowledge considerably greater than Thoreau's. He embraced a comprehension of both botany and geology compared to which Thoreau's observations on the flora and geological structure of Walden Pond are quite elementary. But Muir's scientific knowledge was only a foundation for an extensive and intricate teleology. Like Thoreau and Emerson, he saw design everywhere. Unlike them, he did not believe that the evidence of creation was intended primarily for the sight of man alone. He believed, with Oriental religions, that man has the right, as every animal has, to partake of the perfections of creation, if he so wishes.

Beyond that, his morality included not only the retention and preservation of this beauty from those who would destroy it in the name of commodity, but also his right and purpose to urge others to partake of it with himself.

One need not go to Muir for a criticism of life. Muir can be considered merely as a charming writer about nature. His books may, indeed, ought, to be read by anyone planning a tour of the Sierra Nevada, the Yosemite, or the coast of Alaska. But hidden beneath that apparently innocuous surface of description mingled with personal narration lies—like the nine-tenths of the icebergs which he described so well—a moral idealism that can puncture the materialistic assurance of an unsuspecting reader. It could cause him to reject his position at the bank, the broom factory, or the brokerage house in order to seek the sublimity of a mystic experience dawning upon him with the suddenness of a new moral law. We can grant Muir the finest accolade for a writer in modern society: his work can be "dangerous," for it does not pander to the accepted social norms. (pp. 145-47)

> *Herbert F. Smith, in his* John Muir, *Twayne Publishers, Inc., 1965, 158 p.*

**THOMAS J. LYON**    (essay date 1972)

[*In the following excerpt, Lyon examines the rhetorical devices Muir used to vivify his nature studies.*]

One of Muir's great gifts as a writer is to create and vivify the wilderness perspective from which absurd cultural values can be perceived as absurd and, hopefully, can be reversed. But such a process cannot be established by declaration and it is impotent as a mere abstraction: it has to be dramatized and made physically and emotionally real. Wilderness is more than an idea. In fact, its very power in cultural and philosophical revelation depends upon its being felt fully. The reader has to *be there* before he can look back on civilization.

Muir's chief vehicle for conveying a living sense of the natural, wild world was himself, perhaps dramatized or modified slightly into a "persona." The benefits of thus locating his writing in his own authentic experience are many. First, the device establishes a point of view with which a reader can identify; in Muir's work, there are some grand overviews, to be sure, but they are made live by the documentary proof of the author's having personally walked over the ground he surveys. For instance, he begins *The Mountains of California* with a long view of the mountain topography of the state, encompassing hundreds of miles. But he moves swiftly, on the second page, to his own first view of the mighty Sierra, "one glowing April day," when he stood at the summit of a pass in the Coast Range and looked eastward. This is typical of all his works; what emerges is the certain sense of a man's actually having been there, in the wilderness, where we can follow.

The sense of movement, perhaps the most effective philosophy-proving ingredient in Muir's style, is also enhanced by his dramatizing scenes through himself. He drifts through the wilderness, taking in through free and vibrant senses the endless, moving drama of seasons, of daybreak, of storm, of the births and deaths of flowers and birds and bears, and of what it is like to be alive and aware, in this ever-changing and beautiful matrix. The quality which imbues his writing is not observation, then, but participation. His life, like his writing which is conveying it, is characterized by engagement, by a dynamic awareness. This is why his prose is so much more effective than carefully wrought, "set-piece" nature writing.

Good examples of this sense of movement are to be found on practically every page of Muir's work. Here is one from **"The Glacier Meadows,"** in *The Mountains of California*:

> Bees hum as in a harvest noon, butterflies waver above the flowers, and like them you lave in the vital sunshine, too richly and homogenously joy-filled to be capable of partial thought. You are all eye, sifted through and through with light and beauty. Sauntering along the brook that meanders silently through the meadow from the east, special flowers call you back to discriminating consciousness. The sod comes curving down to the water's edge, forming bossy out-swelling banks, and in some places overlapping counter-sunk boulders and forming bridges. Here you find mats of the curious dwarf willow scarce an inch high, yet sending up a multitude of gray silk catkins, illumined here and there with the purple cups and bells of bryanthus and vaccinium.

Among the butterflies and bees and flowers, and served deliciously by the same bathing light, the consciousness of the reader is guided carefully from wonder to wonder, from expansive joy to close attention. Although Muir here uses the construction "you," there is really no doubt that the experiences are his own; he is only guiding, demonstrating that "you" can have the same experiences. It should be noted that the activity or movement here is not limited to the roving visitor: the "sod comes curving down," in some places "forming bridges," and the tiny willows are "sending up a multitude of gray silk catkins." The life here is in the total scene; the consciousness is alive and moving, and the "objects" of consciousness are alive and moving, too.

Thus subtly, Muir defines and describes the human place: a non-condescending, in fact non-hierarchical, faculty of beholding beauty . . . a free-roving, constantly changing engagement with other manifestations of the grand harmony, all moving together.

But the tendency toward bliss, so obvious in the quoted passage, means "nature-faking" (the phrase was Theodore Roosevelt's) for many readers. They want data: exact detail, clinical description. This, too, can be found in Muir's works, although his facts, to use Thoreau's metaphor, are always carefully helped to flower into truths. But the empirical observation is there, and it is careful. In **"Wild Wool,"** for example, Muir's most explicit and complete comparison of civilization and wilderness, he describes the hair and wool on a wild mountain sheep:

> The hairs are from about two to four inches long, mostly of a dull bluish-gray color, though varying somewhat with the seasons. In general characteristics they are closely related to the hairs of the deer and antelope, being light, spongy, and elastic, with a highly polished surface, and though somewhat ridged and spiraled, like wool, they do not manifest the slightest tendency to felt or become taggy. A hair two and a half inches long, which is perhaps near the average length, will stretch about one fourth of an inch before breaking. . . . The number of hairs growing upon a square inch is about ten thousand; the number of wool fibers is about twenty-five thousand, or two and a half times that of the hairs.

He goes on, after this description, to point out that increasing the proportion of wool to hair, which is what man has done

in breeding his tame sheep, has certain negative effects. While it does make profit for the sheep owner, it makes the sheep itself less able to cope with rain, predation, and disease. Here the purely quantitative orientation has produced an abnormality, and has been ethically and ecologically irresponsible. The innocent sheep has been modified for man's benefit, despite Muir's assertion that in nature he "never yet happened upon a trace of evidence that seemed to show that any one animal was ever made for another as much as it was made for itself." The interpretation derives from close observation, with a magnifying glass, of the wild sheep; Muir seemed to know instinctively that mere assertion of wild superiority—the sort of thing Thoreau ventured in the early "A Natural History of Massachusetts," for example—was not enough. One needed, in America, the facts. To show that the same man who held the magnifying glass could also rove and revel in the wild meadows was Muir's almost-unique genius. What he does, in effect, is to put science and transcendental ecstasy together, to form the basis of a true ecology. Data-gathering alone is merely mechanical; there is no life force to it. Bliss alone is impotent. But the combination makes felt thought, and on the level Muir practiced and dramatized it, this was something new.

To convey this vision, Muir concentrated on words which emphasized flow and words which emphasized the particular, individualized qualities of things, simultaneously. In this area, the glaciers, with their inexorable, stately flow over great periods of time, were almost his favorite image-metaphors. Writing about glaciers, he developed rhythms in his prose which suggested his subject matter, and he was also able to suggest the perspective of tremendously long cycles, a perspective which is essential to the wilderness orientation. One illustration among many is his description of the ancient Yosemite Creek Glacier, written in 1880:

> The broad, many-fountained glacier to which the basin of Yosemite Creek belonged, was about fourteen miles in length by four in width, and in many places was not less than a thousand feet in depth. Its principal tributaries issued from lofty amphitheatres laid well back among the northern spurs of the Hoffman range. These at first pursued a westerly course; then, uniting with each other and absorbing a series of small affluents from the Tuolumne divide, the trunk thus formed swept round to the south in a magnificent curve, and poured its ice into Yosemite in cascades two miles wide. . . . As the ice-water drew near a close, the main trunk, becoming torpid, at length wholly disappeared in the sun, and a waiting multitude of plants and animals entered the new valley to inhabit the mansions prepared for them.

The foreshortening of time in this description, which speeds and animates the actually ponderous and slow-moving glacier, is accomplished by "swept round to the south in a magnificent curve, and poured its ice into Yosemite in cascades two miles wide. . . ." Muir's grasp of the long view, laid out previously in the glacier essays, was firm enough that he could speed up time and motion without distorting the true perspective.

But the perfect guiding image for flow and unity was light. Describing light, he rose to some of his most rapt and mystical writing. Here he seems to have hit upon the most basic characteristic of life itself, a fundamental cosmic necessity.

> Light. I know not a single word fine enough for Light. Its currents pour, but it is a heavy material word not applicable to holy, beamless, bodiless, inaudible floods of Light.

Again, "God's love covers his world like a garment of light," he wrote in his journal for October 7, 1871. But perhaps the most dramatic treatment of light in Muir's work occurs in his famous description of climbing to the top of a 100-foot Douglas Spruce and riding there in a wild Sierra windstorm. The wind itself is a beautiful and common figure for flow in Muir's work, and here from the tree-top view the wind and the light join in rhythmic passage through the forest wilderness:

> In its widest sweeps my tree-top described an arc from twenty to thirty degrees, but I felt sure of its elastic temper, having seen others of the same species still more severely tried—bent almost to the ground indeed, in heavy snows—without breaking a fiber. I was therefore safe, and free to take the wind into my pulses and enjoy the excited forest from my superb outlook. The view from here must be extremely beautiful in any weather. Now my eye roved over the piny hills and dales as over fields of waving grain, and felt the light running in ripples and broad swelling undulations across the valleys from ridge to ridge, as the shining foliage was stirred by corresponding waves of air. Oftentimes these waves of reflected light would break up suddenly into a kind of beaten foam, and again, after chasing one another in regular order, they would seem to bend forward in concentric curves, and disappear on some hillside, like seawaves on a shelving shore. The quantity of light reflected from the bent needles was so great as to make whole groves appear as if covered with snow, while the black shadows beneath the trees greatly enhanced the effect of the silvery splendor.

Besides the precision and appropriateness of the descriptive metaphors, and the quietly suggestive embodiment of consciousness in the free-roving eye, so that the human point of view is effectually merged in the natural scene, the management of tone toward the end of the paragraph should also be noted. As Muir completes his sea-wave metaphor, he seems to realize that the poetic height cannot be maintained longer without becoming self-conscious or precious. So he switches abruptly to "quantity" and to sober description, then modulates the tone back upward a bit with an "effect" (a secondary perception), and gracefully concludes. Such a passage is good evidence of Muir's *carefulness* as a writer—his restraint with powerful romantic materials. This ought to be given as much attention as his evocation of ecstasy.

Though Muir's writing generally lacks the self-ironic dimension, it makes frequent use of an ironic tone for satiric purposes. He is well known for denunciations of commercialism, but he can also be quite artful in juxtaposing the two elements which form the mainspring of his world: the wild and the tame. The classic example here is his gentle disparagement of painter's-eye views—hence all framed or static views of nature—in **"A Near View of the Sierra"** in *The Mountains of California*. Muir had guided some painters into the Sierra to a place where their expectations of a rather stereotyped alpine scene would be gratified. Then, alone, he struck off on a ramble that would take him on the first ascent of Mt. Ritter, two days away from the painters, and give him a frameless, unbounded view of the wilderness from the summit. The comparison is left pretty much implicit, being mainly developed through a description of the city-bred painters' worry at his absence. "They seemed unreasonably glad to see me. I had been absent only three days. . . ."

In **"Wild Wool,"** one of Muir's best essays, his contrasts are more forthright, yet they are built upon very close observation and upon subtle discriminations. **"Wild Wool"** offers his most complete definition of wildness, and here in this prime area his care is exemplary.

We are accustomed to thinking that "wild" means "untamed" or "out of control." Our great accomplishment, we think, is that we have ordered the out-of-control to create "progress." Perhaps there is no more central shibboleth in human thought. But Muir subverts this self-satisfaction by changing the definitions of its foundation terms. The "wild," to Muir, means the self-controlling, ultimately harmonious interworkings of a vast web of relationships. It is the steady-state, not in stagnation but in an always changing modulation of parts. He says that

> we are governed more than we know, and most when we are wildest. Plants, animals, and stars are all kept in place, bridled along appointed ways, *with* one another, and *through the midst* of one another—killing and being killed, eating and being eaten, in harmonious proportions and quantities. And it is right that we should thus reciprocally make use of one another, rob, cook, and consume, to the utmost of our healthy abilities and desires.

This constant reciprocity, in fact, is *culture,* according to Muir's terminology.

What is wrong about man, then, must be not that he desires to eat other creatures, but that he refuses to let them work out their own evolutionary destinies: he alters them through breeding—taking over their evolution—and in the process aggrandizes himself, removes himself from the natural culture, and makes himself arrogant. Thus there is a large negative aspect to what is called "progress," though it ordinarily goes unexamined. Furthermore, since man attempts to escape restraint—since humanist utilitarianism has in fact no inherent self-restraint, but puts its potentially reflective energy into self-justification—man is "out of control."

It would be hard too find a more complete inversion of civilized values. In wilderness, there is complex, many-faceted control: culture. In civilization, there is simplicity and linearity inspired by "the barbarous notion . . . that there is in all the manufacturers of Nature something essentially coarse which can and must be eradicated. . . ."

Muir's writings indicate that the clearest avenue to the ecological position is beauty. In the perception of beauty, we overcome civilization and participate in God—"no synonym for God is so perfect as Beauty"—and affirm our own "most richly Divine" nature. For Muir, beauty was no effete concept, and not a casual activity for leisure time: it was the key to wild nature and thus self-nature. The purely anthropocentric mind is closed to beauty on this level; a "streaming," open consciousness is required.

Muir's chief technique for inspiring this border-crossing kind of consciousness is to show all nature as alive and moving, so that the ordinary Lockeian theory of mind—a separate "subject" perceiving "objects"—is transcended. Here, his most often-criticized tool comes into play: the "pathetic fallacy." A passage from *The Mountains of California* will demonstrate its importance in developing the wild viewpoint. Muir is here describing his first venture out into the Central Valley of California. The valley was wild, and it was covered with flowers:

> Sauntering in any direction, hundreds of these happy sun-plants brushed against my feet at every step, and closed over them as if I were wading in liquid gold. The air was sweet with fragrance, the larks sang their

blessed songs, rising on the wing as I advanced, then sinking out of sight in the polleny sod, while myriads of wild bees stirred the lower air with their monotonous hum—monotonous, yet forever fresh and sweet as everyday sunshine.

The great yellow days circled by uncounted, while I drifted toward the north, observing the countless forms of life thronging about me, lying down almost anywhere on the approach of night. And what glorious botanical beds I had! Oftentimes on awakening I would find several new species leaning over me and looking me full in the face, so that my studies would begin before rising.

If all nature is a living system, and human consciousness a dynamic and flowing part of it, then there is no pathetic fallacy, because there is no distinct boundary on one side of which is "all that is human," and on the other side, the "natural." "The power of imagination makes us infinite," Muir wrote in his journal in 1875; hard and fast boundaries, based on the exaggeration of separate entity-hood, do not exist in natural reality, and it is precisely our imaginative consciousness which shows us this. We are, then, natural.

Approaching the problem from this direction—naturalizing man—is more fruitful, I think, than concentrating upon the apparent "humanizing" of nature which the "pathetic fallacy" seems to entail. Now we are free to appreciate what sort of happiness Muir means when he describes the "happy sunplants," and we can see their faces as they look at his face in the morning. From Muir's point of view, entity-bound logic is dangerously narrow, and ultimately self-defeating.

But in our heavily dualized culture the effectiveness of animating and sensitizing nature depends upon subtlety. When John Ruskin coined the phrase, "the pathetic fallacy," he was talking mainly about over-use and over-emphasis. On this point, Muir will be variously judged, but I think in general he is wise and skillful. In the passage quoted, which is from his most carefully written yet ecologically revolutionary book, he seems restrained enough, and at any rate the Edenic general tone— the depiction of a lone, new man drifting through a perfectly glorious and wild creation—would probably justify an even more obvious attribution of feeling to the flowers. In *Stickeen*, his famous story of a surpassingly intelligent dog who bravely followed him across a narrow ice bridge in Alaska, Muir is extremely careful to found all his judgments in observed fact, and to phrase them in language replete with qualifications. He knew the territory on both sides of the human/natural divide, as it were, and knew how to guide over the passes.

Muir's great creative period as a writer came after his baptism in the "Range of Light," as he called the Sierra. His earlier writings, with the exception of parts of *A Thousand-Mile Walk to the Gulf* describing his 1867 trip, are not distinguished by especially complex thinking, sharp imagery, or straightforward, un-precious writing. . . . But after his "loving study" of the glaciers and his immersion in the wilderness, a growing control of his materials and insights becomes evident. For freshness of vision combined with ecological revelation, *My First Summer in the Sierra* is perhaps his best work; for ability to convey wilderness to unbelievers, *The Mountains of California.* The later books, such as *Our National Parks, The Yosemite, Travels in Alaska,* and *The Cruise of the Corwin,* contain passages of great beauty and passages of subtle contrast between the wild and the civilized, to be sure, but they are much more the documents of a public figure in their tone and diction. By comparison with his earlier writings, they seem tame—

despite the urgent conservationist message in *Our National Parks* and *The Yosemite,* for example.

However, any of Muir's books or articles, seen against the mainstream of American literature, is an adventure in wildness, and talking of his "early period" or his "late period" may tend to obscure his uniqueness and his real contribution to culture. For Muir is probably our wildest writer, literally and philosophically, and it is his ability to convey a whole, living sense of wilderness—and to hold up the natural mirror to man— that marks his greatness. Being vibrantly aware himself, and able to keep the sense of this flow alive in his writing, he inspired—and inspires—his readers to recapture a dimension that often remains buried. (pp. 34-44)

> *Thomas J. Lyon, in his* John Muir, *Boise State College, 1972, 48 p.*

## DONALD WESLING   (essay date 1977)

[*In the following excerpt, Wesling examines the techniques and aims of Muir's descriptive prose, comparing his moral sensibility to that of the English Romantics and John Ruskin.*]

John Muir did not write his first book until he was sixty. The delay was largely, I believe, because the writing was in itself a testimony of decline: of a retreat from the unmediated connection with the natural scene which was his just after entering the Yosemite Valley in 1869. While he was able to live in and with nature in the Sierra there was no need to write about nature, no need to make books; though his letters and journals of this ecstatic time are finer than anything else he did. And the writing itself, at best, contains little human society, but is rather the record of an extraordinary seeing and feeling eye in its perceptual encounters with the world, each new glance a new name.

Muir's is a late, positive version of Romanticism. His descriptive prose, like that of John Ruskin (another writer of émigré Calvinist Scottish stock), catalogues and celebrates things in the world. Muir knew Ruskin's work, and *My First Summer in the Sierra* does for California's mountains what *Modern Painters* did for the English Lake District and the Swiss Alps: never before (or again) was the earth regarded so keenly as a kind of salvation, very likely because it was just at this mid-to-end century moment in the history of ideas that landscape could act as a bridge between faith and unfaith. Descriptive prose in Ruskin and Muir is a displaced version of the Evangelicism of their youth. Just when the wilderness is being settled and humanised, in Muir it becomes the focus for all the values in the universe. Like Ruskin his work is thus a protest, in the teeth of the industrial revolution, that the natural world is not to be ground up and used, but lived in, lived with, morally individuated. They affirm the importance of the non-human to the human world, the necessity of the idiosyncratic eye to the social eye, the necessity of absolute wilderness to civilisation.

Since I want to suggest the method of this descriptive prose, and the reason for its rise and decline within his lifetime, there is room for but a single passage from Muir: I take from *The Yosemite* a set-piece, not his most splendid writing but both famous and very characteristic. Muir wallowed through snow to get a view from the top of the Yosemite Valley, at 8000 feet, of snow-banners waving off the peaks of the Merced Range:

> I reached the top of the ridge in four or five hours, and through an opening in the woods the most im-

posing wind-storm effect I ever beheld came full in sight; unnumbered mountains rising sharply into the cloudless sky, their bases solid white, their sides plashed with snow, like ocean rocks with foam, and on every summit a magnificent silvery banner, from two thousand to six thousand feet in length, slender at the point of attachment, and widening gradually until about a thousand or fifteen hundred feet in breadth, and as shapely and as substantial looking in texture as the banners of the finest silk, all streaming and waving free and clear in the sun-glow with nothing to blur the sublime picture they made.

Fancy yourself standing beside me on this Yosemite ridge. There is a strange garish glitter in the air and the gale drives wildly overhead, but you feel nothing of its violence, for you are looking out through a sheltered opening in the woods, as through a window. In the immediate foreground there is a forest of silver firs, their foliage warm yellow-green, and the snow beneath them is strewn with their plumes, plucked off by the storm; and beyond a broad, ridgy, canyon-furrowed, dome-dotted middle ground, darkened here and there with belts of pines, you behold the lofty snow-laden mountains in glorious array, waving their banners with jubilant enthusiasm as if shouting aloud for joy. They are twenty miles away, but you would not wish them nearer, for every feature is distinct, and the whole wonderful show is seen in its right proportions, like a painting on the sky.

Nature has organised this "wonderful show" with the instincts of an artist so the writer, accordingly, uses technical terms from aesthetics to animate the scene ("sublime," "middle ground," "belts"); if in Ruskin J. M. W. Turner is the artist most like Nature, in Muir Nature is often as painterly as Turner. Here, as often in Ruskin, the segments of a long sentence are laid on in strokes of perception; and when Muir goes on, he follows Ruskin's habit of ostension ("behold . . . mark . . . see"), through the movement of his prose trying, in Ruskin's own words, "not to detail the facts of the scene, but by any means whatsoever to put my hearer's mind into the same ferment as my mind":

> And now after this general view, mark how sharply the ribs and buttresses and summits of the mountains are defined, excepting the portions veiled by the banners; how gracefully and nobly the banners are waving in accord with the throbbing of the wind-flood; how trimly each is attached to the very summit of its peak like a streamer at a mast-head; how bright and glowing white they are, and how finely their fading fringes are penciled on the sky! See how solid white and opaque they are at the point of attachment and how filmy and translucent toward the end, so that the parts of the peaks past which they are streaming look dim as if seen through a veil of ground glass.

Mountain and ocean, wind and water, rock and cathedral, art and nature, self and world for a moment interfuse in this landscape-in-language.

Such blendings of heavenly and earthly are not rare in Muir's century: like Coleridge, Wordsworth, Shelley, Byron, and Ruskin before him, Muir especially favours the symbolic possibilities of mountain-top vision which turns vanquished difficulty of ascent into moral triumph, space into memory. Muir's books are crowded with top-views like the one quoted, olympian visions of earth, though he imagines nothing so dramatic as Wordsworth's ascent of Mount Snowdon at the end of *The Prelude*—nor so dazzling as Ruskin's much-anthologised passage on the "variegated mosaic of the world's surface which

a bird sees in its migration," beginning: "Let us, for a moment, try to raise ouselves even above the level of their flight, and imagine the Mediterranean lying beneath us like an irregular lake, and all its ancient promontories sleeping in the sun." All such top-views, to the extent that they adopt a nonhuman or multiple perspective, affiliate their author with the radical Emerson of "Nature," who dismisses "all mean egotism" and can "become a transparent eye-ball; I am nothing; I see all; the currents of the Universal Being circulate through me." In fact, the distinction between subject and object is momentarily effaced, and the personality of the speaker-hero is displaced into a series of objects. Descriptive prose of the nineteenth century has as its mechanism a routine of specifying contiguous objects in sequence, and these objects are valued insofar as they are emanations of the voyaging self. No literary genre is therefore more obsessed with the procedures of transition and contiguity, or the rhetoric of metonymy which sets up referential objects as surrogate selves.

Yet to see our own nobility objectified is not, for Ruskin or Muir, to wish to dominate the external scene, whose otherness is always acknowledged. The mountains "gracefully and nobly" waving their banners, "as if shouting aloud for joy," are benign teachers, just as the vast glacier-gouged Yosemite Valley itself is for Muir consciously a Temple. The action and scale of wilderness are constant implicit commentary on the rest of earth, which has been turned into city within Muir's own generation, "seared with trade; bleared, smeared with toil; / And wears man's smudge and shares man's smell": Muir, like his exact contemporary G. M. Hopkins, will affirm by enactive description that "for all this, nature is never spent; / There lives the dearest freshness deep down things" ("God's Grandeur"). The purpose of these descriptions is precisely, then, to subsume the self and to call attention to precious objects of concern, which offer to us our best impulses so that we may read them. One annihilates the self, in truth, in order to read the signs which show the earth as benevolent and teacherly, the earth as in itself the ultimate satire upon technology and greed. "I am hopelessly and forever a mountaineer," Muir said in a letter of the 1870s: "Civilization and fever and all the morbidness that has been hooted at me have not dimmed my glacial eye, and I care to live only to entice people to look at Nature's loveliness. My own special self is nothing." Muir's intense scepticism about the medium of language—he spoke of words as "wind-driven mist-rags"—helps in part to explain his extreme diffidence about beginning to write, but very likely he was also stunned by the size of the Ruskinian project which he had set himself: nothing less than the reconstitution of his readers' sense of fact and of sight through the movement of prose discourse.

The ability to read the signs of the wilderness: sometimes, quite literally, Muir speaks of reading the text of the trees against the sky-line, or the alphabet the great glaciers have carved in long lines down the Sierra; most of the time, more by implication, he shows how the world is a sign-system and we are the interpreters who must understand the meanings of its scale. The structure of his imagination is virtually a semiology of the California mountains, and it should be possible to reconstruct that world by cataloguing the various types of scenes: above all the "living electric rock," made naked or scooped into valleys by glaciers, arranged by earthquakes, more imperceptibly changed by weather and moving water; glaciers themselves, a more slowly-moving form of water; clouds; waterfalls; avalanches; snowstorms and windstorms and snow-banners; alpenglow and aurora-borealis and the "Specter of the Brocken''; lakes and still bodies of water like tarns; sunrise and sunset; trees and animals of the region regarded as ''people.'' What, for example, does a valley like the Yosemite mean to such an intelligence? An enclosure, a vast room, a temple, a motherly protection which prevents his being exposed; but primarily, I think, a sign of the forming powers of Nature, whether in the old glacier or the ''beauty-making business'' of the avalanches or earthquakes of the 1870s. During the great Inyo earthquake of 26 March 1872, which made Yosemite's ''cliffs and domes tremble like jelly,'' Muir ''ran out of my cabin, both glad and frightened, shouting, 'A noble earthquake! A noble earthquake!' feeling sure I was going to learn something.'' What he learned was how rock taluses are formed, how streams are diverted and forests cleared by falling rocks, how the U-shaped valley itself was created: not by dropping its bottom out in some prehistoric cataclysm, but by glacial erosion on a vast scale. Muir's glacial hypothesis, documented by his scrupulous and imaginative noting of the semiology of glaciers and by his discovery of several small still-living glaciers, exploded the catastrophe theory once for all. Yet even without the evidence, Muir would not have accepted that a rift could have appeared in Nature's plenitude: ''When we try to pick out anything by itself,'' he said, ''we find it hitched to everything else in the universe.'' The violence of storm, geyser, earthquake, uprush of sap told for Muir ''the same story . . . each and all are the orderly beauty-making love-beats of Nature's heart.''

Nature was a principle of unity, then, and by implication a critique of industrial society with its fragmentation of the self. At this critical moment of encroaching alienation, the genre of Ruskinian descriptive prose developed as one literary attempt to pretend nineteenth-century society back into a sacred unity. That project was doomed; literature, even stridently programmatic as in the later works of Ruskin, could not solve—could only reflect—that late-century historical situation which is in all essential respects our own. Descriptive prose was a version of primitivism, highly complex in its moral claims and human example. At best it managed evocations of the truth of our perceptions, and showed how under the right conditions it was possible (for moments) to be at home in the world. But it was of course frustrated by the reality that language, while referential, is anamorphic with the world, only after all a secondary modelling system. The limitations of literature are consciously for the practitioners of this prose the limitations of the genre. If we feel, that is, the human complexity of the Ruskinian example, we also must perceive the extreme simplicity of a generic organisation which must work primarily through modes of *ambulation, ostension,* and *anecdote.* It is one of the most discontinuous of literary forms, always liable to be destroyed by interminably precise noticing: one thinks of Thoreau's decline into over-particularity in his later notebooks. Again, there is the danger of implausible transition between anecdotes of perception, or of hectoring the reader into a moral response: it does not diminish that great hymn *Modern Painters* to call it from start to finish a shambles of logic, and happily Muir, less brilliant, less wayward, had a commonsense way of stringing his episodes, making more of a rudimentary narrative. Indeed, Muir's forms have profound kinship with the other, more highly sophisticated fictions of their historical moment: in Hardy, in Proust, long descriptive passages work in novels as a counter-narrative, pleasing the reader by retarding the action, introducing a static or horizontal action which is itself a story. But descriptive prose is perhaps closest to that other rudimentary narrative genre of the same time, the prose poem—whose authors, like Ruskin and Muir, often hold our attention

by the non-clarification of grammar and causality, obscuring the form to prolong the response.

Muir took his premise and method from Ruskin, sharing with the English writer a hope that, even in a technological culture, an implicative description might relate our sense of fact to our sense of value. It is only right to emphasise the Americanness of his version of the Ruskinian nineteenth-century enterprise, because clearly his work engages, as Ruskin's does not, notions of frontier and of wilderness which are geographically specific phenomena of American experience. As the frontier is closed off in the 1880s, and the wilderness is decimated with its savages and fraternal animals (the Sioux, Black Elk, was desolated to hear of Mississippi paddleboats whose sole cargo was buffalo-tongues), these aspects of absolute otherness on the American continent were lost, and with them, it seemed, the possibility of forging an original relation to the universe. Threatened by empty prairies, the frontiersmen imagined and then built cities to comfort themselves; and faced by native Indians they saw less-than-humans, imagining race war, reservations. They could not let the thing alone, or study it, or honour its separateness: the domination of the earth, as William Leiss has recently shown, is a form of aggression encouraged by Christianity as a method of casting out Nature. Within this hegemony of a business civilisation which must colonise the world physically and psychologically, there exist a few voices which enact a non-aggressive relation to the landscape: Thoreau and Muir would define wilderness and frontier as not a place but a frame of mind, a form of attention, a reverence for other kinds of life than ours. For Muir, as a writer of the now-defunct

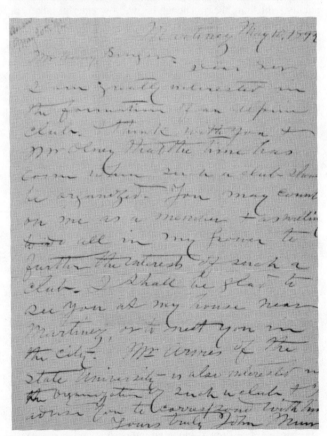

*Muir's 1892 letter to the founders of the Sierra Club expressing his willingness to participate in their organization.*

genre of descriptive prose, the test of the quality of civilisation—its survival possibility—was its ability to protect the
wilderness and keep it wild. (pp. 37-43)

Donald Wesling, "The Poetics of Description: John
Muir and Ruskinian Descriptive Prose," in Prose
Studies, Vol. I, No. 1, 1977, pp. 37-44.

## EDWARD HOAGLAND   (essay date 1985)

[*Hoagland is an American author and critic. While his novels
often focus on the peculiarities of modern urban life, many of his
nonfiction works, such as* The Moose on the Wall: Field Notes
from the Vermont Wilderness *(1974), reflect his avid interest in
wildlife and wilderness exploration. In the following excerpt,
Hoagland discusses Muir's attitudes toward both nature and literature.*]

We must go halfway with John Muir. He was more of an
explorer than a writer, more confident of his abilities in botany
and geology than of what he could do with the eagle-quill pens
he liked to use (while encouraging a friend's year-old baby to
clamber about the floor, lending liveliness to the tedium of a
writer's room). He was a student of glaciers, cloud shapes,
and skyscapes—a lover of Sitka spruce 150 feet tall, of big
sequoias, tiny woods orchids, and great waterfalls. He put
together his books late in life—he was fifty-six before *The
Mountains of California,* his first book, was published—from
magazine articles, most of which had themselves been reconstructed well after the events described, from notes jotted down
in the field with wildfire enthusiasm but little thought of eventually publishing them. Though he was a wonderful talker, he
was never entirely respectful of the written word and was surprised to find that there was an audience willing to read him,
amazed he could earn a living by writing. Being one of those
people "who give the freest and most buoyant portion of their
lives to climbing and seeing for themselves," he doubtless
wished that more of his readers preferred to hike on their own
two feet into the fastnesses he had described.

Henry Thoreau lived to write, but Muir lived to hike. "I will
touch naked God," he wrote once, while glacier-climbing. And
on another jaunt, lunching on his customary dry crust of bread:
"To dine with a glacier on a sunny day is a glorious thing and
makes common feasts of meat and wine ridiculous. The glacier
eats hills and sunbeams." Although he lacked the coherent
artistic passion of a professional writer, he was Emersonianism
personified. There is a time-freeze, a time-warp to a river of
ice, as if God had been caught still alive, in the act and at
work. And because Muir's passions were religious and political
instead of artistic, Muir—unlike Thoreau, who in comfortable
Concord only speculated that his Transcendental intuitions were
right—put his life and his legs on the line in continual tests of
faith in the arduous wilderness of the High Sierras. He believed
if his intuitions were wrong, he would fall, but he didn't ask
himself many questions about what was happening, as Thoreau
would have, and didn't believe such exalted experiences could
be conveyed to the page, anyway. (pp. vii-viii)

Muir as an advocate was a johnny-one-note, but, oh, that note!
"When California was wild, it was one sweet bee-garden
throughout its entire length," he wrote with yearning. "Wherever a bee might fly within the bounds of this virgin wilderness . . . throughout every belt and section of climate up to the
timber line, bee-flowers bloomed in lavish abundance." Wist-
fully he proposed that all of the state might be developed into
a single vast flower palace and honey-hive to the continent,

its principal industry the keeping, herding, and pasturing of
bees.

*When California was wild!* Luckily he'd seen it then. He had
arrived by ship seven years after Mark Twain had appeared by
stagecoach in Nevada, on the other side of the Sierras, to
transcribe the experiences of *Roughing It.* Both Muir and Twain
originally had harbored the hope of lighting out for the Amazon, but Twain got sidetracked into piloting Mississippi riv-
erboats and Muir got seriously sick in Florida and Cuba en
route to South America. Muir—who had reveled in one of the
best adventures of his life in walking south from Louisville to
Georgia—sailed to New York City to recuperate. However,
disliking the city, he caught a packet immediately for San
Francisco, landing in March of 1868, a month before his thir-
tieth birthday.

Unlike Twain, he hadn't gone West as a writer; not till he was
thirty-seven did he resolve to be one. This was "the wild side
of the continent," he said, which was reason enough. Yet he
invariably soft-pedaled its dangers and hardships. Twain, quite
the opposite, and quintessentially "American," celebrated the
bad-men and primitive conditions in marvelously exploitative
tall tales, boasting of how his knees knocked. Twain used the
mountains as a theatrical prop, having abandoned his career
*manqué* as a silver miner as soon as he obtained a job as a
newspaperman in Virginia City. The mountains themselves had
small fascination for him, and he sought companionship with
writerly acquisitiveness at every opportunity, whereas Muir at
that time was grasping at solitude, avoiding "the tyrant of
creation," as Audubon had once described mankind.

But the reason Muir so seldom speaks about the cold rains,
the icebite, and exhaustion he met with in the mountains, the
terror of an avalanche, of breaking through ice in crossing a
waterway, or of the many deer he must have observed starving
to skin and bones after a series of snows, is not simply Scottish
diffidence and asceticism. He loved most of nature's violence—"the jubilee of waters," as he called one particular
winter storm. In the earthquake of 1872, for instance, "disregarding the hard fist of fear in his stomach, he ran out into
the moonlit meadows," according to Linnie Marsh Wolfe, his
biographer [see Additional Bibliography]. "Eagle Rock, high
on the south wall of the valley, was toppling. . . . All fear
forgotten, he bounded toward the descending mass," shouting
exuberantly in the shower of dust and falling fragments, leaping
among the new boulders before they had finished settling into
their resting places on the valley floor.

Besides, when he got around to organizing the journals of his
early wanderings, he had become sharply political. He had
been jotting plant identifications and geological evidence of
glaciation but now was gleaning memories from the same pages,
meaning to write to save the wilderness from obliteration—
and not just by the timber and mining companies. More pervasive a threat at the turn of the century was the injunction in
*Genesis* that any wilderness was a wasteland until tilled, that
man was made in the likeness of God and in opposition to
wilderness and its multitudinous creatures, which were not. It
seems a very old pronouncement; yet it was the revolutionary
edict of a new religion attacking established spiritual values—
monotheism on the offensive against polytheism, which revered or at least incorporated the realities of the wilderness.
Furthermore, later texts and preachers went beyond the objection that certain mountains, forests, springs, and animal races
had been considered gods, to decry the wilderness as actually
Devil-ridden, inimical to the salvation of man.

Muir, like the eastern Transcendentalists, was not advocating polytheism. Nor was he secular. He believed that wilderness, like man, was an expression of one God; that man was part of nature; that nature, fount of the world, remained his natural home, under one God. Like Emerson and Thoreau—and like Twain and Whitman and Melville and Hawthorne—Muir had found Christianity to be a stingy religion in matters vital to him. In his case, it wasn't the Church's vapid response to the issue of slavery or to the mysterious ambiguities of evil or the imperatives of love that swung him toward the perilous experiment of inventing his own religion (for Twain, this became atheism). Polytheism was long dead, yet the wilderness was still perceived as inimical, and so Muir didn't want to increase by even a little the lore that had contributed to such a misreading.

His father had been a free-lance Presbyterian preacher when not working on their Wisconsin farm—a hellfire Presbyterian, fierce with the one flock given into his care, who were his children. The family had immigrated to America when John was eleven, and from then on he worked like an adult, dawn to dusk in the summer, with many beatings. At fifteen, he was set the task of digging a well in sandstone by the light of a candle. Daily for months, except on Sundays, he was lowered alone in a bucket, and once at the eighty-foot level passed out from lack of oxygen. Though he was only just rescued in time, the next morning his father punctually lowered him to the bottom all over again. Not till he was ninety feet down did he hit water.

This amok Presbyterianism helped to estrange Muir from Christianity but not from religion, and paradoxically made him gentler toward everyone but himself. He had encountered kinder treatment from some of the neighbors, and despite his deficiencies in schooling, was welcomed to the university in Madison, where a science professor and Emerson and Agassiz disciple named Ezra Carr (and especially Mrs. Carr) drew him into their household like a son. His education was so hard-won that he seems to have gotten more out of his two and a half years at college in terms of friendships and influences than Thoreau did at Harvard, though both learned to keep an assiduous notebook and to insist that America had a great intellectual role to play in the world.

Muir was one of those people who believe in the rapture of life but who must struggle to find it. He wasn't always blissful in the woods. During the Civil War, when he was twenty-six, he fled to Canada, partly to evade the draft, and wandered the environs of the Great lakes for eight months in intermittent torment. He had already aspired to be a doctor, then had leaned toward natural science, had exhibited a phenomenal knack for inventing machine tools and implements—the kind of talent that has founded family dynasties—and had won his independence from his father without bruising his mother and sisters and brothers unduly. He had had fine friends, had been in love; yet still he wanted to leave "the doleful chambers of civilization, the beaten charts," and search for "the Law that governs the relations between human beings and nature." There was one indispensable lesson he had gained from the brutal schedule of labors of his boyhood. During the next couple of decades when it was essential that he explore, laze, gaze, loaf, muse, listen, climb, and nose about, he was free of any puritan compulsion to "work." After the north-woods sojourn, he put in another two years as a millwright and inventor for wages (not drudgery, because he enjoyed it), before a frightening injury to his right eye in the carriage factory in which he worked bore in upon him the realization that life was short.

Once, finding himself in the metropolis of Chicago, he had passed the five hours between trains by botanizing in vacant lots; and now as he struck off like one of his heroes, Alexander von Humboldt, for the valley of the Amazon, he set a compass course directly through Louisvile so as not to notice the city too much. Beginning this, his earliest journal extant, he signed himself with ecstatic curlicues, "John Muir, Earth-planet, Universe." Later on, in California, he would set off into the radiant high country of "the Range of Light"—as he called the Sierra Nevadas—with his blanket roll and some bread and tea thrown into a sack tossed over his shoulder like "a squirrel's tail." He might scramble up a Douglas fir in spiked boots in a gale to cling to it and ride the wind "like a bobolink on a reed," smelling the flower fields far away and the salt of the sea. "Heaven bless you all," he exclaimed, in his first summer journal from the Sierras—meaning all California's citizenry, including its lizards, grasshoppers, ants, big-horn sheep, grizzly bears, bluebottle flies (who "make all dead flesh fly"), "our horizontal brothers," as he was apt to describe the animal kingdom.

On the giddy cliffs and knife-edges he was not out to test his courage, like the ordinary outdoorsman, but was set upon proving the beneficence of God. More than Thoreau, though less than Emerson, he skewed the evidence. God *was* in the mountains, as he knew from his own sense of joy; and as he gradually discovered that his intuitions were tied in with compass directions, storms brewing, the migration of ice, and the movements of bears, he was preparing to preach the goodness of God to us as well as himself. In even the mildest Christian theology, nature was simply handed over in servitude to man, and the Transcendentalists were trying to bypass not only this destructive anthropocentrism, as they perceived it, but also the emphasis Christianity placed upon an afterlife at the expense of what seemed a proper reverence for life on earth. Such stress upon salvation appeared to isolate people from one another as well, because each person's fate was to be adjudicated separately. Transcendentalists believed in universal links, and while never denying the possibilities of an afterlife, chose to emphasize the miraculous character, the healing divinity, of life here and now.

Emerson admired and communed with Muir during a visit to Yosemite and afterwards encouraged him by correspondence. Other intellectual doyens—Asa Gray, Agassiz, Joseph Le Conte—took up his banner, and he was offered professorships in science in California and Massachusetts, which he turned down. From the start he had seemed a marked man. Like his father's neighbors, his college instructors, and factory mentors, Muir's first employer in the Sierras, a sheepowner named Mr. Delaney predicted that he was going to be famous and "facilitated and encouraged" his explorations, Muir said. Some of the Mormons, too, appear to have noticed him favorably when he descended from the Wasatch Range on one of his larks to hobnob a bit near Salt Lake City. Ardent, outspoken, eloquent in conversation, he wore his heart on his sleeve throughout his life, but although more driven, more energetic than Thoreau, he lacked Thoreau's extraordinary gift of self-containment and single-mindedness. He had more friendships—an intricacy of involvements—and was a "problem-solver," as we say nowadays, a geyser of inventiveness. The trajectory of his career carried him finally to the winsome, wise figure leading day hikes for the Sierra Club or posed on his ample front porch in vest and watch fob with his high-collared daughters and black-garbed wife, to the Muir quarreling publicly and condescendingly with the Hudson River naturalist

John Burroughs, and Muir as a visiting fireman in London, or elected to the American Academy of Arts and Letters in 1909. Yet, for all these amenities and the freedom he won to do as he liked in the world, he never achieved anything like Thoreau's feeling of mastery over it—that easy-wheeling liberty to analyze, criticize, anatomize and summarize society's failings with roosterly pleasure: "the mass of men lead lives of quiet desperation." Compared to Thoreau's spiky commentaries on his neighbors and other townsfolk, on politics, culture, labor, industry, civilization, "Boston," Muir's admonitory remarks sound aloof, stiff, and hostile, as if directed at targets with which he had no firsthand familiarity. For, despite all his friendships, Muir sought the glory of God far from other people; and just as he had had to reinvent Transcendentalism for himself way out on a kind of rim of the world, he devised his own brand of glaciology to explain the landforms of Yosemite—notions at first ridiculed by the academic geologists, then vindicated, though he had taken no account of previous or contemporaneous studies, mainly because he was unacquainted with them. We need to remember that one reason he roamed so high and far was to measure living glaciers and inspect virgin evidence, but he was both too religious and too idiosyncratic to rightly pursue a scientific career, and so he moved on to become a rhapsodist, a polemicist, and a grandfather whitebeard.

He had seen the last of Wisconsin, Appalachian, and California frontiers. Like twenty-one-year-old Francis Parkman on the Oregon Trail in 1846, like twenty-six-year-old Sam Clemens jolting into Fort Bridger in 1861, he had gone West for adventure. But he stayed in the West, stayed exhilarated, witnessing nature on a scale never presented on the Atlantic seaboard. Volcanoes, landslides, glaciers calving, oceans of flowers, forests of devil's-club and Alaskan hemlock. He was thick-skinned to criticism like Mark Twain but more personally peaceable, as exuberant in Alaska as Jack London but indifferent to gold rushes and desperadoes. His favorite bird was the water ouzel, an agile, inoffensive creature living in mountain watercourses, not the golden eagle, and his favorite animals were squirrels.

"The Douglas squirrel is by far the most interesting and influential of the California *sciuridae,* surpassing every other species in force of character. . . . Though only a few inches long, so intense is his fiery vigor and restlessness, he stirs every grove with wild life, and makes himself more important than even the huge bears that shuffle through the tangled underbrush beneath him. Every wind is fretted by his voice, almost every bole and branch feels the sting of his sharp feet. How much the growth of the trees is stimulated by this means is not easy to learn, but . . . Nature has made him master forester and committed most of her coniferous crops to his paws. . . ." This is not the author of *White Fang* talking. (pp. xi-xvii)

As seems to be the case with many wounded-hearts who make a decisive leap away from wherever they were wounded, joy eventually became Muir's strong suit. His joy in the bee-meadows under sun-shot granite and ice, the fir trees and river willows, the tiny water ouzels diving into cold rapids and running on the bottom after insects, ruddering themselves in the current with their half-open wings, was so tactile that he repeatedly experienced episodes of mental telepathy. He lived recklessly and efficiently enough to have done as much scrambling, ambling, trekking, and roaming as he sensibly could have, but at the age of seventy still had published just two

books. His most delicious volumes—*A Thousand Mile Walk to the Gulf* and *My First Summer in the Sierra*—were reconstructed from his youthful journals only after that, journals by then forty years old. His true story of the brave loyal mongrel *Stickeen,* which may be the best of all dog stories, took seventeen years to see print in a magazine after the night they shared on a glacier. And he postponed work on what might have been his finest book, *Travels in Alaska,* until the last year of his life, when his energies were not up to the task. He died of pneumonia in a Los Angeles hospital with his Alaska notes beside his bed; a collaborator had to finish jiggling them into narrative form.

Although Muir helped to invent the conservation movement, he was a tender soul, not merely a battling activist, and lived with the conviction that God was in the sky. Yet the Transcendentalists, in revering the spark of life wherever it occurred, were groping toward a revolutionary concept of survival for Western man: that we must live together with the rest of nature or we will die together with the rest of nature. Centrist churchmen over the years had issued apologias for Inquisitions, wars of racial and sectarian extermination, slavery, child labor, and so on, and their ethics were proving inadequate once again. And because Muir is such an endearing individual, to grow to care for him is all the sadder because the crusade failed. We lead a scorched-earth existence; so much of what he loved about the world is nearly gone. Naturalists themselves are turning into potted plants, and mankind is re-creating itself quite in the way that a born-again Fundamentalist does, who once went to school and learned some smattering of geology, biology, and human history, but who abruptly shuts all that out of his mind, transfixed instead by the idea that the Earth is only six thousand years old, that practically every species that ever lived is right here with us now for our present service and entertainment. So it is with our preternatural assumption that the world was invented by Thomas Edison and Alexander Graham Bell. (pp. xviii-xix)

> *Edward Hoagland, in an introduction to* The Mountains of California *by John Muir, Penguin Books, 1985, pp. vii-xxi.*

---

**ADDITIONAL BIBLIOGRAPHY**

Badé, William Frederick. *The Life and Letters of John Muir.* 2 vols. Boston: Houghton Mifflin, 1924.
    Noncritical biography by the executor of Muir's literary estate.

Bicknell, Percy F. "Chapters from a Naturalist's Early Life." *The Dial* LIV, No. 643 (April 1913): 293-94.
    Reviews *The Story of My Boyhood and Youth.* Bicknell states: "There is a freshness and truth and simple sincerity about [this book] that go far toward making it one of the great pieces of writing of its kind."

Brooks, Van Wyck. "The Plains and the Mountains." In his *The Times of Melville and Whitman,* pp. 410-28. New York: Dutton, 1947.
    Biographical essay.

Clarke, James Mitchell. *The Life and Adventures of John Muir.* New York: Alfred A. Knopf, 1945, 364 p.
    Biography which focuses upon the development of Muir's attitude toward nature.

Cohen, Michael P. *The Pathless Way: John Muir and American Wilderness.* Madison: University of Wisconsin Press, 1984, 408 p.
    Comprehensive biography. Cohen concentrates in particular on the evolution of Muir's conservationist ideology.

Earle, Alice Morse. "The Mountains of California." *Dial* 18 (1 February 1895): 75-7.
    Favorable review of *The Mountains of California*.

Elder, John C. "John Muir and the Literature of Wilderness." *Massachusetts Review* XXII, No. 2 (Summer 1981): 375-86.
    Finds the legacy of Muir's highly personal literary approach in the writings of contemporary "naturalist autobiographers" Aldo Leopold, Loren Eiseley, Edward Abbey, Gary Snyder, and Annie Dillard.

Fleck, Richard F. *Henry Thoreau and John Muir Among the Indians*. Hamden, Conn.: Archon, 1985, 128 p.
    Examines the evolution of Muir's regard for native Americans, noting his increasing sympathy for such groups and a parallel development in the attitude of Henry David Thoreau.

Hansen, Arlen J. "Right Men in the Right Places: The Meeting of Ralph Waldo Emerson and John Muir." *Western Humanities Review* XXXIX, No. 2 (Summer 1985): 165-72.
    Suggests that Emerson supported Muir's contention that glacial erosion was responsible for many of the geological features of the Sierra range.

Johnson, Robert Underwood. "John Muir." In *Commemorative Tributes of the American Academy of Arts and Letters*, pp. 63-70. 1942. Reprint. Freeport, N.Y.: Books for Libraries, 1968.
    Reminiscences by Muir's editor.

Kilmer, Joyce. "Mr. Muir and Spring." *The New York Times Book Review* (23 March 1913): 158.
    Reviews *The Story of My Boyhood and Youth*, noting: "To this book . . . belongs a singular charm, the charm of brilliant, adventurous, and wholesome boyhood."

Kimes, William F., and Kimes, Maymie B. *John Muir: A Reading Bibliography*. Fresno: Panorama West Books, 1986, 179 p.
    Complete, annotated bibliography of Muir's writings.

Osborn, Henry Fairfield. "John Muir." In his *Impressions of Great Naturalists*, pp. 199-205. New York: Charles Scribner's Sons, 1924.
    Reminiscences by a close friend.

Powell, Lawrence Clark. "The Mountains of California: John Muir." In his *California Classics*, pp. 142-50. Los Angeles: Ward Ritchie Press, 1971.
    Praises the power and eloquence of Muir's descriptions in *The Mountains of California*.

Roosevelt, Theodore. "John Muir: An Appreciation." *The Outlook* 109 (6 January 1915): 27-8.
    Memorial tribute. Roosevelt states: "Not only are his books delightful, not only is he the author to whom all men turn when they think of the Sierras and the northern glaciers, and the giant trees of the California slope, but he was also . . . a man able to influence contemporary thought and action on the subjects to which he had devoted his life."

Simonson, Harold P. "The Tempered Romanticism of John Muir." *Western American Literature* XIII, No. 3 (Fall 1978): 227-41.
    Examines Muir's personal philosophy, concentrating on his attempt to reconcile the opposing tenets of Calvinism and Romanticism.

Swett, John. "John Muir." *Century* 46, No. 1 (May 1893): 120-23.
    Biographical sketch. Swett was one of Muir's closest friends during the latter portion of both men's lives.

Turner, Frederick. *Rediscovering America: John Muir in His Time and Ours*. New York: Viking, 1985, 417 p.
    Comprehensive biography.

Wolfe, Linnie Marsh. *Son of the Wilderness: The Life of John Muir*. New York: Alfred A Knopf, 1945, 364 p.
    Biography. Wolfe's account was the most comprehensive available before the publication of Michael P. Cohen's *The Pathless Way* in 1984 and was long considered the standard biography of Muir.

Young, S. Hall. *Alaska Days with John Muir*. New York: Fleming H. Revell, 1915, 226 p.
    Reminiscences of Young's 1897 trip to Alaska with Muir, including an account of the events that inspired Muir's book *Stickeen*.

# Liviu Rebreanu

## 1885-1944

Rumanian novelist, short story writer, dramatist, and essayist.

Rebreanu is considered the preeminent Rumanian author of the interwar period. He is best known for his epic novels *Pădurea spînzuraţilor (Forest of the Hanged), Răscoala (The Uprising),* and *Ion,* all of which document in a comprehensive and realistic fashion the turbulent nature of Rumanian life in the early twentieth century.

Rebreanu was born the son of an impoverished teacher in the Transylvania region of Rumania, which was at that time part of the Austro-Hungarian empire. After studying at Rumanian, German, and Hungarian schools, he attended the Budapest Military Academy; upon graduating in 1906 he served for a short time in the Austro-Hungarian army. Rebreanu then settled in Bucharest, where he worked as a journalist and literary secretary in addition to writing short stories. His first collection of short stories, *Frămîntări,* was published in 1912, and throughout the decade he continued to write short fiction. He also wrote his first novel during this period, and with the publication of *Ion* in 1920 he was immediately hailed as the foremost Rumanian novelist. While he subsequently published dramas, literary criticism, and essays, Rebreanu concentrated on the novel form during the remainder of his career, which ended abruptly with his suicide in 1944.

Rebreanu's fiction consistently reflects his early background in the poor farming region of Transylvania and his concern for the social, economic, and spiritual problems of the Rumanian peasantry. In *Ion,* for example, Rebreanu depicts the circumscribed existence of a Transylvanian farmer, focusing on the conflict between the farmer's physical drives and his Christian morality, while *The Uprising* is based on a peasant revolt of 1907. Synthesizing the techniques of European Realism and its offspring, Naturalism, Rebreanu attempted to provide not only an objective and accurate account of the events he narrated, but also some sense of the larger forces that control human destiny and create human conflict, whether personal, racial, or international. As a result, critics find in his fiction an element of scientific determinism which links Rebreanu with such Western European authors as Emile Zola and Thomas Hardy.

Rebreanu's works were critically acclaimed during his lifetime, and *The Uprising* is widely considered the masterpiece of Rumanian fiction. In addition, his oeuvre is regarded as a watershed in the development of Rumanian literature, marking the transition from nineteenth-century Romanticism to more modern literary theories and techniques. Finally, with the translation of his works into French, English, Spanish, German, and Russian, Rebreanu brought international attention to the literature of his native region, earning him continuing respect and admiration in Rumania.

## PRINCIPAL WORKS

*Frămîntări* (short stories) 1912
*Golanii* (short stories) 1916
*Calvarul* (novel) 1919

*Răfuiala* (short stories) 1919
*Ion* (novel) 1920
  [*Ion,* 1967]
*Pădurea spînzuraţilor* (novel) 1922
  [*Forest of the Hanged,* 1930]
*\*Plicul* (drama) 1923
*Adam şi Eva* (novel) 1925
*\*Apostolii* (drama) 1926
*Ciuleandra* (novel) 1927
*Crăişorul* (novel) 1929
*Răscoala* (novel) 1932
  [*The Uprising,* 1964]
*Jar* (novel) 1934
*Gorila* (novel) 1938
*Amîndoi* (novel) 1940
*Amalgam* (essays and interviews) 1943
*Jurnal* (journals) 1984

\*Date of composition.

---

***THE NEW YORK TIMES BOOK REVIEW*** (essay date 1930)

[*In the following review of* Forest of the Hanged, *the critic praises the technical skill manifested in that novel while noting that the tragic potential of the story is insufficiently realized.*]

*Forest of the Hanged* introduces to the American public the work of a veteran Rumanian novelist, author of several successful books and plays. It reveals a fine and mature talent and a polished technique. Although it is set against a background of the war, *Forest of the Hanged* is not, strictly speaking, a war book. The views of the war which it contains are novel and interesting. This in itself is no small feat, when one considers the exhaustive thoroughness with which the war material has been covered in the past two years. But, in general, the war appears rather as an underlying motive than an immediate factor in the adventures of Apostol Bologa.

The conflict upon which the novel is based is one which must actually have occurred countless times in the action on the Eastern Front. In its depth and reality it is material suitable to tragic writing of the highest order. Apostol Bologa, a young Rumanian student, was betrothed at the outbreak of the war to a pretty and well-dowered young woman with a romantic taste for military uniforms. Twinged by jealousy, Apostol waived his exemption and joined the Hungarian Army. He discovered a remarkable talent for military life, fought creditably on the Russian front, was twice promoted and decorated. Then he was called to serve as a member of a court-martial to try a deserter. Bologa declared himself for a verdict of guilty, and, since the officer on trial had been carrying maps and papers at the time of his desertion, for military degradation and a dishonorable death by hanging. The case seemed clear enough, but Bologa's conscience was uneasy. He flinched at sight of the execution and the serenity of the condemned man's countenance haunted him reproachfully. Then he learned that the man's father had been hanged by the Hungarian authorities during his absence at the front. This circumstance, which would not in the least have altered the judicial aspects of the case, increased a hundredfold Bologa's inner torment.

Bologa carried back to the lines his growing doubt, not only of the essential justice of the sentence he had passed, but of the whole situation which had made possible such a sentence. Then he learned unofficially that his brigade was to be transferred to the Rumanian front. With his dead father's injunction ringing in his ears—"Never forget that you are a Rumanian"—Bologa knew that he himself would have to desert. The conflict dragged on for weeks. He had to await official confirmation of the news. He tried to obtain a transfer to a division bound for the Italian front, but this he recognized as an unworthy expedient. Twice he was prevented from deserting—once by a wound and later by an illness which resulted from it. In his torturing indecision, faced with the loss of his honor on the one hand or with almost certain capture and a shameful death on the other, Bologa was spurred to action only by a summons to appear for service at another court-martial.

The story of Bologa is movingly told. Rebreanu attains an impression of overmastering horror in his descriptions of the executions and of the "forest of the hanged," where deserters who had paid for their crimes were left as examples to their comrades. But the book as a whole does not quite realize the possibilities for tragedy which it contains. Bologa's conflict, deep and inescapable though it is, lacks something of the fundamental balance and clarity which the reader has a right to expect. This may be due less to Rebreanu's fault as an artist than to the existence of a national psychology which defies translation. If so, we may regret the circumstance, but we can hardly quarrel with it.

> *"A Rumanian Novel,"* in The New York Times Book Review, *September 28, 1930, p. 6.*

## DINU PILLAT   (essay date 1976)

*[In the following excerpt, Pillat discusses the influence of Fedor Dostoevsky on Rebreanu's works.]*

Liviu Rebreanu includes among his favourite books *Crime and Punishment* and *The Brothers Karamazov,* "the most terrible moment of Dostoyevsky." A zealous researcher of Rebreanu's literary beginnings informs us, among other things, that before the outbreak of the First World War the writer translated after a German intermediary the well known story "Krotkaya" given by Dostoyevsky in *An Author's Diary,* a story under whose influence he was to create some time later one of his early short-stories, **"The Swan Song" ("Cîntecul lebedei"),** as can be seen in "some similarities" of "atmosphere" and even of the "plot." Although there can be no affinity with the Russian novelist in *The Forest of the Hanged (Pădurea spînzuraţilor),* Radu Dragnea considers it as the first Romanian novel belonging to an "integral realism," like that established by Dostoyevsky with a "complete vision of the world," that approaches both "the seen realities" and "the spiritual ones," represents "mankind in its most varied and contradictory aspects," fathoms "the individual's psychology," abolishes "the aesthetics of types common to both romanticism and Balzac." As an ideologic exponent of "Gîndirea," the essayist shares the conviction that the "new conception" of the generation of novelists after the First World War, a conception based on a complex understanding of man, "starting from Dostoyevsky" can remain only "at the surface of certain creative devices" if it has not also appropriated the human significance of orthodoxy in its moral substance." Implicitly expressing his desideratum that by a novel of Dostoyevsky's Christian spirituality Romanian literature should rise to the dimensions of the eternal and the universal," Radu Dragnea takes the occasion to suggest that *The Forest of the Hanged* is the only book of the time meaning the first step to an achievement in this respect. More cautious in his affirmations, Pompiliu Constantinescu confines himself to point in *The Forest of the Hanged* to "insignificant deviations of ecstatic states, of subjective mysticism, over which hovers Dostoyevsky's giant shadow." In Al. Piru's relatively more recent opinion, the writer seems to have used in *The Forest of the Hanged,* unlike in *Ion,* "a novel in the manner of Tolstoy," "the analytical technique of Dostoyevsky's novel." Nicolae Balotă, one of the latest commentators, in a note to his survey *Liviu Rebreanu or the Vocation of the Tragic (Liviu Rebreanu sau vocatia tragicului)* briefly makes the most evident reference to Dostoyevsky, in connection with *The Forest of the Hanged.* "We recognize in Rebreanu's novel the psychic oppression, the mystic élans, the falls, the hallucinating quasi-hypnotic progress to be met with in Dostoyevsky's novels. As a matter of fact Dostoyevsky was the only literary master Rebreanu could have for projecting an unhappy, really tragic, consciousness." (pp. 243-45)

> *Dinu Pillat, "Dostoyevsky in Romanian Literary Consciousness," translated by Monica Pillat and Ileana Verzea, in* Revista de Istorie si Theori Literara, *Vol. 25, No. 2, 1976, pp. 243-45.*

## NICOLAE MANOLESCU   (essay date 1979)

*[In the following excerpt, Manolescu assesses the degree to which Rebreanu's novels exemplify the essential characteristics of nineteenth-century Realism. The critic provides translations for the titles of several Rebreanu works that have not been translated into English.]*

While speaking of the difficulties he had met with when writing his novel *Ion*, Liviu Rebreanu recalls one night of August 1916, when he wrote down "the whole first chapter, the longest one in the novel, and the beginning of the second," finding at last, after several attempts, "the rhythm and the tone" of his novel. "I think that now, when everything is over, I could offer an explanation for that extraordinary fertility," said he in some *Confessions* in 1932; "almost all the display in the first chapter is in fact the recollection of the first memories of my childhood. But I shall immediately add that, when writing that chapter, I haven't even dreamt of writing the memories of my childhood; and I believe that nobody could find subjective notes in the objective depiction of everything taking place there. And yet! The action takes place in the village of Prislop, near Năsăud: Pripas in the novel. In order to locate the places, I start, together with the reader, from the highway and, north of Armadia, I turn to a byway across the Someş; then, through the village of Jidoviţa, it reaches Pripas." And he adds: "The description of the road to Pripas, and even of the village and its surroundings, corresponds, to a great extent, to reality." But how did the biographical element pass into the imaginary and how did the memories from childhood become novelistic? The "road" at the beginning of *Ion* was said to make a connection between the real world and the world of fiction: by following it, we go in and out of the novel, as through a gate. It is a way of access: doesn't it remind us of the strange journey of Alain Fournier's hero (in *Le Grand Meaulnes*), who lost the way to Vierzon and found himself in an unmapped region, unknown by the natives? The place of Meaulnes' adventure is situated on another plane than the places of his previous life, and the road that took him there is not an ordinary road. As if the real (the school, the road to Vierzon, the map) would be at one end and the imaginary (the Castle, Yvonne de Galais, the children's feast) at the other: two worlds, similar and different, contiguous and yet irremediably apart. The thing that separates them is the same thing that connects them: the road. On the road to Vierzon there is a discontinuity of the space. Let us read the first page in *Ion*: is the road to Pripas the same one with the road to Prislop? does it belong to the novel or to the childhood of the author? is it invented or recalled? Meanwhile, it seems to be a character, the first one in the novel, young, lively and eager to reach its destination: "On the road from Cîrlibaba, which accompanies the Someş, now on its right, now on its left, up to Cluj and even farther, a white road branches off north of Amaradia, crosses the river on the old wooden bridge covered with musty shingle, goes through the village of Jidoviţa and runs towards Bistriţa, where it gets lost in the other highway which comes down from Bucovina by the pass of Bîrgău.

Leaving Jidoviţa behind, the road first mounts with difficulty until it makes its way among the crowded hills, but then it advances, gay and even, now hiding among the young beeches of Pădurea-Domnească, now making a short halt at Cişmeaua-Mortului, where the cool water of the spring drips unceasingly, then it suddenly turns under Rîpele-Dracului, to rush then into Pripas, which lies hidden in a joint of hillocks."

Five hundred pages further, some characters go in the opposite direction, leaving the village for ever. The feeling of the passage of time is very intense. The last character in the novel will be the same "road," yet presented at another age: old, well-worn, rolling lazily "like a grey ribbon in the cool twilight," on which the wheels of the carriage rattle "monotonously-monotonously, like the course of time itself: The road goes through Jidoviţa, on the covered wooden bridge over the Someş, and then it gets lost in the great highway, without a beginning. . . ."

With Rebreanu, the fictitious life is lost the same way in the great life without a beginning. The novel being a closed and round world, it resembles an artificial succedaneum of the open and infinite reality: it seems to flow, both at one end and at the other, into life; but it is isolated from it. "To me, reality was only a pretext," Rebreanu wrote in the same *Confessions,* "so that I could create another world, a new one, with its own laws, with its own events." Between those worlds, one way of access: the road. But it does not only connect, but also isolate that new world, with its laws and events: it suggests an absence of bounds, although it is a bound, a frame and a constituent part of the imaginary. (pp. 111-12)

At the beginning of the novel *Adam Bede,* by George Eliot, there is a rider coming on the road to Hayslope: on the road to Pripas, nobody is coming at the beginning of Rebreanu's novel. The village seems to be dead, the surroundings, deserted. There is a stifling silence. Our ear does not even catch the dripping of the water a Cişmeaua-Mortului. Only from time to time, the leaves rustle in the trees. That immobility and the silence are a remarkable intuition of the novelist: they are a kind of break in the great show of the world, which permits the imaginary period to be set up. In the classic realistic novel, which seems to continue life in a direct way, such pauses are absolutely necessary, although they usually remain imperceptible to the ordinary ear. The time of life is suspended for a few moments: the time of fiction begins. During that period, the discontinuity occurs: we look around and everything seems familiar, although we have the feeling that we took the wrong road; we were coming from Cîrlibaba to Prislop, but the inert village, scorched by the heat of the summer afternoon, at the same time is Prislop, and it is not; it seems familiar, and yet strange. Like the spiral of Möbins, the road led us to another side of reality, similar in every detail to the one from which we started, and yet completely different. We are in the power of an illusion. The realistic novelist enjoys the part of an illusionist. A dog dozes on the road, another one comes trotting lazily, a third one gnaws bones among the weeds. A cat as white as milk treads gracefully on the dust. Two lying cows chew, and, under the apple-trees in the garden, some hens bathe in the hot dust. The teacher's house peers to the heart of the village through two windows. Some chemises hang on a line, and a small greenish earthenware pot, lays on the sill of the verandah. The physical nature, the animals and the things precede the people, who do not hurry to take their places among them. The old woman on the porch is "as if she was made of wood," in other words, part of the inventory, together with everything around her. Only at the inn one can feel that the village is alive. So, the novelist takes possession by himself of his world, depicting it meticulously, populating it with beings and objects. He does not wonder who sees the places, the houses, the dogs, the hens and the earthenware pot. All these *exist* purely and simply: they purely and simply seem to have always been there. The eye which reflects them is as comprehensive and objective as the eye of God. The secret of the novelist's objectivity (and of the illusion he maintains) is not independent of that way of looking upon the things of his fiction as if they existed irrespectively of the onlooker, absolute and eternal: to the author of *Ion,* the world of fiction is but *another real world*. Nobody discovers it, nobody invents it. If we can speak of "creation," in that case it does not resemble the Biblical one, as it implies an anteriority. The omniscient novelist does not deal with the primordial chaos; he does not try to persuade us that he made everything which exists. He became more experienced, he improved his techniques of suggestion: his world has always *been there*. And that is all. The greatest similitude with the real world results from there. One of the aspects not sufficiently emphasized with Rebreanu is the richness of toponymy and onomatology. The places and the people that populate the picture exist from the first moment, together with their names. That simultaneity is one of the main conventions of the realistic prose. To create a world out of chaos means to give it a name: to introduce the reader in an already existing world means to "recognize" the things, and their names as well. The road to Pripas passes among names of places. In the novels of George Eliot or Hardy, in the northern epics (well-known by Rebreanu, who once placed the Norwegian Johan Bojer beside Proust), with Balzac and Tolstoy, the plot is always "drawn out" of a certain time and place, as of an original point which the author identifies, without creating, and localizes in an eternity of the world which precedes him and which continues after him.

The realistic novelist, somehow superficially identified with The Creator, actually hides his ambition to create a world behind the ambition to make it resemble, as alike as two peas, the real world. But here, there is something more than just spirit of imitation. The realistic novel aims at a *trompe l'oeil* where the impression that fiction repeats life is not so important like the one that life prolongs, both at one end and at the other, fiction. At first, an illusion is inculcated upon the reader: that it is sufficient to stretch his hand innocently, to touch the reliefs on the canvas: he is then driven to look for the images on the canvas in the reality and, naturally, he remains as puzzled as Malcolm Lowry's hero in *Under the Volcano* when realizing that the American highway ends in a mysterious Mexican path. Thomas Hardy was astonished to find out that the name of Wessex, used by him to designate a purely novelistic geography, passed into the daily language, designating the South-Western counties of Great Britain in the period of Queen Victoria. Several generations of curious persons followed the traces of Rebreanu's heroes, wishing to verify on the spot, every event in the novels. The realistic novelist is a cartographer who intends to persuade us that his "Yoknapatawpha" is completely real: registered in atlases and history books. After all, that is an essential element of the realistic poetics: the world "in relief," human and natural, threedimensional or, in other words, Euclidean. The whole secret of the novelist is to obtain perfect similitude, using the 1:1 scale. But it is not a matter of copying, as it is not a matter of inventing; the procedure is rather a gradual discovering; only that the things somehow discover themselves. At the beginning, an empty road itself leads us to the core of the imaginary. That road is a metaphor of the novelistic. Let us remember that it plays a double part: it secures a natural continuity between the "outside" world and the "inside" one; and it achieves a convergence of the latter, in other words, it opens and closes a world. The paradox of the road actually reflects a paradox of the novel: that of giving itself up to similitude, placing its fictitious world in the great tide of the real world, and, at the same time, of forming itself as a duplicate, comparatively autonomous, governed by its own laws, and convergent. In other words, the novel is an *imago mundi* and a structure; a "piece of life," as the Zolists pretended, and a logical substitute of life. The most important thing is that, due to that logical and convergent structure, the model of the world appears inverted in the novel. Within the process of the imaginary structuring, an inversion of sign takes place: while the real life is a progress which contains its causes and ignores its aims, the fictitious life in a novel is a progress which ignores its causes and contains its aims. That inversion is in fact valid for all the human works endowed with a structure, as structure means *pre-established direction*. In realism, it is more obvious than anywhere.

First, instead of objects and beings characterized by a mere existence, we have characters and plots characterized by a certain meaning; they are not individualities but types; before being individual presences, they show general meanings. Society, morals, history or heredity form, in a realistic novel, the real causality, which explains what the characters are or do, and which is transcendental to the characters' existence and actions. From that point of view, the realistic novel is not an image, but an *interpretation:* for a character or an action is a result, an indication or a symptom; the realistic novel is rather a symptomatology of the real, than its mirror. Didn't Engels say that he learned more from Balzac than from the economists or from the historians of his time? There is a nightmare of causality in the novel of that type (to use Borges' term for the fantastic prose): nothing, no piece of any being, no part of reality, not one particle of the human or object-world which the realist invents is relevant in itself, in its full and intrinsic freedom to exist, but only as "representing" an extrinisic generality. The realistic novel illustrates the general by the particular, it exemplifies the historical law or the economic notion. It is not the novel of the individual named Birotteau, but of his grandeur and decay: behind the perfumer invented by Balzac, and wearing his mask, there is the Martyr of commercial honesty. Rastignac, Rubempré are not what they are, but what they illustrate: ambitious provincials, fighting with Paris. And Rebreanu's Ion is the peasant obsessed by the land.

Secondly, transcending the causality, the novel immanentizes the finality. The realistic novelist's hand is guided by intentionality, as he always places the end before the beginning. Instead of understanding reality as a succession or as a confusion of events—inexpressible and unforseeable—he looks upon it as a completed process—explainable and predictable; his world is a logical world, made logical. The realistic novelist is a Creator who starts from the ultimate causes, like a finalizing deity. Any reality, says Camus in *L'homme révolté,* is, for the ones who live in it, an endless flowing, like that of Tantalus' water, towards an unknown river-mouth. The classical novelist stops Tantalus' water course, giving it a river-mouth: he turns the life of his characters into fate. All realistic and naturalistic novels are images of fate, rather than of life. Almost nothing exists in itself, but for an aim known by the author. The signs of predestination are everywhere around the hero, in his biography, in his deeds and features. He is not "free." Hazard, chance, exception, in fact singularity are forbidden to him: for the meeting of his fate imposes on him the law, the necessity, the generating and, in fact, the medium. In that kind of novel, nothing being accidental, everything becomes necessary: there is a tyranny of the significant. Everything anticipates, warns. It is not a world of people, but of signs. "Signs are made" to every hero (but also to the reader). The classical realistic novel is that inverted world: the most familiar and the most strange of worlds, by its inhumanity and coherence. Isn't the inferno actually a world of transcendental causes and of immanent aims? The greatest pleasure of the Devil is not to "depict," nor to "invent", but to "build." The classical novelist is much more like the Devil than like God.

In those novels, "the building" represents almost a triumph of the unnatural. In *The Uprising,* the journalist Titu Herdela shakes hands with Petre Petre, the peasant: "Petre's hand was as heavy and rough as the earth.'' A handshake which is not a mere handshake. The young landlady Nadina exchanges one glance with the same one. A glance which is not a mere glance. On the first page of the novel, Ilie Rogojinaru, the tenant, says: ''You don't know the Romanian peasant if you speak like that.'' Rebreanu himself will consider that sentence ''salutary,'' as ''to me, the first sentence and the first chapter are the greatest pains'' (*How I Wrote the Uprising*). In fact, Rogojinaru's sentence should have been in the beginning, so that the character could say in the end: ''Didn't I tell you that the peasants are wicked? . . . Do you remember?'' So, a sentence which is not an ordinary sentence. The difficulty to begin— the first sentence, the first chapter—is, with Rebreanu, at the same time, the difficulty to conclude: the first accord must be necessarily responded, after hundreds of pages, by another one. The ends put pressure on the rest. That can be better noticed in *The Uprising* than in *Ion*. Grigore Iuga and his father, the landowner Miron, part: ''Going out through the gates, Grigore turns his head. The old man was standing in the same place, like a pillar poked into the earth. . . .'' It is not an ordinary parting: it is the final parting. In the writer's sentences, a foreboding music resounds: we know, by their strain or by other signs, what will follow. We know that Peter's hand, rough like the earth, is a symbol of the revolt of those without land. We know that the one who glances that way at Nadina loves her and will kill her. We know that Miron Iuga will die. I do not take into account the second reading, for those signs appear at the first one. It is now the moment to make clear one matter. There has been always recognized the author's great objectivity in describing the uprising (that is the uprising of the Romanian peasants in 1907). If we interpret the matter from an ethical point of view, then Rebreanu is beyond doubt an objective artist. None of his realistic predecessors is capable of such a detachment. With Ioan Slavici (the first great Romanian novelist), there is always a ''voice'' of the people which judges the events and may sometimes be identified with the voice of certain characters like Ghiță's mother-in-law in *The Mill of Good-Luck*. Another novelist of the time, Ion Agîrbiceanu, less of an artist, frequently resorts to the author's judging comments, even in *The Archangels*, his most objective novel. With Rebreanu, the cruelty of the observation never becomes caricatural, for he is not moralistic. Before Marin Preda—the main contemporary Romanian writer who devotes himself to the village—nobody in the Romanian novel, described the peasants with a cooler objectivity than the author of *The Uprising*.

The objectivity being extraordinary in that sense of the attitude towards the characters, it does not remain less obvious that it is revealed in many other scenes, because of the note of anticipation of the characters' gestures or words. The anticipation reflects an intentionality which the structure of the novel emphasizes. The episodes in the chapter ''Flames'' of the novel *The Uprising* were quoted many times, as they seem to be in a succession without artifices, samples of daily life in the village of Amara. The reality seems to be filmed as such, as in the episode of the inquiry. There are two successive sequences:

> ''Hello, hello, Trifon!'' shouted Leonte Orbisor from the street, stopping a little, his hoe on the shoulder. ''You started working?''

> ''What can we do? Around the house—'' answered Trifon Guju, staying on the porch and going on hammering.

''You sharpen the scythe, or . . .?'' asked Leonte without wonder.

''I sharpen it, so that it would be sharp!'' said Trifon without raising his head.

''It seems to me that you want to mow without sowing.''

''If I should . . . Well!''

. . . . .

The cart turned to the permanently opened gate. Marin Stan, a kind of whip in his hand, shouted from behind the cart to the children playing in the front yard:

''Go away, boys, from among the oxen's legs! . . . Step aside!''

Then, suddenly angry, he rushed in front of the cattle who were running over stock and block, towards the back of the yard:

''Damn you, crazy animals, where are you going? . . . Stop! . . . Stop! . . . Or I'll beat you! . . . Stop! . . . You went mad? You play the gentlemen, don't you? . . . All right, I'll show you!''

He hit their muzzles with the handle of the whip, first one of them, then the other, growling out:

''Don't play the gentlemen, or I'll show you!''

The thing that ''deprives'' those fragments of objectivity is the perspective from which they are narrated. Before interesting the author as facts of life, the sharpening of the scythe and the hitting of the oxen interest him as symptoms of the increasing popular anger. Certainly that in a novel, nothing can be completely ''innocent.'' But, in the traditional realism, the convention usually lies in hiding the convention. But in such scenes like the ones quoted above, the meaning can be immediately noticed. Leonte Orbisor wonders that Trifon Guju sharpens the scythe when he doesn't have anything to mow: instantaneously, the ordinary event is pulled out of the natural course of events and it is transformed into a metaphor. The promised mowing is a metaphor for the killing of the landlords. When hitting his oxen, Marin Stan also has in view the landlords. There appears a sense which directs things. That *sui generis* epiphany shows that the object of the novel no longer consists of the ordinary or extraordinary events which made the uprising break out, but of the uprising itself. Necessity nestled in the less significant detail. The realistic objectivity reveals itself as tendentiousness.

In *Ion*, at a higher artistic level, where the most gloomy fatality occurs, the finality circle closes and the novel becomes identical with Tragedy. Here, there is teleology, too. When, at page 15, Savista, the cripple, turns up and the main characters hear her say their names, the tragic quintet is made up. The *hora* in the first chapter is a round dance of fate. The rich Vasile Baciu, Ana's father, exclaims: ''I've got only one daughter, and I don't like the daughter I've got.'' The plot is already sketched. The scuffle at the inn between Ion al Glanetaşului, a peasant without land, and George, his rival to Ana's hand, is a kind of dress rehearsal of the crime. The death of such characters as Moarcăş, or Avrum foretells Ana's suicide. But they are not mere foreboding signs, but elements of an essential pace of existence. In *The Uprising*, the generality is only allegorical, as it suggests a bitter, rough poetry of life. The faithful transcription of daily life does not miss. The wakening of the Glanetaşu family, in the second chapter, is so minutely shown, that the author renders even the morning crow of the rooster (''At that moment, from the porch, the rooster

replied, more coarse and imperious: cock-a-doodle-doo . . .''),
or completely harmless words (''—All right, all right, I'll get
up, grumbled the youth sleepily''). But in the second part of
the chapter, the symbolism takes the place of naturalism:

> Everywhere on the estate, the people, like white bee-
> tles, were toiling with terrible efforts to draw out the
> fruits of the earth. The young man's sweat was drip-
> ping on his cheeks, on his breast, on his back, and
> some drop from the forehead trickled on his brows
> and, felling down, was absorbed by the clay, seeming
> to unite more deeply the man with the earth. His legs
> were aching from knee to foot, his back was burning
> and his arms were hanging like lead weights.

Let us notice the ''high'' perspective in the first lines: the eye
of the narrator no longer reflects identifiable beings, but the
people as species, the labourers, unindividualized, reduced to
the dimensions of diligent beetles that studded the place. Afterwards, it is an illusion that the perspective becomes normal
again: the man who mows impetuously is not Ion, but the
archetype of the peasant, a generic being, whose fight with
nature seems to be the effort of a giant. We are far from the
descriptive realism in the first part of the chapter. The man
fraternizes with the earth in a ritual of possession. The critic
G. Călinescu was right when asserting that ''*Ion* is an epic
poem,'' including ''moments of the sempiternal calendar of
the village, touching by their elementary quality'' *(The History
of Romanian Literature)*. He noticed an epic character in the
novel. At the end of *The Uprising:* ''The voices mixed, blended,
continuously got lost in the greater and greater noise of the
world.'' The voices in *Ion* also mix and blend in the noise of
the world: ''Over the frettings of the world, the time passes
carelessly and wipes away all traces. The little or great pains,
sufferings and aspirations get lost in a painfully vast mystery,
like some feeble trembles in a huge hurricane.'' R. M. Albérès
asserted: ''Realism will also give birth to an epic, to a new
form of sensibility . . . a *positivist* form of tragedy, in which
biological and historical fatalities replace the ones of the passion and sin and the hostility of gods'' *(The History of the
Modern Novel, 1962)*. The epic means, above all, epic spirit,
outsized characters, who receive a ''heroical'' size, and action.
Not even in the most remarkable moments in *The Uprising*,
the realistic view does reach the majesty it has in *Ion*. Here
the characters resemble some huge forces of nature, their existence is pathetic, regarded without relativism and without
irony, comprised in a slow temporariness, which seems to pass
over history, including it. In the peasants' epos, the history of
the people has, from Bojer and Reymont to Steinbeck and
Caldwell, an elementary quality, governed by simple and fundamental symbols: love, blood, earth. It is a so-called naturalistic history, that is, returned to nature, after the novel tried
to secularize it, separating it from the almost sacred environment in which it had its roots. The epos is a realism resacral-
ized. Not by depriving the novel of truth or cruelty and not by
making history less barbarous, but rising from a violence expressing only the instinct of the individuals, with its accidental
and often pathological character, to one expressing the instinct
of mankind, governed by laws, like nature itself. Tragedy is
rediscovered in its full purity. An implacable necessity masters
the man. To assert that, in the centre of *Ion,* there is ''the
problem of land,'' the social machinery of the fight for land,
is insufficient: in the centre of the novel there is the passion
of Ion, the peasant without land, for the land: ''He felt such
a great pleasure when he saw his land, that he felt like kneeling
and embracing it'': we are at the first pages of the novel, and
the theme of the fate can already be heard as in Beethoven's

symphony. That simple and colossal being, underlining, in all
the social and historical determination given by the reality of
the social inequalities in the Transylvanian village at the beginning of the 20th century, the instinct of possession, does
not face that land, as economic means, which Tănase Scatiu
or Dinu Păturică, heroes of our first social novels, exploit in
order to make money, but a land-primary element, as alive as
man, seeming to have, in its bowels, a gigantic *anima:*

> Under the kiss of the dawn, the whole earth, split
> into thousands of pieces, according to the fancies and
> necessities of so many dead and living souls, seemed
> to breathe and live. The cornfields, the wheat and
> oatfields, the hempfields, the gardens, the houses,
> the forests, they all hummed, whispered, rustled,
> speaking in a hoarse voice, understanding one an-
> other and enjoying the light which was getting more
> and more glorious and fertile. The voice of the earth
> was penetrating impetuously into the young man's
> soul, like a call, overwhelming him. He felt small
> and feeble, like a worm trampled under foot or like
> a leaf which the wind whirls to and fro. He sighed
> deeply, humble and frightened in front of the giant:
>
> ''My God, how much land! . . .''

In his fight with the giant, the man himself feels greater and
conqueror of the world:

> But, at the same time, the mowed and wet grass
> seemed to start fretting under his feet. A blade pricked
> his ankle, above his peasant sandals. The laid swath
> was looking helplessly at him, subdued, suddenly
> filling his heart with a master's pride. And then he
> saw himself growing greater and greater. The strange
> whirrings seemed to be songs of submission. Leaning
> upon the scythe, his breast swells, his back straight-
> ens and his eyes begin to shine with triumph. He felt
> as strong as to reign over the whole area.

To see in Ion the ambitious slyness (a ''Stendhalian hero,'' E.
Lovinescu says, ''in the limits of his obscure and reduced
ideation'') or the blamable brutality is equally wrong, as that
implies a conscious moral criterion. Ion lives in the prehistory
of morals, in a very cruel innocence. As a matter of fact, a
characteristic of Rebreanu is a kind of sensualism which excludes ideality. The relations among individuals are as possessive as those between man and his natural environment. Ion
or Petre Petre ''possess'' the world, in the sense that they
participate in it with all their senses. That cosmical sensualism
is, naturally, not the same as the hedonist sensuality in other
novels of the writer, in *Embers,* for example: there it is the
matter of a simple *esartz.* In *Adam and Eve,* the sensualism is
metaphysically substantiated. But the novel is confined to a
cold, clinical treatment of bestiality or passion. Unable to conceive ideality, the novelist distorts it both in its meaning (as
the reincarnations of the initial couple are reduced to the aspiration for the merely animal copulation), and in the Flemish
academism of the description. In *Ciuleandra,* the impression
of the pathological is strong, for Puiu Faranga is a degenerate.
Ion's obsession is inherent, Faranga's one is regressive. What
is elementariness in the first novel, becomes, here or in *Embers,*
vulgarity. In fact, Rebreanu, by changing the environment,
cannot conceive adequate heroes. What becomes, in those novels, of the fresco realism of the writer? Or, maybe, the notion
itself should be reconsidered in his case. His literary work with
urban subject proves a partially inconstant feeling of the pre-
cariousness of this life. Maybe that the town seems to him an
epiphenomenon lacking the tradition and depth of the village.
The town has no law: it may form the object of the journalistic

description, like in another novel, *The Gorilla,* but not of the novel which, with Rebreanu, is remarkable only as a variant of the epic. It is not possible to pass directly from the subhistory in *Ion,* to the politics in *The Gorilla.* The inconstant contempt of the novelist, to whom the poetry of the elementary and sempiternal morality is inherent, towards the superficial institutions of the town prevents him to write good urban novels. The title of being realistic, in the narrow sense of the word, which Rebreanu was given from the beginning, must be cautiously considered. In *Ion,* he is rather a *naturalist,* if we accept R. M. Albérès' definition: "Maybe we should name *naturalism* that huge and cruel novelistic vision universally characteristic of the second half of the 19th century: the vastness of the picture, the almost epic breath of a history which remains purely human and sociological, and especially the sharp biological sense of the individual crushed by society or destroyed by history, who radiates a latent stoicism and compassion. . . . In that inspiration and in that strength, all the great novels in half a century are gathered: preceded by George Sand, George Eliot, Charlotte Brontë, by some aspects in Hugo, Flaubert, Maupassant, there are Zola, Verga, Th. Hardy, Selma Lagerlöf, Tolstoy (who, in the main, was however an anti-naturalist), then their successors, R. Martin du Gard, Martin Andersen Nexö, Sigrid Undset. The human destiny is completely restored socially and historically, collective drama and individual drama are in a perfect equilibrium, and the author presents that drama like an epic tragedy. . .". By entering Rebreanu's name in the list of the French essayist, I shall add that, understood in that way, naturalism is not different from realism, but one which turned away from its initial attitude and aims. The realistic novel corresponds to an epoch, the first half of the 19th century, of a relative social optimism, in which the novelist, like the bourgeois in full rising, is an energetic, enterprising and indefatigable spirit. Balzac himself is a Rastignac and a Vautrin, a Birotteau and a Hulot. The author and his heroes have the makings of conquerors, who live their destinies, trying to master it. The vitality of that type is extraordinary. In the Romanian novel, we find it in Nicolae Filimon's Păturică, in Duiliu Zamfirescu's Scatiu, and in Mara, the protagonist of the homonymous novel by Ioan Slavici, characters belonging to the first stage of the realism in our country. One or two generations later, the enthusiasm of the class disappearing together with its strength, the bourgeoisie begins to produce its disillusioned and sceptical heroes, lacking their vital tonus. The great epoch of scepticism coincides with the one of naturalism and its myths, of which the most lasting one proved to be the one on heredity. Marked from the beginning by a baneful heredity, the naturalistic heroes are, in a way, lived by their own destinies. The conqueror is replaced by the victim. The vainglorious orphan, like Manoil in D. Bolintineanu's novel (1855), by the degenerate, like Faranga. In contrast to Rastignac, Hardy's Jude will remain an obscure all his life. The ambition, even if it is not atrophied, does not succeed in impelling any longer. The definition of the novel, as a narration of a failure, never corresponds better to the truth than in that epoch which ends shortly after the first world war in our country as well as in the West. All Rebreanu's novels narrate failures. *Ion* is, of course, the most significant. There is almost no character in that novel who does not become a victim. Ana, one of the most impressive characters in the whole Romanian novel, moves, from the beginning to the end, in a vicious circle. Her reiterated lament invokes a non-existing good luck: "My good luck, my good luck!" Her only fault is the fact that, at birth, she had taken the miserable lot of being a rich girl, who is wanted not for herself, but for her wealth.

The naturalistic novel takes its majesty out of cultivating those people without chance and those destinies without salvation. Balzac did not refuse even his most insignificant heroes a chance, for society, history, the whole universe still seemed to be marked by chance. Together with the skepticism characterizing the involution of the European bourgeosie after the revolutions at the middle of the century, the novel relies completely on the opposite card: ill-luck. Every time when, beyond the picturesque of the fresco or the social description, the naturalistic novel strikes the major chord of ill-luck, it rises at a dignity of tragedy which no novelist achieved before. And seldom after; are there, in our country, more gloomily, tragical novels than *Ion?* Is there anything similar to the episode in which Vasile Baciu beats Ana black and blue, or to the one in which Ana goes to Ion's home, hoping to tame him after he had raped her and trembling with terror, while the young man, who knows that, in fact, he had carried out his plan to get, through Ana, to Baciu's fortune, cuts indifferently the onion with his penknife, then wipes it "with great care" on his trousers and looks at the woman, "examining her belly with a triumphant look"? Or, finally, than the scene, at the end of the novel, or Ana's suicide, in which every detail seems to be filmed in slow motion ("slowly, leisurely, she took off her kerchief and put it on the pole which separated Joiana and Dumana"), and her death does not find an echo, not even in the feelings of the animals in the stable, as indifferent as nature itself?

> Joiana, feeling no movement, turned its head and looked puzzled. It wagged its tail and touched, with its tuft, Ana's skirt. And, as Ana was lifeless, Joiana heavily shoved its greenish tongue first into one nostril, then into the other one, and, bored, it began to chew slowly.

(pp. 113-23)

*Nicolae Manolescu, "Liviu Rebreanu or The Tragic Novel," in* Romanian Review, *Vol. XXXIII, No. 9, 1979, pp. 111-23.*

**ION DODU BĂLAN**    (essay date 1981)

[*In the following excerpt, Bălan discusses Rebreanu's contribution to the development of Rumanian fiction.*]

Rebreanu's vast oeuvre covers a wide spectrum of subjects and social environments in the novels *Pădurea spînzuraţilor (The Forest of the Hanged),* describing the tragedy of Romanian soldiers forced to fight in the Austrian-Hungarian army against their brethren during the First World War; *Adam şi Eva (Adam and Eve),* a symbolic-mythological novel; *Crăişortil (The Prince of the Mountains),* drawing upon the life of the Transylvanian revolutionary leader Horea in the late 18th century; *Jar (Embers); Gorila (The Gorilla); Amîndoi (Both of Them);* and *Ciuleandra.* The essence of the novelist's epic force is to be found in all these works, apparently very diverse but relying on accurate observation and structural realism. (p. 87)

Rebreanu brought into Romanian literature the idea of achieving a unitary fresco, an épopée of exceptional narrative vigour mirroring the life of the various Romanian provinces in those aspects which best defined it. Feeling closely bound to history, traditions, to the land and the people of his country, Rebreanu confessed in one of his interviews: "I can hardly believe that the human beings who preceded me left no trace upon my soul . . . Could I—a ploughman's son—assert that I feel no odour of the sacred sward within myself? A tree feels its roots struck deep into the earth, for it is from the soil that it draws its sap for its climbing branches. I feel all toilers of the earth stirring within me.'' It was that belief that prompted him to portray unforgettable personages of disturbing authenticity in his short-stories **"Coasa" ("The Scythe"), "Dintele" ("The Tooth"), "Ofilire" ("Wilting"), "Nevasta" ("The Wife"), "Răfuiala" ("Settling Accounts").**

His novel *Ion,* an epic of Transylvania at the beginning of this century, a highly moving tragedy of self-willed characters, brought forth the memorable figure of Ion al Glanetaşului, whose love of nature blends with his passionate drive to acquire land—the only means he can conceive of to struggle out of his poverty:

> His heart was overflowed with joy. He laboured under the impression of having nothing more to wish for, that there was nothing else in the whole world beside his happiness. Land was fawning on him, all the land that there was . . . And everything was his, now, his alone . . . He stopped in the midst of his field. The black, gluey clods stuck to his feet, making them as heavy as the arms of a lovesick mistress. Ion's eyes were laughing downright, and all his face was bathed in a hot sweat of passion. He was seized with a savage lust for embracing the world, for tearing it to bits under his kisses. He stretched out his hands towards the straight furrows, damp and brittle. Their acrid odour, fresh and vivifying, kindled his blood. He stopped, took a clod in his two hands and turned it to crumbles with frightening pleasure. His hands were left sticky, smeared by the gluey earth, looking like mourning gloves. He breathed in the odour, rubbing his palms. Then, gently, piously, unaware of his gesture, he knelt down, lowered his forehead and voluptuously glued his lips to the damp earth. And his hasty embrace sent through him a cold shiver, which made him almost faint . . . He got up abruptly, full of shame, and looked all around him to make sure nobody had seen him. Yet, his face was radiant with infinite pleasure. . . .

Set in Wallachia, *Răscoala* (*The Uprising*) is another grandiose work reflecting with amazing realistic force one of the most painful moments in the hard existence of the Romanian peasantry—the 1907 uprising. A master of perfect epic construction (cyclic in *Răscoala*), Rebreanu was a fine social observer and a penetrating analyst. Conscious of the writer's moral responsibility, Rebreanu continued the already established tradition, lending new brilliance to Romanian novel-writing and thus raising it on a par with the world's most valuable creations of the time. More deeply concerned with the complex and full expression of truth than with niceties of style, the novelist conveyed a forceful impression of reality. In that connection poet Octavian Goga later wrote: "I can see myself in a vast freshly ploughed field. Large black clods of earth, upturned from the depth, are looking at me. That is Rebreanu's prose. Land is talking.''

Rebreanu's writing displays the solid and impressive architecture of objective fiction, capable to overwhelm reality itself. He even used to impress literary critics with the idea that he was the least poetical of all Romanian prose-writers. Indeed, his approach was not lyrical in the form established by tradition. His metaphors do not vibrate like a song upon the quiver of a leaf, but emerge slowly from the heart of things like the magic which on autumn mornings causes haze to rise from the fields. His artistic universe is focused on the earth, just as Eminescu's was on the moon, and Alecsandri's on the sun. If there are solar and selenary writers, then Rebreanu certainly is a telluric one. The universe of Liviu Rebreanu's creation, his epic force, his key metaphors, his harsh and vigorous personages include something telluric. Land is an existential entity for Rebreanu, integrated into a system of social and human categories of his own. (pp. 88-90)

> *Ion Dodu Bălan, "Liviu Rebreanu," in his* A Concise History of Romanian Literature, *translated by Andrei Bantaş, Editura Ştiinţifică şi Enciclopedică, 1981, pp. 87-90.*

---

## ADDITIONAL BIBLIOGRAPHY

Niculescu, Ionuţ. "Liviu Rebreanu: *The Envelope.*" *Romanian Review* 31, No. 2 (1977): 129-31.
   Reviews a performance of Rebreanu's satirical drama *The Envelope,* noting: "*The Envelope* is the grave, overwhelming comedy of corruption in its ravaging, distorted forms bordering on the grotesque."

Philippide, A. "The Spirit and Tradition of Modern Romanian Literature." *Romanian Review* XXI, No. 2 (1967): 5-10.
   Mentions Rebreanu as "a first-class epic talent."

Review of *Forest of the Hanged. The Times Literary Supplement,* No. 1500 (30 October 1930): 892-93.
   Brief discussion of the plot of *Forest of the Hanged* in which the critic notes the similarity between that novel and much Russian fiction.

# Sax Rohmer

## 1883-1959

(Pseudonym of Arthur Henry [Sarsfield] Ward; also wrote under the pseudonym Michael Furey) English novelist, short story writer, and dramatist.

Rohmer was a prolific author of mystery and suspense fiction who is best known for his novels and stories featuring the Chinese villain Fu Manchu. Published from 1913 to 1959, this series was at the height of its popularity during the 1930s. Allied to a subclass of popular literature known as "Yellow Peril" fiction, which originated during the late nineteenth century, the Fu Manchu stories epitomize the xenophobic spirit of this genre, both reflecting and promulgating the fear in the West of domination by Eastern countries. More relevant to the enduring popularity of Rohmer's works are the skill and imagination he displayed in creating one of the most successful series of thrillers ever written.

Rohmer was born near Birmingham in the English Midlands. As a child he enjoyed adventure stories, particularly admiring those of Alexandre Dumas and Mark Twain. His youthful interests included ancient Egyptian hieroglyphics and collecting books on Egyptian history. After completing his formal schooling in 1901, Rohmer's intense interest in Egypt led him to take a civil service exam with the hope of gaining an appointment in the Middle East. Failing the test, Rohmer spent the next several years pursuing and abandoning a succession of careers. In an attempt to earn his living as a fiction writer, Rohmer published his first story, "The Mysterious Mummy," when he was twenty-one. Although this and subsequent short stories gained him a degree of recognition over the next two years, Rohmer left England in what has been described as a "mild panic" when asked to produce a serialized version of one of his stories. On returning, he worked briefly as a journalist but lost his job due to his habit of embellishing articles with falsehoods. He subsequently held several positions, and met with some success as an illustrator, before taking a job as a music hall composer, an experience considered crucial to his development as a writer. Rohmer was influenced by the broad caricatures created by vaudeville performers, especially those of the Chinese and Japanese illusionists who enjoyed a wide popularity during the first three decades of the twentieth century. One critic has argued that Rohmer's primary source of inspiration for Fu Manchu came from the escape techniques, illusions, and disguises of these vaudeville performers.

Rohmer returned to writing fiction in 1912, when he adopted the pseudonym Sax Rohmer, of which he later explained: "In ancient Saxon, 'sax' means 'blade,' 'rohmer' equals 'roamer'." He then wrote the short story "The Zayat Kiss," which introduced Fu Manchu as "the Yellow Peril incarnate in one man." Evoking the fear of the unknown, Rohmer took advantage of the fact that before World War II, most English people from a middle-class background had a limited knowledge of the Orient. The stories Rohmer published in such popular magazines as *Collier's* were widely read and appreciated; according to Robert Briney, the Fu Manchu stories are as "firmly wedded to their period as the Sherlock Holmes stories are to the late Victorian era." Although Rohmer "concluded" the series in 1918, after three collections of his stories had been published,

he was commissioned to revive the Fu Manchu series in the 1930s, when the stories gained a wide audience in the United States; the popularity of these works made him one of the highest paid writers of the period. Despite his lucrative career, however, he was a spendthrift who periodically found himself in debt. In 1955, he misguidedly sold all television, radio, and film rights to the Fu Manchu stories for far less than they were worth. When his rights were restored two years later following litigation, he revived the Fu Manchu stories for a third time, with *Emperor Fu Manchu*. Throughout his career, Rohmer also produced numerous works of popular fiction in addition to the Fu Manchu series, including the Moris Klaw detective stories collected in *The Dream Detective;* the Sumuru adventure series, featuring the female villain who appears in *Sinister Madonna* and other novels; and fantasy novels such as *Brood of the Witch Queen*. In 1957, Rohmer contracted Asian flu, an illness from which he never fully recovered. He died in 1959.

The Fu Manchu series developed as individually published short stories that were later collected to form episodic novels. With the first three of these novels, Rohmer established the basic characterization and plot formula for the series. In *The Mystery of Dr. Fu-Manchu, The Return of Dr. Fu-Manchu,* and *The Si-Fan Mysteries,* the 160-year-old Fu Manchu is portrayed as a shrewd and diabolical Chinese criminal whose mysterious Eastern powers are joined to a fiendish intellect. His learning is well-illustrated by his invention of strange chemical compounds, such as the potion with which he injects himself annually in order to maintain a youthful appearance. His other biochemical experiments include poisonous draughts, mutant insects, and new plague germs with which he eliminates his enemies. Fu Manchu is assisted in his plans by numerous agents, including thugs, dwarfs, and exotic henchmen. Perhaps the most colorful of his henchmen are the dacoits, trained Burmese killers who are strong, squat, ugly, and squint-eyed. Each wears a religious brand called "the mark of Kali" and a loincloth, yet they are such masters of stealth that they are able to move undetected in British society. While Fu Manchu has been described as an independent operator, he is associated with the Si-Fan, a secret organization devoted to world domination. In these early stories, Fu Manchu and the Si-Fan are opposed by an investigative team made up of Nayland Smith, a colonial police officer from Burma who has dedicated his life to capturing Fu Manchu, and Dr. Petrie, a figure who has been compared to Dr. Watson in the Sherlock Holmes stories. It has been suggested that the racial bigotry represented by Nayland Smith's condemnation of Fu Manchu is counterposed by the more moderate position of Dr. Petrie, the narrator of these early novels.

In the later Fu Manchu novels, various detective duos oppose the insidious doctor, including Max and Bluett, Dunbar and Sowerby, and Kerry and Coombes. The action of the novels shifts from England to such locales as France, Venice, Haiti, and America. The most dramatic change, however, is in the characterization of Fu Manchu himself, who becomes the subject of a public relations campaign with the ultimate goal of making him president of the United States. Whereas in the early stories Fu Manchu was the formidable nemesis of Western civilization, in the later series he is more often portrayed in the role of defender of democracy. As Rohmer noted in 1942: "He's still villainous and unscrupulous, but he's flat out against the Communists and trying to help democracy. In the old days, you know, he was still all for personal power."

While commentators have generally regarded Rohmer's stories favorably, contention has arisen over his portrayal of Fu Manchu. Some critics regard the character as a racial stereotype; as Colin Watson has written: "Had there not existed in the minds of many thousands of people an innate fear or dislike of foreigners—oriental foreigners, in particular—Sax Rohmer never would have become a bestselling author." Those who disagree with this view claim that Rohmer's portrayal of Fu Manchu was not motivated by racial prejudice and that his characterization of Fu Manchu resulted in a compelling figure who took on a mythical stature more attractive than that of the detectives appearing in the same stories. Whether critics praise or condemn the oriental arch-villain, it is widely recognized that Fu Manchu has continued to serve as the primary source of interest in Rohmer's fiction. As Alan Brien wrote in 1985: "the devilish Doctor is the reason why we can still read Rohmer, one of those great good-bad writers."

(See also *Contemporary Authors*, Vol. 108.)

## PRINCIPAL WORKS

*The Mystery of Dr. Fu Manchu* (novel) 1913; also published as *The Insidious Dr. Fu-Manchu*, 1913
*The Romance of Sorcery* (nonfiction) 1914; also published as *The Romance of Sorcery* [abridged edition], 1923

*The Sins of Séverac Bablon* (novel) 1914
*The Yellow Claw* (novel) 1915
*The Devil Doctor* (novel) 1916; also published as *The Return of Dr. Fu Manchu*, 1916
*The Exploits of Captain O'Hagan* (short stories) 1916
*The Si-Fan Mysteries* (novel) 1917; also published as *The Hand of Fu Manchu*, 1917
*Brood of the Witch Queen* (novel) 1918
*The Orchard of Tears* (novel) 1918
*Tales of Secret Egypt* (short stories) 1918
*Dope* (novel) 1919
*The Dream Detective* (short stories) 1920
*Bat Wing* (novel) 1921
*Tales of Chinatown* (short stories) 1922
*Grey Face* (novel) 1924
*Yellow Shadows* (novel) 1925
*The Emperor of America* (novel) 1929
*The Day the World Ended* (novel) 1930
*Daughter of Fu Manchu* (novel) 1931
*The Mask of Fu Manchu* (novel) 1932
*Tales of East and West* (short stories) 1932
*Yu'an Hee See Laughs* (novel) 1932
*Fu Manchu's Bride* (novel) 1933; also published as *The Bride of Fu Manchu*, 1933
*The Trail of Fu Manchu* (novel) 1934
*The Bat Flies Low* (novel) 1935
*President Fu Manchu* (novel) 1936
*White Velvet* (novel) 1936
*The Drums of Fu Manchu* (novel) 1939
*The Island of Fu Manchu* (novel) 1941
*Egyptian Nights* (novel) 1943
*Bimbâshi Barûk of Egypt* (novel) 1944
*Shadow of Fu Manchu* (novel) 1948
*Hangover House* (novel) 1949
*Nude in Mink* (novel) 1950; also published as *Sins of Sumuru*, 1950
*Sumuru* (novel) 1951; also published as *Slaves of Sumuru*, 1952
*The Fire Goddess* (novel) 1952; also published as *Virgin in Flames*, 1953
*The Moon is Red* (novel) 1954
*Sinister Madonna* (novel) 1956
*Re-Enter Dr. Fu Manchu* (novel) 1957; also published as *Re-Enter Fu Manchu*, 1957
*Emperor Fu Manchu* (novel) 1959

---

## RALPH HOBART PHILLIPS (essay date 1913)

[*The following is a review of the first novel in the Fu Manchu series.*]

China, the vast and mysterious, as a source from which criminals of uncanny powers and fell designs can overrun the Western world, is a safe card to play for a writer of mystery and adventure stories. No one really knows anything about China's innermost nature, and therefore no one can contradict the writer if he is a little careful in his statements. The author of the adventures of the mysterious Dr. Fu-Manchu and his tireless foe, Wayland Smith of the Burmese Government Service, builded wisely in making his criminal a Chinese emissary. There's been so much said recently in the press about the stupidity of criminals in general that the writer of detective stories is hard put to it to give his shrewd discoverers of crime an opportunity truthfully to show their mettle. A Chinese criminal, clothed with all the powers of Western learning and Eastern knowledge, is a direct inspiration. And his creator, Mr. Sax Rohmer, has proved his ability to profit by his inspiration. After all, what is demanded of the writer of mystery and detective stories is first of all imagination to create situations and then the ability to handle his theme in a way that shall keep the reader breathless from beginning to end of the story. These qualities are all apparent in the narrative of Dr. Fu-Manchu's dread doings [in *The Insidious Dr. Fu-Manchu*]. A series of mysterious sudden deaths, the secret connection of which is not at first comprehended either by the police or the public, startles official England. One by one men who have had dealings with the Orient and proved themselves apt representatives of Occidental progress, drop out of the ranks of the living; [by] sudden death always, but sometimes by a manner of death so natural that no suspicion attaches to it at first. One man only, Wayland Smith, who is not a detective but a hard-working official of the British Government in Colonial Service, realises that these deaths are wrought by Fu-Manchu, a mysterious Chinese scholar who has dreamed a dream of China ruler of the world and attempts to make the dream an actuality. The appearance of the stories in book form has lost no interest by the publication of occasional chapters in a weekly. The volume is not a book of short stories but a well-connected narrative starting with the return to England of Wayland Smith, on the trail of his dangerous antagonist, and ending with the spectacular death or disappearance—the reader is left in doubt—of Dr. Fu-Manchu. The thrills are piled up skilfully, the style is simple and direct. A few affectations in the quieter passages are forgotten when things begin to happen. There is a touch of the supernatural that lends the final element of gruesomeness to the story, a reminder of *Dracula*, which comes as a surprise after the ultra modernity of the rest of the tale. In a word, the book is a very creditable specimen of its kind, and fulfils all the requirements the most exacting reader of that type of fiction could demand. (pp. 305-06)

> *Ralph Hobart Phillips, "Sax Rohmer's 'The Insidious Dr. Fu-Manchu'," in* The Bookman, *New York, Vol. XXXVIII, No. 3, November, 1913, pp. 305-06.*

### THE NEW YORK TIMES BOOK REVIEW    (essay date 1915)

[*In the following essay, the reviewer praises* The Yellow Claw *as a well-written detective story.*]

A detective story with new and weird settings is *The Yellow Claw,* fearsome as well as mystifying. Its action takes place in London, but much of it deals with an underground region of mystery, crime, and gorgeous trappings. From that hidden corner Oriental vice reaches out a yellow claw and touches, numbs, and kills people of high station, sending a stream of poison through streets and homes.

A famous novelist is sitting in his study hard at work in the middle of the night, when his door bell rings and in rushes a woman who tries to tell him something, but faints in the middle of the sentence. He hurries out for help and in five minutes returns to find the woman choked to death beside his study table, where she had tried to write her message but had left only some disconnected words, "your wife" and "Mr. King." Who this "Mr. King" is and what he is doing, it is soon perceived, furnish the mystery of the story. A little later it is found that he has some connection with what the detective calls

"a swell dope shop," which after much labor and nosing about is unearthed in what had purported to be the premises of a ginger importing concern. A labyrinth of cellars, which in centuries past had been the vaults or crypts of a monastery, has been fitted up with Oriental luxury and magnificence, and the Chinese master of the place has sent out his lures and gathered in customers from the social circles of wealth and position. So much they find, but "Mr. King" is still a mystery.

It is a good detective story, having the necessary swift action, perilous and complicated happenings, and plot of mystery. But, in addition to these things, it has uncanny developments, touches of the lore of mystic Eastern cults, Oriental color in the midst of drab London, that gives it a certain exotic, horrifying atmosphere.

> *"The Yellow Claw," in* The New York Times Book Review, *May 9, 1915, p. 182.*

### THE NEW YORK TIMES BOOK REVIEW    (essay date 1919)

[*In the following essay, the reviewer compares Rohmer's short story collection* Tales of Secret Egypt *to his Fu Manchu series.*]

These [*Tales of Secret Egypt*] are described on the cover of the book as "stories of the sinister and mysterious East by the author of the famous Fu Manchu stories." Unfortunately this description leads you to anticipate more thrills and eerie sensations than are realized on investigation. The "Insidious Dr. Fu Manchu," Sax Rohmer's earlier creation, is a much more uncanny and awesome personage than Abû Tabâh, the hero of the first six tales in the book. Abû Tabâh, secret agent of the Egyptian Government and keeper of Egyptian morals, has access to all the closed doors of Cairo and is regarded by the poorer class as a magician, having dealings with the djinn and the efreets. The chief habit of this white-turbaned, black-garbed creature seems to be gliding in like a snake, when least expected, and slipping out again in the same mysterious manner. His aim in life is to foil the plans of those who would despoil Egypt of her ancient treasures or corrupt the morale of the people. Truly a worthy ambition, but Abû impresses one as being far from a worthy character.

The first six stories are similar in that they delineate the pitting of the wits and fighting blood of an Englishman against the subtlety and mysterious powers of the Egyptian, with the latter invariably the victor. The Englishman is the Hon. Neville Karnaby, who relates the stories. He is agent for dealers in Egyptian relics, and is not above double-crossing both his own employers and the natives for his own profit. Abû Tabâh's mission is to prevent the Hon. Neville from securing the relics and costly jewels which the English firm that he represents wants to duplicate for European markets. Wily and scheming as the Englishman is, the Egyptian always manages to defeat him at his own game. We have no objection to his defeating the Englishman, but we should like to know just how it was done, and Sax Rohmer does not elucidate. He simply gives an O. Henryesque twist to the plot at the end of the story, leaving the Englishman defeated and baffled. Now, being told that Abû has turned the tables on Karnaby is not enough. The fun is in watching the wheels go round. Sax Rohmer does not afford you an opportunity to do this, and the stories lose accordingly.

The other six tales, composing the second half of the book, do not concern Abû Tabâh and Karnaby. Each one has a different set of characters and a different plot. They remind one more of the Arabian Nights tales, and are more successful than the first half of the book, which is rather monotonous. The inclusion of some leading European character with wholly commercial interests, such as stealing some costly jewel from a fabulously wealthy Arab or Egyptian or excavating the tomb of an ancient ruler for priceless relics, precludes the atmosphere of passion and voluptuousness permeating tales of the Arabian Nights variety from becoming stifling or even oppressive for the most puritanical reader. There is enough local color to lend romance to the stories, however.

The titles of the tales are masterpieces for rousing the curiosity and suggesting those characteristics of mystery and romance generally attributed to the East by all Occidental writers, for instance **"The Death Ring of Sneferu," "The Lady of the Lattice," "Breath of Allah,"** The Whispering Mummy," **"Lord of the Jackals," "Lure of Souls,"** &c. **"The Whispering Mummy"** is the best tale of the first half, and **"Pomegranate Flower"** is the best of the second half. If you like to dream over the fascinating Orient, with its hashish and perfumes, its veiled ladies and eunuchs, its harems and lattices, its bazaars and mosques, its tombs and its mummies, you will revel in these Eastern tales of Sax Rohmer's.

> *"Secret Egypt," in* The New York Times Book Review, *July 6, 1919, p. 358.*

## J. C. SQUIRE (essay date 1921)

[*Squire was an English man of letters who, as a poet, lent his name to the "Squire-archy," a group of poets who struggled to maintain the Georgian poetry movement of the early twentieth century. In reaction against Victorian prolixity, turn-of-the-century decadence, and contemporary urban realism, Squire and the Georgians concerned themselves primarily with the traditional subjects and themes of English pastoral verse. Squire was also a prolific critic who was involved with many important English periodicals; he served as literary and, later, acting editor of the* New Statesman, *founded and edited the* London Mercury, *and contributed frequently to the* Illustrated London News *and the* Observer. *His criticism, like his poetry, is considered traditional and good natured. In the following excerpt, Squire defines Rohmer's strengths and weaknesses as a fiction writer.*]

A year or two ago I drew, or attempted to draw, attention to the peculiar qualities of Mr. Sax Rohmer. Only in a casual and parenthetical way, however, for I was ostensibly writing about something else. A holiday, during which my brain has required and received rest, has brought me back to him. I unfortunately left at home half-read—if this personal interpolation may be pardoned—his latest work. I saw enough of it to be relieved of my fear, engendered by the last I had read (**The Orchard of Tears**), that Mr. Rohmer was going to desert his natural province and attempt to emulate Miss Corelli, an operation for which he is not designed. But the advantage of liking a really popular author like Mr. Rohmer is that one can find his books, in cheap editions, on even the most Philistine of railway bookstalls, where Chesterton, Richard Jefferies, and even Dickens are names at which the clerk gapes in bewilderment or boredom. I had therefore no difficulty, at various stopping-places, in furnishing myself with the old familiar friends, **The Mystery of Dr. Fu-Manchu, The Yellow Claw, Tales of Secret Egypt, The Devil Doctor,** and **The Si-Fan Mysteries.** This last I am now reading. How, I wonder again, can any man with a taste for the nightmarish and phantasmagorial, and the desire of an occasional escape from the necessity of exerting his own intellect, deny that Mr. Rohmer is as competent a merchant of shocks as exists?

**The Si-Fan Mysteries** is good all through. It even does what all good shockers do when their villains are too good to waste, disposes of its villain in such a manner that, although presumably dead, he may well turn up again—like Sherlock Holmes. It begins in a London hotel, where a diplomat, worn to a shadow by a horrible secret, lies dying. It ends in a cave of the sea with pursuers hot on the heels of pursued, the lot frustrated, the last diabolical weapon foiled. Between this beginning and this end we have met the man with the Limp and the deadly Flower of Silence. We have spent agitated hours in the Chinatown joy-shop, watched burglaries and poisonings, chased cabs, and heard strange knockings. We have learned the secret of the Golden Pomegranates and waited while Sir Baldwin Frazer operated, under compulsion, on Fu-Manchu's brain. We have rushed from the empty little house by the Baldwin, to the house at Wadsworth, the *café* in Soho, the Room with a Golden Door, and the dungeons of Greywater Park. No ingenuity, no method of transport, and no adjective has been spared. And if we notice, we notice with gratitude and a compliment, that almost the whole of the book's long action has been conducted at night, or, failing night, in thick fog.

There are, to put it politely, distinct flaws in Mr. Rohmer's style. His sentences are often so spasmodic, his words so repetitive, that one sometimes suspects him of dictation. In several of his books, including **The Si-Fan Mysteries,** there is a character named Nayland-Smith. His status is odd: he appears to be a Burmese civil servant who gets, whenever Mr. Rohmer wants him, indefinite leave from some undefined authority in order to tackle problems that are a little abstruse for Scotland Yard. He is tall, lean, long of jaw; he has a habit, on almost every page, of either "loading" his pipe or letting fall the match with which he is about to light it. A careful artist would not repeat these things so often as Mr. Rohmer does; even the most patient reader is apt sometimes to wish that, for once, Nayland-Smith would break the monotony by employing, on the one hand, a cigar or a cigarette, or, on the other, a patent lighter. Nayland-Smith's mode of expressing himself is as little varied as his "business with hands and pipe." I extract a few specimens from . . . **The Si-Fan Mysteries:**

> "Take my hand," he snapped energetically.
>
> "Sit tight and catch," rapped Smith.
>
> "Come on, Weymouth!" rapped Nayland-Smith.
>
> "You don't have to," snapped Smith.

Very seldom indeed does Nayland-Smith say, cry, continue, resume, observe, rejoin, remark, reply, or interject. I find him occasionally muttering or jerking, but the immense majority of his sentences are either rapped or snapped. This, quite apart from the fact that it might well have put his companions off their game, becomes so irritating that the reader would welcome anything, anything, for a change—even the "he husked" and "he hoarsed" of Mr. Leacock's celebrated burlesque.

Here are some of Mr. Rohmer's defects; I suppose I had better add, though I personally am corrupt enough to delight in them, the truly terrible words that he invents. In one of his books, all the well-known shuddery words having been worn to rags, he finds it necessary, in order to get one more thrill out of the exhausted nerves, to begin describing things as "beetlesque." His shadows are "cloisteresque," his music is "luresome," and the trackers on the roof of the Café de l'Egypte look down on "the teemful streets of Soho." But what of that? Words are Mr. Rohmer's slaves, not his masters. He uses them as a great painter uses his colours; he is bound by no conventions, but thinks only of the effects at which he is aiming. And he achieves them. There are many writers of cheap shockers as reckless of English, as untrammelled by considerations of "verisimilitude," as resolved to get six thrills to the page, as debonair in the constant use of old materials which themselves or others have found satisfactory, as Mr. Rohmer. We know elsewhere—oh! how plentifully elsewhere—these mysterious Chinese, these oriental brass boxes, these opium dens—hells, I should say—these wharves by the foggy Thames, these police boats and floating corpses, these palatial hotels (I should say khans or caravanserais) with their suave managers, these underground tunnels, these furtive servants, these rope-ladders and blow-pipes, these rooms in the Temple, these boomings of Big Ben at midnight. We know, how well, that distraught girl in the rain with the black scarf over her head and that other hussy, dark-eyed, with the voluptuous lips and the snake bangle, who is "probably a Eurasian." But when we meet them in Mr. Rohmer they have an extra touch of vividness that they lack elsewhere. It is he, and not his rivals, who has left permanently impressed on my imagination the picture of a man shamming sleep in an opium den whilst the local siren, with death in her hands, lifts his eyelids to test him; the picture of a bony yellow arm thrust into the moonlight in a high room. And, to do him justice, he has not left the shocker-maker's cabinet of properties where he found it. The Chinese scientific genius who kidnaps illustrious English doctors, hypnotises them and makes them work for the dominance of the Yellow Race is, I think, a novel conception. The wholesale importation of Oriental spiders, scorpions, and snakes into an English baronet's premises has not, I believe, been done before. And some of Dr. Fu-Manchu's scientific inventions are indisputably new, notably that memorable cross between a fungus and a microbe, used in that case where the fungus fell like dust on the explorers and instantaneously began to spread cankerously over all their flesh. I could give others, only one should not queer the pitch. But I have said enough, I hope, to indicate that Mr. Rohmer—though his morals are uniformly as sound as those of all melodramatists—has as vivid and unwholesome an imagination, as fecund a spring of morbid invention, as any writer in the cheap series or out of them. Of course, if one examines his plots and his machinery with the cold eye of a scientific investigator one will very probably arrive at the conclusion that all would not have happened just as he says it does, that his characters would not in all cases have behaved as he makes them, and, particularly, that the idiocies committed in these, as in all mystery books, by the paladins fighting on the side of the angels, in order to give the villains a good run, might in most cases have been avoided. But readers who examine the art of the fabulist in this manner should avoid Mr. Rohmer. He is not for the pedant. He is for those who can fall under his spell sufficiently to believe whatever he says. Of that company I am one.

The book is open before me. The last sentences on the page catch my eye. The trapdoor is softly closed. The men stand over the panes of the skylight:

"Look," he said, "there is the house of hashish"—

I shall stop writing this, and go on from there. (pp. 203-09)

> *J. C. Squire, "Rohmer," in his* Life and Letters, *George H. Doran Company, 1921, pp. 203-09.*

### THE NEW YORK TIMES BOOK REVIEW (essay date 1924)

[*In the following review of* Grey Face, *the critic discusses Rohmer's exceptional facility as a mystery writer.*]

Sax Rohmer has at his fingertips a type of mystery story that is never-failing in its appeal if it be handled with the slightest degree of actuality. This type includes the introduction of the exoticisms of supernatural mysticism, the delving into Hindu. Chinese or Egyptian secrets or so-called secrets. In *Grey Face,* his most recent attempt at this sort of thing, he has built up a story that is, of course, quite impossible viewed in cold blood, but during the actual reading the reader is apt to fall under the spell of the author and accept his premises. Black magic is, perhaps, the best name for this sort of thing. Mr. Rohmer introduces spectral faces, phantasmal figures, and all sorts of such queer and blood-curdling things, but wisely enough he drapes them in a veil of psuedo-scientific explanation.

In *Grey Face,* for instance, the hero, a sort of private investigator, and his fiancée and his fiancée's father, a doctor who has developed psychoanalysis into a strong weapon of research, struggle against a malign and inexplicable power that can steal the minds of other people and make them do things against their wills. This power, represented by the monstrous de Trepniak, who, Mr. Sax Rohmer even suggests, is a reincarnation of the famous Dr. Cagliostro, can also see what is happening at a distance, apparently through a development of mind-waves that register in a crystal. He is also an alchemist and a savant of medieval mysteries who can enlarge diamonds. Thus Mr. Rohmer, who is anything if not generous, centres in his villain about all the secret knowledge that was supposed to be available to the adepts of the Middle Ages. It is against such a ferocious and apparently invulnerable power that the virtuous types in the book must fight, and, as usual, he piles thrill upon thrill, climax upon climax, until the whole thing rises to a Poesque finish that ought to give the most callous reader a thrill and spine shiver.

Mr. Rohmer rears his structure with the ease and confidence of a past master at this sort of thing. He knows exactly where to make a semi-explanation, how to keep his readers' interest highly sustained, and when to indulge in a little rationalizing in order to drug their skepticism. Too much should not be set down about the actual development of *Grey Face,* for a great part of its value rests in the unexpectedness of the various situations that arise. But it may be stated that Mr. Rohmer is among the few concocters of mystery tales who manage to inject some degree of varied characterization into their tales. Most mystery story writers fail altogether in suggesting reality. Their heroes are always too perfect and their heroines too beautiful. It is true that Mr. Rohmer's people are violently drawn and with but scant regard for complexities, but he is consistent, and he imbues his characters with individual attributes and unexpected traits. De Trepniak, for instance, is a type, but he is a type raised to an individual plane of wickedness. Sir Provost Hope, the psychoanalyst, and Dr. Torrington both suggest reality, perhaps more than the hero, Douglas Carey. But it is always difficult to make a hero in such a well-defined type of story anything else but a hero. His bravery and coolheadedness and shrewdness are an integral part of the scheme.

> *"Black Magic," in* The New York Times Book Review, *December 14, 1924, p. 16.*

### EDWARD FRANK ALLEN (essay date 1948)

[*In the following excerpt, Allen reviews one of the later novels in the Fu Manchu series.*]

Three decades of nefarious activity have not impaired the orneriness of the Chinese superman Fu Manchu. Now [in *Shadow*

*Sample of Rohmer's handwriting. By permission of Bowling Green State University Popular Press.*

*of Fu Manchu*] he has added hypocrisy to his already bulging bag of tricks, which isn't becoming, and fools nobody. He announces that his mission is to save the world from the leprosy of communism. "Morris Craig, a physicist touched with genius," he says, "is perfecting a device which, in the hands of warmongers, would wreck what Hitler left." Nayland Smith, Fu's thus-far indecisive nemesis, replies, with his usual British understatement, "I appreciate your aims; I don't like your methods."

The device, which Craig has brought almost to perfection, embraces all the better known advantages of atomic energy plus refinements heretofore undreamed of (such as utter disintegration). It is financed by one Michael Frobisher, a man of great wealth who married a dumb wife—or was she?

A gorgeous redhead with a rich scientific background and an appearance that adds a romantic interest to the story is Craig's assistant and secretary. She helps to parry the thrusts made against the enterprise; and she makes passes at her employer with telling effect. Fu Manchu's resources include a monster called M'goyna, who can climb like an ape. He was created in Fu's Cairo laboratory from the body of a Turkish criminal executed for strangling women, and supplied with an elementary brain a trifle superior to that of a seal. There are other somewhat higher types on the staff, and there are further aids

to melodrama: a pet cheetah, a crystal ball radio-video-telephone, hypnotism, psychiatry, exotic drugs, and a speaking knowledge of every civilized language.

Fu Manchu gets away after he has provided several hours of escape for the reader, which seems reasonable. Some day our Government will trap him for evading the income-tax law.

*Edward Frank Allen, in a review of "Shadow of Fu Manchu," in* The New York Times Book Review, *August 8, 1948, p. 15.*

**ROBERT E. BRINEY**   (essay date 1971)

[*Briney is an American educator and critic. In the following excerpt, he surveys Rohmer's works.*]

The name "Fu Manchu" has long since been absorbed into the popular vocabulary. As a synonym for old-time Oriental villainy, the name is recognized—and used—by people who probably have never heard of the man responsible for it: Sax Rohmer.

In addition to the chronicles of Dr. Fu Manchu, Rohmer wrote some three dozen other books, populated with a variety of memorable characters, sinister and otherwise. There is much in this body of work to interest the *aficionado* of mystery, as well as the devotee of fantasy and the supernatural. The best of Rohmer's stories display, in addition to their full quota of action and suspense, a seemingly boundless inventiveness of exotic detail and a genuine atmosphere of strangeness and menace. (p. 42)

Fu-Manchu was not the first Oriental arch-criminal in fiction, but he epitomized the breed to such an extent that earlier representatives are all but forgotten. Later examples, from such pulp magazine imitations as Dr. Yen Sin and Wu Fang to Ian Fleming's Dr. No, seem only pale imitations of Rohmer's "Devil Doctor."

The exploits of Fu-Manchu and his battles with his would-be Nemesis, Nayland Smith of Scotland Yard, are chronicled in thirteen books and three short stories which span almost the whole of Rohmer's literary career. The first book to carry the Rohmer byline was *The Mystery of Dr. Fu-Manchu,* published in England in June, 1913, and issued later that year in the United States as *The Insidious Dr. Fu-Manchu*; Rohmer's last book was *Emperor Fu Manchu,* published less than two months before the author's death. In the intervening years the "evil yellow doctor" was featured not only in books but in comic strips, in radio and television serials, and in several motion pictures. (In one of the latter, Boris Karloff gave a memorable performance as Fu Manchu.) In 1947, Rohmer wrote a play about Fu Manchu, in which he wanted Basil Rathbone to star (because, as he said, Rathbone was "appropriately tall, cold, and suave, and masterful even in pyjamas"). The play was never produced, but later formed the basis for the novel *Shadow of Fu Manchu.* The three Fu Manchu short stories themselves are little more than footnotes to the saga.

The Fu-Manchu history was originally intended to consist of only three books. These first appeared as a series of related short stories in *Collier's Weekly*: the ten episodes of the first book in the Spring of 1913, those of *The Return of Dr. Fu-Manchu* between November 1914 and December 1915, and the nine episodes of *The Hand of Fu-Manchu* between April 1916 and June 1917. Each of the twenty-nine stories follows one of three patterns: Nayland Smith and his companion Dr.

Petrie, who narrates the stories, are either a) menaced by one of Fu-Manchu's exotic death-traps, b) captured by his agents, or c) engaged in trying to foil a murderous attempt on the life of someone who Knows Too Much. In about half of the episodes the protagonists triumph either by good luck or by their own efforts; in the rest they are aided by the beautiful Kâramanèh, one of Fu-Manchu's company who has fallen in love with Petrie.

These stories are populated by dacoits and Thugs and less nameable creatures, and are overflowing with mysterious poisons, mutated insects, and other death-dealing agencies bearing such names as "The Zayat Kiss," "The Coughing Horror," and "The Flower of Silence." The locale is pre-World War I London and its surrounding countryside. (These stories are as firmly wedded to their period as the Sherlock Holmes stories are to the late Victorian era.) And over everything broods the shadow of the seemingly omnipresent and omniscient Dr. Fu-Manchu.

At the end of each of the three books, Fu-Manchu is apparently killed—trapped in a burning house in the first, shot through the head (by Kâramanèh) in the second. The third death was, at the time, intended to be permanent. Fu-Manchu had been disowned and sentenced to death by the Si-Fan, the secret organization which he had employed to further his own plans for conquest. The Si-Fan was broken up by Scotland Yard, and in an attempt to flee the country by sea Fu-Manchu was caught by a storm in the English Channel, shipwrecked, and presumably drowned. Petrie married Kâramanèh and retired to Egypt, and Nayland Smith set off in pursuit of less colorful and undoubtedly less dangerous foes.

Three of Smith's "extracurricular" cases are recounted in minor short stories. Here Smith is even more of a stick-figure than he appears in the Fu-Manchu books. It is clear that much of his stature in the latter is merely a reflection of the quality of his opponent: a man who has survived against such a foe as the Doctor, and who is held in such esteem by him, *must* have unusual capabilities, even though there is little solid evidence of them in the books. In effect, we are taking Fu-Manchu's word for Smith's abilities. That we are willing to do so is a measure of Rohmer's success in realizing his chief villain.

The Doctor was allowed to rest (with one exception, to be noted later) for thirteen years. During this period seventeen other books by Rohmer were published and three of his plays were produced on the London stage. With the serialization of *Daughter of Fu Manchu* in 1930, it became clear that drowning at sea had been no more fatal to the durable Oriental than had his earlier "deaths." In this book, Fu Manchu's daughter Fah Lo Suee has set about reviving and reorganizing the Si-Fan. She causes so much trouble that at last Fu Manchu himself, old and lame, emerges from retirement to join forces with Nayland Smith and bring about her downfall. The renewed taste of power stimulates the Doctor's own ambitions, and in *The Mask of Fu Manchu* he is once again scheming for world domination in the old familiar way. He has also managed to grow younger, with the help of an elixir developed in his secret laboratories. This book and the previous one are set mainly in the Near East, and are narrated by a young archaeologist named Shan Greville. Petrie and Inspector Weymouth, from the earlier books, play subsidiary roles.

In *Fu Manchu's Bride* the Doctor's activities move to the French Riviera. He is experimenting with hybrid insects and with new strains of plague germs, which he tries out on unsuspecting human subjects. Petrie, who has acquired a considerable reputation as an expert on tropical diseases, is called in by the French authorities to investigate the plague. He soon learns all too much about it from first-hand experience. The book is narrated by Alan Sterling, the son of an old friend of Petrie, and an orchid hunter by profession. The damsel in distress, who fortunately never quite manages to deserve the appellation in the book's title, is named Fleurette. She turns out to be the long-lost daughter of Petrie and Kâramanèh, kidnapped by Fu Manchu when she was a baby. Sterling and Fleurette are featured again in *The Trail of Fu Manchu*. Here Fu Manchu becomes particularly fiendish. He operates a large blast-furnace in a cavern under Limehouse, where he uses human bodies as fuel in an alchemical process for making gold. One of the bodies he feeds to the furnace is that of his rebellious daughter, Fah Lo Suee. (But fear not, she is as durable as he is!) In *President Fu Manchu* the scene shifts to the New World; the plot is a faint foreshadowing of Richard Condon's *The Manchurian Candidate*. At the end of the book, Fu Manchu is again "killed"—swept over Niagara Falls in a small boat. This in no way inhibits his appearance in the next volume, *The Drums of Fu Manchu*, which is set in England, Paris, and Venice. This is one of the weaker books in the series, and seems in part nothing more than a mechanical reprise of earlier adventures. Indeed, the opening scene of *Drums* is virtually a copy of that of *The Insidious Dr. Fu-Manchu*. In place of Petrie as narrator we have Bart Kerrigan, a journalist. His love-interest is a latter-day Kâramanèh named Ardatha. These two are also the featured players in *The Island of Fu Manchu*. (The Doctor never relinquishes control over one of his beautiful victims after only a single book. . . .) Here the locale shifts to Haiti, and zombies and voodoo rites are added to the more traditional ingredients of Fu Manchu's arsenal. The infusion of new blood, as it were, has a revitalizing effect on quality. *Bride, Trail,* and *Island* provide some of the most exiting and most readily enjoyable parts of the entire series. The old shadows-in-the-fog mood has been replaced by a more cosmopolitan and at the same time more fantastic atmosphere. The writing is smoother, the pace faster, the exotic locales and weird inventions more plentiful and more vividly described than in the previous books. The elaborate biological laboratory on the Riviera and the cavern-world beneath Haiti are a far cry from the dingy Chinatown haunts of the first three books in the series.

Fu Manchu hibernated during the war years, but returned in 1948 in *Shadow of Fu Manchu*. Having mellowed somewhat in his old age (of one hundred plus), he is now fighting on the side of the good guys: "My mission is to save the world from the leprosy of Communism." His methods, however, have not changed. He is still served by dacoits and zombies and beautiful but love-starved girls, and still uses the poisoned darts (tipped with "B.W. 63, of which I had a little left") with which he tried to kill Nayland Smith at their first meeting in the Burmese jungle more than thirty-five years earlier. On the whole, the book is routine, although the writing is livelier than usual, and there are touches of humor. Some of the latter is unintentional, as when Fu Manchu instructs a hypnotized girl, "Tonight you will seduce him with your hair. The rest I shall leave to him. . . ."

It is easy to believe that by this time Rohmer had become heartily tired of his most famous creation. Nine years passed before the Doctor appeared again in print. *Re-Enter Fu Manchu,* published as a Gold Medal Original paperback in the U.S. and in hard covers in England, is a weary re-telling of the typical Fu Manchu plot. The action moves (but just barely) from London to Cairo to New York, and the "hero" stands around doing nothing except complain that he is doing nothing, and staring in stupefaction when practically everyone turns out to be someone else in disguise. The final Fu Manchu book, *Emperor Fu Manchu,* is unlike the others both in style and in atmosphere. Parts of it resemble an unsuccessful pastiche of previous stories. The principle defect of the book is that present-day Communist China, where much of the action takes place, is an unsuitable locale for the kind of story-book Oriental menace which was one of the charms of the earlier books. The Cold Men—Fu Manchu's army of zombies—inspire no dread, and the Doctor himself has been reduced to the two extreme postures of quiet menace and maniacal rage. It is a poor quietus for so honorable a villain; in the words of Nayland Smith, "an assassin, a torturer, the most dangerous criminal the law has ever known; but always an aristocrat." (pp. 47-51)

On any list of "the worst of Sax Rohmer" *The Emperor of America* would come very near the top. In places it verges on self-parody. It was written in the familiar form of a series of related short stories (stretching through nine and a half months in *Collier's*), simply placed end-to-end for the book version. Each story ends with a suitable punchline ("Unless I am greatly mistaken," Roscoe replied, "M. Pascal is *Head Centre*"), and the first few paragraphs of the following chapter are devoted to setting a new scene, reintroducing the characters, and summarizing the plot situation. The latter does not change all that much during the course of the book, and Rohmer was able to carry over short passages virtually intact from one episode to the next.

The forces of law and order are represented by Commander Drake Roscoe of the U.S. Navy (almost a dead ringer for Nayland Smith) and Dr. Stopford, a ship's doctor on the Cunard line (fashioned from the same mold as Dr. Petrie, even to the apparent lack of a first name). Opposing them is an elaborate subversive organization known as The Zones. Head Centre, one of its controlling officers, turns out to be an ex-Governor of New York and current Presidential candidate, although the mastermind, Great Head Centre, is a mere duchess with delusions of grandeur. The goal of The Zones is the overthrow of the United States government and the establishment of an American Empire. Comparison with Fu Manchu and the Si-Fan is inevitable. However, there is no Oriental touch here. The minions of Great Head Centre are not Chinamen or dacoits, but representatives of most of the non-Anglo-Saxon races in the Western world.

The concoction is topped off with dialogue in pure comic-book-British. ("Cheery ho," Stopford murmured. "Failin' dalliance with the fair, there's nothing I enjoy more than a spot of danger.") There is one memorable scene—the trip through the caverns underneath Manhattan in the company of mad Tom Flynn—but it is scarcely worth suffering through the rest of the book.

*The Emperor of America* was published in 1929. Some twenty years later, in his last series of books, Rohmer resurrected Drake Roscoe (now an American Secret Service agent) to battle against the Order of Our Lady, the inevitable secret organization threatening world peace. The Order is the creation of Marquise Sumuru, otherwise known as The Madonna, and is dedicated to "purging the world of ugliness, and destroying the rule of brute force." This is to be accomplished by placing women in control of everything—especially men. ("Women were designed by their Creator to be not men's mistresses but their masters.") Sumuru's main weapon in this crusade is sex, and for those important men whose control she cannot trust to

any of the lesser Sisters of the Order, she reserves the ultimate refinement of this weapon: herself. For some reason never made clear, she includes Roscoe in this select group, so that when, in the concluding pages of *Sumuru,* he bursts into her hideout, he finds her waiting for him. (She has been whiling away the time with her favorite diversion—skinny-dipping in her penthouse pool with a pet barracuda named Satan.) There is a quick tumble among the mink rugs, and when reinforcements arrive a short time later, they find the apartment empty.

When next encountered, in *The Fire Goddess,* Roscoe is known only as Drakos, a faithful but not-too-satisfied member of the Order of Our Lady. The locale this time is Jamaica, where Sumuru has to contend not only with the local police and an Inspector from Scotland Yard, but also with a rebellion in her own ranks. One of her disciples, Sister Melisande, has revived old voodoo practices and employed them to usurp Our Lady's authority. In the end, Sumuru deals with the recalcitrant Sister by having her body turned into a chryselephantine statue and presented as a gift to the people of the island. More by accident than design, Roscoe manages to betray Sumuru. She is forced to flee Jamaica, and he is released from his bondage.

However, he never learns. In the next book, *Return of Sumuru,* he invades Our Lady's Egyptian headquarters to rescue the daughter of an American millionaire, whom Sumuru has kidnapped. He succeeds in this objective, but in the process he falls in love with Sister Dolores, Sumuru's second-in-command. The book ends as he leaves the rescued girl and her lover, and prepares to rejoin the Order. It seems that his reception is somewhat less than satisfactory, for the final book, *Sinister Madonna,* opens with Roscoe, near death from having been beaten and tortured, babbling in delirium in a hospital room. He recovers, physically at least, and there is some foofaraw as he foils Sumuru's attempts to obtain the legendary Seal of Solomon. At the end of the book he again departs to rejoin Dolores and the Order. This is the last we hear of either of them, or of Sumuru.

The preceding summary omits the first book in the Sumuru series, *Nude in Mink.* This book takes place in England, and does not involve Roscoe. The plots of all five books are roughly the same, and they can be read in any order with little loss of continuity. Of them all, only *The Fire Goddess* has enough inventiveness or intriguing detail to make a lasting impression. (pp. 51-4)

Neither Nayland Smith nor Drake Roscoe is in any sense a detective. (The villainies they encounter are seldom subtle enough to require any detection.) Rohmer did, however, create several fictional detectives. In his first novel, *The Sins of Séverac Bablon,* Rohmer makes reference to "the three great practical investigators of the world." The greatest of these, M. Victor Lemage of the Paris Sûreté, appears in person in the latter half of the book, while a second is merely mentioned by name: Mr. Brinsley Monro of Dearborn Street, Chicago. The third member of the trio, Mr. Paul Harley of Chancery Lane, performs some off-stage investigations in the book; he was later featured in a series of novels and short stories.

The first of Rohmer's detectives to have a book of his own was Gaston Max, also of the Paris Sûreté. Max is a younger version of Lemage; it is as if Rohmer regretted the latter's retirement at the end of *Séverac Bablon* and decided to let him continue his career under another name. Like Lemage and all of Rohmer's other detectives, Max is a master of disguise and mimicry, and makes heavy use of both skills in his pursuit of

criminals. Max's first appearance was in *The Yellow Claw*. . . .
The malefactor in this novel is a mysterious "Mr. King," agent
of a Sublime Order which is suspiciously like the Si-Fan. In
Max's second adventure, *The Golden Scorpion*, the villain is
revealed at the end to be an agent of Fu Manchu himself, and
the latter makes a brief anonymous appearance in the book.

Like Fu Manchu, Max was allowed to rest during the 1920's.
He reappeared in 1930 in *The Day the World Ended*. This is
one of the relatively small number of Rohmer's books in which
the fantastic or science-fictional element is dominant. The action takes place in and near the Black Forest in Germany,
whither reporter Brian Woodville has been sent to investigate
rumors of an outbreak of vampirism: bodies of men and animals
drained of blood, and huge bat-like creatures seen flying over
the countryside at night. Woodville is warned by a disembodied
voice to leave the area. He himself sees one of the flying
creatures, watching it land and disappear among the tombs in
the local cemetery. He investigates the ruined castles of Fel-
senweir, and finds its crumbling walls patrolled by seven-foot
men in armor—and at this point the plot comes tumbling back
(almost) to earth. Gaston Max makes his appearance, by the
simple expedient of removing the disguise behind which he
has been hiding for seventy-five pages, and reveals that the
weird goings-on are not supernatural in nature but are the work
of a genuine Mad Scientist, complete with death-ray, Buck
Rogers-type flying suits, and plans to conquer and/or destroy
the world. Happily, this more mundane explanation does nothing to diminish the excitement and suspense of the book.

After this adventure, Max retires for another thirteen years,
returning for the last time in *Seven Sins* to track down a Nazi
spy ring in wartime London. His investigations this time are
complicated by a titled Englishman who dabbles in the occult,
and by an impossibly all-American-boyish Air Force lieutenant
("Put up your hands, because I am going to thrash you until
I am tired"), but with the help of half a dozen well-chosen
disguises, he emerges victorious.

The Tongs which are lacking in the Chinatown episodes of the
Fu Manchu and Gaston Max books are present in full force in
the stories involving Daniel "Red" Kerry, Chief Inspector
(later Superintendent) of the C.I.D. The two short stories **"The
Daughter of Huang Chow"** and **"Kerry's Kid,"** from *Tales
of Chinatown*, and the novels *Dope* and *Yellow Shadows*, are
set in London's Limehouse, and are replete with opium dens,
Tong wars, dope smuggling, and white slavery. Rohmer may
not have invented the notion of the "wily Chinee," but these
books epitomize the idea. Perhaps the sinister, fog-shrouded
Limehouse of which he writes never existed, but it takes on
vivid life in the pages of these stories. Rohmer's xenophobia
is unusually obtrusive, and Chief Inspector Kerry is a cold and
unpleasant character, but even these defects cannot entirely
destroy the appeal of the stories. (pp. 54-6)

Paul Harley was a closer approximation to the traditional fictional detective. He was a private investigator whose services
were sought not only by individuals but also by the Government. He maintained a suite of offices in Chancery Lane,
staffed with a private secretary and a typist, decorated with
Oriental artifacts and an engraved portrait of Edgar Allan Poe,
and supplied with secret exits and a fully-equipped theatrical
dressing room wherein he assumed and discarded his numerous
disguises. In conversations with his friend Malcolm Knox, who
accompanied him on several of his cases, he compared himself
half-facetiously to C. Auguste Dupin. He was selective in his
choice of client ("I have intimated to that distressed noble-

man . . . that a laundry is the proper place to take his dirty
linen"), but any touch of the strange or abnormal was certain
to catch his attention.

Some years after serving as an off-stage presence in *The Sins
of Séverac Bablon*, Harley appeared in a succession of short
stories. Three of these formed part of a connected sequence
which was included in the collection *Tales of Chinatown*. His
best known cases are recounted in the novels *Bat Wing* and
*Fire-Tongue*. The former is essentially a straightforward and
fairly good murder mystery. Sandwiched in the middle of it is
an episode with strong fantasy elements, centering around West
Indian voodoo. As John Dickson Carr was later to do in such
books as *He Who Whispers*, Rohmer threw in this fantasy
episode as a red herring; the mystery turns out to have an
entirely rational solution. In *Fire-Tongue*, the better of the two
novels, Harley is involved with a sect of Indian fire-worship-
pers on the loose in England. He also appeared in a short novel,
*The Black Mandarin*, set in the same Chinatown locale as three
of the early short stories. The play *The Eye of Siva* is also part
of the Harley canon, and there are a number of other short
stories featuring Harley. One of the earliest of them, **"The
Red Mist,"** was included as an advertising device in certain
British editions of the book *The Quest of the Sacred Slipper*.
(That novel itself does not involve Harley.) Three further "investigations of Paul Harley" were included in *Salute to Bazarada, and Other Stories*. One of these, **"Skull Face,"** is the
result of self-plagiarism on Rohmer's part. It is a rewritten
version of an earlier story, **"The Man with the Shaven Skull,"**
with the locale and the characters' names changed. The mystery
is why the author bothered.

Predictably enough, in view of his interest in occult subjects,
Rohmer at one time turned his hand to the creation of a psychic
detective. The result is one of his most satisfying books, *The
Dream Detective*, published in England in 1920 and in the
United States five years later. It consists of ten episodes in
which Moris Klaw employs his method of "odic photography"
to investigate cases of haunting, possession, and other occult
phenomena, as well as a couple of ordinary murders. Klaw is
one of Rohmer's most fascinating characters: tall and stoop-
shouldered, "a very old man who carries his many years lightly,
or a younger man prematurely aged; none can say which." He
poses as an antiquarian, and keeps a musty curio shop near
Wapping Old Stairs. The shop is cluttered with broken statuary
and old books, and inhabited by canaries, white rats, a pet
owl, and at times by hedgehogs and armadilloes. The door is
guarded by a parrot who invariably reacts to the arrival of
visitors with the cry "Moris Klaw! Moris Klaw! The Devil's
come for you!" Klaw lives in the back of the shop, sharing a
small apartment with his beautiful daughter, Isis. Klaw's true
identity and personality are things on which no two of his
acquaintances agree, for he is adept at assuming many roles.
Although his cases are less well known than those of such
confrères as John Silence, Carnacki the Ghost-Finder, and Jules
de Grandin, they are no less fascinating. **"The Headless Mummies"** is an amusing crime story, and **"The Veil of Isis"** is an
eerily effective fantasy.

The last of Rohmer's family of detectives to appear in book
form was Major Mohammed Ibrahîm Brian Barûk, an Anglo-
Egyptian. The ten short stories about Barûk, collected in 1944
under the title *Bimbâshi Barûk of Egypt*, are equally divided
between detective stories with an English setting and stories
of espionage and international intrigue in the Near East. Of
either type, they are smoothly written, entertaining, and for-
gettable.

One other of Rohmer's series characters deserves notice, if only because of the number of stories in which he appears. He is Bernard De Treville—adventurer, Secret Service agent, and tracker-down of lost treasures. Between 1937 and 1945, sixteen short stories featuring De Treville were published in *This Week* magazine. Many of them are variations on the same theme— the search for a stolen jewel or other valuable item hidden in an unusual place—which may explain why they have never been collected in book form. Several of them, such as **"The Mystery of the Paneled Room"** and **"The Secret of the Ruins,"** have appeared more than once in anthologies. (pp. 56-8)

Sax Rohmer's first novel, *The Sins of Séverac Bablon*, is a peculiar affair. What attractions it once had have largely been eroded by the years, and it now appears heavy-handed and crudely written. It was serialized in *Cassell's Magazine* in 1912, before the first Fu Manchu stories were published, but did not appear in book form until 1914. Although it remained in print in England into the mid-1930s, it was not published in the U.S. until 1967, when a limited edition was made available to collectors.

Séverac Bablon was a descendant of the Royal House of Israel, the pure line of descent having been preserved in secret since the break-up of the Kingdom after the time of Solomon. He could command the allegiance of (most of) the world's eight million Jews. In appearance he was young, dark, and handsome. He was given to smoking opium cigarettes, which he carefully left burning in ashtrays as "calling cards." He was filled with noble ideals—or at any rate, one noble ideal—but aside from this he appears not to have been cut from the same pattern as Rohmer's other Oriental villains. He possessed enormous wealth and secret influence, was attended by deferential Arab servitors, and had hordes of silent henchmen who climbed up the sides of buildings and used an eerie minor-key whistle as their signal. Bablon was also, judging by his actions, slightly simple-minded.

Bablon has been described by Rohmer as a Jewish Robin Hood. His victims were always rich, miserly Jews. Sometimes he robbed them outright; more often, by trickery, threats, or blackmail, he forced them to donate vast sums to charities and "worthy projects." As he at one point stated his purpose to one of his victims:

> "You are found guilty, Israel Hagar, of dragging through the mire of greed a name once honored among nations. It is such as you that have earned for the Jewish people a repute it ill deserves. You have succeeded in staining [the Jewish name]. I have a mission. It is to erase that stain."

One of Bablon's worthy projects was the building of an airfleet for Britain. Another involved alleviating the suffering of the poor and unemployed by going out into the slum sections of London and throwing handfuls of gold coins into the crowds (thereby starting riots in which several people were injured). But perhaps his greatest achievement was the prevention of the First World War: by frightening and blackmailing the Jewish financiers involved, he prevented a loan to Germany with which that country had intended to wage war on Britain. "For this will be forgotten all my errors, forgiven all my sins!" (pp. 58-60)

*The Sins of Séverac Bablon* retains today mostly curiosity value. Had it been written entirely in the style of a thriller, in which vein Rohmer from the first showed considerable facility, it would have fared better. Instead, the book continually attempted to treat in a serious manner an essentially ludicrous theme. This combined with a pervasive infelicity of style ("Zoe

Oppner entered the room, regally carrying her small head") to produce an almost total debacle.

*The Orchard of Tears* is an entirely different matter. It is the closest that Rohmer ever came to writing a "serious" novel. It is a near-fantasy, but is written in a quiet and restrained style. All the occult forces and Unseen Powers are kept firmly in the background.

The protagonist is Paul Mario, a successful poet and playwright who, after years of meditation and study of ancient manuscripts, has built up certain Egyptian and other pre-Christian teachings into a religio-philosophical system for the modern world. This system bears more than a slight resemblance to Theosophy, and includes everything from "the Hermetic concept of God and Creation" to a belief in reincarnation. Mario is doubtful about publishing his philosophy, but is urged to do so by an influential neighbor, a financier named Jules Thessaly. The publication of "The Gates," the first section of Mario's manuscript, has widespread consequences not only in literary and political circles throughout the world, but also on the populace at large. (Unfortunately we are only told about these consequences at second hand; they are never shown or described in detail.) These consequences cause Mario to doubt the wisdom of publishing further sections of his book. He comes to realize that he has "given life to something which has lain dormant, occult, for untold ages," that he has created a thing which already has outgrown his control. He begins to suspect that Thessaly may have urged publication of the book precisely for the purpose of unleashing this unspecified occult force.

There is a wandering sub-plot concerning a young artist named Flamby Duveen, Mario's protégé. As the book progresses, her life and Mario's become more and more intertwined, and the situation builds up to a genuinely tragic ending.

The novel is full of unrelieved anti-German sentiment, which is natural, considering that it was published less than three weeks before the Armistice in 1918. Aside from this, the overall impression is one of restraint. Never again did Rohmer exercise such discipline over his imagination.

In fact, with the publication of *The Quest of the Sacred Slipper* a year later, it was loose and in full flight again. This one is about the Hashishin, the ancient Order of Assassins, who are sent to England to punish in bloody fashion the theft from Mecca of a slipper believed to have been worn by Mohammed. The story of the attempts to regain the sacred relic makes a suspenseful Oriental thriller.

Thrills, together with virtually everything else of interest, are conspicuously missing from *Moon of Madness*. This is an inane love story, combined with a tale of Communist agents (vintage 1927) plotting evil doings in Madeira and London. It has a witless heroine, sinister South Americans, compromising letters, a couple of cryptograms, coincidences galore, and a cast of inert clods.

*She Who Sleeps* offers a distinct contrast. It revolves around a perfect fantasy situation: in an ancient Egyptian manuscript is found the record of a young captive princess in the court of Seti I, who was placed in a state of suspended animation and entombed, to awake in a later age as a living advertisement of the greatness of Seti and his kingdom. The manuscript not only gives the location of the princess' tomb and the recipe for awakening her from her age-long sleep, but also contains codicils added at intervals during a three-hundred-year period following the entombment, recording several trial awakenings. Guided by this manuscript, millionaire Egyptologist John Cumberland sets out to uncover the tomb of Zalithea, "She Who Sleeps But Who Will Awaken." The tomb is discovered and opened, the ancient reawakening ritual is performed, and Zalithea awakens. . . .

Unfortunately, *She Who Sleeps* is not a fantasy. Zalithea and her tomb turn out to be part of an elaborate hoax, and the story which opened on a note of supernatural mystery and continued in the unreal atmosphere of a fantasy ends on a thoroughly mundane level. However, this does not detract in the least from the effectiveness of the middle portion of the book, which describes the excavation of the tomb and the awakening of Zalithea. This entire episode is brought to life in vivid and meticulous detail, pleasantly leavened with humor. There is, for example, the problem of how to obtain a passport for a girl whose legal guardians have been dead for three thousand years. . . .

Despite the let-down at the end, this remains one of Rohmer's best books. The annoying elements of his style are at a minimum and the virtues at a maximum.

Although *Yu'an Hee See Laughs* opens in the midst of fog-shrouded Limehouse, the action quickly shifts to warmer climes: via Paris and Marseilles to Port Said, and finally to a small island in the Red Sea, off the coast of Yemen. It is to this island that the Marquis Yu'an Hee See has summoned his criminal employees from all over Europe and the Orient for some unspecified large-scale operation; and it is to this island that several of these employees have been traced by Scotland Yard inspector Dawson Haig. His suspicions having first been aroused by the Marquis' activities in fencing stolen goods in London, Haig soon learns that much more is involved: narcotics smuggling, and both black and white slave traffic. But even these are only sidelines, and the real purpose behind the gathering in the Red Sea remains a secret until too late.

Yu'an Hee See is known to his employees as "Mr. King," the same alias used by the never-identified mastermind in *The Yellow Claw*; however, there is no overt connection between the two books. Rohmer may have been trying to start a new series to rival the Fu Manchu books: Yu'an is referred to as "perhaps the most evil man in the civilized world." He is certainly a far more vicious and unpleasant creation than Fu Manchu. However, even though he escapes unscathed at the end of the book, he never reappears in any further stories.

The book has possibly the most annoying heroine in the Rohmer *opera*, even more tiresome than Nanette in *Moon of Madness*. She has been provided with such idiotic dialogue that the moment she opens her mouth one becomes impatient for the villains to come along and shut her up.

There are similarities in locale and plot situations between *Yu'an Hee See Laughs* and the novel *White Velvet*. In the latter, Rohmer attempted a more serious work than his usual thriller, and succeeded in creating characters who were not exotic stereotypes or mere bundles of eccentricities. The first half of the book centers around The Kofmanns, a vaudeville troupe performing at the Folies Egyptiennes in Port Said. The troupe consists of Pa Kofmann, the domineering but slow-witted head of the family, who cannot understand why the customers would rather ogle the girls in the chorus than watch him lift weights; Ma Kofmann, colorless, quiet, and hardworking, who alone of the family does not hate or despise Pa; "Little Miss" Sally, their granddaughter, an accomplished acrobat, dancer, and mimic

at the age of seven; and Musette (née Elizabeth Morton), a husky-voiced singer whom Pa hired when she was stranded and out of work and who is kept busy dodging his heavy-handed advances. These, and other members of the family, are brought vividly and interestingly to life. However, habit proved too strong to Rohmer, and he set his characters down in the midst of a melodramatic tangle of narcotics smugglers and Secret Service agents, kidnapping and murder. Musette falls in love with Lawrence Tabrer, who is on the trail of the kingpin of a drug syndicate. The latter is known only as "Snow Rat." One of the syndicate members persuades Tabrer that Musette is a member of the gang and has tried to have him killed; at the same time, Musette is tricked into believing that Tabrer has deserted her. She leaves the Kofmanns and goes off to Istanbul. The latter half of the book chronicles her adventures there, where she plays a part in the eventual break-up of the syndicate. The revelation of the true identity of "Snow Rat" is no surprise to any mildly attentive reader, but it gives the concluding scenes of the book an enjoyably ironic flavor. The Near Eastern atmosphere is evoked with uncommon skill and economy, and the book contains some of Rohmer's best writing.

The last Rohmer novel to be serialized in *Collier's*, and the last of Rohmer's books to appear in hard covers in the United States, was *Hangover House*. Like *Shadow of Fu Manchu*, this book originated as a stage play, but was never produced. It is a fair detective novel in the classic English tradition: an assorted cast of characters assembles in a fog-bound country house, and very quickly one of their number turns up in a pool of blood, stabbed with a silver dagger. Enter Scotland Yard, and the deduction is on. Apparently out of a sense of obligation to his readers, Rohmer included in the cast a mysterious Egyptian, who pops up occasionally to quote bad proverbs and give advice. He is quite properly ignored by everybody. A startling moment occurs halfway through the book, when the corpse suddenly decides to get up and walk around (promptly to expire once more of a heart attack). Even this is explained in a relatively reasonable manner at the dénouement.

*The Moon Is Red* was the last of Rohmer's non-series novels. It was published only in England, in 1954. The American publishers who have so far ignored it have missed a bet. It is certainly one of the best of Rohmer's later novels. The locale is the east coast of Florida, and the framework is that of a detective novel. Simultaneously with the escape from the Ringbarn Circus of an intractable male gorilla, there occurs the first of a series of brutal murders. The escaped gorilla is the natural suspect, until it is learned that two similar murders had occurred months earlier in Paris and London. The first victim was the estranged wife of a Parisian acrobat named Gene Marat; Marat was in London at the time of the second killing, and is now in Florida. All the victims were young, beautiful, red-haired women; all had been strangled and then savagely stripped and beaten; all had been found in rooms locked from the inside, and having windows accessible only to some abnormally acrobatic creature. Around the bodies were strewn shreds of paper and clothing, torn by strong teeth. And the killings all occurred on nights when the moon was full. . . .

At this point the reader crosses his fingers and begins hoping that the ending will not be a disappointment. It isn't. Several wild hints in the early part of the book, which seem at the time to be red herrings, turn out to be all too pertinent. The ending fully lives up to expectations. (pp. 60-5)

It is appropriate to discuss Rohmer's sole non-fiction book, *The Romance of Sorcery,* in connection with his fantasy novels. Here are found many of the occult and supernatural impedimenta which later turn up in fictional form: the legendary Egyptian *Book of Thoth,* the elemental spirits, the Theosophical beliefs, Cagliostro's experiments in sorcery.... It is obvious that the book was written by a believer. There are ritual gestures in the direction of impartiality (''If I have formed any opinion on this matter, I will not state it here'') and even skepticism, but one feels that they are not meant to convince, and they do not. In addition to a rambling and diffuse history of sorcery, there are biographical chapters devoted to five noted practitioners of the art: Apollonius of Tyana, Nostradamus, Dr. John Dee, Cagliostro, and Madame Blavatsky. (Many of these same persons figure in the excellent volume *Spirits, Stars and Spells* by L. Sprague de Camp and Catherine C. de Camp. It is amusing and instructive to compare the treatments in the two books.) Rohmer's prose in this book has a fake-scholarly stateliness which slides frequently into pomposity. Many impressively convoluted passages turn out on closer examination to be virtually without meaning. But in spite of such drawbacks in content and style, the book does have value, both as entertainment and as a compendium of anecdotes and quotations from obscure sources.

Rohmer's first fantasy novel, *Brood of the Witch Queen,* made its appearance in 1914, the same year as *The Romance of Sorcery.*... The novel divides readily into nine episodes, each centered around one particular bit of ancient Egyptian sorcery at work in the modern world. The third of these episodes is virtually unconnected with the remainder of the book, and constitutes in its own right an excellent tale of vampirism. In the rest of the episodes Antony Ferrara, a young man of mysterious antecedents, employs ancient witchcraft to murder his adoptive father, the Egyptologist Sir Michael Ferrara, and attempts to gain control of the latter's estate. He is opposed by Sir Michael's life-long friend Dr. Bruce Cairn, and the latter's son. The Cairns are the only people who know of Ferrara's sorcerous activities, and even though they have witnessed his experiments in anthropomancy and even less pleasant arts, they have no legal proof with which to enlist the aid of the law. It is ultimately left to Dr. Cairn to use his own knowledge of arcane matters to defeat the fire elemental which Ferrara sends against him, and to bring about the sorcerer's destruction.

*Brood of the Witch Queen* is probably the best known of Rohmer's books outside of the Fu Manchu series and, in spite of the recent appearance of a paperback edition, the one most eagerly sought in second-hand book stores. It is unlike many of Rohmer's later books in that the supernatural is accepted on its own terms, and there is no attempt to explain it away as hoax, coincidence, or the product of as-yet-unknown scientific principles. The book remains today as suspenseful and exciting as when it was first published.

*The Green Eyes of Bâst* was Rohmer's contribution to the literature of the were-animal. It begins as newspaperman Jack Addison finds himself followed to his home one evening by a shadowy figure, and watched through the window by a pair of enormous glittering cat-like eyes. When the grounds are examined the next morning, the only signs of the nocturnal visitor are several deep imprints of a woman's high-heeled shoes. This is Addison's introduction to Nahémah, the cat-woman. She is not a were-cat in the traditional sense, but a teratological sport whose feline tendencies and attributes become dominant only at certain times of the year (corresponding to the Sothic month

of Phanoi, sacred to the Egyptian cat-headed goddess Bâst). Nahémah is engaged in terrorizing (and decimating) the Coverly family, for which she has conceived a deep hatred. Her guardian, a mad-scientist-type named Dr. Damar Greefe, is forced to aid her in this program. He is finally done in when Nahémah goes wild and escapes his control, but before the end he manages to deliver a three-chapter dying confession which reveals the secret of Nahémah's birth and the reason for her vendetta against the Coverlys. (A quotation from Éliphas Levi in *The Romance of Sorcery* explains Rohmer's apt choice of her name.) The fantastic elements of the plot are partially rationalized away, and the concluding chapters do not live up to the promise of the early part of the book.

There are interesting similarities between Rohmer's novel *Grey Face* and Barré Lyndon's play *The Man in Half Moon Street.* The central figure in both works is a man who has succeeded in renewing his youth and prolonging his life beyond the normal span with the help of certain glandular secretions taken from young, healthy, and usually unwilling donors. Lyndon developed about this figure a suspenseful melodrama, with few further ramifications to the plot. For Rohmer, however, a mere elixir of youth was not nearly enough to fill a book. His professor Hadrian von Gühl is, in a quite literal sense, a spiritual successor to Cagliostro—a successful alchemist, an occult Adept, and a flamboyant criminal mastermind. He has the secret of manufacturing gold and of growing jewels of gigantic size, with one of which he is able to control people's minds at a distance. Another of his toys is a ''temporal eavesdropper,'' with which he can hear and reproduce any conversation or sound out of the past.

A more disciplined or more restrained writer might have turned this accumulation of improbabilities into a coherent book. As it stands, however, *Grey Face* is confused, disjointed, full of loose ends—and utterly fascinating to read.

In *The Bat Flies Low* the fantastic element concerns the secret of producing cheap power and light, a secret recorded in the *Book of Thoth* and guarded through the ages by an ancient Order having its headquarters at the Temple of Light, hidden in the deserts of Upper Egypt. The manuscript containing the secret is stolen from the Temple and sold to Lincoln Hayes, president of a large utilities company in the United States. The First Prophet traces the manuscript to New York and manages to steal it back before it has been fully translated. The document shuttles back and forth between New York and Egypt, changing hands a few more times, and the process it describes is finally put into practice. And:

> In the darkest hours of a very dark night, there appeared an unnatural dawn. Seismic instruments all over the world registered an earthquake in the West. Towering buildings in New York rocked on their foundations....

In spite of this impressive climax, the book seems both slow-moving and dull. The rapid-fire inventiveness and furious action, which in other books often served to distract attention from the ''funny hat'' characterizations, are missing here, and nothing substantial has taken their place. (pp. 66-9)

Two of Rohmer's volumes of short stories have already been discussed: *The Dream Detective* and *Bimbâshi Barûk of Egypt.* Each of these is a collection of stories centered around a single leading character. A third volume of the same type is *The Exploits of Captain O'Hagan.* This was Rohmer's first short story collection, published in England in 1916.... The stories are full of labored humor and show their age badly. Captain the Honourable Bernard O'Hagan, V.C., D.S.O., as his calling card modestly identifies him, is a demented Irishman who stalks about London in a satin-lined cape, staring rudely through his monocle and interfering in other people's business. In his first "exploit" he befriends a young lady song-writer, comments on what an unusual name she has for a person of the lower classes, beats up her fiancé (who he decides is not good enough for her), and at gun-point forces a lecherous publisher to purchase her songs. She, poor thing, is pathetically grateful. O'Hagan, "never for a moment presuming upon his superiority of blood," kisses her hand, claps her father patronizingly on the back, and strides on to further triumphs.

The other short story collections are more bearable. The next to appear was *Tales of Secret Egypt*. Of the twelve stories included, six concern the enigmatic *Imám* Abû Tabâh. The narrator of these stories is a dealer in bogus Egyptian antiques. His schemes for turning a dishonest profit invariably land him in trouble—witness the affairs of **"The Death-Ring of Sneferu"** and **"The Whispering Mummy"**—from which he is extricated with engaging insouciance by the *imám*. The remaining stories include two fine fantasies, **"Lord of the Jackals"** and **"In the Valley of the Sorceress,"** and an amusing Arabian Nights tall tale called **"Pomegranate Flower."**

The third collection, *The Haunting of Low Fennel*, appeared under this name only in England. However, six of its seven stories were reprinted in the American edition of *Tales of East and West* in 1933. Of the three fantasies included, **"The Curse of a Thousand Kisses"** is the best and the most widely known; it has been reprinted at least half a dozen times in magazines and anthologies. One of the other stories, **"The Master of Hollow Grange,"** is an excellent borderline horror story. The one story in the collection which has not been reprinted is **"The Blue Monkey,"** a brief and not very believable murder mystery. It is worth mention only because it is the first of the three stories in which Nayland Smith appears without his usual enemy, Fu Manchu. Although not referred to by name, Smith and Dr. Petrie, who narrates the story, are readily recognizable.

Rohmer's best short story collection is probably *Tales of Chinatown*. Six of its ten stories form a loosely connected sequence; two of these have "Red" Kerry as the protagonist and three others involve Paul Harley. All are good, the best being **"The Daughter of Huang Chow."** The remaining stories are even more memorable. **"Tchériapin"** is an excellent fantasy, possibly the best story that Rohmer ever wrote; certainly it is the most widely reprinted of all his stories. **"The Hand of the Mandarin Quong"** and **"The Dance of the Veils"** are highly effective exotic tales.

The British and American editions of *Tales of East and West* are quite different books. The British edition appeared first, in 1932, and contained ten stories. Among them are the two Nayland Smith short stories **"Mark of the Monkey"** and **"The Turkish Yataghan."** In the former, Smith and Petrie visit Devonshire for a short holiday (to recuperate after the events of *The Hand of Fu Manchu*) and encounter a murderer who dispatches his victims with a poisonous fungus (of Oriental origin, of course). In the latter story, the narrator of *The Daughter of Fu Manchu* and *The Mask of Fu Manchu* returns to London's Chinatown for a nostalgic visit, accompanied by Smith, who is now Assistant Commissioner of Police. The two men are immediately involved in a murder investigation. The murder turns out to be a quite ordinary crime of passion, and is solved

in off-hand fashion by Smith. Another story in the collection is **"The M'Villin,"** a lively historical adventure. (pp. 69-71)

Rohmer's last short story collection was *Salute to Bazarada, and Other Stories*. This is another of the titles published only in England, and is probably the rarest of all the author's books. The title story is a "novel" cobbled together out of six short stories which were published in *Collier's* in 1937-8. The central character is a stage magician and adventurer named Bazarada. (The book is dedicated to "my friend, Harry Houdini.") Both Bazarada and his adventures are unmemorable. As has already been noted, *Salute* also contains three Paul Harley stories. The remaining two stories are **"Sheba's Love-Pearls"** and an excellent "mood" story, **"Limehouse Rhapsody."**

In addition to the stories which are included in the various collections, Rohmer wrote an undetermined number of stories that have appeared only in magazines and newspapers. Some of these are very good: ghost stories like **"Affair of Honor"** from *This Week* and **"The Broken Blade"** from *Blue Book*, and mood-pieces and character studies such as **"Jamaican Rose"** from *This Week* (which was rewritten and included as an episode in the Sumuru novel, *The Fire Goddess*), **"Midnight Rendezvous"** from *Collier's*, and **"Narky"** from *Ellery Queen's Mystery Magazine*. An enterprising publisher may yet give these stories, and others like them, a deserved home in book form. (pp. 71-2)

> *Robert E. Briney, "Sax Rohmer: An Informal Survey," in* The Mystery Writer's Art, *edited by Francis M. Nevins, Jr., Bowling Green University Popular Press, 1971, pp. 42-78.*

## ARTHUR PRAGER  (essay date 1971)

[*Prager is an American critic. In the following excerpt, he surveys the major characters and plot devices that appeared in the Fu Manchu series.*]

The general pattern of the [Fu Manchu] series changed through the years. In the early books . . . the action took place in what seemed to be a string of short stories, loosely connected by some thread of plot, like *The Arabian Nights*, or perhaps like *The Adventures of Sherlock Holmes*. Nayland Smith would arrive out of nowhere, bursting into Dr. Petrie's consulting room in a shower of italics and exclamation points, exhorting his friend to take his Browning automatic and head for Limehouse. *"Come Petrie—for God's sake! HE is in London! Providence grant that we get there in time!"* Smith's knowledge of the evil Doctor's arrival usually stemmed from a recent brush with one of Fu Manchu's weird minions. (p. 51)

Sometimes [Smith and Petrie] made it and sometimes they didn't, but they could always be depended on to stumble into an obvious trap, where they were faced with horrible death at the hands of the fiendish Fu Manchu. Of course last-minute escape was inevitable, with the assistance of a beautiful half-caste slave girl who had fallen helplessly in love with one or both of them or with one of the juveniles introduced in the later books when the aging pair had to be replaced in the love scenes. (Petrie was eventually dropped altogether.) Sometimes Rohmer would write himself into a corner, and people would escape by "a method at which I dare not guess" or some similar evasion.

At the end of each book, Fu Manchu was observed by a crowd of witnesses to be perishing in a fire, explosion, sinking ship,

*Rohmer in his study. By permission of Bowling Green State University Popular Press.*

or similar catastrophe, but he was always back in good form for the next volume.

The murderous Doctor never used simple weapons like guns or knives to carry out his dirty work. He had an inexhaustible arsenal of bizarre weapons and hideous servants, dacoits, thugs with strangling cords, trained apes, dwarfs, snakes, spiders . . . you never knew what was coming next. Unfortunately, by the late 1930s Rohmer had run dry and the Doctor began to repeat himself. His methods and hideouts became predictable. To find his headquarters, Smith had only to look for an opium den in Limehouse (or, later, New York's Chinatown) that connected through underground tunnels with the river. Failing that, he could be found in any remote country house with secret panels, passages, and trapdoors. He depended heavily on his favorite weapon, the Golden Elixir, even after Petrie had found the antidote. The Elixir produced artificial catalepsy, simulating all the symptoms of death. The victims were buried by mourning relatives, and after their funerals Fu Manchu would dig them up, revive them, and keep them in slavery for the rest of their lives!

Let's have a look at the fiendish Doctor in action. An example is the murder of Sir Gregory Hale, "whilom attaché at the British Embassy, Peking, who knew the answer to the hitherto unsolved riddle of Tibet." Hale had barricaded himself into his suite at the fashionable New Louvre Hotel on Smith's advice, but our heroes arrived too late to save him. They forced their way into the suite . . .

. . . from the direction of the bedroom came a most horrible mumbling and gurgling sound—a sound utterly indescribable. . . . On the bed a man lay writhing. His eyes seemed starting from their sockets as he lay on his back uttering inarticulate sounds and plucking with skinny fingers at his lips. . . . He continued to babble, rolling his eyes from side to side hideously . . . and now with his index finger pointed to his mouth.

(***The Hand of Fu Manchu***)

As anyone can see, it was the "Flower of Silence" that got him. This flower was a rare jungle blossom which concealed under its petals a small thorn charged with deadly venom. Fu Manchu had lowered it through a hole in the ceiling until it rested on the sleeping man's cheek. He had attempted to brush it away, and you can guess the rest. (pp. 53-4)

What about the "Coughing Horror" that tried to eliminate Smith himself when he made the mistake of sleeping with his window open? As he later said to Petrie:

What kind of thing, what unnatural distorted creature laid hands upon my throat tonight? I owe my life to . . . the fact that I was awakened, just before the attack—by the creature's *coughing*—by its vile, high-pitched *coughing!* Then came a death grip on my throat, and instinctively my hands shot out in search of my attacker. I could not reach him, my hands came in contact with nothing palpable. Therefore I

clutched at the fingers which were dug into my wind-pipe, and found them to be small . . . and *hairy!*
                                    (*The Return of Fu Manchu*)

The thing was a *Cynocephalus hamadryas,* the sacred baboon of the Amharûn tribe of Abyssinia, an animal whose predominant trait was an unreasoning malignity toward man. It had a tiny dog-like head, little malevolent eyes, and arms fully four feet long that could reach halfway across a bedroom and strangle an unsuspecting sleeper. The coughing? It seems the creatures contracted phthisis in the cold, damp climate of England.

If you were twelve years old how would you have felt after dark? Fortunately my mother subscribed to the school of thought, prevalent at that time, that "the night air is bad for you." She raised no objection to my closing and locking the window at bedtime, but she firmly drew the line at nailing it shut.

Who can forget the Reverend Eltham, the beloved, fighting "Parson Dan," courageous missionary who had been active in the interior during the Boxer Rebellion? He had seen things, a little more than was good for him, and Fu Manchu had reserved the "Wire Jacket" for the good clergyman.

> . . . I saw Eltham stripped to the waist and tied, with his arms upstretched, to a rafter in the ancient ceiling. . . . The appearance of his chest puzzled me momentarily, then I realized that a sort of *tourniquet* of wire netting was screwed so tightly about him that the flesh swelled out in knobs through the mesh. . . .
>                                    (*The Return of Fu Manchu*)

One of the Doctor's evil Chinese servants stood by with a razor-sharp knife, cutting off the knobs, one by one.

Surely the "Six Gates of Joyful Wisdom" took the prize. It was a sort of coffin-shaped box, six feet long, two feet high and two feet wide; covered with fine wire netting but opened at the bottom. It was divided into five sections by four sliding, arched partitions which could be raised and lowered at will. Smith was placed in this contrivance and the partitions were fitted over his body. The plan was to empty a leather bag full of starving rats through the first "gate" where they could devour his feet and ankles. Then the next partition would be raised, and they could eat up to his knees. Then the next and the next and so on. Petrie was immobilized nearby and given a samurai sword on a chain just long enough to reach Smith's heart. He could watch his friend's death agonies or put him out of his misery.

These were only a few of the Doctor's toys. There were the bacilli, and the drugs; the elixir that turned Inspector Weymouth of Scotland Yard into a gibbering idiot and another that reduced lovely Kâramenèh to a wrinkled hag. There were the poisonous mushrooms that reacted to light by swelling to enormous size and smothering a whole detachment of Scotland Yard's Flying Squad when they made the mistake of turning on their flashlights. Who can forget the giant, flying bubonic plague flea, developed by cross-breeding with the African tsetse fly? What about poor Forsyth, who met his end when he walked under a tree that sheltered a dacoit holding an ordinary alley cat whose claws had been dipped in curare. The dacoit attracted his attention and dropped the animal on his upturned face. And Swazi Pasha, the Turkish statesman? A murderous dwarf in a suitcase was dropped down the chimney of his hotel suite while he slept. (pp. 55-7)

Who was the evil genius that contrived these horrors, nurturing them in his laboratories or collecting them from their noisome native jungles? In Smith's terms, he was the most fantastic criminal intelligence the world has ever known.

> "This man, whether a fanatic or a duly appointed agent is unquestionably the most malign and formidable personality existing in the known world today. He is a linguist who speaks with almost equal facility in any of the civilized languages and in most of the barbaric ones. He is an adept in all the arts and sciences which a great university could teach him. He also is an adept in certain obscure arts and sciences which *no* university of today can teach. He has the brains of any three men of genius. Petrie, he is a mental giant."
>                                    (*The Insidious Dr. Fu Manchu*)

Fu Manchu was tall, well over six feet, physically very strong, and trained in all the Oriental arts of hand-to-hand combat to the extent that he was able to overcome Inspector Weymouth in a fist fight, the only time in my memory that a villain overcame a Scotland Yard man. His brow was high and domed, and his face (as Rohmer repeatedly informed us) "strongly resembled the mummy of the Pharaoh Seti I." He always dressed in a plain yellow robe (sometimes sporting the insignia of the Order of the White Peacock, the highest honor his nation could bestow) and a small black skullcap with the coral button that denoted the rank of mandarin. Outdoors he affected an astrakhan coat, a tweed motoring cap, and dark glasses. His eyes were uncanny. They were narrow, long, slightly oblique, and of a brilliant green, and they shone in the dark. Their "unique horror" according to Petrie, lay in "a certain filminess that made me think of the *membrana nictitans* in a bird." They were also hypnotic, and on many occasions he reduced a character to helplessness with a glance. Once he almost got Petrie to shoot Smith under the influence of post-hypnotic suggestion, but Smith had taken the precaution of unloading Petrie's Browning, just in case.

He had "an indescribable gait, cat-like yet awkward" walking with his high shoulders slightly hunched. His hands were large, bony, and parchment-like, with long, narrow fingernails. His voice, in any of the languages he spoke with such facility, was both sibilant and guttural.

In the first books he was a member of "an old Kiangsi family," but by the eighth book he was described as a relative of the Imperial family with the rank of Prince. He also had the right to and frequently used the title of Marquis. In spite of these advantages, he was not the head man of his organization, the Si-Fan (or "The Seven"), but was merely a kind of European regional director, his mission being (as Smith put it) "to *pave the way!*" For this purpose he had unlimited funds at his disposal. On one occasion when the Doctor lost out in a struggle of office politics and the Si-Fan cut off his credit, he unearthed an ancient formula for making pure gold out of base metal, and in doing so precipitated (although only a select few knew about it) the financial chaos of the 1930s. The only problem he had with his gold formula was that he needed human bodies for fuel. This was no hardship for Fu Manchu, but it did make an unpleasant smell around John Ki's Joy Shop in Limehouse, and led Smith and Scotland Yard to his underground refinery.

He was a superb toxicologist, and his knowledge of insect life, especially the venomous kind, was unparalleled. He knew all about fungus growths, and developed several new species of his own. Before becoming an arch-criminal, he had administered the province of Ho-Nan under the Dowager Empress, and he held degrees from four universities, both as a Doctor of Philosophy and a Doctor of Medicine. He was adept at several branches of medical specialization, and was able to direct Petrie and Sir Baldwin Frazer, the finest brain surgeon in Harley Street, in an operation on his own brain, after his slave girl Kârameneh had fired a .38 slug into his head (Petrie and Frazer were blackmailed into saving his life).

By Smith's calculations, Fu Manchu was 160 years old. He kept himself alive by annual infusions of a strange compound which (Rohmer said) was made of such simple, readily obtainable ingredients that you would laugh in amazement if you knew what they were. However, it wasn't the ingredients, but what you *did* to them that gave them their power.

Toward the end of the series, the Doctor began to abandon his weird insects and plants in favor of electronic marvels. He was able to create life (e.g. the terrible Hairless Man), and he was one of the first fictional villains to use wire tapping and concealed television cameras for surveillance. He knew all about explosives and on two occasions escaped by blasting his enemies with an aerial torpedo of advanced design dropped from a Si-Fan bombing plane.

For all his miracles, the Doctor was one of the great bunglers. Time and again he was foiled by simple police methods and by marvels no more advanced than Petrie's Browning. Women were a great cross for him to bear, and no one ever had a larger staff of beautiful but treacherous half-caste slave girls working in his household. The girls always set his captives free with stolen keys, warned Petrie and Smith of his next move, and tipped off Scotland Yard about the location of his secret laboratories. He never caught on. The girls' underhanded actions left him open to a great deal of criticism from his own superiors in the Si-Fan, but he never seemed to realize that they were disloyal. Even his own daughter, the wickedly beautiful Fah Lo Suee, betrayed him again and again.

At the age of 158 the Doctor decided that he would like to perpetuate his dynasty, and chose a bride whom he had kidnapped when she was six months old and trained carefully in the proper attributes of an arch-criminal-cum-world-emperor's wife. Fleurette was just nineteen and the banns had been posted when, like all half-caste girls, she fell madly in love with one of Petrie and Smith's young aides and the project fell through, to the accompaniment of much sibilant, guttural invective.

In one of the later books the Doctor went through an entire public relations campaign with a Si-Fan trained candidate who very nearly became President of the United States (Smith was able to swing the electorate with a last-minute revelation that the candidate was an unfrocked priest). The Doctor went on and on, agelessly welding the forces of wickedness into tools for his search for power, and in 1957 he was ready to come out of retirement in yet another book, while Smith and Petrie got grayer and grayer and younger juveniles and half-caste girls who could have been their grandchildren took over the leading roles.

In the opposite corner was Nayland Smith, an obscure colonial police official (''Burmese commissioner'') who dedicated his life to foiling the Doctor and the Si-Fan. Smith was tall and lean, and had the kind of crisp, graying, English hair that every boy imagines he will have when he is older. He wore a long leather coat and a well-worn tweed suit throughout the whole series. He was a pipe smoker, and had a favorite charred old briar that was always clenched between his firm white teeth. Petrie called him ''the most untidy smoker I ever knew,'' and he was constantly spraying burning bits of tobacco and ash over the carpet in Petrie's consulting room.

At first Smith had no fixed address. He would appear suddenly, with an out-of-season tan, and camp in Petrie's quarters for a few hundred pages. Later, when his anti-Fu Manchu activities had earned him a knighthood and a baronetcy, Sir Denis Nayland Smith would stay at the New Louvre or some other fashionable hotel; and when he had been transferred from Burma to head up a secret division in Scotland Yard (with the rank of Assistant Commissioner) he took a house in Whitehall near the Yard and employed a manservant named Fey.

The years were kind to Smith, bringing titles and an O.B.E. Petrie was not as lucky. He had to sell his practice and move to Egypt because he fell in love with and married Kârameneh, a girl with mixed blood. His only reward was that her beauty and his skill as a doctor eventually earned them grudging social acceptance from the British colony in Cairo.

Smith's powers, in spite of his relatively obscure official position, were amazing. Apparently the Crown recognized the peril of the Si-Fan, and Sir Denis had *carte blanche*. He carried in his breast pocket for thirty years a certain letter which we readers were never privileged to see, but which he flashed in times of crisis. This letter enabled him to pressure a French Préfet de Police into summoning naval forces to prevent the yacht *Lola* from leaving port, so Smith could search it for the Doctor. On one occasion he leaped into the middle of a London street and commandeered a chauffeur-driven Rolls-Royce. One glance at the letter and the affluent citizen in the tonneau surrendered his place to Sir Denis and continued his journey by bus. Petrie notes on another occasion that ''Dreadful crimes had marked Fu Manchu's passage through the land. Not one-half of the truth (and nothing of the later developments) had been made public. Nayland Smith's authority was sufficient to control the press.''

He stopped people's luggage in customs, commandeered and rerouted railway trains, and played fast and loose with Scotland Yard and the British Navy. In America he carried a simple card that said *Federal Agent 56*, but written across the bottom of it was the signature of the President of the United States.

Even the frigidly correct Home Secretary was not immune to Smith's powers. Sir Denis burst into the Cabinet Minister's sitting room one foggy night demanding that Scotland Yard send a detachment to break into a cemetery and disinter a corpse that had been buried that afternoon (the Golden Elixir again). The Home Secretary replied that the whole business was ''irregular—wholly irregular. I shall be bothered by the Roman Catholic authorities, and you know how troublesome they can be.''

> ''It is perhaps unfair of me to remind you that I can bring pressure to bear.''
>
> ''You are not suggesting that you would bother the Prime Minister with this trivial but complicated affair?''
>
> ''I am suggesting nothing. I only ask for your signature. I should not be here if the matter were as trivial as you suppose.''
>
> ''Really—really, Smith. . . .''
>
> Five minutes later the police car was stealing through a mist, yellow, stifling, which closed in remorselessly, throttling London.
>
> (*The Trail of Fu Manchu*)

Smith's background was always a mystery to his fans. Where he came from, and how he got to the Far East in the first place no one ever knew. There were hints of a scandal, a broken love affair out there, a woman. Whatever happened, Smith came off badly, and it left him a lifelong misogynist. "She's only a woman, old boy, and women are very much alike—very much alike from Charing Cross to Pagoda Road" he would say to Petrie whenever Kâramenèh turned nasty under the influence of one of the Doctor's drugs. Under the mask, the bitter, hard, authoritarian baronet had Heart. One day when Fleurette, Petrie's daughter, was left alone in Smith's study and browsed through his books, she found that:

> Those works which were not technical were of a character to have delighted a schoolboy. Particularly Fleurette was intrigued by a hard-bitten copy of *Tom Sawyer Abroad,* which had obviously been read and reread. Despite his great brain and his formidable personality, what a simple soul he was at heart!
>
> *(The Trail of Fu Manchu)*

Smith was no desk soldier. Whenever it became necessary to raid the Doctor's premises, as it did two or three times per book, he was always the first to enter, regardless of the danger. Scotland Yard always waited outside for the signal to break in. In order to carry out these penetrations, Smith (and Petrie) resorted to a number of clever disguises. Thus we find him dressed as a "rough-looking citizen" in a Limehouse pub, and later as a "man with a claret-colored nose." On a visit to the Cafe de l'Égypte, "a hang-out of artists and Bohemians," he and Petrie were "transformed into a pair of Futurists, oddly unlike our actual selves. No wigs, no false mustaches had been employed; a change of costume and a few deft touches of water color paint had rendered us unrecognizable by our most intimate friends."

To the end Smith battled the Si-Fan, always a little ahead, always winning, pulling the lobe of his left ear (a habit of his when mulling over the best countermove to a Fu Manchu gambit) and chaffing Petrie good naturedly. Over a period of some thirty years he and the Yellow Doctor came to have a grudging respect for each other, and in the crises they shared one noble trait. Each of them was as good as his word, and on many occasions Smith and Petrie were set free after facing horrible death, because the Doctor had made some inviolable promise.

Dr. Petrie was as faceless and as heartily bumbling as the good Watson. In all the books there is only one actual description of him, and that is limited to the simple sentence "He was definitely a handsome man, gray at the temples and well set-up." No charred old briar or well-worn tweeds for him. No yellow robe or astrakhan coat. He was a cipher, and could have been made of pure cardboard for all Rohmer cared, but it was he who was the love interest, not Smith, and he whose heart "fluttered like a captive bird" in the throes of tender emotion. It was well set-up old Petrie who turned Kâramenèh's knees to water the first time she set eyes on him, and made her risk her life repeatedly to save him over several thousand pages. He was dependable and gave off a kind of sense of security. At first he was an impecunious practitioner, but in later volumes he became an expert in rare tropical diseases and was able to vie with the evil Doctor himself in the affair of the flying bubonic plague flea.

The early books were written in the first person, with Petrie as narrator, but after the fourth book Rohmer began to introduce new blood, on the grounds that Petrie was getting old. Young American and Canadian juveniles took over and Petrie's appearances got fewer and fewer until he dropped out of sight. We missed him. He was the perfect foil for the nervous, snappish, asexual Smith who would readily have consigned a lovely ingenue to the "Green Mist" or the "Scarlet Brides" if it meant getting Fu Manchu before the Assizes. Petrie was a sentimental fool sometimes, but the stories badly needed him. Imagine Holmes without Watson.

Kâramenèh, delicious half-Bedouin slave girl, who was forced to serve Fu Manchu because he kept her brother in a constant state of artificial catalepsy, was Petrie's love and later his wife. The first time Petrie saw her, his "heart fluttering like a child" he describes her . . .

> A girl wrapped in a hooded opera cloak stood at my elbow, and as she glanced up at me, I thought that I never had seen a face so seductively lovely nor of so unusual a type. With the skin of a perfect blonde, she had eyes and lashes as black as a Creole's, which, together with her full red lips, told me that this beautiful stranger, whose touch had so startled me, was not a child of our northern shores.
>
> *(The Insidious Dr. Fu Manchu)*

Around the house she affected gauzy harem costumes, and little red high-heeled slippers. Rohmer saw to it that all pretty girls in the books wore little red high-heeled slippers, although Fah Lo Suee once switched to green. Zarmi of the Joyshop wore them, as did Fleurette. They were as much a personal insignia as white hats in a cowboy film.

Kâramenèh was a confusing character. She was constantly tricking Smith and Petrie into some disastrous situation, and then appearing at the last minute to get them out again. This habit irritated the waspish Smith:

> "She is one of the finest weapons in the enemy's armory, Petrie. But a woman is a two-edged sword, and treacherous. To our great good fortune, she has formed a sudden predilection, characteristically Oriental, for yourself. Oh you may scoff, but it is evident."
>
> *(The Insidious Dr. Fu Manchu)*

She was my first introduction to Oriental women and I liked what I read. The girls I knew never formed a sudden predilection for oneself. They had an irritating habit of looking through you as though you were invisible. What wouldn't I have given for a subteen Kâramenèh with velvet eyes and a fascinating musical accent, who would say, clasping her hands in wild abandon, "Throw me into prison, kill me if you like for what I have done, but do not torture me, try to drive me mad, with your reproaches!"

Kâramenèh and Petrie lived happily in Cairo after their marriage, and she stayed just as lovely as ever although Petrie's hair got progressively grayer. Their union was blessed with a little daughter, Fleurette, who died at the age of six months to their great grief. Petrie never suspected that it was the Golden Elixir again. Fleurette was exhumed and spirited to Fu Manchu's island headquarters near Monte Carlo, where she was carefully trained to be the evil Doctor's bride and the eventual Empress of the World. This plan was frustrated when she fell in love with Alan Sterling, a junior Petrie-surrogate. She was a carbon-copy of Kâramenèh except that she had blue eyes instead of velvety black ones. Petrie, who hadn't seen her in nineteen years, recognized her immediately as his daughter.

Fah Lo Suee was Fu Manchu's daughter, and she too had been educated for a special purpose, to be the "Lady of the Si-Fan," a half-legendary character, a kind of female Dalai Lama. Once again love intervened, when she fell head over heels ("in true

Oriental fashion'') with Smith. This infatuation caused her to betray her sinister father on at least fifteen occasions, and resulted in her untimely death, when he fed her into the blast furnace he used for his gold transmutation experiments. Poor Fah Lo Suee (the name meant ''sweet perfume'' according to Rohmer) was no better than she should have been, and she was the only sexually inclined character in the series. She attempted to seduce not only Smith, but Alan Sterling as well, and even Sir Bertram Morgan, Governor of the Bank of England. She was also the only nude in any of the books, and was hung up by the thumbs to have her smooth, ivory body whipped by one of her father's dacoits after one unusually blatant betrayal.

The evil Doctor's servants deserve some notice here. The wrinkled, pigtailed little old Chinese, John Ki, also called ''Singapore Charlie'' and a number of other names, who always kept an opium den for the Doctor's headquarters, turns out to have been the governor of a province under the Dowager Empress. The dacoits were Burmans, squat, ugly, squint-eyed, and physically very powerful. Between their eyes they bore a religious brand called ''the mark of Kali.'' They could climb like monkeys, and were trained stranglers. Before each kill they uttered the weird, minor key call that froze Petrie's marrow again and again. Their most endearing trait was the ability to sneak about the crowded corridors of fashionable London hotels, dressed only in Ghandiesque loincloths, without attracting notice. For special duties, the Doctor also had *thugs, phansigars* (the dwarf in the suitcase was one), *hashishin*, and for maritime activities, sea-Dyaks from Malaya.

A good many years after my first adventure with the Doctor and his minions, when my pre-teens were behind me and I was old enough for military service, I found myself in London, bored, lonely, but wearing the smug assurance that olive drab carried in those days. With time on my hands, I hailed a taxi and directed the driver to take me to Limehouse, so that I could see for myself the locale of the Doctor's sinister machinations. The driver looked me over carefully. ''I wouldn't go down there if I was you, mate,'' he said (olive drab or no I was still a man taxi drivers called ''mate'' at that period). I persisted, but he would not be moved. When I asked him what was lurking there that was so dangerous to curious American soldiers he could not explain. He just ''wouldn't go down there'' if he were I. I no longer pressed the point. He knew best. By mutual consent we turned and headed for the Rainbow Corner and the blacked-out lights of Mayfair. From behind me, the direction of the East End docks, I dimly heard what could have been a weird, minor key call, and something flapped against the rear window of the cab that just might have been a giant flying bubonic plague flea. Thirty years after the Doctor's appearance, Limehouse was still a place to stay away from. I never did get there. Perhaps it was for the best. You never can tell. (pp. 58-69)

> *Arthur Prager, ''The Mark of Kali,'' in his* Rascals at Large, or, The Clue in the Old Nostalgia, *Doubleday & Company, Inc., 1971, pp. 45-69.*

## CAY VAN ASH  (essay date 1972)

[*An American novelist, Van Ash became a close friend of Rohmer and lived for a time with Rohmer and his wife. Van Ash's* Ten Years Beyond Baker Street *(1984) reveals the influence of Rohmer, particularly in its inclusion of the characters Fu Manchu and Dr. Petrie. In the following excerpt from a biography of Rohmer co-written with Rohmer's wife, Van Ash discusses the realism of Rohmer's fiction.*]

One feature which emerges prominently, but unexpectedly, from any close study of Sax Rohmer's work is its authenticity. In view of the fact that he wrote deliberately to mystify—this being what his readers wanted—this is rather surprising. A good portion of the ''thrills'' obtained in reading Sax Rohmer comes from being brought face to face with the unknown, perhaps the unknowable. Yet he did not stoop to create this effect by sheer invention. Many writers do, and regard it as entirely legitimate. But when Sax Rohmer wrote familiarly of exotic curiosities such as ''the Well of Zem-zem'' or ''*tsan ihang,* sweet perfume of Tibet,'' readers could take for gospel that these things existed.

Although he drew the line at spreading misinformation, he did not object to a little misdirection. While restricting himself to the facts, he made much use of the mysterious-sounding. He would usually prefer the Assyrian ''Bel'' to the better-known ''Baal'' of the Old Testament. Again, when he refers to something being ''black as the rocks of Shellal,'' one is tempted to think of a location in Hell. Shellal, in fact, lies on the Nile, not far from Aswan.

Once his sardonic sense of humor prompted him to play a trick on the reader. With suitable gravity and impressiveness, he mentioned ''a character resembling the Arab letter *'alif.''* There were no comments. No one, apparently, realized that *'alif* is a vertical straight line.

But apart from these half whimsical excursions into mystery making, Sax Rohmer relied honestly upon references to exotic oddities dug up in a never-ending program of research. His storehouse of these, and his exact knowledge of them, were alike staggering.

''What on earth,'' I asked him, on one occasion, ''is the Deadly Honey of Trebizond?''

''Honey gathered from a species of poisonous azalea native to that region,'' he said promptly, looking at me rather as if everybody ought to know.

In his fictional employment of poisons, and, particularly, of poisonous insects, he was more scrupulously accurate than many authors of his day. During his youthful days in London, many of his friends had been medical students. He lost no chance of acquiring useful information from them, sometimes even accompanying them on their hospital rounds.

When, for dramatic purposes, he occasionally allowed Fu Manchu to make use of some notably outlandish horror, he was always careful to observe that it was an *unknown* species. But where matters of everyday life were concerned, he stuck doggedly to the facts, to the extent that he would not have one of his characters board a train till he had checked its existence in the railway timetable. Here, moreover, he did his utmost to avoid that most subtle of all pitfalls, the temptation to take things for granted. How many writers, I wonder, have assumed, without checking, that the origin of a call made on a dial telephone may later be traced by the police? Sax Rohmer knew it to be impossible, because he took the trouble to find out.

Loath to take anything for granted, he hated to write of any place he had not visited and, short of murder, to describe anything he had not done. He did once go to the length of trying opium, but got nothing out of it. It simply made him sick.

On the odd occasions when mistakes crept into Sax Rohmer's work, they were usually the result of his working methods, going hell-for-leather to get something on paper, to keep up with the rapid pace of his imagination. The subsequent polishing, to which he devoted so much time and energy, was chiefly concerned with stylistics, so that, once in half a million words or so some mis-statement might slip through unnoticed.

I once took him up on the fact that a certain police constable mentioned in one of his stories had become a police sergeant three chapters later.

"H'm!" he said, darkly. "Somewhat rapid promotion!"

When Sax Rohmer first began to write the Fu Manchu series, he had not the faintest idea that he would still be writing it forty years later. Even when it was well under way he did not—as many authors have done—set up dossiers and card-index systems to keep track of what he had said. He continued to keep everything in his head.

One minor detail worth noting is that the names which Sax Rohmer chose for his characters are not examples of careless mistakes. He was perfectly well aware, from the outset, that "Fu Manchu" was impossible. (It is a combination of two Chinese surnames.)

His policy with regard to names shows a marked influence of the writing world in which he had been brought up. At the turn of the century, authors felt an exaggerated fear of libel. This led, on the one hand, to that oft-seen declaration that "all characters are fictitious" and, on the other, to the unlikely and frequently absurd names favored by many writers of that period.

As a matter of fact, neither of these hopeful devices represents any defense in law. Sax Rohmer and his contemporaries had sense enough to know that, but by then the practice had become a convention. Within his own limits, he adhered to it. His personal method of dealing with foreign names was to create names which were non-existent but true to type.

Sax Rohmer's earliest stories are as eminently readable today as they were fifty years ago, and as they will be fifty years hence. They are founded on the elements of wonder, charm, and suspenseful storytelling that have appealed naturally to readers throughout the ages. But in this very fact there lies a certain risk. The casual reader, carried along by the pace of the story, is sometimes apt to think of it as taking place at the present day. Then, coming across something which fails to check with his experience, he criticizes it, unjustly and to his own loss. Lacking an appreciation of the social background, no reader can hope to obtain the maximum pleasure from his reading. Sax Rohmer's stories were not written long enough ago for them to have become period pieces, which makes the tendency to this kind of anachronistic approach all the more common. We tend to forget that customs and beliefs have changed rapidly during the past half century, and precipitously during the past two decades. What Sax Rohmer wrote accurately represented the ideas current among his readers at that time. (pp. 291-94)

[His] attitude towards sex was anything but puritanical. Nor had he any objections to sex in fiction. In the latter part of his life, his unwillingness to match up with the standards of a more permissive age was due to something quite different. He objected to sex as a *substitute* for good writing.

Today's readers may be staggered to learn that, in the 1920's and even later, his stories were often regarded as rather shocking. The codes which they expressed were not simply in line with those of his day, but usually a jump ahead of them. In 1936, with *White Velvet,* he gave his approval to premarital relations between engaged couples, to the marked disapproval of the Bishop of London.

Sax Rohmer moved with the times, both in outlook and expression. But, in the sense that his work never lost the color and charm of an Arabian Nights fantasy, he remained conservative. He deplored the brash, rough-hewn creations of postwar "art" whether in music, painting or literature, and no prospect of financial reward could induce him to join what he termed "the cult of ugliness."

In 1935, with the enthusiastic extravagance of youth, I described Sax Rohmer as "the last great master of the English language." Certainly he exhibited, from his earliest work onward, a profound knowledge of the language. He came into the fiction market along with a group of other authors who were seeking to break away from the over-elaborated styles of Victorian literature, while still maintaining a deep respect for English prose. This respect he retained all his life. As fashions changed, he adapted himself to them so that throughout the 1920's and 1930's his work continued to present a mirror of prevailing trends in the first rank of popular fiction.

At what date twentieth century tendencies toward simplification passed over into the debit column is a point to be hotly disputed according to one's personal tastes. But for Sax Rohmer the point came shortly after the Second World War, when popular "style" ceased to have any visible relationship with language.

Popular fiction today has fallen upon hard times. But when twentieth century popular literature receives the attention which it merits, prominent on the bookshelves of the future will be the collected works of Sax Rohmer. (pp. 294-95)

> *Cay Van Ash, in an afterword to* Master of Villainy: A Biography of Sax Rohmer *by Cay Van Ash and Elizabeth Sax Rohmer, edited by Robert E. Briney, Bowling Green University Popular Press, 1972, pp. 291-95.*

### CHRISTOPHER FRAYLING   (essay date 1973)

[*Frayling is an English educator and critic who has written several books on popular culture. Advocating the avoidance of cultural and racial stereotypes in literature, he has stated: "I feel strongly that cultural historians and writers in the latter part of the twentieth century should attempt to fight against the barriers which cultural chauvinism has traditionally erected: an English person who has addressed a French audience on the subject of Napoleon, an American audience on the subject of westerns, or a Romanian audience on the subject of vampires will know exactly what I mean." In the following excerpt, Frayling discusses Rohmer's vaudeville experience as an important inspiration for his later Fu Manchu novels.*]

Of the forty-one full-length novels, eleven collections of short stories, and three non-fiction books written by Arthur Ward (Sax Rohmer) between 1904 and 1959, only the thirteen Fu Manchu stories are still widely read. The devil doctor also made guest appearances in *The Golden Scorpion* and in four short stories, including **"The Secret of the Flying Saucer"** (also known as **"The Mind of Fu Manchu"**), but these never proved as popular.

In America, Robert Briney's *Rohmer Review* (crammed with well researched, but faintly improbable articles such as *Dantean Allusions in the* Trail of Fu Manchu *by J. R. Christopher*) comes out bi-annually. And Christopher Lee continues the cinematic tradition of Agar Lyons, Oland, Karloff and Brandon in a series of curious low-budget Anglo-German co-productions. Scores of imitations and parodies—including, in recent years, *Dr No* (Fleming admitted to being influenced by Rohmer "in my childhood," in *For Bond Lovers Only* (1965), *Madame Sin* (the name comes from Rohmer's *Dope,* 1919) and Fred Fu Manchu (from the Goons' *China Story*)—have kept the character alive, to cast doubt on Julian Symons' recent assertion in *The Sunday Times,* that people under thirty live in "almost complete ignorance of Dr Fu Manchu."

Probably for ideological reasons, Rohmer's books have always had a bad Press in this country: the La Cour and Mogensen *Murder Book* fails even to mention them, Colin Watson in *Snobbery With Violence* writes that "serious criticism" of Rohmer's work is needed and then proceeds flippantly to dismiss Rohmer's output as "racial vituperation," while Julian Symons concludes that all the Fu Manchu stories are "absolute rubbish." It has become a critical commonplace to categorize Rohmer's work as the lowest form of racist propaganda, a humourless version of the mid-Victorian penny-dreadfuls. Nevertheless, apart from the Second World War years (when Rohmer expressed his disappointment at the BBC's shabby treatment of his work by hinting at Nazi infiltration into broadcasting circles in *Seven Sins,* the Fu Manchu stories have seldom been out of print in this country since first publication, and Tom Stacey have just started to reissue an excellent set of photographic reprints. This article will try to suggest some alternative ways of approaching Rohmer's books: through his Music Hall apprenticeship as a writer, his attitude to the police force, his use of narrators, and his fascination with the idea that the situations created by nineteenth-century writers of romantic adventure stories (such as Dumas, Verne, Rider Haggard and Leroux) could still (conceivably) be used—in the most mundane London settings.

Before *The Mystery of Dr Fu Manchu*—his first full-length novel to appear in book form—was published in England Rohmer had ghost-written two short books about music hall performers, *Pause* (based on an idea by George Robey), and *Little Tich.* He had also produced music and lyrics for various Vaudeville personalities. *The Camel's Parade, a Desert Arabesque* ("introducing the original Bedouin melody, the Mizmoune") is a characteristic example:

> Show'r thy blessings Allah: then shall each heart be glad.
> Be ye, Lord, with our Caravan, bound for Old Baghdad.

Only two of Rohmer's songs (**"Bang Went the Chance of a Lifetime"** recorded by Robey and **"The Gas Inspector"** recorded by Tich) have outlived him. Little Tich claimed in 1911 that "many of my more recent characters have been from the pen of the Abbé Sax Rohmer. This ascetic has provided me with a number of remarkable theses." In 1909, Ward had married Rose Elizabeth Knox (sister of Teddy Knox, later of "Crazy Gang" fame): they had met at a time when she was performing a juggling turn with one of her six brothers.

Not surprisingly, many of the incidents, characters, and stylistic trademarks of the first three Fu Manchu stories, *The Mystery . . . , The Devil Doctor,* and *The Si-Fan Mysteries,* all of which were first published as serials in *Colliers* and the *Story-Teller,* are strongly reminiscent of the music hall world in which Rohmer was mixing. As late as 1918, when Rohmer published *The Orchard of Tears*—his attempt to write a "serious" theosophical novel—he peppered the text with references to George Robey, Vesta Tilley, Little Tich and Charlie Chaplin.

From the 1880s to the first decade of this century, Ching Ling Foo ("Court Conjuror to the Empress of China") had been topping variety bills on both sides of the Atlantic. In January 1905, while Ching was performing at the Empire, his rival Chung Ling Soo ("a rare bit of Old China") was filling the Hippodrome. Troupes of Chinese and Japanese illusionists, jugglers and acrobats were to be found in halls all over the country. When Chung introduced the popular DEFYING THE BULLETS into his act, he began to attract Ching's audiences. In March 1918, at the Wood Green Empire, the indestructible Chung was shot in the chest: at the Cottage Hospital, surgeons discovered that although he had been using interpreters and Chinese assistants for over ten years, Chung was in fact American. Unlike his literary counterpart, Chung Ling Soo had no one of Dr Petrie's calibre to save him. The indestructible Fu Manchu, complete with performing marmoset, "impossible" Chinese name and surreal sense of the dramatic, clearly belongs on the same stage: the *origins* of Rohmer's supervillain should be sought less in newspaper headlines about the overthrow of the Manchu dynasty by Dr Sun Yat-sen and Yu'an Shih-kai, or about the kidnapping of a Chinese dignatory in London, than in Rohmer's apprenticeship years as a music hall composer and lyricist, and in his ambition to become a theatrical impresario.

Great emphasis is laid, in the first three Fu Manchu stories, on Fu's elaborate stage-management of illusions, on the finer points of the art of disguise and make-up, on techniques of escapology (Rohmer corresponded with Harry Houdini from 1915 onwards), on reductionist explanations of apparently supernatural phenomena, and on colourful villains with prominent national or racial characteristics; melodramatic situations are strung together with a minimum of explanation, and Rohmer sustains the reader's interest by constant repetition of reassuring stylistic landmarks (almost signature tunes), also by a trenchant and rhetorical use of words.

The irrepressible Nayland Smith can disguise himself as an Oriental sailor, the inscrutable Fu as an English professor working in the British Museum. The devil doctor convinces various potential buyers that a house is haunted by bell-ringing phantoms, Smith discovers the mice (with bells tied to their tails) which have been trained to run along the wainscoting to cause these manifestations. Smith's classic description of "the Yellow Peril incarnate in one man" is repeated by Petrie (almost word for word) at the beginning of all three stories. When Fu actually speaks, we can be sure that the adjectives "sibilant" and "guttural" will be employed to describe the sound; Smith can be depended on to "snap" or "rap" his staccato speeches; Petrie, by way of contrast, tends to indulge in repetitive and self-consciously florid expositions of the story so far. By 1917, Rohmer had discovered his winning formula; the plots of all the early stories contain a selection of the following ingredients:

> (i) an initial show of force by the Burmese dacoits, in a London setting;
>
> (ii) the attempted murder of a prominent Orientalist or Government scientist;
>
> (iii) a scene in Shen Yan's or John Ki's Limehouse opium den;
>
> (iv) the capture (and complicated escape) of Smith and Petrie;
>
> (v) evidence of Smith's knowledge of the East, Fu's refined sense of honour and expertise in "certain . . . obscure sciences which no university of today can

teach,'' and Petrie's medical skills (misjudged by Fu to be those of a near-genius);

(vi) a contrast between Smith's and Fu's codes of civilization;

(vii) an elaborate machine of torture, described in meticulous detail, but seldom fully used;

(viii) a not-so-subtle hint of Karamaneh's divided loyalties and finally

(ix) a chase, followed by Fu Manchu's ''death.''

There is one obvious ingredient which thriller addicts of a later age of bedridden spies and kinky villains would miss, namely sex. In the Fu Manchu stories, the coy relationships between Petrie and Karamaneh, Smith and Fah Lo Suee seem merely plot mechanisms, and Fu's intentions towards Fleurette are based strictly on dynastic considerations. (pp. 65-70)

The limited (but highly successful) formula of the early Fu Manchu stories was altered when Rohmer continued the series—after a thirteen-year gap—with *Daughter of Fu Manchu*: in future, Petrie was to be replaced as narrator by Shan Greville, Alan Sterling and Bart Kerrigan (the remaining stories being told in the third person), the action was to shift from England to France, North Africa, Venice, Haiti or America (and in the final story *Emperor Fu Manchu* to Communist China) and on only two further occasions was Fu supposed to have ''died'' at the end of the story.

The narrative of each book takes place roughly at the time of first publication (i.e. in the ''present''), and Rohmer gradually infused more political background into the cycle, to keep pace with current events: Dr Fu Manchu promotes himself from small-time Limehouse crook (*The Mystery [of Dr. Fu Manchu]*), to head of the Council of Seven (*Daughter [of Fu Manchu]*), then from self-styled controller of the balance of power in Europe against the new dictatorships (*The Drums [of Fu Manchu]*) to potential world dominator, armed with various ultimate deterrents (*The Island [of Fu Manchu]*). By 1959, Fu Manchu, like his creator, was intent on saving China from Maoist rule. Although at no time are Fu's aims specifically stated, the series evidently reflects the development of Rohmer's own political awareness (compare, for example, the descriptions of war-time London contained in *The Orchard of Tears* and in *Seven Sins*).

But, despite his apparent interest in racial archetypes (Nayland Smith = Wayland the Smith, the Anglo-Saxon folk-warrior—possibly via Kipling and *Puck of Pook's Hill*—and Fu belongs to the recently overthrown Manchu dynasty, widely thought in the English Press to have been the most inventively sadistic regime in recent Chinese history), on the evidence of the early stories at least, Rohmer was less concerned with politics and race-war, than with the law versus organized crime. Whether Fu was specifically a ''fanatic or a duly appointed agent'' did not matter. What mattered was the sensational fact that he was the ''most malign and formidable personality . . . in the known world today.'' Rohmer's law-enforcers, most of whom are baptized with solidly recognizable English, Irish or Scottish placenames (Weymouth, Kerry, Fife, Dunbar, etc.), or else with Vaudeville ''foreign'' names (for example, Gaston Max—incidentally, a prototype, in all but nationality, for Hercule Poirot, who first appeared in 1919-20), invariably see events in terms of the normal pattern of crime in London's dockland areas. Smith himself, an ex-DC ''late of Mandalay,'' relies somewhat naively on Scotland Yard rather than Government

spies or the military. And Fu Manchu can justifiably laugh at the amateurish and inept antics of his adversaries:

> There is such a divine simplicity in the English mind that one may lay one's plans with mathematical precision, and rely on the Nayland Smiths and Dr Petries to play their allotted parts. . . . Mr Commissioner Nayland Smith . . . is less than a child, since he has twice rashly precipitated himself into a chamber charged with an anaesthetic prepared, by a process of my own, from the lycoperdon, or Common Puff-ball.

Smith's efficiency is impaired by an obsessive need to *talk* about the Yellow Peril: Petrie (the narrator) is constantly trying to keep ''Smith, old man'' under control, to act as referee when his partner's fanaticism leads to unforgiveable breaches of etiquette, and to present a balanced assessment of the odds. They both interpret Fu's ''malignancy'' in very different ways: Dr Petrie diagnoses that ''the man is a dangerous homicidal maniac.'' Smith will only agree with half of that statement: He ''shook his head grimly.'' ''Dangerous, yes, I agree,'' he muttered; ''his existence is a danger to the entire white race. . . .''

When Smith confronts another fanatic—namely the Rev J. D. Eltham, alias ''Parson Dan, the Fighting Missionary''—all hell breaks loose:

> ''The class of missionary work which you favour, sir, is injurious to international peace. . . . I insist that you abandon your visit to the interior of China.''
>
> ''You insist, Mr Smith?''
>
> ''As your guest, I regret the necessity for reminding you that I hold authority to enforce it.''
>
> . . . the tone of the conversation was growing harsh and the atmosphere of the library portentous with brewing storms. . . .
>
> ''The phantom Yellow Peril,'' said Nayland Smith, ''today materializes under the very eyes of the Western World!''
>
> ''The 'Yellow Peril'!''
>
> ''You scoff, sir, and so do others. . . . The peace of the world is at stake, Mr Eltham!''

Eventually, much to Petrie's relief, ''Parson Dan'' steps down (''thus, then, the storm blew over . . .'').

Throughout the series, Smith is presented as something of a buffoon: he is forever impressing the urgency of the situation on his assistants (''Time is of the essence''), then lighting up his briar pipe, and pacing up and down for minutes on end. ''You must have worn tracks in more carpets than any man in England,'' says one of his long-suffering colleagues. On such occasions, Smith is prone to self-pity (''I am a child, striving to cope with a mental giant!''), and to long bouts of reminiscence concerning his years in Burma. As Fu Manchu frequently points out, whenever Smith actually *does* anything, his achievement is negligible.

Occasionally, in his evident relish for a well turned phrase, Petrie guys the style and vocabulary of his unstable colleague, and, in the absence of the usual corrective, the stories become one-sided and humourless. But as a rule, Petrie cannot bring himself to give his whole hearted support to Smith's gushing bigotry, particularly when all this talk either postpones action (such as rescuing Karamaneh), or else causes ill feeling (for example, with Eltham, or the future Mrs Petrie).

Are we supposed to agree with Smith's political and social views? Rohmer stresses that Fu Manchu is a freelance operator, working without the backing of the Chinese (or any other) government: there is a tension, throughout the series, between the middle of the road views of the narrators, and the extremism of Nayland Smith. In later years (roughly from *The Drums [of Fu Manchu]* onwards) Sax Rohmer toned down his presentation of Sir Denis; if he had a sneaking admiration for Smith's unashamed jingoism up to the early 'thirties, he subsequently outgrew this—to the noticeable detriment of sales in England. Mrs Sax Rohmer recently told me that her late husband could not sit through the film versions of his work: certainly, the Karloff adaptation (*The Mask of Fu Manchu*) is more blatantly racist than anything Rohmer ever wrote ("Kill all the white men and take their women!"), and the Henry Brandon serials (*The Drums of Fu Manchu*) rather prejudice the case by introducing the Burmese dacoits as vampire-fanged zombies, complete with lobotomy scars on their foreheads.

If the comedy double-acts representing the police-force in Rohmer's books (Smith/Petrie, Max/Bluett, Dunbar/Sowerby, Kerry/Coombes, etc.) sometimes seem, to such "giant intellects" as Fu Manchu, to be behaving like knockabout turns, his villains bear the same stamp. Both Little Tich and George Robey specialized in impressions of eccentric foreigners (particularly Chinamen), and Rohmer devoted a chapter of Tich's "autobiography" to a running gag about "my Chinese correspondent."

*Yu'an Hee See* (alias Mr King, also known as *The White Slaver*) speaks in a weird, falsetto voice, and when he laughs, he sounds like a squeaky bat: this is because his throat has been shot away. His speciality is commandeering U-Boats, to assist in his own personal variations on the *Lusitania* disaster. Sin-Sin Wa (*Dope*) is (ostensibly) a one-eyed Chinaman, with a one-eyed talking raven perched permanently on his shoulder. In fact, of course, Sin-Sin has two eyes: he is just trying to fool the police. Mr de Trepniak (*Grey Face*) is a red-haired albino, with a face like Nero and a pathological fear of death; he refuses to possess any object which will outlast him. In these and other cases Rohmer piles on the gruesome attributes with such surrealistic abandon that it is impossible to believe that we are supposed to take his villains seriously: the supporting acts are always caught by the police, but the star comedian is normally allowed to escape by the stage door. In the case of his most famous creation, Rohmer allowed the devil doctor to take top billing ("Just heaven," moans Smith, "why is retribution delayed?") and in *The Shadow of Fu Manchu*—an adapted stage play—could not bring himself to award Smith the final curtain-call

> "Cease fire there!" he shouted angrily. . . . "You fool!"
>
> Nayland Smith's words came as a groan, "This was no end for the greatest brain in the world!"

So Fu Manchu yet again escapes from an impossible situation, to fight (in future on the side of the angels) in *Re-Enter Fu Manchu,* and as *Emperor Fu Manchu.*

Sax Rohmer's pedantic style ("It is me, or rather it is I," says Smith during one tense scene), which was compounded of elegantly phrased, but by today's standards excessively formal, descriptions and speeches, with lengthy, over-written parentheses in both, was obviously evolved during his apprentice years working for Robey and Tich. In *Little Tich,* the "Abbé Sax Rohmer" satirizes his own stylistic peculiarities: although

these had been ideally suited to Robey's patter-songs, musical monologues, and Little Tich's polysyllabic nonsense-rhymes, they required some explanation in an "autobiography" (even Tich's). Rohmer writes of "ships of the desert (I refer to camels)," and adds a footnote to the phrase "untramelled by the baser conventionalities," which reads: "I told you my style was looking up." In chapter sixteen ("My impression of the Great Pyramid"), the conversation between the Old Man and Tich is funny *because* Tich has never set eyes on the pyramid, and is trying to cover up with a series of meaningless (and long-winded) platitudes, repeated *ad nauseam.*

With the exception of *Emperor Fu Manchu,* Rohmer never wrote stories set in locations he had not either visited or researched in detail: but it is clear from *The Brood of the Witch Queen* (written shortly after his trip to the Meydum pyramid), and from *The Day the World Ended* (written in 1928, after his visit to Baden-Baden) that he was interested only in presenting an aggressively cavalier version of what he had seen. Like Little Tich, he was giving an *impression* of these exotic locales; his imaginative reconstruction, based on limited evidence, of what the Limehouse dope traffic must have been like (*The Yellow Claw, Dope*) was popular, and evidently appealed to Rohmer's view of himself as a latter day romantic, but belonged more to the worlds of *Edwin Drood* and Sherlock Holmes than to the columns of the weekly Press. No wonder he decided to abandon his career as an in-depth journalist. Judging by the recent biography (*Master of Villainy*) Rohmer was the sort of man who could not go to the shops, without returning some hours later with a whole string of (suitably colorful) anecdotes about his exploits. The music hall scene in *The Yellow Claw* is fresh and authentic; in the rest of the story, Limehouse simply provides a garishly decorated backdrop, a contrast to the drab predictability of life in Mayfair high society. When it suited his purposes, Rohmer was quite capable of describing other parts of London (Brixton, Clapham, Dulwich, Bloomsbury) in balanced, almost "prosaic" terms.

George Robey's stage-act (which, as well as "The Chinese Laundryman," included "Clarence, the last of the Dandies"—a clear precursor of Rohmer's *Captain O'Hagan*—in its repertoire of impressions) was famous for its pompous use of euphemism:

> ". . . a coarsening of the auricular appendage. In other words, a thick ear." (Robey).
>
> "A thick voice inquired, brutally, why the sanguinary hell . . . he had had his blood-stained slumbers disturbed in this gory manner, and who was the vermilion blighter responsible." (Rohmer, *The Yellow Claw*).
>
> ". . . and said I might expeditiously migrate. In other words, buzz off." (Robey).
>
> "Twice to redouble the lure of My Lady Nicotine would be but loosely to estimate the seductiveness of the Spirit of the Poppy." (Rohmer, *Dope*).

Watching George Robey, with his "in other words" routine, and Little Tich, with his "so to speak" line in patter, as well as earning a meagre living writing for them both, seems to have had a permanent effect both on Sax Rohmer's prose style, and on his attitude to the mystery story genre.

At first sight, this version of the genesis of Fu Manchu seems to differ considerably from Rohmer's own account. Apparently he had been sent on a magazine assignment (probably for *Tit-Bits*) to cover the dope-smuggling and white-slaving activities of a Mr King in Chinatown. Although he was unable to get anyone to talk about this man, he did claim to have caught a glimpse of a tall, lean and feline Chinaman, who was entering a shabby doorway in Limehouse, accompanied by a stunning Arab girl ("she was like something from an Edmund Dulac illustration to *The Thousand and One Nights*"):

> As I walked on through the fog, I imagined that inside that cheap-looking dwelling, unknown to all but a chosen few, unvisited by the police, were luxurious apartments, Orientally furnished, cushioned and perfumed.

The key words here are "I imagined" and "chosen few." For Rohmer, whose earliest ambition as a writer was to recreate a fantasy world, peopled with characters out of Dumas (see, for example, the "dream" sequence in *The Orchard of Tears*) was always intrigued by the idea that the most wildly romantic adventure stories could still be re-told using everyday London locations. This sense of *incongruity*, combined with the conviction that his individual experience both of Limehouse and the East was unique, runs through all Rohmer's early works. Captain O'Hagan's advice to the long-suffering Raymond sums up the wishful thinking (and, to an extent, the disillusionment) of Arthur Ward:

> "Alas, O'Hagan," I say, "this world of ours is a grey place."
>
> "How can you say so, Raymond? Have I not repeatedly demonstrated that Romance lurks in hiding amid the most prosaic surroundings? Adventure, my boy, is for the adventurous! It is only the blind who deny the existence of fauns. I will undertake to find you a nymph in any wood. Villains profound as the darkest dreams of Tolstoy regularly take tea in the drawing-rooms of Mayfair; heroes loftier than Charlemagne jostle one in the Strand!"

Behind the Limehouse shop-front, within a stone's throw of the Strand ("Oh, my God!" I groaned, "can this be England?"), in a London taxi (a favourite Rohmer motif), or even on Clapham Common, the yellow peril may strike at any time. "Into my humdrum suburban life," writes Petrie, "Nayland Smith had brought fantasy of the wildest." (pp. 71-8)

Arthur Ward's lurid imagination, combined with his apprenticeship in the music halls, created a mental picture of Limehouse which remained in focus for at least thirty years: the social attitudes and the over-written descriptions contained in the Fu Manchu stories are now part of their "period" atmosphere. If quoted out of their Vaudeville context, Rohmer's "asides" about the ghetto areas of London, and his attempts to endow his heroes and villains with easily recognizable national characteristics seem very suspect indeed. But it is all too easy to dismiss his complete works as "racial vituperation" without bothering to study his specific contribution to the mystery story genre. Rohmer was equally happy writing comedy short stories such as **"Narky"** (about an incompetent amateur cracksman who tries to do the *Raffles* thing), and nostalgic countryhouse detective stories such as *Hangover House,* as he was churning out Oriental thrillers: he never conceived the Fu Manchu stories as a *series*. This is not to suggest that Rohmer's predominantly middle-class readership did not wallow in the jingoistic nonsense. On the contrary, they did just that, and in the process (largely as a result of cinema adaptations and cheap jacket designs) invented a moustache for their favourite Chinese villain which is never once mentioned in the books. The spy stories of Rohmer's early contemporaries, such as Le Queux, Sapper, Horler and Oppenheim, are only accessible today via

the shelves of antiquarian bookshops: the first three Fu Manchu stories are always being reprinted, both here and in the States. For better or for worse—most critics today would consider for worse—the devil doctor's shadow lies upon us all. (pp. 79-80)

> Christopher Frayling, "Criminal Tendencies—II: Sax Rohmer and the Devil Doctor," in London Magazine, Vol. 13, No. 2, June-July, 1973, pp. 65-80.

**COLIN WATSON    (essay date 1979)**

[*Watson is an English critic specializing in crime and detective fiction. In the following excerpt, he examines the Fu Manchu stories in the social and political context of English relations with China and the attitudes toward Chinese immigrants living in England.*]

Perhaps the most extravagant invention in the long gallery of crime fiction's bogeyman-villains is Fu-Manchu, the Oriental devil-doctor created by Sax Rohmer.

> Of him it has been fitly said that he had a brow like Shakespeare and a face like Satan. Something serpentine, hypnotic, was in his very presence. . . . He came forward with an indescribable gait, cat-like yet awkward, carrying his high shoulders almost hunched. He placed the lantern in a niche in the wall never turning away the reptilian gaze of those eyes which must haunt my dreams for ever. They possessed a viridescence which hitherto I had only supposed possible in the eye of a cat. . . . I had never supposed, prior to meeting Fu-Manchu, that so intense a force of malignancy could radiate from any human being.

The original *Mystery of Doctor Fu-Manchu* appeared in 1913 and for the next thirty years sequels continued to be published in response to steady demand. They varied little from the prototype and the only serious problem they would seem to have presented their author was the devising, with every book, of some explanation of how the doctor had managed to escape the end so graphically described in the previous one. Rohmer, however, was sufficiently audacious a melodramatist to be able to make short work of such matters. When he ran out of ingenuity, he unashamedly improvised with a casual reference to "certain methods that defy Western science" or to "a secret of which Fu-Manchu alone was the master."

The plots, such as they are, of the Fu-Manchu novels would be quite meaningless in paraphrase. They are a jumble of incredible encounters, pursuits, traps and escapes. Who is trying to accomplish what, and why—this is never explained. All that seems certain is that a titanic struggle is being waged by a man called Nayland Smith to thwart the designs of Fu-Manchu.

> At last they truly were face to face—the head of the great Yellow movement, and the man who fought on behalf of the entire white race. . . .

Smith is in some unspecified way an agent of the British Government, whose interests he once served in Burma, Egypt and certain other countries. The police appear to be at his command and even an inspector must expect Smith to address him somewhat peremptorily:

> "Too late!" rapped my friend. "Jump in a taxi and pick up two good men to leave for China at once! Then go and charter a special train to Tilbury to leave in twenty-five minutes. Order another cab to wait outside for me."

A man with authority to dispatch a pair of Scotland Yard operatives to China at twenty-five minutes' notice is a magnificent example of the sort of fictional go-getter that must have delighted readers who had no reason to hope that their own lives would ever cease to be hedged with petty prohibitions.

But what is Fu-Manchu up to that measures so drastic have to be taken by the indomitable Nayland Smith? The only answer to this question is rhetorical generalization pregnant with hints about a "Yellow Peril." Here is a typical reflection by the narrator, Dr Petrie:

> The mere thought that our trifling error of judgement tonight in tarrying a moment too long might mean the victory of Fu-Manchu might mean the turning of the balance which a wise providence had adjusted between the white and yellow races, was appalling. To Smith and me, who knew something of the secret influences at work to overthrow the Indian Empire, to place, it might be, the whole of Europe and America beneath an Eastern rule, it seemed that a great yellow hand was stretched out over London. Dr Fu-Manchu was a menace to the civilized world.

Passages like this abound throughout Rohmer's work. They link the action sequences and provide spurious justification for them. Credible motives are entirely lacking. Here is the forerunner—perhaps even the progenitor—of Ian Fleming and the espionage fiction of the 1950s and 1960s, the ancestor of the thriller of unreason.

It often has been said that stories of the Fu-Manchu type were devised purely as entertainment and that any attempt to subject them to serious criticism is misconceived. There is something too pat about this argument. No man writes entirely in a mental vacuum; however slight, however apparently automatic his work, it must proceed from ideas, traces at least of which will be carried to the reader. It is to instant rapport between these conveyed notions and the reader's existing prejudices, quite as much as to any quality of story-telling, that a book's success is attributable. The Fu-Manchu novels went into edition after edition. Their only clear message was one of racial vituperation. Had there not existed in the minds of many thousands of people an innate fear or dislike of foreigners—oriental foreigners, in particular—Sax Rohmer never would have become a bestselling author.

Before the second world war, the average middle-class man and woman in England had never seen a Chinaman. The few Chinese who lived and worked in Britain were to be found only in certain areas of the big cities and seaports, generally dockland districts such as London's Limehouse. Their communities were small, unobtrusive and industrious. They also had their own high standards of respectability and cleanliness. Chinese rarely came into conflict with the law and when they did it was as often as not in consequence of some trivial neighbourhood quarrel.

Such was the unexciting reality. No opium dens. No pad-footed assassins. No Tong wars nor kidnapping nor torture chambers. Seldom in the history of racial intolerance had a minority shown itself so uncooperative in the matter of getting hated. Fortunately for the great "fiendish Oriental" myth, the majority of the British public had never walked down the neat, if dull, little streets of Limehouse nor had occasion to penetrate the harbour districts of Liverpool, South Shields or Cardiff. It did become briefly fashionable in the 1930s for groups of wealthy young Londoners to "go slumming" in the East End, where

they supposed that only their daring and their inbred superiority protected them from being doped, robbed or murdered, but they understandably refrained from admitting afterwards that nothing in the least degree thrilling had happened. Nor was the legend contradicted by the provincial and suburban sightseers whose charabanc tours of "Chinatown" proved so consistently and disappointingly uneventful. They preferred to imagine that they had been into dangerous and forbidden territory, which doubtless they had glimpsed through eyes not unlike those of Rohmer's Doctor Petrie:

> The mantle of dusk had closed about the squalid activity of the East End streets as we neared our destination. Aliens of every shade of colour were in the glare of the lamps upon the main road about us now, emerging from burrow-like alleys. In the short space of the drive we had passed from the bright world of the West into the dubious underworld of the East.

The vehemence of this prose is interesting. It is occasioned by nothing in the story itself, and indeed seems unrelated to experience of any kind. Why should street activity in a particular area be described as "squalid" as if rendered so by a mere compass bearing? Why are alleys inhabited by "aliens" specifically "burrow-like"? And what has geography got to do with the distinction between "world" and "underworld?" Even the verb "emerge," with its suggestion of secret and evil purpose, would seem a curious choice if the scene were not to yield at least one specific act of wickedness. But nothing happens. Rohmer's narrative, like the Limehouse touring coach, rolls on elsewhere. The readers have not been thrilled; they simply have been prompted to feel superior.

Historically, the British had been well conditioned to accept the myth of Asiatic guile. In common with other European countries during the nineteenth century, Britain had seized upon every commercial advantage offered by China's vast size and the divisions and weaknesses of her government. China was not colonized, but it was virtually partitioned. The Treaty Ports constituted an effective apparatus of exploitation, and Britain derived additional and special benefit from her control of the Chinese Customs with a consequent vested interest in the opium trade. Like all indefensible arrangements, this called for a virtuous attitude on the part of the beneficiary and a campaign of vilification against the unwilling benefactor—especially after the Opium Wars, in which the Christian forces of Queen Victoria had appeared to be compelling the Heathen Chinese to step up his drug consumption. By the turn of the century, the British had managed to convince themselves that with the exception of a handful of quaint converts, the Chinese were corrupt, untrustworthy, dirty, vicious and cunning. Connoisseurs prized their ancient art, of course, and chinoiserie continued to be a fashionable feature of middle and upper class drawing-rooms, but aesthetic appreciation was quite separate in the public mind from a dislike that verged on loathing for the race which had created that art.

Of all the fields of missionary endeavour that helped gratify the Victorians' desire to patronize the rest of mankind, China seems to have been regarded as presenting a special challenge. Its wickedness was not something negative, like the poor African's failure to realize that God was pained by the sight of a bare backside, but a conscious and systematic adherence to non-Christian—and therefore Satanic—traditions. The various rival churches, whose Missions to China unashamedly blackguarded one another and did as much poaching as proselytizing, were united in one respect: their propaganda had the common aim of destroying the idea that a civilization as ancient as the Chinese might actually possess enough merit to warrant its being left alone for a few more centuries. Congregations and, in particular, children at Sunday schools, were treated to harrowing accounts of a land of famine, banditry, infanticide and opium smoking, where only in the beleaguered mission compounds was there to be found enlightenment and joy. The theme was pursued in countless pamphlets and parish magazines, illustrated in magic lantern lectures, and worked into that peculiarly British manifestation of sadism, the literature of the Sunday School Prize. Thus—and not for the first or the last time—did actions dictated by political expediency receive the retrospective sanction of religion.

Before the nineteenth century, it was the traveller's tale that had provided people with their ideas about China. They pictured it much as the first readers of Marco Polo must have done—rich, strange and utterly remote. It inspired awe but also respect. The imperialist and religious propaganda of Victorian times rendered the mystery sinister and the writers of popular literature grasped eagerly this new opportunity of "preaching to the nerves." After the shock of the Boxer uprising in 1900, the reading public was ready to believe anything of the "treacherous" yellow men, with their slant eyes and funny pigtails and evil secret societies. For the next forty years, the "Yellow Peril" was a constantly recurrent theme of adventure and mystery fiction. Because China was so far away and was represented in Britain by only a tiny, scattered and uncommunicative immigrant population, it was possible to chill the blood of the credulous with the wildest inventions and the most absurd racial libels without fear of disproof or even contradiction.

The Chinaman-villain was a figure that might have been tailor-made for the use of crime novelists. He was readily associated in the minds of uninformed, insular people with vices that they conceived to be endemic in the East. He was what all the writers described as "inscrutable"—in other words, a repository of unspoken thoughts and therefore dangerous. He was a drug addict himself and almost certainly a supplier of drugs to others (did not every newspaper reader in the 1920s know about "Brilliant Chang" whose gang provided dope for the Society habitués of Mrs Kate Meyrick's "43" Club in the West End of London?). Worse still, it was part of the fiendish character of the yellow men to desire sexual intercourse with white girls; this they accomplished by abducting their victims and putting them aboard junks that plied between Wapping and the water-front brothels of China. An intriguing incidental to this aspect of oriental villainy was the widespread belief that the labial plane of a Chinese vagina was horizontal instead of vertical and consequently less prized by native sensualists.

Sax Rohmer set a fashion that was to persist for thirty years when he fixed upon the Thames and the poverty-stricken Eastern boroughs of London as the main scene of the operations of his Chinese criminals. This was the sort of thing whereby the Limehouse thriller school sought to horrify their readers:

> We stood in a bare and very dirty room, which could only claim kinship with a civilized shaving saloon by virtue of the grimy towel thrown across the back of the solitary chair. A Yiddish theatrical bill of some kind, illustrated, adorned one of the walls, and another bill, in what may have been Chinese, completed the decorations. From behind a curtain heavily brocaded with filth a little Chinaman appeared, dressed in a loose smock, black trousers and thick-soled slippers, and, advancing, shook his head vigorously. "No shavee, no shavee," he chattered, simian fash-

ion, squinting from one to the other of us with his twinkling eyes. "Too late! Shuttee shop!"

(pp. 114-21)

*Colin Watson, "The Orientation of Villainy," in his* Snobbery with Violence: English Crime Stories and Their Audience, *1971. Reprint by Eyre Methuen, 1979, pp. 109-21.*

### WILLIAM F. WU  (essay date 1982)

[*Wu is an American science fiction writer, dramatist, and critic. Concerning his work, he has written: "My principal interest is in Asian Americans and their specific identity as a group that is neither Asian nor white American." His major critical work,* The Yellow Peril: Chinese Americans in American Fiction, 1850-1940, *argues that the fear of an Asian takeover was "the overwhelmingly dominant theme in American fiction about Chinese Americans" from 1850 to 1940. In the following excerpt from that study, Wu examines the image of Asians presented to American readers by Rohmer's fiction.*]

The Fu Manchu character is the first Asian role of prominence in modern literature to have a large American readership. Technically, the Fu Manchu series belongs to English literature, since author Sax Rohmer was English; however, the adoption of the Fu Manchu novels by the American public has established Fu Manchu as a major figure in American popular culture. Millions of copies of the Fu Manchu books have been sold in the United States, signaling a popularity that has led to adaptations in film, radio, television, and comics. The tremendous popularity of Fu Manchu has also meant a great deal of literary influence, as the image of Fu Manchu has been absorbed into American consciousness as the archetypal Asian villain. For this reason the particular literary elements of the Fu Manchu novels will be examined for what they present to the American public, and for what subsequent American writers found desirable to emulate. This is done with the understanding that Fu Manchu may have a different significance in English culture.

All together, Rohmer wrote thirteen novels, three short stories, and one novelette about Fu Manchu and his arch-foe, British agent Sir Denis Nayland Smith. The first three novels constitute one unit, including *The Insidious Dr. Fu-Manchu* (1913), *The Return of Fu-Manchu* (1916), and *The Hand of Fu-Manchu* (1917), which stood for fourteen years as the complete series. (The character's name was hyphenated only in the first three novels.) All three works were serialized in British magazines prior to their appearance in the United States in book form. Throughout the 1920s, Rohmer wrote a variety of novels and short stories dealing with suspense, the occult, and with the Chinese in England. A few had at most a marginal relation to the Fu Manchu novels, in the form of minor characters and references. In the late 1920s, Rohmer went to New York to write a Fu Manchu serial for Collier's magazine, which eventually appeared in book form as *Daughter of Fu Manchu* (1931). This and the rest of the novels constitute a second group which appeared at intervals until 1959. However, the two main characters, the prevailing theme, and the type of plot devices used are all established in the first three novels, which will be considered first as a group.

Rohmer introduces Fu Manchu unequivocally as the representative of the Asian threat to the West.

> Imagine a person, tall, lean and feline, high-shouldered, with a brow like Shakespeare and a face like Satan, a close-shaven skull, and long, magnetic eyes

of true cat-green. Invest him with all the cruel cunning of an entire Eastern race, accumulated in one giant intellect, with all the resources, if you will, of a wealthy government which, however, already has denied all knowledge of his existence. Imagine that awful being, and you have a mental picture of Dr. Fu-Manchu, the yellow peril incarnate in one man.

Rohmer strengthens this image of the exotic, evil Asian by the use of three types of plot devices in these early novels. The most evocative device for the exotic aura around the character is an array of complex, original assassination techniques, which are usually successful. The development of the evil taint in Fu Manchu's personality is also achieved through his perpetration of nonfatal tortures and occasional assassination attempts that fail. The qualities of being exotic and evil are bound together by repeated statements to the effect that Fu Manchu represents a rising tide of Asian politics, and that his behavior is determined by his Asian culture and race.

In *The Insidious Doctor Fu-Manchu,* the plot consists of various efforts by Smith to prevent or solve certain murders and disappearances. First, Smith and his friend Dr. Petrie attempt to stop the latest in a rash of assassinations. Urgency heightens the suspense in this endeavor; however, in order to build the potency of the villain, Rohmer makes this attack on an undeveloped character successful. The killing is accomplished by the use of a scorpion, in an incident containing elements of both horror and mystery stories. First a letter is mailed to the victim, dipped in a certain perfume. The night after its arrival, one of Fu Manchu's servants introduces into the victim's study an unknown type of scorpion that locates the victim's hand through the perfume that has rubbed off the letter. The scorpion stings the hand fatally. The delicate planning required for this operation emphasizes the intricate lengths to which Fu Manchu will go and the scorpion itself, discovered in London, signifies the entry into England of the exotic, suggesting the jungle, Asia, and the foreign nature of Fu Manchu and his associates.

The murders committed by "The Call of Siva" offer the most challenge to the reader, as they present a locked-room mystery, where all the facts are presented long before the solution is disclosed. These deaths occur when victims, in upper-story rooms, are found lying on the ground beneath their windows, dead from the fall. In some incidents, they fell from rooms where the doors were locked and the windows completely inaccessible from the ground. One witness in the room actually has seen a victim yanked out the window, though no tangible means for causing this has been found. The only clue is a strange howling or cry outside the building, heard by some witnesses shortly before the victim's death. Smith is familiar with the mystery from his earlier days fighting the forces of Fu Manchu in Burma, where the cry was called "the Call of Siva" by a religious group. An element of mysticism is added to the deaths by this use of the worshippers of Siva and the apparently disembodied voice. The Burmese origin of the phenomenon reinforces in the reader's mind Fu Manchu's status as a leader specifically of Asian people. The solution to the mystery clinches this reminder: in each murder, a member of the Indian religious cult *Thuggee* climbed to the roof of the building, and cried out to attract the victim to the window. When the victim's head was outside the window, looking around, the *Thug* would drop a fixed loop of silken cord over it, yank the victim out of the window, then pull up the cord as the victim fell out of the loop to the ground. The use of silk for the cord and a *Thug* for the crime itself maintain the Asian flavor of this crime, and by now, the reader begins to realize

that crime by Asian people or objects means the presence of Fu Manchu behind the scenes.

In *The Return of Fu Manchu,* the assassination techniques are no longer specifically related to Asia, but are simply unusual and unpleasant. One character is known for carrying a cane with a knob in the shape of a snake's head. To eliminate him, a servant of Fu Manchu replaces it with a hollow tube holding a live adder, with its head in the place of the knob. Other killings are done by an Abyssinian half-man, half-baboon with the intelligence of a human and the strength and agility of the animal. Fu Manchu's use of the adder and the half-baboon represent a widening of his control from creatures of Asia to those of Australia and Africa. The breeding of the special scorpion and ape are gimmicks used here for the sake of mystery and suspense, but they are also the seeds of what blooms into clearly defined science fiction by the end of the third novel.

The last assassinations in the second novel are deaths by fright at the Gables mansion. Mysterious lights and ringing bells literally scare selected residents and guests to death. In this case, the servants of Fu Manchu have attached bells to mice and have released them within the walls of the building where they run in prescribed areas. The strange lights are accomplished with a flashlight, which at that time had not yet become a common item.

Only two assassination techniques appear in *The Hand of Fu Manchu.* The first is the "flower of silence," which produces poison. Since the poison affects the tongue very quickly, clear enunciation of complex words is early proof that one is not contaminated. Tradition states that saying "Sâkya Muni" is a charm against the poison, when of course it is actually just an indication that one has not yet been poisoned at all. By using one of the names of Buddha for this test and by giving India as the origin of the flower, Rohmer again focuses on Asia. A chest with a needle in the handle and a hidden syringe of poison inside has no connection with Asia, but—like the scorpion, the adder, the half-baboon, and the belled mice—it continues the association of sly, complex evil with the name of Fu Manchu.

The nonfatal crimes also heighten this sense of villainy. An attempt to kill Egyptologist Sir Lionel Barton involves filling a sarcophagus in his study with an invention of Fu Manchu's similar to chlorine gas. This extremely lethal cloud is described as seeming "to be alive. It moved over the floor, about a foot from the ground, going away from him and towards a curtain at the other end of the study." Smith and Petrie later venture into London's Chinatown, disguised as Chinese, in search of Fu Manchu. When Fu Manchu discovers Petrie, he drops him through a trapdoor into the Thames. As he is carried by the current, he sees an apparent handhold; however, Smith, climbing down to his rescue, prevents him from grabbing it. The wooden beam actually hides the presence of two sharp, upturned sword blades, that sever the fingers of a victim against the pull of the current. The secondary level reasoning that places these blades creates a grudging respect in both the protagonists and the reader for the thoroughness of the villain, and also disgust for him as the perpetrator of such unnecessary and carefully considered cruelty.

The connection of being evil with being Asian does not rely only on symbolism and association. The theme, that Asian hordes are on the verge of sweeping through Europe and North America with only a few British heroes opposing them, runs explicitly throughout the first three novels. Suspects are chosen by racial background, and are always proven guilty. The assumption of Asian guilt and inferiority is open and unembarrassed. Smith finds that even Fu Manchu has lapses into childishness: "We owe our lives, Petrie, to the national childishness of the Chinese! A race of ancestor worshippers is capable of anything. . . ." Petrie, who is the narrator in the first three novels, often identifies suspects on the basis of race in the narrative: "Though highly educated, and possibly an American citizen, *Van Roon was a Chinaman*." Another killer's disguise was that of "a benevolent old gentleman whose ancestry was not wholly innocent of Oriental strains. . . ." In regard to the struggle against these villains, Petrie gives the reader frequent reminders to the effect that "the swamping of the White world by Yellow hordes might well be the price of our failure."

The other novels and short stories in the series continue Fu Manchu's efforts to conquer the white world through science-fiction methods, to be foiled by Smith and his secret-agent allies. After the third book, Petrie no longer narrates, though he occasionally still appears as a character. His replacements, like him, all act as viewpoint characters, sidekicks to Smith, and romantic leads; some also narrate. The next three novels in succession are *Daughter of Fu Manchu* (1931), *The Mask of Fu Manchu* (1932), and *The Bride of Fu Manchu* (1933). These three are narrated by Shan Greville, who is English; the first two continue to use England as a setting, while the third takes place on the French Riviera. The next two novels seem to indicate an awareness on Rohmer's part of an American audience; *The Trail of Fu Manchu* (1934), told in third person and set in London, features an American sidekick and romantic lead named Alan Sterling. Rohmer handles the fact that he is not British carefully, emphasizing his ancestry. He is introduced as

> a lean young man, marked by an intense virility. His
> features were too irregular for him to be termed hand-
> some, but he had steadfast Scottish eyes, and one
> would have said that tenacity of purpose was his chief
> virtue . . . despite his Scottish name, a keen observer
> might have deduced from his intonation that Sterling
> was a citizen of the United States.

In *President Fu Manchu* (1936), also written in third person, Smith goes to the United States to prevent Fu Manchu's engineering the election of one of his rare Caucasian servants to the presidency. His partner here is Mark Hepburn, a captain in the U.S. Marine Corps on special duty. He, too, has impeccable white ancestry, as a third-generation Quaker with a half-Celtic mother.

The action returns to London in *The Drums of Fu Manchu* (1939), which is narrated by Englishman Bart Kerrigan. However, this is the last wholly British novel; in *The Island of Fu Manchu* (1941), Kerrigan and Smith follow Fu Manchu to the Caribbean, where he is creating an army of zombies, or walking dead, who will obey his commands and staff a powerful, technologically advanced navy. The last three novels all feature Americans as viewpoint characters written about in third person. *The Shadow of Fu Manchu* (1948), set in New York, includes an American named Dr. Morris Craig, whose credentials are not only a British surname, but a manner of speech "particularly English," from his training as "one of the most brilliant physicists Oxford University had ever turned out." Suspicion of the Asian race has not slackened any in this later novel; another of Smith's American colleagues complains to a Harvard-educated secretary of his club about seeing an "Asiatic" in the building and is assured, "Your complaint is before me . . . I can only assure you that not only have we no

Asiatic members, honorary or otherwise, but no visitor such as you describe has been in the club. . . ." The Asian in the building, of course, is a spy in the employ of Fu Manchu, and so justifies such complaints based on racial grounds. In *Re-enter Fu Manchu* (1957), Smith is aided by Brian Merrick, the son of a United States senator and a graduate of Oxford. Finally, in *Emperor Fu Manchu* (1959), finished several weeks before Rohmer died, Smith has another American colleague of Scottish ancestry, U.S. government agent Tony McKay.

The increasing emphasis on American companions for Smith and on settings in the western hemisphere may partly result from a desire of Rohmer's to offer more variety of plot and setting. Also, *Collier's* magazine in the U.S. had revived the series by commissioning *Daughter of Fu Manchu* and *The Mask of Fu Manchu*. In fact, *Collier's* purchased not only several of the other Fu Manchu novels, but also the bulk of Rohmer's fiction from 1913 to 1946. The size of the potential reading market in the United States was probably at least a consideration; Nayland Smith's presence in every story maintains the British flavor and origin of the adventures, while occasional American companions may increase the attraction of the novels for American readers. Rohmer's friend and biographer Cay Van Ash writes that Rohmer decided in 1935 "to reward his American supporters by transferring the activities of Fu Manchu to the United States." The first novel to follow this decision was *President Fu Manchu*. Fu Manchu's success as a character was thus launched in a strictly British framework and was possibly boosted in the United States by certain conscious decisions by Rohmer along the way.

Prior to 1932, the people of China and their cousins throughout the world are not on record as objecting to the image of Fu Manchu as their representative in English-language fiction. Earlier complaints from China are understandably lacking; Fu Manchu first appeared between 1913 and 1917, when the nascent Republic of China, having overthrown the Manchu Dynasty in 1911, was degenerating into a titular government whose land was in reality governed piecemeal by various warlords. Incessant civil strife continued until early 1928, when the Kuomintang under Chiang Kai-shek defeated the other warlords and sent the Chinese Communists into the Long March, near extinction. While the Kuomintang never eliminated all their enemies nor regained all the foreign concessions, they did make the first substantial claim to being the national government of China that the world had seen for many years, so that the international situation had changed from 1917 to 1931, when *Daughter of Fu Manchu* resumed the series in *Collier's*.

In 1932, while *The Mask of Fu Manchu* was running in *Collier's*, Metro-Goldwyn-Mayer began production of a film by that title, starring Boris Karloff as Fu Manchu, Myrna Loy as his daughter, and Lewis Stone as Nayland Smith. The film was a hit, like its British predecessors, and MGM intended to produce sequels. However:

> They were curiously obstructed by urgent protests
> from the Chinese Embassy in Washington. The
> Chinese diplomats took a humorless view of Fu Man-
> chu, whom they considered damaging to their "im-
> age." At this time, the West in general, and America
> in particular, was becoming alarmed by the rapid
> expansion of Japan in the Far East, and rather inclined
> to encourage China as a potential ally against this
> threat. Consequently, the protest received closer at-
> tention than it might otherwise have done.

> The Chinese were unable to influence the publication
> of the Fu Manchu stories (at that time; later, they

were able, and did) but they were successful in hold-ing up the production of further films. Sax's rather questionable financial advisers were furious, and ac-tually suggested bringing an injunction against the Chinese government for "loss of revenue." But Sax, who considered the complaint understandable, even if absurd, refused to give his consent to any such proceeding [Cay Van Ash and Elizabeth Sax Roh-mer, *Master of Villainy*].

Nayland Smith apparently does come to admire Fu Manchu's abilities in the course of the series, though this change appears to be unrelated to any outside pressure. The change in attitude involves Smith's apparent growth of admiration for his foe's abilities during his endeavors to stop the encroachment of the Yellow Peril. At the same time, Fu Manchu develops a similar respect for the abilities of Smith and his associates who con-tinually foil his designs for world domination. The mixture of all-out war between them and their recognition of each other's capabilities heightens the sense of spectacle when the two meet.

On several occasions in the early novels, Smith attempts, and urges his cohorts to attempt, killing Fu Manchu; in ***The Insid-ious Doctor Fu Manchu***, from 1913, he screams at Petrie, "*It's Fu-Manchu!* Cover him! Shoot him dead if—" The sentence is cut off by the falling of a trapdoor beneath Petrie. However, Smith's attitude is entirely different in 1948, when Fu Manchu makes his escape at the end of ***The Shadow of Fu Manchu***. A colleague named Sam has fired three times after what he be-lieves to be Fu Manchu's fleeing form, despite orders from Smith to cease fire. "'You fool!' Nayland Smith's words came as a groan. 'This was no end for the greatest brain in the world!'" However, Sam has in fact only shot one of Fu Man-chu's servants dressed like his master. Fu Manchu's escape has merely allowed Smith to voice his change in attitude toward his adversary. In ***Re-enter Fu Manchu***, however, he expresses a doubt about this new consideration. At one point, Fu Manchu introduces a double for Smith into their intrigue; after the dou-ble is killed, the real Smith reports back to Fu Manchu, posing as his own double. He leaves without harming Fu Manchu, in order to convey his information about Fu Manchu's widespread plans to the authorities. He assumes that he will capture Fu Manchu when the plot as a whole is dismantled. At the end of the novel, when the plan has been foiled but Fu Manchu has escaped, Smith says, "I haven't settled down yet to the fact that that cunning fiend has escaped me again. In my crazy overconfidence I missed my chance. It was my duty to the world when I stood before him to shoot him. . . ." These changes, superficial and waffling, do not ultimately alter the depiction of Fu Manchu's image or character.

The four short works about Fu Manchu are a novelette, **"The Wrath of Fu Manchu"** (1952), the most significant, which appeared in the *Star Weekly* of Toronto; and three short stories, **"The Eyes of Fu Manchu"** (1957), **"The Word of Fu Man-chu"** (1958), and **"The Mind of Fu Manchu"** (1959), all of which appeared in *This Week* magazine. The last three are minor pieces relying on the reader's prior knowledge of Fu Manchu for their full impact. They were severely constrained by the length limitations of the magazine, and so utilize es-tablished parts of the Smith-Fu Manchu conflicts without ex-panding upon them. **"The Wrath of Fu Manchu"** is a much more ambitious tale involving Smith's personal infiltration of Fu Manchu's advisory council. While it adds little new material to the saga, it does contain greater suspense and characteriza-tion, including the final appearance of Fu Manchu's daughter, Fah Lo Suee.

Sax Rohmer altogether wrote fiction consisting of forty-one novels, eleven collections of short fiction, and many other uncollected short stories. Beyond those about Fu Manchu, few of these works involved the Chinese or the Yellow Peril. The novels *The Yellow Claw* (1915), set in London and Paris, and *Yüan Hee See Laughs,* set in London, involve mysteries sur-rounding Chinese mandarins in England. They never gained the popularity of the Fu Manchu stories, possibly because, appearing later, their crimes, techniques, and overall image seem to be mere spin-offs. While interesting, they seem weak compared to the image created in Fu Manchu.

*The Golden Scorpion* (1936) deals with Fu Manchu's secret organization, the Si-Fan, without including him or Nayland Smith. *Dope* (1919) and *Yellow Shadows* (1925) also involve crime in London's Chinatown, as do the short-story collections *Tales of Chinatown* (1922) and *Tales of East and West* (1932). In these stories, the emphasis is on the individual activities of Chinese criminals without the elements of science fiction or of maniacal mandarins in charge of worldwide organizations that help define the threat of Fu Manchu. Instead they are more mundane stories of crimes involving the Chinese in London. The contribution of these stories to the image of the Chinese is Rohmer's portrayal of all Chinatown inhabitants as morally depraved, dangerous, and degenerate. Similar figures appear in the Fu Manchu stories as the servants who actually commit the crimes he designs. None of these works approximate the popularity or impact of the Fu Manchu stories, but they can serve to illuminate further Sax Rohmer's vision of the Chinese. In this capacity, they confirm that his presentation of the moral nature of the Chinese in the West was consistent in his works throughout the many decades in which he wrote.

The greatest impact of Fu Manchu as a character derives from his function as a leader. Prior to his creation, the Chinese in the United States are pictured with variety in their scattered roles throughout the frontier, in their small hamlets, and in their Chinatowns. They are depicted as victims and rogues; they appear as servants, opium smokers, violent criminals, and passive laborers. Their evil characteristics are well established and dominate their image in American fiction during the last half of the nineteenth century. Yet, these characteristics are given to the Chinese as a group, without compelling charac-terization. Even Harte's memorable See Yup and Ah Fes are shown as representatives of the Chinese, not as outstanding personalities. The lack of powerful individual personalities among the Chinese is clearest in the stories of invasion, where the activity of the infiltrating Chinese is presented as the result of an inhumanly strict obedience to shadowy figures in China. When leaders do appear, such as Woltor's Prince Tsa, their function is primarily symbolic.

By contrast, Rohmer places Fu Manchu atop the Chinatown in London, which represents the Chinese communities in the American West to American readers. Fu Manchu's tools are those same scum of the Chinatown opium dens, rough water-fronts, secret societies, and heathen religions whom earlier American fiction has already made familiar. His methods not only utilize, but actually rely on, the secrecy for which the Chinese had become known to white observers in the United States from the time of Bret Harte. He is not a remote leader, however. Like Robert W. Chambers's Yue-Laou and Dr. Doyle's Quong Lung, he supervises his programs personally, lending a profound and powerful, if slightly mad, character of genius to the adventures. As the leader and focal point of Chinese people in Western Europe and North America, Fu Manchu draws upon the old established images of the Chinese for the minor villains who obey his will. Simultaneously, he increases the impact of their images by using these servants and his own scientific genius for carefully organized, large-scale programs. Their individual crimes and depravity grow in stature by becoming parts of an international whole.

In a sense, Fu Manchu fills a power vacuum that had existed in the tales of Chinese immigration and infiltration; with his presence as "the yellow peril incarnate," the evils of Chinatown are seen as a clearly intelligent malevolence rather than as either a random one, or an inevitable one. His character, like those of Sherlock Holmes, Tarzan, and Superman, becomes greater than any particular work of fiction in which he appears. By associating Fu Manchu with every evil aspect of the Chinese image that existed in the early twentieth century, Rohmer ensured that future Chinese villains would evoke memories of Fu Manchu for many years to come, in every wandering wisp of opium smoke, every fugitive trailing a queue, every dark, damp alley of Chinatown, and every sharp-taloned mandarin's silhouette. (pp. 164-74)

> *William F. Wu, "Fu Manchu and Charlie Chan," in his* The Yellow Peril: Chinese Americans in American Fiction 1850-1940, *Archon Books, 1982, pp. 164-84.*

---

## ADDITIONAL BIBLIOGRAPHY

Brien, Alan. "My Enemy's Enemies." *New Statesman* 109, No. 2827 (24 May 1985): 32.
Left-wing political perspective on Rohmer's fiction, observing that Rohmer was "a dedicated righty. Like almost all of his fellow entertainers, from Buchan to Sapper, routinely anti-Semitic, he never questioned the white Anglo-Saxon's right to rule anybody anywhere."

Carson, Anthony. "Yellow Peril." *New Statesman* 74, No. 1909 (13 October 1967): 475-76.
Review of *President Fu Manchu.* Carson observes: "Fu Manchu is a cardboard character, devoid of poetry, and imbued with the sentimental cruelty of Western guilt and pulp-fiction appetite."

"The Doctor's Blade." *New Yorker* (29 November 1947): 36-7.
Interview with Rohmer.

Perelman, S. J. "Cloudland Revisited: Why, Doctor, What Big Green Eyes You Have!" In his *The Ill-Tempered Clavichord*, pp. 37-48. New York: Simon and Schuster, 1952.
Discussion of *The Mystery of Dr. Fu-Manchu* that focuses on the lack of plot in the novel.

Shanks, Edward. "The Drama: A Shocker." *The Outlook* LII, No. 1335 (1 September 1923): 174.
Review of *The Eye of Siva.* While Shanks considers the play dramatically successful, he finds it flawed by too many improbabilities, concluding: "Mr. Rohmer might have made out of this a really first-rate shocker; but he has not taken the trouble."

Thomson, H. Douglas. "The Thriller." In his *Masters of Mystery*, pp. 212-37. London: W. Collins Sons & Co., 1978.
Brief discussion of the genre known as "Yellow Peril" fiction, concluding that Fu Manchu is the greatest Chinese villain ever portrayed.

# Gertrude Stein

## 1874-1946

American novelist, poet, essayist, autobiographer, and dramatist.

A controversial figure during her lifetime, Stein is now regarded as a major literary Modernist and one of the most influential writers of the twentieth century. Working against the naturalistic conventions of nineteenth-century fiction, she developed an abstract manner of expression that was a counterpart in language to the work of the Post-Impressionists and Cubists in the visual arts. Stein wrote prolifically in many genres, composing novels, poetry, plays, and literary portraits. Her radical approach to these forms was admired and emulated by other writers of her era, including Ernest Hemingway, Thornton Wilder, and Sherwood Anderson, and has served as a key inspiration for such Postmodernist writers as the French New Novelists and William H. Gass.

The youngest daughter of a wealthy Jewish-American family, Stein spent most of her childhood in Oakland, California. Biographers describe her mother as a weak, ineffectual woman, and her father as an irrational tyrant; a few have inferred that this family situation is the origin of Stein's lifelong aversion to patriarchal cultural values. Lacking a satisfactory relationship with her parents, she grew very close to her brother Leo. When Leo went to Harvard in 1892, she enrolled in the all-female Harvard Annex—soon to become Radcliffe—the following year. Radcliffe, and in particular her favorite professor there, the psychologist William James, proved a decisive influence on her intellectual development. Many of James's teachings, including his theories of perception and personality types, would inspire her own theories of literary aesthetics. With James's encouragement, Stein decided to become a psychologist, and began medical studies at Johns Hopkins University as part of her training. However, in 1902, after several years of study, she grew disaffected with medicine and left the university without completing her degree. In the months that followed, Stein devoted herself to the study of literary classics. Inspired by her reading, particularly the works of Gustave Flaubert and Henry James, she began to write her first novels.

In 1903, after travels in Europe and Africa, she and Leo settled in Paris, where they began to collect work by the new Modernist painters and became personally acquainted with many of them, including Paul Cézanne, Henri Matisse, and Pablo Picasso. The Steins' apartment at 27 rue de Fleurus became a salon where numerous artists and literary figures, such as Guillaume Apollinaire, Marie Laurencin, and Max Jacob, met regularly. Stein particularly enjoyed the company of Picasso, who in 1906 painted a portrait of her that would become one of his best-known works, and she greatly admired his artistic style, as well as that of such other painters as Cézanne and Juan Gris, who experimented in their works with ways of conveying a more profound and truthful vision of reality than that allowed by the naturalistic techniques of the nineteenth century. The Cubist painters broke a subject down to its essential geometric forms, then reassembled those forms in ways that offer the viewer startling new perceptions of the subject. This revolution in the visual arts encouraged Stein to formulate a literary aesthetic that would, similarly, violate existing formal conventions

in order to allow the reader to experience language and ideas in provocative new ways. Leo, however, who was not enthusiastic about Cubist painting, responded to his sister's work with scorn, causing her anxiety and self-doubt. Stein found a much more appreciative audience in her friend Alice Toklas, a young woman from California who was staying in Paris. In 1909 Stein invited Toklas to live with her, and the women developed a close and affectionate relationship that Stein referred to as a marriage; they remained together for the rest of their lives. Toklas was not only Stein's devoted friend and lover but a vital part of her literary work, helping her to prepare manuscripts and providing her with much-needed encouragement. Because commercial publishers initially rejected her work, Stein was forced to subsidize the printing of her first books. However, many of her distinguished and influential friends, most notably art patron Mabel Dodge, critic Carl Van Vechten, and poet Edith Sitwell, admired and promoted her writings, and by the outbreak of World War I she was regarded as a central figure in the Modernist movement.

Stein remained in Paris for most of the war, winning commendation for her volunteer work as a medical supply driver and befriending many American servicemen. After the war, she became the friend and mentor of a number of young writers from the United States, notably Ernest Hemingway. She encouraged his early attempts at writing fiction; he, in turn, was instrumental in arranging for the publication of Stein's epic novel *The Making of Americans*. As an epigraph to his 1926 novel *The Sun Also Rises*, Hemingway quoted Stein's remark, "You are all a lost generation," which came to refer to Hemingway, F. Scott Fitzgerald, and other young American writers gathered in Paris during the 1920s. At this time Stein was as well known for her many friendships with talented, wealthy, and famous persons as for her innovative literary work. At a publisher's urging, she wrote a memoir, *The Autobiography of Alice B. Toklas,* which became a bestseller and made her an international celebrity. Stein at first feared that personal notoriety might spoil her as an artist. As it happened, however, she used the publicity to her advantage, especially in a series of lectures she delivered at American universities in 1934. Explaining her literary theories not only increased her confidence in and understanding of her own methods, but also provided readers and scholars with valuable keys for interpreting her work.

During World War II, Stein and Toklas remained in Nazi-occupied France. As Jews, both women were at risk of being deported to concentration camps, but they were protected from the Nazis by collaborationist friends such as the French scholar Bernard Faÿ. After the liberation of Paris, Stein was once again visited by many admiring American soldiers. She maintained an active social and literary life until her death, in 1946, from cancer. In a famous anecdote from her autobiography *What Is Remembered,* Toklas recalled a conversation she had with Stein just before her death. "She said to me early in the afternoon, What is the answer? I was silent. In that case, she said, what is the question?"

Some commentators, including Stein herself, divide her career into three phases: early, middle, and late. Her early works, according to critics, are among her most accessible. Her first novel, *Q.E.D.,* written in 1903, is an apparently autobiographical study of a young woman's unhappy relationship with a fickle female lover. Because of its taboo subject matter, the novel was not published until after Stein's death. Her next major work, *Three Lives,* consists of three novella-length stories concerning the lives of ordinary women: "The Good Anna" and "The Gentle Lena," about two German-American servants, and "Melanctha," which, commentators note, is essentially a reworking of the love story in *Q.E.D.,* this time presenting it as a heterosexual affair between two black characters. Although critics now recognize "Melanctha" as an inaccurate, stereotyped depiction of black American life, it was virtually unprecedented as a serious attempt by a white author to portray realistic black characters. Both *Q.E.D.* and *Three Lives,* although relatively conventional, contain some traces of Stein's later, experimental style, such as minimal punctuation, lack of emphasis on plot, and the depiction of characters as psychological types rather than as unique individuals.

Stein regarded *The Making of Americans,* the 925-page epic novel that initiated the next phase in her career, as her masterpiece, a revolutionary work on the scale of James Joyce's *Ulysses* (1922) or Marcel Proust's *À la recherche du temps perdu* (1913-27; *Remembrance of Things Past*). Stein's approach to the psychology of her characters became even more abstract and clinical in this novel, which she intended to illustrate personality types, revealing the "bottom nature," or essential type, of individuals by depicting their patterns of behavior. In addition to its psychological plan, *The Making of Americans* is an autobiographical work which chronicles the lives of three generations of the Herslands, a German-American family modeled after the Steins. The text also contains numerous digressions in which Stein records her thoughts, often anxious and doubtful, about the process of writing *The Making of Americans.* In other works, such as her literary portraits of Picasso and Mabel Dodge, she further developed her characteristic middle style: long sentences made up of simple words and repeated phrases, stripped of subordinate clauses and of all punctuation except periods. Because many of Stein's prose works of this period are written in this dense, ruminative style, with little conventional narrative continuity to sustain reader interest, many critics have pronounced them virtually unreadable.

Stein developed her avant-garde style one step further in *Tender Buttons,* a collection of prose poems. Presented in three sections, "Objects," "Food," and "Rooms," the poems are written in language not meant to evoke emotional or intellectual associations in readers, but to focus their attention on the things described and on the language of the poem itself. While many supporters of Modernism hailed *Tender Buttons* as a brilliant achievement, others derided it as incomprehensible. Some critics compared the hermetic style of these poems to the deliberate absurdities of the Dadaists or to the experiments in automatic writing conducted by the Surrealists. In fact, Stein disliked the deliberate irrationality of Dadaism; although her writings are often frustratingly complex or obscure, they are never purely nonsensical. Stein used psychological theory as a basis for her writings, as did the Surrealists, but she was interested in the dynamics of the conscious mind, not the subconscious. The writings of her middle period reflect theories of consciousness that she learned from William James at Radcliffe. According to James, the individual perceives the world not in discrete temporal segments of past, present, and future, but as a continuous awareness of the moment being presently lived. In her long, static narratives, Stein sought to evoke this atemporal sense of a continuous present. In her *Geographical History of America,* she explains this concept in detail. She divides the conscious self into two parts: human nature and human mind. Human nature governs spoken language, identity, memory, and awareness of time; "I am I because my little dog knows me" is an attitude of human nature. Human mind, conversely, embodies the essential nature of the individual, the awareness of the continuous present.

Throughout the 1920s, Stein continued to develop and implement her theories. Her writings became less accessible to readers, not only because of the increasingly complex intellectual plans behind their composition but also because Stein used so many words and phrases that had meanings only she or close friends could understand. Her poem "Lifting Belly," for instance, while not at all explicit, has been interpreted as an erotic love poem filled with private references to her relationship with Toklas. By this time, the anxiety expressed in Stein's early writings had given way to a mood of serenity, good humor, and confidence. Many of her writings of this era, such as *Lucy Church Amiably,* reflect the pleasant domestic life she shared with Toklas. Stein characterized *Lucy Church Amiably* as a "landscape"; while this particular work is, literally, a description of the scenic area in southern France where she and Toklas spent their summers, she also used the term metaphorically to refer to some of her plays, such as *Four Saints in Three Acts.* Stein's landscape plays, like the prose of her middle period, depict the relations between static elements in a static situation, rather than focusing on plot progression or character development. Composer Virgil Thomson, intrigued by the nonrepresentational, musical quality of Stein's language, adapted *Four Saints* as a successful opera. Stein later collaborated with Thomson on *The Mother of Us All*, an opera based on the life of feminist Susan B. Anthony.

With *The Autobiography of Alice B. Toklas*, Stein proved to her critics that she was capable of writing a relatively conventional, commercially successful work. While most reviewers were charmed by the autobiography's wit and engaging conversational style, not all were pleased. A group of Stein's friends from the art world, including Tristan Tzara and Henri Matisse, published "Testimony against Gertrude Stein," in which they condemned the *Autobiography* as a shallow, distorted portrayal of their lives and work. "Miss Stein understood nothing of what went on around her," protested painter Georges Braque. Stein nevertheless followed the popular success of the *Autobiography* with other memoirs, *Everybody's Autobiography* and *Wars I Have Seen*. She also published her *Lectures in America* and *Narration*, theoretical writings which have proved invaluable to students of her work in explaining her often esoteric style. While she continued to write such avant-garde narratives as the novels *Ida* and *Mrs. Reynolds*, her last works reflect an awareness of current social and political realities absent from the introspective writings of her early and middle period. Her play *Yes Is For a Very Young Man*, for instance, deals with the French Resistance movement, while *Brewsie and Willie*, a set of fictional dialogues between American soldiers and nurses, deals with the atomic bomb and other issues relevant to the post-World War II era.

From the time she started to publish her writings, Stein has proved a challenge to critics. Because much of her work violates basic formal and thematic conventions, certain interpretative methods, such as the close textual analysis practiced by the New Critics, are of no use in approaching her writings. It is partly for this reason that much of the commentary on Stein from 1910 through the 1950s is evaluative rather than interpretative, either arguing her merits, as does Carl Van Vechten, or deriding her, in the case of Wyndham Lewis and B. L. Reid. The linguistically based critical methods of structuralism and deconstruction that emerged in the 1960s and 1970s offered readers of Stein a critical method better suited to understanding her work as she had conceived it. Feminist critics have also provided a fresh perspective on Stein, discussing such issues as Stein's treatment of sexuality and her defiance of patriarchal literary traditions. An additional topic often raised by commentators is Stein's relation to the Post-Impressionists and Cubists. As with other Modernists, such as Cézanne and Picasso, Stein was at first attacked by those who did not accept the validity of her artistic methods. However, as her innovations became institutionalized by succeeding generations of writers, such attacks have given way to more temperate discussions of her work. Although critics acknowledge her as one of the leading literary Modernists, her often cryptic style has made her works less accessible than those of her contemporaries Joyce and Virginia Woolf; her true worth as an artist, many commentators note, has been felt more strongly in her influence on other writers than in the appreciation of her works for their own sake. "I think it can be said," observes Thornton Wilder, "that the fundamental occupation of Miss Stein's life was not the work of art but the shaping of a theory of knowledge, a theory of time, and a theory of the passions."

(See also *TCLC*, Vols. 1 and 6; *Contemporary Authors*, Vol. 104; *Dictionary of Literary Biography*, Vol. 4: *American Writers in Paris, 1920-1939* and Vol. 54: *American Poets, 1880-1945*.)

## PRINCIPAL WORKS

*Three Lives* (novellas) 1909
*Tender Buttons* (poetry) 1914
*Geography and Plays* (dramas and prose) 1922
*\*The Making of Americans: Being a History of a Family's Progress* (novel) 1925; also published as *The Making of Americans: The Hersland Family* [abridged edition], 1934
*Composition as Explanation* (essay) 1926
*Lucy Church Amiably* (prose) 1930
*How to Write* (prose) 1931
*Operas and Plays* (dramas) 1932
*The Autobiography of Alice B. Toklas* (autobiography) 1933
*Matisse, Picasso, and Gertrude Stein with Two Shorter Stories* (portraits) 1933
*Four Saints in Three Acts* (drama) 1934
*Lectures in America* (lectures) 1935
*Narration* (lectures) 1935
*The Geographical History of America; or, The Relation of Human Nature to the Human Mind* (prose) 1936
*Everybody's Autobiography* (autobiography) 1937
*Ida* (novel) 1941
*Wars I Have Seen* (prose) 1945
*Brewsie and Willie* (prose) 1946
*Four in America* (prose) 1947
*The Mother of Us All* (libretto) 1947
*Last Operas and Plays* (prose, dramas, and librettos) 1949
*†Things as They Are* (novel) 1950; also published as *Q.E.D.*, 1971
*The Yale Edition of the Unpublished Writings of Gertrude Stein*. 8 vols. (novels, poetry, and novellas) 1951-58

*This work was written between 1903 and 1911.

†This work was written in 1903.

---

### CARL VAN VECHTEN (essay date 1914)

[*Van Vechten, an American critic, novelist, and essayist, began his career as a music and drama critic for the* New York Times. *During the 1920s he wrote several novels, including* Peter Whiffle *(1922) and* The Blind Bow-Boy *(1923), that display his urbane wit and appreciation for the arts. A friend of Stein, he was editor of the Yale series of her previously unpublished works issued after her death. In the following excerpt from an essay originally published in 1914, Van Vechten praises the freshness and sensuous appeal of Stein's language and offers brief assessments of* Three Lives, The Portrait of Mabel Dodge, *and* Tender Buttons.]

The English language is a language of hypocrisy and evasion. How not to say a thing has been the problem of our writers from the earliest times. The extraordinary fluidity and even naivete of French makes it possible for a writer in that language to babble like a child; de Maupassant is only possible in French, a language in which the phrase, "Je t'aime" means everything. But what does "I love you" mean in English? Donald Evans, of our poets, has realized this peculiar quality of English and he is almost the first of the poets in English to say unsuspected and revolting things, because he so cleverly avoids saying them.

Miss Stein discovered the method before Mr. Evans. In fact his Patagonian Sonnets were an offshoot of her later manner, just as Miss Kenton's superb story, "Nicknames," derives its style from Miss Stein's **Three Lives**. She has really turned language into music, really made its sound more important than its sense. And she has suggested to the reader a thousand channels for his mind and sense to drift along, a thousand, instead of a stupid only one.

Miss Stein has no explanations to offer regarding her work. I have often questioned her, but I have met with no satisfaction. She asks you to read. Her intimate connection with the studies of William James have been commented upon; some say that the "fringe of thought," so frequently referred to by that writer, may dominate her working consciousness. Her method of work is unique. She usually writes in the morning, and she sets down the words as they come from her pen; they bubble, they flow; they surge through her brain and she sets them down. You may regard them as nonsense, but the fact remains that effective imitations of her style do not exist. John Reed tells me that, while he finds her stimulating and interesting, an entity, he feels compelled to regard her work as an offshoot, something that will not be concluded by followers. She lives and dies alone, a unique example of a strange art. (p. 34)

In **Three Lives** Miss Stein attained at a bound an amount of literary facility which a writer might strive in vain for years to acquire. Simplicity is a quality one is born with, so far as literary style is concerned, and Miss Stein was born with that. But to it she added, in this work, a vivid note of reiteration, a fascinatingly complete sense of psychology and the workings of minds one on the other, which at least in **"Melanctha: Each as She May"** reaches a state of perfection which might have satisfied such masters of craft as Turgenev, or Balzac, or Henry James. . . .

To those who know Mrs. Dodge [her portrait in **The Portrait of Mabel Dodge**] may seem to be a true one; it has intention, that is even obvious to those who do not know what the intention is. There is nothing faint or pale about Miss Stein's authority. It is as complete in its way as the authority of Milton. You may not like the words, but you are forced to admit, after, perhaps, a struggle that no other words will do. (p. 36)

There are several theories extant relating to **Tender Buttons**. I may say that one I upheld stoutly for a few hours, that the entire book had a physical application, I have since rejected, at least in part. The three divisions which comprise the book in a way explain the title. They are "Food; Objects; Rooms," all things which fasten our lives together, and whose complications may be said to make them "tender."

The majestic rhythm of the prose in this book; the virtuosity with which Miss Stein intertwines her words, are qualities which strike the ear at once. And **Tender Buttons** benefits by reading aloud. Onomatopœa, sound echoing sense, is a favorite figure of speech with Miss Stein; so is alliteration which is fatally fascinating when mingled with reiteration, and Miss Stein drops repeated words upon your brain with the effect of Chopin's B minor prelude, which is popularly supposed to represent the raindrops falling on the roof at Majorka on one of those George Sand days.

The mere sensuous effect of the words is irresistible and often as in the section labelled, **"Eating,"** or **"A Seltzer Bottle,"** the mere pronunciation of the words gives the effect of the act or the article. On the other hand, **"A Little Called Pauline"** seems to me perfect in the way of a pretty description, a Jap-

anese print of a charming creature. **"Suppose an Eyes"** is similarly a picture, but more postery.

It would seem to me that the inspiration offered to writers in this book was an enormous incentive to read it. What writer after reading **Tender Buttons** but would strive for a fresher phrase, a more perfect rhythmic prose? Gertrude Stein to me is one of the supreme stylists.

In case one is not delighted, amused, or appealed to in any way by the sensuous charm of her art then, of course, there is the sense to fall back on; the ideas expressed. Here one floats about vaguely for a key to describe how to tell what Miss Stein means. Her vagueness is innate and one of her most positive qualities. I have already said how much she adds to language by it. You may get the idea of it if you close your eyes and imagine yourself awaking from the influence of ether, as you gasp to recall some words and ideas, while new ones surge into your brain. A certain sleepy consciousness. Or you may read sense through the fingers as they flit rapidly—almost word by word—through your brain. It is worthy of note that almost everyone tries to make sense out of Miss Stein just as everyone insists on making photographs out of drawings by Picabia, when the essential of his art is that he is getting away from the photographic. (p. 37)

*Carl Van Vechten, "How to Read Gertrude Stein,"* in Critical Essays on Gertrude Stein, *edited by Michael J. Hoffman, G. K. Hall & Co., 1986, pp. 34-7.*

## LAURA RIDING AND ROBERT GRAVES (essay date 1927)

[*Riding is an American critic, essayist, novelist, and poet. Graves was a prolific English man of letters who is considered one of the most accomplished minor poets of the twentieth century. Although his subject matter is traditional, he is credited with ingenious structural and linguistic experimentation. In addition to his achievements in verse and other creative genres, notably the historical novel* I, Claudius *(1934), Graves is equally esteemed for his theoretical and critical works. Riding and Graves together ran the Seizin Press, which in 1926 published Stein's* An Acquaintance with Description; *they are also the co-authors of* A Survey of Modernist Poetry. *In the following excerpt from the conclusion to that work, Riding and Graves comment on what they consider Stein's literary "barbarism" as reflected in her approach to language and composition.*]

The modernist poet . . . has an exaggerated preoccupation with criticism. He has a professional conscience forced on him by the encroachments and pressure of new period activities; and this is understandable. When the prestige of any organization is curtailed—the army or navy for example—a greater internal discipline, morality and study of tactics results, a greater sophistication and up-to-date-ness. In poetry this discipline means the avoidance of all the wrongly-conceived habits and tactics of the past: poetry becomes so sophisticated that it seems to know at last how it should be written and written at the very moment. The more definitely activities like religion, science, psychology and philosophy, which once existed in poetry as loose sentiment, are specialized and confined to their proper departmental technique, the more pure and sharp the technique of poetry itself seems bound to become. It ceases to be civilized in the sense of becoming more and more cultured with loose sentiment; everything in it is particular and strict. It is, indeed, as if poetry were beginning as at the beginning; using all its civilized sophistications to inaugurate a carefully calculated, censored primitiveness. (pp. 262-63)

Gertrude Stein is perhaps the only artisan of language who has ever succeeded in practising scientific barbarism literally. Her words are primitive in the sense that they are bare, immobile, mathematically placed, abstract: so primitive indeed that the theorists of the new barbarism have repudiated her work as a romantic vulgar barbarism, expressing the personal crudeness of a mechanical age rather than a refined historical effort to restore a lost absolute to a community of co-ordinated poets. Mr. Eliot has said of her work that "it is not improving, it is not amusing, it is not interesting, it is not good for one's mind. But its rhythms have a peculiar hypnotic power not met with before. It has a kinship with the saxophone. If this is the future then the future is, as it very likely is, of the barbarians. But this is the future in which we ought not to be interested." Mr. Eliot was for the moment speaking for civilization. He was obliged to do this because it seemed suddenly impossible to reconcile the philosophy of the new barbarism with the historical state of the poetic mind and with the professional dignity of poetry which the new barbarism was invented to restore: a sincere attempt to do so was at once crude and obscure like the work of Miss Stein. Except for such whole-hog literalness as hers, professional modernist poetry has lacked the co-ordination which professional modernist criticism implies: and this contradiction between criticism and workmanship makes it incoherent. It has been too busy being civilized, varied, intellectual—too socially and poetically energetic—to take advantage of the privileged consistency of the new barbarism. (pp. 274-75)

[While] a philosophical tangle was forcing modernist poets into an unwitting romanticism, Gertrude Stein went on—and kept going on for twenty years—quietly, patiently and successfully practising an authentic barbarism; quite by herself and without encouragement. Her only fault, from the practical point of view, was that she took primitiveness too literally, so literally that she made herself incomprehensible to the exponents of primitivism—to everyone for that matter. She exercised perfect discipline over her creative faculties and she was able to do this because she was completely without originality. Everybody being unable to understand her thought that this was because she was too original or was trying hard to be original. But she was only divinely inspired in ordinariness: her creative originality, that is, was original only because it was so grossly, so humanly, all-inclusively ordinary. She used language automatically to record pure ultimate obviousness. She made it capable of direct communication not by caricaturing contemporary language—attacking decadence with decadence—but by purging it completely of its false experiences. None of the words Miss Stein uses ever had experience. They are no older than the use she makes of them, and she has been herself no older than her age conceived barbarically.

> Put it there in there where they have it
> Put it there in there there and they halve it
> Put it there in there there and they have it
> Put it there in there there and they halve it

These words have had no history, and the design that Miss Stein has made of them is literally "abstract" and mathematical because they are commonplace words without any hidden etymology; they are mechanical and not eccentric. If they possess originality it is that of mass-automatism.

Miss Stein in her *Composition as Explanation* has written:

> Nothing changes from generation to generation except the thing seen, and that makes a composition.

Her admission that there are generations does not contradict her belief in an unvarying first principle. Time does not vary, only the sense of time.

> Automatically with the acceptance of the time-sense comes the recognition of the beauty, and once the beauty is accepted the beauty never fails anyone.

Beauty has no history, according to Miss Stein, nor has time: only the time-sense has history. When the time-sense acclaims a beauty that was not at first recognized, the finality of this beauty is at once established; it is as though it had never been denied. All beauty is equally final. The reason why the time-sense if realized reveals the finality or classicalness of beauty, is that it is the feeling of beginning, of primitiveness and freshness which is each age's or each generation's version of time.

> Beginning again and again and again explaining composition and time is a natural thing. It is understood by this time that everything is the same except composition and time, composition and the time of the composition and the time in the composition.

Orginality of vision, then, is invented, she holds, not by the artist but by the collective time-sense. The artist does not see things "as no one else sees them." He sees those objective "things" by which the age repeatedly verifies and represents the absolute. He sees concretely and expressibly what everyone else possessed of the time-sense has an unexpressed intuition of: the time-sense may not be generally and particularly universal; but this does not mean that the artist's vision, even his originality of vision, is less collective or less universal.

> The composition is the thing seen by everyone living in the living they are doing, they are the composing of the composition that at the time they are living is the composition of the time in which they are living. It is that that makes living a thing they are doing. Nothing else is different, of that almost anyone can be certain. The time when and the time of and the time in that composition is the natural phenomena of that composition and of that perhaps everyone can be certain.

All this Gertrude Stein has understood and executed logically because of the perfect simplicity of her mind. Believing implicitly in an absolute, she has not been bothered to doubt the bodily presence of a first principle in her own time. Since she is alive and everybody around her seems to be alive, of course there is an acting first principle, there is composition. This first principle provides a theme for composition because there is time, and everybody, and the beginning again and again and again, and composition. In her primitive good-humour she has not found it necessary to trouble about defining the theme. The theme is to be inferred from the composition. The composition is clear because the language means nothing but what it means through her using of it. The composition is final because it is "a more and more continuous present including more and more using of everything and continuing more and more beginning and beginning and beginning." She creates this atmosphere of continuousness principally by her progressive use of the tenses of verbs, by intense and unflagging repetitiousness and an artificially assumed and regulated child-mentality: the child's time-sense is so vivid that an occurrence is always consecutive to itself, it goes on and on, it has been going on and on, it will be going on and on (a child does perhaps feel the passage of time, does to a certain extent feel itself older than it was yesterday because yesterday was already to-morrow even while it was yesterday). (pp. 280-84)

Repetition has the effect of breaking down the possible historical senses still inherent in the words. So has the infantile jingle of rhyme and assonance. So has the tense-changing of verbs, because restoring to them their significance as a verbal mathematics of motion. Miss Stein's persistence in her own continuousness is astonishing: this is how she wrote in 1926, and in 1906. She has achieved a continuous present by always beginning again, for this keeps everything different and everything the same. It creates duration but makes it absolute by preventing anything from happening in the duration.

> And after that what changes what changes after that,
> after that what changes and what changes after that
> and after that and what changes and after that and
> what changes after that.

The composition has a theme because it has no theme. The words are a self-pursuing, tail-swallowing series and are thus thoroughly abstract. They achieve what Hulme called but could not properly envisage—not being acquainted, it seems, with Miss Stein's work—a "perpendicular," an escape from the human horizontal plane. They contain no reference; no meaning, no caricatures, no jokes, no despairs. They are ideally automatic, creating one another. The only possible explanation of lines like the following is that one word or combination of words creates the next.

> Anyhow means furls furls with a chance chance with
> a change change with as strong strong with as will

*Stein in her student years.*

will with as sign sign with as west west with as most most with as in in with as by by with as change change with as reason reason to be lest lest they did when when they did for for they did there and then. Then does not celebrate the there and then.

This is repetition and continuousness and beginning again and again and again.

Nothing that we have said here should be understood as disrespectful to Gertrude Stein. She has had courage, clarity, sincerity, simplicity. She has created a human mean in language, a mathematical equation of ordinariness which leaves one with a tender respect for that changing and unchanging slowness that is humanity and Gertrude Stein. (pp. 285-87)

> *Laura Riding and Robert Graves, "Conclusion," in*
> *their* A Survey of Modernist Poetry, *William Hei-*
> *nemann Ltd., 1927, pp. 258-91.*

### WYNDHAM LEWIS (essay date 1928)

[*Lewis was an English novelist who, with T. S. Eliot, Ezra Pound, and T. E. Hulme, was instrumental in establishing the anti-Romantic movement in literature during the first decades of the twentieth century. He also emerged as a leader of the Vorticist movement, founded by Pound. Although its principles are vague, critical consensus holds that Vorticism is related to Imagism in poetry and to Cubism in painting, and that one of its primary characteristics is a belief in the total impersonality of art, achieved by fragmenting and reordering the elements of experience into a new and more meaningful existence. Lewis's savage, satiric fiction has been compared to the work of Jonathan Swift and Alexander Pope. His best-known novel,* The Apes of God *(1930), is a long and aggressive satire on the cultural life of England in the 1920s. Some critics believe he will eventually be ranked with Eliot, Pound, and James Joyce as one of the most fascinating, controversial, and influential writers of the early twentieth century. In the following excerpt from his* Time and Western Man, *which uses examples from the works of Stein and other artists and writers to illustrate philosophical concepts of time, Lewis decries her work for what he considers its feigned naivete and "deadness."*]

*In the beginning was the Word* should rather be, *in the beginning was Time,* according to Miss Stein (as also according to Bergson, Prof. Alexander, Einstein, Whitehead, Minkowski, etc. etc.). And she is one of the most eminent writers of what I have described as our *musical society;* that is our time-society, the highly-intellectualized High-Bohemia.

> In the beginning there was the time in the composition
> that naturally was in the composition but time in the
> composition comes now and this is what is now trou-
> bling every one the time in the composition is now
> a part of distribution and equilibration.

In Miss Stein's composition there is above all *time,* she tells us as best she can. As best she can, as you see; for she is not able to tell us this or anything else clearly and simply; first of all because a time-obsession, it seems, interferes, so we are given to understand. The other reason is that she is not simple at all, although she writes usually so like a child—like a confused, stammering, rather "soft" (bloated, acromegalic, squinting and spectacled, one can figure it as) child. Miss Stein you might innocently suppose from her naïf stuttering to be, if not a child, simple, at least, in spite of maturity. But that is not so; though, strangely enough, she would like it to be thought that it is. That is only the old story of people wanting to be things they are not; or else, either as strategy or out of pure caprice, enjoying any disguise that reverses and contradicts the personality. (p. 49)

In [*Composition as Explanation*] you have the announcement that "The time of the composition is the time of the composition." But simple as that sounds, it is only roguishness on the part of its authoress, all the while. That is her fun only. She is just pretending, with a face of solemn humbug, not to be able to get out the word; what this verbal inhibition results in is something *funny*, that will make you laugh. It is a form of clowning, in short; she will disarm and capture you by her absurdity.

But *Time,* you are told, is at the bottom of the matter; though that you could have guessed, since it has been so for a very long time, from beginning of the present period; from the birth of Bergson, shall we say? (Bergson was supposed by all of us to be dead, but Relativity, oddly enough at first sight, has recently resuscitated him; for the *time-spacer* has turned out to be the old-timer, or timist, after all.)

Miss Stein announces her time-doctrine in character, as it were. She gives you an "explanation" and illustrations, side by side; but the explanation is done in the same way as the examples that follow it. A further "explanation" would be required of the "explanation," and so on. And in that little, perhaps unregarded, fact, we have, I believe, one of the clues to this writer's mind. It tells us that her mind is a sham, to some extent.

In doing her "explanation" of her compositions in the same manner as her compositions (examples of which she gives), she is definitely making-believe that it is impossible for her to write in any other way. She is making a claim, in fact, that suggests a lack of candour on her part; and she is making it with an air of exaggerated candour. Supposing that the following line represented a typical composition of yours:—

FugfuggFFF-fewg:fugfug-Fug-fugue-fffffffuuuuuuG

Supposing, having become celebrated for that, you responded to a desire on the part of the public to know what you were driving at. Then the public would be justified in estimating your sincerity of a higher order if you sat down and tried to "explain" according to the canons of plain speech (no doubt employed by you in ordering your dinner, or telling the neighbouring newsagent to send you the *Herald, Tribune,* or *Daily Express* every morning), your verbal experiments, than if you affected to be unable to use that kind of speech at all.

Every painter who has experimented in abstract design, for example, has often been put into that situation; he must often have been asked the familiar question: "But do you really *see* things like that, Mr. So-and-So?" Were Miss Stein that painter, we know now what would happen. She would roll her eyes, squint, point in a frenzy at some object, and, of course, stammer hard. She would play up to the popular ignorance as to the processes by which her picture had been arrived at, in short. She would answer "in character," implying that she was cut off from the rest of the world entirely by an exclusive and peculiar sensibility. Yet every one knows who engages in experiments of any sort, verbal or pictorial, that that is not at all the point of the matter. It is a *deliberate* adjustment of things to some formula which transforms what is treated into an organism, strange according to the human norm, though it might appear normal enough to the senses of some other animal. Normal speech, or normal vision, are not interfered with, on the one hand; nor does what in the result has an abnormal appearance arise *literally* in an abnormal experience, or an experience without a normal, non-visionary, basis.

For these reasons Miss Stein's illustrations would have been much more impressive if she had not pretended, to start with, that, as to the explanation, she "could not do it in any other way." In this fact, that "explanation" and "composition" are both done in the same stuttering dialect, you have the proof that you are in the presence of a *faux-naïf*, not the real article. Miss Stein's merits elsewhere are not cancelled by this—people are often gifted without being able to lay any claim to being "sincere," as we say. But it is a little difficult to understand how she could be so stupid. Her assumption that any advantage was to be gained by this studied obscurity, where it was, after all, pointless, is that. Perhaps, however, it was only conceit.

Should my ensuing remarks sting Miss Stein into a rejoinder, then I think you would see something like the situation that would be created if some beggar shamming blindness observed a person about to disappear with his offertory box. The "blind" under such conditions would *see* at once, and rush after the robber. It is the classic test case in the everyday world of everyday sham. I am afraid, however, that Miss Stein is too cunning a stammerer to be so easily unmasked. Miss Stein's stutter in her *explanation* even of her other celebrated stutterings, is a proof, then, to my mind, that she is a homologue of the false-blind; that, in some measure, she is a sham.

Still, what we can retain from that little affected treatise, is that *Time* is at the bottom of her mind, the treasured key to her technical experiments. And so she is working in the strictest conformity with all the other "time"-doctrinaires, who have gathered in such disciplined numbers, so fanatically disciplined, as though to the beating of a ritualistic drum.

With a trick like Miss Stein's, every one, I think, should have to pay a fee for using it. It is quite certain that it would never have occurred to most of those who use it more or less, like the editor of the *Q.*, for instance, without the promptings of the jazz-sibyl. This habit of speech, like a stuttering infection, is very contagious. Mr. Joyce even has caught it, and, one of the most pedagogically careful of men, has thrown overboard a great deal of laboriously collected cargo, and romps along at the head of the fashionable literary world, hand in hand with Gertrude Stein, both outdoing all children in jolly quaintnesses. (pp. 49-52)

• • • • •

It is in a thick, monotonous prose-song that Miss Stein characteristically expresses her fatigue, her energy, and the bitter fatalism of her nature. Her stories are very often long—all the longer, too, because everything has to be repeated half a dozen times over. In the end the most wearisome dirge it is possible to imagine results, as slab after slab of this heavy, insensitive, common prose-song churns and lumbers by.

To an Antheil tempest of jazz it is the entire body that responds, after all. The executant tires; its duration does not exceed ten minutes or so, consecutively. But it is *the tongue*—only the poor, worried, hard-worked tongue—inside the reader's head, or his laryngeal apparatus, that responds to the prose-song of Miss Stein.

At present I am referring to what I have read of Miss Stein at the *Three Lives* stage of her technical evolution. What is the matter with it is, probably, that it is so *dead*. Gertrude Stein's prose-song is a cold, black suet-pudding. We can represent it as a cold suet-roll of fabulously-reptilian length. Cut it at any point, it is the same thing; the same heavy, sticky, opaque mass all through, and all along. It is weighted, projected, with a sibylline urge. It is mournful and monstrous, composed of dead and inanimate material. It is all fat, without nerve. Or the evident vitality that informs it is vegetable rather than animal. Its life is a low-grade, if tenacious, one; of the sausage, by-the-yard, variety.

That is one aspect of the question, the technical one. There is another which has a certain reference to [political ideology]. . . . In adopting the simplicity, the illiterateness, of the mass-average of the Melancthas and Annas, Miss Stein gives proof of all the false "revolutionary," propagandist *plainmanism* of her time. The monstrous, desperate, soggy *lengths* of primitive mass-life, chopped off and presented to us as a never-ending prose-song, are undoubtedly intended as an epic contribution to the present mass-democracy. The texture of the language has to be jumbled, cheap, slangy and thick to suit. It must be written in a slovenly, straight-off fashion, so that it may appear to be more "real." Only the metre of an obsessing *time* has to be put into it. It has to be rhythmatized; and this proclivity both of Miss Stein, and of all the characteristic fashions of those for whom she writes, destroys the "reality" at least, giving to the life it patronizes the mechanical bias of its creator.

Next we will take up the fashionable child-factor as it is found in the work of Miss Stein, and in most art to-day, from Sir James Barrie to Charlie Chaplin. Her latest book, a vast one, I hear, I have not read. But many slighter, or at least shorter, more recent pieces, I know. In these, where she is not personifying a negress or some small American bourgeoise, but playing her own personal literary game (she may be described as the reverse of Patience sitting on a monument—she appears, that is, as a Monument sitting upon patience), this capable, colossal authoress relapses into the rôle and mental habits of childhood. Fact is thrown to the winds; the irresponsible, lighthearted madness of ignorance is wooed, and the full-fledged *Child* emerges. This child (often an idiot-child as it happens, but none the less sweet to itself for that) throws big, heavy words up and catches them; or letting them slip through its fingers, they break in pieces; and down it squats with a grunt, and begins sticking them together again. Else this far-too-intellectual infant chases the chosen word, like a moth, through many pages, worrying the delicate life out of it. The larynx and tongue of the reader meantime suffer acutely. Every word uttered threatens to obsess and stick to his tongue. Having come, wrongly spelt, wrongly pronounced, or wrongly according to usage, it refuses to move till it has been put right; yet will not come right in Miss Stein's hands.

It is in these occasional pieces that the *child-personality* of Miss Stein is discovered in its acutest form. But *the child* with her is always overshadowed by the imbecile. That is to say, that very clever, very resourceful Gertrude Stein is heavily indebted to the poor honest lunatic for her mannerisms. All the regions between the dull stupor of complete imbecility— which is splendidly portrayed in Picasso's pneumatic giantesses—and the relatively disciplined, alert, fixed condition, which is humanly regarded as the other pole to imbecility, she has thoroughly explored. The massive silence of the full idiot is, unfortunately, out of her reach, of course. In her capacity of writer, or word-knitter, she has to stop short of that, and leave it to her friend Picasso. For words, idle words, have one terrible limitation—they must represent human speech in some form. The silent canvas is their master there.

That, very briefly, is Miss Stein's rôle in the child-cult, and the kindred one (Freud-inspired or not) of *the demented*. She is herself a robust intelligence, a colossus among the practitioners of infancy; a huge, lowering, dogmatic Child. (pp. 61-3)

My general objection, then, to the work of Miss Stein is that it is *dead*. My second objection is that it is *romantic*. As to the latter count, for all its force I feel it to be *unreal* in the same way that I feel Conrad or Zola to be, but without the rationale of the fictionist. It is the personal rhythm, the obvious bias, that of a peculiar rather than a universal nature, that produces this sensation. The dull frantic vitality of Zola is that of an inferior, a brutal, not a highly-organized, nature. The chocolate-cream richness of Conrad, the *romance* laid on with a shovel—best revealed where Mr. Hueffer helped him in the book specifically named *Romance*—all this excess, this tropical unreality, I find (of course, to some extent concealed in an elaborate intellectualist technique) in Miss Stein. (p. 63)

In Miss Stein you get a temperament on the grand scale, as you do in Picasso; they both enjoy the colossal. But if you compare one of Picasso's giantesses (the first born about 1920, I believe) with a giant from the Sistine Ceiling, you will at once find that the Picasso figure is a beautifully executed, imposing, human *doll*. Its fixed imbecility of expression, its immense, bloated eunuchoid limbs, suggest the mental clinic immediately. They are all opaque fat, without nerve or muscle. The figures of Michelangelo, on the other hand—the most supremely noble and terrible creations of the dramatic genius of the West—are creatures of an infectious life. Between the outstretched forefinger of Adam and the finger of the hurrying Jehovah, there is an electric force in suspense of a magnitude that no vegetative imbecility, however well done or however colossal, on one side and on the other, would be able to convey.

The *weight*, then, that is characteristic of the work of Miss Stein—like the sluggish weight of the figures, or the sultry oppressiveness of the chocolate-cream tropics in which they move, of Conrad; or of the unintelligent, catastrophic heaviness of Zola—is, to me, of a dead order of things. (pp. 63-4)

> *Wyndham Lewis, "Tests for Counterfeit in the Arts" and "The Prose-Song of Gertrude Stein," in his* Time and Western Man, *Harcourt, Brace and Company, 1928, pp. 49-52, 61-5.*

### WILLIAM CARLOS WILLIAMS   (essay date 1931)

[*Williams was one of America's most renowned poets of the twentieth century. Rejecting as overly academic the Modernist poetic style established by T. S. Eliot, he sought a more natural poetic expression, endeavoring to replicate the idiomatic cadences of American speech. Perhaps Williams's greatest accomplishment is* Paterson *(1946), a collection of poems depicting urban America. He is best known, however, for such individual poems as "The Red Wheelbarrow," "To Waken an Old Lady," and "Danse Russe." In the following excerpt from an essay originally published in 1931, Williams examines the nature of Stein's artistic achievement.*]

Let it be granted that whatever is new in literature the germ of it will be found somewhere in the writings of other times; only the modern emphasis gives work a present distinction.

The necessity for this modern focus and the meaning of the changes involved are, however, another matter, the everlasting stumbling block to criticism. Here is a theme worth development in the case of Gertrude Stein—yet signally neglected. (p. 113)

Did my father, mother, uncle, aunt, brothers or sisters, ever see a white bear? What would they give?. . . How would they behave? How would the white bear have behaved? Is he wild? Tame? Terrible? Rough? Smooth?

Note the play upon *rough* and *smooth* (though it is not certain that this was intended), *rough* seeming to apply to the bear's deportment, *smooth* to surface, presumably the bear's coat. In any case the effect is that of a comparison relating primarily not to any qualities of the bear himself but to the words rough and smooth. . . .

> Is the white bear worth seeing?
>
> Is there any sin in it?
>
> Is it better than a black one?

In this manner ends Chapter 43 of [Laurence Sterne's] *The Life and Opinions of Tristram Shandy*. The handling of the words and to some extent the imaginative quality of the sentence is a direct forerunner of that which Gertrude Stein has woven today into a synthesis of its own. It will be plain, in fact, on close attention, that Sterne exercises not only the play (or music) of sight, sense and sound contrast among the words themselves which Stein uses, but their grammatical play also. . . . It would not be too much to say that Stein's development over a lifetime is anticipated completely with regard to subject matter, sense and grammar—in Sterne.

Starting from scratch we get, possibly, thatch; just as they have always done in poetry.

Then they would try to connect it up by something like—The mice scratch, beneath the thatch.

Miss Stein does away with all that. The free-versists on the contrary used nothing else. They saved—The mice, under the . . . ,

It is simply the skelton, the "formal " parts of writing, those that make form, that she has to do with, apart from the "burden" which they carry. The skeleton, important to acknowledge where confusion of all knowledge of the "soft parts" reigns as at the present day in all intellectual fields.

Stein's theme is writing. But in such a way as to be writing envisioned as the first concern of the moment, dragging behind it a dead weight of logical burdens, among them a dead criticism which broken through might be a gap by which endless other enterprises of the understanding should issue—for refreshment.

It is a revolution of some proportions that is contemplated, the exact nature of which may be no more than sketched here but whose basis is humanity in a relationship with literature hitherto little contemplated.

And at the same time it is a general attack on the scholastic viewpoint, that medieval remnant with whose effects from generation to generation literature has been infested to its lasting detriment. It is a break-away from that paralyzing vulgarity of logic for which the habits of science and philosophy coming over into literature (where they do not belong) are to blame.

It is this logicality as a basis for literary action which in Stein's case, for better or worse, has been wholly transcended.

She explains her own development in connection with *Tender Buttons*. "It was my first conscious struggle with the problem of correlating sight, sound and sense, and eliminating rhythm;—now I am trying grammar and eliminating sight and sound."

Having taken the words to her choice, to emphasize further what she has in mind she has completely unlinked them (in her most recent work) from their former relationships in the sentence. This was absolutely essential and unescapable. Each under the new arrangement has a quality of its own, but not conjoined to carry the burden science, philosophy and every higgledy-piggledy figment of law and order have been laying upon them in the past. They are like a crowd at Coney Island, let us say, seen from an airplane.

Whatever the value of Miss Stein's work may turn out finally to be, she has at least accomplished her purpose of getting down on paper this much that is decipherable. She has placed writing on a plane where it may deal unhampered with its own affairs, unburdened with scientific and philosophic lumber.

For after all, science and philosophy are today, in their effect upon the mind, little more than fetishes of unspeakable abhorrence. And it is through a subversion of the art of writing that their grip upon us has assumed its steel-like temper.

What are philosophers, scientists, religionists, they that have filled up literature with their pap? Writers, of a kind. Stein simply erases their stories, turns them off and does without them, their logic (founded merely on the limits of the perceptions) which is supposed to transcend the words, along with them. Stein denies it. The words, in writing, she discloses, transcend everything. (pp. 114-17)

There remains to be explained the bewildering volume of what Miss Stein has written, the quantity of her work, its very apparent repetitiousness, its iteration, what I prefer to call its extension, the final clue to her meaning.

It is, of course, a progression (not a progress) beginning, conveniently, with **"Melanctha"** from *Three Lives,* and coming up to today.

How in a democracy, such as the United States, can writing which has to compete with excellence elsewhere and in other times remain in the field and be at once objective (true to fact) intellectually searching, subtle and instinct with powerful additions to our lives? It is impossible, without invention of some sort, for the very good reason that observation about us engenders the very opposite of what we seek: triviality, crassness and intellectual bankruptcy. And yet what we do see can in no way be excluded. Satire and flight are two possibilities but Miss Stein has chosen otherwise.

But if one remain in a place and reject satire, what then? To be democratic, local (in the sense of being attached with integrity to actual experience) Stein, or any other artist, must for subtlety ascend to a plane of almost abstract design to keep alive. To writing, then, as an art in itself. Yet what actually impinges on the senses must be rendered as it appears, by use of which, only, and under which, untouched, the significance has to be disclosed. It is one of the major problems of the artist.

**"Melanctha"** is a thrilling clinical record of the life of a colored woman in the present-day United States, told with directness and truth. It is without question one of the best bits of characterization produced in America. It is universally admired. This is where Stein began. But for Stein to tell a story of that sort, even with the utmost genius, was not enough under the conditions in which we live, since by the very nature of its composition such a story does violence to the larger scene which would be portrayed.

True, a certain way of delineating the scene is to take an individual like Melanctha and draw her carefully. But this is what happens. The more carefully the drawing is made, the greater the genius involved and the greater the interest that attaches, therefore, to the character as an individual, the more exceptional that character becomes in the mind of the reader and the less typical of the scene.

It was no use for Stein to go on with *Three Lives*. There that phase of the work had to end. See *Useful Knowledge,* the parts on the U.S.A.

Stein's pages have become like the United States viewed from an airplane—the same senseless repetitions, the endless multiplications of toneless words, with these she had to work.

No use for Stein to fly to Paris and forget it. The thing, the United States, the unmitigated stupidity, the drab tediousness of the democracy, the overwhelming number of the offensively ignorant, the dull nerve—is there in the artist's mind and cannot be escaped by taking a ship. She must resolve it if she can, if she is to be.

That must be the artist's articulation with existence.

Truly, the world is full of emotion—more or less—but it is caught in bewilderment to a far more important degree. And the purpose of art, so far as it has any, is not at least to copy that, but lies in the resolution of difficulties to its own comprehensive organization of materials. And by so doing, in this case, rather than by copying, it takes its place as most human.

To deal with Melanctha, with characters of whomever it may be, the modern Dickens, is not therefore human. To write like that is not in the artist, to be human at all, since nothing is resolved, nothing is done to resolve the bewilderment which makes of emotion an inanity: That, is to overlook the gross instigation and with all subtlety to examine the object minutely for "the truth"—which if there is anything more commonly practiced or more stupid, I have yet to come upon it.

To be most useful to humanity, or to anything else for that matter, an art, writing, must stay art, not seeking to be science, philosophy, history, the humanities, or anything else it has been made to carry in the past. It is this enforcement which underlies Gertrude Stein's extension and progression to date. (pp. 118-20)

*William Carlos Williams, "The Work of Gertrude Stein," in his* Selected Essays of William Carlos Williams, *Random House, 1954, pp. 113-20.*

**GERTRUDE STEIN   (interview date 1946)**

*[In the following excerpt from an interview with Robert Bartlett Haas conducted in 1946, Stein traces her literary development from* Three Lives *to* Wars I Have Seen.*]*

Everything I have done has been influenced by Flaubert and Cézanne, and this gave me a new feeling about composition. Up to that time composition had consisted of a central idea, to which everything else was an accompaniment and separate but was not an end in itself, and Cézanne conceived the idea that in composition one thing was as important as another thing. Each part is as important as the whole, and that impressed me enormously, and it impressed me so much that I began to write *Three Lives* under this influence and this idea of composition and I was more interested in composition at that moment, this background of word-system, which had come to me from this reading that I had done. I was obsessed by this idea of composition, and the Negro story ("**Melanctha**" in *Three Lives*) was a quintessence of it.

You see I tried to convey the idea of each part of a composition being as important as the whole. It was the first time in any language that anyone had used that idea of composition in literature. Henry James had a slight inkling of it and was in some senses a forerunner, while in my case I made it stay on the page quite composed. You see he made it sort of like an atmosphere, and it was not solely the realism of the characters but the realism of the composition which was the important thing, the realism of the composition of my thoughts.

After all, to me one human being is as important as another human being, and you might say that the landscape has the same values, a blade of grass has the same value as a tree. Because the realism of the people who did realism before was a realism of trying to make people real. I was not interested in making the people real but in the essence or, as a painter would call it, value. One cannot live without the other. This was an entirely new idea and had been done a little by the Russians but had not been conceived as a reality until I came along, but I got it largely from Cézanne. Flaubert was there as a theme. He, too, had a little of the feeling about this thing, but they none of them conceived it as an entity, no more than any painter had done other than Cézanne. They all fell down on it, because the supremacy of one interest overcame them, while the Cézanne thing I put into words came in the *Three Lives* and was followed by the *Making of Americans*.

In the *Making of Americans* I began the same thing. In trying to make a history of the world my idea here was to write the life of every individual who could possibly live on the earth. I hoped to realize that ambition. My intention was to cover every possible variety of human type in it. I made endless diagrams of every human being, watching people from windows and so on until I could put down every type of human being that could be on the earth. I wanted each one to have the same value. I was not at all interested in the little or big men but to realize absolutely every variety of human experience that it was possible to have, every type, every style and nuance. I have always had this obsession, and that is why I enjoy talking to every GI. I must know every possible nuance.

Conception of this has to be based on a real feeling for every human being. The surprises of it are endless. Still there are the endless surprises, the combination that you don't expect, the relation of men to character that you do not expect. It never ends. All the time in it you see what I am singling out is that one thing has the same value as another. There are of course people who are more important than others in that they have more importance in the world, but this is not essential, and it ceases to be. I have no sense of difference in this respect, because every human being comprises the combination form. Just as everybody has the vote, including the women, I think children should, because as soon as a child is conscious of itself, then it has to me an existence and has a stake in what happens. Everybody who has that stake has that quality of interest, and in the *Making of Americans* that is what I tried to show.

In writing the *Three Lives* I was not particularly conscious of the question of style. The style which everybody shouted about surprised me. I was only interested in these other things. In the beginning gradually I became more conscious of the way you did this thing and I became gradually more conscious of it and at that time particularly of a need for evenness. At this time I threw away punctuation. My real objection to it was that it threw away this balance that I was trying to get, this evenness of everybody having a vote, and that is the reason I am impatient with punctuation. Finally I got obsessed with these enormously long sentences and long paragraphs. All that was an effort to get this evenness, and this went on until it sort of exhausted itself.

On the *Making of Americans* I had written about one thousand pages, and I finished the thing with a sort of rhapsody at the end. Then I started in to write *Matisse, Picasso, and Gertrude Stein.* You will see in each one of these stories that they began in the character of *Making of Americans,* and then in about the middle of it words began to be for the first time more important than the sentence structure or the paragraphs. Something happened. I mean I felt a need. I had thought this thing out and felt a need of breaking it down and forcing it into little pieces. I felt that I had lost contact with the words in building up these Beethovian passages. I had lost that idea gained in my youth from the Seventeenth Century writers, and the little rhymes that used to run through my head from Shakespeare, who was always a passion, got lost from the overall pattern. I recognized and I recognize (if you look at the *Long Gay Book*) this something else I knew would guide that.

I began to play with words then. I was a little obsessed by words of equal value. Picasso was painting my portrait at that time, and he and I used to talk this thing over endlessly. At this time he had just begun on cubism. And I felt that the thing I got from Cézanne was not the last composition. You had to recognize words had lost their value in the Nineteenth Century, particularly towards the end, they had lost much of their variety, and I felt that I could not go on, that I had to recapture the value of the individual word, find out what it meant and act within it.

Also the fact that as an American my mind was fresher towards language than the average English mind, as we had more or less renewed the word structure in our language. All through that middle period the interest was with that largely, ending up with *Tender Buttons.* In this I think that there are some of the best uses of words that there are. The movement is simple and holds by little words. I had at the same time a new interest in portraiture. I began then to want to make a more complete picture of each word, and that is when the portrait business started. I wait until each word can intimate some part of each little mannerism. In each one of them I was not satisfied until the whole thing formed, and it is very difficult to put it down, to explain, in words.

While during that middle period I had these two things that were working back to the compositional idea, the idea of portraiture and the idea of the recreation of the word. I took individual words and thought about them until I got their weight and volume complete and put them next to another word, and at this same time I found out very soon that there is no such thing as putting them together without sense. It is impossible to put them together without sense. I made innumerable efforts to make words write without sense and found it impossible. Any human being putting down words had to make sense out of them.

All these things interested me very strongly through the middle years from about after the *Making of Americans* until 1911, leading up to *Tender Buttons,* which was the apex of that. That was the culmination. Then came the war, and through the war I was traveling a great deal.

After the war the form of the thing, the question of the play form, began to interest me very much. I did very little work during the war. As soon as the war was over I settled down and wrote the whole of the *Geography and Plays.* That turned into very strong interest in play form, and then I began to be slowly impressed by the idea of narration.

After all, human beings are interested in two things. They are interested in the reality and interested in telling about it. I had struggled up to that time with the creation of reality, and then I became interested in how you could tell this thing in a way that anybody could understand and at the same time keep true to your values, and the thing bothered me a great deal at that time. I did quite a few plays and portraits, and that ended roughly with the *Four Saints,* 1932. Most of the things that are in the *Useful Knowledge,* including a book of poetry which was not printed, were constant effort, and after that I was beginning the narration consisting in plays at first, ending with the *Four Saints.*

After the *Four Saints* the portrait narration began, and I went back to the form of narration, and at that time I had a certain reputation, no success, but a certain reputation, and I was asked to write a biography, and I said "No." And then as a joke I began to write the *Autobiography of Alice Toklas,* and at that moment I had made a rather interesting discovery. A young French poet had begun to write, and I was asked to translate his poems, and there I made a rather startling discovery that other people's words are quite different from one's own, and that they can not be the result of your internal troubles as a writer. They have a totally different sense than when they are your own words. This solved for me the problem of Shakespeare's sonnets, which are so unlike any of his other work. These may have been his own idea, undoubtedly they were, but the words have none of the violence that exists in any of the poems, in any of the plays. They have a roughness and violence in their juxtaposition which the sonnets do not have, and this brought me to a great deal of illumination of narrative, because most narrative is based not about your opinions but upon someone else's.

Therefore narrative has a different concept than poetry or even exposition, because, you see, the narrative in itself is not what is in your mind but what is in somebody else's. Plays use it less, and so I did a tour de force with the *Autobiography of Alice Toklas,* and when I sent the first half to the agent, they sent back a telegram to see which one of us had written it! But still I had done what I saw, what you do in translation or in a narrative. I had recreated the point of view of somebody else. Therefore the words ran with a certain smoothness. Shakespeare never expressed any feelings of his own in those sonnets. They have too much smoothness. He did not feel "This is my emotion, I will write it down." If it is your own feeling, one's words have a fullness and violence.

Then I became more and more interested in the subject of narration, and my work since this, the bulk of my work since then, has been largely narration, and I had done children's stories. I think *Paris, France* and *Wars I Have Seen* are the most successful of this. I thought I had done it in *Everybody's Autobiography.* I worked very hard on that and was often very exhausted, but it is often confused and not clarified. But in *Wars I Have Seen* and in *Paris, France,* to my feeling, I have done it more completely.

I have done the narration, because in narration your great problem is the problem of time in telling a story of anybody. And that is why newspaper people never become writers, because they have a false sense of time. They have to consider not the time in which to write but the time in which the newspaper is coming out. Three senses of time to struggle with, the time the event took place, the time they are writing, and the time it has to come out. Their sense of time can not be but false. Hemingway, on account of his newspapeer training, has a false sense of time. One will sooner or later get this falsity of time, and that is why newspapers cannot be read later out of their published time.

I found out that in the esssence of narration is this problem of time. You have as a person writing, and all the really great narration has it, you have to denude yourself of time so that writing time does not exist. If time exists, your writing is ephemeral. You can have a historical time, but for you the time does not exist, and if you are writing about the present, the time element must cease to exist. I did it unconsciously in the *Autobiography of Alice Toklas,* but I did it consciously in *Everybody's Autobiography* and in the last thing *Wars I Have Seen.* In it I described something momentous happening under my eyes and I was able to do it without a great sense of time. There should not be a sense of time, but an existence suspended in time. That is really where I am at the present moment, I am still largely meditating about this sense of time.

Words hold an interest that you never lose, but usually at one moment one is more preoccupied with one thing than another, the parts mould into the whole. (pp. 15-20)

> *Gertrude Stein, "A Transatlantic Interview," in her* A Primer for the Gradual Understanding of Gertrude Stein, *edited by Robert Bartlett Haas, Black Sparrow Press, 1971, pp. 13-35.*

**THORNTON WILDER**   (essay date 1947)

[*Wilder was a popular and critically acclaimed American dramatist and novelist. He received the Pulitzer Prize for three of his works:* The Bridge of San Luis Rey *(1927), a novel, and his dramas* Our Town *(1938) and* The Skin of Our Teeth *(1942). Commentators find his writings sophisticated, even experimental at times, yet note that they are informed by a fundamentally conventional, optimistic philosophy. Wilder drew upon a wide range of sources for inspiration, including classical Roman theater and the work of his friend Gertrude Stein. He served on the advisory committee for the publication of Stein's previously unpublished writings from the Yale collection. In the following excerpt from his introduction to Stein's* Four in America, *published in 1947, Wilder examines Stein's literary goals and the theoretical and philosophical bases of her writings.*]

Miss Gertrude Stein, answering a question about her line

> Rose is a rose is a rose is a rose,

once said with characteristic vehemence:

> Now listen! I'm no fool. I know that in daily life we don't go around saying "is a . . . is a . . . is a. . . ."

She knew that she was a difficult and an idiosyncratic author. She pursued her aims, however, with such conviction and intensity that occasionally she forgot that the results could be difficult to others. At such times the achievements she had made in writing, in "telling what she knew" (her most frequent formulization of the aim of writing), had to her the character of self-evident beauty and clarity. A friend, to whom she showed

recently completed examples of her poetry, was frequently driven to reply sadly: "But you forget that I don't understand examples of your extremer styles." To this she would reply with a mixture of bewilderment, distress, and exasperation:

> But what's the difficulty? Just read the words on the paper. They're in English. Just read them. Be simple and you'll understand these things.

Now let me quote the whole speech from which the opening remark in this introduction has been extracted. A student in her seminar at the University of Chicago had asked her for an "explanation" of the famous line. She leaned forward, giving all of herself to the questioner in that unforgettable way which has endeared her to hundreds of students and to hundreds of soldiers in two wars, trenchant, humorous, but above all urgently concerned over the enlightenment of even the most obtuse questioner:

> Now listen! Can't you see that when the language was new—as it was with Chaucer and Homer—the poet could use the name of a thing and the thing was really there? He could say "O moon," "O sea," "O love" and the moon and the sea and love were really there. And can't you see that after hundreds of years had gone by and thousands of poems had been written, he could call on those words and find that they were just worn-out literary words? The excitingness of pure being had withdrawn from them; they were just rather stale literary words. Now the poet has to work in the excitingness of pure being; he has to get back that intensity into the language. We all know that it's hard to write poetry in a late age; and we know that you have to put some strangeness, something unexpected, into the structure of the sentence in order to bring back vitality to the noun. Now it's not enough to be bizarre; the strangeness in the sentence structure has to come from the poetic gift, too. That's why it's doubly hard to be a poet in a late age. Now you all have seen hundreds of poems about roses and you know in your bones that the rose is not there. All those songs that sopranos sing as encores about "I have a garden; oh, what a garden!" Now I don't want to put too much emphasis on that line, because it's just one line in a longer poem. But I notice that you all know it; you make fun of it, but you know it. Now listen! I'm no fool. I know that in daily life we don't go around saying "is a . . . is a . . . is a. . . ." Yes, I'm no fool; but I think that in that line the rose is red for the first time in English poetry for a hundred years.

*Four in America* is full of that "strangeness which must come from the poetic gift" in order to restore intensity to images dusted over with accustomedness and routine. It is not required in poetry alone; for Miss Stein all intellectual activities—philosophical speculation, literary criticism, narration—had to be refreshed at the source.

There are certain of her idiosyncrasies which by this time should not require discussion—for example, her punctuation and her recourse to repetition. Readers who still balk at these should not attempt to read [*Four in America*], for it contains idiosyncrasies far more taxing to conventional taste. The majority of readers ask of literature the kind of pleasure they have always received; they want "more of the same"; they accept idiosyncrasy in author and period only when it has been consecrated by a long-accumulated prestige, as in the cases of the earliest and the latest of Shakespeare's styles, and in the poetry of Donne, Gerard Manley Hopkins, or Emily Dickinson. They arrogate to themselves a superiority in condemning the novels of Kafka or of the later Joyce or the later Henry James, forgetting that they allow a no less astonishing individuality to Laurence Sterne and to Rabelais.

This work is for those who not only largely accord to others "another's way," but who rejoice in the diversity of minds and the tension of difference.

Miss Stein once said:

> Every masterpiece came into the world with a measure of ugliness in it. That ugliness is the sign of the creator's struggle to say a new thing in a new way, for an artist can never repeat yesterday's success. And after every great creator there follows a second man who shows how it can be done easily. Picasso struggled and made his new thing and then Braque came along and showed how it could be done without pain. The Sistine Madonna of Raphael is all over the world, on grocers' calendars and on Christmas cards; everybody thinks it's an easy picture. It's our business as critics to stand in front of it and recover its ugliness.

[*Four in America*] is full of that kind of ugliness. It is perhaps enough to say: "Be simple and you will understand these things"; but it is necessary to say: "Relax your predilection for the accustomed, the received, and be ready to accept an extreme example of idiosyncratic writing."

Distributed throughout Miss Stein's books and in the *Lectures in America* can be found an account of her successive discoveries and aims as a writer. She did not admit that the word "experiments" be applied to them.

> Artists do not experiment. Experiment is what scientists do; they initiate an operation of unknown factors in order to be instructed by its results. An artist puts down what he knows and at every moment it is what he knows at that moment. If he is trying things out to see how they go he is a bad artist.

A brief recapitulation of the history of her aims will help us to understand her work. (pp. 193-96)

[At Radcliffe College], as a research problem, her professor gave her a study of automatic writing. For this work she called upon her fellow students—the number ran into the hundreds—to serve as experimental subjects. Her interest, however, took an unexpected turn; she became more absorbed in the subjects' varying approach to the experiments than in the experiments themselves. They entered the room with alarm, with docility, with bravado, with gravity, with scorn, or with indifference. This striking variation re-awoke within her an interest which had obsessed her even in very early childhood—the conviction that a description could be made of all the types of human character and that these types could be related to two basic types (she called them independent-dependents and dependent-independents). She left the university and, settling in Paris, applied herself to the problem. The result was the novel of one thousand pages, *The Making of Americans,* which is at once an account of a large family from the time of the grandparents' coming to this country from Europe and a description of "everyone who is, or has been, or will be." She then went on to give in *A Long Gay Book* an account of all possible relations of two persons. This book, however, broke down soon after it began. Miss Stein had been invaded by another compelling problem: How, in our time, do you describe anything? In the previous centuries writers had managed pretty well by assembling a number of adjectives and adjectival clauses side by side; the reader "obeyed" by furnishing images and

concepts in his mind and the resultant "thing" in the reader's mind corresponded fairly well with that in the writer's. Miss Stein felt that that process did not work any more. Her painter friends were showing clearly that the corresponding method of "description" had broken down in painting and she was sure that it had broken down in writing.

In the first place, words were no longer precise; they were full of extraneous matter. They were full of "remembering"—and describing a thing in front of us, an "objective thing," is no time for remembering. Even vision (a particularly over-charged word), even sight had been dulled by remembering. The painters of the preceding generation, the Impressionists, had shown that. Hitherto people had known that, close to, a whitewashed wall had no purple in it; at a distance it might have a great deal of purple, but many painters had not allowed themselves to see purple in a distant whitewashed wall because they remembered that close to it was uniformly white. The Impressionists had shown us the red in green trees; the Post-Impressionists showed us that our entire sense of form, our very view of things, was all distorted and distorting and "educated" and adjusted by memory. Miss Stein felt that writing must accomplish a revolution whereby it could report things as they were in themselves before our minds had appropriated them and robbed them of their objectivity "in pure existing." To this end she went about her house describing the objects she found there in the series of short "poems" which make up the volume called *Tender Buttons*. (pp. 196-98)

Miss Stein had now entered upon a period of excited discovery, intense concentration, and enormous productivity. She went on to writing portraits of her friends and of places. She revived an old interest in drama and wrote scores of plays, many of which are themselves portraits of friends and of places. Two of her lectures in *Lectures in America* describe her aims in these kinds of work. She meditated long on the nature of narration and wrote the novel *Lucy Church Amiably.* This novel is a description of a landscape near Bilignin, her summer home in the south of France. Its subtitle and epigraph are: "A Novel of Romantic Beauty and Nature and which Looks Like an Engraving . . . *'and with a nod she turned her head toward the falling water. Amiably.'*" (p. 198)

And always with her great relish for human beings she was listening to people. She was listening with genial absorption to the matters in which they were involved.

> Everybody's life is full of stories; your life is full of stories; my life is full of stories. They are very occupying, but they are not really interesting. What is interesting is the way everyone tells their stories.

and at the same time she was listening to the tellers' revelation of their "basic nature."

> If you listen, really listen, you will hear people repeating themselves. You will hear their pleading nature or their attacking nature or their asserting nature. People who say that I repeat too much do not really listen; they cannot hear that every moment of life is full of repeating. There is only one repeating that is really dead and that is when a thing is taught.
>
> (pp. 199-200)

It can easily be understood that the questions she was asking concerning personality and the nature of language and concerning "how you tell a thing" would inevitably lead to the formulization of a metaphysics. In fact, I think it can be said that the fundamental occupation of Miss Stein's life was not the work of art but the shaping of a theory of knowledge, a theory of time, and a theory of the passions. These theories finally converged on the master question: What are the various ways in which creativity works in everyone? That is the subject of [*Four in America*]. It is a subject which she was to develop more specifically in . . . *The Geographical History of America or The Relation of Human Nature to the Human Mind*. It led also to a reconsideration of all literature, reflected in the beautiful lecture **"What Are Masterpieces and Why Are There So Few of Them?"**

Miss Stein held a doctrine which permeates this book, which informs her theory of creativity, which plays a large part in her demonstration of what an American is, and which helps to explain some of the great difficulty which we feel in reading her work. It is the Doctrine of Audience; its literary aspect is considered in the Theory of the Moment of Recognition. In *The Geographical History of America* it is made to illustrate a Theory of Identity.

Let me enter into the subject by again quoting from her words in a conversation:

> Why is it that no preachers, no teachers, no orators, no parliamentary debaters ever have any ideas after the age of thirty-five? It is because when they talk they only hear what the audience is hearing. They get mixed up in their head and think that it is possible for one person to agree totally with another person; and when you think *that* you are lost and never have any ideas any more. Now what we know is formed in our head by thousands of small occasions in the daily life. By "what we know" I do not mean, of course, what we learn from books, because that is of no importance at all. I mean what we really know, like our assurance about how we know anything, and what we know about the validity of the sentiments, and things like that. All the thousands of occasions in the daily life go into our head to form our ideas about these things. Now if we write, we write; and these things we know flow down our arm and come out on the page. The moment before we wrote them we did not really know we knew them; if they are in our head in the shape of words then that is all wrong and they will come out dead; but if we did not know we knew them until the moment of writing, then they come to us with a shock of surprise. That is the Moment of Recognition. Like God on the Seventh Day we look at it and say it is good. That is the moment that some people call inspiration, but I do not like the word inspiration, because it suggests that someone else is blowing that knowledge into you. It is not being blown into you; it is very much your own and was acquired by you in thousands of tiny occasions in your daily life. Now, of course, there is no audience at that moment. There is no one whom you are instructing, or fighting, or improving, or pleasing, or provoking. To others it may appear that you are doing all those things to them, but of course you are not. At that moment you are totally alone at this recognition of what you know. And of that thing which you have written you are the first and last audience. This thing which you have written is bought by other people and read by them. It goes through their eyes into their heads and they say they agree with it. But, of course, they cannot agree with it. The things they know have been built up by thousands of small occasions which are different from yours. They *say* they agree with you; what they mean is that they are aware that your pages have the vitality of a thing which sounds to them like someone else's knowing; it is consistent to its own world of what

one person has really known. That is a great pleasure and the highest compliment they can pay it is to say that they agree with it.

Now these preachers and orators may have had such moments of recognition when they were young; they may even have had them when they are addressing an audience—though that is very rare. After they have faced a great many audiences they begin to think that the audiences are literally understanding, literally agreeing with them, instead of merely being present at the vitality of these moments of recognition, at their surprising themselves with their own discovery of what they know. Then they gradually slip in more of the kind of ideas that people can agree with, ideas which are not really ideas at all, which are soothing but not exciting—oh, yes, they may be exciting as oratory, but they are not exciting as creation—after a while they dry up and then they do not have any real ideas any more.

A portion of the ideas expressed above is found in the "Henry James" section of [*Four in America*].

> Mr. Owen Young made a mistake, he said the only thing he wished his son to have was the power of clearly expressing his ideas. Not at all. It is not clarity that is desirable but force.

> Clarity is of no importance because nobody listens and nobody knows what you mean no matter what you mean, nor how clearly you mean what you mean. But if you have vitality enough of knowing enough of what you mean, somebody and sometime and sometimes a great many will have to realise that you know what you mean and so they will agree that you mean what you know, what you know you mean, which is as near as anybody can come to understanding any one.

Miss Stein never claimed that these doctrines were new. She delighted in finding them in the great works of the past. She was never tired of saying that all real knowledge is common knowledge; it lies sleeping within us; it is awakened in us when we hear it expressed by a person who is speaking or writing in a state of recognition.

From consciousness of audience, then, come all the evils of thinking, writing, and creating. In *The Geographical History of America* she illustrates the idea by distinguishing between our human nature and our human mind. Our human nature is a serpents' nest, all directed to audience; from it proceed self-justification, jealousy, propaganda, individualism, moralizing, and edification. How comforting it is, and how ignobly pleased we are when we see it expressed in literature. The human mind, however, gazes at experience and without deflection by the insidious pressures from human nature tells what it sees and knows. Its subject matter is indeed human nature; to cite two of Miss Stein's favorites, *Hamlet* and *Pride and Prejudice* are about human nature, but not of it. The survival of masterpieces, and there are very few of them, is due to our astonishment that certain minds can occasionally report life without adulterating the report with the gratifying movements of their own self-assertion, their private quarrel with what it has been to be a human being.

Miss Stein pushed to its furthest extreme this position that at the moment of writing one rigorously excludes from the mind all thought of praise and blame, of persuasion or conciliation. In the early days she used to say: "I write for myself and strangers." Then she eliminated the strangers; then she had a great deal of trouble with the idea that one is an audience to oneself, which she solves in this book with the far-reaching concept: "I am not I when I see."

It has often seemed to me that Miss Stein was engaged in a series of spiritual exercises whose aim was to eliminate during the hours of writing all those whispers into the ear from the outside and inside world where audience dwells. She knew that she was the object of derision to many and to some extent the knowledge fortified her. Yet it is very moving to learn that on one occasion when a friend asked her what a writer most wanted, she replied, throwing up her hands and laughing, "Oh, praise, praise, praise!" Some of the devices that most exasperate readers—such as the capricious headings of subdivisions in her work, such sequences as Book IV, Book VII, Book VIII, Volume I—though in part they are there to make fun of pompous heads who pretend to an organic development and have no development, are at bottom merely attempts to nip in the bud by a drastic intrusion of apparent incoherence any ambition she may have felt within herself to woo for acceptance as a "respectable" philosopher. It should be noted that another philosopher who wrestled with the problem of restating the mind of man in the terms of our times and who has emerged as perhaps the most disturbing and stimulating voice of the nineteenth century—Søren Kierkegaard—delayed his recognition and "put off" his readers by many a mystification and by an occasional resort to almost Aristophanic buffoonery.

There is another evidence of Miss Stein's struggle to keep her audience out of her mind. *Four In America* is not a book which is the end and summary of her thoughts about the subjects she has chosen; it is the record of her thoughts, from the beginning, as she "closes in" on them. It is *being written* before our eyes; she does not, as other writers do, suppress and erase the hesitations, the recapitulations, the connectives, in order to give us the completed fine result of her meditations. She gives us the process. From time to time we hear her groping toward the next idea; we hear her cry of joy when she has found it; sometimes it seems to me that we hear her reiterating the already achieved idea and, as it were, pumping it in order to force out the next development that lies hidden within it. We hear her talking to herself about the book that is growing and glowing (to borrow her often irritating habit of rhyming) within her. Many readers will not like this, but at least it is evidence that she is ensuring the purity of her indifference as to whether her readers will like it or not. It is as though she were afraid that if she went back and weeded out all these signs of groping and shaping and reassembling, if she gave us only the completed thoughts in their last best order, the truth would have slipped away like water through a sieve because such a final marshaling of her thoughts would have been directed toward audience. Her description of existence would be, like so many hundreds of thousands of descriptions of existence, like most literature—dead. (pp. 200-05)

> Thornton Wilder, "Gertrude Stein's 'Four in America'," in his *American Characteristics and Other Essays*, *edited by Donald Gallup, Harper & Row, Publishers, 1979, pp. 193-222.*

## B. L. REID  (essay date 1958)

[*An American critic and educator, Reid is the author of* Art by Subtraction: A Dissenting Opinion of Gertrude Stein, *a critical study that he calls "an essay in decapitation." In the following excerpt from that work, he issues an outright condemnation of Stein, arguing that none of her writings, with the exception of* Three Lives, *deserve to be called art.*]

*Stein in her sitting room beneath the portrait of her by Pablo Picasso. Pictorial Parade Inc.*

It would be a great deal easier to measure Gertrude Stein if she would let us alone. It would be much easier if she would let us weigh her as a minor writer rather than a major one, or as a scientist-philosopher rather than a creative artist, or as a follower of a bypath rather than of the highroad of literature. I am suggesting, obviously, that these alternatives seem to be the essential truths about her, but she will have none of them. The critic has to cut his way through a jungle of Miss Stein's ponderous pronouncements on the subject of herself, backed by all the weight of her full assurance and supported in some degree by the evidences of her wholly real independence and intelligence and the acclamation of eloquent and respectable friends.

Gertrude Stein's ego is one of the great egos of all time. It is monumental; it is heroic. Flat assertion of her own genius is a leitmotiv in virtually all her books. (pp. 168-69)

It may be true . . . that Miss Stein needs to be seen as a genius to be seen at all. That is, we evaluate her as a being essentially not measurable at all, as apart, unique. When we try to fit her into a context involving normality or moderate supranormality, she does not fit; there is no common yardstick; the scales refuse to function. Perhaps we must agree with Julian Sawyer's judgment of her "absolute perspicacity." If she has that, she is beyond us; we cannot know her—and the critic's job is simplified into one of awe.

If Gertrude Stein is a genius, she is one in the vulgar sense of the term: perversely elevated, isolated, inhuman. Hers is not the friendly, communicative genius of her masters, James and Whitehead, or even Picasso, pulling us gently or roughly up to the heights of their new insight. She is a genius with a tragic flaw, one curiously like the old flaw of Oedipus and Lear—

the fatal combination of pride and power and blindness. We must say this with the full knowledge that Gertrude Stein seemed all her life to be trying to communicate to us, that she worked with sweat and occasional humility to make us know her mind. That, however, is her colossal blindness and her arrogance; convinced of the absolute rightness of her vision and of her literary record of that insight, she refused all moderation or compromise.

It seems to me that Miss Stein is a vulgar genius talking to herself, and if she is talking to herself, she is not an artist. It is because she does talk to herself that she offers insuperable difficulties to both reader and critic. I suggest, therefore, that she be defined out of existence as an artist. To be an artist, she must talk to us, not to the dullest or the most tradition bound or the most unsympathetic of us, but to those of us who are flexible, those willing to be fruitfully led. There is not world enough or time enough for Gertrude Stein's kind of writing; too much in literature is both excellent and knowable.

What I am trying to say is that most of the confusion about Gertrude Stein seems the result of trying to understand her in a mistaken context. The original mistake is Miss Stein's; it happened when she defined herself as an artist, thereby obscuring from herself and her readers the fact that both her ends and her means pointed toward philosophy by way of science. The whole cast and capability of her mind was scientific, reflective, rational, philosophic. Of the truly creative ability to fabricate and counterfeit, to excite and to move and to instruct by fact or fiction conceived as dramatic, narrative, or lyric, she had only a rudimentary portion, and this she studiously suppressed until it was very nearly dead. Her works are not, properly speaking, art at all. Her aim was to "describe reality," but description alone is not art but science. In her aesthetics she reflects on reality as well, and it becomes philosophy.

Her "art" is one of subtraction and narrowing throughout. In her art she does not reflect, for reflection entails consciousness of identity and audience, an awareness fatal to the creative vision. She rules out the imagination because it is the hunting ground of secondary talent. She rules out logical, cause-effect relations: "Question and answer make you know time is existing." She rules out distinctions of right and wrong: "Write and right. Of course they have nothing to do with one another." She will have no distinctions of true and false: "The human mind is not concerned with being or not being true." She abjures beauty, emotion, association, analogy, illustration, metaphor. Art by subtraction finally subtracts art itself. What remains as the manner and matter of the specifically "creative" works of Gertrude Stein is the artist and an object vis-à-vis. This is not art; this is science. Miss Stein would turn the artist into a recording mechanism, a camera that somehow utters words rather than pictures.

It is vastly ironic that in a century in which the arts have been in pell-mell flight from the camera, she, who thought herself always galloping in the van of "contemporaneousness," has fled toward the camera. That hers is an eccentric camera, a literal camera obscura, does not make it less a camera. That in her early writing she was interested in what was under the surface, in the "inside," does not make her less a photographer. There she may be operating an X ray, but even its function is to take the picture, not to comment upon it, clothe it, or give it life in beauty or ugliness. Hers is still the "intellectual passion for exactitude in description."

Gertrude Stein's mistake, one must think, lies in conceiving as a sufficient ideal the thing William James handed her as a tool, the tool of rigidly objective scientific observation. She was conscious of this orientation toward science to some degree at one point in her work, *The Making of Americans*; after that she thought she had lost it and embarked upon a purely creative tack. But it seems that she never truly lost the scientific point of view. Whatever her subject, her "art" remained, within its idiosyncrasy, photographic in intention and in method.

Miss Stein makes a passing observation about painting in *The Autobiography of Alice B. Toklas* that is highly significant for an insight into her own work:

> One of the things that always worries her about painting is the difficulty that the artist feels and which sends him to painting still lifes, that after all the human being essentially is not paintable . . . if you do not solve your painting problem in painting human beings you do not solve it at all.

Yet she "always made her chief study people." Thus her chief study is people, who essentially are not paintable, and she is committed by the terms of her creed to painting them. One of the critical verities about Gertrude Stein is that she would never be instructed by impossibility, and one suspects that this particular impossibility is the focal dilemma of her work. It is her commitment to this impossibility, more than any of her ostensible dilemmas—the realization of "the complete actual present" or "the sense of immediacy"—that makes her twist and turn, that "made me try so many ways to tell my story" as she puts it.

True, "abjectly true," as William James would say, the human being is not paintable. Nor is he photographable; no matter whether one snaps his exterior or X-rays his bones and his liver and lights, one still does not have a human being. All great artists have recognized this abject truth; it is the reason they have set about apprehending the "poor, bare, forked animal"—still imperfectly, of course—by a means other than painting or by a means in addition to painting, by all the proliferation of the resources of language and thought and imagination they could command.

Gertrude Stein never effectively admitted that she could not paint or photograph man. She continued to try as long as she lived. And she, like the painters, was driven, in a very curious and retributively just way, into the retreat of still life. There was the difference, however, that the retreat became for her not occasional but chronic, not therapy but the disease itself. She retreated into the outright still life of the unpopulated *Tender Buttons,* or she sterilized and transfixed man until he was virtually a still-life element, no more humanly alive than Cézanne's apples or Braque's guitars. Why else should a play resemble a landscape, as she insists it should? In a very real sense, all the later works of Gertrude Stein, with the exception of those that are in some way autobiographical, are still lifes. To become an artist in the true sense of the word, Miss Stein would have had to surrender to the impossibility of apprehending man by unaided science.

It is significant, surely, that the one work of Gertrude Stein's with real artistic structure is the one that is least exclusively painterly. *Three Lives* is written as one feels, vaguely, a work of art should be written. It is written, that is, by a process of imagination applied to life experienced and directed by an informing philosophical theme and purpose; it is long and thoughtful in gestation; it envisions a reader to be enlightened and moved, and therefore it proceeds with a consciousness of form applied to part and whole, of language to be shaped and disciplined to delight and clarify. In a word, it is art achieved by the addition or multiplication of the tools of the writer. *Three Lives* was written, too, before experience became "sheer phenomenon" to Gertrude Stein, while she yet retained the desire to select and evaluate and be herself moved by her experience, before the encroachment of science upon her art imposed the necessity of removing herself emotionally from her subject and enjoined her to see mechanically rather than qualitatively. (pp. 169-75)

The real content, the root matter of communication in Gertrude Stein's creative writing, may be said in general to be pathetically thin. For a writer of her supposed stature, it is quite unbelievably thin. . . . [In addition to *Three Lives,* a] thin but still perceptible content persists in *Ida, The Making of Americans, Things as They Are,* and *Brewsie and Willie,* but this list leaves a score of volumes, the great bulk of her creative work, that have, one feels, very nearly nothing to say. When we are confronted with this fact, it is very difficult for us to understand the quantity of admiration that has been tendered Miss Stein. The truth is, one suspects, that the great mass of those who profess to admire the writings of Gertrude Stein, as apart from the personality of their creator, are unconsciously testifying not to the excellence of these writings, but to an abstract ideal, to their commitment to the civil liberty of the artist, to the premise that the artist has the right to be as eccentric as he pleases. They do not really understand what she is saying, but they wish to make very sure she is not denied the right to say it.

Few critics today would deny this right. But the reader has civil liberties, too. He has the right to deny the title of art to work that remains, after long and sympathetic immersion, unknowable and unpleasurable. There is degree in all things, including idiosyncrasy. Art moves ahead by idiosyncrasy. The strangeness of a Shakespeare, a Donne, a Coleridge, a Rabelais, a Swift, a Melville, a Proust, a Joyce—this strangeness enriches and advances literature. The strangeness of a Gertrude Stein debilitates and paralyzes. When art turns in on its creator, it may still be creation, but it is not art.

If one accepts every premise of Gertrude Stein, beginning with the great parent premise of her genius, "in english literature in her time the only one," and acquiescing all the way down through the corollaries of her complex aesthetics, there still remains the bar of language. This barrier remains final and fatal because it is the medium she has chosen, the only one through which we can apprehend her. Like her subject matter and her form, but to an even greater degree, her language is private. Gertrude Stein chose words by two main criteria: they had to have for her "existing being"—they had to be privately alive and exciting—and they did not need to be words that in general possessed objective application to the subject at hand in order to be the words that "described that thing." All of this means, practically, for the reader a vocabulary of impenetrable, esoteric abstractions. Miss Stein clearly hopes to inaugurate an art uniquely possessed of accuracy and sensitivity, evoked by words stripped of their received meanings and laid bare and new on the page—a language as new as Homer's.

It is almost incredible that a woman of Gertrude Stein's intelligence could fail to see the fallacy inherent in this position. Yet she does fail to see it, and it is this colossal blind spot that ultimately condemns her to a stillborn art. Just as her "insistence" is to us inevitably repetition, so this abstraction that she looks upon as a bright new concretion seems to us a concretion foreign to hers, based on the received meanings of the words rather than on the meanings she arbitrarily and privately assigns them. The matter is as simple as this: the words do not mean the same things to us that they mean to her; she is writing in one language, we are reading in another.

Gertrude Stein could never bring herself to see that words are the least amenable to abstraction of all the artistic media. To a far greater degree than the musician's medium, sound, or the painter's medium, color, line, and volume, words are unseverably connected in our minds with things. When we see or hear the word, we see an image of the thing, and there is not much Miss Stein can do to make us see something else. That is why, when we read a characteristic Stein page and find that it relates itself to nothing we know, we find it easy to assume the truth of the superstition that she is aiming at abstract painterly or musical effects. Because she was inept at painting and music and because she was convinced that it was her mission to create a great abstract art—concretion by divinely inspired abstraction—she was driven to attempt an impossible degree of abstraction in the only medium left to her. She died believing she had succeeded.

The pathos and paradox of all this, as I see it, lies in the fact that the whole preoccupation with an abstract language is really unnecessary. Our language is not the abject, inadequate vessel Gertrude Stein found it to be. The real innovators—Joyce, Proust, Kafka, Hopkins, Virginia Woolf—all are constantly making the language perform new acrobatics of color, nuance, and intelligibility by sensitively exploiting with new virtuosity its ancient resources. Very fundamental questions about the quality of Miss Stein's mind therefore arise. We can dismiss her distortion of language, as Leo Stein does, as compensation for a root inadequacy with language at its everyday level, but this solution seems oversimple. There is a more complex pathology inhabiting a mind that could pursue so long and so blindly a course so pointless and so perverse.

But even if we surrender entirely, if we go not only the second mile with Gertrude Stein, but the third as well, if we grant the possibility of struggling through her words to a vague approximation of her meaning, or, failing that, of closing upon some other poor literary remnant such as "mood" or "tone," there nevertheless remains the utterly insuperable barrier of her repetition. Gertrude Stein is a ruminant animal, not with the four stomachs of the cow, but with four hundred. Committed to the doctrine that the artist must record his ongoing present knowledge of his subject, she lays each moment's perception on the page, endless repeating or minutely varying that of the previous moment. To say that this becomes tiresome is the grossest understatement; it is deadly, it is not art, and it is not fit fare for a sane reader. (pp. 196-200)

If Gertrude Stein would only admit the poverty of her content and admit that its essential quality is vague suggestion, she would be a great deal more respectable. But she would confess neither. Because the content of her writing was the content of the genius vision, it was to be considered always dense and ponderable. She stubbornly insisted that her object was always concretely present on the page; if communication was imperfect, that was the fault of the reader. So she grumbles, "Mostly those to whom I am explaining are not completely hearing," and, more heatedly, "But what's the difficulty? Just read the words on the paper. They're in English. Just read them. Be simple and you'll understand these things."

The amazing thing is that this is perfectly honest mystification and outrage. Gertrude Stein seems never to have understood certain elementary facts: that it is impossible to be "simple" with English words because they are loaded with meaning; that she is speaking one language, we another; that it is never possible for one mind to know another really well, impossible for one to know another at all without help. Therefore, it is accurate to say that throughout her creative life, Gertrude Stein practiced a kind of cultivated schizophrenia. By an act that may have been will, or stupidity, or some curious pathological quirk, she convinced herself first of the inevitable rightness of her position and then of the inevitable communicability of her vision through the chosen language. Willfully, or stupidly, or pathologically, she blinded herself to the crusted connotativeness of language and to the insularity of sensibilities foreign to her own. She sealed these unpalatable truths in a compartment of her brain that she never again entered. She takes an idea that could be made clear and cold in expository prose, or clear and warm in narrative-dramatic prose, or warm and vaguely—perhaps more meaningfully—clear in intelligible abstraction, and makes it cold and unclear—dead—in unintelligible abstraction. So I see the matter.

I am inclined to contend, then, that Gertrude Stein's creative writings are undernourished in intrinsic matter, that even this poverty fails of communication by being cast in a foreign language, and that her works are therefore practically worthless as art. (pp. 201-03)

To maintain integrity, Miss Stein felt that she had to make herself not merely honest but unique; being unique, she is unknowable, and her creation is stillborn. To maintain the "presentness" of the creative vision, she threw away the archives, closed her mind and her conscience, fixed her lens in a static position, photographed reality as a still-life succession, and then ran the film through a warped projector onto the standard screen of the printed page. The result is a flawed art by subtraction and abstraction.

Gertrude Stein is not alone, of course, in being concerned with the illumination of the present moment of consciousness. This might with justice be called the characteristic preoccupation of prose writers in our time. The greatest of her contemporaries devoted major portions of their careers to its solution. Compared with them, she is pathetic—no other word suffices. To her pathetic narrowing must be compared their burgeoning inclusiveness; to her fortuitous form, their organic form; to her art-for-art insulation from life, their hot immersion in it; to her drab, cacophonous emptiness, their proliferation of the possibilities for beauty, meaning, and passion in the language. Gertrude Stein is right, as the others are right, in believing that it is important that art illuminate the "complete actual present," but in her method she is terrifically, fatally wrongheaded. Joyce once suggested that readers should devote their lives to his works, and his suggestion is less than absurd. But the feeling that remains after reading Gertrude Stein is not one of illumination and profit, but one of darkness and waste.

After writing *The Making of Americans*, Gertrude Stein should have made the great confession and begun anew. Instead, she burrowed blindly, molewise, deeper into a cul-de-sac. Now, reading her books, one lists the good things of literature and crosses them off one by one: her works possess no beauty, no instruction, no passion. All that is finally there is Gertrude Stein mumbling to herself. Everything in her writing returns upon the self for value. All that is left of literature is its function as delight to its creator—which perhaps justifies its writing, but not its being put in print.

Gertrude Stein, it seems to me, is already effectively dead as a writer. Nobody really reads her, but everybody continues to talk knowingly and concernedly about her. Her "importance" is a myth. She is enormously interesting as a phenomenon of the power of personality and as a symptom of a frantic, fumbling, nightmare age—our present—and it is as such that she will live. Later ages will gather about the corpus of her work like a cluster of horrified medical students around a biological sport. (pp. 205-07)

> *B. L. Reid, in his* Art by Subtraction: A Dissenting Opinion of Gertrude Stein, *University of Oklahoma Press, 1958, 224 p.*

## TONY TANNER (essay date 1965)

[*Tanner is an English critic and scholar specializing in American literature. In the following excerpt, he analyzes Stein's attempt to express a fresh vision of reality through stylistic innovations and assesses the effectiveness of these innovations.*]

After Mark Twain, the naive vernacular narrator reappears constantly in American fiction, from the crude and derivative efforts of Don Marquis (*Danny's Own Story*) and Edgar Lee Masters (*Mitch Miller*), up to the sophisticated successes of J. D. Salinger (*Catcher in the Rye*) and Saul Bellow (*Adventures of Augie March*). But a more interesting line of development leads from Twain to Hemingway and it is a development which depends for its success on the separation of the vernacular from the young narrator. The naive vernacular ceases to be an adopted voice and develops into an achieved style; instead of appearing to be spontaneous unarranged talk it is subjected to a rigorous and careful stylization. In this line of development Gertrude Stein played the part of the indispensable provoking theorist. (p. 187)

Few people these days are greatly moved by much of Stein's work, and yet in her time she attracted a reverence and respect which at least attest to an unusually original and stimulating mind. . . . [She] had an unusually penetrating insight into the intellectual climate of her time and a gift for the clarification of ideas and novel experiment. Her ideas ventured beyond what she took from William James, just as her prose changes considerably between the felicitous Henry James imitation of her first novel (which she called *Q.E.D.* and which was [also] . . . published as *Things As They Are*) and the post-experimental clarity of *The Autobiography of Alice B. Toklas.* She is more an innovator than an imitator. One forgets, perhaps, how early she was with her ideas and experiments. Her first important experimental work, *Three Lives,* was published in 1905. *The Making of Americans* followed between 1906 and 1908: her important and understanding book on *Picasso* appeared in 1909 while her own work had achieved almost a maximum of experimentation in *Tender Buttons* in 1910-12. For good or bad she was truly original. (pp. 188-89)

Curiously enough her little book on Picasso contains an unusually lucid statement of certain notions which, no matter how relevant they are to Picasso, are certainly very relevant to American literature. The book is based on the premise that "nothing changes in people from one generation to another except the way of seeing and being seen" and that "another vision than that of all the world is very rare. That is why geniuses are rare, to complicate things in a new way that is easy, but to see the things in a new way that is really difficult, everything prevents one, habits, schools, daily life, reason, necessities of daily life, indolence, everything prevents one, in fact there are very few geniuses in the world." That the artist awakes us out of dulled perceptual habits and offers and enforces new ways of looking at the world, new visual attitudes towards reality, seems to me an insight of perennial relevance: but in this case it is peculiarly relevant in that it leads Stein to take up a question . . . raised by earlier American writers: namely, what is the most rewarding way to look at the world, the best mode of vision. (p. 189)

She first compares his way of regarding reality with the way of the child who sees only vivid fragments (one side of its mother's face) and has not learnt to infer the whole. Picasso's struggle was difficult because "no one had ever tried to express things seen not as one knows them but as they are when one sees them without remembering having looked at them." But "he was right, one sees what one sees, the rest is a reconstruction from memory and painters have nothing to do with reconstruction, nothing to do with memory, they concern themselves only with visible things." The difference between what one can see and what one knows is there, is crucial for Stein and she sees the aim of art as an effort to capture the former: an effort continually interrupted and foiled by reminiscences of the latter. She maintains that, like Picasso, she is trying to look at things as though for the first time and for this reason she works to exclude memory and knowledge from her work.

> In the beginning when Picasso wished to express heads and bodies not like every one could see them, which was the problem of other painters, but as he saw them, *as one can see when one had not the habit of knowing what one is looking at,* inevitably when he commenced he had the tendency to paint them as a mass as sculptors do or in profile as children do [my italics].

The ideas here relate to Thoreau's notion of "seeing without looking," Whitman's "first step," and the general American interest in a recovered naivety of vision. All these ideas are the result of the inquiry: how can man establish an authentic first hand relationship with existing reality? Stein too is addressing herself to the problem of how we can establish contact with the "reality of things that exist." She thought that the greatest hindrances to this contact were memories of other comparable impressions which blur the uniqueness of the present perceptual instant, and all the associations and thoughts which our minds discharge as soon as we are confronted with an object which we want to recognize and classify. What she wanted, and found in Picasso, were "things seen without association but simply as things seen" and she comments approvingly that "only the things seen are knowledge for Picasso." She wants no interpretation, no reference to other previous "things seen," no contributions from the storehouse of the mind. For Picasso, she asserts, and we feel her agreement, "remembered things are not things seen, therefore they are not things known."

More extreme than Thoreau, Stein has an ideal of what we may call seeing without remembering, without associating, without thinking. She wants the eye to open to the reality of the material world as though it had never opened before: for then we catch reality at its "realest," unfiltered through the schemata of the sophisticated eye which is dimmed from too long domestication in the world. And even though she does not develop or push the comparison she clearly cites the child's way of looking as exemplary: naivety must be cultivated in order that we may see reality as it is and not as we remember it to be. This takes us back to the problem of how a child does in fact perceive reality. More basically, whether one can in fact see anything clearly at all without the aid of memory, the subtle reawakening of innumerable past visual experiences, is

open to doubt. Certainly, words are full of memories—are perhaps pure memory—and the impressions gained by the unremembering eye could never be transmitted by the unremembering voice. For without memory there is no metaphor; and without metaphor we would never have had language. Stein avoids live metaphors but to communicate at all she has to use those dead ones we all use continually in our daily speech. Her ideal properly carried out, if it did not lead to a visual confusion akin to blindness, would certainly lead to silence.

To draw these inferences is perhaps unfair. In fact what Stein wants is to purify the eye, to break old visual habits, to initiate a more vivid commerce between the senses and the real world. That Picasso himself managed to do this is indisputable: that Stein's interest in this relates her to a number of American writers from Emerson onwards is my contention. Perhaps all art ultimately contributes to an endless rediscovery of the world around us and within us. American writing in particular has shown a consistent interest in scraping the grime of old emotions from reality, in shedding complex habits of vision, in cleansing words of those clusters of associations which may produce dullness as often as they contribute richness. To equate seeing things as though for the first time with knowledge as Stein does, is a peculiarly American idea. And having described Picasso in these terms, having dismissed memory as an aid to vision, she adds a further idea which makes us think more of Anderson and Hemingway than Picasso. "And so then always and always Picasso commenced his attempt to express not things felt, not things remembered, not established in relations but things which are there, really everything a human being can know *at each moment of his existence and not an assembling of all his experiences*" (my italics). A preference for a moment-by-moment notation of impressions is clearly discernible in Anderson and Hemingway: the "assembling" of experience reveals itself in generalizations and abstractions, just as an interest in the "relations" between things tends to produce a complex syntax: and it is precisely these two things which their prose attempts to avoid. And of course the naive eye which refuses to remember anything can ill afford to pass by anything: hence the detailed inclusiveness of this way of writing, its moment-by-moment quality. Needless to say a more or less subtle sense of selection must be at work, but the close itemizing contact with the concrete world and the predominantly paratactic syntax which we have remarked in much American writing must be related to this preferred mode of seeing, a mode which separates sensations out rather than assembling them together.

Stein's attack on memory and her related preference for a moment-by-moment notation of experience is also in evidence in her *Lectures in America,* particularly in the one entitled **"Portraits and Repetition."** She discusses what she had attempted in some of her prose portraits and revealingly she turns to the cinema to explain how she managed to make portraits of people "as they are existing" without having recourse to "remembering":

> Funnily enough the cinema has offered a solution of this thing. By a continuously moving picture of any one there is no memory of any other thing and there is that thing existing. . . . I was doing what the cinema was doing, I was making a continuous succession of the statement of what that person was until I had not many things but one thing.

Just as life never repeats itself, and the cinema doesn't quite repeat itself, so her prose, she claims, does not really repeat itself: rather there is a series of small additions and modifications in her prose, just as there are minute differences in each successive picture flashed on a cinema screen. ''As I told you in comparing it to a cinema picture one second was never the same as the second before or after.'' She maintains that ''existing as a human being . . . is never repetition'' and goes on to say that ''remembering is the only repetition'' just as ''remembering is the only confusion.'' The confusion comes from allowing the past to get mixed up with the present, presumably a sullying intrusion which mars the accuracy of our perception of what is actually there in the present. Her ideal is a continuously developing present—complete and actual at any given moment—which is yet a whole, just as an existing thing is a whole or even as a single frame of a film is a whole, although both are made up of many minute parts. What she is against is ''letting remembering mix itself with looking'': what she is in favour of is ''moment to moment emphasizing.'' As before, the two go together. In a later lecture she makes a simple remark which succinctly hints at her whole theory of prose. ''After all the natural way to count is not that one and one make two but to go on counting by one and one. . . . One and one and one and one and one. That is the natural way to go on counting.'' Applied to prose this would mean no ''assembling,'' no complex ''relating,'' no accumulation, no interpretation, no comparison, no increasing density of significance. It would mean a prose that, literally, was not additive. Rather language would have to adapt itself to registering the ''complete and actual present'' again and again and again: now and now and now—one and one and one. If we hold on to the cinema for an analogy we can see that this will mean a series of still pictures: reading her prose is at times like holding a strip of movie film and looking at each frame separately. Understandably Stein sometimes uses the idea of the still life to explain her intentions and this whole relation between movement and stillness, and their relation in turn to the twin ideas of rejection of memory and the refusal of assembling, must now be looked at rather carefully.

In her lectures on narration Stein took up a very clear hostile attitude towards traditional narrative habits. (pp. 189-94)

[Stein takes] issue with narrative which concerns itself with giving an account of purposive action, narrative like a chain of causes and effects leading to a final crisis, narrative which deals with successive things and not existing things. It seems to me that she fails to demonstrate that the existence of a thing cannot be revealed by showing it in action but her intention in making these into mutually exclusive alternatives is fairly clear. It is part of the modern rebellion against conventional plot—it is in Anderson as well—which, it was felt, slighted reality by its habit of erecting a spurious superstructure of eventfulness. Old narrative, so the argument would run, forces the attention to inquire, what has happened, what will happen next, to what resolution does all this tend: it never concentrates on the more basic miracle of what *is*. It ignores the man standing still. Stein's dislike of ''successive'' action is not a distrust of all movement: ''it is something strictly American to conceive a space that is filled with moving, a space of time that is filled always filled with moving'' she asserts. Movement is inherent in the existing thing, even in its stillness: but in successive narrative, reality is wrenched, suppressed and ignored to fit the traditional arc of beginning, middle and end. Stein is against narrative which fosters a causal time sense, which forces us to ask of the material in front of us—what is happening and why? Better, she would maintain, to develop an art which makes us ponder what is existing, now and for itself. The present participle—the standing man. Memory deflects our attention into

the past and thence to the future. Better to seize the moment—in its fullness and in its stillness, a stillness throbbing with latent movement. Her fondness for art is relevant here and it is worth noting that *Lucy Church Amiably* is subtitled ''A Novel of Romantic beauty and nature and which Looks Like an Engraving.'' More to the point we should recall that she wrote *Three Lives,* so she tells us, ''looking and looking'' at a Cézanne portrait of a woman. Cézanne would indeed seem to exemplify the attitude to reality which Stein spent so much time and care trying to define.

In turning away from academic and classical subjects and preferring the challenge of still-life painting he spoke revealingly of ''the heroism of the real'' and went on to formulate his magnificent phrase about ''the immensity, the torrent of the world in a little bit of matter.'' This perfectly explains why his still lives are not still. He needs no reference to heroic actions to convey a dynamic sense of movement and charged reality. Presumably Stein had something like this in mind when she wrote in favour of a style of writing which could catch and hold the existing thing and exclude the successive thing. She wanted a writing that would give, not the thing in history, but the thing-in-itself. It is perhaps illustrative of this strain in her thinking that she could write in one of her lectures: ''I wonder now if it is necessary to stand still to live if it is not necessary to stand still to live, and if it is if that is not perhaps to be a new way to write a novel.''

It is when we come to Stein's specific ideas about writing that we see not only what she was really getting at, but also perhaps why it was that she never really managed to write a work that came up to her ideals. She once wrote ''description is explanation''—a phrase very relevant to Hemingway—but in her later lectures, particularly **''Poetry and Grammar,''** she redefines description in a way which separates it from the activity as we might understand it. In **''Portraits and Repetition''** she tells of looking at something and then trying to find words that looked like the thing under observation:

> I became more and more excited about how words which were the words that made whatever I looked at look like itself were not the words that had in them any quality of description. . . . And the thing that excited me so very much at that time and still does is that the words or words that make what I looked at be itself were always words that to me very exactly related themselves to that thing the thing at which I was looking, but as often as not had as I say nothing whatever to do with what any words would do that described that thing.

The idea here—if I understand it correctly—is that if you want to convey a sense of reality, catch the very quality of the thing seen, it is not sufficient to name the object and list its properties. Recreation is not description. Her portraits seem to me for the most part idiosyncratic and unintelligible—too arcane, too subjective, or merely too full of private jokes to communicate any recognizable reality. Similarly the prose studies of ''Objects: food: rooms'' which make up *Tender Buttons* resist most attempts to find any conventional meaning in them. What is clear is that Stein is not interested in conventional ways of transmitting sense and impressions: rather she seems to want to try and find out how she can manipulate the patterning of the sounds of words to create a verbal still-life so that we may receive the proferred thing itself and not the thing summed up. This example has some novel quality:

> A table means does it not my dear it means a whole steadiness. Is it likely that a change.

> A table means more than a glass even a looking glass
> is tall. A table means necessary places and a revision
> a revision of a little thing it means it does mean that
> there has been a stand, a stand where it did shake.

However, some recognizable statements are discernible there. In the following example we have mere word play (though it may be fair to say that by playing, literally, with words, writers often discover forgotten properties in them which are later available for more serious employment).

> Go red go red laugh white.
> Suppose a collapse in rubbed purr, in rubbed purr get.
> Little sales ladies little sales ladies little saddles of mutton.
> Little sales of leather and such beautiful, beautiful, beautiful.

These attempts are obviously too private in their associations and too arbitrary in their procedure: but it seems that a new and careful look is being taken at words themselves, even at the cost of all communicated meaning. And had Gertrude Stein's work matured into real significance she would not have been the first modern artist who had to descend into apparent meaninglessness to emerge with new meanings. Certainly it is worth considering the motivating ideas behind these attempts.

These emerge more clearly in **"Poetry and Grammar."** Her first, and most significant, attack, is on the use of nouns. And here she both makes a valid point and overstates it:

> A noun is a name of anything, why after a thing is
> named write about it. . . . Nouns are the names of
> anything and just naming names is alright when you
> want to call a roll but is it any good for anything
> else. . . . As I say a noun is the name of a thing, and
> therefore slowly if you feel what is inside that thing
> you do not call it by the name by which it is known.
> Everybody knows that by the way they do when they
> are in love and a writer should always have that
> intensity of emotion about whatever is the object
> about which he writes. And therefore and I say it
> again more and more one does not use nouns.

Adjectives, since their job is to affect nouns, are also "not really and truly interesting." From this extreme point of view nouns, with all their qualifying adjuncts, appear as barriers which interpose themselves between the passionate perceiver and the thing perceived. This is valid only if you are considering that crude use of nouns which makes them opaque; mere utilitarian gestures uninhabited by reality. As in a roll call or inventory. There are indeed ways of naming and describing which inhibit, even prohibit, awareness and discourage all sensitivity of response. But to hypothesize an ideal of prose unfurnished with any nouns and adjectives is to recommend a banishment of reality from language which language could not survive. Stein's aim is, however, not so fantastic as that. This is how she phrases her problem: "Was there not a way of naming things that would not invent names, but mean names without naming them." She is here lamenting a common phenomenon whereby once we have named a thing (and as always in Stein's use of the word "thing" she means emotions as well as objects), we tend to forget the reality which lurks or dances beyond the name. Of course there is a way of naming things which embraces and discloses and celebrates that reality—poetry, says Stein. "So I say poetry is essentially the discovery, the love, the passion for the name of anything." But—so her argument trends—as the names become dull, common, and opaque, new ways of access to the reality of things must be sought. "After all one had known its name anything's name for so long, and so the name was not new but the thing being alive was always new." In face of a continually self-renewing

reality we must retain an ever renewed sense of wonder. Look at things as for the first time. Here nouns impede us, they have been around too long. So Stein tries "looking at anything until something that was not the name of that thing but was in a way that actual thing would come to be written." Her point is that the name of a thing (the conventional, accredited name) and the actual thing are inevitably separate and different; the former an impoverished substitute for the latter. After looking at something she tries "creating it without naming it" and so she "struggled desperately with the recreation and the avoidance of nouns as nouns." Walt Whitman is singled out for praise—"He wanted really wanted to express the thing and not call it by its name"—and Stein finishes her lecture with her clear conviction that "the noun must be replaced by the thing in itself." To answer that words never are nor ever can be things is of course too crude and unsympathetic to Stein's point. We could recall Emerson's distinction between language which is heavy with the bullion of nature and language which has become a false paper currency. Stein's ambition is a manifestation of that compelling reality-hunger which we have seen to be a motivating power in many American writers. Stein wants to create verbal models or constructs which do not point to reality but somehow simulate it and evoke the sheer quality of existing things. It is her method, her idea of banishing the noun, which is open to question. Consider language as a reticulated transparent screen through which we look at the world: the reticulations provide relatively stable shapes—names, notions, species, etc.—which help us to bring into focus and thereby recognize a relatively unstable reality continually in flux. The screen is not reality, but without it reality remains undifferentiated and, to that extent, unseen. Without language we would suffer reality: it would beset us. To perceive the thing we need the word. The word is not the thing, but the word lasts longer than the thing. Stein's idea would seem to be to remove much of this reticulated screen, this patchwork of old names, and to substitute an improvised vocabulary which communicates the present feel of reality without identifying it by recourse to accepted nomenclature. Because names, by virtue of their very acceptance, refer back to the past: and Stein would like to get the past out of language, cleanse words of their dark history, cut them off from those roots which anchor and nourish. Ideally she wants the impossible. (pp. 194-200)

It is because so much of the past lies dormant but available in words that we can orient ourselves in current reality. Language is occasionally added to and subtracted from: for the most part it is simply endlessly reshuffled. The great writer manages this reshuffling in such a way as to recall us vividly to reality. He might seek to give us a complete actual present, but he will do it with materials which are saturated with past identifications and insights. The writer brings the past to bear on the present in a new way: indeed it is only by using the old that we can ascertain what is new. It seems to me that Stein confused two separate issues: she wanted to look at reality *as if* for the first time—she then thought it necessary to write about the reality thus perceived without using words which contained dense evidence of previous realities witnessed and wondered at, suffered and seen. Nouns are obviously the main bearers of these past realities—for the word table always refers to yesterday's table—so she struggled to avoid them. Yet we may borrow a Falstaffian reproach for the vast assembly of exiled nouns and imagine them saying to Stein—banish us and you banish the whole world.

Her error was to relegate nouns, theoretically, to poetry. For here she has a point. Concerning her famous phrase she wrote in her lecture:

When I said.

A rose is a rose is a rose is a rose.

And then later made that into a ring I made poetry
and what did I do I caressed completely caressed and
addressed a noun.

The function of the repetition, I would say, is to take us away
from the common word towards the rare reality. It is a way of
reasserting what is miraculous in the commonplace. It represents Emerson's wisdom of wondering at the usual. Each time
the word is repeated a bit of inertia and impercipience is shaken
loose off the noun until the blooming petalled perfumed reality
is brought into our minds. This would be a way of ridding
language of the dulling encrustations of custom and second-
hand reference: being made to hear the word as for the first
time we will come to see the rose as for the first time. This
sort of repetition aims at replacing habit with wonder. Just so
we shall find in some of Hemingway that very simple assertions
of the existence of reality—"The river was there."—can have
a tremendously forceful impact. We rediscover the world.

Of course although Stein's theories moved towards a renunciation of nouns and not a forceful re-use of them, in practice
she uses them frequently: in a fairly orthodox way in the clear
style of *The Autobiography of Alice B. Toklas,* and both in the
more conventional statements and the more patterned and stylized parts of *Lucy Church Amiably.* No written style could
endure the impoverishment consequent upon a total exclusion
of nouns. However it is true that her interest in sheer word-
patterning tends to make of her prose a perverse and personal
unballasted flow which gives us very little reality. It is as
though she experiments nearly all her life and never really puts
the results of those experiments to any very fruitful use. Her
most famous work is the early story "**Melanctha**" which appeared in *Three Lives.* Here there is a true originality and the
words, though patterned and arranged in the interests of calculated repetitions, etc., address themselves directly to palpable realities. It is perhaps one way of commenting on her life's
work to say that though she went on to make many more daring
experiments she never created a better work of art. Looking
back at "**Melanctha**" in *Composition as Explanation* Stein wrote
this:

> In the beginning writing I wrote a book called *Three
> Lives* this was written in 1905, I wrote a negro story
> called *Melanctha.* In that there was a constant re-
> curring and beginning there was a marked direction
> in the direction of being in the present although nat-
> urally I had been accustomed to past present and
> future, and why, because the composition forming
> around me was a prolonged present. A composition
> of a prolonged present is a natural composition in
> the world as it has been these thirty years it was more
> and more a prolonged present. I created then a pro-
> longed present naturally I knew nothing of a contin-
> uous present but it came naturally to me to make one,
> it was simple it was clear to me and nobody knew
> why it was done like that, I did not myself although
> naturally to me it was natural.

In fact the story has a fairly simple narrative line and covers
the life of a passionate, confused and suffering negro woman.
But it is not presented "successively" but rather as a series of
"stills"—as Anderson was to address himself to arrested moments. Great use is made of slightly modified repetitions, echoing phrases, and refrains which both serve to organize the
prose, and have an incremental effect as more and more of
Melanctha's sad experience attaches itself to them (e.g. "Al-

ways Melanctha Herbert wanted peace and quiet, and always
she could only find new ways to get excited." The material
of the story happened in time—it deals mainly with painful
love affairs—but the story itself does not give the effect of
being a trajectory through time. It deposits instants, complete
moments, relevant fractions of experience: it describes the past
as a series of separate presents so that the feeling is more of
"now and now and now" (the word is used at the start of ten
consecutive sentences at one stage) rather than "then and then
and then." The naive narrating eye is full of wonder (and
compassion), not much given to comment and interpretation
but more intent on focusing on emotional moments and separating their complexity out into their simple component parts.
One and one and one and one.

> Jeff Campbell then began again on the old papers.
> He sat there on the steps just above where Melanctha
> was sitting, and he went on with his reading, and his
> head went moving up and down, and sometimes he
> was reading, and sometimes he was thinking about
> all the things he wanted to be doing, and then he
> would rub the back of his dark hand over his mouth,
> and in between he would be frowning over his think-
> ing, and sometimes he would be rubbing his head
> hard to help his thinking. And Melanctha just sat still
> and watched the lamp burning, and sometimes she
> turned it down a little, when the wind caught it and
> it would begin to get to smoking.
>
> Jefferson sighed, and then he smiled, and then they
> were quiet a long time together, and then after some
> more kindness, it was late, and then Jeff left her.
>
> And they loved it always, more and more, together,
> with this new feeling they had now, in these long
> summer days so warm; they, always together now,
> just these two so dear, more and more to each other
> always, and the summer evenings when they wan-
> dered, and the noises in the full streets, and the music
> of the organs, and the dancing, and the warm smell
> of the people, and of dogs and of the horses, and all
> the joy of the strong, sweet, pungent, dirty, moist,
> warm negro southern summer.

Syntax and punctuation here are not used for relating and "assembling" but rather for separating out each moment of existence. The words work outwards to touch and disentangle
reality. Here we have a maintained simplicity, a deliberate
naivety with no simple first-person narrator present to persuade
us to accept the words and point of view as plausible. There
is no attempt to catch the audible accents of a personal address:
care instead is paid to the subtle control of pace, phrase length,
and paragraph organization. The sustained evenness of the narrating tone clearly conceals an intense sympathy, but its main
task is to secure and maintain a simple clarity of vision and
notation. Sometimes, indeed, it becomes a pure naivety, an
almost excessive spelling out of details which nevertheless
plays its part in bringing home the reality of the situation to
us. "Sometimes Jem Richards would be betting and would be
good and lucky, and be getting lots of money. Sometimes Jem
would be betting badly, and then he would not be having any
money."

The story is genuinely moving and reveals Stein's considerable
psychological insight; a talent we must regard as sadly neglected in her subsequent work. For all her theorizing about
the need to establish relationships with existent reality, her
own prose, mainly because of her distrust of nouns, etc., lost
its ability to grope carefully out into the stuff of the world. In
one of her lectures she asserts that the American language

exhibits a "lack of connection" with material daily living, and in another lecture she insists that in American writing words "began to detach themselves from the solidity of anything"; to my mind these estimates are only applicable to Stein's own later writing (and possibly to James's later work as she suggests). Her case as a writer and theorizer then presents a contradiction. Obsessed by the need to find a language that would convey directly the existing real thing in itself, she developed a highly mannered style, complicatedly simple yet curiously weightless, full of subtle movement yet fatally uninhabited. Her new way of writing was not a successful communication of her new way of seeing and, as I have tried to suggest, there are certain aspects of her theories which can go some way to explain this failure. Yet many of her ideas were influential, some of her discoveries were put to good effect by later writers, and her intentions place her in a major American tradition of writing and aspiration. She was genuinely aware of the "seduction (and) ecstasy of things seen" and worked hard to write a prose which could convey "the rhythm of the visible world": in one of her own good phrases we can say that she herself was moved by "the emotion of reality." (pp. 200-04)

> Tony Tanner, "Gertrude Stein and the Complete Actual Present," in his *The Reign of Wonder: Naivety and Reality in American Literature, Cambridge at the University Press, 1965, pp. 187-204.*

## BRUCE F. KAWIN (essay date 1972)

[*An American poet and critic, Kawin is the author of essays and several books that he describes as "works of speculative criticism, most of them having to do with the metaphysics of narration in literature and film." In the following excerpt, he examines the function of repetition in Stein's attempt to reproduce human perception of time.*]

"Gertrude Stein," she wrote of herself, "has always been possessed by the intellectual passion for exactitude in the description of inner and outer reality." Yet her descriptions seem totally unrelated to their objects. We naturally ask, what does the description of Oranges in **Tender Buttons**, "Build is all right," have to do with oranges? Gertrude Stein rejected ordinary speech—which is full of irrelevant associations, connotations, and evocations—in favor of what she considered an accurate, directed, and consistent language, both objective and abstract, whose words and movements would be in her absolute control, and which would not refer obliquely to the associations of old poetry. Stein's manner of recording exactly what she sees—or the movements of her consciousness in relation to its object of attention—in a language that means only what it means *now*, is a discipline of objectivity that her audience has tended to receive as incomprehensibly subjective, if not decadent. For Stein, experience itself "was objective to the point of being indistinguishable from reality."

It is not enough to reinvent language; the act of recording itself must be clear and alive. Gertrude Stein attempted, through simultaneously observing and recording, and by beginning again with each new instant of observing and recording, to make her carefully, consciously chosen individual and nonevocative words record what she actually saw. In her "portraits" particularly, it was important to see each thing, each person, in its or his uniqueness, apart from any resemblance to other things or persons. The success of these observations depended on her being able to see only the present, to write only in the present, to educate her audience to read only in the present.

The effect of Stein's unfamiliar syntax on our spoken-language-oriented ears is to make us consider each word in the relations which it imposes on the words around it. Every mental observation has its own syntax, or manner of organization. Language changes with its object and subject. As we pay attention to each word, our idealized concentration reveals the exact image these exact words here generate; to what else *can* we relate them but to their simple meaning in their immediate context? Another way of putting this is to say that these words do not "remember" how they have been used before, that their author puts them down as if this were the first time she had ever seen them, as if their present context—since the present is the only existing time, and this syntax defies relation to ordinary syntax or to earlier moments in its own world—were the only context that could ever be important for these words. Each word begins its history in this particular usage.

Her mind free of old associations, literal or otherwise, Stein lets words come together in new ways, as they are appropriate and forceful and interesting, in the spontaneous and deliberate act of writing.

> There is nothing that anyone creating needs more than that there is no time sense inside them no past present or future.

The author must allow her work to take shape in front of her, with all her concentration. She must move with the progress of the work, keeping not the past or future of the work in mind, but only its present; not the past usages of her words, but her words; not what she remembers the subject looks like, but how it looks. If she concentrates completely in the moment of writing she must also concentrate completely in the simultaneous moment of observation, seeing the object for what it exactly is, not what it has been compared to or considered. If the grass under the pigeons becomes shorter then longer then yellow, she can see it and write it.... She must see in the present, and see the present completely. What is "recollected in tranquility" is falsified.

In the overfamous line "A rose is a rose is a rose...," for example, we find what looks very like repetition playing an important part in making a dead word ("rose") real again, removing the word from its "history," and insisting on its existence in advancing time. The difficulty of writing poetry in a "late age," as she explains, is precisely that of giving words life, in the face of all their remembering.... Nevertheless Stein denied that repetition had anything to do with the success of that line. She insisted in fact that her writing contained no repetitions.

In her verbal portraits Stein was reproached with being repetitious, and her defense of her method, the lecture **"Portraits and Repetition"**—informed perhaps even on her part by a confusion between "repetitive" and "repetitious"—makes quite clear her belief that where there is life, there is no repetition. Her use of the term is strict; for her it means identical recurrence with no increase in force, with none of the slight differences in composition that constitute life. Something that is being taught (a piece of knowledge with the excitement of discovery taken out of it) can be repeated in drill; an artwork that simply copies another work can be said to be a repetition; but in her writing there is no repetition. We can see what she means from those portraits.

If we do not pay complete attention to the person before us, we cannot write an accurate portrait of that exact person. To produce these abstract verbalizations of her experience of her subjects, Gertrude Stein trained herself to observe people without caring whom else they were like, and to write with that same concentration, faithful to the integrity of her subject. Each of us is unique, and each of our instants is unique. No matter how many times something happens to us, it is real each time. And each ideal Steinian statement—each new instant of writing synchronized with the subject's fresh movement of consciousness—is unique, and real each time.

Stein preferred to call her near-repetitions "insistence." In this succession of simultaneously observed and recorded instants she felt progress; remaining in phase with her subject, she believed she accurately experienced and transcribed its identity, its assurance, its "excitingness of pure being."

> Exciting as a human being, that is being listening and hearing is never repetition. It is not repetition if it is that which you are actually doing because naturally each time the emphasis is different just as the cinema has each time a slightly different thing to make it all be moving.

In comparing the slight differentiation between the successive frames of a motion picture to the differences among her statements and observations—asserting that the differences keep both images moving, just as they constitute the life of the subject—Gertrude Stein makes clear one reason why it is so futile to skim her writing and clarifies her definition of repetition. A motion picture in which each frame was identical would not move. The near-repetition of similar frames, when properly projected, communicates life. If you take a yard of film out of the can and just look at it, you cannot see the movement although you might possibly infer it; the frames look identical. You certainly cannot see how the slight changes act on each other, or feel the movement they produce. Scanning the frames is like skimming Stein; it isn't possible to feel her work without putting yourself in its present. Like each frame of a film, each Steinian statement fills the reader's ideal attention, excluding (by baffling) memory, until the object of her attention is insisted into complex and coherent existence:

> Funnily enough the cinema has offered a solution of this thing. By a continuously moving picture of any one there is no memory of any other thing and there is that thing existing. . . . I was doing what the cinema was doing, I was making a continuous succession of the statement of what that person was until I had not many things but one thing.

It appears to be the act of saying what something is that divides the perception into instants: observe and record, then begin observing again without any memory of the earlier observation that might obscure or misdirect this observation. In a process not of emphasis but of beginning again and again, she describes what something is, and what it is now, and what it is now, until it is.

Just as the primitive kept his world new by yearly returning to the moment of the creation, and by making his life the repetition of archetypal actions gave himself the feeling that time was not irreversibly accumulating, Gertrude Stein's beginnings again keep her writing in its continuous present, keep it alive. She was interested in history, but she resisted "remembering," and felt that "the first time" was "of no importance." While the primitive believed in unbuilding time by returning to Time Zero every year, Gertrude Stein returns to the time of the beginning with each statement, so that there is never any accumulation of building time but an abstract, objective, and jerky continuing.

Implicit in this method of capturing the instant is the assumption that the instant could be looked at hard and precisely. If we hold to the simile of the sequence of motion picture frames, we must see Miss Stein's "film" as like Chris Marker's *La Jetée* (1962), which with one exception is a sequence of tableaux, and there is time to take a good look at each frame—or like the progressing freeze-frames which show one character's memory of the assassination in Costa-Gavras' *Z*. Twenty-four frames a second (normal projection speed) is too fast for precise apprehension of each image. Stein's attention slows time: her attention is her time. In reaction to William James's "flow" or "stream" of consciousness, Frederick Hoffman notes,

> Miss Stein was much more interested in the fact of an *arrested* consciousness, apparently static and fixed and sacrificing motion or flow to precision. . . . She did not ignore "flow," but found it very difficult to attend to, and dangerous as well, for attention to it ran the risk of losing the integrity and precision of the word-object nexus.

There is progress in Gertrude Stein's narration, but it is slow; and plot, of course ("What Happened"), is not very important. The progress is among the instants, toward complete expression, not, as Reid has put it, toward "the collapse of the artist's attention to his subject." A lecture is over when its audience has experienced its meaning, a portrait when its image is complete, a life when the subject has reached the present or has died. Here are some endings:

> Now that is all.
> 
> ["**Composition as Explanation**"]
> 
> Through to you.
> 
> [*Four in America*]
> 
> And now it is today.
> 
> [*Everybody's Autobiography*]
> 
> And she has and this is it.
> 
> [*The Autobiography of Alice B. Toklas*]
> (pp. 117-28)

> *Bruce F. Kawin, "The Continuous Present," in his* Telling It Again and Again: Repetition in Literature and Film, *Cornell University Press, 1972, pp. 108-64.*

**WILLIAM H. GASS** (essay date 1973)

[*Gass is an American fiction writer and critic. Widely praised for the virtuosity of his prose style, he is among the most conspicuous modern proponents of the view that literature's sole meaning lies in the aesthetic forms an author creates with language. This position is developed in two collections of critical essays,* Fiction and the Figures of Life *(1971) and* The World within the Word *(1978), and forms the creative principle of the stories of* In the Heart of the Heart of the Country *(1968), the novel* Omensetter's Luck *(1966), and the long essay* On Being Blue *(1976). As opposed to the representational theory of art, which holds that literature should be a rendering of human experience more or less in the manner of history or journalism, such essays as "The Medium of Fiction" and "Philosophy and the Form of Fiction" disclaim the injunction that fiction should, or indeed is able to, present anything to the reader except an aesthetic pattern composed of rhetorical devices and the poetic qualities of words themselves. This is exemplified by Gass's demonstration in "The Concept of Character in Fiction" that a character may be defined as a series of verbal strategies focusing on a proper noun which in turn serves as one element among many in a larger aesthetic design. Applied to a given work of literature, this critical approach dispenses with psychological, social, moral, or any other consideration which would attempt to offer the meaning of that work in nonliterary terms. While such an abstract account of Gass's work might suggest that his is a purely decorative form of literature, one exclusive of human emotion, he has in fact criticized such writers as Samuel Beckett and Jorge Luis Borges for just such a lack of feeling, and he has made it clear in many of his works that for him the rhetorical substance of literature is perfectly capable of embodying, in aesthetic form, all the passions of life. In the following excerpt from an essay originally published in 1973, Gass interprets and evaluates Stein's literary innovations, particularly the hermetic approach to language she inroduced in* Tender Buttons.]

When Gertrude Stein was a young girl, the twentieth century was approaching like a distant train whose hoot you could only just hear. A whole age was about to end. Nations would re-dedicate themselves, an entire generation bite into a fresh loaf, turn over a new leaf . . . tremble, pray. Despite this threat from the realm of number, though, most of the world went on as before, repeating itself over and over in every place, beginning and rebeginning, again and again and again. (p. 63)

We can only guess whether the calendar had any influence on her, although later no one was to champion the new century more wholeheartedly, or attempt to identify America with modernity. The United States was the oldest country in the world, she said, because it had been in the twentieth century longer. In any case, Gertrude Stein, at age fifteen, thought frequently of death and change and time. Young girls can. She did not think about dying, which is disagreeable, even to young girls, but about death, which is luxurious, like a hot soak. The thought would appear as suddenly as moist grass in the morning, very gently, often after reading, on long reflective walks; and although it distressed her to think that there were civilizations which had perished altogether, she applauded the approaching turn. It was mostly a matter of making room. "I was there to begin to kill what was not dead, the nineteenth century which was so sure of evolution and prayers, and esperanto and their ideas," she said. (pp. 65-6)

Chapter V. In the old books there were chapters and verses, sections, volumes, scenes, parts, lines, divisions which had originated with the Scriptures ("chapter," for instance, a word for the head like *tête* and "title"); there were sentences, paragraphs, and numbered pages to measure the beat of each heart, the course of a life, every inference of reason, and the march, as they say, of time.

In *Four in America* she exposed the arbitrary conventionality of these often awkward cuts of meat. (p. 67)

I do not believe she had any knowledge of Frederick Jackson Turner's frontier hypothesis, but her understanding of American history was based on something very like it: "In the United States there is more space where nobody is than where anybody is." There is no question that she, like Turner, thought human behavior was in great part a function of the amount of free land available. On the frontier, Turner believed, civilization was regularly being reborn. When westward the course of empire no longer took its way, Americans moved "in" and went east to Paris in order to go west within the mind—a land like their own without time. And Gertrude Stein believed Americans were readier than Europeans, consequently, to be the new cultural pioneers. The mind . . . The human mind went on like the prairie, on and on without limit.

It is characteristic of her method by and large that every general thought find exact expression in the language of her own life;

that every general thought in fact be the outcome of a repeated consideration of solidly concrete cases—both wholly particular and thoroughly personal—and further, that these occasions be examined, always, in the precise form of their original occurrence, in which, then, they continue to be contained as if they were parts of a sacred text that cannot be tampered with substantially, only slightly rearranged, as a musician might lengthen the vowels slightly or repeat the words of a lyric to compose a song, skip a little now and then, or call for an extensive reprise. "I was there to begin to kill what was not dead. . . ." (pp. 70-1)

Gertrude Stein blew "the American trumpet as though it were the whole of Sousa's band" and always spoke European brokenly; she was perhaps the last of our serious writers to, in the square sense, love her country, and she moved her writing even through her own enthusiasms (Henry James and Richardson and Eliot), as painfully as through a thicket, straight into the present where it became, in every sense of this she understood, "American" and "measureless."

But not in a moment was this accomplished. In a life. The resolution required would be heroic. Shortly after she began living in Paris with her brother, she completed a manuscript which was not published for nearly fifty years: a curiously wooden work of relentless and mostly tiresome psychological analysis which she called, with crushing candor, *Quod Erat Demonstrandum.* However, in this brief novel about the personal relationships between three depersonalized paper women, plotted as a triangle on which the lines are traveled like a tramway, the points incessantly intersected—in which, though much is shown, nothing's proved, and everyone is exhausted—Gertrude Stein's sexual problem surfaces. Clearly, she has had a kind of love affair with another woman. Clearly, too, the circumstances of her life were now combining against her, compelling her to rely more and more upon a self she did not have. . . . The problem of personal identity, which is triumphantly overcome in *The Geographical History,* would occupy her henceforth, particularly in the most ambitious work of her career, *The Making of Americans.*

Furthermore her brother was beginning to ridicule her writing.

Still she listened to Leo; she looked at Cézanne; she translated Flaubert; and this subordination of ear, eye, and mind eventually released her, because Flaubert and Cézanne taught the same lesson; and as she examined the master's portrait of his wife, she realized that the reality of the model had been superseded by the reality of the composition. Everything in the painting was related to everything else in the painting, and to everything else equally (there were no lesser marks or moments), while the relation of any line or area of color in the painting to anything outside the painting (to a person in this case) was accidental, superfluous, illusory. The picture was of Mme. Cézanne. It had been painted by her husband. It was owned by the Steins. Thus the picture had an *identity.* But the painting was an *entity.* So a breast was no more important than a button, gray patch, or green line. Breasts might be more important than buttons to a vulgar observer, but in biology, where a mouse and a man were equal, in art, in our experience of how things are presented to us in any present moment, in mathematics—indeed, in any real whole or well-ordered system—there was a wonderful and democratic equality of value and function. There was, she said, no "up" in American religion either, no hierarchy, no ranking of dominions and powers.

Identities were what you needed to cash a check or pass a border guard. Identities had neighbors, relatives, husbands, and wives. Pictures were similarly authenticated. Poems were signed. Identities were the persons hired, the books and buildings bought and sold, the famous "things," the stars. She drew the distinction very early. In *The Geographical History* she would describe it as the difference between human nature and the human mind.

Gertrude Stein liked to begin things in February. Henry James has written *The Golden Bowl* and it will take a war to end the century, not the mere appearance of a pair of zeros on the mileage indicator. Never mind. Although the novel as it had been known was now complete, and Gertrude has meanwhile doubled her fifteen years without appreciable effect, still there was in what was being written (*Nostromo*, last year; *The House of Mirth*, just out; and *The Man of Property*, forthcoming), for instance, that socially elevated tone, the orotund authorial voice, the elegant drawing-room diction, that multitude of unfunctional details like flour to thicken gravy; there were those gratuitous posturings, nonsensical descriptions, empty conversations, hollow plots, both romance and Grub Street realism; and there so often remained the necessity, as Howells complained, to write with the printer at one's heels, therefore the need to employ suspense like a drunken chauffeur, Chapter Vs and other temporal divisions as though the author commanded an army, and all of the rest of the paraphernalia required by serialization and the monthly purchase of magazines.

She saw how the life of the model had been conferred upon the portrait. And in the central story of *Three Lives* (they were still stories), she captured the feeling she wanted in words.

> All that long day, with the warm moist young spring stirring in him, Jeff Campbell worked, and thought, and beat his breast, and wandered, and spoke aloud, and was silent, and was certain, and then in doubt and then keen to surely feel, and then all sodden in him; and he walked, and he sometimes ran fast to lose himself in his rushing, and he bit his nails to pain and bleeding, and he tore his hair so that he could be sure he was really feeling, and he never could know what it was right, he now should be doing.

The rhythms, the rhymes, the heavy monosyllabic beat, the skillful rearrangements of normal order, the carefully controlled pace, the running on, the simplicity, exactness, the passion . . . in the history of language no one had written like this before, and the result was as striking in its way, and as successful, as *Ulysses* was to be.

Neither *Three Lives* nor *The Making of Americans* eliminated the traditional novel's endless, morally motivated, psychological analyses, though she would manage that eventually. *A Long Gay Book* was begun as another investigation of the relationships between people, in this case mainly pairs, but it gradually wandered from that path into pure song. "I sing," she said, "and I sing and the tunes I sing are what are tunes if they come and I sing. I sing I sing." For instance:

> Wet weather, wet pen, a black old tiger skin, a shut in shout and a negro coin and the best behind and the sun to shine.

She was readying herself for *Tender Buttons*. But what would never disappear from her work, despite her revolutionary zeal, was her natural American bent toward self-proclamation and her restless quest for truth—especially that, because it would cause her to render some aspects of reality with a ruthlessness

*Stein and Alice B. Toklas on board the "S.S. Champlain" in 1934. The Bettmann Archive, Inc.*

rare in any writer, and at a greater risk to her art than most. (pp. 73-6)

Buttons fasten, and because tender buttons are the buttons we unbutton and press, touch and caress to make love, we can readily see why they fasten. These extraordinary pieces of prose, which Gertrude perversely called poems, do much more than simply resemble the buttons she liked to collect and sort, though they are indeed verbal objects, and their theoretical affinity with the paintings of advanced cubism is profound. Like many of the canvases of Cézanne, Matisse, and Braque, each piece is a domestic still. They employ many of the methods of collage, too, as well as those of Dada disassociation.

Thematically, they are composed of the implements, activities, colors and pleasures of home life, its quiet dangers, its unassertive thrills: cooking, cleaning, eating, loving, visiting, entertaining, and it is upon this base that the embossing of these buttons takes place. Plates are broken, pots and tables polished, meat sliced, food chopped, objects are repaired, arranged, contained. The highest metaphysical categories of sameness and difference, permanence and change, are invoked, as are the concerns of epistemology, of clarity and obscurity, certainty and doubt.

Like a cafeteria tray, *Tender Buttons* has three sorting sections (Objects, Food, Rooms)), but it is also built with three floors, so that its true shape is a cube. Objects are things external to us, which we perceive, manipulate, and confront. Next are the things which nourish us, which we take into ourselves: information, feeling, food. Finally, there are things which enclose us as our body does our consciousness, like a lover's arms, or as people are embraced by rooms. If the X-axis is divided as I've described, the Y-axis is marked off into Work, or household chores, Love, or the complicated emotional exchanges between those who spend their daily life together, and Art, or in this case, the composition of odd, brilliant, foolish, accidental, self-conscious, beautiful, confused, or whimsical sentences. (pp. 77-8)

Throughout, the crucial word is *change*. Some processes, like cleaning and mending, are basically restorative. They remove the present in order to return to and conserve the past. Others, like sewing, decorating, and cooking, principally through operations which alter *quantity* (by shaping, enlarging, reducing, juxtaposing, mingling, and so on), create *qualities* which have not previously existed. Many times these qualities are positive, but naturally not always. In the human sphere, to which these activities are precisely proportional, similar consequences occur. Finally, both these areas are metaphorically measured against the art of writing and found to be structurally the same. Words can be moved about like furniture in their sentences; they can be diced like carrots (Stein cuts up a good number); they can be used in several different ways simultaneously, like wine; they can be brushed off, cleaned and polished; they can be ingeniously joined, like groom and bed, anxiety and bride. Every sentence is a syntactical space (a room) in which words (things, people) act (cook, clean, eat, or excrete) in order to produce quite special and very valuable qualities of feeling. Cleaning a room can be a loving or a vengeful act, a spontaneous tidying, mere routine, or a carefully planned Spring Scrub, and one's engagement to the task can be largely mindless or intensely meant. Similarly, not a few of these buttons are as accidental as kicked stones (my typewriter writes "spoiled cushions" instead of "soiled" and I wonder whether I shouldn't leave the phrase that way), others are painfully self-conscious and referential, as planned as a political coup, while a few seem wholly momentary whims whose consequences have been self-indulgently allowed to stand.

Although the "poems" do not avoid nouns, as their author suggests she was trying to do, and have nice tasty titles ("SINGLE FISH," "SAUSAGE," "CELERY," "VEAL"), they avoid naming. Picasso's hermetic *The Clarinet Player*, for instance, painted during the same period *Tender Buttons* was being composed, offers no comment, visual or otherwise, on clarinet playing, players, or the skill of playing. After the motif has been analyzed into its plastic elements, these are modified and recombined according to entirely abstract schemes in which colors and forms predominate and respond solely to one another. The world is a source of suggestions, nothing more, and every successful work supersedes its model and renders the world superfluous to it.

Yet we are already in a tangle of terminology, because Gertrude Stein was always doing "descriptions," and she furthermore felt that naming was the special function of the poet. *Tender Buttons* is, she insists, a book of poems; poems are based, she claims, on the noun; and tender buttons are portraits, as she puts it, not of living people like Mabel Dodge and Sherwood Anderson, but of ordinary objects and common processes and simple spaces. Naming and not naming, describing and not describing, subject or sign: can we straighten this out?

In the first place, nouns are full of remembrance since they represent collections of past experience, and although it may seem reasonable to encounter the present well-padded by the past, this tends to give to every meeting of bell and clapper

the same dull clonk: ah, there you are again, Socrates. We cease to listen, cease to see. So we must rid ourselves of the old titles and properties, recover a tutored innocence, and then, fresh as a new-scrubbed Adam, reword the world. (pp. 79-80)

When she did her portraits, Gertrude Stein spent a great deal of her time listening, because each of her subjects was, as we all are, a talking machine, and of course what she listened to was in part a response to herself, to her talking. Now she wanted to stress seeing, because, of course, though frying pans speak and one might mutter to one's knitting, objects mainly spangled space with color and reflection. (p. 81)

Now [in *Tender Buttons*] I (the poet, the perceiver, the namer, the praiser) reflect: not upon the Object but upon the pattern I've made of my words and how they space themselves, for their space is inside them, not openly disposed upon the page as poetry normally is. I notice that my verbal combinations are, on that account, unusual (I shall brag about it), and that, although they resemble nothing else which passes for poetry, they are nevertheless not without their own system and order . . . these sentences which form triangles, crowds, or squares, go verbless as one goes naked, or which wind around Being like a fateful spindle. (p. 83)

So these poems are opaque containers. They have been made to fasten us through pleasure together . . . and most household objects and the acts which center on them: pots, pans, pillows, cooking, cleaning, love. The difference between these buttons and other swatches of language is going to deepen, she says, and there are going to be more and more of them, not only because the book will pour them out on us, but because the principles of their composition will be widely imitated. (p. 84)

Although the text is, I think, overclued, the language plain, and the syntax so Spartan as to be peculiar, naked as a Dukhobor whose cause we cannot yet comprehend; nevertheless, the "total altogether of it" remains cryptic, and we are likely to feel that our interpretations are forced unless they are confirmed by readings from another direction. Some knowledge of Gertrude Stein's daily life and obsessive concerns is essential, as well as familiarity with the usual associations she makes among words, and the in-common subjects of her works. Then, not only must we fasten ourselves to Webster, as Empson chained himself to the OED, and avail ourselves of slang dictionaries too, we must go to Skeat or Partridge as eagerly as a cat for cover on a cool day.

Thus this is certainly not an airtight text. It leaks. But where? and why should we care? It will not tell us what day the bridge is to be bombed, the safe rifled, or buck passed. We must set to work without reward or hope of any, and submit ourselves to the boredom of an etymological narrative. (pp. 89-90)

Words, of course, were tender buttons, to be sorted and played with, admired and arranged, and she felt that language in English literature had become increasingly stiff and resistant, and that words had to be pried out of their formulas, freed, and allowed to regain their former Elizabethan fluidity, but it is now evident, I think, that she had other motives, indeed the same ones which had driven her into writing in the first place: the search for and discovery of Gertrude Stein, and the recording of her daily life, her thoughts, her passions. (p. 100)

Although, in a few works—the popular public ones like Alice's and Everybody's autobiographies, *Brewsie and Willie*, and *Wars I Have Seen*—Stein's style is as simple and open and even giddy as we might imagine the letters of a young girl to be, much of her work is written, like *Tender Buttons,* in a kind of code, even when, as in *How to Write,* the subject does not appear to require it; and there is no question whatever that the coding dangerously confounds the surface; for even if a passage effects a concealment, as when a body is covered by clothing, from the artistic point of view, those clothes had better dazzle us as much as the truth would, unless the concealment is only gestural and temporary, and we are expected to penetrate it at once, because the object of art is to make more beautiful that which is, and since that which is is rarely beautiful, often awkward and ugly and ill-arranged, it must be sometimes sheeted like a corpse, or dissolved into its elements and put together afresh, aright, and originally. Stein is painfully aware of the problem. Coming clean is best. "Certainly glittering is handsome and convincing." (p. 105)

In *Tender Buttons* the conflict between concealment and expression is especially intense. This kind of contest can sometimes lead to the most beautiful and powerful of consequences, so long as the victory of concealment remains incomplete, so long as the drapery leads us to dream and desire and demand the body we know it covers, so long as passion speaks through rectitude, so long as impulse laughs with the lips of duty. We can, of course, rip the clothing off anyway, as I·have; but it is the promise of the nipple through the slip, the tender button, which matters to us here, and is the actual action of art; it is the hint of the hollow which holds us, and the way a stone arm encircles nothing but atmosphere so lovingly we want to believe in our being there, also surrounded, and only then as alive in our life as that stone.

"Celery tastes tastes where" (she asks) "in curled lashes and little bits and mostly in remains." It is a careful observation. "A cup is neglected in being full of size." It is a rich saying. Many of these buttons are as tender as tusks, but Gertrude Stein also wrote densely and brilliantly and beautifully and perversely and with intense contrivance and deep care and a skill which no one could recognize. (pp. 107-08)

*The Geographical History of America* is a culminating work, though not the outcome of her meditations. Those she summed up in an essay, **"What Are Masterpieces?"** written a year later. This book is the stylized presentation of the process of meditation itself, with many critical asides. In the manner of her earliest piece, *Q.E.D.,* it demonstrates far more than it proves, and although it is in no sense a volume of philosophy (Gertrude Stein never "argues" anything), it is, philosophically, the most important of her texts. If we follow her thought as Theseus did the thread of Ariadne, I think we find at the end the justice, if not the total truth, of her boast that the most serious thinking about the nature of literature in the twentieth century has been done by a woman. (p. 111)

The range of our sensations, our thoughts, our feelings, is generally fixed, and so is our experience of relations. Make an analysis, draw up a list. Life is rearrangement, and in a dozen different ways Gertrude Stein set out to render it. We are not clocks, designed to repeat without remainder, to mean nothing by a tick, not even the coming tock, and so we must distinguish between merely mechanical repetition, in which there is no progress of idea, no advance or piling up of wealth, and that which seriously defines our nature, describes the central rhythms of our lives.

Almost at once she realized that language itself is a complete analogue of experience because it, too, is made of a large but finite number of relatively fixed terms which are then allowed to occur in a limited number of clearly specified relations, so that it is not the appearance of a word that matters but *the manner of its reappearance,* and that an unspecifiable number of absolutely unique sentences can in this way be composed, as, of course, life is also continuously refreshing itself in a similar fashion. (p. 112)

Sometimes she treats a sentence as if it were a shopping list, and rearranges every item in happier orders, much as we might place knicknacks on a shelf, considering whether the spotted china dog might be seen to better advantage in front of the jade lizard and nearer the window, or beside the tin cup borrowed from a beggar in Beirut.

Sometimes she lets us see and follow every step, but often she neglects to give us the sentences she began with, and we find ourselves puzzled by distant results.

Think next what might happen if we considered the sentence to be composed of various voices: in short, a play. For what else is a play? It simply cites the separate sources of its sentences. . . . A musician would have no trouble in seeing how a single sentence might be treated as the consequence of a chorus, nor would a modern painter find it hard to imagine the dissolution of his plate, bread, vase, and fish, into plastic elements he then rearranged in a new, more pleasing way.

Gertrude Stein did more with sentences, and understood them better, than any writer ever has. Not all her manipulations are successful, but even at their worst, most boring, most mechanical, they are wonderfully informative. And constantly she thought of them as things in space, as long and wiggling and physical as worms. Here is a description of some of them from **"Poetry and Grammar"**:

> . . . my sentences . . . had no longer the balance of sentences because they were not the parts of a paragraph nor were they a paragraph but they had made in so far as they had come to be so long and with the balance of their own that they had they had become something that was a whole thing and in so being they had a balance which was the balance of a space completely not filled but created by something moving as moving is not as moving should be.

She understood reading, for instance. She sometimes read straight on, touching the page as lightly as a fly, but even as her mind moved there would be a halt, a turning, the eyes rising and falling in a wave, and she realized that the page, itself, was artificial, arbitrary with respect to the text, so she included it in the work as well, not as a thing or an action, but as an idea.

| j. l. | Page one. | Pump. Pump ump. |
|---|---|---|
| | Page two. | In the middle. |
| | Page three. | P  p. |
| | Page four. | Um, there's a bin. |
| | Page five. | Pumpkin. |

The understanding was, as she read, not only tormented by the physical makeup of the book, it was often troubled, too, by the content, which it had difficulty in making out. The poem does not repeat itself, but I do. I read the first four lines, and then I reread the first two. Now I am ready to go on, and I jump without a qualm to the second quatrain. Soon, however, I am back at the beginning again. There are interruptions, too. Alice asks me what I would like for dinner. Company comes. Time passes. Other texts may even intervene, many strange words from all directions. Why not, she thought, formalize all this, create something new, not only from the stops and starts and quarrels of normal thought, but from the act of attention itself, and all its snarls and tangles, leaps and stumbles.

She is not always satisfied merely to render the phenomenon. Sometimes she chooses to involve us in it. By removing punctuation, for instance. I am reading her sentence about her sentences, which I quoted above, and sliding over words as though through mud:

> . . . not filled but created by something moving as moving is not as moving . . .

I must pick myself up. Reread until I get the hang:

> . . . not filled, but created by something moving, as moving *is*, not as moving should be.

By the time I understand what she means, *I* have been composed. Thus the repetitions which mimic my own when I read make me repeat even more when I read them written down.

Listen. We converse as we live—by repeating, by combining and recombining a few elements over and over again just as nature does when of elementary particles it builds a world. Gertrude Stein had a wonderful ear and she listened as she listened to Leo—for years—not so she could simply reproduce the talk, that sort of thing was never her intention, but so she could discover the patterns in speech, the *forms* of repetition, and exploit them. At first she saw these shapes as signs of the character of the speaker, but later her aim was to confer upon the words themselves the quality she once traced to the owner of the tongue. That was Cézanne's method—the method of the human mind.

We not only repeat when we see, stand, communicate; we repeat when we think. There's no other way to hold a thought long enough to examine it except to say its words over and over, and the advance of our mind from one notion to another is similarly filled with backs and forths, erasures and crossings-out. The style of *The Geographical History of America* is often a reflection of this mental condition. (pp. 115-18)

Furthermore, Gertrude Stein knew that masterpieces were, like life itself is everywhere, perfect engines of repetition. Just as leaves multiply along a limb, and limbs alike thicket a trunk, a work of art suffers simultaneous existence in many places, and eventually is read again and again, sometimes loved by the same lips. As Borges has demonstrated so well, when that inspired madman, Pierre Menard, succeeded in writing a chapter or two of *Don Quixote*, word for word the same, his version was both richer and more complex than that of Cervantes. The reverse can also be the case: *Three Lives,* written by any of us now, would not be nearly so remarkable as it was then. (p. 118)

When Gertrude Stein wrote that there was little use in being born a little boy if you were going to grow up to be a man, she did not intend to deny causality or the influence of the past. She did mean to say that when we look at our own life, we are looking at the history of another; we are like a little dog licking our own hand, because our sense of ourselves at any time does not depend upon such data, only our "idea" of ourselves does, and this "idea," whether it's our own or that of another, is our identity. Identities depend upon appearances and papers. Appearances can be imitated, papers forged.

She also said: I am not I any longer when I see. Normally, as Schopenhauer first and Bergson later argued so eloquently, we see like an animal. We see prey, danger, comfort, security. Our words are tags which signify our interest: chairs, bears, sunshine, sex; each is seen in relation to our impulses, instincts,

aims, in the light of our passions, and our thought about these things is governed entirely by what we consider their utility to be. Words are therefore weapons like the jaws of the crocodile or the claws of the cat. We use them to hold our thought as we hold a bone; we use them to communicate with the pack, dupe our enemies, manipulate our friends; we use them to club the living into food.

When, for instance, we give ourselves to a piece of music—not to drink, daydream, or make love, but to listen—we literally lose ourselves, and as our consciousness is captured by the music, we are in dreamless sleep, as Hume says, and are no more. We become, in becoming music, that will-less subject of knowing of which Schopenhauer spoke so convincingly.

Human nature is incapable of objectivity. It is viciously anthropocentric, whereas the human mind leaves all personal interest behind. It sees things as entities, not as identities. It is concerned, in the Kantian sense, with things-in-themselves. The human mind knows that men must die that others may live; one epoch go that another may take its place; that ideas, fashions, feelings, pass. The human mind neither forgets nor remembers; it neither sorrows nor longs; it never experiences fear or disappointment. In the table headed Human Nature there is, therefore, time and memory, with all their beginnings, their middles, and their ends; there is habit and identity, storms and hilly country, acting, audience, speaking and adventure, dogs and other animals, politics, propaganda, war, place, practice and its guiding truths, its directing sciences, while in the table of the Human Mind there's contact rather than connection, plains, space, landscape, math and money, not nervousness but excitement, not saying but showing, romance rather than mystery, masterpieces moreover, and above all, Being.

Gertrude Stein was no longer merely explaining herself. She had begun to wonder what it was inside her which had written *Three Lives* rather than the novels of Lew Wallace; what it was that made masterpieces. Besant's books had sold very well and he had been admired. But he had sold to people of principally the same sort and had been read during a fingersnap of time. Masterpieces escaped both country and climate, every condition of daily life; they hurdled history; and it was not because daily life, climate, country, and history were not contents, as if in those sweetly beautiful Angelicos there were no angels. What accounted for it? in reader? writer? work? Her conclusions were not original, although their largely Kantian character is a little surprising for a student of William James and Santayana.

It was not because she was a woman or was butch—her poodles or her Fords, her vests, her friends, her sober life, her so-called curious ways, her Jewishness, none counted. Allegheny, Pennsylvania, had nothing to do with it. Her "scientific" aim in writing *The Making of Americans,* her desire to define "the bottom nature" of everyone who had or could or would be living, was mistaken and had to do with human nature, not the human mind. She had gone on repeating because she thought the world did. The world did, but what the world did, did not matter. *Tender Buttons* was pure composition, like Cézanne, or at least one could pretend it was, but the *Autobiographies* and *A Long Gay Book, Three Lives, The Making of Americans,* many of the portraits and the plays, although they were about human nature, were fortunately written by the human mind. And it took another human mind to understand them.

There were people who were no more than their poodles. If their little dog didn't know them, who would they be? Like mirrors they reflected what fell into them, and when the room was empty, when the walls were removed and the stars pinched back in the sky, they were nothing, not even glass.

Naïvely, she thought free people formed themselves in terms of an Emersonian self-reliance; she believed in the frontier, and in the ethic of the pioneer. After all she was one. Naïvely she thought that the average man, here in America, understood the spiritual significance of space, and was less a slave to human nature. Consequently here the human mind should flourish, the masterpiece emerge, the animal sleep. However, *Finnegans Wake* would demonstrate best the endless roundness she had in mind, and the perfect description of her ideal had long ago appeared, in 1894: Paul Valéry's *Monsieur Teste*.

Just as the order of numbers in a sum makes no difference, just as there is no special sequence to towns on a map, the mind and the masterpiece may pass back and forth between thoughts as often and as easily as trains between Detroit, Duluth, and Denver, and chapter headings are, in fact, only the names of places. Oral literature had to be sequential (like music before tape), but type made possible a reading which began at the rear, which repeated preferred passages, which skipped. As in an atlas, the order was one of convenience, and everything was flat. A geographical history rolls time out like that. Of course, there are stories still; an evening's entertainment, that's all human nature asks for; but masterpieces have to bear repeating and repeating. There are no surprises, no suspense, no tears, no worries in them. We know what will happen to Ahab. Duncan's dead, and Anna's under her train. I can tell you the page. *The Wings of the Dove* lies spread before us now as openly as Iowa. Literature in the eyes of the human mind is like land seen from a plane. And so is Gertrude Stein when we find her. Macbeth shall murder sleep again, Tom Jones receive a beating, Heathcliff . . . ah, well . . . "Oblige me," she says, "by not beginning." Netherfield Park is let at last. Mr. Gradgrind is still proceeding on the principle that two and two are four, and nothing over. Bloom is carrying a piece of soap about. The next century is approaching like a distant train. John Barth has just written *Chimera*, Beckett has brought out *The Lost Ones*, Nabokov a book called *Transparent Things*. And they are reissuing *The Geographical History of America* almost a hundred years from the author's birthday. Oblige me, she says, "Also by not ending." (pp. 120-23)

> William H. Gass, "Gertrude Stein and the Geography of the Sentence," in his The World within the Word, Alfred A. Knopf, 1978, pp. 63-123.

## MICHAEL J. HOFFMAN (essay date 1976)

[*Hoffman, an American critic and professor of English literature, is the editor of* Critical Essays on Gertrude Stein *(1986) and author of the critical studies* The Development of Abstractionism in the Writings of Gertrude Stein *(1965) and* Gertrude Stein *(1976). In the following excerpt from the latter work, he discusses the novels and novel-like prose works written by Stein after 1925.*]

For someone who began her career as a novelist and is still associated in the public's mind primarily with the writing of novels and memoirs, Gertrude Stein wrote surprisingly few full-length works of fiction after the prolific period of *The Making of Americans, Two,* and *A Long Gay Book.* For more than a decade she produced hermetic, experimental works, very few of which were of a sustained length and all of which derived their styles from her previous experiments in portraiture and still lifes. The first book-length work not simply a collection

of shorter pieces that Stein wrote after 1912 was *A Novel of Thank You,* which was begun in 1925. After that, she produced only half a dozen long works that we could consider novels; for one of them, *The World Is Round,* is a book for children.

As usual, Stein's handling of a traditional literary form raises basic questions about the genre. Even during decades in which the word "plot" had become taboo, Stein uses less plot than any novelist of her era. She writes books with no dramatic development—books in which one event follows another in much the same way that events follow one another in everyday life. Even more, she creates works in which her characters simply inhabit a verbal landscape and do nothing at all.

The novels, like the plays of this period, exemplify the shifts from the middle to the later phase of Stein's development. *A Novel of Thank You* and *Lucy Church Amiably* are written primarily in the hermetic style to which we are accustomed. But in the detective story, *Blood on the Dining-Room Floor,* and later in her children's novel, *The World Is Round,* we see a transition into greater continuity and communicability that is continued with many variations through *Ida, A Novel, Mrs. Reynolds,* and *Brewsie and Willie.* Within this larger context of stylistic continuity, however, Stein tackles different problems in every one of her works; but she maintains the attitude she shared with other Modernist artists of seeing each new phase of her work as posing problems to be solved—and of feeling the constant necessity to "make it new." In the course of this attempt, Stein wrote a few novels that deserve to be considered among her most impressive achievements.

Although it remained unpublished until 1958, *A Novel of Thank You* was written during 1925 and 1926, a period Carl Van Vechten has described as being "not very prolific years for our author." According to Van Vechten, Stein had decided "to write in a more obscure vein than she had employed hitherto in her career"; and the book she actually produced more than adequately fulfills that expectation. I can think of no work of Stein's that the unaccustomed reader is more likely to read with such total incomprehension, and to call it a novel is to redefine our conception of that genre. While *A Novel of Thank You* does have a kind of a buried narrative that Richard Bridgman locates in Stein's relationship with Alice Toklas, that story is almost impossible for us to follow; and I shall not even attempt to summarize its "plot." What the book seems most like is a hermetic diary-commonplace book. Stein includes the names of many of her friends, much in the manner of *A Long Gay Book*; and, in Van Vechten's "Introduction" to *A Novel of Thank You,* he lists Alice Toklas's identifications of these people. In some ways this work is the most personal longer one that Stein wrote, although the story's emotional effect is controlled, as usual, through the abstractness of the narrative presentation.

The book consists largely of remembered conversations and short experiences, and the contents have little narrative continuity or story line. It is as though Stein recorded every night the few new things that had happened to her during the day or listed what she might have remembered from the past. The styles used are largely those developed in the portraits and in *Tender Buttons,* styles she repeated and refined during her middle period. There are occasional reflections on the nature of fiction: "What is a surprise. A continued story is a surprise. This is a continued story, this is a surprise this is a continued story. What is a surprise, a continued story is a surprise. This is a continued story, a surprise a continued story is a surprise."

But such remarks in their fictional context often have the ring of a rationalization. Stein uses her narrator the way she has ever since *The Making of Americans*—to comment on the action and to speak in the author's voice as she records the immediate thoughts and directions that emanate from her consciousness. The chapters are all very short and are often numbered eccentrically; for instance, part 1 of the novel contains 316 such chapters in 237 pages; part 2, which is a little over a page, has three chapters, and part 3 contains one two-page chapter. As usual, Stein is telling us with such idiosyncrasies that numerical divisions in longer works of literature are both arbitrary and meaningless.

The language is full of puns ("Minnie Singer"), clichés ("Hanging fire"), familiar definitions ("Action and reaction are equal and opposite."), and phrases that sound like conventional apothegms but are coinages of Stein's ("A novel of thank you is historic."). The reason for this *mélange* of linguistic game-playing is that the tone of *A Novel of Thank You* is primarily that of dialogue, spoken, overheard, remembered, familiar. This tone takes over almost completely in the last third of the book where the more formal tone disappears. Also in this section the book's main repetitive motif takes over, that of "Thank you." This phrase is repeated again and again in many contexts and phrasings. It is almost as though the purpose of the book is to define its title by incantation. Stein also uses for the first time one of her more famous phrases: "Before the flowers of friendship faded friendship faded."

Even though the chapters from the middle of the book onward often seem to describe self-contained episodes abstractly, there is little continuity short of the verbal contents of Stein's consciousness as they are spilled onto the page. To the student of Stein, the contents of her consciousness might be quite interesting; but, to the less committed reader, *A Novel of Thank You* has very little to offer. It is important to us because it marks Stein's return to the longer forms of prose with which she began her career and in which she was to work intermittently from the middle 1920s on.

Stein's next full-length "novel" *Lucy Church Amiably* is a "landscape" very much in the mode of *Four Saints in Three Acts* which was written at the same time. A "pastoral," *Lucy Church Amiably* is surely one of the gentlest works Stein ever wrote, as well as one of her most difficult. On the title page, Stein appended the following description: "A Novel of Romantic beauty and nature and which Looks Like an Engraving." A further indication of the book's elegiac tone is given by its epigraph: "And with a nod she turned her head toward the falling water. Amiably." The language of *Lucy Church* is as unstrained as the simplest kinds of thoughts a saint might have while experiencing enlightenment or a union with God and nature. In this regard, the work is much like Stein's other writings about saints; and her identification with the Lucy Church of the title shows her basic religious orientation.

*Lucy Church Amiably,* while it is a full-length work of prose fiction, is not really a novel; it is an extended meditation on the meaning of a particular place, which is why Gertrude Stein described it as a "landscape." Although there is a series of characters, none is given more flesh in the book than a mere name. A number of localities in that part of provincial France are mentioned, as are many of the plants grown in the area; but none of these adds up to a continuous narrative. *Lucy Church Amiably* is more like an extended prose poem; or, as Richard Bridgman has best described it, "The book is essentially a long, lyric diary, begun in May, lackadaisical as a vacation, and little more than what she herself called it, a landscape . . . in which there are some people."

The landscape qualities of this book, its position as one of Stein's full-length "geographies," become apparent with even a cursory reading. The title character is named after a "little church with a pagoda-like steeple at Lucey in the region of Belley," an area where Stein and Alice Toklas had a summer home for many years. Local characters figure prominently in the narrative as does the region's vegetation and topography. The strong sense of place is aided by what John Malcolm Brinnin describes as "an increased melodiousness in the line-to-line composition of the language." We feel, often without knowing why, what it must be like to be in that particular spot or even, in fact, to *be* that particular spot. In that sense, *Lucy Church Amiably* is in strong contrast to *A Novel of Thank You* in which we have no real sense of place but know somehow what it is like to be inside the head of characters, hearing what they say, think, remember.

*Lucy Church* also has a greater sense of novelistic continuity than its predecessor. It is concerned, at least nominally, with the same set of characters all the way through; and its chapters have a relatively standard length (around fifteen pages) throughout the first three-quarters of the book. Toward the end, as is often the case, Stein seems to have lost some of her vital interest in the project; and the chapters often dwindle to only a page or two, and occasionally to just three or four lines. The characters most continually in evidence are Lucy Church, Simon Therese, John Mary, Albert Bigelow, and Lilian Ann St. Peter Stanhope. Many of them obviously bear the names of both sexes, a phenomenon that not only reveals the author's sexual ambivalence but, more important, creates for the reader a sense of the a-sexual quality of the saintly or the ideally religious. Surely a saint is someone beyond the potential torments of sexuality, whether epicene, like a Della Robia figure of Christ, or serene, like a meditative Boddhisattva.

The continuities of fictional narrative are limited in *Lucy Church,* however, even with the book's continued focus on the same named people and its continuous reference to the setting of the church and to the vegetational topography. For, once again, there is no really discernible plot here. If this "novel" were one of Stein's "plays," it could be used by a scenarist like Maurice Grosser just as open-endedly as was the text of *Four Saints.* Stein does not return to chronological continuity until *The Autobiography of Alice B. Toklas.* (pp. 91-5)

*Lucy Church* can be characterized as a lyrical, easygoing work that depends on the usual Stein word play, including rhymes, puns, and the author's incurably pseudo-aphoristic style. What is striking, however, especially after *A Novel of Thank You,* is the way *Lucy Church* seems to verge on comprehensibility.

While its plot is almost nonexistent and while its characters are little more than names, the book has a genuine continuity of theme and of phrase as well as a style of elegant grammatical linkage. The words seem ready to be explicit on almost every occasion. *A Novel of Thank You* makes no pretense about its hermeticism, and we immediately feel in reading it that comprehensibility is a false expectation, but with *Lucy Church* we constantly expect meaning to emerge. (p. 95)

Stein's lifelong interest in detective stories and her concern during this time over her threatened sense of identity led to her next "novel," a detective story with the marvelously melodramatic title, *Blood on the Dining-Room Floor.* The story, whose melodrama ends with its title, arose from an incident that occurred at a hotel in Belley where Stein and Alice Toklas had taken summer vacations for the past seven years. One day the manager's wife, a Madame Pernollet, fell out of one of the hotel windows onto the courtyard; and her body was removed so quickly that the hotel guests did not even know what happened. For the bourgeois mind so dear to Stein, particularly that of the French bourgeoisie, sentiment must never interfere with business. The dead are dead. Stein was quite fascinated by how the mystery of whether the lady's death was accidental, suicidal, or homicidal was never solved nor even seriously investigated.

As we might imagine, *Blood on the Dining-Room Floor* is a mystery story without any genuine sense of mystery; and, since the mystery was never solved about the real-life counterpart, Stein's fictional version has no solution. But, by the end, the reader does not care; we have been privy to an extended Stein meditation about French provincial families and about the way a violent death can have consequences for them, especially when the people who know about it are discreet. The story is only eighty pages long, but it has twenty chapters. Since the first one has twenty pages, it is apparent that Stein, as usual, lost interest in her project and sustained her energies through fragmentation.

The style of *Blood on the Dining-Room Floor* is comprehensible and informal; it echoes the rhythms of speech and contains the usual directions from the author to herself and her readers. The sentences are short, noncinematic, and only occasionally lyrical or poetic. The major reader interest is not linquistic but generic; it lies in watching Stein take a traditional, ritualistic form like the detective story and violate almost all of its conventions while still maintaining somehow the basic tone and concerns familiar to it. Although *Blood on the Dining-Room Floor* is like no other detective story, it quite definitely falls within that genre, and it points out by its irreverence the artificiality of many of the "whodunit's" conventional concerns.

Except for a few shorter works of fiction, some of which were published in the Yale Edition volumes *As Fine as Melanctha* and *Mrs. Reynolds and Earlier Novelettes,* Stein's next full-length narrative was the children's novel *The World Is Round.* This short book should be read within the context of Stein's contemplations of identity, human nature, and human mind, such as *The Geographical History of America* and *Four in America.* Both the children about whom the book is written, a little girl named Rose and her cousin Willie, are extremely conscious of who they are and what relation their names have to their sense of themselves. It is doubly interesting to consider that the girl's name is Rose and that Stein's most famous line, "A rose is a rose is a rose" (only three roses this time), appears as the book's motto above the dedication in a circle strongly suggestive of a mandala. It is no coincidence that Stein was heavily concerned with the threat to her identity caused by her becoming a celebrity and that a similar device appeared at the top of Stein's personal stationery. Little Rose is both fascinated and disturbed by the fact that the world is round, that one can walk round and round on it, much, as Richard Bridgman suggests, like the serpent of the uroboric circle who has his tale in his mouth. The connection between this concern and the mandala of roses is obvious. As Erich Neumann has indicated, such concerns in primitive cultures have much to do with the process of individuation. In a Modernist primitive, they no doubt have much to do with the same process. Bridgman gives a good capsule summary of the plot of *The World Is Round*:

> Rose is a rather willful, disturbed girl who . . . questions for herself who she is. Particularly depressed

to discover that everything goes round, when she sings, she cries. Her cousin Willie is an adventurous boy who becomes excited when he sings. At the conclusion of their adventures, they are revealed to be unrelated, which permits them to marry, have children, and live happily ever after. But before that traditional close, they undergo several enigmatic experiences, the first involving a lion, the second, the climbing of a mountain. The conquering of fears, self-exploration, aspiration, and success are all components of the story.

The story is composed of a series of readily understandable episodes concerning the adventures, more psychological than is usual in children's books, of Rose and Willie. What I wish to suggest is that this is one of Stein's most successful works, particularly in its unification of style and subject. Like Matisse who wished to paint with the eyes of a child, Stein combines primitivistically simple diction with interlocking repetitions, as well as a humorous tone that mixes the pretense of seriousness with the fun of writing.

This combination works admirably in conveying the consciousness of a child as she tries to locate a place for herself within the world. For a woman who never had children of her own, Stein seems remarkably in touch with a child's mind, perhaps because in one side of her personality she kept the child in herself very active. And, from personal experience, I can attest that children find the book delightful. It is warm and serious, funny and sad; it is consistent with Stein's basic concerns about the nature of personality and identity; and it is very much in the direct line of her stylistic development. No one, even though it is clearly a tale for children written in an easily understandable style and containing a recognizable story, could mistake the author of this book.

Written in a more serious vein, although still full of fun, *Ida, A Novel,* was written in 1940. . . . It reminds me at least of the shorter tales in *Three Lives* ("**The Good Anna**" and "**The Gentle Lena**") because of the stylized discontinuities of its prose and its mock-gentle treatment of the heroine. This novel, however, is much more difficult than the earlier stories because more than thirty years of Stein's mature abstractionism have molded its style.

Supposedly based, at least initially, on the life of Wallis Warfield Simpson, the Baltimore divorcee who had recently married King Edward, the final version of *Ida* has little to do with the Duchess of Windsor. It is, as Donald Sutherland has suggested, "the story of what Gertrude Stein called a 'publicity saint,' that is a person who neither does anything nor is connected with anything but who by sheer force of existence in being there holds the public attention and becomes a legend." As was common in the works Stein wrote after *The Autobiography of Alice B. Toklas,* the main emphasis in *Ida* is on the problem of identity—and most particularly that of the author. As Sutherland also says, "Ida is a sort of combination of Helen of Troy, Dulcinea, Garbo, the Duchess of Windsor, and in particular 'Gertrude Stein'." The last named is in quotation marks because it is the image of herself in publicity that was at this time most threatening to Stein's sense of herself. The material of *Ida* draws on incidents from Stein's own past, some from as far back as her childhood, that were first mentioned in themes she wrote at Radcliffe; she also fills the book with a lot of her negative feelings about men. The specific allusions to the Duchess of Windsor that remain seem limited to the fact that Ida is married and divorced a number of times.

To all the bizarre incidents that occur in her life, Ida reacts with little emotion. She merely questions occasionally what everything means in relation to her sense of self. Like Joyce's Stephen Dedalus who wishes to be his own father, Ida tries to control her own identity to the point of wishing herself a twin sister. We are told at the beginning that Ida did indeed have a twin, Ida-Ida; but we see nothing of this second self until Ida herself is eighteen, at which time she decides how pleasant it would be to have a twin. In singing to one of her many dogs, Ida says: "Oh dear oh dear Love, that was her dog, if I had a twin well nobody would know which one I was and which one she was and so if anything happened nobody could tell anything and lots of things are going to happen and oh Love I felt it yes I know it I have a twin."

When Ida wins a beauty contest, the twin becomes a major factor in her life because she now has a "publicity" half; and, in order to combat the threat to her identity, she names her twin "Winnie" because she is always winning. She uses her twin basically as an object on which to project her alienated self; but after a time Winnie disappears, and, as Bridgman suggests, the novel becomes "tedious." Sutherland proposes that *Ida* is an existentialist novel whose main character is more "contingent" than any in Franz Kafka. "Much of the book," he says, "is an account of her search for her essence, for self-realization." Because of the way in which Ida adjusts to all situations without feeling her personality destroyed, she ironically represents Gertrude Stein's concept of the "human mind." She has, in fact, no personality; and, as Stein claimed in *The Geographical History of America,* personality has nothing to do with the human mind; it is a manifestation of human nature.

*Ida* is composed of a series of incidents that do not develop into a plot. These incidents function primarily as a set of examples of how publicity can create an identity that has nothing to do with personality and yet also has nothing positive to offer in the way of a sense of self to the main character, the author, or the reader. *Ida* is a bleak novel in this regard; it is more specifically autobiographical than any plotted work of fiction Stein had written in thirty years, but it contains just as dark a view of humanity as any of her early books. And yet, the bleakness of Stein's ultimate vision is counterbalanced by some of the most humorous writing she has done, at least in the lighter sections early in the book. It is too much to claim *Ida* to be an existentialist masterpiece, but the book is in many ways one of the more successful productions of Stein's later years. However, it is not so fine a work as *Mrs. Reynolds,* Stein's first fictional response to World War II.

*Mrs. Reynolds* is the longest work of fiction Stein composed after *The Making of Americans*; and, while it is not so difficult as some pieces of Stein's middle period, it is written in a much more difficult and discontinuous style than was *Ida* just a year earlier. Although the setting of *Mrs. Reynolds* is never really specified, Richard Bridgman is right in suggesting that the novel takes place in occupied France. The characters have English names, as do the two centrally evil presences in the book, Angel Harper—meant to be Adolph Hitler—and Joseph Lane—supposed to represent Joseph Stalin.

Although we never get to meet either of the evil men, they are major figures in the novel, particularly Angel Harper, whose increasing age as the book goes on is meant to represent the growing menace of Nazi Germany and the continued ascendancy of the troubled dictator. Juxtaposed against the quiet domesticity of Mr. and Mrs. Reynolds are quick flashes into the mind of Angel Harper as he remembers his life, particularly during his adolescence. As Harper grows older, Mrs. Reynolds in her seemingly endless conversations becomes more and more disturbed at his increasing age. By contrast, Joseph Lane diminishes rapidly; and, by the end, he is merely an occasional name. But the sense of fear and helplessness conveyed through juxtaposing the simple Mrs. Reynolds (we never learn her first name) and the evil Angel Harper gives us an effective sense of how many people felt as they watched with unbelieving eyes the accession to power of the obviously demented German *Führer.* In her flashbacks to Harper's youth, Stein manages to convey the sense of a disturbed childhood, the kind of background that would adequately have given rise to the kind of madness Hitler often displayed. And yet the portrait of Harper is not drawn without sympathy. He is a complex person, not merely a figure from nineteenth-century melodrama; and the fact of his psychic complexity, when combined with the terror of Mrs. Reynolds, has a subtle but powerful effect on the reader.

The echoes of Gertrude Stein that appear in Mrs. Reynolds make it clear that this is a personal book. As Bridgman says, "Mrs. Reynolds is not altogether an autobiographical figure, even though she is 'heavy' and 'quite plump,' has dogs, meditates on George Washington, reads detective stories, takes walks, gardens, talks with the neighbors, and generally engages in those activities that Alice Toklas and Gertrude Stein did when they were in the country, including contemplating flight, then deciding against it. . . . Mr. and Mrs. Reynolds seem to be composites of Gertrude Stein and Alice Toklas."

Stein herself spent the war in the French provinces, tending her garden, thinking her thoughts, writing *Wars I Have Seen,* and feeling confused about how the solid middle-class world she treasured so much had broken down. The quiet heroism of her own wartime endurance is mirrored in Mrs. Reynolds, just as Stein's sense of the continuity of ordinary life throughout all the vicissitudes of a world war is mirrored in the fact that life goes on as usual in the little village where the Reynoldses live with "the oppressive cloud of Angel Harper" hanging over all.

In a short epilogue to the book, Stein clarifies her intentions: "This book is an effort to show the way anybody could feel these years. It is a perfectly ordinary couple living an ordinary life and having ordinary conversations and really not suffering personally from everything that is happening but over them, all over them is the shadow of two men, and then the shadow of one of the two men gets bigger and then blows away and there is no other. There is nothing historical about this book except the state of mind." Stein is toughminded and persistent in following the simplicity of her vision, and the reader is left with an overwhelming sense of the "state of mind" that she has wished to convey—that of an ordinary life of quiet desperation lived without undue consternation but on a continuous level of terror.

The reader who tries to get through *Mrs. Reynolds* in a few long sittings the way he would an ordinary novel is making a mistake, for Stein includes as usual in her narrative a continuous repetition of daily events that only bore someone who is waiting for events to "happen." But the reader who limits himself to thirty or forty pages at a sitting will find that he has read one of the most disturbing books to have come out of the war. Although Stein's novel is rarely discussed, *Mrs. Reynolds* is surely her finest one since *The Making of Americans.*

Not so much can be said, however, for the last full-length work of fiction that Stein wrote, *Brewsie and Willie,* although in a more limited way it is still a successful performance. The book is a record of the extreme partisanship Stein developed for the American soldiers who came into France with the army of liberation. Primarily a series of conversations rather than a novel, the chapters of dialogue seem almost to have been recorded by a tape recorder, and they demonstrate the good ear for speech Stein had.

The young foot soldiers of *Brewsie and Willie* talk of world affairs in conversations that reflect their regional backgrounds, their colloquialisms, their arrogance at having conquered the German army. Stein's instinct for slang is usually good, but her use of it in relation to some of the characters is occasionally stilted. Brewsie and Willie are intentionally contrasted according to both their concerns and sensitivities, although they do not disagree on a really fundamental level. Willie is a loudmouth, a blusterer, a stubborn and sarcastic man; Brewsie seems to think more before he speaks and is involved with issues. Although the other characters express many opinions, Brewsie seems to have thought about matters more seriously than anyone else. As the book proceeds, however, Willie undergoes some mellowing.

Richard Bridgman has suggested that Stein found the dialogue form congenial to her in *Brewsie and Willie* because it gave her the opportunity to vent her spleen without obligating her to develop any position logically. Stein expresses her hostility toward the American economic system by letting her characters talk about it with contempt and yet by allowing their immaturity to give credence to her feelings that too much prosperity has caused the development of a coddled American male who can not think for himself. The recent Depression is still in the minds of the characters who find much of the evil in America to be symbolized by the Gallup Poll, industrialism, and labor unions.

It is difficult for us today to take Stein's presentation of the issues as seriously as did the early reviewers of *Brewsie and Willie.* Stein has no solutions to suggest, and the dialogue rarely sheds much light on the matters discussed; thus the book is interesting only as a work of fiction. The portraits of "G.I.'s" are among the best we have, but Stein's hostility toward men is obvious throughout the book. Perhaps the most unfortunate thing about *Brewsie and Willie* is the epilogue entitled "To Americans." This peroration on the subject of patriotism that is rampant with unblushing clichés is forgiveable, I suppose, only when we realize that Stein had lived through the occupation of France and had discovered thereby how deeply American she really was.

The conventional novel was never a form in which Stein could work with complete success, however, for her conception of plot and character development was too static. That is why her ritualized pieces, such as **"Melanctha,"** *The Making of Americans, The World Is Round,* and *Mrs. Reynolds* are her best works of fiction; they never lead us to expect anything to "happen." Stein's gift for dialogue, for the evocation of place, and for the rendering of inner psychic realities are most successfully evoked by the incantations of her experimental prose in the novel as well as in the drama. (pp. 96-103)

> *Michael J. Hoffman, in his* Gertrude Stein, *Twayne Publishers, 1976, 159 p.*

**JAYNE L. WALKER** (essay date 1984)

[*Walker is the author of* The Making of a Modernist: Gertrude Stein from "Three Lives" to "Tender Buttons." *In the following*

*excerpt from that work, she comments on the theoretical bases of the innovative narrative techniques developed by Stein in her early works.*]

From *Three Lives* to *Tender Buttons,* Gertrude Stein created a series of texts that engage, early and radically, what we have come to recognize as the most crucial issue of modernist art— the problem of representation. *Three Lives* was her first major assault on the conventions governing literary representation in the nineteenth century. This text, in which the halting, repetitive uncertainties of colloquial speech supplant the authoritative voice of conventional narrative discourse, gradually came to be regarded as a central force in reshaping the tradition of American fiction in the twentieth century. Long before *Three Lives* received that belated recognition, however, Stein had gone on to invent far more radical ways of manipulating language to create ever-closer approximations of "reality" as she defined and redefined it. By 1912 her uncompromising efforts to embody her sense of reality in language culminated in *Tender Buttons,* the iconoclastic text in which "real is only, only excreate, only excreate a no since."

*Tender Buttons* is both a manifesto and a demonstration of the new mode of writing that it announces. "Act so that there is no use in a center"—this imperative produces a text that enacts the principles of fragmentation and difference and celebrates the freeplay of writing as a combinative game limited only by the systemic laws of language. If these principles seem to echo the post-structuralist characterizations of the modernist text that have already become clichés of contemporary literary criticism, it is no less remarkable to find them so explicitly thematized and so rigorously enacted in Stein's 1912 text. By the time she wrote *Tender Buttons,* she had already embraced the major premises that would shape most of her subsequent work: the epistemological model of present-tense vision, unmediated by memory or habitual associations, and the literary strategy of subverting, defying, or simply denying the normal discursive order of language. Although she continued to write prolifically for more than thirty years, inventing countless ways to "excreate a no since," no subsequent period of her work exhibits either the range of formal invention or the intense reexamination of fundamental aesthetic principles that impelled the extreme and rapid stylistic changes in her work from *Three Lives* to *Tender Buttons.*

Precisely how and why did this writer who set a new standard for colloquial realism in *Three Lives* come to flaunt the radical iconoclasm of *Tender Buttons* only a few years later? Surely this is the single most compelling question posed by Stein's career as a modernist writer. In her later theoretical writings, Stein herself always claimed that everything she wrote was equally motivated by an "intellectual passion for exactitude in the description of inner and outer reality." But she was equally adamant in her insistence that "reality" is a dynamic configuration that changes from one century—and one generation— to the next: "One must never forget that the reality of the twentieth century is not the reality of the nineteenth century, not at all."

This is the kind of polemical appeal to the "real" that has characterized avant-garde art since the mid-nineteenth century, as successive assaults on artistic conventions have been launched in the name of the uncoded "reality" that lies outside *vraisemblance.* Both challenged and reassured by these claims, the viewing public long ago learned to recognize the images that Cézanne, Picasso, and other painters created as new ways of seeing and rendering the world. In the case of Stein's writings, however, readers who encounter so little in the texts she wrote after *Three Lives* that they can *recognize* as realistic find it extremely difficult to understand what "realities" her increasingly unconventional texts engage and how they do it.

The more radically a literary text departs from familiar conventions, the more actively the reader must struggle to determine how to read it. How does it "work"? What are the theoretical premises that shape its formal strategies? Nowhere is the question of artistic intention, in this sense, such a pressing concern as in the encounter with a new artistic work that systematically refuses to conform to traditional expectations. Faced with the extreme unconventionality of Stein's texts, many readers have simply declared them "meaningless." The more intrepid have generally sought the keys to their significance elsewhere—in Stein's later theoretical writings or, even more frequently, in cubist painting or Jamesian psychology.

Both the retrospective theoretical statements that Stein began to issue in the twenties and the ever-popular legend of her intimate involvement with modernist painting and Jamesian psychology have frequently been mined for evidence of the "influences" that shaped her work during the early years of her career. No study of her literary production fails to acknowledge these affinities or to suggest that, somehow, one or another of these extrinsic models will explain the difficulties of her enigmatic texts. As early as 1912, Alfred Stieglitz, who published Stein's portraits of Picasso and Matisse in his influential magazine *Camera Work,* suggested that her texts proffered a "Rosetta stone of comparison; a decipherable clew to that intellectual and esthetic attitude which underlies and inspires the [modernist] movement." Instead of approaching Stein's texts in this way, as "decipherable clews" that could elucidate the premises of modernism, Stein's critics have generally employed the opposite procedure, turning to modernist painting and Jamesian psychology for clues to the intentions that inform Stein's texts. This procedure, which has dominated the history of reception of Stein's writings, has given rise to strikingly different—and sometimes mutually contradictory—accounts of her intentions, all of which equally short-circuit any serious effort to decipher her texts in their own terms.

Until recently, many of Stein's critics simply ignored her professed commitment to "reality" in favor of the assumption that she was emulating the premises and methods of "abstract," nonobjective painting. This historically untenable assumption, which went virtually unchallenged until a few years ago, long served as the most serious impediment to deciphering Stein's difficult texts. The opposite approach has long been to endorse Stein's claims to "realism" by regarding her most unconventional texts as direct notations—or faithful re-creations—of the Jamesian stream of consciousness. Although Jamesian psychology can help to clarify the epistemological assumptions that Stein's writings explore, it has evident limitations as an interpretative model. Purporting to offer a global explanation of her writings, it tends to discourage interpretation as effectively as the model of nonobjective painting. While the one assumes that the language of the text is totally opaque, the other posits the ideal transparency of pure naturalism. But that assumed transparency is equally uninterpretable, because this model locates the meaning of these surface manifestations in the irrecoverable private associations of the moment—and the mind—that created it. Even when Stein's writings are regarded as more general demonstrations of the operations of consciousness, this psychological approach tends toward the conclusion that they belong to the "phenomenology of mind, not to literature," as Allegra Stewart asserts in her Jungian analysis of Stein's works [see *TCLC*, Vol. 1].

Stein's later theoretical writings, with their relentless emphasis on composition as a present-tense process liberated from the preconceptions of memory, lend some support to this account of her texts as naturalistic renderings of the movements of consciousness. But in her equally strong insistence that "[l]anguage as a real thing is not imitation either of sound or colors or emotions it is an intellectual recreation and there is no possible doubt about it," she clearly acknowledges that her commitment to the reality of immediate experience was always matched by—if not mastered by—her intense awareness of the separate but equal reality of language.

The lectures and other theoretical works Stein began to write in the late twenties have been among the most popular and influential of her literary productions. Many critics have used them as shortcuts to understanding her more difficult texts, which allow them to be read as demonstrations of the theories of composition and time that the essays present in a relatively straightforward style. This approach, too, has its pitfalls, especially as a way of dealing with the texts that preceded Stein's wholehearted embrace of present-tense composition in *Tender*

*Stein, in 1937, singing her favorite song, "On the Trail of the Lonesome Pine." Photograph by W. G. Rogers. Yale Collection of American Literature, The Beinecke Rare Book and Manuscript Library, Yale University.*

*Buttons.* These later writings, which have more polemical force than theoretical precision, systematically refuse to acknowledge how fundamentally both her conception of reality and her evaluation of the powers and limitations of language changed during the early years of her career. For this reason, they tend more to obscure than to clarify the terms of her exploration of the problem of representation from *Three Lives* to *Tender Buttons.*

In these essays, Stein attempted to provide a unifying theoretical framework for all of her writings by reinterpreting her early texts as a steady progress toward the theory and practice of present-tense composition that dominated her writings beginning in 1912. The first essay, **"Composition as Explanation,"** inaugurates this strategy by claiming that as early as *Three Lives* she had "naturally" created a "prolonged present" that prefigures the "continuous present" of *The Making of Americans* and all her subsequent writings. Denying that the seismic changes in her work between *The Making of Americans* and *Tender Buttons* have any particular significance, Stein declares that both are equally "natural" consequences of this uniform immersion in present-tense experience: "if it is all so alike it must be simply different and everything simply different was the natural way of creating it then." In **Portraits and Repetition"** and **"The Gradual Making of *The Making of Americans,"*** she presents a more detailed account of the premises that guided her efforts to render the essential qualities of personality in these early works; but again she refuses to provide an adequate explanation for the radical reversal of these premises by the time she wrote *Tender Buttons.* The latter essay proffers a series of six quotations from *A Long Gay Book,* one of the transitional texts that spans these two phases of her writing, in order to "show how it changed, changed from *Making of Americans* to *Tender Buttons.*" But even while asserting that this was a "necessary change," she again evades the question of why it was necessary, with a flippant refusal to acknowledge the magnitude of the issues that were at stake. Why after years of struggling to render the underlying mechanisms of human character in terms of a totalizing unity did she come to celebrate the principle of pure difference? And what considerations led her to abandon her efforts to make language embody essential truths of human experience for the systematic subversion of sense in *Tender Buttons* and the texts that followed?

It is the evident failure of her later essays to explain this fundamental reorientation that has encouraged so many critics to conclude that it must have been the result of her imitation of modernist painting. . . . [The] most common explanation of Stein's literary evolution . . . regards the modernism of *Tender Buttons* and other texts as at best derivative, dependent upon innovation in another medium, and at worst a failure, predicated upon a naïve or perverse refusal to acknowledge the inherent differences between the resources of painting and those of literature.

Interestingly, one of the few challenges to this negative assessment comes from an art historian. In a little-known 1974 essay David Antin argues that Gertrude Stein was the only thoroughly modernist writer in English, because she was the only one who rigorously practiced what art historians recognize as the central axiom of modernism: "that it is necessary to begin from a radical act of definition or redefinition of the domain of the elements and the operations of the art or of art itself." From this perspective, *Tender Buttons* is not derivative from painting but a logical product of Stein's parallel inves-

tigation of the same fundamental issue that preoccupied first Cézanne and then Picasso and Braque: the problem of representation, redefined in terms of the distinctive resources of their medium. (pp. xi-xvii)

Stein's unpublished notebooks, which record her extensive commentaries on the painters whose work interested her most, amply confirm the crucial role of modernist art as a catalyst for her own investigations of the problem of representation in language. But they reveal that scholarly studies of the impact of painting on her work, which have always focused primarily, if not exclusively, on Picasso's cubism, have been somewhat misdirected. . . . Stein's own notebooks provide persuasive evidence that it was Cézanne's legendary dedication to "realizing" his sensations that served as the seminal model not only for *Three Lives* but for all her subsequent work as well. Even during the years of Stein's greatest intimacy with Picasso, she continued to regard Cézanne as the "great master," while what she admired most in Picasso's work was the extent of his adherence to the aesthetic principles of Cézanne. (pp. xvii-xviii)

The most compelling evidence of the enormous impact of Cézanne's painting on Stein's work is the transformation of her writing from *Q.E.D.* to *Three Lives.* Begun a year after her initial confrontation with Cézanne, *Three Lives* is the first of many texts that resulted from Stein's resolve to reinvent literary realism on new foundations, grounded in "direct" experience and embodied in the material patterning of language. During the next few years this project entailed both a continuing revaluation of the semiotic resources of language and a series of redefinitions of those aspects of language that could be "figured" in language.

By 1912 Stein's relentless pursuit of reality in and through language had led her, with its own inexorable logic, to *Tender Buttons,* her brilliantly subversive demonstration of the unbreachable gulf that separates the chaotic plenitude of the sensory world from the arbitrary order of language. In the same year Picasso's exploration of the conditions and limitations of pictorial representation had reached a similar culmination in cubist *collage,* with its provocative explorations of how far the iconography and syntax of painting can depart from the order of natural appearances and still signify elements of external reality. But the powerful internal coherence of Stein's writings from *Three Lives* to *Tender Buttons* suggests that these similarities cannot be explained merely as Stein's imitations or translations of Picasso's most recent work. They must be understood, instead, as parallel derivations from Cézanne, their common point of departure.

Between 1905 and 1912 Stein was engaged in a monumental struggle with the problem of realism, in which she worked through successive revaluations of the issue of representation that parallel the course of modernist painting from Cézanne to cubist *collage.* In painting, E. H. Gombrich has argued, it was the ideal of the "innocent eye"—the demand for ever-greater fidelity to immediate sensory data—that led, inevitably, to the breakdown of the long tradition of illusionistic painting. Cézanne was the crucial pivotal point in this historical process; it was his techniques of activating the surface patterning of the canvas to encode the multiple and contradictory signs of visual perception that laid the groundwork for the cubists' deliberate attenuation of the connection between pictorial signs and perceptual reality. Unlike Picasso, Stein wholeheartedly embraced Cézanne's legendary ideal of "realizing" his sensations in terms of the material resources of the medium. Far from merely following Picasso's lead during these years, she struggled desperately to retain her faith that language could be manipulated to embody the structures and rhythms of reality. By the time she wrote *Tender Buttons,* she had accepted the inevitable defeat of this ideal and gone on to create a new art from the ruins of this Cézannesque dream of capturing reality in the lineaments of language. As the terms of her successes and her failures are better understood, the trajectory of Stein's writings from *Three Lives* to *Tender Buttons* should come to be regarded as a crucial episode in the history of representation. (pp. xviii-xix)

> *Jayne L. Walker, in her* The Making of a Modernist: Gertrude Stein from ''Three Lives'' to ''Tender Buttons,'' *The University of Massachusetts Press, 1984, 167 p.*

## ELYSE BLANKLEY  (essay date 1986)

[*In the following excerpt, Blankley explains how Stein's works demonstrate her rejection of both feminist dogma and the patriarchal conventions of her time in order to establish her own identity.*]

Long before Gertrude Stein blossomed as a literary iconoclast in Paris, she was a successful American college girl in the 1890s, a time when women strove to master the western intellectual tradition in order to equal their male peers at Harvard or Princeton. In later years Stein would savor the memory of her distinguished undergraduate performance as William James's Radcliffe protégée. But her intellectual achievements did not, and could not, make her sympathetic to the New Woman's crusade for sex equality through education. Stein distrusted the college girl's naive belief that complete parity with men would be won on the battlefield of books: she recognized that intellectual mastery does not automatically bestow the bearer with cultural privilege and power. The New Woman was, in short, derivative; and since Stein wanted to be an original, she had to rid herself of the eager New Woman in order to become her own woman. In her earliest fictions, Stein would work to efface from her imagination the college girl who dines on a diet of western (patriarchal) culture's words. The real revolution of the word would begin with Stein herself. (p. 196)

[Stein's self-absorption] clashed with the Carey Thomas/Bryn Mawr spirit of the 90s that insisted upon the general advancement of women, united by a common goal to compete with men. Whenever Stein does refer to her university days, the evidence is always summoned to buttress the personal Stein myth of the ''brilliant young woman who throws over a promising medical career for literature,'' complete with testimony from the legendary William James. The emphasis falls on Stein the individual, not Stein the New Woman among others. Catharine R. Stimpson speculates that Stein had to reject the New Woman's idealized figure (a fantasy blend of wife, mother, and liberally educated helpmate) in order to begin her lonely assault on ''a male world too strong for most women.'' But the college girl's liberated education was itself at fault and would have paralyzed Stein in Paris had she followed its tenets: she had to erase the New Woman's image because it still functioned within the intellectual paradigms established by men. In her struggle with Miss Bruce, Martha Hersland, and Nancy Redfern (three characters in her earliest works), Stein would kill the New Woman, just as Virginia Woolf had to kill the Angel in the House. Stein's demon was . . . every bit as dangerous for her artistic career as its winged sister was for Woolf's; in order to engender herself through language, Stein had to sacrifice the college girl on the altar of her imagination. For almost a decade, seated at her renaissance table and cloaked

in dark flowing robes, Stein performed the literary rites of exorcism that would bring about her own rebirth/renaissance in Paris.

Nowhere is Stein's contempt for the Carey Thomas philosophy of female equality/superiority more clearly revealed than in *Fernhurst,* an early novella composed in 1905 and later incorporated into *The Making of Americans.* Before beginning *Fernhurst*'s thinly disguised fictional account of the M. Carey Thomas/Mary Gwinn/Alfred Hodder scandal at Bryn Mawr in the mid-1890s, Stein offers her reader an essay condemning the modern college girl's hope that her education will make her man's equal. It is wrong, says Stein, that contemporary young women pass through an athletic childhood and a liberated college education ''as if there were no sex and mankind made all alike and traditional differences mere variations of dress and contour.'' Stein singles out the false promise of the New Woman's liberal education:

> I have seen college women years after graduation still embodying the type and accepting the standard of college girls—who were protected all their days from the struggles of the larger world and lived and died with the intellectual furniture obtained at their college—persisting to the end in their belief that their power was as a man's—and divested of superficial latin and cricket what was their standard but that of an ancient finishing school with courses in classics and liberty replacing the accomplishments of a lady.

Although the narrator concedes that some women ''must do a piece of the man's work,'' most are unqualified or unwilling to make the rough transition between learning and action, between sexless theory and sex-dominated practice:

> I have heard many graduates of this institution [Fernhurst] proclaim this doctrine of equality, with a mental reservation in favor of female superiority, mistaking quick intelligence and acquired knowledge for practical efficiency and a cultured appreciation for vital capacity and who valued more highly the talent of knowing about culture than the power of creating the prosperity of a nation.

What use are intelligence and acquired knowledge to dreamy girls who will not/*can* not share in the power of creating culture? Because there is so little connection between the philosophy of sex equality and its praxis, Dean Helen Thornton's glorious vision ''of a people to remake and all sex to destroy'' is doomed to fail. Stein asks acidly, ''I wonder will the new woman ever relearn the fundamental facts of sex''—the facts, that is, governing the distribution of power between the sexes in a world where educated women's intellectual standards are mismatched with their limited arena of real participation in culture. (pp. 197-99)

The New Woman could never have pleased Stein, who had no desire to be an imitation man in a man's world. Nor, however, could Stein simply speak with a woman's voice, for one senses her dissatisfaction with the purely matriarchal prose, estranged as it is from the power at patriarchal culture's center. Stein had long envisioned herself enshrined in history's pantheon of genius: ''Think of the Bible and Homer think of Shakespeare and think of me,'' she suggests in *The Geographical History of America.* But how would she, a woman who lacked the metaphorical penis of power and creation, place her work in the company of these singularly male masterpieces? Her solution was a strategy of such revolutionary proportions that even the most radical alternatives proposed by her New Woman feminist peers seemed tame by comparison: instead of parodying the *patria*'s worn-out linguistics, Stein started afresh by taking English back to the Word, to the Logos. If Parnassus was the Greek playground of Apollo and the muses, then what better occupation for Stein in Montparnasse than playing God with language?

By the time Stein wrote the extraordinarily daring *Tender Buttons* in 1913, she had begun to revolutionize the mother tongue that she had carried away from the fatherland ten years before. Stein, literally an "expatriate" in Paris, was artistically shaping a distinctly "ex-patriate" vision (in the word's original Latin sense of "away from the father"). But before she could become the verbal anarchist of *Tender Buttons,* she had to write *The Making of Americans* and *Fernhurst,* not just because these works prepared her technically for *Tender Buttons*'s later innovations but also because they helped her discover her power as an artist by letting her confront her own internalized images of female powerlessness that may have prevented her from writing all her later experimental work. Before Stein could sail with authority into uncharted literary seas, two of her college girl doppelgängers—Nancy Redfern and Martha Hersland—had to act out the dangerous submissive female fantasies that still threatened Stein during these crucial early years in Paris.

Nancy Redfern, Stein's *Fernhurst* version of Martha Hersland in *The Making of Americans,* is a free-spirited western college woman whose candor and naïve moral integrity make her a mirror-image of young Gertrude Stein at Radcliffe. Nancy's pathetic beaten figure at the story's end differs dramatically from her initially exuberant character—a contrast so marked that one wonders whether Nancy is the same woman at all or merely a player acting out a poorly realized part in an essentially triangular drama. But one aspect of Nancy's submissive transformation carries Stein's trace: she, like Stein, leaves America and expatriates herself to reforge a new personal identity. The similarities between Nancy and Stein quickly diverge, however; by succumbing to the false promise of Greek and the male intellectual tradition, Nancy acts out a doomed version of the New Woman, whose troubling image still haunted Stein, fresh from eight years at the university. Nancy Redfern, struggling in exile to learn a dead language so that she may become a true citizen of the patriarchal intellectual community, fades in the rarefied but etiolated atmosphere of ancient Athens; Stein, however, expands in the life-giving linguistic possibilities that she creates in Paris. As she would later say in *How To Write,* "Grammar is in our power": she had found the strength to mount a frontal attack on an inherited linguistic system. She had also discovered that "grammar"—*Stein* grammar—is one source of her power to change language: "grammar" is indeed "in" (contained within, part of) our "power."

Like a Prince Charming come to rouse Sleeping Beauty, Stein began shaking language from the torpor in which time and familiarity had placed it. Her famous line "Rose is a rose is a rose is a rose" exemplifies her interest in revivifying language, not to resurrect old ghosts but to transform language in new contexts. As she explained the "rose" phrase during her 1934 American tour, "I think that in that line the rose is red for the first time in English poetry for a hundred years." For Stein, the spell that holds language in suspended animation cannot be broken unless language is forcibly torn from its timeworn patterns. To this end, she introduces her poem "**Patriarchal Poetry**" with a string of long repetitive sentences interrupted by the word "spell":

> As long as it took fasten it back to a place
> where after all he would be carried away, he would
> be carried away as long as it took fasten it back

> to a place where he would be carried away as long
> as it took.
>
> For before let it before to be before *spell* to be
> before to be before to have to be to be for before
> to be tell to be to having held to be to be. . . .
> [emphasis mine].

The poetry of the patriarchy is naturally a study of the past—"their origin and their history," as Stein says later in the poem. Although her language spirals in a series of long incantatory repetitions and rhymes that suggest a movement backward in time, Stein is not trying to locate herself somewhere in this vast cultural snail shell of history that the patriarchy carries on its back; rather, she is moving further back in time, "before spell," where she can "be" and "tell." This is Stein's formula for releasing herself from the burden of the past (including its inherited intellectual and linguistic traditions) by returning language to the free-form primordial mélange in which each word vibrates with the energy it possessed before the spell was cast and language fixed.

Moreover, Stein attributes her discovery of the world/word before "spell" to the fact that she is a woman. "Why is it that in this epoch the only real literary thinking has been done by a woman," she asks in *The Geographical History of America.* She answers that question indirectly in *How To Write*:

> Analysis is a womanly word. It means that they discover there are laws.
>
> It means that she cannot work as long as this.

Analysis ultimately leads anyone ("they"—but especially women here) to laws—that is, things broken down into their component parts will yield a pattern or system governing the whole, in the way that logical Aristotelian discourse, for example, leads to the laws or truths that underlie and govern rational human discourse. Stein finds this process "womanly," not because analysis as a mental discipline is inherently female but because the discovery of laws that *limit* is a particularly female condition. When woman, according to Stein, discovers the laws governing language and culture, she does not find what men perceive as absolute and universal "Truth" but an external system placed on her and restricting her: "she cannot work as long as this" is the "law" that would try to short-circuit Stein, and its unconditional finality resembles Charles Tansley's admonition to Woolf's Lily Briscoe that women "can't paint, can't write."

Women are placed outside the law by culture because men, not women, make those laws, as French feminist Luce Irigaray observes. But their exclusion from the law—the patriarchal order—also gives women the potential for putting that Law into a unique perspective. Had Stein heeded the New Woman's exhortation to study Greek, learn the Law, she might have lost the viewpoint that allowed her to disregard the "laws" governing language. In order to escape the law of the father, she shunned the New Woman and spun the unique Steinian thread that guided her through history's linguistic labyrinth back to the world/word before "spell," a world where she could "be" and "tell."

One final secret self and image of female submission had to be recognized, however, before Stein could break free to the world before "spell." Martha Hersland, a woman caught in the binds of family and culture, is the fictional good girl serving Daddy at home while the real girl (Stein) writes her way out of that prison. Martha's story is borrowed from Nancy Redfern, with the exception that after her failed marriage with Philip,

Martha returns home to California to nurse her ailing elderly father, the man whom she has always distrusted and feared. Only geography separates Martha and Nancy; both characters are essentially the same passive woman sinking in different spots of the cultural quicksand that awaits them. The girl learning Greek and the girl waiting on a demanding patriarch are split images of Milton's daughters who, patiently reading Greek to their imperious blind father, personify western culture's ideal of the woman as man's ministering angel and helpmate. Writers like the Brontës created powerful female characters to act out their authors' internalized feelings of rage against the *patria;* Stein, on the other hand, modeled two submissive handmaidens who would act by proxy in the roles that she no longer wished to play. Moreover, Martha and Nancy may even have helped Stein assuage her guilt at turning away from the role of Daddy's domestic slave or eager intellectual disciple.

It is interesting to note that David Hersland, Martha's father and the unmistakable fictional descendant of Daniel Stein (Gertrude's real father), is also a clear forerunner of another boorish and demanding fictional Daniel/father, Daniel Webster in Stein's play **The Mother of Us All,** a blustering deaf pedant who trips on his own language despite his disclaimer that "there have been men who have stammered and stuttered but not, not I." Webster is both reincarnation and evolutionary refinement of the earlier David/Daniels; moreover, he suggests another father/Webster, Noah Webster, the monolithic father of the dictionary who represents the final threat to a scribbling daughter trying to subvert that institutionalized codification of language. By writing **The Making of Americans,** Stein was both exiling herself from these crippling fathers and preparing for her war on words and on Webster's dictionary. Indeed, before **The Making of Americans** was completed, she had lobbed a missile in the enemy's direction by composing several linguistically revolutionary portraits and prose poems. **The Making of Americans** was the long apprentice piece that hastened Stein's maturation as a modern artist and helped her clarify her goals as a writer. Martha Hersland, trapped in *His*land, let Stein create her own life in Paris.

One other aspect of Martha's story helps shed light on Stein's "expatriation," or movement away from the father: I am referring to the umbrella with which Martha is associated on two key occasions in **The Making of Americans.** As a very young child, Martha one day threatens to throw her umbrella into the mud because of feelings of anger, fright, and despair evoked presumably by some childish quarrel with her friends, who have gone on ahead without her. When she does finally thrust her umbrella into a puddle "in a movement of triumphing," her gesture registers both empty frustration and childish defiance: its "triumph" announces young Martha's first confrontation with the laws of parental authority, which say that little girls should keep their umbrellas for protection from the rain. Later in the novel, Martha witnesses another curious scene involving an umbrella, and this event also carries unmistakable although different Freudian overtones: a man hits an angry, pleading woman with an umbrella in public, and the scene "was for [Martha] the ending of the living I [Stein] have been describing that she had been living. She would go to college, she knew it then and understand everything and know the meaning of the living and the feeling in men and women." This altercation between a man and woman (his wife? a relative? a prostitute?) hints at more than Stein's sexual and emotional awakening away from home; it also introduces Martha to the brutality of the symbolic phallus (umbrella) turned against women. Prior to this incident, young Martha had but dimly

recognized the relationship between sex and power in culture. College life clarified Martha/Stein's understanding of the "fundamental facts of sex"—more specifically, the knowledge that one sex holds power and uses it, quite frequently, against the other.

The umbrella that young Martha throws down and the umbrella used to beat the woman in the road coalesce symbolically in another powerful stylus—the pen—that Stein in exile picks up for good at the age of twenty-nine. When young Martha/Stein throws away her umbrella, the gesture is an empty triumph that leaves her defenseless without even an umbrella/weapon with which to confront man on an equal footing in a public place. (The fencing metaphor is not as strained as it may seem: what was literary modernism if not a series of symbolic duels publicly waged on the pages of little magazines in New York, London, and Paris?) The umbrella signifies power, which takes its symbolic place under the sign of the phallus, the inevitable symbol of power in a patriarchal, indeed a phallogocentric culture, to borrow Derrida's term from *Spurs.* The umbrella/pen does not truly become Stein's tool until she has physically separated herself from the *patria* and psychically wrestled (through Martha and Nancy) with the *patria's* lingering demands. By 1921, when Stein fashions herself as "Little Alice B's" husband, she had become her own phallic pillar dancing across the page: "To be a roman and Julius Caesar and a bridge and a column and a pillar and pure how singularly refreshing." And again: "Lifting belly is so round. / Big Caesars / Two Caesars / Little seize her / Too. / Did I do my duty / Did I wet my knife. / No I Don't mean whet." The phallus is not merely appropriated from the father; it is transformed from the violent weapon/umbrella turned against women to the playful sexual agent, the knife that is "wet," not "whet."

With the expropriated pen in hand, Stein stretched her linguistic expatriation to the limit: the result in 1913 was **Tender Buttons,** which remains one of Stein's most hermetic pieces. Here words create their own *raison d'être,* triumphantly emerging as verbal usurpers that subvert the voice and the underlying linguistic structure of the composition by jamming the syntactical circuits with unfamiliar choices. The audience becomes an enslaved participant in this subversion as soon as it sets its eyes on Stein's prose because the calm omniscient voice narrating these verbal vignettes is at once compelling and mocking, seductive and manipulative. The voice tempts the reader with a promise of perfectly sensible, foursquare prose, and yet everywhere that expectation is overturned.

Stein knows that her audience is trained to respond to an authorial omniscient voice and a rule-bound grammatical/syntactical system. By undermining these two arbiters of meaning, Stein mocks both the system and the audience so dependent on such a system; she offers us, says Neil Schmitz, both "a criticism of definitive discourse and a liberation from it." Whether we as readers throw up our hands in disgust, meekly beg the author for a "clue," or rise above the chaos by creating/interpreting a new order based, for example, on Freudian associative principles, our response is determined by Stein's failure to give us the meaning we demand or expect. We have passed through the looking glass to a world that is neither neatly reversed nor clearly inverted—to a world through whose verbal relativity we grope, lured onward by only one constant, *Stein:* herself now become the Word, the Logos.

**Tender Buttons** became Stein's mark and manifesto, her dissertation (or perhaps we should say, her anti-dissertation), which bestowed upon her no formal degree but the infinitely more subtle initials of influence. Although she was not to enjoy widespread acclaim until *The Autobiography of Alice B. Toklas* was published in 1934, by the mid-20s Stein's early works had helped shape the literary development of Anderson, Fitzgerald, Wilder, and Hemingway, all of whom would later change or had already begun to alter the course of twentieth-century letters. Even Joyce was not immune to Stein's "little sentences." Indeed, the sweeping and fundamental linguistic changes suggested by *Tender Buttons* are echoed in Joyce's final work; but where Joyce's encyclopedic *Finnegans Wake,* the universal dictionary of language, is actually an index of fathers (Sterne, Aristotle, Shakespeare, Vico, etc.) sustained and upheld by a monumental cross-referencing of western civilization, Stein's work refers back to no one but herself. (pp. 201-07)

Perhaps the New Woman's revolution was too young to be of value to Gertrude Stein, for whom the college girl would always be derivative and powerless. Stein achieved the kind of success that her university peers had hoped its generation of educated women might earn, yet she did so without the guidance of the New Woman. By sacrificing that shadow self in her early works, Stein found the power to become her own literary progenitor—the mother and father of us all. (pp. 207-08)

> Elyse Blankley, "Beyond the 'Talent of Knowing': Gertrude Stein and the New Woman," in Critical Essays on Gertrude Stein, *edited by Michael J. Hoffman, G. K. Hall & Co., 1986, pp. 196-209.*

---

## ADDITIONAL BIBLIOGRAPHY

Aldington, Richard. "The Disciples of Gertrude Stein." *Poetry* XVII, No. 1 (October 1920): 35-40.
    Asserts that many modern French poets, including Guillaume Apollinaire, Jean Cocteau, and the Dadaists, were influenced by Stein.

Alkon, Paul K. "Visual Rhetoric in *The Autobiography of Alice B. Toklas.*" *Critical Inquiry* I, No. 4 (June 1975): 849-81.
    Explores the significance of Stein's use of photographs and illustrations in *The Autobiography of Alice B. Toklas.*

Allen, Mary. "Gertrude Stein's Sense of Oneness." *Southwest Review* 65, No. 1 (Winter 1981): 1-10.
    Examines Stein's concept of entity.

Anderson, Sherwood. Introduction to *Geography and Plays,* by Gertrude Stein, pp. 5-8. 1922. Reprint. New York: Haskell House Publishers, 1967.
    Enthusiastic commendation of Stein's work.

Bernstein, Leonard. "Music and Miss Stein." *The New York Times Book Review* (22 May 1949): 4, 22.
    Appreciative review of *Last Operas and Plays* by a major American composer and conductor.

Bloom, Harold, ed. *Gertrude Stein.* New York: Chelsea House, 1986, 215 p.
    Contains essays by fifteen critics, including Sherwood Anderson, Allegra Stewart, Richard Bridgman, Donald Sutherland, Thornton Wilder, and William H. Gass.

Breslin, James E. "Gertrude Stein and the Problems of Autobiography." *The Georgia Review* XXXIII, No. 4 (Winter 1979): 901-13.
    Examines Stein's creative subversion of the conventions of autobiography in her *Autobiography of Alice B. Toklas.*

Bridgman, Richard. "Melanctha." *American Literature* 33, No. 3 (November 1961): 350-59.
    Discusses the origin, style, and structure of *Melanctha.*

———. "Gertrude Stein." In his *The Colloquial Style in America,* pp. 165-94. New York: Oxford University Press, 1966.
    Analyzes the development of Stein's prose style from *Three Lives* to *Tender Buttons.*

———. *Gertrude Stein in Pieces.* London: Oxford University Press, 1970, 411 p.
    Highly regarded criticial study.

Copeland, Carolyn Faunce. *Language and Time and Gertrude Stein.* Iowa City: University of Iowa Press, 1975, 183 p.
    Traces the evolving role of the narrator in Stein's works.

DeKoven, Marianne. *A Different Language: Gertrude Stein's Experimental Writing.* Madison: University of Wisconsin Press, 1983, 175 p.
    Feminist analysis of Stein's experimental writings. DeKoven proposes that Stein developed new modes of expression as an alternative to patriarchal literary traditions.

Doane, Janice L. *Silence and Narrative: The Early Novels of Gertrude Stein.* Westport, Conn.: Greenwood Press, 1986, 162 p.
    Study of narrative strategies in *Q.E.D., Fernhurst, Three Lives,* and *The Making of Americans.*

Dubnick, Randa. *The Structure of Obscurity: Gertrude Stein, Language, and Cubism.* Urbana: University of Illinois Press, 1983, 161 p.
    Structuralist study of the evolution of Stein's abstract style comparing the stages of her literary development to the developmental phases of Cubism.

Dydo, Ulla E. "To Have the Winning Language: Texts and Contexts of Gertrude Stein." In *Coming to Light: American Women Poets in the Twentieth Century,* edited by Diane Wood Middlebrook and Marilyn Yalom. Ann Arbor: University of Michigan Press, 1985, 270 p.
    Reveals autobiographical bases for many of Stein's writings.

———. "Landscape Is Not Grammar: Gertrude Stein in 1928." *Raritan* VII, No. 1 (Summer 1987): 97-113.
    Describes the artistic concerns, particularly the development of a new approach to grammar, that preoccupied Stein during 1928.

Eagleson, Harvey. "Gertrude Stein: Method in Madness." *The Sewanee Review* XLIV (April 1936): 164-77.
    Defends Stein against charges of willful obscurity and elitism, but ultimately dismisses her as more of a technician than an artist.

Fadiman, Clifton. "Gertrude Stein." In his *Party of One: The Selected Writings of Clifton Fadiman,* pp. 85-97. Cleveland, Ohio: World Publishing Co., 1955.
    Humorous essay about Fadiman's inability to appreciate Stein; reprints Fadiman's previously published reviews of *The Autobiography of Alice B. Toklas, Everybody's Autobiography,* and *Ida.*

Fifer, Elizabeth. "Is Flesh Advisable? The Interior Theater of Gertrude Stein." *Signs* 4, No. 3 (Spring 1979): 472-83.
    Identifies allusions to Stein's erotic life in her early poetry.

Forster, E. M. "The Story." In his *Aspects of the Novel,* pp. 25-42. New York: Harcourt, Brace, and Co., 1927.
    Views Stein's abstract style as a failed attempt to abolish chronological continuity.

Gallup, Donald, ed. *The Flowers of Friendship: Letters Written to Gertrude Stein.* New York: Alfred A. Knopf, 1953, 417 p.
    Reprints letters from William James, Leo Stein, Picasso, Mabel Dodge, Carl Van Vechten, Hemingway, and many others in an attempt "to indicate some of the influences which made Gertrude Stein into the woman and the writer she became, and certain aspects of her career and of her personality."

Haas, Robert Bartlett, ed. *A Primer for the Gradual Understanding of Gertrude Stein.* Los Angeles: Black Sparrow Press, 1971, 158 p.
    Contains excerpts from Stein's writings, as well as a 1946 interview with Stein, an essay by critic Donald Sutherland, and commentary by Gertrude Stein Raffel, Stein's niece.

Haines, George, IV. "Gertrude Stein and Composition." *The Sewanee Review* LVII, No. 3 (Summer 1949): 411-24.

Review of Stein's *Selected Writings* which offers appreciative commentary on her theories of literary composition.

Hindus, Milton. "Ethnicity and Sexuality in Gertrude Stein." *Midstream* XX, No. 1 (January 1974): 69-76.

Reflects on how Stein's Judaism and lesbianism may have influenced her writings.

Hobhouse, Janet. *Everybody Who Was Anybody: A Biography of Gertrude Stein*. New York: G. P. Putnam's Sons, 1975, 244 p.

Biography featuring many photographs and reproductions of artworks associated with Stein.

Hoffman, Michael J. *The Development of Abstractionism in the Writings of Gertrude Stein*. Philadelphia: University of Pennsylvania Press, 1965, 229 p.

Traces the development of Stein's abstract style from 1903 to 1913.

————, ed. *Critical Essays on Gertrude Stein*. Boston: G. K. Hall and Co., 1986, 268 p.

Contains essays by thirty-eight critics, including Kenneth Burke, Edmund Wilson, B. F. Skinner, and Thornton Wilder.

Landon, Brooks. "'Not Solve It but Be in It': Gertrude Stein's Detective Stories and the Mystery of Creativity." *American Literature* 53, No. 3 (November 1981): 487-98.

Discusses Stein's writings in the mystery genre, particularly her novel *Blood on the Dining Room Floor*, relating them to her general literary theories.

Loy, Mina. Letter to the editor. *Transatlantic Review* II, Nos. 3, 4 (1924): 305-09, 427-30.

Letter to the editor of *The Transatlantic Review*, Ford Madox Ford, in which Loy offers an interpretation of Stein's literary method.

Mellow, James R. *Charmed Circle: Gertrude Stein and Company*. New York: Praeger, 1974, 528 p.

Biography focusing on Stein as literary celebrity, including many anecdotes about her friendships with Hemingway, F. Scott Fitzgerald, Picasso, and others.

Mencken, H. L. "Holy Writ." *The Smart Set* LXXII, No. 2 (October 1923): 138-44.

Briefly dismisses *Geography and Plays* as "419 pages of drivel."

Miller, Rosalind S. *Gertrude Stein: Form and Intelligibility*. New York: Exposition Press, 1949, 162 p.

General introduction to Stein's works which includes several previously unpublished compositions written by Stein as a student at Radcliffe.

Neuman, S. C. *Gertrude Stein: Autobiography and the Problem of Narration*. Victoria, B.C., Canada: University of Victoria, 1979, 88 p.

Examines Stein's innovative approach to autobiography in *The Autobiography of Alice B. Toklas, Everybody's Autobiography, Paris France*, and *Wars I Have Seen*.

Perloff, Marjorie. "Poetry as Word-System: The Art of Gertrude Stein." *American Poetry Review* 8, Vol. 5 (September-October 1979): 33-43.

Detailed analysis of Stein's use of language.

Rose, Marilyn Gaddis. "Gertrude Stein and Cubist Narrative." *Modern Fiction Studies* 22, No. 4 (Winter 1976-77): 543-55.

Discusses Cubist technique in *Three Lives, Lucy Church Amiably*, and *Ida*.

Ryan, Betsy Alayne. *Gertrude Stein's Theatre of the Absolute*. Ann Arbor, Mich.: UMI Research Press, 1984, 232 p.

Comprehensive survey of Stein's writings for the theater. Ryan describes Stein's approach to drama, classifying her plays into three types: those that present "the essence of what happened," landscape plays, and narrative plays.

Schmitz, Neil. "Gertrude Stein as Post-Modernist: The Rhetoric of *Tender Buttons*." *Journal of Modern Literature* 3, No. 5 (July 1974): 1203-18.

Examines *Tender Buttons* in the context of Postmodernist narrative style.

————. "The Gaiety of Gertrude Stein" and "The Genius of Gertrude Stein." In his *Of Huck and Alice: Humorous Writing in American Literature*, pp. 160-99, 200-40. Minneapolis: University of Minnesota Press, 1983.

Interprets Stein's work in relation to the tradition of subversive humor in American literature.

Secor, Cynthia. "The Question of Gertrude Stein." In *American Novelists Revisited: Essays in Feminist Criticism*, edited by Fritz Fleischmann, pp. 299-310. Boston: G. K. Hall and Co., 1982.

Survey of Stein's works proposing that she invented a new form of writing which would, unlike existing patriarchal literary modes, permit her to express her own ethnic background and sexual orientation.

Sprigge, Elizabeth. *Gertrude Stein: Her Life and Work*. New York: Harper and Brothers, 1957, 277 p.

First full-length biography of Stein.

Steiner, Wendy. *Exact Resemblance to Exact Resemblance: The Literary Portraiture of Gertrude Stein*. New Haven, Conn.: Yale University Press, 1978, 225 p.

Theoretical analysis of Stein's literary portraiture.

Stewart, Allegra. "The Quality of Gertrude Stein's Creativity." *American Literature* XXVIII, No. 4 (January 1957): 488-506.

Examines Stein's literary aesthetics.

Stewart, Lawrence. "Gertrude Stein and the Vital Dead." *The Mystery and Detection Annual* (1972): 102-23.

Explores Stein's fascination with detective fiction.

Sutherland, Donald. "Preface: The Turning Point." In *Stanzas in Meditation and Other Poems (1929-1933)*, by Gertrude Stein, pp. v-xxiv. New Haven: Yale University Press, 1956.

Analyzes the poems collected in *Stanzas in Meditation, and Other Poems (1929-1933)*, focusing on spatial, temporal, and conceptual elements in that volume.

Toklas, Alice B. *What Is Remembered*. New York: Holt, Rinehart, and Winston, 1963, 186 p.

Memoir focusing on Toklas's years with Stein.

Wasserstrom, William. "The Sursymamericubealism of Gertrude Stein." *Twentieth Century Literature* 21, No. 1 (February 1975): 90-106.

Discusses Stein's literary method in relation to Cubism, Surrealism, and other Modernist movements.

# Leo (Nikolaevich) Tolstoy

## 1828-1910

(Also transliterated as Lyof and Leo; also Tolstoi and Tolstoj) Russian novelist, dramatist, short story writer, essayist, and critic.

The following entry presents criticism of Tolstoy's novel *Voina i mir (War and Peace)*. For a discussion of Tolstoy's complete career, see *TCLC*, Volumes 4 and 11; for a comprehensive discussion of his novel *Anna Karenina*, see *TCLC*, Volume 17.

Described by Fyodor Dostoevsky as "a sublime artist," by Virginia Woolf as "the greatest of all novelists," and by Marcel Proust as "a serene god" in literature, Tolstoy was one of the most important figures in modern literary history, and his *War and Peace* is considered one of the greatest novels in world literature. A massive, multidimensional work extending over 1500 pages and featuring more than 500 characters, the novel combines an epic depiction of the military struggle between Russia and Napoleonic France in the early decades of the nineteenth century, a chronicle of the interrelated histories of several families over the course of a generation, and Tolstoy's elaborate and controversial theory of history, set forth in disquisitions within the text and in a lengthy epilogue. Tracing the lives of his main characters from childhood and youth through maturity and death, Tolstoy portrayed with unparalleled fidelity the common events of everyday life, and his novel has been as highly acclaimed for the vividness and insight with which he depicted individual characters and scenes as for the grandeur of its conception. Along with his later novel *Anna Karenina, War and Peace* forms the basis for Tolstoy's immense literary stature.

Tolstoy's vast design for *War and Peace* evolved over more than a decade from what began as a modestly conceived tale set in recent Russian history. In 1856 Tolstoy began a story about a participant in the failed Decembrist rebellion of 1825 who returns to Russia after thirty years of Siberian exile. The hero was named Pierre, his wife, Natasha. Tolstoy abandoned the work after completing only three chapters; when he returned to it seven years later, he sought to more fully explain the character of his protagonist by pushing the setting of the novel first back to 1825, the date of the revolt, then to his hero's youth in 1812, the period of the Russian victory over Napoleon. Noting, however, that he was "ashamed" to write about "our triumph in the struggle against Bonaparte's France without having described our failures and our shame," Tolstoy again abandoned what he had written to begin his novel in the year 1805. He wrote: "If the cause of our victory . . . lay in the essence of the character of the Russian people and army, then that character must be expressed still more clearly in the period of failures and defeats." With the chronological limits of the novel finally set—in its final form, *War and Peace* depicts the years between 1805 and 1814, with an epilogue set in 1820—Tolstoy's work underwent a dramatic thematic evolution, growing from what was essentially a domestic chronicle set against a historical background (and which Tolstoy planned to entitle *All's Well That Ends Well*) to a multilayered national epic. From 1863 to 1869 the author laboriously worked and reworked the complex relationships between his numerous main characters, conducted research on the military history of the period, formulated a theory of history with which he hoped to refute contemporary historiography, and developed his descriptions of historical events on the models of Homer and Goethe. In 1865 and 1866 the opening sections of the novel were published under the title *1805* in the journal *Russky vestik*; the completed novel was published in six volumes under its present title in 1868 and 1869.

From the time of its publication, *War and Peace* has been the subject of widely divergent, often contradictory, critical reactions: in at least one instance the book received both exuberant praise and virulent condemnation from the same critic (Ivan Turgenev, who initially denounced *War and Peace* as "positively bad, boring, and unsuccessful" but later proclaimed it "one of the most remarkable books of our time"). Such a diversity of assessments is in part due to the magnitude of what Tolstoy attempted to create; as a result of the enormous quantity and variety of material comprising the novel, many critics who acclaim the work in its entirety as a masterpiece nevertheless take issue with particular aspects of Tolstoy's art. The multiplicity of *War and Peace* has posed particular problems for critics attempting to classify the work by genre. Anticipating critical consternation at the form of the book, the author wrote: "What is *War and Peace*? It is not a novel, even less is it a poem, and still less a historical chronicle. *War and*

*Peace* is what the author wished and was able to express in the form in which it is expressed.'' Critics have analyzed the novel's affinities with a variety of genres and subgenres, pointing out elements of the classical epic, the English domestic novel, the historical chronicle, the anti-war novel, the patriotic novel, the psychological novel, and the bildungsroman, but generally concede that the work is indeed too multifarious to be neatly classified in any particular category.

While most critics praise Tolstoy for this representation of the variousness of life, many have found fault with the way in which he reconciled the book's diverse elements. Several critics, most notably Percy Lubbock, have found a disunity between the two main strands of the work, the domestic narrative and the historical chronicle. Calling the relationship of the two stories "uncertain and confused," Lubbock complained: "And there is not a sign in the book to show that he knew what he was doing; apparently he was quite unconscious that he was writing two novels at once." Some scholars have disputed this assertion, arguing that the stories are unified through the interrelation of the lives of the fictional and historical characters and through the participation of both groups in the novel's historical events; at the same time, others have objected to Tolstoy's unconventional combination of fiction with philosophy. Formulated largely in response to the historical theories of his era, Tolstoy's philosophy sought to refute the historical approach whereby the shaping of history is attributed to a few isolated, powerful individuals, or "great men"; Tolstoy maintained instead that the course of history is determined by natural laws guiding the collective actions of anonymous masses of individuals. His theory has been among the most controversial aspects of the novel from the first, and has provoked criticism on a variety of grounds: some commentators have objected on a purely aesthetic basis, maintaining that overt philosophizing is detrimental to the art of fiction; others have disputed the actual tenets of Tolstoy's theories, finding little merit in his metaphysics and seeing his arguments as an apology for nihilism; and still others have found an irreconcilable opposition between Tolstoy's apparent denial of individual free will in the philosophical passages and the spirit of moral freedom that pervades the narrative. As a result, critics have traditionally viewed Tolstoy as a great artist but an amateurish philosopher, and have dismissed his theories as unfortunate flaws in a fictional masterwork. Tolstoy, however, considered his philosophy not only an integral part of his novel, but the very focus of his seven years' work. He wrote: "My thoughts about the limits of freedom and necessity and my view of history are not chance paradoxes, which I have taken up for the moment. These thoughts are the fruit of all my mental labor of my life, and they constitute an inseparable part of that world view, which God knows with what labor and suffering I have worked out and which has given me complete peace and happiness." Recent reevaluations of Tolstoy's philosophy of history have found his theories both worthy of consideration on their own merits and compatible with the worldview presented in the fictional narrative. Edward Wasiolek, for example, maintains that Tolstoy's writings did not postulate either absolute freedom or absolute determinism, but rather a sophisticated combination of the two which is easily reconciled with his narrative.

Like the unity of the work as a whole, the unity of the fictional narrative in *War and Peace* has also been the subject of vigorous debate. The novel dispenses with the framework provided by a traditional opening and closing, in which characters are introduced and the action is resolved. Characters are introduced gradually, with no distinctions between the presentation of

those who will play a small role in the events of the novel and those who gradually emerge as primary figures. Neither is there a conventional "hero" who might lend unity to the narrative, but rather a handful of equally sympathetic main characters. Tolstoy's rejection of these common narrative techniques, along with the complexity of his storyline, has traditionally led commentators to view the novel as deliberately formless; many have found it confusing and chaotic. While some see this as a successful rendering of the shapelessness of life itself, others, most notably Henry James, have condemned Tolstoy for a lack of artistry. Characterizing the book as a "large loose baggy monster," James wrote: "we have heard it maintained . . . that such things are 'superior to art'; but we understand least of all what *that* may mean, and we look in vain for the artist, the divine explanatory genius, who will come to our aid and tell us." In recent years several critics have disputed the view of *War and Peace* as unstructured and shapeless: Albert Cook, John Hagan, and Jerome Thale have each found in the novel a subtle but elaborate system of thematic parallels, contrasts, repetitions, and variations through which the various strands of the narrative are united in a meticulously crafted whole. In the words of Hagan, "If the cliché 'art that conceals art' is applicable to one novel more than another, *War and Peace* is that novel."

Despite this belated recognition of the structural artistry of *War and Peace,* the most highly praised aspects of the novel remain Tolstoy's vivid realism and deft characterizations. Critics often note the verisimilitude Tolstoy attained by rejecting a panoramic view of historical events in favor of the limited perspective of the participant, and commend the meticulous detail with which he portrayed episodes of both public and private life. In the words of Percy Lubbock, Tolstoy's "mighty command of spaces and masses is only half his power. He spreads further than anyone else, but he also touches the detail of the scene, the single episode, the fine shade of character, with exquisite lightness and precision." His characters, while exemplifying universal human characteristics, have received unanimous praise for their individuality. It has also often been remarked that Tolstoy's characters grow and change over the course of the novel, and some critics have seen the spiritual development of the characters Andrei, Pierre, Natasha, Marya, and Nikolai as the principal focus of *War and Peace.* At the time of its publication many critics overlooked the spiritual dimension of the work, viewing it primarily as extended social commentary: Tolstoy was decried both by critics of the Right, who saw in his rejection of the "great man" theory of history a mockery of the heroes of the Patriotic War, and by critics of the Left, who considered the book's focus on members of the Russian aristocracy to be an apology for the gentry and a repudiation of social progressivism. Many Soviet critics have also concentrated upon social elements of *War and Peace,* in particular the patriotic struggle between France and Russia and Tolstoy's apparent celebration of the masses over the individual. Most Western critics, however, have tended to locate the focus of the book not in social commentary but in such moral and spiritual issues as the rejection of superficiality and the sublimation of the self.

While critics have debated the technical merits, major themes, and ultimate significance of *War and Peace,* generations of readers have been captivated by the work's profound and compassionate portrayal of human life, and it is this portrait of humanity that Tolstoy declared to be his primary concern as a novelist. In 1865 he wrote: "The aim of the artist is not to solve a problem irrefutably but to make people love life in all its manifestations. If I were told that I could write a novel whereby I might irrefutably establish what seemed to me the correct point of view on all social problems, I would not even devote two hours of work to such a novel; but if I were to be told that what I should write would be read in about twenty years time by those who are now children, and that they would laugh and cry over it and love life, I would devote all my own life and all my energies to it." As R. F. Christian concluded almost a century later, "To make people laugh and cry and love life is a sufficient justification for even the greatest of novels."

(See also *Contemporary Authors*, Vol. 104, and *Something about the Author*, Vol. 26.)

---

**LEO TOLSTOY**   (essay date 1868)

[*The following excerpt is taken from an article in which Tolstoy presented his artistic intentions in* War and Peace *and addressed issues raised by early critics of the novel. For a discussion of some of the most frequent critical objections to* War and Peace *at the time of its publication, see the 1931 excerpt by Boris Eikhenbaum.*]

On publishing this work [*War and Peace*], on which I have spent five years of uninterrupted and exceptionally strenuous labor under the best conditions of life, I wish to express my own view of it and thus counteract misunderstandings which might arise in the reader's mind. I do not want readers of this book to see in it, or look for, what I did not wish, or was unable, to express, and I should like to direct their attention to what I wished to say but owing to the conditions of the work could not enlarge on. Neither my time nor capacity allowed me fully to accomplish what I intended, and I now avail myself of the [opportunity] . . . to state, though but briefly and incompletely, the author's view of his work for those whom it may interest.

(1) What is *War and Peace*? It is not a novel, even less is it a poem, and still less an historical chronicle. *War and Peace* is what the author wished and was able to express in the form in which it is expressed. Such an announcement of disregard of conventional form in an artistic production might seem presumptuous were it premeditated and were there no precedents for it. But the history of Russian literature since the time of Púshkin not merely affords many examples of such deviation from European forms, but does not offer a single example of the contrary. From Gógol's *Dead Souls* to Dostoévski's *House of the Dead,* in the recent period of Russian literature there is not a single artistic prose work rising at all above mediocrity, which quite fits into the form of a novel, epic, or story.

(2) *The character of the period.* When the first part of this book appeared, some readers told me that this is not sufficiently defined in my work. To that reproach I make the following reply: I know what "the characteristics of the period" are that people do not find in my novel—the horrors of serfdom, the immuring of wives, the flogging of grown-up sons, . . . and so on; but I do not think that these characteristics of the period as they exist in our imagination are correct, and I did not wish to reproduce them. On studying letters, diaries, and traditions, I did not find the horrors of such savagery to a greater extent than I find them now, or at any other period. In those days also people loved, envied, sought truth and virtue, and were

carried away by passion; and there was the same complex mental and moral life among the upper classes, who were in some instances even more refined than now. . . . That period had its own characteristics (as every epoch has) which resulted from the predominant alienation of the upper class from other classes, from the religious philosophy of the time, from peculiarities of education, from the habit of using the French language, and so forth. That is the character I tried to depict as well as I could.

(3) *The use of the French language in a Russian book.* Why in my book do Russians as well as Frenchmen sometimes speak Russian and sometimes French? The reproach that in a Russian book people speak and write French is like the reproach of a man who, looking at a portrait, notices black spots (shadows) on it which do not exist in nature. The painter is not to blame if to some people the shadow he has put on the face of the portrait appears as a black spot nonexistent in nature; he is only to blame if such shadows are put on wrongly or coarsely. Dealing with the beginning of the nineteenth century, and depicting the Russians of a certain class and Napoleon and other Frenchmen who had so direct a part in the life of that epoch, I was involuntarily carried away to an unnecessary extent by the form in which they expressed their French way of thought. And so, without denying that the shadows put on by me are probably incorrect and coarse, I would only ask those to whom it seems absurd that Napoleon should speak now Russian and now French, to realize that this seems so to them only because they, like the man looking at the portrait, notice a black spot under the nose instead of observing the face with its lights and shades.

(4) *The names of the people in the book.* Bolkónski, Drubetskóy, Bilíbin, Kurágin, and others suggest well-known Russian names. When confronting fictitious with historical characters I felt it awkward for the ear to make a Count Rostopchín speak to a Prince Prónski, Strélski, or other princes or counts bearing such invented (single or hyphenated) names. Bolkónski or Drubetskóy, though they are neither Volkónski nor Trubetskóy, sound familiar and natural in a Russian aristocratic circle. I was unable to devise for all my characters names which did not sound false to my ear, such as Bezúkhov and Rostóv, and I could not find any other way to overcome this difficulty except by taking at random names quite familiar to a Russian ear and changing some of the letters in them. I should be very sorry if the similarity between the invented names and real ones should suggest to anyone that I wished to describe this or that actual person, more especially as the literary activity which consists of describing real people who exist or have existed has nothing in common with the activity I was engaged in. (pp. 1366-68)

(5) *The divergence between my description of historical events and that given by the historians.* This was not accidental but inevitable. An historian and an artist describing an historic epoch have two quite different tasks before them. As an historian would be wrong if he tried to present an historical person in his entirety, in all the complexity of his relations with all sides of life, so the artist would fail to perform his task were he to represent the person always in his historic significance. Kutúzov did not always hold a telescope, point at the enemy, and ride a white horse. Rostophchín was not always setting fire with a torch to the Voronóvski House (which in fact he never did), and the Empress Márya Fëdorovna did not always stand in an ermine cloak leaning her hand on the code of laws, but that is how the popular imagination pictures them.

For an historian considering the achievement of a certain aim, there are heroes; for the artist treating of man's relation to all sides of life, there cannot and should not be heroes, but there should be men.

An historian is sometimes obliged, by bending the truth, to subordinate all the actions of an historical personage to the one idea he has ascribed to that person. The artist, on the contrary, finds the very singleness of that idea incompatible with his problem, and tries to understand and show not a certain actor but a man.

In the description of the events themselves the difference is still sharper and more essential.

The historian has to deal with the results of an event, the artist with the fact of the event. An historian in describing a battle says: "The left flank of such and such an army was advanced to attack such and such a village and drove out the enemy, but was compelled to retire; then the cavalry, which was sent to attack, overthrew . . ." and so on. But these words have no meaning for an artist and do not actually touch the event itself. Either from his own experience, or from letters, memoirs, and accounts, the artist realizes a certain event to himself, and very often (to take the example of a battle) the deductions the historian permits himself to make as to the activity of such and such armies prove to be the very opposite of the artist's deductions. The difference of the results arrived at is also to be explained by the sources from which the two draw their information. For the historian (to keep to the case of a battle) the chief source is found in the reports of the commanding officers and of the commander in chief. The artist can draw nothing from such sources; they tell him nothing and explain nothing to him. More than that: the artist turns away from them as he finds inevitable falsehood in them. To say nothing of the fact that after any battle the two sides nearly always describe it in quite contradictory ways, in every description of a battle there is a necessary lie, resulting from the need of describing in a few words the actions of thousands of men spread over several miles and subject to most violent moral excitement under the influence of fear, shame, and death. (pp. 1368-69)

But an artist must not forget that the popular conception of historical persons and events is not based on fancy but on historical documents in as far as the historians have been able to group them, and therefore, though he understands and presents them differently, the artist like the historian should be guided by historical material. *Wherever in my novel historical persons speak or act, I have invented nothing, but have used historical material of which I have accumulated a whole library during my work.* (p. 1371)

(6) Finally, the sixth and for me most important consideration relates to the small significance that in my conception should be ascribed to so-called great men in historical events.

Studying so tragic an epoch, so rich in the importance of its events, so near to our own time, and regarding which so many varied traditions survive, I arrived at the evident fact that the causes of historical events when they take place cannot be grasped by our intelligence. To say (which seems to everyone very simple) that the causes of the events of 1812 lay in Napoleon's domineering disposition and the patriotic firmness of the Emperor Alexander I is as meaningless as to say that the causes of the fall of the Roman Empire were that a certain barbarian led his people westward and a certain Roman emperor ruled his state badly, or that an immense hill that was being leveled toppled over because the last laborer struck it with his spade.

The cause of such an event in which millions of people fought one another and killed half a million men cannot be the will of one man. Just as one man could not have leveled the hill, so no single man could cause five hundred thousand to die. But what were the causes? One historian says it was the aggressive spirit of the French and the patriotism of the Russians. Others speak of the democratic element that Napoleon's hordes carried abroad and of Russia's need to form relations with Europe, and so forth. But why did millions of people begin to kill one another? Who told them to do it? It would seem that it was clear to each of them that this could not benefit any of them, but would be worse for them all. Why did they do it? Endless retrospective conjectures can be made, and are made, of the causes of this senseless event, but the immense number of these explanations, and their concurrence in one purpose, only proves that the causes were innumerable and that not one of them deserves to be called the cause.

Why did millions of people kill one another when it has been known since the world began that it is physically and morally bad to do so? Because it was such an inevitable necessity that in doing it men fulfilled the elemental zoological law which bees fulfill when they kill one another in autumn, and which causes male animals to destroy one another. One can give no other reply to that terrible question.

This truth is not only evident, but is so innate in every man's consciousness that it would not be worth while proving it, were there not another sentiment in man which convinces him that he is free at each moment that he commits an action.

Taking a wide view of history we are indubitably convinced of a sempiternal law by which events occur. Looking at it from a personal point of view we are convinced of the opposite.

A man who kills another, Napoleon who orders the crossing of the Niemen, you or I handing in a petition to be admitted to the army or lifting or lowering our arm, are all indubitably convinced that our every action is based on reasonable grounds and on our own free will, and that it depends on us whether we do this or that. This conviction is so inherent in us and so precious to each of us that in spite of the proofs of history and the statistics of crime (which convince us of absence of freedom in the actions of other people) we extend the consciousness of our freedom to all our actions.

The contradiction seems insoluble. When committing an act I am convinced that I do it by my own free will, but considering that action in its connection with the general life of mankind (in its historical significance) I am convinced that this action was predestined and inevitable. Where is the error?

Psychological observations of man's capacity for retrospectively supplying a whole series of supposedly free reasons for something that has been done . . . confirm the assumption that man's consciousness of freedom in the commission of a certain kind of action is erroneous. But the same psychological observations prove that there is another series of actions in which the consciousness of freedom is not retrospective but instantaneous and indubitable. In spite of all that the materialists may say, I can undoubtedly commit an act or refrain from it if the act relates to me alone. I have undoubtedly by my own will just lifted and lowered my arm. I can at once stop writing. You can at once stop reading. I can certainly, by my own will and free from all obstacles, transfer my thoughts to America or to any mathematical problem I choose. Testing my freedom I can lift and forcibly lower my hand in the air. I have done so. But near me stands a child and I raise my hand above him and want to lower it with the same force onto the child. I *cannot* do this. A dog rushes at that child, and I *cannot* refrain from lifting my hand at the dog. I am on parade, and cannot help following the movement of the regiment. In action I cannot refrain from attacking with my regiment or from running when all around me run—I *cannot*. When I appear in court as the defender of an accused person, I cannot help speaking or knowing what I am going to say. I cannot help blinking when a blow is directed at my eye.

So there are two kinds of actions: some that do and others that do not depend on my will. And the mistake causing the contradiction is due only to the fact that I wrongly transfer the consciousness of freedom (which properly accompanies every act relating to my *ego,* to the highest abstractions of my existence) to actions performed in conjunction with others and dependent on the coincidence of other wills with my own. To define the limits of freedom and dependence is very difficult, and the definition of those limits forms the sole and essential problem of psychology, but observing the conditions of the manifestation of our greatest freedom and greatest dependence, we cannot but see that the more abstract and therefore the less connected with the activity of others our activity is, the more free it is; and on the contrary, the more our activity is connected with other people the less free it is.

The strongest, most indissoluble, most burdensome, and constant bond with other men is what is called power over others, which in its real meaning is only the greatest dependence on them.

Having wrongly or rightly become fully convinced of this in the course of my work, I naturally was unable—when describing the historical events of 1805, 1807, and especially of 1812 in which this law of predetermination is most prominently displayed—to attribute importance to the actions of those who thought they controlled the events but who introduced less free human activity into them than did all the other participants. The activity of these people interested me only as an illustration of the law of predetermination which in my opinion guides history, and of that psychological law which compels a man who commits actions under the greatest compulsion, to supply in his imagination a whole series of retrospective reflections to prove his freedom to himself. (pp. 1371-74)

> *Leo Tolstoy, "Some Words about 'War and Peace' by Leo Tolstoy" in "War and Peace" by Leo Tolstoy: The Maude Translation, Backgrounds and Sources, Essays in Criticism, edited by George Gibian, W. W. Norton & Company, Inc., 1966, pp. 1366-74.*

**WILLIAM MORTON PAYNE** (essay date 1886)

[*The longtime literary editor for several Chicago publications, Payne reviewed books for twenty-three years at the* Dial, *one of the most influential American journals of literature and opinion in the early twentieth century. In the following review of the English translation of the first part of* War and Peace, *he comments upon the artistic merits and failings of the work.*]

*War and Peace* has been called a Russian "Human Comedy." It is not often that a single book presents so comprehensive a picture of an epoch in national history as this book presents of Russian society during the Napoleonic period. It begins in the year 1805, and the first part . . . reaches to the Peace of Tilsit

in 1807. The second part carries on the national history, and the fortunes of the fictitious characters of the romance as well, through the period of French invasion and retreat. The writer's military experience enables him to treat with great vividness and precision the campaign of Austerlitz and the scenes preceding and following the French occupation of Moscow. At the same time his penetrative insight coupled with his keen observant faculties enable him to depict with rare sincerity the manifold aspects of Russian private life in the early years of the century. The writer of historical romance, and especially the one who narrates the course of battles, has the choice of two methods, both well approved. He can write from the standpoint of the philosophic observer, who has studied the facts and reduced them to a system, or he can write from the standpoint of the participant, who descries but dimly the issues concerned in the struggle, and sees only what is going on in his immediate vicinity. . . . Count Tolstoï's method is the latter of these. He takes us to the field of Austerlitz, and we see the battle with the eyes of those who are contesting it. Of the struggle as a whole, we receive only the confused ideas of a few individuals who are engaged in it, but the loss of perspective is compensated for by the vividness of those scenes at which we thus play the part of actual spectators. After all, it is peace rather than war to which our attention is chiefly called. In this rich and complex symphony of interwoven human relations, the great national stir of resistance appears as the bass, always present, but only at intervals giving to the movement its dominant character. So various are the types of character which appear, and so shifting are the scenes, that we do not feel at home among them until we are well along in the story. Having reached the point at which they seem familiar, it would not be a bad idea to begin over again. The work is certainly open to criticism upon this point. It attempts to do more than any single work ought to attempt, and a certain confusion is inevitable. Our state of mind is that of a visitor in a strange country, who is introduced to all sorts of people and hurried from place to place with hardly time to look around and get his bearings. After a while the surroundings become intelligible, and he begins to understand the relations of these people to each other. But the novelist ought to do more than reproduce this common experience. He ought to smooth the way, and make the world of his creation more intelligible than the everyday world in which we actually live. All this, however, does not prevent the work of Count Tolstoï from being very remarkable, and, what with the reader of jaded appetites is more to the point, very stimulating in its fresh novelty. (pp. 299-300)

> *William Morton Payne, in a review of "War and Peace," in The Dial, Vol. VI, No. 71, March, 1886, pp. 299-300.*

**VIRGINIA M. CRAWFORD** (essay date 1899)

[*In the following excerpt, Crawford examines qualities that* War and Peace *shares with the classical epic, discusses Tolstoy's depiction of war, and analyzes the main characters.*]

When Tolstoi wrote *War and Peace,* he wrote the great prose epic of the nineteenth century. It is only from Russia that such an epic could come. It is only the Slav race that in our own day could provide the material for a work at once so vast in its proportions and so heroic in its incidents. *War and Peace* presents all the characteristics of the true epic; it is an imaginative work based on a great national upheaval, permeated by an intense patriotism. It is something much more than an historical romance. It has given voice to a national ideal, and it has placed on permanent record in a popular form the deeds of valour on which the power of an Empire is based. Tolstoi has celebrated the first emergence of his country from Asiatic barbarism, the first entry of the great Slav Empire into the conclave of European nations. He has painted a war which in magnitude both actual and potential far outweighs any other war of modern times, and he has painted it in all its far-reaching effects on the life and development of the people, in all its spiritual significance. And this history of his nation is typified in the life-history of a number of imaginary personages, men and women so real and so human, that they break down the barriers that divide race from race, and render intelligible to the outside world a national life of strongly marked characteristics. Surely in such a scheme there is something little short of Homeric.

*War and Peace,* though it occupied many years in writing, belongs in its entirety to the earlier portion of the novelist's career. . . . The period of composition coincided with years of doubt, and inquiry, and mental growth in the life of the author, years that led up to the final evolution of his later philosophy of life, the philosophy founded on the words, ''Resist not Evil.'' Towards the close of his epic there are indications that his theories have taken on a more definite shape, but throughout the greater part of the work they exist only in a latent condition. They give colour and atmosphere to his pictures and life; they give vigour to his grasp of social problems, but they are subordinate to the artistic intention. . . . *War and Peace,* like *Anna Karenina,* is, above all, a superb work of art, and it is surely worth while putting aside for the moment those philosophic considerations that spring from his writings to inquire into the special gifts of perception and style and construction which entitle him to a foremost place among the imaginative writers of the century.

It is customary to place *War and Peace* as a work of art on a lower level than its successor. In reality, no comparison is possible between them. *Anna Karenina* takes undisputed rank among the half-dozen greatest novels of the century. *War and Peace* must be judged by an entirely different standard. The very title itself—unless we accept it as a presumptuous misnomer—is a guarantee that the book is something more than a *roman de moeurs* [''novel of manners'']. If we once accept the view that it is an epic and not a novel, the main accusation brought against it, its inordinate length, falls to the ground. For an epic is of necessity long. *The Iliad, The Æneid, The Divina Commedia,* are all of exceeding length. True, in *War and Peace* there are certain *longueurs* [''lengthy passages''] with which all but the most enthusiastic disciples of Tolstoi would gladly dispense, pages of philosophy . . . and descriptive interludes such as the hunting episodes at Otradnoë, which do not help forward the story in any appreciable manner. Yet bearing in mind the vast scope of the enterprise—the presentment of a great nation in war-time and in peace—there are few scenes which do not complete in one direction or another the author's scheme.

Again, we can dispense with unity of interest more easily in a prose epic than in a novel. . . . An epic gives us a certain march of events seen both in their general effects and in their individual application. This is precisely what Tolstoi has done in *War and Peace.* There is no plot properly so called. He takes us from the drawing-room to the battlefield, and back again to the peaceful routine of country-house life. He conducts us through several campaigns, and shows how in the brief inter-

vals of peace the nation returned with avidity to its normal occupations. The history of the various characters introduced is closely interwoven with the course of public affairs; each is treated in turn. Thus the reader roams necessarily over an exceedingly wide field. There are centres of interest in different parts of the Russian Empire, bound together by very slender threads; there is the circle of society at Moscow and the circle at St. Petersburg; there are at least three heroes, Pierre Besukov, Nicolas Rostov, and Prince André; and if there is but one heroine, Natasha—for who can approach Natasha in interest?—there are several other ladies, Sonia, Elena Besukov, and the Princess Marie, who each claim a considerable share of our attention. Side by side with the fictitious characters there is a long list of historical personages—the Emperor and his entourage and all the generals and aides-de-camp who figure in the campaign. This numerous company is handled by the author with an amazing freedom and sureness of touch. Each one is endowed with an individual humanity, with an elaborate network of qualities and emotions, the threads of which are never allowed to tangle. Nothing could be more admirable in technique than the opening chapter in which the elegant crowd that thronged the salons of Anna Pavlovna at her evening party is introduced to the reader. The inane futility of society gossip is laid bare, but it is done without a sneer, with a wide toleration and comprehension of human frailty. (pp. 276-82)

The trait which more than any other seems to me to distinguish Tolstoi from the successful French novelists of the day is, that whereas their first effort is to explain their characters to their readers, to make them logical, to account for all their actions, Tolstoi realises from the first that human nature can never be explained in its entirety; that behind all that can be seen and accounted for there lie unseen forces which may act at times with volcanic results. He realises that every human soul is to a great extent, to the outside world, a *terra incognita,* that it is wrapped in mystery, that the element of certainty in respect to it is in very small proportion to the element of uncertainty. It is just because Tolstoi professes to understand so much less than the average novelist that we know that he understands so much more; he does not attempt the impossible, but he throws flashes of light into the prevailing darkness; and what he reveals to us, he reveals with all the more convincing effect because of the surrounding gloom.

What is true of his character-drawing is equally true of his pictures of war. The ordinary military historian is ready to point out how every operation, every manœuvre, is the result of some carefully prepared plan. He reduces the science of war to a mathematical calculation, and affects at least to believe that a general holds his army in the palm of his hand to do with it as he lists. For Tolstoi war is, above all things, the clashing of blind forces; and a great battle is a catastrophe precipitated, not by the deliberate scheming of tacticians, but by the resistless action of vast bodies of men, impelled to butcher one another by some common sentiment. (pp. 282-84)

A thousand unexpected chances intervene between plans and their execution. Soldiers—even German soldiers—are not machines, and the battlefield is not a chess-board, and high above all the proposals of man there hovers inexorable fate, which plays in the Slav imagination of to-day almost as commanding a *rôle* as in the Greek imagination of old. And so Tolstoi does not attempt to account for that which is unaccountable; but he conveys a sense of the grandeur and the awfulness of war, and of the helplessness of the individual units engaged in it, with far greater effect than the most competent expert on military tactics could achieve. He sees it, not only in its physical aspects, but in its moral and historical significance, and the least impressionable of readers must carry away from his epic a fuller and truer conception of war than he had before. For myself, I confess that I have never been able to follow intelligently the description of a campaign in any history. For me, Tolstoi alone possesses the art of making military operations both comprehensible and attractive. And one of the reasons is his wonderful faculty for disintegrating an army, for making us realise individually the human atoms of which it is composed, instead of allowing us to regard it merely as a compact mass of human material. . . . Tolstoi's usual method in dealing with a campaign is to give, on the one hand, a general impression in a few broad decisive lines; and, on the other, to fill in the picture here and there with a number of detached personal experiences, sometimes trivial in themselves, but related in great detail, and invariably selected to bring out the human side of the situation. In this way the campaign of 1805, with all its complicated manœuvres, leading up to the battle of Austerlitz, which forms the central episode of the first volume, is rendered extraordinarily dramatic. We have a series of photographic views of the Emperor Alexander, of Kutusov, of Bagration; and we follow in turn the fortunes of Nicholas Rostov and Prince André on the battlefield, culminating in the meeting of Rostov with the Russian Emperor in the moment of defeat, and the interview of André with Napoleon in the hour of his triumph.

The whole of the third volume centres round the battle of Borodino and the burning of Moscow. The appalling nature of the event, and the vastness of the issues at stake, inspire the author with a passionate defence of his country. He shows us how the calamity worked in the end for good, and how it marked a turning-point in the history of the Empire. He makes us realise that the invasion of Russia by a foreign foe, and the destruction of her capital, depended on something far deeper than the personal ambition of Napoleon, or the jealousies and blundering of the Russian headquarter staff. He shows us the inevitableness of the French retreat, their helplessness in the face of Russian patriotism, which, in their work of mere aggression, they could oppose with no corresponding sentiment. He devotes many pages to the philosophy of Borodino—a battle concerning which military critics have never arrived at an agreement—and sums up the meaning of the fight in a paragraph, instinct with his wide vision of life:—

> The victory which the Russians won at Borodino . . . was one of those victories which force upon the soul of the aggressor the double conviction of the moral superiority of his adversary and of his own weakness. The French invading army was like some wild beast that had burst its chains, and had received a mortal wound in its flank; it knew that it was hurrying to its death, but the momentum had been given, and at all risks it was bound to reach Moscow. The Russian army, on the other hand, although twice as weak, was driven inexorably into further resistance. There at Moscow, still bleeding from the wounds of Borodino, its renewed efforts resulted inevitably in the flight of Napoleon, in his retreat by the same road along which he had advanced, in the almost total loss of the 500,000 men who had followed him, and in the destruction of Napoleonic France, upon whom there had descended at Borodino the hand of an adversary, possessed of superior moral worth!

Mingled with the fate of the Empire we have the fate of the main characters of the book. Princess Marie is driven from her home at Lissy-Gory by the invaders; and the Rostov family takes part in the flight from Moscow, which resulted in Napoleon waiting in vain at the gates of the city for the Boyars to come and do obeisance before him. Much of the campaign is related through the personal experiences of Prince André Bolkonski and Pierre Besukov. They represent the military and the civil element in the great struggle for national liberty. Prince André, a typical soldier, intelligent, self-confident, and a little hard, is wounded at Borodino; and we have a long description of his sufferings, of his treatment in the ambulance tent, of his sensations during the retreat. But side by side with the realistic details there is the thread of his spiritual experiences, which we are never allowed to lose sight of. Pain, suffering, the near approach of death, are all appointed means of spiritual enlightenment. Bit by bit the mystery of life becomes revealed to the wounded officer, as he is jolted in his travelling carriage out of Moscow, in that hasty flight of a whole city at the approach of the invader, or as he lies at night on his camp-bed in his temporary halting-places. The infinite pettiness of this life is made plain to him; he becomes detached from all earthly interests, and a strange and radiant sense of wellbeing takes possession of his soul. His resentment against Natasha is at an end, and it is she who sits by his side and ministers to his wants while he awaits the advent of death. The luminous pages describing the last supreme struggle are as full of spiritual consciousness as an essay by Maeterlinck; the majesty of death reigns over all, so imposing that the personal grief of sister and of *fiancée* is hushed before it, and they await the inevitable in silence. Only a supreme artist could have disentangled the essential meaning of events from out of the strife and turmoil of a campaign; and from the artistic point of view, Tolstoi has written nothing more admirable than these pages.

Pierre Besukov is in all respects the opposite of his friend Prince André. In him Tolstoi has combined many of the essential characteristics of the Slav race, and he is the mouthpiece of Tolstoi's most cherished convictions on life and morals. We feel that between Pierre and the author there is on many points so complete an assimilation of ideas as to confer upon the former something of an autobiographical interest. It is through him that the great moral lessons of the book are taught. For a hero, he is a strange clumsy figure; but we realise from the first that behind his apparent timidity there lies a latent energy which in due time will take effect. He is full of faults, he is careless, selfish, addicted to drink and gambling; but in his nature there are infinite possibilities of goodness and gentleness and all-embracing charity, without which, as the author teaches us, there can be no true greatness. Pierre is a dreamer, and while pondering over the mystery of life he stumbles badly in his temporal affairs. He drifts, he hardly knows why, into a marriage with Elena Kuragine, the most beautiful woman in St. Petersburg. He does not love her, but her beauty has appealed to his lower instincts, and his will is paralysed by a sense of the fatality of life. Tolstoi describes the scenes preceding the betrothal with an almost brutal candour; we know that hundreds of marriages are made so, but no one save Tolstoi has shown the repulsive features so clearly through the gilding of conventional society. The marriage turns out a ghastly failure; Pierre fights a duel with his wife's lover; and in a moment of blind rage, to which his great physical strength renders him liable, he almost threatens to kill Elena herself. Travelling from Moscow to St. Petersburg, he is detained at a posting-house, and falls into conversation with one Basdaiev, a Freemason. Basdaiev, with unerring candour, tells Pierre some home truths; and we feel that the questions he puts to him were questions that Tolstoi must have asked of himself at a certain stage of his career, and have felt himself unable to supply the answer.

"If you look with horror on your life," declares Basdaiev, "change it, purify yourself, and as fast as you succeed in reforming yourself you will learn to know wisdom. How have you spent your life? In orgies, in debauchery, in immorality, taking everything from society and giving nothing in exchange. How have you spent the fortune that you inherited? What have you done for your neighbour? Have you given a thought to your tens of thousands of serfs? Have you come to their assistance either morally or materially? No! you know you have not. You have merely profited by their labour to lead a corrupt existence. You have spent your life in idleness."

This conversation is a first turning-point in Pierre's career. Henceforeward, although in many respects he leads the same life as before, continuing to drink and gamble and frequent low company, he never again is able to stifle the inner voice of conscience. He becomes a Freemason; he practises philanthropy; he tries to ameliorate the condition of his serfs. It is of no avail. He cannot rid himself of his evil habits; and, above all, he cannot rid himself of the hideous incubus of his marriage and of the false position in which he is placed by his wife's conduct. His chivalrous love for Natasha is the one bright spot in his life of failure and disappointment. It is only when Elena dies, when the great national crisis of 1812 opens his eyes to much to which he had been blind before, and, finally, when he lives in daily intimacy with Karataiev, during the long weeks when he is dragged as a prisoner in the rear of the French army, that his spiritual conversion is definitely effected. Karataiev, even more than Pierre, is a character difficult for the Western mind to grasp. He is a typical Russian peasant, with all the simplicity and affectionate goodness and strong religious faith of his class at its best. He combines absolute stoicism under suffering with an imperturbable gaiety of mind. "Why make yourself miserable?" he asks Pierre, as they lie side by side on the floor of the crowded prison. "We suffer an hour, and we live a century." His insensibility to material wants is not the insensibility which pertains to a lower order of nature; he has acquired it, because he has raised himself above that which is temporary and unessential in life. His days in prison are spent in little acts of unostentatious kindness; his charity is all-embracing; he does not even neglect a stray cur that has crept in among the prisoners. When he dies—shot down by the French because he is too weak to follow the retreating army—he dies in silence, with an expression of grave serenity in his eyes. Tolstoi is penetrated by a sense of the beauty of Karataiev's nature. The little peasant moves through the pages of *War and Peace* as though crowned with a halo; and he seems to belong, not to our materialistic nineteenth century, but rather to the same plane of spiritual existence as the band of ecstatic Franciscans who gathered round the Saint of Assisi in the beautiful Umbrian plain. He personifies all that the Count holds highest and best in human nature; and it is in keeping with the author's whole attitude towards society that this supreme example should be met with among the untaught Russian peasantry. Karataiev has all the passive vritues; pride and self-seeking have no part in him. Pierre meets with him at a critical moment in his life, when the sufferings he had gone through, and the horrors he had witnessed, had filled his soul with despair, and had extinguished his faith in God. Contact with essential goodness is more persuasive than any sermon, and Pierre learns from Karataiev what no one else had been able to teach him. It is as a prisoner, deprived not only of the luxuries to which he was accustomed, but even of the very necessaries

of life, that he acquires the peace of mind that he has sought for in vain all his life. And he finds it in the renunciation of the things of this world, in the renunciation of his own will, and in the identification of himself, his interests, his aspirations with those of the great human family around him. This is the moral teaching of *War and Peace*; but it is conveyed so eloquently in the progress of the epic, in the gradual evolution of the character of Besukov, that the author has no need to enforce it by deliberate argument. It pervades the whole story, and to it is owing a portion at least of that lofty grandeur of conception which gives to the work its unique place in literature. (pp. 285-96)

But the book before us is not all war and moral philosophy; it has its lighter, almost its frivolous side. Tolstoi's wide outlook on life does not blind him to the details of domestic life, to the characteristic futilities of social intercourse. Not Jane Austen herself chronicles the small talk of her characters with greater zest and accuracy than the seer of Yasnaia Poliana. Even so banal a subject as a girl's first ball he invests with a delightfully fresh aspect. The doings and sayings of quite young people possess a special charm for him; his sympathy with their aspirations is complete and intuitive; and his description of the schoolroom party in the Rostov mansion, their quarrels and flirtations and innocent escapades, while written with no apparent motive save that of the *raconteur,* serve as a valuable basis for his masterly studies of character. He has a wonderful faculty, a supreme gift in a novelist, of winning our sympathies for his characters almost with a word. His few touches describing Lisa Bolkonski, the "little princess" at Anna Pavlovna's evening party, her gay smile, her childish manner, her bewitching upper lip, with the slight down upon it, endear her to us straightway. He paints her with all the tenderness of one who knows that a great tragedy is to befall her. Lisa in reality is an uninteresting, frivolous little person, and Tolstoi is quite conscious of the fact; yet when she dies in childbirth with a scared interrogative expression on her upturned face, as though she were asking of one and all, "What have you done to me?" we understand, better perhaps than we understood before, the capacity for suffering that is inherent in even the most trivial human soul. (pp. 298-99)

It is Tolstoi's intense humanity, his capacity for putting himself in the place of each of his characters in turn, for seeing life from their point of view, that gives to them their appealing charm. They are so real, so like ourselves, that we can enter into all their feelings, all their follies and temptations. (p. 300)

There is no need for Tolstoi to award praise or blame to his characters; he never explains when they should be deserving of either; they speak for themselves. His sinners are as human as his saints; and there is not one for whom, almost unconsciously, he does not enlist some measure of our sympathy. Often his silence will enlighten as much as the speech of another. Of Elena he paints nothing save the beautiful exterior; we understand, without being told, that her nature is rotten to the core, that there is no soul to illuminate the exquisitely chiselled mask of her face. Even to Dologhor and Anatole he allows a few elementary virtues; his sense of the universal frailty of mankind is too keen for him to indulge in harsh judgments. He sees with unerring perception the double nature that is in each one of us. Nothing is more masterly in its very slightness than his analysis of the character of Prince Basil, the father of Anatole and Elena. The ordinary novelist would have shown him merely as a worldly intriguer; but somehow Tolstoi makes us feel that there was in him some subtle personal element which gave him distinction, and we are almost ready to forgive him his unscrupulous scheming. Yet we know that in his three worthless children he has the punishment he deserves.

That the author of two such books as *War and Peace* and *Anna Karenina* should have relinquished novel-writing for any other work, however engrossing and important, cannot but be a matter of regret for all lovers of romantic literature. It is a sacrifice on the altar of duty with which in this instance it is difficult to feel in sympathy; for Count Tolstoi takes his place among the very greatest of novelists. . . . He has put behind him the writing of romances as unworthy dilettantism, as a dangerous tampering with the evil things in our social system. And yet— so different are the ultimate judgments of posterity from our own, and from those of our contemporaries—it may well be as the author of *Anna Karenina,* and the writer of the greatest prose epic of his century, that the would-be social reformer will receive the permanent homage of mankind. (pp. 305-08)

> Virginia M. Crawford, *"War and Peace," in her* Studies in Foreign Literature, *1899. Reprint by Kennikat Press, 1970, pp. 276-308.*

### HENRY JAMES   (essay date 1908)

[*As a novelist James is valued for his psychological acuity and complex sense of artistic form. Throughout his career, he also wrote literary criticism in which he developed his artistic ideals and applied them to the works of others. Among the numerous dictums he formed to clarify the nature of fiction was his definition of the novel as "a direct impression of life." The quality of this impression—the degree of moral and intellectual development— and the author's ability to communicate this impression in an effective and artistic manner were the two principal criteria by which James estimated the worth of a literary work. James admired the self-consciously formalistic manner of contemporary French writers, particularly Gustave Flaubert, which stood in contrast to the loose, less formulated standards of English novelists. On the other hand, he favored the moral concerns of English writing over the often amoral and cynical vision that characterized much of French literature in the second half of the nineteenth century. His literary aim was to combine the qualities of each country's literature that most appealed to his temperament. In the following excerpt, one of the most famous assessments of* War and Peace, *James criticizes the structure of the novel.*]

A picture without composition slights its most precious chance for beauty, and is moreover not composed at all unless the painter knows *how* that principle of health and safety, working as an absolutely premeditated art, has prevailed. There may in its absence be life, incontestably, as *The Newcomes* has life, as *Les Trois Mousquetaires,* and Tolstoi's *Peace and War,* have it; but what do such large loose baggy monsters, with their queer elements of the accidental and the arbitrary, artistically *mean*? We have heard it maintained, we will remember, that such things are "superior to art"; but we understand least of all what *that* may mean, and we look in vain for the artist, the divine explanatory genius, who will come to our aid and tell us. (p. 84)

> Henry James, *"Preface to 'The Tragic Muse',"* in *his* The Art of the Novel: Critical Prefaces, *Charles Scribner's Sons, 1934, pp. 79-97.*

### BORIS EIKHENBAUM   (essay date 1931)

[*Eikhenbaum was one of the most prominent theorists of Russian Formalism, a critical movement of the 1920s whose members studied the intrinsic characteristics of literary language in an attempt to establish a scientific approach to poetics. After Formalism was banned by the Soviet government in the 1930s, Eikhenbaum turned to traditional academic criticism and literary scholarship, and much of his later work is social and biographical in nature. Among his most highly regarded works are two critical studies of Tolstoi:* Molodoi Tolstoi *(1922;* The Young Tolstoi) *and* Lev Tolstoi *(3 vols., 1928-60; translated as* Tolstoi in the Fifties, Tolstoi in the Sixties, *and* Tolstoi in the Seventies). *In the following excerpt from* Tolstoi in the Sixties, *Eikhenbaum notes the ideological and aesthetic evolution of* War and Peace *during its seven-year period of composition and surveys negative commentary by early critics of the novel.*]

The history of Tolstoi's work on his novel, as it progressed from 1863 to 1867-68, clearly shows the gradual growth of the author and with it, the growth of the novel. What was written in 1868, was very far from what had been written in the years 1864, 1865, and 1866. As it approached completion, the novel acquired new directions in genre and ideology. The exclusive emphasis on domesticity and the rudimentary publicistic orientation of the original drafts both receded into the background. On the one hand, the material began to acquire an aesthetic shape, assuming the qualities of "a psychological analysis" which was unconstrained by the need to oppose contemporary historicism; and, on the other hand, with the general elevation of the novel's genre and ideology, what had originally been crudely negative anti-historicism was elevated, without being softened, to the status of a "philosophy of history" of sorts. This did not evolve until 1868-9 and was introduced as an ideological and compositional element when Tolstoi was making the transition from 1805 to 1812. This was when Tolstoi finally clarified and established the relationship between the two plans which had originally impeded one another. The domestic plan was given the function of "a picture of morals," i.e. a historical function, although the material used in this picture was largely taken not from the early nineteenth century but from Yasnaya Polyana of the 1850s and 1860s. And the other, military-historical plan was given a genre function, turning a novel-chronical into a *"poema,"* an *"epic."* English novels (by Trollope, Thackeray, and Braddon) helped Tolstoi to deal with the family plot, while Homer and Goethe inspired him and gave him courage to introduce and develop not only battle scenes but philosophical material as well as markers of the *"epic"* genre. (p. 195)

[The] process of publishing the novel did not give Tolstoi the opportunity to rework the earlier parts so that they would correspond to what the later parts were becoming. Only the journal text of *The Russian Herald* was subjected to a certain amount of reworking when it was published as a separate edition. A full *revision* of the text was never done; consequently the attentive reader may notice that between the first three volumes which were published in 1867 and, for example, the fifth volume, published in 1869, there is a definite difference of style and genre. This is not especially noticeable only because of the fact that the novel has an episodic, "montage" structure. Nevertheless, critics and readers of the most varied tastes and values have complained almost unanimously of the fact that Tolstoi introduced discourses about war and philosophy into the novel and thereby pushed his heroes to one side. These complaints were provoked by the sense of a *change* which had occurred in the novel's design, a change which had not been prepared or motivated by the earlier volumes.

It is significant that these complaints began to be heard after the publication of the fourth volume. Thus, in the newspaper,

*The Voice* (1868) the reviewer complains of the fact that in this volume the plot has not moved forward an inch:

> The absence of novelistic development noted in the first three volumes is even more sharply apparent in the fourth. Not only does the author not develop his heroes further, but even when, yielding to necessity, he does speak of them in connection with the novel's main novelistic design, then, contrary to all the conventions of artistic creation, he only repeats episodes which the characters have already experienced and which are already known to the reader. For example, relations between Pierre Bezukhov and Natasha Rostova, which were begun in the final pages of the third volume and which promised to be so interesting, have not moved a step forward, even though Natasha has managed to recover from her illness and has calmed down somewhat from the agitation which carried her away.... Generally, historical events occupy too much of the foreground in Count Tolstoi's book; they constrain the flow of the novel. Meanwhile, the author does not fulfill the task he has set himself: he does not give us a full description of Alexander's wars with Napoleon, but only certain moments from these wars. He does not describe the full course of any one battle (neither Austerlitz nor Borodino); he only represents their separate episodes. Carried away by the masterful artistic representation of these moments, these episodes, readers involuntarily lose sight of the threads of the novel itself; they involuntarily forget about them. Readers therefore look that much more anxiously in the book for fullness of historical description; they look for a complete picture of Austerlitz or Borodino; and, of course, they do not find it. Disappointed, they return to the novel, but there is no novel; the author himself has forgotten about it. This is the cause of a certain dissatisfaction, a certain ill-defined impression. Count Tolstoi's book contains neither a novel nor a history, and more important, it has no unity. One could expand the number of volumes to infinity but one could also decrease them to two, to one, which would be a loss of course for the reader's enjoyment (because they would lose several masterful scenes), but there would not be the slightest loss as far as the completion of the plot is concerned. The essential ingredients are lacking for the novelistic plot proper, and they are also lacking in the rendering of historical events. The author rushes from one episode to another without establishing any internal connection between them.

The reviewer's final statement refers to what we would call the "montage" structure. Other critics also spoke about this. A certain M-n wrote in *The Illustrated Gazette* (1868):

> It is difficult to interpret *War and Peace* because this quasi-novel does not have any one unity. It divides into separate parts—historical and domestic. The historical part consists of poor synopses or fatalistic and mystical conclusions or original letters, written in French with an interlinear translation. Not only is all of this badly knit together with the other part, but it hinders one's reading and deprives one of the possibility of following the course of the novel, which, despite this, is sewn with living thread.

The critic for the *Kharkov News* (1868) wrote about the same fourth volume:

> The whole volume consists of a series of episodes taken, first, from historical events, and then from lives of Russian society's elite. There is so little internal connection between these episodes which follow one after another, that half of the scenes (of

course, those that are not historical) could be placed anywhere in the work, and the novelistic action would proceed undisturbed in its lazy, half-asleep development.

The final volumes (V and VI) only strengthened this impression and provoked even harsher criticism:

> It is apparent that the author has just managed to drag out to its obligatory conclusion a work which is beyond his powers. A significant part of the book, the part which concerns historical events, is filled with quotes from documents and memoirs of that period. These are familiar to the reading public, partly from the rich appendices in Mr. Bogdanovich's works on the patriotic war of 1812, and partly from articles in *Russian Archives*, but they have no guiding connection between them in Count Tolstoi's work. His philosophy is one of those foggy and mystical apparitions which appear to the mind before it has embarked on a period of research, gradually disappear, the closer one approaches and the closer one gets to know them, and finally collapse into the dust the first time they are touched by the living truth. One should not refrain from advising Count Tolstoi to leave the gulfs and abysses of philosophy in peace and to redirect his talent toward that realm of objective, artistic description in which he is so strong. (*The Russian Invalid*, 1869)

Another example of the critics' response:

> Clearly the novel has completely exhausted the author's creative imagination, and he has finally decided to finish it no matter what, as quickly as possible, and as briefly as possible. In the sixth volume, which consists of 290 pages, a little more than half of these are devoted to the novel proper; the rest is taken up with some sort of political-historical-philosophical commentary. Not satisfied as before with providing a certain amount of commentary haphazardly along with his novel, the author has now designated the whole second half of the epilogue as the place for a dissertation on various questions concerning the philosophy of history. (*The Novorossiia Telegraph*, 1869, A. Voshchinnikov)

Not only were the most well-meaning critics (like N. Akhsharumov [see *TCLC*, Vol. 4] and even N. Strakhov) disappointed, other critics reacted with extreme anger—anger at the substance of Tolstoi's military and philosophical views, which, in the opinion of these critics, completely distorted the picture of the Patriotic War and turned it into a "lampoon." Some pointed out Tolstoi's factual mistakes, which were evidence that he was not well acquainted with the historical sources. This was true of statements by specialists and "veterans" of 1812—P. Vyazemsky, A. S. Norov, M. Dragomirov, and A. Vitmer. To this list we should add an article by P. Demenkov which was published by Bartenev in 1911, but was written as early as 1876. These articles are almost unanimous in interpreting the novel as an unpatriotic attack against the heroes of the Patriotic War and against the gentry of that period. Even the characterization of Kutuzov was perceived as a caricature, a lampoon. Vyazemsky relegated Tolstoi's novel directly to "the school which negates and degrades history while ostensibly interpreting it"; and he relegated the author to that number of "historical *wreckers*." He accused Tolstoi of turning all the people of the 1812 era into Dobchinskys, Bobchinskys, and Lyapkin-Tyapkins:

> Don't forget that Gogol has already worked over and utterly exhausted the theme of our *poshlost*. Just as

after Homer there is no point in writing a new *Iliad*, after *The Inspector General* and *Dead Souls* there is no point chasing after the *Ilya Andreiches*, the Bezukhovs and the old-man magnates. . . . In a fit of humor (which incidentally is of dubious quality) why does he populate the meeting of July 15th (which remains a historical date) with old men who are weak-sighted, toothless, bald, and are either rolling in yellow fat or are wrinkled and skinny? Of course it is pleasant to keep all of one's teeth and one's hair: we old men even become envious looking at such a sight. But how are they at fault—these old men, among whom some were possibly, even probably, comrades-in-arms in Catherine the Great's time? How are they at fault and what is funny about the fact that God willed them to live until 1812 and Napoleon's invasion?

Demenkov, who also took offense at these old men, saw in the novel a direct "spiteful parody" of the era, "a spitefully satirical tale," "a chaotic and anti-patriotic fairy tale."

The veterans were sometimes joined by certain critics like P. Shchebalsky. . . . Following Vyazemsky, his article bore the very typical title "Nihilism in History." He pointed out that between the publication of the first three volumes and the fourth:

> Prince Tolstoi conceived the idea of revising his contemporaries' views not only on the period which he was describing, but on history in general. For this purpose, he strung a didactic thread through his novel and endowed the fourth and fifth volumes with a special coloring, a peculiar tendentiousness. . . . His views have provoked a multitude of protests: people who participated in the events of 1812 have protested, offended by the fact that the author seemed to degrade the glory of the Patriotic War; soldiers have protested, finding the author too unfamiliar with military affairs to criticize Kutuzov and Napoleon; in a word, a great many protests have rained down on the author. Considered separately, none of these protests has any significance in our eyes: it is so bad, really, that a novelist does not know military strategy! But insofar as he denies the glory of 1812 and degrades the service rendered to the country by the Russian Army, we cannot agree with him. It seems to us that Count Tolstoi is negative toward *everything* and is attempting to destroy everything. He negates Napoleon and Kutuzov; he negates major historical figures and the masses of humanity; and he negates individual free will and the significance of historical events. Perhaps even without suspecting it, he is admitting utter nihilism in history.

Tolstoi was relegated to the "Leftist" camp by this kind of negative criticism. Vyazemsky's and Demenkov's implication that Tolstoi was a leftist was perfectly transparent. On the other hand, "leftists" came out with articles showing that Tolstoi's philosophy was a "philosophy of stagnation" (N. Shelgunov); that his novel was "an apology for the overfed gentry, for sanctimoniousness, hypocrisy, and depravity"; that the author's sympathy for his heroes and heroines depended on "a feeling of regret about the loss of the *obrok* ["quit-rent"] payments" (Mr. M-n), and finally that "the whole novel was a disordered heap of accumulated material," and the author viewed military affairs "in the same way that it is viewed by drunken marauders" (S. Navalikhin). Thus, as it turned out, Tolstoi was not accepted by the right or the left; and this was inevitable. It is significant that he was attacked from the right primarily for the scenes about war and history, and from the

left he was attacked for scenes dealing with everyday life in the home and on the estate. This was a perfectly normal distribution. A follower of Riehl and a social anarchist, Tolstoi satirically represented the court and military aristocracy (as Saltykov said, "the Count has really made it hot for our so-called 'high society'"); he gave a sympathetic rendering of the landed gentry, the landowners; and following Riehl's theory, he merged the landed gentry and the peasantry into one whole. The uprising at Bogucharovo was described only in order to conclude an apparently ominous picture of "class struggle" with a comic scene in which all misunderstanding between gentry and peasants would be resolved:

> "Don't put it in so clumsily," said one of the peasants, a tall man with round, smiling face, as he took a trunk from one of the housemaids. "After all, it cost money too. How can you throw it in like that, or shove it under the rope where it'll get rubbed? I don't like that way of doing things. It should all be done right, according to rule. Here, like that; cover it with hay, that's the important thing."

Tolstoi's position in contemporary ideology was so unique that with one side of his novel he could be in tune with the trend toward exposé literature and therefore be interpreted as a "nihilist," a representative of leftist "negativism," while with the other side of his novel he appeared to be one of the "advocates of serfdom," one of the old "lords of the manor." N. Strakhov, speaking of Tolstoi's merciless penchant for analysis, admitted:

> If one looks at *War and Peace* from this point of view, then the book may be taken as a fierce *unmasking* of Alexander's era, as a dauntless *exposé* of all the ulcers from which it suffered. Exposed are the self-interest, emptiness, falsity, depravity, and stupidity of that circle; the senseless, lazy, greedy life of Moscow society and of rich landowners like the Rostovs; and beyond that, maximum disorder everywhere, especially in the army during the war. Everywhere people are shown who even amidst bloody battles are guided by their own personal interests, and who sacrifice the general good for the sake of those interests. The book reveals terrible poverty which is caused by disagreements and petty vanity among the leaders, by the absence of a firm hand in government. A whole crowd of cowards, scoundrels, thieves, profligates, and card-sharps are led out on stage; the vulgarity and savagery of the people are shown (for example, in Smolensk, the man who beats his wife; the peasant uprising at Bogucharovo). So, if one were to decide to write an article about *War and Peace* similar to Dobroliubov's "Dark Kingdom," then one would find abundant material to write about this theme in Count Tolstoi's work. N. Ogarev, one of the writers of our literature's foreign section, once categorized all of our contemporary literature and exposé writing: he said that Turgenev was the exposer of the landowners, Ostrovsky of the merchants, and Nekrasov of the bureaucrats. Following such a view we should rejoice at the appearance of a new writer of exposé, and say: Count Tolstoi exposes the military men; he exposes all our military exploits, all of our glory in history.

Strakhov later presented his own point of view, which was that the satirical exposé aspect of the novel was not important. This qualification is significant as far as Strakhov is concerned, but the fact remains that in this aspect of the novel, Tolstoi was a "man-of-the-sixties," even though he was also an "archaist." He was an archaist precisely in the sense that he did not retreat from contemporary life, but struggled against it, and sometimes even used its means. The exposer of the military and of court circles, who "really made it hot" for the elite, did at the same time admire Nikolai Rostov and opposed all of the ideas and theories of contemporary life by valuing the family life of the working landowner, who knew how to crush peasant uprisings. (pp. 233-38)

Among all the critical responses to *War and Peace* the articles by specialists in military affairs most affected Tolstoi, especially those which were businesslike and sensible, like the articles by A. Norov and A. Vitmer which pointed out serious factual mistakes, inconsistencies, and Tolstoi's unfamiliarity with important sources, etc. Following the publication of Volume IV, Tolstoi published an article [see excerpt dated 1868] . . . which answered his critics, but after that he did not come out with any more refutations of the critics or defenses of his own position. But one article which seemed to have been written by a specialist in military affairs elicited a curious response from Tolstoi in the form of a letter addressed to the editor of *The Russian Invalid*. An article entitled "Concerning the Latest Novel by Count Tolstoi" (signed N.L.) had appeared in this paper in 1868, and the author of the article, while recognizing the great merits of Tolstoi's novel, criticized its statements about history and military history and pointed out its mistakes. While writing about Tolstoi's views on military science, he seemed to hint at the obsolescence of the Urusovian method which Tolstoi had followed:

> It should be noted that the time has passed irrevocably for mathematical and geometrical computations in military affairs. Most people now think that success in war depends on the total effect of a great many conditions, among which not a single one, no matter how important it may be, should be given primacy and cause one to neglect the others. No doubt, morale is the most important among a series of conditions, but this should make one recognize even more the influence of other factors (the commander's orders, the position which the troops occupy, and the number of troops) both because the army's morale depends directly on these conditions and because they have an independent effect on the course of the battle.

Tolstoi wrote to the editor of *The Russian Invalid* on April 11, 1868:

> I just read in issue No. 96 of your newspaper an article by Mr. N.L. concerning the fourth volume of my work. May I ask you to convey to the author of this article my profound gratitude and tell him of the joyous feeling which his article gave me. Please ask him to reveal his name to me, and, as a special honor, to allow me to enter into correspondence with him. I must confess I never dared hope for such indulgent criticism on the part of military men (the author is, no doubt, a military specialist). I am in complete agreement with many of his arguments (where his opinion is contrary to mine), of course, and I disagree with many others. If during my work I had been able to avail myself of such a person's advice, I would have avoided many mistakes. The author of this article would oblige me very much if he were to inform me of his name and address.

This letter (which apparently was never sent) shows that Tolstoi himself was not at all as sure about the correctness of his views as would appear when reading his novel. Much had been cast aside, much had been dictated by the polemics of the day, much had been used and put into the novel without making any special effort to check the sources. Therefore some of the

critics's responses compelled Tolstoi to look at his own work a second time, after it had been finished and published as a separate edition. It turns out that the history of the text and, in part, the genre of *War and Peace* did not end in 1869. Ultimately, Tolstoi had to rework the whole novel and "de-Urusovize" it to a significant extent. Even Strakhov (whom Tolstoi met and became close to after he wrote his article on *War and Peace*) said, without denying the value of Tolstoi's philosophy:

> [I must] admit in all sincerity that the one thing hinders the other. In and of themselves, Count Tolstoi's philosophical arguments are extremely good; if he had published them in a separate book one would have to acknowledge him as an outstanding thinker and the book would be one of that select number which fully deserve the title of philosophy. But next to the chronicle of *War and Peace*, beside its stirring canvases, these arguments appear weak, they lack interest, and do not correspond to the greatness and profundity of the subject. In this respect Count Tolstoi has committed a serious violation of artistic tact: his chronicle seems to overwhelm his philosophy, and his philosophy gets in the way of his chronicle.

Clearly, Strakhov did not understand Tolstoi's intention to turn his novel-chronicle into an epic, just as other critics did not understand it, and this was because the novel's new orientation appeared unexpectedly only in the sixth volume, seemed unmotivated, and contradicted the original genre. Vyazemsky seems to have vaguely sensed this orientation, but only alluded to it ironically: "After Homer, there is no point in writing a new *Iliad*!" In fact, that was precisely Tolstoi's intention. (pp. 238-39)

> *Boris Eikhenbaum, "Part Four: 'War and Peace',"*
> *in his* Tolstoi in the Sixties, *translated by Duffield*
> *White, Ardis, 1982, pp. 175-243.*

### JAMES T. FARRELL   (essay date 1945)

[*Farrell was an American novelist, short story writer, and critic who is best known for his Studs Lonigan trilogy, a series of novels depicting the life of a lower middle-class man of Chicago. Influenced primarily by the author's own Irish-Catholic upbringing on Chicago's rough South Side, and by the writings of Theodore Dreiser, Marcel Proust, and James Joyce, Farrell's fiction is a naturalistic, angry portrait of urban life. His writings explore—from a compassionate, moralistic viewpoint—the problems spawned of poverty, circumstance, and spiritual sterility. In the following excerpt from an essay written in 1945, Farrell analyzes the theory of history presented in the epilogue to* War and Peace *and the expression of that theory in the narrative of the novel.*]

*War and Peace* is a historical novel which includes a formal presentation of Tolstoy's theory of history. The theory is developed in a long essay closing the epilogue, and it is additionally referred to and discussed in various parts of the narrative. "The subject of history is the life of peoples and of humanity. To catch and pin down in words—that is, to describe directly the life, not only of humanity, but even of a single people, appears to be impossible."

Ancient historians, Tolstoy continues, attempting to describe the life of a people, recounted the actions of individual rulers and explained these actions as being guided by the will of the Deity. Problems of historical causation were solved by the assumption that the Deity directly participated in "the affairs of mankind." The Greek idea involved the concept of Nemesis or Fate, which differs from the medieval idea of God, but it is not necessary to go into these detailed distinctions here. By and large, Tolstoy is correct in his broad statement. He then points out that modern historical theory rejects the idea of Deity as guiding the course of events and substitutes the wills and actions of great men, of leading personalities, monarchs, generals, journalists, and ideologues.

> Modern history has rejected the faiths of the ancients, without putting any new conviction in their place; and the logic of the position has forced the historians, leaving behind them the rejected, divine right of kings and fate of the ancients, to come back by a different path to the same point again: to the recognition, that is (1), that peoples are led by individual persons; and (2) that there is a certain goal towards which humanity and the peoples constituting it are moving.

And modern history, in accepting this assumption, "is like a deaf man answering questions which no one has asked him."

The real problem of historiography, assuming that the subject of history is the story of humanity, is that of force. What force moves nations? What force moves humanity?

The aim of historiography is thus the discovery of the laws of motion of history. The human mind, however, cannot conceive of motion as being absolutely continuous. The laws of motion of history can be studied only if arbitrary selections are made. But the arbitrary selection of units of motion renders continuous motion discontinuous and thereby leads to error. The historian must arbitrarily assume some beginning of an event when, in fact, there is no beginning. Tolstoy then argues that after the historian has selected a point of departure he examines the will of one person—a sovereign, for example—as if this could be equated with the wills of all those over whom he rules. And historical science, as it has developed, has taken smaller and smaller units for analysis, thereby striving to approximate the truth. Yet every conclusion arrived at in this way can be dissipated like dust merely by taking a different unit, a different point of departure.

What then is to be done?

> For the investigation of the laws of history, we must completely change the subject of observations, must let kings and ministers and generals alone, and study the homogeneous, infinitesimal elements by which masses are led. No one can say how far it has been given to man to advance in that direction in understanding of the laws of history. But it is obvious that only in that direction lies any possibility of discovering historical laws; and that the human intellect has hitherto not devoted to that method of research one millionth part of the energy that historians have put into the description of the doings of various kings, ministers, and generals, and the exposition of their own views on those doings.

If this direction is taken in the study of history—that of studying the masses rather than the leader and through them seeking the laws of motion of history—some laws can be discovered while others cannot be discovered. This poses the two essential questions of history:

1. What is power?

2. What force produces the movements of peoples?

Tolstoy comes to the conclusion that these questions are, in the final analysis, unanswerable. Power is a relationship between people. Its exercise is based on the agreement of the masses. The man who expresses the opinions, theories, and

*Tolstoy as an officer, circa 1856.*

justifications of the combined acts of the masses of people has the least direct share in the action. The general, for instance, who gives orders and is removed on a hill during battle takes a less direct share in the movements of the armies back and forth than the soldiers who charge with guns and bayonets and the opposing soldiers who meet the charge and resist it.

The movement of people is not a consequence of the exercise of power. It is, rather, a consequence of the combined wills of all the peoples who make up the mass of people in motion. In this connection Tolstoy dismisses the idea of a social contract—indeed, he dismisses all assumptions which relate to the delegation of will by the masses to one man or to a few men. He holds that such theories are merely circular: they explain nothing. According to them, power is the cause of historical events and that power is the combined will of the masses vested in a leader. The condition for this exercise of power is that the leader express the will of the masses. ". . . power is power . . . a word the meaning of which is beyond our comprehension."

These problems are reducible to the question of freedom and necessity. Does man have free will or does he not? The "great man theory" of history obviously attributes freedom of will to the leader. Tolstoy rejects this assumption. Rather than polarize freedom and necessity, he sees them as interrelated. Freedom is content; necessity is form. Man exists only in time and space. All men participate in the historical action of a given period; that is, the actions of all men are part of the total history of that given period. If a man is restricted in his actions by even one law, then he is not totally free. But we have already seen that Tolstoy admits the validity of the concept of historical law; thus he rejects the concept of absolute freedom of the will. Further, in order for a man to be absolutely free, he would have to exist beyond the bonds of time and space; but if he did, he would not be a man living on the plane of history. And if he is outside the plane of history, his actions have no bearing on this problem.

The fact is, then, that man is controlled by necessity. The expression of necessity is found in the concept of law. Some laws are known; others are unknown, and some can never be known. Since man lives in time and place and is an actor on the stage of history, he is part of history. For him to know all would be for the part to be greater than the whole.

Yet man, in his consciousness, does not feel in bondage to necessity: he has a consciousness of freedom. "Consciousness says: I alone am . . . . I measure moving time. . . . I am outside of cause. . . ." This view is based on and embodies a bifurcation. Reason permits man to grasp and express the laws of necessity; consciousness provides man with his conviction of "the reality of free will." Man in his consciousness holds to the idea of unlimited freedom of will. With his reason he examines—examines free will. There are thus two sources of knowledge and "only by their synthesis is a clear conception of the life of man gained." Ergo: consciousness is content; necessity is form.

This problem, in relation to history, is different from what it is in theology: ". . . The question relates, not to the essential nature of the will of man, but to the representation of the manifestations of that will in the past and under certain conditions." Tolstoy is here generalizing what he concretely embodies in the narrative of *War and Peace*. This fact casts a different light on his theory. It shows his utter sincerity and purity of motives, his responsible effort to put all his cards on the table for the reader.

Tolstoy was a contemporary of Marx and Engels. In *What Is Art?* he dismissed Marxian economics in a rather casual way, to say the least; however, many of his denunciations of capitalism, written after his change in the 1880's, can be easily and consistently harmonized with Marxian economics. Marx and Engels also posed the problem of history. Listen to Engels on this same problem:

> Men make their own history, whatever its outcome may be, in that each person follows his own consciously desired end, and it is precisely the resultant of these many wills operating in different directions and of their manifold effects upon the outer world that constitutes history. Thus it is . . . a question of what many individuals desire. The will is determined by passion or deliberation. But the levers which immediately determine passion or deliberation are of very different kinds. Partly they may be external objects, partly ideal motives, ambition, "enthusiasm for truth and justice," personal hatred or purely individual whims of all kinds. But, on the one hand, we have seen that the many individual wills active in history for the most part produce results quite other than those intended—often quite the opposite; their motives therefore in relation to the total result are likewise of only secondary significance. On the other hand, the further question arises: what driving forces in turn stand behind these motives: What are the historical causes which transform themselves into these motives in the brains of the actors?

The statement reads like a general characterization of the problem dealt with in *War and Peace*. Not only does it formally

parallel Tolstoy's statement of the problem in his Epilogue; it also generalizes the concrete events in the narrative, most particularly those relating to Tolstoy's characterization of Napoleon. Tolstoy clearly posed the problem of history in his own time. (pp. 214-19)

Tolstoy defeats the idea of a science of history with the militant, insistent use of a truism. There can be no doubt that the subject of history is what happens to all of humanity. The complete historical representation of a period would be one which told everything that happened to every human being living in the period. The final consequences of Tolstoy's position can only be fatalism and also, perhaps, a nebulous morality of mysticism. If one strictly accepts and applies conclusions such as Tolstoy's, then the road to freedom lies within us. The solutions, not only of the problems of past history but, more importantly, of the problems of living history, which we call political, must then be moral and not political.

Essentially, this was the conclusion at which Tolstoy arrived, and it constitutes the reactionary side or content of his life and work as distinguished from the progressive aspect. The theory of history formulated in *War and Peace* is easily correlated with many of the doctrines which later became known as Tolstoyism. The end result of such a doctrine of fatalism can well be seen as leading to an emphasis on death: for if freedom is merely the content, and if it is constricted on every side by the admittedly large variety of the laws of necessity, then death can be a liberation from necessity. Death is the final controlling law of necessity to which the consciousness of man, believing in absolute freedom, must submit. Prince Andrey, we note, accepts—in fact he welcomes—death as a liberation, and he does this at a time when his body is suffering agonies which can be explained by laws of necessity. (pp. 219-20)

At the very least, one can say that Tolstoy's theory of history is ingenious. It predicates his future and more developed moral doctrine. In this sense it is more interesting to us today for its autobiographical connotations than as a contemporarily valid contribution to historiography.

In effect, Tolstoy renders the problem of historical causation insoluble because one cannot know everything. This seems to me to be similar to saying that the problem of causation in physical science is also insoluble because (a) a man is always in only one place at one time, and (b) every event in the universe is connected with every other event, and one is incapable of seeing every event at one time. The very assumptions of scientific method take limitations of this order into account. Science *isolates*. By isolating, it can gain a sense of some processes. This knowledge permits one to predict, and to make instruments which give man greater control over nature. The purpose of a scientific investigation of history is to give man knowledge so that he may predict and obtain greater mastery over his own destiny.

The major problem of history is the problem of change. How does change occur? What are the conditions which can be seen as the prerequisites of change? Problems of causation in history do not necessarily demand as solutions the proving of ironbound laws that show *absolutely* that "a" *caused* "b." Rather, the problem of historic causation is that of discovering what kinds of conditions in a given period help us to explain what happened in that given period. Tolstoy himself grants that some historical laws are discoverable. If some are discoverable, then more are, also. History is senseless only so long as we don't know enough to describe what happens with relative accuracy, and in terms of a tapestried sequence of events that reveal the elements of change. The definition of problems is an *important* factor in determining what data are *essential*. Tolstoy, by generalizing the problem as he does, confuses it. He dismisses all explanations of the War of 1812 as partial and concludes by telling us that what happened happened and that every event that occurred was causal.

In presenting his theory of history, Tolstoy clearly posed a general problem, one which interested the best minds of his time. The subject of his essay, however, is more properly the philosophy of history than history as a science. His argument is developed in terms of a series of generalizations, and his illustrations are broad and sweeping. He does not concern himself with a close or detailed consideration of precise methodological problems, but sees tendencies in history only in terms of the broadest generalizations. He is much too sweeping here, just as he was in his account of esthetic theories in *What Is Art?*

Tolstoy generalizes on history in an unhistorical manner. He does not make sufficient distinction beween different historical conceptions at different periods. Prior to what is generally called the modern period, he says, historians accepted the idea that the Deity was the cause of events; in the modern period, historians say that great men will history. But there is a difference between the assumption that Greek gods or the God of triumphant feudal Christianity willed history and the assumption that Napoleon Bonaparte willed history. Tolstoy claims that Gibbon and other historians inevitably end up in the same positions as the ancients. He makes no attempt to distinguish the changes and advances in methodology which were conditioned by more fundamental social changes.

In the final analysis, Tolstoy is unable to make sense out of history because he attempts to explain causation on the basis of an assumption similar to that of the Bonapartist and the other historians he criticizes. He attempts to explain history in terms of ideology, of the content of consciousness. He rejects the idea that the will of one or of a few leaders causes history. But he substitutes the will of all humanity. Every human being in an epoch wills, thinking himself free, but what is willed does not always happen. Somehow or other, in terms of necessity, what happens, happens. But Tolstoy explains this in terms of consciousness, and then it develops that it is not consciousness. To say that consciousness is content and necessity is form is to leave unsolved what we have called the problem of history. This problem is, how does consciousness change? What conditions of necessity develop so that there are changes? Empirically, Tolstoy sees changes and he sees differentiations in consciousness. But he does not bridge the gap between empirical observation and theoretical generalization. (pp. 220-23)

Hegel described freedom as the recognition of necessity. Marx and Engels attempted to formulate precisely what are the important "laws of necessity," how these induce changes in consciousness, and how, by trying to understand necessity and its consequences in consciousness, man can arm himself with the knowledge that will enable him to gain greater freedom. Engels saw this understanding as the means whereby mankind could eventually rise from the kingdom of necessity and enter into the kingdom of freedom. Tolstoy's concern in his theory is really the kingdom of freedom. For him, however, freedom remains merely a moral orientation. At times, as in the cases of Platon Karataev and Pierre Bezuhov, this moral orientation becomes an ecstatic consciousness of freedom. Freedom, to

repeat, is resident in the human consciousness: it is merely a moral discovery. This is the heart, the core, of his theory. Its fatalism denies the possibility of prediction and thus helps to cut the nerves of action.

Is Tolstoy's formal theory of history irrelevant to *War and Peace*? The foregoing analysis should help to answer this question. By examining his theory on its own terms, we have arrived at clues concerning his thought. Thus the meaning of Prince Andrey's welcoming of death as a liberation is clarified. Thus the characterizations are given greater depth. There is no evidence that Tolstoy set out deliberately to write a moral critique, a moral renunciation, a moral attack on Tsarist society in a class sense that can be called Marxian. His moral revelations are the consequences of his empirical observations and his own moral needs. A mere tapestry of characters would have been meaningless, especially in the Russia of his day. Fettered by Tsarism and autocracy, aware and sensitive persons felt the problems of life in nineteenth-century Russia so acutely that a genius like Tolstoy could not be satisfied to write nothing more than a tapestry. Further, a novel of this scope had to have depth of meaning. It is one thing to conclude a methodological and theoretical discussion with the assertion that history—destiny—is senseless; it is something else to write a historical novel hundreds upon hundreds of pages long and make it senseless. That would have been impossible for Tolstoy.

One of the major links between theory and concrete action in *War and Peace* is Pierre. . . . [It has] been noted that he has more contacts than any other character in the novel. He tries in many ways to find an objective in life. The pattern of his experience becomes clearer, however, when it is correlated with Tolstoy's theory. In a practical sense, Pierre's problem presents the problem of freedom and necessity in a concrete form. . . . [He] has discovered that the road to freedom is moral: he first becomes conscious of a glowing feeling of freedom when he is most unfree, a prisoner of necessity, represented by the French army. Moreover, he is inspired by Platon, one of the mass of humanity, part of the "swarm" that, according to Tolstoy, constitutes the subject matter of history. Platon, a peasant, has never been free in the worldly, social sense. It is clear that no character in *War and Peace* has been more constrained by necessity. And yet he, too, has the consciousness of freedom. And Natasha, who represents humanity, laughs and sings with a joyful consciousness of freedom until her period of sorrows. Her sorrows are induced by necessity, expressed in the force and prejudice of class conventions. When Pierre, Platon, Natasha, and Andrey on his deathbed possess this consciousness of freedom, they are most happy. Their virtues are sincerity, good nature, kindness—the virtues Tolstoy admired. It is only by giving expression to these virtues that his characters are happy and give happiness to others. These virtues are identified with humanity. Platon is the man of the human "swarm"; Pierre finds humanity through Platon and then, with marriage to Natasha, in family happiness.

Tolstoy's theory emphasizes humanity rather than class or leader. All humanity, he asserts, possesses the innate consciousness of freedom. What is important to humanity is this consciousness. Moral freedom, virtue, happiness, love—all this—in so far as there is an object in life—is the object. This is the means of achieving peace. Both on the empirical level of behavior and on the formal level of theory, Tolstoy stresses correlated points: the action and the theory of the novel are synchronized. This synchronization is in turn a synthesis of the mutual relationship between freedom and necessity, form and content.

The title poses the problem—the problem of man. War is the most constraining of all necessities: it is an all-engulfing and inevitable historical earthquake. And peace is the peace man feels, the peace he discovers in his own soul.

It is well known that Tolstoy was a soldier with battle experience, in fact, a brave soldier. Influenced by Stendhal, he wrote his realistic masterpiece on war, *Sevastopol.* At one time he sought a career in the Russian army and was deeply disappointed that he did not win the Cross of St. George, which he apparently merited for his bravery.

Thus he wrote about war as one who had seen its horrors. The realism of his accounts of battle and of the emotions and attitudes before and during battle is constantly vouched for by military men and others who have had experience in the field. He has often been called the greatest of all creative writers who have dealt with war in fiction. Certainly the battle scenes in *War and Peace* leave an unforgettable impression. Even to one who has had no war experience, his descriptions create the illusion that one has, like Pierre at Borodino, seen, felt, heard, and smelled battle. (pp. 223-26)

The same naturalness and transparency of style which introduces us into the drawing room of Anna Pavlovna and the heart of Natasha, permits us . . . to see war, all phases of Napoleonic war. The description of the war is marked by the same complexity of scenes and contrasts. We are told what the ordinary soldiers say and do; we see them in battle close up and afar; we know how they feel about it. We see officers. We watch cavalry, infantry, artillery, and partisans. Generals appear on the battlefield and in council. Napoleon and his marshals move before our eyes. We watch the routed army and see the victors, and then Bonaparte among the wounded. We are permitted to see Denisov, Rostov, and others in bivouac. Soldiers and officers are described relaxed, tense in battle, camping after battle. The army draws up on parade for the Emperor. The French disintegrate as they flee over frozen Russian snows. Officers on leave move before our eyes. The wounded are glimpsed, alone and groaning on the field, in carts on the road, shrieking and dying in temporary hospital tents, bored, some recuperating and some turning green and gangrenous in permanent hospitals. The plans of battle, with details of strategy and tactics, are discussed, and while old Kutuzov falls alseep more than one plan is presented. Just as there are many types of soldiers and under-officers characterized, so are there many generals. Battles are described in terms of changing situations. One grasps concretely a sense of that chance to which Clausewitz referred as one of the outstanding elements of war. The factor of morale is illustrated not only by understanding comment but also by characterization of individual soldiers and descriptions of groups. As if by miracle, the gestures of officers in "that moment . . . of moral vacillation which decides the fate of battles" seem as absolutely right as does Natasha's laughter when she first scampers into the novel. And despite the efforts of the officers, the soldiers run "shooting into the air and not listening to the word of command. The moral balance . . . was unmistakably falling on the side of panic."

The vigorousness and variety of contrasts is further stamped emotionally. Fear, terror, romantic heroism, cold-bloodedness, the struggle within a man to be merciful or brutal because of practical military reasons, cowardice, nostalgia for home and the past, bitterness, disillusionment, craftiness—the emotional range is as wide as in the scenes of aristocratic social life. And the emotional meanings of war are detailed before, during, and after battle.

The impression of war emerging from this bloodied tapestry is one of waste, of terrible and senseless waste. "On account of personal and court considerations were tens of thousands of lives to be risked. . . ." In blood, death, pain, the author's conception of the senselessness of history and destiny is most dramatically focused on his account of the War of 1812. But Tolstoy was not yet a pacifist when he wrote *War and Peace.* In fact, the narrative now and then includes a sentence or two which glows with the suggestion of the kind of patriotic feeling Tolstoy was later to denounce as immoral and un-Christian. But however balanced his account of war is, he did not like war. He did not glorify it. It is clear that he regarded war to be in contravention of reason and of the best in humanity. The unchaining and progress of the War of 1812 is characterized as follows:

> On the 12th of June the forces of Western Europe crossed the frontier, and the war began, that is, an event took place opposed to human reason and all human nature. Millions of men perpetrated against one another so great a mass of crime—fraud, swindling, robbery, forgery, issue of counterfeit money, plunder, incendiarism, and murder—that the annals of all the criminal courts of the world could not muster such a sum of wickedness in whole centuries, though the men who committed those deeds did not at that time look on them as crimes.

And nobody caused this carnage. "The acts of Napoleon and Alexander . . . were as little voluntary as the act of each soldier, forced to march out by the drawing of a lot or by conscription." The war, so described, is a major example of Tolstoy's theory of history. (pp. 228-30)

> *James T. Farrell, "History and War in Tolstoy's 'War and Peace'," in his* Literature and Morality, *Vanguard Press, 1974, pp. 214-30.*

**ALBERT COOK**  (essay date 1958)

[*Cook is an American man of letters whose criticism has been praised for its erudition and versatility. In the following excerpt from an essay originally published in 1958, he disputes the assertion that* War and Peace *lacks thematic unity, demonstrating that the disparate narrative strands of the novel are unified around Tolstoy's moral vision.*]

If fiction is essentially concerned with the commitment of its characters to moral ideas, its main stream is more to be traced in moral observation than in the tributary of figurative implication. As the instinct of Leavis has shown us, the great tradition of English—as of any—fiction is a moral tradition.

Each original novelist, by virtue of the uniqueness of the world he creates, has a distinct kind of moral observation. We find that Hemingway analyzes the moral gestures of courage, Trollope of sincerity, Jane Austen of altruistic social insight, Defoe of economic and sexual scruple, Stendhal of crassness or fineness.

Tolstoi's world, for all its breadth, is no less single in its moral outlook. It is a truism that the greater the novelist the more sweeping his vision. We tend to combine the persuasive universality of the moral abstraction with the wide scope of the major novelist and attribute to Tolstoi a representation of all life. This ascription, praiseworthy as a tribute to the commanding imagination of a superb writer, has the pernicious critical result of disarming in advance the attempt to define the theme of *War and Peace.* Even so responsible a critic as Forster [in *Aspects of the Novel;* see *TCLC,* Vol. 4] seems almost captiously, and at the same time indolently, content merely to gape at the masterpiece, leaving unchallenged Lubbock's equally imperceptive assertion [see *TCLC,* Vol. 4] of thematic disunity in the novel.

The meaning of *War and Peace* is, however large, single and coherent. It creates its characters and builds its panoramic universe of moral meaning out of a sequence of observed and analyzed moral gestures:

> Prince Vassily always spoke languidly, like an actor repeating his part in an old play. Anna Pavlovna Scherer, in spite of her forty years, was on the contrary brimming over with excitement and impulsiveness. To be enthusiastic had become her pose in society, and at times even when she had, indeed, no inclination to be so, she was enthusiastic so as not to disappoint the expectations of those who knew her. The affected smile which played continually about Anna Pavlovna's face, out of keeping as it was with her faded looks, expressed a spoilt child's continual consciousness of a charming failing of which she had neither the wish nor the power to correct herself, which, indeed, she saw no need to correct.

The surface of social life in the *soirée* of this chapter is presented as a kind of play. Most prominent are the most acting, the most hypocritical (Greek, actors); there are moving at the same time shyly and clumsily in the background, of this scene as throughout Book One, those dedicated beings we will come to know as the agents of a real moral life. Not that they yet know to what they are dedicated. Prince Vassily and Anna Pavlovna know; but their knowledge is not a true superiority; as here rendered, it is only the superficial skill of the actor. Their limit is that they know all they are to do; so they have chosen it.

In the keen individuation of Tolstoi's moral analysis, these two hypocrites are distinguished from one another: Prince Vassily is languid, Anna Pavlovna "brimming over with excitement and impulsiveness." These traits in turn are subjected to analysis. Every nuance of behavior undergoes a moral scrutiny.

What is the domain of Tolstoi's analysis? It is so perfectly fused with the theme of the novel that a short definition is not possible, but, roughly, he is always analyzing a character's attitude toward his own destiny, his own tempo, his own potentialities. Gesture always has become or is becoming moral habit in Tolstoi. He analyzes the certitude of the become, the hesitance of the becoming. Habit is subjected to time, transmuted and retransmuted, in a number of ways whose diversity his moral analysis renders, whose underlying interdependence the plot coordinates. The plot's grand scale of social process changes each phase's moral appearance into a new reality. To keep up with the times, with Time, to be morally real, a character must meet a challenge which faces everyone equally as it faces each at his own individual angle. What makes Anna Pavlovna Scherer and Prince Vassily superficial is their dedication to surface, implied in the meaning Tolstoi analyzes into their almost ritual gestures. Oriented toward mere appearance, they commit themselves toward their temporary social masks. This commitment affords them a certain adroitness, but it cuts them out of all the profounder resurrections of the years to come. Nine years and a thousand pages later the bumbling Pierre of the first scene of the novel will have become spiritually baptized and rebaptized into a moral giant. But Anna Pavlovna, withdrawn from the horribly contrasting background of devastated Moscow, will be giving the identical Petersburg

*soirée,* politely and coldly ignoring the cataclysm that is to be the death through which the best will be reborn. And who is her honored guest but the same Prince Vassily, unchanged in his diabolical superficiality.

In *War and Peace,* the analyzed gestures of the characters find their stated meaning in what will become their final destiny. The appearance of detail is being compounded with the reality of the whole. The constant relevance of these analyzed components to the reflected whole lends, to detail and overall canvas alike, a uniformity and proportionateness which recalls the realism of Vermeer or Caravaggio or better, Velasquez: what Blackmur has called the "buoyancy and sanity of Tolstoi's novels."

The fifteen books and epilog of the novel are orchestrated into an almost contrapuntal order, war and peace being not, as Lubbock thought, disorganized strands, but the basic alternation, each defining the other, of the plot's form and the characters' evolution. War is repeated, and peace. A new stage of peace varies the war epoch immediately preceding it, and vice versa. Each book has a prevailing mood, a phase of the common life to which every character responds in the very act of contributing to create it. The mood of one person is, with the variation of destined personality, the temporary mood of all, a mood to be resmelted from phase to phase till the final temper of the whole novel's vision has been enunciated.

There is a dominance of superficies in the peaceful Book One. Anna Pavlovna's ostentatious *soirée* sets the tone for the preliminary interests of all the characters. Pierre—first shy, then tactlessly professing Bonapartism, finally deferring abashedly as he parts from Anna Pavlovna—goes on to assert his mere surface in the very frankness of his subsequent talk with Prince Andrey, in the sociable inconsequence of his early morning tomfoolery. Prince Andrey on the surface of his mind can express no more probing reason for his military departure than that peacetime life is not to his taste. His unconscious reason is that so far life is as superficial as his first marriage seems to him here. Natasha is likewise enmeshed in surface. At her name day she impulsively wakens to the world of the opposite sex in Boris Drubetskoi, the very puppet-like incarnation of surface, though her keen insight leads her to ask him, symbolically, to kiss her doll before kissing her. Boris' mother makes an abrupt shift of allegiance from the superficial service rendered by Prince Vassily to the superficial hope that Pierre's naïveté can be prevailed on to assume the burdens of a merely external patronage. The death of Count Bezuhov entails not the soul searching of the novel's subsequent deaths but a mere squabble over an inheritance, a manipulation of surfaces about money. Marya's devoutness, as yet a mere form, presses on her departing brother an ikon to which he is indifferent. She has been corresponding with the stultified, pretentious Julie Karagina, not yet sufficiently awakened to cast off this mere husk of a friendship. Dolokhov's bravado is confined to mere surface acting in this book. Marya Dmitrievna's "terrible dragon" frankness is merely another social form, here analyzed in terms of its effect on polite society; its real effectiveness will come into its own only when it saves Natasha in the deeper Book Eight.

Yet Tolstoi is all the while individuating these people, analyzing attitudes of a specific bent and tempo which will recombine for deeper and deeper meaning. Even in the superficiality of Book One, sudden insight into destiny can pierce through the decorum of such shallow characters as the crudely, shamelessly driving Anna Mihalovna, and the bewildered

Countess Rostov, friends from girlhood who ''wept because they were friends, and because they were soft-hearted, and that they, who had been friends in youth, should have to think of anything so base as money, and that their youth was over. . . . But the tears of both were sweet to them.''

In these tears, and throughout Book One, there is a meaning portentously present. People are brought mysteriously into each other's orbits; as Prince Vassily carries on the conversation which will culminate in Anatole's unsuccessful overture for Marya, the stupid Julie Karagina writes portentously of Nikolai Rostov, a man unknown to her correspondent, who will at last, through the transformations of war, become Marya's fitting husband. The circumstances of the Duc d'Enghien's death discussed in the very first chapter's *soirée*—what do they foreshadow but La Belle Hélène's death in Book Twelve as the outcome of a parallel adulterous triangle? Pierre will then be liberated to marry the girl he will love from Book Eight on, though here, in Book One, he scarcely dreams, sitting across from her at a dinner party, that the thin thirteen year old is to become of such absorbing interest. Yet he must have some intimation of this future, or why at her look has he ''felt an impulse to laugh himself without knowing why''? Why does her look keep straying from Boris to him; why does she feel so amused in his presence and go up to ask him for a dance (at her mother's prompting, to be sure) ''laughing and blushing''?

The peaceful surface of Book One can give us only such hints as these. The foreboding grows and the breach between people widens in Book Two, where war displays its surface. In Book One we approached society from the outside in, at a *soirée*. Here we approach panoramically, from above, the campaign of 1805, which will turn out to have been war's mere surface in the later light of 1812. Parade, strategy, honor: surfaces and abstractions crowd the stage; the wretchedness of the ill-shod soldiers is only an uncomfortable logistic detail, and a death at the Enns bridge will occasion a joke more brutal but of the same kind that Bilibin regales his comrades with at staff headquarters. Here superficial discipline, finding in Dolokhov a lack of punctilio, demotes him to the ranks, when in the total upheaval of Book Fourteen he will be elevated to guerrilla command.

Peacetime superficiality is replaced in Book Two by the wartime superficiality of mere military reputation: Bagration, Zherkov, the jocular but impassive Nesvitski sweeping his field glasses across the walled nunnery, the nameless regimental commander whose ''quivering strut seemed to say that, apart from his military interest, he had plenty of warmth in his heart for the attractions of social life and the fair sex.'' Kutuzov turns away sadly from this show to avoid having his deep disillusionment, here incongruous, bewilder his subordinates. Nikolai, dreamily content or dreamily fearful, eats up surface, proud of his initiation into what his shallow mind takes for the reality of military life (the Telyanin incident), of battle (Schoen Grabern). We know no more here of Denisov but his function, that he is an honorable captain. And Andrey is here superficially disillusioned by war, just as he had been by marriage and social life in Book One. A slight wound sends him to the manipulators of this surface, the headquarters staff at Bruenn, where Bilibin's interpretations of diplomacy and strategy will invest these battles with all the meaning they can yet have. Significances are more portentous here; such is the nature of war. But no one can guess why. Tushin parts from Andrey at Schoen Grabern ''with tears, which for some unknown reason

started suddenly into his eyes.'' Seeing the unjust and uncomprehending disgrace of the hero Tushin ''Prince Andrey felt bitter and melancholy. It was all so strange, so unlike what he had been hoping for.'' Nikolai's sorrowful dreaminess confuses the meaninglessness of the many wounded with disjunct recollections of peace, bringing the book to a close.

The surface of war in Book Two looks back to Book One; its note of frustration is the first of a chord which looks ahead to the frustrated life of Book Three. Nikolai's family misses him all the more for his wound. Natasha refrains from writing Boris, to whom her brother is telling falsehoods about heroism. Pierre frustrates himself for seven years by yoking himself to the voluptuous, heartless Hélène.

Here mere surface, as a frustrating influence, asserts its fullest power. The sheer spell of Hélène's body shakes Pierre. Nikolai huzzahs the Czar and evaporates into dreams more confused than those of Book Two (''Natache . . . sabretache.''). Boris' God, surface, empowers him with an understanding of that unwritten code of confident tact which makes a lieutenant superior to a general. Andrey abandons all his illusions as he lies wounded under the sky at Austerlitz, his hero Napoleon dwindled to insignificance. He will await no longer his own Toulon; his depression more than his physical condition has classified him as a hopeless case. But Austerlitz, in all its dominance, is a mere surface beside the Moscow of Book Twelve; it is meaninglessness that Andrey feels under this sky. His frustration with surface is his own special descant to the mood of this book.

Book One: peace; Book Two: war; Book Three: war and peace. These three books state the thesis, antithesis, and synthesis which the rest of the novel works out. The frustration of war in Book Three breaks up after the truce of Austerlitz; in Book Four it invades peace with all the backwashing sterility of war ill concluded. There come from the battlefront a searing fusion of wastes, a series of false notes.

''All Moscow was repeating the words of Prince Dolgorukov: 'Chop down trees enough and you're bound to cut your finger'.'' Berg is falsely supposed a hero, Andrey falsely thought dead, till he returns in time to witness the puzzling waste of his wife's death. Hélène takes the abrupt, brutal Dolokhov as a lover, and Pierre challenges him to a duel that drains both men. Denisov proposes to Natasha, who has burned her arm as a proof of love to Sonya. And when Sonya rejects Dolokhov's absurd proposal, his desperate, wasteful revenge is to entice Nikolai into the waste of heavy losses at cards.

The waste of Book Four plays itself out into the mechanism and flatness of Book Five. After Pierre's duel, ''Everything within himself and around him struck him as confused, meaningless, and loathsome.'' ''It was as though the chief screw in his brain upon which his whole life rested were loose. The screw moved no forwarder, no backwarder, but still it turned, catching on nothing, always in the same groove, and there was no making it cease turning.'' The mechanical image of stagnation receives a mechanical answer, the rational religion of Masonry. This book introduces the novel's flattest character, the Mason Bazdeev, who converts Pierre. The crotchety, obsessively mechanical old Prince Bolkonsky moves to the fore as director of conscription. Colorless Boris Drubetskoi dominates Anna Pavlovna's salon to become the lover of a ''misunderstood'' Hélène. Nikolai candidly recognizes the place of his military profession and returns to find the hospitalized Denisov strangely stagnating at his calamity. Denisov presses a petition on him; he abandons it in order to join a crowd cheering the emperor, and he gets drunk in the last scene of the book. Prince Andrey likewise stagnates, unmoved by Pierre's convert enthusiasm. Still the sight of the sky over the flat ferry raft where they have been talking reminds him of Austerlitz and awakens intimations of "new life in his inner world," the mood of Book Six beginning to gather force.

Against Book Five's stagnated winter rises the burgeoning spring of Book Six. As the flatness of Book Five brought dull Prince Bolkonsky to the political fore, the vitality of Book Six marks the sudden rise of the charismatic Speranski. Andrey, with the rest of society, is to be renewed like the apparently dead oak— "seared with old scars," on his ride out, throwing out a profusion of green shoots on his ride back. Natasha does not burn her arm for love here, as in Book Four; instead she dresses in a yellow gown to set off her black eyes and stays awake ecstatic at the moon through the open window, where Andrey hears her. All draw to her vitality; even Boris gives up Hélène to court her. Happily immersed in his Masonry, Pierre takes a joyfully melancholy consolation in urging Andrey to press his own suit, and the engagement is brought about in the general matchmaking spirit which also unites Vera and Berg. Out at Bogutchorovo Princess Marya, weeping in an excess of love, "felt that she was a sinner, that she loved her father and her nephew more than God," losing herself in the joy of raising Nikolushka and entertaining "God's folk," the vital itinerant pilgrims.

Books Four and Five, waste and flatness, form a pair; so do Books Six and Seven: vitality and unearthly joy. In Book Seven Natasha is riding too high even for her earlier moon ecstasy. The incredible joy, the magically perfect success of a day's hunt, evokes from her a prolonged unearthly shriek:

> At the same moment Natasha, without drawing breath, screamed joyously, ecstatically, and so piercingly that it set everyone's ear tingling. By that shriek she expressed what the others expressed by all talking at once, and it was so strange that she must herself have been ashamed of so wild a cry and everyone else would have been amazed at any other time.

Hunting, dancing, food, moonlight—all of an unearthly perfection. The general elation has roused Nikolai home from the army where he has previously felt willing to vegetate.

This joy is too intense to be more than a phase. "It would be too happy," Natasha feels, if her engagement to Prince Andrey concluded in marriage. The unreality of this momentary joy is exemplified in the falseness of Nikolai's engagement to Sonya. It had been set off by a mere play, the moonlight masquerade ride with burnt cork moustaches and transvestite costumes. "Madagascar, Madagascar," Natasha surrealistically mulls to herself after a transvestite buffoon has told her that her children will be "fleas, and dragonflies, and grasshoppers."

The unearthly joy, at its moment, brings clairvoyant powers that forecast the final reality. In the crystal ball of her looking glasses Sonya sees the real future mirrored:

> "No, I saw. . . . At first there was nothing; then I saw him lying down."

> "Andrey lying down? Is he ill?" Natasha asked, fixing her eyes of terror on her friend.

> "No, on the contrary,—on the contrary, his face was cheerful, and he turned to me"; and at the moment she was saying this, it seemed to herself that she really had seen what she described.

> "Well, and then, Sonya? . . ."

> "Then I could make out more; something blue and red. . . ."

Not only Prince Andrey's ultimate deathbed vision is foretold here, but also Natasha's marriage to Pierre. For when the joy of Book Six sent her in curl papers and pyjamas to her mother's bedroom, Natasha said surrealistically of Pierre: "Bezuhov now—he's blue, dark blue and red, and he's quadrangular. . . . He's jolly, dark blue and red; how am I to explain to you? . . ." But her fear and her poise on the crest of the moment make Natasha here pass by the real significance of "blue and red," and she goes on to query Sonya about Prince Andrey's future calamity.

Unearthly joy, having forecast the future at its zenith of vision, gives way to the next stage. Peace is spent, and Book Eight is dominated by the crass pain of coming war, searing and wasteful in the manner of Book Four. Everyone is involved more deeply than he had been in Book Four, and consequently loss is more durable. Natasha quarrels with her future sister-in-law. Old Prince Bolkonsky flouts his devoted daughter and fanatically flirts with the heartless Mlle. Bourienne, who had drawn Anatole away from Marya in Book Three. Boris Drubetskoi contracts a loveless marriage with Julie Karagina. But the coldest horror comes when Natasha is nearly seduced by Anatole, at the perhaps jealous instigation of his sister Hélène. Natasha's attunement to the mood of this book brings her into spellbound fascination with this unholy pair. Prince Andrey breaks off their engagement, and the coming war will permanently widen the breach till the presence of death unites them. Pierre, leaving Natasha in consternation at the end of the book, sees the comet of 1812.

Book Five's flatness follows the searing waste of Book Four; so after the crass pain of Book Eight comes the abstract mechanism of war in Book Nine. German strategy, formidably competent and colossally stupid, dominates the war planning of this book. Even Pierre supplies soldiers and contrives a Masonic abstraction to explain Napoleon as the 666 of the Apocalypse. The profoundly intuitive Andrey can only turn from the abstractions of this phase to find life again meaningless, while Natasha, on the heels of illness, embraces religion, for her an almost mechanical ritual (her true religious life going on through the high rightness of her acts earlier in Book Six, later when she is a wife and mother).

In Book Six, vitality followed a phase of mechanism; so Book Nine's abstract mechanism leads to creative destruction, the keynote of Book Ten. Pierre weeps with forgiveness for the badly wounded Dolokhov at Borodino. Andrey, wounded, sees the creatively swarming white bodies of soldiers as cannon fodder; he contemplates the creativity inherent in children who run for green plums through the threatened orchard. The death of her father is a creative release for Princess Marya. Into threatened Bogucharovo rides the gallantly rescuing Nikolai, led by the emotions this role arouses to become Princess Marya's only possible husband. The destruction of Borodino brings Anatole to creative atonement, Andrey to creative forgiveness. And the physical destruction of defeat, at the end of the book, is declared to have been a creative moral victory for the Russians.

In Book Eleven the destructiveness of Book Ten descends to an empty horror, as not Smolensk but now Moscow itself is under siege. Toward the end of this book the counterbalancing creation in Book Ten is transmuted to a growing joy. Horror holds sway as Princess Hélène takes two lovers at once, as the innocent Vereschagin is torn to pieces by the crowd, as Moscow is captured and bursts into blaze. Pierre wanders dazed in the empty house of his dead master Bazdeev, Andrey lies wounded on a cart. But growth predominates: Andrey's cart is moved into the procession of the evacuating Rostovs; Natasha comes to him, and they forgive each other in a new, deepened devotion. At the end of the book Pierre saves a child from the fire.

In Books Ten and Eleven destruction and creation counterbalance each other. In Book Eleven they have already been separated as well as transmuted: the horror of the beginning had to wait till the end for a growing gladness. Book Twelve transmutes only the horror into a rigor under which Hélène dies from physical exhaustion of her simultaneous lovers. Andrey dies. Natasha is speechless, Pierre a prisoner, Nikolai perplexed, Marya misunderstood in the train of the Rostovs.

Book Thirteen, however, transforms the gladness of Book Eleven into a philosophical joy, as Napoleon's army moves out of Moscow and Pierre learns the meaning of Russian folk life from Platon Karataev's total reconciliation to process.

In Book Fourteen, recalling the mood of Books Four and Eight, a surreal cruelty emerges as the back thrust of war. Dolokhov in his weirdly correct garb leads guerrillas against the ragged retreating French. The saturnine Denisov, too, comes into his own as a guerrilla commander. And Petya, induced to enlist in the general surface dedication of Book Nine, is grotesquely seduced (Tolstoi develops the notion through a horrible kiss Dolokhov gives him) toward his death.

Book Fifteen establishes for good a calm reconciling joy. Marya marries Nikolai, Pierre, a Natasha so transformed he does not at first recognize her.

In the epilog, process evens off. A retransmuting is hinted in Nikolinka, hiding in the shadow as his elders reveal their fixity in the lax rambling of their manners and conversation. He combines the nobility of his real father with the strength of his adopted father and the sensitivity of his adopted mother. Existence can only remain substantially the same, appearance and reality one, for the middle life of our major characters.

I have deliberately exaggerated the unity of each book to bring out its dominant mood. There are in every book, in every episode, many strands which lead back or ahead. The more stultified characters—Anna Pavlovna, Prince Vassily, Berg, Boris—are out of tune entirely with the later developments of the novel and often act in contrast to the prevailing mood. Yet the over-all pattern of the plot is one of successive dominances orchestrated into unity.

Into this structured time, this process of phases, grow the individual rhythms of the various characters. Each phase subjects to itself the destinies of all. What separates Andrey from Natasha is as much 1812 as the baseness of Anatole; and the titanic force of national events, into which the individual destinies flow, parts Andrey from the Anatole he has desperately been seeking till the moment when, as destiny exacts, he will feel deeply enough to forgive him. Without the siege of Moscow he could never have plumbed the marvel of Natasha's love: but death follows reunion.

Through the phases, the individual destinies realize the tempo of their own development. Present is appearance, future is reality, till the time when there will be no real future. Neither society nor self get beyond appearances until their reality can

be embodied in time. Pierre's gradual maturation takes him through no fewer than nine stages: first, the flouted bastard, then the wealthy cuckold, then the stern, confused victor over Dolokhov, then the dedicated Mason; then the hopeless lover of Natasha, followed by the courageous dreamer at the siege of Moscow. Already he has worked up to such stamina that he can pull out of the dream and save his own life by looking Davoust square in the eye, but he has still to have a philosophical revelation of life from Platon Karataev, and thereafter a final calm happiness, distinct from that of his revelation. To Natasha, at last, he looks "exactly as though he had come . . . out of a moral bath."

The tempo of each character is peculiar to each. To Pierre's gradual, unaware changes, Andrey counterposes the abrupt, somewhat repetitive, self-torturing resurgences of his vast spiritual capacities. First one disillusionment with social life; then another under the sky of Austerlitz. Then the strange joy at the blossoming oak tree, the engagement. Then another bout of disgust, leading to the post-Borodino feeling where, at his death, all is subdued under the light of the Gospels, a light so faint, though intense, that Andrey cannot get the full word out.

Natasha is so sympathetic to phases that she develops only at the innermost heart of her spirit. In the superficies of the beginning she is frivolous, a would-be dancer. Hers is the psyche delicate enough to suffer each prevailing mood into symbolic expression: a burned arm in Book Four, moon-gazing in Book Six, a prolonged unearthly shriek in Book Seven, in Book Nine a rote religion. But her sacrifice to the spiritual demands of war is to submerge this real sensitivity into the appearance of a most ordinary woman—for her the halo of an even more extreme phase than any of the others, one so absolute that Pierre does not recognize her. "No one would have recognized her at the moment when he entered, because when he first glanced at her there was no trace of a smile in the eyes that in old days had always beamed with a suppressed smile of the joy of life. They were intent, kindly eyes, full of mournful inquiry, and nothing more." Yet "Pierre's embarrassment was not reflected in a corresponding embarrassment in Natasha, but only in a look of pleasure that faintly lighted up her whole face." The light has gone out of her eyes for the radiance of a wholly inner light.

Nikolai combines the Rostov dreaminess with the Rostov practicality. He drifts with the tide, and the depth of its currents more than his own blind will conveys him at last to his true destiny, gentleman farming. Marya is enough like him to be his true wife; her religious passivity merely undergoes—though willingly—the ennobling phases. She seems to derive consolation from misunderstanding, first with her father, then with her husband. And at the end, "she felt a submissive, tender love for this man, who could never understand all that she understood; and she seemed, for that very reason, to love him the more, with a shade of passionate tenderness."

The real life of the novel transcends what it must grow out of, the harrowing appearances of war. What marks the stupidity of a public character like Napoleon is his failure to understand these deeper currents. Kutuzov's signal heroism is the sad realization of his own submission to process, of his underlings' opportunistic blindness to it. The national destiny is expressed by Tolstoi not only through the plot but through the historical characters on the top; on the bottom by the anonymous masses, or by characters who, like Platon Karataev or Lavrushka, are too low for responsive will. Top meets bottom only once, in

Napoleon's brief conversation with Lavrushka; this is a mutual deception, though on the whole Lavrushka prevails.

The meaning of this novel, for all its vastness and variety, is so articulately single that it is hard to see how critics could see in it either thematic disjunction or vague grandeur. As Hugh Walpole says, "Its final effect is as concrete and symbolic as a sonnet by Keats; its theme is as simple and singlehearted as the theme of a story by Chekhov." (pp. 179-95)

> Albert Cook, "The Moral Vision: Tolstoi," in his *The Meaning of Fiction, Wayne State University Press,* 1960, pp. 179-201.

## GEORGE STEINER   (essay date 1959)

[*Steiner is a French-born American critic, poet, and fiction writer. He has described his approach to literary criticism as "a kind of continuous inquiry into and conjecture about the relations between literature and society, between poetic value and humane conduct." A central concern of his critical thought is whether or not literature can survive the barbarism of the modern world, particularly in view of the Holocaust. Steiner has written, "We now know that a man can read Goethe or Rilke in the evening, that he can play Bach or Schubert and go to his day's work at Auschwitz in the morning." Steiner's work encompasses a wide range of subjects including social and literary criticism, linguistics, philosophy, and chess. Though some commentators have found fault with his sometimes exuberant prose style, Steiner is generally regarded as a perceptive and extremely erudite critic. In the following excerpt, he analyzes form and meaning in three passages from* War and Peace, *examining the effect of Tolstoy's moral and philosophical didacticism on the artistry of the narrative.*]

I would like to consider three passages from *War and Peace.* The first is the famous portrayal of Prince Andrew in the moment in which he is struck down at Austerlitz:

> "What's this? Am I falling? My legs are giving way," thought he, and fell on his back. He opened his eyes, hoping to see how the struggle of the Frenchmen with the gunners ended, and whether the cannon had been captured or saved. But he saw nothing. Above him there was nothing but the sky—the lofty sky, not clear yet immeasurably lofty, with grey clouds gliding slowly across it. "How quiet, peaceful, and solemn, not at all as it was when I ran," thought Prince Andrew—"not as we ran, shouting and fighting, not at all as the gunner and the Frenchman with frightened and angry faces struggled for the mop: how differently do those clouds glide across that lofty infinite sky! How was it that I did not see that lofty sky before? And how happy am I to have found it at last! Yes! All is vanity, all falsehood, except that infinite sky. There is nothing, nothing but that. But even it does not exist, there is nothing but quiet and peace. Thank God! . . ."

The second passage (from the twenty-second chapter of Book VIII) is an account of Pierre's feelings as he drives home in his sledge after assuring Natasha that she is worthy of love and that life lies all before her:

> It was clear and frosty. Above the dirty ill-lit streets, above the black roofs, stretched the dark starry sky. Only looking up at the sky did Pierre cease to feel how sordid and humiliating were all mundane things compared to the heights to which his soul had just been raised. At the entrance to the Arbat Square an immense expanse of dark starry sky presented itself to his eyes. Almost in the centre of it, above the Perchistenka Boulevard, surrounded and sprinkled on

all sides by stars but distinguished from them all by its nearness to the earth, its white light, and its long uplifted tail, shone the enormous and brilliant comet of the year 1812—the comet which was said to portend all kinds of woes and the end of the world. In Pierre, however, that comet, with its long luminous tail aroused no feeling of fear. On the contrary he gazed joyfully, his eyes moist with tears, at this bright comet which, having travelled in its orbit with inconceivable velocity through immeasurable space, seemed suddenly—like an arrow piercing the earth—to remain fixed in a chosen spot, vigorously holding its tail erect, shining, and displaying its white light amid countless other scintillating stars. It seemed to Pierre that this comet fully responded to what was passing in his own softened and uplifted soul, now blossoming into a new life.

Finally, I want to cite a short passage from the relation of Pierre's captivity in Book XIII:

> The huge endless bivouac that had previously resounded with the crackling of camp-fires and the voices of many men had grown quiet, the red camp-fires were growing paler and dying down. High up in the lit sky hung the full moon. Forests and fields beyond the camp, unseen before, were now visible in the distance. And farther still, beyond those forests and fields the bright, oscillating, limitless distance lured one to itself. Pierre glanced up at the sky and the twinkling stars in its far-away depths. "And this is me, and all that is within me, and it is all I!" thought Pierre. "And they caught all that and put it into a shed boarded up with planks!" He smiled, and went and lay down to sleep beside his companions.

These three passages illustrate how "in the novel, as elsewhere in the literary arts, what is called technical or executive form has as its final purpose to bring into being—to bring into performance, for the writer and for the reader—an instance of the feeling of what life is about" [R. P. Blackmur]. In all three the technical form is a great curve of motion speeding outward from a conscious centre—the eye of the character through which the scene is ostensibly perceived—and returning decisively to earth. This motion is allegorical. It communicates plot-values and visual actualities in its own right; but it is at the same time a stylistic trope, a means of conveying a movement of the soul. Two gestures mirror one another: the upward vision of the eye and the downward gathering of the human consciousness. This duality aims at a conceit which is characteristically Tolstoyan: the three passages draw a closed figure, they return to their point of departure—but that point itself has been immensely widened. The eye has returned inward to find that the vast, exterior spaces have entered into the soul.

All three episodes articulate around a separation between earth and sky. The vastness of the sky extends above the fallen prince; "dark" and "starry," it fills Pierre's eyes as he tilts his head against his fur collar; the full moon hangs in it and draws his glance into faraway depths. The Tolstoyan world is curiously Ptolemaic. Celestial bodies surround the earth and reflect the emotions and destinies of men. The image is not unlike that of medieval cosmography, with its stellar portents and symbolic projections. The comet is like an arrow transpiercing the earth, and this image hints at the perennial symbolism of desire. The earth is emphatically at the centre. The moon hangs above it like a lamp and even the distant stars appear to be a reflection of the camp-fires. And central to the earth is man. The entire vision is anthropomorphic. The comet, "vigorously holding its tail erect," suggests a horse in a terrestrial landscape.

The thematic movement, after reaching the "immeasurably lofty" sky, the "immense expanse of the night," or the "oscillating" distances, is brought downward, to earth. It is as if a man had widely cast his net and were drawing it in. The vastness of the sky collapses into Prince Andrew's bruised consciousness, and his physical position is nearly that of burial, of enclosedness in the earth. The same is true of the third example: the "shed boarded up with planks" stands for more than the hut in which Pierre is being held captive—it evokes the image of a coffin. The implication is reinforced by Pierre's gesture: he lies down beside his companions. The effect of contraction in the second passage is richer and more oblique: we pass rapidly from the comet to Pierre's "softened and uplifted soul, now blossoming into a new life." Softened and uplifted like newly turned earth; blossoming like an earth-rooted plant. All the implicit contrasts, between celestial motion and earthbound growth, between the uncontrollable play of natural phenomena and the ordered, humanized cycles of agriculture, are relevant. In the macrocosm, the tail of the comet is uplifted; in the microcosm, the soul is uplifted. And then, through a crucial transformation of values, we are given to realize that that universe of the soul is the larger.

In each instance, a natural phenomenon moves the observing mind towards some form of insight or revelation. The sky and the grey clouds gliding over Austerlitz tell Prince Andrew that all is vanity; his numbed senses cry out in the voice of Ecclesiastes. The splendour of the night rescues Pierre from the trivialities and malevolence of mundane society. His soul is literally raised to the heights of his belief in Natasha's innocence. There is irony in the motif of the comet. It did portend "all kinds of woes" to Russia. And yet, though Pierre cannot know it, these woes will prove to be his salvation. He has just told Natasha that if they were both free he would offer her his love. When the comet shall have vanished into the depths of the sky and the smoke have settled over Moscow, Pierre is destined to realize his impulse. Thus the comet has the classical ambiguity of oracles and Pierre is both prophetic and mistaken in his interpretation of it. In the final passage the expanding spectacle of forests and fields and shimmering horizons evokes in him a sense of all-inclusiveness. Outward from his captive person radiate concentric circles of awareness. Momentarily, Pierre is hypnotized by the magic of sheer distance—like Keats in the *Ode to a Nightingale*, he feels his soul ebbing away towards dissolution. The net drags the fisherman after it. But then there flashes upon him the insight—"all that is within me," the joyous affirmation that outward reality is born of self-awareness.

This progress through outward motion and the threat of dissolution to solipsism is arch-romantic. Byron scoffed at it in *Don Juan*:

> What a sublime discovery 't was to make the
> Universe universal egotism,
> That's all ideal—*all ourselves*. . . .

In the art of Tolstoy, however, this "discovery" has social and ethical implications. The calmness of the cloud-blown sky, the cold clarity of the night, the unfolding grandeur of field and forest reveal the sordid irreality of mundane affairs. They show up the cruel stupidity of war and the cruel emptiness of the social conventions which have brought Natasha to grief. With dramatic freshness they proclaim two ancient pieces of morality: that no man can be altogether another man's captive,

and that forests shall murmur long after the armies of invading conquerors have gone to dust. The circumstances of weather and physical setting in Tolstoy act both as a reflection of human behaviour and as a commentary upon it—as do those scenes of pastoral repose with which Flemish painters surrounded their depictions of mortal violence or agony.

But in each of these three passages, so illustrative of Tolstoy's genius and of his principal beliefs, we experience a sense of limitation. Lamb wrote a famous gloss on the funeral dirge in Webster's *The White Devil*:

> I never saw anything like this Dirge, except the Ditty which reminds Ferdinand of his drowned Father in the Tempest. As that is of water, watery; so this is of the earth, earthy. Both have the intenseness of feeling, which seems to resolve itself into the elements which it contemplates.

*War and Peace* and *Anna Karenina* are "of the earth, earthy." This is their power and their limitation. Tolstoy's groundedness in material fact, the intransigence of his demand for clear perceptions and empirical assurance, constitute both the strength and the weakness of his mythology and of his aesthetics. In Tolstoyan morality there is something chill and flat; the claims of the ideal are presented with impatient finality. This, perhaps, is why Bernard Shaw took Tolstoy for his prophet. In both men there were a muscular vehemence and a contempt for bewilderment which suggest a defect of charity and of imagination. Orwell remarked on Tolstoy's leaning towards "spiritual bullying."

In the three examples cited, we come to a point at which the tone falters and the narrative loses something of its rhythm and precision. This occurs as we pass from the portrayal of action to the interior monologue. Every time, the monologue itself strikes one as inadequate. It takes on a forensic note, a neutral resonance, as if a second voice were intruding. The stunned uncertainty of Prince Andrew's consciousness, his attempt to rally the sudden *débâcle* of his thoughts, are beautifully rendered. Suddenly the narrative lapses into the abstract pronouncement of a moral and philosophical maxim: "Yes! All is vanity, all falsehood, except that infinite sky. There is nothing, nothing, but that." The change of focus is important: it tells much of Tolstoy's inability to convey genuine disorder, to commit his style to the portrayal of mental chaos. Tolstoy's genius was inexhaustibly literal. In the margin of his copy of *Hamlet*, he placed a question mark after the stage direction "Enter Ghost." His critique of *Lear* and his presentation of Prince Andrew's collapse into unconsciousness are of a piece. When he approached an episode or condition of mind not susceptible to lucid account, he inclined to evasion or abstraction.

The sight of the comet and the immediate impressions arising out of his meeting with Natasha provoke a complex response in Pierre's mentality and in his vision of things. The proposal of love, which he made out of an impulse at once generous and prophetic, is already exerting influence over Pierre's feelings. But little light is thrown on these changes by Tolstoy's flat assertion that the soul of his hero was "now blossoming into a new life." Consider how Dante or Proust would have conveyed the inner drama. Tolstoy was perfectly capable of suggesting mental processes before they reach the simplification of awareness: one need only refer to the famous instance of Anna Karenina's sudden revulsion at the sight of her husband's ears. But in all too many cases he conveyed a psychological truth through a rhetorical, external statement, or by putting in the minds of his characters a train of thought which impresses one as prematurely didactic. The moralizing generality of the image—the soul as a blossoming plant—fails to convey responsibly the delicacy and complication of the underlying action. The technique is impoverished by the thinness of the metaphysics.

Knowing Tolstoy's approach to the theory of knowledge and to the problem of sense perception, we can reconstruct the genesis of Pierre's declaration: "And all that is me, all that is within me, and it is all I!" But in the narrative context (and the latter alone is decisive), Pierre's assertion has an intrusive finality and a ring of platitude. So great a surge of emotion should, one supposes, culminate in a moment of greater complexity and in language more charged with the individuality of the speaker. This applies to the entire treatment of Pierre's relations with Platon Karataev:

> But to Pierre he always remained what he had seemed
> that first night: an unfathomable, rounded, eternal
> personification of the spirit of simplicity and truth.

The weak writing here is revelatory. The figure of Platon and his effect on Pierre are motifs of a "Dostoevskyan" character. They lie on the limits of Tolstoy's domain. Hence the series of abstract epithets and the notion of "personification." What is not altogether of this earth, what is to be found on either hand of normality—the subconscious or the mystical—seemed to Tolstoy unreal or subversive. When it forced itself upon his art, he tended to neutralize it through abstraction and generality.

These failings are not solely, or even primarily, matters of inadequate technique. They are consequential on Tolstoyan philosophy. This can be clearly seen when we examine one of the main objections put forward to Tolstoy's conception of the novel. It is often argued that the characters in Tolstoyan fiction are incarnations of their author's own ideas and immediate reflections of his own nature. They are his puppets; he knew and had mastered every inch of their being. Nothing is seen in the novels that is not seen through Tolstoy's eyes. There are novelists who believe that such narrative omnipotence violates cardinal principles of their craft. One would cite Henry James as the foremost example. In the Preface to *The Golden Bowl,* he recorded his predilection.

> for dealing with my subject-matter, for "seeing my
> story," through the opportunity and the sensibility
> of some more or less detached, some not strictly
> involved, though thoroughly interested and intelli-
> gent, witness or reporter, some person who contrib-
> utes to the case mainly a certain amount of criticism
> and interpretation of it.

The Jamesian "point of view" implies a particular conception of the novel. In this conception the supreme virtue is dramatization and the author's ability to remain "outside" his work. In contrast, the Tolstoyan narrator is omniscient and tells his story with unconcealed directness. Nor is this an accident of literary history. At the time when *War and Peace* and *Anna Karenina* were being written, the Russian novel had developed a high sophistication of style and had exemplified various modes of indirection. Tolstoy's relation to his characters arose out of his rivalry with God and out of his philosophy of the creative act. Like the Deity, he breathed his own life into the mouths of his personages.

The result is a matchless amplitude of presentation and a directness of tone which recall the archaic liberties of "primi-

tive" art. Percy Lubbock, himself an exponent of Jamesian obliquity, writes:

> With less hesitation apparently, than another man
> might feel in setting the scene of a street or parish,
> Tolstoy proceeds to make his world. Daylight seems
> to well out of his page and to surround his characters
> as fast as he sketches them; the darkness lifts from
> their lives, their conditions, their outlying affairs,
> and leaves them under an open sky. In the whole of
> fiction no scene is so continually washed by the com-
> mon air, free to us all, as the scene of Tolstoy.

But the cost was considerable, especially in terms of explored depths.

In each of the three passages we have been examining, Tolstoy passes from the exterior to the interior of the particular character; with each inward movement there occurs a loss of intensity and a certain naïveté of realization. There is something disturbing about the effortless manner in which Tolstoy addresses himself to the notion of the soul. He enters too lucidly into the consciousness of his creations and his own voice pierces through their lips. The fairy-tale conceit, "from that day on he was a new man," plays too broad and uncritical a role in Tolstoyan psychology. We are required to grant a good deal regarding the simplicity and openness of mental processes. On the whole, we do grant it because Tolstoy enclosed his characters with such massiveness of circumstance and elaborated their lives for us with such patient warmth that we believe all he says of them.

But there are effects and depths of insight to which these splendidly rounded creations do not lend themselves. Generally, they are effects of drama. The dramatic arises out of the margin of opaqueness between a writer and his personages, out of their potential for the unexpected. In the full dramatic character lurks the unforeseen possibility, the gift for disorder. Tolstoy was omniscient at a price; the ultimate tension of unreason and the spontaneity of chaos eluded his grasp. There is a snatch of dialogue between Pyotr Stepanovich Verkhovensky and Stavrogin in *The Possessed:*

> "I am a buffoon, but I don't want you, my better
> half, to be one! Do you understand me?"
>
> Stavrogin did understand, though perhaps no one else
> did. Shatov, for instance, was astonished when Stav-
> rogin told him that Pyotr Stepanovich had enthusi-
> asm.
>
> "Go to the devil now, and tomorrow perhaps I may
> wring something out of myself. Come tomorrow."
>
> "Yes? Yes?"
>
> "How can I tell! . . . Go to hell. Go to hell." And
> he walked out of the room.
>
> "Perhaps, after all, it may be for the best," Pyotr
> Stepanovich muttered to himself as he hid the re-
> volver.

The intensities achieved here lie outside Tolstoy's range. The tightness, the high pitch of drama, are brought on by the interplay of ambiguous meanings, of partial ignorance with partial insight. Dostoevsky conveys the impression of being a spectator at his own contrivings; he is baffled and shocked, as we are meant to be, by the unfolding of events. At all times he keeps his distance from "backstage." For Tolstoy this distance did not exist. He viewed his creations as some theologians believe that God views His: with total knowledge and impatient love.

In the moment in which Prince Andrew falls to the ground, Tolstoy enters into him; he is with Pierre in the sleigh and in the encampment. The words spoken by the characters spring only in part from the context of action. And this brings us once again to the main problem in Tolstoyan criticism—what Professor Poggioli has described as the reflection of Molière's moralizing and didactic Alceste in Tolstoy's own nature.

No aspect of Tolstoy's art has been more severely condemned than its didacticism. Whatever he wrote seems to have, in Keats's phrase, a "palpable design" upon us. The act of invention and the impulse towards instruction were inseparable, and the technical forms of the Tolstoyan novel clearly reproduce this duality. When Tolstoy's poetic faculties worked at highest pressure, they brought in their wake the abstract generality or the fragment of theory. His distrust of art came sharply to life where the narrative, through its energy or lyric warmth, threatened to become an end in itself. Hence the sudden breaks of mood, the failures of tone, the downgradings of emotion. Instead of being realized through the aesthetic forms, the metaphysics made their own rhetorical demands on the poem.

This occurs in the instances which we are considering. The downward shift is delicate, and the pressure of Tolstoy's imagination is so constant that we scarcely notice the fracture. But it is there—in Prince Andrew's meditations, in the flat assertion about Pierre's soul, and in Pierre's sudden conversion to a philosophic doctrine which, as we know, represented a specific strain in Tolstoyan metaphysics. In this regard the third passage is the most instructive. The outward movement of vision is arrested and drawn back abruptly to Pierre's consciousness. He exclaims to himself: "And all that is me, all that is within me, and it is all I!" As a piece of epistemology this statement is rather problematic. It expresses one of a number of possible suppositions about the relations between perception and the sensible world. But does it arise out of the imaginative context? I think not, and the proof is that the idea which Pierre expounds runs counter to the general tone of the scene and to its intended lyric effect. This effect is latent in the contrast between the calm eternity of physical nature—the moon in the lofty sky, forests and fields, the bright limitless expanse—and the trivial cruelties of man. But the contrast vanishes if we assume that nature is a mere emanation of individual perception. If "all that" is inside Pierre, if solipsism is the most legitimate interpretation of reality, then the French have succeeded in putting "all" into "a shed boarded up with planks." The explicit philosophic statement runs against the grain of the narrative. Tolstoy has sacrificed to the speculative bent of his mind the logic and particular colouring of the fictional episode.

I realize that Pierre's language may be read more loosely, that it may be interpreted as a moment of vague pantheism or Rousseauist communion with nature. But the change of pace is unmistakable, and even if we take the end of the passage in the most general sense, the voice would seem to be Tolstoy's rather than Pierre's.

When a mythology is realized in painting or sculpture or choreography, thought is translated from language into the relevant material. The actual medium is radically transformed. But when a mythology is embodied in literary expression, a part of the underlying medium remains constant. Both metaphysics and poetry are incarnate in language. This raises a crucial problem: there are linguistic habits and techniques historically appropriate to the discourse of metaphysics even as there are linguistic habits and techniques more naturally appropriate to the discourse of imagination or fancy. When a poem or a novel is expressive of a specific philosophy, the verbal modes of that philosophy tend to encroach on the purity of the poetic form. Thus we are inclined to say of certain passages in the *Divine Comedy* or *Paradise Lost* that in them the language of technical theology or cosmography overlies the language of poetry and poetic immediacy. It is this kind of interposition which De Quincey had in mind when he distinguished between the "literature of knowledge" and the "literature of power." Such encroachments occur whenever an explicit world view is argued and set forth in a poetic medium—when one agency of language is translated into another. They occur with particular acuity in the case of Tolstoy.

Didacticism and the bias towards hortatory argument appeared in Tolstoyan fiction from the time that he began writing. Little he wrote later on was more of a tract than **"The Morning of a Landed Proprietor"** or the early story **"Lucerne."** It was scarcely conceivable to Tolstoy that a serious man should publish a piece of fiction for no purpose but entertainment or in the service of no cause better than the free play of invention. That his own novels and tales should convey so much to readers who neither know nor care about his philosophy is an ironic wonder. The supreme and notorious instance of a divergence of attitudes between Tolstoy and his public arises over the parts of historiography and philosophic disquisition in *War and Peace*. In a well-known letter to Annenkov, the literary critic and editor of Pushkin, Turgeniev denounced these sections of the novel as "farcical." Flaubert exclaimed: *"Il philosophise"* ["he philosophizes"] and suggested that nothing could be more alien to the economy of fiction [see *TCLC*, Vol. 4]. And most of Tolstoy's Russian critics, from Botkin to Biryukov, have considered the philosophical chapters in *War and Peace* as an intrusion—valuable or worthless, as the case might be—on the proper fabric of the novel. And yet, as Isaiah Berlin says,

> there is surely a paradox here. Tolstoy's interest in history and the problem of historical truth was passionate, almost obsessive, both before and during the writing of *War and Peace*. No one who reads his journals and letters, or indeed *War and Peace* itself, can doubt that the author himself, at any rate, regarded this problem as the heart of the entire matter—the central issue around which the novel is built.

Unquestionably this is so. The ponderous and unadorned statements of a theory of history weary most readers or seem to them extrinsic; to Tolstoy (at least at the time that he was writing *War and Peace*) they were the pivot of the novel. . . . [Moreover], the problem of history is only one of the philosophic questions raised in the work. Of comparable significance are the search for the "good life"—dramatized in the sagas of Pierre and Nicholas Rostov—the gathering of material towards a philosophy of marriage, the program of agrarian reform, and Tolstoy's life-long meditation on the nature of the state.

Why is it, then, that the intrusion of metaphysic practices on literary rhythms and the consequent failures of realization—such as occur in the three passages under discussion—do not constitute a more drastic barrier to the success of the novel as a whole? The answer lies in its dimensions and in the relation of individual parts to the complete structure. *War and Peace* is so spaciously conceived, it generates so strong an impetus and forward motion, that momentary weaknesses are submerged in the general splendour; the reader can skim over ample sections—such as the essays on historiography and tactics—without feeling that he has lost the primary thread. Tolstoy would have regarded such selectivity as an affront to his purpose even more than to his craft. Much of his later rancour towards his own novels, the state of mind which induced him to describe *War and Peace* and *Anna Karenina* as representative instances of "bad art," reflects his recognition that they had been written in one key and were being read in another. They had partly been conceived in a cold agony of doubt and in haunted bewilderment at the stupidity and inhumanity of worldly affairs; but they were being taken as images of a golden past or as affirmations of the fineness of life. In this controversy, Tolstoy may well have been mistaken; he may have been blinder than his critics. As Stephen Crane wrote in February 1896:

> Tolstoy's aim is, I suppose—I believe—to make him-self good. It is an incomparably quixotic task for any man to undertake. He will not succeed; but he will succeed more than he can ever himself know, and so at his nearest point to success he will be propor-tionately blind. This is the pay of this kind of great-ness.
>
> (pp. 268-82)

*George Steiner, in an excerpt from his* Tolstoy or Dostoevsky: An Essay in the Old Criticism, *1959. Reprint by Alfred A. Knopf, 1971, pp. 268-85.*

### R. F. CHRISTIAN   (essay date 1962)

[*Christian is an English educator, translator, and critic special-izing in Russian literature. His* Tolstoy's "War and Peace" *is the only book-length study in English devoted to the novel. In the following excerpt from that work, Christian analyzes character-ization in* War and Peace.]

The subject [of characterization in *War and Peace*] is compli-cated by the sheer number and variety of the dramatis personae, but we can narrow it down from the very start by drawing a general distinction between the treatment of historical and non-historical characters in the novel. It is a fact that the generals and statesmen, the great historical names of the period of the Napoleonic wars, are almost without exception flat and static figures. Little or nothing is revealed of their private lives. We do not see them in intimate relationships with other people. Their loves, their hobbies, their personal dramas are a closed book to us. This is not accidental. As Prince Andrei reflects at Drissa in 1812:

> Not only does a good commander not need genius or any special qualities; on the contrary, he needs the absence of the highest and best human qualities— love, poetry, tenderness, and philosophic, inquiring doubt. He must be limited. . . . God forbid that he should be humane, love anyone, pity anyone, or think about what is right and what is not.

Their thoughts are rarely scrutinized either through interior monologue or by extended description from the author. Some characters, such as Arakcheev, for example, use only direct speech. Nothing is conveyed of their thought processes or the motives behind the words they utter. Nor do they develop with the action of the story. The statesmen and the generals in *War and Peace* are either bearers of a message or bureaucratic Aunt-Sallies for Tolstoy to knock down. This fact illustrates the unity which exists between Tolstoy's ideas and their expression through his characters. Static characters generally speaking deserve static treatment. Theme and style are as one.

An exception to the rule that generals are flat characters might be made in the case of Kutuzov. Although he is a general, he

is not, as Tolstoy understands him, arrogant or self-satisfied. The Kutuzov of *War and Peace* has some claim to be three-dimensional. It is not that he is shown by Tolstoy to have grown sufficiently in stature with the course of events to justify the remark—true though it may well have been in real life— that "In 1805 Kutuzov is still only a general of the Suvorov school; in 1812 he is the father of the Russian people." But his little acts of kindness, his friendly words to the soldiers who fought with him in his earlier campaigns, his unaffected behaviour in the company of his inferiors, his present of some sugar lumps to the little girl at Fili, his request to have some poems read to him—all these small things reveal positive and humane qualities which more than balance his lethargy and lechery. Again it is in keeping with Tolstoy's purpose that a general who is not a *poseur* or an egoist or a careerist should emerge as a more rounded personality than any of his profes-sional colleagues. (pp. 167-68)

[Our] remarks will be confined to the fictitious or, rather, non-historical characters. Here again the range is enormous, and in order to restrict it as much as possible we shall concentrate mainly on the men and women who figure most prominently in *War and Peace*. . . . Tolstoy's first step as a novelist was to draw thumbnail sketches of his future heroes and group their main characteristics together under such headings as wealth, social attributes, mental faculties, artistic sensibilities and at-titudes to love. In this respect, incidentally, his rough notes and plans are very different from those left by Dostoevsky, and illustrate an important difference of approach. Dostoevsky in the preliminary stages of his work is concerned with how to formulate his ideas (a generation earlier, Pushkin had tended to jot down first of all the details of his plots). But Tolstoy was interested primarily in the personalities of his characters— in the fact, for example, that Nikolai "is very good at saying the obvious"; that Natasha is "suddenly sad, suddenly terribly happy"; or that Berg has no poetical qualities "except the poetry of accuracy and order."

The problem of actually bringing his major characters on to the stage was one to which Tolstoy attached the greatest im-portance, and one which, as we have seen, gave him a great deal of difficulty. Broadly speaking, the problem was tackled in a fairly uniform manner, and the technique employed is clearly recognizable, though not of course invariable. All the main characters are introduced very early on. They are intro-duced with a minimum of biography and with a minimum of external detail (but such as there is is typical and important, and likely to recur). Attention is drawn to their features, the expression on their faces, the expression in their eyes and in their smile, their way of looking or not looking at a person. This is a fact which has attracted the notice of most critics of Tolstoy's novels, and inspired Merezhkovsky to make his much-quoted *mot* "with Tolstoy we hear because *we see*" (and its corollary "with Dostoevsky we see because *we hear*"). From the very beginning, the fundamental characteristics of the men and women as they then are are enunciated. There is little or no narration to elaborate these characteristics. Almost at once the men and women say something or make an impression on somebody, so that the need for any further direct description from the author disappears. Pierre, for example, is introduced with one sentence about his appearance (stout, heavily built, close cropped hair, spectacles); one sentence about his social status, and one sentence about his life to date. He is then portrayed through the impression he makes on other people present. He is summed up by four epithets which all refer to his *expression* (*vzglyad*)—clever, shy, observant, natural—and which at the same time distinguish him from the rest of the company and reveal the essence of his character as it then is. Similarly Prince Andrei is given a sentence or two of "author's description"—handsome, clear-cut, dry features, measured step, bored expression (*vzglyad*)—while the impression he makes on the company and his reaction to them is at once sharply contrasted with the mutual response of Prince Andrei and Pierre to one another. Virtually nothing is said about the earlier lives of these two men. What did Pierre do in Paris? Why did Prince Andrei marry Lisa? We are not told. Both men immediately catch the eye, for both are bored and ill at ease. They are introduced in fact into an environment which is essentially foreign to their real natures, although their way of life requires that they should move in this environment. Despite the fact that the manner of their first appearances attracts attention, there is nothing to suggest that they will be the main heroes of the novel, in the sense that no extra length or detail goes into their description.

By contrast, Natasha and Nikolai are both introduced in their own domestic environment—home-loving creatures on their home ground—integrated in the family and, as it were, part of the furniture. But again they are presented with a minimum of external description (in which facial expressions are conspicuous); again their salient characteristics—Natasha's charm and vivacity, Nikolai's frankness, enthusiasm and impetuosity—are conveyed from the very start; and again we are told nothing about their earlier lives (for example, Nikolai's student days). This lack of biographical information is important in the sense that it enables us to be introduced to the characters as we usually meet people in real life—that is to say, as they now are, and without any knowledge of the forces which shaped them before we met them and made them what they are. It could even be argued that a novelist who introduces his heroes by reconstructing their past when that past plays no direct part in the novel, actually risks sacrificing, by the accumulation of historical detail such as we do not have about people whom we are meeting for the first time, that immediate lifelikeness which, in the case of Tolstoy's greatest characters, is so strikingly impressive.

Once the men and women have made their entrances the author has to face another problem. Are they to remain substantially as they are, with the reader's interest diverted towards the details of the plot? Or are they to grow and change as the plot progresses? If they are to develop, must they do so because the passage of time and the inner logic of their own personalities dictate it? Or because of the pressure of the events which form the plot? Or because the author wishes to express an idea of his own through their medium? In *War and Peace* the main characters do grow and change, and they do so for all these reasons. In the course of the time span of the novel the adolescents grow to maturity and the mature men reach early middle age. War and marriage make their impact on men and women alike, and experience teaches them what they failed to understand before. The Pierre of the opening chapter of the novel, with his self-indulgence, his agnosticism and his admiration for Napoleon, is very different from the spiritually rejuvenated middle-aged man who has discovered a focus for his restless and dissipated energies, and who no longer has any illusions about the grandeur of power. The course of events brings Prince Andrei round from a cynical disillusionment in life, through a feeling of personal embitterment, to a belief in the reality of happiness and love; in the face of death his vanity and ambition are humbled by the realization of the insignificance of this world, and he acquires a hitherto unknown peace

of mind. Natasha acquires an unsuspected strength of character after her younger brother's death, and an unaccustomed staidness as the wife of Pierre—to some readers an astonishing violation of her nature, but to others a change which is fully comprehensible in the transition from adolescence to motherhood. Even Nikolai's impetuosity is curbed and experience gives him greater solidity and stability. These changes do not result from the fact that our knowledge of the main heroes gradually increases throughout the novel, as it inevitably does, and the picture of them grows fuller and fuller with each successive episode. They are changes of substance, qualitative rather than quantitative changes. Tolstoy's achievement in contriving the development of his main characters lies in the fact that all the reasons mentioned above for their development are so carefully interwoven that the reader is not conscious of many strands but only one. The characters change because they grow older and wiser. But the events which form the plot, and in particular the Napoleonic invasion, give them greater wisdom and experience, for characters and events are organically connected. And the state to which the main heroes come at the end of the novel—marriage, and the simple round of family life—the state which is the ultimate expression of Tolstoy's basic idea—is the natural outcome of the impact on them of the events they have experienced as they have grown older and their realization of the shallowness of society and the vainglory of war. The profoundly subjective basis of Tolstoy's art may be seen in the fact that Pierre and Natasha, Nikolai and Princess Marya all achieve the state which he himself had achieved, however imperfectly, and which he sincerely believed to be the most desirable of all states. But this does not mean that their characters are distorted in order to force them into the channels which for him were the right ones. Pierre has so much of Tolstoy in him that he needs no forcing. Natasha, we may remember, was from the very earliest draft of *War and Peace* "crying out for a husband," and needing "children, love, bed." Nikolai and Princess Marya, for all the difference between their personalities, interests and intellectual attainments, never seem likely to stray far from the family nest or to be seduced from the family estate by the allurements of *le monde* ["the world"].

Change and development are at the centre of Tolstoy's characterization, and the process is a consistent and logical one. But however great the changes in his main heroes may seem to be, it must not be forgotten that they occur within certain well-defined bounds, and that the characters themselves remain in the camp to which they have always belonged and continue to be what they have always been—some of the finest and most sympathetic representatives of the Russian landowning aristocracy.

There is no need to labour the point that Tolstoy's principal heroes change and develop. We can turn instead to the question how he achieved the effects he desired by the devices of characterization at his disposal. It seems to me that the essence of Tolstoy's technique is to show that at every stage in the life of his heroes the likelihood of change is always present, so that at no time are they static, apathetic or inert, but constantly liable to respond to some new external or internal stimulus. Very often the stimulus is provided by a person from the opposite camp—a "negative" character, a selfish, complacent or *static* man or woman. These people act as temptations to the heroes; they are obstacles in their path which have to be overcome. Pierre, for example, is momentarily blinded by the apparent greatness of Napoleon. He is trapped into marriage with Hélène, with whom he has nothing in common, and is in danger of being drawn into the Kuragin net. After their separation he is reconciled with her again, only to bemoan his fate once more as a retired gentleman-in-waiting, a member of the Moscow English Club and a universal favourite in Moscow society. Prince Andrei, like Pierre, is deceived by the symbol of Napoleon, and like Pierre he finds himself married to a woman who is as much his intellectual inferior as Hélène is morally beneath Pierre. Natasha for her part is attracted at first by the social climber Boris Drubetskoy and later infatuated by the same Anatole Kuragin who had actually begun to turn Princess Marya's head. Julie Karagina looms for a while on Nikolai's horizon. From all these temptations and involvements the heroes and heroines are saved, not by their own efforts but by the timely workings of Providence. Prince Andrei's wife dies. Pierre is provoked by Dolokhov into separating from his wife, and after their reconciliation he is eventually released by Hélène's death. Natasha is saved from herself by the solicitude of her friends. By chance Princess Marya catches Anatole unawares as he flirts with Mlle Bourienne. (Nikolai, to his credit, is never likely to obey his mother's wishes and marry Julie.) It seems as if fate is working to rescue them from the clutches of egocentricity. But it is not only external circumstances such as personal associations with people of the opposite camp which are a challenge to Tolstoy's heroes and heroines. There are internal obstacles against which they have to contend, without any help from Providence. Tolstoy made it a main object of his characterization to show his positive heroes at all important moments "becoming" and not just "being," beset with doubts, tormented by decisions, the victims of ambivalent thoughts and emotions, eternally restless. As a result, their mobility, fluidity and receptivity to change are constantly in evidence, as they face their inner problems. Princess Marya has to overcome her instinctive aversion to Natasha. Nikolai has to wage a struggle between love and duty until he finds in the end that they can both be reconciled in one and the same person. Pierre's inner disquiet and spiritual striving express his determination, now weak, now strong, to overcome in himself the very qualities of selfishness and laziness which he despises in other people. Outward and inward pressures are continually being exerted on Pierre, Prince Andrei, Princess Marya, Natasha and Nikolai, and their lives are lived in a state of flux.

And yet Tolstoy felt himself bound to try and resolve their conflicts and bring them to a state which, if not final and irreversible, is a new and higher stage in their life's development. It is not a solution to all their problems, a guarantee that they will not be troubled in future. The peace of mind which Prince Andrei attains before his death might not have lasted long if he had lived. Pierre's uneasy religious equilibrium may not be of long duration. The very fact that we can easily foresee new threats to their security, new stimuli and new responses, is a proof of the depth, integrity and lifelikeness of the two finest heroes of Tolstoy's novel. But although there is not and cannot be any absolute finality about the state to which Tolstoy's men and women are brought, there is nevertheless an ultimate harmony, charity, and sense of purpose in their lives which represent the highest ideals of which they are capable, given the personalities with which they have been endowed and the beliefs of the author who created them.

The novelist who wishes to create a vivid illusion of immediacy and mobility in his heroes must avoid exhaustive character studies and biographical reconstructions concentrated in a chapter or series of chapters in his novels, whether at the beginning, in the middle or at the end. Many novelists begin with lengthy narrative descriptions of their main heroes. . . . But Tolstoy by dispensing largely with "pre-history" and allowing his men and women to reveal themselves little by little as the novel progresses, avoids the necessity for set characterization pieces, static and self-contained as they often are in other writers.

Another factor which aids the illusion of reality—and movement—is the continued interaction of all the elements which make up Tolstoy's novel—men and women, nature, and the world of inanimate objects. Very seldom is a person seen or described in isolation—just as in real life, human beings cannot be divorced from the infinite number of animate and inanimate phenomena which make them what they are and determine what they do. Tolstoy is at pains, therefore, in striving after truthfulness to life in his characterization, to show the interdependence and interpenetration of man and nature. The stars, the sky, the trees, and the fields, the moonlight, the thrill of the chase, the familiar objects of the home all affect the mood and the actions of the characters no less than the rational processes of the mind or the persuasions of other human beings. That this is so in life is a commonplace; but there have been few authors with Tolstoy's power to show the multiplicity of interacting phenomena in the lives of fictitious men and women.

Movement is the essence of Pierre, Prince Andrei and Natasha and this is shown both externally and internally. Externally their eyes, their lips, their smile are mobile and infectious; their expressions continually alter. Internally their thoughts are in a state of turbulence and their mood is liable to swing violently from one extreme to another—from joy to grief, despair to elation, enthusiasm to boredom. There are times indeed when two incompatible emotions coexist uneasily and the character does not know whether he or she is sad or happy.

Princess Marya is not such a forceful or impulsive character as her brother or sister-in-law. Her qualities of gentleness, deep faith, long-suffering, humility and addiction to good works are not combined with a searching mind or a vivacious personality. But she is, nevertheless, a restless person, and as such is clearly a favourite of Tolstoy (she even quotes his beloved Sterne!). The anxieties and disturbances in her relations with Anatole Kuragin, Mlle Bourienne and Natasha are evidence that she is a rounded and dynamic figure, and not, as it were, conceived in one piece. In the presence of Nikolai she is brought to life with all the magic of Tolstoy's art. Nikolai too, for all his apparent complacency and limited horizons, does not stand still. He has his moments of doubt, uncertainty and fear just as he has his outbursts of uninhibited enthusiasm and emperor worship. He is given his own inner crisis to surmount when at Tilsit "a painful process was at work in his mind" as he tried to reconcile the horrors of the hospital he had recently visited, the amputated arms and legs and the stench of dead flesh, with his hero the Emperor Alexander's evident liking and respect for the self-satisfied Napoleon. The crisis, it is true, soon passes after a couple of bottles of wine. But it could never have been allowed to come to a head at all by his friend Boris Drubetskoy.

By contrast, the less prominent figures in *War and Peace* are not shown in the critical stages of their change and development. Even Sonya's conflict (she is described in an early portrait sketch in typically Tolstoy fashion as "generous and mean")—the conflict between her loyalty to the family and her love for Nikolai—emerges rather through Tolstoy's description of it than through the inner workings and sudden vacillations of her mind. Vera and Berg, Akhrosimova, Bolkonsky and many other minor figures, however vital and many-sided they might be as individuals, are fundamentally static characters who are fully-grown from the beginning. The ability to respond to change, the qualities of restlessness, curiosity, flexibility and dynamism are essentially the perquisites of the main heroes of the novel, and in particular Pierre, Prince Andrei and Natasha. And one may add that it is the growth and development of precisely these three people which reflects above all the changes in Tolstoy himself and those closest to him at Yasnaya Polyana, and is a convincing proof of the personal basis of Tolstoy's art.

In examining the characters of a novel with an historical setting, three questions immediately spring to mind. In the first place, do they emerge as individuals? Secondly, do they unmistakably belong to the historical environment in which they are made to move? And thirdly, do they embody universal characteristics which make them readily comprehensible to people of a different country and a different age? If we apply these questions to Pierre, Prince Andrei and Natasha, the answer to the first is indisputably yes. There is nothing bookish, contrived or externally manipulated about their actions. They can never be confused with any other characters. They have an outward presence and an inner life which mark them off as highly individualized personalities. To the second question the answer is less obvious and critical opinion is divided. For my own part I am inclined to think that there is nothing about them specifically representative of their own age, which is not also representative of Tolstoy's own generation. They are the products of a class and a way of life which had not materially altered when Tolstoy began to write. That they experienced the impact in their homes of a great patriotic war is a fact which distinguishes their lives from the lives of Tolstoy's own contemporaries, but the development of their characters cannot be explained solely in terms of that particular war. Pierre might ask different questions from Levin or put the same questions in a different way, but his spiritual journey is fundamentally the same. Prince Andrei's reactions to war could have been those of one of the many obscure defenders of Sevastopol. Natasha's progress to motherhood, while it is not identical with Kitty's, is not peculiar to the first half rather than to the second half of the nineteenth century. The third question, however, like the first, is easily answered. In Tolstoy's heroes in *War and Peace* there is a basic denominator of human experience which is common to all men and women regardless of class, country, age and intellectual attainment. Their mental, spiritual and emotional problems, their pleasures and pursuits, their enthusiasms and their aversions are as relevant to England today as they ever were to Tolstoy's Russia. And it is ultimately this fact which ensures that *War and Peace* and especially the main heroes of *War and Peace* will always be a part of the literary heritage of the reading public throughout the world.

Characterization cannot be considered in isolation from the many other sides of a novelist's art. . . . First there are the changes which occur in Tolstoy's characters themselves as the successive draft versions are written and discarded. Then there are the features which they inherit from their various historical and living prototypes. There are the ideas of the novelist himself which are transmitted to his heroes and heroines, so that they in turn express his own prejudices and beliefs and in Pierre's case, the gulf between what Tolstoy was and what he wanted himself to be. There is the question of the composition of the novel which is so designed that the character development should proceed *pari passu* ["at an equal pace"] with the development of the plot, and not fortuitously or independently of the main action. Finally there are the different linguistic devices at Tolstoy's disposal which play their part in charac-

terization—interior monologue, the contrasting use of the French and Russian languages, speech mannerisms, irony. (pp. 168-77)

In the final analysis it is the characters which a novelist creates which are the greatest and most memorable part of his achievement. In *War and Peace* they range over the scale of good and evil and they are treated by the author with varying degrees of sympathy and dislike. In later life Tolstoy wrote to the artist N. N. Gay that in order to compose a work of art: "It is necessary for a man to know clearly and without doubt what is good and evil, to see plainly the dividing line between them and consequently to paint not what is, but what should be. And he should paint what should be as though it already was, so that for him what should be might already be."

This opinion was expressed some twenty years after *War and Peace* was written, but the first part of it at least is applicable to that novel. Tolstoy knew, as well as any man can, the dividing line between good and evil, although in *War and Peace* he devoted much more time to painting things as they are than as they should be. For a novelist, however, to know what is right and what is wrong is not the same thing as to concentrate virtue in one character and vice in another, or to pass an unqualified moral judgement on any of the people he creates. "The Gospel words 'judge not'," Tolstoy wrote in 1857, "are profoundly true in art: relate, portray, but do not judge." Tolstoy's purpose in his first novel, as a creator of living characters, was to entertain and not to judge. One of the most interesting pronouncements he made about the function of an artist occurs in a letter which he wrote in 1865 while actively engaged on his novel, but which he never sent. . . . The letter was addressed to the minor novelist Boborykin and contains some mild strictures on the latter's two latest novels. Tolstoy wrote:

> Problems of the Zemstvo, literature and the emancipation of women obtrude with you in a polemical manner, but these problems are not only not interesting in the world of art; they have no place there at all. Problems of the emancipation of women and of literary parties inevitably appear to you important in your literary Petersburg milieu, but all these problems splash about in a little puddle of dirty water which only seems like an ocean to those whom fate has set down in the middle of the puddle. The aims of an artist are incommensurate (as the mathematicians say) with social aims. The aim of an artist is not to solve a problem irrefutably but to make people love life in all its countless inexhaustible manifestations. If I were to be told that I could write a novel whereby I might irrefutably establish what seemed to me the correct point of view on all social problems, I would not even devote two hours work to such a novel; but if I were to be told that what I should write would be read in about twenty years time by those who are now children, and that they would laugh and cry over it and love life, I would devote all my own life and all my energies to it.

To make people laugh and cry and love life is a sufficient justification for even the greatest of novels. (pp. 177-79)

*R. F. Christian, in his* Tolstoy's "War and Peace": A Study, *Clarendon Press, Oxford, 1962, 184 p.*

**JEROME THALE**   (essay date 1966)

[*Thale is an American critic who specializes in nineteenth- and twentieth-century English literature. In the following excerpt, he examines narrative structure in* War and Peace.]

*War and Peace* needs no tribute. Everyone has admired it, but few have tried to do more. Lionel Trilling, echoing Matthew Arnold, once said that criticism, faced with the overwhelming life in Tolstoy's fiction, could only lay down its arms. And for a long time it has seemed that criticism in English has done so. In the past few years, however, there have been two attempts to go beyond routine repetitions of praise: Albert Cook's ingenious but strained attempt to bring the novel together under a single formula [see excerpt dated 1958]; and John Hagan's essay, the best argument so far for the overall unity of *War and Peace* [see Additional Bibliography].

What benumbs and bedazzles the critical faculties in dealing with *War and Peace* is, of course, its overwhelming lifelikeness and prodigality. This isn't just a matter of the length or the number of characters. In the very first chapter, and indeed in any chapter, we are struck by the profusion of life. But we wonder exactly what Tolstoy is up to. The history of Russia goes on; the individual lives go on, and in interesting and plausible ways; but where is the novel going? (p. 398)

I would like to talk about three things: the sources of our sense of prodigality in *War and Peace;* the reasons for our confusion about its structure; and some of the kinds of structuring that do operate in it.

The effects of richness, of variousness, and of disorganization are well known and memorable. Consider a fairly typical scene, Chapter XX of Book I, which presents part of the name-day festivities at the Rostóvs. Here we see Tolstoy restless and impatient, moving from a song to a political conversation to a love affair. The first paragraph of the chapter gives a quick outline of the placing of the guests at the party. The second begins with Count Rostóv fending off sleep, moves to the young people, to Julie Karágina playing on the harp, to the other girls, and then shows Julie joining them to persuade Natásha and Nicholas to sing. In the next paragraph they decide on a song. At this point we would seem to have closed in on the scene to which the first paragraphs are preparatory. Suddenly Natásha says, "but where is Sónya?" and she runs off to look for her. What follows is a scene of two pages, largely dialogue, in which we see Sónya heartbroken because she fears that she may lose Nicholas. Natásha consoles her, and the scene ends with the two hopeful and laughing. We return for a paragraph in which the song promised earlier is dismissed in one sentence, and we get the words of another song which Nicholas sings. There is a quick transition to Pierre and then to Natásha, feeling very grown-up and dancing with the awkward Pierre. Finally there is another shift of focus, and for the remainder of the chapter Tolstoy closes in on the old Count surprising and delighting everyone with the energy with which he dances. And so the chapter ends on a climax of vitality.

But a climax of what or to what? There are in the chapter of six pages four distinct centres of attention. There is no particular connection among them by way of contrast, progression, or common motif. The Count is torpid at the beginning of the scene and lively at the end, but the material in between—Sónya's grief, the singing—seems unrelated, And if the chapter is designed to present the variousness of a party, then the proportions seem wrong in devoting so much of a chapter to Sónya's grief, and in any case the scene with Sónya is oddly sandwiched between the sections dealing with the singing. There is in the chapter a certain muted coherence around the contrast between age and youth (a contrast in which age comes off quite well). Still our first and strongest impression is of the richness of the chapter and of its disorganization, its lack of dramatic or thematic centre.

It is, of course, true that things actually happen in this disordered and unfocussed way. And the praise of the life in Tolstoy very often implies the familiar and dubious disjunction between life and art. But *War and Peace* is a novel, not life, and in fact it is not as vast and confusing as experience. We need to look a little deeper at how and where this sense of profusion arises.

I suggest that the sense of profusion in *War and Peace* comes not simply from the amount of material but from the absence of many of the obvious and familiar resources of art. In *War and Peace* we do not seem to have a great deal of connection-making, of putting things together so that they equal more than their arithmetical sum. Tolstoy fails to do—or deliberately chooses not to do—the things that the novelist usually does to organize his material and direct his reader: the focus on a single mood or scene, the purposeful shifts and contrasts of point of view, the juxtaposition of events. We do not see the novelist as connecter and pattern maker. (Indeed this seems to have been Tolstoy's intention: speaking of *Anna Karenina,* he says, "I am proud of the architecture—the arches have been constructed in such a way that it is impossible to see where the keystone is." Rather everything seems simply to happen—as the great commonplace of Tolstoy criticism has it, like life itself.

This sense of prodigality is very closely related to my second problem, our confusion about the structure of *War and Peace.* Ordinarily we think of a novel, or indeed of a scene, as an organization and arrangement of parts or elements into a whole, not necessarily a whole of logical meaning but a whole of some kind. This means that any given part of a novel has a double character; it is both a part of the total work and a thing in itself. Ivan Karamazov or Mr. Micawber—each is and is meant to be interesting in his own right, but at the same time each is part of and subject to the larger whole, the novel. Literary works, in Ransom's metaphor, are neither anarchies with no overall control nor dictatorships with everything rigidly controlled from the top; they are more like republics, combining control from above with a measure of local autonomy. Our attention towards the parts of a novel—characters, scenes—then, is both intransitive (as we see them as interesting objects of contemplation) and transitive (as we are aware of them as functioning parts of the whole).

Since the function in the whole determines the amount of space a character or scene should receive, we can usually recognize the most familiar of the novelist's difficulties, namely, the case in which he is carried away by a character, a scene, an effect, and gives it a disproportionate amount of space. In *War and Peace,* it would seem, Tolstoy has much more sense of his characters and scenes as objects in their own right than as parts of the whole, and with respect to proportion he sins repeatedly and triumphantly. When he presents the name-day party at which Pierre is being pushed into Hélène's arms, he finds the party, the host, the guests, immensely interesting, so that what ought to be background becomes a spectacle in itself; what ought to be subordinated to Pierre's history occupies more space than Pierre. Or consider the case of Prince Vasíli in the same scene: he is an agent in Pierre's fate, but Tolstoy and the reader find him interesting in his own right, and his character and his manipulations occupy more space than they call for within the scene. So also with the battles: they are background for the development of two of the major characters, Nicholas and Andrew, but they are presented with a fullness and fascination that seems to offer them not as subordinate parts but as spectacles in themselves.

This violation of the ordinary rules of proportion is certainly one of the chief features that give *War and Peace* its special character, at once rich and lifelike and structurally unclear. But if it were only that Tolstoy was a "putter-inner," we should have no great difficulty with the structure of *War and Peace*. The problem is much larger and deeper than a matter of proportion. There is much in the manner of treatment that determines whether an incident functions almost wholly as an object in itself or in a dual way as object in itself and as part of the total design.

Tolstoy's art is, to borrow a metaphor from grammar, an art of non-subordination, an art of incoherence. Just as in sentences a change in order or in a connective makes or alters the relationships among the parts without basically altering the elements themselves—so in novels there is, in addition to proportion, a set of devices by which relationships are indicated. To pursue the grammatical analogy, we might think of individual scenes or incidents in *War and Peace* as being like parts of sentences, with individual meanings and centres of interest, but without any of the common devices of arrangement or connection which indicate the mutual relations. We may be able to perceive the relationships (as we can often put a series of clauses together into a sentence), but in *War and Peace* Tolstoy has made it difficult. (pp. 398-402)

[The] lack of subordination, the absence of the devices for coherence, for making relationships clear, manifests itself on the level of the chapter or scene in three different ways.

First and most basic: the focus in *War and Peace* is shifting and unselective, and does not always coincide with thematic or dramatic importance. Tolstoy does not within a chapter or scene choose a single attitude, character, or idea from which to look at things consistently. He shifts repeatedly within a section, and even within a paragraph.

Second, there is in *War and Peace* an absence of those arrangements of material which make relationships clear: juxtaposition, parallelism, repetition, progression. Tolstoy is not apt to make those pointed shifts back and forth between characters with related problems or contrasted temperaments, nor does he regularly follow a development in one character with sufficient continuity to make us aware of a progression. (These relationships are very much a part of the novel, but frequently so much intervenes between related matters that the connections are not easily perceived.)

Third, Tolstoy does not give us explicit signals of relationships. Often when connections are not immediately apparent in the material a novelist will remind us—explicitly or through a character's thought or speech—of a connection. Time connections, pointing back to an earlier stage in a novel, are an obvious example. Most novels don't need too many such signals since the arrangement of the material makes many connections obvious. Tolstoy's multiple plots, his vast array of characters, his habit of shifting, make such signals most urgent; yet he provides them almost in inverse proportion to their necessity.

The result of all this is that in reading individual scenes in *War and Peace* we are not particularly aware of where we are going within the scene or of how an action or character relates to other parts of the novel. And what is true of the individual scene is all the more true of the novel as a whole.

These points need illustration. A simple case of the first problem, that of focus, can be seen in Pierre's engagement to Hélène, mentioned earlier. The proportions do not indicate that Pierre is the centre of the section. The marriage is central to Pierre's character and to the novel as a whole. But Tolstoy refuses to present it in this way: instead a great part of the section focusses on Prince Vasíli, sometimes on lesser characters, sometimes on Pierre. Similarly, in the sections on the old Count's death, the focus is on the struggle for his inheritance, on the spectacle of his followers—on everything and everybody except Pierre, who is not only the heir but the only major character in these scenes. It is, of course, true that Pierre is a very passive character at this point, but the passages dealing with other people are not designed to demonstrate Pierre's passivity. Again, with the battles, the focus seems to be curiously divided between the battles and the commanders on the one hand, and the major characters on the other.

The same scenes illustrate the second problem, that of structure: the action in Book I, Chapters XV-XVI and XXI-XXIV, seems to be organized in terms of the old Count's dying; one might expect it to be structured in terms of Pierre's expectations, his beginning not the Count's end. Similarly the battles are high points for Nicholas and Andrew, but there is little to indicate that this is the direction of the action, and the crucial events happen almost as facts among others of equal importance. In another instance, Book V, Chapter XII, Andrew has a kind of illumination in the last few paragraphs of a chapter that has given very little indication of leading up to his sudden awareness. Tolstoy, after following Pierre on a tour of his estates, has him visit Prince Andrew in the country: they discuss the meaning of life; the focus shifts to Andrew; and we learn suddenly that Pierre's visit has marked a new stage in Andrew's growth. The crisis is described in a few sentences. And than we return to Pierre and his impression of his visit to the Bolkónskis.

The lack of signals, the third problem, is not easily illustrated, since it is an absence rather than a presence. In the instances cited above, where there is some question of focus or of direction, Tolstoy, unlike the typical novelist, frequently gives us no statement that might point out a relationship or direct our attention. (One recalls by way of contrast the opening generalization of *Anna Karenina,* "Happy families are all alike; every unhappy family is unhappy in its own way.") (pp. 402-04)

The result of Tolstoy's method in *War and Peace* is that the coherence of a scene often goes unperceived. The dinner scene at the Rostóvs is a good example: it is a microcosm of Book I and of the entire novel. Book I, written before the design of *War and Peace* had been fully settled, is probably the richest and most varied in the novel; almost all the major characters appear, and a simple enumeration of the things that happen is staggering.

The dinner party, one of a number of scenes describing the name-day festivities, appears at first only a smaller version of all this profusion, the work of a man with a gifted eye and a desire to get it all in. Beyond the fascination with all the surfaces observed, there is apparent no purpose or direction, no governing focus of character or theme. The eye seems to skip from item to item, controlled only by its own delight with the spectacle. We feel that the effect of the scene is one of range and variety, an evoking of the possibilities of life. What else can we make of talk about war, flirtations, concern with wine, patriotism, the arrangement of a table, a young man's awkwardness, and so on? (pp. 405-06)

[There] is, although Tolstoy does not call attention to it, a fairly simple thematic principle governing it. The section is centred on youth and age, not on the contrast between the two—although there are contrasts—but on the varieties of youth and age. Thus at the beginning of the section the cynical old courtier Shinshín lets the solemn youth Berg talk on enthusiastically about his career in the army. If the initial effect is one of contrast between the experience of Shinshín and the inexperience of Berg, there is also a similarity: both are immensely self-absorbed.

Pierre enters and we find another kind of youthful awkwardness. He is uncertain what to do or say, he replies gracelessly to polite questions. If he is inexperienced, there is none of the calculating attitude of Berg: he has too much generosity and simplicity of heart. Immediately Pierre is posed against Márya Dmítrievna, the "dragon," who has long terrified society by her "frank plainness of speech." Her confidence is in contrast to Pierre's diffidence, yet she presents a mature version of much of his honesty.

After a brief section describing the disposition of the guests at the table, we focus on the middle section of the table where the younger people sit, and we see various forms of youthful spirits, Berg speaking of love to Véra, Pierre eating and drinking everything, Borís "exchanging glances with Natásha." Immediately, however, the scene shifts to the men's end of the table where the German colonel is delivering, in response to the cynicism of Shinshín, an overenthusiastic speech on patriotism. Youth joins age when Nicholas seconds the Colonel with his own burst of enthusiasm. But the last word on the subject is given to Márya Dmítrievna, who is calm and realistic: we may be saved in battle, we may die in bed. But this is a name-day, and the end of the chapter is given to the high spirits of the children persuading Natásha to ask about dessert.

Within the framework of gaiety at a party, the chapter presents neither a generalized contrast between age and youth, nor a contrast in terms of any specific item, but more nearly a parallel exploration of the possibilities of age and of youth: age encompasses experience in Shinshín, blustery manly conviction and patriotism in the Colonel; honesty in Márya Dmítrievna; and youth encompasses enthusiasm in Nicholas and Natásha, self-importance in Berg, awkwardness in Pierre, Nicholas, and Natásha, patriotism in Nicholas.

The panorama of age and youth is, of course, apt for the beginning of a novel which is going to be about people growing up; all that youth can be, all that age can become, is suggested here. Furthermore the scene has some connection with a gathering near the end of the book in which we see Nicholas, Natásha, Pierre sliding into middle age. But Tolstoy does nothing to announce or point up this thematic concern, and there is nothing in the scene which will make us recall it later as a point of departure. Rather it stays in our minds as a scene about a dinner party. (pp. 408-09)

The characteristics which we have seen in the smaller units of *War and Peace* also exist in the novel as a whole. I should like to indicate in a general way what some of these are.

In the early part of *War and Peace* we do not have any clear indication—by means of proportion and focus—of who the major characters are. Not until Chapters VI and VII does Tolstoy close in on Pierre and Andrew and thus indicate that they are major. And for a long time we do not realize that Natásha is any more important than Sónya or Borís, who become subsidiary. In fact a good deal of space is given in the early sections

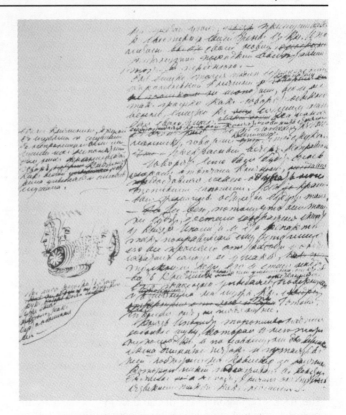

*A page from the manuscript of* War and Peace.

to minor characters: some of the early chapters deal at length with Borís's mother. We see her begging Prince Vasíli to get her son transferred; sympathizing with the Countess Rostóva and hinting that she needs money; scheming to be included in Count Bezúkhov's will. Yet she is dropped after Book I. And the name-day is seen in the early chapters to a great extent in terms of the Countess Rostóva. (p. 412)

Andrew is disillusioned and on a quest, and Pierre, Nicholas, and Natásha are unformed; but Tolstoy does not raise expectations and hint at directions (except in a vague way with Andrew); nor does he ever make explicit the common element in all their problems. (Indeed it is possible to read the novel without particularly adverting to the similarities and contrasts among the three men.) Rather the characters simply grow as in real life. The limitation of this method is that it is possible to read the novel without adequately perceiving the shape and meaning of those absorbing histories.

Those histories do have a shape and meaning, and their design is related to Tolstoy's most deeply felt attitudes towards life. But he is most interested in what is going on at the moment, and not very interested in giving us a sufficient sense of where things are going and how events are related. He seems to take no thought of the morrow; or rather he does, but he does not help the reader to do so.

In this respect Tolstoy seems unique. Those novelists who are like him in using multiple plots and many characters—Dickens, George Eliot, Sholokhov, Manzoni—take great pains in making clear to the reader the overall shape and multifarious relationships in their works. To find novels in which the reader must make all the connections himself, we must go to those twentieth-century novels in which dramatic presentation is carried to the point where almost all connection is unindicated.

*War and Peace,* however, looks so much like the explicitly articulated nineteenth-century novel that we inevitably look for the structural and signalling features of that kind of novel.

*War and Peace* is an "endless labyrinth of connections." It is ironic that Tolstoy has succeeded so well in effacing the traces of art—"the invisible keystone"—that with all our admiration for the book we have not known how to look for its design. (pp. 413-14)

> Jerome Thale, "'War and Peace': The Art of Incoherence," in Essays in Criticism, Vol. XVI, No. 4, October, 1966, pp. 398-415.

## JOHN BAYLEY    (essay date 1966)

[*An English poet and novelist, Bayley is best known for his critical studies of Tolstoy, Alexander Pushkin, and Thomas Hardy. In the following excerpt from his* Tolstoy and the Novel, *Bayley discusses the depiction of characters and historical events and the themes of life and death in* War and Peace.]

Pushkin's tale, *The Captain's Daughter,* which describes the great rebellion of Pugachev in 1773, during Catherine's reign, is the first imagined relation of an episode from Russian history, but it is no more a historical novel than is *War and Peace.* It strikes us at first as a rather baffling work, with nothing very memorable about it. Tolstoy himself commented, as if uneasily, on its bareness, and observes that writers cannot be so straightforward and simple any more. Certainly Pushkin's way of imagining the past is the very opposite of Tolstoy's. *War and Peace* has a remarkable appearance of simplicity, but this simplicity is the result of an emphasis so uniform and so multitudinous that we sometimes feel that there is nothing left for us to think or to say, and that we cannot notice anything that Tolstoy has not. The simplicity of Tolstoy is overpowering: that of Pushkin is neither enigmatic nor evasive, but rapid and light. He writes about the past as if he were writing a letter home about his recent experiences. The horrors of the rebellion cause him neither to heighten, nor deliberately to lower, his style. And he is just as prepared to "comment" as Tolstoy himself, though he does it through the narrator, who composes the book as a memoir. The Captain, Commandant of a fortress in the rebel country, is interrogating a Bashkir.

> The Bashkir crossed the threshold with difficulty (he was wearing fetters) and, taking off his tall cap, stood by the door. I glanced at him and shuddered. I shall never forget that man. He seemed to be over seventy. He had neither nose nor ears. His head was shaven; instead of a beard, a few grey hairs stuck out; he was small, thin and bent, but his narrow eyes still had a gleam in them.
>
> "Aha," said the Commandant, recognising by the terrible marks one of the rebels punished in 1741. "I see you are an old wolf and have been in our snares. Rebelling must be an old game to you, to judge by the look of your head. Come nearer; tell me, who sent you?"
>
> The old Bashkir was silent and gazed at the Commandant with an utterly senseless expression.
>
> "Why don't you speak?" Ivan Kuzmich went on. "Don't you understand Russian? Yulay, ask him in your language who sent him to our fortress."
>
> Yulay repeated Ivan Kuzmich's question in Tartar. But the Bashkir looked at him with the same expression and did not answer a word.

> "Very well," the Commandant said. "I will make you speak! Lads, take off his stupid striped gown and streak his back. Mind you do it thoroughly, Yulay!"
>
> Two soldiers began undressing the Bashkir. The unfortunate man's face expressed anxiety. He looked about him like some wild creature caught by children. But when the old man was made to put his hands round the soldier's neck and was lifted off the ground and Yulay brandished the whip, the Bashkir groaned in a weak, imploring voice, and, nodding his head, opened his mouth in which a short stump could be seen instead of a tongue.
>
> When I recall that this happened in my lifetime, and that now I have lived to see the gentle reign of the Emperor Alexander, I cannot but marvel at the rapid progress of enlightenment and the diffusion of humane principles. Young man! If ever my notes fall into your hands, remember that the best and most permanent changes are those due to the softening of manners and morals, and not to any violent upheavals.
>
> It was a shock to all of us.

The tone of the commentary, and the lack of exaggerated horror, are exactly right. In his late story, *Hadji Murad,* Tolstoy has the same unobtrusive brilliance of description, but—too intent on the art that conceals art—he is careful to avoid the commentary, and so he does not achieve the historical naturalness and anonymity of this narrative. He is too careful in a literary way—almost a Western way—to avoid being shocked. (pp. 66-8)

[The] passage gives us an insight, too, into the reason why all the great nineteenth-century Russians are so good on their history. They feel continuingly in touch with it—horrors and all—in a direct and homely way. They neither romanticise it nor cut themselves off from it, but are soberly thankful (as Shakespeare and the Elizabethans were thankful) if they are spared a repetition in their own time of the same sort of events. Scott subtitled his account of the '45 "'Tis Sixty Years Since," and Pushkin was almost exactly the same distance in time from Pugachev, but their attitudes to the rebellion they describe could hardly be more different. Pushkin borrows greatly from Scott. . . . But he does not borrow Scott's presentation of rebellion as Romance, safely situated in the past and hence to be seen—in contrast to the prosaic present—as something delightful and picturesque. Nor does he see the past as something over and done with, and thus the novelist's preserve. Unemphatically placed as it is, the comment of the narrator in the penultimate chapter—"God save us from seeing a Russian revolt, senseless and merciless!"—strikes like a hammerblow. It is a comment out of Shakespeare's histories, not Scott's novels.

Tolstoy also borrows from Scott, in particular from the device of coincidence as used in historical romance ("Great God! Can it really be Sir Hubert, my own father?") without which the enormous wheels of *War and Peace* could hardly continue to revolve. Tolstoy avails himself of coincidence without drawing attention to it. It is a convenience, and not, as it has become in that distinguished descendant of Tolstoy's novel—*Dr Zhivago*—a quasi-symbolic method. Princess Mary's rescue by Nicholas Rostov, and Pierre's by Dolokhov, are obvious instances, and Tolstoy's easy and natural use of the device makes a satisfying contrast to the expanse of the book, the *versts* that stretch away from us in every direction. It also shows us that the obverse of this boundless geographical space is the narrow dimension of a self-contained class; the rulers of *War and Peace,* its *deux cents familles* ["two hundred families"], are in fact all known to one another (we are told halfway through that Pierre "knew everyone in Moscow and St Petersburg") and meet all over Russia as if at a *soirée* or a club. Kutuzov and Andrew's father are old comrades in arms; Kutuzov is an admirer of Pierre's wife; and hence Andrew gets the *entrée* to Austerlitz and Pierre to Borodino—and we with them.

Yet Tolstoy's domestication by coincidence gives us an indication why we have from *The Captain's Daughter* a more authentic feel of history than from *War and Peace.* Pushkin respects history, and is content to study it and to exercise his intelligence upon it: to Tolstoy it represents a kind of personal challenge—it must be attacked, absorbed, taken over. And in **"Some Words about *War and Peace*"** [see excerpt dated 1868] Tolstoy reveals the two ways in which this takeover of history is to be achieved. First, human characteristics are invariable, and "in those days also people loved, envied, sought truth and virtue, and were carried away by passion"—i.e. all the things I feel were felt by people in the past, and consequently they are all really *me*. Second, "There was the same complex mental and moral life among the upper classes, who were in some instances even more refined than now"—i.e. my own class (which chiefly interests me) and which was even more important then, enjoyed collectively the conviction that I myself do now: that everything stems from and depends upon our own existence. To paraphrase in this way is, of course, unfair, but I am not really misrepresenting Tolstoy. All his historical theories, with their extraordinary interest, authority and illumination, do depend upon these two swift annexatory steps, after which his historical period is at his feet, as Europe was at Napoleon's.

Let us return for a moment to the extract from *The Captain's Daughter* quoted above. The day after the events described, the fortress is taken by Pugachev, and the old Bashkir sits astride the gallows and handles the rope while the Commandant and his lieutenant are hanged. Nothing is said about the Bashkir's sentiments, or whether this was his revenge on the Russian colonial methods the Commandant stood for, and whether it pleased him. The hero, Ensign Grinyov, is himself about to be hanged, but is saved by the intervention of his old servant; he sees the Commandant's wife killed, and finally "having eaten my supper with great relish, went to sleep on a bare floor, exhausted both in mind and body." Next day he observes in passing some rebels pulling off and appropriating the boots of the hanged men.

I have unavoidably given these details more emphasis than they have in the text: the point is that this conveys exactly what the hero's reaction to such events would have been at that time. It is not necessarily Pushkin's reaction, but he has imagined— so lightly and completely that it hardly looks like imagination at all: it is more like Defoe and Richardson than Scott—the reactions of a young man of Grinyov's upbringing, right down to the fervent plea that manners and methods may continue to soften and improve. Now let us take a comparable episode in *War and Peace,* the shooting of the alleged incendiarists by the French in Moscow. Pierre, like Grinyov, is waiting—as he thinks—for execution; and his eye registers with nightmare vividness the appearance and behaviour of the people round him. He ceases to be any sort of character at all, but is merely a vehicle for the overpowering precision of Tolstoyan detail, and Tolstoy concedes this by saying "he lost the power of

thinking and understanding. He could only hear and see." But here Tolstoy is not being quite truthful. Pierre is also to feel an immense and generalised incredulity and horror, which his creator compels the other participants to share. "On the faces of all the Russians, and of the French soldiers and officers without exception, he read the same dismay, horror, and conflict that were in his own heart." Even the fact that he has himself been saved means nothing to him.

> The fifth prisoner, the one next to Pierre, was led away—alone. Pierre did not understand that he was saved, that he and the rest had been brought there only to witness the execution. With ever-growing horror, and no sense of joy or relief, he gazed at what was taking place. The fifth man was the factory lad in the loose cloak. The moment they laid hands on him, he sprang aside in terror and clutched at Pierre. (Pierre shuddered and shook himself free.) The lad was unable to walk. They dragged him along holding him up under the arms, and he screamed. When they got him to the post he grew quiet, as if he had suddenly understood something. Whether he understood that screaming was useless, or whether he thought it incredible that men should kill him, at any rate he took his stand at the post, waiting to be blindfolded like the others, and like a wounded animal looked around him with glittering eyes.

> Pierre was no longer able to turn away and close his eyes. His curiosity and agitation, like that of the whole crowd, reached the highest pitch at this fifth murder. Like the others this fifth man seemed calm; he wrapped his loose cloak closer and rubbed one bare foot with the other.

> When they began to blindfold him he himself adjusted the knot which hurt the back of his head; then when they propped him against the bloodstained post, he leaned back and, not being comfortable in that position, straightened himself, adjusted his feet, and leaned back again more comfortably. Pierre did not take his eyes from him and did not miss his slightest movement.

> Probably a word of command was given and was followed by the reports of eight muskets; but try as he would Pierre could not afterwards remember having heard the slightest sound of the shots. He only saw how the workman suddenly sank down on the cords that held him, how blood showed itself in two places, how the ropes slackened under the weight of the hanging body, and how the workman sat down, his head hanging unnaturally and one leg bent under him. Pierre ran up to the post. No one hindered him. Pale frightened people were doing something around the workman. The lower jaw of an old Frenchman with a thick moustache trembled as he untied the ropes. The body collapsed. The soldiers dragged it awkwardly from the post and began pushing it into the pit.

> They all plainly and certainly knew that they were criminals who must hide the traces of their guilt as quickly as possible.

The concluding comment is not that of a man of the age, but that of Tolstoy himself (it shows, incidentally, how impossible it is to separate Tolstoy the moralist from Tolstoy the novelist at any stage of life) and though the description is one of almost mesmeric horror, yet it is surely somehow not completely moving, or satisfactory. This has nothing to do with the moral comment however. I think the explanation is that it is not seen by a real character, or rather by a character who retains his reality at this moment. It is at such moments that we are aware of Pierre's lack of a body, and of a past—the two things are connected—and we are also aware of Tolstoy's need for such a person, with these assets, at these moments. If any member of the Rostov or Bolkonsky families had been the spectator, the scene would have been very different. It would have been anchored firmly to the whole selfhood of such a spectator, as are the deeds of the guerrillas which Petya hears about in their camp. (pp. 68-72)

The point is that a character like this makes us aware of the necessary multiplicity of human response, of the fact that even at such a scene some of the soldiers and spectators must in the nature of things have been bored, phlegmatic, or actively and enjoyingly curious. But Tolstoy wants to achieve a dramatic and metaphoric *unity* of response, as if we were all absorbed in a tragic spectacle; to reduce the multiplicity of reaction to one sensation—the sensation that he had himself felt on witnessing a public execution in Paris. For this purpose Pierre is his chosen instrument. He never *becomes* Tolstoy, but at these moments his carefully constructed physical self—his corpulence, spectacles, good-natured hang-dog look, etc.—become as it were the physical equivalent of Tolstoy's powerful abstract singlemindedness—they are there not to give Pierre a true self, but to persuade us that the truths we are being told are as solid as the flesh, and are identified with it. We find the same sort of physical counterpart of an insistent Tolstoyan point in Karataev's *roundness*. It is one of the strange artificialities of this seemingly so natural book that Tolstoy can juggle with the flesh as with truth and reason, forcing it to conform to the same kind of willed simplicity.

For Pierre's size and corpulence, Karataev's roundness, are not true characteristics of the flesh, the flesh that dominates the life of Tolstoy's novels. The process makes us realise how little a sense of the flesh has to do with description of physical appearance. It is more a question of intuitive and involuntary sympathy. Theoretically, we know much more about the appearance of Pierre and Karataev than about, say, that of Nicholas Rostov and Anatole Kuragin. But it is the latter whom we know in the flesh. And bad characters, like Napoleon and Anatole, retain the sympathy of the flesh. Napoleon, snorting and grunting with pleasure as he is massaged with a brush by his valet; unable to taste the punch on the evening before Borodino because of his cold; above all, at Austerlitz, when "his face wore that special look of confident, self-complacent happiness that one sees on the face of a boy happily in love"— the tone is overtly objective, satirical, even disgusted, but in fact Tolstoy cannot withhold his intuitive sympathy with, and understanding of, the body. Physically we feel as convinced by, and as *comfortable* with, these two, as we feel physically uncommitted with Pierre and Karataev.

> Anatole was not quick-witted, nor ready or eloquent in conversation, but he had the faculty, so invaluable in society, of composure and imperturbable self possession. If a man lacking in self-confidence remains dumb on a first introduction and betrays a consciousness of the impropriety of such silence and an anxiety to find something to say, the effect is bad. But Anatole was dumb, swung his foot, and smilingly examined the Princess's hair. It was evident that he could be silent in this way for a very long time. "If anyone finds this silence inconvenient, let him talk, but I don't want to," he seemed to say.

Inside Anatole, as it were, we "sit with arms akimbo before a table on the corner of which he smilingly and absentmindedly

fixed his large and handsome eye"; we feel his sensations at the sight of the pretty Mlle Bourrienne; and when his "large white plump leg" is cut off in the operating tent after Borodino, we seem to feel the pang in our own bodies.

But with Prince Andrew, who is lying wounded in the same tent, we have no bodily communication.

> After the sufferings he had been enduring Prince Andrew enjoyed a blissful feeling such as he had not experienced for a long time. All the best and happiest moments of his life—especially his earliest childhood, when he used to be undressed and put to bed, and when leaning over him his nurse sang him to sleep and he, burying his head in the pillow, felt happy in the mere consciousness of life—returned to his memory, not merely as something past but as something present.

We assent completely, but it is from our own experience, not from our knowledge of Prince Andrew. Like Pierre, he does not have a true body: there is this difference between both of them and the other characters, and it is not a difference we can simply put down to their being aspects of Tolstoy himself. The difference is not total, . . . but it is significant, for no other novel can show such different and apparently incompatible kinds of character living together. It is as if Becky Sharp and David Copperfield, Waverley and Tom Jones and Tristram Shandy, together with Onegin and Julien Sorel, Rousseau's Emile and Voltaire's Candide and Goethe's Wilhelm Meister and many more, were all meeting in the same book, taking part in the same plot, communicating freely with one another. For in addition to drawing on his own unparalleled resources of family and class experience, Tolstoy has borrowed every type of character from every kind of novel: not only does he know a lot of people at first-hand—he has absorbed all the artificial ways of describing them.

Moreover, his genius insensibly persuades us that we do actually in life apprehend people in all these different ways, the ways imagined by each kind of novel, so that we feel that Pierre and Andrew are bound to be seekers and questioners because the one has no past and the other no roots in life, forgetting that Tolstoy has deprived them of these things precisely in order that they should conform to the fictional, *Bildungsroman*, type of the seeker. Andrew is a son from a *Bildungsroman* with a father from a historical novel, from Scott or *The Captain's Daughter*. Old Bolkonsky (who was closely modelled on Tolstoy's own grandfather, together with recollections he had heard about Field-Marshal Kamensky) is entirely accessible to us, as much in what we imagine of his old military days, "in the hot nights of the Crimea," as in what we see of his patriarchal life at Bald Hills. But his son, as does happen in life, is distant. We receive vivid perceptions through him (see the chidhood passage) but they remain generalized Tolstoy: they are not connected specifically with him. What was he like as a child at Bald Hills? When did he meet the Little Princess, and how did his courtship of her proceed?

We share this uncertainty about Andrew with Natasha, and— more significantly—with her mother. Embedded in life, the Rostovs cannot really believe that the marriage will take place, any more than they can believe they will die. When Natasha sings, her mother remembers her own youth and reflects that "there was something unnatural and dreadful in this impending marriage of Natasha and Prince Andrew." It is like a marriage of life with death.

Like Death, Andrew remains a stranger to the Rostovs. They cannot see him as a complete being any more than we can—any more than his own son can on the last page of the novel. He has become a symbolic figure, by insensible stages and without any apparent intention on Tolstoy's part. Natasha fights for his life, as life struggles against death, and when he dies old Count Rostov—that champion of the flesh—has to realise death too, and is never the same again. Not only death is symbolised in him, but dissatisfaction, aspiration, change, all the cravings of the spirit, all the changes that undermine the solid kingdom of the flesh, the ball, the supper, the bedroom. Tolstoy's distrust of the spirit, and of the changes it makes, appears in how he handles Andrew, and how he confines him with the greatest skill and naturalness to a particular *enclave*.

This naturalness conceals Tolstoy's laborious and uncertain construction of Andrew, which is intimately connected with the construction of the whole plot. First he was to have died at Austerlitz. Tolstoy decided to keep him alive, but that it was a risk to do so is shown by the uncertainty and hesitations of the ensuing drafts. His attitude of controlled exasperation towards the Little Princess was originally one of settled rudeness, culminating in a burst of fury when she receives a *billet* from Anatole. His rudeness is that of Lermontov's Pechorin and Pushkin's Onegin; it must have been difficult to head him off from being a figure of that kind. When he first sees Natasha he is bewitched because she is in fancy dress as a boy (an incident later transferred to Nicholas and Sonya) but in another version he takes no notice of her at all. Tolstoy's bother is to avoid nailing down Andrew with the kinds of *aperçu* he is so good at: he must not be open to the usual Tolstoyan "discoveries." (It would be out of the question, for instance, for Pierre to perceive that Andrew doesn't *really* care about the beauties of nature, as the "I" of *Boyhood and Youth* suddenly realises about his great friend and hero Nekhludyov who is something of a Prince Andrew figure.) Such stages of illumination would be all wrong, as would be any particular aspect of Natasha (fancy dress, etc.) which would reveal something further about him by their attraction for him. Her attraction must be symbolic of life itself.

At last Tolstoy—remembering an experience of his own—hit on the way to convey this. Andrew hears Natasha and Sonya talking together at night as they lean out of the window below his, and in this way her reality—her sense of her family and her happy sense of herself that make up this reality—comes before him in the right abstract and ideal way, in a way that could not have been conveyed by Natasha herself in a direct confrontation with him. Natasha's own reactions presented an equal difficulty. In one version she is made to tell Sonya that Prince Andrew was such a charming creature that she has never seen and could never imagine anyone comparable! This clearly will not do, and neither will another version in which she says she doesn't like him, that "there is something proud, something dry about him." In the final version the magical ball takes over, and removes the need for any coherent comment from her. Indeed, Tolstoy ingeniously increases her reality by this method, implying her readiness for life that can take even the shadowy Prince Andrew in its stride; that is then dashed by the prospect of a year's delay; and finally pours itself helplessly into an infatuation with a "real man" (real both for us and for her)—Anatole Kuragin.

Natasha's mode of love presents a marked contrast with that of Pushkin's Tatiana, so often compared with her as the same type of vital Russian heroine. Natasha's love is generalised, founded on her own sense of herself and—less consciously—on her almost explosive expectancy, her need not to be *wasted*. Onegin, whom Tatiana loves, is like Andrew an unintimate figure, but for quite different reasons. He gets what reality he has from the delighted scrutiny of Pushkin, and the devoted scrutiny of Tatiana. His own consciousness is nothing. As Nabokov observes, "Onegin grows fluid and flaccid as soon as he starts to feel, as soon as he departs from the existence he had acquired from his maker in terms of colourful parody." Significantly, Natasha's love is solipsistic, in herself, typical of Tolstoyan *samodovolnost* ["self-satisfaction"], it does not need to know its object, and its object is correspondingly unknowable in terms of objective scrutiny. But when Tatiana sees the marks that Onegin's fingernail has scratched in the margins of his books and realises that he is nothing but a parody, a creature of intellectual and social fashion—it does not destroy her love for him, it actually increases it! Finding the loved person's underlinings in a book is almost as intimate as watching them asleep. The two heroines are alike in the vigour of their affections, but it is a very different kind of affection for all that. In Onegin, Pushkin presents an *object* for us to enjoy, and for his heroine to love. In Andrew, Tolstoy creates the symbolic figure of a spectator of life, in the presence of whom Natasha can show what life there is in herself.

Andrew is created for death. He looks towards death as something true and real at last; and after all the false starts, alterations and reprieves, he achieves his right end. Of course this is something of a Tolstoyan *post hoc ergo propter hoc* ["faulty reasoning"], but it is a fact that all the characters in **War and Peace**—from the greatest to the least—get exactly what their natures require. The book is a massive feat of arbitration, arrived at after countless checks and deliberations: though its huge scale gives an effect of all the random inevitability of life, it also satisfies an ideal. It is an immensely audacious and successful attempt to compel the whole area of living to acknowledge the rule of art, proportion, of what is "right." What Henry James deprecatingly called "a wonderful mass of life" is in fact a highly complex patterning of human fulfilment, an allotment of fates on earth as authoritative as Dante's in the world to come. It is significant that the first drafts of the novel carried the title "All's well that ends well."

In his old age Tolstoy said, "when the characters in novels and stories do what from their spiritual nature they are unable to do, it is a terrible thing." To live, as the novel understands and conveys life, is what Prince Andrew would not have been able to do. It is impossible to imagine him developing a relation with Natasha, or communicating with her as Pierre and Natasha communicate in the last pages of the novel. For him Natasha represents life. It is his destiny as a character to conceptualise what others embody. He perceives through metaphor and symbol, as he sees the great oak-tree, apparently bare and dead, coming again into leaf. A much more moving instance of this, to my mind, than the rather grandiloquent image of the oak-tree, is his glimpse of the two little girls as he visits the abandoned house at Bald Hills on his retreat with his regiment.

> . . . two little girls, running out from the hot-house carrying in their skirts plums they had plucked from the trees there, came upon Prince Andrew. On seeing the young master, the elder one, with frightened look, clutched her younger companion by the hand and hid with her behind a birch tree, not stopping to pick up some green plums they had dropped.
>
> Prince Andrew turned away with startled haste, unwilling to let them see that they had been observed.

He was sorry for the pretty frightened little girl, was afraid of looking at her, and yet felt an irresistible desire to do so. A new sensation of comfort and relief came over him when, seeing these girls, he realized the existence of other human interests entirely aloof from his own and just as legitimate as those that occupied him. Evidently these girls passionately desired one thing—to carry away and eat those green plums without being caught—and Prince Andrew shared their wish for the success of their enterprise. He could not resist looking at them once more. Believing their danger past, they sprang from their ambush, and chirruping something in their shrill little voices and holding up their skirts, their bare little sunburnt feet scampered merrily and quickly across the meadow grass.

We can see from this passage exactly why Andrew "loved" Natasha—it resembles the scene where he hears the two of them talking by the window—and why the word "love" in the novel has no meaning of its own apart from the continuous demands and rights of life. He loves the idea of life more than the actuality. When he rejoins his soldiers he finds them splashing about naked in a pond, and he is revolted at the sight of "all that healthy white flesh," doomed to the chances of war. Nor do we ever have a greater sense, by contrast, of what life means, than when Andrew, after all his intimations of death, "the presence of which he had felt continually all his life"— in the clouds above the battlefield of Austerlitz and in the birchtree field before Borodino—confronts Natasha and the Princess Mary on his deathbed.

> In one thin, translucently white hand he held a handkerchief, while with the other he stroked the delicate moustache he had grown, moving his fingers slowly. His eyes gazed at them as they entered.

> On seeing his face and meeting his eyes Princess Mary's pace suddenly slackened, she felt her tears dry up and her sobs ceased. She suddenly felt guilty and grew timid on catching the expression of his face and eyes.

> "But in what am I to blame?" she asked herself. "Because you are alive and thinking of the living, while I . . ." his cold stern look replied.

> In the deep gaze that seemed to look not outwards but inwards there was an almost hostile expression as he slowly regarded his sister and Natasha.

I have suggested that Andrew is not subject to "discoveries," and to Tolstoy's intimate kinds of examination, but this is not entirely true. Tolstoy's genius for character, as comprehensive and apparently involuntary as Shakespeare's, and with far more opportunity for detailed development than Shakespeare has within the limits of a play, could not avoid Andrew's becoming more than a centre of reflection and of symbol. The sheer worldliness of Tolstoy's observation keeps breaking in. We learn, for example, that Andrew befriends Boris, whom he does not much care for, because it gives him an apparently disinterested motive for remaining in touch with the inner ring where preferment is organised and high-level gossip exchanged. And Tolstoy notes that his exasperated criticism of the Russian military leadership both masks and gives an outlet to the tormenting jealousy that he feels about Natasha and Kuragin. But these are perceptions that could relate to someone else: they are not wholly him. What is? I observed that the scene with the two little girls reveals his attitude to life, and so it does; but the deeper and less demonstrated veracity in it is Andrew's *niceness*, a basic quality that we recognise and respond to here,

though we have hardly met it before at first-hand. In the same way the deathbed quotation above shows something else about him that we recognise—in spite of the change in him he is still the same man who used to treat the Little Princess with such cold sarcasm: The life he disliked in her he is fond of in his sister and adores in Natasha, but now that it is time to leave it his manner is much the same as of old. Though he has only grown a moustache on his deathbed we seem to recognise that coldly fastidious gesture of stroking it.

> "There, you see how strangely fate has brought us together," said he, breaking the silence and pointing to Natasha. "She looks after me all the time."

> Princess Mary heard him and did not understand how he could say such a thing. He, the sensitive, tender Prince Andrew, how could he say that, before her whom he loved and who loved him? Had he expected to live he could not have said those words in that offensively cold tone. If he had not known that he was dying, how could he have failed to pity her and how could he speak like that in her presence? The only explanation was that he was indifferent, because something else, much more important, had been revealed to him.

> The conversation was cold and disconnected, and continually broke off.

> "Mary came by way of Ryazan," said Natasha.

> Prince Andrew did not notice that she called his sister *Mary,* and only after calling her so in his presence did Natasha notice it herself.

> "Really?" he asked.

> "They told her that all Moscow has been burnt down, and that . . ."

> Natasha stopped. It was impossible to talk. It was plain he was making an effort to listen, but could not do so.

> "Yes, they say it's burnt," he said. "It's a great pity," and he gazed straight before him absently stroking his moustache with his fingers.

> "And so you have met Count Nicholas, Mary?" Prince Andrew suddenly said, evidently wishing to speak pleasantly to them. "He wrote here that he took a great liking to you," he went on simply and calmly, evidently unable to understand all the complex significance his words had for living people.

Apart from the theme of death, the passage is full of the multitudinous meaning—like the significance of Natasha's use of the name *Mary*—which has been building up throughout the book. It is checked once by Tolstoy's remark—"he was indifferent because something else, much more important, had been revealed to him." Certainly Andrew may think so, but Tolstoy announces the fact with just a shade too much determination: the surface of almost helpless mastery is disturbed. For where death is concerned, Tolstoy in *War and Peace* was under the spell of Schopenhauer. Life is a sleep and death an awakening. "An awakening from life came to Prince Andrew together with his awakening from sleep. And compared to the duration of life it did not seem to him slower than an awakening from sleep compared to the duration of a dream." As Shestov points out, the second sentence comes almost verbatim from *The World as Will and Idea.* In Andrew, Tolstoy has deliberately created the man who fits this conception of death. With his usual confidence Tolstoy annexes death through Andrew,

*Tolstoy with his wife, Sofia, in his study.*

to show that it must *be* something because life is so much something. Yet life and death cannot understand one another.

> —"Shall I live? What do you think?"
>
> "I am sure of it!—sure!" Natasha almost shouted, taking hold of both his hands in a passionate movement.

Natasha "almost shouts" her belief because she can do nothing else—she cannot believe in anything but life. Even when after the last change in Andrew she sees he is dying, she goes about "with a buoyant step"—a phrase twice repeated. This has a deep tragic propriety, for the two are fulfilling their whole natures. Only old Count Rostov is touching. He cries for himself at Andrew's death, because he "knows he must shortly take the same terrible step"; and he knows this because his old assurance—his *samodovolnost*—has gone.

> He had been a brisk, cheerful, self-assured old man, now he seemed a pitiful, bewildered person . . . he continually looked round as if asking everybody if he was doing the right thing. After the destruction of Moscow and of his property, thrown out of his accustomed groove, he seemed to have lost the sense of his own significance and to feel there was no longer a place for him in life.

As Isaiah Berlin points out, Tolstoy's conception of history resembles in many ways that of Marx, whom he had never heard of at the time he was writing *War and Peace,* and this applies to his sense of personal history as well as the history of nations. His imaginative grasp of the individual life is such that freedom does indeed become the recognition of one's personal necessity, and "to each according to his needs" is not only the ideal of society but seems in *War and Peace* the law of life and death. (pp. 73-82)

> *John Bayley, in his* Tolstoy and the Novel, *1966. Reprint by The Viking Press, 1967, 316 p.*

**KONSTANTIN SIMONOV**   (essay date 1969)

*[A prolific and popular dramatist, poet, and fiction writer, Simonov was one of the most prominent literary figures in the Soviet Union during and after World War II. At various times he served as editor of the journal* Literaturnaya gazeta, *Deputy of the Supreme Soviet, and Secretary of the Union of Soviet Writers. In the latter capacity, Simonov was instrumental in establishing the conservative literary principles imposed on Soviet literature during the Stalin era; however, as editor-in-chief of the journal* Novy mir *from 1954 to 1957, he published several liberal works, including Vladimir Dudintsev's* Ne chlebom yedinym *(1956), for which he was censured by the government and was removed from editorship of the journal. In the following excerpt from an essay written on the one-hundredth anniversary of the first edition of* War and Peace, *Simonov discusses the novel's basis in Tolstoy's military experiences and examines the author's treatment of military themes and figures.]*

What was Tolstoy when he began writing *War and Peace*? Our awareness of him is still heavily overshadowed by Tolstoy in his later years, by the image of him as a wise old man with a long gray beard, standing calmly with his crabbed old hands thrust into the belt of his peasant shirt, by his religious sermons, by Tolstoyism; nonresistance to evil. . . . One must in fact make a certain mental effort in order to prevent that deceptively peaceful image of Tolstoy as an old man from imposing itself, by the law of retroactive inertia, onto the real image of the thirty-year-old Tolstoy who conceived and began writing his great novel, the Tolstoy who rolled up his sleeves to grapple in single combat with the gigantic, hydra-headed concept of *War and Peace,* the Tolstoy who sat down for tens of thousands of hours to write all those drafts and fair copies, all those rejected, altered and completely rewritten variants. The Tolstoy of those years was still young, no graybeard, strong, cunning, capable of challenging someone to a duel in the heat of the moment. He had left the army not long before, and the influence of the service was still alive in many of his habits and memories. . . . Early on in the writing of *War and Peace* there flared up in Poland the war of liberation which was mercilessly suppressed by the czar's government. He had not yet finished his novel when Karakozov first fired a shot at the czar. The sixties of the last century, it might seem, was no time to be writing historical novels, and indeed certain critics were later to reproach Tolstoy for his remoteness from the live issues of the day.

Yet was he remote? I confess I have always been worried by a particular question: why did Tolstoy, who had served nearly five years in the army, who had taken part in many of what were known in those days as "incidents" in the Caucasus, who had seen action on the Danube and during the Crimean War in besieged Sebastopol—in short had served throughout the whole of a war which was of considerable significance for the fate of Russia, a war marked by both shameful defeats and heroic deeds—why did he write nothing else about that war besides the *Tales of Sebastopol*? I know that there are plenty of explanations for this; nevertheless I am still intrigued by Tolstoy's state of mind when, not many years after Sebastopol, he sat down and wrote a novel *not* about the war that he had just lived through, but about another one, as though bypassing his personal experience he turned his gaze back five decades in time to a past world and to a war which had taken place well before he was born. (pp. 209-10)

Nevertheless, the experience of [the Crimean War] had a lasting effect on Tolstoy. Whatever may have been the original idea which gave birth to *War and Peace*—a subject on which whole books have been written—the outcome was a novel whose heart was the War of 1812 and whose heart of hearts was Borodino. But what about Natasha, Pierre, Prince Andrei? Are not they the heart of *War and Peace*? Of course they are—who would dare to contend otherwise? Pierre, Natasha, Prince Andrei, the whole Rostov family, the old prince, Princess Mary, Hélène, Dolokhov, Denisov—all of them are the essence of *War and Peace,* without which it would not live on in the grateful consciousness of all mankind. Yet if none of these characters existed in the novel there would still remain the question of how and why Tolstoy projected his own experience of war backward in time to the Napoleonic wars.

There is no need to point out in detail to what degree Tolstoy's own military experience formed the basis of much, if not most, of his descriptions of warfare in *War and Peace*. To discover this one only has to put the novel alongside the *Tales of Se-*

*bastopol*. Here is the source of such characters as Timokhin and Tushin and of the emotions experienced in war by Nikolai Rostov, by Pierre and by Prince Andrei; it is also the source of his knowledge of how men die, and how the legs of a man killed by a blow on the head continue to twitch after he is dead, knowledge which Tolstoy was to use again describing the death of Petya Rostov. Hence, too, his knowledge of military hospitals and field dressing stations, of how arms and legs are amputated, of what kinds of wounds are lethal, of the smell of wounded men and the smell of death. This too he needed later—both when writing of Natasha nursing the dying Prince Andrei, and when he made the Prince himself suddenly think before the battle: "They'll drag me away by my legs and my head and fling me into a pit, so that I don't stink." All this Tolstoy knew from Sebastopol. But from his service in the Crimea, the Balkans and the Caucasus there was much more that he knew and of which he made very little use in the *Tales of Sebastopol.*

Writers on Tolstoy often stress that he was an artillery officer on the bastions of Sebastopol. This is so. And that if he had not served under fire at Sebastopol he would not have been able to re-create the spirit of Borodino. True. But there was another part of his military career—he also saw a considerable amount of service as a staff officer at headquarters. He was an aristocrat and what is more he was a relative of General Gorchakov, the commander in chief. With the merciless self-analysis so characteristic of Tolstoy, he utilized even his own privileged position as material for many of the most mordant passages of *War and Peace,* where he describes what he regarded as the insulated, artificial life at headquarters where people like Boris Drubetskoy flourished, and where men like Andrei Bolkonsky gradually became aware of the falsity of their position. In saying that Tolstoy did not only serve on the bastions of Sebastopol, I mean to stress that the extent of his military knowledge gave him insight not only into what produces a victory like Borodino, but also into the root causes of a defeat such as Austerlitz. It was the use he made of both kinds of knowledge that gives such depth to his writing.

We should not forget that at the end of the sixties of the last century the six parts of *War and Peace* had only just been published and that Tolstoy was the subject of passionate argument. The critics' views of him varied enormously, and they included some merciless abuse. (pp. 211-12)

But the impression that [*War and Peace*] made was overwhelming. In particular the novel made an enormous impact on Russian military men of the time. Naturally they cursed Tolstoy for his fatalism, for his underestimation of the role of the individual in history as a whole and of the military commander in particular. They abused him for his disrespect for military theory and military science, military planning and tactics. They were angry at Tolstoy's estimation of Napoleon, quarreled with his assessment of Kutuzov and with his theory of partisan warfare, they corrected his errors, real and imagined. But despite all this the majority of his military critics admitted that the book had made a tremendous impression on them. The first edition of *War and Peace* came out at a time when the more progressive among Russian officers were seeking army reforms which would secure Russia against a repetition of the harsh lessons of the Crimean War. It is not surprising that the more intelligent of the novel's military critics made a very close analysis of the lessons on warfare which Tolstoy gave them.

One of the most intelligent soldiers in Russia at that time, General Dragomirov, devoted virtually a complete book to an analysis of *War and Peace* from a military standpoint. In this work, in which Dragomirov largely disagreed with Tolstoy's theoretical premises, he nevertheless wrote: "All this is fiction, yet the people in it are alive. They suffer, die, act, lie, do great deeds and indulge in base cowardice exactly as real people do, and that is why they are so highly instructive. Therefore I have only regret for any military officer who does not take Count Tolstoy's book to heart. . . ." While contesting Tolstoy's military theories, Dragomirov nevertheless considered that Tolstoy had described actual warfare with unsurpassed truth and accuracy, and he made a direct appeal to all his brother officers to draw from Tolstoy's writing the moral conclusions appropriate to their own professional conduct.

Dragomirov's remarks strike me as being far from naïve. On the contrary, I believe they stem directly from a feature of Tolstoy's novel of which Dragomirov was acutely aware. Tolstoy wrote when still fresh from the Crimean War. As he wrote he called to mind everything that he detested about the army and society which had led to the errors and disasters of that war. And I believe that in *War and Peace* one of the things which he meant to put across to his readers was the lesson to be learned from comparing the War of 1812 with the Crimean War.

The Tolstoy of the years when he wrote *War and Peace* was profoundly, indeed at that time quite particularly, concerned with the historic fate of Russia. The fact that his views on this were very different from those of the rulers of Russia is another matter. In his reflections in *War and Peace* on the War of 1812 and the events which followed it, Tolstoy distinguished quite unambiguously between what he regarded as a just war that corresponded to the true national interest and the war which in his view exceeded those legitimate bounds. He analyzed the motives which induced Czar Alexander I to prolong the war after the expulsion of Napoleon from Russia, as a result of which Russian forces, no longer led by Kutuzov but by Alexander himself, fought in Europe for a further eighteen months and marched into Paris. But in describing these motives and considering them quite logical for the czar and the politicians of the czar's entourage, Tolstoy himself did not agree with them for a moment; and he said so in plain terms in the last part of the novel, when he bids farewell to Kutuzov.

These pages of *War and Peace* are both a requiem for Kutuzov and a direct statement of Tolstoy's own views on the point at which, in his opinion, the "people's war" of 1812 came to an end and that other war began for which he had no sympathy and which he did not propose to describe. In the passage about that morning at Vilno when all the officers gathered at Alexander's headquarters realized from what the czar was telling them that "the war was not over," Tolstoy wrote of Kutuzov: "Kutuzov alone refused to understand this and gave his frank opinion that a new war would not improve Russia's position nor add to her glory, but could only make her position worse and lessen the pinnacle of renown on which, in his view, Russia now stood." Later, contrasting Kutuzov with Alexander, Tolstoy added: "Kutuzov did not understand the meaning of such concepts as Europe, the balance of power, Napoleon. He could not grasp them. For the representative of the Russian people, once the enemy had been destroyed, Russia liberated and covered in glory, there was no more for a Russian, as such, to do. There was nothing left for the man who personified the people's war but to die. And he died." Thus Tolstoy closes the theme of Kutuzov and with it the theme of the "people's war." The novel ends some twenty pages later with the meeting

between Pierre and Natasha. Tolstoy has said all he had to say about the war. He finished the book at precisely the point where a war whose necessity he had believed in started to become a war whose necessity he denied.

Alongside this theme of conflict between *raison d'état* and true national interest, in *War and Peace* Tolstoy is also deeply concerned with the problem of the role of the individual in history, the problem of power and its real or imaginary limitations. Reading *War and Peace* now, we should remember that when it was written Europe was monarchical, of varying degrees of absolutism, and that Tolstoy's often bitter strictures against kings and emperors were intended to apply not only to the Napoleonic era but to the Russia and Europe of the sixties. This partly explains, in my view, the special place occupied in *War and Peace* by Napoleon.

It is of course hardly necessary to explain away the sheer amount of space devoted to Napoleon in a novel written about the Napoleonic wars; but that unique fury, that outwardly cold yet passionate sarcasm with which in *War and Peace* Tolstoy not so much wrote about as arraigned Napoleon, is highly significant. Tolstoy strives to prove that Napoleon was simply a plaything in the hands of history, and what is more, an evil and dangerous plaything. On this score critics, historians and military theorists from every country have engaged Tolstoy in savage altercation, and even in Russia there has been no lack of defenders of Napoleon against Tolstoy—principally on the grounds that Napoleon was not a plaything of history but a major figure and a great military commander. Tolstoy's opponents had plenty of arguments on their side. Despite the fascinating power of Tolstoy's mind, it is nevertheless impossible to go all the way with him in his assessment of Napoleon as a historic personality. To me, for instance, even after reading *War and Peace* Napoleon is still a great general, although Tolstoy's withering analysis, his relentlessly methodical unmasking of Napoleon's actions, delight me by their sheer virtuosity every time I reread the novel. In reading it, I don't think about how fair or unfair Tolstoy was to Napoleon, but about something else—the reason for that passionate fury with which Tolstoy lashed out at Napoleon. I believe that the cause of this fury was Tolstoy's determination to refute at all costs the dominant views of his time on the role of the personality in history, on the problem of power in general and of absolute power in particular; since the novel dealt with the Napoleonic era, all such arguments inevitably converged on the figure of Napoleon.

So Tolstoy chose this personage as his target. To demolish Napoleon in those vulnerable moral aspects he felt to be inadequate he was not deterred from tackling the hardest task of all, the attempt to challenge precisely what until then had been regarded as indisputable—Napoleon's military genius. In general, whenever Tolstoy wanted to prove something, he was not afraid of proving it by citing the unlikeliest of examples. When, for instance, he came to the conclusion that art was a lie and a factitious deception which distracted mankind from truth and goodness, he had no hesitation in lashing out not only at Shakespeare but at himself. Art itself suffered no harm from his attacks, but the search for truth and goodness in art was given a new impulse. And when Tolstoy decided to prove that great men in general and great military commanders in particular did not exist, that they were not only thought up by other people but worse, were thought up to the great detriment of the true interests of mankind, he did not shrink from the necessity of taking Napoleon as an example to prove it. The result is not that Napoleon has ceased to remain in our consciousness as a military leader, but that by consistently hammering away at Napoleon from so many aspects, Tolstoy has mounted such a devastating attack on the very idea of absolute power and on the immorality of the supposed superiority of one man over all other men, on reading these savage pages of *War and Peace* a century later one can still feel the whole might, the moral sublimity and the incredible perspicacity of the writer. (pp. 212-15)

In striving for a higher justice, Tolstoy was on occasion unjust and prejudiced. He loved some things and could not abide others. *War and Peace* is full of his prejudices and enthusiasms; it is a book written not by a wise old man, but by a man of ungovernable passions, and it resounds with the echoes of these passions. Tolstoy loved Pierre not only for his goodness, but also for his outbursts of unbridled righteous anger, which he always described in the novel with such pleasure, as though at last able to give free rein not only to Pierre but to himself. With equal prejudice, at times even at odds with himself in the matter, he loved or hated others of his heroes. And it seems to me that not to understand this is to fail to understand Tolstoy. There are also people who do not read the massive philosophical digressions with which Tolstoy interrupts the narrative of *War and Peace* and which form, in essence, a second book within the novel. It is a matter of taste. But to me, without these digressions, shattering in their polemic fury, it is not *War and Peace.* Or more precisely it is *War and Peace* without one of its chief heroes: Tolstoy himself of the sixties—that good, angry, passionate, vital man, actively and painfully obsessed by the question whose answer he sought for himself, for Russian society for the world at large—how are we to live? (pp. 215-16)

> *Konstantin Simonov, ''On Reading Tolstoy: An Essay on the Centenary of the First Edition of 'War and Peace','' in* Partisan Review, *Vol. XXXVIII, No. 2, 1971, pp. 208-16.*

**PAUL DEBRECZENY** (essay date 1971)

[*Debreczeny is a Hungarian-born American critic who specializes in nineteenth-century Russian literature. In the following excerpt, he analyzes the expression in* War and Peace *of Tolstoy's complex and contradictory views on free will.*]

Percy Lubbock was wrong, surely, in claiming that in *War and Peace* Tolstoy had written two novels in one. Rather, as the dialectic of war and peace unfolds in Tolstoy's novel the reader becomes increasingly aware of the essential unity of the private and the public in the Russian author's world. Pierre Bezukhov, who has been the gravitational center of nonmilitary, peaceful endeavors through two-thirds of the novel, comes to Borodino, his huge bulk in civilian clothes cutting an odd figure on the battlefield yet epitomizing the inevitable convergence of the individual and the historical. Subsequently, the French move into Moscow—the very homestead of Russian society—in which Tolstoy's family sagas have developed. And a final synthesis of seemingly antithetic elements—not only structural but philosophical—is achieved in the novel's crucial scene: that of Pierre witnessing the execution of fellow captives and expecting to be executed himself.

This scene—so vividly reminiscent of another mock execution, not fictional but very real, in the history of Russian literature— has as profound an effect on Pierre as the ordeal on Semyonovsky Square had on Dostoevsky. ''That hour's experience,''

Tolstoy comments, ''had extinguished in his soul all faith in the perfection of creation, in the human soul, in his own, in the very existence of God.'' Dostoevsky's hero, Ivan Karamazov, was to couch his despair of divine justice in similar terms some twelve years after the appearance of *War and Peace:* he was to ''return his ticket'' to his creator, for he could not envisage an eschatology that could right the wrong done to the innocent. Even as Tolstoy was writing *War and Peace,* Dostoevsky had begun his search for an answer to the problem of human freedom and responsibility, providing, for the time being, merely a theory in a grotesque garb in his *Notes from Underground.*

For both authors the crucial question is: Who is responsible for the atrocities they recount? As Pierre watches the French soldiers going about their bloody duty he asks himself with horror: ''Whose doing is it? They are all as much sickened as I am. Whose doing is it then?'' Asking this question, Tolstoy unites the private and the public, the individual and the historical in his novel. His groping for a philosophy of history and his analysis of the individual characters are both generated by a desire to find an answer to Pierre's question. Moreover, the question haunted him all his life, and he formulated it even more clearly in *Resurrection.* The hero of that novel, Prince Nekhlyudov, witnesses the march of several hundred convicts from a Moscow prison to the railroad station. The heat, the length and quick pace of the march, and the convicts' rundown state of health—most of them have had no exercise or fresh air for months—cause five of them to die of heart attacks. Nekhlyudov claims they did not just die, they were murdered; but he has difficulty in finding a culprit because the minister of justice ultimately responsible for the proceedings has no idea of what happens in reality and the guards taking the convicts are acting under orders. While Dostoevsky looks for a transcendental answer, Tolstoy blames the social system which exacts greater loyalty toward a bureaucratic order than toward a fellow human being.

Pierre's question is, then, expanded into a novel. During the Napoleonic War, Tolstoy argues, over half a million people were killed. Doubtless, Napoleon alone cannot take the responsibility for all of them, even if he is willing to in his supreme arrogance and lack of conscience. Who, then, was responsible? Could any participants of the war be regarded as free agents? Moral responsibility hinges on freedom of choice; if the latter is lacking, there is clearly no one to blame.

Tolstoy wrote in his article **"A Few Words about *War and Peace*,"** "Why did millions of people kill each other although it has been well known, from the beginning of time, that killing is both physically and morally wrong? They did it, because it was inevitable, because they had to obey an instinctive, zoological law, the same law that makes bees destroy each other in the fall and makes male animals fight." This was written in 1867 when only two-thirds of *War and Peace* had been published. The final formulation of the problem, given in epilog 2 to the novel, begins with a similar statement:

> If the will of every man were free, i.e., if every man could do exactly as he pleased—history would be a mere series of disconnected accidents. If but one man out of several millions had the power, once in a thousand years, to act freely, i.e., entirely according to his own will, it is clear that, should his free action transgress a single law, laws could no longer exist at all for humanity. If, on the other hand, one and the same law were to govern the acts of all humanity,

there could exist no free-will, since the will of all humanity would be subject to that law.

If Tolstoy were to let the matter rest at this, he would remain strictly within the framework of natural science; he would see a causality as overriding in human affairs as in nature. His view of man would hardly differ from that of the scientific positivists of his age: he would regard the human being as a complex organism whose actions are in fact reactions—adjustments to the environment in response to stimuli emanating from the environment. (pp. 185-87)

As one reads further into the epilog, however, it becomes clear that Tolstoy is not satisfied with a scientific view: "The problem lies in the fact that, if we look upon man as a subject for study only (whether from the theological, the historical, the ethical, the philosophical or any other point of view), we come upon a general law of necessity to which he, like everything else in existence, is subject; yet if we look upon him also as something representing our own consciousness, we feel that we are free."

Chernyshevsky also spoke of a consciousness of freedom as an illusion, and some students of Tolstoy have interpreted his statement as referring only to an illusion. R. F. Christian [see excerpt dated 1962] writes that

> the life of these people [the heroes of *War and Peace*] can be rich, many-sided, apparently self-determined—without the conviction on their part that they are free agents life would be intolerable—and yet the consciousness of freedom which permeates it can still be an illusion. Men must have this consciousness to live, and through it they live more fully and more richly, but it is ultimately this very consciousness of freedom and not freedom itself which they enjoy.

This statement has a relative truth within its context, but it would not satisfy Tolstoy as absolute. If he were able to concede such a limited, empirical view of life, he would qualify to be cast with the foxes by Isaiah Berlin; but in truth he has an urge to be a hedgehog, for the salient hedgehog quality, as Berlin sees it, is an urge to create a coherent moral universe. In a historical process of cut-and-dried causes and effects there is no room for moral judgment; the only difficulty of such a process is that an infinite number of causes may be posited for every event. Moreover, such a dry, objective method of study will not allow for the writing of history from a national point of view. Tolstoy indeed wanted to judge, and he was writing history from a patently Russian point of view, despite all his protestations to the contrary.

For this reason he carries his argument about the subjective consciousness of freedom further in his second epilog than he did in his earlier note about the novel. Since life is inconceivable without a subjective consciousness of freedom, he argues, and since reason says freedom is impossible, the inevitable conclusion is that freedom as a concept lies beyond the reach of human reason. In other words, he concedes that the concept of freedom does not submit to rational argument. One could not object to this if Tolstoy were now willing to launch into frankly transcendental considerations; but he is not. Instead he applies, from chapter 9 onward in epilog 2, his admittedly irrational concept of freedom to what purports to be rational argument. He establishes an inverted correlation between knowledge of the circumstances of an event and willingness to allow for an element of freedom in it. He claims a similar relationship between the time that has elapsed since the event and the perception of freedom in it.

This argument has two flaws. One, which I have already mentioned, is that Tolstoy concedes freedom to be an irrational concept, yet he is using it here as if he had succeeded in establishing its rationality. The other objection to his argument is that the amount of knowledge gathered about a particular historical event depends on the abilities of the student of history and is therefore not an objective criterion against which quanta of freedom can be measured.

Tolstoy smuggles in elements of freedom despite his own better judgment, because he is compelled by a propensity to moralize. The contradictions which follow from such theory and practice have been pointed out by critics ever since his own time. Since these contradictions have already been analyzed, there is no need here to enumerate them. A single example will suffice. Tolstoy claims that Napoleon, genius, strategy, tactics, and all, had less to do with the outcome of the military confrontation than his simplest soldier. This much is consistent enough with Tolstoy's general theory; but the question arises: How did it happen that Kutuzov managed to influence the course of events? Tolstoy's answer is that Kutuzov "with his whole Russian being" (rather than with his mere intellect) perceived the inevitable drifting of events in a particular direction, and instead of trying to influence the course of history, he harnessed it. But is an ability to harness history not a mark of genius? Is the full utilization of the geographic properties and natural resources of the Russian land not the best strategy—perhaps not in the formal eighteenth-century sense, but in the sense of modern warfare? It is obvious that Tolstoy longed to glorify Kutuzov and to condemn Napoleon. N. N. Ardens has shown that the shifts of emphasis in Tolstoy's historical views, which one observes as he proceeds from volume to volume of the novel, are due to Tolstoy's increasing awareness of the effect the Russian spirit of self-defense had on the outcome of the war. Battles fought in foreign lands might have been shaped by blind forces, but the defense of Mother Russia was a feat of the people.

Moral judgment is inherent in the portrayal of individual, non-historical characters in the novel—the Anna Sherers, Anatole Kuragins, and Boris Trubetskoys get a full measure of the author's disapproval—from which one concludes that the individual persons in *War and Peace* were conceived as possessing moral freedom and responsibility. One would expect that freedom, which according to Tolstoy is a subjective consciousness of the self, would be more evident in the characters' private lives than in historical events. The tenor of criticism has been that Tolstoy's theories serve beautifully in his art proper, i.e., in his character portraiture, but less successfully in his historical depictions. Yet this is not quite so—at least not in relation to the main characters with whom the author sympathizes. What gives the novel viable organic unity is that principles of historical analysis are applied to the portrayal of individual characters, and a sense of freedom informs the depictions of historical events. The application of individual consciousness to historical phenomena results in the glorification of Kutuzov, and the application of historical principles to individual portrayals leads to a sense of necessity in private existence.

N. Chirkov has shown, among other signs all pointing to the unity of the novel, that the fateful stirrings of history—likened to a stormy sea by Tolstoy—are reflected in the turmoil of Natasha's emotional life. When the war is over—the sea is calm—Natasha has also spent her overflowing energies and has settled down to tame domesticity. Albert Cook, having analyzed the sequence of structural units in the novel, comments: "Into this structured time, this process of phases, grow the individual rhythms of the various characters. Each phase subjects to itself the destinies of all. What separates Andrey from Natasha is as much 1812 as the baseness of Anatole; and the titanic force of national events, into which the individual destinies flow, parts Andrey from the Anatole he has desperately been seeking till the moment when, as destiny exacts, he will feel deeply enough to forgive him" [see excerpt dated 1958].

A sense of historical necessity is present in all the private destinies, and above all in that of Prince Andrey. He was one of the last to enter the novel's portrait gallery, and at first Tolstoy intended to leave him to his fate on the battlefield at Austerlitz. "I need a brilliant young man to die at Austerlitz," he wrote in a letter of 3 May 1865 to L. I. Volkonskaya. Indeed, the cycle of Andrey's life came to completion at Austerlitz; he had been through love, glory, vanity, and had realized the futility of them all. Yet Tolstoy resurrects him in the same way in which Anna Karenina and Vronsky are resurrected in the later novel. Anna could have died in childbirth, and it was really a miracle that Vronsky did not succeed in his suicide attempt. Both had, as it were, completed their destinies, had come to a realization of their guilt and shallowness over Anna's sickbed, and a deity more merciful than their creator would have let them die. But Tolstoy made them live through another cycle and meet their real, incomparably more horrifying ends. Similarly, Prince Andrey is a plaything in the hands of fate; he has to live again certain painful scenes as if the great sky over Austerlitz were not great enough and as if Napoleon—the epitome of earthly vanity and futility—were not shrunk to small enough proportions.

The story of Prince Andrey's revival is one of ruthless necessity, a mockery of free will. Part 3 of volume 2, in which that story is related, begins with a brief description of the peace between Napoleon and Alexander: Russia has entered into alliance with Napoleon against Austria, and according to various rumors, Napoleon may marry one of Alexander's sisters. The paragraphs giving this information stand out strangely from a chapter otherwise wholly devoted to developments in the characters' private lives, but the passage is not there without reason. These odd political developments, which are patently temporary and out of tune with the general trend of history, are meant to alert the reader to the strange, zigzagging path of life. They warn that the new turns the characters encounter in their destinies may be as treacherous and temporary as those in the destiny of the nation.

There follows the description of Andrey's journey to Otradnoe and of his famous encounter with an old oak. As he identifies with the tree, the reader comes to understand that Andrey is as subject to nature's immutable laws as any vegetation. Significantly, his first meeting with Natasha, as he rides up to the Rostovs' house, is an encounter with the symbol of a young girl rather than with a real person; one is never told, he merely assumes, that the slim girl in the yellow dress is really Natasha. She is not important as a person; what is important is Andrey's reaction to a young creature to whom—he painfully realizes—he means nothing and with whom he feels like a hardened relic of the past, like the oak among the young birches. In one of his early drafts Tolstoy intended to let Andrey be swept off his feet by Natasha; in another version he would have been irritated by her. The former draft also shows hesitation as to how Natasha should react to the prince: both a favorable and

an adverse reaction are struck out from the same page. I think Tolstoy came to the eventual solution—having Andrey intrigued but not infatuated and dispensing with Natasha's reaction—because he wanted to underscore the impersonality of Andrey's feelings. Although the reader assumes that Andrey has been introduced to her, he is not seen actually face to face with Natasha; and the most important scene occurs when he is a chance witness to her conversation with Sonya at night—a scene in which Tolstoy, once more, does not say definitely to whom the voices belong. The impression thus created is that Andrey's feelings have been aroused, not by a person, but by a faceless feminine image. When the old oak, all green and sprouting, reappears, the sense of a biological, rather than psychological and individual, rejuvenation is reinforced. And to drive the message home entirely, Tolstoy comments that Andrey has begun casting around for reasons to go to St. Petersburg. With his intellect, he should know that another marriage would only lead to a painful repetition of his relations to Lise and that public life is a Vanity Fair; yet he goes because the restlessness of spring drives him—a force in the face of which he can use his intellect only for rationalizations.

It is very likely that Tolstoy had Prince Andrey in mind when he wrote in epilog 2: "However often reflection and experience may show a man that, given the same conditions and character, he will always, at a given juncture, do precisely what he did before, he will none the less feel assured that he can act as he pleases even though he may be engaging for the thousandth time in action which has hitherto always ended in the same way."

Prince Andrey, like the hypothetical man of this passage, faces familiar circumstances when he decides to reenter life, and not only because of his marriage to Lise and the vainglorious Austrian campaign but also because, close as he is to his father, his father's experiences are in a sense his own. At the beginning of the novel, when he tells his father he has decided to go off to war despite his wife's pregnancy, the old prince welcomes his resoluteness. It is implied that the old man knows the futility of marital relations all too well; he does not even have to be told the full story. Father and son are so much alike that they go through similar and interlocking cycles. When Andrey, vital and energetic, goes off to war, the old Bolkonsky, like a hermit, holds fast to his embittered seclusion; but a year or so later, when Andrey has become the recluse of Bogucharovo, his father bounces back to life, busying himself with the organization of the local militia. Like father, like son—Andrey should draw on his father's experiences as much as on his own. In this sense, he is facing the snares of life, figuratively, for the thousandth time, like the hypothetical man of the epilog. But there the similarity between him and the latter ends. While the man of the epilog decides to act out of a consciousness of freedom, Andrey is pushed into action by nature's inevitable forces. Spring has reawakened vitality in him as it does in the old oak.

Necessity permeates the lives of the other main characters too. As he marches with the prisoners of war, Pierre reflects on his past and decides that his marriage to Hélène was not voluntary. And further, his conversion to freemasonry furnishes a classic example of the way in which a man's spiritual energies come to terminal exhaustion under the weight of an unsuccessful marriage and a successful duel—this latter, an act inexpressibly repulsive to him in its violence.

The theme of necessity recurs even in scenes which, by right, should bear the message of freedom. Natasha's decision to elope wth Anatole Kuragin is a moral choice, yet it is emphasized that she could not help it. Anatole's presence mesmerizes her, she feels no moral barrier between him and herself, she is drawn to him by a magnetic force. She refuses to understand that her choice of Anatole means the loss of Andrey; in fact she refuses to choose altogether. Sonya's remonstrances surprise her unpleasantly and she wonders how her confidante could fail to see that there is no choice. Finally, the outcome of the affair testifies to the decisive influence of her environment, for she lives among people who will not allow her to ruin her life.

The most "existential" situation in the novel occurs on the "last day of Moscow." The Rostovs have loaded all their valuable belongings on carts and are ready to take flight from the city. At this moment wounded officers begin begging the Rostovs to make room for them on the carts. As the number of wounded who want to come rapidly multiplies, the Rostovs face a choice between carrying along their belongings and their fellow countrymen, between self-interest and charity. To be sure, Tolstoy wishes to say that these are Russian patriots, capable of making the right choice. Yet the theme of necessity surfaces even in this scene. Count Rostov gives orders, at first, to make room for only a couple of people, and even those orders he mutters half-heartedly as if he were caught up in an embarrassing social situation rather than one requiring a major moral decision. He does not realize he is making a major decision until the affair nearly overwhelms him and he has to explain it to his wife. And when the decision has been made and the servants are unloading the carts to accommodate the wounded, the inevitability of this course of action is reemphasized: "When she [Natasha] gave the order to unload the vehicles the servants could not believe their ears; they gathered round her and would not do it till the count told them that it was by their mistress's desire. Then they were no less convinced of the impossibility of leaving the wounded than they had been, a few minutes before, of the necessity of carrying away all the property, and they set to work with a will." The implication is that, given their characters as the servants know them, the Rostovs could not have acted otherwise.

Tolstoy's depiction of history, although its guiding principle is claimed to be a theory of necessity, gravitates nevertheless toward expressions of free will and reasserts moral values. Conversely, his characters, who should in theory be the main vehicles of individual moral freedom, tend actually to be clad in iron necessity.

The concept of freedom is necessary to *War and Peace* because without it neither foreign invaders nor Frenchified Russians could be adjudged. But the theory of freedom, as expressed in epilog 2, is not carried over into practice when characters close to Tolstoy's heart are portrayed. Prince Andrey, for example, came out of his seclusion, not with a consciousness of freedom, but because he had been rejuvenated simply by biological forces. If one examines a reverse process in his life—the process of his gradual withdrawal from existence after the battle of Borodino—the conclusion seems inescapable that the problem of freedom is, once more, scarcely relevant.

It might be argued that Andrey's withdrawal from life means a victory of necessity over freedom. He has realized the vainglory of the military existence and the futility of the statesman's reforms: he wishes to have no part of either. He has been through love's treacherous plots twice, and instead of love of woman he gives himself over to love of mankind—a condition that for Tolstoy means love of no one in particular and signifies

lack of life. His realization of how life's forces work has enabled him to rise above life. Life has become for him all cause and effect, clear but totally alien. As John Bayley writes, "it is his destiny to conceptualise what others embody" [see excerpt dated 1966]. He can watch his own destiny in as detached a manner as if he were reading a history book. But history is all necessity, all causality; the element of freedom departs from it as soon as the subject's participation ceases.

If this view of Andrey were true, its truth would be relevant to the process in the reversed direction, which is to say that Andrey would have been revitalized in 1809 by an increased awareness of freedom. But that was not the case; on the contrary, Andrey lost rational control over his actions and was driven by an instinctive force. What Tolstoy must here be referring to, then—at least in practice if not in theory—is vitality rather than freedom. When the great globe of sky opens up above Andrey, and Napoleon shrinks to toy size, the change brought about is not the loss of freedom but the loss of a sense of importance in earthly things. It is not that there are no further choices open to him, but rather that whatever he chooses, it will not matter. From a bird's-eye view the destruction of half a million people may be like a fairy tale; from the detached perspective Andrey acquires in the last phase of his illness, it makes no difference that he is leaving an orphan behind. To participate in life, one must feel that life is important. The lack of this sense of importance is the lack of vitality. To put it in Chernyshevsky's terms, the organism that loses its ability to respond to stimuli—to feel the importance of stimuli, so to speak—is no longer viable. Tolstoy does not prove in his novel that the sensation of life is a consciousness of freedom. Instead, wittingly or unwittingly, he shows that those who exercise their muscles—fight for their country, prepare to elope, chase wolves, go to balls, marry, and multiply—are alive; in other words, the sensation of life is the feeling that one is reacting to the environment, flexibly adjusting to its complex demands.

Andrey's responses grow limp because of a physical cause, his fatal wound. But the somatic process is paralleled by the psychological one of opting out of life. Although this psychological process is brought on by the somatic cause, its components have been present, in a hidden or less developed form, in Andrey's personality before he is wounded. His main traits, as Frank F. Seeley has analyzed them, are a tremendous pride and an equally strong diffidence, leading to disdain. An example Seeley refers to is Andrey's reception at the Austrian Court: "He had been sent post-haste from Krems by Kutuzov to report the reverse inflicted on the French and arrived glowing with patriotic and personal satisfaction, to be received with a polite lack of enthusiasm which cut him to the quick. . . . The coolness of his reception hurts Andrey both in his pride and in his feelings. But instead of reacting with disappointment, which would put him in a position of inferiority, or with anger, which would admit the offenders to be his equals, he avoids the issue and sublimates his pain by withdrawing to a position of assumed superiority."

This well-taken observation is relevant to many other situations in Andrey's life. For instance, when he obviously fails to achieve sexual harmony with his wife, his reaction is to scorn all women rather than to admit his failure or to direct his anger at Lise. If something hurts him, he does not attempt to remove the cause of the pain but tells himself that the cause is so contemptible it cannot possibly bring pain. Natasha's infidelity is an even greater wound to his ego than is his unhappy marriage, yet his main reaction is disdain, a contempt for himself for having ever trusted her. Letting things hurt, refusing to adjust to his environment, disclaiming his emotions—these are the means whereby Andrey opts out of life psychologically. The last phase of this process sets in after he talks with Natasha:

> "Natasha, I love you too much; I love you more than all the world."
>
> "And I—" she looked away an instant. "Why too much?" she asked.
>
> "Why too much? Tell me, from the bottom of your heart, what you think: Shall I live?"
>
> "I am sure of it—sure of it!" cried Natasha, seizing his hands with growing excitement. He did not reply.
>
> "How good that would be!" he sighed, and he kissed her hand.

At first sight, this dialogue hardly reveals the causes that bring on "that thing" as Natasha calls it in bewilderment—the last phase of his withdrawal from life. Yet the elements that comprise the process are subtly there. When he says he loves her "too much" he means that his love is greater than she can ever return, particularly in view of her previous infidelity. She understands the reproach and looks away for an instant, breaking off her reply, guilty. The next moment she comes back with the question: "Why too much?" as if wishing to challenge him to remonstrate aloud, to bring complaints into the open and give her an opportunity to apologize, affirming the greatness of her love. Here is an opportunity for Andrey to respond to a challenge, to clarify and happily resolve the only vital problem which still ties him to life and through which he might be able to reenter life. He hesitates a moment, repeating her question. Then he answers, like a Chekhov character, with an apparently irrelevant question of his own. But in fact he implies that he will probably die, which means he is unwilling to take up the challenge. He would love Natasha as much as life; but he is no longer able to love life. Even the most powerful stimulus—a sincere offer of love from the woman who has meant so much to him—is unable to elicit a response from him.

The quality Andrey gradually loses—vitality—is abundant in Natasha, Nikolay Rostov, Platon Karataev, and others—all curiously unintellectual people. Andrey, the intellectual soldier, is doomed; Pierre, another thinker and seeker, is saved only because his energies are recharged out of Platon's and Natasha's inexhaustible resources of vitality. The intellect is suspect, ineffectual, devoid of life. This idea of Tolstoy's became crystallized a decade later in *A Confession:* "Rational knowledge does not give the meaning of life, but excludes life; while the meaning attributed to life by millions of people, by all humanity, rests on some despised pseudo-knowledge."

Although *War and Peace* was written with polemic intent against *La Paix et la Guerre,* Proudhon's antiintellectualism looms large in it. Certain currents of Russian culture of the second half of the century also reinforce Tolstoy's rejection of intellectualism: slavophilism and populism both conjured up deep-seated emotional forces; for Dostoevsky, intellect was the dwelling place of evil; and Turgenev portrayed the ineffectual Rudin in the framework of a Hamlet-Don Quixote opposition to Insarov.

The antiintellectual features of *War and Peace* have, moreover, a certain connection with its epic qualities. Both George Lukács [see *TCLC*, Vol. 4] and George Steiner have argued its affinity to the ancient epic, particularly to *The Iliad.* Both emphasize the importance of a unified world view which sees objects and people, people and leaders as one organic whole. One of the features of the epic that Steiner lists seems to be especially relevant: "The recognition that energy and aliveness are, of themselves, holy."

The "wholeness" of life is the quality of a patriarchal *ancien régime.* Tolstoy lived in an age when this patriarchal order was being threatened by the advance of an industrialized society, a society in which, as R. P. Blackmur has argued, the problem is not the individual's conflict with the existing moral order, but his need to establish a moral universe for himself since society's former uniform values have crumbled. Western rationalism, advancing natural sciences, these were the torch-bearers in Tolstoy's eyes of this approaching new society, and its hallmark was chaos. In a last-ditch effort to save the secure, comprehensive unity of his world, he attacked the intellect on two fronts. On the one hand, he tried to deny it freedom and effectiveness: military leaders, he argued, only imagine they can win battles by clever strategies; historians who try to explain the causes of events err hopelessly; and so forth. He suspected that the intellect, if it penetrated too far, would open up vistas impossible of integration; alienation would inevitably result. On the other hand, the denial of freedom of action and the establishment of strict causality were precisely the results that modern empirical science was offering on an unprecedented scale. For this reason Tolstoy came to reaffirm freedom on an irrational basis, either unable to comprehend or unwilling to accept that consciousness contemplating itself in its full complexity—what he called the consciousness of freedom—could still be subject to the laws of nature. The tension between Tolstoy's contradictory ideas on freedom and necessity produced the mixed genre—half epic, half novel—that is *War and Peace.* (pp. 187-98)

*Paul Debreczeny, "Freedom and Necessity: A Reconsideration of 'War and Peace'," in* Papers on Language & Literature, *Vol. VII, No. 2, Spring, 1971, pp. 185-98.*

**JESSE BIER** (essay date 1971)

[*Bier is an American author and critic. In the following excerpt, he considers* War and Peace *a technical and thematic failure in which Tolstoy's ambition exceeded his ability.*]

Now that we are safely through the centenary anniversary of *War and Peace,* punctuated by the epic film rendition released by the Russians in 1968, we may be able to look at it undaunted for a change. It is as if we have been playing a long hide-and-seek game with the work and, now that we have counted to 100, we can find the real nook it occupies and what it really is.

Tolstoi's novel now forcibly appears to be a kind of early and extensive soap opera. As such—as a distinctly self-conscious popular epic, putting together an obliquely picaresque story and a strenuous apologia for a people fighting its way blind out of devastating war years and social upheaval—it is frequently inferior to the American *Gone With the Wind*. . . . The irony is that what was undoubtedly a model for Mitchell was itself, by virtue of pretenses and excesses she never entertained, a far more grandiose imposture than the American Southerner could have committed.

But what has led to the overwhelming reputation of *War and Peace,* aside from priority in its genre? More than a people's need for a story of epic self-defense and endurance accounts for the novel's prestige, even in Russia, these past one hundred years. When all is said and done, one must duly credit the scale and ambitions of the work. Measured by *intention*, Tolstoi launched a large and teeming book and then sought profundity as well as breadth. Yet even in its *forte*, human scale, there is a general tentativeness rather than realization of design. That great, famously intimidating cast of characters, for instance, centers only on three main characters, a few more of a second-rank, a compassable number of others whom we can keep track of well enough, and only then treats a plethora of quite minor character types who pop in and out of the story all too indecisively as part of the general human panorama rather than as characters truly integrated in the total action. The stage is brimming full of pre-cinematic "extras," not with a thronging cast of true characters; and of the many extras, those who promise or threaten to take on a full life of their own are cut off promptly and never seen again. This is not Homeric or Shakespearean abundance and individuated life, but a canvass of shadows rather than substantial human beings. In philosophic content, the book works much the same way. Once more there is a set-up for dimension, in this case depth analysis, as in the exploratory probing of the instinctive processes at work in a whole people's abandonment of their capital. But the thrust is not completed, and we are left with gesture rather than performance; there is a semblance of effect again—in this case, profundity—but not the substance of it. Still, the very attempt to portray the inter-related lives of many people—though mainly of the aristocracy—combined with even the adumbrations of serious and grand themes, like historical determinism, and heightened by the zeal of exposé, as in Tolstoi's passionate denunciation of over-dignified leaders and over-glamorized warfare, all these efforts taken together seemed to be artistic braveries that elevated the whole work and recommended it enormously. Moreover, one had one's cake and ate it, too, in having a war novel and a pacifist tract simultaneously. Never mind if the book actually missed what it seemed to aim at; what counted was that it attempted so much.

But for those of us who ask for the hard currency of execution in a work and not the earnest of grand conception or high motive, **War and Peace** is a staggering disappointment. As to the language of the book, I can say nothing. But a great work, it appears to me, can make its value felt across all borders and barriers: Homer, Dante, Shakespeare, etc. To put it the other way around, it is difficult to see how expressiveness alone could redeem so many flaws as Tolstoi's putative masterpiece contains. Not even Shakespeare's hand could transform *Henry VI*. There must be matter as well as manner for greatness.

I propose to consider certain crucial technical failings of the book first and proceed next to the most flagrant inadequacies of narrative and theme. In the first instance I wish to call attention to the jejune, manipulative coincidences of plot in the novel, to Tolstoi's heavyhanded characterizations and reckless exaggerations of relationship, and to his otherwise gross tactics of narrative and structural convenience.

One or two of the myriad coincidences in the novel might be rationalized as deliberate structural reinforcements, but the defense is not strong enough to give us more than momentary pause. The rake, Dólokhov, for example, tries to seduce Sonya but fails and then succeeds in seducing Hélène and still later guides Anatól's siege of Natásha. Some kind of commentary on the vulnerability of upper-class women and the compulsive sexual aggression of *arrivistes* may be meant, perhaps in symbolic conjunction with Napoleon's assault on Mother Russia—but that, it turns out, is *our* possible story not Tolstoi's novel. Such plotting never becomes thematic, integrated, or otherwise significant in the actual book. Furthermore, this technique of doubling or tripling the plot line becomes the merest gratuity since, in the case at hand, Anatól does not at all need Dólokhov's incitement or sponsorship in any way. We are left with unnecessary device, with strained artifice or deceptive literary symmetry. We come to see that such technical over-developments, so to speak, actually mask under-developments. That is true for the most notorious Dickensian coincidence in the whole novel: Prince Andrew's return home from the Austrian front precisely on the evening of his wife's *accouchement*, only to witness her death in child-birth. The potential irony in the contrast of his delivery from an almost certain battlefield death with his wife's totally unexpected death is unavailing, since not only is the point itself undercut by the patent melodramatics but the issue of arbitrary fate remains undeveloped in the larger philosophical context of the novel as a whole. Either an incalculable pedantry or modish sensationalism accounts for such over-loading—or, simply, an inability to accord developed plot to consequential theme.

There is a continuous series of other blatant coincidences which do not even qualify for judicial review. Here are some of Tolstoi's more extravagant soap operatics, the sheerest evanescence or whipped up froth. While Smolensk burns and all is chaos in the flaming city, Prince Andrew is made literally to bump into his father's servant on a street corner. Such things happen maybe, but only occasionally in life and much less so in good fiction. But Tolstoi proceeds apace. He cannot quite contrive bringing back Andrew to his family in order to facilitate their escape from the engulfed estate. Out of the whole Russian landscape, however, Nicholas Rostov is plucked and set galloping coincidentally along the one road where he is needed, arriving to rescue Andrew's sister, Princess Mary, in the nick of time from a small but dangerous revolt of serfs. Never mind that great expanses of territory and whole populations are involved in tumultuous action, the right people will forcibly meet each other at the opportune times. During the massive build-up for the actual battle of Borodino, all sorts of personal meetings occur in a similar spirit of casual inevitability: Andrew and Pierre and Boris and Dólokhov, etc. All Russia reels, and literally hundreds of thousands of lives are hurled into conflict, but a select few are endowed with homing instincts of unparalleled precision. At the end of this battle, wounded Andrew lies in one of hundreds of aid stations; it turns out that he is sharing the tent with the dying Anatól, that same would-be seducer of Andrew's betrothed Natásha, the one man that gentle Andrew vowed to kill but whom he may simply and conveniently pity *in extremis* now. Andrew is now spared a quick death of his own from his mortal wounds, to be allowed removal to Moscow where, by merest accident, he is brought directly into—which particular house and grounds of all possible places in the sprawling city?—the home of the Rostovs. Moreover, he yearns for his Natásha grievously, just exactly at the moment that the real Natásha and not his coincidental vision of her comes forward. Here is one of the world's great novelists rendering his scene:

> He now understood for the first time all the cruelty of his rejection of her, the cruelty of his rupture with her. "If only it were possible for me to see her once more! Just once, looking into those eyes to say. . . ."

Genius has its prerogatives, and we sit quite still for the famous master to complete his effect:

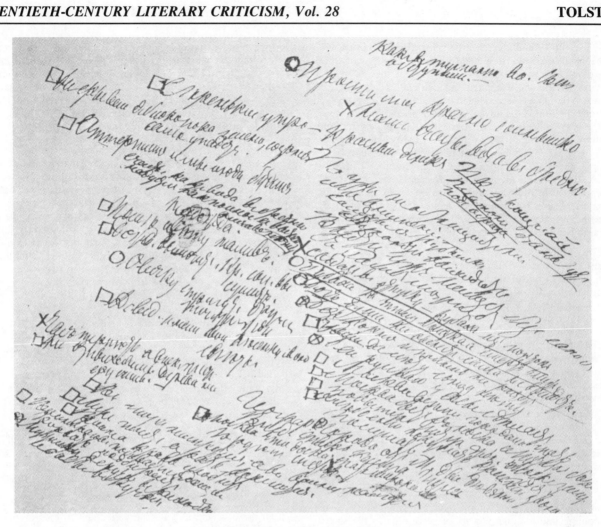

*Proverbs from* War and Peace *in Tolstoy's notes.*

Piti-piti-piti and ti-ti and piti-piti-piti boom! flopped the fly. And his attention was suddenly carried into another world, a world of reality and delirium in which . . . something was . . . stretching out . . . the pale face and shining eyes of the very Natasha of whom he had just been thinking.

There follows an exquisite moment of psychological suspense, during which Andrew thinks he knows that it is all hallucination; but then, along with him, we are brought crashing and weeping into the true world of Tolstoi's actuality, and Andrew now knows for a fact that it *is* his beloved there before him really.

> "You?" he said. "How fortunate!"

And these scenes, these arrangements, these moments are not divagations of the novel but its essential course, not side-effects but prime effects. (pp. 107-11)

Perhaps these weaknesses are more than compensated, however, by depths of character analysis and subtleties of social interplay. But here is only more matter for profound critical regret. One finds himself too often affronted, even appalled, by grossly unconvincing characterization in the putative masterpiece, to say nothing of the extraordinary liberty the author takes with relationships between the central characters, whom he keeps bringing together by a strategy of convenience only excusable if his profundities and subtleties are worth the li-cense. But his delineation of characters is by no stretch of imagination worth the pretexts and tyranny of his plot. What his protagonists do is often incoherent and downright unbelievable.

As a result, Tolstoi's characters keep getting away from him. They are not what he says they are or what he wants them to be. Pierre, for example, is not a great simple soul in the process of finding himself. Pierre is only—and rather steadily—one of the greatest dullards or incredible schizoids in all fiction. His marriage to Hélène is not only unnecessary and insufficiently motivated, it is totally out of character. Since at this particular time of his life his career as a young man about town is dissolute if not wild, Hélène's purely sexual appeal is not overwhelming for him. Moreover at a deeper psychic level, we are told that the alliance, illogical in every way, cannot even be strictly explained as compulsion—it goes against all his instinctual self-awareness. After marriage, of course, he and Hélène fall out with one another quickly and irrevocably, but Pierre's on-and-off cordialities with his unfaithful wife are bizarre and incomprehensible. They are not explained because they are inexplicable—and they are inexplicable because the character is not fundamentally realized.

Now, to argue in defense of Tolstoi's advanced realism that people strangely do not follow the dictates of their own interests and instincts is not only perverse criticism on our part but wholly inaccurate thinking; the curious logic or needs of people may be disguised, even from themselves, but we know by now that a rationale always exists. *That*, in fact, is the reason we have writers—to fathom apparent inconsistencies and to reveal the underlying coherences of human nature. This has always been true and, since the advent of Freud, is a commonplace. At all events to claim that art must simply duplicate the apparently contradictory feelings and confused relations of life itself is only to commit the organic fallacy of a most superficial realism. Where is the hidden and perhaps complex causality that we know governs all characters, for which varied insights the depth-novelist finds his primary reason for existence? But the characterization Tolstoi provides, as for Pierre, is dis-ordered, unconvincing, superficial and evasive. The final effect is one of a curiously pedantic understanding instead of profound realism.

Furthermore, Tolstoi's characterization turns incredible, becoming a sort of wilful outrage on all too many occasions. At such times all vestiges of reality are lost. When, for instance, Pierre is climactically placed in the midst of the Borodino battlefield, the occasion is a culminative event in his life, which should waken every sense in him. Instead, he is practically comatose, a travesty of incognizance, without even the excuse of having been personally hit or instantaneously traumatized. Tolstoi's intention is not to render shell shock but to describe the reactions of a sublimely unbelieving and unbelievable *naif*. What we must accept, then, is the rankest caricature or fantasy:

> He *did not notice the sound of the bullets whistling from every side, or the projectiles that flew over him*, did not see the enemy on the other side of the river, and for a long time *did not notice the killed and the wounded, though many fell near him*. He looked about him with a smile which did not leave his face. (my italics)

We are asked to believe in a simple though sensible Rousseauan hero coming into his own powers of perception in the story, and at this particular climax, but we are given a portrait unmatched by even the clinical records of dissociated schizophrenia. At such critical junctures Tolstoi supplies a species of grotesque parody instead of an ignited or profound characterization. Such effects present the most awkward and pretentious kind of make-believe; this is not the realization of a forthright and potent Russian Shakespeare but the shifts and imposture of a pre-Mitchell epicist.

Tolstoi does not focus his wildest imaginations and evasive characterization exclusively on Pierre any more than he lavished his technique of coincidence on Andrew alone, though both heroes are prime fixations for his respective defects. The book is rife with gross improbabilities or, really, impossibilities of motivation and relationship. When at one point Princess Mary discovers that her paid companion, Mlle. Bourienne, responds wholeheartedly to the clandestine advances and embraces of Anatól, who was supposedly wooing Mary herself, the Princess does not dismiss her household traitor. Later on Mary will have moments when even she is humanly jealous or antagonistic to someone, but now she is her usual long-suffering and impossible self; she is not only moved here to simple forgiveness but, in order to demonstrate her pure and triumphant Christian heart and her tender womanhood, she wants to give Mlle. Bourienne her dowry! Such excess, if credible at all, would be the signal in Dostoyevski's work of a phenomenal but tell-tale neurosis in the character: an extreme compensation for hidden hatred and then guilt for the hatred, a symptom of manic-depressive psychology and repression which

will be progressively developed or explosively uncovered by subsequent events. But that never happens in *War and Peace*, those events and that development never occur. Nothing is further from Tolstoi's mind—because he does not fundamentally understand his characters and so he does not know to what extent he either violates ordinary credibility or misses true motive. (pp. 111-14)

We must add . . . to our demurrals on the technique of *War and Peace* that final resort of romantic scenarios, the ultimate contrivance and wish-fulfillment of simply killing someone off, or not completing a character's story. In the case of Hélène, who quite suddenly dies of either heart failure or quack medication, the end might be poetically just, since her whole neurotic and unpredictable career of despising and yet rejoining her husband and indulging herself in strange love affairs and assorted fads has been largely incomprehensible and futile anyway; her swift convenient demise leaves no real gap in the novel, while it frees Pierre. But when other characters, introduced with the same deliberateness and focused meaningfully for a while, as Vera is, or even developed at some length through most of the book, like Dólokhov, are abruptly dispensed with, we are simply cheated without even the dubious rewards of plot movement. There is an old rule in fiction as well as hunting about not starting a hare, but Tolstoi is clearly pulled off the track by too much else in the book to proceed fully with what he has voluntarily begun on a number of plot lines. And so, even at his imaginative best, in plot, Tolstoi cannot help frustrating us. He wishes that we forget people and relationships he has virtually set up for our subsequent and long-termed concern, hoping perhaps that sheer size and manifoldness will help him. Unfortunately, scale depends somewhat on completion as well as inconclusiveness, and Tolstoi's primary ambition at epic background is consistently flawed by this wishful strategy of elision and forgetfulness.

In all these structural ways the varied sins of commission and omission combine to riddle if not unravel the long book. These are technical failings, the most obvious and injudicious kind, but they lead us on to deeper failures of content, which we have glimpsed through the technique but which we must consider next in their own right.

The quality of Tolstoi's sentimental optimism or humanitarianism looms at once. Monumental and doctrinaire, it is not a willed insensitivity to experience but a desperate concealment of nihilistic doubt.

> Pierre's insanity consisted in not waiting, as he used to, to discover personal attributes which he termed "good qualities" in people before loving them; his heart was now overflowing with love, and by loving people without cause he discovered indubitable causes for loving them.

This sanctification of people-in-general is romantic rather than authentic Christianity and represents a sentimental dismissal of good and sound reasons to love. It is suspect not only because it is a romantically *easy* attitude, but because it suggests, in its desperate generality, a wholesale overcoming of exactly opposite values, namely, misanthropy and nihilism. A fundamentally simplistic national consciousness must go either one whole way or to the direct extreme. Lest we find no one in a turbulent, huge society deserving our love, we love everybody. Never mind that the loving is suspect because it lacks a commensurate object, it is a necessary delusion at an early stage of culture.

Tolstoi writes precisely as a typical unformed Russian, not as someone who has transcended his own national character. He does not see the vacuity of the formula. Even in the terms of his story, what evidence is there at all for the potency of his conviction, for the power of the ideal of loving-kindness? Platón remains a kind of passionate human nullity, and Pierre is really in danger of being killed by Nicholas himself if he persists in his fanciful revolutionary ideas. The world is not converted, by Tolstoi's own narrative admission, to anything but despair and contempt by such compulsive and fundamentally self-serving visionariness as Pierre's. ''Insane'' was the exact word for Tolstoi to use, more accurate than ironic, in finally characterizing the person closest to his heart. For what we see in Tolstoi and in his surrogate is the flaunted and formulated manic side of the covertly depressive vision that characterizes his central psychology: an adolescent or barbaric manic-depression, which stigmatizes the Russians, at least of this date.

Such governing inconsiderations, as it were, like Tolstoi's sentimental and pathological humanitarianism, prompt the modern reader to reject a great deal of the thought and feeling in *War and Peace* as romantic in the worst—that is, softest—senses of the term. If it is not enough that pretentious generalizations turn into the feeblest abstractions, they also grow into outright perversities, as when Tolstoi connects up with the obsessive Russian motif of suffering.

> Harder and more blessed than all else is to love this
> life in one's sufferings, in innocent sufferings.

The concept is an enthusiast's principle, of a piece with the romantic asceticism and self-punishment running throughout the novel and rationalized by the easiest kind of sublime Christian mysticism. We ordinarily love life *despite* our sufferings, not *in* them, lest we fall victim, even in Christian terms, to masochistic pride. Tolstoi's reasoning is perverted, functioning only to authorize Pierre's final position of soft stoicism, which is more a species of self-gratification than it is of profound philosophy. Emotion is neither derived from thought nor allied with it but substituted for it. (pp. 117-20)

The mysticism and the sentimentalism in the novel comprise an especially bare and barren romanticism that crucially dispenses with any objective correlative.

> ''Yes—love,'' he thought again quite clearly. ''But
> not love which loves for something, for some quality,
> for some purpose, or for some reason, but . . . that
> feeling of love which is the very essence of the soul
> and does not require an object. . . .''

What is the true source of such desperate wilfulness in a man with a big enough mind, after all, to have undertaken the enterprise Tolstoi attempts? I contend that it is not an inherent superficiality that holds Tolstoi from a genuine confrontation of experience but an unholy fear of existential absurdity. Now and then Pierre, for instance, is indeed stricken by terror, when the writing turns invariably more particular and forceful than it ever is in the more usual visionary passages of *War and Peace.*

> To Pierre all men seemed like those soldiers, seeking
> refuge . . . some in ambition, some in cards, some
> in framing laws, some in women, some in toys, some
> in horses, some in politics, some in sport, some in
> wine, and some in governmental affairs. ''Nothing
> is trivial, and nothing is important, it's all the same—
> only to save oneself from it as best one can,'' thought
> Pierre. ''Only not to see *it,* that dreadful *it!*''

But instead of such moments becoming the basis of a true plumbing of absurdity and despair, they record only Tolstoi's merest glance over the brink, after which he beats a fearful retreat to concepts of sentimental religiosity, mystical nationalism, and generalized love. To ''save oneself from it as best one can'' means, for Tolstoi, to combine attitudes of soft romanticism and orthodoxy so that the combination will protect him and perhaps prevent him from ever seeing ''it'' again. More than anything else, he lacked the interior courage of his countryman Dostoyevski, that brave will, above all, to look steadily down. I believe that he lacked this essential quality of greatness, that it was fearfulness that headed off greatness in him rather than superficiality that withheld him from it, and that the second weakness derived from the first instead of the other way around.

What we have in *War and Peace* is a presiding contrast: between apparently uncompromising ambition, on one side, and severely compromised thought and deflected will, on the other. There follows a whole series of contradictions that all but destroy the tissue as well as heart of the work.

Most glaring among several book-long contradictions of primary themes is Tolstoi's failure to reconcile the doctrine of pre-determinism with the manifest workings of chance in his novel. He never accords his devout belief that large predetermining forces maneuver for the total good with his frequent view of universal and human chaos or, at the least, of a chancey multitudinous reality which the helpless individual cannot ever fathom, no less control, for his own best interest. Indeed, the latter vision is what is represented so well by warfare and is what led him, after all, to treat the great campaign in Russia as a supremely allegorical and even mythic symbol for human ignorance and powerlessness. In this latter deflationary mood, he is at particular pains to denigrate not only Napoleon, of course, but also Tsar Alexander somewhat—in fact, all figureheads who think they really are directive leaders. No single person, even an emperor, could conceivably direct titanic historical forces; accordingly, Tolstoi sets himself firmly against hero worship, attacking the falsehood of the idea of leadership and attacking specific leaders themselves as either conscious or unconscious impostors. But then again Tolstoi requires a certain number of distinctive human vessels through whom some Divine plan is relentlessly manifesting itself anyhow. They are epitomized in Commander-in-Chief Kutúzov, who can instinctively surrender himself to the great determining forces of History and God. These Kutúzovs paradoxically become invincible great men, not without their own kind of heroic self-denial! The high are brought low, it is true, but a certain percentage of humble persons become the patient, true heroes of historico-religious determinism. The grounds of greatness have been shifted, but the question has not been overturned. Nevertheless Tolstoi and his fervent critics deceive themselves into thinking he has resolved his contradiction into a successful paradox.

Furthermore, while making the case for self-abnegation, Tolstoi also manages to plead for individual moral responsibility. Each of us, although inevitably failing to perceive the whole design of his life and the historical flow of which it is part, must nevertheless act positively and hopefully, placing his will in accord with—what he does not quite know. This is a shade closer to an apparent than to a real and necessary contradiction, but Tolstoi succeeds in making it real. That is because, when he gets right down to things, he portrays the difficulties of coming into one's own as almost overwhelming. For instance, he shows how hard it is to know one's own true taste or most ordinary opinions, as on a harmless enough subject like the opera. The one fine psychological chapter in the novel (Book VIII, Chapter 9)—on the insidious corruption of Natásha's honest reactions to extravagant opera by prevailing public snobbery, the intimidation she suffers from pseudo-sophisticated people around her until she can not be sure of what her real opinions were or are anymore—is Tolstoi's indubitable triumph of subtlety in *War and Peace*. It is also his prime indication of how practically impossible it is to exercise one's autonomy in life. If that is true in the merely social world, then how much less weight must our helpless individualism and tentative responsibility carry in the moral realm? The question is left hanging.

Other matters also become questions that should have been given at least provisional answers. The relation of stoicism and kindness is left completely blurred, for example, especially as the issue is centered in Pierre. What are we to make of Pierre's new-found aloofness when his friend and mentor, Platón Karatáev, dies? Instead of a brave compassion, which Tolstoi has been heading for as a principal theme, Pierre shows the stoniest callousness. His queer indifference is more schizoid than stoical, a pathological *naif's* interpretation of the philosophy of sublime dis-engagement. In a modern view, the character is unable to distinguish self-control from insensitivity.

> Karatáev was still sitting at the side of the road under the birch tree and two Frenchmen were talking over his head. Pierre did not look around again but went limping over the hill.
>
> From behind, where Karatáev had been sitting, came the sound of a shot. Pierre heard it plainly, but at that moment he remembered that he had not yet finished reckoning up how many stages still remained to Smolensk.... And again he started reckoning....
>
> Behind him, where Karatáev had been sitting, the dog began to howl. "What a stupid beast! Why is it howling?" thought Pierre.

Platón's dog is howling because Platón has just been summarily executed, and Pierre knows it. He has not risen above such knowledge, he has refused to face it. But at this point in the story Tolstoi has been taking pains to characterize Pierre as a strong and stolid man now, not dazed or traumatized. Tolstoi, however, can not gauge his effect accurately and presents an evasive and even cowardly character instead of a transcendant figure. We are left with one of the most flagrant perplexities and downright contradictions in the course of the book.

As Pierre marches on figuratively as well as literally into a supposedly climactic state of beatification, he actually sinks deeper into the nirvana of Russian self-annihilation. Fortunately, however, events are stronger than theme—or the theme Tolstoi does not grasp is stronger than the one he wishes to impose on his materials—and Pierre is forced back from visionary passivity to the world of committed action. Then we see, after his marriage and family life with Natásha, that all along Tolstoi had been intending him for a progressively experiential and participative life—from the very first youthful dissipations, through the period of his strenuous allegiance to the Masons, the activist attempt to murder Napoleon, his military capture and rescue, up to his wedding to Natásha. Therefore, the ascetic impulse has been a false lead. Neither the formalized mysticism of the Masons nor the supposed revelations of Platón Karatáev were meant to be truly culminative

in Pierre's story; or, if they were so designed, the rest of his career, including the end Tolstoi insists upon, is not in any real degree coherent with the quiescent state toward which he—with Tolstoi—essentially yearns. The deepest characterization of Pierre is actually that of the dissociated sensibility, which is a perfectly legitimate state of mind to present if the author recognizes it, but he does not. Tolstoi's understanding turns out to be just as unintegrated as Pierre's character. It could not have been otherwise.

Tolstoi did not get unified perspective on Pierre because he could not achieve an over-view of himself, not even a partially objective view of his own philosophic ideals and of the social situation that conditioned them. And that is why he is led to his own towering spiritual perversities. Thus, we know, the long exemplary story told by Platón Karatáev—about the innocent merchant who is wrongly sent to exile and is in later life exonerated, only to be found dead just as the Tsar's order of pardon and apology arrives—moved Tolstoi himself powerfully. He was overwhelmed by this kind of parabolic sentimental fundamentalism, which confounded right and wrong, injustice and mercy in wonderful, simple bafflement. The ways of God to man are more awesome in proportion as they even exceed the story of Job, which at least ends happily, and are just as wicked as they are unreasonable and ineffable. But there is really more of man than of God in the upshot of the modern parable—the Tolstoian and Russian yearning for total moral annihilation. One may guess at least the social motive behind Tolstoi's worshipful acceptance of the abstract, puritanical guilt embodied in the exemplum—the landed aristocrat's spiritual payment for the injustice of serfdom and all the rest. One only regrets that the author himself did not finally see as much and free himself from perverse abstraction as well as superficiality in his "highest" thinking. Rising to such perspective and freedom is what great and exceptional writers are for.

Mostly it is this strategy of pretense rather than real depth-analysis, that puts us off almost all Tolstoi's themes. He does not wish to penetrate the messianic impulse or compulsive Goodness that obsesses many of his leading characters. It rarely if ever occurs to this admiring Russian student of Shakespeare that whole peoples, even one's own, can and do "protest too much." Therefore, he accepts at face value those wandering religious self-mortifiers who regularly stop at Princess Mary's, those obviously neurotic "God's Folk" whose excessive devotion has at least an equal part of anarchic atheism under it. But Tolstoi will not confront the possibility, no less probe it. Once in the long novel (Book IX, Ch. 10) the swift explicit truth about the Russians' sense of futility and nihilism lurking under their compensatory fanaticism emerges, but this happens in practical despite of Tolstoi and never recurs even as an aside, let alone as a motif.

> An Italian is self-assured because he is excitable and easily forgets himself and other people. A Russian is self-assured just because he knows nothing and does not want to know anything, since he does not believe that anything can be known.

Tolstoi is almost constitutionally set against recognizing the force of the negative, though it is to his credit here that at least once the hidden national alter ego comes through and that once or twice, subliminally, a dramatic notation on the evil of serfdom underlying the whole aristocratic Tsarist system or the venality of the favored upper class escapes from his pen also. He cannot totally avoid limning the age's prodigality and oppression in a brief sequence during the famous borzoi hunt:

In the middle of a sober conversation begun by Ilágin about the year's harvest, Nicholas pointed to the red-spotted bitch.

"A fine little bitch, that!" said he in a careless tone. "Is she swift?"

"That one? Yes, she's a good dog, gets what she's after," answered Ilagin indifferently, of the red-spotted bitch Ezra, for which, a year before, he had given a neighbor three families of house serfs. "So, in your parts, too, the harvest is nothing to boast of, Count? . . ."

But Tolstoi cannot and will not proceed along these lines—if, indeed, he actually knows he has struck them. All this would be of less importance, though never devoid of significance, if he did not make the constant pretense of probing Russian and European personality throughout the book. Since he is trying to convince us that his novel is a work of profound interpretation as well as spectacle and human drama, his evasions and gingerliness are all the graver—though it is never hypocrisy but superlative weakness in him that is condemnable.

In addition, Tolstoi's effect often is one of fumbled as well as superficial theme. It has to do with what we have noted in other connections, a certain near-paradoxicality that remains suspended in a state of contradictoriness because Tolstoi simply does not push a potential theme to resolution. For example, opposed to the favored doctrine of self-abnegation is another doctrine he nods to, the possibility of healthily enjoying life. The thought even strikes self-effacing Princess Mary, for whom

listening to Natásha's tales of childhood and early youth, there also opened out a new and hitherto uncomprehended side of life: belief in life and its enjoyment.

Perhaps Tolstoi will here thrust us forward and, as a master writer, modify the former doctrine with the other to give us genuinely transcendant new thematic formulation. But he fumbles the potent reconciliatory theme, though it is there, not far from grasp, for a braver man to have seized and elucidated.

Similar to Tolstoi's failure to reconcile contrasting themes is his failure to unify closely related themes in his book. Certain of his parallel ideas go right on to a theoretical infinity without his ever troubling to bring them together in creative nexus. One of these themes is the virtue of naturalness in character. That is supposed to be the big thing about Pierre and about Natásha and also about Andrew and even Mary and about subsidiary favorites like Denisov; it is meant to be their principal recommendation as protagonists and human beings. On another level of narrative the power of Nature itself informs and even governs the action: Nature, especially as land and weather (winter in particular), is the supra-human antagonist of Napoleon, history's grandest artificer and upstart. We wait for the eventual thematic merging of the two ideas, which we guess are basically one, but the convergence is never made either ideologically or structurally. Is it too much to ask of a great author to detect the potentialities of his closest themes? Is he not responsible for imaginatively fusing and perhaps developing the intellectual and narrative consequences of two great positive ideas like naturalness of character and the role of Nature in men's affairs, especially since he has pointed them for us? But they remain thematic possibilities rather than actualities for him, impotent observations rather than a centered artistic realization that would bestow instead of dissipate energy. No great figure in the world of science or music who failed in this way would have a reputation for excellence, no

less greatness. Why should we celebrate such failure of development in the history of fiction? (pp. 121-28)

I conclude by judging that *War and Peace* does not work. Its big-canvas effect is a much too self-conscious and finally strained technic; its ambitiousness degenerates over and over again to simple, courageless pretense; its details of plot are overly and incessantly contrived; its psychological studies are equally manipulated, superficial and unconvincing at the last; its themes are structurally undeveloped and largely unintegrated; and its general soap-operatics are overflowing. It does not work. *Anna Karenina* does work and holds up through the years—I shall not add my cube of ice to the Cold War by contending that the compact *Scarlet Letter* is still better in its way—but *War and Peace* does not stand the test of time. (p. 135)

*Jesse Bier, "A Century of 'War and Peace'—Gone, Gone with the Wind," in* Genre, *Vol. IV, No. 2, June, 1971, pp. 107-41.*

**ELIZABETH GUNN**  (essay date 1971)

[*Gunn is an English poet, novelist, and critic. In the following excerpt from her study* A Daring Coiffeur: Reflections on Tolstoy's "War and Peace" and "Anna Karenina," *Gunn examines the issues of age and sexuality in* War and Peace.]

I am not [sure I agree with the many readers who consider Natasha the most captivating character in *War and Peace*]. I am not at all sure, that is, that Tolstoy is as successful with Natasha as with Nicholas. But surely, the reader objects, if only as a portrait of a child the thing is unsurpassed? Well, yes, as a child I concede Natasha to be charming. And later she is still brilliantly observed—her behaviour to Anna Dimitrievna after the Anatole Kuràgin débâcle for instance, could not be better done. But she is not, it seems to me, known, felt from inside to the same extent that Nicholas is. Perhaps this is simply because we do in fact see a great deal of her from the outside, through the eyes of other people. Through the eyes of the Countess who exclaims: "Dear, dear! Just look at her!" pointing to Natasha, who, "assuming quite the pose of a society woman," was "fanning herself and smiling over the fan"; through the eyes of the Count and of his servant Simon who admire her riding; of "Uncle" for whom she dances to the balalaika; of Nicholas in the troyka thinking: "How charming this Natasha of mine is. I have no other friend like her, and never shall have. Why should she marry? We might always drive about together"; through the eyes, even, of Helène, who at the height of her beauty, and in the midst of a crowded opera house is made by Tolstoy to glance "attentively" at Natasha.

We see her through the eyes of her lovers, Pierre and Prince Andrew. But everyone in the book loves Natasha and we too are invited to love, to fall in love with her as we are not invited to do with Nicholas. Sonia and Princess Mary may be in love with him but we are not caught up into their feelings, we do not find him romantic; we do not lose our hearts to the hero Pierre. He is patently unromantic; but nor are we in danger of falling for the more heroic Andrew. Even when we are shown Natasha from the inside we are still, we may feel, seeing her as Pierre sees her. (The scene in which half ironically she looks at herself in the glass and thinks: How charming she is that Natasha, pretty, intelligent, graceful, and her voice is excellent, and, yes, she dances too quite divinely—an episode not in itself unlikely or unconvincing, but in which it seems as if Tolstoy were expressing, were unconsciously giving expression to our sense that even when Natasha is alone we are looking on.)

The fact is we cannot without discomfort, without self-praise that is, feel ourselves in Natasha's shoes, as we do in those of Nicholas visiting Boris, for instance. It is not that Tolstoy does not understand women. No one, no woman writer even, has understood them better, as is established by *Anna Karenina,* by his action in writing a book on this subject and by his portrayal of types as different as Anna herself and Dolly. But Natasha is not a woman; she is never allowed to become one. In contrast to the voluptuous Helène, whose appearance at eighteen suggests a woman of thirty, Natasha is maintained in a state of childhood, with her arms hanging down at her sides as she sings or waits to be asked to dance. Natasha, in fact, never leaves the nursery—she is conveyed safely straight from childhood to motherhood, leaving out the bedroom in between.

"All the first impulses of the heart are pure and lofty. Actual life destroys their innocence and charm." It certainly effectually destroys Natasha's charm. But at first for a moment we are incredulous. Can this stout blowzy woman, wearing some loose garment, apparently convenient for breast-feeding, really be that Natasha, that girl who ran past Prince Andrew in the garden, whose existence, whose voice on the balcony, sufficed to awake in him "an unreasoning springtime feeling of joy and renewal"?

We flick back the pages and tot up the dates. The book starts in 1805. In 1805 Natasha was thirteen. At twenty-one, when she marries Pierre, she is still charming. In 1820 she is twenty-eight. But she looks at least forty. "Natasha," we read,

> did not follow the golden rule, advocated by clever folk, especially the French, which says that a girl should not let herself go when she marries. . . . Natasha, on the contrary, had at once abandoned all her witchery, of which her singing had been an unusually powerful part. She gave it up just because it was so powerfully seductive. She took no pains with her manners . . . or with her toilet . . . or to avoid inconveniencing her husband by being too exacting.

She is, in fact, nothing if not exigent. Not only is the way she has let herself go ". . . a habitual subject of jest to those about her," but so too is her jealousy: "She was jealous of Sonya, of the governess, of every woman pretty or plain. Pierre not only dared not flirt with, but dared not even speak smilingly to any other woman; did not dare to dine at the club as a pastime, did not dare to spend money on a whim. The general opinion was that Pierre was under his wife's thumb, which was really true."

We feel as one may feel on returning to a place—to Paris, to some *quartier* we have known, sacred to us by reason of its associations, the names of the poets and artists who have lived there, the colours of the shop fronts, its unique local flavour, its walled gardens—to find it pulled down, its streets erased, its quality gone for ever, replaced by blocks of concrete offices.

For Natasha too has gone for ever; she too has been erased. She who possessed the power to re-awaken in men like Pierre and Prince Andrew new hope, feelings they had thought dead, to bring them back to a sense of the beauty of life, of its joy and fullness, to feel this as one may hear the sound of water running again in brooks that have been frozen, or as those who have lost their hearing may feel on regaining it, and once more hearing Beethoven or Mozart—this Natasha is lost to us. In place of her we now have a Natasha, the reverse of her former

self, a creature wholly occupied with mundane considerations in whom life is reduced to its most basic function, the reproduction of beings who will reproduce themselves, a woman still young, who, the wife of a rich man, can think of nothing better than kopecks and babies' napkins, whose behaviour is devoid of grace or charm, whose existence is a denial of life, contracted to a point where it no longer seems to us worth living.

We are utterly at a loss. We recognise Princess Mary; Nicholas is a coherent character; Pierre is unchanged. But this later Natasha seems to us a wholly arbitrary choice on Tolstoy's part. She might equally well, it seems to us, have turned out quite differently, have filled any one of a dozen different roles. For Natasha, yes, we realise it now (this was her charm), was capable, as Princess Mary was not, of transformation. Hers was the rainbow, chameleon receptivity of youth. Most women are formed by their husbands. And particularly one would have thought, would this be so with Natasha, the wife of a man so much older than herself. If Pierre was in some ways weak he would have been strengthened by marriage. What might not have been made of a Natasha with her quickness, her sensitivity, her capacity for pleasure, her high spirits subdued by her long sadness, a Natasha in love . . .?

But our speculations, our musings are cut short. It dawns on us that Tolstoy is not deploring but actually recommending what seems to us so monstrous. If, for the first few horrified moments we took him to be ironic, to be giving us a dose of reality, to be saying grimly "This, you see, is what happens to your Natashas," we quickly recognise that we are wrong. The tone is not ironic but paradoxical. It is clear that he intends to shock; that he is at his most difficult, in his most perverse mood. Not only does he anticipate our reaction. He is bent on provoking it. The antipathy he feels for us at this moment is, we perceive with amusement, quite equal to the antipathy he feels for historians.

Well, we, at least, can smugly decline to descend to his level. We are sweetly determined to be reasonable. Our impressions, moreover, of what we have read are, we must admit, confused; we feel as if we had been hit on the head with a truncheon. No doubt we have misunderstood. We had better go back. And back we totter, still suffering from shock, still secretly hoping, believing that it will all be different, that we cannot really have seen what we thought we saw—Natasha come striding dishevelled from the nursery in her dressing-gown and with joyful face "show us a yellow instead of a green stain on baby's napkin."

Dutifully then we turn back and force ourselves to swallow the description of the figure "stouter and broader" of this "handsome fertile woman," in whom it is hard "to recognise the slim lively Natasha of former days." We struggle on. But no—it really is too much—here she is at it again with the napkin. We put the book aside and this time we do not muse. Staring blankly before us we ask—"Why?"

The answer, the clue to the early as well as the later Natasha is to be found where we least think of looking for it, in the declaration that sexual love "is something abominable, swinish, which it is horrid and shameful to remember"; that "it is not for nothing that nature has made it disgusting and shameful." These words occur in the *Kreutzer Sonata,* a short book written some twenty years after *War and Peace.*

But I will perhaps make myself clearer if I append one further passage describing the change in Natasha on her marriage.

"To fluff out her curls, put on fashionable dresses, and sing romantic songs to fascinate her husband would have seemed as strange as to adorn herself to attract herself. To adorn herself for others might perhaps have been agreeable—she did not know—but she had no time at all for it. The chief reason for devoting no time either to singing, to dress, or to choosing her words, was that she really had not time to spare for those things.''

It is with something of a shock, the shock of recognition, that we come on this passage in the *Kreutzer Sonata.*

> You see it is only we men who don't know . . . what women know very well, that the most exalted poetic love depends not on moral qualities, but on physical nearness, and on the coiffeur, and on the colour and cut of the dress. Ask an expert coquette who has set herself the task of captivating a man, which she would prefer to risk: to be convicted in his presence of lying, of cruelty, or even dissoluteness, or to appear before him in an ugly or badly made dress—she will always prefer the first. . . .
>
> A woman . . . knows very well that *all the talk about elevated subjects* [my italics] is just talk, but that what a man wants is her body and all that presents it in the most deceptive but alluring light. . . . You say that the women of our society have other interests in life than prostitutes have, but I say no, and will prove it. If people differ in the aims of their lives, by the inner content of their lives, this difference will necessarily be reflected in externals and their externals will be different. But look at those unfortunate despised women and at the highest society ladies: the same costumes, the same fashions, the same perfumes, the same exposure of arms, shoulders and breasts, the same tight skirts over prominent bustles, the same passion for stones, for costly glittering objects, the same amusements, dances, music and singing. As the former employ all means to allure, so do these others.

We no longer ask why Natasha has "abandoned all her witchery." It would place her on a par with a prostitute.

The clue to the child, the girl Natasha, as well as to Pierre's wife, lies, I have said, where we least expect to find it, in the violence of Tolstoy's sexual drives and in the no less violent disgust these aroused in him, a disgust which comes to extend not merely to his own behaviour but to sex itself:

" 'Love? Love is an exclusive preference for one person over everybody else' said the lady.''

" 'Preference for how long? A month, two days, or half an hour?' said the grey-haired man and began to laugh.''

" 'Everyman,' he insisted, 'experiences what you call love for every pretty woman'.''

The fact that after his marriage, he could desire other women, that desire could exist unaccompanied by love, never ceased to revolt Tolstoy.

"It is not merely this impossibility [of exclusive love], but the inevitable satiety. To love one person for a whole lifetime is like saying that one candle will burn a whole life.''

This statement is qualified. It is not that constancy is, in itself, impossible, but that it is made so by debauchery, by the promiscuity regarded as natural for men before marriage.

Thus "I began,'' said the grey-haired man, "to indulge in debauchery as I began to drink and smoke. . . . I had become

what is called a libertine. To be a libertine is a physical condition, like that of a morphinist, a drunkard or a smoker. As a morphinist, a drunkard, or a smoker is no longer normal, so too a man who has known several women for his pleasure is no longer normal, but is a man perverted for ever, a libertine.''

He described his marriage, the honeymoon, and here there occurs one of Tolstoy's most appalling statements:

"Pleasure from smoking, just as from that, if it comes at all, comes later. The husband must cultivate that vice in his wife in order to derive pleasure from it.''

The violence of his sexual urges made Tolstoy fanatical. It is their force that creates the puritan. Not only must men, no less than women, be virgins when they marry, even when married they may not sleep with their wives when they are pregnant or breast-feeding (and his insistence that mothers must breast-feed their children, and not employ wet-nurses, as was the custom in Russia, comes itself to seem like flagellation).

But to return briefly to the text of the *Kreutzer Sonata* at the point where we abandoned it:

" 'Why vice?' I said, 'you are speaking of the most natural human functions.'

" 'Natural?' he said, 'Natural? No, I may tell you that I have come to the conclusion that it is, on the contrary, *un*natural. Yes, quite *un*natural. Ask a child, ask an unperverted girl. . . . It is natural to eat, and to eat is, from the very beginning, enjoyable, easy, pleasant and not shameful; but this is horrid, shameful and painful. . . . And an unspoilt girl, as I have convinced myself, always hates it'.''

It is common practice to regard *War and Peace* as literature and the *Kreutzer Sonata* as a tract. The latter, however, still shocks us. What must its impact have been when it was written? Today it is the tone, less than the matter which shocks, the violence, the unbalance, the desperation.

"But permit me,'' says the lawyer in the *Kreutzer Sonata,* "Facts contradict you . . . many people honourably live long married lives. . . .''

The grey-haired man again laughs. Husbands and wives merely deceive people. They pretend to be monogomists while living polygamously. "That is bad, but still bearable. But when, as most frequently happens, the husband and wife have undertaken the external duty of living together all their lives and begin to hate each other after a month, and wish to part but still continue to live together, it leads to that terrible hell which makes people take to drink, shoot themselves and kill or poison themselves or one another. . . .''

This is a far cry—could one imagine anything further from the tone of *War and Peace?* No wonder the two works are placed in different categories: on the one hand a crackpot sociological outburst—the hysteria, if you like, of a man who has admittedly suffered much in his own domestic life—and on the other the Rostov household. The two things are poles apart.

To my mind they are inseparably connected.

But turning away from Natasha herself, let us look for a moment more closely at her parents, the old Rostovs.

For the first thing that strikes us about them is their antiquity. Countess Rostova married at sixteen. At the start of the book her oldest child Vera is seventeen. Thus the Countess could be thirty-four. Tolstoy makes her older. She is forty-five and worn out with child-bearing; she has borne the Count twelve children of whom four survive. Somehow this fact fails to register, partly perhaps because we are told it too early and too baldly—it comes in our introduction to the Countess, in whom, since we do not yet know her, we feel little interest. But also because our interest is never aroused. For some reason what we are told does not make us sympathetic. It makes us feel that the Countess is a bore.

And it may seem to us that we were right. After some thirteen hundred-odd pages we may feel that we know her little better. And this feeling is doubtless confirmed by our final view of her, irritably playing patience with her companion; by the fact "that she ate, drank, slept and kept awake but did not live," that "life gave her no new impressions." We show her little mercy. If old people are bored or boring they have only themselves to blame. Our harshness may even prompt us to reflect that Tolstoy himself is somewhat harsh in his summary treatment of her.The point, surely, is not that she has *had* twelve children but that out of twelve, eight have died; that the Countess has lived in constant torment. At the time when we come on the scene moreover, Petya is only nine. The Countess's terror when anyone fell ill, the sad time this family has lived through is still recent history. How is it that we find no trace of it? That the shadow which must have darkened the early lives of Nicholas and Natasha is, quite literally, never mentioned?

But wait, no, there is one reference. How was it we overlooked it? It occurs some eight pages on.

> "How plainly all these young people wear their hearts on their sleeves," said Anna Mikhaylovna, pointing to Nicholas as he went out. "*Cousinage—dangereux voisinage*" she added.
>
> "Yes," said the Countess when the brightness these young people had brought into the room had vanished; and as if answering a question which no one had put to her, but which was always on her mind, "and how much suffering, how much anxiety one has had to go through that one might rejoice in them now. And yet really the anxiety is greater now than the joy. One is always, always anxious! Especially just at this age, so dangerous both for girls and boys."

But even here, in this passage, this reference is oblique. The Countess is not so much bemoaning past sorrows, as complaining that things get worse and not better as time goes on. It does not so much remind us of what she has gone through, as have the effect of minimising, making light of this. We do not so much recall as forget her sufferings, which she now replaces with ordinary anxiety, anxiety as common to parents as it is useless. Fresh from our first encounter with the Rostov family, dazzled, intrigued as if in an aviary by our glimpses of all these gay, darting, youthful figures, intoxicated by the air we breathe, that sunlit, buoyant, crystalline air peculiar to the household, the Countess's *douleurs* seem oddly mal à propos.

Tolstoy tells us that she is "languid" and that this gives her an "air of distinction." But if the rate of infant mortality was high, if the Countess's plight is common, this does not make it less painful, less strange that when she confides in an old friend: "Ah, my dear, my life is not all roses either . . ." what she is referring to is money.

It is true that the old Count is feckless and that this comes home to roost. But even the fact that the Rostovs lose their money is, one feels, itself a commendation in Tolstoy's eyes,

part and parcel of their unworldliness, of the old Count's lack of self-interest, of his trusting childlike nature, the penalty rather of virtue than of vice; the penalty of living life as it should be lived, as it is lived in that charming Rostov household, in that simple, lively, unpretentious childhood paradise. . . . And despite the fact that we get to know them in Moscow we do, in fact, if we think of the Rostovs, tend to picture a garden, an unspoilt, overgrown garden in early June, a garden of tangled paths, high with cow-parsley, adazzle with apple-blossom and gay with birds—with children's voices that echo and die, muffled, extinguished like tapers in the tomb-like salons and ante-chambers of the world where old Count Bezhukov lies dying, where Prince Vasili waits, where ambition and corruption dwell.

But how old is Prince Vasili? He is "near sixty." But once again this fact makes no impression. Elegant, urbane, the Prince is the typical courtier; as far as we are concerned he is ageless. His children are all grown up. They are older than the Rostovs. And yet the Prince is never "The old Prince"—whereas Count Rostov is seldom referred to except as "The old Count."

But then the Prince would never "waddle in" to his wife's bedroom with the *sauté de madère* he has been tasting spilt down the front of his evening waistcoat (and which the Countess proceeds to scrub off with her cambric handkerchief).

To suggest that the appellation is one used in the household to distinguish Count Rostov from his sons, as English servants might speak of "The Master" will not do (Prince Vasili has himself two sons). In this case Count Rostov would be known simply as "The Count" and his sons as the young Counts, Count Nicholas and Count Petya.

But how old exactly is the Count, fifty-nine or sixty? On the occasion when he dances the Daniel Cooper, he is expressly referred to as "the amiable old gentleman." This description seems odd for fifty-nine. And he may, of course, be older. But although the performance clearly is an occasion, although everyone stands around to watch and admire the Count's agility, no one seems to think he will have a stroke.

The fact is, if we think about it, that old people are older in the Rostov household than outside it. There they are background figures. Their lives are already over. It is the children whom we, the reader, come to see. This does not strike us as odd as it must do in life were we to visit the houses of people we know not for the sake of the parents, our contemporaries, but for the sake of the children in the school room. The presence of children does not place their parents on the retired list. But let us return to Countess Rostova's drawing-room and listen again, and this time for a little while longer, to the conversation taking place there:

> "One is always, *always* anxious," says the Countess. "Especially at this age, so dangerous, both for girls and boys."
>
> "It all depends on the bringing up," remarked the visitor.
>
> "Yes, you're quite right," continued the Countess. "Till now I have always, thank God, been my children's friend and had their full confidence," said she, repeating the mistake of so many parents who imagine that their children have no secrets from them: "I know I shall always be my daughter's first confidante, and that if Nicholas with his impulsive nature does get into mischief (a boy can't help it) he will

all the same never be like all those Peterbourg young men.''

"Yes, they are splendid, splendid youngsters,'' chimed in the Count, who always solved questions that seemed to him perplexing by deciding that everything was splendid. ''Just fancy: wants to be a hussar. What's one to do, my dear?''

"What a charming creature your younger girl is,'' said the visitor, ''a little volcano!''

"Yes, a regular volcano,'' said the Count, ''Takes after me. And what a voice she has, though she's my daughter I tell the truth when I say she'll be a second Salomoni.''

It is easy to open *War and Peace* and come upon some passage which one has no recollection of ever reading, partly as, in this case, because our interest has flagged, because the young people have left the room, because our interest has followed them out, and partly because what the old people say is so boring, is so exactly what they would say, so that one wonders, really, why they bother to say it. We feel we can take it as read, that we have nothing to learn from it. We do not pause to reflect that our reaction, our boredom even, is itself a tribute to Tolstoy's art, to the lifelike effect he achieves.

The truth is we have entirely forgotten that we are reading. We respond to these people as we would in life. Nor do we reflect that we are ourselves no longer children. For what we have here is again the child's view, not merely that child's unaffectedness and honesty that Tolstoy strove for in himself and in his style, but the child's view of adults as boring. This is a new note. We are not asked to take these people seriously, to treat their problems as on a par with those of a Pierre or Natasha. The Countess's anxiety is stereotyped. If, indeed, Tolstoy struck us as somewhat harsh in his summary treatment of Countess Rostova, may it not be that there is an element of the child's dispassionate cruelty in his attitude? Or is it merely that it is safer, as children themselves find it safer, to dispose of adults in this way?

The answer, as I have said, lies in the *Kreutzer Sonata*. In Tolstoy the cult of the child's view of life, his open preference for children, implies, it must be faced, a rejection of the adult world.

What is the main distinction between adults and children? The dividing line is puberty, the fundamental distinction the procreative function. We cannot but feel the antiquity of the parents as central to Tolstoy's idyll, to the happiness he depicts in the Rostov household. Why do the Count and Countess not ''hate each other''? Why do they not inhabit ''that terrible hell which makes people take to drink, shoot themselves and kill or poison themselves or one another''? Because we are kept at a distance, because they are background figures, because we are not allowed to come too close, to see too much, are not invited to take them seriously. Because the Count is always ''the old Count,'' i.e., because the parents resemble grandparents—they are safely out of the sphere of sexual relations. (pp. 22-38)

> Elizabeth Gunn, ''On 'War and Peace','' in her A Daring Coiffeur: Reflections on ''War and Peace'' and ''Anna Karenina,'' *Chatto and Windus Ltd., 1971, pp. 3-88.*

**ANGUS CALDER**   (essay date 1976)

[*Calder is an English historian and critic. In the following excerpt, he analyzes theme and technique in* War and Peace.]

"It is not a novel,'' Tolstoy wrote, ''even less is it a poem, and still less an historical chronicle. *War and Peace* is what the author wished and was able to express in the form in which it is expressed.'' To Western critics this book and its successor *Anna Karenina* tended to seem formless, if remarkable, productions. (pp. 151-52)

But no one would now seriously suggest that *War and Peace* is not a novel. Tolstoy's achievement, gradually recognized, was to widen the category of the ''novel'' and to establish its capacity to handle every conceivable kind of material with an even unhurried verisimilitude and without Dickensian cranking and creaking of ''plot'' or the kind of neat ''poetic'' finality in which Turgenev specialized. It has been the task of much recent criticism to show that what seemed even to such a distinguished reader as James only a ''loose and baggy monster'' [see excerpt dated 1908] is in fact organized on its own formal principles, both subtle and massive. These can be exposed as we try to find words to define the book as a whole. ''Epic'' is one well-known candidate.

There is no doubt whatever that Tolstoy idealizes his own class and its role in 1812. Of the well-known horrors of social life in Russia at that time—the knouting and sale of serfs, the bedbugs and intellectual backwardness—*War and Peace* contains no trace. Tolstoy's amazing ''authority'' over the history he relates should be wondered at with one ear open to John Bayley's comment that ''Russia belonged to Tolstoy because Russia belonged, literally, to his class.'' In the end he makes Nikolai Rostov—his own father as he ought to have been— into a model Russian landowner, who farms on traditional lines, studies his peasants, banishes the lazy and dissolute ones, and earns gratitude and respect. ''. . . And long after he was dead and gone the peasantry cherished a pious memory of his rule. 'He was a proper master'. . . .''

But if the book draws our attention longest to aristocrats of the best type, we find in it also many representatives of corrupt and frivolous noblemen and women. Against them, Tolstoy poises not only his unconvincing Karataev, but also Tushin, a little captain; that delightful declassed nobleman called ''Uncle''; and that truly complete huntsman, the peasant Danilo. None of his other characters have fuller approval from him. They pull the moral centre in the novel towards the centre of Russian society. They are little, irrelevant folk from the point of view of the high command or of high society, but it is their national culture which Natasha expresses when at Uncle's she dances, Countess though she is, just like a peasant woman. Andrei admires Tushin, Pierre is influenced by Karataev, the young Rostovs adore ''Uncle'' and the old Count lets Danilo, his own serf, reprimand him for incompetence on the hunting field. Tolstoy's favourite aristocratic characters are, in fact, idealized as men and women who are in tune with the little people and can understand what the brittle Petersburg set ignore and sneer at.

So it may seem to make sense to call *War and Peace* a ''national epic.'' In many ways, it recalls the techniques of Homer. Stock epithets and recurrent details—Maria's ''heavy tread,'' Napoleon's ''white hands''—suggest the methods of the *Iliad*, and we know that Tolstoy himself told Gorky ''without false modesty, *War and Peace* is like the *Iliad*.'' George Steiner develops the point strongly:

> . . . There lies behind the literary techniques of the *Iliad* and of Tolstoy a comparable belief in the centrality of the human personage and in the enduring beauty of the natural world. In the case of *War and*

*Peace* the analogy is even more decisive; where the *Iliad* evokes the laws of *Moira*, Tolstoy expounds his philosophy of history. In both works the chaotic individuality of battle stands for the larger randomness in men's lives. And if we consider *War and Peace* as being, in a genuine sense, a heroic epic it is because in it, as in the *Iliad*, war is portrayed in its glitter and joyous ferocity as well as in its pathos.

But even if we acknowledge the combination of scale and intimacy in the battle scenes and the heroic extravagance of Count Rostov's prodigal banquets and wolf-hunt, the word "epic" doesn't connect with most of the novel. Pierre's intellectual self-searchings and Sonia's tremulous, calculating love for Nikolai belong to a different mode. And any word which makes Tolstoy seem to accept "the glitter and joyous ferocity of war" needs to be used with care. Petia Rostov, indeed, is full of joy when he rides with guerrillas against the French; he kills no one and is himself abruptly killed. Not one of Tolstoy's heroes is permitted to kill a man in our presence, not even the bellicose Nikolai. Andrei is twice wounded, never the wounder. Pierre, for all his huge strength and his rages, remains a civilian and is essentially pacific in direction, though paradoxically it is he, wounding Dolokhov, who comes closest to destroying an enemy. It is Dolokhov, man of mischief and sadism, who expresses unwatered relish for killing, and he appalls even the war-like Denisov. Kutuzov, the "historical" hero of the novel is too old and unwell to fight in person and strives to avoid combat. Right at the end, the martial dream of Andrei's son collapses from joy into confusion as the menacing face of Uncle Nikolai appears in it, and the boy's waking hope of fame and glory is an ironic echo of his father's, which Andrei himself came to see as hollow. The book is on the side of the humanitarian Pierre, the defensive Kutuzov, the murdered Karataev, the domesticated Natasha and the lovingly Christian Maria; and it stands against the ambitious aggressor, Napoleon and the viciously destructive Dolokhov. There is no other way of reading it, though we cannot overlook the approval which Tolstoy, and Pierre, give to the self-sacrificing heroism of the Russians in action in *defensive* combat, or Tolstoy's appreciation of the *esprit de corps* of the hussars with whom Nikolai serves; Tolstoy, the old soldier, could not reject as worthless the courage and camaraderie which he had shared at Sevastopol.

The carnage and confusion of the battles must also be weighed against those critics who stress the "idyllic" character of the book. Elizabeth Gunn shrewdly points out that Tolstoy's setting back of his novel in the time of his grandfathers "allowed him his idyll . . . allowed him to minimize the pain of individual experience," because it secured for him a detachment which he couldn't have in relation to his own life and times. Edmund Wilson argues that *War and Peace* falls short of the highest summits of literature "because this idyllic tendency does here get the better of the author. . . ."

As Elizabeth Gunn elsewhere observes [see excerpt dated 1971], it is striking that the Countess Rostova is already forty-five and past childbearing when the novel opens. She and the still-older Count—whose child-likeness is so often stressed—are therefore "safely out of the sphere of sexual relations" and do not confront Tolstoy with the need to lay bare his profound and uncomfortable understanding of the woes that are in marriage. This is a book dominated by young people and the elder Rostovs, even the old Prince Bolkonsky, are rather like children. Whereas *Anna Karenina,* written ten years later, is involved with the boredoms and burdens and compromises of

people past their youth and overshadowed by middle age, *War and Peace* has the radiance of optimistic youth, and the first Epilogue makes the happiest ending we will find in the work of the great nineteenth-century Russian novelists.

But this idyllic quality mustn't be overstressed. It is true that at times leading characters revel in a world of fairy tale—Nikolai as he drives with the disguised and dressed up Sonia through the snow, Anatole Kuragin as he prepares to elope with Natasha, Petia on the eve of battle. But Petia is killed. Anatole is a shallow hedonist. And Nikolai doesn't marry Sonia in the end as he wants to at that time—it is a rather damning point about her that she is never freer, more lively and more beautiful than when she is hiding her "real" self in fancy dress.

In any case, Prince Andrei always dispels, when he appears, the reader's sense of easy, youthful well-being. Andrei, frustrated in and out of marriage, over-intelligent, arrogant, disillusioned, can, it is true, be related to a Romantic stereotype—the bored and remote aristocrat, fascinating to women and cruel to them. But as married man, father, officer, politician and, above all, as wounded and dying man, Andrei inhabits a real and painful "middle-aged" world. And he is very close to Tolstoy himself. Neither Pierre nor Nikolai could have composed the second Epilogue, with its drily satirical flavour, its arrogant rationalism, its aristocratic *hauteur*, but all these are qualities which we find in Andrei.

Andrei, however, seems to have no time for hunting. Tolstoy did. The novelist's own love of life in the open air is expressed above all through Nikolai. Pierre is less completely successful as a characterization than the two other heroes. We are indeed conscious with him of Tolstoy editing out of reality aspects which we would find painful and problematic. We are *told* that Pierre is an obsessive womanizer, but we are not *shown* this side of him in action, so he is left in our eyes boyish, bashful and even "innocent." But Pierre is closer than either of the others to the heroes of Tolstoy's other fiction. The "conscience-stricken nobleman," basically decent but weak-willed and ineffectual, is a type which runs from the Nekhliudov of **"A Billiard Marker's Notes"** through the narrator of *Childhood* and Olenin in *The Cossacks*, then through Pierre and into its finest shaping in Levin in *Anna Karenina*. Since all these stories are autobiographical in their tendency, we aren't likely to be wrong if we identify Pierre also with some aspects of Tolstoy himself.

If we say that Tolstoy participates equally in Andrei's contempt for the trivialities of high society, in Pierre's attraction to the peasants and family life and in Nikolai's gusto and compulsive gambling, we are emphasizing again how vast and well-analysed Tolstoy's own experience had been compared with that of most novelists. But to separate himself, as it were, into three heroes, is to clarify at the cost of simplification. Tolstoy's "wonderful mass of life" is not merely life selected—every novelist has to select—but life simplified, life tidied up. (This charge could not be made against *Anna Karenina*, where Levin's tentativeness is Tolstoy's own.) Dickens's Gothic accumulations of frightening and fantastic detail and Dostoevsky's world of furious intellectual debate force us, as Tolstoy doesn't in *War and Peace*, to question the very basis of our own notions of and about "reality." Tolstoy's glittering clarification is based on the assumption, which we habitually share, that there is a "natural" relationship between man and the inanimate world which is harmonious and "right." Rather more controversially, he in effect proposes that the "natural man" in each of us cannot be at ease or truly himself in the complex structures of the modern State, army or "society." If we accept his vision without question, it is because our thinking is still based, like his, on eighteenth-century ideas which emerged in an aristocratic social order.

*War and Peace* then is best called neither "epic" nor "idyll." It is a "realistic novel" organized so as to persuade us of the correctness of Tolstoy's own view of "reality."

Hussars are moving into battle:

> Tattered violet-grey clouds, reddening in the sunrise, were scudding before the wind. It was getting lighter every moment. The feathery grass which always grows by the roadside in the country could be seen quite plainly, still glistening from the night's rain. The drooping branches of the birch trees, wet too, swayed in the wind and tossed sparkling drops of water aslant across the highway. The soldiers' faces showed more distinctly with the passing of every minute. Rostov, with Ilin who never left him, rode along the side of the road between two rows of birch trees.

This, by Tolstoy's exceptionally high standards, is only a routine piece of description from one of the less intense passages of the novel. We might say that it evokes very well the "beauty" of early morning; but an important thing to notice is that Tolstoy himself would never use the word "beauty" in such a description. We see the landscape from the point of view of someone riding through it, enjoying its freshness, no doubt, but not thinking about its aesthetic properties. It is "naturally" witnessed and conveyed. We are, so to speak, riding along with Nikolai and noticing what he would notice.

But we aren't riding to hunt, we're riding to fight. In one of the most obviously "significant" passages of the novel, Andrei falls wounded on the field of Austerlitz. He sees, as he lies on his back, not men fighting but the sky. "How was it," he asks himself, "I did not see that sky before? And how happy I am to have found it at last! Yes, all is vanity, all is delusion, except these infinite heavens." Here the force of the contrast between "nature" and "war" is obvious. It is not made explicit when Nikolai is moving towards battle, nor, indeed, is the point identical; it is typical of Andrei that he should contrast the loftiest, purest and most empty and alien aspect of nature—the sky—with the vanity of human struggle and ambition. But in both cases we are prodded by Tolstoy to contrast "natural" harmony with "social" conflict.

Karataev and, in their different ways, Nikolai and Natasha, move in unthinking harmony with nature and illustrate how things should be. Tolstoy's assumption that the "natural" self is separable from "society" and is menaced by it (whereas the family, a smaller unit, is "natural" to us) is supported by his technique of "making strange." One aspect of it can be illustrated from the passage above. "The soldiers' faces showed more distinctly with the passing of every minute." Of course they do, we might object, it's dawn. But Tolstoy, as so often, forces us to notice what we might take for granted; he brings it before us as if it were something unusual. Simple, elemental detail, well-chosen, gives us the feeling that we *participate* in the natural world. In descriptions of "social" life detail of the same kind is often used with satiric and destructive purpose to give us the feeling that we are *alien from* the social world.

Mirsky summarizes "making strange" very well:

> It consists in never calling complex things by their accepted name, but always disintegrating a complex action or object into its indivisible components. The

method strips the world of the labels attached to it by habit and by social convention and gives it a "discivilised" appearance, as it might have appeared to Adam on the day of creation. It is easy to see that the method, while it gives unusual freshness to imaginative representation, is in essence hostile to all culture and all social form, and is psychologically akin to anarchism.

Tolstoy develops further a routine which Voltaire had habitually used for satirical purposes. He would carry the technique furthest in *Resurrection*. In *War and Peace* it has its crudest, but most memorable, expression in the scene where Natasha goes to the opera and catches the eye of Anatole Kuragin. Anatole is at home in this "artificial" atmosphere. Natasha isn't, but it takes her over and converts her "natural" sexual drive, which in Tolstoy's view should find expression in marrying and having children, into an immoral and "unnatural" lust which will make her want to have not only a fiancé, Andrei, but a lover, Anatole, as well. She is for a moment perverted by society. This is how Tolstoy describes the stage and how Natasha herself, "fresh from the country" where she has been her "natural" self, initially sees it:

> Smooth boards formed the center of the stage, at the sides stood painted canvases representing trees, and in the background was a cloth stretched over boards. In the middle of the stage sat some girls in red bodices and white petticoats. One extremely fat girl in a white silk dress was sitting apart on a low bench, to the back of which a piece of green cardboard was glued. They were all singing something.

But after the interval, when she has been introduced to Anatole, all that is happening on the stage seems "perfectly natural" to Natasha. Illusion has conquered reality.

We learn of Tolstoy's characters how they seem to others and how they are in themselves, and, especially with the heroes and heroines, the gulf is made obvious. Andrei strikes Nikolai as a stuck-up staff officer, Princess Maria is judged by others to be plain, clumsy and haughty, while her spiteful old father is widely admired. Yet Tolstoy could not be further from denying that the real self does emerge in outward appearance, if uncorrupted eyes are there to observe it. As his heroes enter the *soirée* where the novel begins, Tolstoy emphasizes Pierre's expression, which is diffident and at the same time *natural* and, by contrast, the weary, bored look in Andrei's eyes and the way he expresses his *ennui* by screwing them up. Natasha's light gait expresses her "natural" vivacity and energy and Princess Maria's blotchy blushes suggest her dogged honesty; but the nervous twitch of Prince Vasilli's cheeks when he is alone, which gives his face "an unpleasant expression such as it never had when he was in company," exposes both the nastiness within him and his success in suppressing his true, nasty self when he moves in society. It is a habit of Tolstoy's, and one which can become irritating, to emphasize small gestures which tell us more than the words which the characters use and are, indeed, often at odds with them.

A succession of details of this kind builds up each of the characters in the novel. One exception proves the general rule. Tolstoy introduces and "summarizes" Bilibin, an important minor character, rather as Turgenev or Dostoevsky would have done—we are told what sort of a person he is before we "see" and judge him in action. But what other novelist could have got away with telling us virtually nothing about the previous lives of his heroes? About Pierre's childhood and travels, Andrei's courtship of Liza, the eight little dead Rostov brothers

*Tolstoy in 1895.*

and sisters, we are given no clues around which we can even speculate. We get to know the main characters as in "real" life we get to know "real" people, by watching and listening. When we are given the added knowledge which in "real life" we can only have of ourselves, and are admitted into their thoughts, they only rarely remember things which take us beyond the facts about them which we have observed already. In "real life," people grow familiar with each other by talking about their past experiences—but Tolstoy's characters almost never reminisce. Again, he achieves wonderful clarification at the cost of simplification.

But this technique does ensure that we are never tempted to see the fate of any character as "inevitable." Turgenev's life history of Pavel Kirsanov marks the character out as one already set on a doomed course. Even with the old people in *War and Peace* we have no such sense of fatality. Everyone feels (to us) free. At any moment they may reveal wholly new facets of themselves to us as they respond to fresh experience. It is the most beguiling confidence trick in literature. For, as John Bayley points out [see excerpt dated 1966], Tolstoy has judged them all and decided their fates. "The book (he adds) is a massive feat of arbitration . . . an allotment of fates on earth as authoritative as Dante's in the world to come."

John Bayley goes a bit too far. Tolstoy's vision admits inequity. Good people, like Tushin, suffer injustice. Petia is killed when still too young to have sinned. But Tolstoy certainly judges, incessantly. The basis of Tolstoy's arbitration is, roughly speaking, this: characters who are in touch with nature and with truly Russian culture, and who are themselves "full of life," are approved of and, where possible, rewarded. Those

who "lack something" are judged harshly and "artificial" people are the targets either of broad satire, like that which Tolstoy directs at the ludicrous, scheming Berg and his bride Vera Rostova, or of a more venomous irony.

Those whom Tolstoy approves of are mostly identified with the countryside and with Moscow. Here, he says at one point, "matter" predominates, whereas in Petersburg "form is the prevailing factor." One very minor character says directly, "In Moscow, it is like being in the country." The Rostovs, Moscow people, with their unaffected vitality and rich family life, contrast with the Kuragins, Petersburg people, who are selfish, hedonistic and, in Pierre's view "depraved."

Russian "matter" stands against foreign "form." The French army is a complex, artificial creation led by Napoleon, the prophet of artificiality. German military theorists are at work in the Russian army causing disaster by their "artificial" ideas about war. True Russian-ness emerges in real community and simple natural force. Instinct defeats the schemers. Nature conquers the military machine. Justice is done in the war of 1812, just as it is when Sonia, who schemes to secure Nikolai as her husband, is denied the happiness given to Pierre and Natasha who fall, naturally and instinctively, as it were, into each other's arms.

The reader's sympathies are liable to be with Sonia and have to be carefully prised away from her. Tolstoy can't, perhaps, quite bring it off. But he works cleverly in the scene where Natasha, angrily asking "Are we a lot of wretched Germans?" prevails upon her family to abandon their possessions in Moscow and take wounded men instead, and Sonia, unable to respond to this grand human gesture, busies herself doing her best to get as much of the family property taken with them as possible.

But within Sonia, as with all the richest characterizations in the novel, we find an interesting tension between "nature" and "artificiality" which confounds, as it were, Tolstoy's own rather Napoleonic schemes. He is too honest a writer to avoid, even when he is striving hardest to clarify and simplify human life, the expression of its enigmas and paradoxes. No easy equation of the "natural" with the "good" can cope with Pierre, with Andrei, or the little princess Liza.

The finest and tensest of all the "peace" passages deal with the Bolkonskys, whose relationship to "nature" is ambivalent. The old Prince likes the country and works as a carpenter, with his hands. But he is monstrously dedicated to "routine"—a Frenchified or Germanic trait—and suppresses his natural feelings towards his daughter and son. And even the simple and affectionate Maria has moments where she displays Bolkonsky *hauteur*, while her religion is not, like Natasha's, wholly spontaneous—it is a matter of principle.

Not that Natasha herself is "simple." It is her very spontaneity and thoughtlessness which make her such an easy prey for Anatole. It is natural for children to imitate. It is also, perhaps, part of Pierre's "naturalness" that he doesn't dance at balls and keeps out of that empty glittering ritual. There is a most significant moment at the Rostov's party, very early in the novel, when little Natasha persuades Pierre to dance:

> Natasha was blissful: she was dancing with a *grown-up* man come from *abroad*. She was sitting in view of everyone and talking to him like a grown-up lady. In her hand was a fan which one of the ladies had given her to hold, and assuming quite the air of a society woman (heaven knows when and where she

had learnt it), she talked to her partner, fanning herself and smiling over the fan.

"Dear, dear! Look at her now!" exclaimed the countess as she crossed the ballroom, pointing to Natasha.

Natasha coloured and laughed.

"What do you mean, mamma? Why do you say that? It's quite natural—why shouldn't I?"

Here we can see how the vast novel holds together, how, while it seems to lack any structure, it is all structure. Tolstoy's parenthetical question is, ironically, echoed at the moment when Natasha, at Uncle's, is dancing like a peasant girl. "Where," he asks, "had she picked up that manner which the *pas de châle*, one might have supposed, would have effaced long ago?" We supply the answer without much trouble. This most delightful of all fictional children has at its most highly-developed the childish trait of imitativeness. And Natasha's own question—"It's quite natural—why shouldn't I?"—illustrates already her tendency, which is that of a spoilt child, to excuse herself glibly for doing whatever she feels like doing. This will reappear in her reasoning when she is attempting to elope with Anatole. "If," she tells herself, "I could let things go so far, it means that I fell in love with him at first sight. So he must be kind, noble and splendid, and I could not help loving him."

Anatole, who is so thoughtless and lives for the moment is, after all, rather an apt—one might say "natural"—mate for the thoughtless Natasha whose frustration during Andrei's absence has been so powerfully conveyed. The sensuality of the Kuragins can be branded "unnatural" only if Tolstoy is already anticipating his notorious argument in **The Kreutzer Sonata** that sex itself is not really "natural." He is not quite ready to be so silly yet. Hélène, furthermore, is presented as someone to whom "artificiality" comes "naturally"—she seems, like her father, perfectly "natural" in high society. For a full investigation of the paradoxes of the Kuragin "nature" we will have to wait till **Anna Karenina;** it is much like the Oblonsky "nature" which Anna shares with her brother Stiva. Meanwhile, in order to damn these people, Tolstoy has to invest them with an aura of "unnatural" depravity. Hippolyte Kuragin must flirt with Liza Bolkonskaia when she is pregnant. There must be rumours of an incestuous relationship between Anatole and his sister, though Tolstoy dropped from the finished novel the scene he wrote in draft where he is found in her bedroom holding her hand. Their mother, in her brief appearance, is accorded only one significant emotion and it is a nasty one—"she was tormented by jealousy of her daugher's happiness." Most important of all, Anatole intends to become a bigamist and Hélène refuses to have children.

At this stage Tolstoy still endorses, as "natural," sex as a way of building the monogamous family. Natasha's sexual drive can be excused because it is different from the Kuragins'. She is destined to be the perfect mother and she wants sex not purely for its own sake but so as to have children. Many readers, however, have found it easier to swallow Tolstoy's cunning extinction of Sonia—she lacks natural drive and is "by nature," as it were, an aunt rather than a mother—than his perfectly open treatment of Natasha, who, after all, when we first meet her has in her hand a doll, an imitation baby. Rebecca West accuses him of showing us Natasha "reposing in her family like a sow among its litter." And it is true that not one of all the doctrines ever espoused by Tolstoy is more unworthy of him than his insistence, at this time, that the role of women must be defined and virtually circumscribed by their function as home-makers and child-bearers.

Just as he is forced to discriminate carefully between sexuality enjoyed for its own sake and sexuality meant to produce children, so Tolstoy has to distinguish between offensive and defensive war. The reader, furthermore, must feel the rightness of Napoleon's defeat, but not rejoice over the killing of Frenchmen by Russians. At the moment when Natasha is lifted out of her painful personal griefs by a church service at which the priest reads a special prayer for victory, Tolstoy exposes an issue which is more of a problem for him than for his non-intellectual heroine:

> . . . She prayed to God with all the feeling and fervour with which her heart was overflowing, though she was not really clear what she was asking of God in the prayer. With all her soul she joined in the petition for a right spirit, for the strengthening of her heart by faith and hope and the breathing into them of love. But she could not pray that her enemies might be trampled underfoot when but a few minutes before she had been wishing she had more of them to love and pray for. Yet neither could she doubt the propriety of the prayer that was being read by the priest on his knees.

Many little touches in the novel are designed to convince us that, as Kutuzov puts it in the almost unbearably moving scene where he is shown the captured French colours, the French "are human beings too." "But," he ends up, "with all said and done, who invited them here? It serves them right, the b---b---s!" Like Kutuzov we must welcome the outcome of the war while regretting the slaughter.

Kutuzov is, we are told, "the representative of the Russian people." For Napoleon, the state is himself. Kutuzov knows that events take place irrespective of his own will. Napoleon believes that his will by itself can create events. Tolstoy's portrait of him is often deplored as a travesty. Whether this judgement is fair or not is a question which only historians could decide, and they never will decide it; any attempt to present in a novel the most controversial figure in modern history must annoy one school of thought or another. As a character in a work of fiction, Tolstoy's Napoleon is surely a complete success. He is not crudely satirized. He is given wit and talent. At Austerlitz, as the Russian army founders in the mist and Napoleon from his hill-top sees all clearly, Tolstoy admits that his calculations have been confirmed. But Napoleon's folly in venturing into Russia is beyond dispute and Tolstoy can use such a self-evident fact to undermine the idea that the high command on its eminence can decide the fate of a battle and that a great general can therefore "make" history.

Tolstoy's objections to what can be called for brevity "the Great Man Theory of History" are subtly supported in the very first scene in the novel which describes fighting—the passage recording the crossing and blowing up of the Bridge at Enns. All the main elements of his view are here. The serene beauty of nature is made to contrast with the ugliness of human combat. The handsome and cheerful Nesvitsky, a minor character, is munching a pie on the hill from which the Russian officers have a clear view of what is happening, and the General sends him down with an order that the hussars—with whom Nikolai Rostov is serving—are to cross last and set fire to the bridge. Everything seems very jolly and easy, to us and to him. But down on the bridge itself, all is confusion. Nesvitsky doesn't give the right order. And as the French fire at the bridge Nikolai, having his first taste of war, gazes at the setting sun and the waters of the Danube and wishes that he were anywhere but here, while the good-hearted Nesvitsky, seeing two men fall, exclaims, "If I were Tsar I would never make war."

What this scene has established is that war is palpably "unnatural." At Austerlitz, Andrei learns through suffering that his ambition—to be a second Napoleon—is horribly false. As he broods over his dreams of glory on the night before the battle, he hears one of the orderlies teasing Kutuzov's cook, Tit. The echo some thirty pages later is one that can't be missed. Nikolai Rostov had a much simpler dream of glory—he wanted to be of direct service to the Tsar. An almost comic little scene shows that, while Tolstoy treats Alexander with what one might call formal respect—after all, he lived in a state ruled by that monarch's nephew—his opposition to the Great Man Theory bears sharply on the Tsar as well. Alexander, sunk in despair and unable even to cross a ditch, is helped over by Captain von Toll after Nikolai, who sees this, has let his chance slip by. Later Nikolai hears a groom teasing the same cook, Tit, with the same words. Tolstoy doesn't have to comment directly on the vanity of all military ambition and its irrelevance to the lives of the common people.

In the first half of the novel, in which war goes on far from Russia and domestic life there is rarely touched by it, Tolstoy prepares us with many small touches and broad strokes for the generalizations with which he will confront us in the second half—first in long digressions, finally in his second epilogue. The "particular," his "wonderful mass of life," has been made to seem to precede the "general." In the second half, as the war of 1812 seizes and transforms the lives of all his fictional characters, Tolstoy shows us proportionately less of them and more of Kutuzov and Napoleon. "Historical" and "fictional" people alike are confronted by great and shocking events. Andrei and Petia achieve a vision of the whole of life and die, and this relates to Tolstoy's theoretical demand that we should find the laws of human history and achieve understanding of them. Others, like Kutuzov, accept these laws, which they instinctively apprehend, and bow to necessity. Only Pierre is allowed a whole vision—that given to him by Karataev—and continuing life.

Napoleon, above all, bows to necessity when he flees from Moscow. Nikolai accepts the pressure of family needs which turns him away from Sonia to marriage with Maria. Maria herself accepts her longing for physical love. Natasha accepts her necessary role as wife and mother. Pierre likewise comes to terms with himself as a family man. But again, Tolstoy's clarification serves to expose paradox and complexity. Andrei accepts, not life, but death, and the spinning shell which fascinates him and kills him "echoes" the roundness which Tolstoy so dogmatically makes the main physical characteristic of Karataev. Both in different ways suggest the roundness of the spinning world. Petia's wonderful dream of universal harmony—in which the voices of men and women blend in a march of victory with the mundane "real" sounds of sabre hissing on whetstone and the neighing of horses—takes place on the same night as Pierre's dream when a voice tells him, "Life is everything. Life is God. Everything changes and moves to and fro, and that movement is God. And while there is life there is joy in consciousness of the godhead. To love life is to love God." Pierre sees the round globe as a living thing, and a little old man explains, "in the centre is God and each drop does its best to expand so as to reflect Him to the greatest extent possible. And it grows, and is absorbed and crowded out, disappears from the surface, sinks back into the depths, and emerges again."

Pierre's dream provides a kind of consolation for the death of his namesake Petia. (Both were christened Piotr, and they relate at this point much like Dostoevskian "doubles.") Petia, like the dead Karataev, is a drop which has "overflowed and vanished." He shares, although he is dead, in the coming victory of the Russian people and in the whole of continuing life. As a Rostov he receives full vision not through ideas but through his senses—like Natasha and Nikolai he is naturally musical—whereas Pierre, the intellectual, extracts from what the wholly non-intellectual Karataev has taught him a series of abstract propositions.

The old peasant's wisdom, so much applauded by Pierre as by Tolstoy, essentially consists of *not thinking*. He is at the other extreme to Napoleon, to the German strategists, and to Andrei. Pierre will finally admit to Natasha that while Karataev, he thinks, would have liked their family life, he wouldn't have approved of Pierre's plans to unite all men of good will in a body to reform Russia. Of course not; his "wisdom" is totally passive and therefore totally conservative. It could accept any status quo.

Andrei, of course, is more practical than Pierre. His friend dreams of reform—Andrei actually takes part in the reforms of Speransky, though he comes to see that minister as "unnatural" and hollow, another paltry "Great Man." Andrei actually manages to free his serfs, but they give a neat example of the incompetence of intelligence and human will when in 1812 they revolt against his sister Maria; Andrei if anything seems to have made the Russian class problem worse. Tolstoy must have realized that to spare Andrei, who is mature, capable and experienced, would have made nonsense of any distribution of justice at the end. Married to Natasha—or to anyone else—his intelligence would have given both him and us no peace. His besetting sin, from Tolstoy's point of view, is logicality—that desire which he inherits from his Voltairean father to bring everything within the bounds of Enlightened reason.

There is an element of detachment and study in everything Andrei does—even receiving a mortal wound. While he is to some extent "taken out of himself" by the war of 1812, his mistrust of the flesh, of his own physical nature, keeps him aloof from the soldiers who love him. Pierre can delight in the powerful smell of sweat given off by Karataev, but Andrei is disgusted by the sight of his soldiers bathing in a slimy pool and, rather than join them, souses himself with water alone in a barn. "'Flesh, bodies, *chair à canon* ["cannon fodder"],' he reflected, looking at his own naked body and shuddering, not so much with cold as with aversion and horror, incomprehensible even to himself, aroused by the sight of that immense multitude of bodies splashing about in the dirty lake." The old Countess Rostova is right to feel instinctively that he's the wrong husband for the highly-sexed and naturally self-contented Natasha.

Yet he does love Natasha. And he is Pierre's best friend. And he does understand Kutuzov. He is not remote from Tolstoy's life-embracing characters. He is the most "heroic" hero Tolstoy ever created—the one most fully equipped to participate effectively in life. But Tolstoy mistrusts the most important part of his equipment—that incisive intelligence which is so much like Tolstoy's own.

Andrei, before Borodino, is Tolstoy's spokesman. He explains to Pierre why the theories of German generals have no relevance to a war fought on Russian soil. He stresses Tolstoy's own point about the importance of morale. He says forthrightly that the higher command don't help in a battle but merely hinder their men. He wickedly suggests that no prisoners should be taken, because such chivalrous gestures merely cloak the truth that war, if necessary, is vile and argues (like a realist novelist) that if people only saw war as what it is, they would never go to war.

But if we have read the book before, we know that the argument that no prisoners should be taken might be used as a justification for the barbarities of Dolokhov. This is a good moment to consider Dolokhov, a minor character of major importance. He is the closest Tolstoy came to creating a "Byronic" figure, but he is observed with that minute attention which Tolstoy brings to stereotypes and which dissolves them back into the truth from which they sprang. Though we are surprised to discover at one point that he lives lovingly with a widowed mother, and though he asks Pierre's forgiveness before Borodino with what we must take to be "natural" tears in his eyes, almost everything he does is wicked or unpleasant. Besides becoming Hélène's lover and provoking Pierre into a duel, he fleeces Nikolai Rostov of a fortune at cards and helps Anatole in his attempted abduction of Natasha. His appalling, pointless courage is displayed in that famous scene where we first meet him and he drinks a bottle of rum on a high window sill. But in war no Frenchman behaves so viciously as Dolokhov, no character does more to counteract any impression we might have that Tolstoy is naively nationalistic.

It is, however, important to notice that no character is more like Andrei. It is coldly intelligent rational thought which makes Dolokhov so dangerous. In practice he is a nihilist, brother to Pechorin and close kin to Bazarov and Stavrogin. As we infer from his glibly insincere use of patriotic clichés, he sees through all specious ideals and all social shams, and can act knowingly in accordance with whim and with total lack of consideration for others. What worries Pierre and repels us in the "shrill" voice of Andrei before the battle, when he tells us "I have begun to understand too much," is that his intelligence is bearing him close to nihilism.

Andrei has the same kind of complex fascination that Tolstoy would later create with his lovely adulteress, Anna Karenina. He is potentially evil, though in fact a good man. He is potentially a worldly success, but is in fact doomed to die with his promise unfulfilled. He can appreciate all that is best in the best people in the book, but he cannot be content with them or with himself. And he has in common with Maria, but far more than Pierre, a "religious" temperament. Pierre uses "religion" to find a way of coming to terms with the world as it is. For Andrei, when he hopes for posthumous fame or embraces his own death, what is beyond experience is always crucial. To him it seems that Natasha's soul is "pinioned by her body." And we notice another paradox—this man of the world is in potential a hermit.

Andrei and Pierre express the contrast within Tolstoy himself between the life-lover and the ascetic who despises the limitations of worldly experience. Pierre takes the goodness of all life on trust. Andrei pushes his thoughts, as he lies dying, through to a recognition that "love is life" but feels that his proposition, "Everything is—everything exists—only because I love" is "too intellectual." He dreams that death is pushing at the door, and that he dies. After this dream he "awakens from life" into an unearthly detachment which makes him remote from his son, from Maria and Natasha. He realizes that "death is an awakening."

At first sight it may seem that Andrei's final acceptance of death is the opposite, the inversion, of Karataev's complete acceptance of life. Yet the two amount to the same thing. Both dissolve everything into nothing. "Karataevism" taken seriously would rob life of all significance. Loving all things equally would make any particular love impossible. Karataev's life is a sort of living death in which both consciousness and the exercise of the will are avoided. Andrei's death is an awakening—consciousness and the will, which have pained him so much, are obliterated. So the differences between Andrei and Pierre might seem to be no more than contrasts of temperament—Pierre can accept what Andrei must "see through" and reject. But these different ways of viewing the same all-nothingness do have importantly different implications for the way people live. It would, of course, be inconsistent for a Karataevist to make any choice at all. But Tolstoy himself chooses between Andrei (or Dolokhov) and Pierre (and Natasha). Logic is on Andrei's side, life and morality are on Pierre's.

When Andrei dreams that death stands behind the door, that "death" is at first called "IT." A few pages later, Pierre recognizes as "IT" that "mysterious callous force which drove men against their will to murder their kind." He witnessed IT when French soldiers were executing prisoners, and at the Battle of Borodino. Tolstoy in *Resurrection* would finally identify that IT with the modern State, a structure within which decent people act immorally and which seems to them to relieve them of responsibility for actions they would not undertake if left to their own free will. The way he handles Count Rostopchin, the governor of Moscow, in *War and Peace,* already prefigures his later views.

Pierre's thoughts, we might say, make concrete for us the IT which for Andrei is abstract. We are prodded to identify the death-principle which Andrei accepts with the amoral power of the French military machine; if, like Andrei, we accept death as superior to life, then morality becomes irrelevant and the behaviour of a Dolokhov (which, of course, involves his own life in constant risk) will be acceptable. Tolstoy is a practical moralist asking how men can live well together—and he has not yet given way to the Andrei within him and rejected society, the family and even sex itself.

Sir Isaiah Berlin, in a famous study [see *TCLC,* Vol. 4], has seen within Tolstoy a struggle between the hedgehog, who, according to an old Greek saying, "knows one big thing" and the fox who "knows many things." He argues that "Tolstoy was by nature a fox, but believed in being a hedgehog," that his genius was for depicting the variety of life which, as a thinker, he was determined to simplify and reduce to large, clear laws. By this argument, Tolstoy's theory of history as he expounds it in the second Epilogue to *War and Peace* is a prime piece of hedgehogism. Having extolled instinct at the expense of reason and having explicitly denied that the intellect can solve our problems for us, Tolstoy now attempts to persuade us that history, so far from being dictated by "Great Men," operates in accordance with natural laws akin to those of physics—he runs the risk of reminding us of his own sarcastic picture of the ludicrous but pathetic German military theorist Pfuhl.

The significant force in history, as he hopes he has shown in his presentation of the Battle of Borodino, is not the rulers but the peoples they rule, whose movements the historian must study as he might study those of a herd of cattle. It is in the nature of political power that those who appear to be in charge contribute least to what happens:

> Power is the relation of a given person to other persons, in which the more this person expresses opinions, theories and justifications of the collective action the less is his participation in that action.
>
> The movement of nations is caused not by power, nor by intellectual activity, nor even by a combination of the two, as historians have supposed, but by the activity of *all* the people who participate in the event, and who always combine in such a way that those who take the largest direct share in the event assume the least responsibility, and *vice versa.*

Having reached this impressive, if most debatable, formulation afer many pages of argument, Tolstoy admits the limits of reason, as we have seen Andrei do. "In the last analysis we reach an endless circle—that uttermost limit to which in every domain of thought the human intellect must come if it is not playing with its subject. Electricity produces heat; heat produces electricity." Life is life. History happens as it must happen. The roundness of Karataev and the spinning of the fatal shell alike express in symbol the circularity of the world itself and of every argument about the world. The circle cannot be broken. There is in action a law, which we might as well call the Will of God, which dictates all our behaviour, and this law of life, not the will of Napoleon or Alexander, accounts for everything. Once again (as so often in Russian fiction) we stand with the nihilists confronting a world in which morality seems meaningless. Tolstoy now has to rescue himself from his Andreism. Many decades before the Enlightened philosopher Kant had likewise stood at the limits of reason, and Tolstoy arrives at a conclusion recalling Kant's which salvages morality from the pincer attack of reason and of natural laws.

Man is not free, yet his humanity somehow consists in his being free. Unlike a particle of matter, man can say "I am free":

> A man is only conscious of himself as a living being by the fact that he wills: he is conscious of his volition. And his own will—which is the very essence of his life—he is and cannot but be conscious of as being free.... Man sees his will to be limited just because he is conscious of it in no other way than as being free.

Every human action is both free, because the man undertaking it is conscious of his freedom, and a product of "necessity," because he is subject to the law of Nature. As soon as we stop to think, we are aware of limitations on our freedom. But because our reason is limited, it cannot discover enough causes for our actions to complete the "circle of necessity" and we cannot imagine an action entirely subject to the law of necessity.

If we start adding names of characters to the argument, we see how closely Tolstoy's epilogue relates to the content of his novel. "Reason gives expression to the laws of necessity." Andrei, the reasoner, dies and ceases to be human or free, in accordance with natural law. "Consciousness gives expression to the reality of freewill." Pierre lives, and believes that he and his friends can reform Russia. But in order to increase our understanding of our own lives and to make history a science like astronomy, which the Andrei-like Tolstoy wishes it to be, we "have to renounce a freedom that does not exist and to recognize a dependence of which we are not conscious." It is an act of choice if we "renounce" something, so freedom must exist if we are able to renounce our naive faith in it. Paradoxically, we express our freedom most perfectly when we recognize that our actions are governed by the law of nature.

Tolstoy thinks in terms of simple, unchangeable laws of necessity like those of Newtonian physics. Without Dostoevsky's inherently dialectical cast of mind, and without a vivid interest in the newer sciences, notably biology, which impose on us the view of a constantly changing nature, Tolstoy tends to write as if God really had created the world complete in six days and given it unalterable laws. He doesn't fully see that the existence of what we call "human freedom" indicates a force acting upon and even changing the "law"while acted upon by it.

This helps to explain his conservatism. He extols Kutuzov, old, pacific and expressing what we might call the "eternal reality" of Russia, and Natasha, who is content with a traditional role for women, and Nikolai, the old-fashioned farmer who submits to the existing state of mind of the peasants. If Nikolai had married Sonia he would have defied the prevailing social pattern in which money and property tend as a rule to determine the choice of partners in marriage. Instead, he conforms to it, since the woman he freely chooses to marry is also a rich heiress. Free action, it would seem, is something that you discover, or rediscover, not something which you can create. To behave well is not so much to act rightly as, like Kutuzov, to refrain from acting wrongly. Ideally, we would remain what we are in early childhood, naturally good in harmony with nature.

But Tolstoy was too much of a moralist to be altogether conservative. His contention that we must stop believing ourselves free is directed at historians. As a moralist, he believed in the kind of freedom which can change reality by changing human behaviour. He had to, otherwise all moral distinctions would tend to disappear as Rostopchin (man of the Russian state) at one point wishes they would. We must, for instance, revolt against the "law of nature" which makes us murder our fellow men. The last word of *War and Peace* is left to the "progressives." That dissatisfaction with the limitations of present experience which Andrei represents is inherited by his son, who idolizes Pierre the deluded believer in reform. The story ends with the boy's ringing if pathetic words—"Oh, Father, Father! Yes, I will do something that even *he* would be content with." (pp. 152-68)

*Angus Calder, "Tolstoy to 'War and Peace': Man against History," in his* Russia Discovered: Nineteenth-Century Fiction from Pushkin to Chekhov, *Heinemann Educational Books, 1976, pp. 138-70.*

---

## ADDITIONAL BIBLIOGRAPHY

Benson, Ruth Crego. "Two Natashas." In her *Women in Tolstoy: The Ideal and the Erotic,* pp. 45-75. Urbana: University of Illinois Press, 1973.
    Discusses the various facets of Natasha's personality in relation to Tolstoy's attitude toward women.

Brown, E. K. "Interweaving Themes." In his *Rhythm in the Novel,* pp. 63-86. Toronto: University of Toronto Press, 1950.
    Maintains that upon reading *War and Peace,* "the deepest impression is of a movement, at first very slow, finally almost precipitate, from separateness to union."

Cairns, Huntington; Tate, Allen; and Van Doren, Mark. "Leo Tolstoy: *War and Peace.*" In their *Invitation to Learning,* pp. 152-66. New York: New Home Library, 1941.
    Informal discussion.

Carden, Patricia. "The Recuperative Powers of Memory: Tolstoy's *War and Peace*." In *The Russian Novel from Pushkin to Pasternak,* edited by John Garrard, pp. 81-102. New Haven: Yale University Press, 1983.

Contends that the Platonic doctrine of memory constitutes an important element in the philosophy of *War and Peace*.

Elliott, George P. "A Piece of Lettuce." In his *A Piece of Lettuce,* pp. 246-270. New York: Random House, 1964.

Personal reflections on the meaning of the random and irrational in human life, with frequent references to *War and Peace*. Elliott likens the reading of the novel to "being on a battlefield, where you know the unforeseeable is likely to happen."

Freeborn, Richard. "*War and Peace*." In his *The Rise of the Russian Novel: Studies in the Russian Novel from "Eugene Onegin" to "War and Peace,"* pp. 208-66. Cambridge: Cambridge University Press, 1973.

Detailed analysis in which Freeborn concludes that in *War and Peace* Tolstoy so enlarged "the scale of his fiction that everything which he wrote before it seems both overshadowed and little better than experimental by comparison with the superlative, grandiose achievement of this work."

Gibian, George, ed. *War and Peace: The Maude Translation, Backgrounds and Sources, Essays in Criticism.* New York: W. W. Norton, 1966, 1484 p.

Louise and Aylmer Maude's translation of *War and Peace*, supplemented by secondary information including a chronology of Tolstoy's life, the publication history of *War and Peace*, Tolstoy's own comments on the novel, and essays by sixteen critics.

Golding, William. "Tolstoy's Mountain." In his *The Hot Gates and Other Occasional Pieces,* pp. 121-25. London: Faber and Faber, 1965.

Maintains that although Tolstoy's assessment of war as an essentially unguided movement of masses was accurate during the Napoleonic era, modern advances in technical communications have placed the shaping of history in the hands of individual leaders, or "Great Men."

Greenwood, E. B. "Tolstoy's Poetic Realism in *War and Peace*." *The Critical Quarterly* 11, No. 3 (Autumn 1969): 217-33.

Examines the nature of Tolstoy's realism, maintaining that "Tolstoy is a realist because he is primarily concerned to make the existing human consciousness itself an object of portrayal" and that his "realism is poetic . . . because of the sharpness with which he realizes the consciousness he portrays."

Hagan, John. "On the Craftsmanship of *War and Peace*." *Essays in Criticism* XIII, No. 1 (January 1963): 17-49.

Analyzes structural patterns in *War and Peace* in an attempt to demonstrate the overall unity of the novel.

———. "A Pattern of Character Development in *War and Peace*: Prince Andrej." *The Slavic and East European Journal* n.s. XIII, No. 2 (Summer 1969): 164-90.

Classifies *War and Peace* as "a gigantic novel of education, centering not on one protagonist but on five"—Andrei, Marya, Nikolai, Natasha, and Pierre—and analyzes Andrei's progress "through five distinct cycles of death and rebirth" to "the ultimate peace that passes all understanding."

Hare, Richard. "Tolstoy's Motives for Writing *War and Peace*." *The Russian Review* 15, No. 2 (April 1956): 110-21.

Calls *War and Peace* "a formal protest against that prevalent view of history which isolated certain showy fragments of the past and treated them as if they formed an intelligible and important whole."

Jones, W. Gareth. "A Man Speaking to Men: The Narratives of *War and Peace*. In *New Essays on Tolstoy,* edited by Malcolm Jones, pp. 63-84. Cambridge: Cambridge University Press, 1978.

Notes Tolstoy's conviction that "experience cannot be conveyed directly to another; the paraphernalia of art is necessary for any human communication" and examines the resulting narrative techniques by which the author attempted to both communicate truth

and alert the reader to the ways in which "he was being manipulated by fiction's conventions."

Knowles, A. V. "War over *War and Peace*: Prince Andrey Bolkonsky and Critical Literature of the 1860s and Early 1870s." In *New Essays on Tolstoy,* edited by Malcolm Jones, pp. 39-62. Cambridge: Cambridge University Press, 1978.

Detailed analysis of early critical commentary on Prince Andrei.

Lehrman, Edgar H. *A Guide to the Russian Texts of Tolstoy's "War & Peace."* Ann Arbor: Ardis, 1980, 225 p.

Handbook designed "to help enable the advanced student of Russian . . . to read the original text of *War and Peace* with both pleasure and understanding."

Leon, Philip. "Who Makes History? A Study of Tolstoy's Answer in *War and Peace*." *The Hibbert Journal* XLII, No. 3 (April 1944): 254-58.

Examines the relevance of Tolstoy's theory of history to Western civilization in the era of World War II.

Matlaw, Ralph E. "Mechanical Structure and Inner Form: A Note on *War and Peace* and *Dr. Zhivago*." *Symposium* XVI, No. 4 (Winter 1962): 288-94.

Finds structural parallels between the two novels.

Morgan, Charles. "Tolstoy: *War and Peace*" and "Tolstoy: The Second Epilogue." In his *Reflections in a Mirror,* pp. 192-200 and pp. 201-16. New York: Macmillan, 1945.

General appreciation of *War and Peace* and explication of Tolstoy's theory of history.

Orwin, Donna. "Prince Andrei: The Education of a Rational Man." *Slavic Review* 42, No. 4 (Winter 1983): 620-32.

Traces Prince Andrei's development throughout *War and Peace*. Orwin asserts that reason is the one constant factor in Andrei's life, noting that "wherever Andrei appears, in his attractive and unattractive moments, his rationality molds his passions."

Rolland, Romain. "Marriage." In his *Tolstoy,* pp. 97-114. New York: E. P. Dutton, 1911.

Discusses Tolstoy's family life during the years in which *War and Peace* was written and offers enthusiastic praise for the novel.

Rzhevsky, Nicholas. "Tolstoy's Ideological Order: Herzen and *War and Peace*." In his *Russian Literature and Ideology: Herzen, Dostoevsky, Leontiev, Tolstoy, Fadeyev,* pp. 116-30. Urbana: University of Illinois Press, 1983.

Traces the influence of Alexander Herzen on the ideological perspective of *War and Peace*.

Sampson, R. V. "Leo Tolstoy." In his *The Discovery of Peace,* pp. 108-67. New York: Pantheon Books, 1973.

Discusses literary influences on *War and Peace* and analyzes the novel's main characters in order to determine the principles of Tolstoy's moral philosophy and his attitude toward war.

Simmons, Ernest J. "The Writing of *War and Peace*." In *Slavic Studies,* edited by Alexander Kaun and Ernest J. Simmons, pp. 180-98. Ithaca, N.Y.: Cornell University Press, 1943.

Details the circumstances surrounding the writing of *War and Peace* and briefly assesses the novel.

———. "*War and Peace*." In his *Introduction to Tolstoy's Writings,* pp. 64-82. Chicago: University of Chicago Press, 1968.

Introduction to the principal themes and techniques of the novel.

Strakhov, Nikolai. "Tolstoy's *War and Peace*." In *Literature and National Identity,* edited by Paul Debreczeny and Jesse Zeldin, pp. 119-67. Lincoln: University of Nebraska Press, 1970.

Reprints an extensive excerpt from Strakhov's 1869 review of the first four books of *War and Peace*.

Torgovnick, Marianna. "'Open' and 'Closed' Form in *War and Peace*." In her *Closure in the Novel,* pp. 61-79. Princeton: Princeton University Press, 1981.

Discusses the ending of *War and Peace*, concluding that "the familial . . . epilogue may be seen as an attempt to smother Tolstoy's own doubts about the spiritual value of family life and to convince the reader—and the author himself during the 1860s—that a permanent rather than an interim solution to the problems of existence had been found.''

Warner, Nicholas O. "The Texture of Time in *War and Peace*." *Slavic and East European Journal* n.s. 28, No. 2 (Summer 1984): 192-204.

Challenges the widespread view that time is an element of limited importance in the novel, demonstrating "that time in *War and Peace* acts as a powerful force in the lives of the characters, that it possesses a subtlety and complexity not fully explored by previous criticism, and that it is a major philosophical issue for Tolstoy, anticipating Bergson's theory of *durée* and intersecting with Tolstoy's thought on spiritual development and death.''

————. "Character and Genre in *War and Peace:* The Case of Natasha." *MLN* 100, No. 5 (December 1985): 1012-24.

Notes that *War and Peace* "shares affinities with both the traditional realistic novel and the Homeric epic" and demonstrates that the book's epic and novelistic elements are most successfully combined in the character of Natasha.

Wasiolek, Edward. "The Theory of History in *War and Peace*." *Midway* 9, No. 2 (Autumn 1968): 117-35.

Disputes the widely held assumption that Tolstoy's philosophy of history denies individual free will.

Wilson, Edmund. "The Original of Tolstoy's Natasha." In his *Classics and Commercials: A Literary Chronicle of the Forties,* pp. 442-52. New York: Farrar, Straus and Company, 1950.

Reviews *Tolstoy as I Knew Him,* a memoir by Tolstoy's sister-in-law and model for Natasha, Tatyana Andreyvna Behrs. Wilson also discusses the unhappy romantic entanglements of the Tolstoy men (Leo, his father, and his brother Sergei) with women of lower social classes, and the treatment of similar situations in Tolstoy's fiction.

# Wen I-to

## 1899-1946

(Also transliterated I-tuo) Chinese poet, essayist, and critic.

A pivotal figure in modern Chinese literature, Wen blended Eastern and Western images, symbols, and themes in structured, controlled verse. In both his poetry and his criticism, Wen advocated a return from the formless free verse popular at that time to structured patterns with rhyme, and called for a moderate course between two conflicting visions of literature then prominent in China—pure aestheticism and political propaganda. His poetry, scholarship, and idealism made him one of the most respected figures in twentieth-century Chinese literature.

Born into a scholarly family in the village of Hsia-pa-ho, Wen displayed an early affinity for literature, especially poetry. At the age of twelve he was sent to the Tsing Hua School in Peking, which offered a curriculum incorporating both Eastern and Western philosophy and literature. There Wen was drawn to the poetry of the English Romantics, especially that of John Keats, and published essays and poetry in school journals. In 1922 he graduated from Tsing Hua and traveled to the United States, studying art and literature at the Art Institute of Chicago and at Colorado College. Wen continued to publish essays and poetry in Chinese journals, and in 1923 published his first poetry collection, *Hung-chu (Red Candle)*. After returning to China in 1927, Wen taught Western and Chinese literature at various schools, published a second volume of poetry, *Szu-shui,* and with several other writers began publishing *Crescent,* a monthly literary magazine which advocated aestheticism in art. He abandoned writing poetry in 1931, as the intellectual milieu for writers had become increasingly politicized, and soon after took a position teaching classical Chinese literature at Tsing Hua University.

When the Japanese occupied Peking in 1937, Tsing Hua University set up a temporary campus at Changsha, where Wen taught for a year until the battlefront was again nearing the school. The students and teachers of the university then embarked on a thousand-mile overland journey to Kunming, many of them, Wen included, on foot. The experience deeply moved Wen, and he became involved in politics and began writing poetry again. Although now committed to fighting social injustice, Wen deplored the advocacy and practice of violence by both the Communist Left and the rightist Kuomintang government, and he became an outspoken advocate of social freedom and an opponent of political violence. In 1944 Wen joined the Democratic League, a moderate political organization, and when two years later Li Kung-p'u, the leader of the Democratic League, was assassinated, Wen made a speech at his funeral denouncing political assassinations; he was himself murdered later that day.

Wen's poetic output, though small, was important to the development of Chinese poetry. *Red Candle,* written while Wen was studying in the Tsing Hua school and in America, displays Wen's affinity for English Romanticism, especially in its concern with the themes of love, beauty, and death. The poems written in America also deal with homesickness and the experience of racial discrimination, and idealize China in contrast

By permission of Dr. Catherine Yi-yu Cho Woo

to the United States. The poems in *Szu-shui* contain bleak imagery, are highly concerned with form, and combine Western and Eastern allusions and themes. Wen emphasized structured form and rhyme in reaction to the free verse prevalent in Chinese poetry during the 1920s, arguing that the Chinese language is so adaptable to form and rhyme that free verse loses in structural beauty more than it gains in freedom of expression. Wen, however, did not advocate returning to traditional Chinese forms, but rather suggested the creation of a unique form for each individual poem.

Wen was also involved in disputes between schools of thought advocating opposing relationships between art and politics. While some artists, especially a group known as the Creation Society, advocated a Western "Art for Art's Sake" ideal, leftist associations, especially the radical Sun Society, denounced all writers who did not actively advance radical social change in their work. Wen did not believe that art should be unaffected by politics, but did consider the true artist to be above using his work as a vehicle for propaganda. Wen and his fellow artists of the Crescent School emphasized the aesthetic side of literature, trusting that social issues would of necessity be addressed by an author's attempt to realistically portray life. This attempt to resolve two such conflicting visions of literature drew vehement attacks from theorists on both sides of the issue. At the same time, the Chinese government was taking an increasingly militant stance toward dissenters, and Wen's moderation soon became untenable in the wake of escalating violence between the Chinese Communists and the ruling Kuomintang. Critics believe that his weariness of being attacked on both sides of the political spectrum, as well as his desire for a more stable personal life, led to his abandonment of poetry in the early 1930s. Wen's influence did not decrease with this decision, however, nor with his death: he is still revered and emulated by Chinese authors and intellectuals for his remarkable intellect, moral courage, and brilliant poetry.

## PRINCIPAL WORKS

*Hung-chu* (poetry) 1923
   [*Red Candle*, 1972]
*Szu-shui* (poetry) 1928
*Wen I-to ch'üan-chi.* 4 vols.   (poetry, essays, and criticism)
   1948

Translated selections of Wen's poetry appear in the following collections: H. Acton and Ch'en Shih-hsiang, *Modern Chinese Poetry;* R. Payne, *Contemporary Chinese Poetry;* Kai-Yü Hsü, *Twentieth Century Chinese Poetry.*

---

KAI-YÜ HSÜ   (essay date 1958)

[*Hsü is a Chinese-born American educator, nonfiction writer, and critic specializing in Chinese literature and culture. In the following excerpt, he discusses Wen's artistic progress from his early work to his final poem, published in 1931.*]

Two main currents in Wen I-to's intellectual development—romantic new poetry and scholarly research in Chinese classical literature, particularly poetry, pursued in a romantic spirit—have been apparent throughout his life. In a sense, he worked along both lines simultaneously all the time, with rare side trips into the fields of painting, drama, and finally political pamphleteering. He had been exposed to Western literature during his days at Tsing Hua, and the romantic element in his thought was strengthened and consolidated upon his arrival in America as he gained more confidence in his understanding and grasp of nineteenth-century English romantic poetry. During this period varied themes dominated his thought and writing: "literature for beauty's sake," an attraction to death, a worship of love, an intense preoccupation with color, and at the same time strong strains of nationalism and rebellion.

As soon as he began his classes at the Art Institute of Chicago, he wrote to his friend Liang Shih-ch'iu . . . , later a famed art and literary critic, at Tsing Hua proposing the founding of a literary magazine to promote a school of literature in China—that of the "literature for beauty." In his letter he said, "I feel that I have a mission in literature, so I am anxious to accomplish this mission through a journal." The sense of dedication was clearly revealed in the poem prefacing his *Red Candle:*

> Red candle!
> So red is the candle!
> O, poet!
> Spit out your heart and compare—
> Are they of the same color?

The significance of his first poetic anthology is indicated by its title. As Wen explained in the foreword, "red candle" refers

to a line by Li Shang-yin . . . (813-858), a late T'ang dynasty poet:

> The spring silkworm's thread never ends until
> Time runs out;
> The candle's tear never dries until
> It burns into ashes.

In these lines Li Shang-yin meant to express the unending sadness of parting with a loved one. Wen I-to borrowed the unusual poetic metaphor to pledge unqualified dedication of his life to "romantic ideal beauty."

Li Shang-yin is noted for lyrical poems of great beauty and poignance. Although in his earlier writings he imitated Tu Fu, Li is best remembered as a leading late T'ang poet who, following Li Ho . . . (790-816), eventually turned away from the realism and social consciousness of Tu Fu and Po Chü-i. Like Li Ho, Li Shang-yin stressed personal feeling and insisted that literature have an independent life. "Literature is not a tool for the improvement of society or the destiny of mankind. The highest attainment of literature is beauty; art . . . has no other value than its beauty. . . ." Thus the value of poetry lies in the form, the music, and the language, quite apart from any message. Li Shang-yin carried these points so far that critics often cannot agree on the exact meaning of his poems.

Even toward the end of his life Wen clung to this feeling for the ecstasy of life, expressing it later, however, in different forms. The influence of Li Shang-yin persisted, as did that of the young Keats. His early devotion to Keats is reflected in a letter of March 30, 1923. "After I finished a day's work at painting, I felt like illustrating my own poems upon returning to my room. But as soon as I walked into my room, Byron, Shelley, Keats, Tennyson . . . were waiting for me on the shelf, on the desk, even in bed; and I itched to get close to them again." In a poem from *Red Candle* entitled **"The Loyal Minister of Art,"** Wen first described how the numerous ministers and subjects of the "king of art" surround him like pearls adorning the latter's royal robe, but

> Among them only Keats
> Is the one fiery gem supported by many a dragon;
> His lustre outshines all others.

And then,

> O, you, the poet of poets!
> The entire court can only be
> Famous ministers of Art.
> Only you alone are the loyal minister.
>
> *'Beauty is Truth, Truth Beauty.'*
>         · · · · ·
> You are a true martyr of Art.
> O, your loyal and virtuous soul!
> Your name is not written on water,
> But cast on the precious tripod of the saintly kingdom.

What attracted Wen to Keats was the marriage between truth and beauty, the "prefigurative truth" of Keats's "naive phase." It was precisely this naiveté and dedication that Wen I-to admired.

Another striking feature of this poem is the consistent set of typically Chinese images. The metaphor of "loyal minister" . . . in Chinese suggests a relationship marked by the devotion of a servant to a beloved master. A few lines further Wen used the "truly destined king" . . . to describe art, and quoted a line from the third-century statesman Chu-ko Liang "Your servant (*ch'en*) will exert and exhaust himself (to serve you) until he dies!'' to suggest the artist's (Keats's) dedication. Then there is the idea of self-sacrifice for the sake of the king (art) and of having one's name cast on the precious tripod. Wen believed that the Chinese poet could cull from his own culture rich images to fit new poetic forms with selected Western features. We will discuss this theory later.

Although Wen never ceased to praise life, light, and eternity, his romanticism was characterized at the same time by a fascination with death. On May 15, 1923, he wrote to Liang Shih-ch'iu, who by this time was in Colorado, telling of the suicide of a Chinese student named Sun over his failure at school: "This martyr knew the futility of life and had the resolution to die. He really ended his life. If one wants to die, die. My hat off, my hat off, my hat off... I want to say for the thousandth time, my hat off." Earlier (on Sept. 24, 1922) Wen had written to another friend in China discussing the death of a Chinese student in an automobile accident in Colorado. "This news makes me think of bigger questions—the meaning of life and death—the great puzzle of the universe. The last several days I have been very much absentminded. They say I am losing my mind. But isn't he too senseless who cannot lose his mind over these big questions?" In the poem **"Death"** written in 1922 and included in *Red Candle,* Wen went on to identify death with his ideal—truth and beauty:

> O, my soul's soul!
> My life's life!
> All my failures, all my debts
> Now have to be claimed against you,
> But what can I ask of you?
>
> .    .    .
>
> Let me be drowned in the deep blue of your eyes.
> Let me be burnt in the furnace of your heart.
> Let me die intoxicated in the elixir of your music.
> Let me die of suffocation in the fragrance of your breath.
>
> .    .    .
>
> Death is the only thing I beg of you.
> Death is the most I can offer you.

In this poem the "you" is a personified ideal, a fusion of the young poet's ideal beauty, truth, and a mystical poetic object of worship. Wen found that the only supreme expression of his dedication to this object was death.

Other expressions of death are found in different poems he wrote during the same period. In **"The Death of Li Po,"** also in *Red Candle,* he dramatized the legend that the famous poet drowned while trying to embrace the moon's reflection in a river. This symbolized for Wen the romantic love of a poet for an imaginary ideal beauty. A similar theme is pursued in **"The Sheath."** The sheath is an imaginary work of art wrought to perfection. With "all the jewels" he had, Wen shaped and carved "a Chinese god, a Buddhist god, a Venus, a singing minstrel... all on the sheath." Then, upon finishing it:

> Jade, ruby, white agate, and blue sapphire . . .
> Are pieced into varicolored butterflies.
> Then my work is done!

All this, he said, he did only to "die in the glitter and gleam of this sheath." In addition to the youthful romantic dedication to beauty and to death, the worship of love is another clear theme in Wen's poetry in this period. Like Keats, Wen did not hesitate to use extravagant metaphors in praise of love.

> O, my love, you are the champion;
> But let's play a game of chess.
> My aim is not to win,
> I only wish to lose to you—
> My body and soul,
> And everything mine!

And, using an incense stick as symbol,

> My love!
> Only such pure and refreshing scent
> Is worthy of dedication to you, my saintly one.
> May your hair and eyebrows be forever black;
> May your rosy cheeks be forever young.
> Together with our love may they live a thousand,
> And ten thousand years more.

The fact that Wen included these poems in *Red Candle* under the subtitle "Youth" seems to show that these, and many others like them, were outbursts of the young poet's passionate feeling, the object of this feeling being a combination of his ideal values. Although at this time Wen still seemed to be singing love "for love's sake," the object of his "love" was subject to reidentification, as his later life showed; and once the object was redefined, the poet Wen was capable of the same intense devotion and dedication.

The preoccupation with color which all these poems show is not surprising in view of Wen's childhood passion for painting. Although his transfer to Colorado marked the turn away from a career in painting, he never ceased to study the subject. He must have been something of a campus character at Colorado. Liang Shi-ch'iu wrote in reminiscence years later: "The head of the art school once remarked to me, 'Mr. Wen is certainly a rare artist. Not to speak of his works, he himself is already a work of art. Look at the lines on his face, the smile at the corner of his mouth. There is rhythm in perfection.' I-to has taken up oil here... His smock, a motley of colors, he uses to wipe his nose and his table, and as rain-gear. He is really a perfect picture of a painter-artist." His **"Autumn Colors"** expresses this extreme color-consciousness.

> Water in the creek,
> As purple as ripe grapes,
> Rolls out scales of golden carp,
> Layer upon layer.
> Several scissor-shaped maple leaves,
> Like crimson swallows,
> Whirl and turn, rising and dipping
> On the water.
>
> .    .    .
>
> White pigeons, variegated pigeons,
> Red-eyed, silver gray pigeons,
> Raven-like black pigeons,
> With golden light of violet and green on their backs—
> So many of them, tired of flying,
> Assemble under the steps. . . .

He then apostrophizes the colorful autumn tree:

> I'll ask T'ien Sun to weave you into a robe,
> So that I can wear you;
> Or squeeze you from grapes, oranges, and corn,
> And drink you.

He even wanted to borrow "the words from Li Shang-yin and Keats" to sing the colors and to listen to the colors through "Puccini's *La Bohéme.*" In **"Colors"** Wen I-to compared life to a piece of white paper, innocent and blank at the beginning. He attributed moral feelings, emotions, motion, and rhythm to the various colors that come to be attached to life, and wrote, "Thereafter, I adore my life, because I love its colors." Color remained a joy through his life, although he later gave up painting as a vocation. He wrote treatises on colors in poetry and on colors for book-cover design. He decorated his own study with colors that varied according to his mood; he was even at pains to liven up his lectures on ancient Chinese literature with lavish color, describing the shades and color combination of the costumes worn by the shaman dancers in his lecture on the *Ch'u-tz'u* or painting a landscape in words as background for Tu Fu's poem "The Northern Expedition" (Pei cheng").

Underneath this coat of profuse colors vibrated a stirring nationalistic strain. A nostalgia, easily understandable in a young man alone in a foreign land, was gnawing him. When he mailed his **"Sunshine Rhymes"** to his friends in China on September 24, 1922, he was recording one of the moments of homesickness which caused him acute pain:

> The sunshine pricks and hurts my heart,
> Once again driving away a traveler's home-coming dream,
> Once again condemning him to twelve hours' longing pain.

The whole section in **Red Candle** in which the above poem appears is drenched in nostalgia, as the subtitle **"Lone Swan"** suggests. The "lone swan" is "a solitary soul who leaves his companion and is exiled to a never-never land." Thus, Wen felt that he was an **"Exiled Prisoner"**; and in **"Late Autumn"** he wished to "curl up like a cat in front of the fireplace to dream of my country, home, alma mater, old acquaintances, and the good old days, the thought of which I no longer can bear."

This nostalgia and longing led Wen to idealize his homeland; he was not aware of his over-idealization, however, until his return home. In **"Sunshine Rhymes"** he claimed the sun as China's. In **"Chrysanthemum"** he sang his praise of his homeland, "as beautiful as a flower." Thus home became to the Chinese poet in America the crystallization of beauty.

Wen's nationalism was heightened by anti-Oriental feeling in the United States. In January 1923 he wrote to his family, suggesting that he return to China before he completed his study in America:

> For a Chinese young man with a mind of his own to stay in America, the feeling he experiences defies description. Wait until the end of the year after next, when I return to spend the New Year with you around the fire, I will cry out and pour out my pent-up anger and hatred. I am not a man without a country. We have a history and a culture of five thousand years, what of us is inferior to the Americans? Should we say that because we cannot manufacture guns and cannons for manslaughter therefore we are not as honorable and praiseworthy as they are? In short, the way they look down upon the people from our country cannot be described in one word. After my return I would advocate friendship and alliance between China and Japan against the Americans sooner than I would speak for friendship between China and the United States against Japan.

Wen's homesickness grew, making him doubt the wisdom of having come to the United States at all. "In coming to the Western hemisphere we are not gaining anything besides augmenting the number of 'returned students' for China; but China is not benefiting any," he wrote to Liang Shih-ch'iu on February 15, 1923. The date, the Chinese lunar New Year's Eve, traditionally a sentimental occasion, may have had something to do with his mood.

An expression of his resentment against the humiliation the Chinese were suffering from the Americans took shape in his poem, **"The Laundry Song,"** published shortly before his return to China:

> (One piece, two pieces, three pieces,)
> Washing must be clean.
> (Four pieces, five pieces, six pieces,)
> Ironing must be smooth.

> I can wash handkerchiefs wet with sad tears,
> I can wash shirts soiled in sinful crimes,
> The grease of greed, the dirt of desire . . .
> And all the filthy things at your house,
> Give them to me to wash, give them to me.

> Brass stinks so; blood smells evil,
> Dirty things you have to wash.
> Once washed, they will again be soiled;
> How can you, men of patience, ignore them?
> Wash them (for the Americans), wash them!

> You say the laundry business is too base.
> Only Chinamen are willing to stoop so low?
> It was your preacher who once told me:
> Christ's father used to be a carpenter.
> Do you believe it, don't you believe it?

> There isn't much you can do with soap and water.
> Washing clothes truly can't compare with building warships.
> I, too, say what great prospect lies in this—
> Washing the others' sweat with your own blood and sweat?
> [But] do you want to do it, do you want it?

> Year in year out a drop of homesick tear,
> Midnight, in the depth of night, a laundry lamp. . . .
> Menial or not, you need not bother,
> Just see where is not clean, where is not smooth,
> And ask the Chinaman, ask the Chinaman.

> I can wash handkerchiefs wet with sad tears,
> I can wash shirts soiled in sinful crimes,
> The grease of greed, the dirt of desire . . .
> And all the filthy things at your house,
> Give them to me—I'll wash them, give them to—me!

Wen's own note to this poem explains that because laundry work is the most common occupation of the Chinese in America, Chinese students here are often asked, "Is your father a laundryman?" Wen, however, did not specify whether he ever had to answer this question personally.

Hsiung Fo-hsi . . . , the playwright who collaborated with Wen in 1924 to stage plays in New York under the auspices of the Art Students' League of New York, recalled that Wen often said, "The heaven-endowed nature of a poet is love, for his country and his people." In January 1925 Wen again wrote to Liang Shih-ch'iu, "I am planning to write a series of sketches, depicting the way Chinese are humiliated in this country." Wen said he wanted to write them in free verse, but they never came from his pen. With his New York friends he started a discussion on "cultural nationalism" and considered the publication of a journal to promote this idea. He told his friends that he had decided to study Chinese rather than Western painting after his American sojourn in order to "promote our national culture." Such activities brought him close to a group of more politically conscious students in New York who were organizing a party built around nationalism. This party later was affiliated with the Young China group, later known as the Chinese Youth Party, advocating rightist nationalism. Wen considered himself associated with this party until about two years after his return to China.

Two things prove that Wen was not really committed to this rightist nationalism, and that his feeling of political partisanship was more a poet's way to give vent to his "patriotic" sentiment than a politician's calculated move. First, although his party at that time considered that it was independent from and competing with the Kuomintang, Wen wrote the long poem **"God of the South Sea"** to commemorate the death of Sun Yat-sen in April 1925, organized a memorial service for Sun in New York, and painted a portrait of Sun for the occasion. Second, when Liang Shih-ch'iu suggested that the **"God of the South Sea"** could be published in their party organ, Wen questioned whether this move would "place our party in the awkward position of patting the Kuomintang on the back." All this seems to reflect political naiveté rather than political commitment.

In contrast to the nationalist strain, the rebellious strain was less evident than one might have expected in Wen's early writing. The reason appears to lie in the fact that he was not subject to much direct pressure. Government authority, which his romantic impulse might have prompted him to defy, was kind to him; it sent him abroad to study and thereby assured him a successful career. But latent rebelliousness there was; the "strike" he staged at Tsing Hua prior to his departure for America and his participation in the May 4th Movement were evidence.

The authoritarian atmosphere of Wen's Hupeh home may have planted the seeds of recalcitrance, but as we have seen, in childhood he behaved as a model son. He did not even follow the current fashion among youth of the time in objecting to an arranged marriage. He submitted to his parents' will in everything except the choice of classical texts for study.

After his marriage, however, he began to feel more and more of the pressure of his father's stubborn Confucianism, not so much on himself as on his wife and daughter. Upon his departure for the United States, his wife stayed with his parents, a common practice. The elder Wen's interception of I-to's letters to his wife was bitterly resented; and I-to suffered immeasurably even though he did not openly fight for the right of correspondence for fear that this demand might result in a worse rift in the family. When I-to's first daughter was born, the grandfather withheld the news from him until almost a half year had elapsed and even then only casually mentioned it in a letter. I-to took this to be a clear proof of his father's discrimination against girls; for if it had been a son, I-to was sure the grandfather would have immediately heralded the news with elation. He now worried over the welfare of his wife and child whose position in the old family was obviously anything but happy. How he felt about this situation was revealed in his **"Red Bean"** written during the winter of 1922 at Chicago:

> We are companions,
> First whipped together,
> Then whipped apart.
> O, you, almighty whip!
> Should I sing praises
> Or curses
> Of you?
>
> .  .  .  .  .
>
> Sour, sweet, bitter, and biting
> Are the beans, though all
> Red in color.
> Give the biting ones to tradition,
> Let it taste them first!

This long poem of forty-two stanzas was dedicated to his wife, but she never saw it until it was published in *Red Candle*. After this experience, Wen began to wonder about the validity of many aspects of the Confucian tradition.

To express these themes in poetry Wen had a clear set of tenets to follow. As far back as 1922 he had started to outline his views on rhyme, form, imagery, and Westernization in Chinese poetry. He believed that the Chinese language offered an unusually rich range of rhymes of which the Chinese poet ought to take good advantage. "Rhyming helps to develop rhythm

and to perfect the art of poetry; not to use it would be like starving in front of a royal banquet. Nothing is more foolish than that." He went on to cite his own **"Sunshine Rhymes"** to prove his theory, saying that he felt no strain at all in using the same end rhyme throughout all twelve stanzas.

While accepting *pai-hua* as a promising poetic medium, Wen criticized the vogue of indiscriminate use of colloquialism in poetry. To him, the so-called "natural rhythm" advocated by Hu Shih . . . was not poetry. He urged the poet first to strive to develop a poetic *pai-hua* by "distilling the poetical and musical elements from the ordinary language." "If we don't admit that new poetry with refined rhymes adapted from classical poetry is beauty," said Wen, "then we have only two choices: be contented with bad poetry, or write poetry in a foreign language." He hastened to add that the adaptation he advocated meant critical selection from the classical literary heritage. "The classical Chinese poetry constructs its musical scheme on its own vocabulary, parts of which are dead and can no longer be transplanted into the new poetry." Many writers of new poetry, Wen believed, failed to construct a new prosody when they ineptly borrowed phrases from the classical language.

In his opinion, the form and the rhythm of poetry are but two sides of the same coin. "If we compare poetry to the game of chess, we can easily understand why poetry without form, like a game of chess without rules, must be such a meaningless thing!" But that was exactly how most young poets, hiding themselves behind the banner of romanticism, were parading their "rule-less games" as poetry. That was also the reason why there were "more new poems than the bamboo shoots after a spring rain." He admitted that there was form in nature, but any form copied intact from nature could not be perfect. Perfection in form was achieved only after much patient chiseling. He quoted Goethe's letter to Schiller, and Han Yü's words to support his theory that "The greater the artist, the more he enjoys dancing in fetters." The greatness of an artist lay in his ability to dance gracefully in spite of the shackles. Moreover, the shackles (form) in the hands of a great artist were transformed into effective tools.

As to the essence of form, Wen believed that there were two aspects: the visual and the auditory. Chinese, he insisted, was a visual language; its visual beauty was something European languages did not possess. Therefore he demanded that new poetry must heed the harmony and balance of metrical measures based on the number and quality of syllables in a line. "It is all right to deprive Confucius of his authority, but why blindly worship Christ and Socrates?" asked Wen, and he proposed that if the new poets recognized the beauty in an English sonnet, they should also strive to create forms befitting new Chinese poetry. He opposed a return to the old four-line or eight-line Chinese poetry. "The difference between old and new forms is that the former is a fixed frame into which we are asked to fit all kinds of contents and feelings, while the latter is something we must create to suit each individual subject and image."

The above reference to Confucius and Socrates tells a great deal of Wen's attitude; he championed "calculated but not total Westernization of Chinese poetry." He criticized Kuo Mojo's . . . *Goddess* for its lack of vivid "local color." His own position was that poetry, like any other form of art, is an "embroidery with time as its warp and space its woof," because it is born from life and life is no more than "the footprints of time and space." He felt that although traditional Chinese poetry was outdated and no longer reflected the spirit of the age, the literary revolution had gone too far in its imitation of the West. Kuo Mo-jo's multiple reference to "Venus, Apollo, Cupid, . . . even Christ," made Wen wonder if "the poet is not a Westerner speaking the Chinese language." Wen employed his favorite color metaphor: "one single color is not enough to paint a complete picture. . . . A pencil sketch cannot be compared with a painting of full colors." He sought variety, believing that local colors added to the total picture of art of the entire world. Furthermore, he wrote, "The culture of the Orient is absolutely beautiful . . . it is also the most harmonious culture on earth." In a chauvinist vein, he admonished Kuo to learn to appreciate the intrinsic value of Chinese culture— its quietude and refinement—and not to be scared by the crude outcries of the Westerners.

Wen had something favorable to say about Westernization and Kuo's work when he discussed poetic imagery. In Wen's view, imagery must not be sacrificed for either form or musical effect. Thus he found the poet Yü P'ing-po unjustified in his effort to salvage a few ringing rhymes which resulted in such syntactical chaos that the reader could hardly see any picture in Yü's poems. In contrast Wen cited Kuo to show how a complex and finely drawn image could be achieved by using longer "Europeanized sentence structures." Wen also agreed with Fu Ssu-nien . . . who accused Chinese writers of "manifesting the sterility of their thought" when they tried to write "simply." He suspected that Yü P'ing-po was trying to be "simple" and that this led him to a "degradation of poetry." Here we catch a glimpse of what Wen I-to in his early years thought of the ideal of poetry. Poetry must be a work of refined beauty, worked into artistic perfection as Wen once tried to "carve his bejeweled sheath," even at the risk of making it into an object fit only for the wall of an ivory tower.

Wen expressed these views at a time when new Chinese poetry was, after its "liberation from the old forms," greatly troubled at finding a form of its own. Many had felt that the new poetry was a dead-end street and were already sounding their bugle of retreat to the classical forms. Others were seeking refuge in Western forms. Wen preached and lived up to this gospel of new forms, at least through the 1930's. His poems were a credit to his theory and for a period were regarded as examples of the new Chinese poetry worthy of imitation. We shall elaborate on this when we analyze his **"Dead Water."** Unfortunately he brought to an end his own creative career a little too soon for his new forms to find an assured position in Chinese literary history. Before long many other stronger tides in Chinese literature overtook him, and even he admitted that "form" had become a moot question to be shrugged off during literary debates after the War of Resistance ushered in a new era for China.

After three years in America, Wen I-to was ready to spend his life "not as a creator but a promoter" of art in his own country. In the summer of 1925, having given up painting for literary criticism and without a definite plan for the future, he sailed for home, feeling he was "pursuing a dream."

A short rest at home in Hupeh was followed by his first academic job as dean of instruction at the newly established Art Institute of Peking. There he was immediately involved in campus politics, which, rife in every school in China at that time, disgusted him. He was still nominally connected with the "nationalist" (not to be confused with the Kuomintang) group originally formed in New York, and he expressed a wish to do something about the bloody strife between the Com-

munists and the Kuomintang. Although he became a member of the famous Hsin-yüeh . . . (New Moon, or Crescent) group of poets, he wrote only two poems in the nine months after his return. Nevertheless, he remained active in literary circles. His living quarters became a regular conference room for literary gatherings.

But the poet was greatly disturbed by the ceaseless fighting and the gathering storm of political and social revolution. The glorious homeland that he had dreamed of and longed for while in America was nowhere in sight. This is how he expressed his disappointment:

> I have come, I shout, bursting forth my tortured tears.
> This is not *my China* I longed for through the years.
> I've come because I heard your summoning cry.
> Riding on the wind of time, raising a torch high,
> I came; I knew not this to be unwarranted ecstasy.
> A nightmare I found. You? How could that be!

The misery of his civil-war ravaged homeland was impressed upon his mind. He began to change his conviction that literature was a "beautiful expression of refined human sentiment," and that the poet was a "man of tenderness and kindness." In the **"Deserted Village"** he wrote:

> Where did they go? How has it come to pass?
> On stoves squat frogs, in ladles lilies bloom;
> Tables and chairs float in fields and water ponds;
> Rope-bridges of spider-webs span room on room.
> Coffins are wedged in doorways, rocks block windows.
> What a heart-rendering sight of bleak gloom and doom!

From this disappointment and grief there emerge a strong sense of indignation. Recalling his own experience with the student movement protesting against government authority in 1919, he sympathized with those who participated in the demonstration of March 18, 1926. In **"The T'ien-an Gate,"** he depicted Peking as a city full of the ghosts of the students killed and injured in clashes with the police. Elsewhere he declared that literature must find its life and blood in patriotism and love of freedom. In the excited clamor of patriotism Wen even hinted that "men of letters should do more than preach patriotism with their pens; they themselves must set the patterns for action." The continuing civil war and the government's inaction against foreign encroachment caused him more despair. It was in this moment of bitter frustration that he wrote his famous **"Dead Water"**:

> Here is a ditch of hopelessly dead water.
> No breeze can raise a single ripple on it.
> Might as well throw in rusty metal scraps
> Or even pour left-over food and soup in it.
>
> Perhaps the green on copper will become emeralds.
> Perhaps on tin-cans will peach blossoms bloom.
> Then, let grease weave a layer of silky gauze,
> And germs brew patches of colorful spume.
>
> Let the dead water ferment into jade wine
> Covered with floating pearls of white scum.
> Small pearls, chuckling, become big pearls,
> Only to burst as gnats come to steal this rum.
>
> And so this ditch of hopelessly dead water
> May still claim a touch of something bright.
> And if the frogs cannot bear the silence—
> The dead water will croak its song of delight.
>
> Here is a ditch of hopelessly dead water—
> A region where beauty never can reside.
> Might as well let the devil cultivate it—
> See what sort of world it can provide.

As social protest, this poem is indignant, bitter, and satirical. As art it marked a new height in modern Chinese literature because of the skill with which imagery and feeling were joined to strict prosody, where each line contained the same number of syllables, with the ending rhyme following the standard A-B-C-B scheme. Wen's admirers applauded **"Dead Water"** as an eloquent testimony to the validity of Wen's theory on the form of poetry and praised it as the signal of the dawning of a new era in modern Chinese verse. As an expression of Wen's feeling and thought at that time, however, the poem is negative and pessimistic, and for this he was criticized by many of his younger and more aggressive friends.

Because Wen was first and foremost a romantic poet, his temperament did not permit him easily to join the ranks of revolutionaries, and his first participation in politics was short. Late in 1926 he joined the faculty of the Academy of Political Science founded by Carsun Chang . . . at Wusung (near Shanghai), and the next spring he even accepted the invitation of a friend to assist in propaganda work in the government at Hankow where he painted many political posters. But this assignment was not to his liking and a month later he returned to the Academy of Political Science. Soon the Kuomintang ordered the academy closed and Wen I-to moved on to the Central University (then called the Fourth Sun Yat-sen University) to head the department of foreign languages and literature. Meanwhile, he and his friends founded the *Hsin Yüeh (Crescent)* magazine which was to become famous in the history of modern Chinese literature.

When he went to Wuhan University to take charge of the school of literature in 1928, he had decided that he would devote his time to research in classical Chinese literature. (pp. 139-58)

Wen turned to academic research because his early training had given him a real love of classical Chinese literature. His own statements in the 1930's confirm the revival of this absorbing interest, as we shall see presently. Meanwhile, a combination of his weariness over the ceaseless verbal exchange on what a writer should write, his conviction that there is value in the classical Chinese literature, and a feeling that literature somehow could remain aloof from politics (the last being an inconsistency and a source of perpetual inner conflict) helped Wen I-to to decide on stepping aside, if only temporarily, from active creative writing. He resigned from the editorial board of the *Crescent Monthly* in April 1929.

That Wen thought he was only temporarily retiring from creative writing is seen in the fact that in 1931 he again took up his pen to write what turned out to be his last poem, **"Miracle."** In this poem he expressed his undiminished zeal to seek the "crystallization of the essence of the red of fire and the black of the unfathomable pool under a canopy of peach blossoms." He was still waiting for a "miracle ten thousand times more miraculous than the tenderness of the pigeon and the melancholy of the lyre." But, he explained, he was patient because he had made the pledge to await this miracle many incarnations ago. From the leftist viewpoint, Wen retreated, as Kuo Mo-jo did at least once in his life, to the comparatively safer zone of academic studies. The leftist critics never treated Wen's retreat harshly because while Wen was living, he stayed away from the center of controversy; and after his death, the critics accepted his own belated rationalization (already quoted) in order to complete the picture of a "true democrat," a "martyr," and a courageous "poet of the people" whose name could make political capital for the leftists. (pp. 164-65)

*Kai-Yü Hsü, "The Life and Poetry of Wen I-To," in* The Harvard Journal of Asiatic Studies, *Vol. 21, December, 1958, pp. 134-79.*

## JULIA C. LIN (essay date 1972)

[*Lin is a Chinese-born American educator and critic. In the following excerpt, she examines Wen's espousal of structured verse forms and analyzes images and auditory effects in his poetry.*]

Wen was writing at a time when most new poets were following the trend of writing free verse and adopting the more "natural rhythm" promoted by Hu Shih. The resulting hodgepodge was frequently unappetizing. Wen was appalled by the lack of discipline and the poor performance in the concoctions that appeared. Anxious about the future of the thriving new verse, he became more and more preoccupied with its problems and tirelessly sought solutions for them. The result was his well-known theories of form, which he eloquently defended in **"The Form of Poetry,"** published in 1926.

In this essay Wen declared the inevitability of form in poetry. The poetic act is like playing chess, he maintained: "No game can be played without rules: no poem can be written without form." He further asserted that the greater the poet, the greater pleasure he would receive dancing with chains on his feet. In his analysis of form, Wen I-to focused attention on the two basic patterns in poetry: visual and auditory. The visual pattern with its balanced grouping of characters and lines provides the framework and the structural symmetry of the composition, said Wen, while the auditory pattern with its metrical elements of foot, tone, and rhyme regulates the rhythmic movement of the poem.

Placing emphasis on structural symmetry, Wen urged the new poets to take advantage of their language's linguistic peculiarities to achieve a unique "beauty of architecture." This architectural beauty Wen defined as a visual structural beauty effected through a perfectly balanced and uniform arrangement of characters, lines, and stanzas. This, he pointed out hastily, does not mean a return to the regulated verse forms of the T'ang dynasty, although the latter do possess a limited sort of architectural beauty. "The regulated verse is a 'fixed form' which is forced to accommodate all kinds of themes, situations and emotions. . . . The new forms are infinitely varied, because every single form is created to suit its special content. Therefore, there is an intimate relationship between the form and its content. . . ." What Wen was advocating here is simply the nonce form, which he regarded as ideally flexible, nonarbitrary, and inventive, because it is created to suit a single poetic occasion and experience.

During the early twenties, as in the West, it was the fashion for modern poets to reject conventional metrical schemes in favor of the natural speech rhythm proposed by Hu Shih. Needless to say, Wen was opposed to this "poetic license" and gave as his argument: "Certain poetic rhythm may be accidentally found in our natural speech. But, because of this, to claim that that speech *is* poetic rhythm and thereby determine to dispense with any regulated sound pattern is indeed committing suicide!" Wen's poetic theories are crystallized in the meter he used for **"The Dead Water,"** the poem he considered his most successful experiment. Following is the basic line that opens the poem:

> che shih   i kou   chüeh wang te   ssu shui

The metrical pattern of three two-syllable feet and one three-syllable foot within the line is observed throughout the poem, although the position of these metrical feet varies from line to line. The meter provides a compositional order of sorts, yet allows within that order a variety of sound arrangements.

This compact stanzaic pattern with its end-stopped lines proves particularly congenial to Wen's style, which is more sculpturesque and static than airy or fluid. It offers the structural integrity that Wen strives for. The end-stopped lines here are often deliberately employed to strengthen the syntactical patterns of parallelism in the line units. These stylistic devices produce effects of gravity and restraint, and convey a more formal atmosphere and rhythmic movement.

Wen's indebtedness to both Western and traditional prosody is unmistakable. His general principles are essentially derivative and conservative; nevertheless, they are sound. The meter of **"The Dead Water,"** though it has an affinity with traditional verse forms, is designed to suit the vernacular's looser word order and grammatical construction. Wen's theories failed to solve all the prosodic problems, but they opened up new areas for exploration and at the same time offered a usable prosodic system for the new medium. They were especially meaningful at a time when modern Chinese poetry was desperately in need of order and new direction.

Wen I-to was not a prolific poet. Almost all of his verse was written during the mid-twenties when he was concerned with the problems of form, and his work inevitably reflects this concern. But it does much more. It opens up an extraordinarily lush world interwoven with dazzling colors, startling imageries, and a luxurious sensuousness worthy of his poetic mentors, Keats and Li Shang-yin. Wen attained sensuous effects by means of a richness and variety of imagery unsurpassed by his contemporaries. His poetry not only evokes the animated Keatsian world of "luxuriant vegetation," but also calls forth the inanimate world of sweet incense, red candles, and tinkling jewels that belonged to Li Shang-yin. An artist by instinct and training, Wen was fascinated by works of art whose man-wrought beauty he prized above that of nature. Images, symbols, and descriptive details in his poetry are frequently derived from or associated with the realm of art.

Wen's fondness for the tangible particular and the poised object is seen in the following lines from **"The First Chapter of Spring,"** in which he seeks to recapture an early spring scene:

> Over the bend of the arbor, there are a few lean hard
> Branches of elms that have not quite caught up with spring.
> They are now imprinted in a sky of fish scales
> Like a page of light blue clouded writing paper
> On which monk Huai-ssu has scribbled his
> Cursive script of iron and silver strokes.

Blue clouds like fish scales, hard lean branches of elm, and angular script—these interpenetrating images weave a picture of staid repose in a cold, bleak early spring. All is as serenely poised as a traditional landscape painting. There is no doubt that Wen relies largely on synesthesia to attain the fullest sensuous effect in his poetry. But, like Keats, Wen's pursuit of the sensuous is not an end in itself; it is a means to a more profound and complex poetic experience in which sense, intellect, and emotion are interfused. Again like Keats, Wen's synesthetic imagery holds up the mirror to his own awareness of the relations between nature and man. It reflects, too, Wen's concern with the dualities in life. One feels an emotional, as well as an intellectual, tension in his constant juxtaposition of these opposing forces. It is this tension that distinguishes him

as a modern poet, perceptive and deeply aware of the time and place that give his style its distinctive character and his works their special quality.

Synesthetic imagery is not alien to Chinese traditional poetry. In the poetry of late T'ang times (Li Shang-yin's era) and the *tz'u* verse of early Sung, this kind of imagery is especially abundant. Moonlight is often described as frost, as in the famous quatrain by Li Po that combines both visual and tactual senses in a single image: "Seeing the bright moonlight before my couch / I thought it was frost upon the ground." Here the coolness, the whiteness, and the brightness of the moon are suggested in one image—the frost.

In his depiction of a deserted scene near a temple, Wang Wei, one of the greatest traditional nature poets, combines auditory sensation in one line while mingling the visual and the tactual in the next. The result is cool detachment—the state of mind of the protagonist projected through the synthesis of different sensations: "The sound of stream is echoed by the boulders, / The color of sun chills the green pines." A typical compliment to a beautiful lady is to poetize her as "soft jade and warm perfume," a description that embraces physical sensations of touch, sight, temperature, and smell. Such examples are a common feature in Chinese traditional poetry.

Wen often reinforces a sight or odor image with a kinesthetic one, giving the image added weight: "A patch of slanting sun hangs head down from the eaves." This line is reminiscent of Keats's exquisite blending of images in "Ode to a Nightingale": "Nor what soft incense hangs upon the boughs." It also recalls the line from Tu Fu: "The stars hang over the vast plains." In a love lyric entitled **"Forget Her,"** Wen wishes he could forget his loved one as he would a flower: "That colored morning cloud on the petal, / That thread of fragrance in the heart of a flower."

On certain occasions Wen's interwoven images are the chief contributor to the emotional intensity of a poem. In **"The Tears of Rain,"** Wen compares the youth's tears with the "continuously falling gloomy rains," whose intensity is such that they have even "sprinkled the soil and bitter yellow plum to ripeness."

In still another verse, **"The Red Candle,"** Wen borrows Li Shang-yin's image of a candle melting into tears to suggest the self-consuming passion of the dedicated artist: "O red candle! / Every teardrop you shed has ashened a part of my heart." And in another poem the image is even more explicit: "The red candle ceaselessly sheds its tears of blood." In the first passage, blood is only implied by the color "red." This immediately calls forth a conceit popular in the old poetry when the lover's tears are said to be red because his eyes have been shedding blood. The instantaneous transference from a sight image to an emotional one is strengthened by another sense effect, the ashened heart. This last image, with its connotation of incense burning into ashes (another conceit of self-consuming passion in Li Shang-yin's poetry), completes the highly charged metaphor. Compression and association are the hallmark of Wen's synesthesia.

Like Keats and some traditional Chinese poets, Wen is equally successful at rendering sound more palpable by allying the sound image with some other order of sensation, usually tactual. "The bird sound is as round as a dewdrop." And every word of the song is "a drop of bright pearl / Every word is a drop of hot tear." Or, the children's laughter is crisp, "like a crystal pagoda crashing down."

Perhaps the best illustration of Wen's distinctive technique in fusing divergent sensations is his famous masterpiece, **"The Dead Water,"** which may also serve as the supreme example of Wen's pursuit of stylistic and structural discipline:

> This is a ditch of hopelessly dead water.
> No clear breeze can raise half a ripple on it.
> Why not throw in some rusty metal scraps,
> Or even some of your leftover food and soup?
>
> Perhaps the copper will turn its green patina into jade,
> And on the tin can rust will bloom into peach blossoms;
> Then let grease weave a layer of silk brocade,
> And germs brew out colored clouds.
>
> Let the dead water ferment into a ditch of green wine,
> Filled with the floating pearllike white foam,
> The laughter of small pearls turning into large pearls
> Only to be pierced when gnats come to steal the wine.
>
> Thus, a ditch of hopelessly dead water
> May yet claim some small measure of splendor.
> And if the frogs cannot bear the loneliness,
> Let the dead water burst into song.
>
> This is a ditch of hopelessly dead water,.
> A place where beauty can never live.
> Might as well let vice cultivate it,
> And see what kind of world it can create.

In this elegiac poem written in the late twenties, Wen expressed his feelings about the seemingly hopeless situation in China. It is a sad poem, but not a poem of despair. The formal structure and heavy stresses, the pregnant density, the ponderous movement—all contribute to the somber air and sculpturesque style characteristic of Wen. The use of end-stopped lines supports the syntactical patterns of parallelism and repetition, and thereby secures additional structural balance and unity within the poem.

It is true that Wen tends to overstress the visual at the expense of the auditory. Critics like Chu Hsiang who censured his slipshod use of rhymes would disapprove of Wen's loose rhyme pattern here, but there is justification for Wen's choice. Occurring in irregular order, the rhymes integrate the poem without calling too much notice to themselves; they direct the readers' attention to the content of the poem without being obtrusive. The predominant use of slant rhymes . . . is in perfect congruence with the colloquialism of the vernacular. The poem would risk the monotony of excessive symmetry if the rhyme were too orderly. Wen made abundant use of such devices as alliteration . . . , assonance . . . , and internal rhymes . . . to achieve a subtle unifying effect, at the same time enriching the verbal texture of the poem. Wen's language is a masterful blend of the colloquial . . . and the poetic. . . . The juxtaposition of the rigorous, the commonplace, and even the repulsive with the delicately sensuous and the desirable heightens the dualistic patterns as well as the emotional content of the poem.

**"The Dead Water"** is a prime example of Wen's synesthetic technique. In the third stanza the transformation of the ditch of dead water into luscious green wine produces a swift and exciting shift of sensation. The dead water is no longer stagnant but green—an association with spring which suggests the life force. This visual image is intensified by what it describes—wine, which at once evokes pleasant olfactory and taste sensations. In the next line Wen's favorite pearl image adds form, light, and weight. All these different senses undergo an instantaneous transmutation as the pearls, bursting into laughter, suddenly acquire human qualities. Personification reinforces the fusing of diverse sense images with the new organic feeling. The last line of the stanza brings us back to the initial images

of the dead water and the green wine, thereby providing a final unity to the overall framework.

Wen shared with Keats not only the gift for synesthesia but a fondness for the luxurious world of plants, fruits, and flowers. As early as in his first poem,**"The West Coast,"** one is led to "a small island wearing a headful of flowers and grass," where nature is envisioned in all her lush splendor. Like Keats, Wen favored the joining of the water image with a vegetative image. References to rain or its effects are frequent, as in **"The First Chapter of Spring"**:

> The rain that bathed men's souls has passed.
> The thin mud bites men's shoes everywhere.
> The cool breeze with its moist odor of earth
> Rushes forward to fill our nostrils.

A little later in the same poem, rain again appears:

> The east wind urges the stubborn rush roots
> To open up their newly awakened sprouts.
> The spring rain passes; the sprouts are just one inch long.
> The water in the pond stealthily swallows them.

Wen's unqualified admiration for Keats is apparent in **"The Loyal Minister of Art."** By bestowing such a title on the senior poet, Wen paid him the greatest of compliments. Anyone familiar with Chinese culture will know that one of the highest forms of loyalty is that of a minister to his ruler. In addition to using this traditional symbol, Wen compares Keats's brilliance with the particular pearl on the emperor's robe that surpasses all the rest of the pearls. The piece ends with a couplet: "Your name has not been written on water. / It is cast on the imperial tripod of the sacred reign."

The choice of traditional Chinese symbols here is apt and imaginative; it deepens the sincerity of the sentiment. The inclusion of traditional motifs persists in many of Wen's works, whether they are poems inspired by a Western concept (the quest for beauty, love, and truth), poems dealing with a foreign subject, or descriptive verses. In the following passage Wen joins two old images associated with the moon in order to develop his own image, a device that was habitually cultivated by the traditional Chinese poets.

> O loyal descendants of the Great Cosmos!
> Younger sister of the moon!
> Are you the jade spittle splashed onto the sky?
> Or are you the pearls wept by the mermaid
> And washed up by the waves?

Wen combines here two common images of the moon (goddess and jade) with the verb *t'u* (. . . "to emit" ["splashed"]), which is ordinarily associated with the moon. Tu Fu used the same word to suggest the slow and graceful emergence of the moon from the surrounding mountains in his famous line, "At the fourth watch, the mountains exhale the moon." Wen uses the familiar verb to describe the jade spittle emitted by the moon goddess and splashed onto the horizon. The effect is a bit strained. It needs to be pointed out here that both the words for "emit" . . . and "spittle" . . . escape the unpleasant associations they have in English. On the contrary, they are considered poetically sophisticated in traditional Chinese poetry. In the last two lines, a familiar allusion—the pearls of the mermaid's tears—appears. (The mermaid who weeps tears of pearls comes from a well-known Chinese mythological tale.) Wen customarily employs conventional images in the traditional ways to set the tone or to create a desired atmosphere. Sometimes these images embody a symbolic purpose. In Wen's long narrative poem, **"The Death of Li Po,"** based on the legendary death of the T'ang poet who, when inebriated, drowned himself while trying to catch the image of the moon, the moon becomes the central symbol of the poet's eternal quest for beauty and truth. This quest is a theme important in Wen's works and is traceable to Keats and/or Shelley.

Wen's fondness for the special effect of light filtering through leafy openings is reminiscent of Keats's moon filtering through "opening clouds" in "Endymion":

> And lo! from opening clouds, I saw emerge
> The loveliest moon, that ever silver'd o'er
> A shell for Neptune's goblet. . . .

Compare this with Wen's "The silver tide of moon / Trickled through the leaves' openings to rush into the windows." And his sun is "a laughing blaze—a ray of light / Filtered through the trees' openings to be sprinkled on my forehead."

The moon is sometimes pictured in a more conventional way: "A jade plate hangs on a dark blue sky" has an instinctive rightness about it in a poem with a traditional setting. In the same poem ("**The Death of Li Po,**" mentioned above), the moonlight is similarly depicted as "The dancing silver light sieved through the leaves' openings." The visual image here, enlivened by the blithe and graceful movements of the dance, gives a new personality to the moon. Something cool, precious, and yet quite out of human reach, the moon is now brought down to earth, dancing through the leaves. Toward the last part of the poem, it goes through yet another transformation: "Peeping out behind the shadow of the silken willows by the pond, / Like a beauty drying her hair by the window after her bath." Wen adroitly joins the attenuated image of silken willow strands with the implied vision of the moon's dark tresses, bodied forth by the special effect of the moonlight's being sieved through the willows and cast upon the pond. Here two related sets of descriptions are fused to create a unified vision of the moon that symbolizes not only beauty but love. It becomes a source of inspiration and an ideal to be intensely pursued. The ideal world of beauty and love, however, is illusory and destructive, for it is this very illusion that leads the drunken poet to leap into the water and ironically meet his death trying to save the drowning moon.

"**The Death of Li Po**" perfectly embodies the romantic awareness of the gulf between aspiration and actual fulfillment. The moon is not only an object idealized and pursued, but a symbol of unrealized yearning. Implicit from the beginning and growing in intensity throughout the poem is a sense of human mortality and futility. The ending has a climactic poignancy in the tragic death of Li Po, the great romantic idealist of his day. Li Po, seeing the round moon peacefully pressed against the sky, dies in ecstasy under the delusion that he has succeeded in saving his beloved, while the latter coolly and mockingly watches from above, as unattainable as ever.

The subject of love and beauty is treated more compactly in a purely lyrical piece, "**Beauty and Love**":

> The soft lamplight flickers through the window.
> Rows of saffron-colored squares are inlaid on the walls;
> The shadows of two jujube trees are like coiled snakes
> Spread in all directions and asleep beneath the walls.
>
> Oh that large star, the companion of Chang-o!
> Why do you come within my sight?
> The bird within my heart abruptly stops its spring songs
> When it hears your silent heavenly music.

Listen, it has even forgotten itself,
Determined only to fly away in search of you.
It has crushed open the iron prison.
But in an instant, you vanished.

> The chill wind at the corner of the house sadly sighs.
> Startling the sleepy snakes into motion.
> The moon has turned ghastly pale, perhaps annoyed.
> The window opens its large mouth as if it were laughing aloud.
>
> Poor bird, he is back now.
> Muted, blinded, heart turned to ashes
> And wings dripping with fresh blood.
> Can this be the price of love, the sin of beauty?

It is difficult to discuss "**Beauty and Love**" without recalling Keats, who has influenced Wen in so many ways. One sees interesting parallels with Keats's "Ode to a Nightingale," the chief of which are a somewhat grim outlook on life and a questioning of the true nature of reality. Both poems close with irresolution: Keats asks, "Was it a vision, or a waking dream? . . . Do I wake or sleep?"; Wen's query is, "Can this be the price of love, the sin of beauty?"

But beyond these similarities the two compositions diverge widely. Keats's entire ode concentrates upon the nightingale's song, which seems to offer the only possible relief to "the fever, and the fret" of human life. In "**Beauty and Love,**" although the bird is a prominent figure in its identification with the speaker, Wen centers on the dark and violent nature of reality. Many details are devoted to the mysteriously sinister, almost surrealistic world that confronts the escaped bird. The grotesque appearance of coiled snakes asleep on the ground suggests the potential evil inherent in nature and foreshadows the impending danger. The second stanza opens with an invocation to the large star, the symbol of beauty and love. The bird, hearing the ineffable music of the star, abruptly abandons his singing. The third stanza sees the bird—the human spirit—enthralled by the music, determined to venture forth in search of it. Bursting open its iron prison, it is instantly disappointed in its quest, for the star vanishes. The disconsolate mood deepens in the fourth stanza as the chill wind's sad sigh wakens the snakes by the walls. The window laughs maliciously with gaping mouth. The moon—the object of the bird's quest—turns phantomlike. The concluding stanza discloses the tragic aftermath of the bird's futile search and the speaker's despairing questioning of the experience. This awareness of violence as a condition of human existence is a particularly modern aspect of Wen's works.

One of Wen's early poems, "**Death,**" deals with a theme recurrent in his later works:

> Soul of my soul!
> Life of my life!
> The failures and debts of my whole life
> Now demand their payments from you.
> Yet what do I have?
> What could I ask of you?
> Let me be drowned to death in your eyes' waves.
> Let me be burned to death in the melting stove of your heart.
> Let me be drowned to death in the sweet nectar of your music!
> Let me be suffocated to death in the fragrance of your breath!
> Otherwise, let your dignity shame me to death!
> Let your cold freeze me to death!
> Let that heartless poisonous sword stab me to death!
> If you reward me with happiness,
> I'll die of happiness.
> If you give me suffering,
> I'll die of suffering.
> Death is my only respect from you.
> Death is my ultimate offering to you.

This is a markedly inferior work. Rhetorical indulgences, banalities, and melodramatic gestures are some of its major faults. The word repetition and parallelism of line forecast, but in a relatively crude manner, the subtler technical devices of parallelism and antithesis in Wen's more mature works. The poem is interesting for its disclosure of Wen's concept of death, which he develops in his later verse, **"The Last Day"**:

> The dewdrops sob in the gutters,
> The green tongues of banana trees lick at the window,
> The chalk-white walls are receding from me.
> I cannot fill such an enormous room alone.
>
> With a brazier ablaze in my heart,
> I await quietly the guest from afar.
> I feed the fire with cobwebs and rats' dung.
> I use the scaly snake skins for split wood.
>
> The rooster continues its urging: a heap of ash remains in the
>         pan.
> A gust of chill wind steals over my mouth,
> The guest is already before me;
> I close my eyes and follow after the guest.

One notices a clear advance in Wen's art from the earlier practice to this present performance: the close-knit stanzas, the classical restraint, the dazzling images. The style is more polished too, and phrasings are less awkward and bland. Possibly the most striking surface characteristic is its astonishing empathic responsiveness to nature. Wen's consciousness of the perverse aspects of nature and his gothic sense of the macabre are vividly conveyed through images like snake skins, cobwebs, and rats' dung. Death is humanized as a guest calmly anticipated by the speaker. Despite its quiet air, the poem is tempered by a more formidable note: an ominous foreboding shrouds the closing lines as death inevitably arrives.

To Wen, as to Chu Tzu-ch'ing (in his poem, "Dissolution"), death has an aura of mystery that he finds hard to resist. Perhaps Wen's concept of death is akin to that of Keats—a "luxury" so "easeful" and seductive.

#### "PERHAPS: A DIRGE"

> Perhaps you are indeed too wearied from too much weeping.
> Perhaps, perhaps you wish to fall asleep now.
> Then ask the night owl not to cough,
> The frogs not to croak and bats not to fly.
>
> Let no sunshine pierce your eyelids,
> Let no clear winds touch your brows,
> And whoever he may be, let him not startle you.
> With an umbrella of pine I shall guard your sleep.
>
> Perhaps you hear earthworms turning the soil,
> The grass roots sucking water.
> Perhaps the music you hear now
> Is lovelier than men's cursing voices.
>
> Close tight your eyes then,
> I shall let you sleep, let you sleep.
> I'll gently cover you with yellow earth
> And ask the ashes of paper money to rise slowly.

**"Perhaps"** is a well-controlled poem; the elegiac tone and gentle mood are consistent. The lyrical impulse is unusually light for Wen. Implicit from the initial line is the speaker's assumption that life is wearisome and full of woes (a further reminder of Keats); only in death is ultimate ease achieved. To secure this repose, however, it seems necessary to close out the disturbing elements in life symbolized by the night owl's cough, the frogs' croaking, the bats' flight, and the natural forces, the sunlight and the winds. The serene atmosphere is enhanced in the third stanza by a tranquil delineation of the underground scene. Wen's extraordinary response to nature is here suggested by his ability to hear earthworms turning the soil and roots sucking water and music lovelier than that of the world above. This amazing quality may explain why the poet is drawn to death—he envisions the approach of death as opening up to him a whole new realm of knowledge otherwise inaccessible to men.

Wen composed a number of nature poems, some richly dense and elaborately wrought (such as **"Autumn"**), others spare and taut, as is **"Small Brook"**:

> The lead-gray trees' shadow
> Is a long chapter of nightmare
> Pressing downward on the bosom of
> The small brook in heavy slumber.
> The mountain brook struggles, struggles
> With no result.

This brilliantly compressed verse is as vivid as it is restrained. The mood of stifling oppression is deftly imaged despite the poem's extreme brevity. Like Chu Tzu-ch'ing, Wen often imbues his descriptive verse with his subjective consciousness. By a subtle transference of metaphor the poem is transformed into a stricken vision of life's oppressive burden: in the purity of Wen's lyrical voice is concealed a deep sense of human pathos.

The range of Wen's poetry is quite wide. He has written highly impassioned patriotic verse, in addition to nature poems, occasional verse, and poems of social and political implications. But the essential Wen I-to soars away from the topical and the social to a realm of pure imagination. Behind his poems, be they successes or failures, lies the intense dedication of a wholly committed artist. It seems fitting to conclude here with an earlier poem, **"The Sword Box,"** which is probably the clearest manifestation of Wen the poet.

As a prelude to **"The Sword Box,"** Wen quoted the lines of Tennyson's "Palace of Art":

> . . . I built my soul a lordly pleasure house,
>     Wherein at ease for aye to dwell.
>         . . . . . . . . . . . .
> And while the world runs round and round, I said,
>     "Reign thou apart, a quiet king,
> Still as, while Saturn whirls, his steadfast shade
>     Sleeps on his luminous ring."
> To which my soul made answer readily:
>     "Trust me in bliss I shall abide
> In this great mansion, that is built for me,
>     So royal and rich and wide."

As Tennyson built his soul a "pleasure house," Wen in his poem devotes himself to building a sword box so that his precious sword may have a permanent place to rest.

The poem is not written in Wen's characteristic form, the **"Dead Water"** meter, which evolved later. It is composed of both short and long lines distributed in stanzaic units of unequal length. Although end rhymes are profusely used for patterned effects, the general mode of this verse-narrative is one of flexibility and freedom.

The style is less weighted though no less ornate or intense than his later one. In one of his letters, Wen named this poem together with **"Remembering Chrysanthemum"** and **"Autumn"** as the three works most clearly influenced by Keats and Li Shang-yin. The poem begins: "In the battle of life / I was once a world-famous general." The speaker then narrates how he came to a deserted island to "nurse his battle wounds" and "forget his enemies." In the stanza that follows, he announces his desire to live like a "nameless farmer drinking to the full the brilliant colors of the field," or a fisherman "casting his net of fancy" and dreaming all day long by the sandy beach, or just wandering in the woods collecting precious stones (these are familiar occupations of the recluse poets in traditional poetry). Having collected enough precious stones, he is determined to pursue the humble life of an artisan. He vows to build a box for his sword:

> I shall lay out all the treasures
> And display them before me.
> I shall carve, engrave,
> Rub and grind every single piece.
> Then I shall inlay them on the sword box,
> Using every chapter of my dream as the blueprint.
> I shall design all kinds of wondrous vistas.

The artist proceeds to carve four figures: T'ai I, Venus, Buddha, and a blind musician. They are probably intended as symbols of harmony and permanence, beauty and love, Truth, and Poetry—the quintessence of life that Wen himself seeks in his ideal world of imagination. The four figures are wrought in the most elaborate physical details and sensuous images.

> I shall trace out the white-faced, long-bearded T'ai I,
> Asleep on the pink lotus petals
> And drifting amidst the white clouds of ivory.

The choice of T'ai I, the Supreme Sky God in Chinese mythology, to represent Great Harmony or Permanence is a masterful touch. Wen's personification of him as a "white-faced, long-bearded" old man caught reposing on lotus petals and borne on clouds of ivory imparts an atmosphere of calm and other-worldliness as well as the sense of tranquillity, harmony, and infinity so important to romantic poets of all ages. Wen's choice of Venus as his symbol of love and beauty strikes an incongruous note. Why did he not choose a more traditional Chinese beauty like Yan Kuei-fei or Hsi Shih? Venus certainly looks a bit odd and uncomfortable in the company of so many strangers!

> I shall use ink jade and gold threads
> To build an incense burner inlaid with lines of thunder.
> Over the burner a scriptlike smoke rises gracefully;
> It may be carved out of opaque cat's-eye.
> Above the half-dying smoke,
> A beauty of jade rises dimly.
> Oh how she resembles Venus in flesh:
> This piece of rose jade is just her color!

This dazzling tableau is immediately followed by an equally splendid presentation of the awe-inspiring Buddha:

> I shall carve the Buddha with agate,
> A Buddha of three hands and six arms,
> Riding on an elephant made of fish stone.
> Coral is the fire he holds in his mouth.
> Silver threads are plaited into pythons around his waist,
> And the halo over his head is a round disk of amber.

In all his earlier works, Wen tends to overload his lines with descriptive details. But even in these early attempts he demonstrates an astonishing capability for fusing diverse sense impressions and for attaining strong sensuous effects by transforming a visual image of weight. To invoke an impression of rich ornamentation here, Wen has selected a whole catalogue of precious stones—jade, amber, cat's-eye, coral. These sight images take on an added sense of touch and weight when enforced by words like "carve" or "plaited." The portraiture

of the blind musician playing his ancient instrument on a bamboo raft in the river is just as impressive.

Once these four distinguished personae are carved, the artist-protagonist further embellishes his sword box with intricate decorations. When the project is finally finished, the artist rapturously kisses the sword and cries out:

> I kiss away its rust, its wounds;
> I wash its bloodstains with my tears.
> I cleanse away all traces of sin.
> . . . . . . . . . .
> I then gently place it in the box,
> And singing a soft song,
> I urge it to sleep peacefully in this palace of art.

Having furnished a permanent abode for his cherished sword, the speaker declares that he now wants to "swoon to death in the radiance of the resplendent sword box." This state of swooning to death is repeated in the concluding stanza, when the artist-speaker is so overwhelmed with admiration for his completed masterpiece that he forgets to breathe, "and the blood forgets to flow, / The eyes forget to look." The poem ends in a romantic climax of triumphant death:

> Oh I have killed myself!
> I have killed myself with my self-made sword box!
> My great mission is accomplished!

Despite its seeming ambiguity, the violent ending has an immediate impact on the reader. Wen seems to seek romantic "rapture" in creative imagination and ecstasy, whose intensity is comparable only to that of death itself. Or is Wen thinking of Keats's lines: "Verse, Fame, and Beauty are intense indeed, / But Death intenser—Death is life's high meed"? Wen may very well be attempting to express the tremendous conflict within himself, a conflict accentuated by his feelings of obligation to the modern world. Like other romantics Wen seems torn between an imaginative realm of art and the real world of suffering and pain. He tries to reconcile the two, but with little success. Very likely he feels that art, being useless because its world is an illusion, is ultimately destructive to life.

This feeling again leads us to one pervasive impulse in Wen's poetry: the profound awareness of reality and the preoccupation with the dualities in nature and art—beauty and ugliness, life and death. One senses an emotional, as well as an intellectual, tension in his constant juxtaposition of these opposing forces. It is this tension that distinguishes him as a modern poet, perceptive, sensitive, and keenly conscious of the time and place that give him and his works their special luster. He is a romantic poet living in the twentieth century, not the nineteenth or the tenth. Here is his own confession, in which, despite his disclaimer, he shows himself more a poet than many others of his generation:

### "CONFESSION"

I do not deceive you when I say I am no poet,
Even though I love the integrity of the white rocks,
The green pines and the vast sea, the sunset on the crow's
    back,
The twilight woven with the wings of bats.
You know that I love heroes and tall mountains.
I love, too, the national flag outspread in the breeze,
The chrysanthemums colored from soft yellow to antique
    bronze.
But remember that my food is a pot of bitter tea!
And there is another "I." Will you be afraid to know it?
The flylike thought crawling in the garbage can!

(pp. 80-100)

*Julia C. Lin, "The Formalists," in her* Modern Chinese Poetry: An Introduction, *University of Washington Press, 1972, pp. 75-151.*

**KAI-YÜ HSÜ** (essay date 1980)

[*In the following excerpt, Hsü discusses Wen's poetic theories in the context of the conflicting political and artistic movements in China during the 1920s.*]

As Theophile Gautier, with whom Wen had much in common, had done for French poetry half a century earlier, Wen developed a doctrine for modern Chinese poetry. He theorized on his dedication to poetry and art, which he had expressed in his earlier poems in the **Red Candle**. A poem, he said, must be carved as a sculpture is carved out of a piece of hard stone. In a series of essays published in April-June, 1926, he argued persuasively for the importance of form. "If we compare poetry to the game of chess," he said, "we can easily understand why poetry without form, like a game of chess without rules, must be such a meaningless thing! . . . But most young poets nowadays, in the name of romanticism, regard the ruleless games they are playing as poetry writing." Pursuing his disagreement with the theory of "natural rhythm" or "natural form" advocated by Hu Shih (1891-1962), Wen admitted that there was form in nature, but insisted that very few forms copied intact from nature could be perfect. Perfection in form could be achieved only after much patient chiseling. He quoted Goethe and Han Yü to support his theory that "The greater the artist, the more he enjoys dancing in fetters." That is to say, the greatness of an artist lies in his ability to dance gracefully in spite of the shackles. Moreover, the shackles (form—structural principles) in the hands of a great artist are transformed into effective tools. In this he also found support in Tu Fu's line, "As I grow older I become more particular about poetic rules."

Wen's theory of poetic form stresses mainly the visual and musical effects created by the poetic language. In his typical propensity for structural finesse, he presented a three-point dictum—poetry must possess beauty in three aspects: musical beauty, or the rhythm and melody in a poem; pictorial beauty, or the colors and forms of graphic images bought forth through words; and architectural beauty, or the evenness and neatness of stanza-forms. Making use of the principle of the English prosodic foot, which he had studied with considerable care, he analyzed the stressed and unstressed syllables in *pai-hua* phrases to show the metrical balance that can be achieved in carefully measured lines. Being preoccupied with the graphic and plastic arts, and having mastered the classical Chinese *lü-shih* form, he saw a rich source of aesthetic power in the pictorial quality of written Chinese characters which lend themselves to the architectural structuring of different stanza forms like so many building blocks, each one neat and square. His belief in the convertibility of poetry, painting, sculpture, and music carried him from Gautier's carefully carved *Emaux et Camées* to Mallarmé's graphic *"Un coup de dés jamais n'abolira le hasard."* Although two years later he criticized the forced union of poetry and painting by the pre-Raphaelites, in 1926 he himself planned to decorate his famous studio with three paintings on the themes of three poems by Ch'ü Yüan (343-290 B.C.), Tu Fu, and Lu Yu respectively, and he completed the one on Lu Yu. With all this emphasis on form, however, he hastened to explain that to find new forms was not to return the newly liberated Chinese poetry to a prison. "The difference between the old and new forms is that the former is a fixed frame into which we are asked to fit all kinds of content and feeling, while the latter is something we must create to suit each individual subject and image." Therefore, with all his respect for T'ang poetry, he would not advocate

a revival of writing *lü-shih*, the neatly and strictly structured regulated verse perfected in the T'ang dynasty.

He demonstrated his poetics in what he called his first most successful experiment, a poem entitled **"Dead Water"** which became his best remembered work.

> Chè-shih/ i-kōu/ chüéh-wàng-te/ szŭ-shŭi,
> This is/ a ditch/ hopeless/ dead water
>
> Ch'īng-feng/ ch'ūi-pu-ch'i/ pàn-tien/ ī-lún.
> Light wind/ blow not up/ half point/ ripple
>
> Pù-ju/ tō-jēng-hsieh/ p'ò-t'úng/ làn-t'íeh,
> Better/ more throw some/ broken brass/ torn iron
>
> Shuăng-hsìng/ p'ō-nĭ-te/ shèng-ts'ài/ ts'án-kēng.
> Straightforward nature/ pour your/ leftover food/ unfinished soup

The scansion he himself suggested shows that in this first of five stanzas,—five quatrains—in **"Dead Water,"** each line contains one trisyllabic and three bisyllabic feet, a pattern maintained throughout the poem. The position of the trisyllabic foot may vary from line to line, but the variation does not impede a sustained rhythmic flow, well punctuated by the uniformly bisyllabic foot at the line's end. The end rhyme maintains an *a-b-c-b* pattern, and though when the Chinese sounds are Romanized according to the Wade-Giles system, *lun* and *keng* in the above quoted stanza seem to be imperfect end-rhymes, they are musically pleasing as an experienced Chinese reader declaims the poem in Mandarin.

It has been said that Wen failed to take note of the lack of fixed stress in Chinese syllables, and that scanning a Chinese line presents insoluble problems. But the words in this poem are all taken from natural Chinese speech which, subject to some variation in individual speech habits, could give each syllable equal stress (except the third of a trisyllable foot, in most cases), or carry stress on the first syllable of each foot, making them nearly all trochaic and dactylic. In the above illustration, all unmarked syllables are usually unstressed, and the circled marks indicate secondary or lighter stress. When properly read, the demonstration shows that Wen's theory works, and his discovery of the important function of binomes in the poetic language certainly has made many students of Chinese poetry aware of what they were unconsciously doing or failing to do. Later, it will be seen that his discovery was to have a lasting influence.

Though Wen did not specifically elaborate on this illustration of prosodic features, he did demonstrate in the single sample above the musical qualities achieved by prosodic arrangements, including but not limited to the uniform number of feet in a line and the ringing end-rhymes. There is a pause pattern by sense grouping (meaning of the language) in each line and between stanzas—a slight pause between the second and third foot generally, and a more noticeable pause between each two stanzas. The last feature is particularly noticeable between the third and fourth stanzas, which is introduced with a transitional word, *na-ma*. There is rhythmic repetition of sound units, such as *sheng-ts'ai* / *ts'an-keng* in the fourth line, repeating the rhythm of *p'o-t'ung* / *lan-t'ieh* in the third; they are also syntactical parallels: leftover-food / unfinished-soup and broken-brass / torn-iron. Then, too, there is rhythmic repetition of words and phrases, both for reinforcement of certain images and sound effects. The very first line is repeated at the beginning of the last stanza—the effect is that of a musical refrain as well as, rhetorically, a concluding statement that goes back to the theme, indeed the thematic bar of music.

As Wen said that the new form he was advocating must be wedded to the individual poem's substance, the carefully measured prosody of the **"Dead Water"** poem works well largely because the theme is somber, the tone, one of controlled anger, and the pace smooth but ponderous. For a more lyrical theme, that of mourning the death of his young daughter, Wen designed a different musical and architectural form:

> Wàng-tiao-t'a/ hsìang i-tuo/ wàng-tiao-te hūa
> Forget her/ like-a-bloom/ forgotten flower
>
> Na chāo-hsía/ tsai huā-pàn-shang
> That sunrise/ on flower-petal
>
> Na huā-hsīn-te/ i-lü hsiāng
> That flower-center's/ one-whiff scent
>
> Wàng-tiao-t'a/ hsìang i-tuo/ wàng-tiao-te hūa
> Forget her/ like-a-bloom/ forgotten flower

All seven stanzas of the poem follow the same form, with the same possible scansion, the first and last lines being the same, three feet each, and two feet in the second and third lines. That the scansion depends very much on the stress-and-pause pattern in this poem is quite evident because in some stanzas the lines are so free-flowing and colloquial that the metrical effect can be felt only if they are read with a consciousness of the stressed and unstressed syllables, such as the second and third lines in the sixth stanza:

> Ju-kuo-shih/ yu-jen yao-wen,
> If       there is person ask
>
> Chiu-shuo/ mei-yu na-ko-jen;
> Just say there is no that person

It is very possible to scan both lines into trimeters, but the sense grouping, and the feeling in the poem, call for almost a slurring-over of the second foot in both lines. It's a grief-stricken voice, fighting back tears and trying, almost inaudibly, to dismiss a well-intentioned but nevertheless superfluous question. The refrain effect, at the beginning and end of each stanza, rings a death knell, its sorrow modified only by the mist—

> As a dream in the wind of spring,
> As in a dream, a bell's ring;

—of tears in the eye? or of the evening haze that muffles the sound of the bell?

Even more noticeably demonstrated is the use of the stressed syllables in natural, colloquial speech in the poem "Fei-mao t'ui," which portrays a rickshaw boy, speaking typical Peking colloquial. The neat lengths of the lines, thirteen syllables in every one of the sixteen lines except two, cannot be scanned into regular feet unless the reader grasps the stressed syllables which quite easily define a rather uniform trimetric pattern throughout the poem. One critic has compared this feature with Gerard Manley Hopkins' "sprung rhythm."

In presenting pictorial beauty through his poetry, Wen continued but further refined the colorful images he had used in such poems as **"Autumn Colors"** in the *Red Candle*. The exhilarating jade-green of the autumn pool in that poem becomes the emerald on the oxidized brass in **"Dead Water,"** and the regal splendor of the imperial palace is now reflected in a putrid open sewer. But the poet, in irony, sees peach blooms on rusting tin cans, and ethereal gauze in floating grease. It is at once the influence of the Western grotesque persuasion as well as the Chinese Buddhist-Taoist perception of beauty in what appears ugly to mundane eyes. In **"Spring Light,"** the berries of a nandina are coral beads; in **"Last Day,"** the "green tongue"

of a banana leaf licks the window pane. Here images are also dramatic, when the leaf doesn't just touch but licks. And the little bubbles "chuckle" in the **"Dead Water"** to become big bubbles; the sunshine in the **"Dirge"** "pries" open the sleeping (dead) girl's eyelids. In these and numerous other lines the metaphors are fresh, original, effectively appropriate, bringing to the reader stirringly vivid images both still and in motion.

Unlike in his *wen-yen* days, Wen now rarely employed unfamiliar words. "If anyone should ask / Tell him she never existed" is more natural and colloquial than the vernacular in his *Red Candle,* and yet it fits neatly into the strict prosodic scheme of "Forget Her." The expression *i-lun* in the second line, first stanza of "Dead Water" may be considered a rare exception, but even there it does not sound obtrusive. Wen thus lived up to one of his own poetic dicta; namely, that modern speech can and has to be used in the development of a new Chinese poetic language.

On March 13, 1926, Wen presented his doctrine of form in an essay, **"The Form of Poetry."** The tone, somewhat brash and impatient, clearly reveals that he had been embroiled in a long and drawn-out war of words. "Poetry has never existed without form and rhythm," he said, "this is a universal truth never questioned before by anybody. And yet nowadays all universal truths have to be proven anew before their establishment, right? . . ." His argument was more rhetorically overpowering than exhaustively analytic, and his examples, brief and perfunctory, as though he was saying—all these have been chewed over before, why go into them in detail once again! The essay, indeed, was a frontal counterattack on the prevailing literary trends since the May Fourth Movement.

When Wen sailed for America in 1922, there was an upsurge of literary activity in China. The formation of the Literary Research Society the year before, followed by that of the Creation Society, marked the beginning of a movement to give direction to modern Chinese literature; heretofore, the new literature movement had been encouraging rebellion against traditional literature without offering anything constructive in its place. The Literary Research Society, with Mao Tun (Shen Yen-ping, 1896-  ) as its spokesman, first advocated a "humanistic realism." Mao Tun declared in 1921:

> We are opposed to the "art for life's sake" theory
> of Tolstoy, and we are also definitely opposed to the
> "Art for beauty's sake" type of Chinese literature
> which admittedly divorces itself from life.

Then, to define the purpose of literature and the responsibility of the writer, he said,

> The history of literary development in all countries
> shows that change in literary trends is always such
> as to enable literature more closely to represent life,
> to express the feeling of humanity, to voice man's
> suffering as well as hope, and to fight against the
> evil forces that hold him in bondage.

The Creation Society, led by Kuo Mo-jo, Ch'eng Fang-Wu (1894-  ), and Yü Ta-fu (1896-1945), all of whom Wen I-to admired, was founded on the Western Art-for-Art's-Sake ideal. "We want to pursue the perfection and capture the beauty of literature," said Ch'eng Fang-wu in May, 1923. The same ideal was expressed by Kuo Mo-jo with greater clarity:

> Literature, like the flowers and grass in spring, is the
> expression of the artist's inner wisdom. As the poet
> writes a poem, the composer composes a song, and

the painter paints a picture, their works are the spontaneous flow of their talents; just as the ripples raised by a spring breeze on the water, they have no purpose of their own. . . . Art itself has no purpose!

To be sure, elsewhere in Ch'eng Fang-wu's and Kuo Mo-jo's writings in the early 1920's there were already references to the need for literature sympathetic to the unpropertied class, but the predominating voice of the Creation Society at that time was clearly an expression of the Western "pure literature" ideal which this group of writers had acquired during their study abroad, mainly in Japan.

A major controversy in the new literary movement soon developed between those who continued to argue for the independence of literature, and those who increasingly emphasized the social mission of the writer. The latter group gained in strength. Before long, most of the leading writers agreed that literature had a social mission and that the writer must lead rather than follow social and political developments. To this Wen would consent in part, but not completely. But as soon as the other literary leaders turned to the Russian example which seemed to offer a solution to China's problems, Wen with his political sympathies still on the side of the anticommunist Ta-chiang Society, stood firm to rally his fellow Crescent writers to fight for the cause of "pure literature."

The increasing Kuomintang and warlord pressure speeded the consolidation of the Leftist writers. There was a sharp rise in their influence on the principal publishers and periodicals. The extreme Leftist Sun Society (T'ai-yang She), a small but vociferous group of writers, launched a relentless attack on every writer whose attitude was not clearly radical. When Kuo Mo-jo of the Creation Society first brought up the issue of "revolutionary literature," the Sun Society claimed leadership in this new literary movement. It touched off a race for recognition as the "most progressive and revolutionary" group among the writers. In March, 1926, Kuo Mo-jo said, "the literature we need at present . . . is realist in form, and socialist in content— this I can say with certainty." About a month later he further clarified his new position by writing his celebrated article "Revolution and Literature," calling the youths (with much of the gusto once shown in Ch'en Tu-hsiu's (1879-1942) "Solemn Appeal to Youth" of 1917) to go to "the soldiers, the people, the factories, and the whirlpool of revolution." A series of articles in the same vein appeared, culminating in Ch'eng Fang-wu's "From Literary Revolution to Revolutionary Literature," which exhorted the intelligentsia to band together, denounced neutralism in literature, and urged the writers to grasp dialectical materialism. "Walk toward the proletarian masses," Ch'eng admonished the Chinese bourgeois intellectuals in November, 1927. "Don't worry about losing your chains!" Within a short span of four years, the Creation Society and the trend of modern Chinese literature had reversed their directions completely.

In the literary winds then prevailing, Wen's doctrine of "form" enunciated in May, 1926, was hoisting sail in the opposite direction, because he held that the merit of a literary work should not be judged by its political message. That he was spared the severe criticism of Kuo Mo-jo and Chiang Kuang-tz'u (1901-1931) owed much to the strength of his argument and his poems, but even more to the preoccupation of those "literary revolutionists" with pressing political and social problems, not with strictly literary problems. Those who read Wen's theory most carefully were students of poetry who, since

the beginning of Chinese *pai-hua* literature, had been seeking a suitable new technique. They were impressed by Wen's scholarship and encouraged by his own demonstrations in verse. And Wen, in turn, was emboldened enough to predict that the new poetry would soon enter a new constructive stage, as he declared, "We must admit that this 'form' theory is a strong tide in the development of new poetry." In **"Drama at the Crossroads,"** published in June, 1926, he carried his theory further by maintaining that "the highest goal of art is to attain pure form." In its development toward the highest goal of art, drama was hampered by the prevailing "literary thought" with its exclusive emphasis on "moral, philosophical, and social problems." "One can hardly blame the writers," he said; "Literature, particularly dramatic literature, is easily tinted with philosophical and didactic ideas just as odorous matter readily attracts flies." But over-preoccupation with social messages ruined the art of drama, and he criticized the Chinese imitators of Ibsen and Shaw for merely describing "problems" without writing "plays." He was still an adherent of Arnold's tenet that literature "is criticism of life," but "such great critics of life as Shakespeare and Synge did not rely on problem-plays. Furthermore, merely putting a few fashionable polemical phrases into the mouth of a character is not writing a good problem-play." He was aiming at the Creation Society writers, particularly Kuo Mo-jo, when he said:

> If one, simply by dragging out such ancient characters as Ch'ü Yüan, Cho Wen-chün, and Nieh Cheng, and making them ventriloquize on socialism, democracy, and the emancipation of women, can claim to be writing drama, . . . then, frankly, we would rather not have this sort of drama.

Wen suggested differentiating the content (the thought) from the form of literature (the art of literary writing). He advised the writer to avoid becoming mired in an ideological bog, but to strive for literary excellence. In its emphases, this new argument differed considerably from the view expressed two years before in his essay on Tagore. Then he wanted Tagore to remain close to the flesh-and-blood physical life of man, to sing his joys and bemoan his sorrows, to write *litterature engagée;* now, tired of polemics, he still sought a direct reflection of life in literature, but without preaching social gospels. He did not object to the embodiment of social messages in literature; rather, he opposed writing social messages of no literary quality. This led him to advise a younger writer in February, 1928, as follows,

> Writings that are vague may leave no deep imprint upon the reader, but writings that are too obvious often leave a bad impression with the reader. If a piece of writing is to be too obvious, I would rather have it vague.

He held fast to the supremacy of art in all forms of intellectual expression. But, no matter how he reasoned with himself concerning the theory of literature, the content-form dichotomy remained a source of inner conflict which, according to him, was as serious as the body-soul conflict. Before he found any formula for merging the dichotomy into a single entity, as he once did in Keats' beauty-truth equation and Walter Pater's theory of lyric poetry, he continued to quarrel with himself.

As social dogma without literary art irritated him, so did the dogmatic attitudes of his contemporary writers. In his view they were too self-centered, imitating the theatricality and exhibitionism of Byron without Byron's poetic talent. He felt

that a poet's attitude should be "tender, restrained, and kind,"
in conformity with the advice left supposedly by Confucius.
(pp. 89-99)

*Kai-Yü Hsü, in his* Wen I-To, *Twayne Publishers,
1980, 247 p.*

---

## ADDITIONAL BIBLIOGRAPHY

Allen, Joseph Roe, III. "The Myth Studies of Wen I-to: A Question
of Methodology." *Tamkang Review* XIII, No. 2 (Winter 1982): 137-60.
    Examines Wen's studies of comparative mythology, as compared
    with the theories of British mythologists Friedrich Max Müller
    and Andrew Lang.

# Appendix

The following is a listing of all sources used in Volume 28 of *Twentieth-Century Literary Criticism*. Included in this list are all copyright and reprint rights and acknowledgments for those essays for which permission was obtained. Every effort has been made to trace copyright, but if omissions have been made, please let us know.

**THE EXCERPTS IN TCLC, VOLUME 28, WERE REPRINTED FROM THE FOLLOWING PERIODICALS:**

*The Academy,* January 31, 1874; v. 28, December 12, 1885.

*Annals of the Association of American Geographers,* v. 48, December, 1958.

*The Athenaeum,* n. 3078, October 23, 1886; v. 105, January 19, 1895; n. 4184, January 4, 1908; n. 4229, November 14, 1908.

*The Atlantic Monthly,* v. 177, June, 1946 for "Mr. Dooley and the Same Old World" by John V. Kelleher. Copyright 1946, renewed 1974, by The Atlantic Monthly Company, Boston, MA. Reprinted by permission of the author.

*The Bookman,* London, v. XXI, November, 1901.

*The Bookman,* New York, v. VIII, February, 1899; v. XXXVIII, November, 1913.

*Clues: A Journal of Detection,* v. 6, Spring-Summer, 1985. Copyright 1985 by Pat Browne. Reprinted by permission of the publisher.

*College English,* v. 2, February, 1941.

*The Colored American Magazine,* v. VI, March, 1903.

*The Cornhill Magazine,* n.s. v. 24, March, 1908.

*Critical Quarterly,* v. 5, Summer, 1963 for "In Praise of Scott Fitzgerald" by John Lucas. Reprinted by permission of the author.

*Daily Worker,* May 5, 1934.

*The Dial,* v. VI, March, 1886; v. XLIX, November 1, 1910; v. LVI, January 16, 1914.

*The English Record,* v. XXII, October, 1971. Copyright New York State English Council 1971. Reprinted by permission of the publisher.

*Essays by Divers Hands,* n.s. v. XVIII, 1940.

*The Reprint Bulletin Book Reviews,* v. XXIV, 1979. Reprinted by permission of Glanville Publishers, Inc.

*Revista de Istorie si Theori Literara,* v. 25, 1976.

*Romanian Review,* v. XXXIII, 1979. Reprinted by permission of the publisher.

*The Saturday Review of Literature,* v. IX, October 29, 1922; v. X, April 14, 1934.

*The Saturday Review,* New York, v. XXXV, June 21, 1952.

*Scrutiny,* v. III, December, 1934; v. VII, March, 1939.

*The Spectator,* v. 155, August 2, 1935.

*Studies in Scottish Literature,* v. VII, July-October, 1969; v. XIX, 1984. Copyright © G. Ross Roy 1969, 1984. Both reprinted by permission of the editor.

*Studies in the Novel,* v. V, Fall, 1973. Copyright 1973 by North Texas State University. Reprinted by permission of the publisher.

*Time,* New York, v. LI, May 10, 1948. Copyright 1948, renewed 1975, Time Inc. All rights reserved. Reprinted by permission from *Time.*

*Trend,* v. 7, August, 1914.

*Twentieth Century Literature,* v. 17, April, 1971. Copyright 1971, Hofstra University Press. Reprinted by permission of the publisher.

*The Western Review,* v. 23, Summer, 1958.

Abramson, Doris E. From *Negro Playwrights in the American Theatre: 1925-1959*. Columbia University Press, 1969. Copyright © 1967, 1969 Columbia University Press. Reprinted by permission of the publisher.

Bălan, Ion Dodu. From *A Concise History of Romanian Literature*. Translated by Andrei Bantaş. Editura Ştiinţifică şi Enciclopedică, 1981. Reprinted by permission of the publisher.

Bausani, Alessandro. From "Iqbal: His Philosophy of Religion, and the West," in *Crescent and Green: A Miscellany of Writings on Pakistan*. By Alessandro Bausani and others. Cassell & Company Ltd., 1955.

Bayley, John. From *Tolstoy and the Novel*. Chatto & Windus, 1966. Copyright © 1966 by John Bayley. All rights reserved. Reprinted by permission of the author and Chatto & Windus.

Berman, Jeffrey. From *The Talking Cure: Literary Representations of Psychoanalysis*. New York University Press, 1985. Copyright © 1985 by New York University. All rights reserved. Reprinted by permission of the publisher.

Berzon, Judith R. From *Neither White nor Black: The Mulatto Character in American Fiction*. New York University Press, 1978. Copyright © 1978 by New York University. Reprinted by permission of the publisher.

Bier, Jesse. From *The Rise and Fall of American Humor*. Holt, Rinehart and Winston, 1968. Copyright © 1968 by Jesse Bier. All rights reserved. Reprinted by permission of Henry Holt and Company, Inc.

Blair, Walter. From *Horse Sense in American Humor from Benjamin Franklin to Ogden Nash*. The University of Chicago Press, 1942. Copyright 1942 by The University of Chicago. Renewed 1969 by Walter Blair. All rights reserved. Reprinted by permission of the author.

Blake, George. From *Barrie and the Kailyard School*. Arthur Barker, Ltd., 1951.

Blankley, Elyse. From "Beyond the 'Talent of Knowing': Gertrude Stein and the New Woman," in *Critical Essays on Gertrude Stein*. Edited by Michael J. Hoffman. Hall, 1986. Copyright 1986 by G. K. Hall & Co. All rights reserved. Reprinted with the permission of the publisher.

Bold, Alan. From *Modern Scottish Literature*. Longman, 1983. © Alan Bold 1983. All rights reserved. Reprinted by permission of the publisher.

Braybrooke, Patrick. From *Considerations on Edmund Gosse*. Drane's Limited, 1925.

Briney, Robert E. From "Sax Rohmer: An Informal Survey," in *The Mystery Writer's Art*. Edited by Francis M. Nevins, Jr. Bowling Green University Popular Press, 1971. Copyright © 1970 by the Bowling Green State University Popular Press. Reprinted by permission of the publisher.

Brogan, D. W. From *American Themes*. Harper & Brothers Publishers, 1949.

Brooks, Gwendolyn. From an afterword to *Contending Forces: A Romance Illustrative of Negro Life North and South*. By Pauline Elizabeth Hopkins. Southern Illinois University Press, 1978. Afterword copyright © 1978 by Southern Illinois University Press. All rights reserved. Reprinted by permission of the publisher.

Calder, Angus. From *Russia Discovered: Nineteenth-Century Fiction from Pushkin to Chekhov*. Heinemann Educational Books, 1976. © Angus Calder 1976. Reprinted by permission of A. D. Peters & Co. Ltd.

Campbell, Ian. From *Nineteenth-Century Scottish Fiction: Critical Essays*. Edited by Ian Campbell. Barnes & Noble Books, 1979. Copyright © 1979 by Ian Campbell. All rights reserved. Reprinted by permission of the publisher.

Canby, Henry Seidel. From *Seven Years' Harvest: Notes on Contemporary Literature*. Farrar & Rinehart, Incorporated, 1936. Copyright, 1936, by Henry Seidel Canby. Renewed 1963 by Marion Ponsonby Gause Canby. All rights reserved. Reprinted by permission of Henry Holt and Company, Inc.

Christian, R. F. From *Tolstoy's 'War and Peace': A Study*. Clarendon Press, Oxford, 1962. © Oxford University Press, 1962. Reprinted by permission of Oxford University Press.

Cotter, Joseph S. From *Caleb, the Degenerate: A Study of the Types, Customs, and Needs of the American Negro*. The Bradley & Gilbert Company, 1903.

Cowley, Malcolm. From an introduction to *Tender Is the Night: A Romance*. By F. Scott Fitzgerald. Revised edition. Charles Scribner's Sons, 1951. Copyright, 1948, 1951, by Frances Scott Fitzgerald Lanahan. Renewed 1979 by Frances Scott Fitzgerald Smith and Malcolm Cowley. All rights reserved. Reprinted with the permission of Charles Scribner's Sons, an imprint of Macmillan Publishing Company.

Crawford, Virginia M. From *Studies in Foreign Literature*. Duckworth and Co., 1899.

DeMuth, James. From *Small Town Chicago: The Comic Perspective of Finley Peter Dunne, George Ade, Ring Lardner*. Kennikat Press, 1980. Copyright © 1980 by Kennikat Press Corp. All rights reserved. Reprinted by permission of Associated Faculty Press, Inc., New York, NY.

Eckley, Grace. From *Finley Peter Dunne*. Twayne, 1981. Copyright 1981 by Twayne Publishers. Reprinted with the permission of Twayne Publishers, a division of G. K. Hall & Co., Boston.

Eikhenbaum, Boris. From *Tolstoi in the Sixties*. Translated by Duffield White. Ardis, 1982. Copyright © 1982 by Ardis. All rights reserved. Reprinted by permission of the publisher.

Ellis, Elmer. From *Mr. Dooley's America: A Life of Finley Peter Dunne*. Knopf, 1941. Copyright 1941 by Alfred A. Knopf, Inc. Renewed 1969 by Elmer Ellis. All rights reserved. Reprinted by permission of Alfred A. Knopf, Inc.

Esposito, John L. From *Voices of Resurgent Islam*. Edited by John L. Esposito. Oxford University Press, 1983. Copyright © 1983 by Oxford University Press, Inc. Reprinted by permission of the publisher.

Fanning, Charles. From *Finley Peter Dunne & Mr. Dooley: The Chicago Years*. University Press of Kentucky, 1978. Copyright © 1978 by The University Press of Kentucky. Reprinted by permission of the publisher.

Farrell, James T. From *Literature and Morality*. Vanguard Press, 1947. Copyright 1945, 1946, 1947, renewed 1974, by James T. Farrell. Reprinted by permission of the publisher, Vanguard Press, Inc.

Fine, David. From *Los Angeles in Fiction: A Collection of Original Essays*. Edited by David Fine. University of New Mexico Press, 1984. © 1984 by the University of New Mexico Press. All rights reserved. Reprinted by permission of the publisher.

Finney, Brian. From *The Inner I: British Literary Autobiography of the Twentieth Century*. Oxford University Press, 1985. Copyright © 1985 by Brian Finney. All rights reserved. Reprinted by permission of Oxford University Press, Inc. In Canada by A. D. Peters & Co. Ltd.

Fitzgerald, F. Scott. From "Appendix B," in *The Far Side of Paradise: A Biography of F. Scott Fitzgerald*. By Arthur Mizener. Houghton Mifflin Company, 1951. Copyright, 1949, 1950, 1951, © 1965, renewed 1979, by Arthur Mizener. All rights reserved. Reprinted by permission of Houghton Mifflin Company.

Foerster, Norman. From *Nature in American Literature: Studies in the Modern View of Nature*. The Macmillan Company, 1923.

Forster, E. M. From *Two Cheers for Democracy*. Harcourt Brace Jovanovich, 1951, Edward Arnold, 1951. Copyright 1951 by E. M. Forster. Renewed 1979 by Donald Perry. Reprinted by permission of Harcourt Brace Jovanovich, Inc. In Canada by Edward Arnold Ltd.

Gass, William H. From "Gertrude Stein and the Geography of the Sentence," in *The World within the Word*. Knopf, 1978. Copyright © 1973 by William H. Gass. All rights reserved. Reprinted by permission of Alfred A. Knopf, Inc.

Gloster, Hugh M. From *Negro Voices in American Fiction*. University of North Carolina Press, 1948. Copyright, 1948, by the University of North Carolina Press. Renewed 1975 by Hugh M. Gloster. Reprinted by permission of the publisher.

Gosse, Sir Edmund. From *Silhouettes*. William Heinemann Ltd., 1925.

Gregory, Horace and Marya Zaturenska. From *A History of American Poetry, 1900-1940*. Harcourt Brace Jovanovich, 1946. Copyright, 1942, 1944, 1946, by Harcourt Brace Jovanovich, Inc. Copyright renewed © 1974 by Horace Gregory and Marya Zaturenska. Reprinted by permission of the Estate of Horace Gregory and Marya Zaturenska.

Gunn, Elizabeth. From *A Daring Coiffeur: Reflections on "War and Peace" and "Anna Karenina."* Rowman & Littlefield, 1971, Chatto and Windus, 1971. © Elizabeth Gunn 1971. Reprinted by permission of Rowman & Littlefield. In Canada by the author and Chatto and Windus.

Hart, Francis Russell. From *The Scottish Novel: From Smollett to Spark*. Cambridge, Mass.: Harvard University Press, 1978. Copyright © 1978 by Francis Russell Hart. All rights reserved. Excerpted by permission of the publishers.

Hatch, James V. From *Black Theater, U.S.A.: Forty-Five Plays by Black Americans, 1847-1974*. Edited by James V. Hatch. The Free Press, 1974. Copyright © 1974 by The Free Press. All rights reserved. Reprinted with permission of The Free Press, a Division of Macmillan, Inc.

Hoagland, Edward. From an introduction to *The Mountains of California*. By John Muir. Penguin Books, 1985. Copyright © 1985 by Viking Penguin Inc. All rights reserved. Reprinted by permission of the publisher.

Hoffman, Michael J. From *Gertrude Stein*. Twayne, 1976. Copyright 1976 by Twayne Publishers. All rights reserved. Reprinted with the permission of Twayne Publishers, a division of G. K. Hall & Co., Boston.

Hopkins, Pauline Elizabeth. From *Contending Forces: A Romance Illustrative of Negro Life North and South*. The Colored Co-Operative Publishing Co., 1900.

Hsü, Kai-Yü. From *Wen I-To*. Twayne, 1980. Copyright 1980 by Twayne Publishers. All rights reserved. Reprinted with the permission of Twayne Publishers, a division of G. K. Hall & Co., Boston.

Hussain, Hadi. From "Conception of Poetry and the Poet," in *Iqbal: Poet-Philosopher of Pakistan*. Edited by Hafeez Malik. Columbia University Press, 1971. Copyright © 1971 Columbia University Press. Reprinted by permission of the editor.

Iqbal, Muhammad. From a letter in *The Poet of the East: The Life and Work of Dr. Sir Muhammad Iqbal, the Poet-Philosopher, with a Critical Survey of His Philosophy, Poetical Works and Teachings*. By A. Anwar Beg. Second edition. Khawar Publishing Cooperative Society, 1961.

James, Henry. From *The Tragic Muse, Vol. I*. Charles Scribner's Sons, 1908.

Johnson, Edgar. From *One Mighty Torrent: The Drama of Biography*. Stackpole Sons, 1937.

Joyce, James A. From *The Critical Writings of James Joyce*. Edited by Ellsworth Mason and Richard Ellmann. The Viking Press, 1959. Copyright © 1959 by Harriet Weaver and F. Lionel Monro as Administrators of the Estate of James Joyce. All rights reserved. Reprinted by permission of Viking Penguin Inc.

Kawin, Bruce F. From *Telling It Again and Again: Repetition in Literature and Film*. Cornell University Press, 1972. Copyright © 1972 by Bruce F. Kawin. All rights reserved. Reprinted by permission of the author.

Kerlin, Robert T. From *Negro Poets and Their Poems*. Third edition. The Associated Publishers, Inc., 1940.

Lewis, Wyndham. From *Time and Western Man*. Harcourt, Brace and Company, 1928. Copyright, 1928, by Harcourt, Brace and Company, Inc. Renewed 1955 by Wyndham Lewis. Reprinted by permission of the Literary Estate of Wyndham Lewis.

Lin, Julia C. From *Modern Chinese Poetry: An Introduction*. University of Washington Press, 1972. Copyright © 1972 by the University of Washington Press. All rights reserved. Reprinted by permission of the publisher.

Lyon, Thomas J. From *John Muir*. Boise State College, 1972. Copyright 1972 by the Boise State College Western Writers Series. All rights reserved. Reprinted by permission of the publisher and the author.

Mizener, Arthur. From "On F. Scott Fitzgerald," in *Talks with Authors*. Edited by Charles F. Madden. Southern Illinois University Press, 1968. Copyright © 1968 by Southern Illinois University Press. All rights reserved. Reprinted by permission of the publisher.

Nicolson, Harold. From *The Development of English Biography*. L. & Virginia Woolf, 1927. Copyright 1927 by L. & Virginia Woolf. Renewed 1955 by Harold Nicolson. Reprinted by permission of the Literary Estate of Harold Nicolson and The Hogarth Press.

Parker, W. M. From *Modern Scottish Writers*. W. Hodge & Co., 1917.

Perosa, Sergio. From *The Art of F. Scott Fitzgerald*. Translated by Charles Matz and Sergio Perosa. University of Michigan Press, 1965. Copyright © by The University of Michigan 1965. All rights reserved. Reprinted by permission of the publisher.

Porter, Dorothy. From an introduction to *The House with the Green Shutters*. By George Douglas Brown, edited by Dorothy Porter. Penguin Books, 1985. Introduction copyright © Dorothy Porter, 1985. All rights reserved. Reproduced by permission of Penguin Books Ltd.

Prager, Arthur. From *Rascals at Large, or, The Clue in the Old Nostalgia*. Doubleday & Company, Inc., 1971. Copyright © 1971 by Arthur Prager. All rights reserved. Reprinted by permission of Doubleday, a division of Bantam, Doubleday, Dell Publishing Group, Inc.

Pritchett, V. S. From *The Living Novel & Later Appreciations*. Revised edition. Random House, 1964. Copyright © 1964, 1975 by V. S. Pritchett. All rights reserved. Reprinted by permission of Sterling Lord Literistic, Inc.

Reid, B. L. From *Art by Subtraction: A Dissenting Opinion of Gertrude Stein*. University of Oklahoma Press, 1958. Copyright 1958 by the University of Oklahoma Press. Renewed 1986 by B. L. Reid. Reprinted by permission of the publisher.

Riding, Laura, and Robert Graves. From *A Survey of Modernist Poetry*. William Heinemann Ltd., 1927.

Schaaf, Barbara C. From *Mr. Dooley's Chicago*. Anchor Press/Doubleday, 1977. Copyright © 1977 by Barbara C. Schaaf. All rights reserved. Reprinted by permission of Doubleday, a division of Bantam, Doubleday, Dell Publishing Group, Inc.

Sherman, Joan R. From *Invisible Poets: Afro-Americans of the Nineteenth Century*. University of Illinois Press, 1974. © 1974 by Joan R. Sherman. Reprinted by permission of the publisher and the author.

Singh, Iqbal. From *The Ardent Pilgrim: An Introduction to the Life and Work of Mohammed Iqbal*. Longmans, Green and Co., 1951.

Sinha, Sachchidananda. From *Iqbal: The Poet and His Message*. Ram Narain Lal, 1947.

Smith, Herbert F. From *John Muir*. Twayne, 1965. Copyright 1965 by Twayne Publishers. All rights reserved. Reprinted with the permission of Twayne Publishers, Inc., a division of G. K. Hall & Co., Boston.

Squire, J. C. From *Life and Letters*. Doran, 1921. Copyright 1921 by George H. Doran Company. Renewed 1948 by J. C. Squire. Reprinted by permission of Doubleday, a division of Bantam, Doubleday, Dell Publishing Group, Inc.

Stein, Gertrude. From *A Primer for the Gradual Understanding of Gertrude Stein*. Edited by Robert Bartlett Haas. Black Sparrow Press, 1971. Copyright © 1971 by Robert Bartlett Haas. Reprinted by permission of the Literary Estate of Gertrude Stein.

Steiner, George. From *Tolstoy or Dostoevsky: An Essay in the Old Criticism*. Alfred A. Knopf, Inc., 1959. Copyright © 1959 by George Steiner. All rights reserved. Reprinted by permission of Georges Borchardt, Inc. for the author.

Stern, Milton R. From *The Golden Moment: The Novels of F. Scott Fitzgerald*. University of Illinois Press, 1970. © 1970 by the Board of Trustees of the University of Illinois. Reprinted by permission of the publisher and the author.

Sturak, Thomas. From ''Horace McCoy's Objective Lyricism,'' in *Tough Guy Writers of the Thirties*. Edited by David Madden. Southern Illinois University Press, 1968. Copyright © 1968 by Southern Illinois University Press. All rights reserved. Reprinted by permission of the publisher.

Tanner, Tony. From *The Reign of Wonder: Naivety and Reality in American Literature*. Cambridge at the University Press, 1965. © Cambridge University Press 1965. Reprinted with the permission of the publisher and the author.

Tate, Claudia. From ''Pauline Hopkins: Our Literary Foremother,'' in *Conjuring: Black Women, Fiction, and Literary Tradition*. Edited by Marjorie Pryse and Hortense J. Spillers. Indiana University Press, 1985. © 1985 by Indiana University Press. All rights reserved. Reprinted by permission of the publisher.

Temple, Ruth Zabriskie. From *The Critic's Alchemy: A Study of the Introduction of French Symbolism into England*. Twayne Publishers, Inc., 1953.

Tolstoy, Leo. From *War and Peace, Vol. III*. Oxford University Press, London, 1933.

Tracy, Henry Chester. From *American Naturists*. Dutton, 1930. Copyright, 1930 by E. P. Dutton & Company, Inc. Renewed 1957 by Henry Chester Tracy. All rights reserved. Reprinted by permission of E. P. Dutton, a division of NAL Penguin Inc.

Untermeyer, Louis. From *American Poetry Since 1900*. Henry Holt and Company, 1923. Copyright, 1923, by Henry Holt and Company. Renewed 1951 by Louis Untermeyer. Reprinted by permission of the publisher.

Vahid, Syed Abdul. From *Iqbal: His Art and Thought*. John Murray, 1959. © Syed Abdul Vahid 1959.

Van Ash, Cay. From an afterword to *Master of Villainy: A Biography of Sax Rohmer*. By Cay Van Ash and Elizabeth Sax Rohmer, edited by Robert E. Briney. Bowling Green University Popular Press, 1972. Copyright © 1972 by the Bowling Green State University Popular Press. Reprinted by permission of the publisher.

Walker, Jayne L. From *The Making of a Modernist: Gertrude Stein from ''Three Lives'' to ''Tender Buttons.''* The University of Massachusetts Press, 1984. Copyright © 1976, 1984 by Jayne L. Walker. All rights reserved. Reprinted by permission of the publisher.

Watson, Colin. From *Snobbery with Violence: English Crime and Their Audience*. Eyre & Spottiswoode (Publishers) Ltd, 1971. Copyright © 1971 Colin Watson. All rights reserved. Reprinted by permission of the publisher.

Wilder, Thornton. From an introduction to *Four in America*. By Gertrude Stein. Yale University Press, 1947. Copyright 1947 by Alice B. Toklas. Renewed 1975 by Yale University Press. Reprinted by permission of the publisher.

Williams, William Carlos. From *A Novelette and Other Prose (1921-1931)*. Imprimerie F. Cabasson, 1932.

Winchell, Mark Royden. From *Horace McCoy*. Boise State University, 1982. Copyright 1982 by the Boise State University Western Writers Series. All rights reserved. Reprinted by permission of the publisher and the author.

Woolf, James D. From "'In the Seventh Heaven of Delight': The Aesthetic Sense in Gosse's 'Father and Son'," in *Interspace and the Inward Sphere: Essays on Romantic and Victorian Self*. Edited by Norman A. Anderson and Margene E. Weiss. Western Illinois University, 1978. Copyright © 1978 by Western Illinois University. Reprinted by permission of the publisher.

Woolf, Virginia. From *The Moment and Other Essays*. Hogarth Press, 1947, Harcourt Brace Jovanovich, 1948. Copyright 1948, renewed 1976 by Harcourt Brace Jovanovich and Marjorie T. Parsons. Reprinted by permission of Harcourt Brace Jovanovich, Inc. In Canada by the Literary Estate of Virginia Woolf and The Hogarth Press.

Wu, William F. From *The Yellow Peril: Chinese Americans in American Fiction 1850-1940*. Archon Books, 1982. © 1982 William F. Wu. All rights reserved. Reprinted by permission of Archon Books, an imprint of The Shoe String Press, Inc.

Yates, Norris W. From *The American Humorist: Conscience of the Twentieth Century*. Iowa State University Press, 1964. © 1964 by The Iowa State University Press. All rights reserved. Reprinted by permission of the publisher.

# Twentieth-Century
# Literary Criticism

Cumulative Indexes
Volumes 1-28

# This Index Includes References to Entries in These Gale Series

## Contemporary Literary Criticism

Presents excerpts of criticism on the works of novelists, poets, dramatists, short story writers, scriptwriters, and other creative writers who are now living or who have died since 1960. Cumulative indexes to authors, nationalities, and titles are included. Volumes 1-47 are in print.

## Twentieth-Century Literary Criticism

Contains critical excerpts by the most significant commentators on poets, novelists, short story writers, dramatists, and philosophers who died between 1900 and 1960. Cumulative indexes to authors, nationalities, and titles discussed are included in each new volume. Volumes 1-28 are in print.

## Nineteenth-Century Literature Criticism

Offers significant passages from criticism on authors who died between 1800 and 1899. Cumulative indexes to authors, nationalities, and titles discussed are included in each new volume. Volumes 1-17 are in print.

## Literature Criticism from 1400 to 1800

Compiles significant passages from the most noteworthy criticism on authors of the fifteenth through eighteenth centuries. Cumulative indexes to authors, nationalities, and titles discussed are included in each new volume. Volumes 1-7 are in print.

## Classical and Medieval Literature Criticism

Offers excerpts of criticism on the works of world authors from classical antiquity through the fourteenth century. Cumulative indexes to authors, titles, and critics are included in each volume. Volume 1 is in print.

## Short Story Criticism

Compiles excerpts of criticism on short fiction by writers of all eras and nationalities. Cumulative indexes to authors, nationalities, and titles discussed are included in each new volume. Volume 1 is in print.

## Children's Literature Review

Includes excerpts from reviews, criticism, and commentary on works of authors and illustrators who create books for children. Cumulative indexes to authors, nationalities, and titles discussed are included in each new volume. Volumes 1-15 are in print.

## Contemporary Authors Series

Encompasses five related series. *Contemporary Authors* provides biographical and bibliographical information on more than 90,000 writers of fiction, nonfiction, poetry, journalism, drama, motion pictures, and other fields. Each new volume contains sketches on authors not previously covered in the series. Volumes 1-122 are in print. *Contemporary Authors New Revision Series* provides completely updated information on active authors covered in previously published volumes of *CA*. Only entries requiring significant change are revised for *CA New Revision Series*. Volumes 1-23 are in print. *Contemporary Authors Permanent Series* consists of updated listings for deceased and inactive authors removed from the original volumes 9-36 when these volumes were revised. Volumes 1-2 are in print. *Contemporary Authors Autobiography Series* presents specially commissioned autobiographies by leading contemporary writers. Volumes 1-6 are in print. *Contemporary Authors Bibliographical Series* contains primary and secondary bibliographies as well as analytical bibliographical essays by authorities on major modern authors. Volumes 1-2 are in print.

## Dictionary of Literary Biography

Encompasses three related series. *Dictionary of Literary Biography* furnishes illustrated overviews of authors' lives and works and places them in the larger perspective of literary history. Volumes 1-67 are in print. *Dictionary of Literary Biography Documentary Series* illuminates the careers of major figures through a selection of literary documents, including letters, notebook and diary entries, interviews, book reviews, and photographs. Volumes 1-4 are in print. *Dictionary of Literary Biography Yearbook* summarizes the past year's literary activity with articles on genres, major prizes, conferences, and other timely subjects and includes updated and new entries on individual authors. Yearbooks for 1980-1986 are in print. A cumulative index to authors and articles is included in each new volume.

## Concise Dictionary of American Literary Biography

A six-volume series that collects revised and updated sketches on major American authors that were originally presented in *Dictionary of Literary Biography*. Volumes 1-2 are in print.

## Something about the Author Series

Encompasses two related series. *Something about the Author* contains heavily illustrated biographical sketches on juvenile and young adult authors and illustrators from all eras. Volumes 1-51 are in print. *Something about the Author Autobiography Series* presents specially commissioned autobiographies by prominent authors and illustrators of books for children and young adults. Volumes 1-5 are in print.

## Yesterday's Authors of Books for Children

Contains heavily illustrated entries on children's writers who died before 1961. Complete in two volumes. Volumes 1-2 are in print.

# Literary Criticism Series
# Cumulative Author Index

This index lists all author entries in the Gale Literary Criticism Series and includes cross-references to other Gale sources. For the convenience of the reader, references to the *Yearbook* in the *Contemporary Literary Criticism* series include the page number (in parentheses) after the volume number. References in the index are identified as follows:

Author Index

Box, Edgar   1925-
See Vidal, Gore

Boyd, William   1952-..............CLC 28
See also CA 114, 120

Boyle, Kay   1903-...........CLC 1, 5, 19
See also CAAS 1
See also CA 13-16R
See also DLB 4, 9, 48

Boyle, Patrick   19??-..............CLC 19

Boyle, T. Coraghessan   1948-.......CLC 36
See also CA 120
See also DLB-Y 86

Brackenridge, Hugh Henry
1748-1816...................NCLC 7
See also DLB 11, 37

Bradbury, Edward P.   1939-
See Moorcock, Michael

Bradbury, Malcolm (Stanley)
1932-.......................CLC 32
See also CANR 1
See also CA 1-4R
See also DLB 14

Bradbury, Ray(mond Douglas)
1920-........... CLC 1, 3, 10, 15, 42
See also CANR 2
See also CA 1-4R
See also SATA 11
See also DLB 2, 8
See also AITN 1, 2

Bradley, David (Henry), Jr.
1950-.......................CLC 23
See also CA 104
See also DLB 33

Bradley, Marion Zimmer
1930-.......................CLC 30
See also CANR 7
See also CA 57-60
See also DLB 8

Bradstreet, Anne   1612-1672 ........ LC 4
See also DLB 24

Bragg, Melvyn   1939-..............CLC 10
See also CANR 10
See also CA 57-60
See also DLB 14

Braine, John (Gerard)
1922-1986..............CLC 1, 3, 41
See also CANR 1
See also CA 1-4R
See also obituary CA 120
See also DLB 15
See also DLB-Y 86

Brammer, Billy Lee   1930?-1978
See Brammer, William

Brammer, William   1930?-1978 .....CLC 31
See also obituary CA 77-80

Brancati, Vitaliano
1907-1954.................. TCLC 12
See also CA 109

Brancato, Robin F(idler)   1936-.....CLC 35
See also CANR 11
See also CA 69-72
See also SATA 23

Brand, Millen   1906-1980 ..........CLC 7
See also CA 21-24R
See also obituary CA 97-100

Branden, Barbara   19??-..... CLC 44 (447)

Brandes, Georg (Morris Cohen)
1842-1927................. TCLC 10
See also CA 105

Branley, Franklyn M(ansfield)
1915-.......................CLC 21
See also CANR 14
See also CA 33-36R
See also SATA 4

Brathwaite, Edward   1930-.........CLC 11
See also CANR 11
See also CA 25-28R
See also DLB 53

Brautigan, Richard (Gary)
1935-1984..........CLC 1, 3, 5, 9, 12,
34 (314), 42
See also CA 53-56
See also obituary CA 113
See also DLB 2, 5
See also DLB-Y 80, 84

Brecht, (Eugen) Bertolt (Friedrich)
1898-1956..............TCLC 1, 6, 13
See also CA 104
See also DLB 56

Bremer, Fredrika   1801-1865 ..... NCLC 11

Brennan, Christopher John
1870-1932.................. TCLC 17
See also CA 117

Brennan, Maeve   1917-..............CLC 5
See also CA 81-84

Brentano, Clemens (Maria)
1778-1842 ............... NCLC 1

Brenton, Howard   1942-...........CLC 31
See also CA 69-72
See also DLB 13

Breslin, James   1930-
See Breslin, Jimmy
See also CA 73-76

Breslin, Jimmy   1930- .......... CLC 4, 43
See also Breslin, James
See also AITN 1

Bresson, Robert   1907-.............CLC 16
See also CA 110

Breton, André   1896-1966..... CLC 2, 9, 15
See also CAP 2
See also CA 19-20
See also obituary CA 25-28R

Breytenbach, Breyten
1939-.................... CLC 23, 37
See also CA 113

Bridgers, Sue Ellen   1942-..........CLC 26
See also CANR 11
See also CA 65-68
See also SAAS 1
See also SATA 22
See also DLB 52

Bridges, Robert   1844-1930....... TCLC 1
See also CA 104
See also DLB 19

Bridie, James   1888-1951 ......... TCLC 3
See also Mavor, Osborne Henry
See also DLB 10

Brin, David   1950- .......... CLC 34 (133)
See also CA 102

Brink, André (Philippus)
1935-................... CLC 18, 36
See also CA 104

Brinsmead, H(esba) F(ay)
1922-......................CLC 21
See also CANR 10
See also CA 21-24R
See also SATA 18

Brittain, Vera (Mary)
1893?-1970..................CLC 23
See also CAP 1
See also CA 15-16
See also obituary CA 25-28R

Broch, Hermann   1886-1951...... TCLC 20
See also CA 117

Brock, Rose   1923-
See Hansen, Joseph

Brodsky, Iosif Alexandrovich   1940-
See Brodsky, Joseph
See also CA 41-44R
See also AITN 1

Brodsky, Joseph
1940-................CLC 4, 6, 13, 36
See also Brodsky, Iosif Alexandrovich

Brodsky, Michael (Mark)
1948-......................CLC 19
See also CANR 18
See also CA 102

Bromell, Henry   1947-..............CLC 5
See also CANR 9
See also CA 53-56

Bromfield, Louis (Brucker)
1896-1956.................. TCLC 11
See also CA 107
See also DLB 4, 9

Broner, E(sther) M(asserman)
1930-......................CLC 19
See also CANR 8
See also CA 17-20R
See also DLB 28

Bronk, William   1918-..............CLC 10
See also CA 89-92

Brontë, Anne   1820-1849......... NCLC 4
See also DLB 21

Brontë, Charlotte
1816-1855.................NCLC 3, 8
See also DLB 21

Brontë, (Jane) Emily
1818-1848.................. NCLC 16
See also DLB 21, 32

Brooke, Frances   1724-1789 ......... LC 6
See also DLB 39

Brooke, Henry   1703?-1783 .......... LC 1
See also DLB 39

Brooke, Rupert (Chawner)
1887-1915................. TCLC 2, 7
See also CA 104
See also DLB 19

Brooke-Rose, Christine   1926- ......CLC 40
See also CA 13-16R
See also DLB 14

Brookner, Anita
1938-............... CLC 32, 34 (136)
See also CA 114, 120

Brooks, Cleanth   1906- ...........CLC 24
See also CA 17-20R
See also DLB 63

**Brooks, Gwendolyn**
    1917-............. CLC 1, 2, 4, 5, 15
  See also CANR 1
  See also CA 1-4R
  See also SATA 6
  See also DLB 5
  See also CDALB 1941-1968
  See also AITN 1

**Brooks, Mel** 1926-................CLC 12
  See also Kaminsky, Melvin
  See also CA 65-68
  See also DLB 26

**Brooks, Peter** 1938-........ CLC 34 (519)
  See also CANR 1
  See also CA 45-48

**Brooks, Van Wyck** 1886-1963......CLC 29
  See also CANR 6
  See also CA 1-4R
  See also DLB 45, 63

**Brophy, Brigid (Antonia)**
    1929-.................. CLC 6, 11, 29
  See also CAAS 4
  See also CA 5-8R
  See also DLB 14

**Brosman, Catharine Savage**
    1934-.....................CLC 9
  See also CANR 21
  See also CA 61-64

**Broughton, T(homas) Alan**
    1936-....................CLC 19
  See also CANR 2
  See also CA 45-48

**Broumas, Olga** 1949- .............CLC 10
  See also CANR 20
  See also CA 85-88

**Brown, Claude** 1937- .............CLC 30
  See also CA 73-76

**Brown, Dee (Alexander)**
    1908-.................... CLC 18, 47
  See also CAAS 6
  See also CANR 11
  See also CA 13-16R
  See also SATA 5
  See also DLB-Y 80

**Brown, George Douglas** 1869-1902
  See Douglas, George

**Brown, George Mackay**
    1921-.................... CLC 5, 28
  See also CAAS 6
  See also CANR 12
  See also CA 21-24R
  See also SATA 35
  See also DLB 14, 27

**Brown, Rita Mae** 1944- ....... CLC 18, 43
  See also CANR 2, 11
  See also CA 45-48

**Brown, Rosellen** 1939- ............CLC 32
  See also CANR 14
  See also CA 77-80

**Brown, Sterling A(llen)**
    1901-.................... CLC 1, 23
  See also CA 85-88
  See also DLB 48, 51, 63

**Brown, William Wells**
    1816?-1884.................. NCLC 2
  See also DLB 3, 50

**Browne, Jackson** 1950-...........CLC 21

**Browning, Elizabeth Barrett**
    1806-1861...............NCLC 1, 16
  See also DLB 32

**Browning, Tod** 1882-1962 ........CLC 16
  See also obituary CA 117

**Bruccoli, Matthew J(oseph)**
    1931-................. CLC 34 (416)
  See also CANR 7
  See also CA 9-12R

**Bruce, Lenny** 1925-1966..........CLC 21
  See also Schneider, Leonard Alfred

**Brunner, John (Kilian Houston)**
    1934-.................... CLC 8, 10
  See also CANR 2
  See also CA 1-4R

**Brutus, Dennis** 1924-..............CLC 43
  See also CANR 2
  See also CA 49-52

**Bryan, C(ourtlandt) D(ixon) B(arnes)**
    1936-.....................CLC 29
  See also CANR 13
  See also CA 73-76

**Bryant, William Cullen**
    1794-1878.................. NCLC 6
  See also DLB 3, 43

**Bryusov, Valery (Yakovlevich)**
    1873-1924.................. TCLC 10
  See also CA 107

**Buchanan, George** 1506-1582 ........ LC 4

**Buchheim, Lothar-Günther**
    1918-........................CLC 6
  See also CA 85-88

**Buchwald, Art(hur)** 1925- ........CLC 33
  See also CANR 21
  See also CA 5-8R
  See also SATA 10
  See also AITN 1

**Buck, Pearl S(ydenstricker)**
    1892-1973..............CLC 7, 11, 18
  See also CANR 1
  See also CA 1-4R
  See also obituary CA 41-44R
  See also SATA 1, 25
  See also DLB 9
  See also AITN 1

**Buckler, Ernest** 1908-1984........CLC 13
  See also CAP 1
  See also CA 11-12
  See also obituary CA 114
  See also SATA 47

**Buckley, William F(rank), Jr.**
    1925-................. CLC 7, 18, 37
  See also CANR 1
  See also CA 1-4R
  See also DLB-Y 80
  See also AITN 1

**Buechner, (Carl) Frederick**
    1926-..................CLC 2, 4, 6, 9
  See also CANR 11
  See also CA 13-16R
  See also DLB-Y 80

**Buell, John (Edward)** 1927-........CLC 10
  See also CA 1-4R
  See also DLB 53

**Buero Vallejo, Antonio**
    1916-.................... CLC 15, 46
  See also CA 106

**Bukowski, Charles**
    1920-...............CLC 2, 5, 9, 41
  See also CA 17-20R
  See also DLB 5

**Bulgakov, Mikhail (Afanas'evich)**
    1891-1940................. TCLC 2, 16
  See also CA 105

**Bullins, Ed** 1935-............... CLC 1, 5, 7
  See also CA 49-52
  See also DLB 7, 38

**Bulwer-Lytton, (Lord) Edward (George Earle**
    **Lytton)** 1803-1873 .......... NCLC 1
  See also Lytton, Edward Bulwer
  See also DLB 21

**Bunin, Ivan (Alexeyevich)**
    1870-1953................... TCLC 6
  See also CA 104

**Bunting, Basil**
    1900-1985........CLC 10, 39 (297), 47
  See also CANR 7
  See also CA 53-56
  See also obituary CA 115
  See also DLB 20

**Buñuel, Luis** 1900-1983 ...........CLC 16
  See also CA 101
  See also obituary CA 110

**Bunyan, John** (1628-1688)........... LC 4
  See also DLB 39

**Burgess (Wilson, John) Anthony**
    1917-.....CLC 1, 2, 4, 5, 8, 10, 13, 15,
                       22, 40
  See also Wilson, John (Anthony) Burgess
  See also DLB 14
  See also AITN 1

**Burke, Edmund** 1729-1797 ......... LC 7

**Burke, Kenneth (Duva)**
    1897-.................... CLC 2, 24
  See also CA 5-8R
  See also DLB 45, 63

**Burney, Fanny** 1752-1840 ....... NCLC 12
  See also DLB 39

**Burns, Robert** 1759-1796............ LC 3

**Burns, Tex** 1908?-
  See L'Amour, Louis (Dearborn)

**Burnshaw, Stanley**
    1906-.............CLC 3, 13, 44 (456)
  See also CA 9-12R
  See also DLB 48

**Burr, Anne** 1937-..................CLC 6
  See also CA 25-28R

**Burroughs, Edgar Rice**
    1875-1950................... TCLC 2
  See also CA 104
  See also DLB 8
  See also SATA 41

**Burroughs, William S(eward)**
    1914-.......... CLC 1, 2, 5, 15, 22, 42
  See also CANR 20
  See also CA 9-12R
  See also DLB 2, 8, 16
  See also DLB-Y 81
  See also AITN 2

**Busch, Frederick**
    1941-...............CLC 7, 10, 18, 47
  See also CAAS 1
  See also CA 33-36R
  See also DLB 6

Bush, Ronald  19??-  . . . . . . . . CLC 34 (523)

Butler, Octavia E(stelle)  1947- . . . . . .CLC 38
  See also CANR 12
  See also CA 73-76
  See also DLB 33

Butler, Samuel  1835-1902 . . . . . . . . TCLC 1
  See also CA 104
  See also DLB 18, 57

Butor, Michel (Marie François)
  1926- . . . . . . . . . . . . . CLC 1, 3, 8, 11, 15
  See also CA 9-12R

Buzzati, Dino  1906-1972. . . . . . . . . .CLC 36
  See also obituary CA 33-36R

Byars, Betsy  1928- . . . . . . . . . . . . . .CLC 35
  See also CLR 1
  See also CANR 18
  See also CA 33-36R
  See also SAAS 1
  See also SATA 4, 46
  See also DLB 52

Byatt, A(ntonia) S(usan Drabble)
  1936- . . . . . . . . . . . . . . . . . . . . .CLC 19
  See also CANR 13
  See also CA 13-16R
  See also DLB 14

Byrne, David  1953?- . . . . . . . . . . . . .CLC 26

Byrne, John Keyes  1926-
  See Leonard, Hugh
  See also CA 102

Byron, George Gordon (Noel), Lord Byron
  1788-1824. . . . . . . . . . . . . . .NCLC 2, 12

Caballero, Fernán  1796-1877 . . . . NCLC 10

Cabell, James Branch
  1879-1958. . . . . . . . . . . . . . . . . TCLC 6
  See also CA 105
  See also DLB 9

Cable, George Washington
  1844-1925. . . . . . . . . . . . . . . . . TCLC 4
  See also CA 104
  See also DLB 12

Cabrera Infante, G(uillermo)
  1929- . . . . . . . . . . . . . . . . CLC 5, 25, 45
  See also CA 85-88

Cage, John (Milton, Jr.)  1912- . . . . .CLC 41
  See also CANR 9
  See also CA 13-16R

Cain, G.  1929-
  See Cabrera Infante, G(uillermo)

Cain, James M(allahan)
  1892-1977. . . . . . . . . . . . . CLC 3, 11, 28
  See also CANR 8
  See also CA 17-20R
  See also obituary CA 73-76
  See also AITN 1

Caldwell, Erskine
  1903-1987. . . . . . . . . . . . . . CLC 1, 8, 14
  See also CAAS 1
  See also CANR 2
  See also CA 1-4R
  See also obituary CA 121
  See also DLB 9
  See also AITN 1

Caldwell, (Janet Miriam) Taylor (Holland)
  1900-1985. . . . . . . . .CLC 2, 28, 39 (301)
  See also CANR 5
  See also CA 5-8R
  See also obituary CA 116

Calhoun, John Caldwell
  1782-1850. . . . . . . . . . . . . . . . NCLC 15
  See also DLB 3

Calisher, Hortense
  1911- . . . . . . . . . . . . . . . .CLC 2, 4, 8, 38
  See also CANR 1, 22
  See also CA 1-4R
  See also DLB 2

Callaghan, Morley (Edward)
  1903- . . . . . . . . . . . . . . . . .CLC 3, 14, 41
  See also CA 9-12R

Calvino, Italo
  1923-1985. . . . . . .CLC 5, 8, 11, 22, 33,
                                          39 (305)
  See also CA 85-88
  See also obituary CA 116

Cameron, Peter  1959- . . . . . . . . CLC 44 (33)

Campana, Dino  1885-1932. . . . . . . TCLC 20
  See also CA 117

Campbell, John W(ood), Jr.
  1910-1971. . . . . . . . . . . . . . . . . .CLC 32
  See also CAP 2
  See also CA 21-22
  See also obituary CA 29-32R
  See also DLB 8

Campbell, (John) Ramsey
  1946- . . . . . . . . . . . . . . . . . . . . .CLC 42
  See also CANR 7
  See also CA 57-60

Campbell, (Ignatius) Roy (Dunnachie)
  1901-1957. . . . . . . . . . . . . . . . . TCLC 5
  See also CA 104
  See also DLB 20

Campbell, (William) Wilfred
  1861-1918. . . . . . . . . . . . . . . . . TCLC 9
  See also CA 106

Camus, Albert
  1913-1960. . . . . . CLC 1, 2, 4, 9, 11, 14,
                                          32
  See also CA 89-92

Canby, Vincent  1924- . . . . . . . . . . . .CLC 13
  See also CA 81-84

Canetti, Elias  1905- . . . . . . . . CLC 3, 14, 25
  See also CA 21-24R

Cape, Judith  1916-
  See Page, P(atricia) K(athleen)

Čapek, Karel  1890-1938. . . . . . . . . TCLC 6
  See also CA 104

Capote, Truman
  1924-1984. . . . . . . . .CLC 1, 3, 8, 13, 19,
                                    34 (320), 38
  See also CANR 18
  See also CA 5-8R
  See also obituary CA 113
  See also DLB 2
  See also DLB-Y 80, 84
  See also CDALB 1941-1968

Capra, Frank  1897- . . . . . . . . . . . . .CLC 16
  See also CA 61-64

Caputo, Philip  1941- . . . . . . . . . . . .CLC 32
  See also CA 73-76

Card, Orson Scott
  1951- . . . . . . . . . . . . . CLC 44 (163), 47
  See also CA 102

Cardenal, Ernesto  1925- . . . . . . . . . .CLC 31
  See also CANR 2
  See also CA 49-52

Carey, Ernestine Gilbreth  1908-
  See Gilbreth, Frank B(unker), Jr. and
     Carey, Ernestine Gilbreth
  See also CA 5-8R
  See also SATA 2

Carey, Peter  1943- . . . . . . . . . . . . . .CLC 40

Carleton, William  1794-1869. . . . . . NCLC 3

Carlisle, Henry (Coffin)  1926- . . . . . .CLC 33
  See also CANR 15
  See also CA 13-16R

Carman, (William) Bliss
  1861-1929. . . . . . . . . . . . . . . . . TCLC 7
  See also CA 104

Carpenter, Don(ald Richard)
  1931- . . . . . . . . . . . . . . . . . . . . .CLC 41
  See also CANR 1
  See also CA 45-48

Carpentier (y Valmont), Alejo
  1904-1980. . . . . . . . . . . . . CLC 8, 11, 38
  See also CANR 11
  See also CA 65-68
  See also obituary CA 97-100

Carr, John Dickson  1906-1977 . . . . . .CLC 3
  See also CANR 3
  See also CA 49-52
  See also obituary CA 69-72

Carr, Virginia Spencer
  1929- . . . . . . . . . . . . . . . . CLC 34 (419)
  See also CA 61-64

Carrier, Roch  1937- . . . . . . . . . . . . .CLC 13
  See also DLB 53

Carroll, James (P.)  1943- . . . . . . . . . .CLC 38
  See also CA 81-84

Carroll, Jim  1951- . . . . . . . . . . . . . . .CLC 35
  See also CA 45-48

Carroll, Lewis  1832-1898. . . . . . . . NCLC 2
  See also Dodgson, Charles Lutwidge
  See also CLR 2
  See also DLB 18

Carroll, Paul Vincent
  1900-1968. . . . . . . . . . . . . . . . . .CLC 10
  See also CA 9-12R
  See also obituary CA 25-28R
  See also DLB 10

Carruth, Hayden
  1921- . . . . . . . . . . . . . .CLC 4, 7, 10, 18
  See also CANR 4
  See also CA 9-12R
  See also SATA 47
  See also DLB 5

Carter, Angela (Olive)
  1940- . . . . . . . . . . . . . . . . . . CLC 5, 41
  See also CANR 12
  See also CA 53-56
  See also DLB 14

Carver, Raymond  1938- . . . . . . . CLC 22, 36
  See also CANR 17
  See also CA 33-36R
  See also DLB-Y 84

Cary, (Arthur) Joyce
  1888-1957. . . . . . . . . . . . . . . . . TCLC 1
  See also CA 104
  See also DLB 15

Casares, Adolfo Bioy  1914-
  See Bioy Casares, Adolfo

Casely-Hayford, J(oseph) E(phraim)
  1866-1930. . . . . . . . . . . . . . . . . TCLC 24

**Casey, John** 1880-1964
See O'Casey, Sean

**Casey, Michael** 1947- .............CLC 2
See also CA 65-68
See also DLB 5

**Casey, Warren** 1935-
See Jacobs, Jim and Casey, Warren
See also CA 101

**Cassavetes, John** 1929-...........CLC 20
See also CA 85-88

**Cassill, R(onald) V(erlin)**
1919-.................... CLC 4, 23
See also CAAS 1
See also CANR 7
See also CA 9-12R
See also DLB 6

**Cassity, (Allen) Turner**
1929-.................... CLC 6, 42
See also CANR 11
See also CA 17-20R

**Castaneda, Carlos** 1935?-..........CLC 12
See also CA 25-28R

**Castro, Rosalía de** 1837-1885 ..... NCLC 3

**Cather, Willa (Sibert)**
1873-1947................TCLC 1, 11
See also CA 104
See also SATA 30
See also DLB 9, 54
See also DLB-DS 1

**Catton, (Charles) Bruce**
1899-1978....................CLC 35
See also CANR 7
See also CA 5-8R
See also obituary CA 81-84
See also SATA 2
See also obituary SATA 24
See also DLB 17
See also AITN 1

**Caunitz, William** 1935-....... CLC 34 (35)

**Causley, Charles (Stanley)**
1917-........................CLC 7
See also CANR 5
See also CA 9-12R
See also SATA 3
See also DLB 27

**Caute, (John) David** 1936-........CLC 29
See also CAAS 4
See also CANR 1
See also CA 1-4R
See also DLB 14

**Cavafy, C(onstantine) P(eter)**
1863-1933................TCLC 2, 7
See also CA 104

**Cavanna, Betty** 1909- .............CLC 12
See also CANR 6
See also CA 9-12R
See also SATA 1, 30

**Cayrol, Jean** 1911- ..............CLC 11
See also CA 89-92

**Cela, Camilo José** 1916-........ CLC 4, 13
See also CANR 21
See also CA 21-24R

**Celan, Paul** 1920-1970 ........ CLC 10, 19
See also Antschel, Paul

**Céline, Louis-Ferdinand**
1894-1961...... CLC 1, 3, 4, 7, 9, 15, 47
See also Destouches, Louis-Ferdinand-Auguste

**Cellini, Benvenuto** 1500-1571 ........ LC 7

**Cendrars, Blaise** 1887-1961.......CLC 18
See also Sauser-Hall, Frédéric

**Cervantes (Saavedra), Miguel de**
1547-1616..................... LC 6

**Césaire, Aimé (Fernand)**
1913-.................... CLC 19, 32
See also CA 65-68

**Chabrol, Claude** 1930- ...........CLC 16
See also CA 110

**Challans, Mary** 1905-1983
See Renault, Mary
See also CA 81-84
See also obituary CA 111
See also SATA 23
See also obituary SATA 36

**Chambers, Aidan** 1934- ...........CLC 35
See also CANR 12
See also CA 25-28R
See also SATA 1

**Chambers, James** 1948-
See Cliff, Jimmy

**Chandler, Raymond**
1888-1959................TCLC 1, 7
See also CA 104

**Channing, William Ellery**
1780-1842.................. NCLC 17
See also DLB 1, 59

**Chaplin, Charles (Spencer)**
1889-1977...................CLC 16
See also CA 81-84
See also obituary CA 73-76
See also DLB 44

**Chapman, Graham** 1941?-
See Monty Python
See also CA 116

**Chapman, John Jay**
1862-1933................... TCLC 7
See also CA 104

**Chappell, Fred** 1936- .............CLC 40
See also CAAS 4
See also CANR 8
See also CA 5-8R
See also DLB 6

**Char, René (Emile)**
1907-................ CLC 9, 11, 14
See also CA 13-16R

**Charyn, Jerome** 1937- ....... CLC 5, 8, 18
See also CAAS 1
See also CANR 7
See also CA 5-8R
See also DLB-Y 83

**Chase, Mary Ellen** 1887-1973.......CLC 2
See also CAP 1
See also CA 15-16
See also obituary CA 41-44R
See also SATA 10

**Chateaubriand, François René de**
1768-1848................... NCLC 3

**Chatterji, Saratchandra**
1876-1938.................. TCLC 13
See also CA 109

**Chatterton, Thomas** 1752-1770....... LC 3

**Chatwin, (Charles) Bruce**
1940-........................CLC 28
See also CA 85-88

**Chayefsky, Paddy** 1923-1981.......CLC 23
See also CA 9-12R
See also obituary CA 104
See also DLB 7, 44
See also DLB-Y 81

**Chayefsky, Sidney** 1923-1981
See Chayefsky, Paddy
See also CANR 18

**Chedid, Andrée** 1920-.............CLC 47

**Cheever, John**
1912-1982...... CLC 3, 7, 8, 11, 15, 25
See also SSC 1
See also CANR 5
See also CA 5-8R
See also obituary CA 106
See also CABS 1
See also DLB 2
See also DLB-Y 80, 82
See also CDALB 1941-1968

**Cheever, Susan** 1943-......... CLC 18, 48
See also CA 103
See also DLB-Y 82

**Chekhov, Anton (Pavlovich)**
1860-1904................ TCLC 3, 10
See also CA 104

**Chernyshevsky, Nikolay Gavrilovich**
1828-1889.................. NCLC 1

**Cherry, Caroline Janice** 1942-
See Cherryh, C. J.

**Cherryh, C. J.** 1942-..............CLC 35
See also DLB-Y 80

**Chesnutt, Charles Waddell**
1858-1932.................. TCLC 5
See also CA 106
See also DLB 12, 50

**Chesterton, G(ilbert) K(eith)**
1874-1936................ TCLC 1, 6
See also SSC 1
See also CA 104
See also SATA 27
See also DLB 10, 19, 34

**Ch'ien Chung-shu** 1910-...........CLC 22

**Child, Lydia Maria** 1802-1880 .... NCLC 6
See also DLB 1

**Child, Philip** 1898-1978 ..........CLC 19
See also CAP 1
See also CA 13-14
See also SATA 47

**Childress, Alice** 1920-......... CLC 12, 15
See also CLR 14
See also CANR 3
See also CA 45-48
See also SATA 7, 48
See also DLB 7, 38

**Chislett, (Margaret) Anne**
1943?-................. CLC 34 (144)

**Chitty, (Sir) Thomas Willes** 1926-
See Hinde, Thomas
See also CA 5-8R

**Chomette, René** 1898-1981
See Clair, René
See also obituary CA 103

**Chopin, Kate (O'Flaherty)**
1851-1904 . . . . . . . . . . . . . . TCLC **5, 14**
See also CA 104, 122
See also DLB 12

**Christie, (Dame) Agatha (Mary Clarissa)**
1890-1976 . . . . . . . . . . . CLC **1, 6, 8, 12,**
**39 (436), 48**
See also CANR 10
See also CA 17-20R
See also obituary CA 61-64
See also SATA 36
See also DLB 13
See also AITN 1, 2

**Christie, (Ann) Philippa** 1920-
See Pearce, (Ann) Philippa
See also CANR 4

**Chulkov, Mikhail Dmitrievich**
1743-1792 . . . . . . . . . . . . . . . . . . LC **2**

**Churchill, Caryl** 1938- . . . . . . . . . . . CLC **31**
See also CA 102
See also CANR 22
See also DLB 13

**Churchill, Charles** 1731?-1764 . . . . . . . LC **3**

**Chute, Carolyn** 1947- . . . . . . . . CLC **39 (37)**

**Ciardi, John (Anthony)**
1916-1986 . . . . . . . . CLC **10, 40, 44 (374)**
See also CAAS 2
See also CANR 5
See also CA 5-8R
See also obituary CA 118
See also SATA 1, 46
See also DLB 5
See also DLB-Y 86

**Cimino, Michael** 1943?- . . . . . . . . . . . CLC **16**
See also CA 105

**Clair, René** 1898-1981 . . . . . . . . . . . CLC **20**
See also Chomette, René

**Clampitt, Amy** 19??- . . . . . . . . . . . . . . CLC **32**
See also CA 110

**Clancy, Tom** 1947- . . . . . . . . . . . . . . CLC **45**

**Clare, John** 1793-1864 . . . . . . . . . . . NCLC **9**
See also DLB 55

**Clark, (Robert) Brian** 1932- . . . . . . . CLC **29**
See also CA 41-44R

**Clark, Eleanor** 1913- . . . . . . . . . . . CLC **5, 19**
See also CA 9-12R
See also DLB 6

**Clark, John Pepper** 1935- . . . . . . . . . CLC **38**
See also CANR 16
See also CA 65-68

**Clark, Mavis Thorpe** 1912?- . . . . . . . CLC **12**
See also CANR 8
See also CA 57-60
See also SATA 8

**Clark, Walter Van Tilburg**
1909-1971 . . . . . . . . . . . . . . . . . . CLC **28**
See also CA 9-12R
See also obituary CA 33-36R
See also SATA 8
See also DLB 9

**Clarke, Arthur C(harles)**
1917- . . . . . . . . . . . CLC **1, 4, 13, 18, 35**
See also CANR 2
See also CA 1-4R
See also SATA 13

**Clarke, Austin** 1896-1974 . . . . . . . . CLC **6, 9**
See also CAP 2
See also CANR 14
See also CA 29-32
See also obituary CA 49-52
See also DLB 10, 20, 53

**Clarke, Austin C(hesterfield)**
1934- . . . . . . . . . . . . . . . . . . . . . . CLC **8**
See also CANR 14
See also CA 25-28R
See also DLB 53

**Clarke, Shirley** 1925- . . . . . . . . . . . CLC **16**

**Clash, The** . . . . . . . . . . . . . . . . . . . . CLC **30**

**Claudel, Paul (Louis Charles Marie)**
1868-1955 . . . . . . . . . . . . . . TCLC **2, 10**
See also CA 104

**Clavell, James (duMaresq)**
1924- . . . . . . . . . . . . . . . . . CLC **6, 25**
See also CA 25-28R

**Cleaver, (Leroy) Eldridge**
1935- . . . . . . . . . . . . . . . . . . . . . CLC **30**
See also CANR 16
See also CA 21-24R

**Cleese, John** 1939-
See Monty Python
See also CA 112, 116

**Cleland, John** 1709-1789 . . . . . . . . . . . LC **2**
See also DLB 39

**Clemens, Samuel Langhorne** 1835-1910
See Twain, Mark
See also CA 104
See also YABC 2
See also DLB 11, 12, 23, 64

**Cliff, Jimmy** 1948- . . . . . . . . . . . . . . CLC **21**

**Clifton, Lucille** 1936- . . . . . . . . . . . CLC **19**
See also CLR 5
See also CANR 2
See also CA 49-52
See also SATA 20
See also DLB 5, 41

**Clutha, Janet Paterson Frame** 1924-
See Frame (Clutha), Janet (Paterson)
See also CANR 2
See also CA 1-4R

**Coburn, D(onald) L(ee)** 1938- . . . . . . CLC **10**
See also CA 89-92

**Cocteau, Jean (Maurice Eugene Clement)**
1889-1963 . . . . . . . CLC **1, 8, 15, 16, 43**
See also CAP 2
See also CA 25-28

**Codrescu, Andrei** 1946- . . . . . . . . . . CLC **46**
See also CANR 13
See also CA 33-36R

**Coetzee, J(ohn) M.** 1940- . . . . . . CLC **23, 33**
See also CA 77-80

**Cohen, Arthur A(llen)**
1928-1986 . . . . . . . . . . . . . . . CLC **7, 31**
See also CANR 1, 17
See also CA 1-4R
See also obituary CA 120
See also DLB 28

**Cohen, Leonard (Norman)**
1934- . . . . . . . . . . . . . . . . . CLC **3, 38**
See also CANR 14
See also CA 21-24R
See also DLB 53

**Cohen, Matt** 1942- . . . . . . . . . . . . . . CLC **19**
See also CA 61-64
See also DLB 53

**Colegate, Isabel** 1931- . . . . . . . . . . . CLC **36**
See also CANR 8, 22
See also CA 17-20R
See also DLB 14

**Coleridge, Samuel Taylor**
1772-1834 . . . . . . . . . . . . . . . . . NCLC **9**

**Coles, Don** 1928- . . . . . . . . . . . . . . CLC **46**
See also CA 115

**Colette (Sidonie-Gabrielle)**
1873-1954 . . . . . . . . . . . TCLC **1, 5, 16**
See also CA 104

**Collier, Christopher** 1930-
See Collier, Christopher and Collier, James
L(incoln)
See also CANR 13
See also CA 33-36R
See also SATA 16

**Collier, Christopher** 1930- and
**Collier, James L(incoln)**
1928- . . . . . . . . . . . . . . . . . . . . . CLC **30**

**Collier, James L(incoln)** 1928-
See Collier, Christopher and Collier, James
L(incoln)
See also CLR 3
See also CANR 4
See also CA 9-12R
See also SATA 8

**Collier, James L(incoln)** 1928- and
**Collier, Christopher** 1930-
See Collier, Christopher and Collier, James
L(incoln)

**Collier, Jeremy** 1650-1726 . . . . . . . . . . LC **6**

**Collins, Hunt** 1926-
See Hunter, Evan

**Collins, Linda** 19??- . . . . . . . . CLC **44 (36)**

**Collins, Tom** 1843-1912
See Furphy, Joseph

**Collins, William** 1721-1759 . . . . . . . . . LC **4**

**Collins, (William) Wilkie**
1824-1889 . . . . . . . . . . . . . . NCLC **1, 18**
See also DLB 18

**Colman, George** 1909-1981
See Glassco, John

**Colton, James** 1923-
See Hansen, Joseph

**Colum, Padraic** 1881-1972 . . . . . . . . CLC **28**
See also CA 73-76
See also obituary CA 33-36R
See also SATA 15
See also DLB 19

**Colvin, James** 1939-
See Moorcock, Michael

**Colwin, Laurie** 1945- . . . . . . . CLC **5, 13, 23**
See also CANR 20
See also CA 89-92
See also DLB-Y 80

**Comfort, Alex(ander)** 1920- . . . . . . . CLC **7**
See also CANR 1
See also CA 1-4R

**Crockett, David (Davy)**
1786-1836.................. NCLC 8
See also DLB 3, 11

**Croker, John Wilson**
1780-1857................. NCLC 10

**Cronin, A(rchibald) J(oseph)**
1896-1981..................CLC 32
See also CANR 5
See also CA 1-4R
See also obituary CA 102
See also obituary SATA 25, 47

**Cross, Amanda**  1926-
See Heilbrun, Carolyn G(old)

**Crothers, Rachel**  1878-1953...... TCLC 19
See also CA 113
See also DLB 7

**Crowley, Aleister**  1875-1947 ...... TCLC 7
See also CA 104

**Crumb, Robert**  1943-..............CLC 17
See also CA 106

**Cryer, Gretchen**  1936?-...........CLC 21
See also CA 114

**Csáth, Géza**  1887-1919......... TCLC 13
See also CA 111

**Cudlip, David**  1933- ......... CLC 34 (38)

**Cullen, Countee**  1903-1946 ....... TCLC 4
See also CA 108
See also SATA 18
See also DLB 4, 48, 51

**Cummings, E(dward) E(stlin)**
1894-1962........ CLC 1, 3, 8, 12, 15
See also CA 73-76
See also DLB 4, 48

**Cunha, Euclides (Rodrigues) da**
1866-1909.................. TCLC 24

**Cunningham, J(ames) V(incent)**
1911-1985................ CLC 3, 31
See also CANR 1
See also CA 1-4R
See also obituary CA 115
See also DLB 5

**Cunningham, Julia (Woolfolk)**
1916-.......................CLC 12
See also CANR 4, 19
See also CA 9-12R
See also SAAS 2
See also SATA 1, 26

**Cunningham, Michael**
1952-................... CLC 34 (40)

**Currie, Ellen**  19??- ......... CLC 44 (39)

**Dąbrowska, Maria (Szumska)**
1889-1965..................CLC 15
See also CA 106

**Dabydeen, David**  1956?-..... CLC 34 (147)

**Dagerman, Stig (Halvard)**
1923-1954................. TCLC 17
See also CA 117

**Dahl, Roald**  1916-........... CLC 1, 6, 18
See also CLR 1, 7
See also CANR 6
See also CA 1-4R
See also SATA 1, 26

**Dahlberg, Edward**
1900-1977............... CLC 1, 7, 14
See also CA 9-12R
See also obituary CA 69-72
See also DLB 48

**Daly, Maureen**  1921-..............CLC 17
See also McGivern, Maureen Daly
See also SAAS 1
See also SATA 2

**Däniken, Erich von**  1935-
See Von Däniken, Erich

**Dannay, Frederic**  1905-1982
See Queen, Ellery
See also CANR 1
See also CA 1-4R
See also obituary CA 107

**D'Annunzio, Gabriele**
1863-1938.................. TCLC 6
See also CA 104

**Danziger, Paula**  1944-.............CLC 21
See also CA 112, 115
See also SATA 30, 36

**Darío, Rubén**  1867-1916......... TCLC 4
See also Sarmiento, Felix Ruben Garcia
See also CA 104

**Darley, George**  1795-1846 ....... NCLC 2

**Daryush, Elizabeth**
1887-1977................. CLC 6, 19
See also CANR 3
See also CA 49-52
See also DLB 20

**Daudet, (Louis Marie) Alphonse**
1840-1897.................. NCLC 1

**Daumal, René**  1908-1944 ....... TCLC 14
See also CA 114

**Davenport, Guy (Mattison, Jr.)**
1927-................. CLC 6, 14, 38
See also CA 33-36R

**Davidson, Donald (Grady)**
1893-1968.............. CLC 2, 13, 19
See also CANR 4
See also CA 5-8R
See also obituary CA 25-28R
See also DLB 45

**Davidson, John**  1857-1909 ....... TCLC 24
See also CA 118
See also DLB 19

**Davidson, Sara**  1943-..............CLC 9
See also CA 81-84

**Davie, Donald (Alfred)**
1922-................. CLC 5, 8, 10, 31
See also CAAS 3
See also CANR 1
See also CA 1-4R
See also DLB 27

**Davies, Ray(mond Douglas)**
1944-.......................CLC 21
See also CA 116

**Davies, Rhys**  1903-1978 ...........CLC 23
See also CANR 4
See also CA 9-12R
See also obituary CA 81-84

**Davies, (William) Robertson**
1913-........ CLC 2, 7, 13, 25, 42
See also CANR 17
See also CA 33-36R

**Davies, W(illiam) H(enry)**
1871-1940.................. TCLC 5
See also CA 104
See also DLB 19

**Davis, Rebecca (Blaine) Harding**
1831-1910.................. TCLC 6
See also CA 104

**Davis, Richard Harding**
1864-1916................. TCLC 24
See also CA 114
See also DLB 12, 23

**Davison, Frank Dalby**
1893-1970..................CLC 15
See also obituary CA 116

**Davison, Peter**  1928-..............CLC 28
See also CAAS 4
See also CANR 3
See also CA 9-12R
See also DLB 5

**Davys, Mary**  1674-1732 .............LC 1
See also DLB 39

**Dawson, Fielding**  1930-...........CLC 6
See also CA 85-88

**Day, Clarence (Shepard, Jr.)**
1874-1935................. TCLC 25
See also CA 108
See also DLB 11

**Day Lewis, C(ecil)**
1904-1972................CLC 1, 6, 10
See also CAP 1
See also CA 15-16
See also obituary CA 33-36R
See also DLB 15, 20

**Day, Thomas**  1748-1789.............LC 1
See also YABC 1
See also DLB 39

**Dazai Osamu**  1909-1948........ TCLC 11
See also Tsushima Shūji

**De Crayencour, Marguerite**  1903-
See Yourcenar, Marguerite

**Deer, Sandra**  1940-...............CLC 45

**Defoe, Daniel**  1660?-1731.............LC 1
See also SATA 22
See also DLB 39

**De Hartog, Jan**  1914-.............CLC 19
See also CANR 1
See also CA 1-4R

**Deighton, Len**  1929- ......CLC 4, 7, 22, 46
See also Deighton, Leonard Cyril

**Deighton, Leonard Cyril**  1929-
See Deighton, Len
See also CANR 19
See also CA 9-12R

**De la Mare, Walter (John)**
1873-1956.................. TCLC 4
See also CA 110
See also SATA 16
See also DLB 19

**Delaney, Shelagh**  1939-...........CLC 29
See also CA 17-20R
See also DLB 13

**Delany, Samuel R(ay, Jr.)**
1942-................. CLC 8, 14, 38
See also CA 81-84
See also DLB 8, 33

**De la Roche, Mazo**  1885-1961......CLC 14
See also CA 85-88

**Eckert, Allan W.** 1931-............CLC 17
See also CANR 14
See also CA 13-16R
See also SATA 27, 29

**Eco, Umberto** 1932-..............CLC 28
See also CANR 12
See also CA 77-80

**Eddison, E(ric) R(ucker)**
1882-1945................. TCLC 15
See also CA 109

**Edel, Leon (Joseph)**
1907-.............. CLC 29, 34 (534)
See also CANR 1, 22
See also CA 1-4R

**Eden, Emily** 1797-1869......... NCLC 10

**Edgar, David** 1948-..............CLC 42
See also CANR 12
See also CA 57-60
See also DLB 13

**Edgerton, Clyde** 1944-........ CLC 39 (52)
See also CA 118

**Edgeworth, Maria** 1767-1849 ..... NCLC 1
See also SATA 21

**Edmonds, Helen (Woods)** 1904-1968
See Kavan, Anna
See also CA 5-8R
See also obituary CA 25-28R

**Edmonds, Walter D(umaux)**
1903-........................CLC 35
See also CANR 2
See also CA 5-8R
See also SAAS 4
See also SATA 1, 27
See also DLB 9

**Edson, Russell** 1905-..............CLC 13
See also CA 33-36R

**Edwards, G(erald) B(asil)**
1899-1976...................CLC 25
See also obituary CA 110

**Edwards, Gus** 1939- ..............CLC 43
See also CA 108

**Edwards, Jonathan** 1703-1758 ....... LC 7
See also DLB 24

**Ehle, John (Marsden, Jr.)**
1925-......................CLC 27
See also CA 9-12R

**Ehrenbourg, Ilya (Grigoryevich)** 1891-1967
See Ehrenburg, Ilya (Grigoryevich)

**Ehrenburg, Ilya (Grigoryevich)**
1891-1967.......... CLC 18, 34 (433)
See also CA 102
See also obituary CA 25-28R

**Eich, Guenter** 1907-1971
See also CA 111
See also obituary CA 93-96

**Eich, Günter** 1907-1971..........CLC 15
See also Eich, Guenter

**Eichendorff, Joseph Freiherr von**
1788-1857.................. NCLC 8

**Eigner, Larry** 1927- ..............CLC 9
See also Eigner, Laurence (Joel)
See also DLB 5

**Eigner, Laurence (Joel)** 1927-
See Eigner, Larry
See also CANR 6
See also CA 9-12R

**Eiseley, Loren (Corey)**
1907-1977....................CLC 7
See also CANR 6
See also CA 1-4R
See also obituary CA 73-76

**Ekeloef, Gunnar (Bengt)** 1907-1968
See Ekelöf, Gunnar (Bengt)
See also obituary CA 25-28R

**Ekelöf, Gunnar (Bengt)**
1907-1968...................CLC 27
See also Ekeloef, Gunnar (Bengt)

**Ekwensi, Cyprian (Odiatu Duaka)**
1921-........................CLC 4
See also CANR 18
See also CA 29-32R

**Eliade, Mircea** 1907-1986.........CLC 19
See also CA 65-68
See also obituary CA 119

**Eliot, George** 1819-1880....... NCLC 4, 13
See also DLB 21, 35, 55

**Eliot, John** 1604-1690.............. LC 5
See also DLB 24

**Eliot, T(homas) S(tearns)**
1888-1965...... CLC 1, 2, 3, 6, 9, 10,
13, 15, 24, 34 (387; 523), 41
See also CA 5-8R
See also obituary CA 25-28R
See also DLB 7, 10, 45, 63

**Elkin, Stanley (Lawrence)**
1930-......... CLC 4, 6, 9, 14, 27
See also CANR 8
See also CA 9-12R
See also DLB 2, 28
See also DLB-Y 80

**Elledge, Scott** 19??-........ CLC 34 (425)

**Elliott, George P(aul)**
1918-1980...................CLC 2
See also CANR 2
See also CA 1-4R
See also obituary CA 97-100

**Elliott, Janice** 1931-..............CLC 47
See also CANR 8
See also CA 13-16R
See also DLB 14

**Elliott, Sumner Locke** 1917- .......CLC 38
See also CANR 2, 21
See also CA 5-8R

**Ellis, A. E.** 19??-..................CLC 7

**Ellis, Alice Thomas** 19??-..........CLC 40

**Ellis, Bret Easton** 1964- ...... CLC 39 (55)
See also CA 118

**Ellis, (Henry) Havelock**
1859-1939.................. TCLC 14
See also CA 109

**Ellison, Harlan (Jay)**
1934-.................. CLC 1, 13, 42
See also CANR 5
See also CA 5-8R
See also DLB 8

**Ellison, Ralph (Waldo)**
1914-.................. CLC 1, 3, 11
See also CA 9-12R
See also DLB 2
See also CDALB 1941-1968

**Elman, Richard** 1934-.............CLC 19
See also CAAS 3
See also CA 17-20R

**Éluard, Paul** 1895-1952 ......... TCLC 7
See also Grindel, Eugene

**Elvin, Anne Katharine Stevenson** 1933-
See Stevenson, Anne (Katharine)
See also CA 17-20R

**Elytis, Odysseus** 1911- ...........CLC 15
See also CA 102

**Emecheta, (Florence Onye) Buchi**
1944-................ CLC 14, 48
See also CA 81-84

**Emerson, Ralph Waldo**
1803-1882................... NCLC 1
See also DLB 1

**Empson, William**
1906-1984.......... CLC 3, 8, 19, 33,
34 (335; 538)
See also CA 17-20R
See also obituary CA 112
See also DLB 20

**Enchi, Fumiko (Veda)**
1905-1986...................CLC 31
See also obituary CA 121

**Ende, Michael** 1930-..............CLC 31
See also CLR 14
See also CA 118
See also SATA 42

**Endo, Shusaku** 1923- .......CLC 7, 14, 19
See also CANR 21
See also CA 29-32R

**Engel, Marian** 1933-1985..........CLC 36
See also CANR 12
See also CA 25-28R
See also DLB 53

**Engelhardt, Frederick** 1911-1986
See Hubbard, L(afayette) Ron(ald)

**Enright, D(ennis) J(oseph)**
1920-................... CLC 4, 8, 31
See also CANR 1
See also CA 1-4R
See also SATA 25
See also DLB 27

**Enzensberger, Hans Magnus**
1929-.....................CLC 43
See also CA 116, 119

**Ephron, Nora** 1941- .......... CLC 17, 31
See also CANR 12
See also CA 65-68
See also AITN 2

**Epstein, Daniel Mark** 1948-........CLC 7
See also CANR 2
See also CA 49-52

**Epstein, Jacob** 1956-..............CLC 19
See also CA 114

**Epstein, Joseph** 1937-....... CLC 39 (463)
See also CA 112, 119

**Epstein, Leslie** 1938-..............CLC 27
See also CA 73-76

**Erdman, Paul E(mil)** 1932- ........CLC 25
See also CANR 13
See also CA 61-64
See also AITN 1

**Erdrich, Louise** 1954-....... CLC 39 (128)
See also CA 114

**Erenburg, Ilya (Grigoryevich)** 1891-1967
See Ehrenburg, Ilya (Grigoryevich)

**Eseki, Bruno** 1919-
See Mphahlele, Ezekiel

**Esenin, Sergei (Aleksandrovich)**
1895-1925 .................. TCLC 4
See also CA 104

**Eshleman, Clayton** 1935- .......... CLC 7
See also CAAS 6
See also CA 33-36R
See also DLB 5

**Espriu, Salvador** 1913-1985 ........ CLC 9
See also obituary CA 115

**Estleman, Loren D.** 1952- ......... CLC 48
See also CA 85-88

**Evans, Marian** 1819-1880
See Eliot, George

**Evans, Mary Ann** 1819-1880
See Eliot, George

**Evarts, Esther** 1900-1972
See Benson, Sally

**Everson, Ronald G(ilmour)**
1903- ........................ CLC 27
See also CA 17-20R

**Everson, William (Oliver)**
1912- ................ CLC 1, 5, 14
See also CANR 20
See also CA 9-12R
See also DLB 5, 16

**Evtushenko, Evgenii (Aleksandrovich)** 1933-
See Yevtushenko, Yevgeny

**Ewart, Gavin (Buchanan)**
1916- ................... CLC 13, 46
See also CANR 17
See also CA 89-92
See also DLB 40

**Ewers, Hanns Heinz**
1871-1943 ................. TCLC 12
See also CA 109

**Ewing, Frederick R.** 1918-
See Sturgeon, Theodore (Hamilton)

**Exley, Frederick (Earl)**
1929- .................... CLC 6, 11
See also CA 81-84
See also DLB-Y 81
See also AITN 2

**Ezekiel, Tish O'Dowd**
1943- ................... CLC 34 (46)

**Fagen, Donald** 1948-
See Becker, Walter and Fagen, Donald

**Fagen, Donald** 1948- and
**Becker, Walter** 1950-
See Becker, Walter and Fagen, Donald

**Fair, Ronald L.** 1932- ............ CLC 18
See also CA 69-72
See also DLB 33

**Fairbairns, Zoë (Ann)** 1948- ....... CLC 32
See also CANR 21
See also CA 103

**Fairfield, Cicily Isabel** 1892-1983
See West, Rebecca

**Fallaci, Oriana** 1930- ............ CLC 11
See also CANR 15
See also CA 77-80

**Faludy, George** 1913- ............ CLC 42
See also CA 21-24R

**Fargue, Léon-Paul** 1876-1947 .... TCLC 11
See also CA 109

**Farigoule, Louis** 1885-1972
See Romains, Jules

**Fariña, Richard** 1937?-1966 ....... CLC 9
See also CA 81-84
See also obituary CA 25-28R

**Farley, Walter** 1920- ............. CLC 17
See also CANR 8
See also CA 17-20R
See also SATA 2, 43
See also DLB 22

**Farmer, Philip José** 1918- ...... CLC 1, 19
See also CANR 4
See also CA 1-4R
See also DLB 8

**Farrell, J(ames) G(ordon)**
1935-1979 ................... CLC 6
See also CA 73-76
See also obituary CA 89-92
See also DLB 14

**Farrell, James T(homas)**
1904-1979 ........... CLC 1, 4, 8, 11
See also CANR 9
See also CA 5-8R
See also obituary CA 89-92
See also DLB 4, 9
See also DLB-DS 2

**Farrell, M. J.** 1904-
See Keane, Molly

**Fassbinder, Rainer Werner**
1946-1982 ................... CLC 20
See also CA 93-96
See also obituary CA 106

**Fast, Howard (Melvin)** 1914- ....... CLC 23
See also CANR 1
See also CA 1-4R
See also SATA 7
See also DLB 9

**Faulkner, William (Cuthbert)**
1897-1962 ...... CLC 1, 3, 6, 8, 9, 11,
14, 18, 28
See also SSC 1
See also CA 81-84
See also DLB 9, 11, 44
See also DLB-Y 86
See also DLB-DS 2
See also AITN 1

**Fauset, Jessie Redmon**
1884?-1961 ................... CLC 19
See also CA 109
See also DLB 51

**Faust, Irvin** 1924- ................ CLC 8
See also CA 33-36R
See also DLB 2, 28
See also DLB-Y 80

**Federman, Raymond** 1928- ..... CLC 6, 47
See also CANR 10
See also CA 17-20R
See also DLB-Y 80

**Federspiel, J(ürg) F.** 1931- ........ CLC 42

**Feiffer, Jules** 1929- ............. CLC 2, 8
See also CA 17-20R
See also SATA 8
See also DLB 7, 44

**Feinstein, Elaine** 1930- ........... CLC 36
See also CA 69-72
See also CAAS 1
See also DLB 14, 40

**Feldman, Irving (Mordecai)**
1928- ........................ CLC 7
See also CANR 1
See also CA 1-4R

**Fellini, Federico** 1920- ........... CLC 16
See also CA 65-68

**Felsen, Gregor** 1916-
See Felsen, Henry Gregor

**Felsen, Henry Gregor** 1916- ........ CLC 17
See also CANR 1
See also CA 1-4R
See also SAAS 2
See also SATA 1

**Fenton, James (Martin)** 1949- ...... CLC 32
See also CA 102
See also DLB 40

**Ferber, Edna** 1887-1968 .......... CLC 18
See also CA 5-8R
See also obituary CA 25-28R
See also SATA 7
See also DLB 9, 28
See also AITN 1

**Ferlinghetti, Lawrence (Monsanto)**
1919?- .............. CLC 2, 6, 10, 27
See also CANR 3
See also CA 5-8R
See also DLB 5, 16
See also CDALB 1941-1968

**Ferrier, Susan (Edmonstone)**
1782-1854 .................. NCLC 8

**Feuchtwanger, Lion**
1884-1958 .................. TCLC 3
See also CA 104

**Feydeau, Georges** 1862-1921 ..... TCLC 22
See also CA 113

**Fiedler, Leslie A(aron)**
1917- ................. CLC 4, 13, 24
See also CANR 7
See also CA 9-12R
See also DLB 28

**Field, Andrew** 1938- ........ CLC 44 (463)
See also CA 97-100

**Field, Eugene** 1850-1895 ......... NCLC 3
See also SATA 16
See also DLB 21, 23, 42

**Fielding, Henry** 1707-1754 .......... LC 1
See also DLB 39

**Fielding, Sarah** 1710-1768 .......... LC 1
See also DLB 39

**Fierstein, Harvey** 1954- ........... CLC 33

**Figes, Eva** 1932- ................. CLC 31
See also CANR 4
See also CA 53-56
See also DLB 14

**Finch, Robert (Duer Claydon)**
1900- ........................ CLC 18
See also CANR 9
See also CA 57-60

**Findley, Timothy** 1930- ........... CLC 27
See also CANR 12
See also CA 25-28R
See also DLB 53

**Fink, Janis** 1951-
See Ian, Janis

**Freeman, Mary (Eleanor) Wilkins**
  1852-1930.................... **TCLC 9**
  See also SSC 1
  See also CA 106
  See also DLB 12

**Freeman, R(ichard) Austin**
  1862-1943.................. **TCLC 21**
  See also CA 113

**French, Marilyn** 1929- ........ **CLC 10, 18**
  See also CANR 3
  See also CA 69-72

**Freneau, Philip Morin**
  1752-1832................... **NCLC 1**
  See also DLB 37, 43

**Friedman, B(ernard) H(arper)**
  1926-.......................... **CLC 7**
  See also CANR 3
  See also CA 1-4R

**Friedman, Bruce Jay** 1930- ...... **CLC 3, 5**
  See also CA 9-12R
  See also DLB 2, 28

**Friel, Brian** 1929- ............. **CLC 5, 42**
  See also CA 21-24R
  See also DLB 13

**Friis-Baastad, Babbis (Ellinor)**
  1921-1970.................... **CLC 12**
  See also CA 17-20R
  See also SATA 7

**Frisch, Max (Rudolf)**
  1911-.............**CLC 3, 9, 14, 18, 32,
                          44** (180)
  See also CA 85-88

**Fromentin, Eugène (Samuel Auguste)**
  1820-1876.................. **NCLC 10**

**Frost, Robert (Lee)**
  1874-1963...... **CLC 1, 3, 4, 9, 10, 13,
                 15, 26, 34** (468), **44** (456)
  See also CA 89-92
  See also SATA 14
  See also DLB 54

**Fry, Christopher** 1907-...... **CLC 2, 10, 14**
  See also CANR 9
  See also CA 17-20R
  See also DLB 13

**Frye, (Herman) Northrop**
  1912-..........................**CLC 24**
  See also CANR 8
  See also CA 5-8R

**Fuchs, Daniel** 1909-........... **CLC 8, 22**
  See also CAAS 5
  See also CA 81-84
  See also DLB 9, 26, 28

**Fuchs, Daniel** 1934-........ **CLC 34** (545)
  See also CANR 14
  See also CA 37-40R

**Fuentes, Carlos**
  1928-........**CLC 3, 8, 10, 13, 22, 41**
  See also CANR 10
  See also CA 69-72
  See also AITN 2

**Fugard, Athol**
  1932-........... **CLC 5, 9, 14, 25, 40**
  See also CA 85-88

**Fugard, Sheila** 1932-............. **CLC 48**

**Fuller, Charles (H., Jr.)** 1939- .....**CLC 25**
  See also CA 108, 112
  See also DLB 38

**Fuller, (Sarah) Margaret**
  1810-1850............ **NCLC 5**
  See also Ossoli, Sarah Margaret (Fuller
     marchesa d')
  See also DLB 1

**Fuller, Roy (Broadbent)**
  1912-................ **CLC 4, 28**
  See also CA 5-8R
  See also DLB 15, 20

**Furphy, Joseph** 1843-1912...... **TCLC 25**

**Futrelle, Jacques** 1875-1912..... **TCLC 19**
  See also CA 113

**Gaboriau, Émile** 1835-1873...... **NCLC 14**

**Gadda, Carlo Emilio**
  1893-1973...................**CLC 11**
  See also CA 89-92

**Gaddis, William**
  1922-........**CLC 1, 3, 6, 8, 10, 19, 43**
  See also CAAS 4
  See also CANR 21
  See also CA 17-20R
  See also DLB 2

**Gaines, Ernest J.** 1933- ..... **CLC 3, 11, 18**
  See also CANR 6
  See also CA 9-12R
  See also DLB 2, 33
  See also DLB-Y 80
  See also AITN 1

**Gale, Zona** 1874-1938........... **TCLC 7**
  See also CA 105
  See also DLB 9

**Gallagher, Tess** 1943-............**CLC 18**
  See also CA 106

**Gallant, Mavis** 1922-........ **CLC 7, 18, 38**
  See also CA 69-72
  See also DLB 53

**Gallant, Roy A(rthur)** 1924- .......**CLC 17**
  See also CANR 4
  See also CA 5-8R
  See also SATA 4

**Gallico, Paul (William)**
  1897-1976....................**CLC 2**
  See also CA 5-8R
  See also obituary CA 69-72
  See also SATA 13
  See also DLB 9
  See also AITN 1

**Galsworthy, John** 1867-1933...... **TCLC 1**
  See also CA 104
  See also DLB 10, 34

**Galt, John** 1779-1839 ............ **NCLC 1**

**Galvin, James** 1951- ..............**CLC 38**
  See also CA 108

**Gann, Ernest K(ellogg)** 1910- ......**CLC 23**
  See also CANR 1
  See also CA 1-4R
  See also AITN 1

**García Lorca, Federico**
  1899-1936................ **TCLC 1, 7**
  See also CA 104

**García Márquez, Gabriel (José)**
  1928-.......**CLC 2, 3, 8, 10, 15, 27, 47**
  See also CANR 10
  See also CA 33-36R

**Gardam, Jane** 1928-..............**CLC 43**
  See also CLR 12
  See also CANR 2, 18
  See also CA 49-52
  See also SATA 28, 39
  See also DLB 14

**Gardner, Herb** 1934- ....... **CLC 44** (208)

**Gardner, John (Champlin, Jr.)**
  1933-1982...... **CLC 2, 3, 5, 7, 8, 10,
                      18, 28, 34** (547)
  See also CA 65-68
  See also obituary CA 107
  See also obituary SATA 31, 40
  See also DLB 2
  See also DLB-Y 82
  See also AITN 1

**Gardner, John (Edmund)**
  1926-........................**CLC 30**
  See also CANR 15
  See also CA 103
  See also AITN 1

**Garfield, Leon** 1921-..............**CLC 12**
  See also CA 17-20R
  See also SATA 1, 32

**Garland, (Hannibal) Hamlin**
  1860-1940.................. **TCLC 3**
  See also CA 104
  See also DLB 12

**Garneau, Hector (de) Saint Denys**
  1912-1943.................. **TCLC 13**
  See also CA 111

**Garner, Alan** 1935-..............**CLC 17**
  See also CANR 15
  See also CA 73-76
  See also SATA 18

**Garner, Hugh** 1913-1979..........**CLC 13**
  See also CA 69-72

**Garnett, David** 1892-1981 .........**CLC 3**
  See also CANR 17
  See also CA 5-8R
  See also obituary CA 103
  See also DLB 34

**Garrett, George (Palmer)**
  1929-.................... **CLC 3, 11**
  See also CAAS 5
  See also CANR 1
  See also CA 1-4R
  See also DLB 2, 5
  See also DLB-Y 83

**Garrigue, Jean** 1914-1972 ....... **CLC 2, 8**
  See also CA 5-8R
  See also obituary CA 37-40R

**Gary, Romain** 1914-1980..........**CLC 25**
  See also Kacew, Romain

**Gascar, Pierre** 1916-..............**CLC 11**
  See also Fournier, Pierre

**Gascoyne, David (Emery)**
  1916-........................**CLC 45**
  See also CANR 10
  See also CA 65-68
  See also DLB 20

**Gaskell, Elizabeth Cleghorn**
  1810-1865................. **NCLC 5**
  See also DLB 21

**Gass, William H(oward)**
  1924-.....**CLC 1, 2, 8, 11, 15, 39** (477)
  See also CA 17-20R
  See also DLB 2

Author Index

**Goldbarth, Albert** 1948- ........ **CLC 5, 38**
See also CANR 6
See also CA 53-56

**Goldberg, Anatol**
1910-1982 ............. **CLC 34** (433)
See also obituary CA 117

**Golding, William (Gerald)**
1911- ....... **CLC 1, 2, 3, 8, 10, 17, 27**
See also CANR 13
See also CA 5-8R
See also DLB 15

**Goldman, Emma** 1869-1940 ..... **TCLC 13**
See also CA 110

**Goldman, William (W.)**
1931- .................... **CLC 1, 48**
See also CA 9-12R
See also DLB 44

**Goldmann, Lucien** 1913-1970 ...... **CLC 24**
See also CAP 2
See also CA 25-28

**Goldoni, Carlo** 1707-1793 .......... **LC 4**

**Goldsberry, Steven** 1949- ..... **CLC 34** (54)

**Goldsmith, Oliver** 1728?-1774 ....... **LC 2**
See also SATA 26
See also DLB 39

**Gombrowicz, Witold**
1904-1969 .............. **CLC 4, 7, 11**
See also CAP 2
See also CA 19-20
See also obituary CA 25-28R

**Gómez de la Serna, Ramón**
1888-1963 .................... **CLC 9**
See also obituary CA 116

**Goncharov, Ivan Alexandrovich**
1812-1891 ................... **NCLC 1**

**Goncourt, Edmond (Louis Antoine Huot) de**
1822-1896
See Goncourt, Edmond (Louis Antoine
Huot) de and Goncourt, Jules (Alfred
Huot) de

**Goncourt, Edmond (Louis Antoine Huot) de**
1822-1896 and **Goncourt, Jules (Alfred
Huot) de** 1830-1870 ........ **NCLC 7**

**Goncourt, Jules (Alfred Huot) de** 1830-1870
See Goncourt, Edmond (Louis Antoine
Huot) de and Goncourt, Jules (Alfred
Huot) de

**Goncourt, Jules (Alfred Huot) de** 1830-1870
and **Goncourt, Edmond (Louis Antoine
Huot) de** 1822-1896
See Goncourt, Edmond (Louis Antoine
Huot) de and Goncourt, Jules (Alfred
Huot) de

**Goodman, Paul**
1911-1972 ............. **CLC 1, 2, 4, 7**
See also CAP 2
See also CA 19-20
See also obituary CA 37-40R

**Gordimer, Nadine**
1923- .......... **CLC 3, 5, 7, 10, 18, 33**
See also CANR 3
See also CA 5-8R

**Gordon, Caroline**
1895-1981 ............. **CLC 6, 13, 29**
See also CAP 1
See also CA 11-12
See also obituary CA 103
See also DLB 4, 9
See also DLB-Y 81

**Gordon, Mary (Catherine)**
1949- .................... **CLC 13, 22**
See also CA 102
See also DLB 6
See also DLB-Y 81

**Gordon, Sol** 1923- ................ **CLC 26**
See also CANR 4
See also CA 53-56
See also SATA 11

**Gordone, Charles** 1925- ......... **CLC 1, 4**
See also CA 93-96
See also DLB 7

**Gorenko, Anna Andreyevna** 1889?-1966
See Akhmatova, Anna

**Gorky, Maxim** 1868-1936 ........ **TCLC 8**
See also Peshkov, Alexei Maximovich

**Goryan, Sirak** 1908-1981
See Saroyan, William

**Gosse, Edmund (William)**
1849-1928 ................. **TCLC 28**
See also CA 117
See also DLB 57

**Gotlieb, Phyllis (Fay Bloom)**
1926- .................... **CLC 18**
See also CANR 7
See also CA 13-16R

**Gould, Lois** 1938?- ............ **CLC 4, 10**
See also CA 77-80

**Gourmont, Rémy de**
1858-1915 ................. **TCLC 17**
See also CA 109

**Goyen, (Charles) William**
1915-1983 ............ **CLC 5, 8, 14, 40**
See also CANR 6
See also CA 5-8R
See also obituary CA 110
See also DLB 2
See also DLB-Y 83
See also AITN 2

**Goytisolo, Juan** 1931- ....... **CLC 5, 10, 23**
See also CA 85-88

**Grabbe, Christian Dietrich**
1801-1836 ................... **NCLC 2**

**Gracq, Julien** 1910- .......... **CLC 11, 48**
See also Poirier, Louis

**Grade, Chaim** 1910-1982 ......... **CLC 10**
See also CA 93-96
See also obituary CA 107

**Graham, Jorie** 1951- ............. **CLC 48**
See also CA 111

**Graham, R(obert) B(ontine) Cunninghame**
1852-1936 ................. **TCLC 19**

**Graham, W(illiam) S(ydney)**
1918-1986 .................... **CLC 29**
See also CA 73-76
See also obituary CA 118
See also DLB 20

**Graham, Winston (Mawdsley)**
1910- ...................... **CLC 23**
See also CANR 2
See also CA 49-52
See also obituary CA 118

**Granville-Barker, Harley**
1877-1946 ................. **TCLC 2**
See also CA 104

**Grass, Günter (Wilhelm)**
1927- ....... **CLC 1, 2, 4, 6, 11, 15, 22,
32**
See also CANR 20
See also CA 13-16R

**Grau, Shirley Ann** 1929- ........ **CLC 4, 9**
See also CANR 22
See also CA 89-92
See also DLB 2
See also AITN 2

**Graves, Richard Perceval**
1945- .................. **CLC 44** (474)
See also CANR 9
See also CA 65-68

**Graves, Robert (von Ranke)**
1895-1985 ........... **CLC 1, 2, 6, 11,
39** (320), **44** (474), **45**
See also CANR 5
See also CA 5-8R
See also obituary CA 117
See also SATA 45
See also DLB 20
See also DLB-Y 85

**Gray, Alasdair** 1934- ...............**CLC 41**

**Gray, Amlin** 1946- ................**CLC 29**

**Gray, Francine du Plessix**
1930- ......................**CLC 22**
See also CAAS 2
See also CANR 11
See also CA 61-64

**Gray, John (Henry)**
1866-1934 ................ **TCLC 19**
See also CA 119

**Gray, Simon (James Holliday)**
1936- .................. **CLC 9, 14, 36**
See also CAAS 3
See also CA 21-24R
See also DLB 13
See also AITN 1

**Gray, Thomas** 1716-1771 ............ **LC 4**

**Grayson, Richard (A.)** 1951- .......**CLC 38**
See also CANR 14
See also CA 85-88

**Greeley, Andrew M(oran)**
1928- ......................**CLC 28**
See also CANR 7
See also CA 5-8R

**Green, Hannah** 1932- ........ **CLC 3, 7, 30**
See also Greenberg, Joanne
See also CA 73-76

**Green, Henry** 1905-1974 ....... **CLC 2, 13**
See also Yorke, Henry Vincent
See also DLB 15

**Green, Julien (Hartridge)**
1900- ...................... **CLC 3, 11**
See also CA 21-24R
See also DLB 4

**Green, Paul (Eliot)** 1894-1981 ......**CLC 25**
See also CANR 3
See also CA 5-8R
See also obituary CA 103
See also DLB 7, 9
See also DLB-Y 81
See also AITN 1

**Greenberg, Ivan** 1908-1973
See Rahv, Philip
See also CA 85-88

Hall, (Marguerite) Radclyffe
    1886-1943 .................. TCLC 12
    See also CA 110

Halpern, Daniel  1945- ............ CLC 14
    See also CA 33-36R

Hamburger, Michael (Peter Leopold)
    1924- ....................... CLC 5, 14
    See also CAAS 4
    See also CANR 2
    See also CA 5-8R
    See also DLB 27

Hamill, Pete  1935- ................ CLC 10
    See also CANR 18
    See also CA 25-28R

Hamilton, Edmond  1904-1977 ...... CLC 1
    See also CANR 3
    See also CA 1-4R
    See also DLB 8

Hamilton, Gail  1911-
    See Corcoran, Barbara

Hamilton, Mollie  1909?-
    See Kaye, M(ary) M(argaret)

Hamilton, Virginia (Esther)
    1936- ....................... CLC 26
    See also CLR 1, 11
    See also CANR 20
    See also CA 25-28R
    See also SATA 4
    See also DLB 33, 52

Hammett, (Samuel) Dashiell
    1894-1961 .... CLC 3, 5, 10, 19, 47
    See also CA 81-84
    See also AITN 1

Hammon, Jupiter
    1711?-1800? ................. NCLC 5
    See also DLB 31, 50

Hamner, Earl (Henry), Jr.
    1923- ....................... CLC 12
    See also CA 73-76
    See also DLB 6
    See also AITN 2

Hampton, Christopher (James)
    1946- ........................ CLC 4
    See also CA 25-28R
    See also DLB 13

Hamsun, Knut  1859-1952 ..... TCLC 2, 14
    See also Pedersen, Knut

Handke, Peter
    1942- .......... CLC 5, 8, 10, 15, 38
    See also CA 77-80

Hanley, James
    1901-1985 ............ CLC 3, 5, 8, 13
    See also CA 73-76
    See also obituary CA 117

Hannah, Barry  1942- ........ CLC 23, 38
    See also CA 108, 110
    See also DLB 6

Hansberry, Lorraine (Vivian)
    1930-1965 ................... CLC 17
    See also CA 109
    See also obituary CA 25-28R
    See also DLB 7, 38
    See also CDALB 1941-1968
    See also AITN 2

Hansen, Joseph  1923- ............. CLC 38
    See also CANR 16
    See also CA 29-32R

Hanson, Kenneth O(stlin)
    1922- ....................... CLC 13
    See also CANR 7
    See also CA 53-56

Hardenberg, Friedrich (Leopold Freiherr)
    von  1772-1801
    See Novalis

Hardwick, Elizabeth  1916- ........ CLC 13
    See also CANR 3
    See also CA 5-8R
    See also DLB 6

Hardy, Thomas
    1840-1928 ............ TCLC 4, 10, 18
    See also CA 104
    See also SATA 25
    See also DLB 18, 19

Hare, David  1947- ................ CLC 29
    See also CA 97-100
    See also DLB 13

Harlan, Louis R(udolph)
    1922- ................. CLC 34 (182)
    See also CA 21-24R

Harmon, William (Ruth)  1938- ..... CLC 38
    See also CANR 14
    See also CA 33-36R

Harper, Frances Ellen Watkins
    1825-1911 ................. TCLC 14
    See also CA 111
    See also DLB 50

Harper, Michael S(teven)
    1938- .................... CLC 7, 22
    See also CA 33-36R
    See also DLB 41

Harris, Christie (Lucy Irwin)
    1907- ....................... CLC 12
    See also CANR 6
    See also CA 5-8R
    See also SATA 6

Harris, Frank  1856-1931 ........ TCLC 24
    See also CAAS 1
    See also CA 109

Harris, Joel Chandler
    1848-1908 .................... TCLC 2
    See also CA 104
    See also YABC 1
    See also DLB 11, 23, 42

Harris, John (Wyndham Parkes Lucas)
    Beynon  1903-1969
    See Wyndham, John
    See also CA 102
    See also obituary CA 89-92

Harris, MacDonald  1921- .......... CLC 9
    See also Heiney, Donald (William)

Harris, Mark  1922- ............... CLC 19
    See also CAAS 3
    See also CANR 2
    See also CA 5-8R
    See also DLB 2
    See also DLB-Y 80

Harris, (Theodore) Wilson
    1921- ....................... CLC 25
    See also CANR 11
    See also CA 65-68

Harrison, Harry (Max)  1925- ...... CLC 42
    See also CANR 5, 21
    See also CA 1-4R
    See also SATA 4
    See also DLB 8

Harrison, James (Thomas)  1937-
    See Harrison, Jim
    See also CANR 8
    See also CA 13-16R

Harrison, Jim  1937- ........ CLC 6, 14, 33
    See also Harrison, James (Thomas)
    See also DLB-Y 82

Harrison, Tony  1937- ............. CLC 43
    See also CA 65-68
    See also DLB 40

Harriss, Will(ard Irvin)
    1922- ................. CLC 34 (192)
    See also CA 111

Harte, (Francis) Bret(t)
    1836?-1902 ............... TCLC 1, 25
    See also CA 104
    See also SATA 26
    See also DLB 12, 64

Hartley, L(eslie) P(oles)
    1895-1972 ................. CLC 2, 22
    See also CA 45-48
    See also obituary CA 37-40R
    See also DLB 15

Hartman, Geoffrey H.  1929- ....... CLC 27
    See also CA 117

Haruf, Kent  19??- ........... CLC 34 (57)

Harwood, Ronald  1934- ............ CLC 32
    See also CANR 4
    See also CA 1-4R
    See also DLB 13

Hašek, Jaroslav (Matej Frantisek)
    1883-1923 ................... TCLC 4
    See also CA 104

Hass, Robert  1941- ...... CLC 18, 39 (145)
    See also CA 111

Hastings, Selina  19??- ....... CLC 44 (482)

Hauptmann, Gerhart (Johann Robert)
    1862-1946 ................... TCLC 4
    See also CA 104

Havel, Václav  1936- .............. CLC 25
    See also CA 104

Haviaras, Stratis  1935- ........... CLC 33
    See also CA 105

Hawkes, John (Clendennin Burne, Jr.)
    1925- ...... CLC 1, 2, 3, 4, 7, 9, 14, 15,
                                          27
    See also CANR 2
    See also CA 1-4R
    See also DLB 2, 7
    See also DLB-Y 80

Hawthorne, Julian  1846-1934 .... TCLC 25

Hawthorne, Nathaniel
    1804-1864 ............. NCLC 2, 10, 17
    See also YABC 2
    See also DLB 1

Hayashi, Fumiko  1904-1951 ..... TCLC 27

Haycraft, Anna  19??-
    See Ellis, Alice Thomas

Hayden, Robert (Earl)
    1913-1980 ........... CLC 5, 9, 14, 37
    See also CA 69-72
    See also obituary CA 97-100
    See also CABS 2
    See also SATA 19
    See also obituary SATA 26
    See also DLB 5
    See also CDALB 1941-1968

**Author Index**

Author Index

**McIntyre, Vonda N(eel)** 1948- ......CLC 18
  See also CANR 17
  See also CA 81-84

**McKay, Claude** 1890-1948....... TCLC 7
  See also CA 104
  See also DLB 4, 45

**McKuen, Rod** 1933- ........... CLC 1, 3
  See also CA 41-44R
  See also AITN 1

**McLuhan, (Herbert) Marshall**
    1911-1980...................CLC 37
  See also CANR 12
  See also CA 9-12R
  See also obituary CA 102

**McManus, Declan Patrick** 1955-
  See Costello, Elvis

**McMurtry, Larry (Jeff)**
    1936- .....CLC 2, 3, 7, 11, 27, 44 (253)
  See also CANR 19
  See also CA 5-8R
  See also DLB 2
  See also DLB-Y 80
  See also AITN 2

**McNally, Terrence** 1939- ..... CLC 4, 7, 41
  See also CANR 2
  See also CA 45-48
  See also DLB 7

**McPhee, John** 1931- ..............CLC 36
  See also CANR 20
  See also CA 65-68

**McPherson, James Alan** 1943- .....CLC 19
  See also CA 25-28R
  See also DLB 38

**McPherson, William**
    1939- ............... CLC 34 (85)
  See also CA 57-60

**McSweeney, Kerry** 19??- .... CLC 34 (579)

**Mead, Margaret** 1901-1978 ........CLC 37
  See also CANR 4
  See also CA 1-4R
  See also obituary CA 81-84
  See also SATA 20
  See also AITN 1

**Meaker, M. J.** 1927-
  See Kerr, M. E.
  See Meaker, Marijane

**Meaker, Marijane** 1927-
  See Kerr, M. E.
  See also CA 107
  See also SATA 20

**Medoff, Mark (Howard)**
    1940- .................... CLC 6, 23
  See also CANR 5
  See also CA 53-56
  See also DLB 7
  See also AITN 1

**Megged, Aharon** 1920- .............CLC 9
  See also CANR 1
  See also CA 49-52

**Mehta, Ved (Parkash)** 1934- .......CLC 37
  See also CANR 2
  See also CA 1-4R

**Mellor, John** 1953?-
  See The Clash

**Meltzer, Milton** 1915- .............CLC 26
  See also CA 13-16R
  See also SAAS 1
  See also SATA 1
  See also DLB 61

**Melville, Herman**
    1819-1891................NCLC 3, 12
  See also SSC 1
  See also DLB 3

**Mencken, H(enry) L(ouis)**
    1880-1956................. TCLC 13
  See also CA 105
  See also DLB 11, 29, 63

**Mercer, David** 1928-1980...........CLC 5
  See also CA 9-12R
  See also obituary CA 102
  See also DLB 13

**Meredith, George** 1828-1909..... TCLC 17
  See also CA 117
  See also DLB 18, 35, 57

**Meredith, William (Morris)**
    1919-................. CLC 4, 13, 22
  See also CANR 6
  See also CA 9-12R
  See also DLB 5

**Mérimée, Prosper** 1803-1870...... NCLC 6

**Merkin, Daphne** 1954- ....... CLC 44 (62)

**Merrill, James (Ingram)**
    1926-.......... CLC 2, 3, 6, 8, 13, 18,
                                34 (225)
  See also CANR 10
  See also CA 13-16R
  See also DLB 5
  See also DLB-Y 85

**Merton, Thomas (James)**
    1915-1968...... CLC 1, 3, 11, 34 (460)
  See also CANR 22
  See also CA 5-8R
  See also obituary CA 25-28R
  See also DLB 48
  See also DLB-Y 81

**Merwin, W(illiam) S(tanley)**
    1927-..... CLC 1, 2, 3, 5, 8, 13, 18, 45
  See also CANR 15
  See also CA 13-16R
  See also DLB 5

**Metcalf, John** 1938-...............CLC 37
  See also CA 113
  See also DLB 60

**Mew, Charlotte (Mary)**
    1870-1928.................. TCLC 8
  See also CA 105
  See also DLB 19

**Mewshaw, Michael** 1943-...........CLC 9
  See also CANR 7
  See also CA 53-56
  See also DLB-Y 80

**Meyer-Meyrink, Gustav** 1868-1932
  See Meyrink, Gustav
  See also CA 117

**Meyrink, Gustav** 1868-1932...... TCLC 21
  See also Meyer-Meyrink, Gustav

**Meyers, Jeffrey** 1939-....... CLC 39 (427)
  See also CA 73-76

**Meynell, Alice (Christiana Gertrude**
    **Thompson)** 1847-1922 ....... TCLC 6
  See also CA 104
  See also DLB 19

**Michaels, Leonard** 1933- ....... CLC 6, 25
  See also CANR 21
  See also CA 61-64

**Michaux, Henri** 1899-1984...... CLC 8, 19
  See also CA 85-88
  See also obituary CA 114

**Michener, James A(lbert)**
    1907-................CLC 1, 5, 11, 29
  See also CANR 21
  See also CA 5-8R
  See also DLB 6
  See also AITN 1

**Mickiewicz, Adam** 1798-1855 ..... NCLC 3

**Middleton, Christopher** 1926-......CLC 13
  See also CA 13-16R
  See also DLB 40

**Middleton, Stanley** 1919- ....... CLC 7, 38
  See also CANR 21
  See also CA 25-28R
  See also DLB 14

**Miguéis, José Rodrigues** 1901- .....CLC 10

**Miles, Josephine (Louise)**
    1911-1985......CLC 1, 2, 14, 34 (243),
                                39 (352)
  See also CANR 2
  See also CA 1-4R
  See also obituary CA 116
  See also DLB 48

**Mill, John Stuart** 1806-1873 ..... NCLC 11

**Millar, Kenneth** 1915-1983
  See Macdonald, Ross
  See also CANR 16
  See also CA 9-12R
  See also obituary CA 110
  See also DLB 2
  See also DLB-Y 83

**Millay, Edna St. Vincent**
    1892-1950................... TCLC 4
  See also CA 104
  See also DLB 45

**Miller, Arthur**
    1915-.......CLC 1, 2, 6, 10, 15, 26, 47
  See also CANR 2
  See also CA 1-4R
  See also DLB 7
  See also CDALB 1941-1968
  See also AITN 1

**Miller, Henry (Valentine)**
    1891-1980....... CLC 1, 2, 4, 9, 14, 43
  See also CA 9-12R
  See also obituary CA 97-100
  See also DLB 4, 9
  See also DLB-Y 80

**Miller, Jason** 1939?- ...............CLC 2
  See also CA 73-76
  See also DLB 7
  See also AITN 1

**Miller, Sue** 19??- ............ CLC 44 (67)

**Miller, Walter M(ichael), Jr.**
    1923-..................... CLC 4, 30
  See also CA 85-88
  See also DLB 8

**Millhauser, Steven** 1943- ..........CLC 21
  See also CA 108, 110, 111
  See also DLB 2

**Milne, A(lan) A(lexander)**
1882-1956................. **TCLC 6**
See also CLR 1
See also CA 104
See also YABC 1
See also DLB 10

**Miłosz, Czesław**
1911-.............**CLC 5, 11, 22, 31**
See also CA 81-84

**Miner, Valerie (Jane)** 1947-.......**CLC 40**
See also CA 97-100

**Minot, Susan** 1956-......... **CLC 44 (77)**

**Minus, Ed** 1938-........... **CLC 39 (79)**

**Miró (Ferrer), Gabriel (Francisco Víctor)**
1879-1930................. **TCLC 5**
See also CA 104

**Mishima, Yukio**
1925-1970......... **CLC 2, 4, 6, 9, 27**
See also Hiraoka, Kimitake

**Mistral, Gabriela** 1889-1957 ...... **TCLC 2**
See also CA 104

**Mitchell, James Leslie** 1901-1935
See Gibbon, Lewis Grassic
See also CA 104
See also DLB 15

**Mitchell, Joni** 1943-..............**CLC 12**
See also CA 112

**Mitchell (Marsh), Margaret (Munnerlyn)**
1900-1949................. **TCLC 11**
See also CA 109
See also DLB 9

**Mitchell, W(illiam) O(rmond)**
1914-......................**CLC 25**
See also CANR 15
See also CA 77-80

**Mitford, Mary Russell**
1787-1855.................. **NCLC 4**

**Mitford, Nancy**
1904-1973............. **CLC 44 (482)**
See also CA 9-12R

**Mo, Timothy** 1950-..............**CLC 46**
See also CA 117

**Modarressi, Taghi** 1931-...... **CLC 44 (82)**
See also CA 121

**Modiano, Patrick (Jean)** 1945- .....**CLC 18**
See also CANR 17
See also CA 85-88

**Mofolo, Thomas (Mokopu)**
1876-1948................. **TCLC 22**
See also CA 121

**Mohr, Nicholasa** 1935-...........**CLC 12**
See also CANR 1
See also CA 49-52
See also SATA 8

**Mojtabai, A(nn) G(race)**
1938-...............**CLC 5, 9, 15, 29**
See also CA 85-88

**Molnár, Ferenc** 1878-1952....... **TCLC 20**
See also CA 109

**Momaday, N(avarre) Scott**
1934-................ **CLC 2, 19**
See also CANR 14
See also CA 25-28R
See also SATA 30, 48

**Monroe, Harriet** 1860-1936...... **TCLC 12**
See also CA 109
See also DLB 54

**Montagu, Elizabeth** 1720-1800 .... **NCLC 7**

**Montague, John (Patrick)**
1929-.................. **CLC 13, 46**
See also CANR 9
See also CA 9-12R
See also DLB 40

**Montaigne, Michel (Eyquem) de**
1533-1592..................... **LC 8**

**Montale, Eugenio**
1896-1981.............. **CLC 7, 9, 18**
See also CA 17-20R
See also obituary CA 104

**Montgomery, Marion (H., Jr.)**
1925-.........................**CLC 7**
See also CANR 3
See also CA 1-4R
See also DLB 6
See also AITN 1

**Montgomery, Robert Bruce** 1921-1978
See Crispin, Edmund
See also CA 104

**Montherlant, Henri (Milon) de**
1896-1972................. **CLC 8, 19**
See also CA 85-88
See also obituary CA 37-40R

**Montisquieu, Charles-Louis de Secondat**
1689-1755..................... **LC 7**

**Monty Python**.....................**CLC 21**
See also Cleese, John
See also Gilliam, Terry (Vance)
See also Idle, Eric
See also Jones, Terry
See also Palin, Michael

**Moodie, Susanna (Strickland)**
1803-1885................. **NCLC 14**

**Mooney, Ted** 1951-...............**CLC 25**

**Moorcock, Michael (John)**
1939-................... **CLC 5, 27**
See also CAAS 5
See also CANR 2, 17
See also CA 45-48
See also DLB 14

**Moore, Brian**
1921-.........**CLC 1, 3, 5, 7, 8, 19, 32**
See also CANR 1
See also CA 1-4R

**Moore, George (Augustus)**
1852-1933................. **TCLC 7**
See also CA 104
See also DLB 10, 18, 57

**Moore, Lorrie** 1957- ...... **CLC 39 (82), 45**
See also Moore, Marie Lorena

**Moore, Marianne (Craig)**
1887-1972...... **CLC 1, 2, 4, 8, 10, 13,**
                    **19, 47**
See also CANR 3
See also CA 1-4R
See also obituary CA 33-36R
See also DLB 45
See also SATA 20

**Moore, Marie Lorena** 1957-
See Moore, Lorrie
See also CA 116

**Moore, Thomas** 1779-1852....... **NCLC 6**

**Morand, Paul** 1888-1976.........**CLC 41**
See also obituary CA 69-72

**Morante, Elsa** 1918-1985...... **CLC 8, 47**
See also CA 85-88
See also obituary CA 117

**Moravia, Alberto**
1907-........ **CLC 2, 7, 11, 18, 27, 46**
See also Pincherle, Alberto

**Moréas, Jean** 1856-1910........ **TCLC 18**

**Morgan, Berry** 1919-..............**CLC 6**
See also CA 49-52
See also DLB 6

**Morgan, Edwin (George)**
1920-......................**CLC 31**
See also CANR 3
See also CA 7-8R
See also DLB 27

**Morgan, (George) Frederick**
1922-......................**CLC 23**
See also CANR 21
See also CA 17-20R

**Morgan, Janet** 1945-........ **CLC 39 (436)**
See also CA 65-68

**Morgan, Robin** 1941-..............**CLC 2**
See also CA 69-72

**Morgenstern, Christian (Otto Josef Wolfgang)**
1871-1914................. **TCLC 8**
See also CA 105

**Mori Ōgai** 1862-1922........... **TCLC 14**
See also Mori Rintaro

**Mori Rintaro** 1862-1922
See Mori Ōgai
See also CA 110

**Mörike, Eduard (Friedrich)**
1804-1875................. **NCLC 10**

**Moritz, Karl Philipp** 1756-1793 ...... **LC 2**

**Morris, Julian** 1916-
See West, Morris L.

**Morris, Steveland Judkins** 1950-
See Wonder, Stevie
See also CA 111

**Morris, William** 1834-1896....... **NCLC 4**
See also DLB 18, 35, 57

**Morris, Wright (Marion)**
1910-............. **CLC 1, 3, 7, 18, 37**
See also CA 9-12R
See also DLB 2
See also DLB-Y 81

**Morrison, James Douglas** 1943-1971
See Morrison, Jim
See also CA 73-76

**Morrison, Jim** 1943-1971..........**CLC 17**
See also Morrison, James Douglas

**Morrison, Toni** 1931- ....... **CLC 4, 10, 22**
See also CA 29-32R
See also DLB 6, 33
See also DLB-Y 81

**Morrison, Van** 1945-..............**CLC 21**
See also CA 116

**Mortimer, John (Clifford)**
1923-................... **CLC 28, 43**
See also CANR 21
See also CA 13-16R
See also DLB 13

*Author Index*

**Newman, Edwin (Harold)**
1919-...................CLC 14
See also CANR 5
See also CA 69-72
See also AITN 1

**Newton, Suzanne** 1936-...........CLC 35
See also CANR 14
See also CA 41-44R
See also SATA 5

**Ngugi, James (Thiong'o)**
1938-...............CLC 3, 7, 13, 36
See also Ngugi wa Thiong'o
See also Wa Thiong'o, Ngugi
See also CA 81-84

**Ngugi wa Thiong'o**
1938-...............CLC 3, 7, 13, 36
See also Ngugi, James (Thiong'o)
See also Wa Thiong'o, Ngugi

**Nichol, B(arrie) P(hillip)** 1944- .....CLC 18
See also CA 53-56
See also DLB 53

**Nichols, John (Treadwell)**
1940-.....................CLC 38
See also CAAS 2
See also CANR 6
See also CA 9-12R
See also DLB-Y 82

**Nichols, Peter (Richard)**
1927-..................... CLC 5, 36
See also CA 104
See also DLB 13

**Nicolas, F.R.E.** 1927-
See Freeling, Nicolas

**Niedecker, Lorine**
1903-1970............... CLC 10, 42
See also CAP 2
See also CA 25-28
See also DLB 48

**Nietzsche, Friedrich (Wilhelm)**
1844-1900...............TCLC 10, 18
See also CA 107

**Nightingale, Anne Redmon** 1943-
See Redmon (Nightingale), Anne
See also CA 103

**Nin, Anaïs**
1903-1977........ CLC 1, 4, 8, 11, 14
See also CANR 22
See also CA 13-16R
See also obituary CA 69-72
See also DLB 2, 4
See also AITN 2

**Nissenson, Hugh** 1933-.......... CLC 4, 9
See also CA 17-20R
See also DLB 28

**Niven, Larry** 1938-................CLC 8
See also Niven, Laurence Van Cott
See also DLB 8

**Niven, Laurence Van Cott** 1938-
See Niven, Larry
See also CANR 14
See also CA 21-24R

**Nixon, Agnes Eckhardt** 1927- ......CLC 21
See also CA 110

**Nkosi, Lewis** 1936- ...............CLC 45
See also CA 65-68

**Nordhoff, Charles** 1887-1947..... TCLC 23
See also CA 108
See also SATA 23
See also DLB 9

**Norman, Marsha** 1947-...........CLC 28
See also CA 105
See also DLB-Y 84

**Norris, (Benjamin) Frank(lin)**
1870-1902................. TCLC 24
See also CA 110
See also DLB 12

**Norris, Leslie** 1921-...............CLC 14
See also CANR 14
See also CAP 1
See also CA 11-12
See also DLB 27

**North, Andrew** 1912-
See Norton, Andre

**North, Christopher** 1785-1854
See Wilson, John

**Norton, Alice Mary** 1912-
See Norton, Andre
See also CANR 2
See also CA 1-4R
See also SATA 1, 43

**Norton, Andre** 1912-..............CLC 12
See also Norton, Mary Alice
See also DLB 8, 52

**Norway, Nevil Shute** 1899-1960
See Shute (Norway), Nevil
See also CA 102
See also obituary CA 93-96

**Norwid, Cyprian Kamil**
1821-1883................. NCLC 17

**Nossack, Hans Erich** 1901-1978 .....CLC 6
See also CA 93-96
See also obituary CA 85-88

**Nova, Craig** 1945-............. CLC 7, 31
See also CANR 2
See also CA 45-48

**Novalis** 1772-1801 ............... NCLC 13

**Nowlan, Alden (Albert)** 1933- ......CLC 15
See also CANR 5
See also CA 9-12R
See also DLB 53

**Noyes, Alfred** 1880-1958 ......... TCLC 7
See also CA 104
See also DLB 20

**Nunn, Kem** 19??-............ CLC 34 (94)

**Nye, Robert** 1939-............ CLC 13, 42
See also CA 33-36R
See also SATA 6
See also DLB 14

**Nyro, Laura** 1947-................CLC 17

**Oates, Joyce Carol**
1938-.....CLC 1, 2, 3, 6, 9, 11, 15, 19,
33
See also CA 5-8R
See also DLB 2, 5
See also DLB-Y 81
See also AITN 1

**O'Brien, Darcy** 1939-.............CLC 11
See also CANR 8
See also CA 21-24R

**O'Brien, Edna**
1932-............ CLC 3, 5, 8, 13, 36
See also CANR 6
See also CA 1-4R
See also DLB 14

**O'Brien, Flann**
1911-1966....... CLC 1, 4, 5, 7, 10, 47
See also O Nuallain, Brian

**O'Brien, Richard** 19??-............CLC 17

**O'Brien, (William) Tim(othy)**
1946-...................CLC 7, 19, 40
See also CA 85-88
See also DLB-Y 80

**Obstfelder, Sigbjørn**
1866-1900.................. TCLC 23

**O'Casey, Sean**
1880-1964........ CLC 1, 5, 9, 11, 15
See also CA 89-92
See also DLB 10

**Ochs, Phil** 1940-1976 .............CLC 17
See also obituary CA 65-68

**O'Connor, Edwin (Greene)**
1918-1968.................CLC 14
See also CA 93-96
See also obituary CA 25-28R

**O'Connor, (Mary) Flannery**
1925-1964...... CLC 1, 2, 3, 6, 10, 13,
15, 21
See also SSC 1
See also CANR 3
See also CA 1-4R
See also DLB 2
See also DLB-Y 80
See also CDALB 1941-1968

**O'Connor, Frank**
1903-1966............... CLC 14, 23
See also O'Donovan, Michael (John)

**O'Dell, Scott** 1903- ...............CLC 30
See also CLR 1
See also CANR 12
See also CA 61-64
See also SATA 12
See also DLB 52

**Odets, Clifford** 1906-1963 ...... CLC 2, 28
See also CA 85-88
See also DLB 7, 26

**O'Donovan, Michael (John)** 1903-1966
See O'Connor, Frank
See also CA 93-96

**Ōe, Kenzaburō** 1935- ......... CLC 10, 36
See also CA 97-100

**O'Faolain, Julia** 1932- ...... CLC 6, 19, 47
See also CAAS 2
See also CANR 12
See also CA 81-84
See also DLB 14

**O'Faoláin, Seán**
1900-................CLC 1, 7, 14, 32
See also CANR 12
See also CA 61-64
See also DLB 15

**O'Flaherty, Liam**
1896-1984...........CLC 5, 34 (355)
See also CA 101
See also obituary CA 113
See also DLB 36
See also DLB-Y 84

**Remizov, Alexey (Mikhailovich)**
1877-1957.................. **TCLC 27**

**Renard, Jules**  1864-1910 ....... **TCLC 17**
See also CA 117

**Renault, Mary**
1905-1983............. **CLC 3, 11, 17**
See also Challans, Mary
See also DLB-Y 83

**Rendell, Ruth**  1930- ......... **CLC 28, 48**
See also CA 109

**Renoir, Jean**  1894-1979 .......... **CLC 20**
See also obituary CA 85-88

**Resnais, Alain**  1922- .............. **CLC 16**

**Rexroth, Kenneth**
1905-1982........ **CLC 1, 2, 6, 11, 22**
See also CANR 14
See also CA 5-8R
See also obituary CA 107
See also DLB 16, 48
See also DLB-Y 82
See also CDALB 1941-1968

**Reyes y Basoalto, Ricardo Eliecer Neftali**
1904-1973
See Neruda, Pablo

**Reymont, Władysław Stanisław**
1867-1925................... **TCLC 5**
See also CA 104

**Reynolds, Jonathan**  1942?- ..... **CLC 6, 38**
See also CA 65-68

**Reynolds, Michael (Shane)**
1937-................... **CLC 44** (514)
See also CANR 9
See also CA 65-68

**Reznikoff, Charles**  1894-1976 ....... **CLC 9**
See also CAP 2
See also CA 33-36
See also obituary CA 61-64
See also DLB 28, 45

**Rezzori, Gregor von**  1914-........ **CLC 25**

**Rhys, Jean**
1894-1979........ **CLC 2, 4, 6, 14, 19**
See also CA 25-28R
See also obituary CA 85-88
See also DLB 36

**Ribeiro, Darcy**  1922-........ **CLC 34** (102)
See also CA 33-36R

**Ribeiro, João Ubaldo (Osorio Pimentel)**
1941-.......................... **CLC 10**
See also CA 81-84

**Ribman, Ronald (Burt)**  1932- ....... **CLC 7**
See also CA 21-24R

**Rice, Anne**  1941-................. **CLC 41**
See also CANR 12
See also CA 65-68

**Rice, Elmer**  1892-1967 ............. **CLC 7**
See also CAP 2
See also CA 21-22
See also obituary CA 25-28R
See also DLB 4, 7

**Rice, Tim**  1944-
See Rice, Tim and Webber, Andrew Lloyd
See also CA 103

**Rice, Tim**  1944-  and
**Webber, Andrew Lloyd**
1948-....................... **CLC 21**

**Rich, Adrienne (Cecile)**
1929-......... **CLC 3, 6, 7, 11, 18, 36**
See also CANR 20
See also CA 9-12R
See also DLB 5

**Richard, Keith**  1943-
See Jagger, Mick and Richard, Keith

**Richards, I(vor) A(rmstrong)**
1893-1979................. **CLC 14, 24**
See also CA 41-44R
See also obituary CA 89-92
See also DLB 27

**Richards, Keith**  1943-
See Richard, Keith
See also CA 107

**Richardson, Dorothy (Miller)**
1873-1957................... **TCLC 3**
See also CA 104
See also DLB 36

**Richardson, Ethel**  1870-1946
See Richardson, Henry Handel
See also CA 105

**Richardson, Henry Handel**
1870-1946................... **TCLC 4**
See also Richardson, Ethel

**Richardson, Samuel**  1689-1761 ....... **LC 1**
See also DLB 39

**Richler, Mordecai**
1931-........ **CLC 3, 5, 9, 13, 18, 46**
See also CA 65-68
See also SATA 27, 44
See also DLB 53
See also AITN 1

**Richter, Conrad (Michael)**
1890-1968................. **CLC 30**
See also CA 5-8R
See also obituary CA 25-28R
See also SATA 3
See also DLB 9

**Richter, Johann Paul Friedrich**  1763-1825
See Jean Paul

**Riding, Laura**  1901- ............ **CLC 3, 7**
See also Jackson, Laura (Riding)

**Riefenstahl, Berta Helene Amalia**  1902-
See Riefenstahl, Leni
See also CA 108

**Riefenstahl, Leni**  1902-............ **CLC 16**
See also Riefenstahl, Berta Helene Amalia

**Rilke, Rainer Maria**
1875-1926.............. **TCLC 1, 6, 19**
See also CA 104

**Rimbaud, (Jean Nicolas) Arthur**
1854-1891................... **NCLC 4**

**Ringwood, Gwen(dolyn Margaret) Pharis**
1910-1984................... **CLC 48**
See also obituary CA 112

**Rio, Michel**  19?? ................. **CLC 43**

**Ritsos, Yannis**  1909- ........ **CLC 6, 13, 31**
See also CA 77-80

**Rivers, Conrad Kent**  1933-1968 ..... **CLC 1**
See also CA 85-88
See also DLB 41

**Roa Bastos, Augusto**  1917-........ **CLC 45**

**Robbe-Grillet, Alain**
1922-..... **CLC 1, 2, 4, 6, 8, 10, 14, 43**
See also CA 9-12R

**Robbins, Harold**  1916- ............ **CLC 5**
See also CA 73-76

**Robbins, Thomas Eugene**  1936-
See Robbins, Tom
See also CA 81-84

**Robbins, Tom**  1936- .......... **CLC 9, 32**
See also Robbins, Thomas Eugene
See also DLB-Y 80

**Robbins, Trina**  1938- .............. **CLC 21**

**Roberts, (Sir) Charles G(eorge) D(ouglas)**
1860-1943................... **TCLC 8**
See also CA 105
See also SATA 29

**Roberts, Kate**  1891-1985 .......... **CLC 15**
See also CA 107
See also obituary CA 116

**Roberts, Keith (John Kingston)**
1935-....................... **CLC 14**
See also CA 25-28R

**Roberts, Kenneth**  1885-1957 ..... **TCLC 23**
See also CA 109
See also DLB 9

**Roberts, Michèle (B.)**  1949-........ **CLC 48**
See also CA 115

**Robinson, Edwin Arlington**
1869-1935................... **TCLC 5**
See also CA 104
See also DLB 54

**Robinson, Henry Crabb**
1775-1867................. **NCLC 15**

**Robinson, Jill**  1936-.............. **CLC 10**
See also CA 102

**Robinson, Kim Stanley**
19??-.................. **CLC 34** (105)

**Robinson, Marilynne**  1944- ........ **CLC 25**
See also CA 116

**Robinson, Smokey**  1940- ......... **CLC 21**

**Robinson, William**  1940-
See Robinson, Smokey
See also CA 116

**Robison, Mary**  1949-.............. **CLC 42**
See also CA 113, 116

**Roddenberry, Gene**  1921- ......... **CLC 17**

**Rodgers, Mary**  1931- .............. **CLC 12**
See also CANR 8
See also CA 49-52
See also SATA 8

**Rodgers, W(illiam) R(obert)**
1909-1969.................... **CLC 7**
See also CA 85-88
See also DLB 20

**Rodríguez, Claudio**  1934-......... **CLC 10**

**Roethke, Theodore (Huebner)**
1908-1963...... **CLC 1, 3, 8, 11, 19, 46**
See also CA 81-84
See also CABS 2
See also SAAS 1
See also DLB 5
See also CDALB 1941-1968

**Rogers, Sam**  1943-
See Shepard, Sam

**Rogers, Will(iam Penn Adair)**
1879-1935................... **TCLC 8**
See also CA 105
See also DLB 11

Author Index

**Welch, (Maurice) Denton**
1915-1948................. TCLC 22
See also CA 121

**Weldon, Fay**
1933-........... CLC 6, 9, 11, 19, 36
See also CANR 16
See also CA 21-24R
See also DLB 14

**Wellek, René** 1903-.............CLC 28
See also CANR 8
See also CA 5-8R
See also DLB 63

**Weller, Michael** 1942-.............CLC 10
See also CA 85-88

**Weller, Paul** 1958-................CLC 26

**Wellershoff, Dieter** 1925-..........CLC 46
See also CANR 16
See also CA 89-92

**Welles, (George) Orson**
1915-1985...................CLC 20
See also CA 93-96
See also obituary CA 117

**Wells, H(erbert) G(eorge)**
1866-1946.............TCLC 6, 12, 19
See also CA 110
See also SATA 20
See also DLB 34

**Wells, Rosemary** 1943-............CLC 12
See also CA 85-88
See also SAAS 1
See also SATA 18

**Welty, Eudora (Alice)**
1909-......... CLC 1, 2, 5, 14, 22, 33
See also SSC 1
See also CA 9-12R
See also CABS 1
See also DLB 2
See also CDALB 1941-1968

**Wen I-to** 1899-1946............. TCLC 28

**Werfel, Franz (V.)** 1890-1945..... TCLC 8
See also CA 104

**Wergeland, Henrik Arnold**
1808-1845................... NCLC 5

**Wersba, Barbara** 1932- ..........CLC 30
See also CLR 3
See also CANR 16
See also CA 29-32R
See also SAAS 2
See also SATA 1
See also DLB 52

**Wertmüller, Lina** 1928- ..........CLC 16
See also CA 97-100

**Wescott, Glenway** 1901-1987......CLC 13
See also CA 13-16R
See also obituary CA 121
See also DLB 4, 9

**Wesker, Arnold** 1932-........ CLC 3, 5, 42
See also CANR 1
See also CA 1-4R
See also DLB 13

**Wesley, Richard (Errol)** 1945-.......CLC 7
See also CA 57-60
See also DLB 38

**Wessel, Johan Herman**
1742-1785..................... LC 7

**West, Jessamyn** 1907-1984...... CLC 7, 17
See also CA 9-12R
See also obituary CA 112
See also obituary SATA 37
See also DLB 6
See also DLB-Y 84

**West, Morris L(anglo)**
1916-..................... CLC 6, 33
See also CA 5-8R

**West, Nathanael**
1903?-1940............... TCLC 1, 14
See Weinstein, Nathan Wallenstein
See also DLB 4, 9, 28

**West, Paul** 1930- ............. CLC 7, 14
See also CANR 22
See also CA 13-16R
See also DLB 14

**West, Rebecca** 1892-1983..... CLC 7, 9, 31
See also CA 5-8R
See also obituary CA 109
See also DLB 36
See also DLB-Y 83

**Westall, Robert (Atkinson)**
1929-........................CLC 17
See also CANR 18
See also CA 69-72
See also SAAS 2
See also SATA 23

**Westlake, Donald E(dwin)**
1933-................. CLC 7, 33
See also CANR 16
See also CA 17-20R

**Westmacott, Mary** 1890-1976
See Christie, (Dame) Agatha (Mary Clarissa)

**Whalen, Philip** 1923-........... CLC 6, 29
See also CANR 5
See also CA 9-12R
See also DLB 16

**Wharton, Edith (Newbold Jones)**
1862-1937.............TCLC 3, 9, 27
See also CA 104
See also DLB 4, 9, 12

**Wharton, William** 1925-....... CLC 18, 37
See also CA 93-96
See also DLB-Y 80

**Wheatley (Peters), Phillis**
1753?-1784..................... LC 3
See also DLB 31, 50

**Wheelock, John Hall**
1886-1978...................CLC 14
See also CANR 14
See also CA 13-16R
See also obituary CA 77-80
See also DLB 45

**Whelan, John** 1900-
See O'Faoláin, Seán

**Whitaker, Rodney** 1925-
See Trevanian

**White, E(lwyn) B(rooks)**
1899-1985......... CLC 10, 34 (425),
                                    39 (369)
See also CLR 1
See also CANR 16
See also CA 13-16R
See also obituary CA 116
See also SATA 2, 29
See also obituary SATA 44
See also DLB 11, 22
See also AITN 2

**White, Edmund III** 1940-.........CLC 27
See also CANR 3, 19
See also CA 45-48

**White, Patrick (Victor Martindale)**
1912-............ CLC 3, 4, 5, 7, 9, 18
See also CA 81-84

**White, T(erence) H(anbury)**
1906-1964...................CLC 30
See also CA 73-76
See also SATA 12

**White, Walter (Francis)**
1893-1955.................. TCLC 15
See also CA 115
See also DLB 51

**White, William Hale** 1831-1913
See Rutherford, Mark

**Whitehead, E(dward) A(nthony)**
1933-........................CLC 5
See also CA 65-68

**Whitemore, Hugh** 1936-..........CLC 37

**Whitman, Walt** 1819-1892........ NCLC 4
See also SATA 20
See also DLB 3, 64

**Whitney, Phyllis A(yame)**
1903-........................CLC 42
See also CANR 3
See also CA 1-4R
See also SATA 1, 30
See also AITN 2

**Whittemore, (Edward) Reed (Jr.)**
1919-........................CLC 4
See also CANR 4
See also CA 9-12R
See also DLB 5

**Whittier, John Greenleaf**
1807-1892.................. NCLC 8
See also DLB 1

**Wicker, Thomas Grey** 1926-
See Wicker, Tom
See also CANR 21
See also CA 65-68

**Wicker, Tom** 1926-.................CLC 7
See also Wicker, Thomas Grey

**Wideman, John Edgar**
1941-.............CLC 5, 34 (297), 36
See also CANR 14
See also CA 85-88
See also DLB 33

**Wiebe, Rudy (H.)** 1934-..... CLC 6, 11, 14
See also CA 37-40R
See also DLB 60

**Wieland, Christoph Martin**
1733-1813.................. NCLC 17

**Wieners, John** 1934-................CLC 7
See also CA 13-16R
See also DLB 16

**Wiesel, Elie(zer)**
1928-................CLC 3, 5, 11, 37
See also CAAS 4
See also CANR 8
See also CA 5-8R
See also DLB-Y 1986
See also AITN 1

**Wight, James Alfred** 1916-
See Herriot, James
See also CA 77-80
See also SATA 44

# *TCLC* Cumulative Nationality Index

## AMERICAN

Adams, Henry  **4**
Agee, James  **1, 19**
Anderson, Maxwell  **2**
Anderson, Sherwood  **1, 10, 24**
Atherton, Gertrude  **2**
Austin, Mary  **25**
Barry, Philip  **11**
Baum, L. Frank  **7**
Beard, Charles A.  **15**
Belasco, David  **3**
Benchley, Robert  **1**
Benét, Stephen Vincent  **7**
Benét, William Rose  **28**
Bierce, Ambrose  **1, 7**
Bourne, Randolph S.  **16**
Bromfield, Louis  **11**
Burroughs, Edgar Rice  **2**
Cabell, James Branch  **6**
Cable, George Washington  **4**
Cather, Willa  **1, 11**
Chandler, Raymond  **1, 7**
Chapman, John Jay  **7**
Chesnutt, Charles Waddell  **5**
Chopin, Kate  **5, 14**
Comstock, Anthony  **13**
Cotter, Joseph Seamon, Sr.  **28**
Crane, Hart  **2, 5**
Crane, Stephen  **11, 17**
Crawford, F. Marion  **10**
Crothers, Rachel  **19**
Cullen, Countee  **4**
Davis, Rebecca Harding  **6**
Davis, Richard Harding  **24**
Day, Clarence  **25**
Dreiser, Theodore  **10, 18**
Dunbar, Paul Laurence  **2, 12**

Dunne, Finley Peter  **28**
Fisher, Rudolph  **11**
Fitzgerald, F. Scott  **1, 6, 14, 28**
Forten, Charlotte L.  **16**
Freeman, Douglas Southall  **11**
Freeman, Mary Wilkins  **9**
Futrelle, Jacques  **19**
Gale, Zona  **7**
Garland, Hamlin  **3**
Gilman, Charlotte Perkins  **9**
Glasgow, Ellen  **2, 7**
Goldman, Emma  **13**
Grey, Zane  **6**
Hall, James Norman  **23**
Harper, Frances Ellen Watkins  **14**
Harris, Joel Chandler  **2**
Harte, Bret  **1, 25**
Hawthorne, Julian  **25**
Hearn, Lafcadio  **9**
Henry, O.  **1, 19**
Hergesheimer, Joseph  **11**
Hopkins, Pauline Elizabeth  **28**
Howard, Robert E.  **8**
Howe, Julia Ward  **21**
Howells, William Dean  **7, 17**
James, Henry  **2, 11, 24**
James, William  **15**
Jewett, Sarah Orne  **1, 22**
Johnson, James Weldon  **3, 19**
Kornbluth, C. M.  **8**
Kuttner, Henry  **10**
Lardner, Ring  **2, 14**
Lewis, Sinclair  **4, 13, 23**
Lewisohn, Ludwig  **19**
Lindsay, Vachel  **17**
London, Jack  **9, 15**
Lovecraft, H. P.  **4, 22**

Lowell, Amy  **1, 8**
Marquis, Don  **7**
Masters, Edgar Lee  **2, 25**
McCoy, Horace  **28**
McKay, Claude  **7**
Mencken, H. L.  **13**
Millay, Edna St. Vincent  **4**
Mitchell, Margaret  **11**
Monroe, Harriet  **12**
Muir, John  **28**
Nathan, George Jean  **18**
Nordhoff, Charles  **23**
Norris, Frank  **24**
O'Neill, Eugene  **1, 6, 27**
Porter, Gene Stratton  **21**
Rawlings, Majorie Kinnan  **4**
Reed, John  **9**
Roberts, Kenneth  **23**
Robinson, Edwin Arlington  **5**
Rogers, Will  **8**
Rölvaag, O. E.  **17**
Rourke, Constance  **12**
Runyon, Damon  **10**
Saltus, Edgar  **8**
Sherwood, Robert E.  **3**
Slesinger, Tess  **10**
Steffens, Lincoln  **20**
Stein, Gertrude  **1, 6, 28**
Sterling, George  **20**
Stevens, Wallace  **3, 12**
Tarkington, Booth  **9**
Teasdale, Sara  **4**
Thurman, Wallace  **6**
Twain, Mark  **6, 12, 19**
Van Dine, S. S.  **23**
Van Doren, Carl  **18**
Washington, Booker T.  **10**
West, Nathanael  **1, 14**
Wharton, Edith  **3, 9, 27**

White, Walter  **15**
Wister, Owen  **21**
Wolfe, Thomas  **4, 13**
Woollcott, Alexander  **5**
Wylie, Elinor  **8**

## ARGENTINIAN

Lugones, Leopoldo  **15**
Storni, Alfonsina  **5**

## AUSTRALIAN

Brennan, Christopher John  **17**
Franklin, Miles  **7**
Furphy, Joseph  **25**
Lawson, Henry  **27**
Richardson, Henry Handel  **4**

## AUSTRIAN

Broch, Hermann  **20**
Hofmannsthal, Hugo von  **11**
Kafka, Franz  **2, 6, 13**
Kraus, Karl  **5**
Kubin, Alfred  **23**
Meyrink, Gustav  **21**
Musil, Robert  **12**
Schnitzler, Arthur  **4**
Steiner, Rudolf  **13**
Trakl, Georg  **5**
Werfel, Franz  **8**
Zweig, Stefan  **17**

## BELGIAN

Bosschère, Jean de  **19**
Lemonnier, Camille  **22**
Maeterlinck, Maurice  **3**
Verhaeren, Émile  **12**

## BRAZILIAN

Cunha, Euclides da  **24**
Lima Barreto  **23**

**Nationality Index**

# *TCLC* Cumulative Title Index

Title Index

Title Index

Title Index

Title Index

Title Index

*Title Index*

*A Fine Gentleman* 3:505
"A Fine Summer Evening" 22:164
*The Finer Grain* 2:246, 258
"Finger Man" 7:172
"The Fingers" 27:352-53
"The Finish of Patsy Barnes" 12:120
*Finished* 11:246, 254-55
*Finita comoedia* 23:269
*Finn and His Companions* 5:348, 352, 355-56
*Finnegans Wake* 3:259-63, 268-77, 280-82; **8**:160-62, 167, 169-70, 172; **16**:208, 227-28, 233, 237, 241
*Fiorenza* 14:341, 350, 354
*Fir-Flower Tablets* 8:226, 229, 237
"The Fir Woods" 8:314
"Firdausi in Exile" 28:132, 140
*Firdausi in Exile* 28:132
"Fire!" 22:160
"Fire and Sleet and Candlelight" 8:521
"A Fire at Tranter Sweattey's" 4:152
*The Fire Bird* 21:267
"Fire by Night" 11:209, 212-13
*The Fire-Cantata*
　　See *Die Fever-Kantate*
*The Fire Goddess* 28:281, 286
*The Fire in the Flint* 15:473-75, 480-81, 483-86
"Fire in the Heavens" 17:43
*Fire in the Olive Grove*
　　See *L'incendio nell' oliveto*
*Fire in the Opera House*
　　See *Der Brand im Opernhaus*
"The Fire in the Wood" 22:446, 456
*The Fire of Egliswyl*
　　See *Der Brand von Egliswyl*
*The Fire of Things*
　　See *Ogon' veshchei*
*Fire-Tongue* 28:282
*The Fire Within*
　　See *Le feu follet*
*The Firebird*
　　See *Zhar-ptitsa*
"The Firemen's Ball" 17:222, 224-25, 227
"Firenze" 20:85
*The Fires of Saint Dominic*
　　See *Ogni svyatogo Dominika*
"Fireworks" 8:230
*The Fireworks*
　　See *Ilotulitus*
*The Firm Desire to Endure* 7:260-61
*First and Last Things: A Confession of Faith and Rule of Life* 6:529; **12**:490; **19**:436, 436
"The First Chapter of Spring" 28:414-15
"The First Day of an Immigrant" 4:142
"First Elegy" 1:412, 419-20
*The First Encounter*
　　See *Pervoe svidanie*
"A First Family of Tasajara" 25:223
"First Fruit" 12:299
"The First Game" 14:300-01
*The First Gentleman of America* 6:76-7
"The First Idea Is Not Our Own" 3:448
*The First Lady Chatterley* 9:228
"First Love" (Babel) 2:28; **13**:22-3, 34
"First Love" (Pavese) 3:340
*The First Man* 1:384; 6:325
"The First Meetings" 7:47

*The First Men in the Moon* 6:524, 533, 539, 542, 544-45, 547, 554; **12**:487-88, 505-06, 510-11, 515; **19**:423, 426, 428-29, 434, 436, 438-39, 441-42, 446-47, 449-50, 423, 426, 428-29, 434, 436, 438-39, 441-42, 446-47, 449-50
"First Night in the Churchyard" 5:249
"The First of Spring" 10:458
*First Person Singular* 28:10
*First Plays* 6:306
"The First Ploughing" 8:321
*First Poems* 1:312
*First Reader* 6:412
*The First Rescue Party* 6:86
"The First Snow" 6:393
*The First Terrorists* 18:378
*The First Trilogy* 1:142
"Fisches Nachtgesang" 8:305, 308
"The Fish" (Brooke) 2:51, 60; 7:120-21, 124
"Fish" (Lawrence) 9:229
*A Fish Dinner in Memison* 15:53-4, 56-7, 60, 62
*The Fisher Maiden* 7:105-07
"A Fisher of Men" (Freeman)
　　See "The Blue Diamond Mystery"
"The Fisher of Men" (Zamyatin)
　　See "Lovets chelovekov"
"The Fisherman" 18:446
"The Fisherman and His Soul" 1:503
*Fisherman of the Seine* 17:458
"Fishmonger's Fiddle" 5:180
*Fishmonger's Fiddle* 5:177, 179-81
"A Fit of Madness" 24:272
"A Fit of the Blues" 8:85
*The Fitzgerald Reader* 1:264
*Five Great Odes*
　　See *Cinq grandes odes*
*The Five Jars* 6:207
*Five Men and Pompey* 7:78
"Five Men at Random" 13:365
*Five O'Clock Tea* 7:387
"The Five Orange Pips" 7:216
*The Five Red Herrings (Suspicious Characters)* 15:371, 393
"The Five-Storied Pagoda"
　　See "Gojū no tō"
*The Five-Syllables and the Pathetic Whispers* 5:385
*Five Tales* (Galsworthy) 1:294
*Five Tales* (Verhaeren)
　　See *Cinq récits*
*Five Weeks in a Balloon*
　　See *Cinq semaines en ballon*
"The Five White Mice" 11:140, 155, 160, 164
*Five Women* 12:252
"Five Years of It" 28:7
*Fjalla-Eyvindur*
　　See *Bjærg-Ejvind og hans hustru*
"Le flacon" 10:81
"The Flag" 21:113
*The Flag*
　　See *Flagget*
*Det flager i byen og på havnen (The Flags Are Flying in Town and Port; The Flags Are Out in Town and Harbour; The Heritage of the Kurts)* 7:107-08, 114, 117
*Flagget (The Flag)* 10:209
"The Flags Are Flying in Town and Port"
　　See *Det flager i byen og på havnen*

*The Flags Are Out in Town and Harbour*
　　See *Det flager i byen og paa havnen*
*Les flamandes* 12:458, 460, 462-63, 465-66, 468, 470-71, 473
*Les flambeaux noirs* 12:460, 462-63, 465-66, 469-70
"The Flamboyant Architecture of the Valley of the Somme" 20:299
"The Flame"
　　See "La llama"
*Flame and Shadow* 4:425, 427-28, 430
"Flame-Heart" 7:456-57
*The Flame of Life*
　　See *Il fuoco*
"Flames"
　　See "Tüzek"
*The Flames* 22:323, 336-38
"Flames Flicker" 16:419
*The Flaming Circle*
　　See *Plamennyi krug*
*The Flaming Terrapin* 5:115-19, 123, 125-26
"Flammonde" 5:403, 408
"Flanagan and His Short Filibustering Adventure" 11:125, 160
*Flappers and Philosophers* 6:161
"The Flashlight" 6:398
*Flaubert* 9:327
"Flavia and Her Artists" 11:92, 100-01
"The Flaw in the Crystal" 11:420-21
*The Fleas; or, The Dance of Pain*
　　See *Die Flöhe; oder, Der Schmerzentanz*
*Fledermäuse* 21:232
*The Fledgling* 23:56, 71
*Fleet Street, and Other Poems* 24:172, 191-92
*Fleet Street Eclogues* 24:159, 162, 164, 175-76
"A Fleeting Wonder" 5:203
"Fleisch" 3:112
*Fleisch* 3:104, 106
"Fletcher McGee" 25:298, 308, 313
"Fleur de cing pierres" 20:320, 323
"La fleur de Napoléon" 20:201-02
"Fleurs de jadis" 17:129
*Fleurs d'ennui* 11:353, 368
*Fleurs d'exil* 11:356
"Flick" 3:288
"Der Fliegende Holländer" 9:142
"Flies"
　　See "Las moscas"
*The Flies*
　　See *Las moscas*
"Flight" (Brooke) 2:60
"The Flight" (Roberts) 8:319
"The Flight" (Scott) 6:386
"The Flight" (Teasdale) 4:426
*Flight* (Bulgakov)
　　See *Beg*
*Flight* (White) 15:475-76, 480, 483-86
"Flight at Sunrise" 28:226
*Flight into Darkness* 4:393
"The Flight of Betsey Lane" 1:361; 22:147
*A Flight of Cranes*
　　See *Balākā*
*The Flight of the Eagle* 5:348-49, 352, 354
*The Flight of the Marseillaise* 6:381
*The Flight of the Shadow* 9:292
"The Flight of the Wild Geese" 3:503
*Flight to Arras*
　　See *Pilote de guerre*

Title Index

Title Index

Title Index

Title Index

Title Index

Title Index

Title Index

Title Index

Title Index

Title Index

Title Index

Title Index

*Title Index*

Title Index

591

Title Index

Title Index

Title Index

Title Index

Title Index

Title Index

Title Index

Title Index

*Title Index*

Title Index

Title Index

Title Index